# THE HEXADECIMAL CHRONICLES

By
**Don Lancaster**

Howard W. Sams & Co., Inc.
4300 WEST 62ND ST. INDIANAPOLIS, INDIANA 46268 USA

International Standard Book Number: 0-672-21802-X
Library of Congress Catalog Card Number: 81-50563


*Printed in the United States of America.*

# Preface

Have you ever gone through a microcomputer's BASIC program and found something mysterious like this. . .

```
14410 POKE 2,173: POKE 3,48: POKE
      4,192: POKE 5,136: POKE 6,208
      : POKE 7,4: POKE 8,198: POKE
      9,1: POKE 10,240

14420 POKE 11,8: POKE 12,202: POKE
      13,208: POKE 14,246: POKE 15
      ,166: POKE 16,0: POKE 17,76
      : POKE 18,2: POKE 19,0: POKE
      20,96: RETURN
```

This POKEing process is one easy yet crude way for the BASIC program to create its own private machine language sequence. You drop down into machine language any time you want to do something much faster or more compactly than you can do in BASIC. You also use machine language when you want to tap some of the built-in features of your micro such as sound, color animation, or other resources. Since machine language is usually better for things like animation and business sorts, many of the better programs you will write and use will have a mix of machine language and BASIC or another high-level language.

So far, so good. But go down inside your machine where you thought all those POKEs were going, get a listing, and you'll find something like this instead:

```
0000 FF FF AD 30 C0 88 D0 04
0008 C6 01 F0 08 CA D0 F6 A6
0010 00 4C 02 00 60
```

At first glance, things look totally different. There's all those funny letters, and they are all only two places long.

It turns out that the BASIC program is using plain old *decimal*, or base ten notation, while the innards of the microcomputer are busy working with a number system called *hexadecimal*. Hexidecimal, or hex for short, is a convenient way of showing *binary*, or base-two numbers based on on-off, or 1-0 states.

To understand how other people's programs work, and to be able to write really fast and useful programs of your own, you have to be able to work with *both* the decimal numbers of the BASIC program and the hexadecimal numbers of the computer. You also have to learn to think in both number sets and be able to get quickly from one to the other.

Suppose you are running through an Integer BASIC program on an Apple computer and see a line like this:

```
26710 CALL −1052
```

This line asks the BASIC program to stop and go ahead and jump to a machine language subroutine that starts at location −1052. But, why the minus? And why, when you try to move this program from an *Apple II*, to say, a *Northstar*, do we get exactly this far and then the machine suddenly hangs up, stops entirely, or else gets violently ill?

Even if you knew that this CALL −1052 instruction tells an Apple II to beep its speaker once, how do you know how to change the number of beeps, or alter the length or pitch of the beeps? What else changes in the computer when you use this subroutine?

This time around, the BASIC program is using a code called *Apple Inverted Decimal*, that is used in most all *Apple* Integer BASIC programs. Once again, the innards of the computer are in hexadecimal. What clue do you have that a CALL −1052 goes to hex location FBE4?

If you are going to understand the program, and especially if you are going to change it, you have to be able to get between the codes quickly and easily.

One more example. You decide to cheat on an *Adventure* program and look into the machine to find a clue on how to get out of a bind. You snoop down into the file where you think the answer lies, and you find. . .

```
4F 59 53 54 45 52 20 4D 41 4B 45 53 20
41 20 53 4C 4F 42 42 45 52 49 4E 47 20
4E 4F 49 53 45 2E 0D
```

if you are looking in hexadecimal, or maybe something like

```
207 217 211 212 197 210 160 205 193 203 197 211 160
193 160 211 204 207 194 194 197 210 201 206 199 160
206 207 201 211 197 174 141
```

If you are busy PEEKing from BASIC. Now both of these are "correct" and either can give you the answer you are after. But, what we want are letters and numbers that spell out something, not code. It turns out the message is in *ASCII*, a standard way of stashing letters and numbers in computers. Here is yet another code that you will have to learn. How do you get from ASCII to hexidecimal? Or, ASCII to decimal?

Now, sure, if you know what you are doing, all you need for a number or base conversion is a pencil and paper. Or, use a pocket calculator. There are even special hexadecimal ones available. You'll also find lots of conversion programs that work with your micro, and it's a simple enough matter to write your own. Or, why not print out a complete conversion? Fire up *Excederin Headache* number ASR-33, and three short days and half a mile of paper later, out comes a complete table of all possible conversions. That assumes, of course, that the ribbon didn't jump the track at 3 am, and that the final printout was actually legible, and that the paper would last through a few uses without self-destructing.

All of these ways of converting numbers, codes, and bases will work. But they are a hassle. Each and every one of these methods forces you to stop what you are really doing, and then makes you take time out and go find a conversion.

I needed something better, faster, and simplier than these obvious methods. A way to immediately do conversions, without tieing up machines or interrupting the vibes and thought processes of whatever I was working on. A way of right-now saying decimal 23621 is hexadecimal 5C45, or that an ASCII backspace is the same as hexadecimal 08.

Hence the HEXADECIMAL CHRONICLES.

The hex chronicles immediately give you fifty-two of the most important number, code, and base conversions and calcualtions you are likely to need in microcomputer work. You will find the chronicles arranged as six tables. These tables let you do instant...

● 8-bit conversions of ASCII, BINARY, DECIMAL, HEXADECIMAL, and OCTAL

● 16-bit conversions of DECIMAL, BINARY, DECIMAL, HEXADECIMAL, and OCTAL

● 24-bit conversions of DECIMAL and EXTENDED HEXADECIMAL

Plus, the sixth chronicle is a special calculator that instantly does

● 8-bit calculations of HEX ADDITION, HEX SUBTRACTION, RELATIVE BRANCH CALCULATION, COMPLEMENTS, and 2s COMPLEMENTS

For most of the conversions, you flip down through the pages, find a value, and immediately read the answer. For the hex calculations, you simply spin Chronicle Six and read the sum difference, relative branch value, or complement.

That fast and that easy. A few of the more oddball conversions need a simple subtraction or an intermediate step, but even these are quick and easy to do. We have tried to present things as attractively, conveniently, and as easily used as possible.

You'll find out why the chronicles are sideways when you start to use them. Each chronicle is both tab and block indexed for fast searching.

I hope you will find the Hex Chronicles as useful, essential, convenient, and as hassle-free as I have.

DON LANCASTER

# Contents

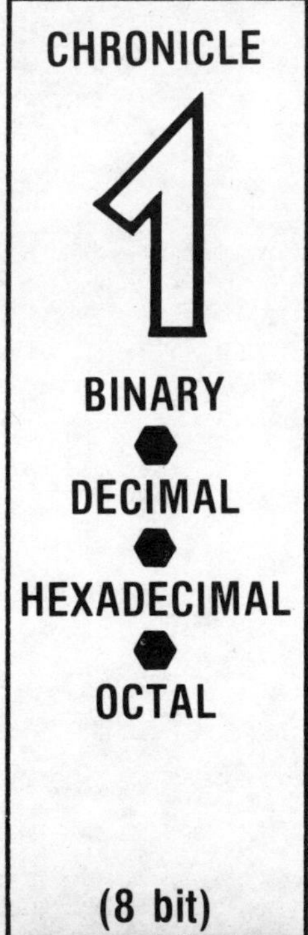



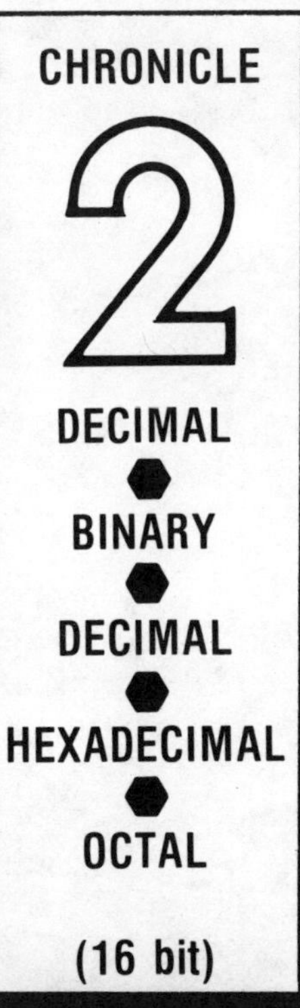



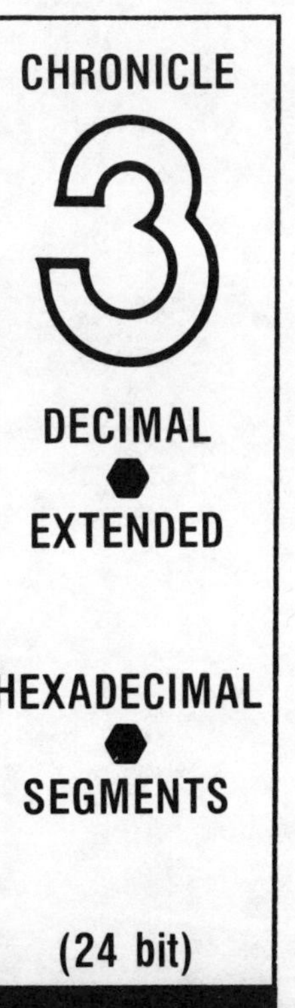



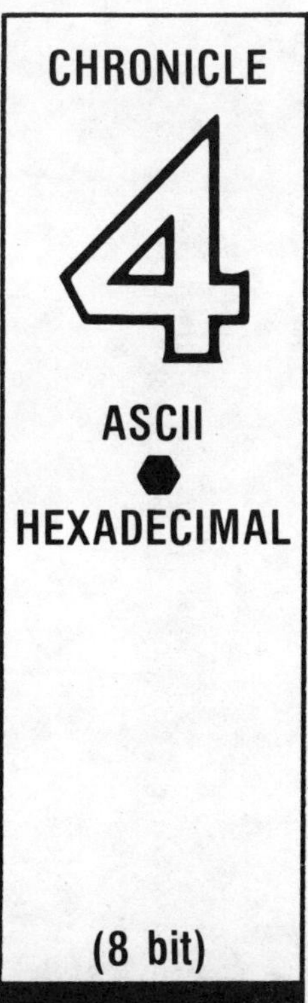

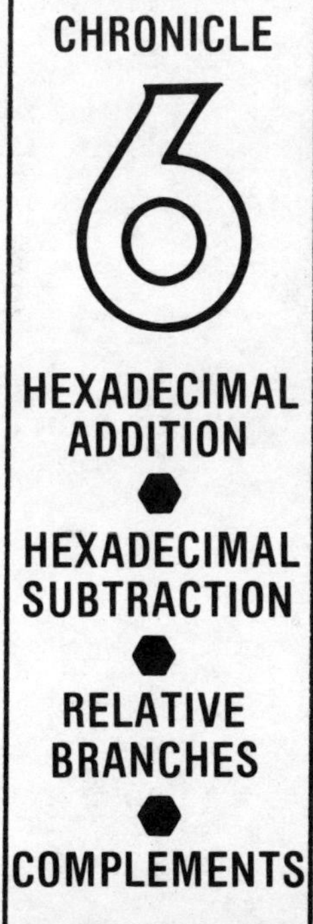

# How to Use the Chronicles

# The Codes

 **Decimal** — This is a special and very popular code used in Apple II Integer BASIC programs. Integer BASIC only recognizes the decimal numbers from − 32768 to + 32767. Ordinary decimal numbers are remapped so that values from 0 to 32767 stay the same. Above that, things run both negative and backwards. For instance, decimal 65535 is  decimal − 1; decimal 65534 is  decimal − 2; and so on down to decimal 32769, which is  decimal − 32767; and decimal 32768, which is  decimal − 32768.

In hex, values from 0000 to 7FFF convert to positive decimal numbers, while values from 8000 to FFFF become the *negative* decimal numbers, counting down from the top.

**ASCII** — ASCII is the standard way of showing letters, numbers, and control codes in the microcomputing world. ASCII only uses the lower seven bits of an 8-bit data word. These seven bits represent 128 possible characters, arranged as four groups of 32 characters each. One character group consists of numbers and symbols. A second group is the upper-case characters and common punctuation. The third group is the lower-case letters and lesser-used punctuation, while the final group is made up of *control characters*. These control characters usually do not appear in print. Instead, they do things like return carriages, ring bells, stop and start things, and so on.

The eighth, or most significant, bit is left over in the ASCII code. Traditionally this bit was used for error checking, but today it is more often used as a keypressed flag, a cursor symbol, or as an "invert the display" command. Since the use of this eighth bit depends on the system, an ASCII character can appear in one of *two* ways, as decided by what the final bit is doing

**Binary** — Binary is the fundamental, base-two arithmetic used in all computers. A single device or line in a computer will have two possible states. These states are usually called on or off, or *one* and *zero*. Binary puts its ones and zeros down just like dec-

imal puts its digits down, with the heavier stuff to the left. For instance, binary 1011 has a value of 8 + 0 + 2 + 1 = decimal 11. Binary 0111 0001 1110 1101 has a decimal value of 29165.

Although all computers actually work in binary, the binary notation is very hard to read and very hard to use. Most often, binary bits are grouped into more significant and easier to read values in either the *hexadecimal* or obsolete *octal* number systems. "Strung out" binary notation is usually avoided, unless you are worrying about what each bit line in a micro is up to or are interested in specific one-zero code patterns.

**Complement** — The complement of binary number has all its ones made into zeros and vice versa. The complement of a hexadecimal or octal number is the number that results when all the equivalent binary ones and zeros are interchanged. The complement of binary 0011 1010 is 1100 0101. The complement of hexadecimal C5 is 3A.

Complements are useful for ports that have active-low or negative logic involved.

**2s Complement** — The 2s complement of a binary number is one more than its complement. To get from a number to its 2s complement, complement the number and ADD one. To get from a 2s complement to its equivalent number, you *also* complement the number and ADD one.

2s complements let you subtract by *adding*. To subtract C − D, add the 2s complement of D to C.

**Decimal** — Decimal is plain old everyday base ten numbering. The digits zero through nine go in the rightmost column, ten through ninety in the next left column, and so on. Besides being the number system that everyone knows and uses, you'll often find decimal inside BASIC programs when specific computer addresses need to be called out, such as in PEEK, POKE, or CALL instructions.

# Examples

There are at least 52 different conversions and calculations you can make using your *Hex Chronicles.* Here are some detailed use examples shown in alphabetical order:

### EIGHT-BIT CONVERSIONS

NOTE: **ASCII conversions can yield one of two values, depending on the use of the most significant code bit. These two values always differ by decimal 128, Hex 80, or binary 1000 0000. Check your system to see which value to use.**

**ASCII to Binary: (4) ⟶ (1)**

Use Chronicle FOUR. Locate the ASCII symbol and then read the second hex value off the row and the first hex value off the column. Record this hex value. Then go to Chronicle ONE. Enter Chronicle ONE at the row set by the second hex value and the column set by the first hex value. Where the row and column cross, read the binary value at the THIRD or LOWEST entry.

**EXAMPLE — ASCII lower case "k" reads as hex 6B or binary 0100 1101.**

**ASCII to Decimal: (5)**

Use Chronicle FIVE. Locate the ASCII symbol and then read the corresponding decimal value.

**EXAMPLE — ASCII semicolon (;) is decimal 59**

**ASCII to Hexadecimal: (4)**

Use Chronicle FOUR. Locate the ASCII symbol and then read the second hex value off the row and the first hex value off the column.

**EXAMPLE: — ASCII control command ESCAPE (ESC) is hex 1B**

**ASCII to Octal: (4) ⟶ (1)**

Use Chronicle FOUR. Locate the ASCII symbol and then read the second hex value off the row and the first hex value off the column. Record this hex value. Then go to Chronicle ONE. Enter Chronicle ONE at the row set by the second hex value and the column set by the first hex value. Where the row and column cross, read the octal value at the SECOND or CENTER entry.

**EXAMPLE: — ASCII upper case "M" is hex 4D or octal 115**

**Binary to ASCII: (1) ⟶ (4)**

Use Chronicle ONE. Find the binary value at the THIRD or LOWEST entry. Then read the second hex value off the row and the first hex value off the column. Record this hex value. Then go to Chronicle FOUR. Enter Chronicle FOUR at the row set by the second hex value and the column set by the first hex value. Read the ASCII value where row and column cross.

**EXAMPLE** — Binary 0111 1010 is hex 7A which is ASCII lower case "z"

## Binary to Decimal: ①

Use Chronicle ONE. Find the binary value at the THIRD or LOWEST entry. Then read the FIRST or HIGHEST entry in the same position.

**EXAMPLE** — Binary 0101 0111 is decimal 87

## Binary to Hexadecimal: ①

Use Chronicle ONE. Find the binary value at the THIRD or LOWEST entry. Then read the second hex value off the row and the first hex value off the column.

**EXAMPLE** — Binary 1100 0011 is hexadecimal C3

## Binary to Octal: ①

Use Chronicle ONE. Find the binary value at the THIRD or LOWEST entry. Then read the octal value from the SECOND or CENTER entry in the same position.

**EXAMPLE** — Binary 1000 0100 is octal 204

## Decimal to ASCII: ⑤

Use Chronicle FIVE. Locate the decimal value and read the corresponding ASCII symbol.

**EXAMPLE** — Decimal 160 is an ASCII space

## Decimal to Binary: ①

Use Chronicle ONE. Locate the decimal value at the FIRST or HIGHEST entry. Then read the THIRD or LOWEST entry in the same position.

**EXAMPLE** — Decimal 237 is binary 1110 1101.

## Decimal to Hexadecimal: ①

Use Chronicle ONE. Locate the decimal value at the FIRST or HIGHEST entry. Then read the second hex value off the row and the first hex value off the column.

**EXAMPLE** — Decimal 45 is hexadecimal 2D

## Decimal to Octal: ①

Use Chronicle ONE. Locate the decimal value from the FIRST or HIGHEST entry. Then read the octal value from the SECOND or CENTER entry in the same position.

**EXAMPLE** — Decimal 55 is octal 067

## Hex to ASCII: (4)

Use Chronicle FOUR. Go to the row corresponding to the second hex value and the column corresponding to the first hex value. Read the ASCII symbol where row and column cross.

**EXAMPLE** — Hexadecimal 7F is the ASCII (DEL) or delete command.

## Hex to Binary: (1)

Use Chronicle ONE. Go to the row corresponding to the second hex value and the column corresponding to the first hex value. Read the binary value at the THIRD or LOWEST entry where row and column cross.

**EXAMPLE** — Hexadecimal BB is binary 1011 1011

## Hex to Decimal: (1)

Use Chronicle ONE. Go to the row corresponding to the second hex value and the column corresponding to the first hex value. Read the decimal value at the FIRST or HIGHEST entry where row and column cross.

**EXAMPLE** — Hexadecimal 0C is decimal 12

## Hex to Octal: (1)

Use Chronicle ONE. Go to the row corresponding to the second hex value and the column corresponding to the first hex value. Read the octal value at the SECOND or CENTER entry where row and column cross.

**EXAMPLE** — Hexadecimal F2 is octal 362.

## Octal to ASCII: (1) ⟶ (4)

Use Chronicle ONE. Locate the octal value at the SECOND or CENTER entry. Then read the second hex value off the row and the first hex value off the column. Record this hex value. Then go to Chronicle FOUR. Enter Chronicle FOUR at the row set by the second hex value and the column set by the first hex value. Read the ASCII value where row and column cross.

**EXAMPLE** — Octal 076 is an ASCII "greater than" or ">" symbol. (Hexadecimal 3E)

## Octal to Binary: (1)

Use Chronicle ONE. Locate the octal value at the SECOND or CENTER entry. Then read the binary value from the THIRD or LOWEST entry in the same position.

**EXAMPLE** — Octal 121 is binary 0101 0001

**Octal to Decimal:** ⬡①

Use Chronicle ONE. Locate the octal value at the SECOND or CENTER entry. Then read the decimal value from the FIRST or HIGHEST entry in the same position.



**Octal to Hexadecimal:** ⬡①

Use Chronicle ONE. Locate the octal value at the SECOND or CENTER entry. Then read the second hex value off the row and the first hex value off the column.



## SIXTEEN-BIT CONVERSIONS

NOTE: Chronicle TWO is much longer than the others. Use the index boxes to get to the needed page.

**⌘ Decimal to Binary:** ②  ⟶  ①

Use Chronicle TWO. Find the SECOND or CENTER entry equal to the ⌘ decimal coding. Write down the value in the BINARY box. This value equals the eight most significant binary bits needed. Next, read the second hex value off the row and the first hex value off the column. Record this hex value. Then go to Chronicle ONE. Enter Chronicle ONE at the row set by the second hex value and the column set the the first hex value. Read the lower eight binary bits at the THIRD of LOWEST entry where row and column cross.



**⌘ Decimal to Decimal:** ⬡②

Use Chronicle TWO. Find the SECOND or CENTER entry equal to the ⌘ decimal coding. Then read the decimal value from the FIRST or HIGHEST entry in the same position.



**⌘ Decimal to Hexadecimal:** ⬡②

Use Chronicle TWO. Find the SECOND or CENTER entry equal to the ⌘ decimal coding. Next, note the page number as the most significant two hex digits. Then read the second hex value off the row and the first hex value off the column, and record these as the two least significant hex digits.



**⌘ Decimal to Octal** ⬡②

Use Chronicle TWO. Find the SECOND or CENTER entry equal to the ⌘ decimal coding. Then read the octal value from the THIRD or LOWEST entry in the same position.

**Binary to  Decimal:** ① ⟶ ②

Use Chronicle ONE. Find the binary value equal to the least significant eight bits at the THIRD or LOWEST entry. Then read the second hex value off the row and the first hex value off the column. Record this hex value. Then go to the Chronicle TWO page whose binary prefix is the same as the most significant eight bits. Enter Chronicle TWO at the row set by the second hex value and the column set by the first hex value. Read the  decimal value at the SECOND or CENTER entry where row and column cross.

> **EXAMPLE** — Binary 1011 0111 1110 1101 takes you to hex entry ED of page B7. The  decimal value is − 18451

**Binary to Decimal:** ① ⟶ ②

Use Chronicle ONE. Find the binary value equal to the least significant eight bits at the THIRD or LOWEST entry. Then read the second hex value off the row and the first hex value off the column. Record this hex value. Then go to the Chronicle TWO page whose binary prefix is the same as the most significant eight bits. Enter Chronicle TWO at the row set by the second hex value and the column set by the first hex value. Read the decimal value at the FIRST or HIGHEST entry where row and column cross.

> **EXAMPLE** — Binary 0010 0100 1000 1001 takes you to hex entry 89 on page 24. The decimal value is 9353.

**Binary to Hexadecimal:** ① ⟶ ②

Use Chronicle ONE. Find the binary value equal to the least signifi-

---

cant eight bits at the THIRD or LOWEST entry. Then read the second hex value off the row and the first hex value off the column. Record this hex value. Then go to the Chronicle TWO pages whose binary box is the same as the most significant eight bits. The hex page number is the fourth and third hex digits, while the value you recorded takes care of the second and first hex digits.

> **EXAMPLE** — Binary 1000 1011 0100 0111 is hexadecimal 8B47.

**Binary to Octal:** ① ⟶ ②

Use Chronicle ONE. Find the binary value equal to the least significant eight bits at the THIRD or LOWEST entry. Then read the second hex value off the row and the first hex value off the column. Record this hex value. Then go to the Chronicle TWO page whose binary box is the same as the most significant eight bits. Enter Chronicle TWO at the row set by the second hex value and the column set by the first hex value. Read the octal value at the THIRD or LOWEST entry where row and column cross.

> **EXAMPLE** — Binary 1101 1011 1110 0000 is octal 333 340

**Decimal to  Decimal:** ②

Use Chronicle TWO. Find the FIRST or HIGHEST entry equal to the decimal coding. Then read the  decimal value from the SECOND or CENTER entry in the same position.

> **EXAMPLE** — Decimal 32771 is  decimal − 32765

to the first hex value of the two least significant hexadecimal digits. Read the decimal value at the FIRST or HIGHEST entry where row and column cross.



**Hexadecimal to Octal:** 

Use Chronicle TWO. Find the page corresponding to the two most significant (fourth and third) hexadecimal digits. Go to the row corresponding to the second hex value and the column corresponding to the first hex value of the two least significant hex digits. Read the octal value at the THIRD or LOWEST entry where row and column cross.



**Octal to**  **Decimal:**

Use Chronicle TWO. Find the THIRD or LOWEST entry equal to the octal coding. Then read the  decimal value from the SECOND or CENTER entry in the same position.



**Octal to Binary:** 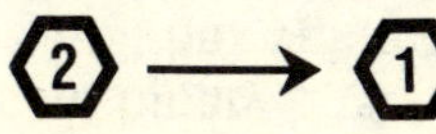

Use Chronicle TWO. Find the THIRD or LOWEST entry equal to the octal coding. Write down the value of the BINARY box as the eight most significant binary bits. Next, read the second hex value off the row and the first hex value off the column. Record this hex value. Then go to Chronicle ONE. Enter Chronicle ONE at the row set by the second hex value and the column set by the first hex value. Read the lower eight binary bits at the THIRD or LOWEST entry where row and column cross.



**Octal to Decimal:** 

Use Chronicle TWO. Find the THIRD or LOWEST entry equal to the octal coding. Then read the decimal value from the FIRST or HIGHEST entry in the same position.



**Octal to Hexadecimal:** 

Use Chronicle TWO. Find the THIRD or LOWEST entry equal to the octal coding. Then read the hex page number as the upper (fourth and third) hex digits, the row as the second hex digit, and the column as the first hex digit.

**Decimal to Binary:** 

Use Chronicle TWO. Find the FIRST or HIGHEST entry equal to the decimal coding. Write down the value of the BINARY box as the eight most significant binary bits. Next, read the second hex value off the row and the first hex value off the column. Record this hex value. Then go to Chronicle ONE. Enter Chronicle ONE at the row set by the second hex value and the column set by the first hex value. Read the lower eight binary bits at the THIRD or LOWEST entry where the row and column cross.

EXAMPLE — Decimal 12526 has a binary prefix of 0011 0000 on hex page 30. Hex values for that page are EE, which converts to binary 1110 1110. The final value is 0011 0000 1110 1110

**Decimal to Hexadecimal:** 

Use Chronicle TWO. Find the FIRST or HIGHEST entry equal to the decimal coding. Next, note the page number as the most significant (fourth and third) hex digits. Then read the second hex value off the row and the first hex value off the column and record these as the two least significant hex digits.

EXAMPLE — Decimal 1698 is hex 06A2

**Decimal to Octal:** 

Use Chronicle TWO. Find the FIRST or HIGHEST entry equal to the decimal coding. Then read the octal value from the THIRD or LOWEST entry in the same position.

EXAMPLE — Decimal 10949 is octal 052 305

**Hexadecimal to  Decimal:** 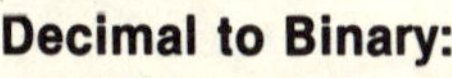

Use Chronicle TWO. Find the page corresponding to the two most significant (fourth and third) hexadecimal digits. Go to the row corresponding to the second hex value and the column corresponding to the first hex value of the two least significant hexadecimal digits. Read the  decimal value at the SECOND or CENTER entry where row and column cross.

EXAMPLE — Hexadecimal 88EB is  decimal — 30485

**Hexadecimal to Binary:**

Use Chronicle TWO. Find the page corresponding to the two most significant (fourth and third) hexadecimal digits. Record the BINARY box as the eight most significant binary bits. Then find the page corresponding to the two *least* significant (second and first) hexadecimal digits. Record the BINARY box as the eight least significant binary bits.

EXAMPLE — Hexadecimal BEEF is binary 1011 1110 1110 1111

**Hexadecimal to Decimal:**

Use Chronicle TWO. Find the page corresponding to the two most significant (fourth and third) hexadecimal digits. Go to the row corresponding to the second hex value and the column corresponding

## TWENTY-FOUR BIT CONVERSIONS

NOTE: **A pocket calculator is a help for the single add or subtract needed in some 24-bit conversions.**

**Decimal to Hexadecimal:** ⬡3 ⟶ ⬡2

Use Chronicle THREE. Find the decimal adder equal to or just less than your value as the SECOND or LOWER entry. Record the row as the sixth hex digit and the column as the fifth hex digit. Subtract the decimal adder from your value, which should leave a decimal *residue* in the range of 0 to 65535. Go to Chronicle TWO and convert this decimal residue into its hexadecimal equivalent. Combine the results.

> EXAMPLE — Decimal 8543901 is larger than adder 8519680 which corresponds to hex 82. The decimal residue is 24221, which converts to hex 5E9D. The result is hexadecimal 82 5E9D.

**Decimal to Segments:** ⬡3

Use Chronicle THREE. Find the decimal adder equal to or just less than your value as the SECOND or LOWER entry. Read the segment number at the FIRST or HIGHER entry in the same position.

> EXAMPLE — Decimal 2166902 is in segment 33

**Hexadecimal to Decimal:** ⬡3 ⟶ ⬡2

Use Chronicle THREE. Find the decimal adder equal to the

SECOND or LOWER entry on the row set by the sixth hex digit and on the column set by the fifth hex digit. Go to Chronicle TWO. Find the decimal value of the four least significant hex digits. Add the results.

> EXAMPLE — Hexadecimal 1E 0A19 has a decimal adder of 917504 to a residue of 2585 for a total of 920089.

**Hexadecimal to Segment:** ⬡3

Use Chronicle THREE. Find the FIRST or HIGHER value on the row set by the sixth hex digit and on the column set by the fifth hex digit.

> EXAMPLE — Hexadecimal DF 012B lies in segment 223.

**Segment to Decimal:** ⬡3

Use Chronicle THREE. Find the FIRST or HIGHER value that equals the segment number. Read the decimal adder as the SECOND or LOWER value immediately below.

> EXAMPLE — Segment 23 decimal values range from 1507328 to (1507328 + 65535) = 1572863

**Segment to Hexadecimal:** ⬡3

Use Chronicle THREE. Find the FIRST or HIGHER value that equals the segment number. Record the row as the sixth hex digit and the column as the fifth hex digit.

EXAMPLE — Segment 76 hex values range from
4C 0000 to 4C FFFF

## EIGHT-BIT CALCULATIONS

NOTE: Chronicle SIX may be left bound in the back of the book or removed and cut out around the hex box for greater ease in using.

**Hexadecimal Addition:** (6)

Use Chronicle SIX. To add A + B, put the pointer on A. Twist the calculator CLOCKWISE till a BLACK number on the dial equal to B is pointing to A. The pointer points to the sum. If the pointer went past 00, a carry resulted from the addition.

EXAMPLE — Hex 3A + 1D = 57 with no carry
Hex 3A + CD = 07 with a carry

**Hexadecimal Subtraction:** (6)

Use Chronicle SIX. To subtract X − Y put the pointer on X. Twist the calculator COUNTERCLOCKWISE till a RED number on the dial equal to Y is pointing to X. The pointer points to the difference Z. If the pointer passed FF, a borrow is needed to complete the subtraction.

EXAMPLES — Hex 7B − 3F = 3C with no borrow
Hex 3F − 7B = C4 with a borrow

**Forward Relative Branch:** (6)

Use Chronicle SIX. Put the pointer on the number that you will go to if the branch IS taken. Find the number on the OUTSIDE that you would go to if the branch IS NOT taken. Read the relative branch value at this position. Forward branches are limited to +00 to +7F, or the WHITE portion of the inner disc.

EXAMPLE — You want to forward branch to address 17AD. If the branch is NOT taken you will go to address 1786. Put the pointer at AD and locate 86 on the outside. Read the relative branch value of 27 on the inside. This is a legal branch since it is in the WHITE.

**Reverse Relative Branch:** (6)

Use Chronicle SIX. Put the pointer on the number that you will go to if the branch IS taken. Find the number on the OUTSIDE that you would go to if the branch IS NOT taken. Read the relative branch value at this position. Reverse branches are limited to FF through 80 or the BLACK portion of the inner disc.

EXAMPLE — You want to reverse branch to address 176C. if the branch is NOT taken you will go to address 1786. Put the pointer at 6C and locate 86 on the outside. Read the relative branch value of E6 on the inside. This also is a legal branch since it is in the BLACK.

Note that the only difference between doing a forward branch and a reverse branch is that forward branches have to end up in the

WHITE and reverse branches have to end up in the BLACK. If you cannot do this, your branch is out of range.

## Complement: 

Use Chronicle SIX. To complement a hex number, set the arrow to "FF". Find the value you want to complement in BLACK on the HEX. Read the complement of that value in BLACK on the DISC.

**EXAMPLE — The complement of Hex 1B is E4**

For a binary or octal complement, convert to hexadecimal first.

## 2s Complement:

Use Chronicle SIX. To find the 2s complement of a hex number, set the arrow to "00". Find the VALUE you want the 2s complement of in BLACK on the HEX. Read the 2s complement of that value in BLACK on the DISC.

**EXAMPLE — The 2s complement of Hex 1B is E5.**

For a binary or octal complement, convert to hexadecimal first.

## ADDITIONAL HINTS

● You'll find most of the really useful and important conversions are done in a single step. As you gain experience, you should be able to immediately go from hexadecimal to binary and back again, without needing or using the chronicles. This will simplify things further and make just about every conversion a "single look" event.

● Your hexadecimal calculator of chronicle SIX can also be used for 16- and 24-bit conversions and the new long relative branches. Just use the calculator over again two or three times, starting with the LEAST significant pair of hex digits. Be sure to allow for carrys and borrows when you pick up the more significant digits.

● Some of the lesser used ASCII control codes and punctuation are sometimes redefined for special uses. Thus, you might find graphics control commands replacing the "forms" commands FS through GS, or you might find cursor direction arrows in the four slots after capital "Z", at hex 5B through 5E.

# CHRONICLE

**BINARY — DECIMAL — HEXADECIMAL — OCTAL**

**(EIGHT BIT)**

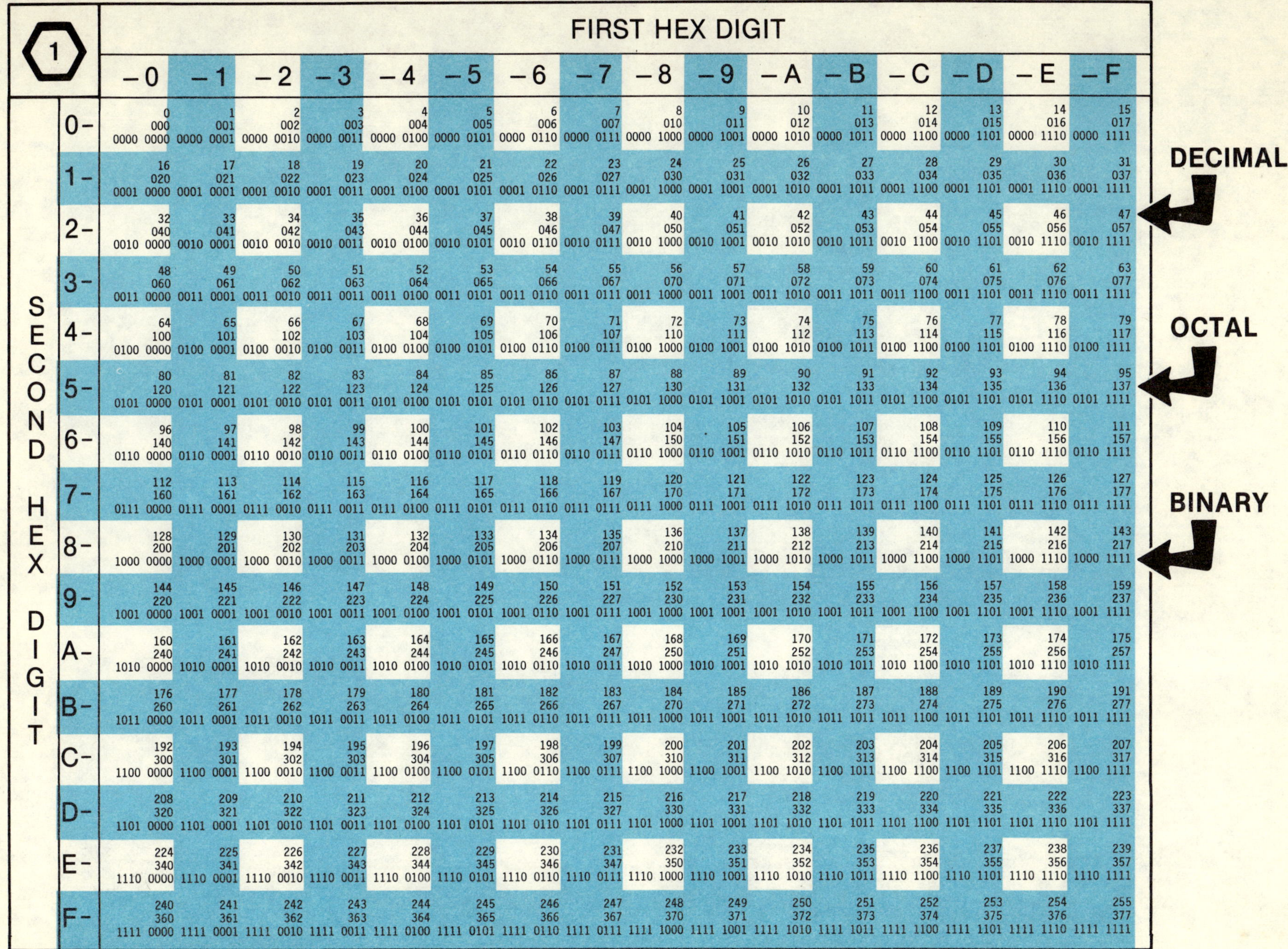



| | −0 | −1 | −2 | −3 | −4 | −5 | −6 | −7 | −8 | −9 | −A | −B | −C | −D | −E | −F |
|---|---|---|---|---|---|---|---|---|---|---|---|---|---|---|---|---|
| **0−** | 0<br>000<br>0000 0000 | 1<br>001<br>0000 0001 | 2<br>002<br>0000 0010 | 3<br>003<br>0000 0011 | 4<br>004<br>0000 0100 | 5<br>005<br>0000 0101 | 6<br>006<br>0000 0110 | 7<br>007<br>0000 0111 | 8<br>010<br>0000 1000 | 9<br>011<br>0000 1001 | 10<br>012<br>0000 1010 | 11<br>013<br>0000 1011 | 12<br>014<br>0000 1100 | 13<br>015<br>0000 1101 | 14<br>016<br>0000 1110 | 15<br>017<br>0000 1111 |
| **1−** | 16<br>020<br>0001 0000 | 17<br>021<br>0001 0001 | 18<br>022<br>0001 0010 | 19<br>023<br>0001 0011 | 20<br>024<br>0001 0100 | 21<br>025<br>0001 0101 | 22<br>026<br>0001 0110 | 23<br>027<br>0001 0111 | 24<br>030<br>0001 1000 | 25<br>031<br>0001 1001 | 26<br>032<br>0001 1010 | 27<br>033<br>0001 1011 | 28<br>034<br>0001 1100 | 29<br>035<br>0001 1101 | 30<br>036<br>0001 1110 | 31<br>037<br>0001 1111 |
| **2−** | 32<br>040<br>0010 0000 | 33<br>041<br>0010 0001 | 34<br>042<br>0010 0010 | 35<br>043<br>0010 0011 | 36<br>044<br>0010 0100 | 37<br>045<br>0010 0101 | 38<br>046<br>0010 0110 | 39<br>047<br>0010 0111 | 40<br>050<br>0010 1000 | 41<br>051<br>0010 1001 | 42<br>052<br>0010 1010 | 43<br>053<br>0010 1011 | 44<br>054<br>0010 1100 | 45<br>055<br>0010 1101 | 46<br>056<br>0010 1110 | 47<br>057<br>0010 1111 |
| **3−** | 48<br>060<br>0011 0000 | 49<br>061<br>0011 0001 | 50<br>062<br>0011 0010 | 51<br>063<br>0011 0011 | 52<br>064<br>0011 0100 | 53<br>065<br>0011 0101 | 54<br>066<br>0011 0110 | 55<br>067<br>0011 0111 | 56<br>070<br>0011 1000 | 57<br>071<br>0011 1001 | 58<br>072<br>0011 1010 | 59<br>073<br>0011 1011 | 60<br>074<br>0011 1100 | 61<br>075<br>0011 1101 | 62<br>076<br>0011 1110 | 63<br>077<br>0011 1111 |
| **4−** | 64<br>100<br>0100 0000 | 65<br>101<br>0100 0001 | 66<br>102<br>0100 0010 | 67<br>103<br>0100 0011 | 68<br>104<br>0100 0100 | 69<br>105<br>0100 0101 | 70<br>106<br>0100 0110 | 71<br>107<br>0100 0111 | 72<br>110<br>0100 1000 | 73<br>111<br>0100 1001 | 74<br>112<br>0100 1010 | 75<br>113<br>0100 1011 | 76<br>114<br>0100 1100 | 77<br>115<br>0100 1101 | 78<br>116<br>0100 1110 | 79<br>117<br>0100 1111 |
| **5−** | 80<br>120<br>0101 0000 | 81<br>121<br>0101 0001 | 82<br>122<br>0101 0010 | 83<br>123<br>0101 0011 | 84<br>124<br>0101 0100 | 85<br>125<br>0101 0101 | 86<br>126<br>0101 0110 | 87<br>127<br>0101 0111 | 88<br>130<br>0101 1000 | 89<br>131<br>0101 1001 | 90<br>132<br>0101 1010 | 91<br>133<br>0101 1011 | 92<br>134<br>0101 1100 | 93<br>135<br>0101 1101 | 94<br>136<br>0101 1110 | 95<br>137<br>0101 1111 |
| **6−** | 96<br>140<br>0110 0000 | 97<br>141<br>0110 0001 | 98<br>142<br>0110 0010 | 99<br>143<br>0110 0011 | 100<br>144<br>0110 0100 | 101<br>145<br>0110 0101 | 102<br>146<br>0110 0110 | 103<br>147<br>0110 0111 | 104<br>150<br>0110 1000 | 105<br>151<br>0110 1001 | 106<br>152<br>0110 1010 | 107<br>153<br>0110 1011 | 108<br>154<br>0110 1100 | 109<br>155<br>0110 1101 | 110<br>156<br>0110 1110 | 111<br>157<br>0110 1111 |
| **7−** | 112<br>160<br>0111 0000 | 113<br>161<br>0111 0001 | 114<br>162<br>0111 0010 | 115<br>163<br>0111 0011 | 116<br>164<br>0111 0100 | 117<br>165<br>0111 0101 | 118<br>166<br>0111 0110 | 119<br>167<br>0111 0111 | 120<br>170<br>0111 1000 | 121<br>171<br>0111 1001 | 122<br>172<br>0111 1010 | 123<br>173<br>0111 1011 | 124<br>174<br>0111 1100 | 125<br>175<br>0111 1101 | 126<br>176<br>0111 1110 | 127<br>177<br>0111 1111 |
| **8−** | 128<br>200<br>1000 0000 | 129<br>201<br>1000 0001 | 130<br>202<br>1000 0010 | 131<br>203<br>1000 0011 | 132<br>204<br>1000 0100 | 133<br>205<br>1000 0101 | 134<br>206<br>1000 0110 | 135<br>207<br>1000 0111 | 136<br>210<br>1000 1000 | 137<br>211<br>1000 1001 | 138<br>212<br>1000 1010 | 139<br>213<br>1000 1011 | 140<br>214<br>1000 1100 | 141<br>215<br>1000 1101 | 142<br>216<br>1000 1110 | 143<br>217<br>1000 1111 |
| **9−** | 144<br>220<br>1001 0000 | 145<br>221<br>1001 0001 | 146<br>222<br>1001 0010 | 147<br>223<br>1001 0011 | 148<br>224<br>1001 0100 | 149<br>225<br>1001 0101 | 150<br>226<br>1001 0110 | 151<br>227<br>1001 0111 | 152<br>230<br>1001 1000 | 153<br>231<br>1001 1001 | 154<br>232<br>1001 1010 | 155<br>233<br>1001 1011 | 156<br>234<br>1001 1100 | 157<br>235<br>1001 1101 | 158<br>236<br>1001 1110 | 159<br>237<br>1001 1111 |
| **A−** | 160<br>240<br>1010 0000 | 161<br>241<br>1010 0001 | 162<br>242<br>1010 0010 | 163<br>243<br>1010 0011 | 164<br>244<br>1010 0100 | 165<br>245<br>1010 0101 | 166<br>246<br>1010 0110 | 167<br>247<br>1010 0111 | 168<br>250<br>1010 1000 | 169<br>251<br>1010 1001 | 170<br>252<br>1010 1010 | 171<br>253<br>1010 1011 | 172<br>254<br>1010 1100 | 173<br>255<br>1010 1101 | 174<br>256<br>1010 1110 | 175<br>257<br>1010 1111 |
| **B−** | 176<br>260<br>1011 0000 | 177<br>261<br>1011 0001 | 178<br>262<br>1011 0010 | 179<br>263<br>1011 0011 | 180<br>264<br>1011 0100 | 181<br>265<br>1011 0101 | 182<br>266<br>1011 0110 | 183<br>267<br>1011 0111 | 184<br>270<br>1011 1000 | 185<br>271<br>1011 1001 | 186<br>272<br>1011 1010 | 187<br>273<br>1011 1011 | 188<br>274<br>1011 1100 | 189<br>275<br>1011 1101 | 190<br>276<br>1011 1110 | 191<br>277<br>1011 1111 |
| **C−** | 192<br>300<br>1100 0000 | 193<br>301<br>1100 0001 | 194<br>302<br>1100 0010 | 195<br>303<br>1100 0011 | 196<br>304<br>1100 0100 | 197<br>305<br>1100 0101 | 198<br>306<br>1100 0110 | 199<br>307<br>1100 0111 | 200<br>310<br>1100 1000 | 201<br>311<br>1100 1001 | 202<br>312<br>1100 1010 | 203<br>313<br>1100 1011 | 204<br>314<br>1100 1100 | 205<br>315<br>1100 1101 | 206<br>316<br>1100 1110 | 207<br>317<br>1100 1111 |
| **D−** | 208<br>320<br>1101 0000 | 209<br>321<br>1101 0001 | 210<br>322<br>1101 0010 | 211<br>323<br>1101 0011 | 212<br>324<br>1101 0100 | 213<br>325<br>1101 0101 | 214<br>326<br>1101 0110 | 215<br>327<br>1101 0111 | 216<br>330<br>1101 1000 | 217<br>331<br>1101 1001 | 218<br>332<br>1101 1010 | 219<br>333<br>1101 1011 | 220<br>334<br>1101 1100 | 221<br>335<br>1101 1101 | 222<br>336<br>1101 1110 | 223<br>337<br>1101 1111 |
| **E−** | 224<br>340<br>1110 0000 | 225<br>341<br>1110 0001 | 226<br>342<br>1110 0010 | 227<br>343<br>1110 0011 | 228<br>344<br>1110 0100 | 229<br>345<br>1110 0101 | 230<br>346<br>1110 0110 | 231<br>347<br>1110 0111 | 232<br>350<br>1110 1000 | 233<br>351<br>1110 1001 | 234<br>352<br>1110 1010 | 235<br>353<br>1110 1011 | 236<br>354<br>1110 1100 | 237<br>355<br>1110 1101 | 238<br>356<br>1110 1110 | 239<br>357<br>1110 1111 |
| **F−** | 240<br>360<br>1111 0000 | 241<br>361<br>1111 0001 | 242<br>362<br>1111 0010 | 243<br>363<br>1111 0011 | 244<br>364<br>1111 0100 | 245<br>365<br>1111 0101 | 246<br>366<br>1111 0110 | 247<br>367<br>1111 0111 | 248<br>370<br>1111 1000 | 249<br>371<br>1111 1001 | 250<br>372<br>1111 1010 | 251<br>373<br>1111 1011 | 252<br>374<br>1111 1100 | 253<br>375<br>1111 1101 | 254<br>376<br>1111 1110 | 255<br>377<br>1111 1111 |

## CHRONICLE ONE ·· BINARY-DECIMAL-HEXADECIMAL-OCTAL (8 BIT)

# CHRONICLE

**DECIMAL — BINARY — DECIMAL — HEXADECIMAL — OCTAL**

**(SIXTEEN BIT)**

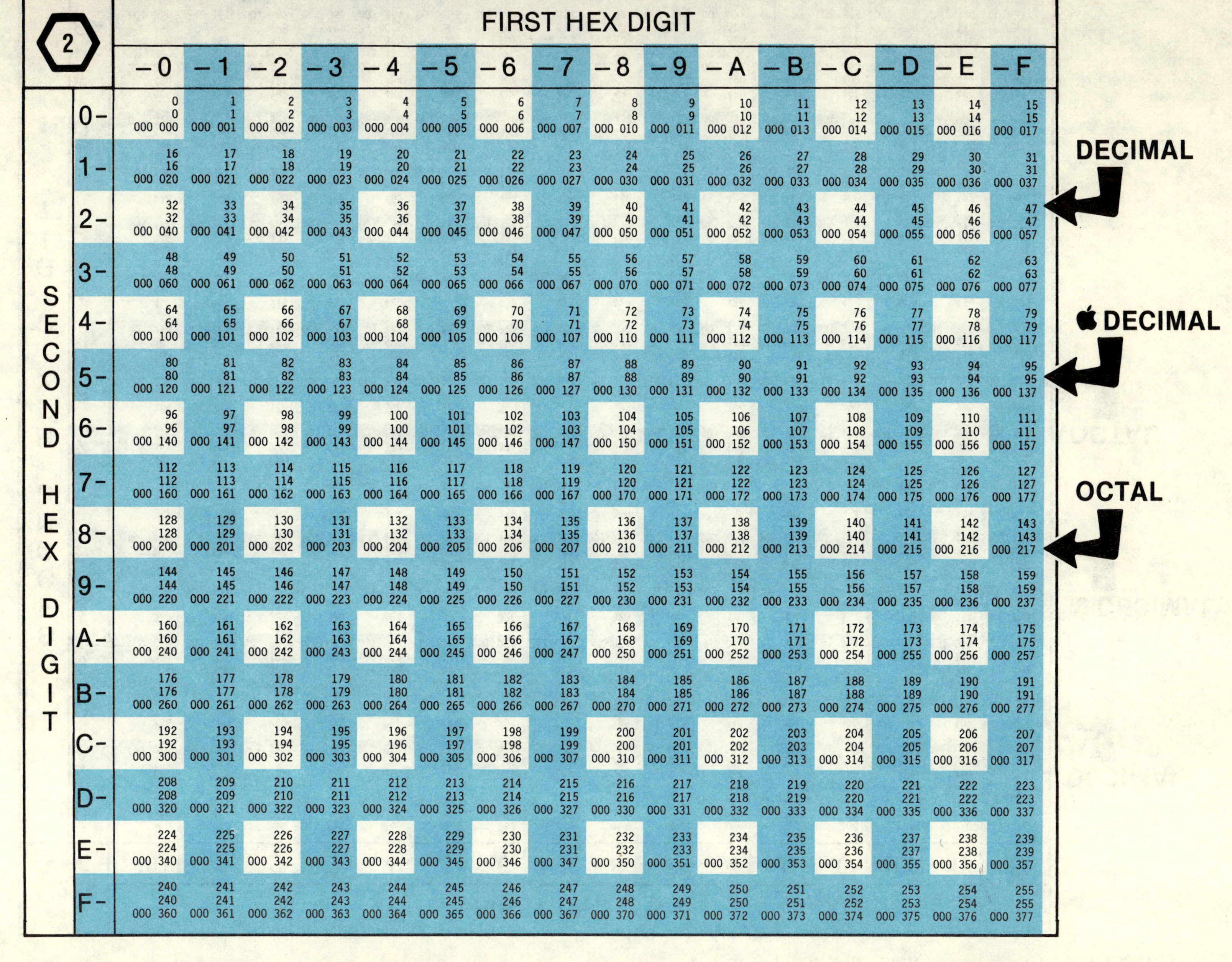



| ② | −0 | −1 | −2 | −3 | −4 | −5 | −6 | −7 | −8 | −9 | −A | −B | −C | −D | −E | −F |
|---|---|---|---|---|---|---|---|---|---|---|---|---|---|---|---|---|
| 0− | 0<br>0<br>000 000 | 1<br>1<br>000 001 | 2<br>2<br>000 002 | 3<br>3<br>000 003 | 4<br>4<br>000 004 | 5<br>5<br>000 005 | 6<br>6<br>000 006 | 7<br>7<br>000 007 | 8<br>8<br>000 010 | 9<br>9<br>000 011 | 10<br>10<br>000 012 | 11<br>11<br>000 013 | 12<br>12<br>000 014 | 13<br>13<br>000 015 | 14<br>14<br>000 016 | 15<br>15<br>000 017 |
| 1− | 16<br>16<br>000 020 | 17<br>17<br>000 021 | 18<br>18<br>000 022 | 19<br>19<br>000 023 | 20<br>20<br>000 024 | 21<br>21<br>000 025 | 22<br>22<br>000 026 | 23<br>23<br>000 027 | 24<br>24<br>000 030 | 25<br>25<br>000 031 | 26<br>26<br>000 032 | 27<br>27<br>000 033 | 28<br>28<br>000 034 | 29<br>29<br>000 035 | 30<br>30<br>000 036 | 31<br>31<br>000 037 |
| 2− | 32<br>32<br>000 040 | 33<br>33<br>000 041 | 34<br>34<br>000 042 | 35<br>35<br>000 043 | 36<br>36<br>000 044 | 37<br>37<br>000 045 | 38<br>38<br>000 046 | 39<br>39<br>000 047 | 40<br>40<br>000 050 | 41<br>41<br>000 051 | 42<br>42<br>000 052 | 43<br>43<br>000 053 | 44<br>44<br>000 054 | 45<br>45<br>000 055 | 46<br>46<br>000 056 | 47<br>47<br>000 057 |
| 3− | 48<br>48<br>000 060 | 49<br>49<br>000 061 | 50<br>50<br>000 062 | 51<br>51<br>000 063 | 52<br>52<br>000 064 | 53<br>53<br>000 065 | 54<br>54<br>000 066 | 55<br>55<br>000 067 | 56<br>56<br>000 070 | 57<br>57<br>000 071 | 58<br>58<br>000 072 | 59<br>59<br>000 073 | 60<br>60<br>000 074 | 61<br>61<br>000 075 | 62<br>62<br>000 076 | 63<br>63<br>000 077 |
| 4− | 64<br>64<br>000 100 | 65<br>65<br>000 101 | 66<br>66<br>000 102 | 67<br>67<br>000 103 | 68<br>68<br>000 104 | 69<br>69<br>000 105 | 70<br>70<br>000 106 | 71<br>71<br>000 107 | 72<br>72<br>000 110 | 73<br>73<br>000 111 | 74<br>74<br>000 112 | 75<br>75<br>000 113 | 76<br>76<br>000 114 | 77<br>77<br>000 115 | 78<br>78<br>000 116 | 79<br>79<br>000 117 |
| 5− | 80<br>80<br>000 120 | 81<br>81<br>000 121 | 82<br>82<br>000 122 | 83<br>83<br>000 123 | 84<br>84<br>000 124 | 85<br>85<br>000 125 | 86<br>86<br>000 126 | 87<br>87<br>000 127 | 88<br>88<br>000 130 | 89<br>89<br>000 131 | 90<br>90<br>000 132 | 91<br>91<br>000 133 | 92<br>92<br>000 134 | 93<br>93<br>000 135 | 94<br>94<br>000 136 | 95<br>95<br>000 137 |
| 6− | 96<br>96<br>000 140 | 97<br>97<br>000 141 | 98<br>98<br>000 142 | 99<br>99<br>000 143 | 100<br>100<br>000 144 | 101<br>101<br>000 145 | 102<br>102<br>000 146 | 103<br>103<br>000 147 | 104<br>104<br>000 150 | 105<br>105<br>000 151 | 106<br>106<br>000 152 | 107<br>107<br>000 153 | 108<br>108<br>000 154 | 109<br>109<br>000 155 | 110<br>110<br>000 156 | 111<br>111<br>000 157 |
| 7− | 112<br>112<br>000 160 | 113<br>113<br>000 161 | 114<br>114<br>000 162 | 115<br>115<br>000 163 | 116<br>116<br>000 164 | 117<br>117<br>000 165 | 118<br>118<br>000 166 | 119<br>119<br>000 167 | 120<br>120<br>000 170 | 121<br>121<br>000 171 | 122<br>122<br>000 172 | 123<br>123<br>000 173 | 124<br>124<br>000 174 | 125<br>125<br>000 175 | 126<br>126<br>000 176 | 127<br>127<br>000 177 |
| 8− | 128<br>128<br>000 200 | 129<br>129<br>000 201 | 130<br>130<br>000 202 | 131<br>131<br>000 203 | 132<br>132<br>000 204 | 133<br>133<br>000 205 | 134<br>134<br>000 206 | 135<br>135<br>000 207 | 136<br>136<br>000 210 | 137<br>137<br>000 211 | 138<br>138<br>000 212 | 139<br>139<br>000 213 | 140<br>140<br>000 214 | 141<br>141<br>000 215 | 142<br>142<br>000 216 | 143<br>143<br>000 217 |
| 9− | 144<br>144<br>000 220 | 145<br>145<br>000 221 | 146<br>146<br>000 222 | 147<br>147<br>000 223 | 148<br>148<br>000 224 | 149<br>149<br>000 225 | 150<br>150<br>000 226 | 151<br>151<br>000 227 | 152<br>152<br>000 230 | 153<br>153<br>000 231 | 154<br>154<br>000 232 | 155<br>155<br>000 233 | 156<br>156<br>000 234 | 157<br>157<br>000 235 | 158<br>158<br>000 236 | 159<br>159<br>000 237 |
| A− | 160<br>160<br>000 240 | 161<br>161<br>000 241 | 162<br>162<br>000 242 | 163<br>163<br>000 243 | 164<br>164<br>000 244 | 165<br>165<br>000 245 | 166<br>166<br>000 246 | 167<br>167<br>000 247 | 168<br>168<br>000 250 | 169<br>169<br>000 251 | 170<br>170<br>000 252 | 171<br>171<br>000 253 | 172<br>172<br>000 254 | 173<br>173<br>000 255 | 174<br>174<br>000 256 | 175<br>175<br>000 257 |
| B− | 176<br>176<br>000 260 | 177<br>177<br>000 261 | 178<br>178<br>000 262 | 179<br>179<br>000 263 | 180<br>180<br>000 264 | 181<br>181<br>000 265 | 182<br>182<br>000 266 | 183<br>183<br>000 267 | 184<br>184<br>000 270 | 185<br>185<br>000 271 | 186<br>186<br>000 272 | 187<br>187<br>000 273 | 188<br>188<br>000 274 | 189<br>189<br>000 275 | 190<br>190<br>000 276 | 191<br>191<br>000 277 |
| C− | 192<br>192<br>000 300 | 193<br>193<br>000 301 | 194<br>194<br>000 302 | 195<br>195<br>000 303 | 196<br>196<br>000 304 | 197<br>197<br>000 305 | 198<br>198<br>000 306 | 199<br>199<br>000 307 | 200<br>200<br>000 310 | 201<br>201<br>000 311 | 202<br>202<br>000 312 | 203<br>203<br>000 313 | 204<br>204<br>000 314 | 205<br>205<br>000 315 | 206<br>206<br>000 316 | 207<br>207<br>000 317 |
| D− | 208<br>208<br>000 320 | 209<br>209<br>000 321 | 210<br>210<br>000 322 | 211<br>211<br>000 323 | 212<br>212<br>000 324 | 213<br>213<br>000 325 | 214<br>214<br>000 326 | 215<br>215<br>000 327 | 216<br>216<br>000 330 | 217<br>217<br>000 331 | 218<br>218<br>000 332 | 219<br>219<br>000 333 | 220<br>220<br>000 334 | 221<br>221<br>000 335 | 222<br>222<br>000 336 | 223<br>223<br>000 337 |
| E− | 224<br>224<br>000 340 | 225<br>225<br>000 341 | 226<br>226<br>000 342 | 227<br>227<br>000 343 | 228<br>228<br>000 344 | 229<br>229<br>000 345 | 230<br>230<br>000 346 | 231<br>231<br>000 347 | 232<br>232<br>000 350 | 233<br>233<br>000 351 | 234<br>234<br>000 352 | 235<br>235<br>000 353 | 236<br>236<br>000 354 | 237<br>237<br>000 355 | 238<br>238<br>000 356 | 239<br>239<br>000 357 |
| F− | 240<br>240<br>000 360 | 241<br>241<br>000 361 | 242<br>242<br>000 362 | 243<br>243<br>000 363 | 244<br>244<br>000 364 | 245<br>245<br>000 365 | 246<br>246<br>000 366 | 247<br>247<br>000 367 | 248<br>248<br>000 370 | 249<br>249<br>000 371 | 250<br>250<br>000 372 | 251<br>251<br>000 373 | 252<br>252<br>000 374 | 253<br>253<br>000 375 | 254<br>254<br>000 376 | 255<br>255<br>000 377 |

 DECIMAL [ 0 ]　BINARY [ 0000 0000 ]　DECIMAL [ 0 ]　HEXADECIMAL ⬡ 00　OCTAL [ 000 000 ]

FOURTH HEX DIGIT　　THIRD HEX DIGIT

FIRST HEX DIGIT

| ⬡2 | −0 | −1 | −2 | −3 | −4 | −5 | −6 | −7 | −8 | −9 | −A | −B | −C | −D | −E | −F |
|---|---|---|---|---|---|---|---|---|---|---|---|---|---|---|---|---|
| 0− | 256 / 001 000 | 257 / 001 001 | 258 / 001 002 | 259 / 001 003 | 260 / 001 004 | 261 / 001 005 | 262 / 001 006 | 263 / 001 007 | 264 / 001 010 | 265 / 001 011 | 266 / 001 012 | 267 / 001 013 | 268 / 001 014 | 269 / 001 015 | 270 / 001 016 | 271 / 001 017 |
| 1− | 272 / 001 020 | 273 / 001 021 | 274 / 001 022 | 275 / 001 023 | 276 / 001 024 | 277 / 001 025 | 278 / 001 026 | 279 / 001 027 | 280 / 001 030 | 281 / 001 031 | 282 / 001 032 | 283 / 001 033 | 284 / 001 034 | 285 / 001 035 | 286 / 001 036 | 287 / 001 037 |
| 2− | 288 / 001 040 | 289 / 001 041 | 290 / 001 042 | 291 / 001 043 | 292 / 001 044 | 293 / 001 045 | 294 / 001 046 | 295 / 001 047 | 296 / 001 050 | 297 / 001 051 | 298 / 001 052 | 299 / 001 053 | 300 / 001 054 | 301 / 001 055 | 302 / 001 056 | 303 / 001 057 |
| 3− | 304 / 001 060 | 305 / 001 061 | 306 / 001 062 | 307 / 001 063 | 308 / 001 064 | 309 / 001 065 | 310 / 001 066 | 311 / 001 067 | 312 / 001 070 | 313 / 001 071 | 314 / 001 072 | 315 / 001 073 | 316 / 001 074 | 317 / 001 075 | 318 / 001 076 | 319 / 001 077 |
| 4− | 320 / 001 100 | 321 / 001 101 | 322 / 001 102 | 323 / 001 103 | 324 / 001 104 | 325 / 001 105 | 326 / 001 106 | 327 / 001 107 | 328 / 001 110 | 329 / 001 111 | 330 / 001 112 | 331 / 001 113 | 332 / 001 114 | 333 / 001 115 | 334 / 001 116 | 335 / 001 117 |
| 5− | 336 / 001 120 | 337 / 001 121 | 338 / 001 122 | 339 / 001 123 | 340 / 001 124 | 341 / 001 125 | 342 / 001 126 | 343 / 001 127 | 344 / 001 130 | 345 / 001 131 | 346 / 001 132 | 347 / 001 133 | 348 / 001 134 | 349 / 001 135 | 350 / 001 136 | 351 / 001 137 |
| 6− | 352 / 001 140 | 353 / 001 141 | 354 / 001 142 | 355 / 001 143 | 356 / 001 144 | 357 / 001 145 | 358 / 001 146 | 359 / 001 147 | 360 / 001 150 | 361 / 001 151 | 362 / 001 152 | 363 / 001 153 | 364 / 001 154 | 365 / 001 155 | 366 / 001 156 | 367 / 001 157 |
| 7− | 368 / 001 160 | 369 / 001 161 | 370 / 001 162 | 371 / 001 163 | 372 / 001 164 | 373 / 001 165 | 374 / 001 166 | 375 / 001 167 | 376 / 001 170 | 377 / 001 171 | 378 / 001 172 | 379 / 001 173 | 380 / 001 174 | 381 / 001 175 | 382 / 001 176 | 383 / 001 177 |
| 8− | 384 / 001 200 | 385 / 001 201 | 386 / 001 202 | 387 / 001 203 | 388 / 001 204 | 389 / 001 205 | 390 / 001 206 | 391 / 001 207 | 392 / 001 210 | 393 / 001 211 | 394 / 001 212 | 395 / 001 213 | 396 / 001 214 | 397 / 001 215 | 398 / 001 216 | 399 / 001 217 |
| 9− | 400 / 001 220 | 401 / 001 221 | 402 / 001 222 | 403 / 001 223 | 404 / 001 224 | 405 / 001 225 | 406 / 001 226 | 407 / 001 227 | 408 / 001 230 | 409 / 001 231 | 410 / 001 232 | 411 / 001 233 | 412 / 001 234 | 413 / 001 235 | 414 / 001 236 | 415 / 001 237 |
| A− | 416 / 001 240 | 417 / 001 241 | 418 / 001 242 | 419 / 001 243 | 420 / 001 244 | 421 / 001 245 | 422 / 001 246 | 423 / 001 247 | 424 / 001 250 | 425 / 001 251 | 426 / 001 252 | 427 / 001 253 | 428 / 001 254 | 429 / 001 255 | 430 / 001 256 | 431 / 001 257 |
| B− | 432 / 001 260 | 433 / 001 261 | 434 / 001 262 | 435 / 001 263 | 436 / 001 264 | 437 / 001 265 | 438 / 001 266 | 439 / 001 267 | 440 / 001 270 | 441 / 001 271 | 442 / 001 272 | 443 / 001 273 | 444 / 001 274 | 445 / 001 275 | 446 / 001 276 | 447 / 001 277 |
| C− | 448 / 001 300 | 449 / 001 301 | 450 / 001 302 | 451 / 001 303 | 452 / 001 304 | 453 / 001 305 | 454 / 001 306 | 455 / 001 307 | 456 / 001 310 | 457 / 001 311 | 458 / 001 312 | 459 / 001 313 | 460 / 001 314 | 461 / 001 315 | 462 / 001 316 | 463 / 001 317 |
| D− | 464 / 001 320 | 465 / 001 321 | 466 / 001 322 | 467 / 001 323 | 468 / 001 324 | 469 / 001 325 | 470 / 001 326 | 471 / 001 327 | 472 / 001 330 | 473 / 001 331 | 474 / 001 332 | 475 / 001 333 | 476 / 001 334 | 477 / 001 335 | 478 / 001 336 | 479 / 001 337 |
| E− | 480 / 001 340 | 481 / 001 341 | 482 / 001 342 | 483 / 001 343 | 484 / 001 344 | 485 / 001 345 | 486 / 001 346 | 487 / 001 347 | 488 / 001 350 | 489 / 001 351 | 490 / 001 352 | 491 / 001 353 | 492 / 001 354 | 493 / 001 355 | 494 / 001 356 | 495 / 001 357 |
| F− | 496 / 001 360 | 497 / 001 361 | 498 / 001 362 | 499 / 001 363 | 500 / 001 364 | 501 / 001 365 | 502 / 001 366 | 503 / 001 367 | 504 / 001 370 | 505 / 001 371 | 506 / 001 372 | 507 / 001 373 | 508 / 001 374 | 509 / 001 375 | 510 / 001 376 | 511 / 001 377 |

SECOND HEX DIGIT

DECIMAL

 DECIMAL

OCTAL

# FIRST HEX DIGIT

Hexagon label: **2**

Arrows (right side): DECIMAL, DECIMAL, OCTAL

Each cell lists: (Apple) DECIMAL / DECIMAL / OCTAL

| SECOND HEX DIGIT | −0 | −1 | −2 | −3 | −4 | −5 | −6 | −7 | −8 | −9 | −A | −B | −C | −D | −E | −F |
|---|---|---|---|---|---|---|---|---|---|---|---|---|---|---|---|---|
| 0− | 512 512 002 000 | 513 513 002 001 | 514 514 002 002 | 515 515 002 003 | 516 516 002 004 | 517 517 002 005 | 518 518 002 006 | 519 519 002 007 | 520 520 002 010 | 521 521 002 011 | 522 522 002 012 | 523 523 002 013 | 524 524 002 014 | 525 525 002 015 | 526 526 002 016 | 527 527 002 017 |
| 1− | 528 528 002 020 | 529 529 002 021 | 530 530 002 022 | 531 531 002 023 | 532 532 002 024 | 533 533 002 025 | 534 534 002 026 | 535 535 002 027 | 536 536 002 030 | 537 537 002 031 | 538 538 002 032 | 539 539 002 033 | 540 540 002 034 | 541 541 002 035 | 542 542 002 036 | 543 543 002 037 |
| 2− | 544 544 002 040 | 545 545 002 041 | 546 546 002 042 | 547 547 002 043 | 548 548 002 044 | 549 549 002 045 | 550 550 002 046 | 551 551 002 047 | 552 552 002 050 | 553 553 002 051 | 554 554 002 052 | 555 555 002 053 | 556 556 002 054 | 557 557 002 055 | 558 558 002 056 | 559 559 002 057 |
| 3− | 560 560 002 060 | 561 561 002 061 | 562 562 002 062 | 563 563 002 063 | 564 564 002 064 | 565 565 002 065 | 566 566 002 066 | 567 567 002 067 | 568 568 002 070 | 569 569 002 071 | 570 570 002 072 | 571 571 002 073 | 572 572 002 074 | 573 573 002 075 | 574 574 002 076 | 575 575 002 077 |
| 4− | 576 576 002 100 | 577 577 002 101 | 578 578 002 102 | 579 579 002 103 | 580 580 002 104 | 581 581 002 105 | 582 582 002 106 | 583 583 002 107 | 584 584 002 110 | 585 585 002 111 | 586 586 002 112 | 587 587 002 113 | 588 588 002 114 | 589 589 002 115 | 590 590 002 116 | 591 591 002 117 |
| 5− | 592 592 002 120 | 593 593 002 121 | 594 594 002 122 | 595 595 002 123 | 596 596 002 124 | 597 597 002 125 | 598 598 002 126 | 599 599 002 127 | 600 600 002 130 | 601 601 002 131 | 602 602 002 132 | 603 603 002 133 | 604 604 002 134 | 605 605 002 135 | 606 606 002 136 | 607 607 002 137 |
| 6− | 608 608 002 140 | 609 609 002 141 | 610 610 002 142 | 611 611 002 143 | 612 612 002 144 | 613 613 002 145 | 614 614 002 146 | 615 615 002 147 | 616 616 002 150 | 617 617 002 151 | 618 618 002 152 | 619 619 002 153 | 620 620 002 154 | 621 621 002 155 | 622 622 002 156 | 623 623 002 157 |
| 7− | 624 624 002 160 | 625 625 002 161 | 626 626 002 162 | 627 627 002 163 | 628 628 002 164 | 629 629 002 165 | 630 630 002 166 | 631 631 002 167 | 632 632 002 170 | 633 633 002 171 | 634 634 002 172 | 635 635 002 173 | 636 636 002 174 | 637 637 002 175 | 638 638 002 176 | 639 639 002 177 |
| 8− | 640 640 002 200 | 641 641 002 201 | 642 642 002 202 | 643 643 002 203 | 644 644 002 204 | 645 645 002 205 | 646 646 002 206 | 647 647 002 207 | 648 648 002 210 | 649 649 002 211 | 650 650 002 212 | 651 651 002 213 | 652 652 002 214 | 653 653 002 215 | 654 654 002 216 | 655 655 002 217 |
| 9− | 656 656 002 220 | 657 657 002 221 | 658 658 002 222 | 659 659 002 223 | 660 660 002 224 | 661 661 002 225 | 662 662 002 226 | 663 663 002 227 | 664 664 002 230 | 665 665 002 231 | 666 666 002 232 | 667 667 002 233 | 668 668 002 234 | 669 669 002 235 | 670 670 002 236 | 671 671 002 237 |
| A− | 672 672 002 240 | 673 673 002 241 | 674 674 002 242 | 675 675 002 243 | 676 676 002 244 | 677 677 002 245 | 678 678 002 246 | 679 679 002 247 | 680 680 002 250 | 681 681 002 251 | 682 682 002 252 | 683 683 002 253 | 684 684 002 254 | 685 685 002 255 | 686 686 002 256 | 687 687 002 257 |
| B− | 688 688 002 260 | 689 689 002 261 | 690 690 002 262 | 691 691 002 263 | 692 692 002 264 | 693 693 002 265 | 694 694 002 266 | 695 695 002 267 | 696 696 002 270 | 697 697 002 271 | 698 698 002 272 | 699 699 002 273 | 700 700 002 274 | 701 701 002 275 | 702 702 002 276 | 703 703 002 277 |
| C− | 704 704 002 300 | 705 705 002 301 | 706 706 002 302 | 707 707 002 303 | 708 708 002 304 | 709 709 002 305 | 710 710 002 306 | 711 711 002 307 | 712 712 002 310 | 713 713 002 311 | 714 714 002 312 | 715 715 002 313 | 716 716 002 314 | 717 717 002 315 | 718 718 002 316 | 719 719 002 317 |
| D− | 720 720 002 320 | 721 721 002 321 | 722 722 002 322 | 723 723 002 323 | 724 724 002 324 | 725 725 002 325 | 726 726 002 326 | 727 727 002 327 | 728 728 002 330 | 729 729 002 331 | 730 730 002 332 | 731 731 002 333 | 732 732 002 334 | 733 733 002 335 | 734 734 002 336 | 735 735 002 337 |
| E− | 736 736 002 340 | 737 737 002 341 | 738 738 002 342 | 739 739 002 343 | 740 740 002 344 | 741 741 002 345 | 742 742 002 346 | 743 743 002 347 | 744 744 002 350 | 745 745 002 351 | 746 746 002 352 | 747 747 002 353 | 748 748 002 354 | 749 749 002 355 | 750 750 002 356 | 751 751 002 357 |
| F− | 752 752 002 360 | 753 753 002 361 | 754 754 002 362 | 755 755 002 363 | 756 756 002 364 | 757 757 002 365 | 758 758 002 366 | 759 759 002 367 | 760 760 002 370 | 761 761 002 371 | 762 762 002 372 | 763 763 002 373 | 764 764 002 374 | 765 765 002 375 | 766 766 002 376 | 767 767 002 377 |

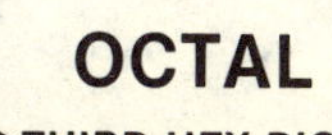 DECIMAL `512`   BINARY `0000 0010`   DECIMAL `512`   HEXADECIMAL `02`   OCTAL `002 000`

FOURTH HEX DIGIT → `0` ← THIRD HEX DIGIT

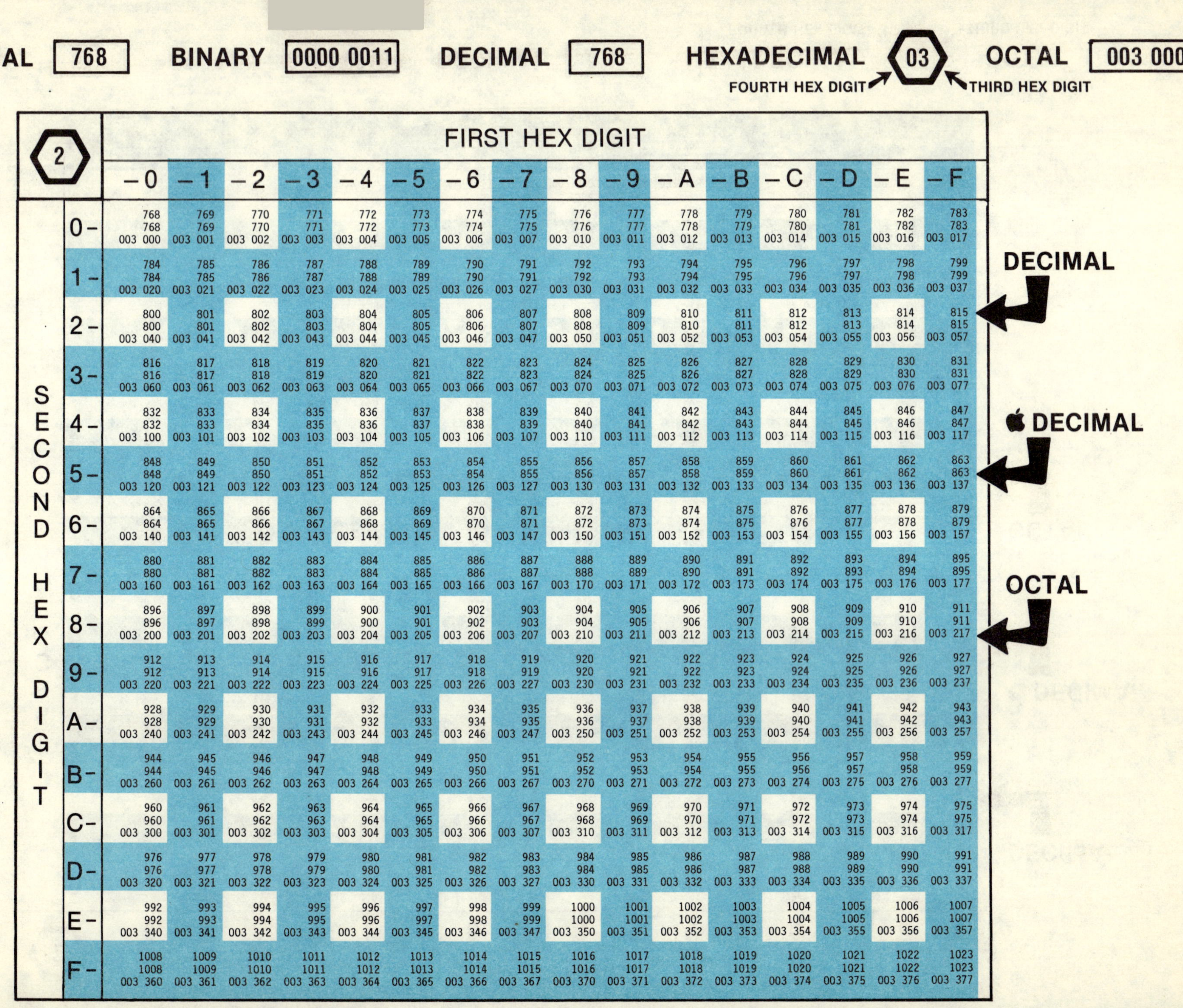



| (2) | FIRST HEX DIGIT | | | | | | | | | | | | | | | |
|---|---|---|---|---|---|---|---|---|---|---|---|---|---|---|---|---|
| | −0 | −1 | −2 | −3 | −4 | −5 | −6 | −7 | −8 | −9 | −A | −B | −C | −D | −E | −F |
| 0− | 768<br>768<br>003 000 | 769<br>769<br>003 001 | 770<br>770<br>003 002 | 771<br>771<br>003 003 | 772<br>772<br>003 004 | 773<br>773<br>003 005 | 774<br>774<br>003 006 | 775<br>775<br>003 007 | 776<br>776<br>003 010 | 777<br>777<br>003 011 | 778<br>778<br>003 012 | 779<br>779<br>003 013 | 780<br>780<br>003 014 | 781<br>781<br>003 015 | 782<br>782<br>003 016 | 783<br>783<br>003 017 |
| 1− | 784<br>784<br>003 020 | 785<br>785<br>003 021 | 786<br>786<br>003 022 | 787<br>787<br>003 023 | 788<br>788<br>003 024 | 789<br>789<br>003 025 | 790<br>790<br>003 026 | 791<br>791<br>003 027 | 792<br>792<br>003 030 | 793<br>793<br>003 031 | 794<br>794<br>003 032 | 795<br>795<br>003 033 | 796<br>796<br>003 034 | 797<br>797<br>003 035 | 798<br>798<br>003 036 | 799<br>799<br>003 037 |
| 2− | 800<br>800<br>003 040 | 801<br>801<br>003 041 | 802<br>802<br>003 042 | 803<br>803<br>003 043 | 804<br>804<br>003 044 | 805<br>805<br>003 045 | 806<br>806<br>003 046 | 807<br>807<br>003 047 | 808<br>808<br>003 050 | 809<br>809<br>003 051 | 810<br>810<br>003 052 | 811<br>811<br>003 053 | 812<br>812<br>003 054 | 813<br>813<br>003 055 | 814<br>814<br>003 056 | 815<br>815<br>003 057 |
| 3− | 816<br>816<br>003 060 | 817<br>817<br>003 061 | 818<br>818<br>003 062 | 819<br>819<br>003 063 | 820<br>820<br>003 064 | 821<br>821<br>003 065 | 822<br>822<br>003 066 | 823<br>823<br>003 067 | 824<br>824<br>003 070 | 825<br>825<br>003 071 | 826<br>826<br>003 072 | 827<br>827<br>003 073 | 828<br>828<br>003 074 | 829<br>829<br>003 075 | 830<br>830<br>003 076 | 831<br>831<br>003 077 |
| 4− | 832<br>832<br>003 100 | 833<br>833<br>003 101 | 834<br>834<br>003 102 | 835<br>835<br>003 103 | 836<br>836<br>003 104 | 837<br>837<br>003 105 | 838<br>838<br>003 106 | 839<br>839<br>003 107 | 840<br>840<br>003 110 | 841<br>841<br>003 111 | 842<br>842<br>003 112 | 843<br>843<br>003 113 | 844<br>844<br>003 114 | 845<br>845<br>003 115 | 846<br>846<br>003 116 | 847<br>847<br>003 117 |
| 5− | 848<br>848<br>003 120 | 849<br>849<br>003 121 | 850<br>850<br>003 122 | 851<br>851<br>003 123 | 852<br>852<br>003 124 | 853<br>853<br>003 125 | 854<br>854<br>003 126 | 855<br>855<br>003 127 | 856<br>856<br>003 130 | 857<br>857<br>003 131 | 858<br>858<br>003 132 | 859<br>859<br>003 133 | 860<br>860<br>003 134 | 861<br>861<br>003 135 | 862<br>862<br>003 136 | 863<br>863<br>003 137 |
| 6− | 864<br>864<br>003 140 | 865<br>865<br>003 141 | 866<br>866<br>003 142 | 867<br>867<br>003 143 | 868<br>868<br>003 144 | 869<br>869<br>003 145 | 870<br>870<br>003 146 | 871<br>871<br>003 147 | 872<br>872<br>003 150 | 873<br>873<br>003 151 | 874<br>874<br>003 152 | 875<br>875<br>003 153 | 876<br>876<br>003 154 | 877<br>877<br>003 155 | 878<br>878<br>003 156 | 879<br>879<br>003 157 |
| 7− | 880<br>880<br>003 160 | 881<br>881<br>003 161 | 882<br>882<br>003 162 | 883<br>883<br>003 163 | 884<br>884<br>003 164 | 885<br>885<br>003 165 | 886<br>886<br>003 166 | 887<br>887<br>003 167 | 888<br>888<br>003 170 | 889<br>889<br>003 171 | 890<br>890<br>003 172 | 891<br>891<br>003 173 | 892<br>892<br>003 174 | 893<br>893<br>003 175 | 894<br>894<br>003 176 | 895<br>895<br>003 177 |
| 8− | 896<br>896<br>003 200 | 897<br>897<br>003 201 | 898<br>898<br>003 202 | 899<br>899<br>003 203 | 900<br>900<br>003 204 | 901<br>901<br>003 205 | 902<br>902<br>003 206 | 903<br>903<br>003 207 | 904<br>904<br>003 210 | 905<br>905<br>003 211 | 906<br>906<br>003 212 | 907<br>907<br>003 213 | 908<br>908<br>003 214 | 909<br>909<br>003 215 | 910<br>910<br>003 216 | 911<br>911<br>003 217 |
| 9− | 912<br>912<br>003 220 | 913<br>913<br>003 221 | 914<br>914<br>003 222 | 915<br>915<br>003 223 | 916<br>916<br>003 224 | 917<br>917<br>003 225 | 918<br>918<br>003 226 | 919<br>919<br>003 227 | 920<br>920<br>003 230 | 921<br>921<br>003 231 | 922<br>922<br>003 232 | 923<br>923<br>003 233 | 924<br>924<br>003 234 | 925<br>925<br>003 235 | 926<br>926<br>003 236 | 927<br>927<br>003 237 |
| A− | 928<br>928<br>003 240 | 929<br>929<br>003 241 | 930<br>930<br>003 242 | 931<br>931<br>003 243 | 932<br>932<br>003 244 | 933<br>933<br>003 245 | 934<br>934<br>003 246 | 935<br>935<br>003 247 | 936<br>936<br>003 250 | 937<br>937<br>003 251 | 938<br>938<br>003 252 | 939<br>939<br>003 253 | 940<br>940<br>003 254 | 941<br>941<br>003 255 | 942<br>942<br>003 256 | 943<br>943<br>003 257 |
| B− | 944<br>944<br>003 260 | 945<br>945<br>003 261 | 946<br>946<br>003 262 | 947<br>947<br>003 263 | 948<br>948<br>003 264 | 949<br>949<br>003 265 | 950<br>950<br>003 266 | 951<br>951<br>003 267 | 952<br>952<br>003 270 | 953<br>953<br>003 271 | 954<br>954<br>003 272 | 955<br>955<br>003 273 | 956<br>956<br>003 274 | 957<br>957<br>003 275 | 958<br>958<br>003 276 | 959<br>959<br>003 277 |
| C− | 960<br>960<br>003 300 | 961<br>961<br>003 301 | 962<br>962<br>003 302 | 963<br>963<br>003 303 | 964<br>964<br>003 304 | 965<br>965<br>003 305 | 966<br>966<br>003 306 | 967<br>967<br>003 307 | 968<br>968<br>003 310 | 969<br>969<br>003 311 | 970<br>970<br>003 312 | 971<br>971<br>003 313 | 972<br>972<br>003 314 | 973<br>973<br>003 315 | 974<br>974<br>003 316 | 975<br>975<br>003 317 |
| D− | 976<br>976<br>003 320 | 977<br>977<br>003 321 | 978<br>978<br>003 322 | 979<br>979<br>003 323 | 980<br>980<br>003 324 | 981<br>981<br>003 325 | 982<br>982<br>003 326 | 983<br>983<br>003 327 | 984<br>984<br>003 330 | 985<br>985<br>003 331 | 986<br>986<br>003 332 | 987<br>987<br>003 333 | 988<br>988<br>003 334 | 989<br>989<br>003 335 | 990<br>990<br>003 336 | 991<br>991<br>003 337 |
| E− | 992<br>992<br>003 340 | 993<br>993<br>003 341 | 994<br>994<br>003 342 | 995<br>995<br>003 343 | 996<br>996<br>003 344 | 997<br>997<br>003 345 | 998<br>998<br>003 346 | 999<br>999<br>003 347 | 1000<br>1000<br>003 350 | 1001<br>1001<br>003 351 | 1002<br>1002<br>003 352 | 1003<br>1003<br>003 353 | 1004<br>1004<br>003 354 | 1005<br>1005<br>003 355 | 1006<br>1006<br>003 356 | 1007<br>1007<br>003 357 |
| F− | 1008<br>1008<br>003 360 | 1009<br>1009<br>003 361 | 1010<br>1010<br>003 362 | 1011<br>1011<br>003 363 | 1012<br>1012<br>003 364 | 1013<br>1013<br>003 365 | 1014<br>1014<br>003 366 | 1015<br>1015<br>003 367 | 1016<br>1016<br>003 370 | 1017<br>1017<br>003 371 | 1018<br>1018<br>003 372 | 1019<br>1019<br>003 373 | 1020<br>1020<br>003 374 | 1021<br>1021<br>003 375 | 1022<br>1022<br>003 376 | 1023<br>1023<br>003 377 |

| | −0 | −1 | −2 | −3 | −4 | −5 | −6 | −7 | −8 | −9 | −A | −B | −C | −D | −E | −F |
|---|---|---|---|---|---|---|---|---|---|---|---|---|---|---|---|---|
| **0−** | 1024<br>1024<br>004 000 | 1025<br>1025<br>004 001 | 1026<br>1026<br>004 002 | 1027<br>1027<br>004 003 | 1028<br>1028<br>004 004 | 1029<br>1029<br>004 005 | 1030<br>1030<br>004 006 | 1031<br>1031<br>004 007 | 1032<br>1032<br>004 010 | 1033<br>1033<br>004 011 | 1034<br>1034<br>004 012 | 1035<br>1035<br>004 013 | 1036<br>1036<br>004 014 | 1037<br>1037<br>004 015 | 1038<br>1038<br>004 016 | 1039<br>1039<br>004 017 |
| **1−** | 1040<br>1040<br>004 020 | 1041<br>1041<br>004 021 | 1042<br>1042<br>004 022 | 1043<br>1043<br>004 023 | 1044<br>1044<br>004 024 | 1045<br>1045<br>004 025 | 1046<br>1046<br>004 026 | 1047<br>1047<br>004 027 | 1048<br>1048<br>004 030 | 1049<br>1049<br>004 031 | 1050<br>1050<br>004 032 | 1051<br>1051<br>004 033 | 1052<br>1052<br>004 034 | 1053<br>1053<br>004 035 | 1054<br>1054<br>004 036 | 1055<br>1055<br>004 037 |
| **2−** | 1056<br>1056<br>004 040 | 1057<br>1057<br>004 041 | 1058<br>1058<br>004 042 | 1059<br>1059<br>004 043 | 1060<br>1060<br>004 044 | 1061<br>1061<br>004 045 | 1062<br>1062<br>004 046 | 1063<br>1063<br>004 047 | 1064<br>1064<br>004 050 | 1065<br>1065<br>004 051 | 1066<br>1066<br>004 052 | 1067<br>1067<br>004 053 | 1068<br>1068<br>004 054 | 1069<br>1069<br>004 055 | 1070<br>1070<br>004 056 | 1071<br>1071<br>004 057 |
| **3−** | 1072<br>1072<br>004 060 | 1073<br>1073<br>004 061 | 1074<br>1074<br>004 062 | 1075<br>1075<br>004 063 | 1076<br>1076<br>004 064 | 1077<br>1077<br>004 065 | 1078<br>1078<br>004 066 | 1079<br>1079<br>004 067 | 1080<br>1080<br>004 070 | 1081<br>1081<br>004 071 | 1082<br>1082<br>004 072 | 1083<br>1083<br>004 073 | 1084<br>1084<br>004 074 | 1085<br>1085<br>004 075 | 1086<br>1086<br>004 076 | 1087<br>1087<br>004 077 |
| **4−** | 1088<br>1088<br>004 100 | 1089<br>1089<br>004 101 | 1090<br>1090<br>004 102 | 1091<br>1091<br>004 103 | 1092<br>1092<br>004 104 | 1093<br>1093<br>004 105 | 1094<br>1094<br>004 106 | 1095<br>1095<br>004 107 | 1096<br>1096<br>004 110 | 1097<br>1097<br>004 111 | 1098<br>1098<br>004 112 | 1099<br>1099<br>004 113 | 1100<br>1100<br>004 114 | 1101<br>1101<br>004 115 | 1102<br>1102<br>004 116 | 1103<br>1103<br>004 117 |
| **5−** | 1104<br>1104<br>004 120 | 1105<br>1105<br>004 121 | 1106<br>1106<br>004 122 | 1107<br>1107<br>004 123 | 1108<br>1108<br>004 124 | 1109<br>1109<br>004 125 | 1110<br>1110<br>004 126 | 1111<br>1111<br>004 127 | 1112<br>1112<br>004 130 | 1113<br>1113<br>004 131 | 1114<br>1114<br>004 132 | 1115<br>1115<br>004 133 | 1116<br>1116<br>004 134 | 1117<br>1117<br>004 135 | 1118<br>1118<br>004 136 | 1119<br>1119<br>004 137 |
| **6−** | 1120<br>1120<br>004 140 | 1121<br>1121<br>004 141 | 1122<br>1122<br>004 142 | 1123<br>1123<br>004 143 | 1124<br>1124<br>004 144 | 1125<br>1125<br>004 145 | 1126<br>1126<br>004 146 | 1127<br>1127<br>004 147 | 1128<br>1128<br>004 150 | 1129<br>1129<br>004 151 | 1130<br>1130<br>004 152 | 1131<br>1131<br>004 153 | 1132<br>1132<br>004 154 | 1133<br>1133<br>004 155 | 1134<br>1134<br>004 156 | 1135<br>1135<br>004 157 |
| **7−** | 1136<br>1136<br>004 160 | 1137<br>1137<br>004 161 | 1138<br>1138<br>004 162 | 1139<br>1139<br>004 163 | 1140<br>1140<br>004 164 | 1141<br>1141<br>004 165 | 1142<br>1142<br>004 166 | 1143<br>1143<br>004 167 | 1144<br>1144<br>004 170 | 1145<br>1145<br>004 171 | 1146<br>1146<br>004 172 | 1147<br>1147<br>004 173 | 1148<br>1148<br>004 174 | 1149<br>1149<br>004 175 | 1150<br>1150<br>004 176 | 1151<br>1151<br>004 177 |
| **8−** | 1152<br>1152<br>004 200 | 1153<br>1153<br>004 201 | 1154<br>1154<br>004 202 | 1155<br>1155<br>004 203 | 1156<br>1156<br>004 204 | 1157<br>1157<br>004 205 | 1158<br>1158<br>004 206 | 1159<br>1159<br>004 207 | 1160<br>1160<br>004 210 | 1161<br>1161<br>004 211 | 1162<br>1162<br>004 212 | 1163<br>1163<br>004 213 | 1164<br>1164<br>004 214 | 1165<br>1165<br>004 215 | 1166<br>1166<br>004 216 | 1167<br>1167<br>004 217 |
| **9−** | 1168<br>1168<br>004 220 | 1169<br>1169<br>004 221 | 1170<br>1170<br>004 222 | 1171<br>1171<br>004 223 | 1172<br>1172<br>004 224 | 1173<br>1173<br>004 225 | 1174<br>1174<br>004 226 | 1175<br>1175<br>004 227 | 1176<br>1176<br>004 230 | 1177<br>1177<br>004 231 | 1178<br>1178<br>004 232 | 1179<br>1179<br>004 233 | 1180<br>1180<br>004 234 | 1181<br>1181<br>004 235 | 1182<br>1182<br>004 236 | 1183<br>1183<br>004 237 |
| **A−** | 1184<br>1184<br>004 240 | 1185<br>1185<br>004 241 | 1186<br>1186<br>004 242 | 1187<br>1187<br>004 243 | 1188<br>1188<br>004 244 | 1189<br>1189<br>004 245 | 1190<br>1190<br>004 246 | 1191<br>1191<br>004 247 | 1192<br>1192<br>004 250 | 1193<br>1193<br>004 251 | 1194<br>1194<br>004 252 | 1195<br>1195<br>004 253 | 1196<br>1196<br>004 254 | 1197<br>1197<br>004 255 | 1198<br>1198<br>004 256 | 1199<br>1199<br>004 257 |
| **B−** | 1200<br>1200<br>004 260 | 1201<br>1201<br>004 261 | 1202<br>1202<br>004 262 | 1203<br>1203<br>004 263 | 1204<br>1204<br>004 264 | 1205<br>1205<br>004 265 | 1206<br>1206<br>004 266 | 1207<br>1207<br>004 267 | 1208<br>1208<br>004 270 | 1209<br>1209<br>004 271 | 1210<br>1210<br>004 272 | 1211<br>1211<br>004 273 | 1212<br>1212<br>004 274 | 1213<br>1213<br>004 275 | 1214<br>1214<br>004 276 | 1215<br>1215<br>004 277 |
| **C−** | 1216<br>1216<br>004 300 | 1217<br>1217<br>004 301 | 1218<br>1218<br>004 302 | 1219<br>1219<br>004 303 | 1220<br>1220<br>004 304 | 1221<br>1221<br>004 305 | 1222<br>1222<br>004 306 | 1223<br>1223<br>004 307 | 1224<br>1224<br>004 310 | 1225<br>1225<br>004 311 | 1226<br>1226<br>004 312 | 1227<br>1227<br>004 313 | 1228<br>1228<br>004 314 | 1229<br>1229<br>004 315 | 1230<br>1230<br>004 316 | 1231<br>1231<br>004 317 |
| **D−** | 1232<br>1232<br>004 320 | 1233<br>1233<br>004 321 | 1234<br>1234<br>004 322 | 1235<br>1235<br>004 323 | 1236<br>1236<br>004 324 | 1237<br>1237<br>004 325 | 1238<br>1238<br>004 326 | 1239<br>1239<br>004 327 | 1240<br>1240<br>004 330 | 1241<br>1241<br>004 331 | 1242<br>1242<br>004 332 | 1243<br>1243<br>004 333 | 1244<br>1244<br>004 334 | 1245<br>1245<br>004 335 | 1246<br>1246<br>004 336 | 1247<br>1247<br>004 337 |
| **E−** | 1248<br>1248<br>004 340 | 1249<br>1249<br>004 341 | 1250<br>1250<br>004 342 | 1251<br>1251<br>004 343 | 1252<br>1252<br>004 344 | 1253<br>1253<br>004 345 | 1254<br>1254<br>004 346 | 1255<br>1255<br>004 347 | 1256<br>1256<br>004 350 | 1257<br>1257<br>004 351 | 1258<br>1258<br>004 352 | 1259<br>1259<br>004 353 | 1260<br>1260<br>004 354 | 1261<br>1261<br>004 355 | 1262<br>1262<br>004 356 | 1263<br>1263<br>004 357 |
| **F−** | 1264<br>1264<br>004 360 | 1265<br>1265<br>004 361 | 1266<br>1266<br>004 362 | 1267<br>1267<br>004 363 | 1268<br>1268<br>004 364 | 1269<br>1269<br>004 365 | 1270<br>1270<br>004 366 | 1271<br>1271<br>004 367 | 1272<br>1272<br>004 370 | 1273<br>1273<br>004 371 | 1274<br>1274<br>004 372 | 1275<br>1275<br>004 373 | 1276<br>1276<br>004 374 | 1277<br>1277<br>004 375 | 1278<br>1278<br>004 376 | 12/9<br>1279<br>004 377 |

Row label column: **SECOND HEX DIGIT**

Legend (right side): **DECIMAL** →,  **DECIMAL** →, **OCTAL** →

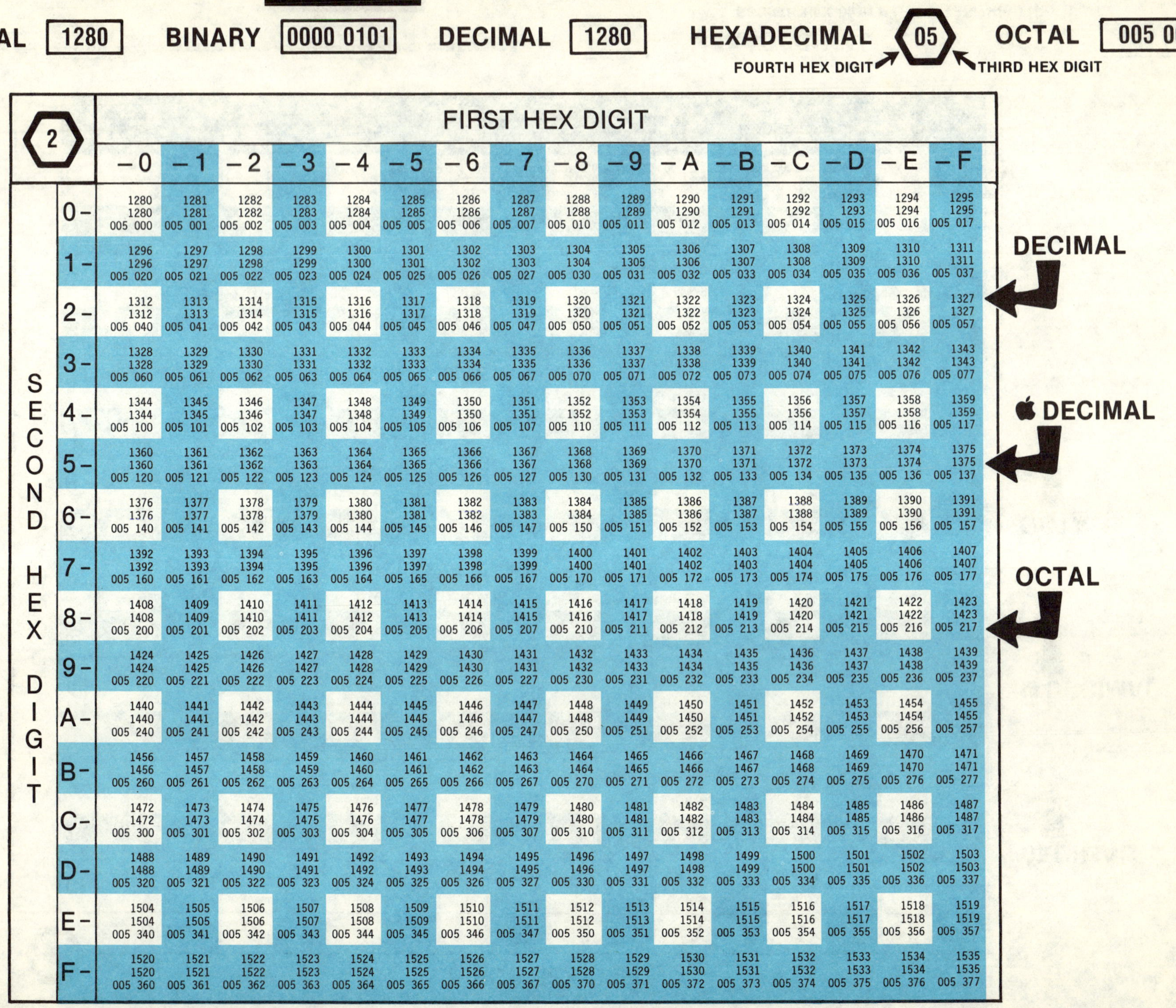

 DECIMAL [1280]  BINARY [0000 0101]  DECIMAL [1280]  HEXADECIMAL ⬡05  OCTAL [005 000]

FOURTH HEX DIGIT → ⬡ ← THIRD HEX DIGIT

⬡2

DECIMAL · DECIMAL · OCTAL

| SECOND HEX DIGIT | FIRST HEX DIGIT | | | | | | | | | | | | | | | |
|---|---|---|---|---|---|---|---|---|---|---|---|---|---|---|---|---|
| | −0 | −1 | −2 | −3 | −4 | −5 | −6 | −7 | −8 | −9 | −A | −B | −C | −D | −E | −F |
| 0− | 1280 / 005 000 | 1281 / 005 001 | 1282 / 005 002 | 1283 / 005 003 | 1284 / 005 004 | 1285 / 005 005 | 1286 / 005 006 | 1287 / 005 007 | 1288 / 005 010 | 1289 / 005 011 | 1290 / 005 012 | 1291 / 005 013 | 1292 / 005 014 | 1293 / 005 015 | 1294 / 005 016 | 1295 / 005 017 |
| 1− | 1296 / 005 020 | 1297 / 005 021 | 1298 / 005 022 | 1299 / 005 023 | 1300 / 005 024 | 1301 / 005 025 | 1302 / 005 026 | 1303 / 005 027 | 1304 / 005 030 | 1305 / 005 031 | 1306 / 005 032 | 1307 / 005 033 | 1308 / 005 034 | 1309 / 005 035 | 1310 / 005 036 | 1311 / 005 037 |
| 2− | 1312 / 005 040 | 1313 / 005 041 | 1314 / 005 042 | 1315 / 005 043 | 1316 / 005 044 | 1317 / 005 045 | 1318 / 005 046 | 1319 / 005 047 | 1320 / 005 050 | 1321 / 005 051 | 1322 / 005 052 | 1323 / 005 053 | 1324 / 005 054 | 1325 / 005 055 | 1326 / 005 056 | 1327 / 005 057 |
| 3− | 1328 / 005 060 | 1329 / 005 061 | 1330 / 005 062 | 1331 / 005 063 | 1332 / 005 064 | 1333 / 005 065 | 1334 / 005 066 | 1335 / 005 067 | 1336 / 005 070 | 1337 / 005 071 | 1338 / 005 072 | 1339 / 005 073 | 1340 / 005 074 | 1341 / 005 075 | 1342 / 005 076 | 1343 / 005 077 |
| 4− | 1344 / 005 100 | 1345 / 005 101 | 1346 / 005 102 | 1347 / 005 103 | 1348 / 005 104 | 1349 / 005 105 | 1350 / 005 106 | 1351 / 005 107 | 1352 / 005 110 | 1353 / 005 111 | 1354 / 005 112 | 1355 / 005 113 | 1356 / 005 114 | 1357 / 005 115 | 1358 / 005 116 | 1359 / 005 117 |
| 5− | 1360 / 005 120 | 1361 / 005 121 | 1362 / 005 122 | 1363 / 005 123 | 1364 / 005 124 | 1365 / 005 125 | 1366 / 005 126 | 1367 / 005 127 | 1368 / 005 130 | 1369 / 005 131 | 1370 / 005 132 | 1371 / 005 133 | 1372 / 005 134 | 1373 / 005 135 | 1374 / 005 136 | 1375 / 005 137 |
| 6− | 1376 / 005 140 | 1377 / 005 141 | 1378 / 005 142 | 1379 / 005 143 | 1380 / 005 144 | 1381 / 005 145 | 1382 / 005 146 | 1383 / 005 147 | 1384 / 005 150 | 1385 / 005 151 | 1386 / 005 152 | 1387 / 005 153 | 1388 / 005 154 | 1389 / 005 155 | 1390 / 005 156 | 1391 / 005 157 |
| 7− | 1392 / 005 160 | 1393 / 005 161 | 1394 / 005 162 | 1395 / 005 163 | 1396 / 005 164 | 1397 / 005 165 | 1398 / 005 166 | 1399 / 005 167 | 1400 / 005 170 | 1401 / 005 171 | 1402 / 005 172 | 1403 / 005 173 | 1404 / 005 174 | 1405 / 005 175 | 1406 / 005 176 | 1407 / 005 177 |
| 8− | 1408 / 005 200 | 1409 / 005 201 | 1410 / 005 202 | 1411 / 005 203 | 1412 / 005 204 | 1413 / 005 205 | 1414 / 005 206 | 1415 / 005 207 | 1416 / 005 210 | 1417 / 005 211 | 1418 / 005 212 | 1419 / 005 213 | 1420 / 005 214 | 1421 / 005 215 | 1422 / 005 216 | 1423 / 005 217 |
| 9− | 1424 / 005 220 | 1425 / 005 221 | 1426 / 005 222 | 1427 / 005 223 | 1428 / 005 224 | 1429 / 005 225 | 1430 / 005 226 | 1431 / 005 227 | 1432 / 005 230 | 1433 / 005 231 | 1434 / 005 232 | 1435 / 005 233 | 1436 / 005 234 | 1437 / 005 235 | 1438 / 005 236 | 1439 / 005 237 |
| A− | 1440 / 005 240 | 1441 / 005 241 | 1442 / 005 242 | 1443 / 005 243 | 1444 / 005 244 | 1445 / 005 245 | 1446 / 005 246 | 1447 / 005 247 | 1448 / 005 250 | 1449 / 005 251 | 1450 / 005 252 | 1451 / 005 253 | 1452 / 005 254 | 1453 / 005 255 | 1454 / 005 256 | 1455 / 005 257 |
| B− | 1456 / 005 260 | 1457 / 005 261 | 1458 / 005 262 | 1459 / 005 263 | 1460 / 005 264 | 1461 / 005 265 | 1462 / 005 266 | 1463 / 005 267 | 1464 / 005 270 | 1465 / 005 271 | 1466 / 005 272 | 1467 / 005 273 | 1468 / 005 274 | 1469 / 005 275 | 1470 / 005 276 | 1471 / 005 277 |
| C− | 1472 / 005 300 | 1473 / 005 301 | 1474 / 005 302 | 1475 / 005 303 | 1476 / 005 304 | 1477 / 005 305 | 1478 / 005 306 | 1479 / 005 307 | 1480 / 005 310 | 1481 / 005 311 | 1482 / 005 312 | 1483 / 005 313 | 1484 / 005 314 | 1485 / 005 315 | 1486 / 005 316 | 1487 / 005 317 |
| D− | 1488 / 005 320 | 1489 / 005 321 | 1490 / 005 322 | 1491 / 005 323 | 1492 / 005 324 | 1493 / 005 325 | 1494 / 005 326 | 1495 / 005 327 | 1496 / 005 330 | 1497 / 005 331 | 1498 / 005 332 | 1499 / 005 333 | 1500 / 005 334 | 1501 / 005 335 | 1502 / 005 336 | 1503 / 005 337 |
| E− | 1504 / 005 340 | 1505 / 005 341 | 1506 / 005 342 | 1507 / 005 343 | 1508 / 005 344 | 1509 / 005 345 | 1510 / 005 346 | 1511 / 005 347 | 1512 / 005 350 | 1513 / 005 351 | 1514 / 005 352 | 1515 / 005 353 | 1516 / 005 354 | 1517 / 005 355 | 1518 / 005 356 | 1519 / 005 357 |
| F− | 1520 / 005 360 | 1521 / 005 361 | 1522 / 005 362 | 1523 / 005 363 | 1524 / 005 364 | 1525 / 005 365 | 1526 / 005 366 | 1527 / 005 367 | 1528 / 005 370 | 1529 / 005 371 | 1530 / 005 372 | 1531 / 005 373 | 1532 / 005 374 | 1533 / 005 375 | 1534 / 005 376 | 1535 / 005 377 |

# FIRST HEX DIGIT

**(2)**

| SECOND HEX DIGIT | −0 | −1 | −2 | −3 | −4 | −5 | −6 | −7 | −8 | −9 | −A | −B | −C | −D | −E | −F |
|---|---|---|---|---|---|---|---|---|---|---|---|---|---|---|---|---|
| **0−** | 1536<br>006 000 | 1537<br>006 001 | 1538<br>006 002 | 1539<br>006 003 | 1540<br>006 004 | 1541<br>006 005 | 1542<br>006 006 | 1543<br>006 007 | 1544<br>006 010 | 1545<br>006 011 | 1546<br>006 012 | 1547<br>006 013 | 1548<br>006 014 | 1549<br>006 015 | 1550<br>006 016 | 1551<br>006 017 |
| **1−** | 1552<br>006 020 | 1553<br>006 021 | 1554<br>006 022 | 1555<br>006 023 | 1556<br>006 024 | 1557<br>006 025 | 1558<br>006 026 | 1559<br>006 027 | 1560<br>006 030 | 1561<br>006 031 | 1562<br>006 032 | 1563<br>006 033 | 1564<br>006 034 | 1565<br>006 035 | 1566<br>006 036 | 1567<br>006 037 |
| **2−** | 1568<br>006 040 | 1569<br>006 041 | 1570<br>006 042 | 1571<br>006 043 | 1572<br>006 044 | 1573<br>006 045 | 1574<br>006 046 | 1575<br>006 047 | 1576<br>006 050 | 1577<br>006 051 | 1578<br>006 052 | 1579<br>006 053 | 1580<br>006 054 | 1581<br>006 055 | 1582<br>006 056 | 1583<br>006 057 |
| **3−** | 1584<br>006 060 | 1585<br>006 061 | 1586<br>006 062 | 1587<br>006 063 | 1588<br>006 064 | 1589<br>006 065 | 1590<br>006 066 | 1591<br>006 067 | 1592<br>006 070 | 1593<br>006 071 | 1594<br>006 072 | 1595<br>006 073 | 1596<br>006 074 | 1597<br>006 075 | 1598<br>006 076 | 1599<br>006 077 |
| **4−** | 1600<br>006 100 | 1601<br>006 101 | 1602<br>006 102 | 1603<br>006 103 | 1604<br>006 104 | 1605<br>006 105 | 1606<br>006 106 | 1607<br>006 107 | 1608<br>006 110 | 1609<br>006 111 | 1610<br>006 112 | 1611<br>006 113 | 1612<br>006 114 | 1613<br>006 115 | 1614<br>006 116 | 1615<br>006 117 |
| **5−** | 1616<br>006 120 | 1617<br>006 121 | 1618<br>006 122 | 1619<br>006 123 | 1620<br>006 124 | 1621<br>006 125 | 1622<br>006 126 | 1623<br>006 127 | 1624<br>006 130 | 1625<br>006 131 | 1626<br>006 132 | 1627<br>006 133 | 1628<br>006 134 | 1629<br>006 135 | 1630<br>006 136 | 1631<br>006 137 |
| **6−** | 1632<br>006 140 | 1633<br>006 141 | 1634<br>006 142 | 1635<br>006 143 | 1636<br>006 144 | 1637<br>006 145 | 1638<br>006 146 | 1639<br>006 147 | 1640<br>006 150 | 1641<br>006 151 | 1642<br>006 152 | 1643<br>006 153 | 1644<br>006 154 | 1645<br>006 155 | 1646<br>006 156 | 1647<br>006 157 |
| **7−** | 1648<br>006 160 | 1649<br>006 161 | 1650<br>006 162 | 1651<br>006 163 | 1652<br>006 164 | 1653<br>006 165 | 1654<br>006 166 | 1655<br>006 167 | 1656<br>006 170 | 1657<br>006 171 | 1658<br>006 172 | 1659<br>006 173 | 1660<br>006 174 | 1661<br>006 175 | 1662<br>006 176 | 1663<br>006 177 |
| **8−** | 1664<br>006 200 | 1665<br>006 201 | 1666<br>006 202 | 1667<br>006 203 | 1668<br>006 204 | 1669<br>006 205 | 1670<br>006 206 | 1671<br>006 207 | 1672<br>006 210 | 1673<br>006 211 | 1674<br>006 212 | 1675<br>006 213 | 1676<br>006 214 | 1677<br>006 215 | 1678<br>006 216 | 1679<br>006 217 |
| **9−** | 1680<br>006 220 | 1681<br>006 221 | 1682<br>006 222 | 1683<br>006 223 | 1684<br>006 224 | 1685<br>006 225 | 1686<br>006 226 | 1687<br>006 227 | 1688<br>006 230 | 1689<br>006 231 | 1690<br>006 232 | 1691<br>006 233 | 1692<br>006 234 | 1693<br>006 235 | 1694<br>006 236 | 1695<br>006 237 |
| **A−** | 1696<br>006 240 | 1697<br>006 241 | 1698<br>006 242 | 1699<br>006 243 | 1700<br>006 244 | 1701<br>006 245 | 1702<br>006 246 | 1703<br>006 247 | 1704<br>006 250 | 1705<br>006 251 | 1706<br>006 252 | 1707<br>006 253 | 1708<br>006 254 | 1709<br>006 255 | 1710<br>006 256 | 1711<br>006 257 |
| **B−** | 1712<br>006 260 | 1713<br>006 261 | 1714<br>006 262 | 1715<br>006 263 | 1716<br>006 264 | 1717<br>006 265 | 1718<br>006 266 | 1719<br>006 267 | 1720<br>006 270 | 1721<br>006 271 | 1722<br>006 272 | 1723<br>006 273 | 1724<br>006 274 | 1725<br>006 275 | 1726<br>006 276 | 1727<br>006 277 |
| **C−** | 1728<br>006 300 | 1729<br>006 301 | 1730<br>006 302 | 1731<br>006 303 | 1732<br>006 304 | 1733<br>006 305 | 1734<br>006 306 | 1735<br>006 307 | 1736<br>006 310 | 1737<br>006 311 | 1738<br>006 312 | 1739<br>006 313 | 1740<br>006 314 | 1741<br>006 315 | 1742<br>006 316 | 1743<br>006 317 |
| **D−** | 1744<br>006 320 | 1745<br>006 321 | 1746<br>006 322 | 1747<br>006 323 | 1748<br>006 324 | 1749<br>006 325 | 1750<br>006 326 | 1751<br>006 327 | 1752<br>006 330 | 1753<br>006 331 | 1754<br>006 332 | 1755<br>006 333 | 1756<br>006 334 | 1757<br>006 335 | 1758<br>006 336 | 1759<br>006 337 |
| **E−** | 1760<br>006 340 | 1761<br>006 341 | 1762<br>006 342 | 1763<br>006 343 | 1764<br>006 344 | 1765<br>006 345 | 1766<br>006 346 | 1767<br>006 347 | 1768<br>006 350 | 1769<br>006 351 | 1770<br>006 352 | 1771<br>006 353 | 1772<br>006 354 | 1773<br>006 355 | 1774<br>006 356 | 1775<br>006 357 |
| **F−** | 1776<br>006 360 | 1777<br>006 361 | 1778<br>006 362 | 1779<br>006 363 | 1780<br>006 364 | 1781<br>006 365 | 1782<br>006 366 | 1783<br>006 367 | 1784<br>006 370 | 1785<br>006 371 | 1786<br>006 372 | 1787<br>006 373 | 1788<br>006 374 | 1789<br>006 375 | 1790<br>006 376 | 1791<br>006 377 |

DECIMAL

DECIMAL

OCTAL

**DECIMAL** 1536    **BINARY** 0000 0110    **DECIMAL** 1536    **HEXADECIMAL** 〈06〉 **OCTAL** 006 000

FOURTH HEX DIGIT → 〈06〉 ← THIRD HEX DIGIT

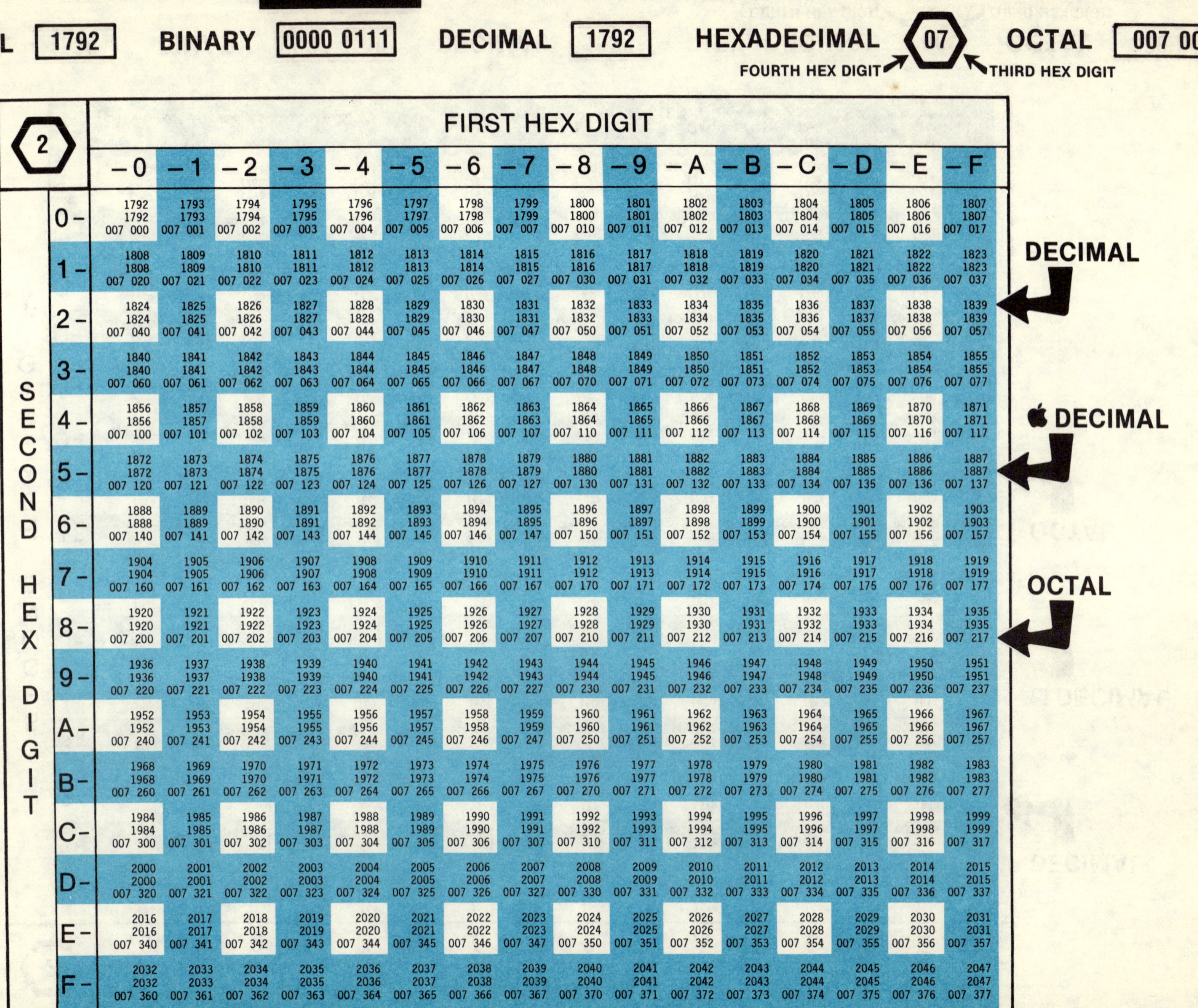



### FIRST HEX DIGIT

| (2) | −0 | −1 | −2 | −3 | −4 | −5 | −6 | −7 | −8 | −9 | −A | −B | −C | −D | −E | −F |
|---|---|---|---|---|---|---|---|---|---|---|---|---|---|---|---|---|
| 0− | 1792<br>1792<br>007 000 | 1793<br>1793<br>007 001 | 1794<br>1794<br>007 002 | 1795<br>1795<br>007 003 | 1796<br>1796<br>007 004 | 1797<br>1797<br>007 005 | 1798<br>1798<br>007 006 | 1799<br>1799<br>007 007 | 1800<br>1800<br>007 010 | 1801<br>1801<br>007 011 | 1802<br>1802<br>007 012 | 1803<br>1803<br>007 013 | 1804<br>1804<br>007 014 | 1805<br>1805<br>007 015 | 1806<br>1806<br>007 016 | 1807<br>1807<br>007 017 |
| 1− | 1808<br>1808<br>007 020 | 1809<br>1809<br>007 021 | 1810<br>1810<br>007 022 | 1811<br>1811<br>007 023 | 1812<br>1812<br>007 024 | 1813<br>1813<br>007 025 | 1814<br>1814<br>007 026 | 1815<br>1815<br>007 027 | 1816<br>1816<br>007 030 | 1817<br>1817<br>007 031 | 1818<br>1818<br>007 032 | 1819<br>1819<br>007 033 | 1820<br>1820<br>007 034 | 1821<br>1821<br>007 035 | 1822<br>1822<br>007 036 | 1823<br>1823<br>007 037 |
| 2− | 1824<br>1824<br>007 040 | 1825<br>1825<br>007 041 | 1826<br>1826<br>007 042 | 1827<br>1827<br>007 043 | 1828<br>1828<br>007 044 | 1829<br>1829<br>007 045 | 1830<br>1830<br>007 046 | 1831<br>1831<br>007 047 | 1832<br>1832<br>007 050 | 1833<br>1833<br>007 051 | 1834<br>1834<br>007 052 | 1835<br>1835<br>007 053 | 1836<br>1836<br>007 054 | 1837<br>1837<br>007 055 | 1838<br>1838<br>007 056 | 1839<br>1839<br>007 057 |
| 3− | 1840<br>1840<br>007 060 | 1841<br>1841<br>007 061 | 1842<br>1842<br>007 062 | 1843<br>1843<br>007 063 | 1844<br>1844<br>007 064 | 1845<br>1845<br>007 065 | 1846<br>1846<br>007 066 | 1847<br>1847<br>007 067 | 1848<br>1848<br>007 070 | 1849<br>1849<br>007 071 | 1850<br>1850<br>007 072 | 1851<br>1851<br>007 073 | 1852<br>1852<br>007 074 | 1853<br>1853<br>007 075 | 1854<br>1854<br>007 076 | 1855<br>1855<br>007 077 |
| 4− | 1856<br>1856<br>007 100 | 1857<br>1857<br>007 101 | 1858<br>1858<br>007 102 | 1859<br>1859<br>007 103 | 1860<br>1860<br>007 104 | 1861<br>1861<br>007 105 | 1862<br>1862<br>007 106 | 1863<br>1863<br>007 107 | 1864<br>1864<br>007 110 | 1865<br>1865<br>007 111 | 1866<br>1866<br>007 112 | 1867<br>1867<br>007 113 | 1868<br>1868<br>007 114 | 1869<br>1869<br>007 115 | 1870<br>1870<br>007 116 | 1871<br>1871<br>007 117 |
| 5− | 1872<br>1872<br>007 120 | 1873<br>1873<br>007 121 | 1874<br>1874<br>007 122 | 1875<br>1875<br>007 123 | 1876<br>1876<br>007 124 | 1877<br>1877<br>007 125 | 1878<br>1878<br>007 126 | 1879<br>1879<br>007 127 | 1880<br>1880<br>007 130 | 1881<br>1881<br>007 131 | 1882<br>1882<br>007 132 | 1883<br>1883<br>007 133 | 1884<br>1884<br>007 134 | 1885<br>1885<br>007 135 | 1886<br>1886<br>007 136 | 1887<br>1887<br>007 137 |
| 6− | 1888<br>1888<br>007 140 | 1889<br>1889<br>007 141 | 1890<br>1890<br>007 142 | 1891<br>1891<br>007 143 | 1892<br>1892<br>007 144 | 1893<br>1893<br>007 145 | 1894<br>1894<br>007 146 | 1895<br>1895<br>007 147 | 1896<br>1896<br>007 150 | 1897<br>1897<br>007 151 | 1898<br>1898<br>007 152 | 1899<br>1899<br>007 153 | 1900<br>1900<br>007 154 | 1901<br>1901<br>007 155 | 1902<br>1902<br>007 156 | 1903<br>1903<br>007 157 |
| 7− | 1904<br>1904<br>007 160 | 1905<br>1905<br>007 161 | 1906<br>1906<br>007 162 | 1907<br>1907<br>007 163 | 1908<br>1908<br>007 164 | 1909<br>1909<br>007 165 | 1910<br>1910<br>007 166 | 1911<br>1911<br>007 167 | 1912<br>1912<br>007 170 | 1913<br>1913<br>007 171 | 1914<br>1914<br>007 172 | 1915<br>1915<br>007 173 | 1916<br>1916<br>007 174 | 1917<br>1917<br>007 175 | 1918<br>1918<br>007 176 | 1919<br>1919<br>007 177 |
| 8− | 1920<br>1920<br>007 200 | 1921<br>1921<br>007 201 | 1922<br>1922<br>007 202 | 1923<br>1923<br>007 203 | 1924<br>1924<br>007 204 | 1925<br>1925<br>007 205 | 1926<br>1926<br>007 206 | 1927<br>1927<br>007 207 | 1928<br>1928<br>007 210 | 1929<br>1929<br>007 211 | 1930<br>1930<br>007 212 | 1931<br>1931<br>007 213 | 1932<br>1932<br>007 214 | 1933<br>1933<br>007 215 | 1934<br>1934<br>007 216 | 1935<br>1935<br>007 217 |
| 9− | 1936<br>1936<br>007 220 | 1937<br>1937<br>007 221 | 1938<br>1938<br>007 222 | 1939<br>1939<br>007 223 | 1940<br>1940<br>007 224 | 1941<br>1941<br>007 225 | 1942<br>1942<br>007 226 | 1943<br>1943<br>007 227 | 1944<br>1944<br>007 230 | 1945<br>1945<br>007 231 | 1946<br>1946<br>007 232 | 1947<br>1947<br>007 233 | 1948<br>1948<br>007 234 | 1949<br>1949<br>007 235 | 1950<br>1950<br>007 236 | 1951<br>1951<br>007 237 |
| A− | 1952<br>1952<br>007 240 | 1953<br>1953<br>007 241 | 1954<br>1954<br>007 242 | 1955<br>1955<br>007 243 | 1956<br>1956<br>007 244 | 1957<br>1957<br>007 245 | 1958<br>1958<br>007 246 | 1959<br>1959<br>007 247 | 1960<br>1960<br>007 250 | 1961<br>1961<br>007 251 | 1962<br>1962<br>007 252 | 1963<br>1963<br>007 253 | 1964<br>1964<br>007 254 | 1965<br>1965<br>007 255 | 1966<br>1966<br>007 256 | 1967<br>1967<br>007 257 |
| B− | 1968<br>1968<br>007 260 | 1969<br>1969<br>007 261 | 1970<br>1970<br>007 262 | 1971<br>1971<br>007 263 | 1972<br>1972<br>007 264 | 1973<br>1973<br>007 265 | 1974<br>1974<br>007 266 | 1975<br>1975<br>007 267 | 1976<br>1976<br>007 270 | 1977<br>1977<br>007 271 | 1978<br>1978<br>007 272 | 1979<br>1979<br>007 273 | 1980<br>1980<br>007 274 | 1981<br>1981<br>007 275 | 1982<br>1982<br>007 276 | 1983<br>1983<br>007 277 |
| C− | 1984<br>1984<br>007 300 | 1985<br>1985<br>007 301 | 1986<br>1986<br>007 302 | 1987<br>1987<br>007 303 | 1988<br>1988<br>007 304 | 1989<br>1989<br>007 305 | 1990<br>1990<br>007 306 | 1991<br>1991<br>007 307 | 1992<br>1992<br>007 310 | 1993<br>1993<br>007 311 | 1994<br>1994<br>007 312 | 1995<br>1995<br>007 313 | 1996<br>1996<br>007 314 | 1997<br>1997<br>007 315 | 1998<br>1998<br>007 316 | 1999<br>1999<br>007 317 |
| D− | 2000<br>2000<br>007 320 | 2001<br>2001<br>007 321 | 2002<br>2002<br>007 322 | 2003<br>2003<br>007 323 | 2004<br>2004<br>007 324 | 2005<br>2005<br>007 325 | 2006<br>2006<br>007 326 | 2007<br>2007<br>007 327 | 2008<br>2008<br>007 330 | 2009<br>2009<br>007 331 | 2010<br>2010<br>007 332 | 2011<br>2011<br>007 333 | 2012<br>2012<br>007 334 | 2013<br>2013<br>007 335 | 2014<br>2014<br>007 336 | 2015<br>2015<br>007 337 |
| E− | 2016<br>2016<br>007 340 | 2017<br>2017<br>007 341 | 2018<br>2018<br>007 342 | 2019<br>2019<br>007 343 | 2020<br>2020<br>007 344 | 2021<br>2021<br>007 345 | 2022<br>2022<br>007 346 | 2023<br>2023<br>007 347 | 2024<br>2024<br>007 350 | 2025<br>2025<br>007 351 | 2026<br>2026<br>007 352 | 2027<br>2027<br>007 353 | 2028<br>2028<br>007 354 | 2029<br>2029<br>007 355 | 2030<br>2030<br>007 356 | 2031<br>2031<br>007 357 |
| F− | 2032<br>2032<br>007 360 | 2033<br>2033<br>007 361 | 2034<br>2034<br>007 362 | 2035<br>2035<br>007 363 | 2036<br>2036<br>007 364 | 2037<br>2037<br>007 365 | 2038<br>2038<br>007 366 | 2039<br>2039<br>007 367 | 2040<br>2040<br>007 370 | 2041<br>2041<br>007 371 | 2042<br>2042<br>007 372 | 2043<br>2043<br>007 373 | 2044<br>2044<br>007 374 | 2045<br>2045<br>007 375 | 2046<br>2046<br>007 376 | 2047<br>2047<br>007 377 |

SECOND HEX DIGIT

## FIRST HEX DIGIT

⬡ 2

Top value = DECIMAL, middle value = ⬥ DECIMAL, bottom value = OCTAL.

| | −0 | −1 | −2 | −3 | −4 | −5 | −6 | −7 | −8 | −9 | −A | −B | −C | −D | −E | −F |
|---|---|---|---|---|---|---|---|---|---|---|---|---|---|---|---|---|
| **0-** | 2048<br>2048<br>010 000 | 2049<br>2049<br>010 001 | 2050<br>2050<br>010 002 | 2051<br>2051<br>010 003 | 2052<br>2052<br>010 004 | 2053<br>2053<br>010 005 | 2054<br>2054<br>010 006 | 2055<br>2055<br>010 007 | 2056<br>2056<br>010 010 | 2057<br>2057<br>010 011 | 2058<br>2058<br>010 012 | 2059<br>2059<br>010 013 | 2060<br>2060<br>010 014 | 2061<br>2061<br>010 015 | 2062<br>2062<br>010 016 | 2063<br>2063<br>010 017 |
| **1-** | 2064<br>2064<br>010 020 | 2065<br>2065<br>010 021 | 2066<br>2066<br>010 022 | 2067<br>2067<br>010 023 | 2068<br>2068<br>010 024 | 2069<br>2069<br>010 025 | 2070<br>2070<br>010 026 | 2071<br>2071<br>010 027 | 2072<br>2072<br>010 030 | 2073<br>2073<br>010 031 | 2074<br>2074<br>010 032 | 2075<br>2075<br>010 033 | 2076<br>2076<br>010 034 | 2077<br>2077<br>010 035 | 2078<br>2078<br>010 036 | 2079<br>2079<br>010 037 |
| **2-** | 2080<br>2080<br>010 040 | 2081<br>2081<br>010 041 | 2082<br>2082<br>010 042 | 2083<br>2083<br>010 043 | 2084<br>2084<br>010 044 | 2085<br>2085<br>010 045 | 2086<br>2086<br>010 046 | 2087<br>2087<br>010 047 | 2088<br>2088<br>010 050 | 2089<br>2089<br>010 051 | 2090<br>2090<br>010 052 | 2091<br>2091<br>010 053 | 2092<br>2092<br>010 054 | 2093<br>2093<br>010 055 | 2094<br>2094<br>010 056 | 2095<br>2095<br>010 057 |
| **3-** | 2096<br>2096<br>010 060 | 2097<br>2097<br>010 061 | 2098<br>2098<br>010 062 | 2099<br>2099<br>010 063 | 2100<br>2100<br>010 064 | 2101<br>2101<br>010 065 | 2102<br>2102<br>010 066 | 2103<br>2103<br>010 067 | 2104<br>2104<br>010 070 | 2105<br>2105<br>010 071 | 2106<br>2106<br>010 072 | 2107<br>2107<br>010 073 | 2108<br>2108<br>010 074 | 2109<br>2109<br>010 075 | 2110<br>2110<br>010 076 | 2111<br>2111<br>010 077 |
| **4-** | 2112<br>2112<br>010 100 | 2113<br>2113<br>010 101 | 2114<br>2114<br>010 102 | 2115<br>2115<br>010 103 | 2116<br>2116<br>010 104 | 2117<br>2117<br>010 105 | 2118<br>2118<br>010 106 | 2119<br>2119<br>010 107 | 2120<br>2120<br>010 110 | 2121<br>2121<br>010 111 | 2122<br>2122<br>010 112 | 2123<br>2123<br>010 113 | 2124<br>2124<br>010 114 | 2125<br>2125<br>010 115 | 2126<br>2126<br>010 116 | 2127<br>2127<br>010 117 |
| **5-** | 2128<br>2128<br>010 120 | 2129<br>2129<br>010 121 | 2130<br>2130<br>010 122 | 2131<br>2131<br>010 123 | 2132<br>2132<br>010 124 | 2133<br>2133<br>010 125 | 2134<br>2134<br>010 126 | 2135<br>2135<br>010 127 | 2136<br>2136<br>010 130 | 2137<br>2137<br>010 131 | 2138<br>2138<br>010 132 | 2139<br>2139<br>010 133 | 2140<br>2140<br>010 134 | 2141<br>2141<br>010 135 | 2142<br>2142<br>010 136 | 2143<br>2143<br>010 137 |
| **6-** | 2144<br>2144<br>010 140 | 2145<br>2145<br>010 141 | 2146<br>2146<br>010 142 | 2147<br>2147<br>010 143 | 2148<br>2148<br>010 144 | 2149<br>2149<br>010 145 | 2150<br>2150<br>010 146 | 2151<br>2151<br>010 147 | 2152<br>2152<br>010 150 | 2153<br>2153<br>010 151 | 2154<br>2154<br>010 152 | 2155<br>2155<br>010 153 | 2156<br>2156<br>010 154 | 2157<br>2157<br>010 155 | 2158<br>2158<br>010 156 | 2159<br>2159<br>010 157 |
| **7-** | 2160<br>2160<br>010 160 | 2161<br>2161<br>010 161 | 2162<br>2162<br>010 162 | 2163<br>2163<br>010 163 | 2164<br>2164<br>010 164 | 2165<br>2165<br>010 165 | 2166<br>2166<br>010 166 | 2167<br>2167<br>010 167 | 2168<br>2168<br>010 170 | 2169<br>2169<br>010 171 | 2170<br>2170<br>010 172 | 2171<br>2171<br>010 173 | 2172<br>2172<br>010 174 | 2173<br>2173<br>010 175 | 2174<br>2174<br>010 176 | 2175<br>2175<br>010 177 |
| **8-** | 2176<br>2176<br>010 200 | 2177<br>2177<br>010 201 | 2178<br>2178<br>010 202 | 2179<br>2179<br>010 203 | 2180<br>2180<br>010 204 | 2181<br>2181<br>010 205 | 2182<br>2182<br>010 206 | 2183<br>2183<br>010 207 | 2184<br>2184<br>010 210 | 2185<br>2185<br>010 211 | 2186<br>2186<br>010 212 | 2187<br>2187<br>010 213 | 2188<br>2188<br>010 214 | 2189<br>2189<br>010 215 | 2190<br>2190<br>010 216 | 2191<br>2191<br>010 217 |
| **9-** | 2192<br>2192<br>010 220 | 2193<br>2193<br>010 221 | 2194<br>2194<br>010 222 | 2195<br>2195<br>010 223 | 2196<br>2196<br>010 224 | 2197<br>2197<br>010 225 | 2198<br>2198<br>010 226 | 2199<br>2199<br>010 227 | 2200<br>2200<br>010 230 | 2201<br>2201<br>010 231 | 2202<br>2202<br>010 232 | 2203<br>2203<br>010 233 | 2204<br>2204<br>010 234 | 2205<br>2205<br>010 235 | 2206<br>2206<br>010 236 | 2207<br>2207<br>010 237 |
| **A-** | 2208<br>2208<br>010 240 | 2209<br>2209<br>010 241 | 2210<br>2210<br>010 242 | 2211<br>2211<br>010 243 | 2212<br>2212<br>010 244 | 2213<br>2213<br>010 245 | 2214<br>2214<br>010 246 | 2215<br>2215<br>010 247 | 2216<br>2216<br>010 250 | 2217<br>2217<br>010 251 | 2218<br>2218<br>010 252 | 2219<br>2219<br>010 253 | 2220<br>2220<br>010 254 | 2221<br>2221<br>010 255 | 2222<br>2222<br>010 256 | 2223<br>2223<br>010 257 |
| **B-** | 2224<br>2224<br>010 260 | 2225<br>2225<br>010 261 | 2226<br>2226<br>010 262 | 2227<br>2227<br>010 263 | 2228<br>2228<br>010 264 | 2229<br>2229<br>010 265 | 2230<br>2230<br>010 266 | 2231<br>2231<br>010 267 | 2232<br>2232<br>010 270 | 2233<br>2233<br>010 271 | 2234<br>2234<br>010 272 | 2235<br>2235<br>010 273 | 2236<br>2236<br>010 274 | 2237<br>2237<br>010 275 | 2238<br>2238<br>010 276 | 2239<br>2239<br>010 277 |
| **C-** | 2240<br>2240<br>010 300 | 2241<br>2241<br>010 301 | 2242<br>2242<br>010 302 | 2243<br>2243<br>010 303 | 2244<br>2244<br>010 304 | 2245<br>2245<br>010 305 | 2246<br>2246<br>010 306 | 2247<br>2247<br>010 307 | 2248<br>2248<br>010 310 | 2249<br>2249<br>010 311 | 2250<br>2250<br>010 312 | 2251<br>2251<br>010 313 | 2252<br>2252<br>010 314 | 2253<br>2253<br>010 315 | 2254<br>2254<br>010 316 | 2255<br>2255<br>010 317 |
| **D-** | 2256<br>2256<br>010 320 | 2257<br>2257<br>010 321 | 2258<br>2258<br>010 322 | 2259<br>2259<br>010 323 | 2260<br>2260<br>010 324 | 2261<br>2261<br>010 325 | 2262<br>2262<br>010 326 | 2263<br>2263<br>010 327 | 2264<br>2264<br>010 330 | 2265<br>2265<br>010 331 | 2266<br>2266<br>010 332 | 2267<br>2267<br>010 333 | 2268<br>2268<br>010 334 | 2269<br>2269<br>010 335 | 2270<br>2270<br>010 336 | 2271<br>2271<br>010 337 |
| **E-** | 2272<br>2272<br>010 340 | 2273<br>2273<br>010 341 | 2274<br>2274<br>010 342 | 2275<br>2275<br>010 343 | 2276<br>2276<br>010 344 | 2277<br>2277<br>010 345 | 2278<br>2278<br>010 346 | 2279<br>2279<br>010 347 | 2280<br>2280<br>010 350 | 2281<br>2281<br>010 351 | 2282<br>2282<br>010 352 | 2283<br>2283<br>010 353 | 2284<br>2284<br>010 354 | 2285<br>2285<br>010 355 | 2286<br>2286<br>010 356 | 2287<br>2287<br>010 357 |
| **F-** | 2288<br>2288<br>010 360 | 2289<br>2289<br>010 361 | 2290<br>2290<br>010 362 | 2291<br>2291<br>010 363 | 2292<br>2292<br>010 364 | 2293<br>2293<br>010 365 | 2294<br>2294<br>010 366 | 2295<br>2295<br>010 367 | 2296<br>2296<br>010 370 | 2297<br>2297<br>010 371 | 2298<br>2298<br>010 372 | 2299<br>2299<br>010 373 | 2300<br>2300<br>010 374 | 2301<br>2301<br>010 375 | 2302<br>2302<br>010 376 | 2303<br>2303<br>010 377 |

(Left margin label: **SECOND HEX DIGIT**)

Right-side pointers: **DECIMAL** · **⬥ DECIMAL** · **OCTAL**

---

**⬥ DECIMAL** `2048`   **BINARY** `0000 1000`   **DECIMAL** `2048`   **HEXADECIMAL** ⬡ `08` **OCTAL** `010 000`

FOURTH HEX DIGIT → ⬡ ← THIRD HEX DIGIT

⟨2⟩ FIRST HEX DIGIT   / SECOND HEX DIGIT

| | −0 | −1 | −2 | −3 | −4 | −5 | −6 | −7 | −8 | −9 | −A | −B | −C | −D | −E | −F |
|---|---|---|---|---|---|---|---|---|---|---|---|---|---|---|---|---|
| 0− | 2304<br>011 000 | 2305<br>011 001 | 2306<br>011 002 | 2307<br>011 003 | 2308<br>011 004 | 2309<br>011 005 | 2310<br>011 006 | 2311<br>011 007 | 2312<br>011 010 | 2313<br>011 011 | 2314<br>011 012 | 2315<br>011 013 | 2316<br>011 014 | 2317<br>011 015 | 2318<br>011 016 | 2319<br>011 017 |
| 1− | 2320<br>011 020 | 2321<br>011 021 | 2322<br>011 022 | 2323<br>011 023 | 2324<br>011 024 | 2325<br>011 025 | 2326<br>011 026 | 2327<br>011 027 | 2328<br>011 030 | 2329<br>011 031 | 2330<br>011 032 | 2331<br>011 033 | 2332<br>011 034 | 2333<br>011 035 | 2334<br>011 036 | 2335<br>011 037 |
| 2− | 2336<br>011 040 | 2337<br>011 041 | 2338<br>011 042 | 2339<br>011 043 | 2340<br>011 044 | 2341<br>011 045 | 2342<br>011 046 | 2343<br>011 047 | 2344<br>011 050 | 2345<br>011 051 | 2346<br>011 052 | 2347<br>011 053 | 2348<br>011 054 | 2349<br>011 055 | 2350<br>011 056 | 2351<br>011 057 |
| 3− | 2352<br>011 060 | 2353<br>011 061 | 2354<br>011 062 | 2355<br>011 063 | 2356<br>011 064 | 2357<br>011 065 | 2358<br>011 066 | 2359<br>011 067 | 2360<br>011 070 | 2361<br>011 071 | 2362<br>011 072 | 2363<br>011 073 | 2364<br>011 074 | 2365<br>011 075 | 2366<br>011 076 | 2367<br>011 077 |
| 4− | 2368<br>011 100 | 2369<br>011 101 | 2370<br>011 102 | 2371<br>011 103 | 2372<br>011 104 | 2373<br>011 105 | 2374<br>011 106 | 2375<br>011 107 | 2376<br>011 110 | 2377<br>011 111 | 2378<br>011 112 | 2379<br>011 113 | 2380<br>011 114 | 2381<br>011 115 | 2382<br>011 116 | 2383<br>011 117 |
| 5− | 2384<br>011 120 | 2385<br>011 121 | 2386<br>011 122 | 2387<br>011 123 | 2388<br>011 124 | 2389<br>011 125 | 2390<br>011 126 | 2391<br>011 127 | 2392<br>011 130 | 2393<br>011 131 | 2394<br>011 132 | 2395<br>011 133 | 2396<br>011 134 | 2397<br>011 135 | 2398<br>011 136 | 2399<br>011 137 |
| 6− | 2400<br>011 140 | 2401<br>011 141 | 2402<br>011 142 | 2403<br>011 143 | 2404<br>011 144 | 2405<br>011 145 | 2406<br>011 146 | 2407<br>011 147 | 2408<br>011 150 | 2409<br>011 151 | 2410<br>011 152 | 2411<br>011 153 | 2412<br>011 154 | 2413<br>011 155 | 2414<br>011 156 | 2415<br>011 157 |
| 7− | 2416<br>011 160 | 2417<br>011 161 | 2418<br>011 162 | 2419<br>011 163 | 2420<br>011 164 | 2421<br>011 165 | 2422<br>011 166 | 2423<br>011 167 | 2424<br>011 170 | 2425<br>011 171 | 2426<br>011 172 | 2427<br>011 173 | 2428<br>011 174 | 2429<br>011 175 | 2430<br>011 176 | 2431<br>011 177 |
| 8− | 2432<br>011 200 | 2433<br>011 201 | 2434<br>011 202 | 2435<br>011 203 | 2436<br>011 204 | 2437<br>011 205 | 2438<br>011 206 | 2439<br>011 207 | 2440<br>011 210 | 2441<br>011 211 | 2442<br>011 212 | 2443<br>011 213 | 2444<br>011 214 | 2445<br>011 215 | 2446<br>011 216 | 2447<br>011 217 |
| 9− | 2448<br>011 220 | 2449<br>011 221 | 2450<br>011 222 | 2451<br>011 223 | 2452<br>011 224 | 2453<br>011 225 | 2454<br>011 226 | 2455<br>011 227 | 2456<br>011 230 | 2457<br>011 231 | 2458<br>011 232 | 2459<br>011 233 | 2460<br>011 234 | 2461<br>011 235 | 2462<br>011 236 | 2463<br>011 237 |
| A− | 2464<br>011 240 | 2465<br>011 241 | 2466<br>011 242 | 2467<br>011 243 | 2468<br>011 244 | 2469<br>011 245 | 2470<br>011 246 | 2471<br>011 247 | 2472<br>011 250 | 2473<br>011 251 | 2474<br>011 252 | 2475<br>011 253 | 2476<br>011 254 | 2477<br>011 255 | 2478<br>011 256 | 2479<br>011 257 |
| B− | 2480<br>011 260 | 2481<br>011 261 | 2482<br>011 262 | 2483<br>011 263 | 2484<br>011 264 | 2485<br>011 265 | 2486<br>011 266 | 2487<br>011 267 | 2488<br>011 270 | 2489<br>011 271 | 2490<br>011 272 | 2491<br>011 273 | 2492<br>011 274 | 2493<br>011 275 | 2494<br>011 276 | 2495<br>011 277 |
| C− | 2496<br>011 300 | 2497<br>011 301 | 2498<br>011 302 | 2499<br>011 303 | 2500<br>011 304 | 2501<br>011 305 | 2502<br>011 306 | 2503<br>011 307 | 2504<br>011 310 | 2505<br>011 311 | 2506<br>011 312 | 2507<br>011 313 | 2508<br>011 314 | 2509<br>011 315 | 2510<br>011 316 | 2511<br>011 317 |
| D− | 2512<br>011 320 | 2513<br>011 321 | 2514<br>011 322 | 2515<br>011 323 | 2516<br>011 324 | 2517<br>011 325 | 2518<br>011 326 | 2519<br>011 327 | 2520<br>011 330 | 2521<br>011 331 | 2522<br>011 332 | 2523<br>011 333 | 2524<br>011 334 | 2525<br>011 335 | 2526<br>011 336 | 2527<br>011 337 |
| E− | 2528<br>011 340 | 2529<br>011 341 | 2530<br>011 342 | 2531<br>011 343 | 2532<br>011 344 | 2533<br>011 345 | 2534<br>011 346 | 2535<br>011 347 | 2536<br>011 350 | 2537<br>011 351 | 2538<br>011 352 | 2539<br>011 353 | 2540<br>011 354 | 2541<br>011 355 | 2542<br>011 356 | 2543<br>011 357 |
| F− | 2544<br>011 360 | 2545<br>011 361 | 2546<br>011 362 | 2547<br>011 363 | 2548<br>011 364 | 2549<br>011 365 | 2550<br>011 366 | 2551<br>011 367 | 2552<br>011 370 | 2553<br>011 371 | 2554<br>011 372 | 2555<br>011 373 | 2556<br>011 374 | 2557<br>011 375 | 2558<br>011 376 | 2559<br>011 377 |

DECIMAL ←

 DECIMAL ←

OCTAL ←

| SECOND HEX DIGIT | −0 | −1 | −2 | −3 | −4 | −5 | −6 | −7 | −8 | −9 | −A | −B | −C | −D | −E | −F |
|---|---|---|---|---|---|---|---|---|---|---|---|---|---|---|---|---|
| 0− | 2560<br>2560<br>012 000 | 2561<br>2561<br>012 001 | 2562<br>2562<br>012 002 | 2563<br>2563<br>012 003 | 2564<br>2564<br>012 004 | 2565<br>2565<br>012 005 | 2566<br>2566<br>012 006 | 2567<br>2567<br>012 007 | 2568<br>2568<br>012 010 | 2569<br>2569<br>012 011 | 2570<br>2570<br>012 012 | 2571<br>2571<br>012 013 | 2572<br>2572<br>012 014 | 2573<br>2573<br>012 015 | 2574<br>2574<br>012 016 | 2575<br>2575<br>012 017 |
| 1− | 2576<br>2576<br>012 020 | 2577<br>2577<br>012 021 | 2578<br>2578<br>012 022 | 2579<br>2579<br>012 023 | 2580<br>2580<br>012 024 | 2581<br>2581<br>012 025 | 2582<br>2582<br>012 026 | 2583<br>2583<br>012 027 | 2584<br>2584<br>012 030 | 2585<br>2585<br>012 031 | 2586<br>2586<br>012 032 | 2587<br>2587<br>012 033 | 2588<br>2588<br>012 034 | 2589<br>2589<br>012 035 | 2590<br>2590<br>012 036 | 2591<br>2591<br>012 037 |
| 2− | 2592<br>2592<br>012 040 | 2593<br>2593<br>012 041 | 2594<br>2594<br>012 042 | 2595<br>2595<br>012 043 | 2596<br>2596<br>012 044 | 2597<br>2597<br>012 045 | 2598<br>2598<br>012 046 | 2599<br>2599<br>012 047 | 2600<br>2600<br>012 050 | 2601<br>2601<br>012 051 | 2602<br>2602<br>012 052 | 2603<br>2603<br>012 053 | 2604<br>2604<br>012 054 | 2605<br>2605<br>012 055 | 2606<br>2606<br>012 056 | 2607<br>2607<br>012 057 |
| 3− | 2608<br>2608<br>012 060 | 2609<br>2609<br>012 061 | 2610<br>2610<br>012 062 | 2611<br>2611<br>012 063 | 2612<br>2612<br>012 064 | 2613<br>2613<br>012 065 | 2614<br>2614<br>012 066 | 2615<br>2615<br>012 067 | 2616<br>2616<br>012 070 | 2617<br>2617<br>012 071 | 2618<br>2618<br>012 072 | 2619<br>2619<br>012 073 | 2620<br>2620<br>012 074 | 2621<br>2621<br>012 075 | 2622<br>2622<br>012 076 | 2623<br>2623<br>012 077 |
| 4− | 2624<br>2624<br>012 100 | 2625<br>2625<br>012 101 | 2626<br>2626<br>012 102 | 2627<br>2627<br>012 103 | 2628<br>2628<br>012 104 | 2629<br>2629<br>012 105 | 2630<br>2630<br>012 106 | 2631<br>2631<br>012 107 | 2632<br>2632<br>012 110 | 2633<br>2633<br>012 111 | 2634<br>2634<br>012 112 | 2635<br>2635<br>012 113 | 2636<br>2636<br>012 114 | 2637<br>2637<br>012 115 | 2638<br>2638<br>012 116 | 2639<br>2639<br>012 117 |
| 5− | 2640<br>2640<br>012 120 | 2641<br>2641<br>012 121 | 2642<br>2642<br>012 122 | 2643<br>2643<br>012 123 | 2644<br>2644<br>012 124 | 2645<br>2645<br>012 125 | 2646<br>2646<br>012 126 | 2647<br>2647<br>012 127 | 2648<br>2648<br>012 130 | 2649<br>2649<br>012 131 | 2650<br>2650<br>012 132 | 2651<br>2651<br>012 133 | 2652<br>2652<br>012 134 | 2653<br>2653<br>012 135 | 2654<br>2654<br>012 136 | 2655<br>2655<br>012 137 |
| 6− | 2656<br>2656<br>012 140 | 2657<br>2657<br>012 141 | 2658<br>2658<br>012 142 | 2659<br>2659<br>012 143 | 2660<br>2660<br>012 144 | 2661<br>2661<br>012 145 | 2662<br>2662<br>012 146 | 2663<br>2663<br>012 147 | 2664<br>2664<br>012 150 | 2665<br>2665<br>012 151 | 2666<br>2666<br>012 152 | 2667<br>2667<br>012 153 | 2668<br>2668<br>012 154 | 2669<br>2669<br>012 155 | 2670<br>2670<br>012 156 | 2671<br>2671<br>012 157 |
| 7− | 2672<br>2672<br>012 160 | 2673<br>2673<br>012 161 | 2674<br>2674<br>012 162 | 2675<br>2675<br>012 163 | 2676<br>2676<br>012 164 | 2677<br>2677<br>012 165 | 2678<br>2678<br>012 166 | 2679<br>2679<br>012 167 | 2680<br>2680<br>012 170 | 2681<br>2681<br>012 171 | 2682<br>2682<br>012 172 | 2683<br>2683<br>012 173 | 2684<br>2684<br>012 174 | 2685<br>2685<br>012 175 | 2686<br>2686<br>012 176 | 2687<br>2687<br>012 177 |
| 8− | 2688<br>2688<br>012 200 | 2689<br>2689<br>012 201 | 2690<br>2690<br>012 202 | 2691<br>2691<br>012 203 | 2692<br>2692<br>012 204 | 2693<br>2693<br>012 205 | 2694<br>2694<br>012 206 | 2695<br>2695<br>012 207 | 2696<br>2696<br>012 210 | 2697<br>2697<br>012 211 | 2698<br>2698<br>012 212 | 2699<br>2699<br>012 213 | 2700<br>2700<br>012 214 | 2701<br>2701<br>012 215 | 2702<br>2702<br>012 216 | 2703<br>2703<br>012 217 |
| 9− | 2704<br>2704<br>012 220 | 2705<br>2705<br>012 221 | 2706<br>2706<br>012 222 | 2707<br>2707<br>012 223 | 2708<br>2708<br>012 224 | 2709<br>2709<br>012 225 | 2710<br>2710<br>012 226 | 2711<br>2711<br>012 227 | 2712<br>2712<br>012 230 | 2713<br>2713<br>012 231 | 2714<br>2714<br>012 232 | 2715<br>2715<br>012 233 | 2716<br>2716<br>012 234 | 2717<br>2717<br>012 235 | 2718<br>2718<br>012 236 | 2719<br>2719<br>012 237 |
| A− | 2720<br>2720<br>012 240 | 2721<br>2721<br>012 241 | 2722<br>2722<br>012 242 | 2723<br>2723<br>012 243 | 2724<br>2724<br>012 244 | 2725<br>2725<br>012 245 | 2726<br>2726<br>012 246 | 2727<br>2727<br>012 247 | 2728<br>2728<br>012 250 | 2729<br>2729<br>012 251 | 2730<br>2730<br>012 252 | 2731<br>2731<br>012 253 | 2732<br>2732<br>012 254 | 2733<br>2733<br>012 255 | 2734<br>2734<br>012 256 | 2735<br>2735<br>012 257 |
| B− | 2736<br>2736<br>012 260 | 2737<br>2737<br>012 261 | 2738<br>2738<br>012 262 | 2739<br>2739<br>012 263 | 2740<br>2740<br>012 264 | 2741<br>2741<br>012 265 | 2742<br>2742<br>012 266 | 2743<br>2743<br>012 267 | 2744<br>2744<br>012 270 | 2745<br>2745<br>012 271 | 2746<br>2746<br>012 272 | 2747<br>2747<br>012 273 | 2748<br>2748<br>012 274 | 2749<br>2749<br>012 275 | 2750<br>2750<br>012 276 | 2751<br>2751<br>012 277 |
| C− | 2752<br>2752<br>012 300 | 2753<br>2753<br>012 301 | 2754<br>2754<br>012 302 | 2755<br>2755<br>012 303 | 2756<br>2756<br>012 304 | 2757<br>2757<br>012 305 | 2758<br>2758<br>012 306 | 2759<br>2759<br>012 307 | 2760<br>2760<br>012 310 | 2761<br>2761<br>012 311 | 2762<br>2762<br>012 312 | 2763<br>2763<br>012 313 | 2764<br>2764<br>012 314 | 2765<br>2765<br>012 315 | 2766<br>2766<br>012 316 | 2767<br>2767<br>012 317 |
| D− | 2768<br>2768<br>012 320 | 2769<br>2769<br>012 321 | 2770<br>2770<br>012 322 | 2771<br>2771<br>012 323 | 2772<br>2772<br>012 324 | 2773<br>2773<br>012 325 | 2774<br>2774<br>012 326 | 2775<br>2775<br>012 327 | 2776<br>2776<br>012 330 | 2777<br>2777<br>012 331 | 2778<br>2778<br>012 332 | 2779<br>2779<br>012 333 | 2780<br>2780<br>012 334 | 2781<br>2781<br>012 335 | 2782<br>2782<br>012 336 | 2783<br>2783<br>012 337 |
| E− | 2784<br>2784<br>012 340 | 2785<br>2785<br>012 341 | 2786<br>2786<br>012 342 | 2787<br>2787<br>012 343 | 2788<br>2788<br>012 344 | 2789<br>2789<br>012 345 | 2790<br>2790<br>012 346 | 2791<br>2791<br>012 347 | 2792<br>2792<br>012 350 | 2793<br>2793<br>012 351 | 2794<br>2794<br>012 352 | 2795<br>2795<br>012 353 | 2796<br>2796<br>012 354 | 2797<br>2797<br>012 355 | 2798<br>2798<br>012 356 | 2799<br>2799<br>012 357 |
| F− | 2800<br>2800<br>012 360 | 2801<br>2801<br>012 361 | 2802<br>2802<br>012 362 | 2803<br>2803<br>012 363 | 2804<br>2804<br>012 364 | 2805<br>2805<br>012 365 | 2806<br>2806<br>012 366 | 2807<br>2807<br>012 367 | 2808<br>2808<br>012 370 | 2809<br>2809<br>012 371 | 2810<br>2810<br>012 372 | 2811<br>2811<br>012 373 | 2812<br>2812<br>012 374 | 2813<br>2813<br>012 375 | 2814<br>2814<br>012 376 | 2815<br>2815<br>012 377 |

DECIMAL

 DECIMAL

OCTAL

 DECIMAL  2560   BINARY  0000 1010   DECIMAL  2560   HEXADECIMAL  0A   OCTAL  012 000

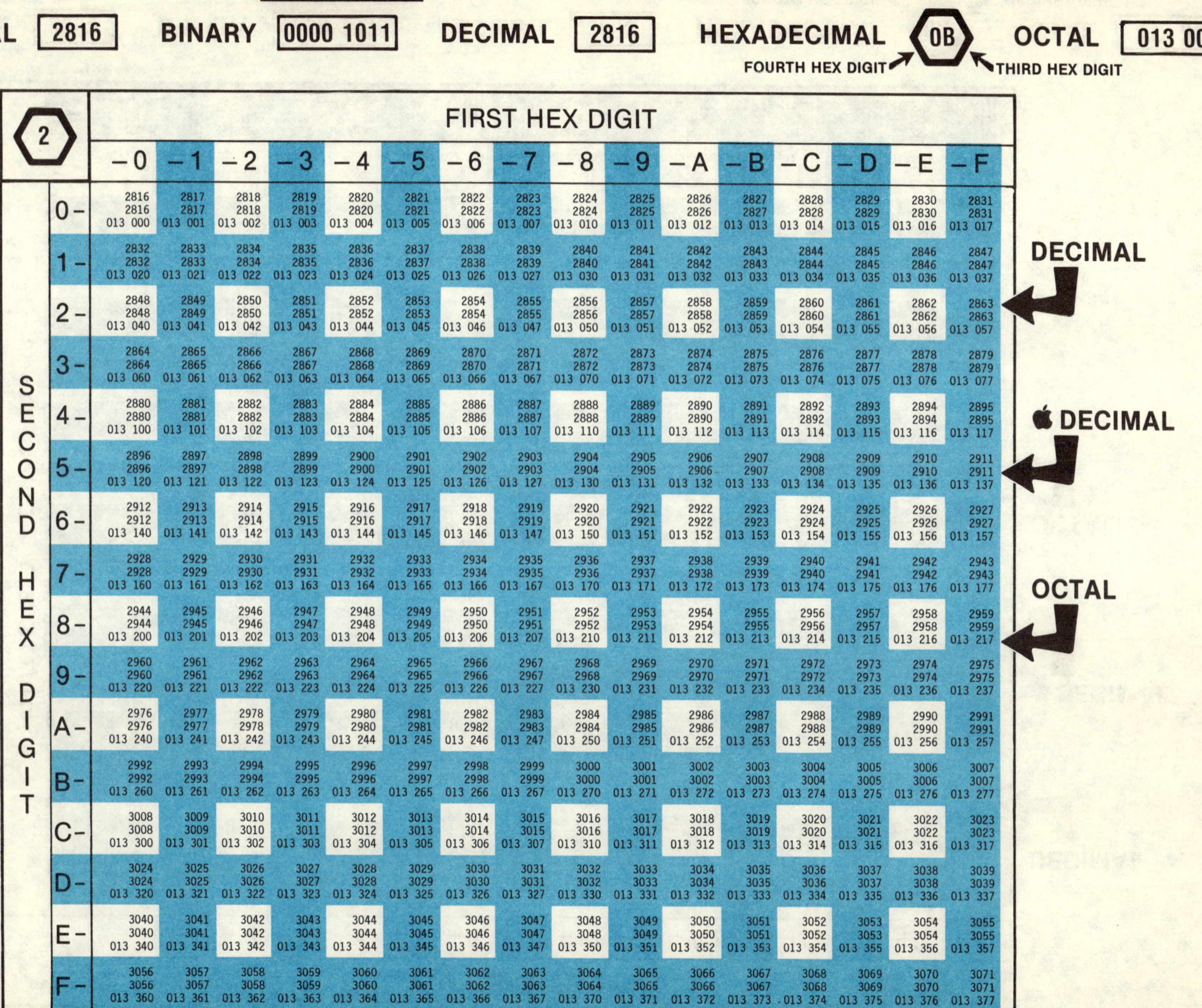



FIRST HEX DIGIT

| 2 | −0 | −1 | −2 | −3 | −4 | −5 | −6 | −7 | −8 | −9 | −A | −B | −C | −D | −E | −F |
|---|---|---|---|---|---|---|---|---|---|---|---|---|---|---|---|---|
| 0− | 2816<br>2816<br>013 000 | 2817<br>2817<br>013 001 | 2818<br>2818<br>013 002 | 2819<br>2819<br>013 003 | 2820<br>2820<br>013 004 | 2821<br>2821<br>013 005 | 2822<br>2822<br>013 006 | 2823<br>2823<br>013 007 | 2824<br>2824<br>013 010 | 2825<br>2825<br>013 011 | 2826<br>2826<br>013 012 | 2827<br>2827<br>013 013 | 2828<br>2828<br>013 014 | 2829<br>2829<br>013 015 | 2830<br>2830<br>013 016 | 2831<br>2831<br>013 017 |
| 1− | 2832<br>2832<br>013 020 | 2833<br>2833<br>013 021 | 2834<br>2834<br>013 022 | 2835<br>2835<br>013 023 | 2836<br>2836<br>013 024 | 2837<br>2837<br>013 025 | 2838<br>2838<br>013 026 | 2839<br>2839<br>013 027 | 2840<br>2840<br>013 030 | 2841<br>2841<br>013 031 | 2842<br>2842<br>013 032 | 2843<br>2843<br>013 033 | 2844<br>2844<br>013 034 | 2845<br>2845<br>013 035 | 2846<br>2846<br>013 036 | 2847<br>2847<br>013 037 |
| 2− | 2848<br>2848<br>013 040 | 2849<br>2849<br>013 041 | 2850<br>2850<br>013 042 | 2851<br>2851<br>013 043 | 2852<br>2852<br>013 044 | 2853<br>2853<br>013 045 | 2854<br>2854<br>013 046 | 2855<br>2855<br>013 047 | 2856<br>2856<br>013 050 | 2857<br>2857<br>013 051 | 2858<br>2858<br>013 052 | 2859<br>2859<br>013 053 | 2860<br>2860<br>013 054 | 2861<br>2861<br>013 055 | 2862<br>2862<br>013 056 | 2863<br>2863<br>013 057 |
| 3− | 2864<br>2864<br>013 060 | 2865<br>2865<br>013 061 | 2866<br>2866<br>013 062 | 2867<br>2867<br>013 063 | 2868<br>2868<br>013 064 | 2869<br>2869<br>013 065 | 2870<br>2870<br>013 066 | 2871<br>2871<br>013 067 | 2872<br>2872<br>013 070 | 2873<br>2873<br>013 071 | 2874<br>2874<br>013 072 | 2875<br>2875<br>013 073 | 2876<br>2876<br>013 074 | 2877<br>2877<br>013 075 | 2878<br>2878<br>013 076 | 2879<br>2879<br>013 077 |
| 4− | 2880<br>2880<br>013 100 | 2881<br>2881<br>013 101 | 2882<br>2882<br>013 102 | 2883<br>2883<br>013 103 | 2884<br>2884<br>013 104 | 2885<br>2885<br>013 105 | 2886<br>2886<br>013 106 | 2887<br>2887<br>013 107 | 2888<br>2888<br>013 110 | 2889<br>2889<br>013 111 | 2890<br>2890<br>013 112 | 2891<br>2891<br>013 113 | 2892<br>2892<br>013 114 | 2893<br>2893<br>013 115 | 2894<br>2894<br>013 116 | 2895<br>2895<br>013 117 |
| 5− | 2896<br>2896<br>013 120 | 2897<br>2897<br>013 121 | 2898<br>2898<br>013 122 | 2899<br>2899<br>013 123 | 2900<br>2900<br>013 124 | 2901<br>2901<br>013 125 | 2902<br>2902<br>013 126 | 2903<br>2903<br>013 127 | 2904<br>2904<br>013 130 | 2905<br>2905<br>013 131 | 2906<br>2906<br>013 132 | 2907<br>2907<br>013 133 | 2908<br>2908<br>013 134 | 2909<br>2909<br>013 135 | 2910<br>2910<br>013 136 | 2911<br>2911<br>013 137 |
| 6− | 2912<br>2912<br>013 140 | 2913<br>2913<br>013 141 | 2914<br>2914<br>013 142 | 2915<br>2915<br>013 143 | 2916<br>2916<br>013 144 | 2917<br>2917<br>013 145 | 2918<br>2918<br>013 146 | 2919<br>2919<br>013 147 | 2920<br>2920<br>013 150 | 2921<br>2921<br>013 151 | 2922<br>2922<br>013 152 | 2923<br>2923<br>013 153 | 2924<br>2924<br>013 154 | 2925<br>2925<br>013 155 | 2926<br>2926<br>013 156 | 2927<br>2927<br>013 157 |
| 7− | 2928<br>2928<br>013 160 | 2929<br>2929<br>013 161 | 2930<br>2930<br>013 162 | 2931<br>2931<br>013 163 | 2932<br>2932<br>013 164 | 2933<br>2933<br>013 165 | 2934<br>2934<br>013 166 | 2935<br>2935<br>013 167 | 2936<br>2936<br>013 170 | 2937<br>2937<br>013 171 | 2938<br>2938<br>013 172 | 2939<br>2939<br>013 173 | 2940<br>2940<br>013 174 | 2941<br>2941<br>013 175 | 2942<br>2942<br>013 176 | 2943<br>2943<br>013 177 |
| 8− | 2944<br>2944<br>013 200 | 2945<br>2945<br>013 201 | 2946<br>2946<br>013 202 | 2947<br>2947<br>013 203 | 2948<br>2948<br>013 204 | 2949<br>2949<br>013 205 | 2950<br>2950<br>013 206 | 2951<br>2951<br>013 207 | 2952<br>2952<br>013 210 | 2953<br>2953<br>013 211 | 2954<br>2954<br>013 212 | 2955<br>2955<br>013 213 | 2956<br>2956<br>013 214 | 2957<br>2957<br>013 215 | 2958<br>2958<br>013 216 | 2959<br>2959<br>013 217 |
| 9− | 2960<br>2960<br>013 220 | 2961<br>2961<br>013 221 | 2962<br>2962<br>013 222 | 2963<br>2963<br>013 223 | 2964<br>2964<br>013 224 | 2965<br>2965<br>013 225 | 2966<br>2966<br>013 226 | 2967<br>2967<br>013 227 | 2968<br>2968<br>013 230 | 2969<br>2969<br>013 231 | 2970<br>2970<br>013 232 | 2971<br>2971<br>013 233 | 2972<br>2972<br>013 234 | 2973<br>2973<br>013 235 | 2974<br>2974<br>013 236 | 2975<br>2975<br>013 237 |
| A− | 2976<br>2976<br>013 240 | 2977<br>2977<br>013 241 | 2978<br>2978<br>013 242 | 2979<br>2979<br>013 243 | 2980<br>2980<br>013 244 | 2981<br>2981<br>013 245 | 2982<br>2982<br>013 246 | 2983<br>2983<br>013 247 | 2984<br>2984<br>013 250 | 2985<br>2985<br>013 251 | 2986<br>2986<br>013 252 | 2987<br>2987<br>013 253 | 2988<br>2988<br>013 254 | 2989<br>2989<br>013 255 | 2990<br>2990<br>013 256 | 2991<br>2991<br>013 257 |
| B− | 2992<br>2992<br>013 260 | 2993<br>2993<br>013 261 | 2994<br>2994<br>013 262 | 2995<br>2995<br>013 263 | 2996<br>2996<br>013 264 | 2997<br>2997<br>013 265 | 2998<br>2998<br>013 266 | 2999<br>2999<br>013 267 | 3000<br>3000<br>013 270 | 3001<br>3001<br>013 271 | 3002<br>3002<br>013 272 | 3003<br>3003<br>013 273 | 3004<br>3004<br>013 274 | 3005<br>3005<br>013 275 | 3006<br>3006<br>013 276 | 3007<br>3007<br>013 277 |
| C− | 3008<br>3008<br>013 300 | 3009<br>3009<br>013 301 | 3010<br>3010<br>013 302 | 3011<br>3011<br>013 303 | 3012<br>3012<br>013 304 | 3013<br>3013<br>013 305 | 3014<br>3014<br>013 306 | 3015<br>3015<br>013 307 | 3016<br>3016<br>013 310 | 3017<br>3017<br>013 311 | 3018<br>3018<br>013 312 | 3019<br>3019<br>013 313 | 3020<br>3020<br>013 314 | 3021<br>3021<br>013 315 | 3022<br>3022<br>013 316 | 3023<br>3023<br>013 317 |
| D− | 3024<br>3024<br>013 320 | 3025<br>3025<br>013 321 | 3026<br>3026<br>013 322 | 3027<br>3027<br>013 323 | 3028<br>3028<br>013 324 | 3029<br>3029<br>013 325 | 3030<br>3030<br>013 326 | 3031<br>3031<br>013 327 | 3032<br>3032<br>013 330 | 3033<br>3033<br>013 331 | 3034<br>3034<br>013 332 | 3035<br>3035<br>013 333 | 3036<br>3036<br>013 334 | 3037<br>3037<br>013 335 | 3038<br>3038<br>013 336 | 3039<br>3039<br>013 337 |
| E− | 3040<br>3040<br>013 340 | 3041<br>3041<br>013 341 | 3042<br>3042<br>013 342 | 3043<br>3043<br>013 343 | 3044<br>3044<br>013 344 | 3045<br>3045<br>013 345 | 3046<br>3046<br>013 346 | 3047<br>3047<br>013 347 | 3048<br>3048<br>013 350 | 3049<br>3049<br>013 351 | 3050<br>3050<br>013 352 | 3051<br>3051<br>013 353 | 3052<br>3052<br>013 354 | 3053<br>3053<br>013 355 | 3054<br>3054<br>013 356 | 3055<br>3055<br>013 357 |
| F− | 3056<br>3056<br>013 360 | 3057<br>3057<br>013 361 | 3058<br>3058<br>013 362 | 3059<br>3059<br>013 363 | 3060<br>3060<br>013 364 | 3061<br>3061<br>013 365 | 3062<br>3062<br>013 366 | 3063<br>3063<br>013 367 | 3064<br>3064<br>013 370 | 3065<br>3065<br>013 371 | 3066<br>3066<br>013 372 | 3067<br>3067<br>013 373 | 3068<br>3068<br>013 374 | 3069<br>3069<br>013 375 | 3070<br>3070<br>013 376 | 3071<br>3071<br>013 377 |

<table>
<tr><td rowspan="2">②</td><td colspan="16" align="center">FIRST HEX DIGIT</td></tr>
<tr><td>–0</td><td>–1</td><td>–2</td><td>–3</td><td>–4</td><td>–5</td><td>–6</td><td>–7</td><td>–8</td><td>–9</td><td>–A</td><td>–B</td><td>–C</td><td>–D</td><td>–E</td><td>–F</td></tr>
<tr><td>0–</td>
<td>3072<br>3072<br>014 000</td><td>3073<br>3073<br>014 001</td><td>3074<br>3074<br>014 002</td><td>3075<br>3075<br>014 003</td><td>3076<br>3076<br>014 004</td><td>3077<br>3077<br>014 005</td><td>3078<br>3078<br>014 006</td><td>3079<br>3079<br>014 007</td><td>3080<br>3080<br>014 010</td><td>3081<br>3081<br>014 011</td><td>3082<br>3082<br>014 012</td><td>3083<br>3083<br>014 013</td><td>3084<br>3084<br>014 014</td><td>3085<br>3085<br>014 015</td><td>3086<br>3086<br>014 016</td><td>3087<br>3087<br>014 017</td></tr>
<tr><td>1–</td>
<td>3088<br>3088<br>014 020</td><td>3089<br>3089<br>014 021</td><td>3090<br>3090<br>014 022</td><td>3091<br>3091<br>014 023</td><td>3092<br>3092<br>014 024</td><td>3093<br>3093<br>014 025</td><td>3094<br>3094<br>014 026</td><td>3095<br>3095<br>014 027</td><td>3096<br>3096<br>014 030</td><td>3097<br>3097<br>014 031</td><td>3098<br>3098<br>014 032</td><td>3099<br>3099<br>014 033</td><td>3100<br>3100<br>014 034</td><td>3101<br>3101<br>014 035</td><td>3102<br>3102<br>014 036</td><td>3103<br>3103<br>014 037</td></tr>
<tr><td>2–</td>
<td>3104<br>3104<br>014 040</td><td>3105<br>3105<br>014 041</td><td>3106<br>3106<br>014 042</td><td>3107<br>3107<br>014 043</td><td>3108<br>3108<br>014 044</td><td>3109<br>3109<br>014 045</td><td>3110<br>3110<br>014 046</td><td>3111<br>3111<br>014 047</td><td>3112<br>3112<br>014 050</td><td>3113<br>3113<br>014 051</td><td>3114<br>3114<br>014 052</td><td>3115<br>3115<br>014 053</td><td>3116<br>3116<br>014 054</td><td>3117<br>3117<br>014 055</td><td>3118<br>3118<br>014 056</td><td>3119<br>3119<br>014 057</td></tr>
<tr><td>3–</td>
<td>3120<br>3120<br>014 060</td><td>3121<br>3121<br>014 061</td><td>3122<br>3122<br>014 062</td><td>3123<br>3123<br>014 063</td><td>3124<br>3124<br>014 064</td><td>3125<br>3125<br>014 065</td><td>3126<br>3126<br>014 066</td><td>3127<br>3127<br>014 067</td><td>3128<br>3128<br>014 070</td><td>3129<br>3129<br>014 071</td><td>3130<br>3130<br>014 072</td><td>3131<br>3131<br>014 073</td><td>3132<br>3132<br>014 074</td><td>3133<br>3133<br>014 075</td><td>3134<br>3134<br>014 076</td><td>3135<br>3135<br>014 077</td></tr>
<tr><td>4–</td>
<td>3136<br>3136<br>014 100</td><td>3137<br>3137<br>014 101</td><td>3138<br>3138<br>014 102</td><td>3139<br>3139<br>014 103</td><td>3140<br>3140<br>014 104</td><td>3141<br>3141<br>014 105</td><td>3142<br>3142<br>014 106</td><td>3143<br>3143<br>014 107</td><td>3144<br>3144<br>014 110</td><td>3145<br>3145<br>014 111</td><td>3146<br>3146<br>014 112</td><td>3147<br>3147<br>014 113</td><td>3148<br>3148<br>014 114</td><td>3149<br>3149<br>014 115</td><td>3150<br>3150<br>014 116</td><td>3151<br>3151<br>014 117</td></tr>
<tr><td>5–</td>
<td>3152<br>3152<br>014 120</td><td>3153<br>3153<br>014 121</td><td>3154<br>3154<br>014 122</td><td>3155<br>3155<br>014 123</td><td>3156<br>3156<br>014 124</td><td>3157<br>3157<br>014 125</td><td>3158<br>3158<br>014 126</td><td>3159<br>3159<br>014 127</td><td>3160<br>3160<br>014 130</td><td>3161<br>3161<br>014 131</td><td>3162<br>3162<br>014 132</td><td>3163<br>3163<br>014 133</td><td>3164<br>3164<br>014 134</td><td>3165<br>3165<br>014 135</td><td>3166<br>3166<br>014 136</td><td>3167<br>3167<br>014 137</td></tr>
<tr><td>6–</td>
<td>3168<br>3168<br>014 140</td><td>3169<br>3169<br>014 141</td><td>3170<br>3170<br>014 142</td><td>3171<br>3171<br>014 143</td><td>3172<br>3172<br>014 144</td><td>3173<br>3173<br>014 145</td><td>3174<br>3174<br>014 146</td><td>3175<br>3175<br>014 147</td><td>3176<br>3176<br>014 150</td><td>3177<br>3177<br>014 151</td><td>3178<br>3178<br>014 152</td><td>3179<br>3179<br>014 153</td><td>3180<br>3180<br>014 154</td><td>3181<br>3181<br>014 155</td><td>3182<br>3182<br>014 156</td><td>3183<br>3183<br>014 157</td></tr>
<tr><td>7–</td>
<td>3184<br>3184<br>014 160</td><td>3185<br>3185<br>014 161</td><td>3186<br>3186<br>014 162</td><td>3187<br>3187<br>014 163</td><td>3188<br>3188<br>014 164</td><td>3189<br>3189<br>014 165</td><td>3190<br>3190<br>014 166</td><td>3191<br>3191<br>014 167</td><td>3192<br>3192<br>014 170</td><td>3193<br>3193<br>014 171</td><td>3194<br>3194<br>014 172</td><td>3195<br>3195<br>014 173</td><td>3196<br>3196<br>014 174</td><td>3197<br>3197<br>014 175</td><td>3198<br>3198<br>014 176</td><td>3199<br>3199<br>014 177</td></tr>
<tr><td>8–</td>
<td>3200<br>3200<br>014 200</td><td>3201<br>3201<br>014 201</td><td>3202<br>3202<br>014 202</td><td>3203<br>3203<br>014 203</td><td>3204<br>3204<br>014 204</td><td>3205<br>3205<br>014 205</td><td>3206<br>3206<br>014 206</td><td>3207<br>3207<br>014 207</td><td>3208<br>3208<br>014 210</td><td>3209<br>3209<br>014 211</td><td>3210<br>3210<br>014 212</td><td>3211<br>3211<br>014 213</td><td>3212<br>3212<br>014 214</td><td>3213<br>3213<br>014 215</td><td>3214<br>3214<br>014 216</td><td>3215<br>3215<br>014 217</td></tr>
<tr><td>9–</td>
<td>3216<br>3216<br>014 220</td><td>3217<br>3217<br>014 221</td><td>3218<br>3218<br>014 222</td><td>3219<br>3219<br>014 223</td><td>3220<br>3220<br>014 224</td><td>3221<br>3221<br>014 225</td><td>3222<br>3222<br>014 226</td><td>3223<br>3223<br>014 227</td><td>3224<br>3224<br>014 230</td><td>3225<br>3225<br>014 231</td><td>3226<br>3226<br>014 232</td><td>3227<br>3227<br>014 233</td><td>3228<br>3228<br>014 234</td><td>3229<br>3229<br>014 235</td><td>3230<br>3230<br>014 236</td><td>3231<br>3231<br>014 237</td></tr>
<tr><td>A–</td>
<td>3232<br>3232<br>014 240</td><td>3233<br>3233<br>014 241</td><td>3234<br>3234<br>014 242</td><td>3235<br>3235<br>014 243</td><td>3236<br>3236<br>014 244</td><td>3237<br>3237<br>014 245</td><td>3238<br>3238<br>014 246</td><td>3239<br>3239<br>014 247</td><td>3240<br>3240<br>014 250</td><td>3241<br>3241<br>014 251</td><td>3242<br>3242<br>014 252</td><td>3243<br>3243<br>014 253</td><td>3244<br>3244<br>014 254</td><td>3245<br>3245<br>014 255</td><td>3246<br>3246<br>014 256</td><td>3247<br>3247<br>014 257</td></tr>
<tr><td>B–</td>
<td>3248<br>3248<br>014 260</td><td>3249<br>3249<br>014 261</td><td>3250<br>3250<br>014 262</td><td>3251<br>3251<br>014 263</td><td>3252<br>3252<br>014 264</td><td>3253<br>3253<br>014 265</td><td>3254<br>3254<br>014 266</td><td>3255<br>3255<br>014 267</td><td>3256<br>3256<br>014 270</td><td>3257<br>3257<br>014 271</td><td>3258<br>3258<br>014 272</td><td>3259<br>3259<br>014 273</td><td>3260<br>3260<br>014 274</td><td>3261<br>3261<br>014 275</td><td>3262<br>3262<br>014 276</td><td>3263<br>3263<br>014 277</td></tr>
<tr><td>C–</td>
<td>3264<br>3264<br>014 300</td><td>3265<br>3265<br>014 301</td><td>3266<br>3266<br>014 302</td><td>3267<br>3267<br>014 303</td><td>3268<br>3268<br>014 304</td><td>3269<br>3269<br>014 305</td><td>3270<br>3270<br>014 306</td><td>3271<br>3271<br>014 307</td><td>3272<br>3272<br>014 310</td><td>3273<br>3273<br>014 311</td><td>3274<br>3274<br>014 312</td><td>3275<br>3275<br>014 313</td><td>3276<br>3276<br>014 314</td><td>3277<br>3277<br>014 315</td><td>3278<br>3278<br>014 316</td><td>3279<br>3279<br>014 317</td></tr>
<tr><td>D–</td>
<td>3280<br>3280<br>014 320</td><td>3281<br>3281<br>014 321</td><td>3282<br>3282<br>014 322</td><td>3283<br>3283<br>014 323</td><td>3284<br>3284<br>014 324</td><td>3285<br>3285<br>014 325</td><td>3286<br>3286<br>014 326</td><td>3287<br>3287<br>014 327</td><td>3288<br>3288<br>014 330</td><td>3289<br>3289<br>014 331</td><td>3290<br>3290<br>014 332</td><td>3291<br>3291<br>014 333</td><td>3292<br>3292<br>014 334</td><td>3293<br>3293<br>014 335</td><td>3294<br>3294<br>014 336</td><td>3295<br>3295<br>014 337</td></tr>
<tr><td>E–</td>
<td>3296<br>3296<br>014 340</td><td>3297<br>3297<br>014 341</td><td>3298<br>3298<br>014 342</td><td>3299<br>3299<br>014 343</td><td>3300<br>3300<br>014 344</td><td>3301<br>3301<br>014 345</td><td>3302<br>3302<br>014 346</td><td>3303<br>3303<br>014 347</td><td>3304<br>3304<br>014 350</td><td>3305<br>3305<br>014 351</td><td>3306<br>3306<br>014 352</td><td>3307<br>3307<br>014 353</td><td>3308<br>3308<br>014 354</td><td>3309<br>3309<br>014 355</td><td>3310<br>3310<br>014 356</td><td>3311<br>3311<br>014 357</td></tr>
<tr><td>F–</td>
<td>3312<br>3312<br>014 360</td><td>3313<br>3313<br>014 361</td><td>3314<br>3314<br>014 362</td><td>3315<br>3315<br>014 363</td><td>3316<br>3316<br>014 364</td><td>3317<br>3317<br>014 365</td><td>3318<br>3318<br>014 366</td><td>3319<br>3319<br>014 367</td><td>3320<br>3320<br>014 370</td><td>3321<br>3321<br>014 371</td><td>3322<br>3322<br>014 372</td><td>3323<br>3323<br>014 373</td><td>3324<br>3324<br>014 374</td><td>3325<br>3325<br>014 375</td><td>3326<br>3326<br>014 376</td><td>3327<br>3327<br>014 377</td></tr>
</table>

SECOND HEX DIGIT

DECIMAL

 DECIMAL

OCTAL

 DECIMAL   3072    **BINARY**   0000 1100    **DECIMAL**   3072    **HEXADECIMAL**   0C    **OCTAL**   014 000

FOURTH HEX DIGIT   THIRD HEX DIGIT

| 2 | FIRST HEX DIGIT | | | | | | | | | | | | | | | |
|---|---|---|---|---|---|---|---|---|---|---|---|---|---|---|---|---|
| SECOND HEX DIGIT | −0 | −1 | −2 | −3 | −4 | −5 | −6 | −7 | −8 | −9 | −A | −B | −C | −D | −E | −F |
| 0− | 3328<br>015 000 | 3329<br>015 001 | 3330<br>015 002 | 3331<br>015 003 | 3332<br>015 004 | 3333<br>015 005 | 3334<br>015 006 | 3335<br>015 007 | 3336<br>015 010 | 3337<br>015 011 | 3338<br>015 012 | 3339<br>015 013 | 3340<br>015 014 | 3341<br>015 015 | 3342<br>015 016 | 3343<br>015 017 |
| 1− | 3344<br>015 020 | 3345<br>015 021 | 3346<br>015 022 | 3347<br>015 023 | 3348<br>015 024 | 3349<br>015 025 | 3350<br>015 026 | 3351<br>015 027 | 3352<br>015 030 | 3353<br>015 031 | 3354<br>015 032 | 3355<br>015 033 | 3356<br>015 034 | 3357<br>015 035 | 3358<br>015 036 | 3359<br>015 037 |
| 2− | 3360<br>015 040 | 3361<br>015 041 | 3362<br>015 042 | 3363<br>015 043 | 3364<br>015 044 | 3365<br>015 045 | 3366<br>015 046 | 3367<br>015 047 | 3368<br>015 050 | 3369<br>015 051 | 3370<br>015 052 | 3371<br>015 053 | 3372<br>015 054 | 3373<br>015 055 | 3374<br>015 056 | 3375<br>015 057 |
| 3− | 3376<br>015 060 | 3377<br>015 061 | 3378<br>015 062 | 3379<br>015 063 | 3380<br>015 064 | 3381<br>015 065 | 3382<br>015 066 | 3383<br>015 067 | 3384<br>015 070 | 3385<br>015 071 | 3386<br>015 072 | 3387<br>015 073 | 3388<br>015 074 | 3389<br>015 075 | 3390<br>015 076 | 3391<br>015 077 |
| 4− | 3392<br>015 100 | 3393<br>015 101 | 3394<br>015 102 | 3395<br>015 103 | 3396<br>015 104 | 3397<br>015 105 | 3398<br>015 106 | 3399<br>015 107 | 3400<br>015 110 | 3401<br>015 111 | 3402<br>015 112 | 3403<br>015 113 | 3404<br>015 114 | 3405<br>015 115 | 3406<br>015 116 | 3407<br>015 117 |
| 5− | 3408<br>015 120 | 3409<br>015 121 | 3410<br>015 122 | 3411<br>015 123 | 3412<br>015 124 | 3413<br>015 125 | 3414<br>015 126 | 3415<br>015 127 | 3416<br>015 130 | 3417<br>015 131 | 3418<br>015 132 | 3419<br>015 133 | 3420<br>015 134 | 3421<br>015 135 | 3422<br>015 136 | 3423<br>015 137 |
| 6− | 3424<br>015 140 | 3425<br>015 141 | 3426<br>015 142 | 3427<br>015 143 | 3428<br>015 144 | 3429<br>015 145 | 3430<br>015 146 | 3431<br>015 147 | 3432<br>015 150 | 3433<br>015 151 | 3434<br>015 152 | 3435<br>015 153 | 3436<br>015 154 | 3437<br>015 155 | 3438<br>015 156 | 3439<br>015 157 |
| 7− | 3440<br>015 160 | 3441<br>015 161 | 3442<br>015 162 | 3443<br>015 163 | 3444<br>015 164 | 3445<br>015 165 | 3446<br>015 166 | 3447<br>015 167 | 3448<br>015 170 | 3449<br>015 171 | 3450<br>015 172 | 3451<br>015 173 | 3452<br>015 174 | 3453<br>015 175 | 3454<br>015 176 | 3455<br>015 177 |
| 8− | 3456<br>015 200 | 3457<br>015 201 | 3458<br>015 202 | 3459<br>015 203 | 3460<br>015 204 | 3461<br>015 205 | 3462<br>015 206 | 3463<br>015 207 | 3464<br>015 210 | 3465<br>015 211 | 3466<br>015 212 | 3467<br>015 213 | 3468<br>015 214 | 3469<br>015 215 | 3470<br>015 216 | 3471<br>015 217 |
| 9− | 3472<br>015 220 | 3473<br>015 221 | 3474<br>015 222 | 3475<br>015 223 | 3476<br>015 224 | 3477<br>015 225 | 3478<br>015 226 | 3479<br>015 227 | 3480<br>015 230 | 3481<br>015 231 | 3482<br>015 232 | 3483<br>015 233 | 3484<br>015 234 | 3485<br>015 235 | 3486<br>015 236 | 3487<br>015 237 |
| A− | 3488<br>015 240 | 3489<br>015 241 | 3490<br>015 242 | 3491<br>015 243 | 3492<br>015 244 | 3493<br>015 245 | 3494<br>015 246 | 3495<br>015 247 | 3496<br>015 250 | 3497<br>015 251 | 3498<br>015 252 | 3499<br>015 253 | 3500<br>015 254 | 3501<br>015 255 | 3502<br>015 256 | 3503<br>015 257 |
| B− | 3504<br>015 260 | 3505<br>015 261 | 3506<br>015 262 | 3507<br>015 263 | 3508<br>015 264 | 3509<br>015 265 | 3510<br>015 266 | 3511<br>015 267 | 3512<br>015 270 | 3513<br>015 271 | 3514<br>015 272 | 3515<br>015 273 | 3516<br>015 274 | 3517<br>015 275 | 3518<br>015 276 | 3519<br>015 277 |
| C− | 3520<br>015 300 | 3521<br>015 301 | 3522<br>015 302 | 3523<br>015 303 | 3524<br>015 304 | 3525<br>015 305 | 3526<br>015 306 | 3527<br>015 307 | 3528<br>015 310 | 3529<br>015 311 | 3530<br>015 312 | 3531<br>015 313 | 3532<br>015 314 | 3533<br>015 315 | 3534<br>015 316 | 3535<br>015 317 |
| D− | 3536<br>015 320 | 3537<br>015 321 | 3538<br>015 322 | 3539<br>015 323 | 3540<br>015 324 | 3541<br>015 325 | 3542<br>015 326 | 3543<br>015 327 | 3544<br>015 330 | 3545<br>015 331 | 3546<br>015 332 | 3547<br>015 333 | 3548<br>015 334 | 3549<br>015 335 | 3550<br>015 336 | 3551<br>015 337 |
| E− | 3552<br>015 340 | 3553<br>015 341 | 3554<br>015 342 | 3555<br>015 343 | 3556<br>015 344 | 3557<br>015 345 | 3558<br>015 346 | 3559<br>015 347 | 3560<br>015 350 | 3561<br>015 351 | 3562<br>015 352 | 3563<br>015 353 | 3564<br>015 354 | 3565<br>015 355 | 3566<br>015 356 | 3567<br>015 357 |
| F− | 3568<br>015 360 | 3569<br>015 361 | 3570<br>015 362 | 3571<br>015 363 | 3572<br>015 364 | 3573<br>015 365 | 3574<br>015 366 | 3575<br>015 367 | 3576<br>015 370 | 3577<br>015 371 | 3578<br>015 372 | 3579<br>015 373 | 3580<br>015 374 | 3581<br>015 375 | 3582<br>015 376 | 3583<br>015 377 |

DECIMAL

DECIMAL

OCTAL

Hex / Decimal / Octal Conversion Table — 2

| | −0 | −1 | −2 | −3 | −4 | −5 | −6 | −7 | −8 | −9 | −A | −B | −C | −D | −E | −F |
|---|---|---|---|---|---|---|---|---|---|---|---|---|---|---|---|---|
| **0−** | 3584<br>016 000 | 3585<br>016 001 | 3586<br>016 002 | 3587<br>016 003 | 3588<br>016 004 | 3589<br>016 005 | 3590<br>016 006 | 3591<br>016 007 | 3592<br>016 010 | 3593<br>016 011 | 3594<br>016 012 | 3595<br>016 013 | 3596<br>016 014 | 3597<br>016 015 | 3598<br>016 016 | 3599<br>016 017 |
| **1−** | 3600<br>016 020 | 3601<br>016 021 | 3602<br>016 022 | 3603<br>016 023 | 3604<br>016 024 | 3605<br>016 025 | 3606<br>016 026 | 3607<br>016 027 | 3608<br>016 030 | 3609<br>016 031 | 3610<br>016 032 | 3611<br>016 033 | 3612<br>016 034 | 3613<br>016 035 | 3614<br>016 036 | 3615<br>016 037 |
| **2−** | 3616<br>016 040 | 3617<br>016 041 | 3618<br>016 042 | 3619<br>016 043 | 3620<br>016 044 | 3621<br>016 045 | 3622<br>016 046 | 3623<br>016 047 | 3624<br>016 050 | 3625<br>016 051 | 3626<br>016 052 | 3627<br>016 053 | 3628<br>016 054 | 3629<br>016 055 | 3630<br>016 056 | 3631<br>016 057 |
| **3−** | 3632<br>016 060 | 3633<br>016 061 | 3634<br>016 062 | 3635<br>016 063 | 3636<br>016 064 | 3637<br>016 065 | 3638<br>016 066 | 3639<br>016 067 | 3640<br>016 070 | 3641<br>016 071 | 3642<br>016 072 | 3643<br>016 073 | 3644<br>016 074 | 3645<br>016 075 | 3646<br>016 076 | 3647<br>016 077 |
| **4−** | 3648<br>016 100 | 3649<br>016 101 | 3650<br>016 102 | 3651<br>016 103 | 3652<br>016 104 | 3653<br>016 105 | 3654<br>016 106 | 3655<br>016 107 | 3656<br>016 110 | 3657<br>016 111 | 3658<br>016 112 | 3659<br>016 113 | 3660<br>016 114 | 3661<br>016 115 | 3662<br>016 116 | 3663<br>016 117 |
| **5−** | 3664<br>016 120 | 3665<br>016 121 | 3666<br>016 122 | 3667<br>016 123 | 3668<br>016 124 | 3669<br>016 125 | 3670<br>016 126 | 3671<br>016 127 | 3672<br>016 130 | 3673<br>016 131 | 3674<br>016 132 | 3675<br>016 133 | 3676<br>016 134 | 3677<br>016 135 | 3678<br>016 136 | 3679<br>016 137 |
| **6−** | 3680<br>016 140 | 3681<br>016 141 | 3682<br>016 142 | 3683<br>016 143 | 3684<br>016 144 | 3685<br>016 145 | 3686<br>016 146 | 3687<br>016 147 | 3688<br>016 150 | 3689<br>016 151 | 3690<br>016 152 | 3691<br>016 153 | 3692<br>016 154 | 3693<br>016 155 | 3694<br>016 156 | 3695<br>016 157 |
| **7−** | 3696<br>016 160 | 3697<br>016 161 | 3698<br>016 162 | 3699<br>016 163 | 3700<br>016 164 | 3701<br>016 165 | 3702<br>016 166 | 3703<br>016 167 | 3704<br>016 170 | 3705<br>016 171 | 3706<br>016 172 | 3707<br>016 173 | 3708<br>016 174 | 3709<br>016 175 | 3710<br>016 176 | 3711<br>016 177 |
| **8−** | 3712<br>016 200 | 3713<br>016 201 | 3714<br>016 202 | 3715<br>016 203 | 3716<br>016 204 | 3717<br>016 205 | 3718<br>016 206 | 3719<br>016 207 | 3720<br>016 210 | 3721<br>016 211 | 3722<br>016 212 | 3723<br>016 213 | 3724<br>016 214 | 3725<br>016 215 | 3726<br>016 216 | 3727<br>016 217 |
| **9−** | 3728<br>016 220 | 3729<br>016 221 | 3730<br>016 222 | 3731<br>016 223 | 3732<br>016 224 | 3733<br>016 225 | 3734<br>016 226 | 3735<br>016 227 | 3736<br>016 230 | 3737<br>016 231 | 3738<br>016 232 | 3739<br>016 233 | 3740<br>016 234 | 3741<br>016 235 | 3742<br>016 236 | 3743<br>016 237 |
| **A−** | 3744<br>016 240 | 3745<br>016 241 | 3746<br>016 242 | 3747<br>016 243 | 3748<br>016 244 | 3749<br>016 245 | 3750<br>016 246 | 3751<br>016 247 | 3752<br>016 250 | 3753<br>016 251 | 3754<br>016 252 | 3755<br>016 253 | 3756<br>016 254 | 3757<br>016 255 | 3758<br>016 256 | 3759<br>016 257 |
| **B−** | 3760<br>016 260 | 3761<br>016 261 | 3762<br>016 262 | 3763<br>016 263 | 3764<br>016 264 | 3765<br>016 265 | 3766<br>016 266 | 3767<br>016 267 | 3768<br>016 270 | 3769<br>016 271 | 3770<br>016 272 | 3771<br>016 273 | 3772<br>016 274 | 3773<br>016 275 | 3774<br>016 276 | 3775<br>016 277 |
| **C−** | 3776<br>016 300 | 3777<br>016 301 | 3778<br>016 302 | 3779<br>016 303 | 3780<br>016 304 | 3781<br>016 305 | 3782<br>016 306 | 3783<br>016 307 | 3784<br>016 310 | 3785<br>016 311 | 3786<br>016 312 | 3787<br>016 313 | 3788<br>016 314 | 3789<br>016 315 | 3790<br>016 316 | 3791<br>016 317 |
| **D−** | 3792<br>016 320 | 3793<br>016 321 | 3794<br>016 322 | 3795<br>016 323 | 3796<br>016 324 | 3797<br>016 325 | 3798<br>016 326 | 3799<br>016 327 | 3800<br>016 330 | 3801<br>016 331 | 3802<br>016 332 | 3803<br>016 333 | 3804<br>016 334 | 3805<br>016 335 | 3806<br>016 336 | 3807<br>016 337 |
| **E−** | 3808<br>016 340 | 3809<br>016 341 | 3810<br>016 342 | 3811<br>016 343 | 3812<br>016 344 | 3813<br>016 345 | 3814<br>016 346 | 3815<br>016 347 | 3816<br>016 350 | 3817<br>016 351 | 3818<br>016 352 | 3819<br>016 353 | 3820<br>016 354 | 3821<br>016 355 | 3822<br>016 356 | 3823<br>016 357 |
| **F−** | 3824<br>016 360 | 3825<br>016 361 | 3826<br>016 362 | 3827<br>016 363 | 3828<br>016 364 | 3829<br>016 365 | 3830<br>016 366 | 3831<br>016 367 | 3832<br>016 370 | 3833<br>016 371 | 3834<br>016 372 | 3835<br>016 373 | 3836<br>016 374 | 3837<br>016 375 | 3838<br>016 376 | 3839<br>016 377 |

SECOND HEX DIGIT (rows) · DECIMAL · DECIMAL · OCTAL

 DECIMAL 3584 — BINARY 0000 1110 — DECIMAL 3584 — HEXADECIMAL 0E — OCTAL 016 000

FOURTH HEX DIGIT → ← THIRD HEX DIGIT

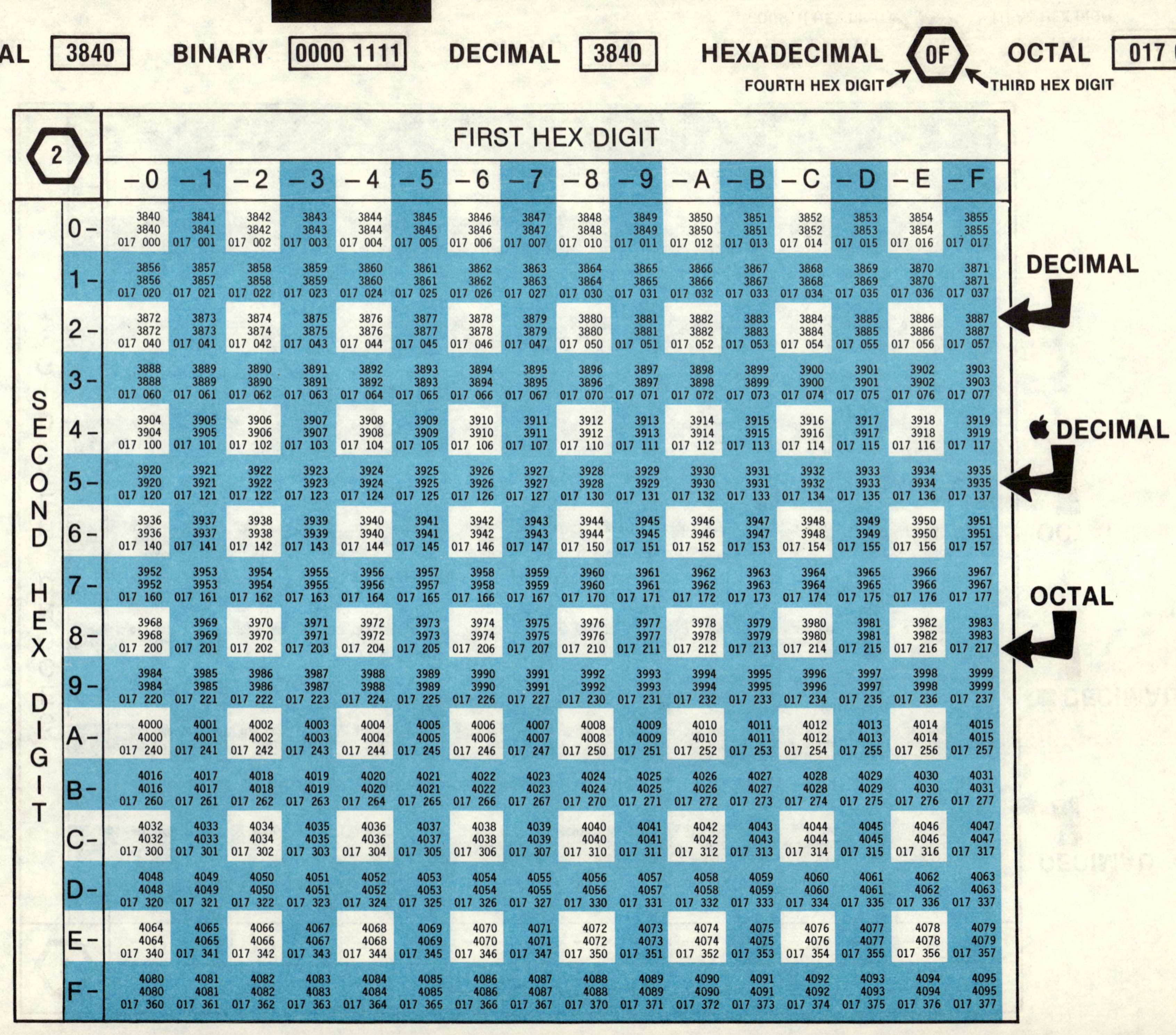


FIRST HEX DIGIT

| 2 | −0 | −1 | −2 | −3 | −4 | −5 | −6 | −7 | −8 | −9 | −A | −B | −C | −D | −E | −F |
|---|---|---|---|---|---|---|---|---|---|---|---|---|---|---|---|---|
| **0−** | 3840<br>017 000 | 3841<br>017 001 | 3842<br>017 002 | 3843<br>017 003 | 3844<br>017 004 | 3845<br>017 005 | 3846<br>017 006 | 3847<br>017 007 | 3848<br>017 010 | 3849<br>017 011 | 3850<br>017 012 | 3851<br>017 013 | 3852<br>017 014 | 3853<br>017 015 | 3854<br>017 016 | 3855<br>017 017 |
| **1−** | 3856<br>017 020 | 3857<br>017 021 | 3858<br>017 022 | 3859<br>017 023 | 3860<br>017 024 | 3861<br>017 025 | 3862<br>017 026 | 3863<br>017 027 | 3864<br>017 030 | 3865<br>017 031 | 3866<br>017 032 | 3867<br>017 033 | 3868<br>017 034 | 3869<br>017 035 | 3870<br>017 036 | 3871<br>017 037 |
| **2−** | 3872<br>017 040 | 3873<br>017 041 | 3874<br>017 042 | 3875<br>017 043 | 3876<br>017 044 | 3877<br>017 045 | 3878<br>017 046 | 3879<br>017 047 | 3880<br>017 050 | 3881<br>017 051 | 3882<br>017 052 | 3883<br>017 053 | 3884<br>017 054 | 3885<br>017 055 | 3886<br>017 056 | 3887<br>017 057 |
| **3−** | 3888<br>017 060 | 3889<br>017 061 | 3890<br>017 062 | 3891<br>017 063 | 3892<br>017 064 | 3893<br>017 065 | 3894<br>017 066 | 3895<br>017 067 | 3896<br>017 070 | 3897<br>017 071 | 3898<br>017 072 | 3899<br>017 073 | 3900<br>017 074 | 3901<br>017 075 | 3902<br>017 076 | 3903<br>017 077 |
| **4−** | 3904<br>017 100 | 3905<br>017 101 | 3906<br>017 102 | 3907<br>017 103 | 3908<br>017 104 | 3909<br>017 105 | 3910<br>017 106 | 3911<br>017 107 | 3912<br>017 110 | 3913<br>017 111 | 3914<br>017 112 | 3915<br>017 113 | 3916<br>017 114 | 3917<br>017 115 | 3918<br>017 116 | 3919<br>017 117 |
| **5−** | 3920<br>017 120 | 3921<br>017 121 | 3922<br>017 122 | 3923<br>017 123 | 3924<br>017 124 | 3925<br>017 125 | 3926<br>017 126 | 3927<br>017 127 | 3928<br>017 130 | 3929<br>017 131 | 3930<br>017 132 | 3931<br>017 133 | 3932<br>017 134 | 3933<br>017 135 | 3934<br>017 136 | 3935<br>017 137 |
| **6−** | 3936<br>017 140 | 3937<br>017 141 | 3938<br>017 142 | 3939<br>017 143 | 3940<br>017 144 | 3941<br>017 145 | 3942<br>017 146 | 3943<br>017 147 | 3944<br>017 150 | 3945<br>017 151 | 3946<br>017 152 | 3947<br>017 153 | 3948<br>017 154 | 3949<br>017 155 | 3950<br>017 156 | 3951<br>017 157 |
| **7−** | 3952<br>017 160 | 3953<br>017 161 | 3954<br>017 162 | 3955<br>017 163 | 3956<br>017 164 | 3957<br>017 165 | 3958<br>017 166 | 3959<br>017 167 | 3960<br>017 170 | 3961<br>017 171 | 3962<br>017 172 | 3963<br>017 173 | 3964<br>017 174 | 3965<br>017 175 | 3966<br>017 176 | 3967<br>017 177 |
| **8−** | 3968<br>017 200 | 3969<br>017 201 | 3970<br>017 202 | 3971<br>017 203 | 3972<br>017 204 | 3973<br>017 205 | 3974<br>017 206 | 3975<br>017 207 | 3976<br>017 210 | 3977<br>017 211 | 3978<br>017 212 | 3979<br>017 213 | 3980<br>017 214 | 3981<br>017 215 | 3982<br>017 216 | 3983<br>017 217 |
| **9−** | 3984<br>017 220 | 3985<br>017 221 | 3986<br>017 222 | 3987<br>017 223 | 3988<br>017 224 | 3989<br>017 225 | 3990<br>017 226 | 3991<br>017 227 | 3992<br>017 230 | 3993<br>017 231 | 3994<br>017 232 | 3995<br>017 233 | 3996<br>017 234 | 3997<br>017 235 | 3998<br>017 236 | 3999<br>017 237 |
| **A−** | 4000<br>017 240 | 4001<br>017 241 | 4002<br>017 242 | 4003<br>017 243 | 4004<br>017 244 | 4005<br>017 245 | 4006<br>017 246 | 4007<br>017 247 | 4008<br>017 250 | 4009<br>017 251 | 4010<br>017 252 | 4011<br>017 253 | 4012<br>017 254 | 4013<br>017 255 | 4014<br>017 256 | 4015<br>017 257 |
| **B−** | 4016<br>017 260 | 4017<br>017 261 | 4018<br>017 262 | 4019<br>017 263 | 4020<br>017 264 | 4021<br>017 265 | 4022<br>017 266 | 4023<br>017 267 | 4024<br>017 270 | 4025<br>017 271 | 4026<br>017 272 | 4027<br>017 273 | 4028<br>017 274 | 4029<br>017 275 | 4030<br>017 276 | 4031<br>017 277 |
| **C−** | 4032<br>017 300 | 4033<br>017 301 | 4034<br>017 302 | 4035<br>017 303 | 4036<br>017 304 | 4037<br>017 305 | 4038<br>017 306 | 4039<br>017 307 | 4040<br>017 310 | 4041<br>017 311 | 4042<br>017 312 | 4043<br>017 313 | 4044<br>017 314 | 4045<br>017 315 | 4046<br>017 316 | 4047<br>017 317 |
| **D−** | 4048<br>017 320 | 4049<br>017 321 | 4050<br>017 322 | 4051<br>017 323 | 4052<br>017 324 | 4053<br>017 325 | 4054<br>017 326 | 4055<br>017 327 | 4056<br>017 330 | 4057<br>017 331 | 4058<br>017 332 | 4059<br>017 333 | 4060<br>017 334 | 4061<br>017 335 | 4062<br>017 336 | 4063<br>017 337 |
| **E−** | 4064<br>017 340 | 4065<br>017 341 | 4066<br>017 342 | 4067<br>017 343 | 4068<br>017 344 | 4069<br>017 345 | 4070<br>017 346 | 4071<br>017 347 | 4072<br>017 350 | 4073<br>017 351 | 4074<br>017 352 | 4075<br>017 353 | 4076<br>017 354 | 4077<br>017 355 | 4078<br>017 356 | 4079<br>017 357 |
| **F−** | 4080<br>017 360 | 4081<br>017 361 | 4082<br>017 362 | 4083<br>017 363 | 4084<br>017 364 | 4085<br>017 365 | 4086<br>017 366 | 4087<br>017 367 | 4088<br>017 370 | 4089<br>017 371 | 4090<br>017 372 | 4091<br>017 373 | 4092<br>017 374 | 4093<br>017 375 | 4094<br>017 376 | 4095<br>017 377 |

SECOND HEX DIGIT

<table>
<thead>
<tr><th>②</th><th colspan="16">FIRST HEX DIGIT</th></tr>
<tr><th></th><th>−0</th><th>−1</th><th>−2</th><th>−3</th><th>−4</th><th>−5</th><th>−6</th><th>−7</th><th>−8</th><th>−9</th><th>−A</th><th>−B</th><th>−C</th><th>−D</th><th>−E</th><th>−F</th></tr>
</thead>
<tbody>
<tr><td>0−</td><td>4096<br>4096<br>020 000</td><td>4097<br>4097<br>020 001</td><td>4098<br>4098<br>020 002</td><td>4099<br>4099<br>020 003</td><td>4100<br>4100<br>020 004</td><td>4101<br>4101<br>020 005</td><td>4102<br>4102<br>020 006</td><td>4103<br>4103<br>020 007</td><td>4104<br>4104<br>020 010</td><td>4105<br>4105<br>020 011</td><td>4106<br>4106<br>020 012</td><td>4107<br>4107<br>020 013</td><td>4108<br>4108<br>020 014</td><td>4109<br>4109<br>020 015</td><td>4110<br>4110<br>020 016</td><td>4111<br>4111<br>020 017</td></tr>
<tr><td>1−</td><td>4112<br>4112<br>020 020</td><td>4113<br>4113<br>020 021</td><td>4114<br>4114<br>020 022</td><td>4115<br>4115<br>020 023</td><td>4116<br>4116<br>020 024</td><td>4117<br>4117<br>020 025</td><td>4118<br>4118<br>020 026</td><td>4119<br>4119<br>020 027</td><td>4120<br>4120<br>020 030</td><td>4121<br>4121<br>020 031</td><td>4122<br>4122<br>020 032</td><td>4123<br>4123<br>020 033</td><td>4124<br>4124<br>020 034</td><td>4125<br>4125<br>020 035</td><td>4126<br>4126<br>020 036</td><td>4127<br>4127<br>020 037</td></tr>
<tr><td>2−</td><td>4128<br>4128<br>020 040</td><td>4129<br>4129<br>020 041</td><td>4130<br>4130<br>020 042</td><td>4131<br>4131<br>020 043</td><td>4132<br>4132<br>020 044</td><td>4133<br>4133<br>020 045</td><td>4134<br>4134<br>020 046</td><td>4135<br>4135<br>020 047</td><td>4136<br>4136<br>020 050</td><td>4137<br>4137<br>020 051</td><td>4138<br>4138<br>020 052</td><td>4139<br>4139<br>020 053</td><td>4140<br>4140<br>020 054</td><td>4141<br>4141<br>020 055</td><td>4142<br>4142<br>020 056</td><td>4143<br>4143<br>020 057</td></tr>
<tr><td>3−</td><td>4144<br>4144<br>020 060</td><td>4145<br>4145<br>020 061</td><td>4146<br>4146<br>020 062</td><td>4147<br>4147<br>020 063</td><td>4148<br>4148<br>020 064</td><td>4149<br>4149<br>020 065</td><td>4150<br>4150<br>020 066</td><td>4151<br>4151<br>020 067</td><td>4152<br>4152<br>020 070</td><td>4153<br>4153<br>020 071</td><td>4154<br>4154<br>020 072</td><td>4155<br>4155<br>020 073</td><td>4156<br>4156<br>020 074</td><td>4157<br>4157<br>020 075</td><td>4158<br>4158<br>020 076</td><td>4159<br>4159<br>020 077</td></tr>
<tr><td>4−</td><td>4160<br>4160<br>020 100</td><td>4161<br>4161<br>020 101</td><td>4162<br>4162<br>020 102</td><td>4163<br>4163<br>020 103</td><td>4164<br>4164<br>020 104</td><td>4165<br>4165<br>020 105</td><td>4166<br>4166<br>020 106</td><td>4167<br>4167<br>020 107</td><td>4168<br>4168<br>020 110</td><td>4169<br>4169<br>020 111</td><td>4170<br>4170<br>020 112</td><td>4171<br>4171<br>020 113</td><td>4172<br>4172<br>020 114</td><td>4173<br>4173<br>020 115</td><td>4174<br>4174<br>020 116</td><td>4175<br>4175<br>020 117</td></tr>
<tr><td>5−</td><td>4176<br>4176<br>020 120</td><td>4177<br>4177<br>020 121</td><td>4178<br>4178<br>020 122</td><td>4179<br>4179<br>020 123</td><td>4180<br>4180<br>020 124</td><td>4181<br>4181<br>020 125</td><td>4182<br>4182<br>020 126</td><td>4183<br>4183<br>020 127</td><td>4184<br>4184<br>020 130</td><td>4185<br>4185<br>020 131</td><td>4186<br>4186<br>020 132</td><td>4187<br>4187<br>020 133</td><td>4188<br>4188<br>020 134</td><td>4189<br>4189<br>020 135</td><td>4190<br>4190<br>020 136</td><td>4191<br>4191<br>020 137</td></tr>
<tr><td>6−</td><td>4192<br>4192<br>020 140</td><td>4193<br>4193<br>020 141</td><td>4194<br>4194<br>020 142</td><td>4195<br>4195<br>020 143</td><td>4196<br>4196<br>020 144</td><td>4197<br>4197<br>020 145</td><td>4198<br>4198<br>020 146</td><td>4199<br>4199<br>020 147</td><td>4200<br>4200<br>020 150</td><td>4201<br>4201<br>020 151</td><td>4202<br>4202<br>020 152</td><td>4203<br>4203<br>020 153</td><td>4204<br>4204<br>020 154</td><td>4205<br>4205<br>020 155</td><td>4206<br>4206<br>020 156</td><td>4207<br>4207<br>020 157</td></tr>
<tr><td>7−</td><td>4208<br>4208<br>020 160</td><td>4209<br>4209<br>020 161</td><td>4210<br>4210<br>020 162</td><td>4211<br>4211<br>020 163</td><td>4212<br>4212<br>020 164</td><td>4213<br>4213<br>020 165</td><td>4214<br>4214<br>020 166</td><td>4215<br>4215<br>020 167</td><td>4216<br>4216<br>020 170</td><td>4217<br>4217<br>020 171</td><td>4218<br>4218<br>020 172</td><td>4219<br>4219<br>020 173</td><td>4220<br>4220<br>020 174</td><td>4221<br>4221<br>020 175</td><td>4222<br>4222<br>020 176</td><td>4223<br>4223<br>020 177</td></tr>
<tr><td>8−</td><td>4224<br>4224<br>020 200</td><td>4225<br>4225<br>020 201</td><td>4226<br>4226<br>020 202</td><td>4227<br>4227<br>020 203</td><td>4228<br>4228<br>020 204</td><td>4229<br>4229<br>020 205</td><td>4230<br>4230<br>020 206</td><td>4231<br>4231<br>020 207</td><td>4232<br>4232<br>020 210</td><td>4233<br>4233<br>020 211</td><td>4234<br>4234<br>020 212</td><td>4235<br>4235<br>020 213</td><td>4236<br>4236<br>020 214</td><td>4237<br>4237<br>020 215</td><td>4238<br>4238<br>020 216</td><td>4239<br>4239<br>020 217</td></tr>
<tr><td>9−</td><td>4240<br>4240<br>020 220</td><td>4241<br>4241<br>020 221</td><td>4242<br>4242<br>020 222</td><td>4243<br>4243<br>020 223</td><td>4244<br>4244<br>020 224</td><td>4245<br>4245<br>020 225</td><td>4246<br>4246<br>020 226</td><td>4247<br>4247<br>020 227</td><td>4248<br>4248<br>020 230</td><td>4249<br>4249<br>020 231</td><td>4250<br>4250<br>020 232</td><td>4251<br>4251<br>020 233</td><td>4252<br>4252<br>020 234</td><td>4253<br>4253<br>020 235</td><td>4254<br>4254<br>020 236</td><td>4255<br>4255<br>020 237</td></tr>
<tr><td>A−</td><td>4256<br>4256<br>020 240</td><td>4257<br>4257<br>020 241</td><td>4258<br>4258<br>020 242</td><td>4259<br>4259<br>020 243</td><td>4260<br>4260<br>020 244</td><td>4261<br>4261<br>020 245</td><td>4262<br>4262<br>020 246</td><td>4263<br>4263<br>020 247</td><td>4264<br>4264<br>020 250</td><td>4265<br>4265<br>020 251</td><td>4266<br>4266<br>020 252</td><td>4267<br>4267<br>020 253</td><td>4268<br>4268<br>020 254</td><td>4269<br>4269<br>020 255</td><td>4270<br>4270<br>020 256</td><td>4271<br>4271<br>020 257</td></tr>
<tr><td>B−</td><td>4272<br>4272<br>020 260</td><td>4273<br>4273<br>020 261</td><td>4274<br>4274<br>020 262</td><td>4275<br>4275<br>020 263</td><td>4276<br>4276<br>020 264</td><td>4277<br>4277<br>020 265</td><td>4278<br>4278<br>020 266</td><td>4279<br>4279<br>020 267</td><td>4280<br>4280<br>020 270</td><td>4281<br>4281<br>020 271</td><td>4282<br>4282<br>020 272</td><td>4283<br>4283<br>020 273</td><td>4284<br>4284<br>020 274</td><td>4285<br>4285<br>020 275</td><td>4286<br>4286<br>020 276</td><td>4287<br>4287<br>020 277</td></tr>
<tr><td>C−</td><td>4288<br>4288<br>020 300</td><td>4289<br>4289<br>020 301</td><td>4290<br>4290<br>020 302</td><td>4291<br>4291<br>020 303</td><td>4292<br>4292<br>020 304</td><td>4293<br>4293<br>020 305</td><td>4294<br>4294<br>020 306</td><td>4295<br>4295<br>020 307</td><td>4296<br>4296<br>020 310</td><td>4297<br>4297<br>020 311</td><td>4298<br>4298<br>020 312</td><td>4299<br>4299<br>020 313</td><td>4300<br>4300<br>020 314</td><td>4301<br>4301<br>020 315</td><td>4302<br>4302<br>020 316</td><td>4303<br>4303<br>020 317</td></tr>
<tr><td>D−</td><td>4304<br>4304<br>020 320</td><td>4305<br>4305<br>020 321</td><td>4306<br>4306<br>020 322</td><td>4307<br>4307<br>020 323</td><td>4308<br>4308<br>020 324</td><td>4309<br>4309<br>020 325</td><td>4310<br>4310<br>020 326</td><td>4311<br>4311<br>020 327</td><td>4312<br>4312<br>020 330</td><td>4313<br>4313<br>020 331</td><td>4314<br>4314<br>020 332</td><td>4315<br>4315<br>020 333</td><td>4316<br>4316<br>020 334</td><td>4317<br>4317<br>020 335</td><td>4318<br>4318<br>020 336</td><td>4319<br>4319<br>020 337</td></tr>
<tr><td>E−</td><td>4320<br>4320<br>020 340</td><td>4321<br>4321<br>020 341</td><td>4322<br>4322<br>020 342</td><td>4323<br>4323<br>020 343</td><td>4324<br>4324<br>020 344</td><td>4325<br>4325<br>020 345</td><td>4326<br>4326<br>020 346</td><td>4327<br>4327<br>020 347</td><td>4328<br>4328<br>020 350</td><td>4329<br>4329<br>020 351</td><td>4330<br>4330<br>020 352</td><td>4331<br>4331<br>020 353</td><td>4332<br>4332<br>020 354</td><td>4333<br>4333<br>020 355</td><td>4334<br>4334<br>020 356</td><td>4335<br>4335<br>020 357</td></tr>
<tr><td>F−</td><td>4336<br>4336<br>020 360</td><td>4337<br>4337<br>020 361</td><td>4338<br>4338<br>020 362</td><td>4339<br>4339<br>020 363</td><td>4340<br>4340<br>020 364</td><td>4341<br>4341<br>020 365</td><td>4342<br>4342<br>020 366</td><td>4343<br>4343<br>020 367</td><td>4344<br>4344<br>020 370</td><td>4345<br>4345<br>020 371</td><td>4346<br>4346<br>020 372</td><td>4347<br>4347<br>020 373</td><td>4348<br>4348<br>020 374</td><td>4349<br>4349<br>020 375</td><td>4350<br>4350<br>020 376</td><td>4351<br>4351<br>020 377</td></tr>
</tbody>
</table>

Row label (left margin): **SECOND HEX DIGIT**

Annotations (right side): **DECIMAL** → ;  **DECIMAL** → ; **OCTAL** →

 **DECIMAL** | 4096 |   **BINARY** | 0001 0000 |   **DECIMAL** | 4096 |   **HEXADECIMAL** ⬡ 10   **OCTAL** | 020 000 |

FOURTH HEX DIGIT →   ← THIRD HEX DIGIT

# DECIMAL `4352` BINARY `0001 0001` DECIMAL `4352` HEXADECIMAL (11) OCTAL `021 000`

FOURTH HEX DIGIT → ← THIRD HEX DIGIT

(2) / FIRST HEX DIGIT

Each cell shows: decimal value (top), decimal value (middle), octal value (bottom).

| SECOND HEX DIGIT | −0 | −1 | −2 | −3 | −4 | −5 | −6 | −7 | −8 | −9 | −A | −B | −C | −D | −E | −F |
|---|---|---|---|---|---|---|---|---|---|---|---|---|---|---|---|---|
| 0− | 4352 / 021 000 | 4353 / 021 001 | 4354 / 021 002 | 4355 / 021 003 | 4356 / 021 004 | 4357 / 021 005 | 4358 / 021 006 | 4359 / 021 007 | 4360 / 021 010 | 4361 / 021 011 | 4362 / 021 012 | 4363 / 021 013 | 4364 / 021 014 | 4365 / 021 015 | 4366 / 021 016 | 4367 / 021 017 |
| 1− | 4368 / 021 020 | 4369 / 021 021 | 4370 / 021 022 | 4371 / 021 023 | 4372 / 021 024 | 4373 / 021 025 | 4374 / 021 026 | 4375 / 021 027 | 4376 / 021 030 | 4377 / 021 031 | 4378 / 021 032 | 4379 / 021 033 | 4380 / 021 034 | 4381 / 021 035 | 4382 / 021 036 | 4383 / 021 037 |
| 2− | 4384 / 021 040 | 4385 / 021 041 | 4386 / 021 042 | 4387 / 021 043 | 4388 / 021 044 | 4389 / 021 045 | 4390 / 021 046 | 4391 / 021 047 | 4392 / 021 050 | 4393 / 021 051 | 4394 / 021 052 | 4395 / 021 053 | 4396 / 021 054 | 4397 / 021 055 | 4398 / 021 056 | 4399 / 021 057 |
| 3− | 4400 / 021 060 | 4401 / 021 061 | 4402 / 021 062 | 4403 / 021 063 | 4404 / 021 064 | 4405 / 021 065 | 4406 / 021 066 | 4407 / 021 067 | 4408 / 021 070 | 4409 / 021 071 | 4410 / 021 072 | 4411 / 021 073 | 4412 / 021 074 | 4413 / 021 075 | 4414 / 021 076 | 4415 / 021 077 |
| 4− | 4416 / 021 100 | 4417 / 021 101 | 4418 / 021 102 | 4419 / 021 103 | 4420 / 021 104 | 4421 / 021 105 | 4422 / 021 106 | 4423 / 021 107 | 4424 / 021 110 | 4425 / 021 111 | 4426 / 021 112 | 4427 / 021 113 | 4428 / 021 114 | 4429 / 021 115 | 4430 / 021 116 | 4431 / 021 117 |
| 5− | 4432 / 021 120 | 4433 / 021 121 | 4434 / 021 122 | 4435 / 021 123 | 4436 / 021 124 | 4437 / 021 125 | 4438 / 021 126 | 4439 / 021 127 | 4440 / 021 130 | 4441 / 021 131 | 4442 / 021 132 | 4443 / 021 133 | 4444 / 021 134 | 4445 / 021 135 | 4446 / 021 136 | 4447 / 021 137 |
| 6− | 4448 / 021 140 | 4449 / 021 141 | 4450 / 021 142 | 4451 / 021 143 | 4452 / 021 144 | 4453 / 021 145 | 4454 / 021 146 | 4455 / 021 147 | 4456 / 021 150 | 4457 / 021 151 | 4458 / 021 152 | 4459 / 021 153 | 4460 / 021 154 | 4461 / 021 155 | 4462 / 021 156 | 4463 / 021 157 |
| 7− | 4464 / 021 160 | 4465 / 021 161 | 4466 / 021 162 | 4467 / 021 163 | 4468 / 021 164 | 4469 / 021 165 | 4470 / 021 166 | 4471 / 021 167 | 4472 / 021 170 | 4473 / 021 171 | 4474 / 021 172 | 4475 / 021 173 | 4476 / 021 174 | 4477 / 021 175 | 4478 / 021 176 | 4479 / 021 177 |
| 8− | 4480 / 021 200 | 4481 / 021 201 | 4482 / 021 202 | 4483 / 021 203 | 4484 / 021 204 | 4485 / 021 205 | 4486 / 021 206 | 4487 / 021 207 | 4488 / 021 210 | 4489 / 021 211 | 4490 / 021 212 | 4491 / 021 213 | 4492 / 021 214 | 4493 / 021 215 | 4494 / 021 216 | 4495 / 021 217 |
| 9− | 4496 / 021 220 | 4497 / 021 221 | 4498 / 021 222 | 4499 / 021 223 | 4500 / 021 224 | 4501 / 021 225 | 4502 / 021 226 | 4503 / 021 227 | 4504 / 021 230 | 4505 / 021 231 | 4506 / 021 232 | 4507 / 021 233 | 4508 / 021 234 | 4509 / 021 235 | 4510 / 021 236 | 4511 / 021 237 |
| A− | 4512 / 021 240 | 4513 / 021 241 | 4514 / 021 242 | 4515 / 021 243 | 4516 / 021 244 | 4517 / 021 245 | 4518 / 021 246 | 4519 / 021 247 | 4520 / 021 250 | 4521 / 021 251 | 4522 / 021 252 | 4523 / 021 253 | 4524 / 021 254 | 4525 / 021 255 | 4526 / 021 256 | 4527 / 021 257 |
| B− | 4528 / 021 260 | 4529 / 021 261 | 4530 / 021 262 | 4531 / 021 263 | 4532 / 021 264 | 4533 / 021 265 | 4534 / 021 266 | 4535 / 021 267 | 4536 / 021 270 | 4537 / 021 271 | 4538 / 021 272 | 4539 / 021 273 | 4540 / 021 274 | 4541 / 021 275 | 4542 / 021 276 | 4543 / 021 277 |
| C− | 4544 / 021 300 | 4545 / 021 301 | 4546 / 021 302 | 4547 / 021 303 | 4548 / 021 304 | 4549 / 021 305 | 4550 / 021 306 | 4551 / 021 307 | 4552 / 021 310 | 4553 / 021 311 | 4554 / 021 312 | 4555 / 021 313 | 4556 / 021 314 | 4557 / 021 315 | 4558 / 021 316 | 4559 / 021 317 |
| D− | 4560 / 021 320 | 4561 / 021 321 | 4562 / 021 322 | 4563 / 021 323 | 4564 / 021 324 | 4565 / 021 325 | 4566 / 021 326 | 4567 / 021 327 | 4568 / 021 330 | 4569 / 021 331 | 4570 / 021 332 | 4571 / 021 333 | 4572 / 021 334 | 4573 / 021 335 | 4574 / 021 336 | 4575 / 021 337 |
| E− | 4576 / 021 340 | 4577 / 021 341 | 4578 / 021 342 | 4579 / 021 343 | 4580 / 021 344 | 4581 / 021 345 | 4582 / 021 346 | 4583 / 021 347 | 4584 / 021 350 | 4585 / 021 351 | 4586 / 021 352 | 4587 / 021 353 | 4588 / 021 354 | 4589 / 021 355 | 4590 / 021 356 | 4591 / 021 357 |
| F− | 4592 / 021 360 | 4593 / 021 361 | 4594 / 021 362 | 4595 / 021 363 | 4596 / 021 364 | 4597 / 021 365 | 4598 / 021 366 | 4599 / 021 367 | 4600 / 021 370 | 4601 / 021 371 | 4602 / 021 372 | 4603 / 021 373 | 4604 / 021 374 | 4605 / 021 375 | 4606 / 021 376 | 4607 / 021 377 |

## FIRST HEX DIGIT

|  | −0 | −1 | −2 | −3 | −4 | −5 | −6 | −7 | −8 | −9 | −A | −B | −C | −D | −E | −F |
|---|---|---|---|---|---|---|---|---|---|---|---|---|---|---|---|---|
| **0−** | 4608<br>4608<br>022 000 | 4609<br>4609<br>022 001 | 4610<br>4610<br>022 002 | 4611<br>4611<br>022 003 | 4612<br>4612<br>022 004 | 4613<br>4613<br>022 005 | 4614<br>4614<br>022 006 | 4615<br>4615<br>022 007 | 4616<br>4616<br>022 010 | 4617<br>4617<br>022 011 | 4618<br>4618<br>022 012 | 4619<br>4619<br>022 013 | 4620<br>4620<br>022 014 | 4621<br>4621<br>022 015 | 4622<br>4622<br>022 016 | 4623<br>4623<br>022 017 |
| **1−** | 4624<br>4624<br>022 020 | 4625<br>4625<br>022 021 | 4626<br>4626<br>022 022 | 4627<br>4627<br>022 023 | 4628<br>4628<br>022 024 | 4629<br>4629<br>022 025 | 4630<br>4630<br>022 026 | 4631<br>4631<br>022 027 | 4632<br>4632<br>022 030 | 4633<br>4633<br>022 031 | 4634<br>4634<br>022 032 | 4635<br>4635<br>022 033 | 4636<br>4636<br>022 034 | 4637<br>4637<br>022 035 | 4638<br>4638<br>022 036 | 4639<br>4639<br>022 037 |
| **2−** | 4640<br>4640<br>022 040 | 4641<br>4641<br>022 041 | 4642<br>4642<br>022 042 | 4643<br>4643<br>022 043 | 4644<br>4644<br>022 044 | 4645<br>4645<br>022 045 | 4646<br>4646<br>022 046 | 4647<br>4647<br>022 047 | 4648<br>4648<br>022 050 | 4649<br>4649<br>022 051 | 4650<br>4650<br>022 052 | 4651<br>4651<br>022 053 | 4652<br>4652<br>022 054 | 4653<br>4653<br>022 055 | 4654<br>4654<br>022 056 | 4655<br>4655<br>022 057 |
| **3−** | 4656<br>4656<br>022 060 | 4657<br>4657<br>022 061 | 4658<br>4658<br>022 062 | 4659<br>4659<br>022 063 | 4660<br>4660<br>022 064 | 4661<br>4661<br>022 065 | 4662<br>4662<br>022 066 | 4663<br>4663<br>022 067 | 4664<br>4664<br>022 070 | 4665<br>4665<br>022 071 | 4666<br>4666<br>022 072 | 4667<br>4667<br>022 073 | 4668<br>4668<br>022 074 | 4669<br>4669<br>022 075 | 4670<br>4670<br>022 076 | 4671<br>4671<br>022 077 |
| **4−** | 4672<br>4672<br>022 100 | 4673<br>4673<br>022 101 | 4674<br>4674<br>022 102 | 4675<br>4675<br>022 103 | 4676<br>4676<br>022 104 | 4677<br>4677<br>022 105 | 4678<br>4678<br>022 106 | 4679<br>4679<br>022 107 | 4680<br>4680<br>022 110 | 4681<br>4681<br>022 111 | 4682<br>4682<br>022 112 | 4683<br>4683<br>022 113 | 4684<br>4684<br>022 114 | 4685<br>4685<br>022 115 | 4686<br>4686<br>022 116 | 4687<br>4687<br>022 117 |
| **5−** | 4688<br>4688<br>022 120 | 4689<br>4689<br>022 121 | 4690<br>4690<br>022 122 | 4691<br>4691<br>022 123 | 4692<br>4692<br>022 124 | 4693<br>4693<br>022 125 | 4694<br>4694<br>022 126 | 4695<br>4695<br>022 127 | 4696<br>4696<br>022 130 | 4697<br>4697<br>022 131 | 4698<br>4698<br>022 132 | 4699<br>4699<br>022 133 | 4700<br>4700<br>022 134 | 4701<br>4701<br>022 135 | 4702<br>4702<br>022 136 | 4703<br>4703<br>022 137 |
| **6−** | 4704<br>4704<br>022 140 | 4705<br>4705<br>022 141 | 4706<br>4706<br>022 142 | 4707<br>4707<br>022 143 | 4708<br>4708<br>022 144 | 4709<br>4709<br>022 145 | 4710<br>4710<br>022 146 | 4711<br>4711<br>022 147 | 4712<br>4712<br>022 150 | 4713<br>4713<br>022 151 | 4714<br>4714<br>022 152 | 4715<br>4715<br>022 153 | 4716<br>4716<br>022 154 | 4717<br>4717<br>022 155 | 4718<br>4718<br>022 156 | 4719<br>4719<br>022 157 |
| **7−** | 4720<br>4720<br>022 160 | 4721<br>4721<br>022 161 | 4722<br>4722<br>022 162 | 4723<br>4723<br>022 163 | 4724<br>4724<br>022 164 | 4725<br>4725<br>022 165 | 4726<br>4726<br>022 166 | 4727<br>4727<br>022 167 | 4728<br>4728<br>022 170 | 4729<br>4729<br>022 171 | 4730<br>4730<br>022 172 | 4731<br>4731<br>022 173 | 4732<br>4732<br>022 174 | 4733<br>4733<br>022 175 | 4734<br>4734<br>022 176 | 4735<br>4735<br>022 177 |
| **8−** | 4736<br>4736<br>022 200 | 4737<br>4737<br>022 201 | 4738<br>4738<br>022 202 | 4739<br>4739<br>022 203 | 4740<br>4740<br>022 204 | 4741<br>4741<br>022 205 | 4742<br>4742<br>022 206 | 4743<br>4743<br>022 207 | 4744<br>4744<br>022 210 | 4745<br>4745<br>022 211 | 4746<br>4746<br>022 212 | 4747<br>4747<br>022 213 | 4748<br>4748<br>022 214 | 4749<br>4749<br>022 215 | 4750<br>4750<br>022 216 | 4751<br>4751<br>022 217 |
| **9−** | 4752<br>4752<br>022 220 | 4753<br>4753<br>022 221 | 4754<br>4754<br>022 222 | 4755<br>4755<br>022 223 | 4756<br>4756<br>022 224 | 4757<br>4757<br>022 225 | 4758<br>4758<br>022 226 | 4759<br>4759<br>022 227 | 4760<br>4760<br>022 230 | 4761<br>4761<br>022 231 | 4762<br>4762<br>022 232 | 4763<br>4763<br>022 233 | 4764<br>4764<br>022 234 | 4765<br>4765<br>022 235 | 4766<br>4766<br>022 236 | 4767<br>4767<br>022 237 |
| **A−** | 4768<br>4768<br>022 240 | 4769<br>4769<br>022 241 | 4770<br>4770<br>022 242 | 4771<br>4771<br>022 243 | 4772<br>4772<br>022 244 | 4773<br>4773<br>022 245 | 4774<br>4774<br>022 246 | 4775<br>4775<br>022 247 | 4776<br>4776<br>022 250 | 4777<br>4777<br>022 251 | 4778<br>4778<br>022 252 | 4779<br>4779<br>022 253 | 4780<br>4780<br>022 254 | 4781<br>4781<br>022 255 | 4782<br>4782<br>022 256 | 4783<br>4783<br>022 257 |
| **B−** | 4784<br>4784<br>022 260 | 4785<br>4785<br>022 261 | 4786<br>4786<br>022 262 | 4787<br>4787<br>022 263 | 4788<br>4788<br>022 264 | 4789<br>4789<br>022 265 | 4790<br>4790<br>022 266 | 4791<br>4791<br>022 267 | 4792<br>4792<br>022 270 | 4793<br>4793<br>022 271 | 4794<br>4794<br>022 272 | 4795<br>4795<br>022 273 | 4796<br>4796<br>022 274 | 4797<br>4797<br>022 275 | 4798<br>4798<br>022 276 | 4799<br>4799<br>022 277 |
| **C−** | 4800<br>4800<br>022 300 | 4801<br>4801<br>022 301 | 4802<br>4802<br>022 302 | 4803<br>4803<br>022 303 | 4804<br>4804<br>022 304 | 4805<br>4805<br>022 305 | 4806<br>4806<br>022 306 | 4807<br>4807<br>022 307 | 4808<br>4808<br>022 310 | 4809<br>4809<br>022 311 | 4810<br>4810<br>022 312 | 4811<br>4811<br>022 313 | 4812<br>4812<br>022 314 | 4813<br>4813<br>022 315 | 4814<br>4814<br>022 316 | 4815<br>4815<br>022 317 |
| **D−** | 4816<br>4816<br>022 320 | 4817<br>4817<br>022 321 | 4818<br>4818<br>022 322 | 4819<br>4819<br>022 323 | 4820<br>4820<br>022 324 | 4821<br>4821<br>022 325 | 4822<br>4822<br>022 326 | 4823<br>4823<br>022 327 | 4824<br>4824<br>022 330 | 4825<br>4825<br>022 331 | 4826<br>4826<br>022 332 | 4827<br>4827<br>022 333 | 4828<br>4828<br>022 334 | 4829<br>4829<br>022 335 | 4830<br>4830<br>022 336 | 4831<br>4831<br>022 337 |
| **E−** | 4832<br>4832<br>022 340 | 4833<br>4833<br>022 341 | 4834<br>4834<br>022 342 | 4835<br>4835<br>022 343 | 4836<br>4836<br>022 344 | 4837<br>4837<br>022 345 | 4838<br>4838<br>022 346 | 4839<br>4839<br>022 347 | 4840<br>4840<br>022 350 | 4841<br>4841<br>022 351 | 4842<br>4842<br>022 352 | 4843<br>4843<br>022 353 | 4844<br>4844<br>022 354 | 4845<br>4845<br>022 355 | 4846<br>4846<br>022 356 | 4847<br>4847<br>022 357 |
| **F−** | 4848<br>4848<br>022 360 | 4849<br>4849<br>022 361 | 4850<br>4850<br>022 362 | 4851<br>4851<br>022 363 | 4852<br>4852<br>022 364 | 4853<br>4853<br>022 365 | 4854<br>4854<br>022 366 | 4855<br>4855<br>022 367 | 4856<br>4856<br>022 370 | 4857<br>4857<br>022 371 | 4858<br>4858<br>022 372 | 4859<br>4859<br>022 373 | 4860<br>4860<br>022 374 | 4861<br>4861<br>022 375 | 4862<br>4862<br>022 376 | 4863<br>4863<br>022 377 |

**SECOND HEX DIGIT** (row labels, left side)

DECIMAL →
 DECIMAL →
OCTAL →

---

 DECIMAL 4608  BINARY 0001 0010  DECIMAL 4608  HEXADECIMAL ⬡ 12  OCTAL 022 000

FOURTH HEX DIGIT → ← THIRD HEX DIGIT

| | DECIMAL | BINARY | DECIMAL | HEXADECIMAL | OCTAL |
|---|---|---|---|---|---|
|  DECIMAL | 4864 | 0001 0011 | 4864 | 13 | 023 000 |

FOURTH HEX DIGIT → 13 ← THIRD HEX DIGIT

**FIRST HEX DIGIT** (⬡ 2) / **SECOND HEX DIGIT**

| | −0 | −1 | −2 | −3 | −4 | −5 | −6 | −7 | −8 | −9 | −A | −B | −C | −D | −E | −F |
|---|---|---|---|---|---|---|---|---|---|---|---|---|---|---|---|---|
| **0−** | 4864<br>023 000 | 4865<br>023 001 | 4866<br>023 002 | 4867<br>023 003 | 4868<br>023 004 | 4869<br>023 005 | 4870<br>023 006 | 4871<br>023 007 | 4872<br>023 010 | 4873<br>023 011 | 4874<br>023 012 | 4875<br>023 013 | 4876<br>023 014 | 4877<br>023 015 | 4878<br>023 016 | 4879<br>023 017 |
| **1−** | 4880<br>023 020 | 4881<br>023 021 | 4882<br>023 022 | 4883<br>023 023 | 4884<br>023 024 | 4885<br>023 025 | 4886<br>023 026 | 4887<br>023 027 | 4888<br>023 030 | 4889<br>023 031 | 4890<br>023 032 | 4891<br>023 033 | 4892<br>023 034 | 4893<br>023 035 | 4894<br>023 036 | 4895<br>023 037 |
| **2−** | 4896<br>023 040 | 4897<br>023 041 | 4898<br>023 042 | 4899<br>023 043 | 4900<br>023 044 | 4901<br>023 045 | 4902<br>023 046 | 4903<br>023 047 | 4904<br>023 050 | 4905<br>023 051 | 4906<br>023 052 | 4907<br>023 053 | 4908<br>023 054 | 4909<br>023 055 | 4910<br>023 056 | 4911<br>023 057 |
| **3−** | 4912<br>023 060 | 4913<br>023 061 | 4914<br>023 062 | 4915<br>023 063 | 4916<br>023 064 | 4917<br>023 065 | 4918<br>023 066 | 4919<br>023 067 | 4920<br>023 070 | 4921<br>023 071 | 4922<br>023 072 | 4923<br>023 073 | 4924<br>023 074 | 4925<br>023 075 | 4926<br>023 076 | 4927<br>023 077 |
| **4−** | 4928<br>023 100 | 4929<br>023 101 | 4930<br>023 102 | 4931<br>023 103 | 4932<br>023 104 | 4933<br>023 105 | 4934<br>023 106 | 4935<br>023 107 | 4936<br>023 110 | 4937<br>023 111 | 4938<br>023 112 | 4939<br>023 113 | 4940<br>023 114 | 4941<br>023 115 | 4942<br>023 116 | 4943<br>023 117 |
| **5−** | 4944<br>023 120 | 4945<br>023 121 | 4946<br>023 122 | 4947<br>023 123 | 4948<br>023 124 | 4949<br>023 125 | 4950<br>023 126 | 4951<br>023 127 | 4952<br>023 130 | 4953<br>023 131 | 4954<br>023 132 | 4955<br>023 133 | 4956<br>023 134 | 4957<br>023 135 | 4958<br>023 136 | 4959<br>023 137 |
| **6−** | 4960<br>023 140 | 4961<br>023 141 | 4962<br>023 142 | 4963<br>023 143 | 4964<br>023 144 | 4965<br>023 145 | 4966<br>023 146 | 4967<br>023 147 | 4968<br>023 150 | 4969<br>023 151 | 4970<br>023 152 | 4971<br>023 153 | 4972<br>023 154 | 4973<br>023 155 | 4974<br>023 156 | 4975<br>023 157 |
| **7−** | 4976<br>023 160 | 4977<br>023 161 | 4978<br>023 162 | 4979<br>023 163 | 4980<br>023 164 | 4981<br>023 165 | 4982<br>023 166 | 4983<br>023 167 | 4984<br>023 170 | 4985<br>023 171 | 4986<br>023 172 | 4987<br>023 173 | 4988<br>023 174 | 4989<br>023 175 | 4990<br>023 176 | 4991<br>023 177 |
| **8−** | 4992<br>023 200 | 4993<br>023 201 | 4994<br>023 202 | 4995<br>023 203 | 4996<br>023 204 | 4997<br>023 205 | 4998<br>023 206 | 4999<br>023 207 | 5000<br>023 210 | 5001<br>023 211 | 5002<br>023 212 | 5003<br>023 213 | 5004<br>023 214 | 5005<br>023 215 | 5006<br>023 216 | 5007<br>023 217 |
| **9−** | 5008<br>023 220 | 5009<br>023 221 | 5010<br>023 222 | 5011<br>023 223 | 5012<br>023 224 | 5013<br>023 225 | 5014<br>023 226 | 5015<br>023 227 | 5016<br>023 230 | 5017<br>023 231 | 5018<br>023 232 | 5019<br>023 233 | 5020<br>023 234 | 5021<br>023 235 | 5022<br>023 236 | 5023<br>023 237 |
| **A−** | 5024<br>023 240 | 5025<br>023 241 | 5026<br>023 242 | 5027<br>023 243 | 5028<br>023 244 | 5029<br>023 245 | 5030<br>023 246 | 5031<br>023 247 | 5032<br>023 250 | 5033<br>023 251 | 5034<br>023 252 | 5035<br>023 253 | 5036<br>023 254 | 5037<br>023 255 | 5038<br>023 256 | 5039<br>023 257 |
| **B−** | 5040<br>023 260 | 5041<br>023 261 | 5042<br>023 262 | 5043<br>023 263 | 5044<br>023 264 | 5045<br>023 265 | 5046<br>023 266 | 5047<br>023 267 | 5048<br>023 270 | 5049<br>023 271 | 5050<br>023 272 | 5051<br>023 273 | 5052<br>023 274 | 5053<br>023 275 | 5054<br>023 276 | 5055<br>023 277 |
| **C−** | 5056<br>023 300 | 5057<br>023 301 | 5058<br>023 302 | 5059<br>023 303 | 5060<br>023 304 | 5061<br>023 305 | 5062<br>023 306 | 5063<br>023 307 | 5064<br>023 310 | 5065<br>023 311 | 5066<br>023 312 | 5067<br>023 313 | 5068<br>023 314 | 5069<br>023 315 | 5070<br>023 316 | 5071<br>023 317 |
| **D−** | 5072<br>023 320 | 5073<br>023 321 | 5074<br>023 322 | 5075<br>023 323 | 5076<br>023 324 | 5077<br>023 325 | 5078<br>023 326 | 5079<br>023 327 | 5080<br>023 330 | 5081<br>023 331 | 5082<br>023 332 | 5083<br>023 333 | 5084<br>023 334 | 5085<br>023 335 | 5086<br>023 336 | 5087<br>023 337 |
| **E−** | 5088<br>023 340 | 5089<br>023 341 | 5090<br>023 342 | 5091<br>023 343 | 5092<br>023 344 | 5093<br>023 345 | 5094<br>023 346 | 5095<br>023 347 | 5096<br>023 350 | 5097<br>023 351 | 5098<br>023 352 | 5099<br>023 353 | 5100<br>023 354 | 5101<br>023 355 | 5102<br>023 356 | 5103<br>023 357 |
| **F−** | 5104<br>023 360 | 5105<br>023 361 | 5106<br>023 362 | 5107<br>023 363 | 5108<br>023 364 | 5109<br>023 365 | 5110<br>023 366 | 5111<br>023 367 | 5112<br>023 370 | 5113<br>023 371 | 5114<br>023 372 | 5115<br>023 373 | 5116<br>023 374 | 5117<br>023 375 | 5118<br>023 376 | 5119<br>023 377 |

| SECOND HEX DIGIT | −0 | −1 | −2 | −3 | −4 | −5 | −6 | −7 | −8 | −9 | −A | −B | −C | −D | −E | −F |
|---|---|---|---|---|---|---|---|---|---|---|---|---|---|---|---|---|
| 0− | 5120<br>5120<br>024 000 | 5121<br>5121<br>024 001 | 5122<br>5122<br>024 002 | 5123<br>5123<br>024 003 | 5124<br>5124<br>024 004 | 5125<br>5125<br>024 005 | 5126<br>5126<br>024 006 | 5127<br>5127<br>024 007 | 5128<br>5128<br>024 010 | 5129<br>5129<br>024 011 | 5130<br>5130<br>024 012 | 5131<br>5131<br>024 013 | 5132<br>5132<br>024 014 | 5133<br>5133<br>024 015 | 5134<br>5134<br>024 016 | 5135<br>5135<br>024 017 |
| 1− | 5136<br>5136<br>024 020 | 5137<br>5137<br>024 021 | 5138<br>5138<br>024 022 | 5139<br>5139<br>024 023 | 5140<br>5140<br>024 024 | 5141<br>5141<br>024 025 | 5142<br>5142<br>024 026 | 5143<br>5143<br>024 027 | 5144<br>5144<br>024 030 | 5145<br>5145<br>024 031 | 5146<br>5146<br>024 032 | 5147<br>5147<br>024 033 | 5148<br>5148<br>024 034 | 5149<br>5149<br>024 035 | 5150<br>5150<br>024 036 | 5151<br>5151<br>024 037 |
| 2− | 5152<br>5152<br>024 040 | 5153<br>5153<br>024 041 | 5154<br>5154<br>024 042 | 5155<br>5155<br>024 043 | 5156<br>5156<br>024 044 | 5157<br>5157<br>024 045 | 5158<br>5158<br>024 046 | 5159<br>5159<br>024 047 | 5160<br>5160<br>024 050 | 5161<br>5161<br>024 051 | 5162<br>5162<br>024 052 | 5163<br>5163<br>024 053 | 5164<br>5164<br>024 054 | 5165<br>5165<br>024 055 | 5166<br>5166<br>024 056 | 5167<br>5167<br>024 057 |
| 3− | 5168<br>5168<br>024 060 | 5169<br>5169<br>024 061 | 5170<br>5170<br>024 062 | 5171<br>5171<br>024 063 | 5172<br>5172<br>024 064 | 5173<br>5173<br>024 065 | 5174<br>5174<br>024 066 | 5175<br>5175<br>024 067 | 5176<br>5176<br>024 070 | 5177<br>5177<br>024 071 | 5178<br>5178<br>024 072 | 5179<br>5179<br>024 073 | 5180<br>5180<br>024 074 | 5181<br>5181<br>024 075 | 5182<br>5182<br>024 076 | 5183<br>5183<br>024 077 |
| 4− | 5184<br>5184<br>024 100 | 5185<br>5185<br>024 101 | 5186<br>5186<br>024 102 | 5187<br>5187<br>024 103 | 5188<br>5188<br>024 104 | 5189<br>5189<br>024 105 | 5190<br>5190<br>024 106 | 5191<br>5191<br>024 107 | 5192<br>5192<br>024 110 | 5193<br>5193<br>024 111 | 5194<br>5194<br>024 112 | 5195<br>5195<br>024 113 | 5196<br>5196<br>024 114 | 5197<br>5197<br>024 115 | 5198<br>5198<br>024 116 | 5199<br>5199<br>024 117 |
| 5− | 5200<br>5200<br>024 120 | 5201<br>5201<br>024 121 | 5202<br>5202<br>024 122 | 5203<br>5203<br>024 123 | 5204<br>5204<br>024 124 | 5205<br>5205<br>024 125 | 5206<br>5206<br>024 126 | 5207<br>5207<br>024 127 | 5208<br>5208<br>024 130 | 5209<br>5209<br>024 131 | 5210<br>5210<br>024 132 | 5211<br>5211<br>024 133 | 5212<br>5212<br>024 134 | 5213<br>5213<br>024 135 | 5214<br>5214<br>024 136 | 5215<br>5215<br>024 137 |
| 6− | 5216<br>5216<br>024 140 | 5217<br>5217<br>024 141 | 5218<br>5218<br>024 142 | 5219<br>5219<br>024 143 | 5220<br>5220<br>024 144 | 5221<br>5221<br>024 145 | 5222<br>5222<br>024 146 | 5223<br>5223<br>024 147 | 5224<br>5224<br>024 150 | 5225<br>5225<br>024 151 | 5226<br>5226<br>024 152 | 5227<br>5227<br>024 153 | 5228<br>5228<br>024 154 | 5229<br>5229<br>024 155 | 5230<br>5230<br>024 156 | 5231<br>5231<br>024 157 |
| 7− | 5232<br>5232<br>024 160 | 5233<br>5233<br>024 161 | 5234<br>5234<br>024 162 | 5235<br>5235<br>024 163 | 5236<br>5236<br>024 164 | 5237<br>5237<br>024 165 | 5238<br>5238<br>024 166 | 5239<br>5239<br>024 167 | 5240<br>5240<br>024 170 | 5241<br>5241<br>024 171 | 5242<br>5242<br>024 172 | 5243<br>5243<br>024 173 | 5244<br>5244<br>024 174 | 5245<br>5245<br>024 175 | 5246<br>5246<br>024 176 | 5247<br>5247<br>024 177 |
| 8− | 5248<br>5248<br>024 200 | 5249<br>5249<br>024 201 | 5250<br>5250<br>024 202 | 5251<br>5251<br>024 203 | 5252<br>5252<br>024 204 | 5253<br>5253<br>024 205 | 5254<br>5254<br>024 206 | 5255<br>5255<br>024 207 | 5256<br>5256<br>024 210 | 5257<br>5257<br>024 211 | 5258<br>5258<br>024 212 | 5259<br>5259<br>024 213 | 5260<br>5260<br>024 214 | 5261<br>5261<br>024 215 | 5262<br>5262<br>024 216 | 5263<br>5263<br>024 217 |
| 9− | 5264<br>5264<br>024 220 | 5265<br>5265<br>024 221 | 5266<br>5266<br>024 222 | 5267<br>5267<br>024 223 | 5268<br>5268<br>024 224 | 5269<br>5269<br>024 225 | 5270<br>5270<br>024 226 | 5271<br>5271<br>024 227 | 5272<br>5272<br>024 230 | 5273<br>5273<br>024 231 | 5274<br>5274<br>024 232 | 5275<br>5275<br>024 233 | 5276<br>5276<br>024 234 | 5277<br>5277<br>024 235 | 5278<br>5278<br>024 236 | 5279<br>5279<br>024 237 |
| A− | 5280<br>5280<br>024 240 | 5281<br>5281<br>024 241 | 5282<br>5282<br>024 242 | 5283<br>5283<br>024 243 | 5284<br>5284<br>024 244 | 5285<br>5285<br>024 245 | 5286<br>5286<br>024 246 | 5287<br>5287<br>024 247 | 5288<br>5288<br>024 250 | 5289<br>5289<br>024 251 | 5290<br>5290<br>024 252 | 5291<br>5291<br>024 253 | 5292<br>5292<br>024 254 | 5293<br>5293<br>024 255 | 5294<br>5294<br>024 256 | 5295<br>5295<br>024 257 |
| B− | 5296<br>5296<br>024 260 | 5297<br>5297<br>024 261 | 5298<br>5298<br>024 262 | 5299<br>5299<br>024 263 | 5300<br>5300<br>024 264 | 5301<br>5301<br>024 265 | 5302<br>5302<br>024 266 | 5303<br>5303<br>024 267 | 5304<br>5304<br>024 270 | 5305<br>5305<br>024 271 | 5306<br>5306<br>024 272 | 5307<br>5307<br>024 273 | 5308<br>5308<br>024 274 | 5309<br>5309<br>024 275 | 5310<br>5310<br>024 276 | 5311<br>5311<br>024 277 |
| C− | 5312<br>5312<br>024 300 | 5313<br>5313<br>024 301 | 5314<br>5314<br>024 302 | 5315<br>5315<br>024 303 | 5316<br>5316<br>024 304 | 5317<br>5317<br>024 305 | 5318<br>5318<br>024 306 | 5319<br>5319<br>024 307 | 5320<br>5320<br>024 310 | 5321<br>5321<br>024 311 | 5322<br>5322<br>024 312 | 5323<br>5323<br>024 313 | 5324<br>5324<br>024 314 | 5325<br>5325<br>024 315 | 5326<br>5326<br>024 316 | 5327<br>5327<br>024 317 |
| D− | 5328<br>5328<br>024 320 | 5329<br>5329<br>024 321 | 5330<br>5330<br>024 322 | 5331<br>5331<br>024 323 | 5332<br>5332<br>024 324 | 5333<br>5333<br>024 325 | 5334<br>5334<br>024 326 | 5335<br>5335<br>024 327 | 5336<br>5336<br>024 330 | 5337<br>5337<br>024 331 | 5338<br>5338<br>024 332 | 5339<br>5339<br>024 333 | 5340<br>5340<br>024 334 | 5341<br>5341<br>024 335 | 5342<br>5342<br>024 336 | 5343<br>5343<br>024 337 |
| E− | 5344<br>5344<br>024 340 | 5345<br>5345<br>024 341 | 5346<br>5346<br>024 342 | 5347<br>5347<br>024 343 | 5348<br>5348<br>024 344 | 5349<br>5349<br>024 345 | 5350<br>5350<br>024 346 | 5351<br>5351<br>024 347 | 5352<br>5352<br>024 350 | 5353<br>5353<br>024 351 | 5354<br>5354<br>024 352 | 5355<br>5355<br>024 353 | 5356<br>5356<br>024 354 | 5357<br>5357<br>024 355 | 5358<br>5358<br>024 356 | 5359<br>5359<br>024 357 |
| F− | 5360<br>5360<br>024 360 | 5361<br>5361<br>024 361 | 5362<br>5362<br>024 362 | 5363<br>5363<br>024 363 | 5364<br>5364<br>024 364 | 5365<br>5365<br>024 365 | 5366<br>5366<br>024 366 | 5367<br>5367<br>024 367 | 5368<br>5368<br>024 370 | 5369<br>5369<br>024 371 | 5370<br>5370<br>024 372 | 5371<br>5371<br>024 373 | 5372<br>5372<br>024 374 | 5373<br>5373<br>024 375 | 5374<br>5374<br>024 376 | 5375<br>5375<br>024 377 |

Legend (right side): DECIMAL — DECIMAL — OCTAL

 DECIMAL 5120   BINARY 0001 0100   DECIMAL 5120   HEXADECIMAL ⬡14 OCTAL 024 000

FOURTH HEX DIGIT → ⬡ ← THIRD HEX DIGIT

| $\bullet$ DECIMAL | 5376 | BINARY | 0001 0101 | DECIMAL | 5376 | HEXADECIMAL | 15 | OCTAL | 025 000 |
| --- | --- | --- | --- | --- | --- | --- | --- | --- | --- |

FOURTH HEX DIGIT → ⬡ ← THIRD HEX DIGIT

## FIRST HEX DIGIT

⬡ 2 — SECOND HEX DIGIT

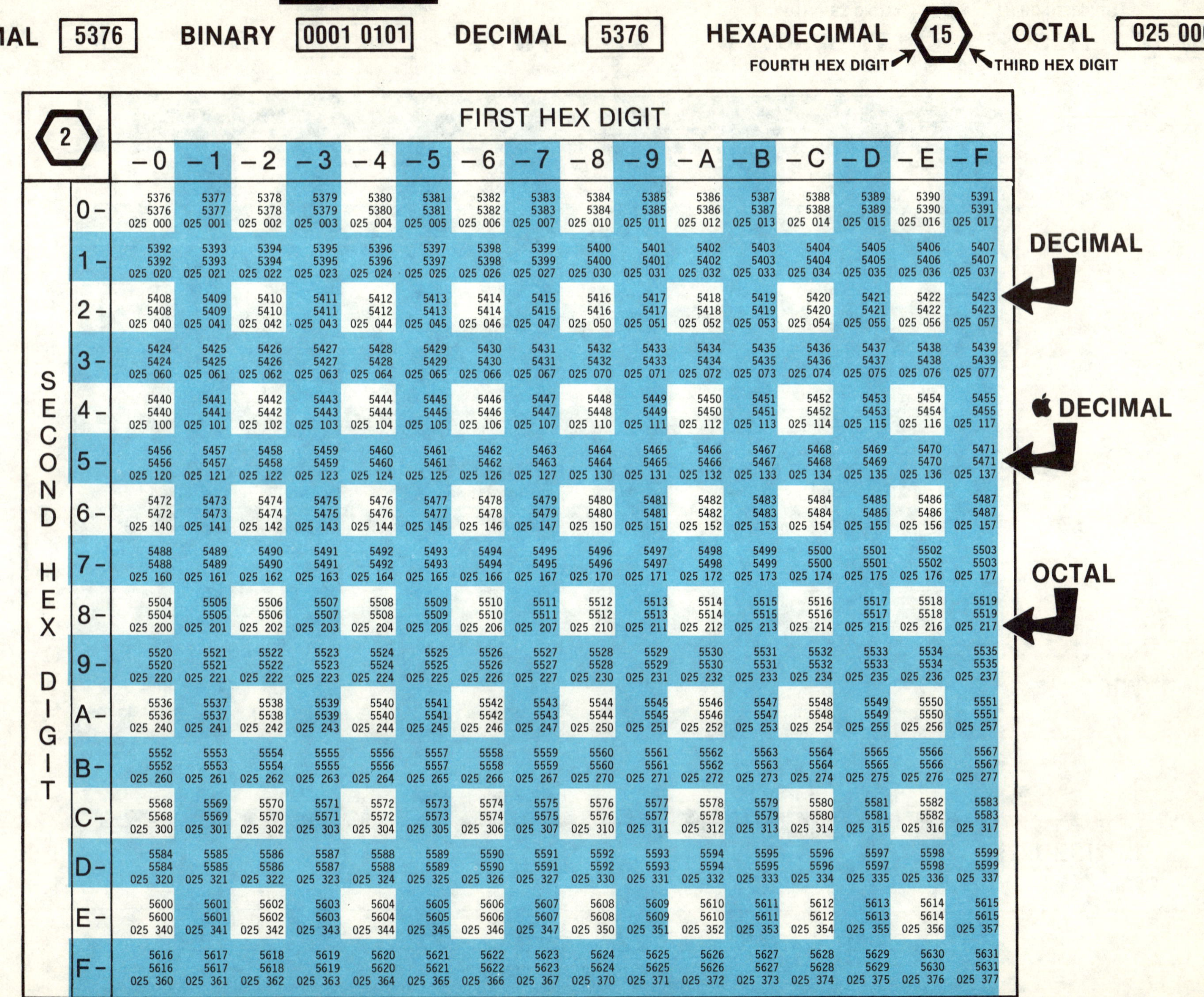

| | -0 | -1 | -2 | -3 | -4 | -5 | -6 | -7 | -8 | -9 | -A | -B | -C | -D | -E | -F |
| --- | --- | --- | --- | --- | --- | --- | --- | --- | --- | --- | --- | --- | --- | --- | --- | --- |
| 0- | 5376<br>025 000 | 5377<br>025 001 | 5378<br>025 002 | 5379<br>025 003 | 5380<br>025 004 | 5381<br>025 005 | 5382<br>025 006 | 5383<br>025 007 | 5384<br>025 010 | 5385<br>025 011 | 5386<br>025 012 | 5387<br>025 013 | 5388<br>025 014 | 5389<br>025 015 | 5390<br>025 016 | 5391<br>025 017 |
| 1- | 5392<br>025 020 | 5393<br>025 021 | 5394<br>025 022 | 5395<br>025 023 | 5396<br>025 024 | 5397<br>025 025 | 5398<br>025 026 | 5399<br>025 027 | 5400<br>025 030 | 5401<br>025 031 | 5402<br>025 032 | 5403<br>025 033 | 5404<br>025 034 | 5405<br>025 035 | 5406<br>025 036 | 5407<br>025 037 |
| 2- | 5408<br>025 040 | 5409<br>025 041 | 5410<br>025 042 | 5411<br>025 043 | 5412<br>025 044 | 5413<br>025 045 | 5414<br>025 046 | 5415<br>025 047 | 5416<br>025 050 | 5417<br>025 051 | 5418<br>025 052 | 5419<br>025 053 | 5420<br>025 054 | 5421<br>025 055 | 5422<br>025 056 | 5423<br>025 057 |
| 3- | 5424<br>025 060 | 5425<br>025 061 | 5426<br>025 062 | 5427<br>025 063 | 5428<br>025 064 | 5429<br>025 065 | 5430<br>025 066 | 5431<br>025 067 | 5432<br>025 070 | 5433<br>025 071 | 5434<br>025 072 | 5435<br>025 073 | 5436<br>025 074 | 5437<br>025 075 | 5438<br>025 076 | 5439<br>025 077 |
| 4- | 5440<br>025 100 | 5441<br>025 101 | 5442<br>025 102 | 5443<br>025 103 | 5444<br>025 104 | 5445<br>025 105 | 5446<br>025 106 | 5447<br>025 107 | 5448<br>025 110 | 5449<br>025 111 | 5450<br>025 112 | 5451<br>025 113 | 5452<br>025 114 | 5453<br>025 115 | 5454<br>025 116 | 5455<br>025 117 |
| 5- | 5456<br>025 120 | 5457<br>025 121 | 5458<br>025 122 | 5459<br>025 123 | 5460<br>025 124 | 5461<br>025 125 | 5462<br>025 126 | 5463<br>025 127 | 5464<br>025 130 | 5465<br>025 131 | 5466<br>025 132 | 5467<br>025 133 | 5468<br>025 134 | 5469<br>025 135 | 5470<br>025 136 | 5471<br>025 137 |
| 6- | 5472<br>025 140 | 5473<br>025 141 | 5474<br>025 142 | 5475<br>025 143 | 5476<br>025 144 | 5477<br>025 145 | 5478<br>025 146 | 5479<br>025 147 | 5480<br>025 150 | 5481<br>025 151 | 5482<br>025 152 | 5483<br>025 153 | 5484<br>025 154 | 5485<br>025 155 | 5486<br>025 156 | 5487<br>025 157 |
| 7- | 5488<br>025 160 | 5489<br>025 161 | 5490<br>025 162 | 5491<br>025 163 | 5492<br>025 164 | 5493<br>025 165 | 5494<br>025 166 | 5495<br>025 167 | 5496<br>025 170 | 5497<br>025 171 | 5498<br>025 172 | 5499<br>025 173 | 5500<br>025 174 | 5501<br>025 175 | 5502<br>025 176 | 5503<br>025 177 |
| 8- | 5504<br>025 200 | 5505<br>025 201 | 5506<br>025 202 | 5507<br>025 203 | 5508<br>025 204 | 5509<br>025 205 | 5510<br>025 206 | 5511<br>025 207 | 5512<br>025 210 | 5513<br>025 211 | 5514<br>025 212 | 5515<br>025 213 | 5516<br>025 214 | 5517<br>025 215 | 5518<br>025 216 | 5519<br>025 217 |
| 9- | 5520<br>025 220 | 5521<br>025 221 | 5522<br>025 222 | 5523<br>025 223 | 5524<br>025 224 | 5525<br>025 225 | 5526<br>025 226 | 5527<br>025 227 | 5528<br>025 230 | 5529<br>025 231 | 5530<br>025 232 | 5531<br>025 233 | 5532<br>025 234 | 5533<br>025 235 | 5534<br>025 236 | 5535<br>025 237 |
| A- | 5536<br>025 240 | 5537<br>025 241 | 5538<br>025 242 | 5539<br>025 243 | 5540<br>025 244 | 5541<br>025 245 | 5542<br>025 246 | 5543<br>025 247 | 5544<br>025 250 | 5545<br>025 251 | 5546<br>025 252 | 5547<br>025 253 | 5548<br>025 254 | 5549<br>025 255 | 5550<br>025 256 | 5551<br>025 257 |
| B- | 5552<br>025 260 | 5553<br>025 261 | 5554<br>025 262 | 5555<br>025 263 | 5556<br>025 264 | 5557<br>025 265 | 5558<br>025 266 | 5559<br>025 267 | 5560<br>025 270 | 5561<br>025 271 | 5562<br>025 272 | 5563<br>025 273 | 5564<br>025 274 | 5565<br>025 275 | 5566<br>025 276 | 5567<br>025 277 |
| C- | 5568<br>025 300 | 5569<br>025 301 | 5570<br>025 302 | 5571<br>025 303 | 5572<br>025 304 | 5573<br>025 305 | 5574<br>025 306 | 5575<br>025 307 | 5576<br>025 310 | 5577<br>025 311 | 5578<br>025 312 | 5579<br>025 313 | 5580<br>025 314 | 5581<br>025 315 | 5582<br>025 316 | 5583<br>025 317 |
| D- | 5584<br>025 320 | 5585<br>025 321 | 5586<br>025 322 | 5587<br>025 323 | 5588<br>025 324 | 5589<br>025 325 | 5590<br>025 326 | 5591<br>025 327 | 5592<br>025 330 | 5593<br>025 331 | 5594<br>025 332 | 5595<br>025 333 | 5596<br>025 334 | 5597<br>025 335 | 5598<br>025 336 | 5599<br>025 337 |
| E- | 5600<br>025 340 | 5601<br>025 341 | 5602<br>025 342 | 5603<br>025 343 | 5604<br>025 344 | 5605<br>025 345 | 5606<br>025 346 | 5607<br>025 347 | 5608<br>025 350 | 5609<br>025 351 | 5610<br>025 352 | 5611<br>025 353 | 5612<br>025 354 | 5613<br>025 355 | 5614<br>025 356 | 5615<br>025 357 |
| F- | 5616<br>025 360 | 5617<br>025 361 | 5618<br>025 362 | 5619<br>025 363 | 5620<br>025 364 | 5621<br>025 365 | 5622<br>025 366 | 5623<br>025 367 | 5624<br>025 370 | 5625<br>025 371 | 5626<br>025 372 | 5627<br>025 373 | 5628<br>025 374 | 5629<br>025 375 | 5630<br>025 376 | 5631<br>025 377 |

**⬡ 2**

SECOND HEX DIGIT

| | −0 | −1 | −2 | −3 | −4 | −5 | −6 | −7 | −8 | −9 | −A | −B | −C | −D | −E | −F |
|---|---|---|---|---|---|---|---|---|---|---|---|---|---|---|---|---|
| 0− | 5632<br>5632<br>026 000 | 5633<br>5633<br>026 001 | 5634<br>5634<br>026 002 | 5635<br>5635<br>026 003 | 5636<br>5636<br>026 004 | 5637<br>5637<br>026 005 | 5638<br>5638<br>026 006 | 5639<br>5639<br>026 007 | 5640<br>5640<br>026 010 | 5641<br>5641<br>026 011 | 5642<br>5642<br>026 012 | 5643<br>5643<br>026 013 | 5644<br>5644<br>026 014 | 5645<br>5645<br>026 015 | 5646<br>5646<br>026 016 | 5647<br>5647<br>026 017 |
| 1− | 5648<br>5648<br>026 020 | 5649<br>5649<br>026 021 | 5650<br>5650<br>026 022 | 5651<br>5651<br>026 023 | 5652<br>5652<br>026 024 | 5653<br>5653<br>026 025 | 5654<br>5654<br>026 026 | 5655<br>5655<br>026 027 | 5656<br>5656<br>026 030 | 5657<br>5657<br>026 031 | 5658<br>5658<br>026 032 | 5659<br>5659<br>026 033 | 5660<br>5660<br>026 034 | 5661<br>5661<br>026 035 | 5662<br>5662<br>026 036 | 5663<br>5663<br>026 037 |
| 2− | 5664<br>5664<br>026 040 | 5665<br>5665<br>026 041 | 5666<br>5666<br>026 042 | 5667<br>5667<br>026 043 | 5668<br>5668<br>026 044 | 5669<br>5669<br>026 045 | 5670<br>5670<br>026 046 | 5671<br>5671<br>026 047 | 5672<br>5672<br>026 050 | 5673<br>5673<br>026 051 | 5674<br>5674<br>026 052 | 5675<br>5675<br>026 053 | 5676<br>5676<br>026 054 | 5677<br>5677<br>026 055 | 5678<br>5678<br>026 056 | 5679<br>5679<br>026 057 |
| 3− | 5680<br>5680<br>026 060 | 5681<br>5681<br>026 061 | 5682<br>5682<br>026 062 | 5683<br>5683<br>026 063 | 5684<br>5684<br>026 064 | 5685<br>5685<br>026 065 | 5686<br>5686<br>026 066 | 5687<br>5687<br>026 067 | 5688<br>5688<br>026 070 | 5689<br>5689<br>026 071 | 5690<br>5690<br>026 072 | 5691<br>5691<br>026 073 | 5692<br>5692<br>026 074 | 5693<br>5693<br>026 075 | 5694<br>5694<br>026 076 | 5695<br>5695<br>026 077 |
| 4− | 5696<br>5696<br>026 100 | 5697<br>5697<br>026 101 | 5698<br>5698<br>026 102 | 5699<br>5699<br>026 103 | 5700<br>5700<br>026 104 | 5701<br>5701<br>026 105 | 5702<br>5702<br>026 106 | 5703<br>5703<br>026 107 | 5704<br>5704<br>026 110 | 5705<br>5705<br>026 111 | 5706<br>5706<br>026 112 | 5707<br>5707<br>026 113 | 5708<br>5708<br>026 114 | 5709<br>5709<br>026 115 | 5710<br>5710<br>026 116 | 5711<br>5711<br>026 117 |
| 5− | 5712<br>5712<br>026 120 | 5713<br>5713<br>026 121 | 5714<br>5714<br>026 122 | 5715<br>5715<br>026 123 | 5716<br>5716<br>026 124 | 5717<br>5717<br>026 125 | 5718<br>5718<br>026 126 | 5719<br>5719<br>026 127 | 5720<br>5720<br>026 130 | 5721<br>5721<br>026 131 | 5722<br>5722<br>026 132 | 5723<br>5723<br>026 133 | 5724<br>5724<br>026 134 | 5725<br>5725<br>026 135 | 5726<br>5726<br>026 136 | 5727<br>5727<br>026 137 |
| 6− | 5728<br>5728<br>026 140 | 5729<br>5729<br>026 141 | 5730<br>5730<br>026 142 | 5731<br>5731<br>026 143 | 5732<br>5732<br>026 144 | 5733<br>5733<br>026 145 | 5734<br>5734<br>026 146 | 5735<br>5735<br>026 147 | 5736<br>5736<br>026 150 | 5737<br>5737<br>026 151 | 5738<br>5738<br>026 152 | 5739<br>5739<br>026 153 | 5740<br>5740<br>026 154 | 5741<br>5741<br>026 155 | 5742<br>5742<br>026 156 | 5743<br>5743<br>026 157 |
| 7− | 5744<br>5744<br>026 160 | 5745<br>5745<br>026 161 | 5746<br>5746<br>026 162 | 5747<br>5747<br>026 163 | 5748<br>5748<br>026 164 | 5749<br>5749<br>026 165 | 5750<br>5750<br>026 166 | 5751<br>5751<br>026 167 | 5752<br>5752<br>026 170 | 5753<br>5753<br>026 171 | 5754<br>5754<br>026 172 | 5755<br>5755<br>026 173 | 5756<br>5756<br>026 174 | 5757<br>5757<br>026 175 | 5758<br>5758<br>026 176 | 5759<br>5759<br>026 177 |
| 8− | 5760<br>5760<br>026 200 | 5761<br>5761<br>026 201 | 5762<br>5762<br>026 202 | 5763<br>5763<br>026 203 | 5764<br>5764<br>026 204 | 5765<br>5765<br>026 205 | 5766<br>5766<br>026 206 | 5767<br>5767<br>026 207 | 5768<br>5768<br>026 210 | 5769<br>5769<br>026 211 | 5770<br>5770<br>026 212 | 5771<br>5771<br>026 213 | 5772<br>5772<br>026 214 | 5773<br>5773<br>026 215 | 5774<br>5774<br>026 216 | 5775<br>5775<br>026 217 |
| 9− | 5776<br>5776<br>026 220 | 5777<br>5777<br>026 221 | 5778<br>5778<br>026 222 | 5779<br>5779<br>026 223 | 5780<br>5780<br>026 224 | 5781<br>5781<br>026 225 | 5782<br>5782<br>026 226 | 5783<br>5783<br>026 227 | 5784<br>5784<br>026 230 | 5785<br>5785<br>026 231 | 5786<br>5786<br>026 232 | 5787<br>5787<br>026 233 | 5788<br>5788<br>026 234 | 5789<br>5789<br>026 235 | 5790<br>5790<br>026 236 | 5791<br>5791<br>026 237 |
| A− | 5792<br>5792<br>026 240 | 5793<br>5793<br>026 241 | 5794<br>5794<br>026 242 | 5795<br>5795<br>026 243 | 5796<br>5796<br>026 244 | 5797<br>5797<br>026 245 | 5798<br>5798<br>026 246 | 5799<br>5799<br>026 247 | 5800<br>5800<br>026 250 | 5801<br>5801<br>026 251 | 5802<br>5802<br>026 252 | 5803<br>5803<br>026 253 | 5804<br>5804<br>026 254 | 5805<br>5805<br>026 255 | 5806<br>5806<br>026 256 | 5807<br>5807<br>026 257 |
| B− | 5808<br>5808<br>026 260 | 5809<br>5809<br>026 261 | 5810<br>5810<br>026 262 | 5811<br>5811<br>026 263 | 5812<br>5812<br>026 264 | 5813<br>5813<br>026 265 | 5814<br>5814<br>026 266 | 5815<br>5815<br>026 267 | 5816<br>5816<br>026 270 | 5817<br>5817<br>026 271 | 5818<br>5818<br>026 272 | 5819<br>5819<br>026 273 | 5820<br>5820<br>026 274 | 5821<br>5821<br>026 275 | 5822<br>5822<br>026 276 | 5823<br>5823<br>026 277 |
| C− | 5824<br>5824<br>026 300 | 5825<br>5825<br>026 301 | 5826<br>5826<br>026 302 | 5827<br>5827<br>026 303 | 5828<br>5828<br>026 304 | 5829<br>5829<br>026 305 | 5830<br>5830<br>026 306 | 5831<br>5831<br>026 307 | 5832<br>5832<br>026 310 | 5833<br>5833<br>026 311 | 5834<br>5834<br>026 312 | 5835<br>5835<br>026 313 | 5836<br>5836<br>026 314 | 5837<br>5837<br>026 315 | 5838<br>5838<br>026 316 | 5839<br>5839<br>026 317 |
| D− | 5840<br>5840<br>026 320 | 5841<br>5841<br>026 321 | 5842<br>5842<br>026 322 | 5843<br>5843<br>026 323 | 5844<br>5844<br>026 324 | 5845<br>5845<br>026 325 | 5846<br>5846<br>026 326 | 5847<br>5847<br>026 327 | 5848<br>5848<br>026 330 | 5849<br>5849<br>026 331 | 5850<br>5850<br>026 332 | 5851<br>5851<br>026 333 | 5852<br>5852<br>026 334 | 5853<br>5853<br>026 335 | 5854<br>5854<br>026 336 | 5855<br>5855<br>026 337 |
| E− | 5856<br>5856<br>026 340 | 5857<br>5857<br>026 341 | 5858<br>5858<br>026 342 | 5859<br>5859<br>026 343 | 5860<br>5860<br>026 344 | 5861<br>5861<br>026 345 | 5862<br>5862<br>026 346 | 5863<br>5863<br>026 347 | 5864<br>5864<br>026 350 | 5865<br>5865<br>026 351 | 5866<br>5866<br>026 352 | 5867<br>5867<br>026 353 | 5868<br>5868<br>026 354 | 5869<br>5869<br>026 355 | 5870<br>5870<br>026 356 | 5871<br>5871<br>026 357 |
| F− | 5872<br>5872<br>026 360 | 5873<br>5873<br>026 361 | 5874<br>5874<br>026 362 | 5875<br>5875<br>026 363 | 5876<br>5876<br>026 364 | 5877<br>5877<br>026 365 | 5878<br>5878<br>026 366 | 5879<br>5879<br>026 367 | 5880<br>5880<br>026 370 | 5881<br>5881<br>026 371 | 5882<br>5882<br>026 372 | 5883<br>5883<br>026 373 | 5884<br>5884<br>026 374 | 5885<br>5885<br>026 375 | 5886<br>5886<br>026 376 | 5887<br>5887<br>026 377 |

DECIMAL ⬅

⬤ DECIMAL ⬅

OCTAL ⬅

⬤ DECIMAL  5632   BINARY  0001 0110   DECIMAL  5632   HEXADECIMAL ⬡ 16  OCTAL  026 000

FOURTH HEX DIGIT →  ← THIRD HEX DIGIT

FIRST HEX DIGIT

SECOND HEX DIGIT

DECIMAL

DECIMAL

OCTAL

Each cell lists: decimal value (printed twice) over octal value.

| 2 | −0 | −1 | −2 | −3 | −4 | −5 | −6 | −7 | −8 | −9 | −A | −B | −C | −D | −E | −F |
|---|---|---|---|---|---|---|---|---|---|---|---|---|---|---|---|---|
| 0− | 5888<br>027 000 | 5889<br>027 001 | 5890<br>027 002 | 5891<br>027 003 | 5892<br>027 004 | 5893<br>027 005 | 5894<br>027 006 | 5895<br>027 007 | 5896<br>027 010 | 5897<br>027 011 | 5898<br>027 012 | 5899<br>027 013 | 5900<br>027 014 | 5901<br>027 015 | 5902<br>027 016 | 5903<br>027 017 |
| 1− | 5904<br>027 020 | 5905<br>027 021 | 5906<br>027 022 | 5907<br>027 023 | 5908<br>027 024 | 5909<br>027 025 | 5910<br>027 026 | 5911<br>027 027 | 5912<br>027 030 | 5913<br>027 031 | 5914<br>027 032 | 5915<br>027 033 | 5916<br>027 034 | 5917<br>027 035 | 5918<br>027 036 | 5919<br>027 037 |
| 2− | 5920<br>027 040 | 5921<br>027 041 | 5922<br>027 042 | 5923<br>027 043 | 5924<br>027 044 | 5925<br>027 045 | 5926<br>027 046 | 5927<br>027 047 | 5928<br>027 050 | 5929<br>027 051 | 5930<br>027 052 | 5931<br>027 053 | 5932<br>027 054 | 5933<br>027 055 | 5934<br>027 056 | 5935<br>027 057 |
| 3− | 5936<br>027 060 | 5937<br>027 061 | 5938<br>027 062 | 5939<br>027 063 | 5940<br>027 064 | 5941<br>027 065 | 5942<br>027 066 | 5943<br>027 067 | 5944<br>027 070 | 5945<br>027 071 | 5946<br>027 072 | 5947<br>027 073 | 5948<br>027 074 | 5949<br>027 075 | 5950<br>027 076 | 5951<br>027 077 |
| 4− | 5952<br>027 100 | 5953<br>027 101 | 5954<br>027 102 | 5955<br>027 103 | 5956<br>027 104 | 5957<br>027 105 | 5958<br>027 106 | 5959<br>027 107 | 5960<br>027 110 | 5961<br>027 111 | 5962<br>027 112 | 5963<br>027 113 | 5964<br>027 114 | 5965<br>027 115 | 5966<br>027 116 | 5967<br>027 117 |
| 5− | 5968<br>027 120 | 5969<br>027 121 | 5970<br>027 122 | 5971<br>027 123 | 5972<br>027 124 | 5973<br>027 125 | 5974<br>027 126 | 5975<br>027 127 | 5976<br>027 130 | 5977<br>027 131 | 5978<br>027 132 | 5979<br>027 133 | 5980<br>027 134 | 5981<br>027 135 | 5982<br>027 136 | 5983<br>027 137 |
| 6− | 5984<br>027 140 | 5985<br>027 141 | 5986<br>027 142 | 5987<br>027 143 | 5988<br>027 144 | 5989<br>027 145 | 5990<br>027 146 | 5991<br>027 147 | 5992<br>027 150 | 5993<br>027 151 | 5994<br>027 152 | 5995<br>027 153 | 5996<br>027 154 | 5997<br>027 155 | 5998<br>027 156 | 5999<br>027 157 |
| 7− | 6000<br>027 160 | 6001<br>027 161 | 6002<br>027 162 | 6003<br>027 163 | 6004<br>027 164 | 6005<br>027 165 | 6006<br>027 166 | 6007<br>027 167 | 6008<br>027 170 | 6009<br>027 171 | 6010<br>027 172 | 6011<br>027 173 | 6012<br>027 174 | 6013<br>027 175 | 6014<br>027 176 | 6015<br>027 177 |
| 8− | 6016<br>027 200 | 6017<br>027 201 | 6018<br>027 202 | 6019<br>027 203 | 6020<br>027 204 | 6021<br>027 205 | 6022<br>027 206 | 6023<br>027 207 | 6024<br>027 210 | 6025<br>027 211 | 6026<br>027 212 | 6027<br>027 213 | 6028<br>027 214 | 6029<br>027 215 | 6030<br>027 216 | 6031<br>027 217 |
| 9− | 6032<br>027 220 | 6033<br>027 221 | 6034<br>027 222 | 6035<br>027 223 | 6036<br>027 224 | 6037<br>027 225 | 6038<br>027 226 | 6039<br>027 227 | 6040<br>027 230 | 6041<br>027 231 | 6042<br>027 232 | 6043<br>027 233 | 6044<br>027 234 | 6045<br>027 235 | 6046<br>027 236 | 6047<br>027 237 |
| A− | 6048<br>027 240 | 6049<br>027 241 | 6050<br>027 242 | 6051<br>027 243 | 6052<br>027 244 | 6053<br>027 245 | 6054<br>027 246 | 6055<br>027 247 | 6056<br>027 250 | 6057<br>027 251 | 6058<br>027 252 | 6059<br>027 253 | 6060<br>027 254 | 6061<br>027 255 | 6062<br>027 256 | 6063<br>027 257 |
| B− | 6064<br>027 260 | 6065<br>027 261 | 6066<br>027 262 | 6067<br>027 263 | 6068<br>027 264 | 6069<br>027 265 | 6070<br>027 266 | 6071<br>027 267 | 6072<br>027 270 | 6073<br>027 271 | 6074<br>027 272 | 6075<br>027 273 | 6076<br>027 274 | 6077<br>027 275 | 6078<br>027 276 | 6079<br>027 277 |
| C− | 6080<br>027 300 | 6081<br>027 301 | 6082<br>027 302 | 6083<br>027 303 | 6084<br>027 304 | 6085<br>027 305 | 6086<br>027 306 | 6087<br>027 307 | 6088<br>027 310 | 6089<br>027 311 | 6090<br>027 312 | 6091<br>027 313 | 6092<br>027 314 | 6093<br>027 315 | 6094<br>027 316 | 6095<br>027 317 |
| D− | 6096<br>027 320 | 6097<br>027 321 | 6098<br>027 322 | 6099<br>027 323 | 6100<br>027 324 | 6101<br>027 325 | 6102<br>027 326 | 6103<br>027 327 | 6104<br>027 330 | 6105<br>027 331 | 6106<br>027 332 | 6107<br>027 333 | 6108<br>027 334 | 6109<br>027 335 | 6110<br>027 336 | 6111<br>027 337 |
| E− | 6112<br>027 340 | 6113<br>027 341 | 6114<br>027 342 | 6115<br>027 343 | 6116<br>027 344 | 6117<br>027 345 | 6118<br>027 346 | 6119<br>027 347 | 6120<br>027 350 | 6121<br>027 351 | 6122<br>027 352 | 6123<br>027 353 | 6124<br>027 354 | 6125<br>027 355 | 6126<br>027 356 | 6127<br>027 357 |
| F− | 6128<br>027 360 | 6129<br>027 361 | 6130<br>027 362 | 6131<br>027 363 | 6132<br>027 364 | 6133<br>027 365 | 6134<br>027 366 | 6135<br>027 367 | 6136<br>027 370 | 6137<br>027 371 | 6138<br>027 372 | 6139<br>027 373 | 6140<br>027 374 | 6141<br>027 375 | 6142<br>027 376 | 6143<br>027 377 |

<table>
<tr><th>②</th><th colspan="16">FIRST HEX DIGIT</th></tr>
<tr><th></th><th>-0</th><th>-1</th><th>-2</th><th>-3</th><th>-4</th><th>-5</th><th>-6</th><th>-7</th><th>-8</th><th>-9</th><th>-A</th><th>-B</th><th>-C</th><th>-D</th><th>-E</th><th>-F</th></tr>
<tr><th>0-</th><td>6144<br>6144<br>030 000</td><td>6145<br>6145<br>030 001</td><td>6146<br>6146<br>030 002</td><td>6147<br>6147<br>030 003</td><td>6148<br>6148<br>030 004</td><td>6149<br>6149<br>030 005</td><td>6150<br>6150<br>030 006</td><td>6151<br>6151<br>030 007</td><td>6152<br>6152<br>030 010</td><td>6153<br>6153<br>030 011</td><td>6154<br>6154<br>030 012</td><td>6155<br>6155<br>030 013</td><td>6156<br>6156<br>030 014</td><td>6157<br>6157<br>030 015</td><td>6158<br>6158<br>030 016</td><td>6159<br>6159<br>030 017</td></tr>
<tr><th>1-</th><td>6160<br>6160<br>030 020</td><td>6161<br>6161<br>030 021</td><td>6162<br>6162<br>030 022</td><td>6163<br>6163<br>030 023</td><td>6164<br>6164<br>030 024</td><td>6165<br>6165<br>030 025</td><td>6166<br>6166<br>030 026</td><td>6167<br>6167<br>030 027</td><td>6168<br>6168<br>030 030</td><td>6169<br>6169<br>030 031</td><td>6170<br>6170<br>030 032</td><td>6171<br>6171<br>030 033</td><td>6172<br>6172<br>030 034</td><td>6173<br>6173<br>030 035</td><td>6174<br>6174<br>030 036</td><td>6175<br>6175<br>030 037</td></tr>
<tr><th>2-</th><td>6176<br>6176<br>030 040</td><td>6177<br>6177<br>030 041</td><td>6178<br>6178<br>030 042</td><td>6179<br>6179<br>030 043</td><td>6180<br>6180<br>030 044</td><td>6181<br>6181<br>030 045</td><td>6182<br>6182<br>030 046</td><td>6183<br>6183<br>030 047</td><td>6184<br>6184<br>030 050</td><td>6185<br>6185<br>030 051</td><td>6186<br>6186<br>030 052</td><td>6187<br>6187<br>030 053</td><td>6188<br>6188<br>030 054</td><td>6189<br>6189<br>030 055</td><td>6190<br>6190<br>030 056</td><td>6191<br>6191<br>030 057</td></tr>
<tr><th>3-</th><td>6192<br>6192<br>030 060</td><td>6193<br>6193<br>030 061</td><td>6194<br>6194<br>030 062</td><td>6195<br>6195<br>030 063</td><td>6196<br>6196<br>030 064</td><td>6197<br>6197<br>030 065</td><td>6198<br>6198<br>030 066</td><td>6199<br>6199<br>030 067</td><td>6200<br>6200<br>030 070</td><td>6201<br>6201<br>030 071</td><td>6202<br>6202<br>030 072</td><td>6203<br>6203<br>030 073</td><td>6204<br>6204<br>030 074</td><td>6205<br>6205<br>030 075</td><td>6206<br>6206<br>030 076</td><td>6207<br>6207<br>030 077</td></tr>
<tr><th>4-</th><td>6208<br>6208<br>030 100</td><td>6209<br>6209<br>030 101</td><td>6210<br>6210<br>030 102</td><td>6211<br>6211<br>030 103</td><td>6212<br>6212<br>030 104</td><td>6213<br>6213<br>030 105</td><td>6214<br>6214<br>030 106</td><td>6215<br>6215<br>030 107</td><td>6216<br>6216<br>030 110</td><td>6217<br>6217<br>030 111</td><td>6218<br>6218<br>030 112</td><td>6219<br>6219<br>030 113</td><td>6220<br>6220<br>030 114</td><td>6221<br>6221<br>030 115</td><td>6222<br>6222<br>030 116</td><td>6223<br>6223<br>030 117</td></tr>
<tr><th>5-</th><td>6224<br>6224<br>030 120</td><td>6225<br>6225<br>030 121</td><td>6226<br>6226<br>030 122</td><td>6227<br>6227<br>030 123</td><td>6228<br>6228<br>030 124</td><td>6229<br>6229<br>030 125</td><td>6230<br>6230<br>030 126</td><td>6231<br>6231<br>030 127</td><td>6232<br>6232<br>030 130</td><td>6233<br>6233<br>030 131</td><td>6234<br>6234<br>030 132</td><td>6235<br>6235<br>030 133</td><td>6236<br>6236<br>030 134</td><td>6237<br>6237<br>030 135</td><td>6238<br>6238<br>030 136</td><td>6239<br>6239<br>030 137</td></tr>
<tr><th>6-</th><td>6240<br>6240<br>030 140</td><td>6241<br>6241<br>030 141</td><td>6242<br>6242<br>030 142</td><td>6243<br>6243<br>030 143</td><td>6244<br>6244<br>030 144</td><td>6245<br>6245<br>030 145</td><td>6246<br>6246<br>030 146</td><td>6247<br>6247<br>030 147</td><td>6248<br>6248<br>030 150</td><td>6249<br>6249<br>030 151</td><td>6250<br>6250<br>030 152</td><td>6251<br>6251<br>030 153</td><td>6252<br>6252<br>030 154</td><td>6253<br>6253<br>030 155</td><td>6254<br>6254<br>030 156</td><td>6255<br>6255<br>030 157</td></tr>
<tr><th>7-</th><td>6256<br>6256<br>030 160</td><td>6257<br>6257<br>030 161</td><td>6258<br>6258<br>030 162</td><td>6259<br>6259<br>030 163</td><td>6260<br>6260<br>030 164</td><td>6261<br>6261<br>030 165</td><td>6262<br>6262<br>030 166</td><td>6263<br>6263<br>030 167</td><td>6264<br>6264<br>030 170</td><td>6265<br>6265<br>030 171</td><td>6266<br>6266<br>030 172</td><td>6267<br>6267<br>030 173</td><td>6268<br>6268<br>030 174</td><td>6269<br>6269<br>030 175</td><td>6270<br>6270<br>030 176</td><td>6271<br>6271<br>030 177</td></tr>
<tr><th>8-</th><td>6272<br>6272<br>030 200</td><td>6273<br>6273<br>030 201</td><td>6274<br>6274<br>030 202</td><td>6275<br>6275<br>030 203</td><td>6276<br>6276<br>030 204</td><td>6277<br>6277<br>030 205</td><td>6278<br>6278<br>030 206</td><td>6279<br>6279<br>030 207</td><td>6280<br>6280<br>030 210</td><td>6281<br>6281<br>030 211</td><td>6282<br>6282<br>030 212</td><td>6283<br>6283<br>030 213</td><td>6284<br>6284<br>030 214</td><td>6285<br>6285<br>030 215</td><td>6286<br>6286<br>030 216</td><td>6287<br>6287<br>030 217</td></tr>
<tr><th>9-</th><td>6288<br>6288<br>030 220</td><td>6289<br>6289<br>030 221</td><td>6290<br>6290<br>030 222</td><td>6291<br>6291<br>030 223</td><td>6292<br>6292<br>030 224</td><td>6293<br>6293<br>030 225</td><td>6294<br>6294<br>030 226</td><td>6295<br>6295<br>030 227</td><td>6296<br>6296<br>030 230</td><td>6297<br>6297<br>030 231</td><td>6298<br>6298<br>030 232</td><td>6299<br>6299<br>030 233</td><td>6300<br>6300<br>030 234</td><td>6301<br>6301<br>030 235</td><td>6302<br>6302<br>030 236</td><td>6303<br>6303<br>030 237</td></tr>
<tr><th>A-</th><td>6304<br>6304<br>030 240</td><td>6305<br>6305<br>030 241</td><td>6306<br>6306<br>030 242</td><td>6307<br>6307<br>030 243</td><td>6308<br>6308<br>030 244</td><td>6309<br>6309<br>030 245</td><td>6310<br>6310<br>030 246</td><td>6311<br>6311<br>030 247</td><td>6312<br>6312<br>030 250</td><td>6313<br>6313<br>030 251</td><td>6314<br>6314<br>030 252</td><td>6315<br>6315<br>030 253</td><td>6316<br>6316<br>030 254</td><td>6317<br>6317<br>030 255</td><td>6318<br>6318<br>030 256</td><td>6319<br>6319<br>030 257</td></tr>
<tr><th>B-</th><td>6320<br>6320<br>030 260</td><td>6321<br>6321<br>030 261</td><td>6322<br>6322<br>030 262</td><td>6323<br>6323<br>030 263</td><td>6324<br>6324<br>030 264</td><td>6325<br>6325<br>030 265</td><td>6326<br>6326<br>030 266</td><td>6327<br>6327<br>030 267</td><td>6328<br>6328<br>030 270</td><td>6329<br>6329<br>030 271</td><td>6330<br>6330<br>030 272</td><td>6331<br>6331<br>030 273</td><td>6332<br>6332<br>030 274</td><td>6333<br>6333<br>030 275</td><td>6334<br>6334<br>030 276</td><td>6335<br>6335<br>030 277</td></tr>
<tr><th>C-</th><td>6336<br>6336<br>030 300</td><td>6337<br>6337<br>030 301</td><td>6338<br>6338<br>030 302</td><td>6339<br>6339<br>030 303</td><td>6340<br>6340<br>030 304</td><td>6341<br>6341<br>030 305</td><td>6342<br>6342<br>030 306</td><td>6343<br>6343<br>030 307</td><td>6344<br>6344<br>030 310</td><td>6345<br>6345<br>030 311</td><td>6346<br>6346<br>030 312</td><td>6347<br>6347<br>030 313</td><td>6348<br>6348<br>030 314</td><td>6349<br>6349<br>030 315</td><td>6350<br>6350<br>030 316</td><td>6351<br>6351<br>030 317</td></tr>
<tr><th>D-</th><td>6352<br>6352<br>030 320</td><td>6353<br>6353<br>030 321</td><td>6354<br>6354<br>030 322</td><td>6355<br>6355<br>030 323</td><td>6356<br>6356<br>030 324</td><td>6357<br>6357<br>030 325</td><td>6358<br>6358<br>030 326</td><td>6359<br>6359<br>030 327</td><td>6360<br>6360<br>030 330</td><td>6361<br>6361<br>030 331</td><td>6362<br>6362<br>030 332</td><td>6363<br>6363<br>030 333</td><td>6364<br>6364<br>030 334</td><td>6365<br>6365<br>030 335</td><td>6366<br>6366<br>030 336</td><td>6367<br>6367<br>030 337</td></tr>
<tr><th>E-</th><td>6368<br>6368<br>030 340</td><td>6369<br>6369<br>030 341</td><td>6370<br>6370<br>030 342</td><td>6371<br>6371<br>030 343</td><td>6372<br>6372<br>030 344</td><td>6373<br>6373<br>030 345</td><td>6374<br>6374<br>030 346</td><td>6375<br>6375<br>030 347</td><td>6376<br>6376<br>030 350</td><td>6377<br>6377<br>030 351</td><td>6378<br>6378<br>030 352</td><td>6379<br>6379<br>030 353</td><td>6380<br>6380<br>030 354</td><td>6381<br>6381<br>030 355</td><td>6382<br>6382<br>030 356</td><td>6383<br>6383<br>030 357</td></tr>
<tr><th>F-</th><td>6384<br>6384<br>030 360</td><td>6385<br>6385<br>030 361</td><td>6386<br>6386<br>030 362</td><td>6387<br>6387<br>030 363</td><td>6388<br>6388<br>030 364</td><td>6389<br>6389<br>030 365</td><td>6390<br>6390<br>030 366</td><td>6391<br>6391<br>030 367</td><td>6392<br>6392<br>030 370</td><td>6393<br>6393<br>030 371</td><td>6394<br>6394<br>030 372</td><td>6395<br>6395<br>030 373</td><td>6396<br>6396<br>030 374</td><td>6397<br>6397<br>030 375</td><td>6398<br>6398<br>030 376</td><td>6399<br>6399<br>030 377</td></tr>
</table>

SECOND HEX DIGIT

DECIMAL

 DECIMAL

OCTAL

 DECIMAL 6144    BINARY 0001 1000    DECIMAL 6144    HEXADECIMAL ⬡ 18    OCTAL 030 000

FOURTH HEX DIGIT →   ← THIRD HEX DIGIT

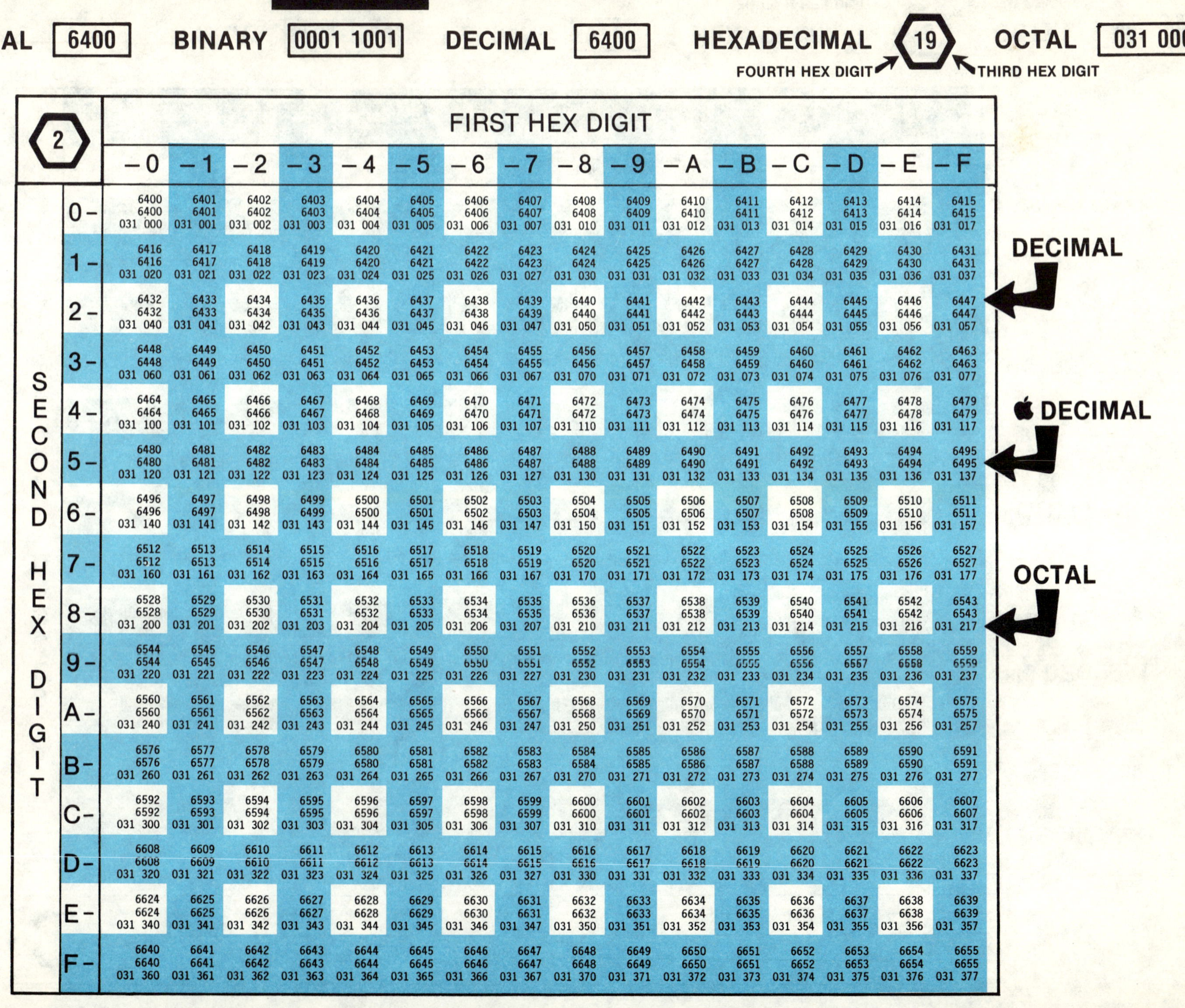



| 2 | −0 | −1 | −2 | −3 | −4 | −5 | −6 | −7 | −8 | −9 | −A | −B | −C | −D | −E | −F |
|---|---|---|---|---|---|---|---|---|---|---|---|---|---|---|---|---|
| 0− | 6400<br>6400<br>031 000 | 6401<br>6401<br>031 001 | 6402<br>6402<br>031 002 | 6403<br>6403<br>031 003 | 6404<br>6404<br>031 004 | 6405<br>6405<br>031 005 | 6406<br>6406<br>031 006 | 6407<br>6407<br>031 007 | 6408<br>6408<br>031 010 | 6409<br>6409<br>031 011 | 6410<br>6410<br>031 012 | 6411<br>6411<br>031 013 | 6412<br>6412<br>031 014 | 6413<br>6413<br>031 015 | 6414<br>6414<br>031 016 | 6415<br>6415<br>031 017 |
| 1− | 6416<br>6416<br>031 020 | 6417<br>6417<br>031 021 | 6418<br>6418<br>031 022 | 6419<br>6419<br>031 023 | 6420<br>6420<br>031 024 | 6421<br>6421<br>031 025 | 6422<br>6422<br>031 026 | 6423<br>6423<br>031 027 | 6424<br>6424<br>031 030 | 6425<br>6425<br>031 031 | 6426<br>6426<br>031 032 | 6427<br>6427<br>031 033 | 6428<br>6428<br>031 034 | 6429<br>6429<br>031 035 | 6430<br>6430<br>031 036 | 6431<br>6431<br>031 037 |
| 2− | 6432<br>6432<br>031 040 | 6433<br>6433<br>031 041 | 6434<br>6434<br>031 042 | 6435<br>6435<br>031 043 | 6436<br>6436<br>031 044 | 6437<br>6437<br>031 045 | 6438<br>6438<br>031 046 | 6439<br>6439<br>031 047 | 6440<br>6440<br>031 050 | 6441<br>6441<br>031 051 | 6442<br>6442<br>031 052 | 6443<br>6443<br>031 053 | 6444<br>6444<br>031 054 | 6445<br>6445<br>031 055 | 6446<br>6446<br>031 056 | 6447<br>6447<br>031 057 |
| 3− | 6448<br>6448<br>031 060 | 6449<br>6449<br>031 061 | 6450<br>6450<br>031 062 | 6451<br>6451<br>031 063 | 6452<br>6452<br>031 064 | 6453<br>6453<br>031 065 | 6454<br>6454<br>031 066 | 6455<br>6455<br>031 067 | 6456<br>6456<br>031 070 | 6457<br>6457<br>031 071 | 6458<br>6458<br>031 072 | 6459<br>6459<br>031 073 | 6460<br>6460<br>031 074 | 6461<br>6461<br>031 075 | 6462<br>6462<br>031 076 | 6463<br>6463<br>031 077 |
| 4− | 6464<br>6464<br>031 100 | 6465<br>6465<br>031 101 | 6466<br>6466<br>031 102 | 6467<br>6467<br>031 103 | 6468<br>6468<br>031 104 | 6469<br>6469<br>031 105 | 6470<br>6470<br>031 106 | 6471<br>6471<br>031 107 | 6472<br>6472<br>031 110 | 6473<br>6473<br>031 111 | 6474<br>6474<br>031 112 | 6475<br>6475<br>031 113 | 6476<br>6476<br>031 114 | 6477<br>6477<br>031 115 | 6478<br>6478<br>031 116 | 6479<br>6479<br>031 117 |
| 5− | 6480<br>6480<br>031 120 | 6481<br>6481<br>031 121 | 6482<br>6482<br>031 122 | 6483<br>6483<br>031 123 | 6484<br>6484<br>031 124 | 6485<br>6485<br>031 125 | 6486<br>6486<br>031 126 | 6487<br>6487<br>031 127 | 6488<br>6488<br>031 130 | 6489<br>6489<br>031 131 | 6490<br>6490<br>031 132 | 6491<br>6491<br>031 133 | 6492<br>6492<br>031 134 | 6493<br>6493<br>031 135 | 6494<br>6494<br>031 136 | 6495<br>6495<br>031 137 |
| 6− | 6496<br>6496<br>031 140 | 6497<br>6497<br>031 141 | 6498<br>6498<br>031 142 | 6499<br>6499<br>031 143 | 6500<br>6500<br>031 144 | 6501<br>6501<br>031 145 | 6502<br>6502<br>031 146 | 6503<br>6503<br>031 147 | 6504<br>6504<br>031 150 | 6505<br>6505<br>031 151 | 6506<br>6506<br>031 152 | 6507<br>6507<br>031 153 | 6508<br>6508<br>031 154 | 6509<br>6509<br>031 155 | 6510<br>6510<br>031 156 | 6511<br>6511<br>031 157 |
| 7− | 6512<br>6512<br>031 160 | 6513<br>6513<br>031 161 | 6514<br>6514<br>031 162 | 6515<br>6515<br>031 163 | 6516<br>6516<br>031 164 | 6517<br>6517<br>031 165 | 6518<br>6518<br>031 166 | 6519<br>6519<br>031 167 | 6520<br>6520<br>031 170 | 6521<br>6521<br>031 171 | 6522<br>6522<br>031 172 | 6523<br>6523<br>031 173 | 6524<br>6524<br>031 174 | 6525<br>6525<br>031 175 | 6526<br>6526<br>031 176 | 6527<br>6527<br>031 177 |
| 8− | 6528<br>6528<br>031 200 | 6529<br>6529<br>031 201 | 6530<br>6530<br>031 202 | 6531<br>6531<br>031 203 | 6532<br>6532<br>031 204 | 6533<br>6533<br>031 205 | 6534<br>6534<br>031 206 | 6535<br>6535<br>031 207 | 6536<br>6536<br>031 210 | 6537<br>6537<br>031 211 | 6538<br>6538<br>031 212 | 6539<br>6539<br>031 213 | 6540<br>6540<br>031 214 | 6541<br>6541<br>031 215 | 6542<br>6542<br>031 216 | 6543<br>6543<br>031 217 |
| 9− | 6544<br>6544<br>031 220 | 6545<br>6545<br>031 221 | 6546<br>6546<br>031 222 | 6547<br>6547<br>031 223 | 6548<br>6548<br>031 224 | 6549<br>6549<br>031 225 | 6550<br>6550<br>031 226 | 6551<br>6551<br>031 227 | 6552<br>6552<br>031 230 | 6553<br>6553<br>031 231 | 6554<br>6554<br>031 232 | 6555<br>6555<br>031 233 | 6556<br>6556<br>031 234 | 6557<br>6557<br>031 235 | 6558<br>6558<br>031 236 | 6559<br>6559<br>031 237 |
| A− | 6560<br>6560<br>031 240 | 6561<br>6561<br>031 241 | 6562<br>6562<br>031 242 | 6563<br>6563<br>031 243 | 6564<br>6564<br>031 244 | 6565<br>6565<br>031 245 | 6566<br>6566<br>031 246 | 6567<br>6567<br>031 247 | 6568<br>6568<br>031 250 | 6569<br>6569<br>031 251 | 6570<br>6570<br>031 252 | 6571<br>6571<br>031 253 | 6572<br>6572<br>031 254 | 6573<br>6573<br>031 255 | 6574<br>6574<br>031 256 | 6575<br>6575<br>031 257 |
| B− | 6576<br>6576<br>031 260 | 6577<br>6577<br>031 261 | 6578<br>6578<br>031 262 | 6579<br>6579<br>031 263 | 6580<br>6580<br>031 264 | 6581<br>6581<br>031 265 | 6582<br>6582<br>031 266 | 6583<br>6583<br>031 267 | 6584<br>6584<br>031 270 | 6585<br>6585<br>031 271 | 6586<br>6586<br>031 272 | 6587<br>6587<br>031 273 | 6588<br>6588<br>031 274 | 6589<br>6589<br>031 275 | 6590<br>6590<br>031 276 | 6591<br>6591<br>031 277 |
| C− | 6592<br>6592<br>031 300 | 6593<br>6593<br>031 301 | 6594<br>6594<br>031 302 | 6595<br>6595<br>031 303 | 6596<br>6596<br>031 304 | 6597<br>6597<br>031 305 | 6598<br>6598<br>031 306 | 6599<br>6599<br>031 307 | 6600<br>6600<br>031 310 | 6601<br>6601<br>031 311 | 6602<br>6602<br>031 312 | 6603<br>6603<br>031 313 | 6604<br>6604<br>031 314 | 6605<br>6605<br>031 315 | 6606<br>6606<br>031 316 | 6607<br>6607<br>031 317 |
| D− | 6608<br>6608<br>031 320 | 6609<br>6609<br>031 321 | 6610<br>6610<br>031 322 | 6611<br>6611<br>031 323 | 6612<br>6612<br>031 324 | 6613<br>6613<br>031 325 | 6614<br>6614<br>031 326 | 6615<br>6615<br>031 327 | 6616<br>6616<br>031 330 | 6617<br>6617<br>031 331 | 6618<br>6618<br>031 332 | 6619<br>6619<br>031 333 | 6620<br>6620<br>031 334 | 6621<br>6621<br>031 335 | 6622<br>6622<br>031 336 | 6623<br>6623<br>031 337 |
| E− | 6624<br>6624<br>031 340 | 6625<br>6625<br>031 341 | 6626<br>6626<br>031 342 | 6627<br>6627<br>031 343 | 6628<br>6628<br>031 344 | 6629<br>6629<br>031 345 | 6630<br>6630<br>031 346 | 6631<br>6631<br>031 347 | 6632<br>6632<br>031 350 | 6633<br>6633<br>031 351 | 6634<br>6634<br>031 352 | 6635<br>6635<br>031 353 | 6636<br>6636<br>031 354 | 6637<br>6637<br>031 355 | 6638<br>6638<br>031 356 | 6639<br>6639<br>031 357 |
| F− | 6640<br>6640<br>031 360 | 6641<br>6641<br>031 361 | 6642<br>6642<br>031 362 | 6643<br>6643<br>031 363 | 6644<br>6644<br>031 364 | 6645<br>6645<br>031 365 | 6646<br>6646<br>031 366 | 6647<br>6647<br>031 367 | 6648<br>6648<br>031 370 | 6649<br>6649<br>031 371 | 6650<br>6650<br>031 372 | 6651<br>6651<br>031 373 | 6652<br>6652<br>031 374 | 6653<br>6653<br>031 375 | 6654<br>6654<br>031 376 | 6655<br>6655<br>031 377 |

| | −0 | −1 | −2 | −3 | −4 | −5 | −6 | −7 | −8 | −9 | −A | −B | −C | −D | −E | −F |
|---|---|---|---|---|---|---|---|---|---|---|---|---|---|---|---|---|
| **0−** | 6656<br>6656<br>032 000 | 6657<br>6657<br>032 001 | 6658<br>6658<br>032 002 | 6659<br>6659<br>032 003 | 6660<br>6660<br>032 004 | 6661<br>6661<br>032 005 | 6662<br>6662<br>032 006 | 6663<br>6663<br>032 007 | 6664<br>6664<br>032 010 | 6665<br>6665<br>032 011 | 6666<br>6666<br>032 012 | 6667<br>6667<br>032 013 | 6668<br>6668<br>032 014 | 6669<br>6669<br>032 015 | 6670<br>6670<br>032 016 | 6671<br>6671<br>032 017 |
| **1−** | 6672<br>6672<br>032 020 | 6673<br>6673<br>032 021 | 6674<br>6674<br>032 022 | 6675<br>6675<br>032 023 | 6676<br>6676<br>032 024 | 6677<br>6677<br>032 025 | 6678<br>6678<br>032 026 | 6679<br>6679<br>032 027 | 6680<br>6680<br>032 030 | 6681<br>6681<br>032 031 | 6682<br>6682<br>032 032 | 6683<br>6683<br>032 033 | 6684<br>6684<br>032 034 | 6685<br>6685<br>032 035 | 6686<br>6686<br>032 036 | 6687<br>6687<br>032 037 |
| **2−** | 6688<br>6688<br>032 040 | 6689<br>6689<br>032 041 | 6690<br>6690<br>032 042 | 6691<br>6691<br>032 043 | 6692<br>6692<br>032 044 | 6693<br>6693<br>032 045 | 6694<br>6694<br>032 046 | 6695<br>6695<br>032 047 | 6696<br>6696<br>032 050 | 6697<br>6697<br>032 051 | 6698<br>6698<br>032 052 | 6699<br>6699<br>032 053 | 6700<br>6700<br>032 054 | 6701<br>6701<br>032 055 | 6702<br>6702<br>032 056 | 6703<br>6703<br>032 057 |
| **3−** | 6704<br>6704<br>032 060 | 6705<br>6705<br>032 061 | 6706<br>6706<br>032 062 | 6707<br>6707<br>032 063 | 6708<br>6708<br>032 064 | 6709<br>6709<br>032 065 | 6710<br>6710<br>032 066 | 6711<br>6711<br>032 067 | 6712<br>6712<br>032 070 | 6713<br>6713<br>032 071 | 6714<br>6714<br>032 072 | 6715<br>6715<br>032 073 | 6716<br>6716<br>032 074 | 6717<br>6717<br>032 075 | 6718<br>6718<br>032 076 | 6719<br>6719<br>032 077 |
| **4−** | 6720<br>6720<br>032 100 | 6721<br>6721<br>032 101 | 6722<br>6722<br>032 102 | 6723<br>6723<br>032 103 | 6724<br>6724<br>032 104 | 6725<br>6725<br>032 105 | 6726<br>6726<br>032 106 | 6727<br>6727<br>032 107 | 6728<br>6728<br>032 110 | 6729<br>6729<br>032 111 | 6730<br>6730<br>032 112 | 6731<br>6731<br>032 113 | 6732<br>6732<br>032 114 | 6733<br>6733<br>032 115 | 6734<br>6734<br>032 116 | 6735<br>6735<br>032 117 |
| **5−** | 6736<br>6736<br>032 120 | 6737<br>6737<br>032 121 | 6738<br>6738<br>032 122 | 6739<br>6739<br>032 123 | 6740<br>6740<br>032 124 | 6741<br>6741<br>032 125 | 6742<br>6742<br>032 126 | 6743<br>6743<br>032 127 | 6744<br>6744<br>032 130 | 6745<br>6745<br>032 131 | 6746<br>6746<br>032 132 | 6747<br>6747<br>032 133 | 6748<br>6748<br>032 134 | 6749<br>6749<br>032 135 | 6750<br>6750<br>032 136 | 6751<br>6751<br>032 137 |
| **6−** | 6752<br>6752<br>032 140 | 6753<br>6753<br>032 141 | 6754<br>6754<br>032 142 | 6755<br>6755<br>032 143 | 6756<br>6756<br>032 144 | 6757<br>6757<br>032 145 | 6758<br>6758<br>032 146 | 6759<br>6759<br>032 147 | 6760<br>6760<br>032 150 | 6761<br>6761<br>032 151 | 6762<br>6762<br>032 152 | 6763<br>6763<br>032 153 | 6764<br>6764<br>032 154 | 6765<br>6765<br>032 155 | 6766<br>6766<br>032 156 | 6767<br>6767<br>032 157 |
| **7−** | 6768<br>6768<br>032 160 | 6769<br>6769<br>032 161 | 6770<br>6770<br>032 162 | 6771<br>6771<br>032 163 | 6772<br>6772<br>032 164 | 6773<br>6773<br>032 165 | 6774<br>6774<br>032 166 | 6775<br>6775<br>032 167 | 6776<br>6776<br>032 170 | 6777<br>6777<br>032 171 | 6778<br>6778<br>032 172 | 6779<br>6779<br>032 173 | 6780<br>6780<br>032 174 | 6781<br>6781<br>032 175 | 6782<br>6782<br>032 176 | 6783<br>6783<br>032 177 |
| **8−** | 6784<br>6784<br>032 200 | 6785<br>6785<br>032 201 | 6786<br>6786<br>032 202 | 6787<br>6787<br>032 203 | 6788<br>6788<br>032 204 | 6789<br>6789<br>032 205 | 6790<br>6790<br>032 206 | 6791<br>6791<br>032 207 | 6792<br>6792<br>032 210 | 6793<br>6793<br>032 211 | 6794<br>6794<br>032 212 | 6795<br>6795<br>032 213 | 6796<br>6796<br>032 214 | 6797<br>6797<br>032 215 | 6798<br>6798<br>032 216 | 6799<br>6799<br>032 217 |
| **9−** | 6800<br>6800<br>032 220 | 6801<br>6801<br>032 221 | 6802<br>6802<br>032 222 | 6803<br>6803<br>032 223 | 6804<br>6804<br>032 224 | 6805<br>6805<br>032 225 | 6806<br>6806<br>032 226 | 6807<br>6807<br>032 227 | 6808<br>6808<br>032 230 | 6809<br>6809<br>032 231 | 6810<br>6810<br>032 232 | 6811<br>6811<br>032 233 | 6812<br>6812<br>032 234 | 6813<br>6813<br>032 235 | 6814<br>6814<br>032 236 | 6815<br>6815<br>032 237 |
| **A−** | 6816<br>6816<br>032 240 | 6817<br>6817<br>032 241 | 6818<br>6818<br>032 242 | 6819<br>6819<br>032 243 | 6820<br>6820<br>032 244 | 6821<br>6821<br>032 245 | 6822<br>6822<br>032 246 | 6823<br>6823<br>032 247 | 6824<br>6824<br>032 250 | 6825<br>6825<br>032 251 | 6826<br>6826<br>032 252 | 6827<br>6827<br>032 253 | 6828<br>6828<br>032 254 | 6829<br>6829<br>032 255 | 6830<br>6830<br>032 256 | 6831<br>6831<br>032 257 |
| **B−** | 6832<br>6832<br>032 260 | 6833<br>6833<br>032 261 | 6834<br>6834<br>032 262 | 6835<br>6835<br>032 263 | 6836<br>6836<br>032 264 | 6837<br>6837<br>032 265 | 6838<br>6838<br>032 266 | 6839<br>6839<br>032 267 | 6840<br>6840<br>032 270 | 6841<br>6841<br>032 271 | 6842<br>6842<br>032 272 | 6843<br>6843<br>032 273 | 6844<br>6844<br>032 274 | 6845<br>6845<br>032 275 | 6846<br>6846<br>032 276 | 6847<br>6847<br>032 277 |
| **C−** | 6848<br>6848<br>032 300 | 6849<br>6849<br>032 301 | 6850<br>6850<br>032 302 | 6851<br>6851<br>032 303 | 6852<br>6852<br>032 304 | 6853<br>6853<br>032 305 | 6854<br>6854<br>032 306 | 6855<br>6855<br>032 307 | 6856<br>6856<br>032 310 | 6857<br>6857<br>032 311 | 6858<br>6858<br>032 312 | 6859<br>6859<br>032 313 | 6860<br>6860<br>032 314 | 6861<br>6861<br>032 315 | 6862<br>6862<br>032 316 | 6863<br>6863<br>032 317 |
| **D−** | 6864<br>6864<br>032 320 | 6865<br>6865<br>032 321 | 6866<br>6866<br>032 322 | 6867<br>6867<br>032 323 | 6868<br>6868<br>032 324 | 6869<br>6869<br>032 325 | 6870<br>6870<br>032 326 | 6871<br>6871<br>032 327 | 6872<br>6872<br>032 330 | 6873<br>6873<br>032 331 | 6874<br>6874<br>032 332 | 6875<br>6875<br>032 333 | 6876<br>6876<br>032 334 | 6877<br>6877<br>032 335 | 6878<br>6878<br>032 336 | 6879<br>6879<br>032 337 |
| **E−** | 6880<br>6880<br>032 340 | 6881<br>6881<br>032 341 | 6882<br>6882<br>032 342 | 6883<br>6883<br>032 343 | 6884<br>6884<br>032 344 | 6885<br>6885<br>032 345 | 6886<br>6886<br>032 346 | 6887<br>6887<br>032 347 | 6888<br>6888<br>032 350 | 6889<br>6889<br>032 351 | 6890<br>6890<br>032 352 | 6891<br>6891<br>032 353 | 6892<br>6892<br>032 354 | 6893<br>6893<br>032 355 | 6894<br>6894<br>032 356 | 6895<br>6895<br>032 357 |
| **F−** | 6896<br>6896<br>032 360 | 6897<br>6897<br>032 361 | 6898<br>6898<br>032 362 | 6899<br>6899<br>032 363 | 6900<br>6900<br>032 364 | 6901<br>6901<br>032 365 | 6902<br>6902<br>032 366 | 6903<br>6903<br>032 367 | 6904<br>6904<br>032 370 | 6905<br>6905<br>032 371 | 6906<br>6906<br>032 372 | 6907<br>6907<br>032 373 | 6908<br>6908<br>032 374 | 6909<br>6909<br>032 375 | 6910<br>6910<br>032 376 | 6911<br>6911<br>032 377 |

SECOND HEX DIGIT

DECIMAL →
 DECIMAL →
OCTAL →

 DECIMAL  | 6656 |  BINARY  | 0001 1010 |  DECIMAL  | 6656 |  HEXADECIMAL  ⬡1A  OCTAL  | 032 000 |

FOURTH HEX DIGIT →  ⬡  ← THIRD HEX DIGIT

⎚ DECIMAL `6912`  BINARY `0001 1011`  DECIMAL `6912`  HEXADECIMAL ⬡ `1B`  OCTAL `033 000`

FOURTH HEX DIGIT → ⬡ ← THIRD HEX DIGIT

| ⟨2⟩ | FIRST HEX DIGIT | | | | | | | | | | | | | | | |
|---|---|---|---|---|---|---|---|---|---|---|---|---|---|---|---|---|
| | −0 | −1 | −2 | −3 | −4 | −5 | −6 | −7 | −8 | −9 | −A | −B | −C | −D | −E | −F |
| 0− | 6912<br>6912<br>033 000 | 6913<br>6913<br>033 001 | 6914<br>6914<br>033 002 | 6915<br>6915<br>033 003 | 6916<br>6916<br>033 004 | 6917<br>6917<br>033 005 | 6918<br>6918<br>033 006 | 6919<br>6919<br>033 007 | 6920<br>6920<br>033 010 | 6921<br>6921<br>033 011 | 6922<br>6922<br>033 012 | 6923<br>6923<br>033 013 | 6924<br>6924<br>033 014 | 6925<br>6925<br>033 015 | 6926<br>6926<br>033 016 | 6927<br>6927<br>033 017 |
| 1− | 6928<br>6928<br>033 020 | 6929<br>6929<br>033 021 | 6930<br>6930<br>033 022 | 6931<br>6931<br>033 023 | 6932<br>6932<br>033 024 | 6933<br>6933<br>033 025 | 6934<br>6934<br>033 026 | 6935<br>6935<br>033 027 | 6936<br>6936<br>033 030 | 6937<br>6937<br>033 031 | 6938<br>6938<br>033 032 | 6939<br>6939<br>033 033 | 6940<br>6940<br>033 034 | 6941<br>6941<br>033 035 | 6942<br>6942<br>033 036 | 6943<br>6943<br>033 037 |
| 2− | 6944<br>6944<br>033 040 | 6945<br>6945<br>033 041 | 6946<br>6946<br>033 042 | 6947<br>6947<br>033 043 | 6948<br>6948<br>033 044 | 6949<br>6949<br>033 045 | 6950<br>6950<br>033 046 | 6951<br>6951<br>033 047 | 6952<br>6952<br>033 050 | 6953<br>6953<br>033 051 | 6954<br>6954<br>033 052 | 6955<br>6955<br>033 053 | 6956<br>6956<br>033 054 | 6957<br>6957<br>033 055 | 6958<br>6958<br>033 056 | 6959<br>6959<br>033 057 |
| 3− | 6960<br>6960<br>033 060 | 6961<br>6961<br>033 061 | 6962<br>6962<br>033 062 | 6963<br>6963<br>033 063 | 6964<br>6964<br>033 064 | 6965<br>6965<br>033 065 | 6966<br>6966<br>033 066 | 6967<br>6967<br>033 067 | 6968<br>6968<br>033 070 | 6969<br>6969<br>033 071 | 6970<br>6970<br>033 072 | 6971<br>6971<br>033 073 | 6972<br>6972<br>033 074 | 6973<br>6973<br>033 075 | 6974<br>6974<br>033 076 | 6975<br>6975<br>033 077 |
| 4− | 6976<br>6976<br>033 100 | 6977<br>6977<br>033 101 | 6978<br>6978<br>033 102 | 6979<br>6979<br>033 103 | 6980<br>6980<br>033 104 | 6981<br>6981<br>033 105 | 6982<br>6982<br>033 106 | 6983<br>6983<br>033 107 | 6984<br>6984<br>033 110 | 6985<br>6985<br>033 111 | 6986<br>6986<br>033 112 | 6987<br>6987<br>033 113 | 6988<br>6988<br>033 114 | 6989<br>6989<br>033 115 | 6990<br>6990<br>033 116 | 6991<br>6991<br>033 117 |
| 5− | 6992<br>6992<br>033 120 | 6993<br>6993<br>033 121 | 6994<br>6994<br>033 122 | 6995<br>6995<br>033 123 | 6996<br>6996<br>033 124 | 6997<br>6997<br>033 125 | 6998<br>6998<br>033 126 | 6999<br>6999<br>033 127 | 7000<br>7000<br>033 130 | 7001<br>7001<br>033 131 | 7002<br>7002<br>033 132 | 7003<br>7003<br>033 133 | 7004<br>7004<br>033 134 | 7005<br>7005<br>033 135 | 7006<br>7006<br>033 136 | 7007<br>7007<br>033 137 |
| 6− | 7008<br>7008<br>033 140 | 7009<br>7009<br>033 141 | 7010<br>7010<br>033 142 | 7011<br>7011<br>033 143 | 7012<br>7012<br>033 144 | 7013<br>7013<br>033 145 | 7014<br>7014<br>033 146 | 7015<br>7015<br>033 147 | 7016<br>7016<br>033 150 | 7017<br>7017<br>033 151 | 7018<br>7018<br>033 152 | 7019<br>7019<br>033 153 | 7020<br>7020<br>033 154 | 7021<br>7021<br>033 155 | 7022<br>7022<br>033 156 | 7023<br>7023<br>033 157 |
| 7− | 7024<br>7024<br>033 160 | 7025<br>7025<br>033 161 | 7026<br>7026<br>033 162 | 7027<br>7027<br>033 163 | 7028<br>7028<br>033 164 | 7029<br>7029<br>033 165 | 7030<br>7030<br>033 166 | 7031<br>7031<br>033 167 | 7032<br>7032<br>033 170 | 7033<br>7033<br>033 171 | 7034<br>7034<br>033 172 | 7035<br>7035<br>033 173 | 7036<br>7036<br>033 174 | 7037<br>7037<br>033 175 | 7038<br>7038<br>033 176 | 7039<br>7039<br>033 177 |
| 8− | 7040<br>7040<br>033 200 | 7041<br>7041<br>033 201 | 7042<br>7042<br>033 202 | 7043<br>7043<br>033 203 | 7044<br>7044<br>033 204 | 7045<br>7045<br>033 205 | 7046<br>7046<br>033 206 | 7047<br>7047<br>033 207 | 7048<br>7048<br>033 210 | 7049<br>7049<br>033 211 | 7050<br>7050<br>033 212 | 7051<br>7051<br>033 213 | 7052<br>7052<br>033 214 | 7053<br>7053<br>033 215 | 7054<br>7054<br>033 216 | 7055<br>7055<br>033 217 |
| 9− | 7056<br>7056<br>033 220 | 7057<br>7057<br>033 221 | 7058<br>7058<br>033 222 | 7059<br>7059<br>033 223 | 7060<br>7060<br>033 224 | 7061<br>7061<br>033 225 | 7062<br>7062<br>033 226 | 7063<br>7063<br>033 227 | 7064<br>7064<br>033 230 | 7065<br>7065<br>033 231 | 7066<br>7066<br>033 232 | 7067<br>7067<br>033 233 | 7068<br>7068<br>033 234 | 7069<br>7069<br>033 235 | 7070<br>7070<br>033 236 | 7071<br>7071<br>033 237 |
| A− | 7072<br>7072<br>033 240 | 7073<br>7073<br>033 241 | 7074<br>7074<br>033 242 | 7075<br>7075<br>033 243 | 7076<br>7076<br>033 244 | 7077<br>7077<br>033 245 | 7078<br>7078<br>033 246 | 7079<br>7079<br>033 247 | 7080<br>7080<br>033 250 | 7081<br>7081<br>033 251 | 7082<br>7082<br>033 252 | 7083<br>7083<br>033 253 | 7084<br>7084<br>033 254 | 7085<br>7085<br>033 255 | 7086<br>7086<br>033 256 | 7087<br>7087<br>033 257 |
| B− | 7088<br>7088<br>033 260 | 7089<br>7089<br>033 261 | 7090<br>7090<br>033 262 | 7091<br>7091<br>033 263 | 7092<br>7092<br>033 264 | 7093<br>7093<br>033 265 | 7094<br>7094<br>033 266 | 7095<br>7095<br>033 267 | 7096<br>7096<br>033 270 | 7097<br>7097<br>033 271 | 7098<br>7098<br>033 272 | 7099<br>7099<br>033 273 | 7100<br>7100<br>033 274 | 7101<br>7101<br>033 275 | 7102<br>7102<br>033 276 | 7103<br>7103<br>033 277 |
| C− | 7104<br>7104<br>033 300 | 7105<br>7105<br>033 301 | 7106<br>7106<br>033 302 | 7107<br>7107<br>033 303 | 7108<br>7108<br>033 304 | 7109<br>7109<br>033 305 | 7110<br>7110<br>033 306 | 7111<br>7111<br>033 307 | 7112<br>7112<br>033 310 | 7113<br>7113<br>033 311 | 7114<br>7114<br>033 312 | 7115<br>7115<br>033 313 | 7116<br>7116<br>033 314 | 7117<br>7117<br>033 315 | 7118<br>7118<br>033 316 | 7119<br>7119<br>033 317 |
| D− | 7120<br>7120<br>033 320 | 7121<br>7121<br>033 321 | 7122<br>7122<br>033 322 | 7123<br>7123<br>033 323 | 7124<br>7124<br>033 324 | 7125<br>7125<br>033 325 | 7126<br>7126<br>033 326 | 7127<br>7127<br>033 327 | 7128<br>7128<br>033 330 | 7129<br>7129<br>033 331 | 7130<br>7130<br>033 332 | 7131<br>7131<br>033 333 | 7132<br>7132<br>033 334 | 7133<br>7133<br>033 335 | 7134<br>7134<br>033 336 | 7135<br>7135<br>033 337 |
| E− | 7136<br>7136<br>033 340 | 7137<br>7137<br>033 341 | 7138<br>7138<br>033 342 | 7139<br>7139<br>033 343 | 7140<br>7140<br>033 344 | 7141<br>7141<br>033 345 | 7142<br>7142<br>033 346 | 7143<br>7143<br>033 347 | 7144<br>7144<br>033 350 | 7145<br>7145<br>033 351 | 7146<br>7146<br>033 352 | 7147<br>7147<br>033 353 | 7148<br>7148<br>033 354 | 7149<br>7149<br>033 355 | 7150<br>7150<br>033 356 | 7151<br>7151<br>033 357 |
| F− | 7152<br>7152<br>033 360 | 7153<br>7153<br>033 361 | 7154<br>7154<br>033 362 | 7155<br>7155<br>033 363 | 7156<br>7156<br>033 364 | 7157<br>7157<br>033 365 | 7158<br>7158<br>033 366 | 7159<br>7159<br>033 367 | 7160<br>7160<br>033 370 | 7161<br>7161<br>033 371 | 7162<br>7162<br>033 372 | 7163<br>7163<br>033 373 | 7164<br>7164<br>033 374 | 7165<br>7165<br>033 375 | 7166<br>7166<br>033 376 | 7167<br>7167<br>033 377 |

SECOND HEX DIGIT

DECIMAL →

⎚ DECIMAL →

OCTAL →

## FIRST HEX DIGIT ⟨2⟩

| SECOND HEX DIGIT | −0 | −1 | −2 | −3 | −4 | −5 | −6 | −7 | −8 | −9 | −A | −B | −C | −D | −E | −F |
|---|---|---|---|---|---|---|---|---|---|---|---|---|---|---|---|---|
| **0−** | 7168 7168 034 000 | 7169 7169 034 001 | 7170 7170 034 002 | 7171 7171 034 003 | 7172 7172 034 004 | 7173 7173 034 005 | 7174 7174 034 006 | 7175 7175 034 007 | 7176 7176 034 010 | 7177 7177 034 011 | 7178 7178 034 012 | 7179 7179 034 013 | 7180 7180 034 014 | 7181 7181 034 015 | 7182 7182 034 016 | 7183 7183 034 017 |
| **1−** | 7184 7184 034 020 | 7185 7185 034 021 | 7186 7186 034 022 | 7187 7187 034 023 | 7188 7188 034 024 | 7189 7189 034 025 | 7190 7190 034 026 | 7191 7191 034 027 | 7192 7192 034 030 | 7193 7193 034 031 | 7194 7194 034 032 | 7195 7195 034 033 | 7196 7196 034 034 | 7197 7197 034 035 | 7198 7198 034 036 | 7199 7199 034 037 |
| **2−** | 7200 7200 034 040 | 7201 7201 034 041 | 7202 7202 034 042 | 7203 7203 034 043 | 7204 7204 034 044 | 7205 7205 034 045 | 7206 7206 034 046 | 7207 7207 034 047 | 7208 7208 034 050 | 7209 7209 034 051 | 7210 7210 034 052 | 7211 7211 034 053 | 7212 7212 034 054 | 7213 7213 034 055 | 7214 7214 034 056 | 7215 7215 034 057 |
| **3−** | 7216 7216 034 060 | 7217 7217 034 061 | 7218 7218 034 062 | 7219 7219 034 063 | 7220 7220 034 064 | 7221 7221 034 065 | 7222 7222 034 066 | 7223 7223 034 067 | 7224 7224 034 070 | 7225 7225 034 071 | 7226 7226 034 072 | 7227 7227 034 073 | 7228 7228 034 074 | 7229 7229 034 075 | 7230 7230 034 076 | 7231 7231 034 077 |
| **4−** | 7232 7232 034 100 | 7233 7233 034 101 | 7234 7234 034 102 | 7235 7235 034 103 | 7236 7236 034 104 | 7237 7237 034 105 | 7238 7238 034 106 | 7239 7239 034 107 | 7240 7240 034 110 | 7241 7241 034 111 | 7242 7242 034 112 | 7243 7243 034 113 | 7244 7244 034 114 | 7245 7245 034 115 | 7246 7246 034 116 | 7247 7247 034 117 |
| **5−** | 7248 7248 034 120 | 7249 7249 034 121 | 7250 7250 034 122 | 7251 7251 034 123 | 7252 7252 034 124 | 7253 7253 034 125 | 7254 7254 034 126 | 7255 7255 034 127 | 7256 7256 034 130 | 7257 7257 034 131 | 7258 7258 034 132 | 7259 7259 034 133 | 7260 7260 034 134 | 7261 7261 034 135 | 7262 7262 034 136 | 7263 7263 034 137 |
| **6−** | 7264 7264 034 140 | 7265 7265 034 141 | 7266 7266 034 142 | 7267 7267 034 143 | 7268 7268 034 144 | 7269 7269 034 145 | 7270 7270 034 146 | 7271 7271 034 147 | 7272 7272 034 150 | 7273 7273 034 151 | 7274 7274 034 152 | 7275 7275 034 153 | 7276 7276 034 154 | 7277 7277 034 155 | 7278 7278 034 156 | 7279 7279 034 157 |
| **7−** | 7280 7280 034 160 | 7281 7281 034 161 | 7282 7282 034 162 | 7283 7283 034 163 | 7284 7284 034 164 | 7285 7285 034 165 | 7286 7286 034 166 | 7287 7287 034 167 | 7288 7288 034 170 | 7289 7289 034 171 | 7290 7290 034 172 | 7291 7291 034 173 | 7292 7292 034 174 | 7293 7293 034 175 | 7294 7294 034 176 | 7295 7295 034 177 |
| **8−** | 7296 7296 034 200 | 7297 7297 034 201 | 7298 7298 034 202 | 7299 7299 034 203 | 7300 7300 034 204 | 7301 7301 034 205 | 7302 7302 034 206 | 7303 7303 034 207 | 7304 7304 034 210 | 7305 7305 034 211 | 7306 7306 034 212 | 7307 7307 034 213 | 7308 7308 034 214 | 7309 7309 034 215 | 7310 7310 034 216 | 7311 7311 034 217 |
| **9−** | 7312 7312 034 220 | 7313 7313 034 221 | 7314 7314 034 222 | 7315 7315 034 223 | 7316 7316 034 224 | 7317 7317 034 225 | 7318 7318 034 226 | 7319 7319 034 227 | 7320 7320 034 230 | 7321 7321 034 231 | 7322 7322 034 232 | 7323 7323 034 233 | 7324 7324 034 234 | 7325 7325 034 235 | 7326 7326 034 236 | 7327 7327 034 237 |
| **A−** | 7328 7328 034 240 | 7329 7329 034 241 | 7330 7330 034 242 | 7331 7331 034 243 | 7332 7332 034 244 | 7333 7333 034 245 | 7334 7334 034 246 | 7335 7335 034 247 | 7336 7336 034 250 | 7337 7337 034 251 | 7338 7338 034 252 | 7339 7339 034 253 | 7340 7340 034 254 | 7341 7341 034 255 | 7342 7342 034 256 | 7343 7343 034 257 |
| **B−** | 7344 7344 034 260 | 7345 7345 034 261 | 7346 7346 034 262 | 7347 7347 034 263 | 7348 7348 034 264 | 7349 7349 034 265 | 7350 7350 034 266 | 7351 7351 034 267 | 7352 7352 034 270 | 7353 7353 034 271 | 7354 7354 034 272 | 7355 7355 034 273 | 7356 7356 034 274 | 7357 7357 034 275 | 7358 7358 034 276 | 7359 7359 034 277 |
| **C−** | 7360 7360 034 300 | 7361 7361 034 301 | 7362 7362 034 302 | 7363 7363 034 303 | 7364 7364 034 304 | 7365 7365 034 305 | 7366 7366 034 306 | 7367 7367 034 307 | 7368 7368 034 310 | 7369 7369 034 311 | 7370 7370 034 312 | 7371 7371 034 313 | 7372 7372 034 314 | 7373 7373 034 315 | 7374 7374 034 316 | 7375 7375 034 317 |
| **D−** | 7376 7376 034 320 | 7377 7377 034 321 | 7378 7378 034 322 | 7379 7379 034 323 | 7380 7380 034 324 | 7381 7381 034 325 | 7382 7382 034 326 | 7383 7383 034 327 | 7384 7384 034 330 | 7385 7385 034 331 | 7386 7386 034 332 | 7387 7387 034 333 | 7388 7388 034 334 | 7389 7389 034 335 | 7390 7390 034 336 | 7391 7391 034 337 |
| **E−** | 7392 7392 034 340 | 7393 7393 034 341 | 7394 7394 034 342 | 7395 7395 034 343 | 7396 7396 034 344 | 7397 7397 034 345 | 7398 7398 034 346 | 7399 7399 034 347 | 7400 7400 034 350 | 7401 7401 034 351 | 7402 7402 034 352 | 7403 7403 034 353 | 7404 7404 034 354 | 7405 7405 034 355 | 7406 7406 034 356 | 7407 7407 034 357 |
| **F−** | 7408 7408 034 360 | 7409 7409 034 361 | 7410 7410 034 362 | 7411 7411 034 363 | 7412 7412 034 364 | 7413 7413 034 365 | 7414 7414 034 366 | 7415 7415 034 367 | 7416 7416 034 370 | 7417 7417 034 371 | 7418 7418 034 372 | 7419 7419 034 373 | 7420 7420 034 374 | 7421 7421 034 375 | 7422 7422 034 376 | 7423 7423 034 377 |

DECIMAL

 DECIMAL

OCTAL

 DECIMAL 7168    BINARY 0001 1100    DECIMAL 7168    HEXADECIMAL ⟨1C⟩    OCTAL 034 000

FOURTH HEX DIGIT → ⟨1C⟩ ← THIRD HEX DIGIT

## FIRST HEX DIGIT

⬡2 — SECOND HEX DIGIT

Each cell lists the decimal value (shown twice on the card) and, below it, the octal value.

| | −0 | −1 | −2 | −3 | −4 | −5 | −6 | −7 | −8 | −9 | −A | −B | −C | −D | −E | −F |
|---|---|---|---|---|---|---|---|---|---|---|---|---|---|---|---|---|
| 0− | 7424<br>035 000 | 7425<br>035 001 | 7426<br>035 002 | 7427<br>035 003 | 7428<br>035 004 | 7429<br>035 005 | 7430<br>035 006 | 7431<br>035 007 | 7432<br>035 010 | 7433<br>035 011 | 7434<br>035 012 | 7435<br>035 013 | 7436<br>035 014 | 7437<br>035 015 | 7438<br>035 016 | 7439<br>035 017 |
| 1− | 7440<br>035 020 | 7441<br>035 021 | 7442<br>035 022 | 7443<br>035 023 | 7444<br>035 024 | 7445<br>035 025 | 7446<br>035 026 | 7447<br>035 027 | 7448<br>035 030 | 7449<br>035 031 | 7450<br>035 032 | 7451<br>035 033 | 7452<br>035 034 | 7453<br>035 035 | 7454<br>035 036 | 7455<br>035 037 |
| 2− | 7456<br>035 040 | 7457<br>035 041 | 7458<br>035 042 | 7459<br>035 043 | 7460<br>035 044 | 7461<br>035 045 | 7462<br>035 046 | 7463<br>035 047 | 7464<br>035 050 | 7465<br>035 051 | 7466<br>035 052 | 7467<br>035 053 | 7468<br>035 054 | 7469<br>035 055 | 7470<br>035 056 | 7471<br>035 057 |
| 3− | 7472<br>035 060 | 7473<br>035 061 | 7474<br>035 062 | 7475<br>035 063 | 7476<br>035 064 | 7477<br>035 065 | 7478<br>035 066 | 7479<br>035 067 | 7480<br>035 070 | 7481<br>035 071 | 7482<br>035 072 | 7483<br>035 073 | 7484<br>035 074 | 7485<br>035 075 | 7486<br>035 076 | 7487<br>035 077 |
| 4− | 7488<br>035 100 | 7489<br>035 101 | 7490<br>035 102 | 7491<br>035 103 | 7492<br>035 104 | 7493<br>035 105 | 7494<br>035 106 | 7495<br>035 107 | 7496<br>035 110 | 7497<br>035 111 | 7498<br>035 112 | 7499<br>035 113 | 7500<br>035 114 | 7501<br>035 115 | 7502<br>035 116 | 7503<br>035 117 |
| 5− | 7504<br>035 120 | 7505<br>035 121 | 7506<br>035 122 | 7507<br>035 123 | 7508<br>035 124 | 7509<br>035 125 | 7510<br>035 126 | 7511<br>035 127 | 7512<br>035 130 | 7513<br>035 131 | 7514<br>035 132 | 7515<br>035 133 | 7516<br>035 134 | 7517<br>035 135 | 7518<br>035 136 | 7519<br>035 137 |
| 6− | 7520<br>035 140 | 7521<br>035 141 | 7522<br>035 142 | 7523<br>035 143 | 7524<br>035 144 | 7525<br>035 145 | 7526<br>035 146 | 7527<br>035 147 | 7528<br>035 150 | 7529<br>035 151 | 7530<br>035 152 | 7531<br>035 153 | 7532<br>035 154 | 7533<br>035 155 | 7534<br>035 156 | 7535<br>035 157 |
| 7− | 7536<br>035 160 | 7537<br>035 161 | 7538<br>035 162 | 7539<br>035 163 | 7540<br>035 164 | 7541<br>035 165 | 7542<br>035 166 | 7543<br>035 167 | 7544<br>035 170 | 7545<br>035 171 | 7546<br>035 172 | 7547<br>035 173 | 7548<br>035 174 | 7549<br>035 175 | 7550<br>035 176 | 7551<br>035 177 |
| 8− | 7552<br>035 200 | 7553<br>035 201 | 7554<br>035 202 | 7555<br>035 203 | 7556<br>035 204 | 7557<br>035 205 | 7558<br>035 206 | 7559<br>035 207 | 7560<br>035 210 | 7561<br>035 211 | 7562<br>035 212 | 7563<br>035 213 | 7564<br>035 214 | 7565<br>035 215 | 7566<br>035 216 | 7567<br>035 217 |
| 9− | 7568<br>035 220 | 7569<br>035 221 | 7570<br>035 222 | 7571<br>035 223 | 7572<br>035 224 | 7573<br>035 225 | 7574<br>035 226 | 7575<br>035 227 | 7576<br>035 230 | 7577<br>035 231 | 7578<br>035 232 | 7579<br>035 233 | 7580<br>035 234 | 7581<br>035 235 | 7582<br>035 236 | 7583<br>035 237 |
| A− | 7584<br>035 240 | 7585<br>035 241 | 7586<br>035 242 | 7587<br>035 243 | 7588<br>035 244 | 7589<br>035 245 | 7590<br>035 246 | 7591<br>035 247 | 7592<br>035 250 | 7593<br>035 251 | 7594<br>035 252 | 7595<br>035 253 | 7596<br>035 254 | 7597<br>035 255 | 7598<br>035 256 | 7599<br>035 257 |
| B− | 7600<br>035 260 | 7601<br>035 261 | 7602<br>035 262 | 7603<br>035 263 | 7604<br>035 264 | 7605<br>035 265 | 7606<br>035 266 | 7607<br>035 267 | 7608<br>035 270 | 7609<br>035 271 | 7610<br>035 272 | 7611<br>035 273 | 7612<br>035 274 | 7613<br>035 275 | 7614<br>035 276 | 7615<br>035 277 |
| C− | 7616<br>035 300 | 7617<br>035 301 | 7618<br>035 302 | 7619<br>035 303 | 7620<br>035 304 | 7621<br>035 305 | 7622<br>035 306 | 7623<br>035 307 | 7624<br>035 310 | 7625<br>035 311 | 7626<br>035 312 | 7627<br>035 313 | 7628<br>035 314 | 7629<br>035 315 | 7630<br>035 316 | 7631<br>035 317 |
| D− | 7632<br>035 320 | 7633<br>035 321 | 7634<br>035 322 | 7635<br>035 323 | 7636<br>035 324 | 7637<br>035 325 | 7638<br>035 326 | 7639<br>035 327 | 7640<br>035 330 | 7641<br>035 331 | 7642<br>035 332 | 7643<br>035 333 | 7644<br>035 334 | 7645<br>035 335 | 7646<br>035 336 | 7647<br>035 337 |
| E− | 7648<br>035 340 | 7649<br>035 341 | 7650<br>035 342 | 7651<br>035 343 | 7652<br>035 344 | 7653<br>035 345 | 7654<br>035 346 | 7655<br>035 347 | 7656<br>035 350 | 7657<br>035 351 | 7658<br>035 352 | 7659<br>035 353 | 7660<br>035 354 | 7661<br>035 355 | 7662<br>035 356 | 7663<br>035 357 |
| F− | 7664<br>035 360 | 7665<br>035 361 | 7666<br>035 362 | 7667<br>035 363 | 7668<br>035 364 | 7669<br>035 365 | 7670<br>035 366 | 7671<br>035 367 | 7672<br>035 370 | 7673<br>035 371 | 7674<br>035 372 | 7675<br>035 373 | 7676<br>035 374 | 7677<br>035 375 | 7678<br>035 376 | 7679<br>035 377 |

DECIMAL →

🍎 DECIMAL →

OCTAL →

# FIRST HEX DIGIT

② 

| SECOND HEX DIGIT | −0 | −1 | −2 | −3 | −4 | −5 | −6 | −7 | −8 | −9 | −A | −B | −C | −D | −E | −F |
|---|---|---|---|---|---|---|---|---|---|---|---|---|---|---|---|---|
| **0−** | 7680<br>7680<br>036 000 | 7681<br>7681<br>036 001 | 7682<br>7682<br>036 002 | 7683<br>7683<br>036 003 | 7684<br>7684<br>036 004 | 7685<br>7685<br>036 005 | 7686<br>7686<br>036 006 | 7687<br>7687<br>036 007 | 7688<br>7688<br>036 010 | 7689<br>7689<br>036 011 | 7690<br>7690<br>036 012 | 7691<br>7691<br>036 013 | 7692<br>7692<br>036 014 | 7693<br>7693<br>036 015 | 7694<br>7694<br>036 016 | 7695<br>7695<br>036 017 |
| **1−** | 7696<br>7696<br>036 020 | 7697<br>7697<br>036 021 | 7698<br>7698<br>036 022 | 7699<br>7699<br>036 023 | 7700<br>7700<br>036 024 | 7701<br>7701<br>036 025 | 7702<br>7702<br>036 026 | 7703<br>7703<br>036 027 | 7704<br>7704<br>036 030 | 7705<br>7705<br>036 031 | 7706<br>7706<br>036 032 | 7707<br>7707<br>036 033 | 7708<br>7708<br>036 034 | 7709<br>7709<br>036 035 | 7710<br>7710<br>036 036 | 7711<br>7711<br>036 037 |
| **2−** | 7712<br>7712<br>036 040 | 7713<br>7713<br>036 041 | 7714<br>7714<br>036 042 | 7715<br>7715<br>036 043 | 7716<br>7716<br>036 044 | 7717<br>7717<br>036 045 | 7718<br>7718<br>036 046 | 7719<br>7719<br>036 047 | 7720<br>7720<br>036 050 | 7721<br>7721<br>036 051 | 7722<br>7722<br>036 052 | 7723<br>7723<br>036 053 | 7724<br>7724<br>036 054 | 7725<br>7725<br>036 055 | 7726<br>7726<br>036 056 | 7727<br>7727<br>036 057 |
| **3−** | 7728<br>7728<br>036 060 | 7729<br>7729<br>036 061 | 7730<br>7730<br>036 062 | 7731<br>7731<br>036 063 | 7732<br>7732<br>036 064 | 7733<br>7733<br>036 065 | 7734<br>7734<br>036 066 | 7735<br>7735<br>036 067 | 7736<br>7736<br>036 070 | 7737<br>7737<br>036 071 | 7738<br>7738<br>036 072 | 7739<br>7739<br>036 073 | 7740<br>7740<br>036 074 | 7741<br>7741<br>036 075 | 7742<br>7742<br>036 076 | 7743<br>7743<br>036 077 |
| **4−** | 7744<br>7744<br>036 100 | 7745<br>7745<br>036 101 | 7746<br>7746<br>036 102 | 7747<br>7747<br>036 103 | 7748<br>7748<br>036 104 | 7749<br>7749<br>036 105 | 7750<br>7750<br>036 106 | 7751<br>7751<br>036 107 | 7752<br>7752<br>036 110 | 7753<br>7753<br>036 111 | 7754<br>7754<br>036 112 | 7755<br>7755<br>036 113 | 7756<br>7756<br>036 114 | 7757<br>7757<br>036 115 | 7758<br>7758<br>036 116 | 7759<br>7759<br>036 117 |
| **5−** | 7760<br>7760<br>036 120 | 7761<br>7761<br>036 121 | 7762<br>7762<br>036 122 | 7763<br>7763<br>036 123 | 7764<br>7764<br>036 124 | 7765<br>7765<br>036 125 | 7766<br>7766<br>036 126 | 7767<br>7767<br>036 127 | 7768<br>7768<br>036 130 | 7769<br>7769<br>036 131 | 7770<br>7770<br>036 132 | 7771<br>7771<br>036 133 | 7772<br>7772<br>036 134 | 7773<br>7773<br>036 135 | 7774<br>7774<br>036 136 | 7775<br>7775<br>036 137 |
| **6−** | 7776<br>7776<br>036 140 | 7777<br>7777<br>036 141 | 7778<br>7778<br>036 142 | 7779<br>7779<br>036 143 | 7780<br>7780<br>036 144 | 7781<br>7781<br>036 145 | 7782<br>7782<br>036 146 | 7783<br>7783<br>036 147 | 7784<br>7784<br>036 150 | 7785<br>7785<br>036 151 | 7786<br>7786<br>036 152 | 7787<br>7787<br>036 153 | 7788<br>7788<br>036 154 | 7789<br>7789<br>036 155 | 7790<br>7790<br>036 156 | 7791<br>7791<br>036 157 |
| **7−** | 7792<br>7792<br>036 160 | 7793<br>7793<br>036 161 | 7794<br>7794<br>036 162 | 7795<br>7795<br>036 163 | 7796<br>7796<br>036 164 | 7797<br>7797<br>036 165 | 7798<br>7798<br>036 166 | 7799<br>7799<br>036 167 | 7800<br>7800<br>036 170 | 7801<br>7801<br>036 171 | 7802<br>7802<br>036 172 | 7803<br>7803<br>036 173 | 7804<br>7804<br>036 174 | 7805<br>7805<br>036 175 | 7806<br>7806<br>036 176 | 7807<br>7807<br>036 177 |
| **8−** | 7808<br>7808<br>036 200 | 7809<br>7809<br>036 201 | 7810<br>7810<br>036 202 | 7811<br>7811<br>036 203 | 7812<br>7812<br>036 204 | 7813<br>7813<br>036 205 | 7814<br>7814<br>036 206 | 7815<br>7815<br>036 207 | 7816<br>7816<br>036 210 | 7817<br>7817<br>036 211 | 7818<br>7818<br>036 212 | 7819<br>7819<br>036 213 | 7820<br>7820<br>036 214 | 7821<br>7821<br>036 215 | 7822<br>7822<br>036 216 | 7823<br>7823<br>036 217 |
| **9−** | 7824<br>7824<br>036 220 | 7825<br>7825<br>036 221 | 7826<br>7826<br>036 222 | 7827<br>7827<br>036 223 | 7828<br>7828<br>036 224 | 7829<br>7829<br>036 225 | 7830<br>7830<br>036 226 | 7831<br>7831<br>036 227 | 7832<br>7832<br>036 230 | 7833<br>7833<br>036 231 | 7834<br>7834<br>036 232 | 7835<br>7835<br>036 233 | 7836<br>7836<br>036 234 | 7837<br>7837<br>036 235 | 7838<br>7838<br>036 236 | 7839<br>7839<br>036 237 |
| **A−** | 7840<br>7840<br>036 240 | 7841<br>7841<br>036 241 | 7842<br>7842<br>036 242 | 7843<br>7843<br>036 243 | 7844<br>7844<br>036 244 | 7845<br>7845<br>036 245 | 7846<br>7846<br>036 246 | 7847<br>7847<br>036 247 | 7848<br>7848<br>036 250 | 7849<br>7849<br>036 251 | 7850<br>7850<br>036 252 | 7851<br>7851<br>036 253 | 7852<br>7852<br>036 254 | 7853<br>7853<br>036 255 | 7854<br>7854<br>036 256 | 7855<br>7855<br>036 257 |
| **B−** | 7856<br>7856<br>036 260 | 7857<br>7857<br>036 261 | 7858<br>7858<br>036 262 | 7859<br>7859<br>036 263 | 7860<br>7860<br>036 264 | 7861<br>7861<br>036 265 | 7862<br>7862<br>036 266 | 7863<br>7863<br>036 267 | 7864<br>7864<br>036 270 | 7865<br>7865<br>036 271 | 7866<br>7866<br>036 272 | 7867<br>7867<br>036 273 | 7868<br>7868<br>036 274 | 7869<br>7869<br>036 275 | 7870<br>7870<br>036 276 | 7871<br>7871<br>036 277 |
| **C−** | 7872<br>7872<br>036 300 | 7873<br>7873<br>036 301 | 7874<br>7874<br>036 302 | 7875<br>7875<br>036 303 | 7876<br>7876<br>036 304 | 7877<br>7877<br>036 305 | 7878<br>7878<br>036 306 | 7879<br>7879<br>036 307 | 7880<br>7880<br>036 310 | 7881<br>7881<br>036 311 | 7882<br>7882<br>036 312 | 7883<br>7883<br>036 313 | 7884<br>7884<br>036 314 | 7885<br>7885<br>036 315 | 7886<br>7886<br>036 316 | 7887<br>7887<br>036 317 |
| **D−** | 7888<br>7888<br>036 320 | 7889<br>7889<br>036 321 | 7890<br>7890<br>036 322 | 7891<br>7891<br>036 323 | 7892<br>7892<br>036 324 | 7893<br>7893<br>036 325 | 7894<br>7894<br>036 326 | 7895<br>7895<br>036 327 | 7896<br>7896<br>036 330 | 7897<br>7897<br>036 331 | 7898<br>7898<br>036 332 | 7899<br>7899<br>036 333 | 7900<br>7900<br>036 334 | 7901<br>7901<br>036 335 | 7902<br>7902<br>036 336 | 7903<br>7903<br>036 337 |
| **E−** | 7904<br>7904<br>036 340 | 7905<br>7905<br>036 341 | 7906<br>7906<br>036 342 | 7907<br>7907<br>036 343 | 7908<br>7908<br>036 344 | 7909<br>7909<br>036 345 | 7910<br>7910<br>036 346 | 7911<br>7911<br>036 347 | 7912<br>7912<br>036 350 | 7913<br>7913<br>036 351 | 7914<br>7914<br>036 352 | 7915<br>7915<br>036 353 | 7916<br>7916<br>036 354 | 7917<br>7917<br>036 355 | 7918<br>7918<br>036 356 | 7919<br>7919<br>036 357 |
| **F−** | 7920<br>7920<br>036 360 | 7921<br>7921<br>036 361 | 7922<br>7922<br>036 362 | 7923<br>7923<br>036 363 | 7924<br>7924<br>036 364 | 7925<br>7925<br>036 365 | 7926<br>7926<br>036 366 | 7927<br>7927<br>036 367 | 7928<br>7928<br>036 370 | 7929<br>7929<br>036 371 | 7930<br>7930<br>036 372 | 7931<br>7931<br>036 373 | 7932<br>7932<br>036 374 | 7933<br>7933<br>036 375 | 7934<br>7934<br>036 376 | 7935<br>7935<br>036 377 |

DECIMAL

 DECIMAL

OCTAL

 DECIMAL | 7680    BINARY | 0001 1110    DECIMAL | 7680    HEXADECIMAL ⬡ 1E    OCTAL | 036 000

FOURTH HEX DIGIT     THIRD HEX DIGIT

FIRST HEX DIGIT ②

| SECOND HEX DIGIT | −0 | −1 | −2 | −3 | −4 | −5 | −6 | −7 | −8 | −9 | −A | −B | −C | −D | −E | −F |
|---|---|---|---|---|---|---|---|---|---|---|---|---|---|---|---|---|
| 0− | 7936<br>7936<br>037 000 | 7937<br>7937<br>037 001 | 7938<br>7938<br>037 002 | 7939<br>7939<br>037 003 | 7940<br>7940<br>037 004 | 7941<br>7941<br>037 005 | 7942<br>7942<br>037 006 | 7943<br>7943<br>037 007 | 7944<br>7944<br>037 010 | 7945<br>7945<br>037 011 | 7946<br>7946<br>037 012 | 7947<br>7947<br>037 013 | 7948<br>7948<br>037 014 | 7949<br>7949<br>037 015 | 7950<br>7950<br>037 016 | 7951<br>7951<br>037 017 |
| 1− | 7952<br>7952<br>037 020 | 7953<br>7953<br>037 021 | 7954<br>7954<br>037 022 | 7955<br>7955<br>037 023 | 7956<br>7956<br>037 024 | 7957<br>7957<br>037 025 | 7958<br>7958<br>037 026 | 7959<br>7959<br>037 027 | 7960<br>7960<br>037 030 | 7961<br>7961<br>037 031 | 7962<br>7962<br>037 032 | 7963<br>7963<br>037 033 | 7964<br>7964<br>037 034 | 7965<br>7965<br>037 035 | 7966<br>7966<br>037 036 | 7967<br>7967<br>037 037 |
| 2− | 7968<br>7968<br>037 040 | 7969<br>7969<br>037 041 | 7970<br>7970<br>037 042 | 7971<br>7971<br>037 043 | 7972<br>7972<br>037 044 | 7973<br>7973<br>037 045 | 7974<br>7974<br>037 046 | 7975<br>7975<br>037 047 | 7976<br>7976<br>037 050 | 7977<br>7977<br>037 051 | 7978<br>7978<br>037 052 | 7979<br>7979<br>037 053 | 7980<br>7980<br>037 054 | 7981<br>7981<br>037 055 | 7982<br>7982<br>037 056 | 7983<br>7983<br>037 057 |
| 3− | 7984<br>7984<br>037 060 | 7985<br>7985<br>037 061 | 7986<br>7986<br>037 062 | 7987<br>7987<br>037 063 | 7988<br>7988<br>037 064 | 7989<br>7989<br>037 065 | 7990<br>7990<br>037 066 | 7991<br>7991<br>037 067 | 7992<br>7992<br>037 070 | 7993<br>7993<br>037 071 | 7994<br>7994<br>037 072 | 7995<br>7995<br>037 073 | 7996<br>7996<br>037 074 | 7997<br>7997<br>037 075 | 7998<br>7998<br>037 076 | 7999<br>7999<br>037 077 |
| 4− | 8000<br>8000<br>037 100 | 8001<br>8001<br>037 101 | 8002<br>8002<br>037 102 | 8003<br>8003<br>037 103 | 8004<br>8004<br>037 104 | 8005<br>8005<br>037 105 | 8006<br>8006<br>037 106 | 8007<br>8007<br>037 107 | 8008<br>8008<br>037 110 | 8009<br>8009<br>037 111 | 8010<br>8010<br>037 112 | 8011<br>8011<br>037 113 | 8012<br>8012<br>037 114 | 8013<br>8013<br>037 115 | 8014<br>8014<br>037 116 | 8015<br>8015<br>037 117 |
| 5− | 8016<br>8016<br>037 120 | 8017<br>8017<br>037 121 | 8018<br>8018<br>037 122 | 8019<br>8019<br>037 123 | 8020<br>8020<br>037 124 | 8021<br>8021<br>037 125 | 8022<br>8022<br>037 126 | 8023<br>8023<br>037 127 | 8024<br>8024<br>037 130 | 8025<br>8025<br>037 131 | 8026<br>8026<br>037 132 | 8027<br>8027<br>037 133 | 8028<br>8028<br>037 134 | 8029<br>8029<br>037 135 | 8030<br>8030<br>037 136 | 8031<br>8031<br>037 137 |
| 6− | 8032<br>8032<br>037 140 | 8033<br>8033<br>037 141 | 8034<br>8034<br>037 142 | 8035<br>8035<br>037 143 | 8036<br>8036<br>037 144 | 8037<br>8037<br>037 145 | 8038<br>8038<br>037 146 | 8039<br>8039<br>037 147 | 8040<br>8040<br>037 150 | 8041<br>8041<br>037 151 | 8042<br>8042<br>037 152 | 8043<br>8043<br>037 153 | 8044<br>8044<br>037 154 | 8045<br>8045<br>037 155 | 8046<br>8046<br>037 156 | 8047<br>8047<br>037 157 |
| 7− | 8048<br>8048<br>037 160 | 8049<br>8049<br>037 161 | 8050<br>8050<br>037 162 | 8051<br>8051<br>037 163 | 8052<br>8052<br>037 164 | 8053<br>8053<br>037 165 | 8054<br>8054<br>037 166 | 8055<br>8055<br>037 167 | 8056<br>8056<br>037 170 | 8057<br>8057<br>037 171 | 8058<br>8058<br>037 172 | 8059<br>8059<br>037 173 | 8060<br>8060<br>037 174 | 8061<br>8061<br>037 175 | 8062<br>8062<br>037 176 | 8063<br>8063<br>037 177 |
| 8− | 8064<br>8064<br>037 200 | 8065<br>8065<br>037 201 | 8066<br>8066<br>037 202 | 8067<br>8067<br>037 203 | 8068<br>8068<br>037 204 | 8069<br>8069<br>037 205 | 8070<br>8070<br>037 206 | 8071<br>8071<br>037 207 | 8072<br>8072<br>037 210 | 8073<br>8073<br>037 211 | 8074<br>8074<br>037 212 | 8075<br>8075<br>037 213 | 8076<br>8076<br>037 214 | 8077<br>8077<br>037 215 | 8078<br>8078<br>037 216 | 8079<br>8079<br>037 217 |
| 9− | 8080<br>8080<br>037 220 | 8081<br>8081<br>037 221 | 8082<br>8082<br>037 222 | 8083<br>8083<br>037 223 | 8084<br>8084<br>037 224 | 8085<br>8085<br>037 225 | 8086<br>8086<br>037 226 | 8087<br>8087<br>037 227 | 8088<br>8088<br>037 230 | 8089<br>8089<br>037 231 | 8090<br>8090<br>037 232 | 8091<br>8091<br>037 233 | 8092<br>8092<br>037 234 | 8093<br>8093<br>037 235 | 8094<br>8094<br>037 236 | 8095<br>8095<br>037 237 |
| A− | 8096<br>8096<br>037 240 | 8097<br>8097<br>037 241 | 8098<br>8098<br>037 242 | 8099<br>8099<br>037 243 | 8100<br>8100<br>037 244 | 8101<br>8101<br>037 245 | 8102<br>8102<br>037 246 | 8103<br>8103<br>037 247 | 8104<br>8104<br>037 250 | 8105<br>8105<br>037 251 | 8106<br>8106<br>037 252 | 8107<br>8107<br>037 253 | 8108<br>8108<br>037 254 | 8109<br>8109<br>037 255 | 8110<br>8110<br>037 256 | 8111<br>8111<br>037 257 |
| B− | 8112<br>8112<br>037 260 | 8113<br>8113<br>037 261 | 8114<br>8114<br>037 262 | 8115<br>8115<br>037 263 | 8116<br>8116<br>037 264 | 8117<br>8117<br>037 265 | 8118<br>8118<br>037 266 | 8119<br>8119<br>037 267 | 8120<br>8120<br>037 270 | 8121<br>8121<br>037 271 | 8122<br>8122<br>037 272 | 8123<br>8123<br>037 273 | 8124<br>8124<br>037 274 | 8125<br>8125<br>037 275 | 8126<br>8126<br>037 276 | 8127<br>8127<br>037 277 |
| C− | 8128<br>8128<br>037 300 | 8129<br>8129<br>037 301 | 8130<br>8130<br>037 302 | 8131<br>8131<br>037 303 | 8132<br>8132<br>037 304 | 8133<br>8133<br>037 305 | 8134<br>8134<br>037 306 | 8135<br>8135<br>037 307 | 8136<br>8136<br>037 310 | 8137<br>8137<br>037 311 | 8138<br>8138<br>037 312 | 8139<br>8139<br>037 313 | 8140<br>8140<br>037 314 | 8141<br>8141<br>037 315 | 8142<br>8142<br>037 316 | 8143<br>8143<br>037 317 |
| D− | 8144<br>8144<br>037 320 | 8145<br>8145<br>037 321 | 8146<br>8146<br>037 322 | 8147<br>8147<br>037 323 | 8148<br>8148<br>037 324 | 8149<br>8149<br>037 325 | 8150<br>8150<br>037 326 | 8151<br>8151<br>037 327 | 8152<br>8152<br>037 330 | 8153<br>8153<br>037 331 | 8154<br>8154<br>037 332 | 8155<br>8155<br>037 333 | 8156<br>8156<br>037 334 | 8157<br>8157<br>037 335 | 8158<br>8158<br>037 336 | 8159<br>8159<br>037 337 |
| E− | 8160<br>8160<br>037 340 | 8161<br>8161<br>037 341 | 8162<br>8162<br>037 342 | 8163<br>8163<br>037 343 | 8164<br>8164<br>037 344 | 8165<br>8165<br>037 345 | 8166<br>8166<br>037 346 | 8167<br>8167<br>037 347 | 8168<br>8168<br>037 350 | 8169<br>8169<br>037 351 | 8170<br>8170<br>037 352 | 8171<br>8171<br>037 353 | 8172<br>8172<br>037 354 | 8173<br>8173<br>037 355 | 8174<br>8174<br>037 356 | 8175<br>8175<br>037 357 |
| F− | 8176<br>8176<br>037 360 | 8177<br>8177<br>037 361 | 8178<br>8178<br>037 362 | 8179<br>8179<br>037 363 | 8180<br>8180<br>037 364 | 8181<br>8181<br>037 365 | 8182<br>8182<br>037 366 | 8183<br>8183<br>037 367 | 8184<br>8184<br>037 370 | 8185<br>8185<br>037 371 | 8186<br>8186<br>037 372 | 8187<br>8187<br>037 373 | 8188<br>8188<br>037 374 | 8189<br>8189<br>037 375 | 8190<br>8190<br>037 376 | 8191<br>8191<br>037 377 |

| SECOND HEX DIGIT | −0 | −1 | −2 | −3 | −4 | −5 | −6 | −7 | −8 | −9 | −A | −B | −C | −D | −E | −F |
|---|---|---|---|---|---|---|---|---|---|---|---|---|---|---|---|---|
| **0-** | 8192<br>8192<br>040 000 | 8193<br>8193<br>040 001 | 8194<br>8194<br>040 002 | 8195<br>8195<br>040 003 | 8196<br>8196<br>040 004 | 8197<br>8197<br>040 005 | 8198<br>8198<br>040 006 | 8199<br>8199<br>040 007 | 8200<br>8200<br>040 010 | 8201<br>8201<br>040 011 | 8202<br>8202<br>040 012 | 8203<br>8203<br>040 013 | 8204<br>8204<br>040 014 | 8205<br>8205<br>040 015 | 8206<br>8206<br>040 016 | 8207<br>8207<br>040 017 |
| **1-** | 8208<br>8208<br>040 020 | 8209<br>8209<br>040 021 | 8210<br>8210<br>040 022 | 8211<br>8211<br>040 023 | 8212<br>8212<br>040 024 | 8213<br>8213<br>040 025 | 8214<br>8214<br>040 026 | 8215<br>8215<br>040 027 | 8216<br>8216<br>040 030 | 8217<br>8217<br>040 031 | 8218<br>8218<br>040 032 | 8219<br>8219<br>040 033 | 8220<br>8220<br>040 034 | 8221<br>8221<br>040 035 | 8222<br>8222<br>040 036 | 8223<br>8223<br>040 037 |
| **2-** | 8224<br>8224<br>040 040 | 8225<br>8225<br>040 041 | 8226<br>8226<br>040 042 | 8227<br>8227<br>040 043 | 8228<br>8228<br>040 044 | 8229<br>8229<br>040 045 | 8230<br>8230<br>040 046 | 8231<br>8231<br>040 047 | 8232<br>8232<br>040 050 | 8233<br>8233<br>040 051 | 8234<br>8234<br>040 052 | 8235<br>8235<br>040 053 | 8236<br>8236<br>040 054 | 8237<br>8237<br>040 055 | 8238<br>8238<br>040 056 | 8239<br>8239<br>040 057 |
| **3-** | 8240<br>8240<br>040 060 | 8241<br>8241<br>040 061 | 8242<br>8242<br>040 062 | 8243<br>8243<br>040 063 | 8244<br>8244<br>040 064 | 8245<br>8245<br>040 065 | 8246<br>8246<br>040 066 | 8247<br>8247<br>040 067 | 8248<br>8248<br>040 070 | 8249<br>8249<br>040 071 | 8250<br>8250<br>040 072 | 8251<br>8251<br>040 073 | 8252<br>8252<br>040 074 | 8253<br>8253<br>040 075 | 8254<br>8254<br>040 076 | 8255<br>8255<br>040 077 |
| **4-** | 8256<br>8256<br>040 100 | 8257<br>8257<br>040 101 | 8258<br>8258<br>040 102 | 8259<br>8259<br>040 103 | 8260<br>8260<br>040 104 | 8261<br>8261<br>040 105 | 8262<br>8262<br>040 106 | 8263<br>8263<br>040 107 | 8264<br>8264<br>040 110 | 8265<br>8265<br>040 111 | 8266<br>8266<br>040 112 | 8267<br>8267<br>040 113 | 8268<br>8268<br>040 114 | 8269<br>8269<br>040 115 | 8270<br>8270<br>040 116 | 8271<br>8271<br>040 117 |
| **5-** | 8272<br>8272<br>040 120 | 8273<br>8273<br>040 121 | 8274<br>8274<br>040 122 | 8275<br>8275<br>040 123 | 8276<br>8276<br>040 124 | 8277<br>8277<br>040 125 | 8278<br>8278<br>040 126 | 8279<br>8279<br>040 127 | 8280<br>8280<br>040 130 | 8281<br>8281<br>040 131 | 8282<br>8282<br>040 132 | 8283<br>8283<br>040 133 | 8284<br>8284<br>040 134 | 8285<br>8285<br>040 135 | 8286<br>8286<br>040 136 | 8287<br>8287<br>040 137 |
| **6-** | 8288<br>8288<br>040 140 | 8289<br>8289<br>040 141 | 8290<br>8290<br>040 142 | 8291<br>8291<br>040 143 | 8292<br>8292<br>040 144 | 8293<br>8293<br>040 145 | 8294<br>8294<br>040 146 | 8295<br>8295<br>040 147 | 8296<br>8296<br>040 150 | 8297<br>8297<br>040 151 | 8298<br>8298<br>040 152 | 8299<br>8299<br>040 153 | 8300<br>8300<br>040 154 | 8301<br>8301<br>040 155 | 8302<br>8302<br>040 156 | 8303<br>8303<br>040 157 |
| **7-** | 8304<br>8304<br>040 160 | 8305<br>8305<br>040 161 | 8306<br>8306<br>040 162 | 8307<br>8307<br>040 163 | 8308<br>8308<br>040 164 | 8309<br>8309<br>040 165 | 8310<br>8310<br>040 166 | 8311<br>8311<br>040 167 | 8312<br>8312<br>040 170 | 8313<br>8313<br>040 171 | 8314<br>8314<br>040 172 | 8315<br>8315<br>040 173 | 8316<br>8316<br>040 174 | 8317<br>8317<br>040 175 | 8318<br>8318<br>040 176 | 8319<br>8319<br>040 177 |
| **8-** | 8320<br>8320<br>040 200 | 8321<br>8321<br>040 201 | 8322<br>8322<br>040 202 | 8323<br>8323<br>040 203 | 8324<br>8324<br>040 204 | 8325<br>8325<br>040 205 | 8326<br>8326<br>040 206 | 8327<br>8327<br>040 207 | 8328<br>8328<br>040 210 | 8329<br>8329<br>040 211 | 8330<br>8330<br>040 212 | 8331<br>8331<br>040 213 | 8332<br>8332<br>040 214 | 8333<br>8333<br>040 215 | 8334<br>8334<br>040 216 | 8335<br>8335<br>040 217 |
| **9-** | 8336<br>8336<br>040 220 | 8337<br>8337<br>040 221 | 8338<br>8338<br>040 222 | 8339<br>8339<br>040 223 | 8340<br>8340<br>040 224 | 8341<br>8341<br>040 225 | 8342<br>8342<br>040 226 | 8343<br>8343<br>040 227 | 8344<br>8344<br>040 230 | 8345<br>8345<br>040 231 | 8346<br>8346<br>040 232 | 8347<br>8347<br>040 233 | 8348<br>8348<br>040 234 | 8349<br>8349<br>040 235 | 8350<br>8350<br>040 236 | 8351<br>8351<br>040 237 |
| **A-** | 8352<br>8352<br>040 240 | 8353<br>8353<br>040 241 | 8354<br>8354<br>040 242 | 8355<br>8355<br>040 243 | 8356<br>8356<br>040 244 | 8357<br>8357<br>040 245 | 8358<br>8358<br>040 246 | 8359<br>8359<br>040 247 | 8360<br>8360<br>040 250 | 8361<br>8361<br>040 251 | 8362<br>8362<br>040 252 | 8363<br>8363<br>040 253 | 8364<br>8364<br>040 254 | 8365<br>8365<br>040 255 | 8366<br>8366<br>040 256 | 8367<br>8367<br>040 257 |
| **B-** | 8368<br>8368<br>040 260 | 8369<br>8369<br>040 261 | 8370<br>8370<br>040 262 | 8371<br>8371<br>040 263 | 8372<br>8372<br>040 264 | 8373<br>8373<br>040 265 | 8374<br>8374<br>040 266 | 8375<br>8375<br>040 267 | 8376<br>8376<br>040 270 | 8377<br>8377<br>040 271 | 8378<br>8378<br>040 272 | 8379<br>8379<br>040 273 | 8380<br>8380<br>040 274 | 8381<br>8381<br>040 275 | 8382<br>8382<br>040 276 | 8383<br>8383<br>040 277 |
| **C-** | 8384<br>8384<br>040 300 | 8385<br>8385<br>040 301 | 8386<br>8386<br>040 302 | 8387<br>8387<br>040 303 | 8388<br>8388<br>040 304 | 8389<br>8389<br>040 305 | 8390<br>8390<br>040 306 | 8391<br>8391<br>040 307 | 8392<br>8392<br>040 310 | 8393<br>8393<br>040 311 | 8394<br>8394<br>040 312 | 8395<br>8395<br>040 313 | 8396<br>8396<br>040 314 | 8397<br>8397<br>040 315 | 8398<br>8398<br>040 316 | 8399<br>8399<br>040 317 |
| **D-** | 8400<br>8400<br>040 320 | 8401<br>8401<br>040 321 | 8402<br>8402<br>040 322 | 8403<br>8403<br>040 323 | 8404<br>8404<br>040 324 | 8405<br>8405<br>040 325 | 8406<br>8406<br>040 326 | 8407<br>8407<br>040 327 | 8408<br>8408<br>040 330 | 8409<br>8409<br>040 331 | 8410<br>8410<br>040 332 | 8411<br>8411<br>040 333 | 8412<br>8412<br>040 334 | 8413<br>8413<br>040 335 | 8414<br>8414<br>040 336 | 8415<br>8415<br>040 337 |
| **E-** | 8416<br>8416<br>040 340 | 8417<br>8417<br>040 341 | 8418<br>8418<br>040 342 | 8419<br>8419<br>040 343 | 8420<br>8420<br>040 344 | 8421<br>8421<br>040 345 | 8422<br>8422<br>040 346 | 8423<br>8423<br>040 347 | 8424<br>8424<br>040 350 | 8425<br>8425<br>040 351 | 8426<br>8426<br>040 352 | 8427<br>8427<br>040 353 | 8428<br>8428<br>040 354 | 8429<br>8429<br>040 355 | 8430<br>8430<br>040 356 | 8431<br>8431<br>040 357 |
| **F-** | 8432<br>8432<br>040 360 | 8433<br>8433<br>040 361 | 8434<br>8434<br>040 362 | 8435<br>8435<br>040 363 | 8436<br>8436<br>040 364 | 8437<br>8437<br>040 365 | 8438<br>8438<br>040 366 | 8439<br>8439<br>040 367 | 8440<br>8440<br>040 370 | 8441<br>8441<br>040 371 | 8442<br>8442<br>040 372 | 8443<br>8443<br>040 373 | 8444<br>8444<br>040 374 | 8445<br>8445<br>040 375 | 8446<br>8446<br>040 376 | 8447<br>8447<br>040 377 |

**DECIMAL** →

 **DECIMAL** →

**OCTAL** →

 **DECIMAL** 8192    **BINARY** 0010 0000    **DECIMAL** 8192    **HEXADECIMAL** 20    **OCTAL** 040 000

FOURTH HEX DIGIT → 20 ← THIRD HEX DIGIT

| 2 | FIRST HEX DIGIT | | | | | | | | | | | | | | | |
| --- | -0 | -1 | -2 | -3 | -4 | -5 | -6 | -7 | -8 | -9 | -A | -B | -C | -D | -E | -F |
| 0- | 8448<br>8448<br>041 000 | 8449<br>8449<br>041 001 | 8450<br>8450<br>041 002 | 8451<br>8451<br>041 003 | 8452<br>8452<br>041 004 | 8453<br>8453<br>041 005 | 8454<br>8454<br>041 006 | 8455<br>8455<br>041 007 | 8456<br>8456<br>041 010 | 8457<br>8457<br>041 011 | 8458<br>8458<br>041 012 | 8459<br>8459<br>041 013 | 8460<br>8460<br>041 014 | 8461<br>8461<br>041 015 | 8462<br>8462<br>041 016 | 8463<br>8463<br>041 017 |
| 1- | 8464<br>8464<br>041 020 | 8465<br>8465<br>041 021 | 8466<br>8466<br>041 022 | 8467<br>8467<br>041 023 | 8468<br>8468<br>041 024 | 8469<br>8469<br>041 025 | 8470<br>8470<br>041 026 | 8471<br>8471<br>041 027 | 8472<br>8472<br>041 030 | 8473<br>8473<br>041 031 | 8474<br>8474<br>041 032 | 8475<br>8475<br>041 033 | 8476<br>8476<br>041 034 | 8477<br>8477<br>041 035 | 8478<br>8478<br>041 036 | 8479<br>8479<br>041 037 |
| 2- | 8480<br>8480<br>041 040 | 8481<br>8481<br>041 041 | 8482<br>8482<br>041 042 | 8483<br>8483<br>041 043 | 8484<br>8484<br>041 044 | 8485<br>8485<br>041 045 | 8486<br>8486<br>041 046 | 8487<br>8487<br>041 047 | 8488<br>8488<br>041 050 | 8489<br>8489<br>041 051 | 8490<br>8490<br>041 052 | 8491<br>8491<br>041 053 | 8492<br>8492<br>041 054 | 8493<br>8493<br>041 055 | 8494<br>8494<br>041 056 | 8495<br>8495<br>041 057 |
| 3- | 8496<br>8496<br>041 060 | 8497<br>8497<br>041 061 | 8498<br>8498<br>041 062 | 8499<br>8499<br>041 063 | 8500<br>8500<br>041 064 | 8501<br>8501<br>041 065 | 8502<br>8502<br>041 066 | 8503<br>8503<br>041 067 | 8504<br>8504<br>041 070 | 8505<br>8505<br>041 071 | 8506<br>8506<br>041 072 | 8507<br>8507<br>041 073 | 8508<br>8508<br>041 074 | 8509<br>8509<br>041 075 | 8510<br>8510<br>041 076 | 8511<br>8511<br>041 077 |
| 4- | 8512<br>8512<br>041 100 | 8513<br>8513<br>041 101 | 8514<br>8514<br>041 102 | 8515<br>8515<br>041 103 | 8516<br>8516<br>041 104 | 8517<br>8517<br>041 105 | 8518<br>8518<br>041 106 | 8519<br>8519<br>041 107 | 8520<br>8520<br>041 110 | 8521<br>8521<br>041 111 | 8522<br>8522<br>041 112 | 8523<br>8523<br>041 113 | 8524<br>8524<br>041 114 | 8525<br>8525<br>041 115 | 8526<br>8526<br>041 116 | 8527<br>8527<br>041 117 |
| 5- | 8528<br>8528<br>041 120 | 8529<br>8529<br>041 121 | 8530<br>8530<br>041 122 | 8531<br>8531<br>041 123 | 8532<br>8532<br>041 124 | 8533<br>8533<br>041 125 | 8534<br>8534<br>041 126 | 8535<br>8535<br>041 127 | 8536<br>8536<br>041 130 | 8537<br>8537<br>041 131 | 8538<br>8538<br>041 132 | 8539<br>8539<br>041 133 | 8540<br>8540<br>041 134 | 8541<br>8541<br>041 135 | 8542<br>8542<br>041 136 | 8543<br>8543<br>041 137 |
| 6- | 8544<br>8544<br>041 140 | 8545<br>8545<br>041 141 | 8546<br>8546<br>041 142 | 8547<br>8547<br>041 143 | 8548<br>8548<br>041 144 | 8549<br>8549<br>041 145 | 8550<br>8550<br>041 146 | 8551<br>8551<br>041 147 | 8552<br>8552<br>041 150 | 8553<br>8553<br>041 151 | 8554<br>8554<br>041 152 | 8555<br>8555<br>041 153 | 8556<br>8556<br>041 154 | 8557<br>8557<br>041 155 | 8558<br>8558<br>041 156 | 8559<br>8559<br>041 157 |
| 7- | 8560<br>8560<br>041 160 | 8561<br>8561<br>041 161 | 8562<br>8562<br>041 162 | 8563<br>8563<br>041 163 | 8564<br>8564<br>041 164 | 8565<br>8565<br>041 165 | 8566<br>8566<br>041 166 | 8567<br>8567<br>041 167 | 8568<br>8568<br>041 170 | 8569<br>8569<br>041 171 | 8570<br>8570<br>041 172 | 8571<br>8571<br>041 173 | 8572<br>8572<br>041 174 | 8573<br>8573<br>041 175 | 8574<br>8574<br>041 176 | 8575<br>8575<br>041 177 |
| 8- | 8576<br>8576<br>041 200 | 8577<br>8577<br>041 201 | 8578<br>8578<br>041 202 | 8579<br>8579<br>041 203 | 8580<br>8580<br>041 204 | 8581<br>8581<br>041 205 | 8582<br>8582<br>041 206 | 8583<br>8583<br>041 207 | 8584<br>8584<br>041 210 | 8585<br>8585<br>041 211 | 8586<br>8586<br>041 212 | 8587<br>8587<br>041 213 | 8588<br>8588<br>041 214 | 8589<br>8589<br>041 215 | 8590<br>8590<br>041 216 | 8591<br>8591<br>041 217 |
| 9- | 8592<br>8592<br>041 220 | 8593<br>8593<br>041 221 | 8594<br>8594<br>041 222 | 8595<br>8595<br>041 223 | 8596<br>8596<br>041 224 | 8597<br>8597<br>041 225 | 8598<br>8598<br>041 226 | 8599<br>8599<br>041 227 | 8600<br>8600<br>041 230 | 8601<br>8601<br>041 231 | 8602<br>8602<br>041 232 | 8603<br>8603<br>041 233 | 8604<br>8604<br>041 234 | 8605<br>8605<br>041 235 | 8606<br>8606<br>041 236 | 8607<br>8607<br>041 237 |
| A- | 8608<br>8608<br>041 240 | 8609<br>8609<br>041 241 | 8610<br>8610<br>041 242 | 8611<br>8611<br>041 243 | 8612<br>8612<br>041 244 | 8613<br>8613<br>041 245 | 8614<br>8614<br>041 246 | 8615<br>8615<br>041 247 | 8616<br>8616<br>041 250 | 8617<br>8617<br>041 251 | 8618<br>8618<br>041 252 | 8619<br>8619<br>041 253 | 8620<br>8620<br>041 254 | 8621<br>8621<br>041 255 | 8622<br>8622<br>041 256 | 8623<br>8623<br>041 257 |
| B- | 8624<br>8624<br>041 260 | 8625<br>8625<br>041 261 | 8626<br>8626<br>041 262 | 8627<br>8627<br>041 263 | 8628<br>8628<br>041 264 | 8629<br>8629<br>041 265 | 8630<br>8630<br>041 266 | 8631<br>8631<br>041 267 | 8632<br>8632<br>041 270 | 8633<br>8633<br>041 271 | 8634<br>8634<br>041 272 | 8635<br>8635<br>041 273 | 8636<br>8636<br>041 274 | 8637<br>8637<br>041 275 | 8638<br>8638<br>041 276 | 8639<br>8639<br>041 277 |
| C- | 8640<br>8640<br>041 300 | 8641<br>8641<br>041 301 | 8642<br>8642<br>041 302 | 8643<br>8643<br>041 303 | 8644<br>8644<br>041 304 | 8645<br>8645<br>041 305 | 8646<br>8646<br>041 306 | 8647<br>8647<br>041 307 | 8648<br>8648<br>041 310 | 8649<br>8649<br>041 311 | 8650<br>8650<br>041 312 | 8651<br>8651<br>041 313 | 8652<br>8652<br>041 314 | 8653<br>8653<br>041 315 | 8654<br>8654<br>041 316 | 8655<br>8655<br>041 317 |
| D- | 8656<br>8656<br>041 320 | 8657<br>8657<br>041 321 | 8658<br>8658<br>041 322 | 8659<br>8659<br>041 323 | 8660<br>8660<br>041 324 | 8661<br>8661<br>041 325 | 8662<br>8662<br>041 326 | 8663<br>8663<br>041 327 | 8664<br>8664<br>041 330 | 8665<br>8665<br>041 331 | 8666<br>8666<br>041 332 | 8667<br>8667<br>041 333 | 8668<br>8668<br>041 334 | 8669<br>8669<br>041 335 | 8670<br>8670<br>041 336 | 8671<br>8671<br>041 337 |
| E- | 8672<br>8672<br>041 340 | 8673<br>8673<br>041 341 | 8674<br>8674<br>041 342 | 8675<br>8675<br>041 343 | 8676<br>8676<br>041 344 | 8677<br>8677<br>041 345 | 8678<br>8678<br>041 346 | 8679<br>8679<br>041 347 | 8680<br>8680<br>041 350 | 8681<br>8681<br>041 351 | 8682<br>8682<br>041 352 | 8683<br>8683<br>041 353 | 8684<br>8684<br>041 354 | 8685<br>8685<br>041 355 | 8686<br>8686<br>041 356 | 8687<br>8687<br>041 357 |
| F- | 8688<br>8688<br>041 360 | 8689<br>8689<br>041 361 | 8690<br>8690<br>041 362 | 8691<br>8691<br>041 363 | 8692<br>8692<br>041 364 | 8693<br>8693<br>041 365 | 8694<br>8694<br>041 366 | 8695<br>8695<br>041 367 | 8696<br>8696<br>041 370 | 8697<br>8697<br>041 371 | 8698<br>8698<br>041 372 | 8699<br>8699<br>041 373 | 8700<br>8700<br>041 374 | 8701<br>8701<br>041 375 | 8702<br>8702<br>041 376 | 8703<br>8703<br>041 377 |

SECOND HEX DIGIT

## FIRST HEX DIGIT

| ② | −0 | −1 | −2 | −3 | −4 | −5 | −6 | −7 | −8 | −9 | −A | −B | −C | −D | −E | −F |
|---|---|---|---|---|---|---|---|---|---|---|---|---|---|---|---|---|
| **0−** | 8704<br>8704<br>042 000 | 8705<br>8705<br>042 001 | 8706<br>8706<br>042 002 | 8707<br>8707<br>042 003 | 8708<br>8708<br>042 004 | 8709<br>8709<br>042 005 | 8710<br>8710<br>042 006 | 8711<br>8711<br>042 007 | 8712<br>8712<br>042 010 | 8713<br>8713<br>042 011 | 8714<br>8714<br>042 012 | 8715<br>8715<br>042 013 | 8716<br>8716<br>042 014 | 8717<br>8717<br>042 015 | 8718<br>8718<br>042 016 | 8719<br>8719<br>042 017 |
| **1−** | 8720<br>8720<br>042 020 | 8721<br>8721<br>042 021 | 8722<br>8722<br>042 022 | 8723<br>8723<br>042 023 | 8724<br>8724<br>042 024 | 8725<br>8725<br>042 025 | 8726<br>8726<br>042 026 | 8727<br>8727<br>042 027 | 8728<br>8728<br>042 030 | 8729<br>8729<br>042 031 | 8730<br>8730<br>042 032 | 8731<br>8731<br>042 033 | 8732<br>8732<br>042 034 | 8733<br>8733<br>042 035 | 8734<br>8734<br>042 036 | 8735<br>8735<br>042 037 |
| **2−** | 8736<br>8736<br>042 040 | 8737<br>8737<br>042 041 | 8738<br>8738<br>042 042 | 8739<br>8739<br>042 043 | 8740<br>8740<br>042 044 | 8741<br>8741<br>042 045 | 8742<br>8742<br>042 046 | 8743<br>8743<br>042 047 | 8744<br>8744<br>042 050 | 8745<br>8745<br>042 051 | 8746<br>8746<br>042 052 | 8747<br>8747<br>042 053 | 8748<br>8748<br>042 054 | 8749<br>8749<br>042 055 | 8750<br>8750<br>042 056 | 8751<br>8751<br>042 057 |
| **3−** | 8752<br>8752<br>042 060 | 8753<br>8753<br>042 061 | 8754<br>8754<br>042 062 | 8755<br>8755<br>042 063 | 8756<br>8756<br>042 064 | 8757<br>8757<br>042 065 | 8758<br>8758<br>042 066 | 8759<br>8759<br>042 067 | 8760<br>8760<br>042 070 | 8761<br>8761<br>042 071 | 8762<br>8762<br>042 072 | 8763<br>8763<br>042 073 | 8764<br>8764<br>042 074 | 8765<br>8765<br>042 075 | 8766<br>8766<br>042 076 | 8767<br>8767<br>042 077 |
| **4−** | 8768<br>8768<br>042 100 | 8769<br>8769<br>042 101 | 8770<br>8770<br>042 102 | 8771<br>8771<br>042 103 | 8772<br>8772<br>042 104 | 8773<br>8773<br>042 105 | 8774<br>8774<br>042 106 | 8775<br>8775<br>042 107 | 8776<br>8776<br>042 110 | 8777<br>8777<br>042 111 | 8778<br>8778<br>042 112 | 8779<br>8779<br>042 113 | 8780<br>8780<br>042 114 | 8781<br>8781<br>042 115 | 8782<br>8782<br>042 116 | 8783<br>8783<br>042 117 |
| **5−** | 8784<br>8784<br>042 120 | 8785<br>8785<br>042 121 | 8786<br>8786<br>042 122 | 8787<br>8787<br>042 123 | 8788<br>8788<br>042 124 | 8789<br>8789<br>042 125 | 8790<br>8790<br>042 126 | 8791<br>8791<br>042 127 | 8792<br>8792<br>042 130 | 8793<br>8793<br>042 131 | 8794<br>8794<br>042 132 | 8795<br>8795<br>042 133 | 8796<br>8796<br>042 134 | 8797<br>8797<br>042 135 | 8798<br>8798<br>042 136 | 8799<br>8799<br>042 137 |
| **6−** | 8800<br>8800<br>042 140 | 8801<br>8801<br>042 141 | 8802<br>8802<br>042 142 | 8803<br>8803<br>042 143 | 8804<br>8804<br>042 144 | 8805<br>8805<br>042 145 | 8806<br>8806<br>042 146 | 8807<br>8807<br>042 147 | 8808<br>8808<br>042 150 | 8809<br>8809<br>042 151 | 8810<br>8810<br>042 152 | 8811<br>8811<br>042 153 | 8812<br>8812<br>042 154 | 8813<br>8813<br>042 155 | 8814<br>8814<br>042 156 | 8815<br>8815<br>042 157 |
| **7−** | 8816<br>8816<br>042 160 | 8817<br>8817<br>042 161 | 8818<br>8818<br>042 162 | 8819<br>8819<br>042 163 | 8820<br>8820<br>042 164 | 8821<br>8821<br>042 165 | 8822<br>8822<br>042 166 | 8823<br>8823<br>042 167 | 8824<br>8824<br>042 170 | 8825<br>8825<br>042 171 | 8826<br>8826<br>042 172 | 8827<br>8827<br>042 173 | 8828<br>8828<br>042 174 | 8829<br>8829<br>042 175 | 8830<br>8830<br>042 176 | 8831<br>8831<br>042 177 |
| **8−** | 8832<br>8832<br>042 200 | 8833<br>8833<br>042 201 | 8834<br>8834<br>042 202 | 8835<br>8835<br>042 203 | 8836<br>8836<br>042 204 | 8837<br>8837<br>042 205 | 8838<br>8838<br>042 206 | 8839<br>8839<br>042 207 | 8840<br>8840<br>042 210 | 8841<br>8841<br>042 211 | 8842<br>8842<br>042 212 | 8843<br>8843<br>042 213 | 8844<br>8844<br>042 214 | 8845<br>8845<br>042 215 | 8846<br>8846<br>042 216 | 8847<br>8847<br>042 217 |
| **9−** | 8848<br>8848<br>042 220 | 8849<br>8849<br>042 221 | 8850<br>8850<br>042 222 | 8851<br>8851<br>042 223 | 8852<br>8852<br>042 224 | 8853<br>8853<br>042 225 | 8854<br>8854<br>042 226 | 8855<br>8855<br>042 227 | 8856<br>8856<br>042 230 | 8857<br>8857<br>042 231 | 8858<br>8858<br>042 232 | 8859<br>8859<br>042 233 | 8860<br>8860<br>042 234 | 8861<br>8861<br>042 235 | 8862<br>8862<br>042 236 | 8863<br>8863<br>042 237 |
| **A−** | 8864<br>8864<br>042 240 | 8865<br>8865<br>042 241 | 8866<br>8866<br>042 242 | 8867<br>8867<br>042 243 | 8868<br>8868<br>042 244 | 8869<br>8869<br>042 245 | 8870<br>8870<br>042 246 | 8871<br>8871<br>042 247 | 8872<br>8872<br>042 250 | 8873<br>8873<br>042 251 | 8874<br>8874<br>042 252 | 8875<br>8875<br>042 253 | 8876<br>8876<br>042 254 | 8877<br>8877<br>042 255 | 8878<br>8878<br>042 256 | 8879<br>8879<br>042 257 |
| **B−** | 8880<br>8880<br>042 260 | 8881<br>8881<br>042 261 | 8882<br>8882<br>042 262 | 8883<br>8883<br>042 263 | 8884<br>8884<br>042 264 | 8885<br>8885<br>042 265 | 8886<br>8886<br>042 266 | 8887<br>8887<br>042 267 | 8888<br>8888<br>042 270 | 8889<br>8889<br>042 271 | 8890<br>8890<br>042 272 | 8891<br>8891<br>042 273 | 8892<br>8892<br>042 274 | 8893<br>8893<br>042 275 | 8894<br>8894<br>042 276 | 8895<br>8895<br>042 277 |
| **C−** | 8896<br>8896<br>042 300 | 8897<br>8897<br>042 301 | 8898<br>8898<br>042 302 | 8899<br>8899<br>042 303 | 8900<br>8900<br>042 304 | 8901<br>8901<br>042 305 | 8902<br>8902<br>042 306 | 8903<br>8903<br>042 307 | 8904<br>8904<br>042 310 | 8905<br>8905<br>042 311 | 8906<br>8906<br>042 312 | 8907<br>8907<br>042 313 | 8908<br>8908<br>042 314 | 8909<br>8909<br>042 315 | 8910<br>8910<br>042 316 | 8911<br>8911<br>042 317 |
| **D−** | 8912<br>8912<br>042 320 | 8913<br>8913<br>042 321 | 8914<br>8914<br>042 322 | 8915<br>8915<br>042 323 | 8916<br>8916<br>042 324 | 8917<br>8917<br>042 325 | 8918<br>8918<br>042 326 | 8919<br>8919<br>042 327 | 8920<br>8920<br>042 330 | 8921<br>8921<br>042 331 | 8922<br>8922<br>042 332 | 8923<br>8923<br>042 333 | 8924<br>8924<br>042 334 | 8925<br>8925<br>042 335 | 8926<br>8926<br>042 336 | 8927<br>8927<br>042 337 |
| **E−** | 8928<br>8928<br>042 340 | 8929<br>8929<br>042 341 | 8930<br>8930<br>042 342 | 8931<br>8931<br>042 343 | 8932<br>8932<br>042 344 | 8933<br>8933<br>042 345 | 8934<br>8934<br>042 346 | 8935<br>8935<br>042 347 | 8936<br>8936<br>042 350 | 8937<br>8937<br>042 351 | 8938<br>8938<br>042 352 | 8939<br>8939<br>042 353 | 8940<br>8940<br>042 354 | 8941<br>8941<br>042 355 | 8942<br>8942<br>042 356 | 8943<br>8943<br>042 357 |
| **F−** | 8944<br>8944<br>042 360 | 8945<br>8945<br>042 361 | 8946<br>8946<br>042 362 | 8947<br>8947<br>042 363 | 8948<br>8948<br>042 364 | 8949<br>8949<br>042 365 | 8950<br>8950<br>042 366 | 8951<br>8951<br>042 367 | 8952<br>8952<br>042 370 | 8953<br>8953<br>042 371 | 8954<br>8954<br>042 372 | 8955<br>8955<br>042 373 | 8956<br>8956<br>042 374 | 8957<br>8957<br>042 375 | 8958<br>8958<br>042 376 | 8959<br>8959<br>042 377 |

**DECIMAL** 8704  **BINARY** 0010 0010  **DECIMAL** 8704  **HEXADECIMAL** ⟨22⟩  **OCTAL** 042 000

FOURTH HEX DIGIT → ⟨ ⟩ ← THIRD HEX DIGIT

**FIRST HEX DIGIT**

| 2 | −0 | −1 | −2 | −3 | −4 | −5 | −6 | −7 | −8 | −9 | −A | −B | −C | −D | −E | −F |
|---|---|---|---|---|---|---|---|---|---|---|---|---|---|---|---|---|
| 0- | 8960<br>8960<br>043 000 | 8961<br>8961<br>043 001 | 8962<br>8962<br>043 002 | 8963<br>8963<br>043 003 | 8964<br>8964<br>043 004 | 8965<br>8965<br>043 005 | 8966<br>8966<br>043 006 | 8967<br>8967<br>043 007 | 8968<br>8968<br>043 010 | 8969<br>8969<br>043 011 | 8970<br>8970<br>043 012 | 8971<br>8971<br>043 013 | 8972<br>8972<br>043 014 | 8973<br>8973<br>043 015 | 8974<br>8974<br>043 016 | 8975<br>8975<br>043 017 |
| 1- | 8976<br>8976<br>043 020 | 8977<br>8977<br>043 021 | 8978<br>8978<br>043 022 | 8979<br>8979<br>043 023 | 8980<br>8980<br>043 024 | 8981<br>8981<br>043 025 | 8982<br>8982<br>043 026 | 8983<br>8983<br>043 027 | 8984<br>8984<br>043 030 | 8985<br>8985<br>043 031 | 8986<br>8986<br>043 032 | 8987<br>8987<br>043 033 | 8988<br>8988<br>043 034 | 8989<br>8989<br>043 035 | 8990<br>8990<br>043 036 | 8991<br>8991<br>043 037 |
| 2- | 8992<br>8992<br>043 040 | 8993<br>8993<br>043 041 | 8994<br>8994<br>043 042 | 8995<br>8995<br>043 043 | 8996<br>8996<br>043 044 | 8997<br>8997<br>043 045 | 8998<br>8998<br>043 046 | 8999<br>8999<br>043 047 | 9000<br>9000<br>043 050 | 9001<br>9001<br>043 051 | 9002<br>9002<br>043 052 | 9003<br>9003<br>043 053 | 9004<br>9004<br>043 054 | 9005<br>9005<br>043 055 | 9006<br>9006<br>043 056 | 9007<br>9007<br>043 057 |
| 3- | 9008<br>9008<br>043 060 | 9009<br>9009<br>043 061 | 9010<br>9010<br>043 062 | 9011<br>9011<br>043 063 | 9012<br>9012<br>043 064 | 9013<br>9013<br>043 065 | 9014<br>9014<br>043 066 | 9015<br>9015<br>043 067 | 9016<br>9016<br>043 070 | 9017<br>9017<br>043 071 | 9018<br>9018<br>043 072 | 9019<br>9019<br>043 073 | 9020<br>9020<br>043 074 | 9021<br>9021<br>043 075 | 9022<br>9022<br>043 076 | 9023<br>9023<br>043 077 |
| 4- | 9024<br>9024<br>043 100 | 9025<br>9025<br>043 101 | 9026<br>9026<br>043 102 | 9027<br>9027<br>043 103 | 9028<br>9028<br>043 104 | 9029<br>9029<br>043 105 | 9030<br>9030<br>043 106 | 9031<br>9031<br>043 107 | 9032<br>9032<br>043 110 | 9033<br>9033<br>043 111 | 9034<br>9034<br>043 112 | 9035<br>9035<br>043 113 | 9036<br>9036<br>043 114 | 9037<br>9037<br>043 115 | 9038<br>9038<br>043 116 | 9039<br>9039<br>043 117 |
| 5- | 9040<br>9040<br>043 120 | 9041<br>9041<br>043 121 | 9042<br>9042<br>043 122 | 9043<br>9043<br>043 123 | 9044<br>9044<br>043 124 | 9045<br>9045<br>043 125 | 9046<br>9046<br>043 126 | 9047<br>9047<br>043 127 | 9048<br>9048<br>043 130 | 9049<br>9049<br>043 131 | 9050<br>9050<br>043 132 | 9051<br>9051<br>043 133 | 9052<br>9052<br>043 134 | 9053<br>9053<br>043 135 | 9054<br>9054<br>043 136 | 9055<br>9055<br>043 137 |
| 6- | 9056<br>9056<br>043 140 | 9057<br>9057<br>043 141 | 9058<br>9058<br>043 142 | 9059<br>9059<br>043 143 | 9060<br>9060<br>043 144 | 9061<br>9061<br>043 145 | 9062<br>9062<br>043 146 | 9063<br>9063<br>043 147 | 9064<br>9064<br>043 150 | 9065<br>9065<br>043 151 | 9066<br>9066<br>043 152 | 9067<br>9067<br>043 153 | 9068<br>9068<br>043 154 | 9069<br>9069<br>043 155 | 9070<br>9070<br>043 156 | 9071<br>9071<br>043 157 |
| 7- | 9072<br>9072<br>043 160 | 9073<br>9073<br>043 161 | 9074<br>9074<br>043 162 | 9075<br>9075<br>043 163 | 9076<br>9076<br>043 164 | 9077<br>9077<br>043 165 | 9078<br>9078<br>043 166 | 9079<br>9079<br>043 167 | 9080<br>9080<br>043 170 | 9081<br>9081<br>043 171 | 9082<br>9082<br>043 172 | 9083<br>9083<br>043 173 | 9084<br>9084<br>043 174 | 9085<br>9085<br>043 175 | 9086<br>9086<br>043 176 | 9087<br>9087<br>043 177 |
| 8- | 9088<br>9088<br>043 200 | 9089<br>9089<br>043 201 | 9090<br>9090<br>043 202 | 9091<br>9091<br>043 203 | 9092<br>9092<br>043 204 | 9093<br>9093<br>043 205 | 9094<br>9094<br>043 206 | 9095<br>9095<br>043 207 | 9096<br>9096<br>043 210 | 9097<br>9097<br>043 211 | 9098<br>9098<br>043 212 | 9099<br>9099<br>043 213 | 9100<br>9100<br>043 214 | 9101<br>9101<br>043 215 | 9102<br>9102<br>043 216 | 9103<br>9103<br>043 217 |
| 9- | 9104<br>9104<br>043 220 | 9105<br>9105<br>043 221 | 9106<br>9106<br>043 222 | 9107<br>9107<br>043 223 | 9108<br>9108<br>043 224 | 9109<br>9109<br>043 225 | 9110<br>9110<br>043 226 | 9111<br>9111<br>043 227 | 9112<br>9112<br>043 230 | 9113<br>9113<br>043 231 | 9114<br>9114<br>043 232 | 9115<br>9115<br>043 233 | 9116<br>9116<br>043 234 | 9117<br>9117<br>043 235 | 9118<br>9118<br>043 236 | 9119<br>9119<br>043 237 |
| A- | 9120<br>9120<br>043 240 | 9121<br>9121<br>043 241 | 9122<br>9122<br>043 242 | 9123<br>9123<br>043 243 | 9124<br>9124<br>043 244 | 9125<br>9125<br>043 245 | 9126<br>9126<br>043 246 | 9127<br>9127<br>043 247 | 9128<br>9128<br>043 250 | 9129<br>9129<br>043 251 | 9130<br>9130<br>043 252 | 9131<br>9131<br>043 253 | 9132<br>9132<br>043 254 | 9133<br>9133<br>043 255 | 9134<br>9134<br>043 256 | 9135<br>9135<br>043 257 |
| B- | 9136<br>9136<br>043 260 | 9137<br>9137<br>043 261 | 9138<br>9138<br>043 262 | 9139<br>9139<br>043 263 | 9140<br>9140<br>043 264 | 9141<br>9141<br>043 265 | 9142<br>9142<br>043 266 | 9143<br>9143<br>043 267 | 9144<br>9144<br>043 270 | 9145<br>9145<br>043 271 | 9146<br>9146<br>043 272 | 9147<br>9147<br>043 273 | 9148<br>9148<br>043 274 | 9149<br>9149<br>043 275 | 9150<br>9150<br>043 276 | 9151<br>9151<br>043 277 |
| C- | 9152<br>9152<br>043 300 | 9153<br>9153<br>043 301 | 9154<br>9154<br>043 302 | 9155<br>9155<br>043 303 | 9156<br>9156<br>043 304 | 9157<br>9157<br>043 305 | 9158<br>9158<br>043 306 | 9159<br>9159<br>043 307 | 9160<br>9160<br>043 310 | 9161<br>9161<br>043 311 | 9162<br>9162<br>043 312 | 9163<br>9163<br>043 313 | 9164<br>9164<br>043 314 | 9165<br>9165<br>043 315 | 9166<br>9166<br>043 316 | 9167<br>9167<br>043 317 |
| D- | 9168<br>9168<br>043 320 | 9169<br>9169<br>043 321 | 9170<br>9170<br>043 322 | 9171<br>9171<br>043 323 | 9172<br>9172<br>043 324 | 9173<br>9173<br>043 325 | 9174<br>9174<br>043 326 | 9175<br>9175<br>043 327 | 9176<br>9176<br>043 330 | 9177<br>9177<br>043 331 | 9178<br>9178<br>043 332 | 9179<br>9179<br>043 333 | 9180<br>9180<br>043 334 | 9181<br>9181<br>043 335 | 9182<br>9182<br>043 336 | 9183<br>9183<br>043 337 |
| E- | 9184<br>9184<br>043 340 | 9185<br>9185<br>043 341 | 9186<br>9186<br>043 342 | 9187<br>9187<br>043 343 | 9188<br>9188<br>043 344 | 9189<br>9189<br>043 345 | 9190<br>9190<br>043 346 | 9191<br>9191<br>043 347 | 9192<br>9192<br>043 350 | 9193<br>9193<br>043 351 | 9194<br>9194<br>043 352 | 9195<br>9195<br>043 353 | 9196<br>9196<br>043 354 | 9197<br>9197<br>043 355 | 9198<br>9198<br>043 356 | 9199<br>9199<br>043 357 |
| F- | 9200<br>9200<br>043 360 | 9201<br>9201<br>043 361 | 9202<br>9202<br>043 362 | 9203<br>9203<br>043 363 | 9204<br>9204<br>043 364 | 9205<br>9205<br>043 365 | 9206<br>9206<br>043 366 | 9207<br>9207<br>043 367 | 9208<br>9208<br>043 370 | 9209<br>9209<br>043 371 | 9210<br>9210<br>043 372 | 9211<br>9211<br>043 373 | 9212<br>9212<br>043 374 | 9213<br>9213<br>043 375 | 9214<br>9214<br>043 376 | 9215<br>9215<br>043 377 |

SECOND HEX DIGIT

DECIMAL

DECIMAL

OCTAL

# FIRST HEX DIGIT

| 2 | | −0 | −1 | −2 | −3 | −4 | −5 | −6 | −7 | −8 | −9 | −A | −B | −C | −D | −E | −F |
|---|---|---|---|---|---|---|---|---|---|---|---|---|---|---|---|---|---|
| **S** | **0−** | 9216<br>044 000 | 9217<br>044 001 | 9218<br>044 002 | 9219<br>044 003 | 9220<br>044 004 | 9221<br>044 005 | 9222<br>044 006 | 9223<br>044 007 | 9224<br>044 010 | 9225<br>044 011 | 9226<br>044 012 | 9227<br>044 013 | 9228<br>044 014 | 9229<br>044 015 | 9230<br>044 016 | 9231<br>044 017 |
| **E** | **1−** | 9232<br>044 020 | 9233<br>044 021 | 9234<br>044 022 | 9235<br>044 023 | 9236<br>044 024 | 9237<br>044 025 | 9238<br>044 026 | 9239<br>044 027 | 9240<br>044 030 | 9241<br>044 031 | 9242<br>044 032 | 9243<br>044 033 | 9244<br>044 034 | 9245<br>044 035 | 9246<br>044 036 | 9247<br>044 037 |
| **C** | **2−** | 9248<br>044 040 | 9249<br>044 041 | 9250<br>044 042 | 9251<br>044 043 | 9252<br>044 044 | 9253<br>044 045 | 9254<br>044 046 | 9255<br>044 047 | 9256<br>044 050 | 9257<br>044 051 | 9258<br>044 052 | 9259<br>044 053 | 9260<br>044 054 | 9261<br>044 055 | 9262<br>044 056 | 9263<br>044 057 |
| **O** | **3−** | 9264<br>044 060 | 9265<br>044 061 | 9266<br>044 062 | 9267<br>044 063 | 9268<br>044 064 | 9269<br>044 065 | 9270<br>044 066 | 9271<br>044 067 | 9272<br>044 070 | 9273<br>044 071 | 9274<br>044 072 | 9275<br>044 073 | 9276<br>044 074 | 9277<br>044 075 | 9278<br>044 076 | 9279<br>044 077 |
| **N** | **4−** | 9280<br>044 100 | 9281<br>044 101 | 9282<br>044 102 | 9283<br>044 103 | 9284<br>044 104 | 9285<br>044 105 | 9286<br>044 106 | 9287<br>044 107 | 9288<br>044 110 | 9289<br>044 111 | 9290<br>044 112 | 9291<br>044 113 | 9292<br>044 114 | 9293<br>044 115 | 9294<br>044 116 | 9295<br>044 117 |
| **D** | **5−** | 9296<br>044 120 | 9297<br>044 121 | 9298<br>044 122 | 9299<br>044 123 | 9300<br>044 124 | 9301<br>044 125 | 9302<br>044 126 | 9303<br>044 127 | 9304<br>044 130 | 9305<br>044 131 | 9306<br>044 132 | 9307<br>044 133 | 9308<br>044 134 | 9309<br>044 135 | 9310<br>044 136 | 9311<br>044 137 |
| | **6−** | 9312<br>044 140 | 9313<br>044 141 | 9314<br>044 142 | 9315<br>044 143 | 9316<br>044 144 | 9317<br>044 145 | 9318<br>044 146 | 9319<br>044 147 | 9320<br>044 150 | 9321<br>044 151 | 9322<br>044 152 | 9323<br>044 153 | 9324<br>044 154 | 9325<br>044 155 | 9326<br>044 156 | 9327<br>044 157 |
| **H** | **7−** | 9328<br>044 160 | 9329<br>044 161 | 9330<br>044 162 | 9331<br>044 163 | 9332<br>044 164 | 9333<br>044 165 | 9334<br>044 166 | 9335<br>044 167 | 9336<br>044 170 | 9337<br>044 171 | 9338<br>044 172 | 9339<br>044 173 | 9340<br>044 174 | 9341<br>044 175 | 9342<br>044 176 | 9343<br>044 177 |
| **E** | **8−** | 9344<br>044 200 | 9345<br>044 201 | 9346<br>044 202 | 9347<br>044 203 | 9348<br>044 204 | 9349<br>044 205 | 9350<br>044 206 | 9351<br>044 207 | 9352<br>044 210 | 9353<br>044 211 | 9354<br>044 212 | 9355<br>044 213 | 9356<br>044 214 | 9357<br>044 215 | 9358<br>044 216 | 9359<br>044 217 |
| **X** | **9−** | 9360<br>044 220 | 9361<br>044 221 | 9362<br>044 222 | 9363<br>044 223 | 9364<br>044 224 | 9365<br>044 225 | 9366<br>044 226 | 9367<br>044 227 | 9368<br>044 230 | 9369<br>044 231 | 9370<br>044 232 | 9371<br>044 233 | 9372<br>044 234 | 9373<br>044 235 | 9374<br>044 236 | 9375<br>044 237 |
| | **A−** | 9376<br>044 240 | 9377<br>044 241 | 9378<br>044 242 | 9379<br>044 243 | 9380<br>044 244 | 9381<br>044 245 | 9382<br>044 246 | 9383<br>044 247 | 9384<br>044 250 | 9385<br>044 251 | 9386<br>044 252 | 9387<br>044 253 | 9388<br>044 254 | 9389<br>044 255 | 9390<br>044 256 | 9391<br>044 257 |
| **D** | **B−** | 9392<br>044 260 | 9393<br>044 261 | 9394<br>044 262 | 9395<br>044 263 | 9396<br>044 264 | 9397<br>044 265 | 9398<br>044 266 | 9399<br>044 267 | 9400<br>044 270 | 9401<br>044 271 | 9402<br>044 272 | 9403<br>044 273 | 9404<br>044 274 | 9405<br>044 275 | 9406<br>044 276 | 9407<br>044 277 |
| **I** | **C−** | 9408<br>044 300 | 9409<br>044 301 | 9410<br>044 302 | 9411<br>044 303 | 9412<br>044 304 | 9413<br>044 305 | 9414<br>044 306 | 9415<br>044 307 | 9416<br>044 310 | 9417<br>044 311 | 9418<br>044 312 | 9419<br>044 313 | 9420<br>044 314 | 9421<br>044 315 | 9422<br>044 316 | 9423<br>044 317 |
| **G** | **D−** | 9424<br>044 320 | 9425<br>044 321 | 9426<br>044 322 | 9427<br>044 323 | 9428<br>044 324 | 9429<br>044 325 | 9430<br>044 326 | 9431<br>044 327 | 9432<br>044 330 | 9433<br>044 331 | 9434<br>044 332 | 9435<br>044 333 | 9436<br>044 334 | 9437<br>044 335 | 9438<br>044 336 | 9439<br>044 337 |
| **I** | **E−** | 9440<br>044 340 | 9441<br>044 341 | 9442<br>044 342 | 9443<br>044 343 | 9444<br>044 344 | 9445<br>044 345 | 9446<br>044 346 | 9447<br>044 347 | 9448<br>044 350 | 9449<br>044 351 | 9450<br>044 352 | 9451<br>044 353 | 9452<br>044 354 | 9453<br>044 355 | 9454<br>044 356 | 9455<br>044 357 |
| **T** | **F−** | 9456<br>044 360 | 9457<br>044 361 | 9458<br>044 362 | 9459<br>044 363 | 9460<br>044 364 | 9461<br>044 365 | 9462<br>044 366 | 9463<br>044 367 | 9464<br>044 370 | 9465<br>044 371 | 9466<br>044 372 | 9467<br>044 373 | 9468<br>044 374 | 9469<br>044 375 | 9470<br>044 376 | 9471<br>044 377 |

SECOND HEX DIGIT

DECIMAL → · DECIMAL → · OCTAL →

DECIMAL  9216   BINARY  0010 0100   DECIMAL  9216   HEXADECIMAL  2 4   OCTAL  044 000

FOURTH HEX DIGIT → · ← THIRD HEX DIGIT

FIRST HEX DIGIT

| 2 | −0 | −1 | −2 | −3 | −4 | −5 | −6 | −7 | −8 | −9 | −A | −B | −C | −D | −E | −F |
|---|---|---|---|---|---|---|---|---|---|---|---|---|---|---|---|---|
| 0− | 9472<br>9472<br>045 000 | 9473<br>9473<br>045 001 | 9474<br>9474<br>045 002 | 9475<br>9475<br>045 003 | 9476<br>9476<br>045 004 | 9477<br>9477<br>045 005 | 9478<br>9478<br>045 006 | 9479<br>9479<br>045 007 | 9480<br>9480<br>045 010 | 9481<br>9481<br>045 011 | 9482<br>9482<br>045 012 | 9483<br>9483<br>045 013 | 9484<br>9484<br>045 014 | 9485<br>9485<br>045 015 | 9486<br>9486<br>045 016 | 9487<br>9487<br>045 017 |
| 1− | 9488<br>9488<br>045 020 | 9489<br>9489<br>045 021 | 9490<br>9490<br>045 022 | 9491<br>9491<br>045 023 | 9492<br>9492<br>045 024 | 9493<br>9493<br>045 025 | 9494<br>9494<br>045 026 | 9495<br>9495<br>045 027 | 9496<br>9496<br>045 030 | 9497<br>9497<br>045 031 | 9498<br>9498<br>045 032 | 9499<br>9499<br>045 033 | 9500<br>9500<br>045 034 | 9501<br>9501<br>045 035 | 9502<br>9502<br>045 036 | 9503<br>9503<br>045 037 |
| 2− | 9504<br>9504<br>045 040 | 9505<br>9505<br>045 041 | 9506<br>9506<br>045 042 | 9507<br>9507<br>045 043 | 9508<br>9508<br>045 044 | 9509<br>9509<br>045 045 | 9510<br>9510<br>045 046 | 9511<br>9511<br>045 047 | 9512<br>9512<br>045 050 | 9513<br>9513<br>045 051 | 9514<br>9514<br>045 052 | 9515<br>9515<br>045 053 | 9516<br>9516<br>045 054 | 9517<br>9517<br>045 055 | 9518<br>9518<br>045 056 | 9519<br>9519<br>045 057 |
| 3− | 9520<br>9520<br>045 060 | 9521<br>9521<br>045 061 | 9522<br>9522<br>045 062 | 9523<br>9523<br>045 063 | 9524<br>9524<br>045 064 | 9525<br>9525<br>045 065 | 9526<br>9526<br>045 066 | 9527<br>9527<br>045 067 | 9528<br>9528<br>045 070 | 9529<br>9529<br>045 071 | 9530<br>9530<br>045 072 | 9531<br>9531<br>045 073 | 9532<br>9532<br>045 074 | 9533<br>9533<br>045 075 | 9534<br>9534<br>045 076 | 9535<br>9535<br>045 077 |
| 4− | 9536<br>9536<br>045 100 | 9537<br>9537<br>045 101 | 9538<br>9538<br>045 102 | 9539<br>9539<br>045 103 | 9540<br>9540<br>045 104 | 9541<br>9541<br>045 105 | 9542<br>9542<br>045 106 | 9543<br>9543<br>045 107 | 9544<br>9544<br>045 110 | 9545<br>9545<br>045 111 | 9546<br>9546<br>045 112 | 9547<br>9547<br>045 113 | 9548<br>9548<br>045 114 | 9549<br>9549<br>045 115 | 9550<br>9550<br>045 116 | 9551<br>9551<br>045 117 |
| 5− | 9552<br>9552<br>045 120 | 9553<br>9553<br>045 121 | 9554<br>9554<br>045 122 | 9555<br>9555<br>045 123 | 9556<br>9556<br>045 124 | 9557<br>9557<br>045 125 | 9558<br>9558<br>045 126 | 9559<br>9559<br>045 127 | 9560<br>9560<br>045 130 | 9561<br>9561<br>045 131 | 9562<br>9562<br>045 132 | 9563<br>9563<br>045 133 | 9564<br>9564<br>045 134 | 9565<br>9565<br>045 135 | 9566<br>9566<br>045 136 | 9567<br>9567<br>045 137 |
| 6− | 9568<br>9568<br>045 140 | 9569<br>9569<br>045 141 | 9570<br>9570<br>045 142 | 9571<br>9571<br>045 143 | 9572<br>9572<br>045 144 | 9573<br>9573<br>045 145 | 9574<br>9574<br>045 146 | 9575<br>9575<br>045 147 | 9576<br>9576<br>045 150 | 9577<br>9577<br>045 151 | 9578<br>9578<br>045 152 | 9579<br>9579<br>045 153 | 9580<br>9580<br>045 154 | 9581<br>9581<br>045 155 | 9582<br>9582<br>045 156 | 9583<br>9583<br>045 157 |
| 7− | 9584<br>9584<br>045 160 | 9585<br>9585<br>045 161 | 9586<br>9586<br>045 162 | 9587<br>9587<br>045 163 | 9588<br>9588<br>045 164 | 9589<br>9589<br>045 165 | 9590<br>9590<br>045 166 | 9591<br>9591<br>045 167 | 9592<br>9592<br>045 170 | 9593<br>9593<br>045 171 | 9594<br>9594<br>045 172 | 9595<br>9595<br>045 173 | 9596<br>9596<br>045 174 | 9597<br>9597<br>045 175 | 9598<br>9598<br>045 176 | 9599<br>9599<br>045 177 |
| 8− | 9600<br>9600<br>045 200 | 9601<br>9601<br>045 201 | 9602<br>9602<br>045 202 | 9603<br>9603<br>045 203 | 9604<br>9604<br>045 204 | 9605<br>9605<br>045 205 | 9606<br>9606<br>045 206 | 9607<br>9607<br>045 207 | 9608<br>9608<br>045 210 | 9609<br>9609<br>045 211 | 9610<br>9610<br>045 212 | 9611<br>9611<br>045 213 | 9612<br>9612<br>045 214 | 9613<br>9613<br>045 215 | 9614<br>9614<br>045 216 | 9615<br>9615<br>045 217 |
| 9− | 9616<br>9616<br>045 220 | 9617<br>9617<br>045 221 | 9618<br>9618<br>045 222 | 9619<br>9619<br>045 223 | 9620<br>9620<br>045 224 | 9621<br>9621<br>045 225 | 9622<br>9622<br>045 226 | 9623<br>9623<br>045 227 | 9624<br>9624<br>045 230 | 9625<br>9625<br>045 231 | 9626<br>9626<br>045 232 | 9627<br>9627<br>045 233 | 9628<br>9628<br>045 234 | 9629<br>9629<br>045 235 | 9630<br>9630<br>045 236 | 9631<br>9631<br>045 237 |
| A− | 9632<br>9632<br>045 240 | 9633<br>9633<br>045 241 | 9634<br>9634<br>045 242 | 9635<br>9635<br>045 243 | 9636<br>9636<br>045 244 | 9637<br>9637<br>045 245 | 9638<br>9638<br>045 246 | 9639<br>9639<br>045 247 | 9640<br>9640<br>045 250 | 9641<br>9641<br>045 251 | 9642<br>9642<br>045 252 | 9643<br>9643<br>045 253 | 9644<br>9644<br>045 254 | 9645<br>9645<br>045 255 | 9646<br>9646<br>045 256 | 9647<br>9647<br>045 257 |
| B− | 9648<br>9648<br>045 260 | 9649<br>9649<br>045 261 | 9650<br>9650<br>045 262 | 9651<br>9651<br>045 263 | 9652<br>9652<br>045 264 | 9653<br>9653<br>045 265 | 9654<br>9654<br>045 266 | 9655<br>9655<br>045 267 | 9656<br>9656<br>045 270 | 9657<br>9657<br>045 271 | 9658<br>9658<br>045 272 | 9659<br>9659<br>045 273 | 9660<br>9660<br>045 274 | 9661<br>9661<br>045 275 | 9662<br>9662<br>045 276 | 9663<br>9663<br>045 277 |
| C− | 9664<br>9664<br>045 300 | 9665<br>9665<br>045 301 | 9666<br>9666<br>045 302 | 9667<br>9667<br>045 303 | 9668<br>9668<br>045 304 | 9669<br>9669<br>045 305 | 9670<br>9670<br>045 306 | 9671<br>9671<br>045 307 | 9672<br>9672<br>045 310 | 9673<br>9673<br>045 311 | 9674<br>9674<br>045 312 | 9675<br>9675<br>045 313 | 9676<br>9676<br>045 314 | 9677<br>9677<br>045 315 | 9678<br>9678<br>045 316 | 9679<br>9679<br>045 317 |
| D− | 9680<br>9680<br>045 320 | 9681<br>9681<br>045 321 | 9682<br>9682<br>045 322 | 9683<br>9683<br>045 323 | 9684<br>9684<br>045 324 | 9685<br>9685<br>045 325 | 9686<br>9686<br>045 326 | 9687<br>9687<br>045 327 | 9688<br>9688<br>045 330 | 9689<br>9689<br>045 331 | 9690<br>9690<br>045 332 | 9691<br>9691<br>045 333 | 9692<br>9692<br>045 334 | 9693<br>9693<br>045 335 | 9694<br>9694<br>045 336 | 9695<br>9695<br>045 337 |
| E− | 9696<br>9696<br>045 340 | 9697<br>9697<br>045 341 | 9698<br>9698<br>045 342 | 9699<br>9699<br>045 343 | 9700<br>9700<br>045 344 | 9701<br>9701<br>045 345 | 9702<br>9702<br>045 346 | 9703<br>9703<br>045 347 | 9704<br>9704<br>045 350 | 9705<br>9705<br>045 351 | 9706<br>9706<br>045 352 | 9707<br>9707<br>045 353 | 9708<br>9708<br>045 354 | 9709<br>9709<br>045 355 | 9710<br>9710<br>045 356 | 9711<br>9711<br>045 357 |
| F− | 9712<br>9712<br>045 360 | 9713<br>9713<br>045 361 | 9714<br>9714<br>045 362 | 9715<br>9715<br>045 363 | 9716<br>9716<br>045 364 | 9717<br>9717<br>045 365 | 9718<br>9718<br>045 366 | 9719<br>9719<br>045 367 | 9720<br>9720<br>045 370 | 9721<br>9721<br>045 371 | 9722<br>9722<br>045 372 | 9723<br>9723<br>045 373 | 9724<br>9724<br>045 374 | 9725<br>9725<br>045 375 | 9726<br>9726<br>045 376 | 9727<br>9727<br>045 377 |

SECOND HEX DIGIT

DECIMAL (→ column −F)

 DECIMAL (→ column −F)

OCTAL (→ row 8−)

## 2

| SECOND HEX DIGIT \ FIRST HEX DIGIT | −0 | −1 | −2 | −3 | −4 | −5 | −6 | −7 | −8 | −9 | −A | −B | −C | −D | −E | −F |
|---|---|---|---|---|---|---|---|---|---|---|---|---|---|---|---|---|
| 0− | 9728<br>9728<br>046 000 | 9729<br>9729<br>046 001 | 9730<br>9730<br>046 002 | 9731<br>9731<br>046 003 | 9732<br>9732<br>046 004 | 9733<br>9733<br>046 005 | 9734<br>9734<br>046 006 | 9735<br>9735<br>046 007 | 9736<br>9736<br>046 010 | 9737<br>9737<br>046 011 | 9738<br>9738<br>046 012 | 9739<br>9739<br>046 013 | 9740<br>9740<br>046 014 | 9741<br>9741<br>046 015 | 9742<br>9742<br>046 016 | 9743<br>9743<br>046 017 |
| 1− | 9744<br>9744<br>046 020 | 9745<br>9745<br>046 021 | 9746<br>9746<br>046 022 | 9747<br>9747<br>046 023 | 9748<br>9748<br>046 024 | 9749<br>9749<br>046 025 | 9750<br>9750<br>046 026 | 9751<br>9751<br>046 027 | 9752<br>9752<br>046 030 | 9753<br>9753<br>046 031 | 9754<br>9754<br>046 032 | 9755<br>9755<br>046 033 | 9756<br>9756<br>046 034 | 9757<br>9757<br>046 035 | 9758<br>9758<br>046 036 | 9759<br>9759<br>046 037 |
| 2− | 9760<br>9760<br>046 040 | 9761<br>9761<br>046 041 | 9762<br>9762<br>046 042 | 9763<br>9763<br>046 043 | 9764<br>9764<br>046 044 | 9765<br>9765<br>046 045 | 9766<br>9766<br>046 046 | 9767<br>9767<br>046 047 | 9768<br>9768<br>046 050 | 9769<br>9769<br>046 051 | 9770<br>9770<br>046 052 | 9771<br>9771<br>046 053 | 9772<br>9772<br>046 054 | 9773<br>9773<br>046 055 | 9774<br>9774<br>046 056 | 9775<br>9775<br>046 057 |
| 3− | 9776<br>9776<br>046 060 | 9777<br>9777<br>046 061 | 9778<br>9778<br>046 062 | 9779<br>9779<br>046 063 | 9780<br>9780<br>046 064 | 9781<br>9781<br>046 065 | 9782<br>9782<br>046 066 | 9783<br>9783<br>046 067 | 9784<br>9784<br>046 070 | 9785<br>9785<br>046 071 | 9786<br>9786<br>046 072 | 9787<br>9787<br>046 073 | 9788<br>9788<br>046 074 | 9789<br>9789<br>046 075 | 9790<br>9790<br>046 076 | 9791<br>9791<br>046 077 |
| 4− | 9792<br>9792<br>046 100 | 9793<br>9793<br>046 101 | 9794<br>9794<br>046 102 | 9795<br>9795<br>046 103 | 9796<br>9796<br>046 104 | 9797<br>9797<br>046 105 | 9798<br>9798<br>046 106 | 9799<br>9799<br>046 107 | 9800<br>9800<br>046 110 | 9801<br>9801<br>046 111 | 9802<br>9802<br>046 112 | 9803<br>9803<br>046 113 | 9804<br>9804<br>046 114 | 9805<br>9805<br>046 115 | 9806<br>9806<br>046 116 | 9807<br>9807<br>046 117 |
| 5− | 9808<br>9808<br>046 120 | 9809<br>9809<br>046 121 | 9810<br>9810<br>046 122 | 9811<br>9811<br>046 123 | 9812<br>9812<br>046 124 | 9813<br>9813<br>046 125 | 9814<br>9814<br>046 126 | 9815<br>9815<br>046 127 | 9816<br>9816<br>046 130 | 9817<br>9817<br>046 131 | 9818<br>9818<br>046 132 | 9819<br>9819<br>046 133 | 9820<br>9820<br>046 134 | 9821<br>9821<br>046 135 | 9822<br>9822<br>046 136 | 9823<br>9823<br>046 137 |
| 6− | 9824<br>9824<br>046 140 | 9825<br>9825<br>046 141 | 9826<br>9826<br>046 142 | 9827<br>9827<br>046 143 | 9828<br>9828<br>046 144 | 9829<br>9829<br>046 145 | 9830<br>9830<br>046 146 | 9831<br>9831<br>046 147 | 9832<br>9832<br>046 150 | 9833<br>9833<br>046 151 | 9834<br>9834<br>046 152 | 9835<br>9835<br>046 153 | 9836<br>9836<br>046 154 | 9837<br>9837<br>046 155 | 9838<br>9838<br>046 156 | 9839<br>9839<br>046 157 |
| 7− | 9840<br>9840<br>046 160 | 9841<br>9841<br>046 161 | 9842<br>9842<br>046 162 | 9843<br>9843<br>046 163 | 9844<br>9844<br>046 164 | 9845<br>9845<br>046 165 | 9846<br>9846<br>046 166 | 9847<br>9847<br>046 167 | 9848<br>9848<br>046 170 | 9849<br>9849<br>046 171 | 9850<br>9850<br>046 172 | 9851<br>9851<br>046 173 | 9852<br>9852<br>046 174 | 9853<br>9853<br>046 175 | 9854<br>9854<br>046 176 | 9855<br>9855<br>046 177 |
| 8− | 9856<br>9856<br>046 200 | 9857<br>9857<br>046 201 | 9858<br>9858<br>046 202 | 9859<br>9859<br>046 203 | 9860<br>9860<br>046 204 | 9861<br>9861<br>046 205 | 9862<br>9862<br>046 206 | 9863<br>9863<br>046 207 | 9864<br>9864<br>046 210 | 9865<br>9865<br>046 211 | 9866<br>9866<br>046 212 | 9867<br>9867<br>046 213 | 9868<br>9868<br>046 214 | 9869<br>9869<br>046 215 | 9870<br>9870<br>046 216 | 9871<br>9871<br>046 217 |
| 9− | 9872<br>9872<br>046 220 | 9873<br>9873<br>046 221 | 9874<br>9874<br>046 222 | 9875<br>9875<br>046 223 | 9876<br>9876<br>046 224 | 9877<br>9877<br>046 225 | 9878<br>9878<br>046 226 | 9879<br>9879<br>046 227 | 9880<br>9880<br>046 230 | 9881<br>9881<br>046 231 | 9882<br>9882<br>046 232 | 9883<br>9883<br>046 233 | 9884<br>9884<br>046 234 | 9885<br>9885<br>046 235 | 9886<br>9886<br>046 236 | 9887<br>9887<br>046 237 |
| A− | 9888<br>9888<br>046 240 | 9889<br>9889<br>046 241 | 9890<br>9890<br>046 242 | 9891<br>9891<br>046 243 | 9892<br>9892<br>046 244 | 9893<br>9893<br>046 245 | 9894<br>9894<br>046 246 | 9895<br>9895<br>046 247 | 9896<br>9896<br>046 250 | 9897<br>9897<br>046 251 | 9898<br>9898<br>046 252 | 9899<br>9899<br>046 253 | 9900<br>9900<br>046 254 | 9901<br>9901<br>046 255 | 9902<br>9902<br>046 256 | 9903<br>9903<br>046 257 |
| B− | 9904<br>9904<br>046 260 | 9905<br>9905<br>046 261 | 9906<br>9906<br>046 262 | 9907<br>9907<br>046 263 | 9908<br>9908<br>046 264 | 9909<br>9909<br>046 265 | 9910<br>9910<br>046 266 | 9911<br>9911<br>046 267 | 9912<br>9912<br>046 270 | 9913<br>9913<br>046 271 | 9914<br>9914<br>046 272 | 9915<br>9915<br>046 273 | 9916<br>9916<br>046 274 | 9917<br>9917<br>046 275 | 9918<br>9918<br>046 276 | 9919<br>9919<br>046 277 |
| C− | 9920<br>9920<br>046 300 | 9921<br>9921<br>046 301 | 9922<br>9922<br>046 302 | 9923<br>9923<br>046 303 | 9924<br>9924<br>046 304 | 9925<br>9925<br>046 305 | 9926<br>9926<br>046 306 | 9927<br>9927<br>046 307 | 9928<br>9928<br>046 310 | 9929<br>9929<br>046 311 | 9930<br>9930<br>046 312 | 9931<br>9931<br>046 313 | 9932<br>9932<br>046 314 | 9933<br>9933<br>046 315 | 9934<br>9934<br>046 316 | 9935<br>9935<br>046 317 |
| D− | 9936<br>9936<br>046 320 | 9937<br>9937<br>046 321 | 9938<br>9938<br>046 322 | 9939<br>9939<br>046 323 | 9940<br>9940<br>046 324 | 9941<br>9941<br>046 325 | 9942<br>9942<br>046 326 | 9943<br>9943<br>046 327 | 9944<br>9944<br>046 330 | 9945<br>9945<br>046 331 | 9946<br>9946<br>046 332 | 9947<br>9947<br>046 333 | 9948<br>9948<br>046 334 | 9949<br>9949<br>046 335 | 9950<br>9950<br>046 336 | 9951<br>9951<br>046 337 |
| E− | 9952<br>9952<br>046 340 | 9953<br>9953<br>046 341 | 9954<br>9954<br>046 342 | 9955<br>9955<br>046 343 | 9956<br>9956<br>046 344 | 9957<br>9957<br>046 345 | 9958<br>9958<br>046 346 | 9959<br>9959<br>046 347 | 9960<br>9960<br>046 350 | 9961<br>9961<br>046 351 | 9962<br>9962<br>046 352 | 9963<br>9963<br>046 353 | 9964<br>9964<br>046 354 | 9965<br>9965<br>046 355 | 9966<br>9966<br>046 356 | 9967<br>9967<br>046 357 |
| F− | 9968<br>9968<br>046 360 | 9969<br>9969<br>046 361 | 9970<br>9970<br>046 362 | 9971<br>9971<br>046 363 | 9972<br>9972<br>046 364 | 9973<br>9973<br>046 365 | 9974<br>9974<br>046 366 | 9975<br>9975<br>046 367 | 9976<br>9976<br>046 370 | 9977<br>9977<br>046 371 | 9978<br>9978<br>046 372 | 9979<br>9979<br>046 373 | 9980<br>9980<br>046 374 | 9981<br>9981<br>046 375 | 9982<br>9982<br>046 376 | 9983<br>9983<br>046 377 |

**DECIMAL** (first line of each cell)

**DECIMAL** (second line of each cell)

**OCTAL** (third line of each cell)

DECIMAL 9728 · BINARY 0010 0110 · DECIMAL 9728 · HEXADECIMAL 26 (FOURTH HEX DIGIT, THIRD HEX DIGIT) · OCTAL 046 000

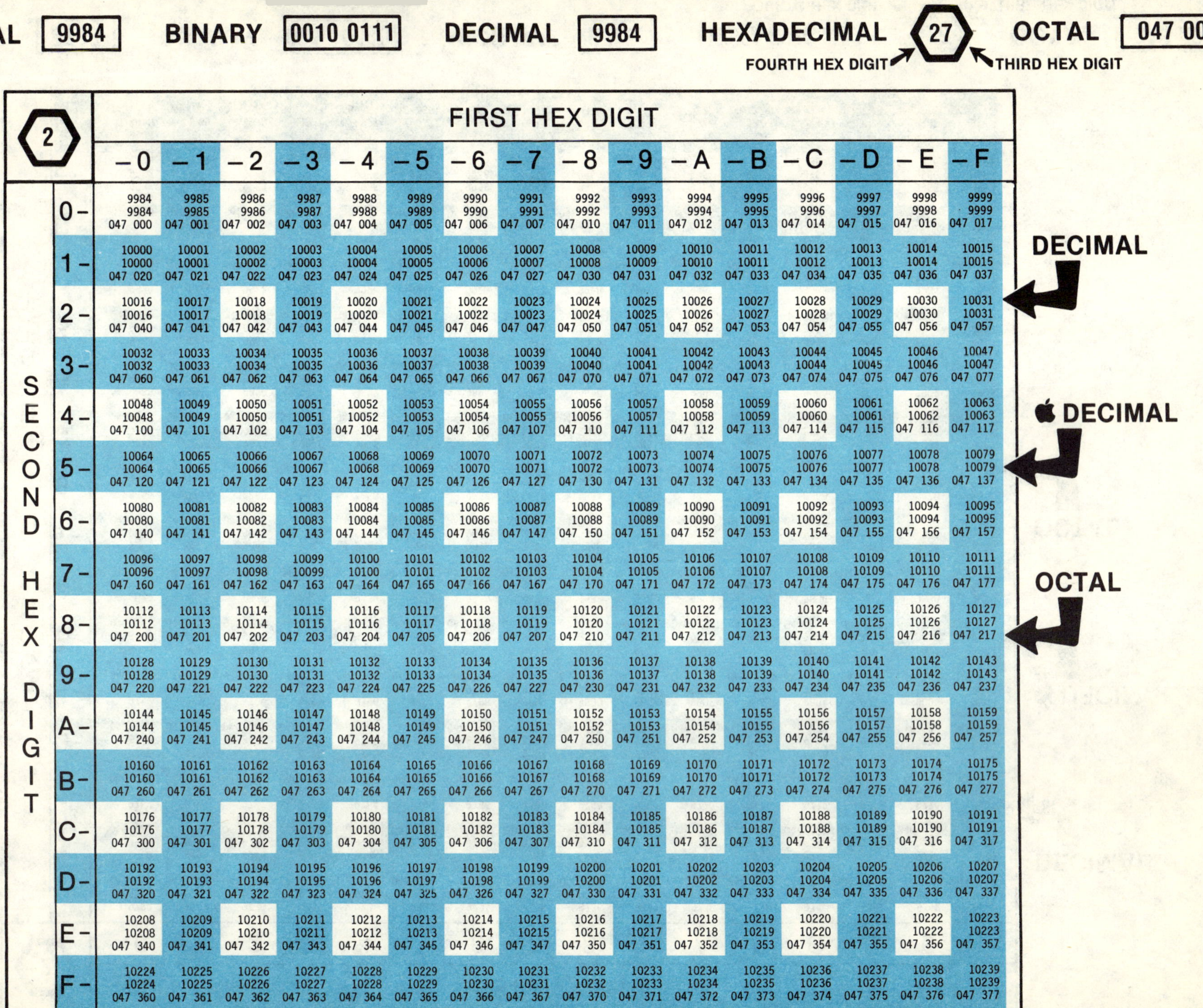

DECIMAL `9984`  BINARY `0010 0111`  DECIMAL `9984`  HEXADECIMAL ⬡`27`  OCTAL `047 000`

FOURTH HEX DIGIT → 27 ← THIRD HEX DIGIT

⬡ 2

FIRST HEX DIGIT / SECOND HEX DIGIT

DECIMAL · DECIMAL · OCTAL

| | −0 | −1 | −2 | −3 | −4 | −5 | −6 | −7 | −8 | −9 | −A | −B | −C | −D | −E | −F |
|---|---|---|---|---|---|---|---|---|---|---|---|---|---|---|---|---|
| 0− | 9984<br>9984<br>047 000 | 9985<br>9985<br>047 001 | 9986<br>9986<br>047 002 | 9987<br>9987<br>047 003 | 9988<br>9988<br>047 004 | 9989<br>9989<br>047 005 | 9990<br>9990<br>047 006 | 9991<br>9991<br>047 007 | 9992<br>9992<br>047 010 | 9993<br>9993<br>047 011 | 9994<br>9994<br>047 012 | 9995<br>9995<br>047 013 | 9996<br>9996<br>047 014 | 9997<br>9997<br>047 015 | 9998<br>9998<br>047 016 | 9999<br>9999<br>047 017 |
| 1− | 10000<br>10000<br>047 020 | 10001<br>10001<br>047 021 | 10002<br>10002<br>047 022 | 10003<br>10003<br>047 023 | 10004<br>10004<br>047 024 | 10005<br>10005<br>047 025 | 10006<br>10006<br>047 026 | 10007<br>10007<br>047 027 | 10008<br>10008<br>047 030 | 10009<br>10009<br>047 031 | 10010<br>10010<br>047 032 | 10011<br>10011<br>047 033 | 10012<br>10012<br>047 034 | 10013<br>10013<br>047 035 | 10014<br>10014<br>047 036 | 10015<br>10015<br>047 037 |
| 2− | 10016<br>10016<br>047 040 | 10017<br>10017<br>047 041 | 10018<br>10018<br>047 042 | 10019<br>10019<br>047 043 | 10020<br>10020<br>047 044 | 10021<br>10021<br>047 045 | 10022<br>10022<br>047 046 | 10023<br>10023<br>047 047 | 10024<br>10024<br>047 050 | 10025<br>10025<br>047 051 | 10026<br>10026<br>047 052 | 10027<br>10027<br>047 053 | 10028<br>10028<br>047 054 | 10029<br>10029<br>047 055 | 10030<br>10030<br>047 056 | 10031<br>10031<br>047 057 |
| 3− | 10032<br>10032<br>047 060 | 10033<br>10033<br>047 061 | 10034<br>10034<br>047 062 | 10035<br>10035<br>047 063 | 10036<br>10036<br>047 064 | 10037<br>10037<br>047 065 | 10038<br>10038<br>047 066 | 10039<br>10039<br>047 067 | 10040<br>10040<br>047 070 | 10041<br>10041<br>047 071 | 10042<br>10042<br>047 072 | 10043<br>10043<br>047 073 | 10044<br>10044<br>047 074 | 10045<br>10045<br>047 075 | 10046<br>10046<br>047 076 | 10047<br>10047<br>047 077 |
| 4− | 10048<br>10048<br>047 100 | 10049<br>10049<br>047 101 | 10050<br>10050<br>047 102 | 10051<br>10051<br>047 103 | 10052<br>10052<br>047 104 | 10053<br>10053<br>047 105 | 10054<br>10054<br>047 106 | 10055<br>10055<br>047 107 | 10056<br>10056<br>047 110 | 10057<br>10057<br>047 111 | 10058<br>10058<br>047 112 | 10059<br>10059<br>047 113 | 10060<br>10060<br>047 114 | 10061<br>10061<br>047 115 | 10062<br>10062<br>047 116 | 10063<br>10063<br>047 117 |
| 5− | 10064<br>10064<br>047 120 | 10065<br>10065<br>047 121 | 10066<br>10066<br>047 122 | 10067<br>10067<br>047 123 | 10068<br>10068<br>047 124 | 10069<br>10069<br>047 125 | 10070<br>10070<br>047 126 | 10071<br>10071<br>047 127 | 10072<br>10072<br>047 130 | 10073<br>10073<br>047 131 | 10074<br>10074<br>047 132 | 10075<br>10075<br>047 133 | 10076<br>10076<br>047 134 | 10077<br>10077<br>047 135 | 10078<br>10078<br>047 136 | 10079<br>10079<br>047 137 |
| 6− | 10080<br>10080<br>047 140 | 10081<br>10081<br>047 141 | 10082<br>10082<br>047 142 | 10083<br>10083<br>047 143 | 10084<br>10084<br>047 144 | 10085<br>10085<br>047 145 | 10086<br>10086<br>047 146 | 10087<br>10087<br>047 147 | 10088<br>10088<br>047 150 | 10089<br>10089<br>047 151 | 10090<br>10090<br>047 152 | 10091<br>10091<br>047 153 | 10092<br>10092<br>047 154 | 10093<br>10093<br>047 155 | 10094<br>10094<br>047 156 | 10095<br>10095<br>047 157 |
| 7− | 10096<br>10096<br>047 160 | 10097<br>10097<br>047 161 | 10098<br>10098<br>047 162 | 10099<br>10099<br>047 163 | 10100<br>10100<br>047 164 | 10101<br>10101<br>047 165 | 10102<br>10102<br>047 166 | 10103<br>10103<br>047 167 | 10104<br>10104<br>047 170 | 10105<br>10105<br>047 171 | 10106<br>10106<br>047 172 | 10107<br>10107<br>047 173 | 10108<br>10108<br>047 174 | 10109<br>10109<br>047 175 | 10110<br>10110<br>047 176 | 10111<br>10111<br>047 177 |
| 8− | 10112<br>10112<br>047 200 | 10113<br>10113<br>047 201 | 10114<br>10114<br>047 202 | 10115<br>10115<br>047 203 | 10116<br>10116<br>047 204 | 10117<br>10117<br>047 205 | 10118<br>10118<br>047 206 | 10119<br>10119<br>047 207 | 10120<br>10120<br>047 210 | 10121<br>10121<br>047 211 | 10122<br>10122<br>047 212 | 10123<br>10123<br>047 213 | 10124<br>10124<br>047 214 | 10125<br>10125<br>047 215 | 10126<br>10126<br>047 216 | 10127<br>10127<br>047 217 |
| 9− | 10128<br>10128<br>047 220 | 10129<br>10129<br>047 221 | 10130<br>10130<br>047 222 | 10131<br>10131<br>047 223 | 10132<br>10132<br>047 224 | 10133<br>10133<br>047 225 | 10134<br>10134<br>047 226 | 10135<br>10135<br>047 227 | 10136<br>10136<br>047 230 | 10137<br>10137<br>047 231 | 10138<br>10138<br>047 232 | 10139<br>10139<br>047 233 | 10140<br>10140<br>047 234 | 10141<br>10141<br>047 235 | 10142<br>10142<br>047 236 | 10143<br>10143<br>047 237 |
| A− | 10144<br>10144<br>047 240 | 10145<br>10145<br>047 241 | 10146<br>10146<br>047 242 | 10147<br>10147<br>047 243 | 10148<br>10148<br>047 244 | 10149<br>10149<br>047 245 | 10150<br>10150<br>047 246 | 10151<br>10151<br>047 247 | 10152<br>10152<br>047 250 | 10153<br>10153<br>047 251 | 10154<br>10154<br>047 252 | 10155<br>10155<br>047 253 | 10156<br>10156<br>047 254 | 10157<br>10157<br>047 255 | 10158<br>10158<br>047 256 | 10159<br>10159<br>047 257 |
| B− | 10160<br>10160<br>047 260 | 10161<br>10161<br>047 261 | 10162<br>10162<br>047 262 | 10163<br>10163<br>047 263 | 10164<br>10164<br>047 264 | 10165<br>10165<br>047 265 | 10166<br>10166<br>047 266 | 10167<br>10167<br>047 267 | 10168<br>10168<br>047 270 | 10169<br>10169<br>047 271 | 10170<br>10170<br>047 272 | 10171<br>10171<br>047 273 | 10172<br>10172<br>047 274 | 10173<br>10173<br>047 275 | 10174<br>10174<br>047 276 | 10175<br>10175<br>047 277 |
| C− | 10176<br>10176<br>047 300 | 10177<br>10177<br>047 301 | 10178<br>10178<br>047 302 | 10179<br>10179<br>047 303 | 10180<br>10180<br>047 304 | 10181<br>10181<br>047 305 | 10182<br>10182<br>047 306 | 10183<br>10183<br>047 307 | 10184<br>10184<br>047 310 | 10185<br>10185<br>047 311 | 10186<br>10186<br>047 312 | 10187<br>10187<br>047 313 | 10188<br>10188<br>047 314 | 10189<br>10189<br>047 315 | 10190<br>10190<br>047 316 | 10191<br>10191<br>047 317 |
| D− | 10192<br>10192<br>047 320 | 10193<br>10193<br>047 321 | 10194<br>10194<br>047 322 | 10195<br>10195<br>047 323 | 10196<br>10196<br>047 324 | 10197<br>10197<br>047 325 | 10198<br>10198<br>047 326 | 10199<br>10199<br>047 327 | 10200<br>10200<br>047 330 | 10201<br>10201<br>047 331 | 10202<br>10202<br>047 332 | 10203<br>10203<br>047 333 | 10204<br>10204<br>047 334 | 10205<br>10205<br>047 335 | 10206<br>10206<br>047 336 | 10207<br>10207<br>047 337 |
| E− | 10208<br>10208<br>047 340 | 10209<br>10209<br>047 341 | 10210<br>10210<br>047 342 | 10211<br>10211<br>047 343 | 10212<br>10212<br>047 344 | 10213<br>10213<br>047 345 | 10214<br>10214<br>047 346 | 10215<br>10215<br>047 347 | 10216<br>10216<br>047 350 | 10217<br>10217<br>047 351 | 10218<br>10218<br>047 352 | 10219<br>10219<br>047 353 | 10220<br>10220<br>047 354 | 10221<br>10221<br>047 355 | 10222<br>10222<br>047 356 | 10223<br>10223<br>047 357 |
| F− | 10224<br>10224<br>047 360 | 10225<br>10225<br>047 361 | 10226<br>10226<br>047 362 | 10227<br>10227<br>047 363 | 10228<br>10228<br>047 364 | 10229<br>10229<br>047 365 | 10230<br>10230<br>047 366 | 10231<br>10231<br>047 367 | 10232<br>10232<br>047 370 | 10233<br>10233<br>047 371 | 10234<br>10234<br>047 372 | 10235<br>10235<br>047 373 | 10236<br>10236<br>047 374 | 10237<br>10237<br>047 375 | 10238<br>10238<br>047 376 | 10239<br>10239<br>047 377 |

# FIRST HEX DIGIT

Table selector: **2** (hexagon)

| SECOND HEX DIGIT | −0 | −1 | −2 | −3 | −4 | −5 | −6 | −7 | −8 | −9 | −A | −B | −C | −D | −E | −F |
|---|---|---|---|---|---|---|---|---|---|---|---|---|---|---|---|---|
| 0− | 10240<br>10240<br>050 000 | 10241<br>10241<br>050 001 | 10242<br>10242<br>050 002 | 10243<br>10243<br>050 003 | 10244<br>10244<br>050 004 | 10245<br>10245<br>050 005 | 10246<br>10246<br>050 006 | 10247<br>10247<br>050 007 | 10248<br>10248<br>050 010 | 10249<br>10249<br>050 011 | 10250<br>10250<br>050 012 | 10251<br>10251<br>050 013 | 10252<br>10252<br>050 014 | 10253<br>10253<br>050 015 | 10254<br>10254<br>050 016 | 10255<br>10255<br>050 017 |
| 1− | 10256<br>10256<br>050 020 | 10257<br>10257<br>050 021 | 10258<br>10258<br>050 022 | 10259<br>10259<br>050 023 | 10260<br>10260<br>050 024 | 10261<br>10261<br>050 025 | 10262<br>10262<br>050 026 | 10263<br>10263<br>050 027 | 10264<br>10264<br>050 030 | 10265<br>10265<br>050 031 | 10266<br>10266<br>050 032 | 10267<br>10267<br>050 033 | 10268<br>10268<br>050 034 | 10269<br>10269<br>050 035 | 10270<br>10270<br>050 036 | 10271<br>10271<br>050 037 |
| 2− | 10272<br>10272<br>050 040 | 10273<br>10273<br>050 041 | 10274<br>10274<br>050 042 | 10275<br>10275<br>050 043 | 10276<br>10276<br>050 044 | 10277<br>10277<br>050 045 | 10278<br>10278<br>050 046 | 10279<br>10279<br>050 047 | 10280<br>10280<br>050 050 | 10281<br>10281<br>050 051 | 10282<br>10282<br>050 052 | 10283<br>10283<br>050 053 | 10284<br>10284<br>050 054 | 10285<br>10285<br>050 055 | 10286<br>10286<br>050 056 | 10287<br>10287<br>050 057 |
| 3− | 10288<br>10288<br>050 060 | 10289<br>10289<br>050 061 | 10290<br>10290<br>050 062 | 10291<br>10291<br>050 063 | 10292<br>10292<br>050 064 | 10293<br>10293<br>050 065 | 10294<br>10294<br>050 066 | 10295<br>10295<br>050 067 | 10296<br>10296<br>050 070 | 10297<br>10297<br>050 071 | 10298<br>10298<br>050 072 | 10299<br>10299<br>050 073 | 10300<br>10300<br>050 074 | 10301<br>10301<br>050 075 | 10302<br>10302<br>050 076 | 10303<br>10303<br>050 077 |
| 4− | 10304<br>10304<br>050 100 | 10305<br>10305<br>050 101 | 10306<br>10306<br>050 102 | 10307<br>10307<br>050 103 | 10308<br>10308<br>050 104 | 10309<br>10309<br>050 105 | 10310<br>10310<br>050 106 | 10311<br>10311<br>050 107 | 10312<br>10312<br>050 110 | 10313<br>10313<br>050 111 | 10314<br>10314<br>050 112 | 10315<br>10315<br>050 113 | 10316<br>10316<br>050 114 | 10317<br>10317<br>050 115 | 10318<br>10318<br>050 116 | 10319<br>10319<br>050 117 |
| 5− | 10320<br>10320<br>050 120 | 10321<br>10321<br>050 121 | 10322<br>10322<br>050 122 | 10323<br>10323<br>050 123 | 10324<br>10324<br>050 124 | 10325<br>10325<br>050 125 | 10326<br>10326<br>050 126 | 10327<br>10327<br>050 127 | 10328<br>10328<br>050 130 | 10329<br>10329<br>050 131 | 10330<br>10330<br>050 132 | 10331<br>10331<br>050 133 | 10332<br>10332<br>050 134 | 10333<br>10333<br>050 135 | 10334<br>10334<br>050 136 | 10335<br>10335<br>050 137 |
| 6− | 10336<br>10336<br>050 140 | 10337<br>10337<br>050 141 | 10338<br>10338<br>050 142 | 10339<br>10339<br>050 143 | 10340<br>10340<br>050 144 | 10341<br>10341<br>050 145 | 10342<br>10342<br>050 146 | 10343<br>10343<br>050 147 | 10344<br>10344<br>050 150 | 10345<br>10345<br>050 151 | 10346<br>10346<br>050 152 | 10347<br>10347<br>050 153 | 10348<br>10348<br>050 154 | 10349<br>10349<br>050 155 | 10350<br>10350<br>050 156 | 10351<br>10351<br>050 157 |
| 7− | 10352<br>10352<br>050 160 | 10353<br>10353<br>050 161 | 10354<br>10354<br>050 162 | 10355<br>10355<br>050 163 | 10356<br>10356<br>050 164 | 10357<br>10357<br>050 165 | 10358<br>10358<br>050 166 | 10359<br>10359<br>050 167 | 10360<br>10360<br>050 170 | 10361<br>10361<br>050 171 | 10362<br>10362<br>050 172 | 10363<br>10363<br>050 173 | 10364<br>10364<br>050 174 | 10365<br>10365<br>050 175 | 10366<br>10366<br>050 176 | 10367<br>10367<br>050 177 |
| 8− | 10368<br>10368<br>050 200 | 10369<br>10369<br>050 201 | 10370<br>10370<br>050 202 | 10371<br>10371<br>050 203 | 10372<br>10372<br>050 204 | 10373<br>10373<br>050 205 | 10374<br>10374<br>050 206 | 10375<br>10375<br>050 207 | 10376<br>10376<br>050 210 | 10377<br>10377<br>050 211 | 10378<br>10378<br>050 212 | 10379<br>10379<br>050 213 | 10380<br>10380<br>050 214 | 10381<br>10381<br>050 215 | 10382<br>10382<br>050 216 | 10383<br>10383<br>050 217 |
| 9− | 10384<br>10384<br>050 220 | 10385<br>10385<br>050 221 | 10386<br>10386<br>050 222 | 10387<br>10387<br>050 223 | 10388<br>10388<br>050 224 | 10389<br>10389<br>050 225 | 10390<br>10390<br>050 226 | 10391<br>10391<br>050 227 | 10392<br>10392<br>050 230 | 10393<br>10393<br>050 231 | 10394<br>10394<br>050 232 | 10395<br>10395<br>050 233 | 10396<br>10396<br>050 234 | 10397<br>10397<br>050 235 | 10398<br>10398<br>050 236 | 10399<br>10399<br>050 237 |
| A− | 10400<br>10400<br>050 240 | 10401<br>10401<br>050 241 | 10402<br>10402<br>050 242 | 10403<br>10403<br>050 243 | 10404<br>10404<br>050 244 | 10405<br>10405<br>050 245 | 10406<br>10406<br>050 246 | 10407<br>10407<br>050 247 | 10408<br>10408<br>050 250 | 10409<br>10409<br>050 251 | 10410<br>10410<br>050 252 | 10411<br>10411<br>050 253 | 10412<br>10412<br>050 254 | 10413<br>10413<br>050 255 | 10414<br>10414<br>050 256 | 10415<br>10415<br>050 257 |
| B− | 10416<br>10416<br>050 260 | 10417<br>10417<br>050 261 | 10418<br>10418<br>050 262 | 10419<br>10419<br>050 263 | 10420<br>10420<br>050 264 | 10421<br>10421<br>050 265 | 10422<br>10422<br>050 266 | 10423<br>10423<br>050 267 | 10424<br>10424<br>050 270 | 10425<br>10425<br>050 271 | 10426<br>10426<br>050 272 | 10427<br>10427<br>050 273 | 10428<br>10428<br>050 274 | 10429<br>10429<br>050 275 | 10430<br>10430<br>050 276 | 10431<br>10431<br>050 277 |
| C− | 10432<br>10432<br>050 300 | 10433<br>10433<br>050 301 | 10434<br>10434<br>050 302 | 10435<br>10435<br>050 303 | 10436<br>10436<br>050 304 | 10437<br>10437<br>050 305 | 10438<br>10438<br>050 306 | 10439<br>10439<br>050 307 | 10440<br>10440<br>050 310 | 10441<br>10441<br>050 311 | 10442<br>10442<br>050 312 | 10443<br>10443<br>050 313 | 10444<br>10444<br>050 314 | 10445<br>10445<br>050 315 | 10446<br>10446<br>050 316 | 10447<br>10447<br>050 317 |
| D− | 10448<br>10448<br>050 320 | 10449<br>10449<br>050 321 | 10450<br>10450<br>050 322 | 10451<br>10451<br>050 323 | 10452<br>10452<br>050 324 | 10453<br>10453<br>050 325 | 10454<br>10454<br>050 326 | 10455<br>10455<br>050 327 | 10456<br>10456<br>050 330 | 10457<br>10457<br>050 331 | 10458<br>10458<br>050 332 | 10459<br>10459<br>050 333 | 10460<br>10460<br>050 334 | 10461<br>10461<br>050 335 | 10462<br>10462<br>050 336 | 10463<br>10463<br>050 337 |
| E− | 10464<br>10464<br>050 340 | 10465<br>10465<br>050 341 | 10466<br>10466<br>050 342 | 10467<br>10467<br>050 343 | 10468<br>10468<br>050 344 | 10469<br>10469<br>050 345 | 10470<br>10470<br>050 346 | 10471<br>10471<br>050 347 | 10472<br>10472<br>050 350 | 10473<br>10473<br>050 351 | 10474<br>10474<br>050 352 | 10475<br>10475<br>050 353 | 10476<br>10476<br>050 354 | 10477<br>10477<br>050 355 | 10478<br>10478<br>050 356 | 10479<br>10479<br>050 357 |
| F− | 10480<br>10480<br>050 360 | 10481<br>10481<br>050 361 | 10482<br>10482<br>050 362 | 10483<br>10483<br>050 363 | 10484<br>10484<br>050 364 | 10485<br>10485<br>050 365 | 10486<br>10486<br>050 366 | 10487<br>10487<br>050 367 | 10488<br>10488<br>050 370 | 10489<br>10489<br>050 371 | 10490<br>10490<br>050 372 | 10491<br>10491<br>050 373 | 10492<br>10492<br>050 374 | 10493<br>10493<br>050 375 | 10494<br>10494<br>050 376 | 10495<br>10495<br>050 377 |

Legend (right side): ■ DECIMAL → ● DECIMAL → ■ OCTAL

**⌘ DECIMAL** `10240`   **BINARY** `0010 1000`   **DECIMAL** `10240`   **HEXADECIMAL** (28)   **OCTAL** `050 000`

FOURTH HEX DIGIT → ← THIRD HEX DIGIT

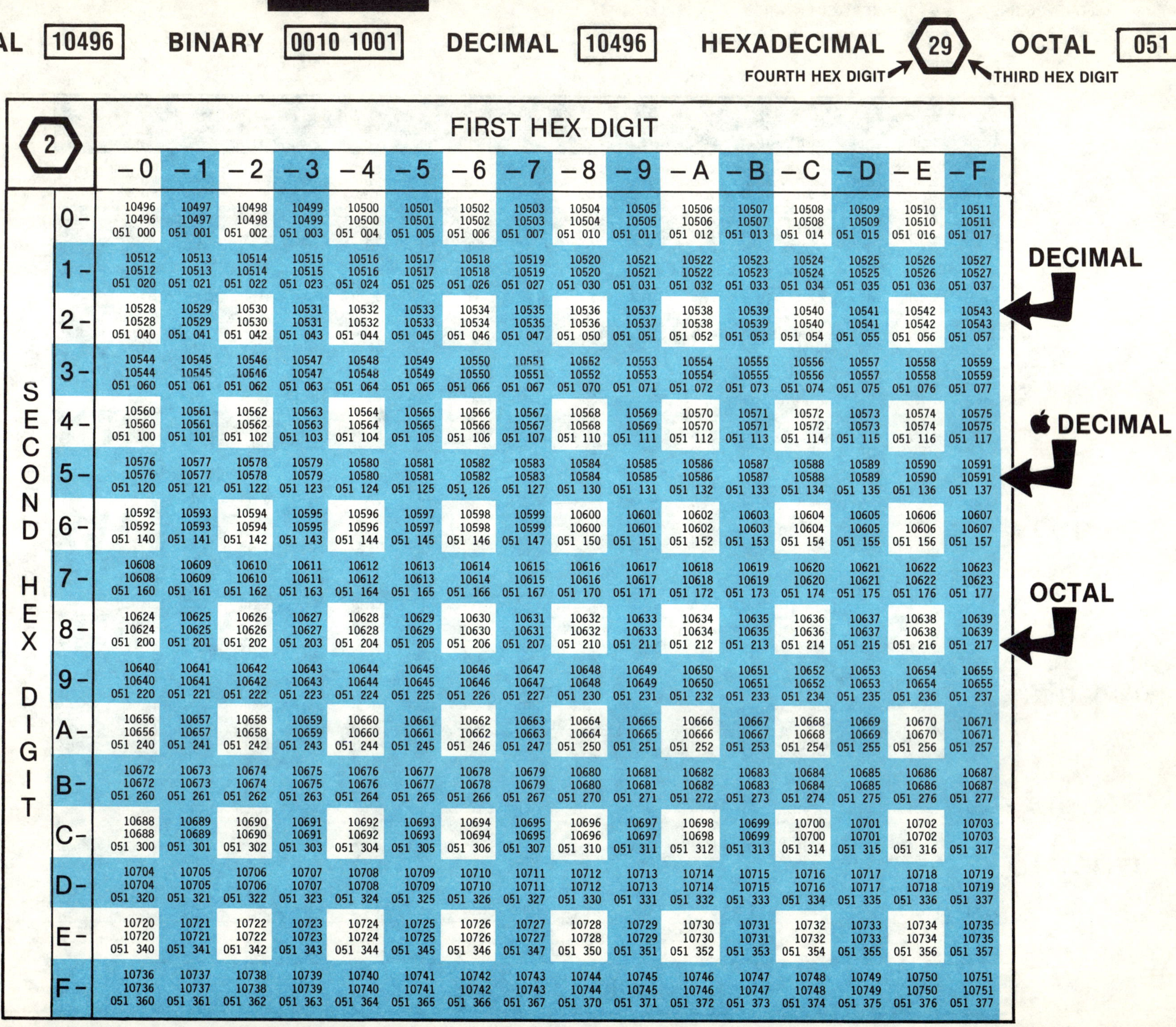

 DECIMAL [10496]   BINARY [0010 1001]   DECIMAL [10496]   HEXADECIMAL (29)   OCTAL [051 000]

FOURTH HEX DIGIT → 29 ← THIRD HEX DIGIT

(2)

| SECOND HEX DIGIT \ FIRST HEX DIGIT | −0 | −1 | −2 | −3 | −4 | −5 | −6 | −7 | −8 | −9 | −A | −B | −C | −D | −E | −F |
|---|---|---|---|---|---|---|---|---|---|---|---|---|---|---|---|---|
| 0− | 10496<br>10496<br>051 000 | 10497<br>10497<br>051 001 | 10498<br>10498<br>051 002 | 10499<br>10499<br>051 003 | 10500<br>10500<br>051 004 | 10501<br>10501<br>051 005 | 10502<br>10502<br>051 006 | 10503<br>10503<br>051 007 | 10504<br>10504<br>051 010 | 10505<br>10505<br>051 011 | 10506<br>10506<br>051 012 | 10507<br>10507<br>051 013 | 10508<br>10508<br>051 014 | 10509<br>10509<br>051 015 | 10510<br>10510<br>051 016 | 10511<br>10511<br>051 017 |
| 1− | 10512<br>10512<br>051 020 | 10513<br>10513<br>051 021 | 10514<br>10514<br>051 022 | 10515<br>10515<br>051 023 | 10516<br>10516<br>051 024 | 10517<br>10517<br>051 025 | 10518<br>10518<br>051 026 | 10519<br>10519<br>051 027 | 10520<br>10520<br>051 030 | 10521<br>10521<br>051 031 | 10522<br>10522<br>051 032 | 10523<br>10523<br>051 033 | 10524<br>10524<br>051 034 | 10525<br>10525<br>051 035 | 10526<br>10526<br>051 036 | 10527<br>10527<br>051 037 |
| 2− | 10528<br>10528<br>051 040 | 10529<br>10529<br>051 041 | 10530<br>10530<br>051 042 | 10531<br>10531<br>051 043 | 10532<br>10532<br>051 044 | 10533<br>10533<br>051 045 | 10534<br>10534<br>051 046 | 10535<br>10535<br>051 047 | 10536<br>10536<br>051 050 | 10537<br>10537<br>051 051 | 10538<br>10538<br>051 052 | 10539<br>10539<br>051 053 | 10540<br>10540<br>051 054 | 10541<br>10541<br>051 055 | 10542<br>10542<br>051 056 | 10543<br>10543<br>051 057 |
| 3− | 10544<br>10544<br>051 060 | 10545<br>10545<br>051 061 | 10546<br>10546<br>051 062 | 10547<br>10547<br>051 063 | 10548<br>10548<br>051 064 | 10549<br>10549<br>051 065 | 10550<br>10550<br>051 066 | 10551<br>10551<br>051 067 | 10552<br>10552<br>051 070 | 10553<br>10553<br>051 071 | 10554<br>10554<br>051 072 | 10555<br>10555<br>051 073 | 10556<br>10556<br>051 074 | 10557<br>10557<br>051 075 | 10558<br>10558<br>051 076 | 10559<br>10559<br>051 077 |
| 4− | 10560<br>10560<br>051 100 | 10561<br>10561<br>051 101 | 10562<br>10562<br>051 102 | 10563<br>10563<br>051 103 | 10564<br>10564<br>051 104 | 10565<br>10565<br>051 105 | 10566<br>10566<br>051 106 | 10567<br>10567<br>051 107 | 10568<br>10568<br>051 110 | 10569<br>10569<br>051 111 | 10570<br>10570<br>051 112 | 10571<br>10571<br>051 113 | 10572<br>10572<br>051 114 | 10573<br>10573<br>051 115 | 10574<br>10574<br>051 116 | 10575<br>10575<br>051 117 |
| 5− | 10576<br>10576<br>051 120 | 10577<br>10577<br>051 121 | 10578<br>10578<br>051 122 | 10579<br>10579<br>051 123 | 10580<br>10580<br>051 124 | 10581<br>10581<br>051 125 | 10582<br>10582<br>051 126 | 10583<br>10583<br>051 127 | 10584<br>10584<br>051 130 | 10585<br>10585<br>051 131 | 10586<br>10586<br>051 132 | 10587<br>10587<br>051 133 | 10588<br>10588<br>051 134 | 10589<br>10589<br>051 135 | 10590<br>10590<br>051 136 | 10591<br>10591<br>051 137 |
| 6− | 10592<br>10592<br>051 140 | 10593<br>10593<br>051 141 | 10594<br>10594<br>051 142 | 10595<br>10595<br>051 143 | 10596<br>10596<br>051 144 | 10597<br>10597<br>051 145 | 10598<br>10598<br>051 146 | 10599<br>10599<br>051 147 | 10600<br>10600<br>051 150 | 10601<br>10601<br>051 151 | 10602<br>10602<br>051 152 | 10603<br>10603<br>051 153 | 10604<br>10604<br>051 154 | 10605<br>10605<br>051 155 | 10606<br>10606<br>051 156 | 10607<br>10607<br>051 157 |
| 7− | 10608<br>10608<br>051 160 | 10609<br>10609<br>051 161 | 10610<br>10610<br>051 162 | 10611<br>10611<br>051 163 | 10612<br>10612<br>051 164 | 10613<br>10613<br>051 165 | 10614<br>10614<br>051 166 | 10615<br>10615<br>051 167 | 10616<br>10616<br>051 170 | 10617<br>10617<br>051 171 | 10618<br>10618<br>051 172 | 10619<br>10619<br>051 173 | 10620<br>10620<br>051 174 | 10621<br>10621<br>051 175 | 10622<br>10622<br>051 176 | 10623<br>10623<br>051 177 |
| 8− | 10624<br>10624<br>051 200 | 10625<br>10625<br>051 201 | 10626<br>10626<br>051 202 | 10627<br>10627<br>051 203 | 10628<br>10628<br>051 204 | 10629<br>10629<br>051 205 | 10630<br>10630<br>051 206 | 10631<br>10631<br>051 207 | 10632<br>10632<br>051 210 | 10633<br>10633<br>051 211 | 10634<br>10634<br>051 212 | 10635<br>10635<br>051 213 | 10636<br>10636<br>051 214 | 10637<br>10637<br>051 215 | 10638<br>10638<br>051 216 | 10639<br>10639<br>051 217 |
| 9− | 10640<br>10640<br>051 220 | 10641<br>10641<br>051 221 | 10642<br>10642<br>051 222 | 10643<br>10643<br>051 223 | 10644<br>10644<br>051 224 | 10645<br>10645<br>051 225 | 10646<br>10646<br>051 226 | 10647<br>10647<br>051 227 | 10648<br>10648<br>051 230 | 10649<br>10649<br>051 231 | 10650<br>10650<br>051 232 | 10651<br>10651<br>051 233 | 10652<br>10652<br>051 234 | 10653<br>10653<br>051 235 | 10654<br>10654<br>051 236 | 10655<br>10655<br>051 237 |
| A− | 10656<br>10656<br>051 240 | 10657<br>10657<br>051 241 | 10658<br>10658<br>051 242 | 10659<br>10659<br>051 243 | 10660<br>10660<br>051 244 | 10661<br>10661<br>051 245 | 10662<br>10662<br>051 246 | 10663<br>10663<br>051 247 | 10664<br>10664<br>051 250 | 10665<br>10665<br>051 251 | 10666<br>10666<br>051 252 | 10667<br>10667<br>051 253 | 10668<br>10668<br>051 254 | 10669<br>10669<br>051 255 | 10670<br>10670<br>051 256 | 10671<br>10671<br>051 257 |
| B− | 10672<br>10672<br>051 260 | 10673<br>10673<br>051 261 | 10674<br>10674<br>051 262 | 10675<br>10675<br>051 263 | 10676<br>10676<br>051 264 | 10677<br>10677<br>051 265 | 10678<br>10678<br>051 266 | 10679<br>10679<br>051 267 | 10680<br>10680<br>051 270 | 10681<br>10681<br>051 271 | 10682<br>10682<br>051 272 | 10683<br>10683<br>051 273 | 10684<br>10684<br>051 274 | 10685<br>10685<br>051 275 | 10686<br>10686<br>051 276 | 10687<br>10687<br>051 277 |
| C− | 10688<br>10688<br>051 300 | 10689<br>10689<br>051 301 | 10690<br>10690<br>051 302 | 10691<br>10691<br>051 303 | 10692<br>10692<br>051 304 | 10693<br>10693<br>051 305 | 10694<br>10694<br>051 306 | 10695<br>10695<br>051 307 | 10696<br>10696<br>051 310 | 10697<br>10697<br>051 311 | 10698<br>10698<br>051 312 | 10699<br>10699<br>051 313 | 10700<br>10700<br>051 314 | 10701<br>10701<br>051 315 | 10702<br>10702<br>051 316 | 10703<br>10703<br>051 317 |
| D− | 10704<br>10704<br>051 320 | 10705<br>10705<br>051 321 | 10706<br>10706<br>051 322 | 10707<br>10707<br>051 323 | 10708<br>10708<br>051 324 | 10709<br>10709<br>051 325 | 10710<br>10710<br>051 326 | 10711<br>10711<br>051 327 | 10712<br>10712<br>051 330 | 10713<br>10713<br>051 331 | 10714<br>10714<br>051 332 | 10715<br>10715<br>051 333 | 10716<br>10716<br>051 334 | 10717<br>10717<br>051 335 | 10718<br>10718<br>051 336 | 10719<br>10719<br>051 337 |
| E− | 10720<br>10720<br>051 340 | 10721<br>10721<br>051 341 | 10722<br>10722<br>051 342 | 10723<br>10723<br>051 343 | 10724<br>10724<br>051 344 | 10725<br>10725<br>051 345 | 10726<br>10726<br>051 346 | 10727<br>10727<br>051 347 | 10728<br>10728<br>051 350 | 10729<br>10729<br>051 351 | 10730<br>10730<br>051 352 | 10731<br>10731<br>051 353 | 10732<br>10732<br>051 354 | 10733<br>10733<br>051 355 | 10734<br>10734<br>051 356 | 10735<br>10735<br>051 357 |
| F− | 10736<br>10736<br>051 360 | 10737<br>10737<br>051 361 | 10738<br>10738<br>051 362 | 10739<br>10739<br>051 363 | 10740<br>10740<br>051 364 | 10741<br>10741<br>051 365 | 10742<br>10742<br>051 366 | 10743<br>10743<br>051 367 | 10744<br>10744<br>051 370 | 10745<br>10745<br>051 371 | 10746<br>10746<br>051 372 | 10747<br>10747<br>051 373 | 10748<br>10748<br>051 374 | 10749<br>10749<br>051 375 | 10750<br>10750<br>051 376 | 10751<br>10751<br>051 377 |

## FIRST HEX DIGIT

| ⬡2 | −0 | −1 | −2 | −3 | −4 | −5 | −6 | −7 | −8 | −9 | −A | −B | −C | −D | −E | −F |
|---|---|---|---|---|---|---|---|---|---|---|---|---|---|---|---|---|
| **0−** | 10752<br>10752<br>052 000 | 10753<br>10753<br>052 001 | 10754<br>10754<br>052 002 | 10755<br>10755<br>052 003 | 10756<br>10756<br>052 004 | 10757<br>10757<br>052 005 | 10758<br>10758<br>052 006 | 10759<br>10759<br>052 007 | 10760<br>10760<br>052 010 | 10761<br>10761<br>052 011 | 10762<br>10762<br>052 012 | 10763<br>10763<br>052 013 | 10764<br>10764<br>052 014 | 10765<br>10765<br>052 015 | 10766<br>10766<br>052 016 | 10767<br>10767<br>052 017 |
| **1−** | 10768<br>10768<br>052 020 | 10769<br>10769<br>052 021 | 10770<br>10770<br>052 022 | 10771<br>10771<br>052 023 | 10772<br>10772<br>052 024 | 10773<br>10773<br>052 025 | 10774<br>10774<br>052 026 | 10775<br>10775<br>052 027 | 10776<br>10776<br>052 030 | 10777<br>10777<br>052 031 | 10778<br>10778<br>052 032 | 10779<br>10779<br>052 033 | 10780<br>10780<br>052 034 | 10781<br>10781<br>052 035 | 10782<br>10782<br>052 036 | 10783<br>10783<br>052 037 |
| **2−** | 10784<br>10784<br>052 040 | 10785<br>10785<br>052 041 | 10786<br>10786<br>052 042 | 10787<br>10787<br>052 043 | 10788<br>10788<br>052 044 | 10789<br>10789<br>052 045 | 10790<br>10790<br>052 046 | 10791<br>10791<br>052 047 | 10792<br>10792<br>052 050 | 10793<br>10793<br>052 051 | 10794<br>10794<br>052 052 | 10795<br>10795<br>052 053 | 10796<br>10796<br>052 054 | 10797<br>10797<br>052 055 | 10798<br>10798<br>052 056 | 10799<br>10799<br>052 057 |
| **3−** | 10800<br>10800<br>052 060 | 10801<br>10801<br>052 061 | 10802<br>10802<br>052 062 | 10803<br>10803<br>052 063 | 10804<br>10804<br>052 064 | 10805<br>10805<br>052 065 | 10806<br>10806<br>052 066 | 10807<br>10807<br>052 067 | 10808<br>10808<br>052 070 | 10809<br>10809<br>052 071 | 10810<br>10810<br>052 072 | 10811<br>10811<br>052 073 | 10812<br>10812<br>052 074 | 10813<br>10813<br>052 075 | 10814<br>10814<br>052 076 | 10815<br>10815<br>052 077 |
| **4−** | 10816<br>10816<br>052 100 | 10817<br>10817<br>052 101 | 10818<br>10818<br>052 102 | 10819<br>10819<br>052 103 | 10820<br>10820<br>052 104 | 10821<br>10821<br>052 105 | 10822<br>10822<br>052 106 | 10823<br>10823<br>052 107 | 10824<br>10824<br>052 110 | 10825<br>10825<br>052 111 | 10826<br>10826<br>052 112 | 10827<br>10827<br>052 113 | 10828<br>10828<br>052 114 | 10829<br>10829<br>052 115 | 10830<br>10830<br>052 116 | 10831<br>10831<br>052 117 |
| **5−** | 10832<br>10832<br>052 120 | 10833<br>10833<br>052 121 | 10834<br>10834<br>052 122 | 10835<br>10835<br>052 123 | 10836<br>10836<br>052 124 | 10837<br>10837<br>052 125 | 10838<br>10838<br>052 126 | 10839<br>10839<br>052 127 | 10840<br>10840<br>052 130 | 10841<br>10841<br>052 131 | 10842<br>10842<br>052 132 | 10843<br>10843<br>052 133 | 10844<br>10844<br>052 134 | 10845<br>10845<br>052 135 | 10846<br>10846<br>052 136 | 10847<br>10847<br>052 137 |
| **6−** | 10848<br>10848<br>052 140 | 10849<br>10849<br>052 141 | 10850<br>10850<br>052 142 | 10851<br>10851<br>052 143 | 10852<br>10852<br>052 144 | 10853<br>10853<br>052 145 | 10854<br>10854<br>052 146 | 10855<br>10855<br>052 147 | 10856<br>10856<br>052 150 | 10857<br>10857<br>052 151 | 10858<br>10858<br>052 152 | 10859<br>10859<br>052 153 | 10860<br>10860<br>052 154 | 10861<br>10861<br>052 155 | 10862<br>10862<br>052 156 | 10863<br>10863<br>052 157 |
| **7−** | 10864<br>10864<br>052 160 | 10865<br>10865<br>052 161 | 10866<br>10866<br>052 162 | 10867<br>10867<br>052 163 | 10868<br>10868<br>052 164 | 10869<br>10869<br>052 165 | 10870<br>10870<br>052 166 | 10871<br>10871<br>052 167 | 10872<br>10872<br>052 170 | 10873<br>10873<br>052 171 | 10874<br>10874<br>052 172 | 10875<br>10875<br>052 173 | 10876<br>10876<br>052 174 | 10877<br>10877<br>052 175 | 10878<br>10878<br>052 176 | 10879<br>10879<br>052 177 |
| **8−** | 10880<br>10880<br>052 200 | 10881<br>10881<br>052 201 | 10882<br>10882<br>052 202 | 10883<br>10883<br>052 203 | 10884<br>10884<br>052 204 | 10885<br>10885<br>052 205 | 10886<br>10886<br>052 206 | 10887<br>10887<br>052 207 | 10888<br>10888<br>052 210 | 10889<br>10889<br>052 211 | 10890<br>10890<br>052 212 | 10891<br>10891<br>052 213 | 10892<br>10892<br>052 214 | 10893<br>10893<br>052 215 | 10894<br>10894<br>052 216 | 10895<br>10895<br>052 217 |
| **9−** | 10896<br>10896<br>052 220 | 10897<br>10897<br>052 221 | 10898<br>10898<br>052 222 | 10899<br>10899<br>052 223 | 10900<br>10900<br>052 224 | 10901<br>10901<br>052 225 | 10902<br>10902<br>052 226 | 10903<br>10903<br>052 227 | 10904<br>10904<br>052 230 | 10905<br>10905<br>052 231 | 10906<br>10906<br>052 232 | 10907<br>10907<br>052 233 | 10908<br>10908<br>052 234 | 10909<br>10909<br>052 235 | 10910<br>10910<br>052 236 | 10911<br>10911<br>052 237 |
| **A−** | 10912<br>10912<br>052 240 | 10913<br>10913<br>052 241 | 10914<br>10914<br>052 242 | 10915<br>10915<br>052 243 | 10916<br>10916<br>052 244 | 10917<br>10917<br>052 245 | 10918<br>10918<br>052 246 | 10919<br>10919<br>052 247 | 10920<br>10920<br>052 250 | 10921<br>10921<br>052 251 | 10922<br>10922<br>052 252 | 10923<br>10923<br>052 253 | 10924<br>10924<br>052 254 | 10925<br>10925<br>052 255 | 10926<br>10926<br>052 256 | 10927<br>10927<br>052 257 |
| **B−** | 10928<br>10928<br>052 260 | 10929<br>10929<br>052 261 | 10930<br>10930<br>052 262 | 10931<br>10931<br>052 263 | 10932<br>10932<br>052 264 | 10933<br>10933<br>052 265 | 10934<br>10934<br>052 266 | 10935<br>10935<br>052 267 | 10936<br>10936<br>052 270 | 10937<br>10937<br>052 271 | 10938<br>10938<br>052 272 | 10939<br>10939<br>052 273 | 10940<br>10940<br>052 274 | 10941<br>10941<br>052 275 | 10942<br>10942<br>052 276 | 10943<br>10943<br>052 277 |
| **C−** | 10944<br>10944<br>052 300 | 10945<br>10945<br>052 301 | 10946<br>10946<br>052 302 | 10947<br>10947<br>052 303 | 10948<br>10948<br>052 304 | 10949<br>10949<br>052 305 | 10950<br>10950<br>052 306 | 10951<br>10951<br>052 307 | 10952<br>10952<br>052 310 | 10953<br>10953<br>052 311 | 10954<br>10954<br>052 312 | 10955<br>10955<br>052 313 | 10956<br>10956<br>052 314 | 10957<br>10957<br>052 315 | 10958<br>10958<br>052 316 | 10959<br>10959<br>052 317 |
| **D−** | 10960<br>10960<br>052 320 | 10961<br>10961<br>052 321 | 10962<br>10962<br>052 322 | 10963<br>10963<br>052 323 | 10964<br>10964<br>052 324 | 10965<br>10965<br>052 325 | 10966<br>10966<br>052 326 | 10967<br>10967<br>052 327 | 10968<br>10968<br>052 330 | 10969<br>10969<br>052 331 | 10970<br>10970<br>052 332 | 10971<br>10971<br>052 333 | 10972<br>10972<br>052 334 | 10973<br>10973<br>052 335 | 10974<br>10974<br>052 336 | 10975<br>10975<br>052 337 |
| **E−** | 10976<br>10976<br>052 340 | 10977<br>10977<br>052 341 | 10978<br>10978<br>052 342 | 10979<br>10979<br>052 343 | 10980<br>10980<br>052 344 | 10981<br>10981<br>052 345 | 10982<br>10982<br>052 346 | 10983<br>10983<br>052 347 | 10984<br>10984<br>052 350 | 10985<br>10985<br>052 351 | 10986<br>10986<br>052 352 | 10987<br>10987<br>052 353 | 10988<br>10988<br>052 354 | 10989<br>10989<br>052 355 | 10990<br>10990<br>052 356 | 10991<br>10991<br>052 357 |
| **F−** | 10992<br>10992<br>052 360 | 10993<br>10993<br>052 361 | 10994<br>10994<br>052 362 | 10995<br>10995<br>052 363 | 10996<br>10996<br>052 364 | 10997<br>10997<br>052 365 | 10998<br>10998<br>052 366 | 10999<br>10999<br>052 367 | 11000<br>11000<br>052 370 | 11001<br>11001<br>052 371 | 11002<br>11002<br>052 372 | 11003<br>11003<br>052 373 | 11004<br>11004<br>052 374 | 11005<br>11005<br>052 375 | 11006<br>11006<br>052 376 | 11007<br>11007<br>052 377 |

SECOND HEX DIGIT *(row labels)*

DECIMAL → (row 2)    DECIMAL → (row 4)    OCTAL → (row 7 / 8)

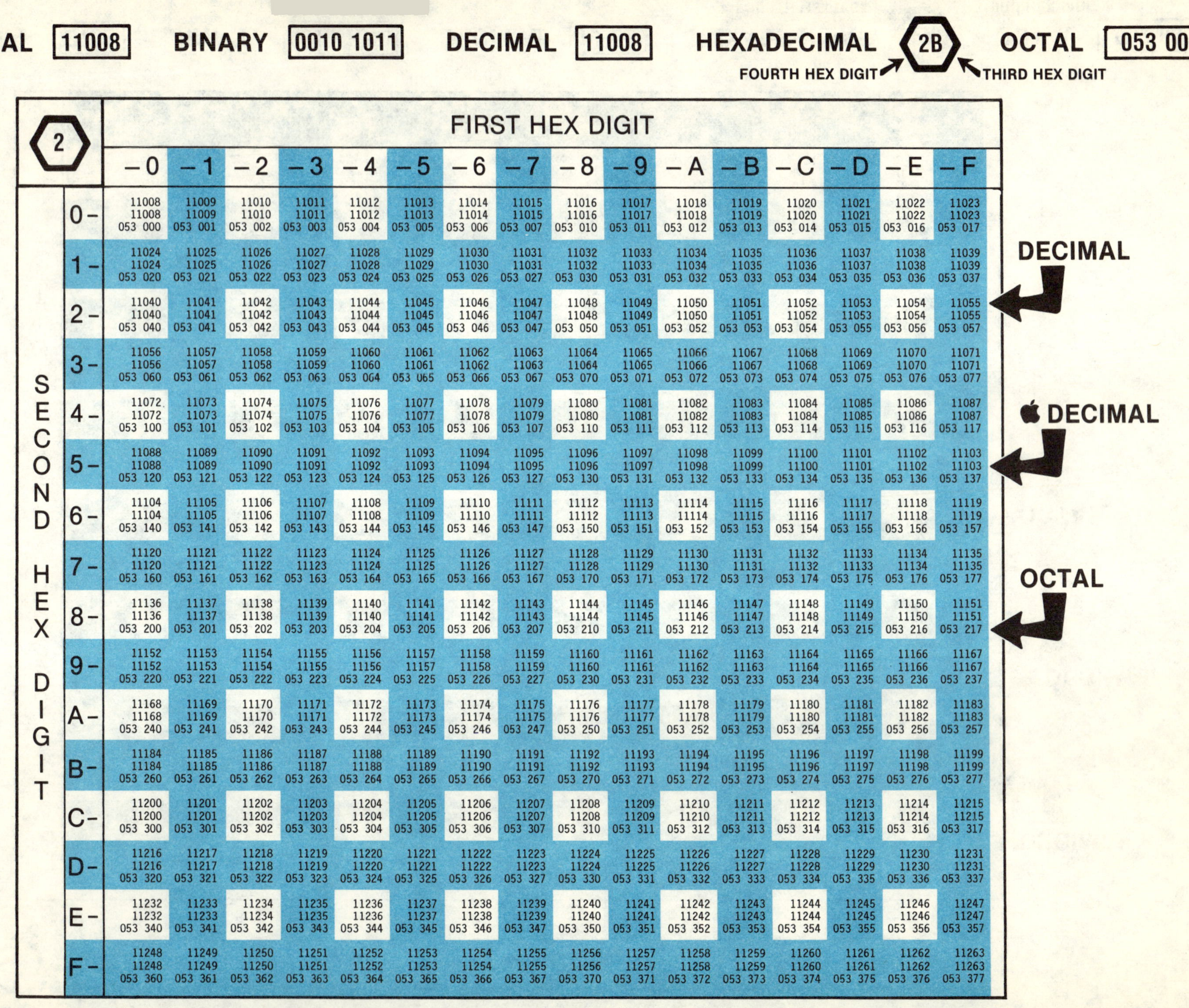

 DECIMAL `11008`  BINARY `0010 1011`  DECIMAL `11008`  HEXADECIMAL ⬡ `2B`  OCTAL `053 000`

FOURTH HEX DIGIT → ⬡ ← THIRD HEX DIGIT

⬡ 2

| SECOND HEX DIGIT | FIRST HEX DIGIT | | | | | | | | | | | | | | | |
|---|---|---|---|---|---|---|---|---|---|---|---|---|---|---|---|---|
| | −0 | −1 | −2 | −3 | −4 | −5 | −6 | −7 | −8 | −9 | −A | −B | −C | −D | −E | −F |
| 0− | 11008<br>11008<br>053 000 | 11009<br>11009<br>053 001 | 11010<br>11010<br>053 002 | 11011<br>11011<br>053 003 | 11012<br>11012<br>053 004 | 11013<br>11013<br>053 005 | 11014<br>11014<br>053 006 | 11015<br>11015<br>053 007 | 11016<br>11016<br>053 010 | 11017<br>11017<br>053 011 | 11018<br>11018<br>053 012 | 11019<br>11019<br>053 013 | 11020<br>11020<br>053 014 | 11021<br>11021<br>053 015 | 11022<br>11022<br>053 016 | 11023<br>11023<br>053 017 |
| 1− | 11024<br>11024<br>053 020 | 11025<br>11025<br>053 021 | 11026<br>11026<br>053 022 | 11027<br>11027<br>053 023 | 11028<br>11028<br>053 024 | 11029<br>11029<br>053 025 | 11030<br>11030<br>053 026 | 11031<br>11031<br>053 027 | 11032<br>11032<br>053 030 | 11033<br>11033<br>053 031 | 11034<br>11034<br>053 032 | 11035<br>11035<br>053 033 | 11036<br>11036<br>053 034 | 11037<br>11037<br>053 035 | 11038<br>11038<br>053 036 | 11039<br>11039<br>053 037 |
| 2− | 11040<br>11040<br>053 040 | 11041<br>11041<br>053 041 | 11042<br>11042<br>053 042 | 11043<br>11043<br>053 043 | 11044<br>11044<br>053 044 | 11045<br>11045<br>053 045 | 11046<br>11046<br>053 046 | 11047<br>11047<br>053 047 | 11048<br>11048<br>053 050 | 11049<br>11049<br>053 051 | 11050<br>11050<br>053 052 | 11051<br>11051<br>053 053 | 11052<br>11052<br>053 054 | 11053<br>11053<br>053 055 | 11054<br>11054<br>053 056 | 11055<br>11055<br>053 057 |
| 3− | 11056<br>11056<br>053 060 | 11057<br>11057<br>053 061 | 11058<br>11058<br>053 062 | 11059<br>11059<br>053 063 | 11060<br>11060<br>053 064 | 11061<br>11061<br>053 065 | 11062<br>11062<br>053 066 | 11063<br>11063<br>053 067 | 11064<br>11064<br>053 070 | 11065<br>11065<br>053 071 | 11066<br>11066<br>053 072 | 11067<br>11067<br>053 073 | 11068<br>11068<br>053 074 | 11069<br>11069<br>053 075 | 11070<br>11070<br>053 076 | 11071<br>11071<br>053 077 |
| 4− | 11072<br>11072<br>053 100 | 11073<br>11073<br>053 101 | 11074<br>11074<br>053 102 | 11075<br>11075<br>053 103 | 11076<br>11076<br>053 104 | 11077<br>11077<br>053 105 | 11078<br>11078<br>053 106 | 11079<br>11079<br>053 107 | 11080<br>11080<br>053 110 | 11081<br>11081<br>053 111 | 11082<br>11082<br>053 112 | 11083<br>11083<br>053 113 | 11084<br>11084<br>053 114 | 11085<br>11085<br>053 115 | 11086<br>11086<br>053 116 | 11087<br>11087<br>053 117 |
| 5− | 11088<br>11088<br>053 120 | 11089<br>11089<br>053 121 | 11090<br>11090<br>053 122 | 11091<br>11091<br>053 123 | 11092<br>11092<br>053 124 | 11093<br>11093<br>053 125 | 11094<br>11094<br>053 126 | 11095<br>11095<br>053 127 | 11096<br>11096<br>053 130 | 11097<br>11097<br>053 131 | 11098<br>11098<br>053 132 | 11099<br>11099<br>053 133 | 11100<br>11100<br>053 134 | 11101<br>11101<br>053 135 | 11102<br>11102<br>053 136 | 11103<br>11103<br>053 137 |
| 6− | 11104<br>11104<br>053 140 | 11105<br>11105<br>053 141 | 11106<br>11106<br>053 142 | 11107<br>11107<br>053 143 | 11108<br>11108<br>053 144 | 11109<br>11109<br>053 145 | 11110<br>11110<br>053 146 | 11111<br>11111<br>053 147 | 11112<br>11112<br>053 150 | 11113<br>11113<br>053 151 | 11114<br>11114<br>053 152 | 11115<br>11115<br>053 153 | 11116<br>11116<br>053 154 | 11117<br>11117<br>053 155 | 11118<br>11118<br>053 156 | 11119<br>11119<br>053 157 |
| 7− | 11120<br>11120<br>053 160 | 11121<br>11121<br>053 161 | 11122<br>11122<br>053 162 | 11123<br>11123<br>053 163 | 11124<br>11124<br>053 164 | 11125<br>11125<br>053 165 | 11126<br>11126<br>053 166 | 11127<br>11127<br>053 167 | 11128<br>11128<br>053 170 | 11129<br>11129<br>053 171 | 11130<br>11130<br>053 172 | 11131<br>11131<br>053 173 | 11132<br>11132<br>053 174 | 11133<br>11133<br>053 175 | 11134<br>11134<br>053 176 | 11135<br>11135<br>053 177 |
| 8− | 11136<br>11136<br>053 200 | 11137<br>11137<br>053 201 | 11138<br>11138<br>053 202 | 11139<br>11139<br>053 203 | 11140<br>11140<br>053 204 | 11141<br>11141<br>053 205 | 11142<br>11142<br>053 206 | 11143<br>11143<br>053 207 | 11144<br>11144<br>053 210 | 11145<br>11145<br>053 211 | 11146<br>11146<br>053 212 | 11147<br>11147<br>053 213 | 11148<br>11148<br>053 214 | 11149<br>11149<br>053 215 | 11150<br>11150<br>053 216 | 11151<br>11151<br>053 217 |
| 9− | 11152<br>11152<br>053 220 | 11153<br>11153<br>053 221 | 11154<br>11154<br>053 222 | 11155<br>11155<br>053 223 | 11156<br>11156<br>053 224 | 11157<br>11157<br>053 225 | 11158<br>11158<br>053 226 | 11159<br>11159<br>053 227 | 11160<br>11160<br>053 230 | 11161<br>11161<br>053 231 | 11162<br>11162<br>053 232 | 11163<br>11163<br>053 233 | 11164<br>11164<br>053 234 | 11165<br>11165<br>053 235 | 11166<br>11166<br>053 236 | 11167<br>11167<br>053 237 |
| A− | 11168<br>11168<br>053 240 | 11169<br>11169<br>053 241 | 11170<br>11170<br>053 242 | 11171<br>11171<br>053 243 | 11172<br>11172<br>053 244 | 11173<br>11173<br>053 245 | 11174<br>11174<br>053 246 | 11175<br>11175<br>053 247 | 11176<br>11176<br>053 250 | 11177<br>11177<br>053 251 | 11178<br>11178<br>053 252 | 11179<br>11179<br>053 253 | 11180<br>11180<br>053 254 | 11181<br>11181<br>053 255 | 11182<br>11182<br>053 256 | 11183<br>11183<br>053 257 |
| B− | 11184<br>11184<br>053 260 | 11185<br>11185<br>053 261 | 11186<br>11186<br>053 262 | 11187<br>11187<br>053 263 | 11188<br>11188<br>053 264 | 11189<br>11189<br>053 265 | 11190<br>11190<br>053 266 | 11191<br>11191<br>053 267 | 11192<br>11192<br>053 270 | 11193<br>11193<br>053 271 | 11194<br>11194<br>053 272 | 11195<br>11195<br>053 273 | 11196<br>11196<br>053 274 | 11197<br>11197<br>053 275 | 11198<br>11198<br>053 276 | 11199<br>11199<br>053 277 |
| C− | 11200<br>11200<br>053 300 | 11201<br>11201<br>053 301 | 11202<br>11202<br>053 302 | 11203<br>11203<br>053 303 | 11204<br>11204<br>053 304 | 11205<br>11205<br>053 305 | 11206<br>11206<br>053 306 | 11207<br>11207<br>053 307 | 11208<br>11208<br>053 310 | 11209<br>11209<br>053 311 | 11210<br>11210<br>053 312 | 11211<br>11211<br>053 313 | 11212<br>11212<br>053 314 | 11213<br>11213<br>053 315 | 11214<br>11214<br>053 316 | 11215<br>11215<br>053 317 |
| D− | 11216<br>11216<br>053 320 | 11217<br>11217<br>053 321 | 11218<br>11218<br>053 322 | 11219<br>11219<br>053 323 | 11220<br>11220<br>053 324 | 11221<br>11221<br>053 325 | 11222<br>11222<br>053 326 | 11223<br>11223<br>053 327 | 11224<br>11224<br>053 330 | 11225<br>11225<br>053 331 | 11226<br>11226<br>053 332 | 11227<br>11227<br>053 333 | 11228<br>11228<br>053 334 | 11229<br>11229<br>053 335 | 11230<br>11230<br>053 336 | 11231<br>11231<br>053 337 |
| E− | 11232<br>11232<br>053 340 | 11233<br>11233<br>053 341 | 11234<br>11234<br>053 342 | 11235<br>11235<br>053 343 | 11236<br>11236<br>053 344 | 11237<br>11237<br>053 345 | 11238<br>11238<br>053 346 | 11239<br>11239<br>053 347 | 11240<br>11240<br>053 350 | 11241<br>11241<br>053 351 | 11242<br>11242<br>053 352 | 11243<br>11243<br>053 353 | 11244<br>11244<br>053 354 | 11245<br>11245<br>053 355 | 11246<br>11246<br>053 356 | 11247<br>11247<br>053 357 |
| F− | 11248<br>11248<br>053 360 | 11249<br>11249<br>053 361 | 11250<br>11250<br>053 362 | 11251<br>11251<br>053 363 | 11252<br>11252<br>053 364 | 11253<br>11253<br>053 365 | 11254<br>11254<br>053 366 | 11255<br>11255<br>053 367 | 11256<br>11256<br>053 370 | 11257<br>11257<br>053 371 | 11258<br>11258<br>053 372 | 11259<br>11259<br>053 373 | 11260<br>11260<br>053 374 | 11261<br>11261<br>053 375 | 11262<br>11262<br>053 376 | 11263<br>11263<br>053 377 |

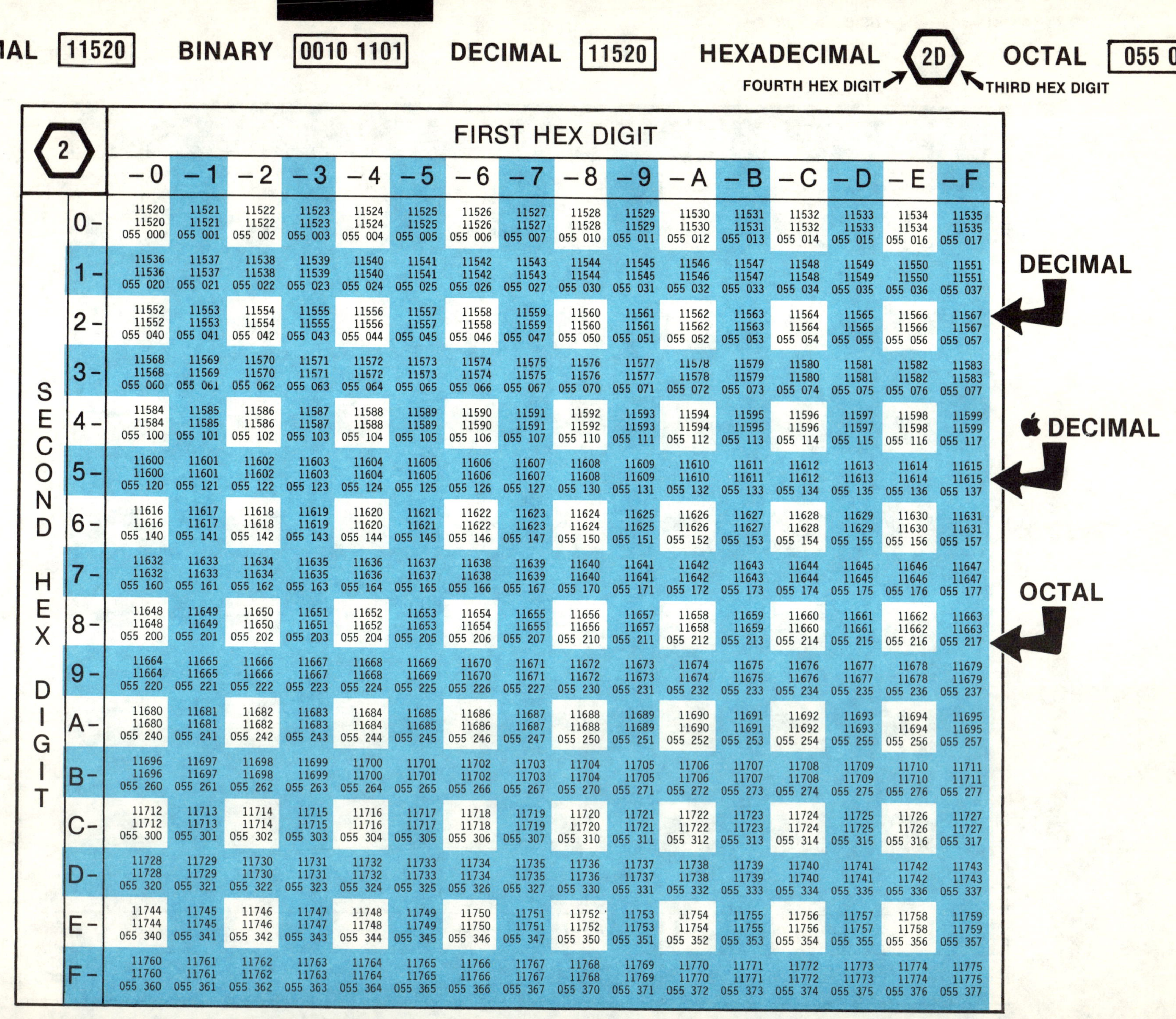

 DECIMAL [11520]   BINARY [0010 1101]   DECIMAL [11520]   HEXADECIMAL (2D)   OCTAL [055 000]

FOURTH HEX DIGIT → (2D) ← THIRD HEX DIGIT

## FIRST HEX DIGIT

| (2) | -0 | -1 | -2 | -3 | -4 | -5 | -6 | -7 | -8 | -9 | -A | -B | -C | -D | -E | -F |
|---|---|---|---|---|---|---|---|---|---|---|---|---|---|---|---|---|
| 0- | 11520<br>055 000 | 11521<br>055 001 | 11522<br>055 002 | 11523<br>055 003 | 11524<br>055 004 | 11525<br>055 005 | 11526<br>055 006 | 11527<br>055 007 | 11528<br>055 010 | 11529<br>055 011 | 11530<br>055 012 | 11531<br>055 013 | 11532<br>055 014 | 11533<br>055 015 | 11534<br>055 016 | 11535<br>055 017 |
| 1- | 11536<br>055 020 | 11537<br>055 021 | 11538<br>055 022 | 11539<br>055 023 | 11540<br>055 024 | 11541<br>055 025 | 11542<br>055 026 | 11543<br>055 027 | 11544<br>055 030 | 11545<br>055 031 | 11546<br>055 032 | 11547<br>055 033 | 11548<br>055 034 | 11549<br>055 035 | 11550<br>055 036 | 11551<br>055 037 |
| 2- | 11552<br>055 040 | 11553<br>055 041 | 11554<br>055 042 | 11555<br>055 043 | 11556<br>055 044 | 11557<br>055 045 | 11558<br>055 046 | 11559<br>055 047 | 11560<br>055 050 | 11561<br>055 051 | 11562<br>055 052 | 11563<br>055 053 | 11564<br>055 054 | 11565<br>055 055 | 11566<br>055 056 | 11567<br>055 057 |
| 3- | 11568<br>055 060 | 11569<br>055 061 | 11570<br>055 062 | 11571<br>055 063 | 11572<br>055 064 | 11573<br>055 065 | 11574<br>055 066 | 11575<br>055 067 | 11576<br>055 070 | 11577<br>055 071 | 11578<br>055 072 | 11579<br>055 073 | 11580<br>055 074 | 11581<br>055 075 | 11582<br>055 076 | 11583<br>055 077 |
| 4- | 11584<br>055 100 | 11585<br>055 101 | 11586<br>055 102 | 11587<br>055 103 | 11588<br>055 104 | 11589<br>055 105 | 11590<br>055 106 | 11591<br>055 107 | 11592<br>055 110 | 11593<br>055 111 | 11594<br>055 112 | 11595<br>055 113 | 11596<br>055 114 | 11597<br>055 115 | 11598<br>055 116 | 11599<br>055 117 |
| 5- | 11600<br>055 120 | 11601<br>055 121 | 11602<br>055 122 | 11603<br>055 123 | 11604<br>055 124 | 11605<br>055 125 | 11606<br>055 126 | 11607<br>055 127 | 11608<br>055 130 | 11609<br>055 131 | 11610<br>055 132 | 11611<br>055 133 | 11612<br>055 134 | 11613<br>055 135 | 11614<br>055 136 | 11615<br>055 137 |
| 6- | 11616<br>055 140 | 11617<br>055 141 | 11618<br>055 142 | 11619<br>055 143 | 11620<br>055 144 | 11621<br>055 145 | 11622<br>055 146 | 11623<br>055 147 | 11624<br>055 150 | 11625<br>055 151 | 11626<br>055 152 | 11627<br>055 153 | 11628<br>055 154 | 11629<br>055 155 | 11630<br>055 156 | 11631<br>055 157 |
| 7- | 11632<br>055 160 | 11633<br>055 161 | 11634<br>055 162 | 11635<br>055 163 | 11636<br>055 164 | 11637<br>055 165 | 11638<br>055 166 | 11639<br>055 167 | 11640<br>055 170 | 11641<br>055 171 | 11642<br>055 172 | 11643<br>055 173 | 11644<br>055 174 | 11645<br>055 175 | 11646<br>055 176 | 11647<br>055 177 |
| 8- | 11648<br>055 200 | 11649<br>055 201 | 11650<br>055 202 | 11651<br>055 203 | 11652<br>055 204 | 11653<br>055 205 | 11654<br>055 206 | 11655<br>055 207 | 11656<br>055 210 | 11657<br>055 211 | 11658<br>055 212 | 11659<br>055 213 | 11660<br>055 214 | 11661<br>055 215 | 11662<br>055 216 | 11663<br>055 217 |
| 9- | 11664<br>055 220 | 11665<br>055 221 | 11666<br>055 222 | 11667<br>055 223 | 11668<br>055 224 | 11669<br>055 225 | 11670<br>055 226 | 11671<br>055 227 | 11672<br>055 230 | 11673<br>055 231 | 11674<br>055 232 | 11675<br>055 233 | 11676<br>055 234 | 11677<br>055 235 | 11678<br>055 236 | 11679<br>055 237 |
| A- | 11680<br>055 240 | 11681<br>055 241 | 11682<br>055 242 | 11683<br>055 243 | 11684<br>055 244 | 11685<br>055 245 | 11686<br>055 246 | 11687<br>055 247 | 11688<br>055 250 | 11689<br>055 251 | 11690<br>055 252 | 11691<br>055 253 | 11692<br>055 254 | 11693<br>055 255 | 11694<br>055 256 | 11695<br>055 257 |
| B- | 11696<br>055 260 | 11697<br>055 261 | 11698<br>055 262 | 11699<br>055 263 | 11700<br>055 264 | 11701<br>055 265 | 11702<br>055 266 | 11703<br>055 267 | 11704<br>055 270 | 11705<br>055 271 | 11706<br>055 272 | 11707<br>055 273 | 11708<br>055 274 | 11709<br>055 275 | 11710<br>055 276 | 11711<br>055 277 |
| C- | 11712<br>055 300 | 11713<br>055 301 | 11714<br>055 302 | 11715<br>055 303 | 11716<br>055 304 | 11717<br>055 305 | 11718<br>055 306 | 11719<br>055 307 | 11720<br>055 310 | 11721<br>055 311 | 11722<br>055 312 | 11723<br>055 313 | 11724<br>055 314 | 11725<br>055 315 | 11726<br>055 316 | 11727<br>055 317 |
| D- | 11728<br>055 320 | 11729<br>055 321 | 11730<br>055 322 | 11731<br>055 323 | 11732<br>055 324 | 11733<br>055 325 | 11734<br>055 326 | 11735<br>055 327 | 11736<br>055 330 | 11737<br>055 331 | 11738<br>055 332 | 11739<br>055 333 | 11740<br>055 334 | 11741<br>055 335 | 11742<br>055 336 | 11743<br>055 337 |
| E- | 11744<br>055 340 | 11745<br>055 341 | 11746<br>055 342 | 11747<br>055 343 | 11748<br>055 344 | 11749<br>055 345 | 11750<br>055 346 | 11751<br>055 347 | 11752<br>055 350 | 11753<br>055 351 | 11754<br>055 352 | 11755<br>055 353 | 11756<br>055 354 | 11757<br>055 355 | 11758<br>055 356 | 11759<br>055 357 |
| F- | 11760<br>055 360 | 11761<br>055 361 | 11762<br>055 362 | 11763<br>055 363 | 11764<br>055 364 | 11765<br>055 365 | 11766<br>055 366 | 11767<br>055 367 | 11768<br>055 370 | 11769<br>055 371 | 11770<br>055 372 | 11771<br>055 373 | 11772<br>055 374 | 11773<br>055 375 | 11774<br>055 376 | 11775<br>055 377 |

| SECOND HEX DIGIT | −0 | −1 | −2 | −3 | −4 | −5 | −6 | −7 | −8 | −9 | −A | −B | −C | −D | −E | −F |
|---|---|---|---|---|---|---|---|---|---|---|---|---|---|---|---|---|
| 0− | 11776 / 056 000 | 11777 / 056 001 | 11778 / 056 002 | 11779 / 056 003 | 11780 / 056 004 | 11781 / 056 005 | 11782 / 056 006 | 11783 / 056 007 | 11784 / 056 010 | 11785 / 056 011 | 11786 / 056 012 | 11787 / 056 013 | 11788 / 056 014 | 11789 / 056 015 | 11790 / 056 016 | 11791 / 056 017 |
| 1− | 11792 / 056 020 | 11793 / 056 021 | 11794 / 056 022 | 11795 / 056 023 | 11796 / 056 024 | 11797 / 056 025 | 11798 / 056 026 | 11799 / 056 027 | 11800 / 056 030 | 11801 / 056 031 | 11802 / 056 032 | 11803 / 056 033 | 11804 / 056 034 | 11805 / 056 035 | 11806 / 056 036 | 11807 / 056 037 |
| 2− | 11808 / 056 040 | 11809 / 056 041 | 11810 / 056 042 | 11811 / 056 043 | 11812 / 056 044 | 11813 / 056 045 | 11814 / 056 046 | 11815 / 056 047 | 11816 / 056 050 | 11817 / 056 051 | 11818 / 056 052 | 11819 / 056 053 | 11820 / 056 054 | 11821 / 056 055 | 11822 / 056 056 | 11823 / 056 057 |
| 3− | 11824 / 056 060 | 11825 / 056 061 | 11826 / 056 062 | 11827 / 056 063 | 11828 / 056 064 | 11829 / 056 065 | 11830 / 056 066 | 11831 / 056 067 | 11832 / 056 070 | 11833 / 056 071 | 11834 / 056 072 | 11835 / 056 073 | 11836 / 056 074 | 11837 / 056 075 | 11838 / 056 076 | 11839 / 056 077 |
| 4− | 11840 / 056 100 | 11841 / 056 101 | 11842 / 056 102 | 11843 / 056 103 | 11844 / 056 104 | 11845 / 056 105 | 11846 / 056 106 | 11847 / 056 107 | 11848 / 056 110 | 11849 / 056 111 | 11850 / 056 112 | 11851 / 056 113 | 11852 / 056 114 | 11853 / 056 115 | 11854 / 056 116 | 11855 / 056 117 |
| 5− | 11856 / 056 120 | 11857 / 056 121 | 11858 / 056 122 | 11859 / 056 123 | 11860 / 056 124 | 11861 / 056 125 | 11862 / 056 126 | 11863 / 056 127 | 11864 / 056 130 | 11865 / 056 131 | 11866 / 056 132 | 11867 / 056 133 | 11868 / 056 134 | 11869 / 056 135 | 11870 / 056 136 | 11871 / 056 137 |
| 6− | 11872 / 056 140 | 11873 / 056 141 | 11874 / 056 142 | 11875 / 056 143 | 11876 / 056 144 | 11877 / 056 145 | 11878 / 056 146 | 11879 / 056 147 | 11880 / 056 150 | 11881 / 056 151 | 11882 / 056 152 | 11883 / 056 153 | 11884 / 056 154 | 11885 / 056 155 | 11886 / 056 156 | 11887 / 056 157 |
| 7− | 11888 / 056 160 | 11889 / 056 161 | 11890 / 056 162 | 11891 / 056 163 | 11892 / 056 164 | 11893 / 056 165 | 11894 / 056 166 | 11895 / 056 167 | 11896 / 056 170 | 11897 / 056 171 | 11898 / 056 172 | 11899 / 056 173 | 11900 / 056 174 | 11901 / 056 175 | 11902 / 056 176 | 11903 / 056 177 |
| 8− | 11904 / 056 200 | 11905 / 056 201 | 11906 / 056 202 | 11907 / 056 203 | 11908 / 056 204 | 11909 / 056 205 | 11910 / 056 206 | 11911 / 056 207 | 11912 / 056 210 | 11913 / 056 211 | 11914 / 056 212 | 11915 / 056 213 | 11916 / 056 214 | 11917 / 056 215 | 11918 / 056 216 | 11919 / 056 217 |
| 9− | 11920 / 056 220 | 11921 / 056 221 | 11922 / 056 222 | 11923 / 056 223 | 11924 / 056 224 | 11925 / 056 225 | 11926 / 056 226 | 11927 / 056 227 | 11928 / 056 230 | 11929 / 056 231 | 11930 / 056 232 | 11931 / 056 233 | 11932 / 056 234 | 11933 / 056 235 | 11934 / 056 236 | 11935 / 056 237 |
| A− | 11936 / 056 240 | 11937 / 056 241 | 11938 / 056 242 | 11939 / 056 243 | 11940 / 056 244 | 11941 / 056 245 | 11942 / 056 246 | 11943 / 056 247 | 11944 / 056 250 | 11945 / 056 251 | 11946 / 056 252 | 11947 / 056 253 | 11948 / 056 254 | 11949 / 056 255 | 11950 / 056 256 | 11951 / 056 257 |
| B− | 11952 / 056 260 | 11953 / 056 261 | 11954 / 056 262 | 11955 / 056 263 | 11956 / 056 264 | 11957 / 056 265 | 11958 / 056 266 | 11959 / 056 267 | 11960 / 056 270 | 11961 / 056 271 | 11962 / 056 272 | 11963 / 056 273 | 11964 / 056 274 | 11965 / 056 275 | 11966 / 056 276 | 11967 / 056 277 |
| C− | 11968 / 056 300 | 11969 / 056 301 | 11970 / 056 302 | 11971 / 056 303 | 11972 / 056 304 | 11973 / 056 305 | 11974 / 056 306 | 11975 / 056 307 | 11976 / 056 310 | 11977 / 056 311 | 11978 / 056 312 | 11979 / 056 313 | 11980 / 056 314 | 11981 / 056 315 | 11982 / 056 316 | 11983 / 056 317 |
| D− | 11984 / 056 320 | 11985 / 056 321 | 11986 / 056 322 | 11987 / 056 323 | 11988 / 056 324 | 11989 / 056 325 | 11990 / 056 326 | 11991 / 056 327 | 11992 / 056 330 | 11993 / 056 331 | 11994 / 056 332 | 11995 / 056 333 | 11996 / 056 334 | 11997 / 056 335 | 11998 / 056 336 | 11999 / 056 337 |
| E− | 12000 / 056 340 | 12001 / 056 341 | 12002 / 056 342 | 12003 / 056 343 | 12004 / 056 344 | 12005 / 056 345 | 12006 / 056 346 | 12007 / 056 347 | 12008 / 056 350 | 12009 / 056 351 | 12010 / 056 352 | 12011 / 056 353 | 12012 / 056 354 | 12013 / 056 355 | 12014 / 056 356 | 12015 / 056 357 |
| F− | 12016 / 056 360 | 12017 / 056 361 | 12018 / 056 362 | 12019 / 056 363 | 12020 / 056 364 | 12021 / 056 365 | 12022 / 056 366 | 12023 / 056 367 | 12024 / 056 370 | 12025 / 056 371 | 12026 / 056 372 | 12027 / 056 373 | 12028 / 056 374 | 12029 / 056 375 | 12030 / 056 376 | 12031 / 056 377 |

DECIMAL

 DECIMAL

OCTAL

**DECIMAL** | 11776 | **BINARY** | 0010 1110 | **DECIMAL** | 11776 | **HEXADECIMAL** ②E 2E **OCTAL** | 056 000

FOURTH HEX DIGIT → ② ← THIRD HEX DIGIT

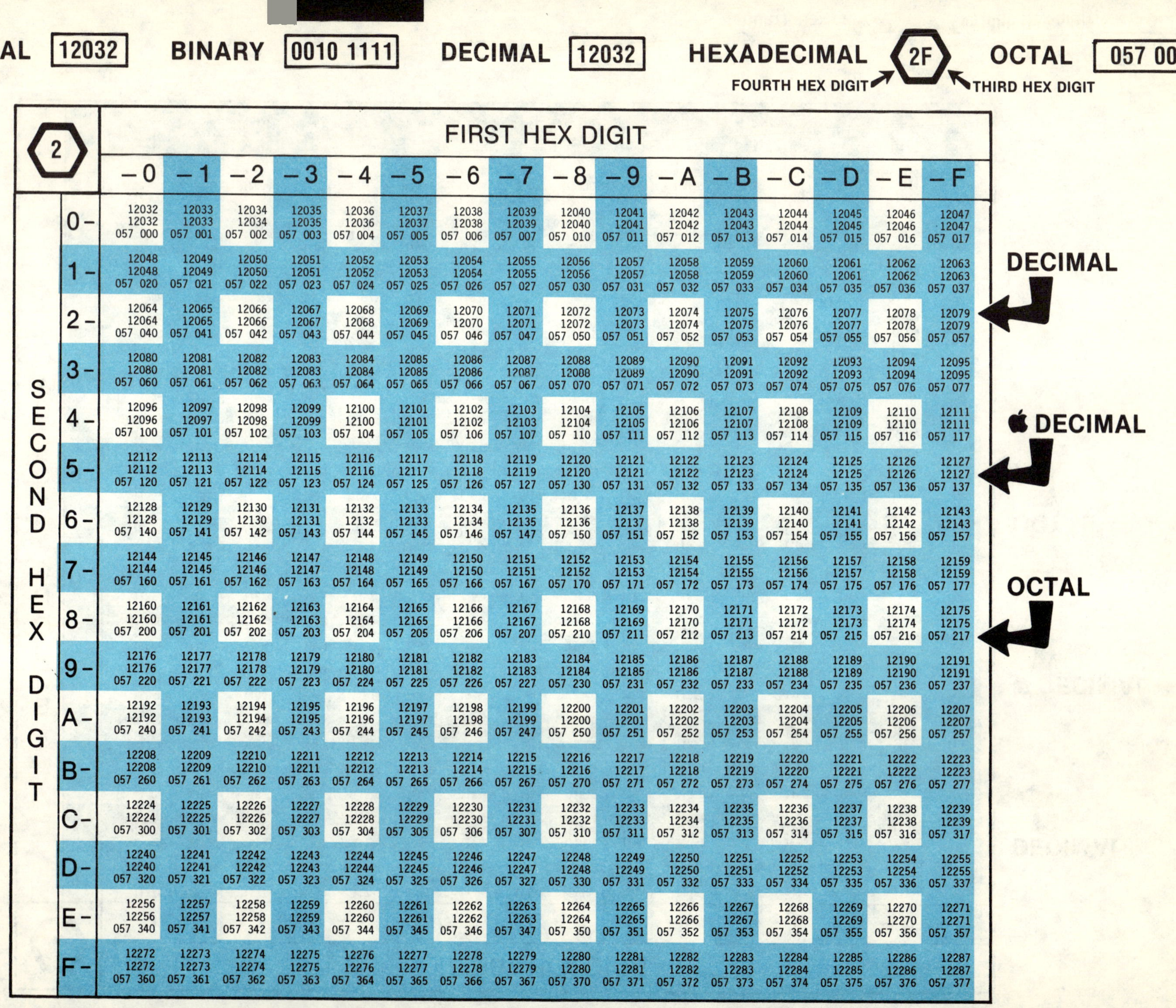

 DECIMAL  12032    BINARY  0010 1111    DECIMAL  12032    HEXADECIMAL  2F    OCTAL  057 000

FOURTH HEX DIGIT → 2F ← THIRD HEX DIGIT

FIRST HEX DIGIT — SECOND HEX DIGIT — OCTAL / DECIMAL

Each cell shows the decimal value over the octal value.

| 2 | −0 | −1 | −2 | −3 | −4 | −5 | −6 | −7 | −8 | −9 | −A | −B | −C | −D | −E | −F |
|---|---|---|---|---|---|---|---|---|---|---|---|---|---|---|---|---|
| 0- | 12032 / 057 000 | 12033 / 057 001 | 12034 / 057 002 | 12035 / 057 003 | 12036 / 057 004 | 12037 / 057 005 | 12038 / 057 006 | 12039 / 057 007 | 12040 / 057 010 | 12041 / 057 011 | 12042 / 057 012 | 12043 / 057 013 | 12044 / 057 014 | 12045 / 057 015 | 12046 / 057 016 | 12047 / 057 017 |
| 1- | 12048 / 057 020 | 12049 / 057 021 | 12050 / 057 022 | 12051 / 057 023 | 12052 / 057 024 | 12053 / 057 025 | 12054 / 057 026 | 12055 / 057 027 | 12056 / 057 030 | 12057 / 057 031 | 12058 / 057 032 | 12059 / 057 033 | 12060 / 057 034 | 12061 / 057 035 | 12062 / 057 036 | 12063 / 057 037 |
| 2- | 12064 / 057 040 | 12065 / 057 041 | 12066 / 057 042 | 12067 / 057 043 | 12068 / 057 044 | 12069 / 057 045 | 12070 / 057 046 | 12071 / 057 047 | 12072 / 057 050 | 12073 / 057 051 | 12074 / 057 052 | 12075 / 057 053 | 12076 / 057 054 | 12077 / 057 055 | 12078 / 057 056 | 12079 / 057 057 |
| 3- | 12080 / 057 060 | 12081 / 057 061 | 12082 / 057 062 | 12083 / 057 063 | 12084 / 057 064 | 12085 / 057 065 | 12086 / 057 066 | 12087 / 057 067 | 12088 / 057 070 | 12089 / 057 071 | 12090 / 057 072 | 12091 / 057 073 | 12092 / 057 074 | 12093 / 057 075 | 12094 / 057 076 | 12095 / 057 077 |
| 4- | 12096 / 057 100 | 12097 / 057 101 | 12098 / 057 102 | 12099 / 057 103 | 12100 / 057 104 | 12101 / 057 105 | 12102 / 057 106 | 12103 / 057 107 | 12104 / 057 110 | 12105 / 057 111 | 12106 / 057 112 | 12107 / 057 113 | 12108 / 057 114 | 12109 / 057 115 | 12110 / 057 116 | 12111 / 057 117 |
| 5- | 12112 / 057 120 | 12113 / 057 121 | 12114 / 057 122 | 12115 / 057 123 | 12116 / 057 124 | 12117 / 057 125 | 12118 / 057 126 | 12119 / 057 127 | 12120 / 057 130 | 12121 / 057 131 | 12122 / 057 132 | 12123 / 057 133 | 12124 / 057 134 | 12125 / 057 135 | 12126 / 057 136 | 12127 / 057 137 |
| 6- | 12128 / 057 140 | 12129 / 057 141 | 12130 / 057 142 | 12131 / 057 143 | 12132 / 057 144 | 12133 / 057 145 | 12134 / 057 146 | 12135 / 057 147 | 12136 / 057 150 | 12137 / 057 151 | 12138 / 057 152 | 12139 / 057 153 | 12140 / 057 154 | 12141 / 057 155 | 12142 / 057 156 | 12143 / 057 157 |
| 7- | 12144 / 057 160 | 12145 / 057 161 | 12146 / 057 162 | 12147 / 057 163 | 12148 / 057 164 | 12149 / 057 165 | 12150 / 057 166 | 12151 / 057 167 | 12152 / 057 170 | 12153 / 057 171 | 12154 / 057 172 | 12155 / 057 173 | 12156 / 057 174 | 12157 / 057 175 | 12158 / 057 176 | 12159 / 057 177 |
| 8- | 12160 / 057 200 | 12161 / 057 201 | 12162 / 057 202 | 12163 / 057 203 | 12164 / 057 204 | 12165 / 057 205 | 12166 / 057 206 | 12167 / 057 207 | 12168 / 057 210 | 12169 / 057 211 | 12170 / 057 212 | 12171 / 057 213 | 12172 / 057 214 | 12173 / 057 215 | 12174 / 057 216 | 12175 / 057 217 |
| 9- | 12176 / 057 220 | 12177 / 057 221 | 12178 / 057 222 | 12179 / 057 223 | 12180 / 057 224 | 12181 / 057 225 | 12182 / 057 226 | 12183 / 057 227 | 12184 / 057 230 | 12185 / 057 231 | 12186 / 057 232 | 12187 / 057 233 | 12188 / 057 234 | 12189 / 057 235 | 12190 / 057 236 | 12191 / 057 237 |
| A- | 12192 / 057 240 | 12193 / 057 241 | 12194 / 057 242 | 12195 / 057 243 | 12196 / 057 244 | 12197 / 057 245 | 12198 / 057 246 | 12199 / 057 247 | 12200 / 057 250 | 12201 / 057 251 | 12202 / 057 252 | 12203 / 057 253 | 12204 / 057 254 | 12205 / 057 255 | 12206 / 057 256 | 12207 / 057 257 |
| B- | 12208 / 057 260 | 12209 / 057 261 | 12210 / 057 262 | 12211 / 057 263 | 12212 / 057 264 | 12213 / 057 265 | 12214 / 057 266 | 12215 / 057 267 | 12216 / 057 270 | 12217 / 057 271 | 12218 / 057 272 | 12219 / 057 273 | 12220 / 057 274 | 12221 / 057 275 | 12222 / 057 276 | 12223 / 057 277 |
| C- | 12224 / 057 300 | 12225 / 057 301 | 12226 / 057 302 | 12227 / 057 303 | 12228 / 057 304 | 12229 / 057 305 | 12230 / 057 306 | 12231 / 057 307 | 12232 / 057 310 | 12233 / 057 311 | 12234 / 057 312 | 12235 / 057 313 | 12236 / 057 314 | 12237 / 057 315 | 12238 / 057 316 | 12239 / 057 317 |
| D- | 12240 / 057 320 | 12241 / 057 321 | 12242 / 057 322 | 12243 / 057 323 | 12244 / 057 324 | 12245 / 057 325 | 12246 / 057 326 | 12247 / 057 327 | 12248 / 057 330 | 12249 / 057 331 | 12250 / 057 332 | 12251 / 057 333 | 12252 / 057 334 | 12253 / 057 335 | 12254 / 057 336 | 12255 / 057 337 |
| E- | 12256 / 057 340 | 12257 / 057 341 | 12258 / 057 342 | 12259 / 057 343 | 12260 / 057 344 | 12261 / 057 345 | 12262 / 057 346 | 12263 / 057 347 | 12264 / 057 350 | 12265 / 057 351 | 12266 / 057 352 | 12267 / 057 353 | 12268 / 057 354 | 12269 / 057 355 | 12270 / 057 356 | 12271 / 057 357 |
| F- | 12272 / 057 360 | 12273 / 057 361 | 12274 / 057 362 | 12275 / 057 363 | 12276 / 057 364 | 12277 / 057 365 | 12278 / 057 366 | 12279 / 057 367 | 12280 / 057 370 | 12281 / 057 371 | 12282 / 057 372 | 12283 / 057 373 | 12284 / 057 374 | 12285 / 057 375 | 12286 / 057 376 | 12287 / 057 377 |

SECOND HEX DIGIT

| | −0 | −1 | −2 | −3 | −4 | −5 | −6 | −7 | −8 | −9 | −A | −B | −C | −D | −E | −F |
|---|---|---|---|---|---|---|---|---|---|---|---|---|---|---|---|---|
| 0− | 12288<br>12288<br>060 000 | 12289<br>12289<br>060 001 | 12290<br>12290<br>060 002 | 12291<br>12291<br>060 003 | 12292<br>12292<br>060 004 | 12293<br>12293<br>060 005 | 12294<br>12294<br>060 006 | 12295<br>12295<br>060 007 | 12296<br>12296<br>060 010 | 12297<br>12297<br>060 011 | 12298<br>12298<br>060 012 | 12299<br>12299<br>060 013 | 12300<br>12300<br>060 014 | 12301<br>12301<br>060 015 | 12302<br>12302<br>060 016 | 12303<br>12303<br>060 017 |
| 1− | 12304<br>12304<br>060 020 | 12305<br>12305<br>060 021 | 12306<br>12306<br>060 022 | 12307<br>12307<br>060 023 | 12308<br>12308<br>060 024 | 12309<br>12309<br>060 025 | 12310<br>12310<br>060 026 | 12311<br>12311<br>060 027 | 12312<br>12312<br>060 030 | 12313<br>12313<br>060 031 | 12314<br>12314<br>060 032 | 12315<br>12315<br>060 033 | 12316<br>12316<br>060 034 | 12317<br>12317<br>060 035 | 12318<br>12318<br>060 036 | 12319<br>12319<br>060 037 |
| 2− | 12320<br>12320<br>060 040 | 12321<br>12321<br>060 041 | 12322<br>12322<br>060 042 | 12323<br>12323<br>060 043 | 12324<br>12324<br>060 044 | 12325<br>12325<br>060 045 | 12326<br>12326<br>060 046 | 12327<br>12327<br>060 047 | 12328<br>12328<br>060 050 | 12329<br>12329<br>060 051 | 12330<br>12330<br>060 052 | 12331<br>12331<br>060 053 | 12332<br>12332<br>060 054 | 12333<br>12333<br>060 055 | 12334<br>12334<br>060 056 | 12335<br>12335<br>060 057 |
| 3− | 12336<br>12336<br>060 060 | 12337<br>12337<br>060 061 | 12338<br>12338<br>060 062 | 12339<br>12339<br>060 063 | 12340<br>12340<br>060 064 | 12341<br>12341<br>060 065 | 12342<br>12342<br>060 066 | 12343<br>12343<br>060 067 | 12344<br>12344<br>060 070 | 12345<br>12345<br>060 071 | 12346<br>12346<br>060 072 | 12347<br>12347<br>060 073 | 12348<br>12348<br>060 074 | 12349<br>12349<br>060 075 | 12350<br>12350<br>060 076 | 12351<br>12351<br>060 077 |
| 4− | 12352<br>12352<br>060 100 | 12353<br>12353<br>060 101 | 12354<br>12354<br>060 102 | 12355<br>12355<br>060 103 | 12356<br>12356<br>060 104 | 12357<br>12357<br>060 105 | 12358<br>12358<br>060 106 | 12359<br>12359<br>060 107 | 12360<br>12360<br>060 110 | 12361<br>12361<br>060 111 | 12362<br>12362<br>060 112 | 12363<br>12363<br>060 113 | 12364<br>12364<br>060 114 | 12365<br>12365<br>060 115 | 12366<br>12366<br>060 116 | 12367<br>12367<br>060 117 |
| 5− | 12368<br>12368<br>060 120 | 12369<br>12369<br>060 121 | 12370<br>12370<br>060 122 | 12371<br>12371<br>060 123 | 12372<br>12372<br>060 124 | 12373<br>12373<br>060 125 | 12374<br>12374<br>060 126 | 12375<br>12375<br>060 127 | 12376<br>12376<br>060 130 | 12377<br>12377<br>060 131 | 12378<br>12378<br>060 132 | 12379<br>12379<br>060 133 | 12380<br>12380<br>060 134 | 12381<br>12381<br>060 135 | 12382<br>12382<br>060 136 | 12383<br>12383<br>060 137 |
| 6− | 12384<br>12384<br>060 140 | 12385<br>12385<br>060 141 | 12386<br>12386<br>060 142 | 12387<br>12387<br>060 143 | 12388<br>12388<br>060 144 | 12389<br>12389<br>060 145 | 12390<br>12390<br>060 146 | 12391<br>12391<br>060 147 | 12392<br>12392<br>060 150 | 12393<br>12393<br>060 151 | 12394<br>12394<br>060 152 | 12395<br>12395<br>060 153 | 12396<br>12396<br>060 154 | 12397<br>12397<br>060 155 | 12398<br>12398<br>060 156 | 12399<br>12399<br>060 157 |
| 7− | 12400<br>12400<br>060 160 | 12401<br>12401<br>060 161 | 12402<br>12402<br>060 162 | 12403<br>12403<br>060 163 | 12404<br>12404<br>060 164 | 12405<br>12405<br>060 165 | 12406<br>12406<br>060 166 | 12407<br>12407<br>060 167 | 12408<br>12408<br>060 170 | 12409<br>12409<br>060 171 | 12410<br>12410<br>060 172 | 12411<br>12411<br>060 173 | 12412<br>12412<br>060 174 | 12413<br>12413<br>060 175 | 12414<br>12414<br>060 176 | 12415<br>12415<br>060 177 |
| 8− | 12416<br>12416<br>060 200 | 12417<br>12417<br>060 201 | 12418<br>12418<br>060 202 | 12419<br>12419<br>060 203 | 12420<br>12420<br>060 204 | 12421<br>12421<br>060 205 | 12422<br>12422<br>060 206 | 12423<br>12423<br>060 207 | 12424<br>12424<br>060 210 | 12425<br>12425<br>060 211 | 12426<br>12426<br>060 212 | 12427<br>12427<br>060 213 | 12428<br>12428<br>060 214 | 12429<br>12429<br>060 215 | 12430<br>12430<br>060 216 | 12431<br>12431<br>060 217 |
| 9− | 12432<br>12432<br>060 220 | 12433<br>12433<br>060 221 | 12434<br>12434<br>060 222 | 12435<br>12435<br>060 223 | 12436<br>12436<br>060 224 | 12437<br>12437<br>060 225 | 12438<br>12438<br>060 226 | 12439<br>12439<br>060 227 | 12440<br>12440<br>060 230 | 12441<br>12441<br>060 231 | 12442<br>12442<br>060 232 | 12443<br>12443<br>060 233 | 12444<br>12444<br>060 234 | 12445<br>12445<br>060 235 | 12446<br>12446<br>060 236 | 12447<br>12447<br>060 237 |
| A− | 12448<br>12448<br>060 240 | 12449<br>12449<br>060 241 | 12450<br>12450<br>060 242 | 12451<br>12451<br>060 243 | 12452<br>12452<br>060 244 | 12453<br>12453<br>060 245 | 12454<br>12454<br>060 246 | 12455<br>12455<br>060 247 | 12456<br>12456<br>060 250 | 12457<br>12457<br>060 251 | 12458<br>12458<br>060 252 | 12459<br>12459<br>060 253 | 12460<br>12460<br>060 254 | 12461<br>12461<br>060 255 | 12462<br>12462<br>060 256 | 12463<br>12463<br>060 257 |
| B− | 12464<br>12464<br>060 260 | 12465<br>12465<br>060 261 | 12466<br>12466<br>060 262 | 12467<br>12467<br>060 263 | 12468<br>12468<br>060 264 | 12469<br>12469<br>060 265 | 12470<br>12470<br>060 266 | 12471<br>12471<br>060 267 | 12472<br>12472<br>060 270 | 12473<br>12473<br>060 271 | 12474<br>12474<br>060 272 | 12475<br>12475<br>060 273 | 12476<br>12476<br>060 274 | 12477<br>12477<br>060 275 | 12478<br>12478<br>060 276 | 12479<br>12479<br>060 277 |
| C− | 12480<br>12480<br>060 300 | 12481<br>12481<br>060 301 | 12482<br>12482<br>060 302 | 12483<br>12483<br>060 303 | 12484<br>12484<br>060 304 | 12485<br>12485<br>060 305 | 12486<br>12486<br>060 306 | 12487<br>12487<br>060 307 | 12488<br>12488<br>060 310 | 12489<br>12489<br>060 311 | 12490<br>12490<br>060 312 | 12491<br>12491<br>060 313 | 12492<br>12492<br>060 314 | 12493<br>12493<br>060 315 | 12494<br>12494<br>060 316 | 12495<br>12495<br>060 317 |
| D− | 12496<br>12496<br>060 320 | 12497<br>12497<br>060 321 | 12498<br>12498<br>060 322 | 12499<br>12499<br>060 323 | 12500<br>12500<br>060 324 | 12501<br>12501<br>060 325 | 12502<br>12502<br>060 326 | 12503<br>12503<br>060 327 | 12504<br>12504<br>060 330 | 12505<br>12505<br>060 331 | 12506<br>12506<br>060 332 | 12507<br>12507<br>060 333 | 12508<br>12508<br>060 334 | 12509<br>12509<br>060 335 | 12510<br>12510<br>060 336 | 12511<br>12511<br>060 337 |
| E− | 12512<br>12512<br>060 340 | 12513<br>12513<br>060 341 | 12514<br>12514<br>060 342 | 12515<br>12515<br>060 343 | 12516<br>12516<br>060 344 | 12517<br>12517<br>060 345 | 12518<br>12518<br>060 346 | 12519<br>12519<br>060 347 | 12520<br>12520<br>060 350 | 12521<br>12521<br>060 351 | 12522<br>12522<br>060 352 | 12523<br>12523<br>060 353 | 12524<br>12524<br>060 354 | 12525<br>12525<br>060 355 | 12526<br>12526<br>060 356 | 12527<br>12527<br>060 357 |
| F− | 12528<br>12528<br>060 360 | 12529<br>12529<br>060 361 | 12530<br>12530<br>060 362 | 12531<br>12531<br>060 363 | 12532<br>12532<br>060 364 | 12533<br>12533<br>060 365 | 12534<br>12534<br>060 366 | 12535<br>12535<br>060 367 | 12536<br>12536<br>060 370 | 12537<br>12537<br>060 371 | 12538<br>12538<br>060 372 | 12539<br>12539<br>060 373 | 12540<br>12540<br>060 374 | 12541<br>12541<br>060 375 | 12542<br>12542<br>060 376 | 12543<br>12543<br>060 377 |

DECIMAL · DECIMAL · OCTAL

 DECIMAL  12288    BINARY  0011 0000    DECIMAL  12288    HEXADECIMAL  ⬡30  OCTAL  060 000

FOURTH HEX DIGIT →  ← THIRD HEX DIGIT

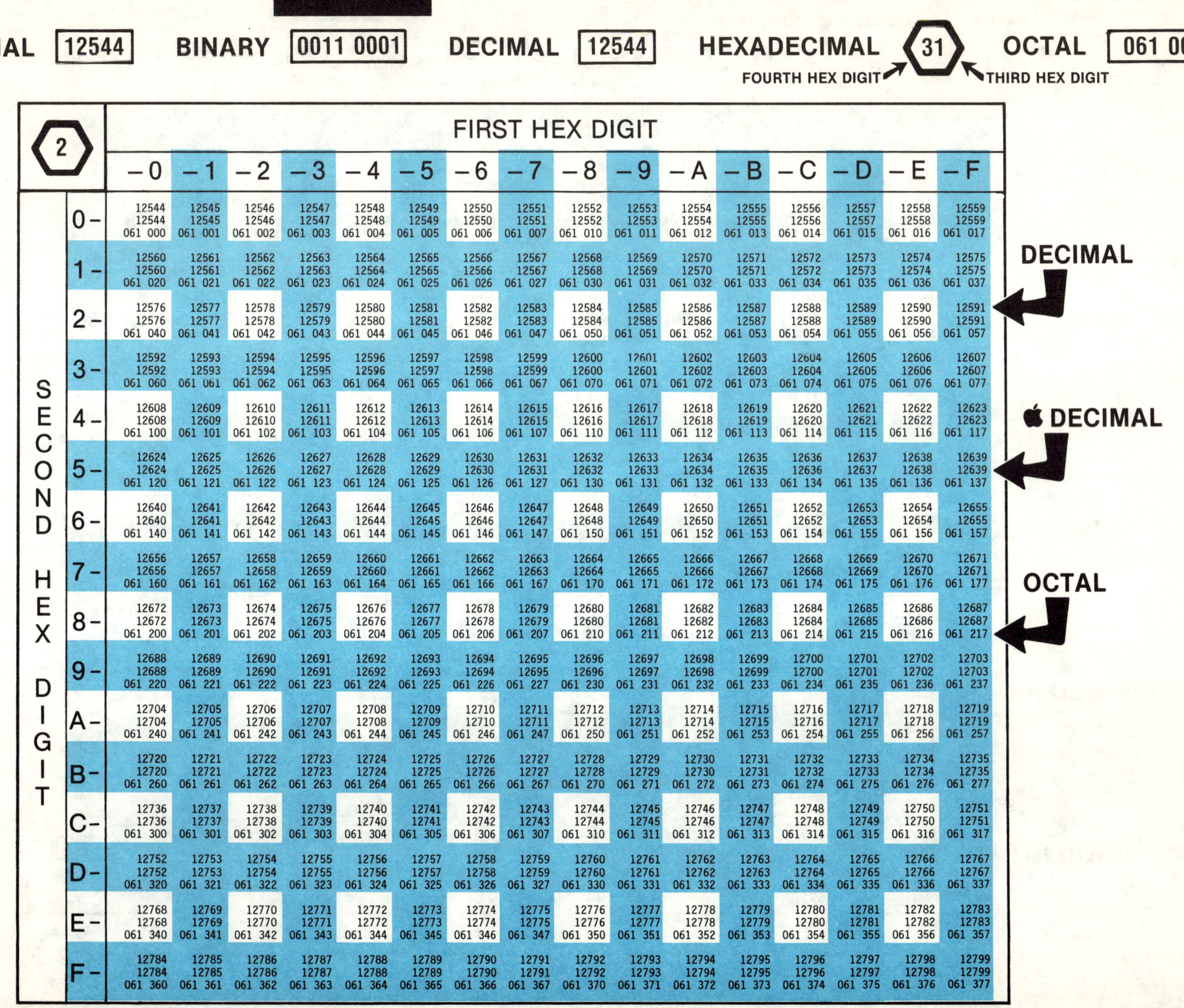



FIRST HEX DIGIT

| 2 | −0 | −1 | −2 | −3 | −4 | −5 | −6 | −7 | −8 | −9 | −A | −B | −C | −D | −E | −F |
|---|---|---|---|---|---|---|---|---|---|---|---|---|---|---|---|---|
| 0− | 12544<br>12544<br>061 000 | 12545<br>12545<br>061 001 | 12546<br>12546<br>061 002 | 12547<br>12547<br>061 003 | 12548<br>12548<br>061 004 | 12549<br>12549<br>061 005 | 12550<br>12550<br>061 006 | 12551<br>12551<br>061 007 | 12552<br>12552<br>061 010 | 12553<br>12553<br>061 011 | 12554<br>12554<br>061 012 | 12555<br>12555<br>061 013 | 12556<br>12556<br>061 014 | 12557<br>12557<br>061 015 | 12558<br>12558<br>061 016 | 12559<br>12559<br>061 017 |
| 1− | 12560<br>12560<br>061 020 | 12561<br>12561<br>061 021 | 12562<br>12562<br>061 022 | 12563<br>12563<br>061 023 | 12564<br>12564<br>061 024 | 12565<br>12565<br>061 025 | 12566<br>12566<br>061 026 | 12567<br>12567<br>061 027 | 12568<br>12568<br>061 030 | 12569<br>12569<br>061 031 | 12570<br>12570<br>061 032 | 12571<br>12571<br>061 033 | 12572<br>12572<br>061 034 | 12573<br>12573<br>061 035 | 12574<br>12574<br>061 036 | 12575<br>12575<br>061 037 |
| 2− | 12576<br>12576<br>061 040 | 12577<br>12577<br>061 041 | 12578<br>12578<br>061 042 | 12579<br>12579<br>061 043 | 12580<br>12580<br>061 044 | 12581<br>12581<br>061 045 | 12582<br>12582<br>061 046 | 12583<br>12583<br>061 047 | 12584<br>12584<br>061 050 | 12585<br>12585<br>061 051 | 12586<br>12586<br>061 052 | 12587<br>12587<br>061 053 | 12588<br>12588<br>061 054 | 12589<br>12589<br>061 055 | 12590<br>12590<br>061 056 | 12591<br>12591<br>061 057 |
| 3− | 12592<br>12592<br>061 060 | 12593<br>12593<br>061 061 | 12594<br>12594<br>061 062 | 12595<br>12595<br>061 063 | 12596<br>12596<br>061 064 | 12597<br>12597<br>061 065 | 12598<br>12598<br>061 066 | 12599<br>12599<br>061 067 | 12600<br>12600<br>061 070 | 12601<br>12601<br>061 071 | 12602<br>12602<br>061 072 | 12603<br>12603<br>061 073 | 12604<br>12604<br>061 074 | 12605<br>12605<br>061 075 | 12606<br>12606<br>061 076 | 12607<br>12607<br>061 077 |
| 4− | 12608<br>12608<br>061 100 | 12609<br>12609<br>061 101 | 12610<br>12610<br>061 102 | 12611<br>12611<br>061 103 | 12612<br>12612<br>061 104 | 12613<br>12613<br>061 105 | 12614<br>12614<br>061 106 | 12615<br>12615<br>061 107 | 12616<br>12616<br>061 110 | 12617<br>12617<br>061 111 | 12618<br>12618<br>061 112 | 12619<br>12619<br>061 113 | 12620<br>12620<br>061 114 | 12621<br>12621<br>061 115 | 12622<br>12622<br>061 116 | 12623<br>12623<br>061 117 |
| 5− | 12624<br>12624<br>061 120 | 12625<br>12625<br>061 121 | 12626<br>12626<br>061 122 | 12627<br>12627<br>061 123 | 12628<br>12628<br>061 124 | 12629<br>12629<br>061 125 | 12630<br>12630<br>061 126 | 12631<br>12631<br>061 127 | 12632<br>12632<br>061 130 | 12633<br>12633<br>061 131 | 12634<br>12634<br>061 132 | 12635<br>12635<br>061 133 | 12636<br>12636<br>061 134 | 12637<br>12637<br>061 135 | 12638<br>12638<br>061 136 | 12639<br>12639<br>061 137 |
| 6− | 12640<br>12640<br>061 140 | 12641<br>12641<br>061 141 | 12642<br>12642<br>061 142 | 12643<br>12643<br>061 143 | 12644<br>12644<br>061 144 | 12645<br>12645<br>061 145 | 12646<br>12646<br>061 146 | 12647<br>12647<br>061 147 | 12648<br>12648<br>061 150 | 12649<br>12649<br>061 151 | 12650<br>12650<br>061 152 | 12651<br>12651<br>061 153 | 12652<br>12652<br>061 154 | 12653<br>12653<br>061 155 | 12654<br>12654<br>061 156 | 12655<br>12655<br>061 157 |
| 7− | 12656<br>12656<br>061 160 | 12657<br>12657<br>061 161 | 12658<br>12658<br>061 162 | 12659<br>12659<br>061 163 | 12660<br>12660<br>061 164 | 12661<br>12661<br>061 165 | 12662<br>12662<br>061 166 | 12663<br>12663<br>061 167 | 12664<br>12664<br>061 170 | 12665<br>12665<br>061 171 | 12666<br>12666<br>061 172 | 12667<br>12667<br>061 173 | 12668<br>12668<br>061 174 | 12669<br>12669<br>061 175 | 12670<br>12670<br>061 176 | 12671<br>12671<br>061 177 |
| 8− | 12672<br>12672<br>061 200 | 12673<br>12673<br>061 201 | 12674<br>12674<br>061 202 | 12675<br>12675<br>061 203 | 12676<br>12676<br>061 204 | 12677<br>12677<br>061 205 | 12678<br>12678<br>061 206 | 12679<br>12679<br>061 207 | 12680<br>12680<br>061 210 | 12681<br>12681<br>061 211 | 12682<br>12682<br>061 212 | 12683<br>12683<br>061 213 | 12684<br>12684<br>061 214 | 12685<br>12685<br>061 215 | 12686<br>12686<br>061 216 | 12687<br>12687<br>061 217 |
| 9− | 12688<br>12688<br>061 220 | 12689<br>12689<br>061 221 | 12690<br>12690<br>061 222 | 12691<br>12691<br>061 223 | 12692<br>12692<br>061 224 | 12693<br>12693<br>061 225 | 12694<br>12694<br>061 226 | 12695<br>12695<br>061 227 | 12696<br>12696<br>061 230 | 12697<br>12697<br>061 231 | 12698<br>12698<br>061 232 | 12699<br>12699<br>061 233 | 12700<br>12700<br>061 234 | 12701<br>12701<br>061 235 | 12702<br>12702<br>061 236 | 12703<br>12703<br>061 237 |
| A− | 12704<br>12704<br>061 240 | 12705<br>12705<br>061 241 | 12706<br>12706<br>061 242 | 12707<br>12707<br>061 243 | 12708<br>12708<br>061 244 | 12709<br>12709<br>061 245 | 12710<br>12710<br>061 246 | 12711<br>12711<br>061 247 | 12712<br>12712<br>061 250 | 12713<br>12713<br>061 251 | 12714<br>12714<br>061 252 | 12715<br>12715<br>061 253 | 12716<br>12716<br>061 254 | 12717<br>12717<br>061 255 | 12718<br>12718<br>061 256 | 12719<br>12719<br>061 257 |
| B− | 12720<br>12720<br>061 260 | 12721<br>12721<br>061 261 | 12722<br>12722<br>061 262 | 12723<br>12723<br>061 263 | 12724<br>12724<br>061 264 | 12725<br>12725<br>061 265 | 12726<br>12726<br>061 266 | 12727<br>12727<br>061 267 | 12728<br>12728<br>061 270 | 12729<br>12729<br>061 271 | 12730<br>12730<br>061 272 | 12731<br>12731<br>061 273 | 12732<br>12732<br>061 274 | 12733<br>12733<br>061 275 | 12734<br>12734<br>061 276 | 12735<br>12735<br>061 277 |
| C− | 12736<br>12736<br>061 300 | 12737<br>12737<br>061 301 | 12738<br>12738<br>061 302 | 12739<br>12739<br>061 303 | 12740<br>12740<br>061 304 | 12741<br>12741<br>061 305 | 12742<br>12742<br>061 306 | 12743<br>12743<br>061 307 | 12744<br>12744<br>061 310 | 12745<br>12745<br>061 311 | 12746<br>12746<br>061 312 | 12747<br>12747<br>061 313 | 12748<br>12748<br>061 314 | 12749<br>12749<br>061 315 | 12750<br>12750<br>061 316 | 12751<br>12751<br>061 317 |
| D− | 12752<br>12752<br>061 320 | 12753<br>12753<br>061 321 | 12754<br>12754<br>061 322 | 12755<br>12755<br>061 323 | 12756<br>12756<br>061 324 | 12757<br>12757<br>061 325 | 12758<br>12758<br>061 326 | 12759<br>12759<br>061 327 | 12760<br>12760<br>061 330 | 12761<br>12761<br>061 331 | 12762<br>12762<br>061 332 | 12763<br>12763<br>061 333 | 12764<br>12764<br>061 334 | 12765<br>12765<br>061 335 | 12766<br>12766<br>061 336 | 12767<br>12767<br>061 337 |
| E− | 12768<br>12768<br>061 340 | 12769<br>12769<br>061 341 | 12770<br>12770<br>061 342 | 12771<br>12771<br>061 343 | 12772<br>12772<br>061 344 | 12773<br>12773<br>061 345 | 12774<br>12774<br>061 346 | 12775<br>12775<br>061 347 | 12776<br>12776<br>061 350 | 12777<br>12777<br>061 351 | 12778<br>12778<br>061 352 | 12779<br>12779<br>061 353 | 12780<br>12780<br>061 354 | 12781<br>12781<br>061 355 | 12782<br>12782<br>061 356 | 12783<br>12783<br>061 357 |
| F− | 12784<br>12784<br>061 360 | 12785<br>12785<br>061 361 | 12786<br>12786<br>061 362 | 12787<br>12787<br>061 363 | 12788<br>12788<br>061 364 | 12789<br>12789<br>061 365 | 12790<br>12790<br>061 366 | 12791<br>12791<br>061 367 | 12792<br>12792<br>061 370 | 12793<br>12793<br>061 371 | 12794<br>12794<br>061 372 | 12795<br>12795<br>061 373 | 12796<br>12796<br>061 374 | 12797<br>12797<br>061 375 | 12798<br>12798<br>061 376 | 12799<br>12799<br>061 377 |

## FIRST HEX DIGIT

| SECOND HEX DIGIT | −0 | −1 | −2 | −3 | −4 | −5 | −6 | −7 | −8 | −9 | −A | −B | −C | −D | −E | −F |
|---|---|---|---|---|---|---|---|---|---|---|---|---|---|---|---|---|
| **0−** | 12800<br>12800<br>062 000 | 12801<br>12801<br>062 001 | 12802<br>12802<br>062 002 | 12803<br>12803<br>062 003 | 12804<br>12804<br>062 004 | 12805<br>12805<br>062 005 | 12806<br>12806<br>062 006 | 12807<br>12807<br>062 007 | 12808<br>12808<br>062 010 | 12809<br>12809<br>062 011 | 12810<br>12810<br>062 012 | 12811<br>12811<br>062 013 | 12812<br>12812<br>062 014 | 12813<br>12813<br>062 015 | 12814<br>12814<br>062 016 | 12815<br>12815<br>062 017 |
| **1−** | 12816<br>12816<br>062 020 | 12817<br>12817<br>062 021 | 12818<br>12818<br>062 022 | 12819<br>12819<br>062 023 | 12820<br>12820<br>062 024 | 12821<br>12821<br>062 025 | 12822<br>12822<br>062 026 | 12823<br>12823<br>062 027 | 12824<br>12824<br>062 030 | 12825<br>12825<br>062 031 | 12826<br>12826<br>062 032 | 12827<br>12827<br>062 033 | 12828<br>12828<br>062 034 | 12829<br>12829<br>062 035 | 12830<br>12830<br>062 036 | 12831<br>12831<br>062 037 |
| **2−** | 12832<br>12832<br>062 040 | 12833<br>12833<br>062 041 | 12834<br>12834<br>062 042 | 12835<br>12835<br>062 043 | 12836<br>12836<br>062 044 | 12837<br>12837<br>062 045 | 12838<br>12838<br>062 046 | 12839<br>12839<br>062 047 | 12840<br>12840<br>062 050 | 12841<br>12841<br>062 051 | 12842<br>12842<br>062 052 | 12843<br>12843<br>062 053 | 12844<br>12844<br>062 054 | 12845<br>12845<br>062 055 | 12846<br>12846<br>062 056 | 12847<br>12847<br>062 057 |
| **3−** | 12848<br>12848<br>062 060 | 12849<br>12849<br>062 061 | 12850<br>12850<br>062 062 | 12851<br>12851<br>062 063 | 12852<br>12852<br>062 064 | 12853<br>12853<br>062 065 | 12854<br>12854<br>062 066 | 12855<br>12855<br>062 067 | 12856<br>12856<br>062 070 | 12857<br>12857<br>062 071 | 12858<br>12858<br>062 072 | 12859<br>12859<br>062 073 | 12860<br>12860<br>062 074 | 12861<br>12861<br>062 075 | 12862<br>12862<br>062 076 | 12863<br>12863<br>062 077 |
| **4−** | 12864<br>12864<br>062 100 | 12865<br>12865<br>062 101 | 12866<br>12866<br>062 102 | 12867<br>12867<br>062 103 | 12868<br>12868<br>062 104 | 12869<br>12869<br>062 105 | 12870<br>12870<br>062 106 | 12871<br>12871<br>062 107 | 12872<br>12872<br>062 110 | 12873<br>12873<br>062 111 | 12874<br>12874<br>062 112 | 12875<br>12875<br>062 113 | 12876<br>12876<br>062 114 | 12877<br>12877<br>062 115 | 12878<br>12878<br>062 116 | 12879<br>12879<br>062 117 |
| **5−** | 12880<br>12880<br>062 120 | 12881<br>12881<br>062 121 | 12882<br>12882<br>062 122 | 12883<br>12883<br>062 123 | 12884<br>12884<br>062 124 | 12885<br>12885<br>062 125 | 12886<br>12886<br>062 126 | 12887<br>12887<br>062 127 | 12888<br>12888<br>062 130 | 12889<br>12889<br>062 131 | 12890<br>12890<br>062 132 | 12891<br>12891<br>062 133 | 12892<br>12892<br>062 134 | 12893<br>12893<br>062 135 | 12894<br>12894<br>062 136 | 12895<br>12895<br>062 137 |
| **6−** | 12896<br>12896<br>062 140 | 12897<br>12897<br>062 141 | 12898<br>12898<br>062 142 | 12899<br>12899<br>062 143 | 12900<br>12900<br>062 144 | 12901<br>12901<br>062 145 | 12902<br>12902<br>062 146 | 12903<br>12903<br>062 147 | 12904<br>12904<br>062 150 | 12905<br>12905<br>062 151 | 12906<br>12906<br>062 152 | 12907<br>12907<br>062 153 | 12908<br>12908<br>062 154 | 12909<br>12909<br>062 155 | 12910<br>12910<br>062 156 | 12911<br>12911<br>062 157 |
| **7−** | 12912<br>12912<br>062 160 | 12913<br>12913<br>062 161 | 12914<br>12914<br>062 162 | 12915<br>12915<br>062 163 | 12916<br>12916<br>062 164 | 12917<br>12917<br>062 165 | 12918<br>12918<br>062 166 | 12919<br>12919<br>062 167 | 12920<br>12920<br>062 170 | 12921<br>12921<br>062 171 | 12922<br>12922<br>062 172 | 12923<br>12923<br>062 173 | 12924<br>12924<br>062 174 | 12925<br>12925<br>062 175 | 12926<br>12926<br>062 176 | 12927<br>12927<br>062 177 |
| **8−** | 12928<br>12928<br>062 200 | 12929<br>12929<br>062 201 | 12930<br>12930<br>062 202 | 12931<br>12931<br>062 203 | 12932<br>12932<br>062 204 | 12933<br>12933<br>062 205 | 12934<br>12934<br>062 206 | 12935<br>12935<br>062 207 | 12936<br>12936<br>062 210 | 12937<br>12937<br>062 211 | 12938<br>12938<br>062 212 | 12939<br>12939<br>062 213 | 12940<br>12940<br>062 214 | 12941<br>12941<br>062 215 | 12942<br>12942<br>062 216 | 12943<br>12943<br>062 217 |
| **9−** | 12944<br>12944<br>062 220 | 12945<br>12945<br>062 221 | 12946<br>12946<br>062 222 | 12947<br>12947<br>062 223 | 12948<br>12948<br>062 224 | 12949<br>12949<br>062 225 | 12950<br>12950<br>062 226 | 12951<br>12951<br>062 227 | 12952<br>12952<br>062 230 | 12953<br>12953<br>062 231 | 12954<br>12954<br>062 232 | 12955<br>12955<br>062 233 | 12956<br>12956<br>062 234 | 12957<br>12957<br>062 235 | 12958<br>12958<br>062 236 | 12959<br>12959<br>062 237 |
| **A−** | 12960<br>12960<br>062 240 | 12961<br>12961<br>062 241 | 12962<br>12962<br>062 242 | 12963<br>12963<br>062 243 | 12964<br>12964<br>062 244 | 12965<br>12965<br>062 245 | 12966<br>12966<br>062 246 | 12967<br>12967<br>062 247 | 12968<br>12968<br>062 250 | 12969<br>12969<br>062 251 | 12970<br>12970<br>062 252 | 12971<br>12971<br>062 253 | 12972<br>12972<br>062 254 | 12973<br>12973<br>062 255 | 12974<br>12974<br>062 256 | 12975<br>12975<br>062 257 |
| **B−** | 12976<br>12976<br>062 260 | 12977<br>12977<br>062 261 | 12978<br>12978<br>062 262 | 12979<br>12979<br>062 263 | 12980<br>12980<br>062 264 | 12981<br>12981<br>062 265 | 12982<br>12982<br>062 266 | 12983<br>12983<br>062 267 | 12984<br>12984<br>062 270 | 12985<br>12985<br>062 271 | 12986<br>12986<br>062 272 | 12987<br>12987<br>062 273 | 12988<br>12988<br>062 274 | 12989<br>12989<br>062 275 | 12990<br>12990<br>062 276 | 12991<br>12991<br>062 277 |
| **C−** | 12992<br>12992<br>062 300 | 12993<br>12993<br>062 301 | 12994<br>12994<br>062 302 | 12995<br>12995<br>062 303 | 12996<br>12996<br>062 304 | 12997<br>12997<br>062 305 | 12998<br>12998<br>062 306 | 12999<br>12999<br>062 307 | 13000<br>13000<br>062 310 | 13001<br>13001<br>062 311 | 13002<br>13002<br>062 312 | 13003<br>13003<br>062 313 | 13004<br>13004<br>062 314 | 13005<br>13005<br>062 315 | 13006<br>13006<br>062 316 | 13007<br>13007<br>062 317 |
| **D−** | 13008<br>13008<br>062 320 | 13009<br>13009<br>062 321 | 13010<br>13010<br>062 322 | 13011<br>13011<br>062 323 | 13012<br>13012<br>062 324 | 13013<br>13013<br>062 325 | 13014<br>13014<br>062 326 | 13015<br>13015<br>062 327 | 13016<br>13016<br>062 330 | 13017<br>13017<br>062 331 | 13018<br>13018<br>062 332 | 13019<br>13019<br>062 333 | 13020<br>13020<br>062 334 | 13021<br>13021<br>062 335 | 13022<br>13022<br>062 336 | 13023<br>13023<br>062 337 |
| **E−** | 13024<br>13024<br>062 340 | 13025<br>13025<br>062 341 | 13026<br>13026<br>062 342 | 13027<br>13027<br>062 343 | 13028<br>13028<br>062 344 | 13029<br>13029<br>062 345 | 13030<br>13030<br>062 346 | 13031<br>13031<br>062 347 | 13032<br>13032<br>062 350 | 13033<br>13033<br>062 351 | 13034<br>13034<br>062 352 | 13035<br>13035<br>062 353 | 13036<br>13036<br>062 354 | 13037<br>13037<br>062 355 | 13038<br>13038<br>062 356 | 13039<br>13039<br>062 357 |
| **F−** | 13040<br>13040<br>062 360 | 13041<br>13041<br>062 361 | 13042<br>13042<br>062 362 | 13043<br>13043<br>062 363 | 13044<br>13044<br>062 364 | 13045<br>13045<br>062 365 | 13046<br>13046<br>062 366 | 13047<br>13047<br>062 367 | 13048<br>13048<br>062 370 | 13049<br>13049<br>062 371 | 13050<br>13050<br>062 372 | 13051<br>13051<br>062 373 | 13052<br>13052<br>062 374 | 13053<br>13053<br>062 375 | 13054<br>13054<br>062 376 | 13055<br>13055<br>062 377 |

DECIMAL

DECIMAL

OCTAL

 **DECIMAL** [12800]  **BINARY** [0011 0010]  **DECIMAL** [12800]  **HEXADECIMAL** (32)  **OCTAL** [062 000]

FOURTH HEX DIGIT → ← THIRD HEX DIGIT

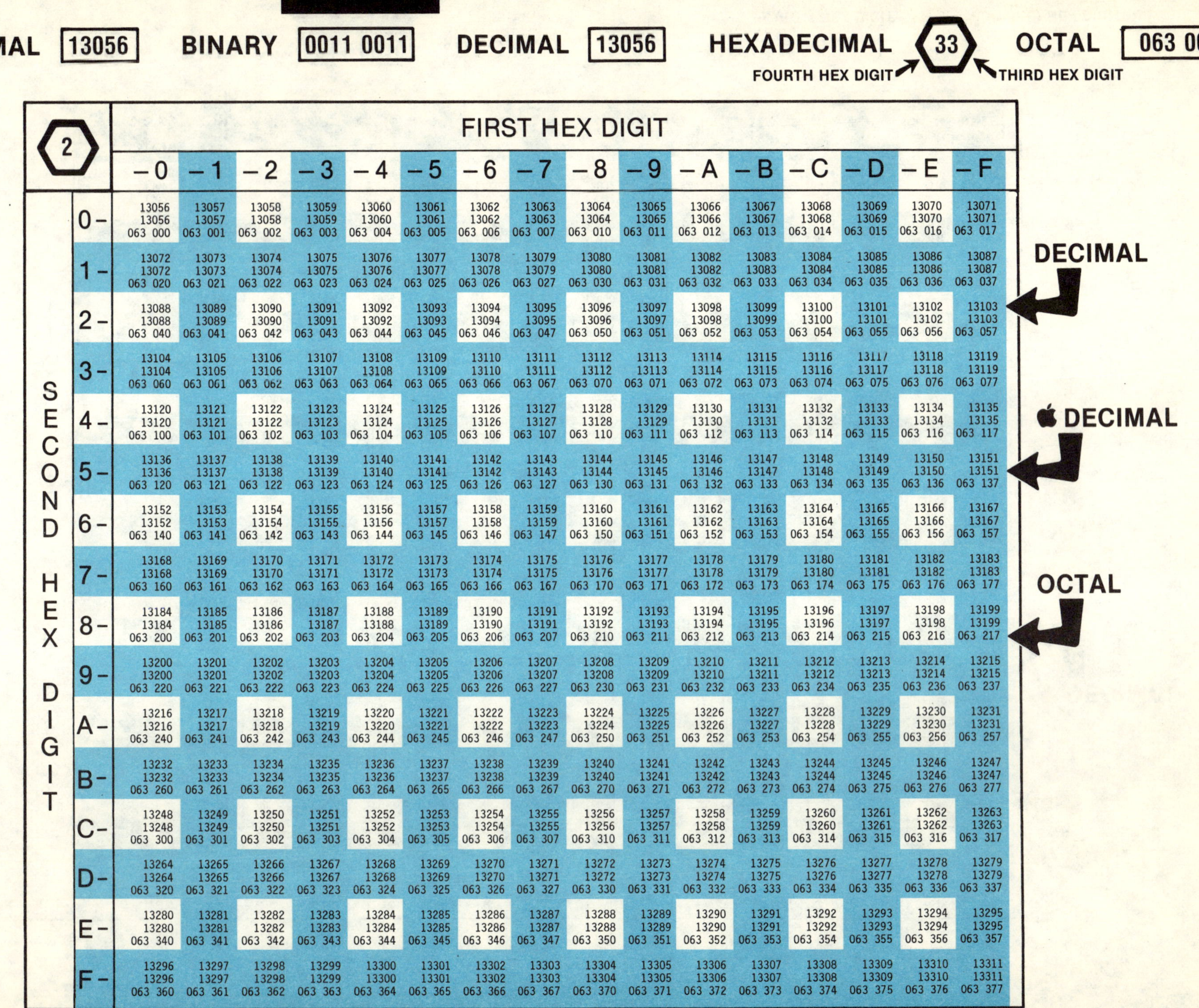

DECIMAL 13056 | BINARY 0011 0011 | DECIMAL 13056 | HEXADECIMAL 33 | OCTAL 063 000

FOURTH HEX DIGIT → ← THIRD HEX DIGIT

2

FIRST HEX DIGIT

SECOND HEX DIGIT

| | −0 | −1 | −2 | −3 | −4 | −5 | −6 | −7 | −8 | −9 | −A | −B | −C | −D | −E | −F |
|---|---|---|---|---|---|---|---|---|---|---|---|---|---|---|---|---|
| 0− | 13056<br>13056<br>063 000 | 13057<br>13057<br>063 001 | 13058<br>13058<br>063 002 | 13059<br>13059<br>063 003 | 13060<br>13060<br>063 004 | 13061<br>13061<br>063 005 | 13062<br>13062<br>063 006 | 13063<br>13063<br>063 007 | 13064<br>13064<br>063 010 | 13065<br>13065<br>063 011 | 13066<br>13066<br>063 012 | 13067<br>13067<br>063 013 | 13068<br>13068<br>063 014 | 13069<br>13069<br>063 015 | 13070<br>13070<br>063 016 | 13071<br>13071<br>063 017 |
| 1− | 13072<br>13072<br>063 020 | 13073<br>13073<br>063 021 | 13074<br>13074<br>063 022 | 13075<br>13075<br>063 023 | 13076<br>13076<br>063 024 | 13077<br>13077<br>063 025 | 13078<br>13078<br>063 026 | 13079<br>13079<br>063 027 | 13080<br>13080<br>063 030 | 13081<br>13081<br>063 031 | 13082<br>13082<br>063 032 | 13083<br>13083<br>063 033 | 13084<br>13084<br>063 034 | 13085<br>13085<br>063 035 | 13086<br>13086<br>063 036 | 13087<br>13087<br>063 037 |
| 2− | 13088<br>13088<br>063 040 | 13089<br>13089<br>063 041 | 13090<br>13090<br>063 042 | 13091<br>13091<br>063 043 | 13092<br>13092<br>063 044 | 13093<br>13093<br>063 045 | 13094<br>13094<br>063 046 | 13095<br>13095<br>063 047 | 13096<br>13096<br>063 050 | 13097<br>13097<br>063 051 | 13098<br>13098<br>063 052 | 13099<br>13099<br>063 053 | 13100<br>13100<br>063 054 | 13101<br>13101<br>063 055 | 13102<br>13102<br>063 056 | 13103<br>13103<br>063 057 |
| 3− | 13104<br>13104<br>063 060 | 13105<br>13105<br>063 061 | 13106<br>13106<br>063 062 | 13107<br>13107<br>063 063 | 13108<br>13108<br>063 064 | 13109<br>13109<br>063 065 | 13110<br>13110<br>063 066 | 13111<br>13111<br>063 067 | 13112<br>13112<br>063 070 | 13113<br>13113<br>063 071 | 13114<br>13114<br>063 072 | 13115<br>13115<br>063 073 | 13116<br>13116<br>063 074 | 13117<br>13117<br>063 075 | 13118<br>13118<br>063 076 | 13119<br>13119<br>063 077 |
| 4− | 13120<br>13120<br>063 100 | 13121<br>13121<br>063 101 | 13122<br>13122<br>063 102 | 13123<br>13123<br>063 103 | 13124<br>13124<br>063 104 | 13125<br>13125<br>063 105 | 13126<br>13126<br>063 106 | 13127<br>13127<br>063 107 | 13128<br>13128<br>063 110 | 13129<br>13129<br>063 111 | 13130<br>13130<br>063 112 | 13131<br>13131<br>063 113 | 13132<br>13132<br>063 114 | 13133<br>13133<br>063 115 | 13134<br>13134<br>063 116 | 13135<br>13135<br>063 117 |
| 5− | 13136<br>13136<br>063 120 | 13137<br>13137<br>063 121 | 13138<br>13138<br>063 122 | 13139<br>13139<br>063 123 | 13140<br>13140<br>063 124 | 13141<br>13141<br>063 125 | 13142<br>13142<br>063 126 | 13143<br>13143<br>063 127 | 13144<br>13144<br>063 130 | 13145<br>13145<br>063 131 | 13146<br>13146<br>063 132 | 13147<br>13147<br>063 133 | 13148<br>13148<br>063 134 | 13149<br>13149<br>063 135 | 13150<br>13150<br>063 136 | 13151<br>13151<br>063 137 |
| 6− | 13152<br>13152<br>063 140 | 13153<br>13153<br>063 141 | 13154<br>13154<br>063 142 | 13155<br>13155<br>063 143 | 13156<br>13156<br>063 144 | 13157<br>13157<br>063 145 | 13158<br>13158<br>063 146 | 13159<br>13159<br>063 147 | 13160<br>13160<br>063 150 | 13161<br>13161<br>063 151 | 13162<br>13162<br>063 152 | 13163<br>13163<br>063 153 | 13164<br>13164<br>063 154 | 13165<br>13165<br>063 155 | 13166<br>13166<br>063 156 | 13167<br>13167<br>063 157 |
| 7− | 13168<br>13168<br>063 160 | 13169<br>13169<br>063 161 | 13170<br>13170<br>063 162 | 13171<br>13171<br>063 163 | 13172<br>13172<br>063 164 | 13173<br>13173<br>063 165 | 13174<br>13174<br>063 166 | 13175<br>13175<br>063 167 | 13176<br>13176<br>063 170 | 13177<br>13177<br>063 171 | 13178<br>13178<br>063 172 | 13179<br>13179<br>063 173 | 13180<br>13180<br>063 174 | 13181<br>13181<br>063 175 | 13182<br>13182<br>063 176 | 13183<br>13183<br>063 177 |
| 8− | 13184<br>13184<br>063 200 | 13185<br>13185<br>063 201 | 13186<br>13186<br>063 202 | 13187<br>13187<br>063 203 | 13188<br>13188<br>063 204 | 13189<br>13189<br>063 205 | 13190<br>13190<br>063 206 | 13191<br>13191<br>063 207 | 13192<br>13192<br>063 210 | 13193<br>13193<br>063 211 | 13194<br>13194<br>063 212 | 13195<br>13195<br>063 213 | 13196<br>13196<br>063 214 | 13197<br>13197<br>063 215 | 13198<br>13198<br>063 216 | 13199<br>13199<br>063 217 |
| 9− | 13200<br>13200<br>063 220 | 13201<br>13201<br>063 221 | 13202<br>13202<br>063 222 | 13203<br>13203<br>063 223 | 13204<br>13204<br>063 224 | 13205<br>13205<br>063 225 | 13206<br>13206<br>063 226 | 13207<br>13207<br>063 227 | 13208<br>13208<br>063 230 | 13209<br>13209<br>063 231 | 13210<br>13210<br>063 232 | 13211<br>13211<br>063 233 | 13212<br>13212<br>063 234 | 13213<br>13213<br>063 235 | 13214<br>13214<br>063 236 | 13215<br>13215<br>063 237 |
| A− | 13216<br>13216<br>063 240 | 13217<br>13217<br>063 241 | 13218<br>13218<br>063 242 | 13219<br>13219<br>063 243 | 13220<br>13220<br>063 244 | 13221<br>13221<br>063 245 | 13222<br>13222<br>063 246 | 13223<br>13223<br>063 247 | 13224<br>13224<br>063 250 | 13225<br>13225<br>063 251 | 13226<br>13226<br>063 252 | 13227<br>13227<br>063 253 | 13228<br>13228<br>063 254 | 13229<br>13229<br>063 255 | 13230<br>13230<br>063 256 | 13231<br>13231<br>063 257 |
| B− | 13232<br>13232<br>063 260 | 13233<br>13233<br>063 261 | 13234<br>13234<br>063 262 | 13235<br>13235<br>063 263 | 13236<br>13236<br>063 264 | 13237<br>13237<br>063 265 | 13238<br>13238<br>063 266 | 13239<br>13239<br>063 267 | 13240<br>13240<br>063 270 | 13241<br>13241<br>063 271 | 13242<br>13242<br>063 272 | 13243<br>13243<br>063 273 | 13244<br>13244<br>063 274 | 13245<br>13245<br>063 275 | 13246<br>13246<br>063 276 | 13247<br>13247<br>063 277 |
| C− | 13248<br>13248<br>063 300 | 13249<br>13249<br>063 301 | 13250<br>13250<br>063 302 | 13251<br>13251<br>063 303 | 13252<br>13252<br>063 304 | 13253<br>13253<br>063 305 | 13254<br>13254<br>063 306 | 13255<br>13255<br>063 307 | 13256<br>13256<br>063 310 | 13257<br>13257<br>063 311 | 13258<br>13258<br>063 312 | 13259<br>13259<br>063 313 | 13260<br>13260<br>063 314 | 13261<br>13261<br>063 315 | 13262<br>13262<br>063 316 | 13263<br>13263<br>063 317 |
| D− | 13264<br>13264<br>063 320 | 13265<br>13265<br>063 321 | 13266<br>13266<br>063 322 | 13267<br>13267<br>063 323 | 13268<br>13268<br>063 324 | 13269<br>13269<br>063 325 | 13270<br>13270<br>063 326 | 13271<br>13271<br>063 327 | 13272<br>13272<br>063 330 | 13273<br>13273<br>063 331 | 13274<br>13274<br>063 332 | 13275<br>13275<br>063 333 | 13276<br>13276<br>063 334 | 13277<br>13277<br>063 335 | 13278<br>13278<br>063 336 | 13279<br>13279<br>063 337 |
| E− | 13280<br>13280<br>063 340 | 13281<br>13281<br>063 341 | 13282<br>13282<br>063 342 | 13283<br>13283<br>063 343 | 13284<br>13284<br>063 344 | 13285<br>13285<br>063 345 | 13286<br>13286<br>063 346 | 13287<br>13287<br>063 347 | 13288<br>13288<br>063 350 | 13289<br>13289<br>063 351 | 13290<br>13290<br>063 352 | 13291<br>13291<br>063 353 | 13292<br>13292<br>063 354 | 13293<br>13293<br>063 355 | 13294<br>13294<br>063 356 | 13295<br>13295<br>063 357 |
| F− | 13296<br>13296<br>063 360 | 13297<br>13297<br>063 361 | 13298<br>13298<br>063 362 | 13299<br>13299<br>063 363 | 13300<br>13300<br>063 364 | 13301<br>13301<br>063 365 | 13302<br>13302<br>063 366 | 13303<br>13303<br>063 367 | 13304<br>13304<br>063 370 | 13305<br>13305<br>063 371 | 13306<br>13306<br>063 372 | 13307<br>13307<br>063 373 | 13308<br>13308<br>063 374 | 13309<br>13309<br>063 375 | 13310<br>13310<br>063 376 | 13311<br>13311<br>063 377 |

## FIRST HEX DIGIT

Each cell lists: DECIMAL (top), DECIMAL (middle), OCTAL (bottom).

| SECOND HEX DIGIT | −0 | −1 | −2 | −3 | −4 | −5 | −6 | −7 | −8 | −9 | −A | −B | −C | −D | −E | −F |
|---|---|---|---|---|---|---|---|---|---|---|---|---|---|---|---|---|
| 0− | 13312<br>13312<br>064 000 | 13313<br>13313<br>064 001 | 13314<br>13314<br>064 002 | 13315<br>13315<br>064 003 | 13316<br>13316<br>064 004 | 13317<br>13317<br>064 005 | 13318<br>13318<br>064 006 | 13319<br>13319<br>064 007 | 13320<br>13320<br>064 010 | 13321<br>13321<br>064 011 | 13322<br>13322<br>064 012 | 13323<br>13323<br>064 013 | 13324<br>13324<br>064 014 | 13325<br>13325<br>064 015 | 13326<br>13326<br>064 016 | 13327<br>13327<br>064 017 |
| 1− | 13328<br>13328<br>064 020 | 13329<br>13329<br>064 021 | 13330<br>13330<br>064 022 | 13331<br>13331<br>064 023 | 13332<br>13332<br>064 024 | 13333<br>13333<br>064 025 | 13334<br>13334<br>064 026 | 13335<br>13335<br>064 027 | 13336<br>13336<br>064 030 | 13337<br>13337<br>064 031 | 13338<br>13338<br>064 032 | 13339<br>13339<br>064 033 | 13340<br>13340<br>064 034 | 13341<br>13341<br>064 035 | 13342<br>13342<br>064 036 | 13343<br>13343<br>064 037 |
| 2− | 13344<br>13344<br>064 040 | 13345<br>13345<br>064 041 | 13346<br>13346<br>064 042 | 13347<br>13347<br>064 043 | 13348<br>13348<br>064 044 | 13349<br>13349<br>064 045 | 13350<br>13350<br>064 046 | 13351<br>13351<br>064 047 | 13352<br>13352<br>064 050 | 13353<br>13353<br>064 051 | 13354<br>13354<br>064 052 | 13355<br>13355<br>064 053 | 13356<br>13356<br>064 054 | 13357<br>13357<br>064 055 | 13358<br>13358<br>064 056 | 13359<br>13359<br>064 057 |
| 3− | 13360<br>13360<br>064 060 | 13361<br>13361<br>064 061 | 13362<br>13362<br>064 062 | 13363<br>13363<br>064 063 | 13364<br>13364<br>064 064 | 13365<br>13365<br>064 065 | 13366<br>13366<br>064 066 | 13367<br>13367<br>064 067 | 13368<br>13368<br>064 070 | 13369<br>13369<br>064 071 | 13370<br>13370<br>064 072 | 13371<br>13371<br>064 073 | 13372<br>13372<br>064 074 | 13373<br>13373<br>064 075 | 13374<br>13374<br>064 076 | 13375<br>13375<br>064 077 |
| 4− | 13376<br>13376<br>064 100 | 13377<br>13377<br>064 101 | 13378<br>13378<br>064 102 | 13379<br>13379<br>064 103 | 13380<br>13380<br>064 104 | 13381<br>13381<br>064 105 | 13382<br>13382<br>064 106 | 13383<br>13383<br>064 107 | 13384<br>13384<br>064 110 | 13385<br>13385<br>064 111 | 13386<br>13386<br>064 112 | 13387<br>13387<br>064 113 | 13388<br>13388<br>064 114 | 13389<br>13389<br>064 115 | 13390<br>13390<br>064 116 | 13391<br>13391<br>064 117 |
| 5− | 13392<br>13392<br>064 120 | 13393<br>13393<br>064 121 | 13394<br>13394<br>064 122 | 13395<br>13395<br>064 123 | 13396<br>13396<br>064 124 | 13397<br>13397<br>064 125 | 13398<br>13398<br>064 126 | 13399<br>13399<br>064 127 | 13400<br>13400<br>064 130 | 13401<br>13401<br>064 131 | 13402<br>13402<br>064 132 | 13403<br>13403<br>064 133 | 13404<br>13404<br>064 134 | 13405<br>13405<br>064 135 | 13406<br>13406<br>064 136 | 13407<br>13407<br>064 137 |
| 6− | 13408<br>13408<br>064 140 | 13409<br>13409<br>064 141 | 13410<br>13410<br>064 142 | 13411<br>13411<br>064 143 | 13412<br>13412<br>064 144 | 13413<br>13413<br>064 145 | 13414<br>13414<br>064 146 | 13415<br>13415<br>064 147 | 13416<br>13416<br>064 150 | 13417<br>13417<br>064 151 | 13418<br>13418<br>064 152 | 13419<br>13419<br>064 153 | 13420<br>13420<br>064 154 | 13421<br>13421<br>064 155 | 13422<br>13422<br>064 156 | 13423<br>13423<br>064 157 |
| 7− | 13424<br>13424<br>064 160 | 13425<br>13425<br>064 161 | 13426<br>13426<br>064 162 | 13427<br>13427<br>064 163 | 13428<br>13428<br>064 164 | 13429<br>13429<br>064 165 | 13430<br>13430<br>064 166 | 13431<br>13431<br>064 167 | 13432<br>13432<br>064 170 | 13433<br>13433<br>064 171 | 13434<br>13434<br>064 172 | 13435<br>13435<br>064 173 | 13436<br>13436<br>064 174 | 13437<br>13437<br>064 175 | 13438<br>13438<br>064 176 | 13439<br>13439<br>064 177 |
| 8− | 13440<br>13440<br>064 200 | 13441<br>13441<br>064 201 | 13442<br>13442<br>064 202 | 13443<br>13443<br>064 203 | 13444<br>13444<br>064 204 | 13445<br>13445<br>064 205 | 13446<br>13446<br>064 206 | 13447<br>13447<br>064 207 | 13448<br>13448<br>064 210 | 13449<br>13449<br>064 211 | 13450<br>13450<br>064 212 | 13451<br>13451<br>064 213 | 13452<br>13452<br>064 214 | 13453<br>13453<br>064 215 | 13454<br>13454<br>064 216 | 13455<br>13455<br>064 217 |
| 9− | 13456<br>13456<br>064 220 | 13457<br>13457<br>064 221 | 13458<br>13458<br>064 222 | 13459<br>13459<br>064 223 | 13460<br>13460<br>064 224 | 13461<br>13461<br>064 225 | 13462<br>13462<br>064 226 | 13463<br>13463<br>064 227 | 13464<br>13464<br>064 230 | 13465<br>13465<br>064 231 | 13466<br>13466<br>064 232 | 13467<br>13467<br>064 233 | 13468<br>13468<br>064 234 | 13469<br>13469<br>064 235 | 13470<br>13470<br>064 236 | 13471<br>13471<br>064 237 |
| A− | 13472<br>13472<br>064 240 | 13473<br>13473<br>064 241 | 13474<br>13474<br>064 242 | 13475<br>13475<br>064 243 | 13476<br>13476<br>064 244 | 13477<br>13477<br>064 245 | 13478<br>13478<br>064 246 | 13479<br>13479<br>064 247 | 13480<br>13480<br>064 250 | 13481<br>13481<br>064 251 | 13482<br>13482<br>064 252 | 13483<br>13483<br>064 253 | 13484<br>13484<br>064 254 | 13485<br>13485<br>064 255 | 13486<br>13486<br>064 256 | 13487<br>13487<br>064 257 |
| B− | 13488<br>13488<br>064 260 | 13489<br>13489<br>064 261 | 13490<br>13490<br>064 262 | 13491<br>13491<br>064 263 | 13492<br>13492<br>064 264 | 13493<br>13493<br>064 265 | 13494<br>13494<br>064 266 | 13495<br>13495<br>064 267 | 13496<br>13496<br>064 270 | 13497<br>13497<br>064 271 | 13498<br>13498<br>064 272 | 13499<br>13499<br>064 273 | 13500<br>13500<br>064 274 | 13501<br>13501<br>064 275 | 13502<br>13502<br>064 276 | 13503<br>13503<br>064 277 |
| C− | 13504<br>13504<br>064 300 | 13505<br>13505<br>064 301 | 13506<br>13506<br>064 302 | 13507<br>13507<br>064 303 | 13508<br>13508<br>064 304 | 13509<br>13509<br>064 305 | 13510<br>13510<br>064 306 | 13511<br>13511<br>064 307 | 13512<br>13512<br>064 310 | 13513<br>13513<br>064 311 | 13514<br>13514<br>064 312 | 13515<br>13515<br>064 313 | 13516<br>13516<br>064 314 | 13517<br>13517<br>064 315 | 13518<br>13518<br>064 316 | 13519<br>13519<br>064 317 |
| D− | 13520<br>13520<br>064 320 | 13521<br>13521<br>064 321 | 13522<br>13522<br>064 322 | 13523<br>13523<br>064 323 | 13524<br>13524<br>064 324 | 13525<br>13525<br>064 325 | 13526<br>13526<br>064 326 | 13527<br>13527<br>064 327 | 13528<br>13528<br>064 330 | 13529<br>13529<br>064 331 | 13530<br>13530<br>064 332 | 13531<br>13531<br>064 333 | 13532<br>13532<br>064 334 | 13533<br>13533<br>064 335 | 13534<br>13534<br>064 336 | 13535<br>13535<br>064 337 |
| E− | 13536<br>13536<br>064 340 | 13537<br>13537<br>064 341 | 13538<br>13538<br>064 342 | 13539<br>13539<br>064 343 | 13540<br>13540<br>064 344 | 13541<br>13541<br>064 345 | 13542<br>13542<br>064 346 | 13543<br>13543<br>064 347 | 13544<br>13544<br>064 350 | 13545<br>13545<br>064 351 | 13546<br>13546<br>064 352 | 13547<br>13547<br>064 353 | 13548<br>13548<br>064 354 | 13549<br>13549<br>064 355 | 13550<br>13550<br>064 356 | 13551<br>13551<br>064 357 |
| F− | 13552<br>13552<br>064 360 | 13553<br>13553<br>064 361 | 13554<br>13554<br>064 362 | 13555<br>13555<br>064 363 | 13556<br>13556<br>064 364 | 13557<br>13557<br>064 365 | 13558<br>13558<br>064 366 | 13559<br>13559<br>064 367 | 13560<br>13560<br>064 370 | 13561<br>13561<br>064 371 | 13562<br>13562<br>064 372 | 13563<br>13563<br>064 373 | 13564<br>13564<br>064 374 | 13565<br>13565<br>064 375 | 13566<br>13566<br>064 376 | 13567<br>13567<br>064 377 |

Legend (right side): DECIMAL · DECIMAL · OCTAL

🍎 DECIMAL 13312  BINARY 0011 0100  DECIMAL 13312  HEXADECIMAL ⬡ 34  OCTAL 064 000

FOURTH HEX DIGIT → ⬡ ← THIRD HEX DIGIT

 DECIMAL [13568]    BINARY [0011 0101]    DECIMAL [13568]    HEXADECIMAL <35>    OCTAL [065 000]

FOURTH HEX DIGIT → 35 ← THIRD HEX DIGIT

| <2> | FIRST HEX DIGIT | | | | | | | | | | | | | | | |
| --- | --- | --- | --- | --- | --- | --- | --- | --- | --- | --- | --- | --- | --- | --- | --- | --- |
| | −0 | −1 | −2 | −3 | −4 | −5 | −6 | −7 | −8 | −9 | −A | −B | −C | −D | −E | −F |
| 0− | 13568<br>13568<br>065 000 | 13569<br>13569<br>065 001 | 13570<br>13570<br>065 002 | 13571<br>13571<br>065 003 | 13572<br>13572<br>065 004 | 13573<br>13573<br>065 005 | 13574<br>13574<br>065 006 | 13575<br>13575<br>065 007 | 13576<br>13576<br>065 010 | 13577<br>13577<br>065 011 | 13578<br>13578<br>065 012 | 13579<br>13579<br>065 013 | 13580<br>13580<br>065 014 | 13581<br>13581<br>065 015 | 13582<br>13582<br>065 016 | 13583<br>13583<br>065 017 |
| 1− | 13584<br>13584<br>065 020 | 13585<br>13585<br>065 021 | 13586<br>13586<br>065 022 | 13587<br>13587<br>065 023 | 13588<br>13588<br>065 024 | 13589<br>13589<br>065 025 | 13590<br>13590<br>065 026 | 13591<br>13591<br>065 027 | 13592<br>13592<br>065 030 | 13593<br>13593<br>065 031 | 13594<br>13594<br>065 032 | 13595<br>13595<br>065 033 | 13596<br>13596<br>065 034 | 13597<br>13597<br>065 035 | 13598<br>13598<br>065 036 | 13599<br>13599<br>065 037 |
| 2− | 13600<br>13600<br>065 040 | 13601<br>13601<br>065 041 | 13602<br>13602<br>065 042 | 13603<br>13603<br>065 043 | 13604<br>13604<br>065 044 | 13605<br>13605<br>065 045 | 13606<br>13606<br>065 046 | 13607<br>13607<br>065 047 | 13608<br>13608<br>065 050 | 13609<br>13609<br>065 051 | 13610<br>13610<br>065 052 | 13611<br>13611<br>065 053 | 13612<br>13612<br>065 054 | 13613<br>13613<br>065 055 | 13614<br>13614<br>065 056 | 13615<br>13615<br>065 057 |
| 3− | 13616<br>13616<br>065 060 | 13617<br>13617<br>065 061 | 13618<br>13618<br>065 062 | 13619<br>13619<br>065 063 | 13620<br>13620<br>065 064 | 13621<br>13621<br>065 065 | 13622<br>13622<br>065 066 | 13623<br>13623<br>065 067 | 13624<br>13624<br>065 070 | 13625<br>13625<br>065 071 | 13626<br>13626<br>065 072 | 13627<br>13627<br>065 073 | 13628<br>13628<br>065 074 | 13629<br>13629<br>065 075 | 13630<br>13630<br>065 076 | 13631<br>13631<br>065 077 |
| 4− | 13632<br>13632<br>065 100 | 13633<br>13633<br>065 101 | 13634<br>13634<br>065 102 | 13635<br>13635<br>065 103 | 13636<br>13636<br>065 104 | 13637<br>13637<br>065 105 | 13638<br>13638<br>065 106 | 13639<br>13639<br>065 107 | 13640<br>13640<br>065 110 | 13641<br>13641<br>065 111 | 13642<br>13642<br>065 112 | 13643<br>13643<br>065 113 | 13644<br>13644<br>065 114 | 13645<br>13645<br>065 115 | 13646<br>13646<br>065 116 | 13647<br>13647<br>065 117 |
| 5− | 13648<br>13648<br>065 120 | 13649<br>13649<br>065 121 | 13650<br>13650<br>065 122 | 13651<br>13651<br>065 123 | 13652<br>13652<br>065 124 | 13653<br>13653<br>065 125 | 13654<br>13654<br>065 126 | 13655<br>13655<br>065 127 | 13656<br>13656<br>065 130 | 13657<br>13657<br>065 131 | 13658<br>13658<br>065 132 | 13659<br>13659<br>065 133 | 13660<br>13660<br>065 134 | 13661<br>13661<br>065 135 | 13662<br>13662<br>065 136 | 13663<br>13663<br>065 137 |
| 6− | 13664<br>13664<br>065 140 | 13665<br>13665<br>065 141 | 13666<br>13666<br>065 142 | 13667<br>13667<br>065 143 | 13668<br>13668<br>065 144 | 13669<br>13669<br>065 145 | 13670<br>13670<br>065 146 | 13671<br>13671<br>065 147 | 13672<br>13672<br>065 150 | 13673<br>13673<br>065 151 | 13674<br>13674<br>065 152 | 13675<br>13675<br>065 153 | 13676<br>13676<br>065 154 | 13677<br>13677<br>065 155 | 13678<br>13678<br>065 156 | 13679<br>13679<br>065 157 |
| 7− | 13680<br>13680<br>065 160 | 13681<br>13681<br>065 161 | 13682<br>13682<br>065 162 | 13683<br>13683<br>065 163 | 13684<br>13684<br>065 164 | 13685<br>13685<br>065 165 | 13686<br>13686<br>065 166 | 13687<br>13687<br>065 167 | 13688<br>13688<br>065 170 | 13689<br>13689<br>065 171 | 13690<br>13690<br>065 172 | 13691<br>13691<br>065 173 | 13692<br>13692<br>065 174 | 13693<br>13693<br>065 175 | 13694<br>13694<br>065 176 | 13695<br>13695<br>065 177 |
| 8− | 13696<br>13696<br>065 200 | 13697<br>13697<br>065 201 | 13698<br>13698<br>065 202 | 13699<br>13699<br>065 203 | 13700<br>13700<br>065 204 | 13701<br>13701<br>065 205 | 13702<br>13702<br>065 206 | 13703<br>13703<br>065 207 | 13704<br>13704<br>065 210 | 13705<br>13705<br>065 211 | 13706<br>13706<br>065 212 | 13707<br>13707<br>065 213 | 13708<br>13708<br>065 214 | 13709<br>13709<br>065 215 | 13710<br>13710<br>065 216 | 13711<br>13711<br>065 217 |
| 9− | 13712<br>13712<br>065 220 | 13713<br>13713<br>065 221 | 13714<br>13714<br>065 222 | 13715<br>13715<br>065 223 | 13716<br>13716<br>065 224 | 13717<br>13717<br>065 225 | 13718<br>13718<br>065 226 | 13719<br>13719<br>065 227 | 13720<br>13720<br>065 230 | 13721<br>13721<br>065 231 | 13722<br>13722<br>065 232 | 13723<br>13723<br>065 233 | 13724<br>13724<br>065 234 | 13725<br>13725<br>065 235 | 13726<br>13726<br>065 236 | 13727<br>13727<br>065 237 |
| A− | 13728<br>13728<br>065 240 | 13729<br>13729<br>065 241 | 13730<br>13730<br>065 242 | 13731<br>13731<br>065 243 | 13732<br>13732<br>065 244 | 13733<br>13733<br>065 245 | 13734<br>13734<br>065 246 | 13735<br>13735<br>065 247 | 13736<br>13736<br>065 250 | 13737<br>13737<br>065 251 | 13738<br>13738<br>065 252 | 13739<br>13739<br>065 253 | 13740<br>13740<br>065 254 | 13741<br>13741<br>065 255 | 13742<br>13742<br>065 256 | 13743<br>13743<br>065 257 |
| B− | 13744<br>13744<br>065 260 | 13745<br>13745<br>065 261 | 13746<br>13746<br>065 262 | 13747<br>13747<br>065 263 | 13748<br>13748<br>065 264 | 13749<br>13749<br>065 265 | 13750<br>13750<br>065 266 | 13751<br>13751<br>065 267 | 13752<br>13752<br>065 270 | 13753<br>13753<br>065 271 | 13754<br>13754<br>065 272 | 13755<br>13755<br>065 273 | 13756<br>13756<br>065 274 | 13757<br>13757<br>065 275 | 13758<br>13758<br>065 276 | 13759<br>13759<br>065 277 |
| C− | 13760<br>13760<br>065 300 | 13761<br>13761<br>065 301 | 13762<br>13762<br>065 302 | 13763<br>13763<br>065 303 | 13764<br>13764<br>065 304 | 13765<br>13765<br>065 305 | 13766<br>13766<br>065 306 | 13767<br>13767<br>065 307 | 13768<br>13768<br>065 310 | 13769<br>13769<br>065 311 | 13770<br>13770<br>065 312 | 13771<br>13771<br>065 313 | 13772<br>13772<br>065 314 | 13773<br>13773<br>065 315 | 13774<br>13774<br>065 316 | 13775<br>13775<br>065 317 |
| D− | 13776<br>13776<br>065 320 | 13777<br>13777<br>065 321 | 13778<br>13778<br>065 322 | 13779<br>13779<br>065 323 | 13780<br>13780<br>065 324 | 13781<br>13781<br>065 325 | 13782<br>13782<br>065 326 | 13783<br>13783<br>065 327 | 13784<br>13784<br>065 330 | 13785<br>13785<br>065 331 | 13786<br>13786<br>065 332 | 13787<br>13787<br>065 333 | 13788<br>13788<br>065 334 | 13789<br>13789<br>065 335 | 13790<br>13790<br>065 336 | 13791<br>13791<br>065 337 |
| E− | 13792<br>13792<br>065 340 | 13793<br>13793<br>065 341 | 13794<br>13794<br>065 342 | 13795<br>13795<br>065 343 | 13796<br>13796<br>065 344 | 13797<br>13797<br>065 345 | 13798<br>13798<br>065 346 | 13799<br>13799<br>065 347 | 13800<br>13800<br>065 350 | 13801<br>13801<br>065 351 | 13802<br>13802<br>065 352 | 13803<br>13803<br>065 353 | 13804<br>13804<br>065 354 | 13805<br>13805<br>065 355 | 13806<br>13806<br>065 356 | 13807<br>13807<br>065 357 |
| F− | 13808<br>13808<br>065 360 | 13809<br>13809<br>065 361 | 13810<br>13810<br>065 362 | 13811<br>13811<br>065 363 | 13812<br>13812<br>065 364 | 13813<br>13813<br>065 365 | 13814<br>13814<br>065 366 | 13815<br>13815<br>065 367 | 13816<br>13816<br>065 370 | 13817<br>13817<br>065 371 | 13818<br>13818<br>065 372 | 13819<br>13819<br>065 373 | 13820<br>13820<br>065 374 | 13821<br>13821<br>065 375 | 13822<br>13822<br>065 376 | 13823<br>13823<br>065 377 |

SECOND HEX DIGIT

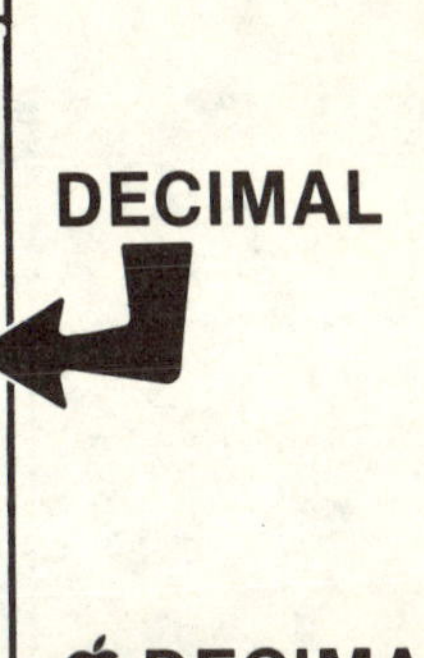

| SECOND HEX DIGIT | −0 | −1 | −2 | −3 | −4 | −5 | −6 | −7 | −8 | −9 | −A | −B | −C | −D | −E | −F |
|---|---|---|---|---|---|---|---|---|---|---|---|---|---|---|---|---|
| 0− | 13824<br>13824<br>066 000 | 13825<br>13825<br>066 001 | 13826<br>13826<br>066 002 | 13827<br>13827<br>066 003 | 13828<br>13828<br>066 004 | 13829<br>13829<br>066 005 | 13830<br>13830<br>066 006 | 13831<br>13831<br>066 007 | 13832<br>13832<br>066 010 | 13833<br>13833<br>066 011 | 13834<br>13834<br>066 012 | 13835<br>13835<br>066 013 | 13836<br>13836<br>066 014 | 13837<br>13837<br>066 015 | 13838<br>13838<br>066 016 | 13839<br>13839<br>066 017 |
| 1− | 13840<br>13840<br>066 020 | 13841<br>13841<br>066 021 | 13842<br>13842<br>066 022 | 13843<br>13843<br>066 023 | 13844<br>13844<br>066 024 | 13845<br>13845<br>066 025 | 13846<br>13846<br>066 026 | 13847<br>13847<br>066 027 | 13848<br>13848<br>066 030 | 13849<br>13849<br>066 031 | 13850<br>13850<br>066 032 | 13851<br>13851<br>066 033 | 13852<br>13852<br>066 034 | 13853<br>13853<br>066 035 | 13854<br>13854<br>066 036 | 13855<br>13855<br>066 037 |
| 2− | 13856<br>13856<br>066 040 | 13857<br>13857<br>066 041 | 13858<br>13858<br>066 042 | 13859<br>13859<br>066 043 | 13860<br>13860<br>066 044 | 13861<br>13861<br>066 045 | 13862<br>13862<br>066 046 | 13863<br>13863<br>066 047 | 13864<br>13864<br>066 050 | 13865<br>13865<br>066 051 | 13866<br>13866<br>066 052 | 13867<br>13867<br>066 053 | 13868<br>13868<br>066 054 | 13869<br>13869<br>066 055 | 13870<br>13870<br>066 056 | 13871<br>13871<br>066 057 |
| 3− | 13872<br>13872<br>066 060 | 13873<br>13873<br>066 061 | 13874<br>13874<br>066 062 | 13875<br>13875<br>066 063 | 13876<br>13876<br>066 064 | 13877<br>13877<br>066 065 | 13878<br>13878<br>066 066 | 13879<br>13879<br>066 067 | 13880<br>13880<br>066 070 | 13881<br>13881<br>066 071 | 13882<br>13882<br>066 072 | 13883<br>13883<br>066 073 | 13884<br>13884<br>066 074 | 13885<br>13885<br>066 075 | 13886<br>13886<br>066 076 | 13887<br>13887<br>066 077 |
| 4− | 13888<br>13888<br>066 100 | 13889<br>13889<br>066 101 | 13890<br>13890<br>066 102 | 13891<br>13891<br>066 103 | 13892<br>13892<br>066 104 | 13893<br>13893<br>066 105 | 13894<br>13894<br>066 106 | 13895<br>13895<br>066 107 | 13896<br>13896<br>066 110 | 13897<br>13897<br>066 111 | 13898<br>13898<br>066 112 | 13899<br>13899<br>066 113 | 13900<br>13900<br>066 114 | 13901<br>13901<br>066 115 | 13902<br>13902<br>066 116 | 13903<br>13903<br>066 117 |
| 5− | 13904<br>13904<br>066 120 | 13905<br>13905<br>066 121 | 13906<br>13906<br>066 122 | 13907<br>13907<br>066 123 | 13908<br>13908<br>066 124 | 13909<br>13909<br>066 125 | 13910<br>13910<br>066 126 | 13911<br>13911<br>066 127 | 13912<br>13912<br>066 130 | 13913<br>13913<br>066 131 | 13914<br>13914<br>066 132 | 13915<br>13915<br>066 133 | 13916<br>13916<br>066 134 | 13917<br>13917<br>066 135 | 13918<br>13918<br>066 136 | 13919<br>13919<br>066 137 |
| 6− | 13920<br>13920<br>066 140 | 13921<br>13921<br>066 141 | 13922<br>13922<br>066 142 | 13923<br>13923<br>066 143 | 13924<br>13924<br>066 144 | 13925<br>13925<br>066 145 | 13926<br>13926<br>066 146 | 13927<br>13927<br>066 147 | 13928<br>13928<br>066 150 | 13929<br>13929<br>066 151 | 13930<br>13930<br>066 152 | 13931<br>13931<br>066 153 | 13932<br>13932<br>066 154 | 13933<br>13933<br>066 155 | 13934<br>13934<br>066 156 | 13935<br>13935<br>066 157 |
| 7− | 13936<br>13936<br>066 160 | 13937<br>13937<br>066 161 | 13938<br>13938<br>066 162 | 13939<br>13939<br>066 163 | 13940<br>13940<br>066 164 | 13941<br>13941<br>066 165 | 13942<br>13942<br>066 166 | 13943<br>13943<br>066 167 | 13944<br>13944<br>066 170 | 13945<br>13945<br>066 171 | 13946<br>13946<br>066 172 | 13947<br>13947<br>066 173 | 13948<br>13948<br>066 174 | 13949<br>13949<br>066 175 | 13950<br>13950<br>066 176 | 13951<br>13951<br>066 177 |
| 8− | 13952<br>13952<br>066 200 | 13953<br>13953<br>066 201 | 13954<br>13954<br>066 202 | 13955<br>13955<br>066 203 | 13956<br>13956<br>066 204 | 13957<br>13957<br>066 205 | 13958<br>13958<br>066 206 | 13959<br>13959<br>066 207 | 13960<br>13960<br>066 210 | 13961<br>13961<br>066 211 | 13962<br>13962<br>066 212 | 13963<br>13963<br>066 213 | 13964<br>13964<br>066 214 | 13965<br>13965<br>066 215 | 13966<br>13966<br>066 216 | 13967<br>13967<br>066 217 |
| 9− | 13968<br>13968<br>066 220 | 13969<br>13969<br>066 221 | 13970<br>13970<br>066 222 | 13971<br>13971<br>066 223 | 13972<br>13972<br>066 224 | 13973<br>13973<br>066 225 | 13974<br>13974<br>066 226 | 13975<br>13975<br>066 227 | 13976<br>13976<br>066 230 | 13977<br>13977<br>066 231 | 13978<br>13978<br>066 232 | 13979<br>13979<br>066 233 | 13980<br>13980<br>066 234 | 13981<br>13981<br>066 235 | 13982<br>13982<br>066 236 | 13983<br>13983<br>066 237 |
| A− | 13984<br>13984<br>066 240 | 13985<br>13985<br>066 241 | 13986<br>13986<br>066 242 | 13987<br>13987<br>066 243 | 13988<br>13988<br>066 244 | 13989<br>13989<br>066 245 | 13990<br>13990<br>066 246 | 13991<br>13991<br>066 247 | 13992<br>13992<br>066 250 | 13993<br>13993<br>066 251 | 13994<br>13994<br>066 252 | 13995<br>13995<br>066 253 | 13996<br>13996<br>066 254 | 13997<br>13997<br>066 255 | 13998<br>13998<br>066 256 | 13999<br>13999<br>066 257 |
| B− | 14000<br>14000<br>066 260 | 14001<br>14001<br>066 261 | 14002<br>14002<br>066 262 | 14003<br>14003<br>066 263 | 14004<br>14004<br>066 264 | 14005<br>14005<br>066 265 | 14006<br>14006<br>066 266 | 14007<br>14007<br>066 267 | 14008<br>14008<br>066 270 | 14009<br>14009<br>066 271 | 14010<br>14010<br>066 272 | 14011<br>14011<br>066 273 | 14012<br>14012<br>066 274 | 14013<br>14013<br>066 275 | 14014<br>14014<br>066 276 | 14015<br>14015<br>066 277 |
| C− | 14016<br>14016<br>066 300 | 14017<br>14017<br>066 301 | 14018<br>14018<br>066 302 | 14019<br>14019<br>066 303 | 14020<br>14020<br>066 304 | 14021<br>14021<br>066 305 | 14022<br>14022<br>066 306 | 14023<br>14023<br>066 307 | 14024<br>14024<br>066 310 | 14025<br>14025<br>066 311 | 14026<br>14026<br>066 312 | 14027<br>14027<br>066 313 | 14028<br>14028<br>066 314 | 14029<br>14029<br>066 315 | 14030<br>14030<br>066 316 | 14031<br>14031<br>066 317 |
| D− | 14032<br>14032<br>066 320 | 14033<br>14033<br>066 321 | 14034<br>14034<br>066 322 | 14035<br>14035<br>066 323 | 14036<br>14036<br>066 324 | 14037<br>14037<br>066 325 | 14038<br>14038<br>066 326 | 14039<br>14039<br>066 327 | 14040<br>14040<br>066 330 | 14041<br>14041<br>066 331 | 14042<br>14042<br>066 332 | 14043<br>14043<br>066 333 | 14044<br>14044<br>066 334 | 14045<br>14045<br>066 335 | 14046<br>14046<br>066 336 | 14047<br>14047<br>066 337 |
| E− | 14048<br>14048<br>066 340 | 14049<br>14049<br>066 341 | 14050<br>14050<br>066 342 | 14051<br>14051<br>066 343 | 14052<br>14052<br>066 344 | 14053<br>14053<br>066 345 | 14054<br>14054<br>066 346 | 14055<br>14055<br>066 347 | 14056<br>14056<br>066 350 | 14057<br>14057<br>066 351 | 14058<br>14058<br>066 352 | 14059<br>14059<br>066 353 | 14060<br>14060<br>066 354 | 14061<br>14061<br>066 355 | 14062<br>14062<br>066 356 | 14063<br>14063<br>066 357 |
| F− | 14064<br>14064<br>066 360 | 14065<br>14065<br>066 361 | 14066<br>14066<br>066 362 | 14067<br>14067<br>066 363 | 14068<br>14068<br>066 364 | 14069<br>14069<br>066 365 | 14070<br>14070<br>066 366 | 14071<br>14071<br>066 367 | 14072<br>14072<br>066 370 | 14073<br>14073<br>066 371 | 14074<br>14074<br>066 372 | 14075<br>14075<br>066 373 | 14076<br>14076<br>066 374 | 14077<br>14077<br>066 375 | 14078<br>14078<br>066 376 | 14079<br>14079<br>066 377 |

Legend (right side): DECIMAL → ; DECIMAL → ; OCTAL →

 DECIMAL `13824`   **BINARY** `0011 0110`   **DECIMAL** `13824`   **HEXADECIMAL** ⬡ 36   **OCTAL** `066 000`

FOURTH HEX DIGIT → ← THIRD HEX DIGIT

### FIRST HEX DIGIT

| ⬡2 | −0 | −1 | −2 | −3 | −4 | −5 | −6 | −7 | −8 | −9 | −A | −B | −C | −D | −E | −F |
|---|---|---|---|---|---|---|---|---|---|---|---|---|---|---|---|---|
| 0− | 14080<br>14080<br>067 000 | 14081<br>14081<br>067 001 | 14082<br>14082<br>067 002 | 14083<br>14083<br>067 003 | 14084<br>14084<br>067 004 | 14085<br>14085<br>067 005 | 14086<br>14086<br>067 006 | 14087<br>14087<br>067 007 | 14088<br>14088<br>067 010 | 14089<br>14089<br>067 011 | 14090<br>14090<br>067 012 | 14091<br>14091<br>067 013 | 14092<br>14092<br>067 014 | 14093<br>14093<br>067 015 | 14094<br>14094<br>067 016 | 14095<br>14095<br>067 017 |
| 1− | 14096<br>14096<br>067 020 | 14097<br>14097<br>067 021 | 14098<br>14098<br>067 022 | 14099<br>14099<br>067 023 | 14100<br>14100<br>067 024 | 14101<br>14101<br>067 025 | 14102<br>14102<br>067 026 | 14103<br>14103<br>067 027 | 14104<br>14104<br>067 030 | 14105<br>14105<br>067 031 | 14106<br>14106<br>067 032 | 14107<br>14107<br>067 033 | 14108<br>14108<br>067 034 | 14109<br>14109<br>067 035 | 14110<br>14110<br>067 036 | 14111<br>14111<br>067 037 |
| 2− | 14112<br>14112<br>067 040 | 14113<br>14113<br>067 041 | 14114<br>14114<br>067 042 | 14115<br>14115<br>067 043 | 14116<br>14116<br>067 044 | 14117<br>14117<br>067 045 | 14118<br>14118<br>067 046 | 14119<br>14119<br>067 047 | 14120<br>14120<br>067 050 | 14121<br>14121<br>067 051 | 14122<br>14122<br>067 052 | 14123<br>14123<br>067 053 | 14124<br>14124<br>067 054 | 14125<br>14125<br>067 055 | 14126<br>14126<br>067 056 | 14127<br>14127<br>067 057 |
| 3− | 14128<br>14128<br>067 060 | 14129<br>14129<br>067 061 | 14130<br>14130<br>067 062 | 14131<br>14131<br>067 063 | 14132<br>14132<br>067 064 | 14133<br>14133<br>067 065 | 14134<br>14134<br>067 066 | 14135<br>14135<br>067 067 | 14136<br>14136<br>067 070 | 14137<br>14137<br>067 071 | 14138<br>14138<br>067 072 | 14139<br>14139<br>067 073 | 14140<br>14140<br>067 074 | 14141<br>14141<br>067 075 | 14142<br>14142<br>067 076 | 14143<br>14143<br>067 077 |
| 4− | 14144<br>14144<br>067 100 | 14145<br>14145<br>067 101 | 14146<br>14146<br>067 102 | 14147<br>14147<br>067 103 | 14148<br>14148<br>067 104 | 14149<br>14149<br>067 105 | 14150<br>14150<br>067 106 | 14151<br>14151<br>067 107 | 14152<br>14152<br>067 110 | 14153<br>14153<br>067 111 | 14154<br>14154<br>067 112 | 14155<br>14155<br>067 113 | 14156<br>14156<br>067 114 | 14157<br>14157<br>067 115 | 14158<br>14158<br>067 116 | 14159<br>14159<br>067 117 |
| 5− | 14160<br>14160<br>067 120 | 14161<br>14161<br>067 121 | 14162<br>14162<br>067 122 | 14163<br>14163<br>067 123 | 14164<br>14164<br>067 124 | 14165<br>14165<br>067 125 | 14166<br>14166<br>067 126 | 14167<br>14167<br>067 127 | 14168<br>14168<br>067 130 | 14169<br>14169<br>067 131 | 14170<br>14170<br>067 132 | 14171<br>14171<br>067 133 | 14172<br>14172<br>067 134 | 14173<br>14173<br>067 135 | 14174<br>14174<br>067 136 | 14175<br>14175<br>067 137 |
| 6− | 14176<br>14176<br>067 140 | 14177<br>14177<br>067 141 | 14178<br>14178<br>067 142 | 14179<br>14179<br>067 143 | 14180<br>14180<br>067 144 | 14181<br>14181<br>067 145 | 14182<br>14182<br>067 146 | 14183<br>14183<br>067 147 | 14184<br>14184<br>067 150 | 14185<br>14185<br>067 151 | 14186<br>14186<br>067 152 | 14187<br>14187<br>067 153 | 14188<br>14188<br>067 154 | 14189<br>14189<br>067 155 | 14190<br>14190<br>067 156 | 14191<br>14191<br>067 157 |
| 7− | 14192<br>14192<br>067 160 | 14193<br>14193<br>067 161 | 14194<br>14194<br>067 162 | 14195<br>14195<br>067 163 | 14196<br>14196<br>067 164 | 14197<br>14197<br>067 165 | 14198<br>14198<br>067 166 | 14199<br>14199<br>067 167 | 14200<br>14200<br>067 170 | 14201<br>14201<br>067 171 | 14202<br>14202<br>067 172 | 14203<br>14203<br>067 173 | 14204<br>14204<br>067 174 | 14205<br>14205<br>067 175 | 14206<br>14206<br>067 176 | 14207<br>14207<br>067 177 |
| 8− | 14208<br>14208<br>067 200 | 14209<br>14209<br>067 201 | 14210<br>14210<br>067 202 | 14211<br>14211<br>067 203 | 14212<br>14212<br>067 204 | 14213<br>14213<br>067 205 | 14214<br>14214<br>067 206 | 14215<br>14215<br>067 207 | 14216<br>14216<br>067 210 | 14217<br>14217<br>067 211 | 14218<br>14218<br>067 212 | 14219<br>14219<br>067 213 | 14220<br>14220<br>067 214 | 14221<br>14221<br>067 215 | 14222<br>14222<br>067 216 | 14223<br>14223<br>067 217 |
| 9− | 14224<br>14224<br>067 220 | 14225<br>14225<br>067 221 | 14226<br>14226<br>067 222 | 14227<br>14227<br>067 223 | 14228<br>14228<br>067 224 | 14229<br>14229<br>067 225 | 14230<br>14230<br>067 226 | 14231<br>14231<br>067 227 | 14232<br>14232<br>067 230 | 14233<br>14233<br>067 231 | 14234<br>14234<br>067 232 | 14235<br>14235<br>067 233 | 14236<br>14236<br>067 234 | 14237<br>14237<br>067 235 | 14238<br>14238<br>067 236 | 14239<br>14239<br>067 237 |
| A− | 14240<br>14240<br>067 240 | 14241<br>14241<br>067 241 | 14242<br>14242<br>067 242 | 14243<br>14243<br>067 243 | 14244<br>14244<br>067 244 | 14245<br>14245<br>067 245 | 14246<br>14246<br>067 246 | 14247<br>14247<br>067 247 | 14248<br>14248<br>067 250 | 14249<br>14249<br>067 251 | 14250<br>14250<br>067 252 | 14251<br>14251<br>067 253 | 14252<br>14252<br>067 254 | 14253<br>14253<br>067 255 | 14254<br>14254<br>067 256 | 14255<br>14255<br>067 257 |
| B− | 14256<br>14256<br>067 260 | 14257<br>14257<br>067 261 | 14258<br>14258<br>067 262 | 14259<br>14259<br>067 263 | 14260<br>14260<br>067 264 | 14261<br>14261<br>067 265 | 14262<br>14262<br>067 266 | 14263<br>14263<br>067 267 | 14264<br>14264<br>067 270 | 14265<br>14265<br>067 271 | 14266<br>14266<br>067 272 | 14267<br>14267<br>067 273 | 14268<br>14268<br>067 274 | 14269<br>14269<br>067 275 | 14270<br>14270<br>067 276 | 14271<br>14271<br>067 277 |
| C− | 14272<br>14272<br>067 300 | 14273<br>14273<br>067 301 | 14274<br>14274<br>067 302 | 14275<br>14275<br>067 303 | 14276<br>14276<br>067 304 | 14277<br>14277<br>067 305 | 14278<br>14278<br>067 306 | 14279<br>14279<br>067 307 | 14280<br>14280<br>067 310 | 14281<br>14281<br>067 311 | 14282<br>14282<br>067 312 | 14283<br>14283<br>067 313 | 14284<br>14284<br>067 314 | 14285<br>14285<br>067 315 | 14286<br>14286<br>067 316 | 14287<br>14287<br>067 317 |
| D− | 14288<br>14288<br>067 320 | 14289<br>14289<br>067 321 | 14290<br>14290<br>067 322 | 14291<br>14291<br>067 323 | 14292<br>14292<br>067 324 | 14293<br>14293<br>067 325 | 14294<br>14294<br>067 326 | 14295<br>14295<br>067 327 | 14296<br>14296<br>067 330 | 14297<br>14297<br>067 331 | 14298<br>14298<br>067 332 | 14299<br>14299<br>067 333 | 14300<br>14300<br>067 334 | 14301<br>14301<br>067 335 | 14302<br>14302<br>067 336 | 14303<br>14303<br>067 337 |
| E− | 14304<br>14304<br>067 340 | 14305<br>14305<br>067 341 | 14306<br>14306<br>067 342 | 14307<br>14307<br>067 343 | 14308<br>14308<br>067 344 | 14309<br>14309<br>067 345 | 14310<br>14310<br>067 346 | 14311<br>14311<br>067 347 | 14312<br>14312<br>067 350 | 14313<br>14313<br>067 351 | 14314<br>14314<br>067 352 | 14315<br>14315<br>067 353 | 14316<br>14316<br>067 354 | 14317<br>14317<br>067 355 | 14318<br>14318<br>067 356 | 14319<br>14319<br>067 357 |
| F− | 14320<br>14320<br>067 360 | 14321<br>14321<br>067 361 | 14322<br>14322<br>067 362 | 14323<br>14323<br>067 363 | 14324<br>14324<br>067 364 | 14325<br>14325<br>067 365 | 14326<br>14326<br>067 366 | 14327<br>14327<br>067 367 | 14328<br>14328<br>067 370 | 14329<br>14329<br>067 371 | 14330<br>14330<br>067 372 | 14331<br>14331<br>067 373 | 14332<br>14332<br>067 374 | 14333<br>14333<br>067 375 | 14334<br>14334<br>067 376 | 14335<br>14335<br>067 377 |

SECOND HEX DIGIT

DECIMAL →

🍎 DECIMAL →

OCTAL →

<table>
<thead>
<tr><th></th><th colspan="16">FIRST HEX DIGIT</th></tr>
<tr><th>2</th><th>–0</th><th>–1</th><th>–2</th><th>–3</th><th>–4</th><th>–5</th><th>–6</th><th>–7</th><th>–8</th><th>–9</th><th>–A</th><th>–B</th><th>–C</th><th>–D</th><th>–E</th><th>–F</th></tr>
</thead>
<tbody>
<tr><td>0–</td><td>14336<br>14336<br>070 000</td><td>14337<br>14337<br>070 001</td><td>14338<br>14338<br>070 002</td><td>14339<br>14339<br>070 003</td><td>14340<br>14340<br>070 004</td><td>14341<br>14341<br>070 005</td><td>14342<br>14342<br>070 006</td><td>14343<br>14343<br>070 007</td><td>14344<br>14344<br>070 010</td><td>14345<br>14345<br>070 011</td><td>14346<br>14346<br>070 012</td><td>14347<br>14347<br>070 013</td><td>14348<br>14348<br>070 014</td><td>14349<br>14349<br>070 015</td><td>14350<br>14350<br>070 016</td><td>14351<br>14351<br>070 017</td></tr>
<tr><td>1–</td><td>14352<br>14352<br>070 020</td><td>14353<br>14353<br>070 021</td><td>14354<br>14354<br>070 022</td><td>14355<br>14355<br>070 023</td><td>14356<br>14356<br>070 024</td><td>14357<br>14357<br>070 025</td><td>14358<br>14358<br>070 026</td><td>14359<br>14359<br>070 027</td><td>14360<br>14360<br>070 030</td><td>14361<br>14361<br>070 031</td><td>14362<br>14362<br>070 032</td><td>14363<br>14363<br>070 033</td><td>14364<br>14364<br>070 034</td><td>14365<br>14365<br>070 035</td><td>14366<br>14366<br>070 036</td><td>14367<br>14367<br>070 037</td></tr>
<tr><td>2–</td><td>14368<br>14368<br>070 040</td><td>14369<br>14369<br>070 041</td><td>14370<br>14370<br>070 042</td><td>14371<br>14371<br>070 043</td><td>14372<br>14372<br>070 044</td><td>14373<br>14373<br>070 045</td><td>14374<br>14374<br>070 046</td><td>14375<br>14375<br>070 047</td><td>14376<br>14376<br>070 050</td><td>14377<br>14377<br>070 051</td><td>14378<br>14378<br>070 052</td><td>14379<br>14379<br>070 053</td><td>14380<br>14380<br>070 054</td><td>14381<br>14381<br>070 055</td><td>14382<br>14382<br>070 056</td><td>14383<br>14383<br>070 057</td></tr>
<tr><td>3–</td><td>14384<br>14384<br>070 060</td><td>14385<br>14385<br>070 061</td><td>14386<br>14386<br>070 062</td><td>14387<br>14387<br>070 063</td><td>14388<br>14388<br>070 064</td><td>14389<br>14389<br>070 065</td><td>14390<br>14390<br>070 066</td><td>14391<br>14391<br>070 067</td><td>14392<br>14392<br>070 070</td><td>14393<br>14393<br>070 071</td><td>14394<br>14394<br>070 072</td><td>14395<br>14395<br>070 073</td><td>14396<br>14396<br>070 074</td><td>14397<br>14397<br>070 075</td><td>14398<br>14398<br>070 076</td><td>14399<br>14399<br>070 077</td></tr>
<tr><td>4–</td><td>14400<br>14400<br>070 100</td><td>14401<br>14401<br>070 101</td><td>14402<br>14402<br>070 102</td><td>14403<br>14403<br>070 103</td><td>14404<br>14404<br>070 104</td><td>14405<br>14405<br>070 105</td><td>14406<br>14406<br>070 106</td><td>14407<br>14407<br>070 107</td><td>14408<br>14408<br>070 110</td><td>14409<br>14409<br>070 111</td><td>14410<br>14410<br>070 112</td><td>14411<br>14411<br>070 113</td><td>14412<br>14412<br>070 114</td><td>14413<br>14413<br>070 115</td><td>14414<br>14414<br>070 116</td><td>14415<br>14415<br>070 117</td></tr>
<tr><td>5–</td><td>14416<br>14416<br>070 120</td><td>14417<br>14417<br>070 121</td><td>14418<br>14418<br>070 122</td><td>14419<br>14419<br>070 123</td><td>14420<br>14420<br>070 124</td><td>14421<br>14421<br>070 125</td><td>14422<br>14422<br>070 126</td><td>14423<br>14423<br>070 127</td><td>14424<br>14424<br>070 130</td><td>14425<br>14425<br>070 131</td><td>14426<br>14426<br>070 132</td><td>14427<br>14427<br>070 133</td><td>14428<br>14428<br>070 134</td><td>14429<br>14429<br>070 135</td><td>14430<br>14430<br>070 136</td><td>14431<br>14431<br>070 137</td></tr>
<tr><td>6–</td><td>14432<br>14432<br>070 140</td><td>14433<br>14433<br>070 141</td><td>14434<br>14434<br>070 142</td><td>14435<br>14435<br>070 143</td><td>14436<br>14436<br>070 144</td><td>14437<br>14437<br>070 145</td><td>14438<br>14438<br>070 146</td><td>14439<br>14439<br>070 147</td><td>14440<br>14440<br>070 150</td><td>14441<br>14441<br>070 151</td><td>14442<br>14442<br>070 152</td><td>14443<br>14443<br>070 153</td><td>14444<br>14444<br>070 154</td><td>14445<br>14445<br>070 155</td><td>14446<br>14446<br>070 156</td><td>14447<br>14447<br>070 157</td></tr>
<tr><td>7–</td><td>14448<br>14448<br>070 160</td><td>14449<br>14449<br>070 161</td><td>14450<br>14450<br>070 162</td><td>14451<br>14451<br>070 163</td><td>14452<br>14452<br>070 164</td><td>14453<br>14453<br>070 165</td><td>14454<br>14454<br>070 166</td><td>14455<br>14455<br>070 167</td><td>14456<br>14456<br>070 170</td><td>14457<br>14457<br>070 171</td><td>14458<br>14458<br>070 172</td><td>14459<br>14459<br>070 173</td><td>14460<br>14460<br>070 174</td><td>14461<br>14461<br>070 175</td><td>14462<br>14462<br>070 176</td><td>14463<br>14463<br>070 177</td></tr>
<tr><td>8–</td><td>14464<br>14464<br>070 200</td><td>14465<br>14465<br>070 201</td><td>14466<br>14466<br>070 202</td><td>14467<br>14467<br>070 203</td><td>14468<br>14468<br>070 204</td><td>14469<br>14469<br>070 205</td><td>14470<br>14470<br>070 206</td><td>14471<br>14471<br>070 207</td><td>14472<br>14472<br>070 210</td><td>14473<br>14473<br>070 211</td><td>14474<br>14474<br>070 212</td><td>14475<br>14475<br>070 213</td><td>14476<br>14476<br>070 214</td><td>14477<br>14477<br>070 215</td><td>14478<br>14478<br>070 216</td><td>14479<br>14479<br>070 217</td></tr>
<tr><td>9–</td><td>14480<br>14480<br>070 220</td><td>14481<br>14481<br>070 221</td><td>14482<br>14482<br>070 222</td><td>14483<br>14483<br>070 223</td><td>14484<br>14484<br>070 224</td><td>14485<br>14485<br>070 225</td><td>14486<br>14486<br>070 226</td><td>14487<br>14487<br>070 227</td><td>14488<br>14488<br>070 230</td><td>14489<br>14489<br>070 231</td><td>14490<br>14490<br>070 232</td><td>14491<br>14491<br>070 233</td><td>14492<br>14492<br>070 234</td><td>14493<br>14493<br>070 235</td><td>14494<br>14494<br>070 236</td><td>14495<br>14495<br>070 237</td></tr>
<tr><td>A–</td><td>14496<br>14496<br>070 240</td><td>14497<br>14497<br>070 241</td><td>14498<br>14498<br>070 242</td><td>14499<br>14499<br>070 243</td><td>14500<br>14500<br>070 244</td><td>14501<br>14501<br>070 245</td><td>14502<br>14502<br>070 246</td><td>14503<br>14503<br>070 247</td><td>14504<br>14504<br>070 250</td><td>14505<br>14505<br>070 251</td><td>14506<br>14506<br>070 252</td><td>14507<br>14507<br>070 253</td><td>14508<br>14508<br>070 254</td><td>14509<br>14509<br>070 255</td><td>14510<br>14510<br>070 256</td><td>14511<br>14511<br>070 257</td></tr>
<tr><td>B–</td><td>14512<br>14512<br>070 260</td><td>14513<br>14513<br>070 261</td><td>14514<br>14514<br>070 262</td><td>14515<br>14515<br>070 263</td><td>14516<br>14516<br>070 264</td><td>14517<br>14517<br>070 265</td><td>14518<br>14518<br>070 266</td><td>14519<br>14519<br>070 267</td><td>14520<br>14520<br>070 270</td><td>14521<br>14521<br>070 271</td><td>14522<br>14522<br>070 272</td><td>14523<br>14523<br>070 273</td><td>14524<br>14524<br>070 274</td><td>14525<br>14525<br>070 275</td><td>14526<br>14526<br>070 276</td><td>14527<br>14527<br>070 277</td></tr>
<tr><td>C–</td><td>14528<br>14528<br>070 300</td><td>14529<br>14529<br>070 301</td><td>14530<br>14530<br>070 302</td><td>14531<br>14531<br>070 303</td><td>14532<br>14532<br>070 304</td><td>14533<br>14533<br>070 305</td><td>14534<br>14534<br>070 306</td><td>14535<br>14535<br>070 307</td><td>14536<br>14536<br>070 310</td><td>14537<br>14537<br>070 311</td><td>14538<br>14538<br>070 312</td><td>14539<br>14539<br>070 313</td><td>14540<br>14540<br>070 314</td><td>14541<br>14541<br>070 315</td><td>14542<br>14542<br>070 316</td><td>14543<br>14543<br>070 317</td></tr>
<tr><td>D–</td><td>14544<br>14544<br>070 320</td><td>14545<br>14545<br>070 321</td><td>14546<br>14546<br>070 322</td><td>14547<br>14547<br>070 323</td><td>14548<br>14548<br>070 324</td><td>14549<br>14549<br>070 325</td><td>14550<br>14550<br>070 326</td><td>14551<br>14551<br>070 327</td><td>14552<br>14552<br>070 330</td><td>14553<br>14553<br>070 331</td><td>14554<br>14554<br>070 332</td><td>14555<br>14555<br>070 333</td><td>14556<br>14556<br>070 334</td><td>14557<br>14557<br>070 335</td><td>14558<br>14558<br>070 336</td><td>14559<br>14559<br>070 337</td></tr>
<tr><td>E–</td><td>14560<br>14560<br>070 340</td><td>14561<br>14561<br>070 341</td><td>14562<br>14562<br>070 342</td><td>14563<br>14563<br>070 343</td><td>14564<br>14564<br>070 344</td><td>14565<br>14565<br>070 345</td><td>14566<br>14566<br>070 346</td><td>14567<br>14567<br>070 347</td><td>14568<br>14568<br>070 350</td><td>14569<br>14569<br>070 351</td><td>14570<br>14570<br>070 352</td><td>14571<br>14571<br>070 353</td><td>14572<br>14572<br>070 354</td><td>14573<br>14573<br>070 355</td><td>14574<br>14574<br>070 356</td><td>14575<br>14575<br>070 357</td></tr>
<tr><td>F–</td><td>14576<br>14576<br>070 360</td><td>14577<br>14577<br>070 361</td><td>14578<br>14578<br>070 362</td><td>14579<br>14579<br>070 363</td><td>14580<br>14580<br>070 364</td><td>14581<br>14581<br>070 365</td><td>14582<br>14582<br>070 366</td><td>14583<br>14583<br>070 367</td><td>14584<br>14584<br>070 370</td><td>14585<br>14585<br>070 371</td><td>14586<br>14586<br>070 372</td><td>14587<br>14587<br>070 373</td><td>14588<br>14588<br>070 374</td><td>14589<br>14589<br>070 375</td><td>14590<br>14590<br>070 376</td><td>14591<br>14591<br>070 377</td></tr>
</tbody>
</table>

SECOND HEX DIGIT

DECIMAL

 DECIMAL

OCTAL

 DECIMAL  14336   BINARY  0011 1000   DECIMAL  14336   HEXADECIMAL  38   OCTAL  070 000

FOURTH HEX DIGIT   THIRD HEX DIGIT

| 2 | FIRST HEX DIGIT | | | | | | | | | | | | | | | |
|---|---|---|---|---|---|---|---|---|---|---|---|---|---|---|---|---|
| | −0 | −1 | −2 | −3 | −4 | −5 | −6 | −7 | −8 | −9 | −A | −B | −C | −D | −E | −F |
| 0− | 14592<br>14592<br>071 000 | 14593<br>14593<br>071 001 | 14594<br>14594<br>071 002 | 14595<br>14595<br>071 003 | 14596<br>14596<br>071 004 | 14597<br>14597<br>071 005 | 14598<br>14598<br>071 006 | 14599<br>14599<br>071 007 | 14600<br>14600<br>071 010 | 14601<br>14601<br>071 011 | 14602<br>14602<br>071 012 | 14603<br>14603<br>071 013 | 14604<br>14604<br>071 014 | 14605<br>14605<br>071 015 | 14606<br>14606<br>071 016 | 14607<br>14607<br>071 017 |
| 1− | 14608<br>14608<br>071 020 | 14609<br>14609<br>071 021 | 14610<br>14610<br>071 022 | 14611<br>14611<br>071 023 | 14612<br>14612<br>071 024 | 14613<br>14613<br>071 025 | 14614<br>14614<br>071 026 | 14615<br>14615<br>071 027 | 14616<br>14616<br>071 030 | 14617<br>14617<br>071 031 | 14618<br>14618<br>071 032 | 14619<br>14619<br>071 033 | 14620<br>14620<br>071 034 | 14621<br>14621<br>071 035 | 14622<br>14622<br>071 036 | 14623<br>14623<br>071 037 |
| 2− | 14624<br>14624<br>071 040 | 14625<br>14625<br>071 041 | 14626<br>14626<br>071 042 | 14627<br>14627<br>071 043 | 14628<br>14628<br>071 044 | 14629<br>14629<br>071 045 | 14630<br>14630<br>071 046 | 14631<br>14631<br>071 047 | 14632<br>14632<br>071 050 | 14633<br>14633<br>071 051 | 14634<br>14634<br>071 052 | 14635<br>14635<br>071 053 | 14636<br>14636<br>071 054 | 14637<br>14637<br>071 055 | 14638<br>14638<br>071 056 | 14639<br>14639<br>071 057 |
| 3− | 14640<br>14640<br>071 060 | 14641<br>14641<br>071 061 | 14642<br>14642<br>071 062 | 14643<br>14643<br>071 063 | 14644<br>14644<br>071 064 | 14645<br>14645<br>071 065 | 14646<br>14646<br>071 066 | 14647<br>14647<br>071 067 | 14648<br>14648<br>071 070 | 14649<br>14649<br>071 071 | 14650<br>14650<br>071 072 | 14651<br>14651<br>071 073 | 14652<br>14652<br>071 074 | 14653<br>14653<br>071 075 | 14654<br>14654<br>071 076 | 14655<br>14655<br>071 077 |
| 4− | 14656<br>14656<br>071 100 | 14657<br>14657<br>071 101 | 14658<br>14658<br>071 102 | 14659<br>14659<br>071 103 | 14660<br>14660<br>071 104 | 14661<br>14661<br>071 105 | 14662<br>14662<br>071 106 | 14663<br>14663<br>071 107 | 14664<br>14664<br>071 110 | 14665<br>14665<br>071 111 | 14666<br>14666<br>071 112 | 14667<br>14667<br>071 113 | 14668<br>14668<br>071 114 | 14669<br>14669<br>071 115 | 14670<br>14670<br>071 116 | 14671<br>14671<br>071 117 |
| 5− | 14672<br>14672<br>071 120 | 14673<br>14673<br>071 121 | 14674<br>14674<br>071 122 | 14675<br>14675<br>071 123 | 14676<br>14676<br>071 124 | 14677<br>14677<br>071 125 | 14678<br>14678<br>071 126 | 14679<br>14679<br>071 127 | 14680<br>14680<br>071 130 | 14681<br>14681<br>071 131 | 14682<br>14682<br>071 132 | 14683<br>14683<br>071 133 | 14684<br>14684<br>071 134 | 14685<br>14685<br>071 135 | 14686<br>14686<br>071 136 | 14687<br>14687<br>071 137 |
| 6− | 14688<br>14688<br>071 140 | 14689<br>14689<br>071 141 | 14690<br>14690<br>071 142 | 14691<br>14691<br>071 143 | 14692<br>14692<br>071 144 | 14693<br>14693<br>071 145 | 14694<br>14694<br>071 146 | 14695<br>14695<br>071 147 | 14696<br>14696<br>071 150 | 14697<br>14697<br>071 151 | 14698<br>14698<br>071 152 | 14699<br>14699<br>071 153 | 14700<br>14700<br>071 154 | 14701<br>14701<br>071 155 | 14702<br>14702<br>071 156 | 14703<br>14703<br>071 157 |
| 7− | 14704<br>14704<br>071 160 | 14705<br>14705<br>071 161 | 14706<br>14706<br>071 162 | 14707<br>14707<br>071 163 | 14708<br>14708<br>071 164 | 14709<br>14709<br>071 165 | 14710<br>14710<br>071 166 | 14711<br>14711<br>071 167 | 14712<br>14712<br>071 170 | 14713<br>14713<br>071 171 | 14714<br>14714<br>071 172 | 14715<br>14715<br>071 173 | 14716<br>14716<br>071 174 | 14717<br>14717<br>071 175 | 14718<br>14718<br>071 176 | 14719<br>14719<br>071 177 |
| 8− | 14720<br>14720<br>071 200 | 14721<br>14721<br>071 201 | 14722<br>14722<br>071 202 | 14723<br>14723<br>071 203 | 14724<br>14724<br>071 204 | 14725<br>14725<br>071 205 | 14726<br>14726<br>071 206 | 14727<br>14727<br>071 207 | 14728<br>14728<br>071 210 | 14729<br>14729<br>071 211 | 14730<br>14730<br>071 212 | 14731<br>14731<br>071 213 | 14732<br>14732<br>071 214 | 14733<br>14733<br>071 215 | 14734<br>14734<br>071 216 | 14735<br>14735<br>071 217 |
| 9− | 14736<br>14736<br>071 220 | 14737<br>14737<br>071 221 | 14738<br>14738<br>071 222 | 14739<br>14739<br>071 223 | 14740<br>14740<br>071 224 | 14741<br>14741<br>071 225 | 14742<br>14742<br>071 226 | 14743<br>14743<br>071 227 | 14744<br>14744<br>071 230 | 14745<br>14745<br>071 231 | 14746<br>14746<br>071 232 | 14747<br>14747<br>071 233 | 14748<br>14748<br>071 234 | 14749<br>14749<br>071 235 | 14750<br>14750<br>071 236 | 14751<br>14751<br>071 237 |
| A− | 14752<br>14752<br>071 240 | 14753<br>14753<br>071 241 | 14754<br>14754<br>071 242 | 14755<br>14755<br>071 243 | 14756<br>14756<br>071 244 | 14757<br>14757<br>071 245 | 14758<br>14758<br>071 246 | 14759<br>14759<br>071 247 | 14760<br>14760<br>071 250 | 14761<br>14761<br>071 251 | 14762<br>14762<br>071 252 | 14763<br>14763<br>071 253 | 14764<br>14764<br>071 254 | 14765<br>14765<br>071 255 | 14766<br>14766<br>071 256 | 14767<br>14767<br>071 257 |
| B− | 14768<br>14768<br>071 260 | 14769<br>14769<br>071 261 | 14770<br>14770<br>071 262 | 14771<br>14771<br>071 263 | 14772<br>14772<br>071 264 | 14773<br>14773<br>071 265 | 14774<br>14774<br>071 266 | 14775<br>14775<br>071 267 | 14776<br>14776<br>071 270 | 14777<br>14777<br>071 271 | 14778<br>14778<br>071 272 | 14779<br>14779<br>071 273 | 14780<br>14780<br>071 274 | 14781<br>14781<br>071 275 | 14782<br>14782<br>071 276 | 14783<br>14783<br>071 277 |
| C− | 14784<br>14784<br>071 300 | 14785<br>14785<br>071 301 | 14786<br>14786<br>071 302 | 14787<br>14787<br>071 303 | 14788<br>14788<br>071 304 | 14789<br>14789<br>071 305 | 14790<br>14790<br>071 306 | 14791<br>14791<br>071 307 | 14792<br>14792<br>071 310 | 14793<br>14793<br>071 311 | 14794<br>14794<br>071 312 | 14795<br>14795<br>071 313 | 14796<br>14796<br>071 314 | 14797<br>14797<br>071 315 | 14798<br>14798<br>071 316 | 14799<br>14799<br>071 317 |
| D− | 14800<br>14800<br>071 320 | 14801<br>14801<br>071 321 | 14802<br>14802<br>071 322 | 14803<br>14803<br>071 323 | 14804<br>14804<br>071 324 | 14805<br>14805<br>071 325 | 14806<br>14806<br>071 326 | 14807<br>14807<br>071 327 | 14808<br>14808<br>071 330 | 14809<br>14809<br>071 331 | 14810<br>14810<br>071 332 | 14811<br>14811<br>071 333 | 14812<br>14812<br>071 334 | 14813<br>14813<br>071 335 | 14814<br>14814<br>071 336 | 14815<br>14815<br>071 337 |
| E− | 14816<br>14816<br>071 340 | 14817<br>14817<br>071 341 | 14818<br>14818<br>071 342 | 14819<br>14819<br>071 343 | 14820<br>14820<br>071 344 | 14821<br>14821<br>071 345 | 14822<br>14822<br>071 346 | 14823<br>14823<br>071 347 | 14824<br>14824<br>071 350 | 14825<br>14825<br>071 351 | 14826<br>14826<br>071 352 | 14827<br>14827<br>071 353 | 14828<br>14828<br>071 354 | 14829<br>14829<br>071 355 | 14830<br>14830<br>071 356 | 14831<br>14831<br>071 357 |
| F− | 14832<br>14832<br>071 360 | 14833<br>14833<br>071 361 | 14834<br>14834<br>071 362 | 14835<br>14835<br>071 363 | 14836<br>14836<br>071 364 | 14837<br>14837<br>071 365 | 14838<br>14838<br>071 366 | 14839<br>14839<br>071 367 | 14840<br>14840<br>071 370 | 14841<br>14841<br>071 371 | 14842<br>14842<br>071 372 | 14843<br>14843<br>071 373 | 14844<br>14844<br>071 374 | 14845<br>14845<br>071 375 | 14846<br>14846<br>071 376 | 14847<br>14847<br>071 377 |

SECOND HEX DIGIT

DECIMAL
DECIMAL
OCTAL

(2) **FIRST HEX DIGIT**

Each cell shows: DECIMAL (top), ❖ DECIMAL (middle), OCTAL (bottom).

| SECOND HEX DIGIT | −0 | −1 | −2 | −3 | −4 | −5 | −6 | −7 | −8 | −9 | −A | −B | −C | −D | −E | −F |
|---|---|---|---|---|---|---|---|---|---|---|---|---|---|---|---|---|
| **0−** | 14848<br>14848<br>072 000 | 14849<br>14849<br>072 001 | 14850<br>14850<br>072 002 | 14851<br>14851<br>072 003 | 14852<br>14852<br>072 004 | 14853<br>14853<br>072 005 | 14854<br>14854<br>072 006 | 14855<br>14855<br>072 007 | 14856<br>14856<br>072 010 | 14857<br>14857<br>072 011 | 14858<br>14858<br>072 012 | 14859<br>14859<br>072 013 | 14860<br>14860<br>072 014 | 14861<br>14861<br>072 015 | 14862<br>14862<br>072 016 | 14863<br>14863<br>072 017 |
| **1−** | 14864<br>14864<br>072 020 | 14865<br>14865<br>072 021 | 14866<br>14866<br>072 022 | 14867<br>14867<br>072 023 | 14868<br>14868<br>072 024 | 14869<br>14869<br>072 025 | 14870<br>14870<br>072 026 | 14871<br>14871<br>072 027 | 14872<br>14872<br>072 030 | 14873<br>14873<br>072 031 | 14874<br>14874<br>072 032 | 14875<br>14875<br>072 033 | 14876<br>14876<br>072 034 | 14877<br>14877<br>072 035 | 14878<br>14878<br>072 036 | 14879<br>14879<br>072 037 |
| **2−** | 14880<br>14880<br>072 040 | 14881<br>14881<br>072 041 | 14882<br>14882<br>072 042 | 14883<br>14883<br>072 043 | 14884<br>14884<br>072 044 | 14885<br>14885<br>072 045 | 14886<br>14886<br>072 046 | 14887<br>14887<br>072 047 | 14888<br>14888<br>072 050 | 14889<br>14889<br>072 051 | 14890<br>14890<br>072 052 | 14891<br>14891<br>072 053 | 14892<br>14892<br>072 054 | 14893<br>14893<br>072 055 | 14894<br>14894<br>072 056 | 14895<br>14895<br>072 057 |
| **3−** | 14896<br>14896<br>072 060 | 14897<br>14897<br>072 061 | 14898<br>14898<br>072 062 | 14899<br>14899<br>072 063 | 14900<br>14900<br>072 064 | 14901<br>14901<br>072 065 | 14902<br>14902<br>072 066 | 14903<br>14903<br>072 067 | 14904<br>14904<br>072 070 | 14905<br>14905<br>072 071 | 14906<br>14906<br>072 072 | 14907<br>14907<br>072 073 | 14908<br>14908<br>072 074 | 14909<br>14909<br>072 075 | 14910<br>14910<br>072 076 | 14911<br>14911<br>072 077 |
| **4−** | 14912<br>14912<br>072 100 | 14913<br>14913<br>072 101 | 14914<br>14914<br>072 102 | 14915<br>14915<br>072 103 | 14916<br>14916<br>072 104 | 14917<br>14917<br>072 105 | 14918<br>14918<br>072 106 | 14919<br>14919<br>072 107 | 14920<br>14920<br>072 110 | 14921<br>14921<br>072 111 | 14922<br>14922<br>072 112 | 14923<br>14923<br>072 113 | 14924<br>14924<br>072 114 | 14925<br>14925<br>072 115 | 14926<br>14926<br>072 116 | 14927<br>14927<br>072 117 |
| **5−** | 14928<br>14928<br>072 120 | 14929<br>14929<br>072 121 | 14930<br>14930<br>072 122 | 14931<br>14931<br>072 123 | 14932<br>14932<br>072 124 | 14933<br>14933<br>072 125 | 14934<br>14934<br>072 126 | 14935<br>14935<br>072 127 | 14936<br>14936<br>072 130 | 14937<br>14937<br>072 131 | 14938<br>14938<br>072 132 | 14939<br>14939<br>072 133 | 14940<br>14940<br>072 134 | 14941<br>14941<br>072 135 | 14942<br>14942<br>072 136 | 14943<br>14943<br>072 137 |
| **6−** | 14944<br>14944<br>072 140 | 14945<br>14945<br>072 141 | 14946<br>14946<br>072 142 | 14947<br>14947<br>072 143 | 14948<br>14948<br>072 144 | 14949<br>14949<br>072 145 | 14950<br>14950<br>072 146 | 14951<br>14951<br>072 147 | 14952<br>14952<br>072 150 | 14953<br>14953<br>072 151 | 14954<br>14954<br>072 152 | 14955<br>14955<br>072 153 | 14956<br>14956<br>072 154 | 14957<br>14957<br>072 155 | 14958<br>14958<br>072 156 | 14959<br>14959<br>072 157 |
| **7−** | 14960<br>14960<br>072 160 | 14961<br>14961<br>072 161 | 14962<br>14962<br>072 162 | 14963<br>14963<br>072 163 | 14964<br>14964<br>072 164 | 14965<br>14965<br>072 165 | 14966<br>14966<br>072 166 | 14967<br>14967<br>072 167 | 14968<br>14968<br>072 170 | 14969<br>14969<br>072 171 | 14970<br>14970<br>072 172 | 14971<br>14971<br>072 173 | 14972<br>14972<br>072 174 | 14973<br>14973<br>072 175 | 14974<br>14974<br>072 176 | 14975<br>14975<br>072 177 |
| **8−** | 14976<br>14976<br>072 200 | 14977<br>14977<br>072 201 | 14978<br>14978<br>072 202 | 14979<br>14979<br>072 203 | 14980<br>14980<br>072 204 | 14981<br>14981<br>072 205 | 14982<br>14982<br>072 206 | 14983<br>14983<br>072 207 | 14984<br>14984<br>072 210 | 14985<br>14985<br>072 211 | 14986<br>14986<br>072 212 | 14987<br>14987<br>072 213 | 14988<br>14988<br>072 214 | 14989<br>14989<br>072 215 | 14990<br>14990<br>072 216 | 14991<br>14991<br>072 217 |
| **9−** | 14992<br>14992<br>072 220 | 14993<br>14993<br>072 221 | 14994<br>14994<br>072 222 | 14995<br>14995<br>072 223 | 14996<br>14996<br>072 224 | 14997<br>14997<br>072 225 | 14998<br>14998<br>072 226 | 14999<br>14999<br>072 227 | 15000<br>15000<br>072 230 | 15001<br>15001<br>072 231 | 15002<br>15002<br>072 232 | 15003<br>15003<br>072 233 | 15004<br>15004<br>072 234 | 15005<br>15005<br>072 235 | 15006<br>15006<br>072 236 | 15007<br>15007<br>072 237 |
| **A−** | 15008<br>15008<br>072 240 | 15009<br>15009<br>072 241 | 15010<br>15010<br>072 242 | 15011<br>15011<br>072 243 | 15012<br>15012<br>072 244 | 15013<br>15013<br>072 245 | 15014<br>15014<br>072 246 | 15015<br>15015<br>072 247 | 15016<br>15016<br>072 250 | 15017<br>15017<br>072 251 | 15018<br>15018<br>072 252 | 15019<br>15019<br>072 253 | 15020<br>15020<br>072 254 | 15021<br>15021<br>072 255 | 15022<br>15022<br>072 256 | 15023<br>15023<br>072 257 |
| **B−** | 15024<br>15024<br>072 260 | 15025<br>15025<br>072 261 | 15026<br>15026<br>072 262 | 15027<br>15027<br>072 263 | 15028<br>15028<br>072 264 | 15029<br>15029<br>072 265 | 15030<br>15030<br>072 266 | 15031<br>15031<br>072 267 | 15032<br>15032<br>072 270 | 15033<br>15033<br>072 271 | 15034<br>15034<br>072 272 | 15035<br>15035<br>072 273 | 15036<br>15036<br>072 274 | 15037<br>15037<br>072 275 | 15038<br>15038<br>072 276 | 15039<br>15039<br>072 277 |
| **C−** | 15040<br>15040<br>072 300 | 15041<br>15041<br>072 301 | 15042<br>15042<br>072 302 | 15043<br>15043<br>072 303 | 15044<br>15044<br>072 304 | 15045<br>15045<br>072 305 | 15046<br>15046<br>072 306 | 15047<br>15047<br>072 307 | 15048<br>15048<br>072 310 | 15049<br>15049<br>072 311 | 15050<br>15050<br>072 312 | 15051<br>15051<br>072 313 | 15052<br>15052<br>072 314 | 15053<br>15053<br>072 315 | 15054<br>15054<br>072 316 | 15055<br>15055<br>072 317 |
| **D−** | 15056<br>15056<br>072 320 | 15057<br>15057<br>072 321 | 15058<br>15058<br>072 322 | 15059<br>15059<br>072 323 | 15060<br>15060<br>072 324 | 15061<br>15061<br>072 325 | 15062<br>15062<br>072 326 | 15063<br>15063<br>072 327 | 15064<br>15064<br>072 330 | 15065<br>15065<br>072 331 | 15066<br>15066<br>072 332 | 15067<br>15067<br>072 333 | 15068<br>15068<br>072 334 | 15069<br>15069<br>072 335 | 15070<br>15070<br>072 336 | 15071<br>15071<br>072 337 |
| **E−** | 15072<br>15072<br>072 340 | 15073<br>15073<br>072 341 | 15074<br>15074<br>072 342 | 15075<br>15075<br>072 343 | 15076<br>15076<br>072 344 | 15077<br>15077<br>072 345 | 15078<br>15078<br>072 346 | 15079<br>15079<br>072 347 | 15080<br>15080<br>072 350 | 15081<br>15081<br>072 351 | 15082<br>15082<br>072 352 | 15083<br>15083<br>072 353 | 15084<br>15084<br>072 354 | 15085<br>15085<br>072 355 | 15086<br>15086<br>072 356 | 15087<br>15087<br>072 357 |
| **F−** | 15088<br>15088<br>072 360 | 15089<br>15089<br>072 361 | 15090<br>15090<br>072 362 | 15091<br>15091<br>072 363 | 15092<br>15092<br>072 364 | 15093<br>15093<br>072 365 | 15094<br>15094<br>072 366 | 15095<br>15095<br>072 367 | 15096<br>15096<br>072 370 | 15097<br>15097<br>072 371 | 15098<br>15098<br>072 372 | 15099<br>15099<br>072 373 | 15100<br>15100<br>072 374 | 15101<br>15101<br>072 375 | 15102<br>15102<br>072 376 | 15103<br>15103<br>072 377 |

Legend (right margin): **DECIMAL** → , ❖ **DECIMAL** → , **OCTAL** →

❖ DECIMAL `14848`  BINARY `0011 1010`  DECIMAL `14848`  HEXADECIMAL ⬡ `3A`  OCTAL `072 000`

FOURTH HEX DIGIT → ⬡ ← THIRD HEX DIGIT

|   2   | FIRST HEX DIGIT | | | | | | | | | | | | | | | |
|---|---|---|---|---|---|---|---|---|---|---|---|---|---|---|---|---|
| SECOND HEX DIGIT | −0 | −1 | −2 | −3 | −4 | −5 | −6 | −7 | −8 | −9 | −A | −B | −C | −D | −E | −F |
| 0− | 15104<br>073 000 | 15105<br>073 001 | 15106<br>073 002 | 15107<br>073 003 | 15108<br>073 004 | 15109<br>073 005 | 15110<br>073 006 | 15111<br>073 007 | 15112<br>073 010 | 15113<br>073 011 | 15114<br>073 012 | 15115<br>073 013 | 15116<br>073 014 | 15117<br>073 015 | 15118<br>073 016 | 15119<br>073 017 |
| 1− | 15120<br>073 020 | 15121<br>073 021 | 15122<br>073 022 | 15123<br>073 023 | 15124<br>073 024 | 15125<br>073 025 | 15126<br>073 026 | 15127<br>073 027 | 15128<br>073 030 | 15129<br>073 031 | 15130<br>073 032 | 15131<br>073 033 | 15132<br>073 034 | 15133<br>073 035 | 15134<br>073 036 | 15135<br>073 037 |
| 2− | 15136<br>073 040 | 15137<br>073 041 | 15138<br>073 042 | 15139<br>073 043 | 15140<br>073 044 | 15141<br>073 045 | 15142<br>073 046 | 15143<br>073 047 | 15144<br>073 050 | 15145<br>073 051 | 15146<br>073 052 | 15147<br>073 053 | 15148<br>073 054 | 15149<br>073 055 | 15150<br>073 056 | 15151<br>073 057 |
| 3− | 15152<br>073 060 | 15153<br>073 061 | 15154<br>073 062 | 15155<br>073 063 | 15156<br>073 064 | 15157<br>073 065 | 15158<br>073 066 | 15159<br>073 067 | 15160<br>073 070 | 15161<br>073 071 | 15162<br>073 072 | 15163<br>073 073 | 15164<br>073 074 | 15165<br>073 075 | 15166<br>073 076 | 15167<br>073 077 |
| 4− | 15168<br>073 100 | 15169<br>073 101 | 15170<br>073 102 | 15171<br>073 103 | 15172<br>073 104 | 15173<br>073 105 | 15174<br>073 106 | 15175<br>073 107 | 15176<br>073 110 | 15177<br>073 111 | 15178<br>073 112 | 15179<br>073 113 | 15180<br>073 114 | 15181<br>073 115 | 15182<br>073 116 | 15183<br>073 117 |
| 5− | 15184<br>073 120 | 15185<br>073 121 | 15186<br>073 122 | 15187<br>073 123 | 15188<br>073 124 | 15189<br>073 125 | 15190<br>073 126 | 15191<br>073 127 | 15192<br>073 130 | 15193<br>073 131 | 15194<br>073 132 | 15195<br>073 133 | 15196<br>073 134 | 15197<br>073 135 | 15198<br>073 136 | 15199<br>073 137 |
| 6− | 15200<br>073 140 | 15201<br>073 141 | 15202<br>073 142 | 15203<br>073 143 | 15204<br>073 144 | 15205<br>073 145 | 15206<br>073 146 | 15207<br>073 147 | 15208<br>073 150 | 15209<br>073 151 | 15210<br>073 152 | 15211<br>073 153 | 15212<br>073 154 | 15213<br>073 155 | 15214<br>073 156 | 15215<br>073 157 |
| 7− | 15216<br>073 160 | 15217<br>073 161 | 15218<br>073 162 | 15219<br>073 163 | 15220<br>073 164 | 15221<br>073 165 | 15222<br>073 166 | 15223<br>073 167 | 15224<br>073 170 | 15225<br>073 171 | 15226<br>073 172 | 15227<br>073 173 | 15228<br>073 174 | 15229<br>073 175 | 15230<br>073 176 | 15231<br>073 177 |
| 8− | 15232<br>073 200 | 15233<br>073 201 | 15234<br>073 202 | 15235<br>073 203 | 15236<br>073 204 | 15237<br>073 205 | 15238<br>073 206 | 15239<br>073 207 | 15240<br>073 210 | 15241<br>073 211 | 15242<br>073 212 | 15243<br>073 213 | 15244<br>073 214 | 15245<br>073 215 | 15246<br>073 216 | 15247<br>073 217 |
| 9− | 15248<br>073 220 | 15249<br>073 221 | 15250<br>073 222 | 15251<br>073 223 | 15252<br>073 224 | 15253<br>073 225 | 15254<br>073 226 | 15255<br>073 227 | 15256<br>073 230 | 15257<br>073 231 | 15258<br>073 232 | 15259<br>073 233 | 15260<br>073 234 | 15261<br>073 235 | 15262<br>073 236 | 15263<br>073 237 |
| A− | 15264<br>073 240 | 15265<br>073 241 | 15266<br>073 242 | 15267<br>073 243 | 15268<br>073 244 | 15269<br>073 245 | 15270<br>073 246 | 15271<br>073 247 | 15272<br>073 250 | 15273<br>073 251 | 15274<br>073 252 | 15275<br>073 253 | 15276<br>073 254 | 15277<br>073 255 | 15278<br>073 256 | 15279<br>073 257 |
| B− | 15280<br>073 260 | 15281<br>073 261 | 15282<br>073 262 | 15283<br>073 263 | 15284<br>073 264 | 15285<br>073 265 | 15286<br>073 266 | 15287<br>073 267 | 15288<br>073 270 | 15289<br>073 271 | 15290<br>073 272 | 15291<br>073 273 | 15292<br>073 274 | 15293<br>073 275 | 15294<br>073 276 | 15295<br>073 277 |
| C− | 15296<br>073 300 | 15297<br>073 301 | 15298<br>073 302 | 15299<br>073 303 | 15300<br>073 304 | 15301<br>073 305 | 15302<br>073 306 | 15303<br>073 307 | 15304<br>073 310 | 15305<br>073 311 | 15306<br>073 312 | 15307<br>073 313 | 15308<br>073 314 | 15309<br>073 315 | 15310<br>073 316 | 15311<br>073 317 |
| D− | 15312<br>073 320 | 15313<br>073 321 | 15314<br>073 322 | 15315<br>073 323 | 15316<br>073 324 | 15317<br>073 325 | 15318<br>073 326 | 15319<br>073 327 | 15320<br>073 330 | 15321<br>073 331 | 15322<br>073 332 | 15323<br>073 333 | 15324<br>073 334 | 15325<br>073 335 | 15326<br>073 336 | 15327<br>073 337 |
| E− | 15328<br>073 340 | 15329<br>073 341 | 15330<br>073 342 | 15331<br>073 343 | 15332<br>073 344 | 15333<br>073 345 | 15334<br>073 346 | 15335<br>073 347 | 15336<br>073 350 | 15337<br>073 351 | 15338<br>073 352 | 15339<br>073 353 | 15340<br>073 354 | 15341<br>073 355 | 15342<br>073 356 | 15343<br>073 357 |
| F− | 15344<br>073 360 | 15345<br>073 361 | 15346<br>073 362 | 15347<br>073 363 | 15348<br>073 364 | 15349<br>073 365 | 15350<br>073 366 | 15351<br>073 367 | 15352<br>073 370 | 15353<br>073 371 | 15354<br>073 372 | 15355<br>073 373 | 15356<br>073 374 | 15357<br>073 375 | 15358<br>073 376 | 15359<br>073 377 |

**DECIMAL** (Apple logo) 15616 **BINARY** 0011 1101 **DECIMAL** 15616 **HEXADECIMAL** 3D **OCTAL** 075 000

FOURTH HEX DIGIT ↗ 3D ↖ THIRD HEX DIGIT

2

| SECOND HEX DIGIT \ FIRST HEX DIGIT | -0 | -1 | -2 | -3 | -4 | -5 | -6 | -7 | -8 | -9 | -A | -B | -C | -D | -E | -F |
|---|---|---|---|---|---|---|---|---|---|---|---|---|---|---|---|---|
| 0- | 15616<br>15616<br>075 000 | 15617<br>15617<br>075 001 | 15618<br>15618<br>075 002 | 15619<br>15619<br>075 003 | 15620<br>15620<br>075 004 | 15621<br>15621<br>075 005 | 15622<br>15622<br>075 006 | 15623<br>15623<br>075 007 | 15624<br>15624<br>075 010 | 15625<br>15625<br>075 011 | 15626<br>15626<br>075 012 | 15627<br>15627<br>075 013 | 15628<br>15628<br>075 014 | 15629<br>15629<br>075 015 | 15630<br>15630<br>075 016 | 15631<br>15631<br>075 017 |
| 1- | 15632<br>15632<br>075 020 | 15633<br>15633<br>075 021 | 15634<br>15634<br>075 022 | 15635<br>15635<br>075 023 | 15636<br>15636<br>075 024 | 15637<br>15637<br>075 025 | 15638<br>15638<br>075 026 | 15639<br>15639<br>075 027 | 15640<br>15640<br>075 030 | 15641<br>15641<br>075 031 | 15642<br>15642<br>075 032 | 15643<br>15643<br>075 033 | 15644<br>15644<br>075 034 | 15645<br>15645<br>075 035 | 15646<br>15646<br>075 036 | 15647<br>15647<br>075 037 |
| 2- | 15648<br>15648<br>075 040 | 15649<br>15649<br>075 041 | 15650<br>15650<br>075 042 | 15651<br>15651<br>075 043 | 15652<br>15652<br>075 044 | 15653<br>15653<br>075 045 | 15654<br>15654<br>075 046 | 15655<br>15655<br>075 047 | 15656<br>15656<br>075 050 | 15657<br>15657<br>075 051 | 15658<br>15658<br>075 052 | 15659<br>15659<br>075 053 | 15660<br>15660<br>075 054 | 15661<br>15661<br>075 055 | 15662<br>15662<br>075 056 | 15663<br>15663<br>075 057 |
| 3- | 15664<br>15664<br>075 060 | 15665<br>15665<br>075 061 | 15666<br>15666<br>075 062 | 15667<br>15667<br>075 063 | 15668<br>15668<br>075 064 | 15669<br>15669<br>075 065 | 15670<br>15670<br>075 066 | 15671<br>15671<br>075 067 | 15672<br>15672<br>075 070 | 15673<br>15673<br>075 071 | 15674<br>15674<br>075 072 | 15675<br>15675<br>075 073 | 15676<br>15676<br>075 074 | 15677<br>15677<br>075 075 | 15678<br>15678<br>075 076 | 15679<br>15679<br>075 077 |
| 4- | 15680<br>15680<br>075 100 | 15681<br>15681<br>075 101 | 15682<br>15682<br>075 102 | 15683<br>15683<br>075 103 | 15684<br>15684<br>075 104 | 15685<br>15685<br>075 105 | 15686<br>15686<br>075 106 | 15687<br>15687<br>075 107 | 15688<br>15688<br>075 110 | 15689<br>15689<br>075 111 | 15690<br>15690<br>075 112 | 15691<br>15691<br>075 113 | 15692<br>15692<br>075 114 | 15693<br>15693<br>075 115 | 15694<br>15694<br>075 116 | 15695<br>15695<br>075 117 |
| 5- | 15696<br>15696<br>075 120 | 15697<br>15697<br>075 121 | 15698<br>15698<br>075 122 | 15699<br>15699<br>075 123 | 15700<br>15700<br>075 124 | 15701<br>15701<br>075 125 | 15702<br>15702<br>075 126 | 15703<br>15703<br>075 127 | 15704<br>15704<br>075 130 | 15705<br>15705<br>075 131 | 15706<br>15706<br>075 132 | 15707<br>15707<br>075 133 | 15708<br>15708<br>075 134 | 15709<br>15709<br>075 135 | 15710<br>15710<br>075 136 | 15711<br>15711<br>075 137 |
| 6- | 15712<br>15712<br>075 140 | 15713<br>15713<br>075 141 | 15714<br>15714<br>075 142 | 15715<br>15715<br>075 143 | 15716<br>15716<br>075 144 | 15717<br>15717<br>075 145 | 15718<br>15718<br>075 146 | 15719<br>15719<br>075 147 | 15720<br>15720<br>075 150 | 15721<br>15721<br>075 151 | 15722<br>15722<br>075 152 | 15723<br>15723<br>075 153 | 15724<br>15724<br>075 154 | 15725<br>15725<br>075 155 | 15726<br>15726<br>075 156 | 15727<br>15727<br>075 157 |
| 7- | 15728<br>15728<br>075 160 | 15729<br>15729<br>075 161 | 15730<br>15730<br>075 162 | 15731<br>15731<br>075 163 | 15732<br>15732<br>075 164 | 15733<br>15733<br>075 165 | 15734<br>15734<br>075 166 | 15735<br>15735<br>075 167 | 15736<br>15736<br>075 170 | 15737<br>15737<br>075 171 | 15738<br>15738<br>075 172 | 15739<br>15739<br>075 173 | 15740<br>15740<br>075 174 | 15741<br>15741<br>075 175 | 15742<br>15742<br>075 176 | 15743<br>15743<br>075 177 |
| 8- | 15744<br>15744<br>075 200 | 15745<br>15745<br>075 201 | 15746<br>15746<br>075 202 | 15747<br>15747<br>075 203 | 15748<br>15748<br>075 204 | 15749<br>15749<br>075 205 | 15750<br>15750<br>075 206 | 15751<br>15751<br>075 207 | 15752<br>15752<br>075 210 | 15753<br>15753<br>075 211 | 15754<br>15754<br>075 212 | 15755<br>15755<br>075 213 | 15756<br>15756<br>075 214 | 15757<br>15757<br>075 215 | 15758<br>15758<br>075 216 | 15759<br>15759<br>075 217 |
| 9- | 15760<br>15760<br>075 220 | 15761<br>15761<br>075 221 | 15762<br>15762<br>075 222 | 15763<br>15763<br>075 223 | 15764<br>15764<br>075 224 | 15765<br>15765<br>075 225 | 15766<br>15766<br>075 226 | 15767<br>15767<br>075 227 | 15768<br>15768<br>075 230 | 15769<br>15769<br>075 231 | 15770<br>15770<br>075 232 | 15771<br>15771<br>075 233 | 15772<br>15772<br>075 234 | 15773<br>15773<br>075 235 | 15774<br>15774<br>075 236 | 15775<br>15775<br>075 237 |
| A- | 15776<br>15776<br>075 240 | 15777<br>15777<br>075 241 | 15778<br>15778<br>075 242 | 15779<br>15779<br>075 243 | 15780<br>15780<br>075 244 | 15781<br>15781<br>075 245 | 15782<br>15782<br>075 246 | 15783<br>15783<br>075 247 | 15784<br>15784<br>075 250 | 15785<br>15785<br>075 251 | 15786<br>15786<br>075 252 | 15787<br>15787<br>075 253 | 15788<br>15788<br>075 254 | 15789<br>15789<br>075 255 | 15790<br>15790<br>075 256 | 15791<br>15791<br>075 257 |
| B- | 15792<br>15792<br>075 260 | 15793<br>15793<br>075 261 | 15794<br>15794<br>075 262 | 15795<br>15795<br>075 263 | 15796<br>15796<br>075 264 | 15797<br>15797<br>075 265 | 15798<br>15798<br>075 266 | 15799<br>15799<br>075 267 | 15800<br>15800<br>075 270 | 15801<br>15801<br>075 271 | 15802<br>15802<br>075 272 | 15803<br>15803<br>075 273 | 15804<br>15804<br>075 274 | 15805<br>15805<br>075 275 | 15806<br>15806<br>075 276 | 15807<br>15807<br>075 277 |
| C- | 15808<br>15808<br>075 300 | 15809<br>15809<br>075 301 | 15810<br>15810<br>075 302 | 15811<br>15811<br>075 303 | 15812<br>15812<br>075 304 | 15813<br>15813<br>075 305 | 15814<br>15814<br>075 306 | 15815<br>15815<br>075 307 | 15816<br>15816<br>075 310 | 15817<br>15817<br>075 311 | 15818<br>15818<br>075 312 | 15819<br>15819<br>075 313 | 15820<br>15820<br>075 314 | 15821<br>15821<br>075 315 | 15822<br>15822<br>075 316 | 15823<br>15823<br>075 317 |
| D- | 15824<br>15824<br>075 320 | 15825<br>15825<br>075 321 | 15826<br>15826<br>075 322 | 15827<br>15827<br>075 323 | 15828<br>15828<br>075 324 | 15829<br>15829<br>075 325 | 15830<br>15830<br>075 326 | 15831<br>15831<br>075 327 | 15832<br>15832<br>075 330 | 15833<br>15833<br>075 331 | 15834<br>15834<br>075 332 | 15835<br>15835<br>075 333 | 15836<br>15836<br>075 334 | 15837<br>15837<br>075 335 | 15838<br>15838<br>075 336 | 15839<br>15839<br>075 337 |
| E- | 15840<br>15840<br>075 340 | 15841<br>15841<br>075 341 | 15842<br>15842<br>075 342 | 15843<br>15843<br>075 343 | 15844<br>15844<br>075 344 | 15845<br>15845<br>075 345 | 15846<br>15846<br>075 346 | 15847<br>15847<br>075 347 | 15848<br>15848<br>075 350 | 15849<br>15849<br>075 351 | 15850<br>15850<br>075 352 | 15851<br>15851<br>075 353 | 15852<br>15852<br>075 354 | 15853<br>15853<br>075 355 | 15854<br>15854<br>075 356 | 15855<br>15855<br>075 357 |
| F- | 15856<br>15856<br>075 360 | 15857<br>15857<br>075 361 | 15858<br>15858<br>075 362 | 15859<br>15859<br>075 363 | 15860<br>15860<br>075 364 | 15861<br>15861<br>075 365 | 15862<br>15862<br>075 366 | 15863<br>15863<br>075 367 | 15864<br>15864<br>075 370 | 15865<br>15865<br>075 371 | 15866<br>15866<br>075 372 | 15867<br>15867<br>075 373 | 15868<br>15868<br>075 374 | 15869<br>15869<br>075 375 | 15870<br>15870<br>075 376 | 15871<br>15871<br>075 377 |

DECIMAL (first line of each cell)

(Apple logo) DECIMAL (second line of each cell)

OCTAL (third line of each cell)

| SECOND HEX DIGIT | −0 | −1 | −2 | −3 | −4 | −5 | −6 | −7 | −8 | −9 | −A | −B | −C | −D | −E | −F |
|---|---|---|---|---|---|---|---|---|---|---|---|---|---|---|---|---|
| 0- | 15872<br>15872<br>076 000 | 15873<br>15873<br>076 001 | 15874<br>15874<br>076 002 | 15875<br>15875<br>076 003 | 15876<br>15876<br>076 004 | 15877<br>15877<br>076 005 | 15878<br>15878<br>076 006 | 15879<br>15879<br>076 007 | 15880<br>15880<br>076 010 | 15881<br>15881<br>076 011 | 15882<br>15882<br>076 012 | 15883<br>15883<br>076 013 | 15884<br>15884<br>076 014 | 15885<br>15885<br>076 015 | 15886<br>15886<br>076 016 | 15887<br>15887<br>076 017 |
| 1- | 15888<br>15888<br>076 020 | 15889<br>15889<br>076 021 | 15890<br>15890<br>076 022 | 15891<br>15891<br>076 023 | 15892<br>15892<br>076 024 | 15893<br>15893<br>076 025 | 15894<br>15894<br>076 026 | 15895<br>15895<br>076 027 | 15896<br>15896<br>076 030 | 15897<br>15897<br>076 031 | 15898<br>15898<br>076 032 | 15899<br>15899<br>076 033 | 15900<br>15900<br>076 034 | 15901<br>15901<br>076 035 | 15902<br>15902<br>076 036 | 15903<br>15903<br>076 037 |
| 2- | 15904<br>15904<br>076 040 | 15905<br>15905<br>076 041 | 15906<br>15906<br>076 042 | 15907<br>15907<br>076 043 | 15908<br>15908<br>076 044 | 15909<br>15909<br>076 045 | 15910<br>15910<br>076 046 | 15911<br>15911<br>076 047 | 15912<br>15912<br>076 050 | 15913<br>15913<br>076 051 | 15914<br>15914<br>076 052 | 15915<br>15915<br>076 053 | 15916<br>15916<br>076 054 | 15917<br>15917<br>076 055 | 15918<br>15918<br>076 056 | 15919<br>15919<br>076 057 |
| 3- | 15920<br>15920<br>076 060 | 15921<br>15921<br>076 061 | 15922<br>15922<br>076 062 | 15923<br>15923<br>076 063 | 15924<br>15924<br>076 064 | 15925<br>15925<br>076 065 | 15926<br>15926<br>076 066 | 15927<br>15927<br>076 067 | 15928<br>15928<br>076 070 | 15929<br>15929<br>076 071 | 15930<br>15930<br>076 072 | 15931<br>15931<br>076 073 | 15932<br>15932<br>076 074 | 15933<br>15933<br>076 075 | 15934<br>15934<br>076 076 | 15935<br>15935<br>076 077 |
| 4- | 15936<br>15936<br>076 100 | 15937<br>15937<br>076 101 | 15938<br>15938<br>076 102 | 15939<br>15939<br>076 103 | 15940<br>15940<br>076 104 | 15941<br>15941<br>076 105 | 15942<br>15942<br>076 106 | 15943<br>15943<br>076 107 | 15944<br>15944<br>076 110 | 15945<br>15945<br>076 111 | 15946<br>15946<br>076 112 | 15947<br>15947<br>076 113 | 15948<br>15948<br>076 114 | 15949<br>15949<br>076 115 | 15950<br>15950<br>076 116 | 15951<br>15951<br>076 117 |
| 5- | 15952<br>15952<br>076 120 | 15953<br>15953<br>076 121 | 15954<br>15954<br>076 122 | 15955<br>15955<br>076 123 | 15956<br>15956<br>076 124 | 15957<br>15957<br>076 125 | 15958<br>15958<br>076 126 | 15959<br>15959<br>076 127 | 15960<br>15960<br>076 130 | 15961<br>15961<br>076 131 | 15962<br>15962<br>076 132 | 15963<br>15963<br>076 133 | 15964<br>15964<br>076 134 | 15965<br>15965<br>076 135 | 15966<br>15966<br>076 136 | 15967<br>15967<br>076 137 |
| 6- | 15968<br>15968<br>076 140 | 15969<br>15969<br>076 141 | 15970<br>15970<br>076 142 | 15971<br>15971<br>076 143 | 15972<br>15972<br>076 144 | 15973<br>15973<br>076 145 | 15974<br>15974<br>076 146 | 15975<br>15975<br>076 147 | 15976<br>15976<br>076 150 | 15977<br>15977<br>076 151 | 15978<br>15978<br>076 152 | 15979<br>15979<br>076 153 | 15980<br>15980<br>076 154 | 15981<br>15981<br>076 155 | 15982<br>15982<br>076 156 | 15983<br>15983<br>076 157 |
| 7- | 15984<br>15984<br>076 160 | 15985<br>15985<br>076 161 | 15986<br>15986<br>076 162 | 15987<br>15987<br>076 163 | 15988<br>15988<br>076 164 | 15989<br>15989<br>076 165 | 15990<br>15990<br>076 166 | 15991<br>15991<br>076 167 | 15992<br>15992<br>076 170 | 15993<br>15993<br>076 171 | 15994<br>15994<br>076 172 | 15995<br>15995<br>076 173 | 15996<br>15996<br>076 174 | 15997<br>15997<br>076 175 | 15998<br>15998<br>076 176 | 15999<br>15999<br>076 177 |
| 8- | 16000<br>16000<br>076 200 | 16001<br>16001<br>076 201 | 16002<br>16002<br>076 202 | 16003<br>16003<br>076 203 | 16004<br>16004<br>076 204 | 16005<br>16005<br>076 205 | 16006<br>16006<br>076 206 | 16007<br>16007<br>076 207 | 16008<br>16008<br>076 210 | 16009<br>16009<br>076 211 | 16010<br>16010<br>076 212 | 16011<br>16011<br>076 213 | 16012<br>16012<br>076 214 | 16013<br>16013<br>076 215 | 16014<br>16014<br>076 216 | 16015<br>16015<br>076 217 |
| 9- | 16016<br>16016<br>076 220 | 16017<br>16017<br>076 221 | 16018<br>16018<br>076 222 | 16019<br>16019<br>076 223 | 16020<br>16020<br>076 224 | 16021<br>16021<br>076 225 | 16022<br>16022<br>076 226 | 16023<br>16023<br>076 227 | 16024<br>16024<br>076 230 | 16025<br>16025<br>076 231 | 16026<br>16026<br>076 232 | 16027<br>16027<br>076 233 | 16028<br>16028<br>076 234 | 16029<br>16029<br>076 235 | 16030<br>16030<br>076 236 | 16031<br>16031<br>076 237 |
| A- | 16032<br>16032<br>076 240 | 16033<br>16033<br>076 241 | 16034<br>16034<br>076 242 | 16035<br>16035<br>076 243 | 16036<br>16036<br>076 244 | 16037<br>16037<br>076 245 | 16038<br>16038<br>076 246 | 16039<br>16039<br>076 247 | 16040<br>16040<br>076 250 | 16041<br>16041<br>076 251 | 16042<br>16042<br>076 252 | 16043<br>16043<br>076 253 | 16044<br>16044<br>076 254 | 16045<br>16045<br>076 255 | 16046<br>16046<br>076 256 | 16047<br>16047<br>076 257 |
| B- | 16048<br>16048<br>076 260 | 16049<br>16049<br>076 261 | 16050<br>16050<br>076 262 | 16051<br>16051<br>076 263 | 16052<br>16052<br>076 264 | 16053<br>16053<br>076 265 | 16054<br>16054<br>076 266 | 16055<br>16055<br>076 267 | 16056<br>16056<br>076 270 | 16057<br>16057<br>076 271 | 16058<br>16058<br>076 272 | 16059<br>16059<br>076 273 | 16060<br>16060<br>076 274 | 16061<br>16061<br>076 275 | 16062<br>16062<br>076 276 | 16063<br>16063<br>076 277 |
| C- | 16064<br>16064<br>076 300 | 16065<br>16065<br>076 301 | 16066<br>16066<br>076 302 | 16067<br>16067<br>076 303 | 16068<br>16068<br>076 304 | 16069<br>16069<br>076 305 | 16070<br>16070<br>076 306 | 16071<br>16071<br>076 307 | 16072<br>16072<br>076 310 | 16073<br>16073<br>076 311 | 16074<br>16074<br>076 312 | 16075<br>16075<br>076 313 | 16076<br>16076<br>076 314 | 16077<br>16077<br>076 315 | 16078<br>16078<br>076 316 | 16079<br>16079<br>076 317 |
| D- | 16080<br>16080<br>076 320 | 16081<br>16081<br>076 321 | 16082<br>16082<br>076 322 | 16083<br>16083<br>076 323 | 16084<br>16084<br>076 324 | 16085<br>16085<br>076 325 | 16086<br>16086<br>076 326 | 16087<br>16087<br>076 327 | 16088<br>16088<br>076 330 | 16089<br>16089<br>076 331 | 16090<br>16090<br>076 332 | 16091<br>16091<br>076 333 | 16092<br>16092<br>076 334 | 16093<br>16093<br>076 335 | 16094<br>16094<br>076 336 | 16095<br>16095<br>076 337 |
| E- | 16096<br>16096<br>076 340 | 16097<br>16097<br>076 341 | 16098<br>16098<br>076 342 | 16099<br>16099<br>076 343 | 16100<br>16100<br>076 344 | 16101<br>16101<br>076 345 | 16102<br>16102<br>076 346 | 16103<br>16103<br>076 347 | 16104<br>16104<br>076 350 | 16105<br>16105<br>076 351 | 16106<br>16106<br>076 352 | 16107<br>16107<br>076 353 | 16108<br>16108<br>076 354 | 16109<br>16109<br>076 355 | 16110<br>16110<br>076 356 | 16111<br>16111<br>076 357 |
| F- | 16112<br>16112<br>076 360 | 16113<br>16113<br>076 361 | 16114<br>16114<br>076 362 | 16115<br>16115<br>076 363 | 16116<br>16116<br>076 364 | 16117<br>16117<br>076 365 | 16118<br>16118<br>076 366 | 16119<br>16119<br>076 367 | 16120<br>16120<br>076 370 | 16121<br>16121<br>076 371 | 16122<br>16122<br>076 372 | 16123<br>16123<br>076 373 | 16124<br>16124<br>076 374 | 16125<br>16125<br>076 375 | 16126<br>16126<br>076 376 | 16127<br>16127<br>076 377 |

DECIMAL

DECIMAL

OCTAL

 DECIMAL [15872]   BINARY [0011 1110]   DECIMAL [15872]   HEXADECIMAL (3E) OCTAL [076 000]

FOURTH HEX DIGIT → ← THIRD HEX DIGIT

(2)

| SECOND HEX DIGIT \ FIRST HEX DIGIT | −0 | −1 | −2 | −3 | −4 | −5 | −6 | −7 | −8 | −9 | −A | −B | −C | −D | −E | −F |
|---|---|---|---|---|---|---|---|---|---|---|---|---|---|---|---|---|
| 0− | 16128<br>077 000 | 16129<br>077 001 | 16130<br>077 002 | 16131<br>077 003 | 16132<br>077 004 | 16133<br>077 005 | 16134<br>077 006 | 16135<br>077 007 | 16136<br>077 010 | 16137<br>077 011 | 16138<br>077 012 | 16139<br>077 013 | 16140<br>077 014 | 16141<br>077 015 | 16142<br>077 016 | 16143<br>077 017 |
| 1− | 16144<br>077 020 | 16145<br>077 021 | 16146<br>077 022 | 16147<br>077 023 | 16148<br>077 024 | 16149<br>077 025 | 16150<br>077 026 | 16151<br>077 027 | 16152<br>077 030 | 16153<br>077 031 | 16154<br>077 032 | 16155<br>077 033 | 16156<br>077 034 | 16157<br>077 035 | 16158<br>077 036 | 16159<br>077 037 |
| 2− | 16160<br>077 040 | 16161<br>077 041 | 16162<br>077 042 | 16163<br>077 043 | 16164<br>077 044 | 16165<br>077 045 | 16166<br>077 046 | 16167<br>077 047 | 16168<br>077 050 | 16169<br>077 051 | 16170<br>077 052 | 16171<br>077 053 | 16172<br>077 054 | 16173<br>077 055 | 16174<br>077 056 | 16175<br>077 057 |
| 3− | 16176<br>077 060 | 16177<br>077 061 | 16178<br>077 062 | 16179<br>077 063 | 16180<br>077 064 | 16181<br>077 065 | 16182<br>077 066 | 16183<br>077 067 | 16184<br>077 070 | 16185<br>077 071 | 16186<br>077 072 | 16187<br>077 073 | 16188<br>077 074 | 16189<br>077 075 | 16190<br>077 076 | 16191<br>077 077 |
| 4− | 16192<br>077 100 | 16193<br>077 101 | 16194<br>077 102 | 16195<br>077 103 | 16196<br>077 104 | 16197<br>077 105 | 16198<br>077 106 | 16199<br>077 107 | 16200<br>077 110 | 16201<br>077 111 | 16202<br>077 112 | 16203<br>077 113 | 16204<br>077 114 | 16205<br>077 115 | 16206<br>077 116 | 16207<br>077 117 |
| 5− | 16208<br>077 120 | 16209<br>077 121 | 16210<br>077 122 | 16211<br>077 123 | 16212<br>077 124 | 16213<br>077 125 | 16214<br>077 126 | 16215<br>077 127 | 16216<br>077 130 | 16217<br>077 131 | 16218<br>077 132 | 16219<br>077 133 | 16220<br>077 134 | 16221<br>077 135 | 16222<br>077 136 | 16223<br>077 137 |
| 6− | 16224<br>077 140 | 16225<br>077 141 | 16226<br>077 142 | 16227<br>077 143 | 16228<br>077 144 | 16229<br>077 145 | 16230<br>077 146 | 16231<br>077 147 | 16232<br>077 150 | 16233<br>077 151 | 16234<br>077 152 | 16235<br>077 153 | 16236<br>077 154 | 16237<br>077 155 | 16238<br>077 156 | 16239<br>077 157 |
| 7− | 16240<br>077 160 | 16241<br>077 161 | 16242<br>077 162 | 16243<br>077 163 | 16244<br>077 164 | 16245<br>077 165 | 16246<br>077 166 | 16247<br>077 167 | 16248<br>077 170 | 16249<br>077 171 | 16250<br>077 172 | 16251<br>077 173 | 16252<br>077 174 | 16253<br>077 175 | 16254<br>077 176 | 16255<br>077 177 |
| 8− | 16256<br>077 200 | 16257<br>077 201 | 16258<br>077 202 | 16259<br>077 203 | 16260<br>077 204 | 16261<br>077 205 | 16262<br>077 206 | 16263<br>077 207 | 16264<br>077 210 | 16265<br>077 211 | 16266<br>077 212 | 16267<br>077 213 | 16268<br>077 214 | 16269<br>077 215 | 16270<br>077 216 | 16271<br>077 217 |
| 9− | 16272<br>077 220 | 16273<br>077 221 | 16274<br>077 222 | 16275<br>077 223 | 16276<br>077 224 | 16277<br>077 225 | 16278<br>077 226 | 16279<br>077 227 | 16280<br>077 230 | 16281<br>077 231 | 16282<br>077 232 | 16283<br>077 233 | 16284<br>077 234 | 16285<br>077 235 | 16286<br>077 236 | 16287<br>077 237 |
| A− | 16288<br>077 240 | 16289<br>077 241 | 16290<br>077 242 | 16291<br>077 243 | 16292<br>077 244 | 16293<br>077 245 | 16294<br>077 246 | 16295<br>077 247 | 16296<br>077 250 | 16297<br>077 251 | 16298<br>077 252 | 16299<br>077 253 | 16300<br>077 254 | 16301<br>077 255 | 16302<br>077 256 | 16303<br>077 257 |
| B− | 16304<br>077 260 | 16305<br>077 261 | 16306<br>077 262 | 16307<br>077 263 | 16308<br>077 264 | 16309<br>077 265 | 16310<br>077 266 | 16311<br>077 267 | 16312<br>077 270 | 16313<br>077 271 | 16314<br>077 272 | 16315<br>077 273 | 16316<br>077 274 | 16317<br>077 275 | 16318<br>077 276 | 16319<br>077 277 |
| C− | 16320<br>077 300 | 16321<br>077 301 | 16322<br>077 302 | 16323<br>077 303 | 16324<br>077 304 | 16325<br>077 305 | 16326<br>077 306 | 16327<br>077 307 | 16328<br>077 310 | 16329<br>077 311 | 16330<br>077 312 | 16331<br>077 313 | 16332<br>077 314 | 16333<br>077 315 | 16334<br>077 316 | 16335<br>077 317 |
| D− | 16336<br>077 320 | 16337<br>077 321 | 16338<br>077 322 | 16339<br>077 323 | 16340<br>077 324 | 16341<br>077 325 | 16342<br>077 326 | 16343<br>077 327 | 16344<br>077 330 | 16345<br>077 331 | 16346<br>077 332 | 16347<br>077 333 | 16348<br>077 334 | 16349<br>077 335 | 16350<br>077 336 | 16351<br>077 337 |
| E− | 16352<br>077 340 | 16353<br>077 341 | 16354<br>077 342 | 16355<br>077 343 | 16356<br>077 344 | 16357<br>077 345 | 16358<br>077 346 | 16359<br>077 347 | 16360<br>077 350 | 16361<br>077 351 | 16362<br>077 352 | 16363<br>077 353 | 16364<br>077 354 | 16365<br>077 355 | 16366<br>077 356 | 16367<br>077 357 |
| F− | 16368<br>077 360 | 16369<br>077 361 | 16370<br>077 362 | 16371<br>077 363 | 16372<br>077 364 | 16373<br>077 365 | 16374<br>077 366 | 16375<br>077 367 | 16376<br>077 370 | 16377<br>077 371 | 16378<br>077 372 | 16379<br>077 373 | 16380<br>077 374 | 16381<br>077 375 | 16382<br>077 376 | 16383<br>077 377 |

| | −0 | −1 | −2 | −3 | −4 | −5 | −6 | −7 | −8 | −9 | −A | −B | −C | −D | −E | −F |
|---|---|---|---|---|---|---|---|---|---|---|---|---|---|---|---|---|
| 0- | 16384<br>16384<br>100 000 | 16385<br>16385<br>100 001 | 16386<br>16386<br>100 002 | 16387<br>16387<br>100 003 | 16388<br>16388<br>100 004 | 16389<br>16389<br>100 005 | 16390<br>16390<br>100 006 | 16391<br>16391<br>100 007 | 16392<br>16392<br>100 010 | 16393<br>16393<br>100 011 | 16394<br>16394<br>100 012 | 16395<br>16395<br>100 013 | 16396<br>16396<br>100 014 | 16397<br>16397<br>100 015 | 16398<br>16398<br>100 016 | 16399<br>16399<br>100 017 |
| 1- | 16400<br>16400<br>100 020 | 16401<br>16401<br>100 021 | 16402<br>16402<br>100 022 | 16403<br>16403<br>100 023 | 16404<br>16404<br>100 024 | 16405<br>16405<br>100 025 | 16406<br>16406<br>100 026 | 16407<br>16407<br>100 027 | 16408<br>16408<br>100 030 | 16409<br>16409<br>100 031 | 16410<br>16410<br>100 032 | 16411<br>16411<br>100 033 | 16412<br>16412<br>100 034 | 16413<br>16413<br>100 035 | 16414<br>16414<br>100 036 | 16415<br>16415<br>100 037 |
| 2- | 16416<br>16416<br>100 040 | 16417<br>16417<br>100 041 | 16418<br>16418<br>100 042 | 16419<br>16419<br>100 043 | 16420<br>16420<br>100 044 | 16421<br>16421<br>100 045 | 16422<br>16422<br>100 046 | 16423<br>16423<br>100 047 | 16424<br>16424<br>100 050 | 16425<br>16425<br>100 051 | 16426<br>16426<br>100 052 | 16427<br>16427<br>100 053 | 16428<br>16428<br>100 054 | 16429<br>16429<br>100 055 | 16430<br>16430<br>100 056 | 16431<br>16431<br>100 057 |
| 3- | 16432<br>16432<br>100 060 | 16433<br>16433<br>100 061 | 16434<br>16434<br>100 062 | 16435<br>16435<br>100 063 | 16436<br>16436<br>100 064 | 16437<br>16437<br>100 065 | 16438<br>16438<br>100 066 | 16439<br>16439<br>100 067 | 16440<br>16440<br>100 070 | 16441<br>16441<br>100 071 | 16442<br>16442<br>100 072 | 16443<br>16443<br>100 073 | 16444<br>16444<br>100 074 | 16445<br>16445<br>100 075 | 16446<br>16446<br>100 076 | 16447<br>16447<br>100 077 |
| 4- | 16448<br>16448<br>100 100 | 16449<br>16449<br>100 101 | 16450<br>16450<br>100 102 | 16451<br>16451<br>100 103 | 16452<br>16452<br>100 104 | 16453<br>16453<br>100 105 | 16454<br>16454<br>100 106 | 16455<br>16455<br>100 107 | 16456<br>16456<br>100 110 | 16457<br>16457<br>100 111 | 16458<br>16458<br>100 112 | 16459<br>16459<br>100 113 | 16460<br>16460<br>100 114 | 16461<br>16461<br>100 115 | 16462<br>16462<br>100 116 | 16463<br>16463<br>100 117 |
| 5- | 16464<br>16464<br>100 120 | 16465<br>16465<br>100 121 | 16466<br>16466<br>100 122 | 16467<br>16467<br>100 123 | 16468<br>16468<br>100 124 | 16469<br>16469<br>100 125 | 16470<br>16470<br>100 126 | 16471<br>16471<br>100 127 | 16472<br>16472<br>100 130 | 16473<br>16473<br>100 131 | 16474<br>16474<br>100 132 | 16475<br>16475<br>100 133 | 16476<br>16476<br>100 134 | 16477<br>16477<br>100 135 | 16478<br>16478<br>100 136 | 16479<br>16479<br>100 137 |
| 6- | 16480<br>16480<br>100 140 | 16481<br>16481<br>100 141 | 16482<br>16482<br>100 142 | 16483<br>16483<br>100 143 | 16484<br>16484<br>100 144 | 16485<br>16485<br>100 145 | 16486<br>16486<br>100 146 | 16487<br>16487<br>100 147 | 16488<br>16488<br>100 150 | 16489<br>16489<br>100 151 | 16490<br>16490<br>100 152 | 16491<br>16491<br>100 153 | 16492<br>16492<br>100 154 | 16493<br>16493<br>100 155 | 16494<br>16494<br>100 156 | 16495<br>16495<br>100 157 |
| 7- | 16496<br>16496<br>100 160 | 16497<br>16497<br>100 161 | 16498<br>16498<br>100 162 | 16499<br>16499<br>100 163 | 16500<br>16500<br>100 164 | 16501<br>16501<br>100 165 | 16502<br>16502<br>100 166 | 16503<br>16503<br>100 167 | 16504<br>16504<br>100 170 | 16505<br>16505<br>100 171 | 16506<br>16506<br>100 172 | 16507<br>16507<br>100 173 | 16508<br>16508<br>100 174 | 16509<br>16509<br>100 175 | 16510<br>16510<br>100 176 | 16511<br>16511<br>100 177 |
| 8- | 16512<br>16512<br>100 200 | 16513<br>16513<br>100 201 | 16514<br>16514<br>100 202 | 16515<br>16515<br>100 203 | 16516<br>16516<br>100 204 | 16517<br>16517<br>100 205 | 16518<br>16518<br>100 206 | 16519<br>16519<br>100 207 | 16520<br>16520<br>100 210 | 16521<br>16521<br>100 211 | 16522<br>16522<br>100 212 | 16523<br>16523<br>100 213 | 16524<br>16524<br>100 214 | 16525<br>16525<br>100 215 | 16526<br>16526<br>100 216 | 16527<br>16527<br>100 217 |
| 9- | 16528<br>16528<br>100 220 | 16529<br>16529<br>100 221 | 16530<br>16530<br>100 222 | 16531<br>16531<br>100 223 | 16532<br>16532<br>100 224 | 16533<br>16533<br>100 225 | 16534<br>16534<br>100 226 | 16535<br>16535<br>100 227 | 16536<br>16536<br>100 230 | 16537<br>16537<br>100 231 | 16538<br>16538<br>100 232 | 16539<br>16539<br>100 233 | 16540<br>16540<br>100 234 | 16541<br>16541<br>100 235 | 16542<br>16542<br>100 236 | 16543<br>16543<br>100 237 |
| A- | 16544<br>16544<br>100 240 | 16545<br>16545<br>100 241 | 16546<br>16546<br>100 242 | 16547<br>16547<br>100 243 | 16548<br>16548<br>100 244 | 16549<br>16549<br>100 245 | 16550<br>16550<br>100 246 | 16551<br>16551<br>100 247 | 16552<br>16552<br>100 250 | 16553<br>16553<br>100 251 | 16554<br>16554<br>100 252 | 16555<br>16555<br>100 253 | 16556<br>16556<br>100 254 | 16557<br>16557<br>100 255 | 16558<br>16558<br>100 256 | 16559<br>16559<br>100 257 |
| B- | 16560<br>16560<br>100 260 | 16561<br>16561<br>100 261 | 16562<br>16562<br>100 262 | 16563<br>16563<br>100 263 | 16564<br>16564<br>100 264 | 16565<br>16565<br>100 265 | 16566<br>16566<br>100 266 | 16567<br>16567<br>100 267 | 16568<br>16568<br>100 270 | 16569<br>16569<br>100 271 | 16570<br>16570<br>100 272 | 16571<br>16571<br>100 273 | 16572<br>16572<br>100 274 | 16573<br>16573<br>100 275 | 16574<br>16574<br>100 276 | 16575<br>16575<br>100 277 |
| C- | 16576<br>16576<br>100 300 | 16577<br>16577<br>100 301 | 16578<br>16578<br>100 302 | 16579<br>16579<br>100 303 | 16580<br>16580<br>100 304 | 16581<br>16581<br>100 305 | 16582<br>16582<br>100 306 | 16583<br>16583<br>100 307 | 16584<br>16584<br>100 310 | 16585<br>16585<br>100 311 | 16586<br>16586<br>100 312 | 16587<br>16587<br>100 313 | 16588<br>16588<br>100 314 | 16589<br>16589<br>100 315 | 16590<br>16590<br>100 316 | 16591<br>16591<br>100 317 |
| D- | 16592<br>16592<br>100 320 | 16593<br>16593<br>100 321 | 16594<br>16594<br>100 322 | 16595<br>16595<br>100 323 | 16596<br>16596<br>100 324 | 16597<br>16597<br>100 325 | 16598<br>16598<br>100 326 | 16599<br>16599<br>100 327 | 16600<br>16600<br>100 330 | 16601<br>16601<br>100 331 | 16602<br>16602<br>100 332 | 16603<br>16603<br>100 333 | 16604<br>16604<br>100 334 | 16605<br>16605<br>100 335 | 16606<br>16606<br>100 336 | 16607<br>16607<br>100 337 |
| E- | 16608<br>16608<br>100 340 | 16609<br>16609<br>100 341 | 16610<br>16610<br>100 342 | 16611<br>16611<br>100 343 | 16612<br>16612<br>100 344 | 16613<br>16613<br>100 345 | 16614<br>16614<br>100 346 | 16615<br>16615<br>100 347 | 16616<br>16616<br>100 350 | 16617<br>16617<br>100 351 | 16618<br>16618<br>100 352 | 16619<br>16619<br>100 353 | 16620<br>16620<br>100 354 | 16621<br>16621<br>100 355 | 16622<br>16622<br>100 356 | 16623<br>16623<br>100 357 |
| F- | 16624<br>16624<br>100 360 | 16625<br>16625<br>100 361 | 16626<br>16626<br>100 362 | 16627<br>16627<br>100 363 | 16628<br>16628<br>100 364 | 16629<br>16629<br>100 365 | 16630<br>16630<br>100 366 | 16631<br>16631<br>100 367 | 16632<br>16632<br>100 370 | 16633<br>16633<br>100 371 | 16634<br>16634<br>100 372 | 16635<br>16635<br>100 373 | 16636<br>16636<br>100 374 | 16637<br>16637<br>100 375 | 16638<br>16638<br>100 376 | 16639<br>16639<br>100 377 |

SECOND HEX DIGIT

DECIMAL · 🍎 DECIMAL · OCTAL

🍎 DECIMAL 16384   BINARY 0100 0000   DECIMAL 16384   HEXADECIMAL ⬡40   OCTAL 100 000

FOURTH HEX DIGIT → ⬡ ← THIRD HEX DIGIT

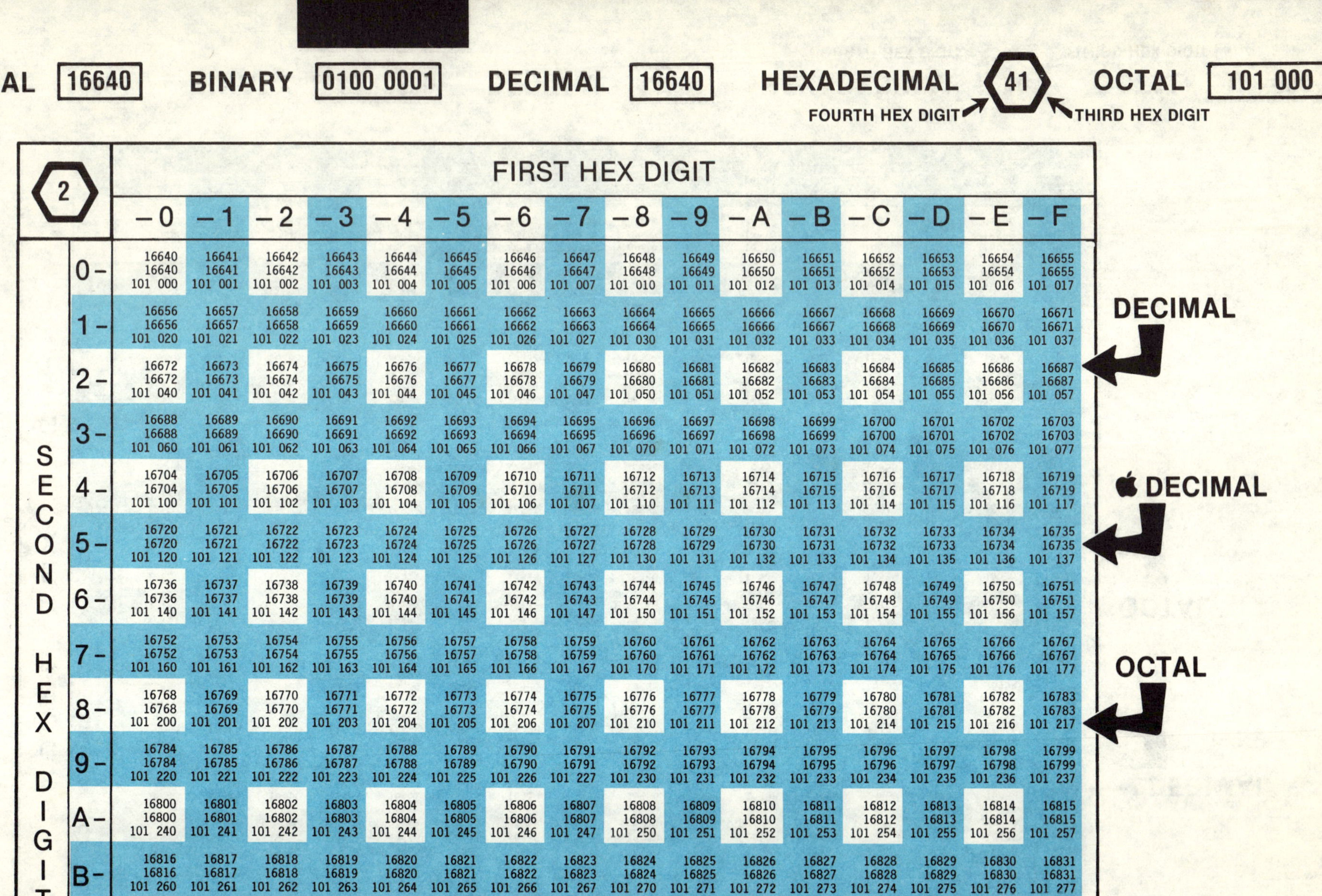

 DECIMAL `16640`    BINARY `0100 0001`    DECIMAL `16640`    HEXADECIMAL (41)    OCTAL `101 000`

FOURTH HEX DIGIT → ← THIRD HEX DIGIT

(2)

| SECOND HEX DIGIT | FIRST HEX DIGIT | | | | | | | | | | | | | | |
| | −0 | −1 | −2 | −3 | −4 | −5 | −6 | −7 | −8 | −9 | −A | −B | −C | −D | −E | −F |
|---|---|---|---|---|---|---|---|---|---|---|---|---|---|---|---|---|
| 0− | 16640<br>101 000 | 16641<br>101 001 | 16642<br>101 002 | 16643<br>101 003 | 16644<br>101 004 | 16645<br>101 005 | 16646<br>101 006 | 16647<br>101 007 | 16648<br>101 010 | 16649<br>101 011 | 16650<br>101 012 | 16651<br>101 013 | 16652<br>101 014 | 16653<br>101 015 | 16654<br>101 016 | 16655<br>101 017 |
| 1− | 16656<br>101 020 | 16657<br>101 021 | 16658<br>101 022 | 16659<br>101 023 | 16660<br>101 024 | 16661<br>101 025 | 16662<br>101 026 | 16663<br>101 027 | 16664<br>101 030 | 16665<br>101 031 | 16666<br>101 032 | 16667<br>101 033 | 16668<br>101 034 | 16669<br>101 035 | 16670<br>101 036 | 16671<br>101 037 |
| 2− | 16672<br>101 040 | 16673<br>101 041 | 16674<br>101 042 | 16675<br>101 043 | 16676<br>101 044 | 16677<br>101 045 | 16678<br>101 046 | 16679<br>101 047 | 16680<br>101 050 | 16681<br>101 051 | 16682<br>101 052 | 16683<br>101 053 | 16684<br>101 054 | 16685<br>101 055 | 16686<br>101 056 | 16687<br>101 057 |
| 3− | 16688<br>101 060 | 16689<br>101 061 | 16690<br>101 062 | 16691<br>101 063 | 16692<br>101 064 | 16693<br>101 065 | 16694<br>101 066 | 16695<br>101 067 | 16696<br>101 070 | 16697<br>101 071 | 16698<br>101 072 | 16699<br>101 073 | 16700<br>101 074 | 16701<br>101 075 | 16702<br>101 076 | 16703<br>101 077 |
| 4− | 16704<br>101 100 | 16705<br>101 101 | 16706<br>101 102 | 16707<br>101 103 | 16708<br>101 104 | 16709<br>101 105 | 16710<br>101 106 | 16711<br>101 107 | 16712<br>101 110 | 16713<br>101 111 | 16714<br>101 112 | 16715<br>101 113 | 16716<br>101 114 | 16717<br>101 115 | 16718<br>101 116 | 16719<br>101 117 |
| 5− | 16720<br>101 120 | 16721<br>101 121 | 16722<br>101 122 | 16723<br>101 123 | 16724<br>101 124 | 16725<br>101 125 | 16726<br>101 126 | 16727<br>101 127 | 16728<br>101 130 | 16729<br>101 131 | 16730<br>101 132 | 16731<br>101 133 | 16732<br>101 134 | 16733<br>101 135 | 16734<br>101 136 | 16735<br>101 137 |
| 6− | 16736<br>101 140 | 16737<br>101 141 | 16738<br>101 142 | 16739<br>101 143 | 16740<br>101 144 | 16741<br>101 145 | 16742<br>101 146 | 16743<br>101 147 | 16744<br>101 150 | 16745<br>101 151 | 16746<br>101 152 | 16747<br>101 153 | 16748<br>101 154 | 16749<br>101 155 | 16750<br>101 156 | 16751<br>101 157 |
| 7− | 16752<br>101 160 | 16753<br>101 161 | 16754<br>101 162 | 16755<br>101 163 | 16756<br>101 164 | 16757<br>101 165 | 16758<br>101 166 | 16759<br>101 167 | 16760<br>101 170 | 16761<br>101 171 | 16762<br>101 172 | 16763<br>101 173 | 16764<br>101 174 | 16765<br>101 175 | 16766<br>101 176 | 16767<br>101 177 |
| 8− | 16768<br>101 200 | 16769<br>101 201 | 16770<br>101 202 | 16771<br>101 203 | 16772<br>101 204 | 16773<br>101 205 | 16774<br>101 206 | 16775<br>101 207 | 16776<br>101 210 | 16777<br>101 211 | 16778<br>101 212 | 16779<br>101 213 | 16780<br>101 214 | 16781<br>101 215 | 16782<br>101 216 | 16783<br>101 217 |
| 9− | 16784<br>101 220 | 16785<br>101 221 | 16786<br>101 222 | 16787<br>101 223 | 16788<br>101 224 | 16789<br>101 225 | 16790<br>101 226 | 16791<br>101 227 | 16792<br>101 230 | 16793<br>101 231 | 16794<br>101 232 | 16795<br>101 233 | 16796<br>101 234 | 16797<br>101 235 | 16798<br>101 236 | 16799<br>101 237 |
| A− | 16800<br>101 240 | 16801<br>101 241 | 16802<br>101 242 | 16803<br>101 243 | 16804<br>101 244 | 16805<br>101 245 | 16806<br>101 246 | 16807<br>101 247 | 16808<br>101 250 | 16809<br>101 251 | 16810<br>101 252 | 16811<br>101 253 | 16812<br>101 254 | 16813<br>101 255 | 16814<br>101 256 | 16815<br>101 257 |
| B− | 16816<br>101 260 | 16817<br>101 261 | 16818<br>101 262 | 16819<br>101 263 | 16820<br>101 264 | 16821<br>101 265 | 16822<br>101 266 | 16823<br>101 267 | 16824<br>101 270 | 16825<br>101 271 | 16826<br>101 272 | 16827<br>101 273 | 16828<br>101 274 | 16829<br>101 275 | 16830<br>101 276 | 16831<br>101 277 |
| C− | 16832<br>101 300 | 16833<br>101 301 | 16834<br>101 302 | 16835<br>101 303 | 16836<br>101 304 | 16837<br>101 305 | 16838<br>101 306 | 16839<br>101 307 | 16840<br>101 310 | 16841<br>101 311 | 16842<br>101 312 | 16843<br>101 313 | 16844<br>101 314 | 16845<br>101 315 | 16846<br>101 316 | 16847<br>101 317 |
| D− | 16848<br>101 320 | 16849<br>101 321 | 16850<br>101 322 | 16851<br>101 323 | 16852<br>101 324 | 16853<br>101 325 | 16854<br>101 326 | 16855<br>101 327 | 16856<br>101 330 | 16857<br>101 331 | 16858<br>101 332 | 16859<br>101 333 | 16860<br>101 334 | 16861<br>101 335 | 16862<br>101 336 | 16863<br>101 337 |
| E− | 16864<br>101 340 | 16865<br>101 341 | 16866<br>101 342 | 16867<br>101 343 | 16868<br>101 344 | 16869<br>101 345 | 16870<br>101 346 | 16871<br>101 347 | 16872<br>101 350 | 16873<br>101 351 | 16874<br>101 352 | 16875<br>101 353 | 16876<br>101 354 | 16877<br>101 355 | 16878<br>101 356 | 16879<br>101 357 |
| F− | 16880<br>101 360 | 16881<br>101 361 | 16882<br>101 362 | 16883<br>101 363 | 16884<br>101 364 | 16885<br>101 365 | 16886<br>101 366 | 16887<br>101 367 | 16888<br>101 370 | 16889<br>101 371 | 16890<br>101 372 | 16891<br>101 373 | 16892<br>101 374 | 16893<br>101 375 | 16894<br>101 376 | 16895<br>101 377 |

## FIRST HEX DIGIT — ②

Legend (right side): DECIMAL / DECIMAL / OCTAL

| SECOND HEX DIGIT | −0 | −1 | −2 | −3 | −4 | −5 | −6 | −7 | −8 | −9 | −A | −B | −C | −D | −E | −F |
|---|---|---|---|---|---|---|---|---|---|---|---|---|---|---|---|---|
| 0- | 16896<br>16896<br>102 000 | 16897<br>16897<br>102 001 | 16898<br>16898<br>102 002 | 16899<br>16899<br>102 003 | 16900<br>16900<br>102 004 | 16901<br>16901<br>102 005 | 16902<br>16902<br>102 006 | 16903<br>16903<br>102 007 | 16904<br>16904<br>102 010 | 16905<br>16905<br>102 011 | 16906<br>16906<br>102 012 | 16907<br>16907<br>102 013 | 16908<br>16908<br>102 014 | 16909<br>16909<br>102 015 | 16910<br>16910<br>102 016 | 16911<br>16911<br>102 017 |
| 1- | 16912<br>16912<br>102 020 | 16913<br>16913<br>102 021 | 16914<br>16914<br>102 022 | 16915<br>16915<br>102 023 | 16916<br>16916<br>102 024 | 16917<br>16917<br>102 025 | 16918<br>16918<br>102 026 | 16919<br>16919<br>102 027 | 16920<br>16920<br>102 030 | 16921<br>16921<br>102 031 | 16922<br>16922<br>102 032 | 16923<br>16923<br>102 033 | 16924<br>16924<br>102 034 | 16925<br>16925<br>102 035 | 16926<br>16926<br>102 036 | 16927<br>16927<br>102 037 |
| 2- | 16928<br>16928<br>102 040 | 16929<br>16929<br>102 041 | 16930<br>16930<br>102 042 | 16931<br>16931<br>102 043 | 16932<br>16932<br>102 044 | 16933<br>16933<br>102 045 | 16934<br>16934<br>102 046 | 16935<br>16935<br>102 047 | 16936<br>16936<br>102 050 | 16937<br>16937<br>102 051 | 16938<br>16938<br>102 052 | 16939<br>16939<br>102 053 | 16940<br>16940<br>102 054 | 16941<br>16941<br>102 055 | 16942<br>16942<br>102 056 | 16943<br>16943<br>102 057 |
| 3- | 16944<br>16944<br>102 060 | 16945<br>16945<br>102 061 | 16946<br>16946<br>102 062 | 16947<br>16947<br>102 063 | 16948<br>16948<br>102 064 | 16949<br>16949<br>102 065 | 16950<br>16950<br>102 066 | 16951<br>16951<br>102 067 | 16952<br>16952<br>102 070 | 16953<br>16953<br>102 071 | 16954<br>16954<br>102 072 | 16955<br>16955<br>102 073 | 16956<br>16956<br>102 074 | 16957<br>16957<br>102 075 | 16958<br>16958<br>102 076 | 16959<br>16959<br>102 077 |
| 4- | 16960<br>16960<br>102 100 | 16961<br>16961<br>102 101 | 16962<br>16962<br>102 102 | 16963<br>16963<br>102 103 | 16964<br>16964<br>102 104 | 16965<br>16965<br>102 105 | 16966<br>16966<br>102 106 | 16967<br>16967<br>102 107 | 16968<br>16968<br>102 110 | 16969<br>16969<br>102 111 | 16970<br>16970<br>102 112 | 16971<br>16971<br>102 113 | 16972<br>16972<br>102 114 | 16973<br>16973<br>102 115 | 16974<br>16974<br>102 116 | 16975<br>16975<br>102 117 |
| 5- | 16976<br>16976<br>102 120 | 16977<br>16977<br>102 121 | 16978<br>16978<br>102 122 | 16979<br>16979<br>102 123 | 16980<br>16980<br>102 124 | 16981<br>16981<br>102 125 | 16982<br>16982<br>102 126 | 16983<br>16983<br>102 127 | 16984<br>16984<br>102 130 | 16985<br>16985<br>102 131 | 16986<br>16986<br>102 132 | 16987<br>16987<br>102 133 | 16988<br>16988<br>102 134 | 16989<br>16989<br>102 135 | 16990<br>16990<br>102 136 | 16991<br>16991<br>102 137 |
| 6- | 16992<br>16992<br>102 140 | 16993<br>16993<br>102 141 | 16994<br>16994<br>102 142 | 16995<br>16995<br>102 143 | 16996<br>16996<br>102 144 | 16997<br>16997<br>102 145 | 16998<br>16998<br>102 146 | 16999<br>16999<br>102 147 | 17000<br>17000<br>102 150 | 17001<br>17001<br>102 151 | 17002<br>17002<br>102 152 | 17003<br>17003<br>102 153 | 17004<br>17004<br>102 154 | 17005<br>17005<br>102 155 | 17006<br>17006<br>102 156 | 17007<br>17007<br>102 157 |
| 7- | 17008<br>17008<br>102 160 | 17009<br>17009<br>102 161 | 17010<br>17010<br>102 162 | 17011<br>17011<br>102 163 | 17012<br>17012<br>102 164 | 17013<br>17013<br>102 165 | 17014<br>17014<br>102 166 | 17015<br>17015<br>102 167 | 17016<br>17016<br>102 170 | 17017<br>17017<br>102 171 | 17018<br>17018<br>102 172 | 17019<br>17019<br>102 173 | 17020<br>17020<br>102 174 | 17021<br>17021<br>102 175 | 17022<br>17022<br>102 176 | 17023<br>17023<br>102 177 |
| 8- | 17024<br>17024<br>102 200 | 17025<br>17025<br>102 201 | 17026<br>17026<br>102 202 | 17027<br>17027<br>102 203 | 17028<br>17028<br>102 204 | 17029<br>17029<br>102 205 | 17030<br>17030<br>102 206 | 17031<br>17031<br>102 207 | 17032<br>17032<br>102 210 | 17033<br>17033<br>102 211 | 17034<br>17034<br>102 212 | 17035<br>17035<br>102 213 | 17036<br>17036<br>102 214 | 17037<br>17037<br>102 215 | 17038<br>17038<br>102 216 | 17039<br>17039<br>102 217 |
| 9- | 17040<br>17040<br>102 220 | 17041<br>17041<br>102 221 | 17042<br>17042<br>102 222 | 17043<br>17043<br>102 223 | 17044<br>17044<br>102 224 | 17045<br>17045<br>102 225 | 17046<br>17046<br>102 226 | 17047<br>17047<br>102 227 | 17048<br>17048<br>102 230 | 17049<br>17049<br>102 231 | 17050<br>17050<br>102 232 | 17051<br>17051<br>102 233 | 17052<br>17052<br>102 234 | 17053<br>17053<br>102 235 | 17054<br>17054<br>102 236 | 17055<br>17055<br>102 237 |
| A- | 17056<br>17056<br>102 240 | 17057<br>17057<br>102 241 | 17058<br>17058<br>102 242 | 17059<br>17059<br>102 243 | 17060<br>17060<br>102 244 | 17061<br>17061<br>102 245 | 17062<br>17062<br>102 246 | 17063<br>17063<br>102 247 | 17064<br>17064<br>102 250 | 17065<br>17065<br>102 251 | 17066<br>17066<br>102 252 | 17067<br>17067<br>102 253 | 17068<br>17068<br>102 254 | 17069<br>17069<br>102 255 | 17070<br>17070<br>102 256 | 17071<br>17071<br>102 257 |
| B- | 17072<br>17072<br>102 260 | 17073<br>17073<br>102 261 | 17074<br>17074<br>102 262 | 17075<br>17075<br>102 263 | 17076<br>17076<br>102 264 | 17077<br>17077<br>102 265 | 17078<br>17078<br>102 266 | 17079<br>17079<br>102 267 | 17080<br>17080<br>102 270 | 17081<br>17081<br>102 271 | 17082<br>17082<br>102 272 | 17083<br>17083<br>102 273 | 17084<br>17084<br>102 274 | 17085<br>17085<br>102 275 | 17086<br>17086<br>102 276 | 17087<br>17087<br>102 277 |
| C- | 17088<br>17088<br>102 300 | 17089<br>17089<br>102 301 | 17090<br>17090<br>102 302 | 17091<br>17091<br>102 303 | 17092<br>17092<br>102 304 | 17093<br>17093<br>102 305 | 17094<br>17094<br>102 306 | 17095<br>17095<br>102 307 | 17096<br>17096<br>102 310 | 17097<br>17097<br>102 311 | 17098<br>17098<br>102 312 | 17099<br>17099<br>102 313 | 17100<br>17100<br>102 314 | 17101<br>17101<br>102 315 | 17102<br>17102<br>102 316 | 17103<br>17103<br>102 317 |
| D- | 17104<br>17104<br>102 320 | 17105<br>17105<br>102 321 | 17106<br>17106<br>102 322 | 17107<br>17107<br>102 323 | 17108<br>17108<br>102 324 | 17109<br>17109<br>102 325 | 17110<br>17110<br>102 326 | 17111<br>17111<br>102 327 | 17112<br>17112<br>102 330 | 17113<br>17113<br>102 331 | 17114<br>17114<br>102 332 | 17115<br>17115<br>102 333 | 17116<br>17116<br>102 334 | 17117<br>17117<br>102 335 | 17118<br>17118<br>102 336 | 17119<br>17119<br>102 337 |
| E- | 17120<br>17120<br>102 340 | 17121<br>17121<br>102 341 | 17122<br>17122<br>102 342 | 17123<br>17123<br>102 343 | 17124<br>17124<br>102 344 | 17125<br>17125<br>102 345 | 17126<br>17126<br>102 346 | 17127<br>17127<br>102 347 | 17128<br>17128<br>102 350 | 17129<br>17129<br>102 351 | 17130<br>17130<br>102 352 | 17131<br>17131<br>102 353 | 17132<br>17132<br>102 354 | 17133<br>17133<br>102 355 | 17134<br>17134<br>102 356 | 17135<br>17135<br>102 357 |
| F- | 17136<br>17136<br>102 360 | 17137<br>17137<br>102 361 | 17138<br>17138<br>102 362 | 17139<br>17139<br>102 363 | 17140<br>17140<br>102 364 | 17141<br>17141<br>102 365 | 17142<br>17142<br>102 366 | 17143<br>17143<br>102 367 | 17144<br>17144<br>102 370 | 17145<br>17145<br>102 371 | 17146<br>17146<br>102 372 | 17147<br>17147<br>102 373 | 17148<br>17148<br>102 374 | 17149<br>17149<br>102 375 | 17150<br>17150<br>102 376 | 17151<br>17151<br>102 377 |

 DECIMAL  16896   BINARY  0100 0010   DECIMAL  16896   HEXADECIMAL  ⟨42⟩   OCTAL  102 000

FOURTH HEX DIGIT → ⟨ ⟩ ← THIRD HEX DIGIT

FIRST HEX DIGIT

⬡2⬡

| SECOND HEX DIGIT | −0 | −1 | −2 | −3 | −4 | −5 | −6 | −7 | −8 | −9 | −A | −B | −C | −D | −E | −F |
|---|---|---|---|---|---|---|---|---|---|---|---|---|---|---|---|---|
| 0− | 17152 17152 103 000 | 17153 17153 103 001 | 17154 17154 103 002 | 17155 17155 103 003 | 17156 17156 103 004 | 17157 17157 103 005 | 17158 17158 103 006 | 17159 17159 103 007 | 17160 17160 103 010 | 17161 17161 103 011 | 17162 17162 103 012 | 17163 17163 103 013 | 17164 17164 103 014 | 17165 17165 103 015 | 17166 17166 103 016 | 17167 17167 103 017 |
| 1− | 17168 17168 103 020 | 17169 17169 103 021 | 17170 17170 103 022 | 17171 17171 103 023 | 17172 17172 103 024 | 17173 17173 103 025 | 17174 17174 103 026 | 17175 17175 103 027 | 17176 17176 103 030 | 17177 17177 103 031 | 17178 17178 103 032 | 17179 17179 103 033 | 17180 17180 103 034 | 17181 17181 103 035 | 17182 17182 103 036 | 17183 17183 103 037 |
| 2− | 17184 17184 103 040 | 17185 17185 103 041 | 17186 17186 103 042 | 17187 17187 103 043 | 17188 17188 103 044 | 17189 17189 103 045 | 17190 17190 103 046 | 17191 17191 103 047 | 17192 17192 103 050 | 17193 17193 103 051 | 17194 17194 103 052 | 17195 17195 103 053 | 17196 17196 103 054 | 17197 17197 103 055 | 17198 17198 103 056 | 17199 17199 103 057 |
| 3− | 17200 17200 103 060 | 17201 17201 103 061 | 17202 17202 103 062 | 17203 17203 103 063 | 17204 17204 103 064 | 17205 17205 103 065 | 17206 17206 103 066 | 17207 17207 103 067 | 17208 17208 103 070 | 17209 17209 103 071 | 17210 17210 103 072 | 17211 17211 103 073 | 17212 17212 103 074 | 17213 17213 103 075 | 17214 17214 103 076 | 17215 17215 103 077 |
| 4− | 17216 17216 103 100 | 17217 17217 103 101 | 17218 17218 103 102 | 17219 17219 103 103 | 17220 17220 103 104 | 17221 17221 103 105 | 17222 17222 103 106 | 17223 17223 103 107 | 17224 17224 103 110 | 17225 17225 103 111 | 17226 17226 103 112 | 17227 17227 103 113 | 17228 17228 103 114 | 17229 17229 103 115 | 17230 17230 103 116 | 17231 17231 103 117 |
| 5− | 17232 17232 103 120 | 17233 17233 103 121 | 17234 17234 103 122 | 17235 17235 103 123 | 17236 17236 103 124 | 17237 17237 103 125 | 17238 17238 103 126 | 17239 17239 103 127 | 17240 17240 103 130 | 17241 17241 103 131 | 17242 17242 103 132 | 17243 17243 103 133 | 17244 17244 103 134 | 17245 17245 103 135 | 17246 17246 103 136 | 17247 17247 103 137 |
| 6− | 17248 17248 103 140 | 17249 17249 103 141 | 17250 17250 103 142 | 17251 17251 103 143 | 17252 17252 103 144 | 17253 17253 103 145 | 17254 17254 103 146 | 17255 17255 103 147 | 17256 17256 103 150 | 17257 17257 103 151 | 17258 17258 103 152 | 17259 17259 103 153 | 17260 17260 103 154 | 17261 17261 103 155 | 17262 17262 103 156 | 17263 17263 103 157 |
| 7− | 17264 17264 103 160 | 17265 17265 103 161 | 17266 17266 103 162 | 17267 17267 103 163 | 17268 17268 103 164 | 17269 17269 103 165 | 17270 17270 103 166 | 17271 17271 103 167 | 17272 17272 103 170 | 17273 17273 103 171 | 17274 17274 103 172 | 17275 17275 103 173 | 17276 17276 103 174 | 17277 17277 103 175 | 17278 17278 103 176 | 17279 17279 103 177 |
| 8− | 17280 17280 103 200 | 17281 17281 103 201 | 17282 17282 103 202 | 17283 17283 103 203 | 17284 17284 103 204 | 17285 17285 103 205 | 17286 17286 103 206 | 17287 17287 103 207 | 17288 17288 103 210 | 17289 17289 103 211 | 17290 17290 103 212 | 17291 17291 103 213 | 17292 17292 103 214 | 17293 17293 103 215 | 17294 17294 103 216 | 17295 17295 103 217 |
| 9− | 17296 17296 103 220 | 17297 17297 103 221 | 17298 17298 103 222 | 17299 17299 103 223 | 17300 17300 103 224 | 17301 17301 103 225 | 17302 17302 103 226 | 17303 17303 103 227 | 17304 17304 103 230 | 17305 17305 103 231 | 17306 17306 103 232 | 17307 17307 103 233 | 17308 17308 103 234 | 17309 17309 103 235 | 17310 17310 103 236 | 17311 17311 103 237 |
| A− | 17312 17312 103 240 | 17313 17313 103 241 | 17314 17314 103 242 | 17315 17315 103 243 | 17316 17316 103 244 | 17317 17317 103 245 | 17318 17318 103 246 | 17319 17319 103 247 | 17320 17320 103 250 | 17321 17321 103 251 | 17322 17322 103 252 | 17323 17323 103 253 | 17324 17324 103 254 | 17325 17325 103 255 | 17326 17326 103 256 | 17327 17327 103 257 |
| B− | 17328 17328 103 260 | 17329 17329 103 261 | 17330 17330 103 262 | 17331 17331 103 263 | 17332 17332 103 264 | 17333 17333 103 265 | 17334 17334 103 266 | 17335 17335 103 267 | 17336 17336 103 270 | 17337 17337 103 271 | 17338 17338 103 272 | 17339 17339 103 273 | 17340 17340 103 274 | 17341 17341 103 275 | 17342 17342 103 276 | 17343 17343 103 277 |
| C− | 17344 17344 103 300 | 17345 17345 103 301 | 17346 17346 103 302 | 17347 17347 103 303 | 17348 17348 103 304 | 17349 17349 103 305 | 17350 17350 103 306 | 17351 17351 103 307 | 17352 17352 103 310 | 17353 17353 103 311 | 17354 17354 103 312 | 17355 17355 103 313 | 17356 17356 103 314 | 17357 17357 103 315 | 17358 17358 103 316 | 17359 17359 103 317 |
| D− | 17360 17360 103 320 | 17361 17361 103 321 | 17362 17362 103 322 | 17363 17363 103 323 | 17364 17364 103 324 | 17365 17365 103 325 | 17366 17366 103 326 | 17367 17367 103 327 | 17368 17368 103 330 | 17369 17369 103 331 | 17370 17370 103 332 | 17371 17371 103 333 | 17372 17372 103 334 | 17373 17373 103 335 | 17374 17374 103 336 | 17375 17375 103 337 |
| E− | 17376 17376 103 340 | 17377 17377 103 341 | 17378 17378 103 342 | 17379 17379 103 343 | 17380 17380 103 344 | 17381 17381 103 345 | 17382 17382 103 346 | 17383 17383 103 347 | 17384 17384 103 350 | 17385 17385 103 351 | 17386 17386 103 352 | 17387 17387 103 353 | 17388 17388 103 354 | 17389 17389 103 355 | 17390 17390 103 356 | 17391 17391 103 357 |
| F− | 17392 17392 103 360 | 17393 17393 103 361 | 17394 17394 103 362 | 17395 17395 103 363 | 17396 17396 103 364 | 17397 17397 103 365 | 17398 17398 103 366 | 17399 17399 103 367 | 17400 17400 103 370 | 17401 17401 103 371 | 17402 17402 103 372 | 17403 17403 103 373 | 17404 17404 103 374 | 17405 17405 103 375 | 17406 17406 103 376 | 17407 17407 103 377 |

DECIMAL →

🍎 DECIMAL →

OCTAL →

# FIRST HEX DIGIT

②   SECOND HEX DIGIT (rows) / FIRST HEX DIGIT (columns). Each cell: DECIMAL (top two) and OCTAL (bottom).

| | −0 | −1 | −2 | −3 | −4 | −5 | −6 | −7 | −8 | −9 | −A | −B | −C | −D | −E | −F |
|---|---|---|---|---|---|---|---|---|---|---|---|---|---|---|---|---|
| **0−** | 17408<br>17408<br>104 000 | 17409<br>17409<br>104 001 | 17410<br>17410<br>104 002 | 17411<br>17411<br>104 003 | 17412<br>17412<br>104 004 | 17413<br>17413<br>104 005 | 17414<br>17414<br>104 006 | 17415<br>17415<br>104 007 | 17416<br>17416<br>104 010 | 17417<br>17417<br>104 011 | 17418<br>17418<br>104 012 | 17419<br>17419<br>104 013 | 17420<br>17420<br>104 014 | 17421<br>17421<br>104 015 | 17422<br>17422<br>104 016 | 17423<br>17423<br>104 017 |
| **1−** | 17424<br>17424<br>104 020 | 17425<br>17425<br>104 021 | 17426<br>17426<br>104 022 | 17427<br>17427<br>104 023 | 17428<br>17428<br>104 024 | 17429<br>17429<br>104 025 | 17430<br>17430<br>104 026 | 17431<br>17431<br>104 027 | 17432<br>17432<br>104 030 | 17433<br>17433<br>104 031 | 17434<br>17434<br>104 032 | 17435<br>17435<br>104 033 | 17436<br>17436<br>104 034 | 17437<br>17437<br>104 035 | 17438<br>17438<br>104 036 | 17439<br>17439<br>104 037 |
| **2−** | 17440<br>17440<br>104 040 | 17441<br>17441<br>104 041 | 17442<br>17442<br>104 042 | 17443<br>17443<br>104 043 | 17444<br>17444<br>104 044 | 17445<br>17445<br>104 045 | 17446<br>17446<br>104 046 | 17447<br>17447<br>104 047 | 17448<br>17448<br>104 050 | 17449<br>17449<br>104 051 | 17450<br>17450<br>104 052 | 17451<br>17451<br>104 053 | 17452<br>17452<br>104 054 | 17453<br>17453<br>104 055 | 17454<br>17454<br>104 056 | 17455<br>17455<br>104 057 |
| **3−** | 17456<br>17456<br>104 060 | 17457<br>17457<br>104 061 | 17458<br>17458<br>104 062 | 17459<br>17459<br>104 063 | 17460<br>17460<br>104 064 | 17461<br>17461<br>104 065 | 17462<br>17462<br>104 066 | 17463<br>17463<br>104 067 | 17464<br>17464<br>104 070 | 17465<br>17465<br>104 071 | 17466<br>17466<br>104 072 | 17467<br>17467<br>104 073 | 17468<br>17468<br>104 074 | 17469<br>17469<br>104 075 | 17470<br>17470<br>104 076 | 17471<br>17471<br>104 077 |
| **4−** | 17472<br>17472<br>104 100 | 17473<br>17473<br>104 101 | 17474<br>17474<br>104 102 | 17475<br>17475<br>104 103 | 17476<br>17476<br>104 104 | 17477<br>17477<br>104 105 | 17478<br>17478<br>104 106 | 17479<br>17479<br>104 107 | 17480<br>17480<br>104 110 | 17481<br>17481<br>104 111 | 17482<br>17482<br>104 112 | 17483<br>17483<br>104 113 | 17484<br>17484<br>104 114 | 17485<br>17485<br>104 115 | 17486<br>17486<br>104 116 | 17487<br>17487<br>104 117 |
| **5−** | 17488<br>17488<br>104 120 | 17489<br>17489<br>104 121 | 17490<br>17490<br>104 122 | 17491<br>17491<br>104 123 | 17492<br>17492<br>104 124 | 17493<br>17493<br>104 125 | 17494<br>17494<br>104 126 | 17495<br>17495<br>104 127 | 17496<br>17496<br>104 130 | 17497<br>17497<br>104 131 | 17498<br>17498<br>104 132 | 17499<br>17499<br>104 133 | 17500<br>17500<br>104 134 | 17501<br>17501<br>104 135 | 17502<br>17502<br>104 136 | 17503<br>17503<br>104 137 |
| **6−** | 17504<br>17504<br>104 140 | 17505<br>17505<br>104 141 | 17506<br>17506<br>104 142 | 17507<br>17507<br>104 143 | 17508<br>17508<br>104 144 | 17509<br>17509<br>104 145 | 17510<br>17510<br>104 146 | 17511<br>17511<br>104 147 | 17512<br>17512<br>104 150 | 17513<br>17513<br>104 151 | 17514<br>17514<br>104 152 | 17515<br>17515<br>104 153 | 17516<br>17516<br>104 154 | 17517<br>17517<br>104 155 | 17518<br>17518<br>104 156 | 17519<br>17519<br>104 157 |
| **7−** | 17520<br>17520<br>104 160 | 17521<br>17521<br>104 161 | 17522<br>17522<br>104 162 | 17523<br>17523<br>104 163 | 17524<br>17524<br>104 164 | 17525<br>17525<br>104 165 | 17526<br>17526<br>104 166 | 17527<br>17527<br>104 167 | 17528<br>17528<br>104 170 | 17529<br>17529<br>104 171 | 17530<br>17530<br>104 172 | 17531<br>17531<br>104 173 | 17532<br>17532<br>104 174 | 17533<br>17533<br>104 175 | 17534<br>17534<br>104 176 | 17535<br>17535<br>104 177 |
| **8−** | 17536<br>17536<br>104 200 | 17537<br>17537<br>104 201 | 17538<br>17538<br>104 202 | 17539<br>17539<br>104 203 | 17540<br>17540<br>104 204 | 17541<br>17541<br>104 205 | 17542<br>17542<br>104 206 | 17543<br>17543<br>104 207 | 17544<br>17544<br>104 210 | 17545<br>17545<br>104 211 | 17546<br>17546<br>104 212 | 17547<br>17547<br>104 213 | 17548<br>17548<br>104 214 | 17549<br>17549<br>104 215 | 17550<br>17550<br>104 216 | 17551<br>17551<br>104 217 |
| **9−** | 17552<br>17552<br>104 220 | 17553<br>17553<br>104 221 | 17554<br>17554<br>104 222 | 17555<br>17555<br>104 223 | 17556<br>17556<br>104 224 | 17557<br>17557<br>104 225 | 17558<br>17558<br>104 226 | 17559<br>17559<br>104 227 | 17560<br>17560<br>104 230 | 17561<br>17561<br>104 231 | 17562<br>17562<br>104 232 | 17563<br>17563<br>104 233 | 17564<br>17564<br>104 234 | 17565<br>17565<br>104 235 | 17566<br>17566<br>104 236 | 17567<br>17567<br>104 237 |
| **A−** | 17568<br>17568<br>104 240 | 17569<br>17569<br>104 241 | 17570<br>17570<br>104 242 | 17571<br>17571<br>104 243 | 17572<br>17572<br>104 244 | 17573<br>17573<br>104 245 | 17574<br>17574<br>104 246 | 17575<br>17575<br>104 247 | 17576<br>17576<br>104 250 | 17577<br>17577<br>104 251 | 17578<br>17578<br>104 252 | 17579<br>17579<br>104 253 | 17580<br>17580<br>104 254 | 17581<br>17581<br>104 255 | 17582<br>17582<br>104 256 | 17583<br>17583<br>104 257 |
| **B−** | 17584<br>17584<br>104 260 | 17585<br>17585<br>104 261 | 17586<br>17586<br>104 262 | 17587<br>17587<br>104 263 | 17588<br>17588<br>104 264 | 17589<br>17589<br>104 265 | 17590<br>17590<br>104 266 | 17591<br>17591<br>104 267 | 17592<br>17592<br>104 270 | 17593<br>17593<br>104 271 | 17594<br>17594<br>104 272 | 17595<br>17595<br>104 273 | 17596<br>17596<br>104 274 | 17597<br>17597<br>104 275 | 17598<br>17598<br>104 276 | 17599<br>17599<br>104 277 |
| **C−** | 17600<br>17600<br>104 300 | 17601<br>17601<br>104 301 | 17602<br>17602<br>104 302 | 17603<br>17603<br>104 303 | 17604<br>17604<br>104 304 | 17605<br>17605<br>104 305 | 17606<br>17606<br>104 306 | 17607<br>17607<br>104 307 | 17608<br>17608<br>104 310 | 17609<br>17609<br>104 311 | 17610<br>17610<br>104 312 | 17611<br>17611<br>104 313 | 17612<br>17612<br>104 314 | 17613<br>17613<br>104 315 | 17614<br>17614<br>104 316 | 17615<br>17615<br>104 317 |
| **D−** | 17616<br>17616<br>104 320 | 17617<br>17617<br>104 321 | 17618<br>17618<br>104 322 | 17619<br>17619<br>104 323 | 17620<br>17620<br>104 324 | 17621<br>17621<br>104 325 | 17622<br>17622<br>104 326 | 17623<br>17623<br>104 327 | 17624<br>17624<br>104 330 | 17625<br>17625<br>104 331 | 17626<br>17626<br>104 332 | 17627<br>17627<br>104 333 | 17628<br>17628<br>104 334 | 17629<br>17629<br>104 335 | 17630<br>17630<br>104 336 | 17631<br>17631<br>104 337 |
| **E−** | 17632<br>17632<br>104 340 | 17633<br>17633<br>104 341 | 17634<br>17634<br>104 342 | 17635<br>17635<br>104 343 | 17636<br>17636<br>104 344 | 17637<br>17637<br>104 345 | 17638<br>17638<br>104 346 | 17639<br>17639<br>104 347 | 17640<br>17640<br>104 350 | 17641<br>17641<br>104 351 | 17642<br>17642<br>104 352 | 17643<br>17643<br>104 353 | 17644<br>17644<br>104 354 | 17645<br>17645<br>104 355 | 17646<br>17646<br>104 356 | 17647<br>17647<br>104 357 |
| **F−** | 17648<br>17648<br>104 360 | 17649<br>17649<br>104 361 | 17650<br>17650<br>104 362 | 17651<br>17651<br>104 363 | 17652<br>17652<br>104 364 | 17653<br>17653<br>104 365 | 17654<br>17654<br>104 366 | 17655<br>17655<br>104 367 | 17656<br>17656<br>104 370 | 17657<br>17657<br>104 371 | 17658<br>17658<br>104 372 | 17659<br>17659<br>104 373 | 17660<br>17660<br>104 374 | 17661<br>17661<br>104 375 | 17662<br>17662<br>104 376 | 17663<br>17663<br>104 377 |

DECIMAL    DECIMAL    OCTAL

DECIMAL  17408    **BINARY**  0100 0100    **DECIMAL**  17408    **HEXADECIMAL**  ⬡44    **OCTAL**  104 000

FOURTH HEX DIGIT → ⬡ ← THIRD HEX DIGIT

**FIRST HEX DIGIT**

⬡2 — SECOND HEX DIGIT

| | −0 | −1 | −2 | −3 | −4 | −5 | −6 | −7 | −8 | −9 | −A | −B | −C | −D | −E | −F |
|---|---|---|---|---|---|---|---|---|---|---|---|---|---|---|---|---|
| 0− | 17664<br>17664<br>105 000 | 17665<br>17665<br>105 001 | 17666<br>17666<br>105 002 | 17667<br>17667<br>105 003 | 17668<br>17668<br>105 004 | 17669<br>17669<br>105 005 | 17670<br>17670<br>105 006 | 17671<br>17671<br>105 007 | 17672<br>17672<br>105 010 | 17673<br>17673<br>105 011 | 17674<br>17674<br>105 012 | 17675<br>17675<br>105 013 | 17676<br>17676<br>105 014 | 17677<br>17677<br>105 015 | 17678<br>17678<br>105 016 | 17679<br>17679<br>105 017 |
| 1− | 17680<br>17680<br>105 020 | 17681<br>17681<br>105 021 | 17682<br>17682<br>105 022 | 17683<br>17683<br>105 023 | 17684<br>17684<br>105 024 | 17685<br>17685<br>105 025 | 17686<br>17686<br>105 026 | 17687<br>17687<br>105 027 | 17688<br>17688<br>105 030 | 17689<br>17689<br>105 031 | 17690<br>17690<br>105 032 | 17691<br>17691<br>105 033 | 17692<br>17692<br>105 034 | 17693<br>17693<br>105 035 | 17694<br>17694<br>105 036 | 17695<br>17695<br>105 037 |
| 2− | 17696<br>17696<br>105 040 | 17697<br>17697<br>105 041 | 17698<br>17698<br>105 042 | 17699<br>17699<br>105 043 | 17700<br>17700<br>105 044 | 17701<br>17701<br>105 045 | 17702<br>17702<br>105 046 | 17703<br>17703<br>105 047 | 17704<br>17704<br>105 050 | 17705<br>17705<br>105 051 | 17706<br>17706<br>105 052 | 17707<br>17707<br>105 053 | 17708<br>17708<br>105 054 | 17709<br>17709<br>105 055 | 17710<br>17710<br>105 056 | 17711<br>17711<br>105 057 |
| 3− | 17712<br>17712<br>105 060 | 17713<br>17713<br>105 061 | 17714<br>17714<br>105 062 | 17715<br>17715<br>105 063 | 17716<br>17716<br>105 064 | 17717<br>17717<br>105 065 | 17718<br>17718<br>105 066 | 17719<br>17719<br>105 067 | 17720<br>17720<br>105 070 | 17721<br>17721<br>105 071 | 17722<br>17722<br>105 072 | 17723<br>17723<br>105 073 | 17724<br>17724<br>105 074 | 17725<br>17725<br>105 075 | 17726<br>17726<br>105 076 | 17727<br>17727<br>105 077 |
| 4− | 17728<br>17728<br>105 100 | 17729<br>17729<br>105 101 | 17730<br>17730<br>105 102 | 17731<br>17731<br>105 103 | 17732<br>17732<br>105 104 | 17733<br>17733<br>105 105 | 17734<br>17734<br>105 106 | 17735<br>17735<br>105 107 | 17736<br>17736<br>105 110 | 17737<br>17737<br>105 111 | 17738<br>17738<br>105 112 | 17739<br>17739<br>105 113 | 17740<br>17740<br>105 114 | 17741<br>17741<br>105 115 | 17742<br>17742<br>105 116 | 17743<br>17743<br>105 117 |
| 5− | 17744<br>17744<br>105 120 | 17745<br>17745<br>105 121 | 17746<br>17746<br>105 122 | 17747<br>17747<br>105 123 | 17748<br>17748<br>105 124 | 17749<br>17749<br>105 125 | 17750<br>17750<br>105 126 | 17751<br>17751<br>105 127 | 17752<br>17752<br>105 130 | 17753<br>17753<br>105 131 | 17754<br>17754<br>105 132 | 17755<br>17755<br>105 133 | 17756<br>17756<br>105 134 | 17757<br>17757<br>105 135 | 17758<br>17758<br>105 136 | 17759<br>17759<br>105 137 |
| 6− | 17760<br>17760<br>105 140 | 17761<br>17761<br>105 141 | 17762<br>17762<br>105 142 | 17763<br>17763<br>105 143 | 17764<br>17764<br>105 144 | 17765<br>17765<br>105 145 | 17766<br>17766<br>105 146 | 17767<br>17767<br>105 147 | 17768<br>17768<br>105 150 | 17769<br>17769<br>105 151 | 17770<br>17770<br>105 152 | 17771<br>17771<br>105 153 | 17772<br>17772<br>105 154 | 17773<br>17773<br>105 155 | 17774<br>17774<br>105 156 | 17775<br>17775<br>105 157 |
| 7− | 17776<br>17776<br>105 160 | 17777<br>17777<br>105 161 | 17778<br>17778<br>105 162 | 17779<br>17779<br>105 163 | 17780<br>17780<br>105 164 | 17781<br>17781<br>105 165 | 17782<br>17782<br>105 166 | 17783<br>17783<br>105 167 | 17784<br>17784<br>105 170 | 17785<br>17785<br>105 171 | 17786<br>17786<br>105 172 | 17787<br>17787<br>105 173 | 17788<br>17788<br>105 174 | 17789<br>17789<br>105 175 | 17790<br>17790<br>105 176 | 17791<br>17791<br>105 177 |
| 8− | 17792<br>17792<br>105 200 | 17793<br>17793<br>105 201 | 17794<br>17794<br>105 202 | 17795<br>17795<br>105 203 | 17796<br>17796<br>105 204 | 17797<br>17797<br>105 205 | 17798<br>17798<br>105 206 | 17799<br>17799<br>105 207 | 17800<br>17800<br>105 210 | 17801<br>17801<br>105 211 | 17802<br>17802<br>105 212 | 17803<br>17803<br>105 213 | 17804<br>17804<br>105 214 | 17805<br>17805<br>105 215 | 17806<br>17806<br>105 216 | 17807<br>17807<br>105 217 |
| 9− | 17808<br>17808<br>105 220 | 17809<br>17809<br>105 221 | 17810<br>17810<br>105 222 | 17811<br>17811<br>105 223 | 17812<br>17812<br>105 224 | 17813<br>17813<br>105 225 | 17814<br>17814<br>105 226 | 17815<br>17815<br>105 227 | 17816<br>17816<br>105 230 | 17817<br>17817<br>105 231 | 17818<br>17818<br>105 232 | 17819<br>17819<br>105 233 | 17820<br>17820<br>105 234 | 17821<br>17821<br>105 235 | 17822<br>17822<br>105 236 | 17823<br>17823<br>105 237 |
| A− | 17824<br>17824<br>105 240 | 17825<br>17825<br>105 241 | 17826<br>17826<br>105 242 | 17827<br>17827<br>105 243 | 17828<br>17828<br>105 244 | 17829<br>17829<br>105 245 | 17830<br>17830<br>105 246 | 17831<br>17831<br>105 247 | 17832<br>17832<br>105 250 | 17833<br>17833<br>105 251 | 17834<br>17834<br>105 252 | 17835<br>17835<br>105 253 | 17836<br>17836<br>105 254 | 17837<br>17837<br>105 255 | 17838<br>17838<br>105 256 | 17839<br>17839<br>105 257 |
| B− | 17840<br>17840<br>105 260 | 17841<br>17841<br>105 261 | 17842<br>17842<br>105 262 | 17843<br>17843<br>105 263 | 17844<br>17844<br>105 264 | 17845<br>17845<br>105 265 | 17846<br>17846<br>105 266 | 17847<br>17847<br>105 267 | 17848<br>17848<br>105 270 | 17849<br>17849<br>105 271 | 17850<br>17850<br>105 272 | 17851<br>17851<br>105 273 | 17852<br>17852<br>105 274 | 17853<br>17853<br>105 275 | 17854<br>17854<br>105 276 | 17855<br>17855<br>105 277 |
| C− | 17856<br>17856<br>105 300 | 17857<br>17857<br>105 301 | 17858<br>17858<br>105 302 | 17859<br>17859<br>105 303 | 17860<br>17860<br>105 304 | 17861<br>17861<br>105 305 | 17862<br>17862<br>105 306 | 17863<br>17863<br>105 307 | 17864<br>17864<br>105 310 | 17865<br>17865<br>105 311 | 17866<br>17866<br>105 312 | 17867<br>17867<br>105 313 | 17868<br>17868<br>105 314 | 17869<br>17869<br>105 315 | 17870<br>17870<br>105 316 | 17871<br>17871<br>105 317 |
| D− | 17872<br>17872<br>105 320 | 17873<br>17873<br>105 321 | 17874<br>17874<br>105 322 | 17875<br>17875<br>105 323 | 17876<br>17876<br>105 324 | 17877<br>17877<br>105 325 | 17878<br>17878<br>105 326 | 17879<br>17879<br>105 327 | 17880<br>17880<br>105 330 | 17881<br>17881<br>105 331 | 17882<br>17882<br>105 332 | 17883<br>17883<br>105 333 | 17884<br>17884<br>105 334 | 17885<br>17885<br>105 335 | 17886<br>17886<br>105 336 | 17887<br>17887<br>105 337 |
| E− | 17888<br>17888<br>105 340 | 17889<br>17889<br>105 341 | 17890<br>17890<br>105 342 | 17891<br>17891<br>105 343 | 17892<br>17892<br>105 344 | 17893<br>17893<br>105 345 | 17894<br>17894<br>105 346 | 17895<br>17895<br>105 347 | 17896<br>17896<br>105 350 | 17897<br>17897<br>105 351 | 17898<br>17898<br>105 352 | 17899<br>17899<br>105 353 | 17900<br>17900<br>105 354 | 17901<br>17901<br>105 355 | 17902<br>17902<br>105 356 | 17903<br>17903<br>105 357 |
| F− | 17904<br>17904<br>105 360 | 17905<br>17905<br>105 361 | 17906<br>17906<br>105 362 | 17907<br>17907<br>105 363 | 17908<br>17908<br>105 364 | 17909<br>17909<br>105 365 | 17910<br>17910<br>105 366 | 17911<br>17911<br>105 367 | 17912<br>17912<br>105 370 | 17913<br>17913<br>105 371 | 17914<br>17914<br>105 372 | 17915<br>17915<br>105 373 | 17916<br>17916<br>105 374 | 17917<br>17917<br>105 375 | 17918<br>17918<br>105 376 | 17919<br>17919<br>105 377 |

| SECOND HEX DIGIT | −0 | −1 | −2 | −3 | −4 | −5 | −6 | −7 | −8 | −9 | −A | −B | −C | −D | −E | −F |
|---|---|---|---|---|---|---|---|---|---|---|---|---|---|---|---|---|
| 0- | 17920<br>17920<br>106 000 | 17921<br>17921<br>106 001 | 17922<br>17922<br>106 002 | 17923<br>17923<br>106 003 | 17924<br>17924<br>106 004 | 17925<br>17925<br>106 005 | 17926<br>17926<br>106 006 | 17927<br>17927<br>106 007 | 17928<br>17928<br>106 010 | 17929<br>17929<br>106 011 | 17930<br>17930<br>106 012 | 17931<br>17931<br>106 013 | 17932<br>17932<br>106 014 | 17933<br>17933<br>106 015 | 17934<br>17934<br>106 016 | 17935<br>17935<br>106 017 |
| 1- | 17936<br>17936<br>106 020 | 17937<br>17937<br>106 021 | 17938<br>17938<br>106 022 | 17939<br>17939<br>106 023 | 17940<br>17940<br>106 024 | 17941<br>17941<br>106 025 | 17942<br>17942<br>106 026 | 17943<br>17943<br>106 027 | 17944<br>17944<br>106 030 | 17945<br>17945<br>106 031 | 17946<br>17946<br>106 032 | 17947<br>17947<br>106 033 | 17948<br>17948<br>106 034 | 17949<br>17949<br>106 035 | 17950<br>17950<br>106 036 | 17951<br>17951<br>106 037 |
| 2- | 17952<br>17952<br>106 040 | 17953<br>17953<br>106 041 | 17954<br>17954<br>106 042 | 17955<br>17955<br>106 043 | 17956<br>17956<br>106 044 | 17957<br>17957<br>106 045 | 17958<br>17958<br>106 046 | 17959<br>17959<br>106 047 | 17960<br>17960<br>106 050 | 17961<br>17961<br>106 051 | 17962<br>17962<br>106 052 | 17963<br>17963<br>106 053 | 17964<br>17964<br>106 054 | 17965<br>17965<br>106 055 | 17966<br>17966<br>106 056 | 17967<br>17967<br>106 057 |
| 3- | 17968<br>17968<br>106 060 | 17969<br>17969<br>106 061 | 17970<br>17970<br>106 062 | 17971<br>17971<br>106 063 | 17972<br>17972<br>106 064 | 17973<br>17973<br>106 065 | 17974<br>17974<br>106 066 | 17975<br>17975<br>106 067 | 17976<br>17976<br>106 070 | 17977<br>17977<br>106 071 | 17978<br>17978<br>106 072 | 17979<br>17979<br>106 073 | 17980<br>17980<br>106 074 | 17981<br>17981<br>106 075 | 17982<br>17982<br>106 076 | 17983<br>17983<br>106 077 |
| 4- | 17984<br>17984<br>106 100 | 17985<br>17985<br>106 101 | 17986<br>17986<br>106 102 | 17987<br>17987<br>106 103 | 17988<br>17988<br>106 104 | 17989<br>17989<br>106 105 | 17990<br>17990<br>106 106 | 17991<br>17991<br>106 107 | 17992<br>17992<br>106 110 | 17993<br>17993<br>106 111 | 17994<br>17994<br>106 112 | 17995<br>17995<br>106 113 | 17996<br>17996<br>106 114 | 17997<br>17997<br>106 115 | 17998<br>17998<br>106 116 | 17999<br>17999<br>106 117 |
| 5- | 18000<br>18000<br>106 120 | 18001<br>18001<br>106 121 | 18002<br>18002<br>106 122 | 18003<br>18003<br>106 123 | 18004<br>18004<br>106 124 | 18005<br>18005<br>106 125 | 18006<br>18006<br>106 126 | 18007<br>18007<br>106 127 | 18008<br>18008<br>106 130 | 18009<br>18009<br>106 131 | 18010<br>18010<br>106 132 | 18011<br>18011<br>106 133 | 18012<br>18012<br>106 134 | 18013<br>18013<br>106 135 | 18014<br>18014<br>106 136 | 18015<br>18015<br>106 137 |
| 6- | 18016<br>18016<br>106 140 | 18017<br>18017<br>106 141 | 18018<br>18018<br>106 142 | 18019<br>18019<br>106 143 | 18020<br>18020<br>106 144 | 18021<br>18021<br>106 145 | 18022<br>18022<br>106 146 | 18023<br>18023<br>106 147 | 18024<br>18024<br>106 150 | 18025<br>18025<br>106 151 | 18026<br>18026<br>106 152 | 18027<br>18027<br>106 153 | 18028<br>18028<br>106 154 | 18029<br>18029<br>106 155 | 18030<br>18030<br>106 156 | 18031<br>18031<br>106 157 |
| 7- | 18032<br>18032<br>106 160 | 18033<br>18033<br>106 161 | 18034<br>18034<br>106 162 | 18035<br>18035<br>106 163 | 18036<br>18036<br>106 164 | 18037<br>18037<br>106 165 | 18038<br>18038<br>106 166 | 18039<br>18039<br>106 167 | 18040<br>18040<br>106 170 | 18041<br>18041<br>106 171 | 18042<br>18042<br>106 172 | 18043<br>18043<br>106 173 | 18044<br>18044<br>106 174 | 18045<br>18045<br>106 175 | 18046<br>18046<br>106 176 | 18047<br>18047<br>106 177 |
| 8- | 18048<br>18048<br>106 200 | 18049<br>18049<br>106 201 | 18050<br>18050<br>106 202 | 18051<br>18051<br>106 203 | 18052<br>18052<br>106 204 | 18053<br>18053<br>106 205 | 18054<br>18054<br>106 206 | 18055<br>18055<br>106 207 | 18056<br>18056<br>106 210 | 18057<br>18057<br>106 211 | 18058<br>18058<br>106 212 | 18059<br>18059<br>106 213 | 18060<br>18060<br>106 214 | 18061<br>18061<br>106 215 | 18062<br>18062<br>106 216 | 18063<br>18063<br>106 217 |
| 9- | 18064<br>18064<br>106 220 | 18065<br>18065<br>106 221 | 18066<br>18066<br>106 222 | 18067<br>18067<br>106 223 | 18068<br>18068<br>106 224 | 18069<br>18069<br>106 225 | 18070<br>18070<br>106 226 | 18071<br>18071<br>106 227 | 18072<br>18072<br>106 230 | 18073<br>18073<br>106 231 | 18074<br>18074<br>106 232 | 18075<br>18075<br>106 233 | 18076<br>18076<br>106 234 | 18077<br>18077<br>106 235 | 18078<br>18078<br>106 236 | 18079<br>18079<br>106 237 |
| A- | 18080<br>18080<br>106 240 | 18081<br>18081<br>106 241 | 18082<br>18082<br>106 242 | 18083<br>18083<br>106 243 | 18084<br>18084<br>106 244 | 18085<br>18085<br>106 245 | 18086<br>18086<br>106 246 | 18087<br>18087<br>106 247 | 18088<br>18088<br>106 250 | 18089<br>18089<br>106 251 | 18090<br>18090<br>106 252 | 18091<br>18091<br>106 253 | 18092<br>18092<br>106 254 | 18093<br>18093<br>106 255 | 18094<br>18094<br>106 256 | 18095<br>18095<br>106 257 |
| B- | 18096<br>18096<br>106 260 | 18097<br>18097<br>106 261 | 18098<br>18098<br>106 262 | 18099<br>18099<br>106 263 | 18100<br>18100<br>106 264 | 18101<br>18101<br>106 265 | 18102<br>18102<br>106 266 | 18103<br>18103<br>106 267 | 18104<br>18104<br>106 270 | 18105<br>18105<br>106 271 | 18106<br>18106<br>106 272 | 18107<br>18107<br>106 273 | 18108<br>18108<br>106 274 | 18109<br>18109<br>106 275 | 18110<br>18110<br>106 276 | 18111<br>18111<br>106 277 |
| C- | 18112<br>18112<br>106 300 | 18113<br>18113<br>106 301 | 18114<br>18114<br>106 302 | 18115<br>18115<br>106 303 | 18116<br>18116<br>106 304 | 18117<br>18117<br>106 305 | 18118<br>18118<br>106 306 | 18119<br>18119<br>106 307 | 18120<br>18120<br>106 310 | 18121<br>18121<br>106 311 | 18122<br>18122<br>106 312 | 18123<br>18123<br>106 313 | 18124<br>18124<br>106 314 | 18125<br>18125<br>106 315 | 18126<br>18126<br>106 316 | 18127<br>18127<br>106 317 |
| D- | 18128<br>18128<br>106 320 | 18129<br>18129<br>106 321 | 18130<br>18130<br>106 322 | 18131<br>18131<br>106 323 | 18132<br>18132<br>106 324 | 18133<br>18133<br>106 325 | 18134<br>18134<br>106 326 | 18135<br>18135<br>106 327 | 18136<br>18136<br>106 330 | 18137<br>18137<br>106 331 | 18138<br>18138<br>106 332 | 18139<br>18139<br>106 333 | 18140<br>18140<br>106 334 | 18141<br>18141<br>106 335 | 18142<br>18142<br>106 336 | 18143<br>18143<br>106 337 |
| E- | 18144<br>18144<br>106 340 | 18145<br>18145<br>106 341 | 18146<br>18146<br>106 342 | 18147<br>18147<br>106 343 | 18148<br>18148<br>106 344 | 18149<br>18149<br>106 345 | 18150<br>18150<br>106 346 | 18151<br>18151<br>106 347 | 18152<br>18152<br>106 350 | 18153<br>18153<br>106 351 | 18154<br>18154<br>106 352 | 18155<br>18155<br>106 353 | 18156<br>18156<br>106 354 | 18157<br>18157<br>106 355 | 18158<br>18158<br>106 356 | 18159<br>18159<br>106 357 |
| F- | 18160<br>18160<br>106 360 | 18161<br>18161<br>106 361 | 18162<br>18162<br>106 362 | 18163<br>18163<br>106 363 | 18164<br>18164<br>106 364 | 18165<br>18165<br>106 365 | 18166<br>18166<br>106 366 | 18167<br>18167<br>106 367 | 18168<br>18168<br>106 370 | 18169<br>18169<br>106 371 | 18170<br>18170<br>106 372 | 18171<br>18171<br>106 373 | 18172<br>18172<br>106 374 | 18173<br>18173<br>106 375 | 18174<br>18174<br>106 376 | 18175<br>18175<br>106 377 |

DECIMAL

 DECIMAL

OCTAL

 DECIMAL [17920]  BINARY [0100 0110]  DECIMAL [17920]  HEXADECIMAL ⬡46  OCTAL [106 000]

FOURTH HEX DIGIT →⬡← THIRD HEX DIGIT

|⟨2⟩| FIRST HEX DIGIT | | | | | | | | | | | | | | | |
|---|---|---|---|---|---|---|---|---|---|---|---|---|---|---|---|---|
| | −0 | −1 | −2 | −3 | −4 | −5 | −6 | −7 | −8 | −9 | −A | −B | −C | −D | −E | −F |
| 0− | 18176<br>18176<br>107 000 | 18177<br>18177<br>107 001 | 18178<br>18178<br>107 002 | 18179<br>18179<br>107 003 | 18180<br>18180<br>107 004 | 18181<br>18181<br>107 005 | 18182<br>18182<br>107 006 | 18183<br>18183<br>107 007 | 18184<br>18184<br>107 010 | 18185<br>18185<br>107 011 | 18186<br>18186<br>107 012 | 18187<br>18187<br>107 013 | 18188<br>18188<br>107 014 | 18189<br>18189<br>107 015 | 18190<br>18190<br>107 016 | 18191<br>18191<br>107 017 |
| 1− | 18192<br>18192<br>107 020 | 18193<br>18193<br>107 021 | 18194<br>18194<br>107 022 | 18195<br>18195<br>107 023 | 18196<br>18196<br>107 024 | 18197<br>18197<br>107 025 | 18198<br>18198<br>107 026 | 18199<br>18199<br>107 027 | 18200<br>18200<br>107 030 | 18201<br>18201<br>107 031 | 18202<br>18202<br>107 032 | 18203<br>18203<br>107 033 | 18204<br>18204<br>107 034 | 18205<br>18205<br>107 035 | 18206<br>18206<br>107 036 | 18207<br>18207<br>107 037 |
| 2− | 18208<br>18208<br>107 040 | 18209<br>18209<br>107 041 | 18210<br>18210<br>107 042 | 18211<br>18211<br>107 043 | 18212<br>18212<br>107 044 | 18213<br>18213<br>107 045 | 18214<br>18214<br>107 046 | 18215<br>18215<br>107 047 | 18216<br>18216<br>107 050 | 18217<br>18217<br>107 051 | 18218<br>18218<br>107 052 | 18219<br>18219<br>107 053 | 18220<br>18220<br>107 054 | 18221<br>18221<br>107 055 | 18222<br>18222<br>107 056 | 18223<br>18223<br>107 057 |
| 3− | 18224<br>18224<br>107 060 | 18225<br>18225<br>107 061 | 18226<br>18226<br>107 062 | 18227<br>18227<br>107 063 | 18228<br>18228<br>107 064 | 18229<br>18229<br>107 065 | 18230<br>18230<br>107 066 | 18231<br>18231<br>107 067 | 18232<br>18232<br>107 070 | 18233<br>18233<br>107 071 | 18234<br>18234<br>107 072 | 18235<br>18235<br>107 073 | 18236<br>18236<br>107 074 | 18237<br>18237<br>107 075 | 18238<br>18238<br>107 076 | 18239<br>18239<br>107 077 |
| 4− | 18240<br>18240<br>107 100 | 18241<br>18241<br>107 101 | 18242<br>18242<br>107 102 | 18243<br>18243<br>107 103 | 18244<br>18244<br>107 104 | 18245<br>18245<br>107 105 | 18246<br>18246<br>107 106 | 18247<br>18247<br>107 107 | 18248<br>18248<br>107 110 | 18249<br>18249<br>107 111 | 18250<br>18250<br>107 112 | 18251<br>18251<br>107 113 | 18252<br>18252<br>107 114 | 18253<br>18253<br>107 115 | 18254<br>18254<br>107 116 | 18255<br>18255<br>107 117 |
| 5− | 18256<br>18256<br>107 120 | 18257<br>18257<br>107 121 | 18258<br>18258<br>107 122 | 18259<br>18259<br>107 123 | 18260<br>18260<br>107 124 | 18261<br>18261<br>107 125 | 18262<br>18262<br>107 126 | 18263<br>18263<br>107 127 | 18264<br>18264<br>107 130 | 18265<br>18265<br>107 131 | 18266<br>18266<br>107 132 | 18267<br>18267<br>107 133 | 18268<br>18268<br>107 134 | 18269<br>18269<br>107 135 | 18270<br>18270<br>107 136 | 18271<br>18271<br>107 137 |
| 6− | 18272<br>18272<br>107 140 | 18273<br>18273<br>107 141 | 18274<br>18274<br>107 142 | 18275<br>18275<br>107 143 | 18276<br>18276<br>107 144 | 18277<br>18277<br>107 145 | 18278<br>18278<br>107 146 | 18279<br>18279<br>107 147 | 18280<br>18280<br>107 150 | 18281<br>18281<br>107 151 | 18282<br>18282<br>107 152 | 18283<br>18283<br>107 153 | 18284<br>18284<br>107 154 | 18285<br>18285<br>107 155 | 18286<br>18286<br>107 156 | 18287<br>18287<br>107 157 |
| 7− | 18288<br>18288<br>107 160 | 18289<br>18289<br>107 161 | 18290<br>18290<br>107 162 | 18291<br>18291<br>107 163 | 18292<br>18292<br>107 164 | 18293<br>18293<br>107 165 | 18294<br>18294<br>107 166 | 18295<br>18295<br>107 167 | 18296<br>18296<br>107 170 | 18297<br>18297<br>107 171 | 18298<br>18298<br>107 172 | 18299<br>18299<br>107 173 | 18300<br>18300<br>107 174 | 18301<br>18301<br>107 175 | 18302<br>18302<br>107 176 | 18303<br>18303<br>107 177 |
| 8− | 18304<br>18304<br>107 200 | 18305<br>18305<br>107 201 | 18306<br>18306<br>107 202 | 18307<br>18307<br>107 203 | 18308<br>18308<br>107 204 | 18309<br>18309<br>107 205 | 18310<br>18310<br>107 206 | 18311<br>18311<br>107 207 | 18312<br>18312<br>107 210 | 18313<br>18313<br>107 211 | 18314<br>18314<br>107 212 | 18315<br>18315<br>107 213 | 18316<br>18316<br>107 214 | 18317<br>18317<br>107 215 | 18318<br>18318<br>107 216 | 18319<br>18319<br>107 217 |
| 9− | 18320<br>18320<br>107 220 | 18321<br>18321<br>107 221 | 18322<br>18322<br>107 222 | 18323<br>18323<br>107 223 | 18324<br>18324<br>107 224 | 18325<br>18325<br>107 225 | 18326<br>18326<br>107 226 | 18327<br>18327<br>107 227 | 18328<br>18328<br>107 230 | 18329<br>18329<br>107 231 | 18330<br>18330<br>107 232 | 18331<br>18331<br>107 233 | 18332<br>18332<br>107 234 | 18333<br>18333<br>107 235 | 18334<br>18334<br>107 236 | 18335<br>18335<br>107 237 |
| A− | 18336<br>18336<br>107 240 | 18337<br>18337<br>107 241 | 18338<br>18338<br>107 242 | 18339<br>18339<br>107 243 | 18340<br>18340<br>107 244 | 18341<br>18341<br>107 245 | 18342<br>18342<br>107 246 | 18343<br>18343<br>107 247 | 18344<br>18344<br>107 250 | 18345<br>18345<br>107 251 | 18346<br>18346<br>107 252 | 18347<br>18347<br>107 253 | 18348<br>18348<br>107 254 | 18349<br>18349<br>107 255 | 18350<br>18350<br>107 256 | 18351<br>18351<br>107 257 |
| B− | 18352<br>18352<br>107 260 | 18353<br>18353<br>107 261 | 18354<br>18354<br>107 262 | 18355<br>18355<br>107 263 | 18356<br>18356<br>107 264 | 18357<br>18357<br>107 265 | 18358<br>18358<br>107 266 | 18359<br>18359<br>107 267 | 18360<br>18360<br>107 270 | 18361<br>18361<br>107 271 | 18362<br>18362<br>107 272 | 18363<br>18363<br>107 273 | 18364<br>18364<br>107 274 | 18365<br>18365<br>107 275 | 18366<br>18366<br>107 276 | 18367<br>18367<br>107 277 |
| C− | 18368<br>18368<br>107 300 | 18369<br>18369<br>107 301 | 18370<br>18370<br>107 302 | 18371<br>18371<br>107 303 | 18372<br>18372<br>107 304 | 18373<br>18373<br>107 305 | 18374<br>18374<br>107 306 | 18375<br>18375<br>107 307 | 18376<br>18376<br>107 310 | 18377<br>18377<br>107 311 | 18378<br>18378<br>107 312 | 18379<br>18379<br>107 313 | 18380<br>18380<br>107 314 | 18381<br>18381<br>107 315 | 18382<br>18382<br>107 316 | 18383<br>18383<br>107 317 |
| D− | 18384<br>18384<br>107 320 | 18385<br>18385<br>107 321 | 18386<br>18386<br>107 322 | 18387<br>18387<br>107 323 | 18388<br>18388<br>107 324 | 18389<br>18389<br>107 325 | 18390<br>18390<br>107 326 | 18391<br>18391<br>107 327 | 18392<br>18392<br>107 330 | 18393<br>18393<br>107 331 | 18394<br>18394<br>107 332 | 18395<br>18395<br>107 333 | 18396<br>18396<br>107 334 | 18397<br>18397<br>107 335 | 18398<br>18398<br>107 336 | 18399<br>18399<br>107 337 |
| E− | 18400<br>18400<br>107 340 | 18401<br>18401<br>107 341 | 18402<br>18402<br>107 342 | 18403<br>18403<br>107 343 | 18404<br>18404<br>107 344 | 18405<br>18405<br>107 345 | 18406<br>18406<br>107 346 | 18407<br>18407<br>107 347 | 18408<br>18408<br>107 350 | 18409<br>18409<br>107 351 | 18410<br>18410<br>107 352 | 18411<br>18411<br>107 353 | 18412<br>18412<br>107 354 | 18413<br>18413<br>107 355 | 18414<br>18414<br>107 356 | 18415<br>18415<br>107 357 |
| F− | 18416<br>18416<br>107 360 | 18417<br>18417<br>107 361 | 18418<br>18418<br>107 362 | 18419<br>18419<br>107 363 | 18420<br>18420<br>107 364 | 18421<br>18421<br>107 365 | 18422<br>18422<br>107 366 | 18423<br>18423<br>107 367 | 18424<br>18424<br>107 370 | 18425<br>18425<br>107 371 | 18426<br>18426<br>107 372 | 18427<br>18427<br>107 373 | 18428<br>18428<br>107 374 | 18429<br>18429<br>107 375 | 18430<br>18430<br>107 376 | 18431<br>18431<br>107 377 |

(Row label column: SECOND HEX DIGIT)

DECIMAL →

🍎 DECIMAL →

OCTAL →

| (2) | | −0 | −1 | −2 | −3 | −4 | −5 | −6 | −7 | −8 | −9 | −A | −B | −C | −D | −E | −F |
|---|---|---|---|---|---|---|---|---|---|---|---|---|---|---|---|---|---|
| | 0− | 18432<br>18432<br>110 000 | 18433<br>18433<br>110 001 | 18434<br>18434<br>110 002 | 18435<br>18435<br>110 003 | 18436<br>18436<br>110 004 | 18437<br>18437<br>110 005 | 18438<br>18438<br>110 006 | 18439<br>18439<br>110 007 | 18440<br>18440<br>110 010 | 18441<br>18441<br>110 011 | 18442<br>18442<br>110 012 | 18443<br>18443<br>110 013 | 18444<br>18444<br>110 014 | 18445<br>18445<br>110 015 | 18446<br>18446<br>110 016 | 18447<br>18447<br>110 017 |
| | 1− | 18448<br>18448<br>110 020 | 18449<br>18449<br>110 021 | 18450<br>18450<br>110 022 | 18451<br>18451<br>110 023 | 18452<br>18452<br>110 024 | 18453<br>18453<br>110 025 | 18454<br>18454<br>110 026 | 18455<br>18455<br>110 027 | 18456<br>18456<br>110 030 | 18457<br>18457<br>110 031 | 18458<br>18458<br>110 032 | 18459<br>18459<br>110 033 | 18460<br>18460<br>110 034 | 18461<br>18461<br>110 035 | 18462<br>18462<br>110 036 | 18463<br>18463<br>110 037 |
| | 2− | 18464<br>18464<br>110 040 | 18465<br>18465<br>110 041 | 18466<br>18466<br>110 042 | 18467<br>18467<br>110 043 | 18468<br>18468<br>110 044 | 18469<br>18469<br>110 045 | 18470<br>18470<br>110 046 | 18471<br>18471<br>110 047 | 18472<br>18472<br>110 050 | 18473<br>18473<br>110 051 | 18474<br>18474<br>110 052 | 18475<br>18475<br>110 053 | 18476<br>18476<br>110 054 | 18477<br>18477<br>110 055 | 18478<br>18478<br>110 056 | 18479<br>18479<br>110 057 |
| | 3− | 18480<br>18480<br>110 060 | 18481<br>18481<br>110 061 | 18482<br>18482<br>110 062 | 18483<br>18483<br>110 063 | 18484<br>18484<br>110 064 | 18485<br>18485<br>110 065 | 18486<br>18486<br>110 066 | 18487<br>18487<br>110 067 | 18488<br>18488<br>110 070 | 18489<br>18489<br>110 071 | 18490<br>18490<br>110 072 | 18491<br>18491<br>110 073 | 18492<br>18492<br>110 074 | 18493<br>18493<br>110 075 | 18494<br>18494<br>110 076 | 18495<br>18495<br>110 077 |
| | 4− | 18496<br>18496<br>110 100 | 18497<br>18497<br>110 101 | 18498<br>18498<br>110 102 | 18499<br>18499<br>110 103 | 18500<br>18500<br>110 104 | 18501<br>18501<br>110 105 | 18502<br>18502<br>110 106 | 18503<br>18503<br>110 107 | 18504<br>18504<br>110 110 | 18505<br>18505<br>110 111 | 18506<br>18506<br>110 112 | 18507<br>18507<br>110 113 | 18508<br>18508<br>110 114 | 18509<br>18509<br>110 115 | 18510<br>18510<br>110 116 | 18511<br>18511<br>110 117 |
| | 5− | 18512<br>18512<br>110 120 | 18513<br>18513<br>110 121 | 18514<br>18514<br>110 122 | 18515<br>18515<br>110 123 | 18516<br>18516<br>110 124 | 18517<br>18517<br>110 125 | 18518<br>18518<br>110 126 | 18519<br>18519<br>110 127 | 18520<br>18520<br>110 130 | 18521<br>18521<br>110 131 | 18522<br>18522<br>110 132 | 18523<br>18523<br>110 133 | 18524<br>18524<br>110 134 | 18525<br>18525<br>110 135 | 18526<br>18526<br>110 136 | 18527<br>18527<br>110 137 |
| | 6− | 18528<br>18528<br>110 140 | 18529<br>18529<br>110 141 | 18530<br>18530<br>110 142 | 18531<br>18531<br>110 143 | 18532<br>18532<br>110 144 | 18533<br>18533<br>110 145 | 18534<br>18534<br>110 146 | 18535<br>18535<br>110 147 | 18536<br>18536<br>110 150 | 18537<br>18537<br>110 151 | 18538<br>18538<br>110 152 | 18539<br>18539<br>110 153 | 18540<br>18540<br>110 154 | 18541<br>18541<br>110 155 | 18542<br>18542<br>110 156 | 18543<br>18543<br>110 157 |
| | 7− | 18544<br>18544<br>110 160 | 18545<br>18545<br>110 161 | 18546<br>18546<br>110 162 | 18547<br>18547<br>110 163 | 18548<br>18548<br>110 164 | 18549<br>18549<br>110 165 | 18550<br>18550<br>110 166 | 18551<br>18551<br>110 167 | 18552<br>18552<br>110 170 | 18553<br>18553<br>110 171 | 18554<br>18554<br>110 172 | 18555<br>18555<br>110 173 | 18556<br>18556<br>110 174 | 18557<br>18557<br>110 175 | 18558<br>18558<br>110 176 | 18559<br>18559<br>110 177 |
| | 8− | 18560<br>18560<br>110 200 | 18561<br>18561<br>110 201 | 18562<br>18562<br>110 202 | 18563<br>18563<br>110 203 | 18564<br>18564<br>110 204 | 18565<br>18565<br>110 205 | 18566<br>18566<br>110 206 | 18567<br>18567<br>110 207 | 18568<br>18568<br>110 210 | 18569<br>18569<br>110 211 | 18570<br>18570<br>110 212 | 18571<br>18571<br>110 213 | 18572<br>18572<br>110 214 | 18573<br>18573<br>110 215 | 18574<br>18574<br>110 216 | 18575<br>18575<br>110 217 |
| | 9− | 18576<br>18576<br>110 220 | 18577<br>18577<br>110 221 | 18578<br>18578<br>110 222 | 18579<br>18579<br>110 223 | 18580<br>18580<br>110 224 | 18581<br>18581<br>110 225 | 18582<br>18582<br>110 226 | 18583<br>18583<br>110 227 | 18584<br>18584<br>110 230 | 18585<br>18585<br>110 231 | 18586<br>18586<br>110 232 | 18587<br>18587<br>110 233 | 18588<br>18588<br>110 234 | 18589<br>18589<br>110 235 | 18590<br>18590<br>110 236 | 18591<br>18591<br>110 237 |
| | A− | 18592<br>18592<br>110 240 | 18593<br>18593<br>110 241 | 18594<br>18594<br>110 242 | 18595<br>18595<br>110 243 | 18596<br>18596<br>110 244 | 18597<br>18597<br>110 245 | 18598<br>18598<br>110 246 | 18599<br>18599<br>110 247 | 18600<br>18600<br>110 250 | 18601<br>18601<br>110 251 | 18602<br>18602<br>110 252 | 18603<br>18603<br>110 253 | 18604<br>18604<br>110 254 | 18605<br>18605<br>110 255 | 18606<br>18606<br>110 256 | 18607<br>18607<br>110 257 |
| | B− | 18608<br>18608<br>110 260 | 18609<br>18609<br>110 261 | 18610<br>18610<br>110 262 | 18611<br>18611<br>110 263 | 18612<br>18612<br>110 264 | 18613<br>18613<br>110 265 | 18614<br>18614<br>110 266 | 18615<br>18615<br>110 267 | 18616<br>18616<br>110 270 | 18617<br>18617<br>110 271 | 18618<br>18618<br>110 272 | 18619<br>18619<br>110 273 | 18620<br>18620<br>110 274 | 18621<br>18621<br>110 275 | 18622<br>18622<br>110 276 | 18623<br>18623<br>110 277 |
| | C− | 18624<br>18624<br>110 300 | 18625<br>18625<br>110 301 | 18626<br>18626<br>110 302 | 18627<br>18627<br>110 303 | 18628<br>18628<br>110 304 | 18629<br>18629<br>110 305 | 18630<br>18630<br>110 306 | 18631<br>18631<br>110 307 | 18632<br>18632<br>110 310 | 18633<br>18633<br>110 311 | 18634<br>18634<br>110 312 | 18635<br>18635<br>110 313 | 18636<br>18636<br>110 314 | 18637<br>18637<br>110 315 | 18638<br>18638<br>110 316 | 18639<br>18639<br>110 317 |
| | D− | 18640<br>18640<br>110 320 | 18641<br>18641<br>110 321 | 18642<br>18642<br>110 322 | 18643<br>18643<br>110 323 | 18644<br>18644<br>110 324 | 18645<br>18645<br>110 325 | 18646<br>18646<br>110 326 | 18647<br>18647<br>110 327 | 18648<br>18648<br>110 330 | 18649<br>18649<br>110 331 | 18650<br>18650<br>110 332 | 18651<br>18651<br>110 333 | 18652<br>18652<br>110 334 | 18653<br>18653<br>110 335 | 18654<br>18654<br>110 336 | 18655<br>18655<br>110 337 |
| | E− | 18656<br>18656<br>110 340 | 18657<br>18657<br>110 341 | 18658<br>18658<br>110 342 | 18659<br>18659<br>110 343 | 18660<br>18660<br>110 344 | 18661<br>18661<br>110 345 | 18662<br>18662<br>110 346 | 18663<br>18663<br>110 347 | 18664<br>18664<br>110 350 | 18665<br>18665<br>110 351 | 18666<br>18666<br>110 352 | 18667<br>18667<br>110 353 | 18668<br>18668<br>110 354 | 18669<br>18669<br>110 355 | 18670<br>18670<br>110 356 | 18671<br>18671<br>110 357 |
| | F− | 18672<br>18672<br>110 360 | 18673<br>18673<br>110 361 | 18674<br>18674<br>110 362 | 18675<br>18675<br>110 363 | 18676<br>18676<br>110 364 | 18677<br>18677<br>110 365 | 18678<br>18678<br>110 366 | 18679<br>18679<br>110 367 | 18680<br>18680<br>110 370 | 18681<br>18681<br>110 371 | 18682<br>18682<br>110 372 | 18683<br>18683<br>110 373 | 18684<br>18684<br>110 374 | 18685<br>18685<br>110 375 | 18686<br>18686<br>110 376 | 18687<br>18687<br>110 377 |

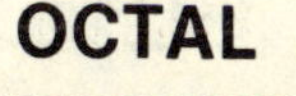

 DECIMAL [18432]　　BINARY [0100 1000]　　DECIMAL [18432]　　HEXADECIMAL (48)　　OCTAL [110 000]

FOURTH HEX DIGIT → (48) ← THIRD HEX DIGIT

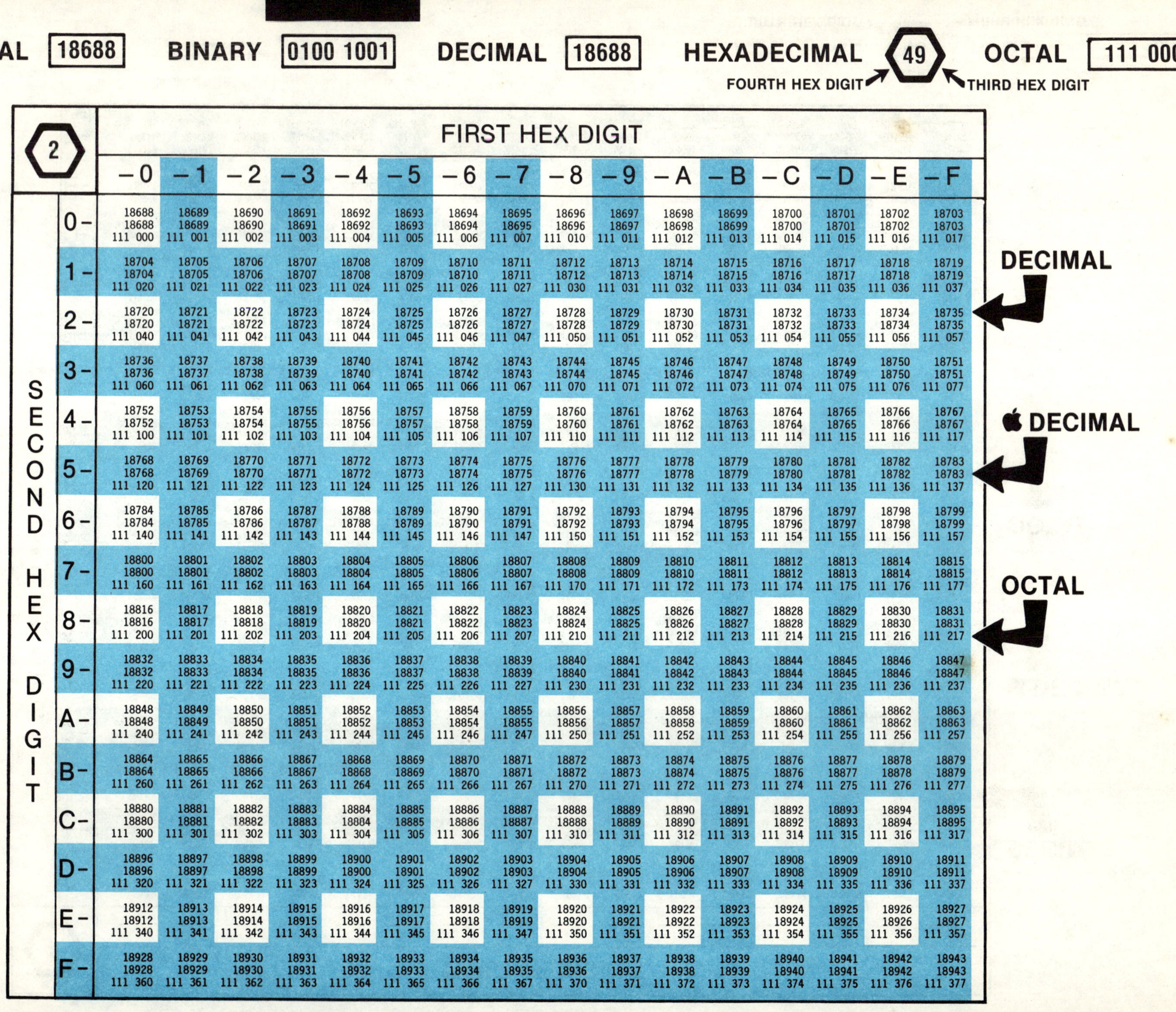



| 2 | -0 | -1 | -2 | -3 | -4 | -5 | -6 | -7 | -8 | -9 | -A | -B | -C | -D | -E | -F |
|---|---|---|---|---|---|---|---|---|---|---|---|---|---|---|---|---|
| 0- | 18688<br>18688<br>111 000 | 18689<br>18689<br>111 001 | 18690<br>18690<br>111 002 | 18691<br>18691<br>111 003 | 18692<br>18692<br>111 004 | 18693<br>18693<br>111 005 | 18694<br>18694<br>111 006 | 18695<br>18695<br>111 007 | 18696<br>18696<br>111 010 | 18697<br>18697<br>111 011 | 18698<br>18698<br>111 012 | 18699<br>18699<br>111 013 | 18700<br>18700<br>111 014 | 18701<br>18701<br>111 015 | 18702<br>18702<br>111 016 | 18703<br>18703<br>111 017 |
| 1- | 18704<br>18704<br>111 020 | 18705<br>18705<br>111 021 | 18706<br>18706<br>111 022 | 18707<br>18707<br>111 023 | 18708<br>18708<br>111 024 | 18709<br>18709<br>111 025 | 18710<br>18710<br>111 026 | 18711<br>18711<br>111 027 | 18712<br>18712<br>111 030 | 18713<br>18713<br>111 031 | 18714<br>18714<br>111 032 | 18715<br>18715<br>111 033 | 18716<br>18716<br>111 034 | 18717<br>18717<br>111 035 | 18718<br>18718<br>111 036 | 18719<br>18719<br>111 037 |
| 2- | 18720<br>18720<br>111 040 | 18721<br>18721<br>111 041 | 18722<br>18722<br>111 042 | 18723<br>18723<br>111 043 | 18724<br>18724<br>111 044 | 18725<br>18725<br>111 045 | 18726<br>18726<br>111 046 | 18727<br>18727<br>111 047 | 18728<br>18728<br>111 050 | 18729<br>18729<br>111 051 | 18730<br>18730<br>111 052 | 18731<br>18731<br>111 053 | 18732<br>18732<br>111 054 | 18733<br>18733<br>111 055 | 18734<br>18734<br>111 056 | 18735<br>18735<br>111 057 |
| 3- | 18736<br>18736<br>111 060 | 18737<br>18737<br>111 061 | 18738<br>18738<br>111 062 | 18739<br>18739<br>111 063 | 18740<br>18740<br>111 064 | 18741<br>18741<br>111 065 | 18742<br>18742<br>111 066 | 18743<br>18743<br>111 067 | 18744<br>18744<br>111 070 | 18745<br>18745<br>111 071 | 18746<br>18746<br>111 072 | 18747<br>18747<br>111 073 | 18748<br>18748<br>111 074 | 18749<br>18749<br>111 075 | 18750<br>18750<br>111 076 | 18751<br>18751<br>111 077 |
| 4- | 18752<br>18752<br>111 100 | 18753<br>18753<br>111 101 | 18754<br>18754<br>111 102 | 18755<br>18755<br>111 103 | 18756<br>18756<br>111 104 | 18757<br>18757<br>111 105 | 18758<br>18758<br>111 106 | 18759<br>18759<br>111 107 | 18760<br>18760<br>111 110 | 18761<br>18761<br>111 111 | 18762<br>18762<br>111 112 | 18763<br>18763<br>111 113 | 18764<br>18764<br>111 114 | 18765<br>18765<br>111 115 | 18766<br>18766<br>111 116 | 18767<br>18767<br>111 117 |
| 5- | 18768<br>18768<br>111 120 | 18769<br>18769<br>111 121 | 18770<br>18770<br>111 122 | 18771<br>18771<br>111 123 | 18772<br>18772<br>111 124 | 18773<br>18773<br>111 125 | 18774<br>18774<br>111 126 | 18775<br>18775<br>111 127 | 18776<br>18776<br>111 130 | 18777<br>18777<br>111 131 | 18778<br>18778<br>111 132 | 18779<br>18779<br>111 133 | 18780<br>18780<br>111 134 | 18781<br>18781<br>111 135 | 18782<br>18782<br>111 136 | 18783<br>18783<br>111 137 |
| 6- | 18784<br>18784<br>111 140 | 18785<br>18785<br>111 141 | 18786<br>18786<br>111 142 | 18787<br>18787<br>111 143 | 18788<br>18788<br>111 144 | 18789<br>18789<br>111 145 | 18790<br>18790<br>111 146 | 18791<br>18791<br>111 147 | 18792<br>18792<br>111 150 | 18793<br>18793<br>111 151 | 18794<br>18794<br>111 152 | 18795<br>18795<br>111 153 | 18796<br>18796<br>111 154 | 18797<br>18797<br>111 155 | 18798<br>18798<br>111 156 | 18799<br>18799<br>111 157 |
| 7- | 18800<br>18800<br>111 160 | 18801<br>18801<br>111 161 | 18802<br>18802<br>111 162 | 18803<br>18803<br>111 163 | 18804<br>18804<br>111 164 | 18805<br>18805<br>111 165 | 18806<br>18806<br>111 166 | 18807<br>18807<br>111 167 | 18808<br>18808<br>111 170 | 18809<br>18809<br>111 171 | 18810<br>18810<br>111 172 | 18811<br>18811<br>111 173 | 18812<br>18812<br>111 174 | 18813<br>18813<br>111 175 | 18814<br>18814<br>111 176 | 18815<br>18815<br>111 177 |
| 8- | 18816<br>18816<br>111 200 | 18817<br>18817<br>111 201 | 18818<br>18818<br>111 202 | 18819<br>18819<br>111 203 | 18820<br>18820<br>111 204 | 18821<br>18821<br>111 205 | 18822<br>18822<br>111 206 | 18823<br>18823<br>111 207 | 18824<br>18824<br>111 210 | 18825<br>18825<br>111 211 | 18826<br>18826<br>111 212 | 18827<br>18827<br>111 213 | 18828<br>18828<br>111 214 | 18829<br>18829<br>111 215 | 18830<br>18830<br>111 216 | 18831<br>18831<br>111 217 |
| 9- | 18832<br>18832<br>111 220 | 18833<br>18833<br>111 221 | 18834<br>18834<br>111 222 | 18835<br>18835<br>111 223 | 18836<br>18836<br>111 224 | 18837<br>18837<br>111 225 | 18838<br>18838<br>111 226 | 18839<br>18839<br>111 227 | 18840<br>18840<br>111 230 | 18841<br>18841<br>111 231 | 18842<br>18842<br>111 232 | 18843<br>18843<br>111 233 | 18844<br>18844<br>111 234 | 18845<br>18845<br>111 235 | 18846<br>18846<br>111 236 | 18847<br>18847<br>111 237 |
| A- | 18848<br>18848<br>111 240 | 18849<br>18849<br>111 241 | 18850<br>18850<br>111 242 | 18851<br>18851<br>111 243 | 18852<br>18852<br>111 244 | 18853<br>18853<br>111 245 | 18854<br>18854<br>111 246 | 18855<br>18855<br>111 247 | 18856<br>18856<br>111 250 | 18857<br>18857<br>111 251 | 18858<br>18858<br>111 252 | 18859<br>18859<br>111 253 | 18860<br>18860<br>111 254 | 18861<br>18861<br>111 255 | 18862<br>18862<br>111 256 | 18863<br>18863<br>111 257 |
| B- | 18864<br>18864<br>111 260 | 18865<br>18865<br>111 261 | 18866<br>18866<br>111 262 | 18867<br>18867<br>111 263 | 18868<br>18868<br>111 264 | 18869<br>18869<br>111 265 | 18870<br>18870<br>111 266 | 18871<br>18871<br>111 267 | 18872<br>18872<br>111 270 | 18873<br>18873<br>111 271 | 18874<br>18874<br>111 272 | 18875<br>18875<br>111 273 | 18876<br>18876<br>111 274 | 18877<br>18877<br>111 275 | 18878<br>18878<br>111 276 | 18879<br>18879<br>111 277 |
| C- | 18880<br>18880<br>111 300 | 18881<br>18881<br>111 301 | 18882<br>18882<br>111 302 | 18883<br>18883<br>111 303 | 18884<br>18884<br>111 304 | 18885<br>18885<br>111 305 | 18886<br>18886<br>111 306 | 18887<br>18887<br>111 307 | 18888<br>18888<br>111 310 | 18889<br>18889<br>111 311 | 18890<br>18890<br>111 312 | 18891<br>18891<br>111 313 | 18892<br>18892<br>111 314 | 18893<br>18893<br>111 315 | 18894<br>18894<br>111 316 | 18895<br>18895<br>111 317 |
| D- | 18896<br>18896<br>111 320 | 18897<br>18897<br>111 321 | 18898<br>18898<br>111 322 | 18899<br>18899<br>111 323 | 18900<br>18900<br>111 324 | 18901<br>18901<br>111 325 | 18902<br>18902<br>111 326 | 18903<br>18903<br>111 327 | 18904<br>18904<br>111 330 | 18905<br>18905<br>111 331 | 18906<br>18906<br>111 332 | 18907<br>18907<br>111 333 | 18908<br>18908<br>111 334 | 18909<br>18909<br>111 335 | 18910<br>18910<br>111 336 | 18911<br>18911<br>111 337 |
| E- | 18912<br>18912<br>111 340 | 18913<br>18913<br>111 341 | 18914<br>18914<br>111 342 | 18915<br>18915<br>111 343 | 18916<br>18916<br>111 344 | 18917<br>18917<br>111 345 | 18918<br>18918<br>111 346 | 18919<br>18919<br>111 347 | 18920<br>18920<br>111 350 | 18921<br>18921<br>111 351 | 18922<br>18922<br>111 352 | 18923<br>18923<br>111 353 | 18924<br>18924<br>111 354 | 18925<br>18925<br>111 355 | 18926<br>18926<br>111 356 | 18927<br>18927<br>111 357 |
| F- | 18928<br>18928<br>111 360 | 18929<br>18929<br>111 361 | 18930<br>18930<br>111 362 | 18931<br>18931<br>111 363 | 18932<br>18932<br>111 364 | 18933<br>18933<br>111 365 | 18934<br>18934<br>111 366 | 18935<br>18935<br>111 367 | 18936<br>18936<br>111 370 | 18937<br>18937<br>111 371 | 18938<br>18938<br>111 372 | 18939<br>18939<br>111 373 | 18940<br>18940<br>111 374 | 18941<br>18941<br>111 375 | 18942<br>18942<br>111 376 | 18943<br>18943<br>111 377 |

**② FIRST HEX DIGIT**

| SECOND HEX DIGIT | −0 | −1 | −2 | −3 | −4 | −5 | −6 | −7 | −8 | −9 | −A | −B | −C | −D | −E | −F |
|---|---|---|---|---|---|---|---|---|---|---|---|---|---|---|---|---|
| 0- | 18944<br>18944<br>112 000 | 18945<br>18945<br>112 001 | 18946<br>18946<br>112 002 | 18947<br>18947<br>112 003 | 18948<br>18948<br>112 004 | 18949<br>18949<br>112 005 | 18950<br>18950<br>112 006 | 18951<br>18951<br>112 007 | 18952<br>18952<br>112 010 | 18953<br>18953<br>112 011 | 18954<br>18954<br>112 012 | 18955<br>18955<br>112 013 | 18956<br>18956<br>112 014 | 18957<br>18957<br>112 015 | 18958<br>18958<br>112 016 | 18959<br>18959<br>112 017 |
| 1- | 18960<br>18960<br>112 020 | 18961<br>18961<br>112 021 | 18962<br>18962<br>112 022 | 18963<br>18963<br>112 023 | 18964<br>18964<br>112 024 | 18965<br>18965<br>112 025 | 18966<br>18966<br>112 026 | 18967<br>18967<br>112 027 | 18968<br>18968<br>112 030 | 18969<br>18969<br>112 031 | 18970<br>18970<br>112 032 | 18971<br>18971<br>112 033 | 18972<br>18972<br>112 034 | 18973<br>18973<br>112 035 | 18974<br>18974<br>112 036 | 18975<br>18975<br>112 037 |
| 2- | 18976<br>18976<br>112 040 | 18977<br>18977<br>112 041 | 18978<br>18978<br>112 042 | 18979<br>18979<br>112 043 | 18980<br>18980<br>112 044 | 18981<br>18981<br>112 045 | 18982<br>18982<br>112 046 | 18983<br>18983<br>112 047 | 18984<br>18984<br>112 050 | 18985<br>18985<br>112 051 | 18986<br>18986<br>112 052 | 18987<br>18987<br>112 053 | 18988<br>18988<br>112 054 | 18989<br>18989<br>112 055 | 18990<br>18990<br>112 056 | 18991<br>18991<br>112 057 |
| 3- | 18992<br>18992<br>112 060 | 18993<br>18993<br>112 061 | 18994<br>18994<br>112 062 | 18995<br>18995<br>112 063 | 18996<br>18996<br>112 064 | 18997<br>18997<br>112 065 | 18998<br>18998<br>112 066 | 18999<br>18999<br>112 067 | 19000<br>19000<br>112 070 | 19001<br>19001<br>112 071 | 19002<br>19002<br>112 072 | 19003<br>19003<br>112 073 | 19004<br>19004<br>112 074 | 19005<br>19005<br>112 075 | 19006<br>19006<br>112 076 | 19007<br>19007<br>112 077 |
| 4- | 19008<br>19008<br>112 100 | 19009<br>19009<br>112 101 | 19010<br>19010<br>112 102 | 19011<br>19011<br>112 103 | 19012<br>19012<br>112 104 | 19013<br>19013<br>112 105 | 19014<br>19014<br>112 106 | 19015<br>19015<br>112 107 | 19016<br>19016<br>112 110 | 19017<br>19017<br>112 111 | 19018<br>19018<br>112 112 | 19019<br>19019<br>112 113 | 19020<br>19020<br>112 114 | 19021<br>19021<br>112 115 | 19022<br>19022<br>112 116 | 19023<br>19023<br>112 117 |
| 5- | 19024<br>19024<br>112 120 | 19025<br>19025<br>112 121 | 19026<br>19026<br>112 122 | 19027<br>19027<br>112 123 | 19028<br>19028<br>112 124 | 19029<br>19029<br>112 125 | 19030<br>19030<br>112 126 | 19031<br>19031<br>112 127 | 19032<br>19032<br>112 130 | 19033<br>19033<br>112 131 | 19034<br>19034<br>112 132 | 19035<br>19035<br>112 133 | 19036<br>19036<br>112 134 | 19037<br>19037<br>112 135 | 19038<br>19038<br>112 136 | 19039<br>19039<br>112 137 |
| 6- | 19040<br>19040<br>112 140 | 19041<br>19041<br>112 141 | 19042<br>19042<br>112 142 | 19043<br>19043<br>112 143 | 19044<br>19044<br>112 144 | 19045<br>19045<br>112 145 | 19046<br>19046<br>112 146 | 19047<br>19047<br>112 147 | 19048<br>19048<br>112 150 | 19049<br>19049<br>112 151 | 19050<br>19050<br>112 152 | 19051<br>19051<br>112 153 | 19052<br>19052<br>112 154 | 19053<br>19053<br>112 155 | 19054<br>19054<br>112 156 | 19055<br>19055<br>112 157 |
| 7- | 19056<br>19056<br>112 160 | 19057<br>19057<br>112 161 | 19058<br>19058<br>112 162 | 19059<br>19059<br>112 163 | 19060<br>19060<br>112 164 | 19061<br>19061<br>112 165 | 19062<br>19062<br>112 166 | 19063<br>19063<br>112 167 | 19064<br>19064<br>112 170 | 19065<br>19065<br>112 171 | 19066<br>19066<br>112 172 | 19067<br>19067<br>112 173 | 19068<br>19068<br>112 174 | 19069<br>19069<br>112 175 | 19070<br>19070<br>112 176 | 19071<br>19071<br>112 177 |
| 8- | 19072<br>19072<br>112 200 | 19073<br>19073<br>112 201 | 19074<br>19074<br>112 202 | 19075<br>19075<br>112 203 | 19076<br>19076<br>112 204 | 19077<br>19077<br>112 205 | 19078<br>19078<br>112 206 | 19079<br>19079<br>112 207 | 19080<br>19080<br>112 210 | 19081<br>19081<br>112 211 | 19082<br>19082<br>112 212 | 19083<br>19083<br>112 213 | 19084<br>19084<br>112 214 | 19085<br>19085<br>112 215 | 19086<br>19086<br>112 216 | 19087<br>19087<br>112 217 |
| 9- | 19088<br>19088<br>112 220 | 19089<br>19089<br>112 221 | 19090<br>19090<br>112 222 | 19091<br>19091<br>112 223 | 19092<br>19092<br>112 224 | 19093<br>19093<br>112 225 | 19094<br>19094<br>112 226 | 19095<br>19095<br>112 227 | 19096<br>19096<br>112 230 | 19097<br>19097<br>112 231 | 19098<br>19098<br>112 232 | 19099<br>19099<br>112 233 | 19100<br>19100<br>112 234 | 19101<br>19101<br>112 235 | 19102<br>19102<br>112 236 | 19103<br>19103<br>112 237 |
| A- | 19104<br>19104<br>112 240 | 19105<br>19105<br>112 241 | 19106<br>19106<br>112 242 | 19107<br>19107<br>112 243 | 19108<br>19108<br>112 244 | 19109<br>19109<br>112 245 | 19110<br>19110<br>112 246 | 19111<br>19111<br>112 247 | 19112<br>19112<br>112 250 | 19113<br>19113<br>112 251 | 19114<br>19114<br>112 252 | 19115<br>19115<br>112 253 | 19116<br>19116<br>112 254 | 19117<br>19117<br>112 255 | 19118<br>19118<br>112 256 | 19119<br>19119<br>112 257 |
| B- | 19120<br>19120<br>112 260 | 19121<br>19121<br>112 261 | 19122<br>19122<br>112 262 | 19123<br>19123<br>112 263 | 19124<br>19124<br>112 264 | 19125<br>19125<br>112 265 | 19126<br>19126<br>112 266 | 19127<br>19127<br>112 267 | 19128<br>19128<br>112 270 | 19129<br>19129<br>112 271 | 19130<br>19130<br>112 272 | 19131<br>19131<br>112 273 | 19132<br>19132<br>112 274 | 19133<br>19133<br>112 275 | 19134<br>19134<br>112 276 | 19135<br>19135<br>112 277 |
| C- | 19136<br>19136<br>112 300 | 19137<br>19137<br>112 301 | 19138<br>19138<br>112 302 | 19139<br>19139<br>112 303 | 19140<br>19140<br>112 304 | 19141<br>19141<br>112 305 | 19142<br>19142<br>112 306 | 19143<br>19143<br>112 307 | 19144<br>19144<br>112 310 | 19145<br>19145<br>112 311 | 19146<br>19146<br>112 312 | 1914/<br>19147<br>112 313 | 19148<br>19148<br>112 314 | 19149<br>19149<br>112 315 | 19150<br>19150<br>112 316 | 19151<br>19151<br>112 317 |
| D- | 19152<br>19152<br>112 320 | 19153<br>19153<br>112 321 | 19154<br>19154<br>112 322 | 19155<br>19155<br>112 323 | 19156<br>19156<br>112 324 | 19157<br>19157<br>112 325 | 19158<br>19158<br>112 326 | 19159<br>19159<br>112 327 | 19160<br>19160<br>112 330 | 19161<br>19161<br>112 331 | 19162<br>19162<br>112 332 | 19163<br>19163<br>112 333 | 19164<br>19164<br>112 334 | 19165<br>19165<br>112 335 | 19166<br>19166<br>112 336 | 19167<br>19167<br>112 337 |
| E- | 19168<br>19168<br>112 340 | 19169<br>19169<br>112 341 | 19170<br>19170<br>112 342 | 19171<br>19171<br>112 343 | 19172<br>19172<br>112 344 | 19173<br>19173<br>112 345 | 19174<br>19174<br>112 346 | 19175<br>19175<br>112 347 | 19176<br>19176<br>112 350 | 19177<br>19177<br>112 351 | 19178<br>19178<br>112 352 | 19179<br>19179<br>112 353 | 19180<br>19180<br>112 354 | 19181<br>19181<br>112 355 | 19182<br>19182<br>112 356 | 19183<br>19183<br>112 357 |
| F- | 19184<br>19184<br>112 360 | 19185<br>19185<br>112 361 | 19186<br>19186<br>112 362 | 19187<br>19187<br>112 363 | 19188<br>19188<br>112 364 | 19189<br>19189<br>112 365 | 19190<br>19190<br>112 366 | 19191<br>19191<br>112 367 | 19192<br>19192<br>112 370 | 19193<br>19193<br>112 371 | 19194<br>19194<br>112 372 | 19195<br>19195<br>112 373 | 19196<br>19196<br>112 374 | 19197<br>19197<br>112 375 | 19198<br>19198<br>112 376 | 19199<br>19199<br>112 377 |

 DECIMAL ← (rows 2-, 5-, 8-)

 DECIMAL

OCTAL ←

 DECIMAL  18944   BINARY  0100 1010   DECIMAL  18944   HEXADECIMAL  ⬡ 4A   OCTAL  112 000

FOURTH HEX DIGIT →     ← THIRD HEX DIGIT

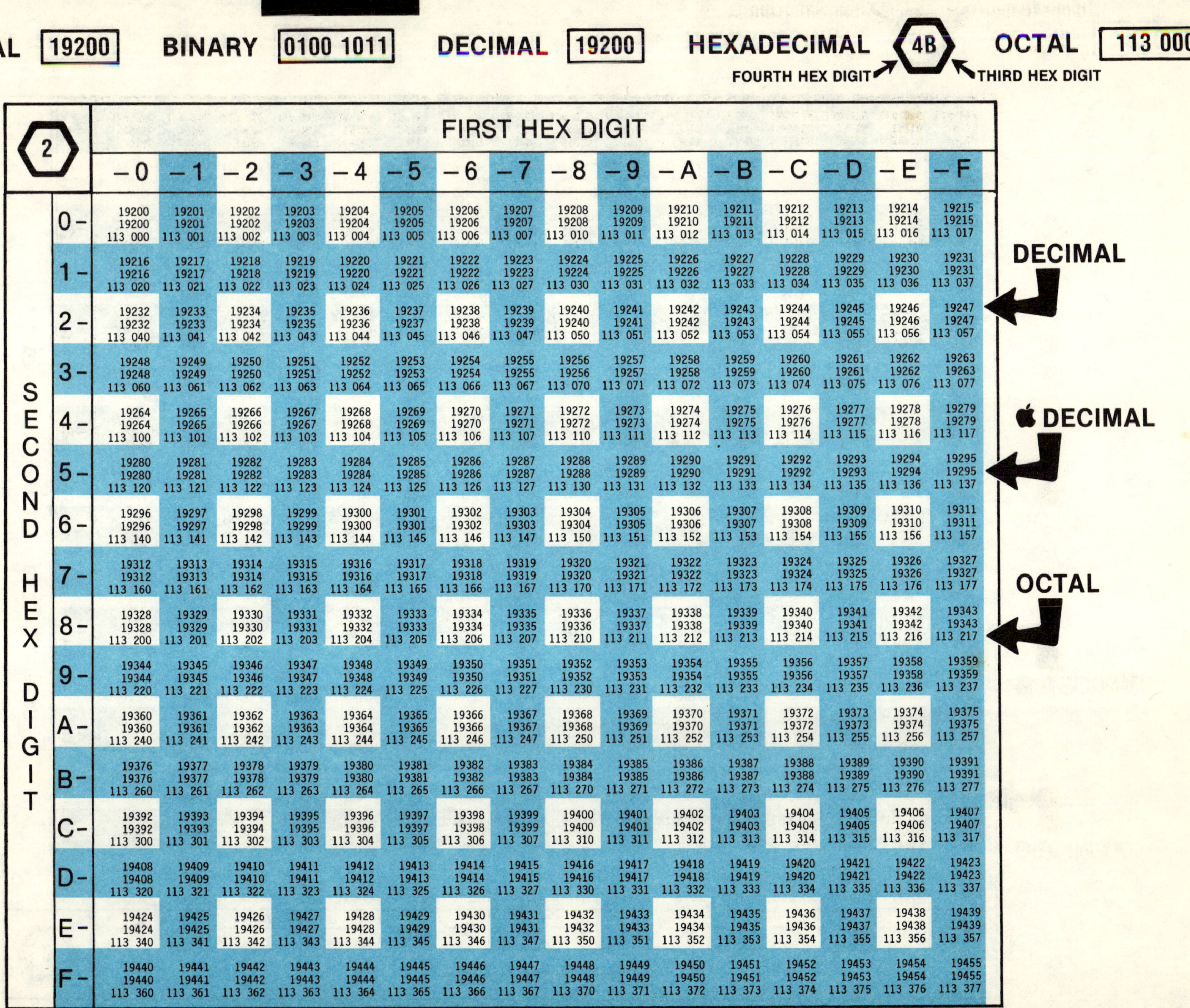

**FIRST HEX DIGIT**

2 (SECOND HEX DIGIT down the side)

Each cell lists: decimal value (printed twice) over the octal value.

| | −0 | −1 | −2 | −3 | −4 | −5 | −6 | −7 | −8 | −9 | −A | −B | −C | −D | −E | −F |
|---|---|---|---|---|---|---|---|---|---|---|---|---|---|---|---|---|
| **0−** | 19200<br>19200<br>113 000 | 19201<br>19201<br>113 001 | 19202<br>19202<br>113 002 | 19203<br>19203<br>113 003 | 19204<br>19204<br>113 004 | 19205<br>19205<br>113 005 | 19206<br>19206<br>113 006 | 19207<br>19207<br>113 007 | 19208<br>19208<br>113 010 | 19209<br>19209<br>113 011 | 19210<br>19210<br>113 012 | 19211<br>19211<br>113 013 | 19212<br>19212<br>113 014 | 19213<br>19213<br>113 015 | 19214<br>19214<br>113 016 | 19215<br>19215<br>113 017 |
| **1−** | 19216<br>19216<br>113 020 | 19217<br>19217<br>113 021 | 19218<br>19218<br>113 022 | 19219<br>19219<br>113 023 | 19220<br>19220<br>113 024 | 19221<br>19221<br>113 025 | 19222<br>19222<br>113 026 | 19223<br>19223<br>113 027 | 19224<br>19224<br>113 030 | 19225<br>19225<br>113 031 | 19226<br>19226<br>113 032 | 19227<br>19227<br>113 033 | 19228<br>19228<br>113 034 | 19229<br>19229<br>113 035 | 19230<br>19230<br>113 036 | 19231<br>19231<br>113 037 |
| **2−** | 19232<br>19232<br>113 040 | 19233<br>19233<br>113 041 | 19234<br>19234<br>113 042 | 19235<br>19235<br>113 043 | 19236<br>19236<br>113 044 | 19237<br>19237<br>113 045 | 19238<br>19238<br>113 046 | 19239<br>19239<br>113 047 | 19240<br>19240<br>113 050 | 19241<br>19241<br>113 051 | 19242<br>19242<br>113 052 | 19243<br>19243<br>113 053 | 19244<br>19244<br>113 054 | 19245<br>19245<br>113 055 | 19246<br>19246<br>113 056 | 19247<br>19247<br>113 057 |
| **3−** | 19248<br>19248<br>113 060 | 19249<br>19249<br>113 061 | 19250<br>19250<br>113 062 | 19251<br>19251<br>113 063 | 19252<br>19252<br>113 064 | 19253<br>19253<br>113 065 | 19254<br>19254<br>113 066 | 19255<br>19255<br>113 067 | 19256<br>19256<br>113 070 | 19257<br>19257<br>113 071 | 19258<br>19258<br>113 072 | 19259<br>19259<br>113 073 | 19260<br>19260<br>113 074 | 19261<br>19261<br>113 075 | 19262<br>19262<br>113 076 | 19263<br>19263<br>113 077 |
| **4−** | 19264<br>19264<br>113 100 | 19265<br>19265<br>113 101 | 19266<br>19266<br>113 102 | 19267<br>19267<br>113 103 | 19268<br>19268<br>113 104 | 19269<br>19269<br>113 105 | 19270<br>19270<br>113 106 | 19271<br>19271<br>113 107 | 19272<br>19272<br>113 110 | 19273<br>19273<br>113 111 | 19274<br>19274<br>113 112 | 19275<br>19275<br>113 113 | 19276<br>19276<br>113 114 | 19277<br>19277<br>113 115 | 19278<br>19278<br>113 116 | 19279<br>19279<br>113 117 |
| **5−** | 19280<br>19280<br>113 120 | 19281<br>19281<br>113 121 | 19282<br>19282<br>113 122 | 19283<br>19283<br>113 123 | 19284<br>19284<br>113 124 | 19285<br>19285<br>113 125 | 19286<br>19286<br>113 126 | 19287<br>19287<br>113 127 | 19288<br>19288<br>113 130 | 19289<br>19289<br>113 131 | 19290<br>19290<br>113 132 | 19291<br>19291<br>113 133 | 19292<br>19292<br>113 134 | 19293<br>19293<br>113 135 | 19294<br>19294<br>113 136 | 19295<br>19295<br>113 137 |
| **6−** | 19296<br>19296<br>113 140 | 19297<br>19297<br>113 141 | 19298<br>19298<br>113 142 | 19299<br>19299<br>113 143 | 19300<br>19300<br>113 144 | 19301<br>19301<br>113 145 | 19302<br>19302<br>113 146 | 19303<br>19303<br>113 147 | 19304<br>19304<br>113 150 | 19305<br>19305<br>113 151 | 19306<br>19306<br>113 152 | 19307<br>19307<br>113 153 | 19308<br>19308<br>113 154 | 19309<br>19309<br>113 155 | 19310<br>19310<br>113 156 | 19311<br>19311<br>113 157 |
| **7−** | 19312<br>19312<br>113 160 | 19313<br>19313<br>113 161 | 19314<br>19314<br>113 162 | 19315<br>19315<br>113 163 | 19316<br>19316<br>113 164 | 19317<br>19317<br>113 165 | 19318<br>19318<br>113 166 | 19319<br>19319<br>113 167 | 19320<br>19320<br>113 170 | 19321<br>19321<br>113 171 | 19322<br>19322<br>113 172 | 19323<br>19323<br>113 173 | 19324<br>19324<br>113 174 | 19325<br>19325<br>113 175 | 19326<br>19326<br>113 176 | 19327<br>19327<br>113 177 |
| **8−** | 19328<br>19328<br>113 200 | 19329<br>19329<br>113 201 | 19330<br>19330<br>113 202 | 19331<br>19331<br>113 203 | 19332<br>19332<br>113 204 | 19333<br>19333<br>113 205 | 19334<br>19334<br>113 206 | 19335<br>19335<br>113 207 | 19336<br>19336<br>113 210 | 19337<br>19337<br>113 211 | 19338<br>19338<br>113 212 | 19339<br>19339<br>113 213 | 19340<br>19340<br>113 214 | 19341<br>19341<br>113 215 | 19342<br>19342<br>113 216 | 19343<br>19343<br>113 217 |
| **9−** | 19344<br>19344<br>113 220 | 19345<br>19345<br>113 221 | 19346<br>19346<br>113 222 | 19347<br>19347<br>113 223 | 19348<br>19348<br>113 224 | 19349<br>19349<br>113 225 | 19350<br>19350<br>113 226 | 19351<br>19351<br>113 227 | 19352<br>19352<br>113 230 | 19353<br>19353<br>113 231 | 19354<br>19354<br>113 232 | 19355<br>19355<br>113 233 | 19356<br>19356<br>113 234 | 19357<br>19357<br>113 235 | 19358<br>19358<br>113 236 | 19359<br>19359<br>113 237 |
| **A−** | 19360<br>19360<br>113 240 | 19361<br>19361<br>113 241 | 19362<br>19362<br>113 242 | 19363<br>19363<br>113 243 | 19364<br>19364<br>113 244 | 19365<br>19365<br>113 245 | 19366<br>19366<br>113 246 | 19367<br>19367<br>113 247 | 19368<br>19368<br>113 250 | 19369<br>19369<br>113 251 | 19370<br>19370<br>113 252 | 19371<br>19371<br>113 253 | 19372<br>19372<br>113 254 | 19373<br>19373<br>113 255 | 19374<br>19374<br>113 256 | 19375<br>19375<br>113 257 |
| **B−** | 19376<br>19376<br>113 260 | 19377<br>19377<br>113 261 | 19378<br>19378<br>113 262 | 19379<br>19379<br>113 263 | 19380<br>19380<br>113 264 | 19381<br>19381<br>113 265 | 19382<br>19382<br>113 266 | 19383<br>19383<br>113 267 | 19384<br>19384<br>113 270 | 19385<br>19385<br>113 271 | 19386<br>19386<br>113 272 | 19387<br>19387<br>113 273 | 19388<br>19388<br>113 274 | 19389<br>19389<br>113 275 | 19390<br>19390<br>113 276 | 19391<br>19391<br>113 277 |
| **C−** | 19392<br>19392<br>113 300 | 19393<br>19393<br>113 301 | 19394<br>19394<br>113 302 | 19395<br>19395<br>113 303 | 19396<br>19396<br>113 304 | 19397<br>19397<br>113 305 | 19398<br>19398<br>113 306 | 19399<br>19399<br>113 307 | 19400<br>19400<br>113 310 | 19401<br>19401<br>113 311 | 19402<br>19402<br>113 312 | 19403<br>19403<br>113 313 | 19404<br>19404<br>113 314 | 19405<br>19405<br>113 315 | 19406<br>19406<br>113 316 | 19407<br>19407<br>113 317 |
| **D−** | 19408<br>19408<br>113 320 | 19409<br>19409<br>113 321 | 19410<br>19410<br>113 322 | 19411<br>19411<br>113 323 | 19412<br>19412<br>113 324 | 19413<br>19413<br>113 325 | 19414<br>19414<br>113 326 | 19415<br>19415<br>113 327 | 19416<br>19416<br>113 330 | 19417<br>19417<br>113 331 | 19418<br>19418<br>113 332 | 19419<br>19419<br>113 333 | 19420<br>19420<br>113 334 | 19421<br>19421<br>113 335 | 19422<br>19422<br>113 336 | 19423<br>19423<br>113 337 |
| **E−** | 19424<br>19424<br>113 340 | 19425<br>19425<br>113 341 | 19426<br>19426<br>113 342 | 19427<br>19427<br>113 343 | 19428<br>19428<br>113 344 | 19429<br>19429<br>113 345 | 19430<br>19430<br>113 346 | 19431<br>19431<br>113 347 | 19432<br>19432<br>113 350 | 19433<br>19433<br>113 351 | 19434<br>19434<br>113 352 | 19435<br>19435<br>113 353 | 19436<br>19436<br>113 354 | 19437<br>19437<br>113 355 | 19438<br>19438<br>113 356 | 19439<br>19439<br>113 357 |
| **F−** | 19440<br>19440<br>113 360 | 19441<br>19441<br>113 361 | 19442<br>19442<br>113 362 | 19443<br>19443<br>113 363 | 19444<br>19444<br>113 364 | 19445<br>19445<br>113 365 | 19446<br>19446<br>113 366 | 19447<br>19447<br>113 367 | 19448<br>19448<br>113 370 | 19449<br>19449<br>113 371 | 19450<br>19450<br>113 372 | 19451<br>19451<br>113 373 | 19452<br>19452<br>113 374 | 19453<br>19453<br>113 375 | 19454<br>19454<br>113 376 | 19455<br>19455<br>113 377 |

**SECOND HEX DIGIT** (row labels at left)

**DECIMAL** ←
**⌘ DECIMAL** ←
**OCTAL** ←

| SECOND HEX DIGIT | −0 | −1 | −2 | −3 | −4 | −5 | −6 | −7 | −8 | −9 | −A | −B | −C | −D | −E | −F |
|---|---|---|---|---|---|---|---|---|---|---|---|---|---|---|---|---|
| **0−** | 19456<br>19456<br>114 000 | 19457<br>19457<br>114 001 | 19458<br>19458<br>114 002 | 19459<br>19459<br>114 003 | 19460<br>19460<br>114 004 | 19461<br>19461<br>114 005 | 19462<br>19462<br>114 006 | 19463<br>19463<br>114 007 | 19464<br>19464<br>114 010 | 19465<br>19465<br>114 011 | 19466<br>19466<br>114 012 | 19467<br>19467<br>114 013 | 19468<br>19468<br>114 014 | 19469<br>19469<br>114 015 | 19470<br>19470<br>114 016 | 19471<br>19471<br>114 017 |
| **1−** | 19472<br>19472<br>114 020 | 19473<br>19473<br>114 021 | 19474<br>19474<br>114 022 | 19475<br>19475<br>114 023 | 19476<br>19476<br>114 024 | 19477<br>19477<br>114 025 | 19478<br>19478<br>114 026 | 19479<br>19479<br>114 027 | 19480<br>19480<br>114 030 | 19481<br>19481<br>114 031 | 19482<br>19482<br>114 032 | 19483<br>19483<br>114 033 | 19484<br>19484<br>114 034 | 19485<br>19485<br>114 035 | 19486<br>19486<br>114 036 | 19487<br>19487<br>114 037 |
| **2−** | 19488<br>19488<br>114 040 | 19489<br>19489<br>114 041 | 19490<br>19490<br>114 042 | 19491<br>19491<br>114 043 | 19492<br>19492<br>114 044 | 19493<br>19493<br>114 045 | 19494<br>19494<br>114 046 | 19495<br>19495<br>114 047 | 19496<br>19496<br>114 050 | 19497<br>19497<br>114 051 | 19498<br>19498<br>114 052 | 19499<br>19499<br>114 053 | 19500<br>19500<br>114 054 | 19501<br>19501<br>114 055 | 19502<br>19502<br>114 056 | 19503<br>19503<br>114 057 |
| **3−** | 19504<br>19504<br>114 060 | 19505<br>19505<br>114 061 | 19506<br>19506<br>114 062 | 19507<br>19507<br>114 063 | 19508<br>19508<br>114 064 | 19509<br>19509<br>114 065 | 19510<br>19510<br>114 066 | 19511<br>19511<br>114 067 | 19512<br>19512<br>114 070 | 19513<br>19513<br>114 071 | 19514<br>19514<br>114 072 | 19515<br>19515<br>114 073 | 19516<br>19516<br>114 074 | 19517<br>19517<br>114 075 | 19518<br>19518<br>114 076 | 19519<br>19519<br>114 077 |
| **4−** | 19520<br>19520<br>114 100 | 19521<br>19521<br>114 101 | 19522<br>19522<br>114 102 | 19523<br>19523<br>114 103 | 19524<br>19524<br>114 104 | 19525<br>19525<br>114 105 | 19526<br>19526<br>114 106 | 19527<br>19527<br>114 107 | 19528<br>19528<br>114 110 | 19529<br>19529<br>114 111 | 19530<br>19530<br>114 112 | 19531<br>19531<br>114 113 | 19532<br>19532<br>114 114 | 19533<br>19533<br>114 115 | 19534<br>19534<br>114 116 | 19535<br>19535<br>114 117 |
| **5−** | 19536<br>19536<br>114 120 | 19537<br>19537<br>114 121 | 19538<br>19538<br>114 122 | 19539<br>19539<br>114 123 | 19540<br>19540<br>114 124 | 19541<br>19541<br>114 125 | 19542<br>19542<br>114 126 | 19543<br>19543<br>114 127 | 19544<br>19544<br>114 130 | 19545<br>19545<br>114 131 | 19546<br>19546<br>114 132 | 19547<br>19547<br>114 133 | 19548<br>19548<br>114 134 | 19549<br>19549<br>114 135 | 19550<br>19550<br>114 136 | 19551<br>19551<br>114 137 |
| **6−** | 19552<br>19552<br>114 140 | 19553<br>19553<br>114 141 | 19554<br>19554<br>114 142 | 19555<br>19555<br>114 143 | 19556<br>19556<br>114 144 | 19557<br>19557<br>114 145 | 19558<br>19558<br>114 146 | 19559<br>19559<br>114 147 | 19560<br>19560<br>114 150 | 19561<br>19561<br>114 151 | 19562<br>19562<br>114 152 | 19563<br>19563<br>114 153 | 19564<br>19564<br>114 154 | 19565<br>19565<br>114 155 | 19566<br>19566<br>114 156 | 19567<br>19567<br>114 157 |
| **7−** | 19568<br>19568<br>114 160 | 19569<br>19569<br>114 161 | 19570<br>19570<br>114 162 | 19571<br>19571<br>114 163 | 19572<br>19572<br>114 164 | 19573<br>19573<br>114 165 | 19574<br>19574<br>114 166 | 19575<br>19575<br>114 167 | 19576<br>19576<br>114 170 | 19577<br>19577<br>114 171 | 19578<br>19578<br>114 172 | 19579<br>19579<br>114 173 | 19580<br>19580<br>114 174 | 19581<br>19581<br>114 175 | 19582<br>19582<br>114 176 | 19583<br>19583<br>114 177 |
| **8−** | 19584<br>19584<br>114 200 | 19585<br>19585<br>114 201 | 19586<br>19586<br>114 202 | 19587<br>19587<br>114 203 | 19588<br>19588<br>114 204 | 19589<br>19589<br>114 205 | 19590<br>19590<br>114 206 | 19591<br>19591<br>114 207 | 19592<br>19592<br>114 210 | 19593<br>19593<br>114 211 | 19594<br>19594<br>114 212 | 19595<br>19595<br>114 213 | 19596<br>19596<br>114 214 | 19597<br>19597<br>114 215 | 19598<br>19598<br>114 216 | 19599<br>19599<br>114 217 |
| **9−** | 19600<br>19600<br>114 220 | 19601<br>19601<br>114 221 | 19602<br>19602<br>114 222 | 19603<br>19603<br>114 223 | 19604<br>19604<br>114 224 | 19605<br>19605<br>114 225 | 19606<br>19606<br>114 226 | 19607<br>19607<br>114 227 | 19608<br>19608<br>114 230 | 19609<br>19609<br>114 231 | 19610<br>19610<br>114 232 | 19611<br>19611<br>114 233 | 19612<br>19612<br>114 234 | 19613<br>19613<br>114 235 | 19614<br>19614<br>114 236 | 19615<br>19615<br>114 237 |
| **A−** | 19616<br>19616<br>114 240 | 19617<br>19617<br>114 241 | 19618<br>19618<br>114 242 | 19619<br>19619<br>114 243 | 19620<br>19620<br>114 244 | 19621<br>19621<br>114 245 | 19622<br>19622<br>114 246 | 19623<br>19623<br>114 247 | 19624<br>19624<br>114 250 | 19625<br>19625<br>114 251 | 19626<br>19626<br>114 252 | 19627<br>19627<br>114 253 | 19628<br>19628<br>114 254 | 19629<br>19629<br>114 255 | 19630<br>19630<br>114 256 | 19631<br>19631<br>114 257 |
| **B−** | 19632<br>19632<br>114 260 | 19633<br>19633<br>114 261 | 19634<br>19634<br>114 262 | 19635<br>19635<br>114 263 | 19636<br>19636<br>114 264 | 19637<br>19637<br>114 265 | 19638<br>19638<br>114 266 | 19639<br>19639<br>114 267 | 19640<br>19640<br>114 270 | 19641<br>19641<br>114 271 | 19642<br>19642<br>114 272 | 19643<br>19643<br>114 273 | 19644<br>19644<br>114 274 | 19645<br>19645<br>114 275 | 19646<br>19646<br>114 276 | 19647<br>19647<br>114 277 |
| **C−** | 19648<br>19648<br>114 300 | 19649<br>19649<br>114 301 | 19650<br>19650<br>114 302 | 19651<br>19651<br>114 303 | 19652<br>19652<br>114 304 | 19653<br>19653<br>114 305 | 19654<br>19654<br>114 306 | 19655<br>19655<br>114 307 | 19656<br>19656<br>114 310 | 19657<br>19657<br>114 311 | 19658<br>19658<br>114 312 | 19659<br>19659<br>114 313 | 19660<br>19660<br>114 314 | 19661<br>19661<br>114 315 | 19662<br>19662<br>114 316 | 19663<br>19663<br>114 317 |
| **D−** | 19664<br>19664<br>114 320 | 19665<br>19665<br>114 321 | 19666<br>19666<br>114 322 | 19667<br>19667<br>114 323 | 19668<br>19668<br>114 324 | 19669<br>19669<br>114 325 | 19670<br>19670<br>114 326 | 19671<br>19671<br>114 327 | 19672<br>19672<br>114 330 | 19673<br>19673<br>114 331 | 19674<br>19674<br>114 332 | 19675<br>19675<br>114 333 | 19676<br>19676<br>114 334 | 19677<br>19677<br>114 335 | 19678<br>19678<br>114 336 | 19679<br>19679<br>114 337 |
| **E−** | 19680<br>19680<br>114 340 | 19681<br>19681<br>114 341 | 19682<br>19682<br>114 342 | 19683<br>19683<br>114 343 | 19684<br>19684<br>114 344 | 19685<br>19685<br>114 345 | 19686<br>19686<br>114 346 | 19687<br>19687<br>114 347 | 19688<br>19688<br>114 350 | 19689<br>19689<br>114 351 | 19690<br>19690<br>114 352 | 19691<br>19691<br>114 353 | 19692<br>19692<br>114 354 | 19693<br>19693<br>114 355 | 19694<br>19694<br>114 356 | 19695<br>19695<br>114 357 |
| **F−** | 19696<br>19696<br>114 360 | 19697<br>19697<br>114 361 | 19698<br>19698<br>114 362 | 19699<br>19699<br>114 363 | 19700<br>19700<br>114 364 | 19701<br>19701<br>114 365 | 19702<br>19702<br>114 366 | 19703<br>19703<br>114 367 | 19704<br>19704<br>114 370 | 19705<br>19705<br>114 371 | 19706<br>19706<br>114 372 | 19707<br>19707<br>114 373 | 19708<br>19708<br>114 374 | 19709<br>19709<br>114 375 | 19710<br>19710<br>114 376 | 19711<br>19711<br>114 377 |

---

**⌘ DECIMAL** `19456`    **BINARY** `0100 1100`    **DECIMAL** `19456`    **HEXADECIMAL** ⬡ `4C`    **OCTAL** `114 000`

FOURTH HEX DIGIT →   ← THIRD HEX DIGIT

| (2) | FIRST HEX DIGIT | | | | | | | | | | | | | | | |
|---|---|---|---|---|---|---|---|---|---|---|---|---|---|---|---|---|
| | −0 | −1 | −2 | −3 | −4 | −5 | −6 | −7 | −8 | −9 | −A | −B | −C | −D | −E | −F |
| 0− | 19712<br>115 000 | 19713<br>115 001 | 19714<br>115 002 | 19715<br>115 003 | 19716<br>115 004 | 19717<br>115 005 | 19718<br>115 006 | 19719<br>115 007 | 19720<br>115 010 | 19721<br>115 011 | 19722<br>115 012 | 19723<br>115 013 | 19724<br>115 014 | 19725<br>115 015 | 19726<br>115 016 | 19727<br>115 017 |
| 1− | 19728<br>115 020 | 19729<br>115 021 | 19730<br>115 022 | 19731<br>115 023 | 19732<br>115 024 | 19733<br>115 025 | 19734<br>115 026 | 19735<br>115 027 | 19736<br>115 030 | 19737<br>115 031 | 19738<br>115 032 | 19739<br>115 033 | 19740<br>115 034 | 19741<br>115 035 | 19742<br>115 036 | 19743<br>115 037 |
| 2− | 19744<br>115 040 | 19745<br>115 041 | 19746<br>115 042 | 19747<br>115 043 | 19748<br>115 044 | 19749<br>115 045 | 19750<br>115 046 | 19751<br>115 047 | 19752<br>115 050 | 19753<br>115 051 | 19754<br>115 052 | 19755<br>115 053 | 19756<br>115 054 | 19757<br>115 055 | 19758<br>115 056 | 19759<br>115 057 |
| 3− | 19760<br>115 060 | 19761<br>115 061 | 19762<br>115 062 | 19763<br>115 063 | 19764<br>115 064 | 19765<br>115 065 | 19766<br>115 066 | 19767<br>115 067 | 19768<br>115 070 | 19769<br>115 071 | 19770<br>115 072 | 19771<br>115 073 | 19772<br>115 074 | 19773<br>115 075 | 19774<br>115 076 | 19775<br>115 077 |
| 4− | 19776<br>115 100 | 19777<br>115 101 | 19778<br>115 102 | 19779<br>115 103 | 19780<br>115 104 | 19781<br>115 105 | 19782<br>115 106 | 19783<br>115 107 | 19784<br>115 110 | 19785<br>115 111 | 19786<br>115 112 | 19787<br>115 113 | 19788<br>115 114 | 19789<br>115 115 | 19790<br>115 116 | 19791<br>115 117 |
| 5− | 19792<br>115 120 | 19793<br>115 121 | 19794<br>115 122 | 19795<br>115 123 | 19796<br>115 124 | 19797<br>115 125 | 19798<br>115 126 | 19799<br>115 127 | 19800<br>115 130 | 19801<br>115 131 | 19802<br>115 132 | 19803<br>115 133 | 19804<br>115 134 | 19805<br>115 135 | 19806<br>115 136 | 19807<br>115 137 |
| 6− | 19808<br>115 140 | 19809<br>115 141 | 19810<br>115 142 | 19811<br>115 143 | 19812<br>115 144 | 19813<br>115 145 | 19814<br>115 146 | 19815<br>115 147 | 19816<br>115 150 | 19817<br>115 151 | 19818<br>115 152 | 19819<br>115 153 | 19820<br>115 154 | 19821<br>115 155 | 19822<br>115 156 | 19823<br>115 157 |
| 7− | 19824<br>115 160 | 19825<br>115 161 | 19826<br>115 162 | 19827<br>115 163 | 19828<br>115 164 | 19829<br>115 165 | 19830<br>115 166 | 19831<br>115 167 | 19832<br>115 170 | 19833<br>115 171 | 19834<br>115 172 | 19835<br>115 173 | 19836<br>115 174 | 19837<br>115 175 | 19838<br>115 176 | 19839<br>115 177 |
| 8− | 19840<br>115 200 | 19841<br>115 201 | 19842<br>115 202 | 19843<br>115 203 | 19844<br>115 204 | 19845<br>115 205 | 19846<br>115 206 | 19847<br>115 207 | 19848<br>115 210 | 19849<br>115 211 | 19850<br>115 212 | 19851<br>115 213 | 19852<br>115 214 | 19853<br>115 215 | 19854<br>115 216 | 19855<br>115 217 |
| 9− | 19856<br>115 220 | 19857<br>115 221 | 19858<br>115 222 | 19859<br>115 223 | 19860<br>115 224 | 19861<br>115 225 | 19862<br>115 226 | 19863<br>115 227 | 19864<br>115 230 | 19865<br>115 231 | 19866<br>115 232 | 19867<br>115 233 | 19868<br>115 234 | 19869<br>115 235 | 19870<br>115 236 | 19871<br>115 237 |
| A− | 19872<br>115 240 | 19873<br>115 241 | 19874<br>115 242 | 19875<br>115 243 | 19876<br>115 244 | 19877<br>115 245 | 19878<br>115 246 | 19879<br>115 247 | 19880<br>115 250 | 19881<br>115 251 | 19882<br>115 252 | 19883<br>115 253 | 19884<br>115 254 | 19885<br>115 255 | 19886<br>115 256 | 19887<br>115 257 |
| B− | 19888<br>115 260 | 19889<br>115 261 | 19890<br>115 262 | 19891<br>115 263 | 19892<br>115 264 | 19893<br>115 265 | 19894<br>115 266 | 19895<br>115 267 | 19896<br>115 270 | 19897<br>115 271 | 19898<br>115 272 | 19899<br>115 273 | 19900<br>115 274 | 19901<br>115 275 | 19902<br>115 276 | 19903<br>115 277 |
| C− | 19904<br>115 300 | 19905<br>115 301 | 19906<br>115 302 | 19907<br>115 303 | 19908<br>115 304 | 19909<br>115 305 | 19910<br>115 306 | 19911<br>115 307 | 19912<br>115 310 | 19913<br>115 311 | 19914<br>115 312 | 19915<br>115 313 | 19916<br>115 314 | 19917<br>115 315 | 19918<br>115 316 | 19919<br>115 317 |
| D− | 19920<br>115 320 | 19921<br>115 321 | 19922<br>115 322 | 19923<br>115 323 | 19924<br>115 324 | 19925<br>115 325 | 19926<br>115 326 | 19927<br>115 327 | 19928<br>115 330 | 19929<br>115 331 | 19930<br>115 332 | 19931<br>115 333 | 19932<br>115 334 | 19933<br>115 335 | 19934<br>115 336 | 19935<br>115 337 |
| E− | 19936<br>115 340 | 19937<br>115 341 | 19938<br>115 342 | 19939<br>115 343 | 19940<br>115 344 | 19941<br>115 345 | 19942<br>115 346 | 19943<br>115 347 | 19944<br>115 350 | 19945<br>115 351 | 19946<br>115 352 | 19947<br>115 353 | 19948<br>115 354 | 19949<br>115 355 | 19950<br>115 356 | 19951<br>115 357 |
| F− | 19952<br>115 360 | 19953<br>115 361 | 19954<br>115 362 | 19955<br>115 363 | 19956<br>115 364 | 19957<br>115 365 | 19958<br>115 366 | 19959<br>115 367 | 19960<br>115 370 | 19961<br>115 371 | 19962<br>115 372 | 19963<br>115 373 | 19964<br>115 374 | 19965<br>115 375 | 19966<br>115 376 | 19967<br>115 377 |

SECOND HEX DIGIT

DECIMAL

 DECIMAL

OCTAL

2

FIRST HEX DIGIT

SECOND HEX DIGIT

| | -0 | -1 | -2 | -3 | -4 | -5 | -6 | -7 | -8 | -9 | -A | -B | -C | -D | -E | -F |
|---|---|---|---|---|---|---|---|---|---|---|---|---|---|---|---|---|
| 0- | 19968<br>19968<br>116 000 | 19969<br>19969<br>116 001 | 19970<br>19970<br>116 002 | 19971<br>19971<br>116 003 | 19972<br>19972<br>116 004 | 19973<br>19973<br>116 005 | 19974<br>19974<br>116 006 | 19975<br>19975<br>116 007 | 19976<br>19976<br>116 010 | 19977<br>19977<br>116 011 | 19978<br>19978<br>116 012 | 19979<br>19979<br>116 013 | 19980<br>19980<br>116 014 | 19981<br>19981<br>116 015 | 19982<br>19982<br>116 016 | 19983<br>19983<br>116 017 |
| 1- | 19984<br>19984<br>116 020 | 19985<br>19985<br>116 021 | 19986<br>19986<br>116 022 | 19987<br>19987<br>116 023 | 19988<br>19988<br>116 024 | 19989<br>19989<br>116 025 | 19990<br>19990<br>116 026 | 19991<br>19991<br>116 027 | 19992<br>19992<br>116 030 | 19993<br>19993<br>116 031 | 19994<br>19994<br>116 032 | 19995<br>19995<br>116 033 | 19996<br>19996<br>116 034 | 19997<br>19997<br>116 035 | 19998<br>19998<br>116 036 | 19999<br>19999<br>116 037 |
| 2- | 20000<br>20000<br>116 040 | 20001<br>20001<br>116 041 | 20002<br>20002<br>116 042 | 20003<br>20003<br>116 043 | 20004<br>20004<br>116 044 | 20005<br>20005<br>116 045 | 20006<br>20006<br>116 046 | 20007<br>20007<br>116 047 | 20008<br>20008<br>116 050 | 20009<br>20009<br>116 051 | 20010<br>20010<br>116 052 | 20011<br>20011<br>116 053 | 20012<br>20012<br>116 054 | 20013<br>20013<br>116 055 | 20014<br>20014<br>116 056 | 20015<br>20015<br>116 057 |
| 3- | 20016<br>20016<br>116 060 | 20017<br>20017<br>116 061 | 20018<br>20018<br>116 062 | 20019<br>20019<br>116 063 | 20020<br>20020<br>116 064 | 20021<br>20021<br>116 065 | 20022<br>20022<br>116 066 | 20023<br>20023<br>116 067 | 20024<br>20024<br>116 070 | 20025<br>20025<br>116 071 | 20026<br>20026<br>116 072 | 20027<br>20027<br>116 073 | 20028<br>20028<br>116 074 | 20029<br>20029<br>116 075 | 20030<br>20030<br>116 076 | 20031<br>20031<br>116 077 |
| 4- | 20032<br>20032<br>116 100 | 20033<br>20033<br>116 101 | 20034<br>20034<br>116 102 | 20035<br>20035<br>116 103 | 20036<br>20036<br>116 104 | 20037<br>20037<br>116 105 | 20038<br>20038<br>116 106 | 20039<br>20039<br>116 107 | 20040<br>20040<br>116 110 | 20041<br>20041<br>116 111 | 20042<br>20042<br>116 112 | 20043<br>20043<br>116 113 | 20044<br>20044<br>116 114 | 20045<br>20045<br>116 115 | 20046<br>20046<br>116 116 | 20047<br>20047<br>116 117 |
| 5- | 20048<br>20048<br>116 120 | 20049<br>20049<br>116 121 | 20050<br>20050<br>116 122 | 20051<br>20051<br>116 123 | 20052<br>20052<br>116 124 | 20053<br>20053<br>116 125 | 20054<br>20054<br>116 126 | 20055<br>20055<br>116 127 | 20056<br>20056<br>116 130 | 20057<br>20057<br>116 131 | 20058<br>20058<br>116 132 | 20059<br>20059<br>116 133 | 20060<br>20060<br>116 134 | 20061<br>20061<br>116 135 | 20062<br>20062<br>116 136 | 20063<br>20063<br>116 137 |
| 6- | 20064<br>20064<br>116 140 | 20065<br>20065<br>116 141 | 20066<br>20066<br>116 142 | 20067<br>20067<br>116 143 | 20068<br>20068<br>116 144 | 20069<br>20069<br>116 145 | 20070<br>20070<br>116 146 | 20071<br>20071<br>116 147 | 20072<br>20072<br>116 150 | 20073<br>20073<br>116 151 | 20074<br>20074<br>116 152 | 20075<br>20075<br>116 153 | 20076<br>20076<br>116 154 | 20077<br>20077<br>116 155 | 20078<br>20078<br>116 156 | 20079<br>20079<br>116 157 |
| 7- | 20080<br>20080<br>116 160 | 20081<br>20081<br>116 161 | 20082<br>20082<br>116 162 | 20083<br>20083<br>116 163 | 20084<br>20084<br>116 164 | 20085<br>20085<br>116 165 | 20086<br>20086<br>116 166 | 20087<br>20087<br>116 167 | 20088<br>20088<br>116 170 | 20089<br>20089<br>116 171 | 20090<br>20090<br>116 172 | 20091<br>20091<br>116 173 | 20092<br>20092<br>116 174 | 20093<br>20093<br>116 175 | 20094<br>20094<br>116 176 | 20095<br>20095<br>116 177 |
| 8- | 20096<br>20096<br>116 200 | 20097<br>20097<br>116 201 | 20098<br>20098<br>116 202 | 20099<br>20099<br>116 203 | 20100<br>20100<br>116 204 | 20101<br>20101<br>116 205 | 20102<br>20102<br>116 206 | 20103<br>20103<br>116 207 | 20104<br>20104<br>116 210 | 20105<br>20105<br>116 211 | 20106<br>20106<br>116 212 | 20107<br>20107<br>116 213 | 20108<br>20108<br>116 214 | 20109<br>20109<br>116 215 | 20110<br>20110<br>116 216 | 20111<br>20111<br>116 217 |
| 9- | 20112<br>20112<br>116 220 | 20113<br>20113<br>116 221 | 20114<br>20114<br>116 222 | 20115<br>20115<br>116 223 | 20116<br>20116<br>116 224 | 20117<br>20117<br>116 225 | 20118<br>20118<br>116 226 | 20119<br>20119<br>116 227 | 20120<br>20120<br>116 230 | 20121<br>20121<br>116 231 | 20122<br>20122<br>116 232 | 20123<br>20123<br>116 233 | 20124<br>20124<br>116 234 | 20125<br>20125<br>116 235 | 20126<br>20126<br>116 236 | 20127<br>20127<br>116 237 |
| A- | 20128<br>20128<br>116 240 | 20129<br>20129<br>116 241 | 20130<br>20130<br>116 242 | 20131<br>20131<br>116 243 | 20132<br>20132<br>116 244 | 20133<br>20133<br>116 245 | 20134<br>20134<br>116 246 | 20135<br>20135<br>116 247 | 20136<br>20136<br>116 250 | 20137<br>20137<br>116 251 | 20138<br>20138<br>116 252 | 20139<br>20139<br>116 253 | 20140<br>20140<br>116 254 | 20141<br>20141<br>116 255 | 20142<br>20142<br>116 256 | 20143<br>20143<br>116 257 |
| B- | 20144<br>20144<br>116 260 | 20145<br>20145<br>116 261 | 20146<br>20146<br>116 262 | 20147<br>20147<br>116 263 | 20148<br>20148<br>116 264 | 20149<br>20149<br>116 265 | 20150<br>20150<br>116 266 | 20151<br>20151<br>116 267 | 20152<br>20152<br>116 270 | 20153<br>20153<br>116 271 | 20154<br>20154<br>116 272 | 20155<br>20155<br>116 273 | 20156<br>20156<br>116 274 | 20157<br>20157<br>116 275 | 20158<br>20158<br>116 276 | 20159<br>20159<br>116 277 |
| C- | 20160<br>20160<br>116 300 | 20161<br>20161<br>116 301 | 20162<br>20162<br>116 302 | 20163<br>20163<br>116 303 | 20164<br>20164<br>116 304 | 20165<br>20165<br>116 305 | 20166<br>20166<br>116 306 | 20167<br>20167<br>116 307 | 20168<br>20168<br>116 310 | 20169<br>20169<br>116 311 | 20170<br>20170<br>116 312 | 20171<br>20171<br>116 313 | 20172<br>20172<br>116 314 | 20173<br>20173<br>116 315 | 20174<br>20174<br>116 316 | 20175<br>20175<br>116 317 |
| D- | 20176<br>20176<br>116 320 | 20177<br>20177<br>116 321 | 20178<br>20178<br>116 322 | 20179<br>20179<br>116 323 | 20180<br>20180<br>116 324 | 20181<br>20181<br>116 325 | 20182<br>20182<br>116 326 | 20183<br>20183<br>116 327 | 20184<br>20184<br>116 330 | 20185<br>20185<br>116 331 | 20186<br>20186<br>116 332 | 20187<br>20187<br>116 333 | 20188<br>20188<br>116 334 | 20189<br>20189<br>116 335 | 20190<br>20190<br>116 336 | 20191<br>20191<br>116 337 |
| E- | 20192<br>20192<br>116 340 | 20193<br>20193<br>116 341 | 20194<br>20194<br>116 342 | 20195<br>20195<br>116 343 | 20196<br>20196<br>116 344 | 20197<br>20197<br>116 345 | 20198<br>20198<br>116 346 | 20199<br>20199<br>116 347 | 20200<br>20200<br>116 350 | 20201<br>20201<br>116 351 | 20202<br>20202<br>116 352 | 20203<br>20203<br>116 353 | 20204<br>20204<br>116 354 | 20205<br>20205<br>116 355 | 20206<br>20206<br>116 356 | 20207<br>20207<br>116 357 |
| F- | 20208<br>20208<br>116 360 | 20209<br>20209<br>116 361 | 20210<br>20210<br>116 362 | 20211<br>20211<br>116 363 | 20212<br>20212<br>116 364 | 20213<br>20213<br>116 365 | 20214<br>20214<br>116 366 | 20215<br>20215<br>116 367 | 20216<br>20216<br>116 370 | 20217<br>20217<br>116 371 | 20218<br>20218<br>116 372 | 20219<br>20219<br>116 373 | 20220<br>20220<br>116 374 | 20221<br>20221<br>116 375 | 20222<br>20222<br>116 376 | 20223<br>20223<br>116 377 |

DECIMAL

DECIMAL

OCTAL

DECIMAL 19968 BINARY 0100 1110 DECIMAL 19968 HEXADECIMAL 4E OCTAL 116 000

FOURTH HEX DIGIT THIRD HEX DIGIT

Each cell lists: decimal, decimal, octal.

| (2) | −0 | −1 | −2 | −3 | −4 | −5 | −6 | −7 | −8 | −9 | −A | −B | −C | −D | −E | −F |
|---|---|---|---|---|---|---|---|---|---|---|---|---|---|---|---|---|
| **FIRST HEX DIGIT** | | | | | | | | | | | | | | | | |
| 0- | 20224<br>20224<br>117 000 | 20225<br>20225<br>117 001 | 20226<br>20226<br>117 002 | 20227<br>20227<br>117 003 | 20228<br>20228<br>117 004 | 20229<br>20229<br>117 005 | 20230<br>20230<br>117 006 | 20231<br>20231<br>117 007 | 20232<br>20232<br>117 010 | 20233<br>20233<br>117 011 | 20234<br>20234<br>117 012 | 20235<br>20235<br>117 013 | 20236<br>20236<br>117 014 | 20237<br>20237<br>117 015 | 20238<br>20238<br>117 016 | 20239<br>20239<br>117 017 |
| 1- | 20240<br>20240<br>117 020 | 20241<br>20241<br>117 021 | 20242<br>20242<br>117 022 | 20243<br>20243<br>117 023 | 20244<br>20244<br>117 024 | 20245<br>20245<br>117 025 | 20246<br>20246<br>117 026 | 20247<br>20247<br>117 027 | 20248<br>20248<br>117 030 | 20249<br>20249<br>117 031 | 20250<br>20250<br>117 032 | 20251<br>20251<br>117 033 | 20252<br>20252<br>117 034 | 20253<br>20253<br>117 035 | 20254<br>20254<br>117 036 | 20255<br>20255<br>117 037 |
| 2- | 20256<br>20256<br>117 040 | 20257<br>20257<br>117 041 | 20258<br>20258<br>117 042 | 20259<br>20259<br>117 043 | 20260<br>20260<br>117 044 | 20261<br>20261<br>117 045 | 20262<br>20262<br>117 046 | 20263<br>20263<br>117 047 | 20264<br>20264<br>117 050 | 20265<br>20265<br>117 051 | 20266<br>20266<br>117 052 | 20267<br>20267<br>117 053 | 20268<br>20268<br>117 054 | 20269<br>20269<br>117 055 | 20270<br>20270<br>117 056 | 20271<br>20271<br>117 057 |
| 3- | 20272<br>20272<br>117 060 | 20273<br>20273<br>117 061 | 20274<br>20274<br>117 062 | 20275<br>20275<br>117 063 | 20276<br>20276<br>117 064 | 20277<br>20277<br>117 065 | 20278<br>20278<br>117 066 | 20279<br>20279<br>117 067 | 20280<br>20280<br>117 070 | 20281<br>20281<br>117 071 | 20282<br>20282<br>117 072 | 20283<br>20283<br>117 073 | 20284<br>20284<br>117 074 | 20285<br>20285<br>117 075 | 20286<br>20286<br>117 076 | 20287<br>20287<br>117 077 |
| 4- | 20288<br>20288<br>117 100 | 20289<br>20289<br>117 101 | 20290<br>20290<br>117 102 | 20291<br>20291<br>117 103 | 20292<br>20292<br>117 104 | 20293<br>20293<br>117 105 | 20294<br>20294<br>117 106 | 20295<br>20295<br>117 107 | 20296<br>20296<br>117 110 | 20297<br>20297<br>117 111 | 20298<br>20298<br>117 112 | 20299<br>20299<br>117 113 | 20300<br>20300<br>117 114 | 20301<br>20301<br>117 115 | 20302<br>20302<br>117 116 | 20303<br>20303<br>117 117 |
| 5- | 20304<br>20304<br>117 120 | 20305<br>20305<br>117 121 | 20306<br>20306<br>117 122 | 20307<br>20307<br>117 123 | 20308<br>20308<br>117 124 | 20309<br>20309<br>117 125 | 20310<br>20310<br>117 126 | 20311<br>20311<br>117 127 | 20312<br>20312<br>117 130 | 20313<br>20313<br>117 131 | 20314<br>20314<br>117 132 | 20315<br>20315<br>117 133 | 20316<br>20316<br>117 134 | 20317<br>20317<br>117 135 | 20318<br>20318<br>117 136 | 20319<br>20319<br>117 137 |
| 6- | 20320<br>20320<br>117 140 | 20321<br>20321<br>117 141 | 20322<br>20322<br>117 142 | 20323<br>20323<br>117 143 | 20324<br>20324<br>117 144 | 20325<br>20325<br>117 145 | 20326<br>20326<br>117 146 | 20327<br>20327<br>117 147 | 20328<br>20328<br>117 150 | 20329<br>20329<br>117 151 | 20330<br>20330<br>117 152 | 20331<br>20331<br>117 153 | 20332<br>20332<br>117 154 | 20333<br>20333<br>117 155 | 20334<br>20334<br>117 156 | 20335<br>20335<br>117 157 |
| 7- | 20336<br>20336<br>117 160 | 20337<br>20337<br>117 161 | 20338<br>20338<br>117 162 | 20339<br>20339<br>117 163 | 20340<br>20340<br>117 164 | 20341<br>20341<br>117 165 | 20342<br>20342<br>117 166 | 20343<br>20343<br>117 167 | 20344<br>20344<br>117 170 | 20345<br>20345<br>117 171 | 20346<br>20346<br>117 172 | 20347<br>20347<br>117 173 | 20348<br>20348<br>117 174 | 20349<br>20349<br>117 175 | 20350<br>20350<br>117 176 | 20351<br>20351<br>117 177 |
| 8- | 20352<br>20352<br>117 200 | 20353<br>20353<br>117 201 | 20354<br>20354<br>117 202 | 20355<br>20355<br>117 203 | 20356<br>20356<br>117 204 | 20357<br>20357<br>117 205 | 20358<br>20358<br>117 206 | 20359<br>20359<br>117 207 | 20360<br>20360<br>117 210 | 20361<br>20361<br>117 211 | 20362<br>20362<br>117 212 | 20363<br>20363<br>117 213 | 20364<br>20364<br>117 214 | 20365<br>20365<br>117 215 | 20366<br>20366<br>117 216 | 20367<br>20367<br>117 217 |
| 9- | 20368<br>20368<br>117 220 | 20369<br>20369<br>117 221 | 20370<br>20370<br>117 222 | 20371<br>20371<br>117 223 | 20372<br>20372<br>117 224 | 20373<br>20373<br>117 225 | 20374<br>20374<br>117 226 | 20375<br>20375<br>117 227 | 20376<br>20376<br>117 230 | 20377<br>20377<br>117 231 | 20378<br>20378<br>117 232 | 20379<br>20379<br>117 233 | 20380<br>20380<br>117 234 | 20381<br>20381<br>117 235 | 20382<br>20382<br>117 236 | 20383<br>20383<br>117 237 |
| A- | 20384<br>20384<br>117 240 | 20385<br>20385<br>117 241 | 20386<br>20386<br>117 242 | 20387<br>20387<br>117 243 | 20388<br>20388<br>117 244 | 20389<br>20389<br>117 245 | 20390<br>20390<br>117 246 | 20391<br>20391<br>117 247 | 20392<br>20392<br>117 250 | 20393<br>20393<br>117 251 | 20394<br>20394<br>117 252 | 20395<br>20395<br>117 253 | 20396<br>20396<br>117 254 | 20397<br>20397<br>117 255 | 20398<br>20398<br>117 256 | 20399<br>20399<br>117 257 |
| B- | 20400<br>20400<br>117 260 | 20401<br>20401<br>117 261 | 20402<br>20402<br>117 262 | 20403<br>20403<br>117 263 | 20404<br>20404<br>117 264 | 20405<br>20405<br>117 265 | 20406<br>20406<br>117 266 | 20407<br>20407<br>117 267 | 20408<br>20408<br>117 270 | 20409<br>20409<br>117 271 | 20410<br>20410<br>117 272 | 20411<br>20411<br>117 273 | 20412<br>20412<br>117 274 | 20413<br>20413<br>117 275 | 20414<br>20414<br>117 276 | 20415<br>20415<br>117 277 |
| C- | 20416<br>20416<br>117 300 | 20417<br>20417<br>117 301 | 20418<br>20418<br>117 302 | 20419<br>20419<br>117 303 | 20420<br>20420<br>117 304 | 20421<br>20421<br>117 305 | 20422<br>20422<br>117 306 | 20423<br>20423<br>117 307 | 20424<br>20424<br>117 310 | 20425<br>20425<br>117 311 | 20426<br>20426<br>117 312 | 20427<br>20427<br>117 313 | 20428<br>20428<br>117 314 | 20429<br>20429<br>117 315 | 20430<br>20430<br>117 316 | 20431<br>20431<br>117 317 |
| D- | 20432<br>20432<br>117 320 | 20433<br>20433<br>117 321 | 20434<br>20434<br>117 322 | 20435<br>20435<br>117 323 | 20436<br>20436<br>117 324 | 20437<br>20437<br>117 325 | 20438<br>20438<br>117 326 | 20439<br>20439<br>117 327 | 20440<br>20440<br>117 330 | 20441<br>20441<br>117 331 | 20442<br>20442<br>117 332 | 20443<br>20443<br>117 333 | 20444<br>20444<br>117 334 | 20445<br>20445<br>117 335 | 20446<br>20446<br>117 336 | 20447<br>20447<br>117 337 |
| E- | 20448<br>20448<br>117 340 | 20449<br>20449<br>117 341 | 20450<br>20450<br>117 342 | 20451<br>20451<br>117 343 | 20452<br>20452<br>117 344 | 20453<br>20453<br>117 345 | 20454<br>20454<br>117 346 | 20455<br>20455<br>117 347 | 20456<br>20456<br>117 350 | 20457<br>20457<br>117 351 | 20458<br>20458<br>117 352 | 20459<br>20459<br>117 353 | 20460<br>20460<br>117 354 | 20461<br>20461<br>117 355 | 20462<br>20462<br>117 356 | 20463<br>20463<br>117 357 |
| F- | 20464<br>20464<br>117 360 | 20465<br>20465<br>117 361 | 20466<br>20466<br>117 362 | 20467<br>20467<br>117 363 | 20468<br>20468<br>117 364 | 20469<br>20469<br>117 365 | 20470<br>20470<br>117 366 | 20471<br>20471<br>117 367 | 20472<br>20472<br>117 370 | 20473<br>20473<br>117 371 | 20474<br>20474<br>117 372 | 20475<br>20475<br>117 373 | 20476<br>20476<br>117 374 | 20477<br>20477<br>117 375 | 20478<br>20478<br>117 376 | 20479<br>20479<br>117 377 |

SECOND HEX DIGIT (left axis, rows 0- through F-)

DECIMAL → (first two rows of each cell)　 DECIMAL →　 OCTAL → (third row of each cell)

# FIRST HEX DIGIT

| SECOND HEX DIGIT | −0 | −1 | −2 | −3 | −4 | −5 | −6 | −7 | −8 | −9 | −A | −B | −C | −D | −E | −F |
|---|---|---|---|---|---|---|---|---|---|---|---|---|---|---|---|---|
| **0−** | 20480<br>20480<br>120 000 | 20481<br>20481<br>120 001 | 20482<br>20482<br>120 002 | 20483<br>20483<br>120 003 | 20484<br>20484<br>120 004 | 20485<br>20485<br>120 005 | 20486<br>20486<br>120 006 | 20487<br>20487<br>120 007 | 20488<br>20488<br>120 010 | 20489<br>20489<br>120 011 | 20490<br>20490<br>120 012 | 20491<br>20491<br>120 013 | 20492<br>20492<br>120 014 | 20493<br>20493<br>120 015 | 20494<br>20494<br>120 016 | 20495<br>20495<br>120 017 |
| **1−** | 20496<br>20496<br>120 020 | 20497<br>20497<br>120 021 | 20498<br>20498<br>120 022 | 20499<br>20499<br>120 023 | 20500<br>20500<br>120 024 | 20501<br>20501<br>120 025 | 20502<br>20502<br>120 026 | 20503<br>20503<br>120 027 | 20504<br>20504<br>120 030 | 20505<br>20505<br>120 031 | 20506<br>20506<br>120 032 | 20507<br>20507<br>120 033 | 20508<br>20508<br>120 034 | 20509<br>20509<br>120 035 | 20510<br>20510<br>120 036 | 20511<br>20511<br>120 037 |
| **2−** | 20512<br>20512<br>120 040 | 20513<br>20513<br>120 041 | 20514<br>20514<br>120 042 | 20515<br>20515<br>120 043 | 20516<br>20516<br>120 044 | 20517<br>20517<br>120 045 | 20518<br>20518<br>120 046 | 20519<br>20519<br>120 047 | 20520<br>20520<br>120 050 | 20521<br>20521<br>120 051 | 20522<br>20522<br>120 052 | 20523<br>20523<br>120 053 | 20524<br>20524<br>120 054 | 20525<br>20525<br>120 055 | 20526<br>20526<br>120 056 | 20527<br>20527<br>120 057 |
| **3−** | 20528<br>20528<br>120 060 | 20529<br>20529<br>120 061 | 20530<br>20530<br>120 062 | 20531<br>20531<br>120 063 | 20532<br>20532<br>120 064 | 20533<br>20533<br>120 065 | 20534<br>20534<br>120 066 | 20535<br>20535<br>120 067 | 20536<br>20536<br>120 070 | 20537<br>20537<br>120 071 | 20538<br>20538<br>120 072 | 20539<br>20539<br>120 073 | 20540<br>20540<br>120 074 | 20541<br>20541<br>120 075 | 20542<br>20542<br>120 076 | 20543<br>20543<br>120 077 |
| **4−** | 20544<br>20544<br>120 100 | 20545<br>20545<br>120 101 | 20546<br>20546<br>120 102 | 20547<br>20547<br>120 103 | 20548<br>20548<br>120 104 | 20549<br>20549<br>120 105 | 20550<br>20550<br>120 106 | 20551<br>20551<br>120 107 | 20552<br>20552<br>120 110 | 20553<br>20553<br>120 111 | 20554<br>20554<br>120 112 | 20555<br>20555<br>120 113 | 20556<br>20556<br>120 114 | 20557<br>20557<br>120 115 | 20558<br>20558<br>120 116 | 20559<br>20559<br>120 117 |
| **5−** | 20560<br>20560<br>120 120 | 20561<br>20561<br>120 121 | 20562<br>20562<br>120 122 | 20563<br>20563<br>120 123 | 20564<br>20564<br>120 124 | 20565<br>20565<br>120 125 | 20566<br>20566<br>120 126 | 20567<br>20567<br>120 127 | 20568<br>20568<br>120 130 | 20569<br>20569<br>120 131 | 20570<br>20570<br>120 132 | 20571<br>20571<br>120 133 | 20572<br>20572<br>120 134 | 20573<br>20573<br>120 135 | 20574<br>20574<br>120 136 | 20575<br>20575<br>120 137 |
| **6−** | 20576<br>20576<br>120 140 | 20577<br>20577<br>120 141 | 20578<br>20578<br>120 142 | 20579<br>20579<br>120 143 | 20580<br>20580<br>120 144 | 20581<br>20581<br>120 145 | 20582<br>20582<br>120 146 | 20583<br>20583<br>120 147 | 20584<br>20584<br>120 150 | 20585<br>20585<br>120 151 | 20586<br>20586<br>120 152 | 20587<br>20587<br>120 153 | 20588<br>20588<br>120 154 | 20589<br>20589<br>120 155 | 20590<br>20590<br>120 156 | 20591<br>20591<br>120 157 |
| **7−** | 20592<br>20592<br>120 160 | 20593<br>20593<br>120 161 | 20594<br>20594<br>120 162 | 20595<br>20595<br>120 163 | 20596<br>20596<br>120 164 | 20597<br>20597<br>120 165 | 20598<br>20598<br>120 166 | 20599<br>20599<br>120 167 | 20600<br>20600<br>120 170 | 20601<br>20601<br>120 171 | 20602<br>20602<br>120 172 | 20603<br>20603<br>120 173 | 20604<br>20604<br>120 174 | 20605<br>20605<br>120 175 | 20606<br>20606<br>120 176 | 20607<br>20607<br>120 177 |
| **8−** | 20608<br>20608<br>120 200 | 20609<br>20609<br>120 201 | 20610<br>20610<br>120 202 | 20611<br>20611<br>120 203 | 20612<br>20612<br>120 204 | 20613<br>20613<br>120 205 | 20614<br>20614<br>120 206 | 20615<br>20615<br>120 207 | 20616<br>20616<br>120 210 | 20617<br>20617<br>120 211 | 20618<br>20618<br>120 212 | 20619<br>20619<br>120 213 | 20620<br>20620<br>120 214 | 20621<br>20621<br>120 215 | 20622<br>20622<br>120 216 | 20623<br>20623<br>120 217 |
| **9−** | 20624<br>20624<br>120 220 | 20625<br>20625<br>120 221 | 20626<br>20626<br>120 222 | 20627<br>20627<br>120 223 | 20628<br>20628<br>120 224 | 20629<br>20629<br>120 225 | 20630<br>20630<br>120 226 | 20631<br>20631<br>120 227 | 20632<br>20632<br>120 230 | 20633<br>20633<br>120 231 | 20634<br>20634<br>120 232 | 20635<br>20635<br>120 233 | 20636<br>20636<br>120 234 | 20637<br>20637<br>120 235 | 20638<br>20638<br>120 236 | 20639<br>20639<br>120 237 |
| **A−** | 20640<br>20640<br>120 240 | 20641<br>20641<br>120 241 | 20642<br>20642<br>120 242 | 20643<br>20643<br>120 243 | 20644<br>20644<br>120 244 | 20645<br>20645<br>120 245 | 20646<br>20646<br>120 246 | 20647<br>20647<br>120 247 | 20648<br>20648<br>120 250 | 20649<br>20649<br>120 251 | 20650<br>20650<br>120 252 | 20651<br>20651<br>120 253 | 20652<br>20652<br>120 254 | 20653<br>20653<br>120 255 | 20654<br>20654<br>120 256 | 20655<br>20655<br>120 257 |
| **B−** | 20656<br>20656<br>120 260 | 20657<br>20657<br>120 261 | 20658<br>20658<br>120 262 | 20659<br>20659<br>120 263 | 20660<br>20660<br>120 264 | 20661<br>20661<br>120 265 | 20662<br>20662<br>120 266 | 20663<br>20663<br>120 267 | 20664<br>20664<br>120 270 | 20665<br>20665<br>120 271 | 20666<br>20666<br>120 272 | 20667<br>20667<br>120 273 | 20668<br>20668<br>120 274 | 20669<br>20669<br>120 275 | 20670<br>20670<br>120 276 | 20671<br>20671<br>120 277 |
| **C−** | 20672<br>20672<br>120 300 | 20673<br>20673<br>120 301 | 20674<br>20674<br>120 302 | 20675<br>20675<br>120 303 | 20676<br>20676<br>120 304 | 20677<br>20677<br>120 305 | 20678<br>20678<br>120 306 | 20679<br>20679<br>120 307 | 20680<br>20680<br>120 310 | 20681<br>20681<br>120 311 | 20682<br>20682<br>120 312 | 20683<br>20683<br>120 313 | 20684<br>20684<br>120 314 | 20685<br>20685<br>120 315 | 20686<br>20686<br>120 316 | 20687<br>20687<br>120 317 |
| **D−** | 20688<br>20688<br>120 320 | 20689<br>20689<br>120 321 | 20690<br>20690<br>120 322 | 20691<br>20691<br>120 323 | 20692<br>20692<br>120 324 | 20693<br>20693<br>120 325 | 20694<br>20694<br>120 326 | 20695<br>20695<br>120 327 | 20696<br>20696<br>120 330 | 20697<br>20697<br>120 331 | 20698<br>20698<br>120 332 | 20699<br>20699<br>120 333 | 20700<br>20700<br>120 334 | 20701<br>20701<br>120 335 | 20702<br>20702<br>120 336 | 20703<br>20703<br>120 337 |
| **E−** | 20704<br>20704<br>120 340 | 20705<br>20705<br>120 341 | 20706<br>20706<br>120 342 | 20707<br>20707<br>120 343 | 20708<br>20708<br>120 344 | 20709<br>20709<br>120 345 | 20710<br>20710<br>120 346 | 20711<br>20711<br>120 347 | 20712<br>20712<br>120 350 | 20713<br>20713<br>120 351 | 20714<br>20714<br>120 352 | 20715<br>20715<br>120 353 | 20716<br>20716<br>120 354 | 20717<br>20717<br>120 355 | 20718<br>20718<br>120 356 | 20719<br>20719<br>120 357 |
| **F−** | 20720<br>20720<br>120 360 | 20721<br>20721<br>120 361 | 20722<br>20722<br>120 362 | 20723<br>20723<br>120 363 | 20724<br>20724<br>120 364 | 20725<br>20725<br>120 365 | 20726<br>20726<br>120 366 | 20727<br>20727<br>120 367 | 20728<br>20728<br>120 370 | 20729<br>20729<br>120 371 | 20730<br>20730<br>120 372 | 20731<br>20731<br>120 373 | 20732<br>20732<br>120 374 | 20733<br>20733<br>120 375 | 20734<br>20734<br>120 376 | 20735<br>20735<br>120 377 |

Legend (right side): DECIMAL →, DECIMAL →, OCTAL →

---

 DECIMAL [ 20480 ]   BINARY [ 0101 0000 ]   DECIMAL [ 20480 ]   HEXADECIMAL  OCTAL [ 120 000 ]

DECIMAL 20736  BINARY 0101 0001  DECIMAL 20736  HEXADECIMAL 51  OCTAL 121 000

FOURTH HEX DIGIT → 51 ← THIRD HEX DIGIT

| 2 | FIRST HEX DIGIT | | | | | | | | | | | | | | | |
|---|−0|−1|−2|−3|−4|−5|−6|−7|−8|−9|−A|−B|−C|−D|−E|−F|
|0−|20736 20736 121 000|20737 20737 121 001|20738 20738 121 002|20739 20739 121 003|20740 20740 121 004|20741 20741 121 005|20742 20742 121 006|20743 20743 121 007|20744 20744 121 010|20745 20745 121 011|20746 20746 121 012|20747 20747 121 013|20748 20748 121 014|20749 20749 121 015|20750 20750 121 016|20751 20751 121 017|
|1−|20752 20752 121 020|20753 20753 121 021|20754 20754 121 022|20755 20755 121 023|20756 20756 121 024|20757 20757 121 025|20758 20758 121 026|20759 20759 121 027|20760 20760 121 030|20761 20761 121 031|20762 20762 121 032|20763 20763 121 033|20764 20764 121 034|20765 20765 121 035|20766 20766 121 036|20767 20767 121 037|
|2−|20768 20768 121 040|20769 20769 121 041|20770 20770 121 042|20771 20771 121 043|20772 20772 121 044|20773 20773 121 045|20774 20774 121 046|20775 20775 121 047|20776 20776 121 050|20777 20777 121 051|20778 20778 121 052|20779 20779 121 053|20780 20780 121 054|20781 20781 121 055|20782 20782 121 056|20783 20783 121 057|
|3−|20784 20784 121 060|20785 20785 121 061|20786 20786 121 062|20787 20787 121 063|20788 20788 121 064|20789 20789 121 065|20790 20790 121 066|20791 20791 121 067|20792 20792 121 070|20793 20793 121 071|20794 20794 121 072|20795 20795 121 073|20796 20796 121 074|20797 20797 121 075|20798 20798 121 076|20799 20799 121 077|
|4−|20800 20800 121 100|20801 20801 121 101|20802 20802 121 102|20803 20803 121 103|20804 20804 121 104|20805 20805 121 105|20806 20806 121 106|20807 20807 121 107|20808 20808 121 110|20809 20809 121 111|20810 20810 121 112|20811 20811 121 113|20812 20812 121 114|20813 20813 121 115|20814 20814 121 116|20815 20815 121 117|
|5−|20816 20816 121 120|20817 20817 121 121|20818 20818 121 122|20819 20819 121 123|20820 20820 121 124|20821 20821 121 125|20822 20822 121 126|20823 20823 121 127|20824 20824 121 130|20825 20825 121 131|20826 20826 121 132|20827 20827 121 133|20828 20828 121 134|20829 20829 121 135|20830 20830 121 136|20831 20831 121 137|
|6−|20832 20832 121 140|20833 20833 121 141|20834 20834 121 142|20835 20835 121 143|20836 20836 121 144|20837 20837 121 145|20838 20838 121 146|20839 20839 121 147|20840 20840 121 150|20841 20841 121 151|20842 20842 121 152|20843 20843 121 153|20844 20844 121 154|20845 20845 121 155|20846 20846 121 156|20847 20847 121 157|
|7−|20848 20848 121 160|20849 20849 121 161|20850 20850 121 162|20851 20851 121 163|20852 20852 121 164|20853 20853 121 165|20854 20854 121 166|20855 20855 121 167|20856 20856 121 170|20857 20857 121 171|20858 20858 121 172|20859 20859 121 173|20860 20860 121 174|20861 20861 121 175|20862 20862 121 176|20863 20863 121 177|
|8−|20864 20864 121 200|20865 20865 121 201|20866 20866 121 202|20867 20867 121 203|20868 20868 121 204|20869 20869 121 205|20870 20870 121 206|20871 20871 121 207|20872 20872 121 210|20873 20873 121 211|20874 20874 121 212|20875 20875 121 213|20876 20876 121 214|20877 20877 121 215|20878 20878 121 216|20879 20879 121 217|
|9−|20880 20880 121 220|20881 20881 121 221|20882 20882 121 222|20883 20883 121 223|20884 20884 121 224|20885 20885 121 225|20886 20886 121 226|20887 20887 121 227|20888 20888 121 230|20889 20889 121 231|20890 20890 121 232|20891 20891 121 233|20892 20892 121 234|20893 20893 121 235|20894 20894 121 236|20895 20895 121 237|
|A−|20896 20896 121 240|20897 20897 121 241|20898 20898 121 242|20899 20899 121 243|20900 20900 121 244|20901 20901 121 245|20902 20902 121 246|20903 20903 121 247|20904 20904 121 250|20905 20905 121 251|20906 20906 121 252|20907 20907 121 253|20908 20908 121 254|20909 20909 121 255|20910 20910 121 256|20911 20911 121 257|
|B−|20912 20912 121 260|20913 20913 121 261|20914 20914 121 262|20915 20915 121 263|20916 20916 121 264|20917 20917 121 265|20918 20918 121 266|20919 20919 121 267|20920 20920 121 270|20921 20921 121 271|20922 20922 121 272|20923 20923 121 273|20924 20924 121 274|20925 20925 121 275|20926 20926 121 276|20927 20927 121 277|
|C−|20928 20928 121 300|20929 20929 121 301|20930 20930 121 302|20931 20931 121 303|20932 20932 121 304|20933 20933 121 305|20934 20934 121 306|20935 20935 121 307|20936 20936 121 310|20937 20937 121 311|20938 20938 121 312|20939 20939 121 313|20940 20940 121 314|20941 20941 121 315|20942 20942 121 316|20943 20943 121 317|
|D−|20944 20944 121 320|20945 20945 121 321|20946 20946 121 322|20947 20947 121 323|20948 20948 121 324|20949 20949 121 325|20950 20950 121 326|20951 20951 121 327|20952 20952 121 330|20953 20953 121 331|20954 20954 121 332|20955 20955 121 333|20956 20956 121 334|20957 20957 121 335|20958 20958 121 336|20959 20959 121 337|
|E−|20960 20960 121 340|20961 20961 121 341|20962 20962 121 342|20963 20963 121 343|20964 20964 121 344|20965 20965 121 345|20966 20966 121 346|20967 20967 121 347|20968 20968 121 350|20969 20969 121 351|20970 20970 121 352|20971 20971 121 353|20972 20972 121 354|20973 20973 121 355|20974 20974 121 356|20975 20975 121 357|
|F−|20976 20976 121 360|20977 20977 121 361|20978 20978 121 362|20979 20979 121 363|20980 20980 121 364|20981 20981 121 365|20982 20982 121 366|20983 20983 121 367|20984 20984 121 370|20985 20985 121 371|20986 20986 121 372|20987 20987 121 373|20988 20988 121 374|20989 20989 121 375|20990 20990 121 376|20991 20991 121 377|

SECOND HEX DIGIT

DECIMAL
DECIMAL
OCTAL

<table>
<tr><td colspan="17" align="center">FIRST HEX DIGIT</td></tr>
<tr><td>(2)</td><td>−0</td><td>−1</td><td>−2</td><td>−3</td><td>−4</td><td>−5</td><td>−6</td><td>−7</td><td>−8</td><td>−9</td><td>−A</td><td>−B</td><td>−C</td><td>−D</td><td>−E</td><td>−F</td></tr>
<tr><td>0−</td><td>20992<br>20992<br>122 000</td><td>20993<br>20993<br>122 001</td><td>20994<br>20994<br>122 002</td><td>20995<br>20995<br>122 003</td><td>20996<br>20996<br>122 004</td><td>20997<br>20997<br>122 005</td><td>20998<br>20998<br>122 006</td><td>20999<br>20999<br>122 007</td><td>21000<br>21000<br>122 010</td><td>21001<br>21001<br>122 011</td><td>21002<br>21002<br>122 012</td><td>21003<br>21003<br>122 013</td><td>21004<br>21004<br>122 014</td><td>21005<br>21005<br>122 015</td><td>21006<br>21006<br>122 016</td><td>21007<br>21007<br>122 017</td></tr>
<tr><td>1−</td><td>21008<br>21008<br>122 020</td><td>21009<br>21009<br>122 021</td><td>21010<br>21010<br>122 022</td><td>21011<br>21011<br>122 023</td><td>21012<br>21012<br>122 024</td><td>21013<br>21013<br>122 025</td><td>21014<br>21014<br>122 026</td><td>21015<br>21015<br>122 027</td><td>21016<br>21016<br>122 030</td><td>21017<br>21017<br>122 031</td><td>21018<br>21018<br>122 032</td><td>21019<br>21019<br>122 033</td><td>21020<br>21020<br>122 034</td><td>21021<br>21021<br>122 035</td><td>21022<br>21022<br>122 036</td><td>21023<br>21023<br>122 037</td></tr>
<tr><td>2−</td><td>21024<br>21024<br>122 040</td><td>21025<br>21025<br>122 041</td><td>21026<br>21026<br>122 042</td><td>21027<br>21027<br>122 043</td><td>21028<br>21028<br>122 044</td><td>21029<br>21029<br>122 045</td><td>21030<br>21030<br>122 046</td><td>21031<br>21031<br>122 047</td><td>21032<br>21032<br>122 050</td><td>21033<br>21033<br>122 051</td><td>21034<br>21034<br>122 052</td><td>21035<br>21035<br>122 053</td><td>21036<br>21036<br>122 054</td><td>21037<br>21037<br>122 055</td><td>21038<br>21038<br>122 056</td><td>21039<br>21039<br>122 057</td></tr>
<tr><td>3−</td><td>21040<br>21040<br>122 060</td><td>21041<br>21041<br>122 061</td><td>21042<br>21042<br>122 062</td><td>21043<br>21043<br>122 063</td><td>21044<br>21044<br>122 064</td><td>21045<br>21045<br>122 065</td><td>21046<br>21046<br>122 066</td><td>21047<br>21047<br>122 067</td><td>21048<br>21048<br>122 070</td><td>21049<br>21049<br>122 071</td><td>21050<br>21050<br>122 072</td><td>21051<br>21051<br>122 073</td><td>21052<br>21052<br>122 074</td><td>21053<br>21053<br>122 075</td><td>21054<br>21054<br>122 076</td><td>21055<br>21055<br>122 077</td></tr>
<tr><td>4−</td><td>21056<br>21056<br>122 100</td><td>21057<br>21057<br>122 101</td><td>21058<br>21058<br>122 102</td><td>21059<br>21059<br>122 103</td><td>21060<br>21060<br>122 104</td><td>21061<br>21061<br>122 105</td><td>21062<br>21062<br>122 106</td><td>21063<br>21063<br>122 107</td><td>21064<br>21064<br>122 110</td><td>21065<br>21065<br>122 111</td><td>21066<br>21066<br>122 112</td><td>21067<br>21067<br>122 113</td><td>21068<br>21068<br>122 114</td><td>21069<br>21069<br>122 115</td><td>21070<br>21070<br>122 116</td><td>21071<br>21071<br>122 117</td></tr>
<tr><td>5−</td><td>21072<br>21072<br>122 120</td><td>21073<br>21073<br>122 121</td><td>21074<br>21074<br>122 122</td><td>21075<br>21075<br>122 123</td><td>21076<br>21076<br>122 124</td><td>21077<br>21077<br>122 125</td><td>21078<br>21078<br>122 126</td><td>21079<br>21079<br>122 127</td><td>21080<br>21080<br>122 130</td><td>21081<br>21081<br>122 131</td><td>21082<br>21082<br>122 132</td><td>21083<br>21083<br>122 133</td><td>21084<br>21084<br>122 134</td><td>21085<br>21085<br>122 135</td><td>21086<br>21086<br>122 136</td><td>21087<br>21087<br>122 137</td></tr>
<tr><td>6−</td><td>21088<br>21088<br>122 140</td><td>21089<br>21089<br>122 141</td><td>21090<br>21090<br>122 142</td><td>21091<br>21091<br>122 143</td><td>21092<br>21092<br>122 144</td><td>21093<br>21093<br>122 145</td><td>21094<br>21094<br>122 146</td><td>21095<br>21095<br>122 147</td><td>21096<br>21096<br>122 150</td><td>21097<br>21097<br>122 151</td><td>21098<br>21098<br>122 152</td><td>21099<br>21099<br>122 153</td><td>21100<br>21100<br>122 154</td><td>21101<br>21101<br>122 155</td><td>21102<br>21102<br>122 156</td><td>21103<br>21103<br>122 157</td></tr>
<tr><td>7−</td><td>21104<br>21104<br>122 160</td><td>21105<br>21105<br>122 161</td><td>21106<br>21106<br>122 162</td><td>21107<br>21107<br>122 163</td><td>21108<br>21108<br>122 164</td><td>21109<br>21109<br>122 165</td><td>21110<br>21110<br>122 166</td><td>21111<br>21111<br>122 167</td><td>21112<br>21112<br>122 170</td><td>21113<br>21113<br>122 171</td><td>21114<br>21114<br>122 172</td><td>21115<br>21115<br>122 173</td><td>21116<br>21116<br>122 174</td><td>21117<br>21117<br>122 175</td><td>21118<br>21118<br>122 176</td><td>21119<br>21119<br>122 177</td></tr>
<tr><td>8−</td><td>21120<br>21120<br>122 200</td><td>21121<br>21121<br>122 201</td><td>21122<br>21122<br>122 202</td><td>21123<br>21123<br>122 203</td><td>21124<br>21124<br>122 204</td><td>21125<br>21125<br>122 205</td><td>21126<br>21126<br>122 206</td><td>21127<br>21127<br>122 207</td><td>21128<br>21128<br>122 210</td><td>21129<br>21129<br>122 211</td><td>21130<br>21130<br>122 212</td><td>21131<br>21131<br>122 213</td><td>21132<br>21132<br>122 214</td><td>21133<br>21133<br>122 215</td><td>21134<br>21134<br>122 216</td><td>21135<br>21135<br>122 217</td></tr>
<tr><td>9−</td><td>21136<br>21136<br>122 220</td><td>21137<br>21137<br>122 221</td><td>21138<br>21138<br>122 222</td><td>21139<br>21139<br>122 223</td><td>21140<br>21140<br>122 224</td><td>21141<br>21141<br>122 225</td><td>21142<br>21142<br>122 226</td><td>21143<br>21143<br>122 227</td><td>21144<br>21144<br>122 230</td><td>21145<br>21145<br>122 231</td><td>21146<br>21146<br>122 232</td><td>21147<br>21147<br>122 233</td><td>21148<br>21148<br>122 234</td><td>21149<br>21149<br>122 235</td><td>21150<br>21150<br>122 236</td><td>21151<br>21151<br>122 237</td></tr>
<tr><td>A−</td><td>21152<br>21152<br>122 240</td><td>21153<br>21153<br>122 241</td><td>21154<br>21154<br>122 242</td><td>21155<br>21155<br>122 243</td><td>21156<br>21156<br>122 244</td><td>21157<br>21157<br>122 245</td><td>21158<br>21158<br>122 246</td><td>21159<br>21159<br>122 247</td><td>21160<br>21160<br>122 250</td><td>21161<br>21161<br>122 251</td><td>21162<br>21162<br>122 252</td><td>21163<br>21163<br>122 253</td><td>21164<br>21164<br>122 254</td><td>21165<br>21165<br>122 255</td><td>21166<br>21166<br>122 256</td><td>21167<br>21167<br>122 257</td></tr>
<tr><td>B−</td><td>21168<br>21168<br>122 260</td><td>21169<br>21169<br>122 261</td><td>21170<br>21170<br>122 262</td><td>21171<br>21171<br>122 263</td><td>21172<br>21172<br>122 264</td><td>21173<br>21173<br>122 265</td><td>21174<br>21174<br>122 266</td><td>21175<br>21175<br>122 267</td><td>21176<br>21176<br>122 270</td><td>21177<br>21177<br>122 271</td><td>21178<br>21178<br>122 272</td><td>21179<br>21179<br>122 273</td><td>21180<br>21180<br>122 274</td><td>21181<br>21181<br>122 275</td><td>21182<br>21182<br>122 276</td><td>21183<br>21183<br>122 277</td></tr>
<tr><td>C−</td><td>21184<br>21184<br>122 300</td><td>21185<br>21185<br>122 301</td><td>21186<br>21186<br>122 302</td><td>21187<br>21187<br>122 303</td><td>21188<br>21188<br>122 304</td><td>21189<br>21189<br>122 305</td><td>21190<br>21190<br>122 306</td><td>21191<br>21191<br>122 307</td><td>21192<br>21192<br>122 310</td><td>21193<br>21193<br>122 311</td><td>21194<br>21194<br>122 312</td><td>21195<br>21195<br>122 313</td><td>21196<br>21196<br>122 314</td><td>21197<br>21197<br>122 315</td><td>21198<br>21198<br>122 316</td><td>21199<br>21199<br>122 317</td></tr>
<tr><td>D−</td><td>21200<br>21200<br>122 320</td><td>21201<br>21201<br>122 321</td><td>21202<br>21202<br>122 322</td><td>21203<br>21203<br>122 323</td><td>21204<br>21204<br>122 324</td><td>21205<br>21205<br>122 325</td><td>21206<br>21206<br>122 326</td><td>21207<br>21207<br>122 327</td><td>21208<br>21208<br>122 330</td><td>21209<br>21209<br>122 331</td><td>21210<br>21210<br>122 332</td><td>21211<br>21211<br>122 333</td><td>21212<br>21212<br>122 334</td><td>21213<br>21213<br>122 335</td><td>21214<br>21214<br>122 336</td><td>21215<br>21215<br>122 337</td></tr>
<tr><td>E−</td><td>21216<br>21216<br>122 340</td><td>21217<br>21217<br>122 341</td><td>21218<br>21218<br>122 342</td><td>21219<br>21219<br>122 343</td><td>21220<br>21220<br>122 344</td><td>21221<br>21221<br>122 345</td><td>21222<br>21222<br>122 346</td><td>21223<br>21223<br>122 347</td><td>21224<br>21224<br>122 350</td><td>21225<br>21225<br>122 351</td><td>21226<br>21226<br>122 352</td><td>21227<br>21227<br>122 353</td><td>21228<br>21228<br>122 354</td><td>21229<br>21229<br>122 355</td><td>21230<br>21230<br>122 356</td><td>21231<br>21231<br>122 357</td></tr>
<tr><td>F−</td><td>21232<br>21232<br>122 360</td><td>21233<br>21233<br>122 361</td><td>21234<br>21234<br>122 362</td><td>21235<br>21235<br>122 363</td><td>21236<br>21236<br>122 364</td><td>21237<br>21237<br>122 365</td><td>21238<br>21238<br>122 366</td><td>21239<br>21239<br>122 367</td><td>21240<br>21240<br>122 370</td><td>21241<br>21241<br>122 371</td><td>21242<br>21242<br>122 372</td><td>21243<br>21243<br>122 373</td><td>21244<br>21244<br>122 374</td><td>21245<br>21245<br>122 375</td><td>21246<br>21246<br>122 376</td><td>21247<br>21247<br>122 377</td></tr>
</table>

SECOND HEX DIGIT

⬅ DECIMAL

⬅ DECIMAL

⬅ OCTAL

 DECIMAL [20992]  BINARY [0101 0010]  DECIMAL [20992]  HEXADECIMAL ⟨52⟩ OCTAL [122 000]

FOURTH HEX DIGIT → ⟨ ⟩ ← THIRD HEX DIGIT

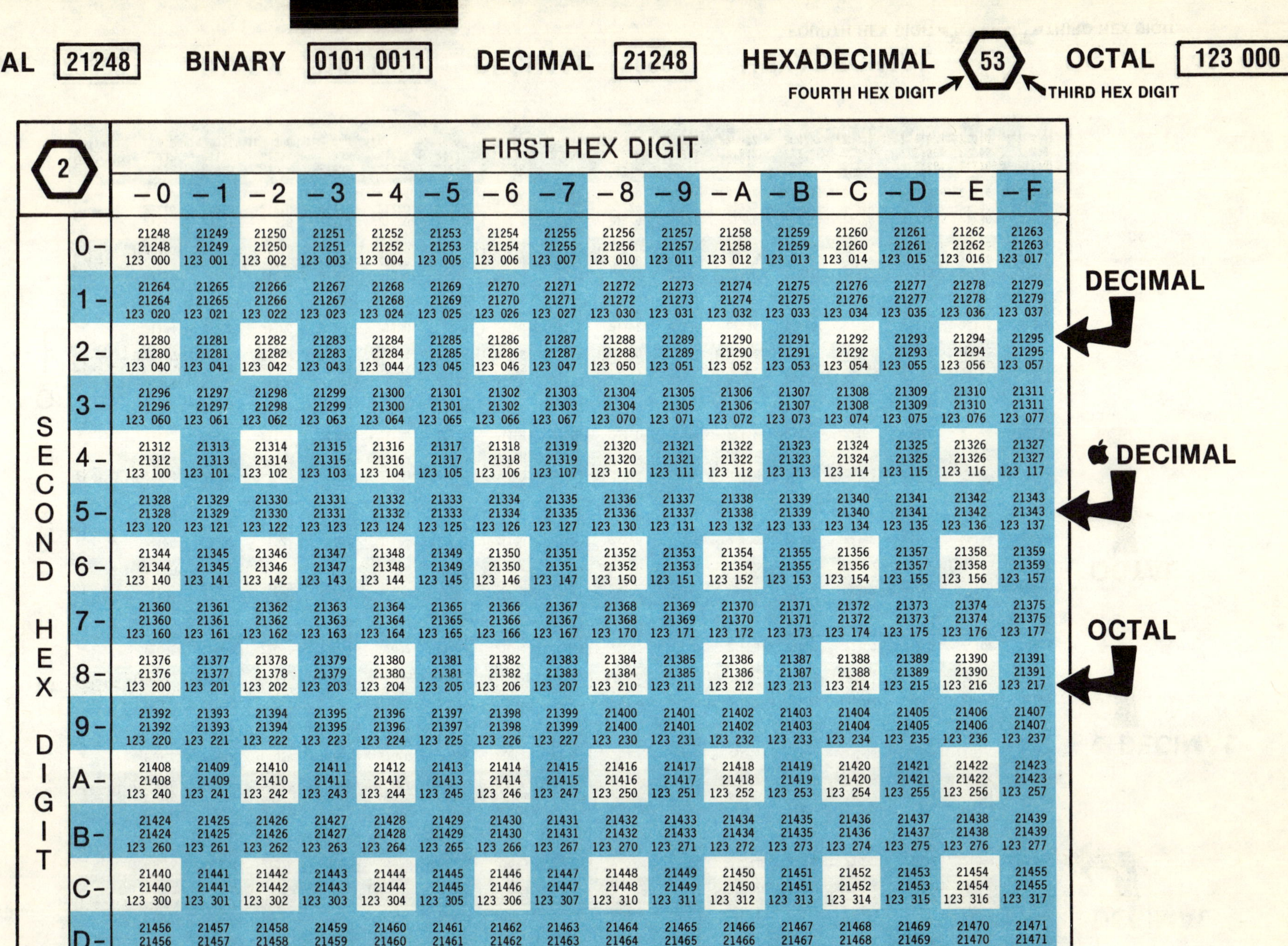



**FIRST HEX DIGIT** (hex value 2 _ _)

Each cell shows: decimal (top), decimal (repeat), octal (bottom).

| SECOND HEX DIGIT | −0 | −1 | −2 | −3 | −4 | −5 | −6 | −7 | −8 | −9 | −A | −B | −C | −D | −E | −F |
|---|---|---|---|---|---|---|---|---|---|---|---|---|---|---|---|---|
| 0− | 21248<br>123 000 | 21249<br>123 001 | 21250<br>123 002 | 21251<br>123 003 | 21252<br>123 004 | 21253<br>123 005 | 21254<br>123 006 | 21255<br>123 007 | 21256<br>123 010 | 21257<br>123 011 | 21258<br>123 012 | 21259<br>123 013 | 21260<br>123 014 | 21261<br>123 015 | 21262<br>123 016 | 21263<br>123 017 |
| 1− | 21264<br>123 020 | 21265<br>123 021 | 21266<br>123 022 | 21267<br>123 023 | 21268<br>123 024 | 21269<br>123 025 | 21270<br>123 026 | 21271<br>123 027 | 21272<br>123 030 | 21273<br>123 031 | 21274<br>123 032 | 21275<br>123 033 | 21276<br>123 034 | 21277<br>123 035 | 21278<br>123 036 | 21279<br>123 037 |
| 2− | 21280<br>123 040 | 21281<br>123 041 | 21282<br>123 042 | 21283<br>123 043 | 21284<br>123 044 | 21285<br>123 045 | 21286<br>123 046 | 21287<br>123 047 | 21288<br>123 050 | 21289<br>123 051 | 21290<br>123 052 | 21291<br>123 053 | 21292<br>123 054 | 21293<br>123 055 | 21294<br>123 056 | 21295<br>123 057 |
| 3− | 21296<br>123 060 | 21297<br>123 061 | 21298<br>123 062 | 21299<br>123 063 | 21300<br>123 064 | 21301<br>123 065 | 21302<br>123 066 | 21303<br>123 067 | 21304<br>123 070 | 21305<br>123 071 | 21306<br>123 072 | 21307<br>123 073 | 21308<br>123 074 | 21309<br>123 075 | 21310<br>123 076 | 21311<br>123 077 |
| 4− | 21312<br>123 100 | 21313<br>123 101 | 21314<br>123 102 | 21315<br>123 103 | 21316<br>123 104 | 21317<br>123 105 | 21318<br>123 106 | 21319<br>123 107 | 21320<br>123 110 | 21321<br>123 111 | 21322<br>123 112 | 21323<br>123 113 | 21324<br>123 114 | 21325<br>123 115 | 21326<br>123 116 | 21327<br>123 117 |
| 5− | 21328<br>123 120 | 21329<br>123 121 | 21330<br>123 122 | 21331<br>123 123 | 21332<br>123 124 | 21333<br>123 125 | 21334<br>123 126 | 21335<br>123 127 | 21336<br>123 130 | 21337<br>123 131 | 21338<br>123 132 | 21339<br>123 133 | 21340<br>123 134 | 21341<br>123 135 | 21342<br>123 136 | 21343<br>123 137 |
| 6− | 21344<br>123 140 | 21345<br>123 141 | 21346<br>123 142 | 21347<br>123 143 | 21348<br>123 144 | 21349<br>123 145 | 21350<br>123 146 | 21351<br>123 147 | 21352<br>123 150 | 21353<br>123 151 | 21354<br>123 152 | 21355<br>123 153 | 21356<br>123 154 | 21357<br>123 155 | 21358<br>123 156 | 21359<br>123 157 |
| 7− | 21360<br>123 160 | 21361<br>123 161 | 21362<br>123 162 | 21363<br>123 163 | 21364<br>123 164 | 21365<br>123 165 | 21366<br>123 166 | 21367<br>123 167 | 21368<br>123 170 | 21369<br>123 171 | 21370<br>123 172 | 21371<br>123 173 | 21372<br>123 174 | 21373<br>123 175 | 21374<br>123 176 | 21375<br>123 177 |
| 8− | 21376<br>123 200 | 21377<br>123 201 | 21378<br>123 202 | 21379<br>123 203 | 21380<br>123 204 | 21381<br>123 205 | 21382<br>123 206 | 21383<br>123 207 | 21384<br>123 210 | 21385<br>123 211 | 21386<br>123 212 | 21387<br>123 213 | 21388<br>123 214 | 21389<br>123 215 | 21390<br>123 216 | 21391<br>123 217 |
| 9− | 21392<br>123 220 | 21393<br>123 221 | 21394<br>123 222 | 21395<br>123 223 | 21396<br>123 224 | 21397<br>123 225 | 21398<br>123 226 | 21399<br>123 227 | 21400<br>123 230 | 21401<br>123 231 | 21402<br>123 232 | 21403<br>123 233 | 21404<br>123 234 | 21405<br>123 235 | 21406<br>123 236 | 21407<br>123 237 |
| A− | 21408<br>123 240 | 21409<br>123 241 | 21410<br>123 242 | 21411<br>123 243 | 21412<br>123 244 | 21413<br>123 245 | 21414<br>123 246 | 21415<br>123 247 | 21416<br>123 250 | 21417<br>123 251 | 21418<br>123 252 | 21419<br>123 253 | 21420<br>123 254 | 21421<br>123 255 | 21422<br>123 256 | 21423<br>123 257 |
| B− | 21424<br>123 260 | 21425<br>123 261 | 21426<br>123 262 | 21427<br>123 263 | 21428<br>123 264 | 21429<br>123 265 | 21430<br>123 266 | 21431<br>123 267 | 21432<br>123 270 | 21433<br>123 271 | 21434<br>123 272 | 21435<br>123 273 | 21436<br>123 274 | 21437<br>123 275 | 21438<br>123 276 | 21439<br>123 277 |
| C− | 21440<br>123 300 | 21441<br>123 301 | 21442<br>123 302 | 21443<br>123 303 | 21444<br>123 304 | 21445<br>123 305 | 21446<br>123 306 | 21447<br>123 307 | 21448<br>123 310 | 21449<br>123 311 | 21450<br>123 312 | 21451<br>123 313 | 21452<br>123 314 | 21453<br>123 315 | 21454<br>123 316 | 21455<br>123 317 |
| D− | 21456<br>123 320 | 21457<br>123 321 | 21458<br>123 322 | 21459<br>123 323 | 21460<br>123 324 | 21461<br>123 325 | 21462<br>123 326 | 21463<br>123 327 | 21464<br>123 330 | 21465<br>123 331 | 21466<br>123 332 | 21467<br>123 333 | 21468<br>123 334 | 21469<br>123 335 | 21470<br>123 336 | 21471<br>123 337 |
| E− | 21472<br>123 340 | 21473<br>123 341 | 21474<br>123 342 | 21475<br>123 343 | 21476<br>123 344 | 21477<br>123 345 | 21478<br>123 346 | 21479<br>123 347 | 21480<br>123 350 | 21481<br>123 351 | 21482<br>123 352 | 21483<br>123 353 | 21484<br>123 354 | 21485<br>123 355 | 21486<br>123 356 | 21487<br>123 357 |
| F− | 21488<br>123 360 | 21489<br>123 361 | 21490<br>123 362 | 21491<br>123 363 | 21492<br>123 364 | 21493<br>123 365 | 21494<br>123 366 | 21495<br>123 367 | 21496<br>123 370 | 21497<br>123 371 | 21498<br>123 372 | 21499<br>123 373 | 21500<br>123 374 | 21501<br>123 375 | 21502<br>123 376 | 21503<br>123 377 |

### FIRST HEX DIGIT

| | −0 | −1 | −2 | −3 | −4 | −5 | −6 | −7 | −8 | −9 | −A | −B | −C | −D | −E | −F |
|---|---|---|---|---|---|---|---|---|---|---|---|---|---|---|---|---|
| **0-** | 21504<br>21504<br>124 000 | 21505<br>21505<br>124 001 | 21506<br>21506<br>124 002 | 21507<br>21507<br>124 003 | 21508<br>21508<br>124 004 | 21509<br>21509<br>124 005 | 21510<br>21510<br>124 006 | 21511<br>21511<br>124 007 | 21512<br>21512<br>124 010 | 21513<br>21513<br>124 011 | 21514<br>21514<br>124 012 | 21515<br>21515<br>124 013 | 21516<br>21516<br>124 014 | 21517<br>21517<br>124 015 | 21518<br>21518<br>124 016 | 21519<br>21519<br>124 017 |
| **1-** | 21520<br>21520<br>124 020 | 21521<br>21521<br>124 021 | 21522<br>21522<br>124 022 | 21523<br>21523<br>124 023 | 21524<br>21524<br>124 024 | 21525<br>21525<br>124 025 | 21526<br>21526<br>124 026 | 21527<br>21527<br>124 027 | 21528<br>21528<br>124 030 | 21529<br>21529<br>124 031 | 21530<br>21530<br>124 032 | 21531<br>21531<br>124 033 | 21532<br>21532<br>124 034 | 21533<br>21533<br>124 035 | 21534<br>21534<br>124 036 | 21535<br>21535<br>124 037 |
| **2-** | 21536<br>21536<br>124 040 | 21537<br>21537<br>124 041 | 21538<br>21538<br>124 042 | 21539<br>21539<br>124 043 | 21540<br>21540<br>124 044 | 21541<br>21541<br>124 045 | 21542<br>21542<br>124 046 | 21543<br>21543<br>124 047 | 21544<br>21544<br>124 050 | 21545<br>21545<br>124 051 | 21546<br>21546<br>124 052 | 21547<br>21547<br>124 053 | 21548<br>21548<br>124 054 | 21549<br>21549<br>124 055 | 21550<br>21550<br>124 056 | 21551<br>21551<br>124 057 |
| **3-** | 21552<br>21552<br>124 060 | 21553<br>21553<br>124 061 | 21554<br>21554<br>124 062 | 21555<br>21555<br>124 063 | 21556<br>21556<br>124 064 | 21557<br>21557<br>124 065 | 21558<br>21558<br>124 066 | 21559<br>21559<br>124 067 | 21560<br>21560<br>124 070 | 21561<br>21561<br>124 071 | 21562<br>21562<br>124 072 | 21563<br>21563<br>124 073 | 21564<br>21564<br>124 074 | 21565<br>21565<br>124 075 | 21566<br>21566<br>124 076 | 21567<br>21567<br>124 077 |
| **4-** | 21568<br>21568<br>124 100 | 21569<br>21569<br>124 101 | 21570<br>21570<br>124 102 | 21571<br>21571<br>124 103 | 21572<br>21572<br>124 104 | 21573<br>21573<br>124 105 | 21574<br>21574<br>124 106 | 21575<br>21575<br>124 107 | 21576<br>21576<br>124 110 | 21577<br>21577<br>124 111 | 21578<br>21578<br>124 112 | 21579<br>21579<br>124 113 | 21580<br>21580<br>124 114 | 21581<br>21581<br>124 115 | 21582<br>21582<br>124 116 | 21583<br>21583<br>124 117 |
| **5-** | 21584<br>21584<br>124 120 | 21585<br>21585<br>124 121 | 21586<br>21586<br>124 122 | 21587<br>21587<br>124 123 | 21588<br>21588<br>124 124 | 21589<br>21589<br>124 125 | 21590<br>21590<br>124 126 | 21591<br>21591<br>124 127 | 21592<br>21592<br>124 130 | 21593<br>21593<br>124 131 | 21594<br>21594<br>124 132 | 21595<br>21595<br>124 133 | 21596<br>21596<br>124 134 | 21597<br>21597<br>124 135 | 21598<br>21598<br>124 136 | 21599<br>21599<br>124 137 |
| **6-** | 21600<br>21600<br>124 140 | 21601<br>21601<br>124 141 | 21602<br>21602<br>124 142 | 21603<br>21603<br>124 143 | 21604<br>21604<br>124 144 | 21605<br>21605<br>124 145 | 21606<br>21606<br>124 146 | 21607<br>21607<br>124 147 | 21608<br>21608<br>124 150 | 21609<br>21609<br>124 151 | 21610<br>21610<br>124 152 | 21611<br>21611<br>124 153 | 21612<br>21612<br>124 154 | 21613<br>21613<br>124 155 | 21614<br>21614<br>124 156 | 21615<br>21615<br>124 157 |
| **7-** | 21616<br>21616<br>124 160 | 21617<br>21617<br>124 161 | 21618<br>21618<br>124 162 | 21619<br>21619<br>124 163 | 21620<br>21620<br>124 164 | 21621<br>21621<br>124 165 | 21622<br>21622<br>124 166 | 21623<br>21623<br>124 167 | 21624<br>21624<br>124 170 | 21625<br>21625<br>124 171 | 21626<br>21626<br>124 172 | 21627<br>21627<br>124 173 | 21628<br>21628<br>124 174 | 21629<br>21629<br>124 175 | 21630<br>21630<br>124 176 | 21631<br>21631<br>124 177 |
| **8-** | 21632<br>21632<br>124 200 | 21633<br>21633<br>124 201 | 21634<br>21634<br>124 202 | 21635<br>21635<br>124 203 | 21636<br>21636<br>124 204 | 21637<br>21637<br>124 205 | 21638<br>21638<br>124 206 | 21639<br>21639<br>124 207 | 21640<br>21640<br>124 210 | 21641<br>21641<br>124 211 | 21642<br>21642<br>124 212 | 21643<br>21643<br>124 213 | 21644<br>21644<br>124 214 | 21645<br>21645<br>124 215 | 21646<br>21646<br>124 216 | 21647<br>21647<br>124 217 |
| **9-** | 21648<br>21648<br>124 220 | 21649<br>21649<br>124 221 | 21650<br>21650<br>124 222 | 21651<br>21651<br>124 223 | 21652<br>21652<br>124 224 | 21653<br>21653<br>124 225 | 21654<br>21654<br>124 226 | 21655<br>21655<br>124 227 | 21656<br>21656<br>124 230 | 21657<br>21657<br>124 231 | 21658<br>21658<br>124 232 | 21659<br>21659<br>124 233 | 21660<br>21660<br>124 234 | 21661<br>21661<br>124 235 | 21662<br>21662<br>124 236 | 21663<br>21663<br>124 237 |
| **A-** | 21664<br>21664<br>124 240 | 21665<br>21665<br>124 241 | 21666<br>21666<br>124 242 | 21667<br>21667<br>124 243 | 21668<br>21668<br>124 244 | 21669<br>21669<br>124 245 | 21670<br>21670<br>124 246 | 21671<br>21671<br>124 247 | 21672<br>21672<br>124 250 | 21673<br>21673<br>124 251 | 21674<br>21674<br>124 252 | 21675<br>21675<br>124 253 | 21676<br>21676<br>124 254 | 21677<br>21677<br>124 255 | 21678<br>21678<br>124 256 | 21679<br>21679<br>124 257 |
| **B-** | 21680<br>21680<br>124 260 | 21681<br>21681<br>124 261 | 21682<br>21682<br>124 262 | 21683<br>21683<br>124 263 | 21684<br>21684<br>124 264 | 21685<br>21685<br>124 265 | 21686<br>21686<br>124 266 | 21687<br>21687<br>124 267 | 21688<br>21688<br>124 270 | 21689<br>21689<br>124 271 | 21690<br>21690<br>124 272 | 21691<br>21691<br>124 273 | 21692<br>21692<br>124 274 | 21693<br>21693<br>124 275 | 21694<br>21694<br>124 276 | 21695<br>21695<br>124 277 |
| **C-** | 21696<br>21696<br>124 300 | 21697<br>21697<br>124 301 | 21698<br>21698<br>124 302 | 21699<br>21699<br>124 303 | 21700<br>21700<br>124 304 | 21701<br>21701<br>124 305 | 21702<br>21702<br>124 306 | 21703<br>21703<br>124 307 | 21704<br>21704<br>124 310 | 21705<br>21705<br>124 311 | 21706<br>21706<br>124 312 | 21707<br>21707<br>124 313 | 21708<br>21708<br>124 314 | 21709<br>21709<br>124 315 | 21710<br>21710<br>124 316 | 21711<br>21711<br>124 317 |
| **D-** | 21712<br>21712<br>124 320 | 21713<br>21713<br>124 321 | 21714<br>21714<br>124 322 | 21715<br>21715<br>124 323 | 21716<br>21716<br>124 324 | 21717<br>21717<br>124 325 | 21718<br>21718<br>124 326 | 21719<br>21719<br>124 327 | 21720<br>21720<br>124 330 | 21721<br>21721<br>124 331 | 21722<br>21722<br>124 332 | 21723<br>21723<br>124 333 | 21724<br>21724<br>124 334 | 21725<br>21725<br>124 335 | 21726<br>21726<br>124 336 | 21727<br>21727<br>124 337 |
| **E-** | 21728<br>21728<br>124 340 | 21729<br>21729<br>124 341 | 21730<br>21730<br>124 342 | 21731<br>21731<br>124 343 | 21732<br>21732<br>124 344 | 21733<br>21733<br>124 345 | 21734<br>21734<br>124 346 | 21735<br>21735<br>124 347 | 21736<br>21736<br>124 350 | 21737<br>21737<br>124 351 | 21738<br>21738<br>124 352 | 21739<br>21739<br>124 353 | 21740<br>21740<br>124 354 | 21741<br>21741<br>124 355 | 21742<br>21742<br>124 356 | 21743<br>21743<br>124 357 |
| **F-** | 21744<br>21744<br>124 360 | 21745<br>21745<br>124 361 | 21746<br>21746<br>124 362 | 21747<br>21747<br>124 363 | 21748<br>21748<br>124 364 | 21749<br>21749<br>124 365 | 21750<br>21750<br>124 366 | 21751<br>21751<br>124 367 | 21752<br>21752<br>124 370 | 21753<br>21753<br>124 371 | 21754<br>21754<br>124 372 | 21755<br>21755<br>124 373 | 21756<br>21756<br>124 374 | 21757<br>21757<br>124 375 | 21758<br>21758<br>124 376 | 21759<br>21759<br>124 377 |

**SECOND HEX DIGIT** (left axis)

DECIMAL →
DECIMAL →
OCTAL →

 DECIMAL  21504   **BINARY**  0101 0100   **DECIMAL**  21504   **HEXADECIMAL** ⬡ 54   **OCTAL**  124 000

**FOURTH HEX DIGIT** → ⬡ ← **THIRD HEX DIGIT**

## FIRST HEX DIGIT

| 2 | −0 | −1 | −2 | −3 | −4 | −5 | −6 | −7 | −8 | −9 | −A | −B | −C | −D | −E | −F |
|---|---|---|---|---|---|---|---|---|---|---|---|---|---|---|---|---|
| 0− | 21760<br>21760<br>125 000 | 21761<br>21761<br>125 001 | 21762<br>21762<br>125 002 | 21763<br>21763<br>125 003 | 21764<br>21764<br>125 004 | 21765<br>21765<br>125 005 | 21766<br>21766<br>125 006 | 21767<br>21767<br>125 007 | 21768<br>21768<br>125 010 | 21769<br>21769<br>125 011 | 21770<br>21770<br>125 012 | 21771<br>21771<br>125 013 | 21772<br>21772<br>125 014 | 21773<br>21773<br>125 015 | 21774<br>21774<br>125 016 | 21775<br>21775<br>125 017 |
| 1− | 21776<br>21776<br>125 020 | 21777<br>21777<br>125 021 | 21778<br>21778<br>125 022 | 21779<br>21779<br>125 023 | 21780<br>21780<br>125 024 | 21781<br>21781<br>125 025 | 21782<br>21782<br>125 026 | 21783<br>21783<br>125 027 | 21784<br>21784<br>125 030 | 21785<br>21785<br>125 031 | 21786<br>21786<br>125 032 | 21787<br>21787<br>125 033 | 21788<br>21788<br>125 034 | 21789<br>21789<br>125 035 | 21790<br>21790<br>125 036 | 21791<br>21791<br>125 037 |
| 2− | 21792<br>21792<br>125 040 | 21793<br>21793<br>125 041 | 21794<br>21794<br>125 042 | 21795<br>21795<br>125 043 | 21796<br>21796<br>125 044 | 21797<br>21797<br>125 045 | 21798<br>21798<br>125 046 | 21799<br>21799<br>125 047 | 21800<br>21800<br>125 050 | 21801<br>21801<br>125 051 | 21802<br>21802<br>125 052 | 21803<br>21803<br>125 053 | 21804<br>21804<br>125 054 | 21805<br>21805<br>125 055 | 21806<br>21806<br>125 056 | 21807<br>21807<br>125 057 |
| 3− | 21808<br>21808<br>125 060 | 21809<br>21809<br>125 061 | 21810<br>21810<br>125 062 | 21811<br>21811<br>125 063 | 21812<br>21812<br>125 064 | 21813<br>21813<br>125 065 | 21814<br>21814<br>125 066 | 21815<br>21815<br>125 067 | 21816<br>21816<br>125 070 | 21817<br>21817<br>125 071 | 21818<br>21818<br>125 072 | 21819<br>21819<br>125 073 | 21820<br>21820<br>125 074 | 21821<br>21821<br>125 075 | 21822<br>21822<br>125 076 | 21823<br>21823<br>125 077 |
| 4− | 21824<br>21824<br>125 100 | 21825<br>21825<br>125 101 | 21826<br>21826<br>125 102 | 21827<br>21827<br>125 103 | 21828<br>21828<br>125 104 | 21829<br>21829<br>125 105 | 21830<br>21830<br>125 106 | 21831<br>21831<br>125 107 | 21832<br>21832<br>125 110 | 21833<br>21833<br>125 111 | 21834<br>21834<br>125 112 | 21835<br>21835<br>125 113 | 21836<br>21836<br>125 114 | 21837<br>21837<br>125 115 | 21838<br>21838<br>125 116 | 21839<br>21839<br>125 117 |
| 5− | 21840<br>21840<br>125 120 | 21841<br>21841<br>125 121 | 21842<br>21842<br>125 122 | 21843<br>21843<br>125 123 | 21844<br>21844<br>125 124 | 21845<br>21845<br>125 125 | 21846<br>21846<br>125 126 | 21847<br>21847<br>125 127 | 21848<br>21848<br>125 130 | 21849<br>21849<br>125 131 | 21850<br>21850<br>125 132 | 21851<br>21851<br>125 133 | 21852<br>21852<br>125 134 | 21853<br>21853<br>125 135 | 21854<br>21854<br>125 136 | 21855<br>21855<br>125 137 |
| 6− | 21856<br>21856<br>125 140 | 21857<br>21857<br>125 141 | 21858<br>21858<br>125 142 | 21859<br>21859<br>125 143 | 21860<br>21860<br>125 144 | 21861<br>21861<br>125 145 | 21862<br>21862<br>125 146 | 21863<br>21863<br>125 147 | 21864<br>21864<br>125 150 | 21865<br>21865<br>125 151 | 21866<br>21866<br>125 152 | 21867<br>21867<br>125 153 | 21868<br>21868<br>125 154 | 21869<br>21869<br>125 155 | 21870<br>21870<br>125 156 | 21871<br>21871<br>125 157 |
| 7− | 21872<br>21872<br>125 160 | 21873<br>21873<br>125 161 | 21874<br>21874<br>125 162 | 21875<br>21875<br>125 163 | 21876<br>21876<br>125 164 | 21877<br>21877<br>125 165 | 21878<br>21878<br>125 166 | 21879<br>21879<br>125 167 | 21880<br>21880<br>125 170 | 21881<br>21881<br>125 171 | 21882<br>21882<br>125 172 | 21883<br>21883<br>125 173 | 21884<br>21884<br>125 174 | 21885<br>21885<br>125 175 | 21886<br>21886<br>125 176 | 21887<br>21887<br>125 177 |
| 8− | 21888<br>21888<br>125 200 | 21889<br>21889<br>125 201 | 21890<br>21890<br>125 202 | 21891<br>21891<br>125 203 | 21892<br>21892<br>125 204 | 21893<br>21893<br>125 205 | 21894<br>21894<br>125 206 | 21895<br>21895<br>125 207 | 21896<br>21896<br>125 210 | 21897<br>21897<br>125 211 | 21898<br>21898<br>125 212 | 21899<br>21899<br>125 213 | 21900<br>21900<br>125 214 | 21901<br>21901<br>125 215 | 21902<br>21902<br>125 216 | 21903<br>21903<br>125 217 |
| 9− | 21904<br>21904<br>125 220 | 21905<br>21905<br>125 221 | 21906<br>21906<br>125 222 | 21907<br>21907<br>125 223 | 21908<br>21908<br>125 224 | 21909<br>21909<br>125 225 | 21910<br>21910<br>125 226 | 21911<br>21911<br>125 227 | 21912<br>21912<br>125 230 | 21913<br>21913<br>125 231 | 21914<br>21914<br>125 232 | 21915<br>21915<br>125 233 | 21916<br>21916<br>125 234 | 21917<br>21917<br>125 235 | 21918<br>21918<br>125 236 | 21919<br>21919<br>125 237 |
| A− | 21920<br>21920<br>125 240 | 21921<br>21921<br>125 241 | 21922<br>21922<br>125 242 | 21923<br>21923<br>125 243 | 21924<br>21924<br>125 244 | 21925<br>21925<br>125 245 | 21926<br>21926<br>125 246 | 21927<br>21927<br>125 247 | 21928<br>21928<br>125 250 | 21929<br>21929<br>125 251 | 21930<br>21930<br>125 252 | 21931<br>21931<br>125 253 | 21932<br>21932<br>125 254 | 21933<br>21933<br>125 255 | 21934<br>21934<br>125 256 | 21935<br>21935<br>125 257 |
| B− | 21936<br>21936<br>125 260 | 21937<br>21937<br>125 261 | 21938<br>21938<br>125 262 | 21939<br>21939<br>125 263 | 21940<br>21940<br>125 264 | 21941<br>21941<br>125 265 | 21942<br>21942<br>125 266 | 21943<br>21943<br>125 267 | 21944<br>21944<br>125 270 | 21945<br>21945<br>125 271 | 21946<br>21946<br>125 272 | 21947<br>21947<br>125 273 | 21948<br>21948<br>125 274 | 21949<br>21949<br>125 275 | 21950<br>21950<br>125 276 | 21951<br>21951<br>125 277 |
| C− | 21952<br>21952<br>125 300 | 21953<br>21953<br>125 301 | 21954<br>21954<br>125 302 | 21955<br>21955<br>125 303 | 21956<br>21956<br>125 304 | 21957<br>21957<br>125 305 | 21958<br>21958<br>125 306 | 21959<br>21959<br>125 307 | 21960<br>21960<br>125 310 | 21961<br>21961<br>125 311 | 21962<br>21962<br>125 312 | 21963<br>21963<br>125 313 | 21964<br>21964<br>125 314 | 21965<br>21965<br>125 315 | 21966<br>21966<br>125 316 | 21967<br>21967<br>125 317 |
| D− | 21968<br>21968<br>125 320 | 21969<br>21969<br>125 321 | 21970<br>21970<br>125 322 | 21971<br>21971<br>125 323 | 21972<br>21972<br>125 324 | 21973<br>21973<br>125 325 | 21974<br>21974<br>125 326 | 21975<br>21975<br>125 327 | 21976<br>21976<br>125 330 | 21977<br>21977<br>125 331 | 21978<br>21978<br>125 332 | 21979<br>21979<br>125 333 | 21980<br>21980<br>125 334 | 21981<br>21981<br>125 335 | 21982<br>21982<br>125 336 | 21983<br>21983<br>125 337 |
| E− | 21984<br>21984<br>125 340 | 21985<br>21985<br>125 341 | 21986<br>21986<br>125 342 | 21987<br>21987<br>125 343 | 21988<br>21988<br>125 344 | 21989<br>21989<br>125 345 | 21990<br>21990<br>125 346 | 21991<br>21991<br>125 347 | 21992<br>21992<br>125 350 | 21993<br>21993<br>125 351 | 21994<br>21994<br>125 352 | 21995<br>21995<br>125 353 | 21996<br>21996<br>125 354 | 21997<br>21997<br>125 355 | 21998<br>21998<br>125 356 | 21999<br>21999<br>125 357 |
| F− | 22000<br>22000<br>125 360 | 22001<br>22001<br>125 361 | 22002<br>22002<br>125 362 | 22003<br>22003<br>125 363 | 22004<br>22004<br>125 364 | 22005<br>22005<br>125 365 | 22006<br>22006<br>125 366 | 22007<br>22007<br>125 367 | 22008<br>22008<br>125 370 | 22009<br>22009<br>125 371 | 22010<br>22010<br>125 372 | 22011<br>22011<br>125 373 | 22012<br>22012<br>125 374 | 22013<br>22013<br>125 375 | 22014<br>22014<br>125 376 | 22015<br>22015<br>125 377 |

SECOND HEX DIGIT

DECIMAL · DECIMAL · OCTAL

## ⬡2  FIRST HEX DIGIT

| SECOND HEX DIGIT | -0 | -1 | -2 | -3 | -4 | -5 | -6 | -7 | -8 | -9 | -A | -B | -C | -D | -E | -F |
|---|---|---|---|---|---|---|---|---|---|---|---|---|---|---|---|---|
| 0- | 22016<br>22016<br>126 000 | 22017<br>22017<br>126 001 | 22018<br>22018<br>126 002 | 22019<br>22019<br>126 003 | 22020<br>22020<br>126 004 | 22021<br>22021<br>126 005 | 22022<br>22022<br>126 006 | 22023<br>22023<br>126 007 | 22024<br>22024<br>126 010 | 22025<br>22025<br>126 011 | 22026<br>22026<br>126 012 | 22027<br>22027<br>126 013 | 22028<br>22028<br>126 014 | 22029<br>22029<br>126 015 | 22030<br>22030<br>126 016 | 22031<br>22031<br>126 017 |
| 1- | 22032<br>22032<br>126 020 | 22033<br>22033<br>126 021 | 22034<br>22034<br>126 022 | 22035<br>22035<br>126 023 | 22036<br>22036<br>126 024 | 22037<br>22037<br>126 025 | 22038<br>22038<br>126 026 | 22039<br>22039<br>126 027 | 22040<br>22040<br>126 030 | 22041<br>22041<br>126 031 | 22042<br>22042<br>126 032 | 22043<br>22043<br>126 033 | 22044<br>22044<br>126 034 | 22045<br>22045<br>126 035 | 22046<br>22046<br>126 036 | 22047<br>22047<br>126 037 |
| 2- | 22048<br>22048<br>126 040 | 22049<br>22049<br>126 041 | 22050<br>22050<br>126 042 | 22051<br>22051<br>126 043 | 22052<br>22052<br>126 044 | 22053<br>22053<br>126 045 | 22054<br>22054<br>126 046 | 22055<br>22055<br>126 047 | 22056<br>22056<br>126 050 | 22057<br>22057<br>126 051 | 22058<br>22058<br>126 052 | 22059<br>22059<br>126 053 | 22060<br>22060<br>126 054 | 22061<br>22061<br>126 055 | 22062<br>22062<br>126 056 | 22063<br>22063<br>126 057 |
| 3- | 22064<br>22064<br>126 060 | 22065<br>22065<br>126 061 | 22066<br>22066<br>126 062 | 22067<br>22067<br>126 063 | 22068<br>22068<br>126 064 | 22069<br>22069<br>126 065 | 22070<br>22070<br>126 066 | 22071<br>22071<br>126 067 | 22072<br>22072<br>126 070 | 22073<br>22073<br>126 071 | 22074<br>22074<br>126 072 | 22075<br>22075<br>126 073 | 22076<br>22076<br>126 074 | 22077<br>22077<br>126 075 | 22078<br>22078<br>126 076 | 22079<br>22079<br>126 077 |
| 4- | 22080<br>22080<br>126 100 | 22081<br>22081<br>126 101 | 22082<br>22082<br>126 102 | 22083<br>22083<br>126 103 | 22084<br>22084<br>126 104 | 22085<br>22085<br>126 105 | 22086<br>22086<br>126 106 | 22087<br>22087<br>126 107 | 22088<br>22088<br>126 110 | 22089<br>22089<br>126 111 | 22090<br>22090<br>126 112 | 22091<br>22091<br>126 113 | 22092<br>22092<br>126 114 | 22093<br>22093<br>126 115 | 22094<br>22094<br>126 116 | 22095<br>22095<br>126 117 |
| 5- | 22096<br>22096<br>126 120 | 22097<br>22097<br>126 121 | 22098<br>22098<br>126 122 | 22099<br>22099<br>126 123 | 22100<br>22100<br>126 124 | 22101<br>22101<br>126 125 | 22102<br>22102<br>126 126 | 22103<br>22103<br>126 127 | 22104<br>22104<br>126 130 | 22105<br>22105<br>126 131 | 22106<br>22106<br>126 132 | 22107<br>22107<br>126 133 | 22108<br>22108<br>126 134 | 22109<br>22109<br>126 135 | 22110<br>22110<br>126 136 | 22111<br>22111<br>126 137 |
| 6- | 22112<br>22112<br>126 140 | 22113<br>22113<br>126 141 | 22114<br>22114<br>126 142 | 22115<br>22115<br>126 143 | 22116<br>22116<br>126 144 | 22117<br>22117<br>126 145 | 22118<br>22118<br>126 146 | 22119<br>22119<br>126 147 | 22120<br>22120<br>126 150 | 22121<br>22121<br>126 151 | 22122<br>22122<br>126 152 | 22123<br>22123<br>126 153 | 22124<br>22124<br>126 154 | 22125<br>22125<br>126 155 | 22126<br>22126<br>126 156 | 22127<br>22127<br>126 157 |
| 7- | 22128<br>22128<br>126 160 | 22129<br>22129<br>126 161 | 22130<br>22130<br>126 162 | 22131<br>22131<br>126 163 | 22132<br>22132<br>126 164 | 22133<br>22133<br>126 165 | 22134<br>22134<br>126 166 | 22135<br>22135<br>126 167 | 22136<br>22136<br>126 170 | 22137<br>22137<br>126 171 | 22138<br>22138<br>126 172 | 22139<br>22139<br>126 173 | 22140<br>22140<br>126 174 | 22141<br>22141<br>126 175 | 22142<br>22142<br>126 176 | 22143<br>22143<br>126 177 |
| 8- | 22144<br>22144<br>126 200 | 22145<br>22145<br>126 201 | 22146<br>22146<br>126 202 | 22147<br>22147<br>126 203 | 22148<br>22148<br>126 204 | 22149<br>22149<br>126 205 | 22150<br>22150<br>126 206 | 22151<br>22151<br>126 207 | 22152<br>22152<br>126 210 | 22153<br>22153<br>126 211 | 22154<br>22154<br>126 212 | 22155<br>22155<br>126 213 | 22156<br>22156<br>126 214 | 22157<br>22157<br>126 215 | 22158<br>22158<br>126 216 | 22159<br>22159<br>126 217 |
| 9- | 22160<br>22160<br>126 220 | 22161<br>22161<br>126 221 | 22162<br>22162<br>126 222 | 22163<br>22163<br>126 223 | 22164<br>22164<br>126 224 | 22165<br>22165<br>126 225 | 22166<br>22166<br>126 226 | 22167<br>22167<br>126 227 | 22168<br>22168<br>126 230 | 22169<br>22169<br>126 231 | 22170<br>22170<br>126 232 | 22171<br>22171<br>126 233 | 22172<br>22172<br>126 234 | 22173<br>22173<br>126 235 | 22174<br>22174<br>126 236 | 22175<br>22175<br>126 237 |
| A- | 22176<br>22176<br>126 240 | 22177<br>22177<br>126 241 | 22178<br>22178<br>126 242 | 22179<br>22179<br>126 243 | 22180<br>22180<br>126 244 | 22181<br>22181<br>126 245 | 22182<br>22182<br>126 246 | 22183<br>22183<br>126 247 | 22184<br>22184<br>126 250 | 22185<br>22185<br>126 251 | 22186<br>22186<br>126 252 | 22187<br>22187<br>126 253 | 22188<br>22188<br>126 254 | 22189<br>22189<br>126 255 | 22190<br>22190<br>126 256 | 22191<br>22191<br>126 257 |
| B- | 22192<br>22192<br>126 260 | 22193<br>22193<br>126 261 | 22194<br>22194<br>126 262 | 22195<br>22195<br>126 263 | 22196<br>22196<br>126 264 | 22197<br>22197<br>126 265 | 22198<br>22198<br>126 266 | 22199<br>22199<br>126 267 | 22200<br>22200<br>126 270 | 22201<br>22201<br>126 271 | 22202<br>22202<br>126 272 | 22203<br>22203<br>126 273 | 22204<br>22204<br>126 274 | 22205<br>22205<br>126 275 | 22206<br>22206<br>126 276 | 22207<br>22207<br>126 277 |
| C- | 22208<br>22208<br>126 300 | 22209<br>22209<br>126 301 | 22210<br>22210<br>126 302 | 22211<br>22211<br>126 303 | 22212<br>22212<br>126 304 | 22213<br>22213<br>126 305 | 22214<br>22214<br>126 306 | 22215<br>22215<br>126 307 | 22216<br>22216<br>126 310 | 22217<br>22217<br>126 311 | 22218<br>22218<br>126 312 | 22219<br>22219<br>126 313 | 22220<br>22220<br>126 314 | 22221<br>22221<br>126 315 | 22222<br>22222<br>126 316 | 22223<br>22223<br>126 317 |
| D- | 22224<br>22224<br>126 320 | 22225<br>22225<br>126 321 | 22226<br>22226<br>126 322 | 22227<br>22227<br>126 323 | 22228<br>22228<br>126 324 | 22229<br>22229<br>126 325 | 22230<br>22230<br>126 326 | 22231<br>22231<br>126 327 | 22232<br>22232<br>126 330 | 22233<br>22233<br>126 331 | 22234<br>22234<br>126 332 | 22235<br>22235<br>126 333 | 22236<br>22236<br>126 334 | 22237<br>22237<br>126 335 | 22238<br>22238<br>126 336 | 22239<br>22239<br>126 337 |
| E- | 22240<br>22240<br>126 340 | 22241<br>22241<br>126 341 | 22242<br>22242<br>126 342 | 22243<br>22243<br>126 343 | 22244<br>22244<br>126 344 | 22245<br>22245<br>126 345 | 22246<br>22246<br>126 346 | 22247<br>22247<br>126 347 | 22248<br>22248<br>126 350 | 22249<br>22249<br>126 351 | 22250<br>22250<br>126 352 | 22251<br>22251<br>126 353 | 22252<br>22252<br>126 354 | 22253<br>22253<br>126 355 | 22254<br>22254<br>126 356 | 22255<br>22255<br>126 357 |
| F- | 22256<br>22256<br>126 360 | 22257<br>22257<br>126 361 | 22258<br>22258<br>126 362 | 22259<br>22259<br>126 363 | 22260<br>22260<br>126 364 | 22261<br>22261<br>126 365 | 22262<br>22262<br>126 366 | 22263<br>22263<br>126 367 | 22264<br>22264<br>126 370 | 22265<br>22265<br>126 371 | 22266<br>22266<br>126 372 | 22267<br>22267<br>126 373 | 22268<br>22268<br>126 374 | 22269<br>22269<br>126 375 | 22270<br>22270<br>126 376 | 22271<br>22271<br>126 377 |

Legend (right side): DECIMAL → , ⌘ DECIMAL → , OCTAL →

 DECIMAL  22016   BINARY  0101 0110   DECIMAL  22016   HEXADECIMAL ⬡ 56   OCTAL  126 000

FOURTH HEX DIGIT →  ⬡  ← THIRD HEX DIGIT

| 2 | −0 | −1 | −2 | −3 | −4 | −5 | −6 | −7 | −8 | −9 | −A | −B | −C | −D | −E | −F |
|---|---|---|---|---|---|---|---|---|---|---|---|---|---|---|---|---|
| **0-** | 22272 / 127 000 | 22273 / 127 001 | 22274 / 127 002 | 22275 / 127 003 | 22276 / 127 004 | 22277 / 127 005 | 22278 / 127 006 | 22279 / 127 007 | 22280 / 127 010 | 22281 / 127 011 | 22282 / 127 012 | 22283 / 127 013 | 22284 / 127 014 | 22285 / 127 015 | 22286 / 127 016 | 22287 / 127 017 |
| **1-** | 22288 / 127 020 | 22289 / 127 021 | 22290 / 127 022 | 22291 / 127 023 | 22292 / 127 024 | 22293 / 127 025 | 22294 / 127 026 | 22295 / 127 027 | 22296 / 127 030 | 22297 / 127 031 | 22298 / 127 032 | 22299 / 127 033 | 22300 / 127 034 | 22301 / 127 035 | 22302 / 127 036 | 22303 / 127 037 |
| **2-** | 22304 / 127 040 | 22305 / 127 041 | 22306 / 127 042 | 22307 / 127 043 | 22308 / 127 044 | 22309 / 127 045 | 22310 / 127 046 | 22311 / 127 047 | 22312 / 127 050 | 22313 / 127 051 | 22314 / 127 052 | 22315 / 127 053 | 22316 / 127 054 | 22317 / 127 055 | 22318 / 127 056 | 22319 / 127 057 |
| **3-** | 22320 / 127 060 | 22321 / 127 061 | 22322 / 127 062 | 22323 / 127 063 | 22324 / 127 064 | 22325 / 127 065 | 22326 / 127 066 | 22327 / 127 067 | 22328 / 127 070 | 22329 / 127 071 | 22330 / 127 072 | 22331 / 127 073 | 22332 / 127 074 | 22333 / 127 075 | 22334 / 127 076 | 22335 / 127 077 |
| **4-** | 22336 / 127 100 | 22337 / 127 101 | 22338 / 127 102 | 22339 / 127 103 | 22340 / 127 104 | 22341 / 127 105 | 22342 / 127 106 | 22343 / 127 107 | 22344 / 127 110 | 22345 / 127 111 | 22346 / 127 112 | 22347 / 127 113 | 22348 / 127 114 | 22349 / 127 115 | 22350 / 127 116 | 22351 / 127 117 |
| **5-** | 22352 / 127 120 | 22353 / 127 121 | 22354 / 127 122 | 22355 / 127 123 | 22356 / 127 124 | 22357 / 127 125 | 22358 / 127 126 | 22359 / 127 127 | 22360 / 127 130 | 22361 / 127 131 | 22362 / 127 132 | 22363 / 127 133 | 22364 / 127 134 | 22365 / 127 135 | 22366 / 127 136 | 22367 / 127 137 |
| **6-** | 22368 / 127 140 | 22369 / 127 141 | 22370 / 127 142 | 22371 / 127 143 | 22372 / 127 144 | 22373 / 127 145 | 22374 / 127 146 | 22375 / 127 147 | 22376 / 127 150 | 22377 / 127 151 | 22378 / 127 152 | 22379 / 127 153 | 22380 / 127 154 | 22381 / 127 155 | 22382 / 127 156 | 22383 / 127 157 |
| **7-** | 22384 / 127 160 | 22385 / 127 161 | 22386 / 127 162 | 22387 / 127 163 | 22388 / 127 164 | 22389 / 127 165 | 22390 / 127 166 | 22391 / 127 167 | 22392 / 127 170 | 22393 / 127 171 | 22394 / 127 172 | 22395 / 127 173 | 22396 / 127 174 | 22397 / 127 175 | 22398 / 127 176 | 22399 / 127 177 |
| **8-** | 22400 / 127 200 | 22401 / 127 201 | 22402 / 127 202 | 22403 / 127 203 | 22404 / 127 204 | 22405 / 127 205 | 22406 / 127 206 | 22407 / 127 207 | 22408 / 127 210 | 22409 / 127 211 | 22410 / 127 212 | 22411 / 127 213 | 22412 / 127 214 | 22413 / 127 215 | 22414 / 127 216 | 22415 / 127 217 |
| **9-** | 22416 / 127 220 | 22417 / 127 221 | 22418 / 127 222 | 22419 / 127 223 | 22420 / 127 224 | 22421 / 127 225 | 22422 / 127 226 | 22423 / 127 227 | 22424 / 127 230 | 22425 / 127 231 | 22426 / 127 232 | 22427 / 127 233 | 22428 / 127 234 | 22429 / 127 235 | 22430 / 127 236 | 22431 / 127 237 |
| **A-** | 22432 / 127 240 | 22433 / 127 241 | 22434 / 127 242 | 22435 / 127 243 | 22436 / 127 244 | 22437 / 127 245 | 22438 / 127 246 | 22439 / 127 247 | 22440 / 127 250 | 22441 / 127 251 | 22442 / 127 252 | 22443 / 127 253 | 22444 / 127 254 | 22445 / 127 255 | 22446 / 127 256 | 22447 / 127 257 |
| **B-** | 22448 / 127 260 | 22449 / 127 261 | 22450 / 127 262 | 22451 / 127 263 | 22452 / 127 264 | 22453 / 127 265 | 22454 / 127 266 | 22455 / 127 267 | 22456 / 127 270 | 22457 / 127 271 | 22458 / 127 272 | 22459 / 127 273 | 22460 / 127 274 | 22461 / 127 275 | 22462 / 127 276 | 22463 / 127 277 |
| **C-** | 22464 / 127 300 | 22465 / 127 301 | 22466 / 127 302 | 22467 / 127 303 | 22468 / 127 304 | 22469 / 127 305 | 22470 / 127 306 | 22471 / 127 307 | 22472 / 127 310 | 22473 / 127 311 | 22474 / 127 312 | 22475 / 127 313 | 22476 / 127 314 | 22477 / 127 315 | 22478 / 127 316 | 22479 / 127 317 |
| **D-** | 22480 / 127 320 | 22481 / 127 321 | 22482 / 127 322 | 22483 / 127 323 | 22484 / 127 324 | 22485 / 127 325 | 22486 / 127 326 | 22487 / 127 327 | 22488 / 127 330 | 22489 / 127 331 | 22490 / 127 332 | 22491 / 127 333 | 22492 / 127 334 | 22493 / 127 335 | 22494 / 127 336 | 22495 / 127 337 |
| **E-** | 22496 / 127 340 | 22497 / 127 341 | 22498 / 127 342 | 22499 / 127 343 | 22500 / 127 344 | 22501 / 127 345 | 22502 / 127 346 | 22503 / 127 347 | 22504 / 127 350 | 22505 / 127 351 | 22506 / 127 352 | 22507 / 127 353 | 22508 / 127 354 | 22509 / 127 355 | 22510 / 127 356 | 22511 / 127 357 |
| **F-** | 22512 / 127 360 | 22513 / 127 361 | 22514 / 127 362 | 22515 / 127 363 | 22516 / 127 364 | 22517 / 127 365 | 22518 / 127 366 | 22519 / 127 367 | 22520 / 127 370 | 22521 / 127 371 | 22522 / 127 372 | 22523 / 127 373 | 22524 / 127 374 | 22525 / 127 375 | 22526 / 127 376 | 22527 / 127 377 |

## FIRST HEX DIGIT

(2)

|  | −0 | −1 | −2 | −3 | −4 | −5 | −6 | −7 | −8 | −9 | −A | −B | −C | −D | −E | −F |
|---|---|---|---|---|---|---|---|---|---|---|---|---|---|---|---|---|
| **0−** | 22528<br>22528<br>130 000 | 22529<br>22529<br>130 001 | 22530<br>22530<br>130 002 | 22531<br>22531<br>130 003 | 22532<br>22532<br>130 004 | 22533<br>22533<br>130 005 | 22534<br>22534<br>130 006 | 22535<br>22535<br>130 007 | 22536<br>22536<br>130 010 | 22537<br>22537<br>130 011 | 22538<br>22538<br>130 012 | 22539<br>22539<br>130 013 | 22540<br>22540<br>130 014 | 22541<br>22541<br>130 015 | 22542<br>22542<br>130 016 | 22543<br>22543<br>130 017 |
| **1−** | 22544<br>22544<br>130 020 | 22545<br>22545<br>130 021 | 22546<br>22546<br>130 022 | 22547<br>22547<br>130 023 | 22548<br>22548<br>130 024 | 22549<br>22549<br>130 025 | 22550<br>22550<br>130 026 | 22551<br>22551<br>130 027 | 22552<br>22552<br>130 030 | 22553<br>22553<br>130 031 | 22554<br>22554<br>130 032 | 22555<br>22555<br>130 033 | 22556<br>22556<br>130 034 | 22557<br>22557<br>130 035 | 22558<br>22558<br>130 036 | 22559<br>22559<br>130 037 |
| **2−** | 22560<br>22560<br>130 040 | 22561<br>22561<br>130 041 | 22562<br>22562<br>130 042 | 22563<br>22563<br>130 043 | 22564<br>22564<br>130 044 | 22565<br>22565<br>130 045 | 22566<br>22566<br>130 046 | 22567<br>22567<br>130 047 | 22568<br>22568<br>130 050 | 22569<br>22569<br>130 051 | 22570<br>22570<br>130 052 | 22571<br>22571<br>130 053 | 22572<br>22572<br>130 054 | 22573<br>22573<br>130 055 | 22574<br>22574<br>130 056 | 22575<br>22575<br>130 057 |
| **3−** | 22576<br>22576<br>130 060 | 22577<br>22577<br>130 061 | 22578<br>22578<br>130 062 | 22579<br>22579<br>130 063 | 22580<br>22580<br>130 064 | 22581<br>22581<br>130 065 | 22582<br>22582<br>130 066 | 22583<br>22583<br>130 067 | 22584<br>22584<br>130 070 | 22585<br>22585<br>130 071 | 22586<br>22586<br>130 072 | 22587<br>22587<br>130 073 | 22588<br>22588<br>130 074 | 22589<br>22589<br>130 075 | 22590<br>22590<br>130 076 | 22591<br>22591<br>130 077 |
| **4−** | 22592<br>22592<br>130 100 | 22593<br>22593<br>130 101 | 22594<br>22594<br>130 102 | 22595<br>22595<br>130 103 | 22596<br>22596<br>130 104 | 22597<br>22597<br>130 105 | 22598<br>22598<br>130 106 | 22599<br>22599<br>130 107 | 22600<br>22600<br>130 110 | 22601<br>22601<br>130 111 | 22602<br>22602<br>130 112 | 22603<br>22603<br>130 113 | 22604<br>22604<br>130 114 | 22605<br>22605<br>130 115 | 22606<br>22606<br>130 116 | 22607<br>22607<br>130 117 |
| **5−** | 22608<br>22608<br>130 120 | 22609<br>22609<br>130 121 | 22610<br>22610<br>130 122 | 22611<br>22611<br>130 123 | 22612<br>22612<br>130 124 | 22613<br>22613<br>130 125 | 22614<br>22614<br>130 126 | 22615<br>22615<br>130 127 | 22616<br>22616<br>130 130 | 22617<br>22617<br>130 131 | 22618<br>22618<br>130 132 | 22619<br>22619<br>130 133 | 22620<br>22620<br>130 134 | 22621<br>22621<br>130 135 | 22622<br>22622<br>130 136 | 22623<br>22623<br>130 137 |
| **6−** | 22624<br>22624<br>130 140 | 22625<br>22625<br>130 141 | 22626<br>22626<br>130 142 | 22627<br>22627<br>130 143 | 22628<br>22628<br>130 144 | 22629<br>22629<br>130 145 | 22630<br>22630<br>130 146 | 22631<br>22631<br>130 147 | 22632<br>22632<br>130 150 | 22633<br>22633<br>130 151 | 22634<br>22634<br>130 152 | 22635<br>22635<br>130 153 | 22636<br>22636<br>130 154 | 22637<br>22637<br>130 155 | 22638<br>22638<br>130 156 | 22639<br>22639<br>130 157 |
| **7−** | 22640<br>22640<br>130 160 | 22641<br>22641<br>130 161 | 22642<br>22642<br>130 162 | 22643<br>22643<br>130 163 | 22644<br>22644<br>130 164 | 22645<br>22645<br>130 165 | 22646<br>22646<br>130 166 | 22647<br>22647<br>130 167 | 22648<br>22648<br>130 170 | 22649<br>22649<br>130 171 | 22650<br>22650<br>130 172 | 22651<br>22651<br>130 173 | 22652<br>22652<br>130 174 | 22653<br>22653<br>130 175 | 22654<br>22654<br>130 176 | 22655<br>22655<br>130 177 |
| **8−** | 22656<br>22656<br>130 200 | 22657<br>22657<br>130 201 | 22658<br>22658<br>130 202 | 22659<br>22659<br>130 203 | 22660<br>22660<br>130 204 | 22661<br>22661<br>130 205 | 22662<br>22662<br>130 206 | 22663<br>22663<br>130 207 | 22664<br>22664<br>130 210 | 22665<br>22665<br>130 211 | 22666<br>22666<br>130 212 | 22667<br>22667<br>130 213 | 22668<br>22668<br>130 214 | 22669<br>22669<br>130 215 | 22670<br>22670<br>130 216 | 22671<br>22671<br>130 217 |
| **9−** | 22672<br>22672<br>130 220 | 22673<br>22673<br>130 221 | 22674<br>22674<br>130 222 | 22675<br>22675<br>130 223 | 22676<br>22676<br>130 224 | 22677<br>22677<br>130 225 | 22678<br>22678<br>130 226 | 22679<br>22679<br>130 227 | 22680<br>22680<br>130 230 | 22681<br>22681<br>130 231 | 22682<br>22682<br>130 232 | 22683<br>22683<br>130 233 | 22684<br>22684<br>130 234 | 22685<br>22685<br>130 235 | 22686<br>22686<br>130 236 | 22687<br>22687<br>130 237 |
| **A−** | 22688<br>22688<br>130 240 | 22689<br>22689<br>130 241 | 22690<br>22690<br>130 242 | 22691<br>22691<br>130 243 | 22692<br>22692<br>130 244 | 22693<br>22693<br>130 245 | 22694<br>22694<br>130 246 | 22695<br>22695<br>130 247 | 22696<br>22696<br>130 250 | 22697<br>22697<br>130 251 | 22698<br>22698<br>130 252 | 22699<br>22699<br>130 253 | 22700<br>22700<br>130 254 | 22701<br>22701<br>130 255 | 22702<br>22702<br>130 256 | 22703<br>22703<br>130 257 |
| **B−** | 22704<br>22704<br>130 260 | 22705<br>22705<br>130 261 | 22706<br>22706<br>130 262 | 22707<br>22707<br>130 263 | 22708<br>22708<br>130 264 | 22709<br>22709<br>130 265 | 22710<br>22710<br>130 266 | 22711<br>22711<br>130 267 | 22712<br>22712<br>130 270 | 22713<br>22713<br>130 271 | 22714<br>22714<br>130 272 | 22715<br>22715<br>130 273 | 22716<br>22716<br>130 274 | 22717<br>22717<br>130 275 | 22718<br>22718<br>130 276 | 22719<br>22719<br>130 277 |
| **C−** | 22720<br>22720<br>130 300 | 22721<br>22721<br>130 301 | 22722<br>22722<br>130 302 | 22723<br>22723<br>130 303 | 22724<br>22724<br>130 304 | 22725<br>22725<br>130 305 | 22726<br>22726<br>130 306 | 22727<br>22727<br>130 307 | 22728<br>22728<br>130 310 | 22729<br>22729<br>130 311 | 22730<br>22730<br>130 312 | 22731<br>22731<br>130 313 | 22732<br>22732<br>130 314 | 22733<br>22733<br>130 315 | 22734<br>22734<br>130 316 | 22735<br>22735<br>130 317 |
| **D−** | 22736<br>22736<br>130 320 | 22737<br>22737<br>130 321 | 22738<br>22738<br>130 322 | 22739<br>22739<br>130 323 | 22740<br>22740<br>130 324 | 22741<br>22741<br>130 325 | 22742<br>22742<br>130 326 | 22743<br>22743<br>130 327 | 22744<br>22744<br>130 330 | 22745<br>22745<br>130 331 | 22746<br>22746<br>130 332 | 22747<br>22747<br>130 333 | 22748<br>22748<br>130 334 | 22749<br>22749<br>130 335 | 22750<br>22750<br>130 336 | 22751<br>22751<br>130 337 |
| **E−** | 22752<br>22752<br>130 340 | 22753<br>22753<br>130 341 | 22754<br>22754<br>130 342 | 22755<br>22755<br>130 343 | 22756<br>22756<br>130 344 | 22757<br>22757<br>130 345 | 22758<br>22758<br>130 346 | 22759<br>22759<br>130 347 | 22760<br>22760<br>130 350 | 22761<br>22761<br>130 351 | 22762<br>22762<br>130 352 | 22763<br>22763<br>130 353 | 22764<br>22764<br>130 354 | 22765<br>22765<br>130 355 | 22766<br>22766<br>130 356 | 22767<br>22767<br>130 357 |
| **F−** | 22768<br>22768<br>130 360 | 22769<br>22769<br>130 361 | 22770<br>22770<br>130 362 | 22771<br>22771<br>130 363 | 22772<br>22772<br>130 364 | 22773<br>22773<br>130 365 | 22774<br>22774<br>130 366 | 22775<br>22775<br>130 367 | 22776<br>22776<br>130 370 | 22777<br>22777<br>130 371 | 22778<br>22778<br>130 372 | 22779<br>22779<br>130 373 | 22780<br>22780<br>130 374 | 22781<br>22781<br>130 375 | 22782<br>22782<br>130 376 | 22783<br>22783<br>130 377 |

Left axis label: **SECOND HEX DIGIT**

 **DECIMAL** [22528]   **BINARY** [0101 1000]   **DECIMAL** [22528]   **HEXADECIMAL** (58)   **OCTAL** [130 000]

FOURTH HEX DIGIT → (58) ← THIRD HEX DIGIT

FIRST HEX DIGIT

| (2) / SECOND HEX DIGIT | −0 | −1 | −2 | −3 | −4 | −5 | −6 | −7 | −8 | −9 | −A | −B | −C | −D | −E | −F |
|---|---|---|---|---|---|---|---|---|---|---|---|---|---|---|---|---|
| 0− | 22784<br>22784<br>131 000 | 22785<br>22785<br>131 001 | 22786<br>22786<br>131 002 | 22787<br>22787<br>131 003 | 22788<br>22788<br>131 004 | 22789<br>22789<br>131 005 | 22790<br>22790<br>131 006 | 22791<br>22791<br>131 007 | 22792<br>22792<br>131 010 | 22793<br>22793<br>131 011 | 22794<br>22794<br>131 012 | 22795<br>22795<br>131 013 | 22796<br>22796<br>131 014 | 22797<br>22797<br>131 015 | 22798<br>22798<br>131 016 | 22799<br>22799<br>131 017 |
| 1− | 22800<br>22800<br>131 020 | 22801<br>22801<br>131 021 | 22802<br>22802<br>131 022 | 22803<br>22803<br>131 023 | 22804<br>22804<br>131 024 | 22805<br>22805<br>131 025 | 22806<br>22806<br>131 026 | 22807<br>22807<br>131 027 | 22808<br>22808<br>131 030 | 22809<br>22809<br>131 031 | 22810<br>22810<br>131 032 | 22811<br>22811<br>131 033 | 22812<br>22812<br>131 034 | 22813<br>22813<br>131 035 | 22814<br>22814<br>131 036 | 22815<br>22815<br>131 037 |
| 2− | 22816<br>22816<br>131 040 | 22817<br>22817<br>131 041 | 22818<br>22818<br>131 042 | 22819<br>22819<br>131 043 | 22820<br>22820<br>131 044 | 22821<br>22821<br>131 045 | 22822<br>22822<br>131 046 | 22823<br>22823<br>131 047 | 22824<br>22824<br>131 050 | 22825<br>22825<br>131 051 | 22826<br>22826<br>131 052 | 22827<br>22827<br>131 053 | 22828<br>22828<br>131 054 | 22829<br>22829<br>131 055 | 22830<br>22830<br>131 056 | 22831<br>22831<br>131 057 |
| 3− | 22832<br>22832<br>131 060 | 22833<br>22833<br>131 061 | 22834<br>22834<br>131 062 | 22835<br>22835<br>131 063 | 22836<br>22836<br>131 064 | 22837<br>22837<br>131 065 | 22838<br>22838<br>131 066 | 22839<br>22839<br>131 067 | 22840<br>22840<br>131 070 | 22841<br>22841<br>131 071 | 22842<br>22842<br>131 072 | 22843<br>22843<br>131 073 | 22844<br>22844<br>131 074 | 22845<br>22845<br>131 075 | 22846<br>22846<br>131 076 | 22847<br>22847<br>131 077 |
| 4− | 22848<br>22848<br>131 100 | 22849<br>22849<br>131 101 | 22850<br>22850<br>131 102 | 22851<br>22851<br>131 103 | 22852<br>22852<br>131 104 | 22853<br>22853<br>131 105 | 22854<br>22854<br>131 106 | 22855<br>22855<br>131 107 | 22856<br>22856<br>131 110 | 22857<br>22857<br>131 111 | 22858<br>22858<br>131 112 | 22859<br>22859<br>131 113 | 22860<br>22860<br>131 114 | 22861<br>22861<br>131 115 | 22862<br>22862<br>131 116 | 22863<br>22863<br>131 117 |
| 5− | 22864<br>22864<br>131 120 | 22865<br>22865<br>131 121 | 22866<br>22866<br>131 122 | 22867<br>22867<br>131 123 | 22868<br>22868<br>131 124 | 22869<br>22869<br>131 125 | 22870<br>22870<br>131 126 | 22871<br>22871<br>131 127 | 22872<br>22872<br>131 130 | 22873<br>22873<br>131 131 | 22874<br>22874<br>131 132 | 22875<br>22875<br>131 133 | 22876<br>22876<br>131 134 | 22877<br>22877<br>131 135 | 22878<br>22878<br>131 136 | 22879<br>22879<br>131 137 |
| 6− | 22880<br>22880<br>131 140 | 22881<br>22881<br>131 141 | 22882<br>22882<br>131 142 | 22883<br>22883<br>131 143 | 22884<br>22884<br>131 144 | 22885<br>22885<br>131 145 | 22886<br>22886<br>131 146 | 22887<br>22887<br>131 147 | 22888<br>22888<br>131 150 | 22889<br>22889<br>131 151 | 22890<br>22890<br>131 152 | 22891<br>22891<br>131 153 | 22892<br>22892<br>131 154 | 22893<br>22893<br>131 155 | 22894<br>22894<br>131 156 | 22895<br>22895<br>131 157 |
| 7− | 22896<br>22896<br>131 160 | 22897<br>22897<br>131 161 | 22898<br>22898<br>131 162 | 22899<br>22899<br>131 163 | 22900<br>22900<br>131 164 | 22901<br>22901<br>131 165 | 22902<br>22902<br>131 166 | 22903<br>22903<br>131 167 | 22904<br>22904<br>131 170 | 22905<br>22905<br>131 171 | 22906<br>22906<br>131 172 | 22907<br>22907<br>131 173 | 22908<br>22908<br>131 174 | 22909<br>22909<br>131 175 | 22910<br>22910<br>131 176 | 22911<br>22911<br>131 177 |
| 8− | 22912<br>22912<br>131 200 | 22913<br>22913<br>131 201 | 22914<br>22914<br>131 202 | 22915<br>22915<br>131 203 | 22916<br>22916<br>131 204 | 22917<br>22917<br>131 205 | 22918<br>22918<br>131 206 | 22919<br>22919<br>131 207 | 22920<br>22920<br>131 210 | 22921<br>22921<br>131 211 | 22922<br>22922<br>131 212 | 22923<br>22923<br>131 213 | 22924<br>22924<br>131 214 | 22925<br>22925<br>131 215 | 22926<br>22926<br>131 216 | 22927<br>22927<br>131 217 |
| 9− | 22928<br>22928<br>131 220 | 22929<br>22929<br>131 221 | 22930<br>22930<br>131 222 | 22931<br>22931<br>131 223 | 22932<br>22932<br>131 224 | 22933<br>22933<br>131 225 | 22934<br>22934<br>131 226 | 22935<br>22935<br>131 227 | 22936<br>22936<br>131 230 | 22937<br>22937<br>131 231 | 22938<br>22938<br>131 232 | 22939<br>22939<br>131 233 | 22940<br>22940<br>131 234 | 22941<br>22941<br>131 235 | 22942<br>22942<br>131 236 | 22943<br>22943<br>131 237 |
| A− | 22944<br>22944<br>131 240 | 22945<br>22945<br>131 241 | 22946<br>22946<br>131 242 | 22947<br>22947<br>131 243 | 22948<br>22948<br>131 244 | 22949<br>22949<br>131 245 | 22950<br>22950<br>131 246 | 22951<br>22951<br>131 247 | 22952<br>22952<br>131 250 | 22953<br>22953<br>131 251 | 22954<br>22954<br>131 252 | 22955<br>22955<br>131 253 | 22956<br>22956<br>131 254 | 22957<br>22957<br>131 255 | 22958<br>22958<br>131 256 | 22959<br>22959<br>131 257 |
| B− | 22960<br>22960<br>131 260 | 22961<br>22961<br>131 261 | 22962<br>22962<br>131 262 | 22963<br>22963<br>131 263 | 22964<br>22964<br>131 264 | 22965<br>22965<br>131 265 | 22966<br>22966<br>131 266 | 22967<br>22967<br>131 267 | 22968<br>22968<br>131 270 | 22969<br>22969<br>131 271 | 22970<br>22970<br>131 272 | 22971<br>22971<br>131 273 | 22972<br>22972<br>131 274 | 22973<br>22973<br>131 275 | 22974<br>22974<br>131 276 | 22975<br>22975<br>131 277 |
| C− | 22976<br>22976<br>131 300 | 22977<br>22977<br>131 301 | 22978<br>22978<br>131 302 | 22979<br>22979<br>131 303 | 22980<br>22980<br>131 304 | 22981<br>22981<br>131 305 | 22982<br>22982<br>131 306 | 22983<br>22983<br>131 307 | 22984<br>22984<br>131 310 | 22985<br>22985<br>131 311 | 22986<br>22986<br>131 312 | 22987<br>22987<br>131 313 | 22988<br>22988<br>131 314 | 22989<br>22989<br>131 315 | 22990<br>22990<br>131 316 | 22991<br>22991<br>131 317 |
| D− | 22992<br>22992<br>131 320 | 22993<br>22993<br>131 321 | 22994<br>22994<br>131 322 | 22995<br>22995<br>131 323 | 22996<br>22996<br>131 324 | 22997<br>22997<br>131 325 | 22998<br>22998<br>131 326 | 22999<br>22999<br>131 327 | 23000<br>23000<br>131 330 | 23001<br>23001<br>131 331 | 23002<br>23002<br>131 332 | 23003<br>23003<br>131 333 | 23004<br>23004<br>131 334 | 23005<br>23005<br>131 335 | 23006<br>23006<br>131 336 | 23007<br>23007<br>131 337 |
| E− | 23008<br>23008<br>131 340 | 23009<br>23009<br>131 341 | 23010<br>23010<br>131 342 | 23011<br>23011<br>131 343 | 23012<br>23012<br>131 344 | 23013<br>23013<br>131 345 | 23014<br>23014<br>131 346 | 23015<br>23015<br>131 347 | 23016<br>23016<br>131 350 | 23017<br>23017<br>131 351 | 23018<br>23018<br>131 352 | 23019<br>23019<br>131 353 | 23020<br>23020<br>131 354 | 23021<br>23021<br>131 355 | 23022<br>23022<br>131 356 | 23023<br>23023<br>131 357 |
| F− | 23024<br>23024<br>131 360 | 23025<br>23025<br>131 361 | 23026<br>23026<br>131 362 | 23027<br>23027<br>131 363 | 23028<br>23028<br>131 364 | 23029<br>23029<br>131 365 | 23030<br>23030<br>131 366 | 23031<br>23031<br>131 367 | 23032<br>23032<br>131 370 | 23033<br>23033<br>131 371 | 23034<br>23034<br>131 372 | 23035<br>23035<br>131 373 | 23036<br>23036<br>131 374 | 23037<br>23037<br>131 375 | 23038<br>23038<br>131 376 | 23039<br>23039<br>131 377 |

| SECOND HEX DIGIT | −0 | −1 | −2 | −3 | −4 | −5 | −6 | −7 | −8 | −9 | −A | −B | −C | −D | −E | −F |
|---|---|---|---|---|---|---|---|---|---|---|---|---|---|---|---|---|
| 0- | 23040<br>23040<br>132 000 | 23041<br>23041<br>132 001 | 23042<br>23042<br>132 002 | 23043<br>23043<br>132 003 | 23044<br>23044<br>132 004 | 23045<br>23045<br>132 005 | 23046<br>23046<br>132 006 | 23047<br>23047<br>132 007 | 23048<br>23048<br>132 010 | 23049<br>23049<br>132 011 | 23050<br>23050<br>132 012 | 23051<br>23051<br>132 013 | 23052<br>23052<br>132 014 | 23053<br>23053<br>132 015 | 23054<br>23054<br>132 016 | 23055<br>23055<br>132 017 |
| 1- | 23056<br>23056<br>132 020 | 23057<br>23057<br>132 021 | 23058<br>23058<br>132 022 | 23059<br>23059<br>132 023 | 23060<br>23060<br>132 024 | 23061<br>23061<br>132 025 | 23062<br>23062<br>132 026 | 23063<br>23063<br>132 027 | 23064<br>23064<br>132 030 | 23065<br>23065<br>132 031 | 23066<br>23066<br>132 032 | 23067<br>23067<br>132 033 | 23068<br>23068<br>132 034 | 23069<br>23069<br>132 035 | 23070<br>23070<br>132 036 | 23071<br>23071<br>132 037 |
| 2- | 23072<br>23072<br>132 040 | 23073<br>23073<br>132 041 | 23074<br>23074<br>132 042 | 23075<br>23075<br>132 043 | 23076<br>23076<br>132 044 | 23077<br>23077<br>132 045 | 23078<br>23078<br>132 046 | 23079<br>23079<br>132 047 | 23080<br>23080<br>132 050 | 23081<br>23081<br>132 051 | 23082<br>23082<br>132 052 | 23083<br>23083<br>132 053 | 23084<br>23084<br>132 054 | 23085<br>23085<br>132 055 | 23086<br>23086<br>132 056 | 23087<br>23087<br>132 057 |
| 3- | 23088<br>23088<br>132 060 | 23089<br>23089<br>132 061 | 23090<br>23090<br>132 062 | 23091<br>23091<br>132 063 | 23092<br>23092<br>132 064 | 23093<br>23093<br>132 065 | 23094<br>23094<br>132 066 | 23095<br>23095<br>132 067 | 23096<br>23096<br>132 070 | 23097<br>23097<br>132 071 | 23098<br>23098<br>132 072 | 23099<br>23099<br>132 073 | 23100<br>23100<br>132 074 | 23101<br>23101<br>132 075 | 23102<br>23102<br>132 076 | 23103<br>23103<br>132 077 |
| 4- | 23104<br>23104<br>132 100 | 23105<br>23105<br>132 101 | 23106<br>23106<br>132 102 | 23107<br>23107<br>132 103 | 23108<br>23108<br>132 104 | 23109<br>23109<br>132 105 | 23110<br>23110<br>132 106 | 23111<br>23111<br>132 107 | 23112<br>23112<br>132 110 | 23113<br>23113<br>132 111 | 23114<br>23114<br>132 112 | 23115<br>23115<br>132 113 | 23116<br>23116<br>132 114 | 23117<br>23117<br>132 115 | 23118<br>23118<br>132 116 | 23119<br>23119<br>132 117 |
| 5- | 23120<br>23120<br>132 120 | 23121<br>23121<br>132 121 | 23122<br>23122<br>132 122 | 23123<br>23123<br>132 123 | 23124<br>23124<br>132 124 | 23125<br>23125<br>132 125 | 23126<br>23126<br>132 126 | 23127<br>23127<br>132 127 | 23128<br>23128<br>132 130 | 23129<br>23129<br>132 131 | 23130<br>23130<br>132 132 | 23131<br>23131<br>132 133 | 23132<br>23132<br>132 134 | 23133<br>23133<br>132 135 | 23134<br>23134<br>132 136 | 23135<br>23135<br>132 137 |
| 6- | 23136<br>23136<br>132 140 | 23137<br>23137<br>132 141 | 23138<br>23138<br>132 142 | 23139<br>23139<br>132 143 | 23140<br>23140<br>132 144 | 23141<br>23141<br>132 145 | 23142<br>23142<br>132 146 | 23143<br>23143<br>132 147 | 23144<br>23144<br>132 150 | 23145<br>23145<br>132 151 | 23146<br>23146<br>132 152 | 23147<br>23147<br>132 153 | 23148<br>23148<br>132 154 | 23149<br>23149<br>132 155 | 23150<br>23150<br>132 156 | 23151<br>23151<br>132 157 |
| 7- | 23152<br>23152<br>132 160 | 23153<br>23153<br>132 161 | 23154<br>23154<br>132 162 | 23155<br>23155<br>132 163 | 23156<br>23156<br>132 164 | 23157<br>23157<br>132 165 | 23158<br>23158<br>132 166 | 23159<br>23159<br>132 167 | 23160<br>23160<br>132 170 | 23161<br>23161<br>132 171 | 23162<br>23162<br>132 172 | 23163<br>23163<br>132 173 | 23164<br>23164<br>132 174 | 23165<br>23165<br>132 175 | 23166<br>23166<br>132 176 | 23167<br>23167<br>132 177 |
| 8- | 23168<br>23168<br>132 200 | 23169<br>23169<br>132 201 | 23170<br>23170<br>132 202 | 23171<br>23171<br>132 203 | 23172<br>23172<br>132 204 | 23173<br>23173<br>132 205 | 23174<br>23174<br>132 206 | 23175<br>23175<br>132 207 | 23176<br>23176<br>132 210 | 23177<br>23177<br>132 211 | 23178<br>23178<br>132 212 | 23179<br>23179<br>132 213 | 23180<br>23180<br>132 214 | 23181<br>23181<br>132 215 | 23182<br>23182<br>132 216 | 23183<br>23183<br>132 217 |
| 9- | 23184<br>23184<br>132 220 | 23185<br>23185<br>132 221 | 23186<br>23186<br>132 222 | 23187<br>23187<br>132 223 | 23188<br>23188<br>132 224 | 23189<br>23189<br>132 225 | 23190<br>23190<br>132 226 | 23191<br>23191<br>132 227 | 23192<br>23192<br>132 230 | 23193<br>23193<br>132 231 | 23194<br>23194<br>132 232 | 23195<br>23195<br>132 233 | 23196<br>23196<br>132 234 | 23197<br>23197<br>132 235 | 23198<br>23198<br>132 236 | 23199<br>23199<br>132 237 |
| A- | 23200<br>23200<br>132 240 | 23201<br>23201<br>132 241 | 23202<br>23202<br>132 242 | 23203<br>23203<br>132 243 | 23204<br>23204<br>132 244 | 23205<br>23205<br>132 245 | 23206<br>23206<br>132 246 | 23207<br>23207<br>132 247 | 23208<br>23208<br>132 250 | 23209<br>23209<br>132 251 | 23210<br>23210<br>132 252 | 23211<br>23211<br>132 253 | 23212<br>23212<br>132 254 | 23213<br>23213<br>132 255 | 23214<br>23214<br>132 256 | 23215<br>23215<br>132 257 |
| B- | 23216<br>23216<br>132 260 | 23217<br>23217<br>132 261 | 23218<br>23218<br>132 262 | 23219<br>23219<br>132 263 | 23220<br>23220<br>132 264 | 23221<br>23221<br>132 265 | 23222<br>23222<br>132 266 | 23223<br>23223<br>132 267 | 23224<br>23224<br>132 270 | 23225<br>23225<br>132 271 | 23226<br>23226<br>132 272 | 23227<br>23227<br>132 273 | 23228<br>23228<br>132 274 | 23229<br>23229<br>132 275 | 23230<br>23230<br>132 276 | 23231<br>23231<br>132 277 |
| C- | 23232<br>23232<br>132 300 | 23233<br>23233<br>132 301 | 23234<br>23234<br>132 302 | 23235<br>23235<br>132 303 | 23236<br>23236<br>132 304 | 23237<br>23237<br>132 305 | 23238<br>23238<br>132 306 | 23239<br>23239<br>132 307 | 23240<br>23240<br>132 310 | 23241<br>23241<br>132 311 | 23242<br>23242<br>132 312 | 23243<br>23243<br>132 313 | 23244<br>23244<br>132 314 | 23245<br>23245<br>132 315 | 23246<br>23246<br>132 316 | 23247<br>23247<br>132 317 |
| D- | 23248<br>23248<br>132 320 | 23249<br>23249<br>132 321 | 23250<br>23250<br>132 322 | 23251<br>23251<br>132 323 | 23252<br>23252<br>132 324 | 23253<br>23253<br>132 325 | 23254<br>23254<br>132 326 | 23255<br>23255<br>132 327 | 23256<br>23256<br>132 330 | 23257<br>23257<br>132 331 | 23258<br>23258<br>132 332 | 23259<br>23259<br>132 333 | 23260<br>23260<br>132 334 | 23261<br>23261<br>132 335 | 23262<br>23262<br>132 336 | 23263<br>23263<br>132 337 |
| E- | 23264<br>23264<br>132 340 | 23265<br>23265<br>132 341 | 23266<br>23266<br>132 342 | 23267<br>23267<br>132 343 | 23268<br>23268<br>132 344 | 23269<br>23269<br>132 345 | 23270<br>23270<br>132 346 | 23271<br>23271<br>132 347 | 23272<br>23272<br>132 350 | 23273<br>23273<br>132 351 | 23274<br>23274<br>132 352 | 23275<br>23275<br>132 353 | 23276<br>23276<br>132 354 | 23277<br>23277<br>132 355 | 23278<br>23278<br>132 356 | 23279<br>23279<br>132 357 |
| F- | 23280<br>23280<br>132 360 | 23281<br>23281<br>132 361 | 23282<br>23282<br>132 362 | 23283<br>23283<br>132 363 | 23284<br>23284<br>132 364 | 23285<br>23285<br>132 365 | 23286<br>23286<br>132 366 | 23287<br>23287<br>132 367 | 23288<br>23288<br>132 370 | 23289<br>23289<br>132 371 | 23290<br>23290<br>132 372 | 23291<br>23291<br>132 373 | 23292<br>23292<br>132 374 | 23293<br>23293<br>132 375 | 23294<br>23294<br>132 376 | 23295<br>23295<br>132 377 |

DECIMAL →
 DECIMAL →
OCTAL →

 DECIMAL  23040    BINARY  0101 1010    DECIMAL  23040    HEXADECIMAL  (5A)  OCTAL  132 000

FOURTH HEX DIGIT →  ← THIRD HEX DIGIT

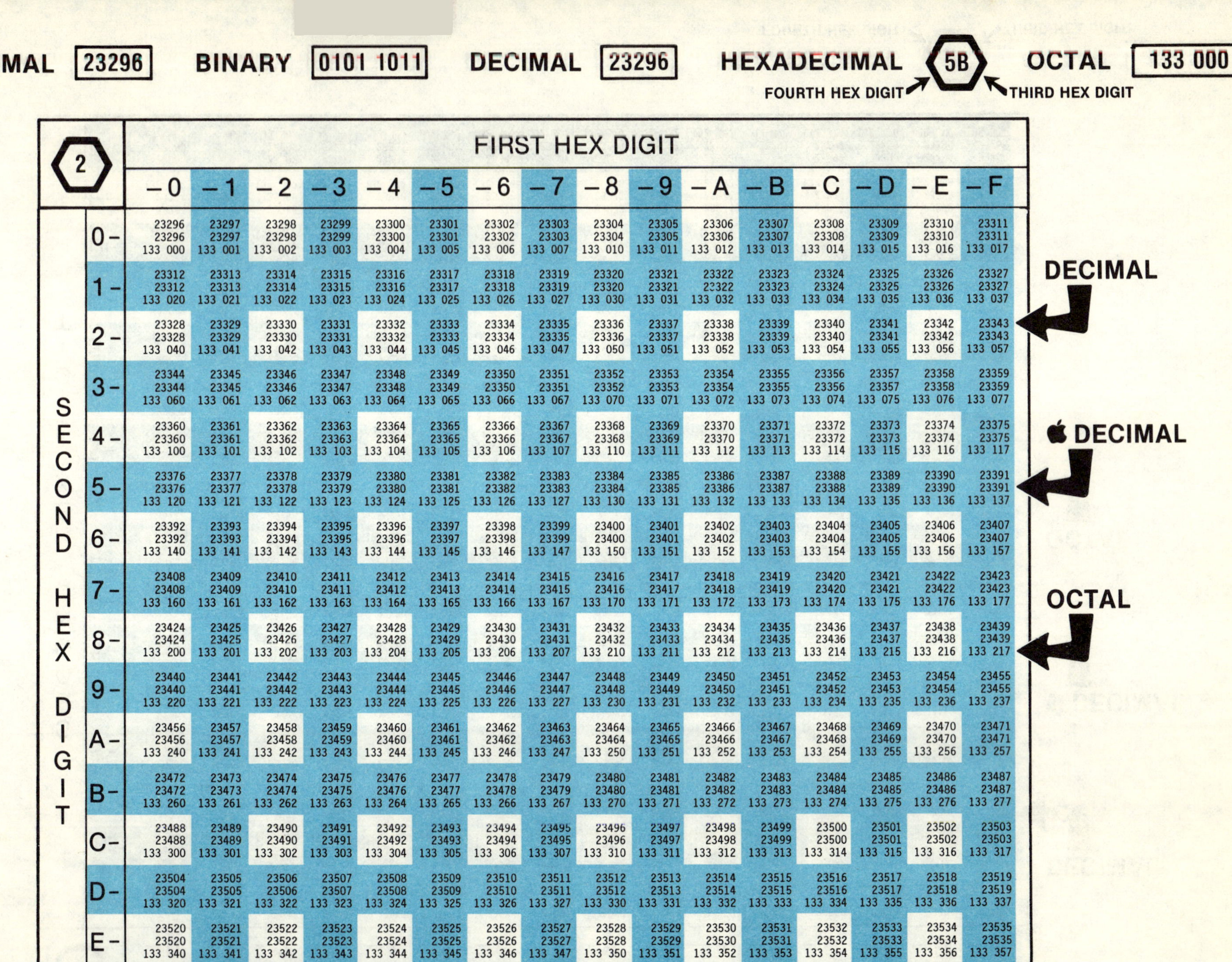

**FIRST HEX DIGIT** — ② (SECOND HEX DIGIT)

| | −0 | −1 | −2 | −3 | −4 | −5 | −6 | −7 | −8 | −9 | −A | −B | −C | −D | −E | −F |
|---|---|---|---|---|---|---|---|---|---|---|---|---|---|---|---|---|
| 0− | 23296<br>23296<br>133 000 | 23297<br>23297<br>133 001 | 23298<br>23298<br>133 002 | 23299<br>23299<br>133 003 | 23300<br>23300<br>133 004 | 23301<br>23301<br>133 005 | 23302<br>23302<br>133 006 | 23303<br>23303<br>133 007 | 23304<br>23304<br>133 010 | 23305<br>23305<br>133 011 | 23306<br>23306<br>133 012 | 23307<br>23307<br>133 013 | 23308<br>23308<br>133 014 | 23309<br>23309<br>133 015 | 23310<br>23310<br>133 016 | 23311<br>23311<br>133 017 |
| 1− | 23312<br>23312<br>133 020 | 23313<br>23313<br>133 021 | 23314<br>23314<br>133 022 | 23315<br>23315<br>133 023 | 23316<br>23316<br>133 024 | 23317<br>23317<br>133 025 | 23318<br>23318<br>133 026 | 23319<br>23319<br>133 027 | 23320<br>23320<br>133 030 | 23321<br>23321<br>133 031 | 23322<br>23322<br>133 032 | 23323<br>23323<br>133 033 | 23324<br>23324<br>133 034 | 23325<br>23325<br>133 035 | 23326<br>23326<br>133 036 | 23327<br>23327<br>133 037 |
| 2− | 23328<br>23328<br>133 040 | 23329<br>23329<br>133 041 | 23330<br>23330<br>133 042 | 23331<br>23331<br>133 043 | 23332<br>23332<br>133 044 | 23333<br>23333<br>133 045 | 23334<br>23334<br>133 046 | 23335<br>23335<br>133 047 | 23336<br>23336<br>133 050 | 23337<br>23337<br>133 051 | 23338<br>23338<br>133 052 | 23339<br>23339<br>133 053 | 23340<br>23340<br>133 054 | 23341<br>23341<br>133 055 | 23342<br>23342<br>133 056 | 23343<br>23343<br>133 057 |
| 3− | 23344<br>23344<br>133 060 | 23345<br>23345<br>133 061 | 23346<br>23346<br>133 062 | 23347<br>23347<br>133 063 | 23348<br>23348<br>133 064 | 23349<br>23349<br>133 065 | 23350<br>23350<br>133 066 | 23351<br>23351<br>133 067 | 23352<br>23352<br>133 070 | 23353<br>23353<br>133 071 | 23354<br>23354<br>133 072 | 23355<br>23355<br>133 073 | 23356<br>23356<br>133 074 | 23357<br>23357<br>133 075 | 23358<br>23358<br>133 076 | 23359<br>23359<br>133 077 |
| 4− | 23360<br>23360<br>133 100 | 23361<br>23361<br>133 101 | 23362<br>23362<br>133 102 | 23363<br>23363<br>133 103 | 23364<br>23364<br>133 104 | 23365<br>23365<br>133 105 | 23366<br>23366<br>133 106 | 23367<br>23367<br>133 107 | 23368<br>23368<br>133 110 | 23369<br>23369<br>133 111 | 23370<br>23370<br>133 112 | 23371<br>23371<br>133 113 | 23372<br>23372<br>133 114 | 23373<br>23373<br>133 115 | 23374<br>23374<br>133 116 | 23375<br>23375<br>133 117 |
| 5− | 23376<br>23376<br>133 120 | 23377<br>23377<br>133 121 | 23378<br>23378<br>133 122 | 23379<br>23379<br>133 123 | 23380<br>23380<br>133 124 | 23381<br>23381<br>133 125 | 23382<br>23382<br>133 126 | 23383<br>23383<br>133 127 | 23384<br>23384<br>133 130 | 23385<br>23385<br>133 131 | 23386<br>23386<br>133 132 | 23387<br>23387<br>133 133 | 23388<br>23388<br>133 134 | 23389<br>23389<br>133 135 | 23390<br>23390<br>133 136 | 23391<br>23391<br>133 137 |
| 6− | 23392<br>23392<br>133 140 | 23393<br>23393<br>133 141 | 23394<br>23394<br>133 142 | 23395<br>23395<br>133 143 | 23396<br>23396<br>133 144 | 23397<br>23397<br>133 145 | 23398<br>23398<br>133 146 | 23399<br>23399<br>133 147 | 23400<br>23400<br>133 150 | 23401<br>23401<br>133 151 | 23402<br>23402<br>133 152 | 23403<br>23403<br>133 153 | 23404<br>23404<br>133 154 | 23405<br>23405<br>133 155 | 23406<br>23406<br>133 156 | 23407<br>23407<br>133 157 |
| 7− | 23408<br>23408<br>133 160 | 23409<br>23409<br>133 161 | 23410<br>23410<br>133 162 | 23411<br>23411<br>133 163 | 23412<br>23412<br>133 164 | 23413<br>23413<br>133 165 | 23414<br>23414<br>133 166 | 23415<br>23415<br>133 167 | 23416<br>23416<br>133 170 | 23417<br>23417<br>133 171 | 23418<br>23418<br>133 172 | 23419<br>23419<br>133 173 | 23420<br>23420<br>133 174 | 23421<br>23421<br>133 175 | 23422<br>23422<br>133 176 | 23423<br>23423<br>133 177 |
| 8− | 23424<br>23424<br>133 200 | 23425<br>23425<br>133 201 | 23426<br>23426<br>133 202 | 23427<br>23427<br>133 203 | 23428<br>23428<br>133 204 | 23429<br>23429<br>133 205 | 23430<br>23430<br>133 206 | 23431<br>23431<br>133 207 | 23432<br>23432<br>133 210 | 23433<br>23433<br>133 211 | 23434<br>23434<br>133 212 | 23435<br>23435<br>133 213 | 23436<br>23436<br>133 214 | 23437<br>23437<br>133 215 | 23438<br>23438<br>133 216 | 23439<br>23439<br>133 217 |
| 9− | 23440<br>23440<br>133 220 | 23441<br>23441<br>133 221 | 23442<br>23442<br>133 222 | 23443<br>23443<br>133 223 | 23444<br>23444<br>133 224 | 23445<br>23445<br>133 225 | 23446<br>23446<br>133 226 | 23447<br>23447<br>133 227 | 23448<br>23448<br>133 230 | 23449<br>23449<br>133 231 | 23450<br>23450<br>133 232 | 23451<br>23451<br>133 233 | 23452<br>23452<br>133 234 | 23453<br>23453<br>133 235 | 23454<br>23454<br>133 236 | 23455<br>23455<br>133 237 |
| A− | 23456<br>23456<br>133 240 | 23457<br>23457<br>133 241 | 23458<br>23458<br>133 242 | 23459<br>23459<br>133 243 | 23460<br>23460<br>133 244 | 23461<br>23461<br>133 245 | 23462<br>23462<br>133 246 | 23463<br>23463<br>133 247 | 23464<br>23464<br>133 250 | 23465<br>23465<br>133 251 | 23466<br>23466<br>133 252 | 23467<br>23467<br>133 253 | 23468<br>23468<br>133 254 | 23469<br>23469<br>133 255 | 23470<br>23470<br>133 256 | 23471<br>23471<br>133 257 |
| B− | 23472<br>23472<br>133 260 | 23473<br>23473<br>133 261 | 23474<br>23474<br>133 262 | 23475<br>23475<br>133 263 | 23476<br>23476<br>133 264 | 23477<br>23477<br>133 265 | 23478<br>23478<br>133 266 | 23479<br>23479<br>133 267 | 23480<br>23480<br>133 270 | 23481<br>23481<br>133 271 | 23482<br>23482<br>133 272 | 23483<br>23483<br>133 273 | 23484<br>23484<br>133 274 | 23485<br>23485<br>133 275 | 23486<br>23486<br>133 276 | 23487<br>23487<br>133 277 |
| C− | 23488<br>23488<br>133 300 | 23489<br>23489<br>133 301 | 23490<br>23490<br>133 302 | 23491<br>23491<br>133 303 | 23492<br>23492<br>133 304 | 23493<br>23493<br>133 305 | 23494<br>23494<br>133 306 | 23495<br>23495<br>133 307 | 23496<br>23496<br>133 310 | 23497<br>23497<br>133 311 | 23498<br>23498<br>133 312 | 23499<br>23499<br>133 313 | 23500<br>23500<br>133 314 | 23501<br>23501<br>133 315 | 23502<br>23502<br>133 316 | 23503<br>23503<br>133 317 |
| D− | 23504<br>23504<br>133 320 | 23505<br>23505<br>133 321 | 23506<br>23506<br>133 322 | 23507<br>23507<br>133 323 | 23508<br>23508<br>133 324 | 23509<br>23509<br>133 325 | 23510<br>23510<br>133 326 | 23511<br>23511<br>133 327 | 23512<br>23512<br>133 330 | 23513<br>23513<br>133 331 | 23514<br>23514<br>133 332 | 23515<br>23515<br>133 333 | 23516<br>23516<br>133 334 | 23517<br>23517<br>133 335 | 23518<br>23518<br>133 336 | 23519<br>23519<br>133 337 |
| E− | 23520<br>23520<br>133 340 | 23521<br>23521<br>133 341 | 23522<br>23522<br>133 342 | 23523<br>23523<br>133 343 | 23524<br>23524<br>133 344 | 23525<br>23525<br>133 345 | 23526<br>23526<br>133 346 | 23527<br>23527<br>133 347 | 23528<br>23528<br>133 350 | 23529<br>23529<br>133 351 | 23530<br>23530<br>133 352 | 23531<br>23531<br>133 353 | 23532<br>23532<br>133 354 | 23533<br>23533<br>133 355 | 23534<br>23534<br>133 356 | 23535<br>23535<br>133 357 |
| F− | 23536<br>23536<br>133 360 | 23537<br>23537<br>133 361 | 23538<br>23538<br>133 362 | 23539<br>23539<br>133 363 | 23540<br>23540<br>133 364 | 23541<br>23541<br>133 365 | 23542<br>23542<br>133 366 | 23543<br>23543<br>133 367 | 23544<br>23544<br>133 370 | 23545<br>23545<br>133 371 | 23546<br>23546<br>133 372 | 23547<br>23547<br>133 373 | 23548<br>23548<br>133 374 | 23549<br>23549<br>133 375 | 23550<br>23550<br>133 376 | 23551<br>23551<br>133 377 |

# FIRST HEX DIGIT

**(2)**

| | −0 | −1 | −2 | −3 | −4 | −5 | −6 | −7 | −8 | −9 | −A | −B | −C | −D | −E | −F |
|---|---|---|---|---|---|---|---|---|---|---|---|---|---|---|---|---|
| **0-** | 23552<br>23552<br>134 000 | 23553<br>23553<br>134 001 | 23554<br>23554<br>134 002 | 23555<br>23555<br>134 003 | 23556<br>23556<br>134 004 | 23557<br>23557<br>134 005 | 23558<br>23558<br>134 006 | 23559<br>23559<br>134 007 | 23560<br>23560<br>134 010 | 23561<br>23561<br>134 011 | 23562<br>23562<br>134 012 | 23563<br>23563<br>134 013 | 23564<br>23564<br>134 014 | 23565<br>23565<br>134 015 | 23566<br>23566<br>134 016 | 23567<br>23567<br>134 017 |
| **1-** | 23568<br>23568<br>134 020 | 23569<br>23569<br>134 021 | 23570<br>23570<br>134 022 | 23571<br>23571<br>134 023 | 23572<br>23572<br>134 024 | 23573<br>23573<br>134 025 | 23574<br>23574<br>134 026 | 23575<br>23575<br>134 027 | 23576<br>23576<br>134 030 | 23577<br>23577<br>134 031 | 23578<br>23578<br>134 032 | 23579<br>23579<br>134 033 | 23580<br>23580<br>134 034 | 23581<br>23581<br>134 035 | 23582<br>23582<br>134 036 | 23583<br>23583<br>134 037 |
| **2-** | 23584<br>23584<br>134 040 | 23585<br>23585<br>134 041 | 23586<br>23586<br>134 042 | 23587<br>23587<br>134 043 | 23588<br>23588<br>134 044 | 23589<br>23589<br>134 045 | 23590<br>23590<br>134 046 | 23591<br>23591<br>134 047 | 23592<br>23592<br>134 050 | 23593<br>23593<br>134 051 | 23594<br>23594<br>134 052 | 23595<br>23595<br>134 053 | 23596<br>23596<br>134 054 | 23597<br>23597<br>134 055 | 23598<br>23598<br>134 056 | 23599<br>23599<br>134 057 |
| **3-** | 23600<br>23600<br>134 060 | 23601<br>23601<br>134 061 | 23602<br>23602<br>134 062 | 23603<br>23603<br>134 063 | 23604<br>23604<br>134 064 | 23605<br>23605<br>134 065 | 23606<br>23606<br>134 066 | 23607<br>23607<br>134 067 | 23608<br>23608<br>134 070 | 23609<br>23609<br>134 071 | 23610<br>23610<br>134 072 | 23611<br>23611<br>134 073 | 23612<br>23612<br>134 074 | 23613<br>23613<br>134 075 | 23614<br>23614<br>134 076 | 23615<br>23615<br>134 077 |
| **4-** | 23616<br>23616<br>134 100 | 23617<br>23617<br>134 101 | 23618<br>23618<br>134 102 | 23619<br>23619<br>134 103 | 23620<br>23620<br>134 104 | 23621<br>23621<br>134 105 | 23622<br>23622<br>134 106 | 23623<br>23623<br>134 107 | 23624<br>23624<br>134 110 | 23625<br>23625<br>134 111 | 23626<br>23626<br>134 112 | 23627<br>23627<br>134 113 | 23628<br>23628<br>134 114 | 23629<br>23629<br>134 115 | 23630<br>23630<br>134 116 | 23631<br>23631<br>134 117 |
| **5-** | 23632<br>23632<br>134 120 | 23633<br>23633<br>134 121 | 23634<br>23634<br>134 122 | 23635<br>23635<br>134 123 | 23636<br>23636<br>134 124 | 23637<br>23637<br>134 125 | 23638<br>23638<br>134 126 | 23639<br>23639<br>134 127 | 23640<br>23640<br>134 130 | 23641<br>23641<br>134 131 | 23642<br>23642<br>134 132 | 23643<br>23643<br>134 133 | 23644<br>23644<br>134 134 | 23645<br>23645<br>134 135 | 23646<br>23646<br>134 136 | 23647<br>23647<br>134 137 |
| **6-** | 23648<br>23648<br>134 140 | 23649<br>23649<br>134 141 | 23650<br>23650<br>134 142 | 23651<br>23651<br>134 143 | 23652<br>23652<br>134 144 | 23653<br>23653<br>134 145 | 23654<br>23654<br>134 146 | 23655<br>23655<br>134 147 | 23656<br>23656<br>134 150 | 23657<br>23657<br>134 151 | 23658<br>23658<br>134 152 | 23659<br>23659<br>134 153 | 23660<br>23660<br>134 154 | 23661<br>23661<br>134 155 | 23662<br>23662<br>134 156 | 23663<br>23663<br>134 157 |
| **7-** | 23664<br>23664<br>134 160 | 23665<br>23665<br>134 161 | 23666<br>23666<br>134 162 | 23667<br>23667<br>134 163 | 23668<br>23668<br>134 164 | 23669<br>23669<br>134 165 | 23670<br>23670<br>134 166 | 23671<br>23671<br>134 167 | 23672<br>23672<br>134 170 | 23673<br>23673<br>134 171 | 23674<br>23674<br>134 172 | 23675<br>23675<br>134 173 | 23676<br>23676<br>134 174 | 23677<br>23677<br>134 175 | 23678<br>23678<br>134 176 | 23679<br>23679<br>134 177 |
| **8-** | 23680<br>23680<br>134 200 | 23681<br>23681<br>134 201 | 23682<br>23682<br>134 202 | 23683<br>23683<br>134 203 | 23684<br>23684<br>134 204 | 23685<br>23685<br>134 205 | 23686<br>23686<br>134 206 | 23687<br>23687<br>134 207 | 23688<br>23688<br>134 210 | 23689<br>23689<br>134 211 | 23690<br>23690<br>134 212 | 23691<br>23691<br>134 213 | 23692<br>23692<br>134 214 | 23693<br>23693<br>134 215 | 23694<br>23694<br>134 216 | 23695<br>23695<br>134 217 |
| **9-** | 23696<br>23696<br>134 220 | 23697<br>23697<br>134 221 | 23698<br>23698<br>134 222 | 23699<br>23699<br>134 223 | 23700<br>23700<br>134 224 | 23701<br>23701<br>134 225 | 23702<br>23702<br>134 226 | 23703<br>23703<br>134 227 | 23704<br>23704<br>134 230 | 23705<br>23705<br>134 231 | 23706<br>23706<br>134 232 | 23707<br>23707<br>134 233 | 23708<br>23708<br>134 234 | 23709<br>23709<br>134 235 | 23710<br>23710<br>134 236 | 23711<br>23711<br>134 237 |
| **A-** | 23712<br>23712<br>134 240 | 23713<br>23713<br>134 241 | 23714<br>23714<br>134 242 | 23715<br>23715<br>134 243 | 23716<br>23716<br>134 244 | 23717<br>23717<br>134 245 | 23718<br>23718<br>134 246 | 23719<br>23719<br>134 247 | 23720<br>23720<br>134 250 | 23721<br>23721<br>134 251 | 23722<br>23722<br>134 252 | 23723<br>23723<br>134 253 | 23724<br>23724<br>134 254 | 23725<br>23725<br>134 255 | 23726<br>23726<br>134 256 | 23727<br>23727<br>134 257 |
| **B-** | 23728<br>23728<br>134 260 | 23729<br>23729<br>134 261 | 23730<br>23730<br>134 262 | 23731<br>23731<br>134 263 | 23732<br>23732<br>134 264 | 23733<br>23733<br>134 265 | 23734<br>23734<br>134 266 | 23735<br>23735<br>134 267 | 23736<br>23736<br>134 270 | 23737<br>23737<br>134 271 | 23738<br>23738<br>134 272 | 23739<br>23739<br>134 273 | 23740<br>23740<br>134 274 | 23741<br>23741<br>134 275 | 23742<br>23742<br>134 276 | 23743<br>23743<br>134 277 |
| **C-** | 23744<br>23744<br>134 300 | 23745<br>23745<br>134 301 | 23746<br>23746<br>134 302 | 23747<br>23747<br>134 303 | 23748<br>23748<br>134 304 | 23749<br>23749<br>134 305 | 23750<br>23750<br>134 306 | 23751<br>23751<br>134 307 | 23752<br>23752<br>134 310 | 23753<br>23753<br>134 311 | 23754<br>23754<br>134 312 | 23755<br>23755<br>134 313 | 23756<br>23756<br>134 314 | 23757<br>23757<br>134 315 | 23758<br>23758<br>134 316 | 23759<br>23759<br>134 317 |
| **D-** | 23760<br>23760<br>134 320 | 23761<br>23761<br>134 321 | 23762<br>23762<br>134 322 | 23763<br>23763<br>134 323 | 23764<br>23764<br>134 324 | 23765<br>23765<br>134 325 | 23766<br>23766<br>134 326 | 23767<br>23767<br>134 327 | 23768<br>23768<br>134 330 | 23769<br>23769<br>134 331 | 23770<br>23770<br>134 332 | 23771<br>23771<br>134 333 | 23772<br>23772<br>134 334 | 23773<br>23773<br>134 335 | 23774<br>23774<br>134 336 | 23775<br>23775<br>134 337 |
| **E-** | 23776<br>23776<br>134 340 | 23777<br>23777<br>134 341 | 23778<br>23778<br>134 342 | 23779<br>23779<br>134 343 | 23780<br>23780<br>134 344 | 23781<br>23781<br>134 345 | 23782<br>23782<br>134 346 | 23783<br>23783<br>134 347 | 23784<br>23784<br>134 350 | 23785<br>23785<br>134 351 | 23786<br>23786<br>134 352 | 23787<br>23787<br>134 353 | 23788<br>23788<br>134 354 | 23789<br>23789<br>134 355 | 23790<br>23790<br>134 356 | 23791<br>23791<br>134 357 |
| **F-** | 23792<br>23792<br>134 360 | 23793<br>23793<br>134 361 | 23794<br>23794<br>134 362 | 23795<br>23795<br>134 363 | 23796<br>23796<br>134 364 | 23797<br>23797<br>134 365 | 23798<br>23798<br>134 366 | 23799<br>23799<br>134 367 | 23800<br>23800<br>134 370 | 23801<br>23801<br>134 371 | 23802<br>23802<br>134 372 | 23803<br>23803<br>134 373 | 23804<br>23804<br>134 374 | 23805<br>23805<br>134 375 | 23806<br>23806<br>134 376 | 23807<br>23807<br>134 377 |

SECOND HEX DIGIT

DECIMAL →   DECIMAL →   OCTAL →

 DECIMAL  `23552`  **BINARY**  `0101 1100`  **DECIMAL**  `23552`  **HEXADECIMAL**  (5C)  **OCTAL**  `134 000`

FOURTH HEX DIGIT →   ← THIRD HEX DIGIT

| 2 / FIRST HEX DIGIT | −0 | −1 | −2 | −3 | −4 | −5 | −6 | −7 | −8 | −9 | −A | −B | −C | −D | −E | −F |
|---|---|---|---|---|---|---|---|---|---|---|---|---|---|---|---|---|
| 0− | 23808<br>23808<br>135 000 | 23809<br>23809<br>135 001 | 23810<br>23810<br>135 002 | 23811<br>23811<br>135 003 | 23812<br>23812<br>135 004 | 23813<br>23813<br>135 005 | 23814<br>23814<br>135 006 | 23815<br>23815<br>135 007 | 23816<br>23816<br>135 010 | 23817<br>23817<br>135 011 | 23818<br>23818<br>135 012 | 23819<br>23819<br>135 013 | 23820<br>23820<br>135 014 | 23821<br>23821<br>135 015 | 23822<br>23822<br>135 016 | 23823<br>23823<br>135 017 |
| 1− | 23824<br>23824<br>135 020 | 23825<br>23825<br>135 021 | 23826<br>23826<br>135 022 | 23827<br>23827<br>135 023 | 23828<br>23828<br>135 024 | 23829<br>23829<br>135 025 | 23830<br>23830<br>135 026 | 23831<br>23831<br>135 027 | 23832<br>23832<br>135 030 | 23833<br>23833<br>135 031 | 23834<br>23834<br>135 032 | 23835<br>23835<br>135 033 | 23836<br>23836<br>135 034 | 23837<br>23837<br>135 035 | 23838<br>23838<br>135 036 | 23839<br>23839<br>135 037 |
| 2− | 23840<br>23840<br>135 040 | 23841<br>23841<br>135 041 | 23842<br>23842<br>135 042 | 23843<br>23843<br>135 043 | 23844<br>23844<br>135 044 | 23845<br>23845<br>135 045 | 23846<br>23846<br>135 046 | 23847<br>23847<br>135 047 | 23848<br>23848<br>135 050 | 23849<br>23849<br>135 051 | 23850<br>23850<br>135 052 | 23851<br>23851<br>135 053 | 23852<br>23852<br>135 054 | 23853<br>23853<br>135 055 | 23854<br>23854<br>135 056 | 23855<br>23855<br>135 057 |
| 3− | 23856<br>23856<br>135 060 | 23857<br>23857<br>135 061 | 23858<br>23858<br>135 062 | 23859<br>23859<br>135 063 | 23860<br>23860<br>135 064 | 23861<br>23861<br>135 065 | 23862<br>23862<br>135 066 | 23863<br>23863<br>135 067 | 23864<br>23864<br>135 070 | 23865<br>23865<br>135 071 | 23866<br>23866<br>135 072 | 23867<br>23867<br>135 073 | 23868<br>23868<br>135 074 | 23869<br>23869<br>135 075 | 23870<br>23870<br>135 076 | 23871<br>23871<br>135 077 |
| 4− | 23872<br>23872<br>135 100 | 23873<br>23873<br>135 101 | 23874<br>23874<br>135 102 | 23875<br>23875<br>135 103 | 23876<br>23876<br>135 104 | 23877<br>23877<br>135 105 | 23878<br>23878<br>135 106 | 23879<br>23879<br>135 107 | 23880<br>23880<br>135 110 | 23881<br>23881<br>135 111 | 23882<br>23882<br>135 112 | 23883<br>23883<br>135 113 | 23884<br>23884<br>135 114 | 23885<br>23885<br>135 115 | 23886<br>23886<br>135 116 | 23887<br>23887<br>135 117 |
| 5− | 23888<br>23888<br>135 120 | 23889<br>23889<br>135 121 | 23890<br>23890<br>135 122 | 23891<br>23891<br>135 123 | 23892<br>23892<br>135 124 | 23893<br>23893<br>135 125 | 23894<br>23894<br>135 126 | 23895<br>23895<br>135 127 | 23896<br>23896<br>135 130 | 23897<br>23897<br>135 131 | 23898<br>23898<br>135 132 | 23899<br>23899<br>135 133 | 23900<br>23900<br>135 134 | 23901<br>23901<br>135 135 | 23902<br>23902<br>135 136 | 23903<br>23903<br>135 137 |
| 6− | 23904<br>23904<br>135 140 | 23905<br>23905<br>135 141 | 23906<br>23906<br>135 142 | 23907<br>23907<br>135 143 | 23908<br>23908<br>135 144 | 23909<br>23909<br>135 145 | 23910<br>23910<br>135 146 | 23911<br>23911<br>135 147 | 23912<br>23912<br>135 150 | 23913<br>23913<br>135 151 | 23914<br>23914<br>135 152 | 23915<br>23915<br>135 153 | 23916<br>23916<br>135 154 | 23917<br>23917<br>135 155 | 23918<br>23918<br>135 156 | 23919<br>23919<br>135 157 |
| 7− | 23920<br>23920<br>135 160 | 23921<br>23921<br>135 161 | 23922<br>23922<br>135 162 | 23923<br>23923<br>135 163 | 23924<br>23924<br>135 164 | 23925<br>23925<br>135 165 | 23926<br>23926<br>135 166 | 23927<br>23927<br>135 167 | 23928<br>23928<br>135 170 | 23929<br>23929<br>135 171 | 23930<br>23930<br>135 172 | 23931<br>23931<br>135 173 | 23932<br>23932<br>135 174 | 23933<br>23933<br>135 175 | 23934<br>23934<br>135 176 | 23935<br>23935<br>135 177 |
| 8− | 23936<br>23936<br>135 200 | 23937<br>23937<br>135 201 | 23938<br>23938<br>135 202 | 23939<br>23939<br>135 203 | 23940<br>23940<br>135 204 | 23941<br>23941<br>135 205 | 23942<br>23942<br>135 206 | 23943<br>23943<br>135 207 | 23944<br>23944<br>135 210 | 23945<br>23945<br>135 211 | 23946<br>23946<br>135 212 | 23947<br>23947<br>135 213 | 23948<br>23948<br>135 214 | 23949<br>23949<br>135 215 | 23950<br>23950<br>135 216 | 23951<br>23951<br>135 217 |
| 9− | 23952<br>23952<br>135 220 | 23953<br>23953<br>135 221 | 23954<br>23954<br>135 222 | 23955<br>23955<br>135 223 | 23956<br>23956<br>135 224 | 23957<br>23957<br>135 225 | 23958<br>23958<br>135 226 | 23959<br>23959<br>135 227 | 23960<br>23960<br>135 230 | 23961<br>23961<br>135 231 | 23962<br>23962<br>135 232 | 23963<br>23963<br>135 233 | 23964<br>23964<br>135 234 | 23965<br>23965<br>135 235 | 23966<br>23966<br>135 236 | 23967<br>23967<br>135 237 |
| A− | 23968<br>23968<br>135 240 | 23969<br>23969<br>135 241 | 23970<br>23970<br>135 242 | 23971<br>23971<br>135 243 | 23972<br>23972<br>135 244 | 23973<br>23973<br>135 245 | 23974<br>23974<br>135 246 | 23975<br>23975<br>135 247 | 23976<br>23976<br>135 250 | 23977<br>23977<br>135 251 | 23978<br>23978<br>135 252 | 23979<br>23979<br>135 253 | 23980<br>23980<br>135 254 | 23981<br>23981<br>135 255 | 23982<br>23982<br>135 256 | 23983<br>23983<br>135 257 |
| B− | 23984<br>23984<br>135 260 | 23985<br>23985<br>135 261 | 23986<br>23986<br>135 262 | 23987<br>23987<br>135 263 | 23988<br>23988<br>135 264 | 23989<br>23989<br>135 265 | 23990<br>23990<br>135 266 | 23991<br>23991<br>135 267 | 23992<br>23992<br>135 270 | 23993<br>23993<br>135 271 | 23994<br>23994<br>135 272 | 23995<br>23995<br>135 273 | 23996<br>23996<br>135 274 | 23997<br>23997<br>135 275 | 23998<br>23998<br>135 276 | 23999<br>23999<br>135 277 |
| C− | 24000<br>24000<br>135 300 | 24001<br>24001<br>135 301 | 24002<br>24002<br>135 302 | 24003<br>24003<br>135 303 | 24004<br>24004<br>135 304 | 24005<br>24005<br>135 305 | 24006<br>24006<br>135 306 | 24007<br>24007<br>135 307 | 24008<br>24008<br>135 310 | 24009<br>24009<br>135 311 | 24010<br>24010<br>135 312 | 24011<br>24011<br>135 313 | 24012<br>24012<br>135 314 | 24013<br>24013<br>135 315 | 24014<br>24014<br>135 316 | 24015<br>24015<br>135 317 |
| D− | 24016<br>24016<br>135 320 | 24017<br>24017<br>135 321 | 24018<br>24018<br>135 322 | 24019<br>24019<br>135 323 | 24020<br>24020<br>135 324 | 24021<br>24021<br>135 325 | 24022<br>24022<br>135 326 | 24023<br>24023<br>135 327 | 24024<br>24024<br>135 330 | 24025<br>24025<br>135 331 | 24026<br>24026<br>135 332 | 24027<br>24027<br>135 333 | 24028<br>24028<br>135 334 | 24029<br>24029<br>135 335 | 24030<br>24030<br>135 336 | 24031<br>24031<br>135 337 |
| E− | 24032<br>24032<br>135 340 | 24033<br>24033<br>135 341 | 24034<br>24034<br>135 342 | 24035<br>24035<br>135 343 | 24036<br>24036<br>135 344 | 24037<br>24037<br>135 345 | 24038<br>24038<br>135 346 | 24039<br>24039<br>135 347 | 24040<br>24040<br>135 350 | 24041<br>24041<br>135 351 | 24042<br>24042<br>135 352 | 24043<br>24043<br>135 353 | 24044<br>24044<br>135 354 | 24045<br>24045<br>135 355 | 24046<br>24046<br>135 356 | 24047<br>24047<br>135 357 |
| F− | 24048<br>24048<br>135 360 | 24049<br>24049<br>135 361 | 24050<br>24050<br>135 362 | 24051<br>24051<br>135 363 | 24052<br>24052<br>135 364 | 24053<br>24053<br>135 365 | 24054<br>24054<br>135 366 | 24055<br>24055<br>135 367 | 24056<br>24056<br>135 370 | 24057<br>24057<br>135 371 | 24058<br>24058<br>135 372 | 24059<br>24059<br>135 373 | 24060<br>24060<br>135 374 | 24061<br>24061<br>135 375 | 24062<br>24062<br>135 376 | 24063<br>24063<br>135 377 |

SECOND HEX DIGIT

# FIRST HEX DIGIT

Each cell shows: DECIMAL / DECIMAL / OCTAL

| 2 | −0 | −1 | −2 | −3 | −4 | −5 | −6 | −7 | −8 | −9 | −A | −B | −C | −D | −E | −F |
|---|---|---|---|---|---|---|---|---|---|---|---|---|---|---|---|---|
| **0−** | 24064 / 24064 / 136 000 | 24065 / 24065 / 136 001 | 24066 / 24066 / 136 002 | 24067 / 24067 / 136 003 | 24068 / 24068 / 136 004 | 24069 / 24069 / 136 005 | 24070 / 24070 / 136 006 | 24071 / 24071 / 136 007 | 24072 / 24072 / 136 010 | 24073 / 24073 / 136 011 | 24074 / 24074 / 136 012 | 24075 / 24075 / 136 013 | 24076 / 24076 / 136 014 | 24077 / 24077 / 136 015 | 24078 / 24078 / 136 016 | 24079 / 24079 / 136 017 |
| **1−** | 24080 / 24080 / 136 020 | 24081 / 24081 / 136 021 | 24082 / 24082 / 136 022 | 24083 / 24083 / 136 023 | 24084 / 24084 / 136 024 | 24085 / 24085 / 136 025 | 24086 / 24086 / 136 026 | 24087 / 24087 / 136 027 | 24088 / 24088 / 136 030 | 24089 / 24089 / 136 031 | 24090 / 24090 / 136 032 | 24091 / 24091 / 136 033 | 24092 / 24092 / 136 034 | 24093 / 24093 / 136 035 | 24094 / 24094 / 136 036 | 24095 / 24095 / 136 037 |
| **2−** | 24096 / 24096 / 136 040 | 24097 / 24097 / 136 041 | 24098 / 24098 / 136 042 | 24099 / 24099 / 136 043 | 24100 / 24100 / 136 044 | 24101 / 24101 / 136 045 | 24102 / 24102 / 136 046 | 24103 / 24103 / 136 047 | 24104 / 24104 / 136 050 | 24105 / 24105 / 136 051 | 24106 / 24106 / 136 052 | 24107 / 24107 / 136 053 | 24108 / 24108 / 136 054 | 24109 / 24109 / 136 055 | 24110 / 24110 / 136 056 | 24111 / 24111 / 136 057 |
| **3−** | 24112 / 24112 / 136 060 | 24113 / 24113 / 136 061 | 24114 / 24114 / 136 062 | 24115 / 24115 / 136 063 | 24116 / 24116 / 136 064 | 24117 / 24117 / 136 065 | 24118 / 24118 / 136 066 | 24119 / 24119 / 136 067 | 24120 / 24120 / 136 070 | 24121 / 24121 / 136 071 | 24122 / 24122 / 136 072 | 24123 / 24123 / 136 073 | 24124 / 24124 / 136 074 | 24125 / 24125 / 136 075 | 24126 / 24126 / 136 076 | 24127 / 24127 / 136 077 |
| **4−** | 24128 / 24128 / 136 100 | 24129 / 24129 / 136 101 | 24130 / 24130 / 136 102 | 24131 / 24131 / 136 103 | 24132 / 24132 / 136 104 | 24133 / 24133 / 136 105 | 24134 / 24134 / 136 106 | 24135 / 24135 / 136 107 | 24136 / 24136 / 136 110 | 24137 / 24137 / 136 111 | 24138 / 24138 / 136 112 | 24139 / 24139 / 136 113 | 24140 / 24140 / 136 114 | 24141 / 24141 / 136 115 | 24142 / 24142 / 136 116 | 24143 / 24143 / 136 117 |
| **5−** | 24144 / 24144 / 136 120 | 24145 / 24145 / 136 121 | 24146 / 24146 / 136 122 | 24147 / 24147 / 136 123 | 24148 / 24148 / 136 124 | 24149 / 24149 / 136 125 | 24150 / 24150 / 136 126 | 24151 / 24151 / 136 127 | 24152 / 24152 / 136 130 | 24153 / 24153 / 136 131 | 24154 / 24154 / 136 132 | 24155 / 24155 / 136 133 | 24156 / 24156 / 136 134 | 24157 / 24157 / 136 135 | 24158 / 24158 / 136 136 | 24159 / 24159 / 136 137 |
| **6−** | 24160 / 24160 / 136 140 | 24161 / 24161 / 136 141 | 24162 / 24162 / 136 142 | 24163 / 24163 / 136 143 | 24164 / 24164 / 136 144 | 24165 / 24165 / 136 145 | 24166 / 24166 / 136 146 | 24167 / 24167 / 136 147 | 24168 / 24168 / 136 150 | 24169 / 24169 / 136 151 | 24170 / 24170 / 136 152 | 24171 / 24171 / 136 153 | 24172 / 24172 / 136 154 | 24173 / 24173 / 136 155 | 24174 / 24174 / 136 156 | 24175 / 24175 / 136 157 |
| **7−** | 24176 / 24176 / 136 160 | 24177 / 24177 / 136 161 | 24178 / 24178 / 136 162 | 24179 / 24179 / 136 163 | 24180 / 24180 / 136 164 | 24181 / 24181 / 136 165 | 24182 / 24182 / 136 166 | 24183 / 24183 / 136 167 | 24184 / 24184 / 136 170 | 24185 / 24185 / 136 171 | 24186 / 24186 / 136 172 | 24187 / 24187 / 136 173 | 24188 / 24188 / 136 174 | 24189 / 24189 / 136 175 | 24190 / 24190 / 136 176 | 24191 / 24191 / 136 177 |
| **8−** | 24192 / 24192 / 136 200 | 24193 / 24193 / 136 201 | 24194 / 24194 / 136 202 | 24195 / 24195 / 136 203 | 24196 / 24196 / 136 204 | 24197 / 24197 / 136 205 | 24198 / 24198 / 136 206 | 24199 / 24199 / 136 207 | 24200 / 24200 / 136 210 | 24201 / 24201 / 136 211 | 24202 / 24202 / 136 212 | 24203 / 24203 / 136 213 | 24204 / 24204 / 136 214 | 24205 / 24205 / 136 215 | 24206 / 24206 / 136 216 | 24207 / 24207 / 136 217 |
| **9−** | 24208 / 24208 / 136 220 | 24209 / 24209 / 136 221 | 24210 / 24210 / 136 222 | 24211 / 24211 / 136 223 | 24212 / 24212 / 136 224 | 24213 / 24213 / 136 225 | 24214 / 24214 / 136 226 | 24215 / 24215 / 136 227 | 24216 / 24216 / 136 230 | 24217 / 24217 / 136 231 | 24218 / 24218 / 136 232 | 24219 / 24219 / 136 233 | 24220 / 24220 / 136 234 | 24221 / 24221 / 136 235 | 24222 / 24222 / 136 236 | 24223 / 24223 / 136 237 |
| **A−** | 24224 / 24224 / 136 240 | 24225 / 24225 / 136 241 | 24226 / 24226 / 136 242 | 24227 / 24227 / 136 243 | 24228 / 24228 / 136 244 | 24229 / 24229 / 136 245 | 24230 / 24230 / 136 246 | 24231 / 24231 / 136 247 | 24232 / 24232 / 136 250 | 24233 / 24233 / 136 251 | 24234 / 24234 / 136 252 | 24235 / 24235 / 136 253 | 24236 / 24236 / 136 254 | 24237 / 24237 / 136 255 | 24238 / 24238 / 136 256 | 24239 / 24239 / 136 257 |
| **B−** | 24240 / 24240 / 136 260 | 24241 / 24241 / 136 261 | 24242 / 24242 / 136 262 | 24243 / 24243 / 136 263 | 24244 / 24244 / 136 264 | 24245 / 24245 / 136 265 | 24246 / 24246 / 136 266 | 24247 / 24247 / 136 267 | 24248 / 24248 / 136 270 | 24249 / 24249 / 136 271 | 24250 / 24250 / 136 272 | 24251 / 24251 / 136 273 | 24252 / 24252 / 136 274 | 24253 / 24253 / 136 275 | 24254 / 24254 / 136 276 | 24255 / 24255 / 136 277 |
| **C−** | 24256 / 24256 / 136 300 | 24257 / 24257 / 136 301 | 24258 / 24258 / 136 302 | 24259 / 24259 / 136 303 | 24260 / 24260 / 136 304 | 24261 / 24261 / 136 305 | 24262 / 24262 / 136 306 | 24263 / 24263 / 136 307 | 24264 / 24264 / 136 310 | 24265 / 24265 / 136 311 | 24266 / 24266 / 136 312 | 24267 / 24267 / 136 313 | 24268 / 24268 / 136 314 | 24269 / 24269 / 136 315 | 24270 / 24270 / 136 316 | 24271 / 24271 / 136 317 |
| **D−** | 24272 / 24272 / 136 320 | 24273 / 24273 / 136 321 | 24274 / 24274 / 136 322 | 24275 / 24275 / 136 323 | 24276 / 24276 / 136 324 | 24277 / 24277 / 136 325 | 24278 / 24278 / 136 326 | 24279 / 24279 / 136 327 | 24280 / 24280 / 136 330 | 24281 / 24281 / 136 331 | 24282 / 24282 / 136 332 | 24283 / 24283 / 136 333 | 24284 / 24284 / 136 334 | 24285 / 24285 / 136 335 | 24286 / 24286 / 136 336 | 24287 / 24287 / 136 337 |
| **E−** | 24288 / 24288 / 136 340 | 24289 / 24289 / 136 341 | 24290 / 24290 / 136 342 | 24291 / 24291 / 136 343 | 24292 / 24292 / 136 344 | 24293 / 24293 / 136 345 | 24294 / 24294 / 136 346 | 24295 / 24295 / 136 347 | 24296 / 24296 / 136 350 | 24297 / 24297 / 136 351 | 24298 / 24298 / 136 352 | 24299 / 24299 / 136 353 | 24300 / 24300 / 136 354 | 24301 / 24301 / 136 355 | 24302 / 24302 / 136 356 | 24303 / 24303 / 136 357 |
| **F−** | 24304 / 24304 / 136 360 | 24305 / 24305 / 136 361 | 24306 / 24306 / 136 362 | 24307 / 24307 / 136 363 | 24308 / 24308 / 136 364 | 24309 / 24309 / 136 365 | 24310 / 24310 / 136 366 | 24311 / 24311 / 136 367 | 24312 / 24312 / 136 370 | 24313 / 24313 / 136 371 | 24314 / 24314 / 136 372 | 24315 / 24315 / 136 373 | 24316 / 24316 / 136 374 | 24317 / 24317 / 136 375 | 24318 / 24318 / 136 376 | 24319 / 24319 / 136 377 |

SECOND HEX DIGIT (row labels at left)

DECIMAL ↙

 DECIMAL ↙

OCTAL ↙

---

 DECIMAL [24064]  BINARY [0101 1110]  DECIMAL [24064]  HEXADECIMAL ⟨5E⟩  OCTAL [136 000]

FOURTH HEX DIGIT →  ← THIRD HEX DIGIT

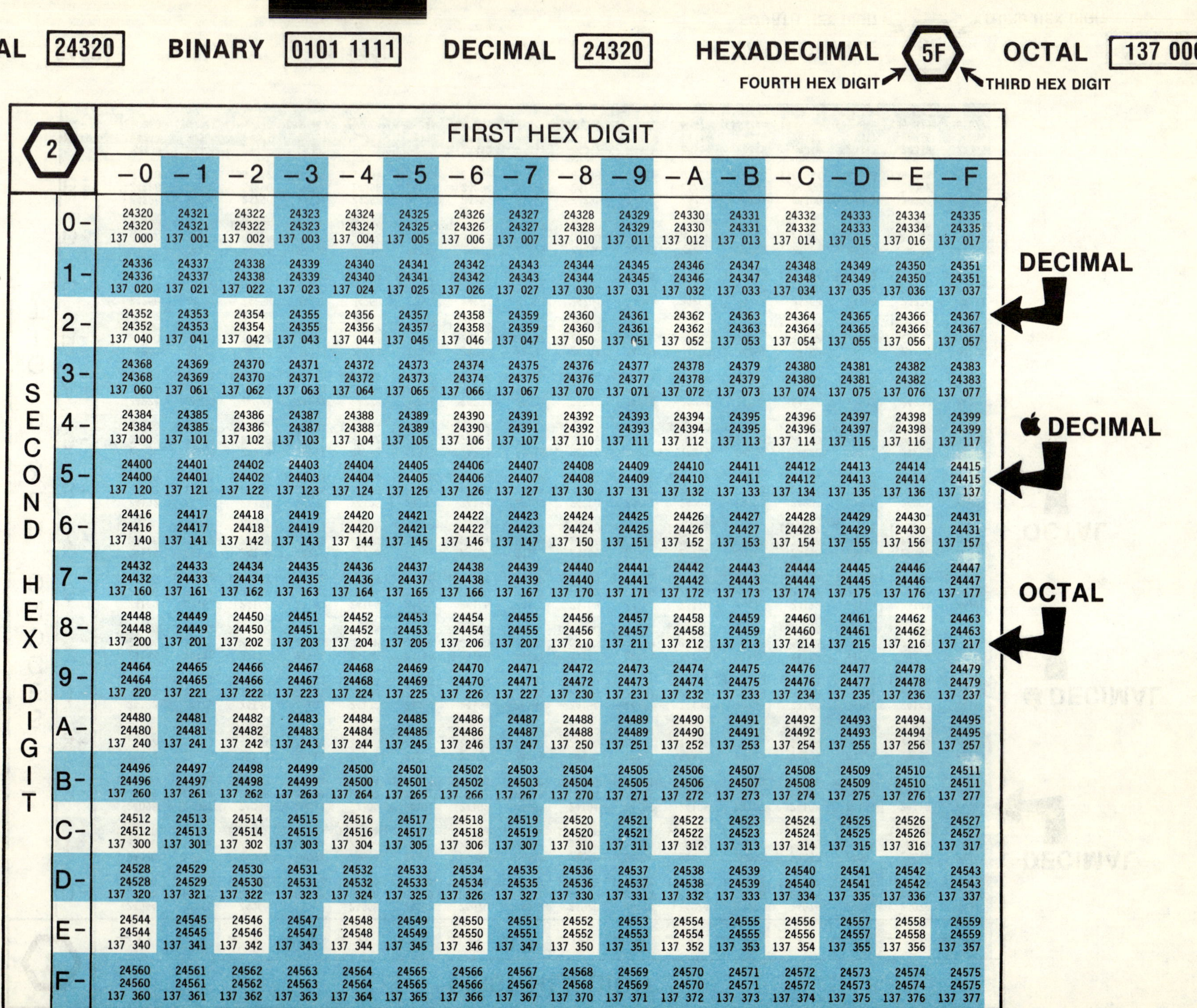

 DECIMAL `24320`　BINARY `0101 1111`　DECIMAL `24320`　HEXADECIMAL ⬡5F　OCTAL `137 000`

FOURTH HEX DIGIT →　← THIRD HEX DIGIT

⬡2

| SECOND HEX DIGIT | FIRST HEX DIGIT | | | | | | | | | | | | | | | |
|---|---|---|---|---|---|---|---|---|---|---|---|---|---|---|---|---|
| | −0 | −1 | −2 | −3 | −4 | −5 | −6 | −7 | −8 | −9 | −A | −B | −C | −D | −E | −F |
| 0− | 24320<br>24320<br>137 000 | 24321<br>24321<br>137 001 | 24322<br>24322<br>137 002 | 24323<br>24323<br>137 003 | 24324<br>24324<br>137 004 | 24325<br>24325<br>137 005 | 24326<br>24326<br>137 006 | 24327<br>24327<br>137 007 | 24328<br>24328<br>137 010 | 24329<br>24329<br>137 011 | 24330<br>24330<br>137 012 | 24331<br>24331<br>137 013 | 24332<br>24332<br>137 014 | 24333<br>24333<br>137 015 | 24334<br>24334<br>137 016 | 24335<br>24335<br>137 017 |
| 1− | 24336<br>24336<br>137 020 | 24337<br>24337<br>137 021 | 24338<br>24338<br>137 022 | 24339<br>24339<br>137 023 | 24340<br>24340<br>137 024 | 24341<br>24341<br>137 025 | 24342<br>24342<br>137 026 | 24343<br>24343<br>137 027 | 24344<br>24344<br>137 030 | 24345<br>24345<br>137 031 | 24346<br>24346<br>137 032 | 24347<br>24347<br>137 033 | 24348<br>24348<br>137 034 | 24349<br>24349<br>137 035 | 24350<br>24350<br>137 036 | 24351<br>24351<br>137 037 |
| 2− | 24352<br>24352<br>137 040 | 24353<br>24353<br>137 041 | 24354<br>24354<br>137 042 | 24355<br>24355<br>137 043 | 24356<br>24356<br>137 044 | 24357<br>24357<br>137 045 | 24358<br>24358<br>137 046 | 24359<br>24359<br>137 047 | 24360<br>24360<br>137 050 | 24361<br>24361<br>137 051 | 24362<br>24362<br>137 052 | 24363<br>24363<br>137 053 | 24364<br>24364<br>137 054 | 24365<br>24365<br>137 055 | 24366<br>24366<br>137 056 | 24367<br>24367<br>137 057 |
| 3− | 24368<br>24368<br>137 060 | 24369<br>24369<br>137 061 | 24370<br>24370<br>137 062 | 24371<br>24371<br>137 063 | 24372<br>24372<br>137 064 | 24373<br>24373<br>137 065 | 24374<br>24374<br>137 066 | 24375<br>24375<br>137 067 | 24376<br>24376<br>137 070 | 24377<br>24377<br>137 071 | 24378<br>24378<br>137 072 | 24379<br>24379<br>137 073 | 24380<br>24380<br>137 074 | 24381<br>24381<br>137 075 | 24382<br>24382<br>137 076 | 24383<br>24383<br>137 077 |
| 4− | 24384<br>24384<br>137 100 | 24385<br>24385<br>137 101 | 24386<br>24386<br>137 102 | 24387<br>24387<br>137 103 | 24388<br>24388<br>137 104 | 24389<br>24389<br>137 105 | 24390<br>24390<br>137 106 | 24391<br>24391<br>137 107 | 24392<br>24392<br>137 110 | 24393<br>24393<br>137 111 | 24394<br>24394<br>137 112 | 24395<br>24395<br>137 113 | 24396<br>24396<br>137 114 | 24397<br>24397<br>137 115 | 24398<br>24398<br>137 116 | 24399<br>24399<br>137 117 |
| 5− | 24400<br>24400<br>137 120 | 24401<br>24401<br>137 121 | 24402<br>24402<br>137 122 | 24403<br>24403<br>137 123 | 24404<br>24404<br>137 124 | 24405<br>24405<br>137 125 | 24406<br>24406<br>137 126 | 24407<br>24407<br>137 127 | 24408<br>24408<br>137 130 | 24409<br>24409<br>137 131 | 24410<br>24410<br>137 132 | 24411<br>24411<br>137 133 | 24412<br>24412<br>137 134 | 24413<br>24413<br>137 135 | 24414<br>24414<br>137 136 | 24415<br>24415<br>137 137 |
| 6− | 24416<br>24416<br>137 140 | 24417<br>24417<br>137 141 | 24418<br>24418<br>137 142 | 24419<br>24419<br>137 143 | 24420<br>24420<br>137 144 | 24421<br>24421<br>137 145 | 24422<br>24422<br>137 146 | 24423<br>24423<br>137 147 | 24424<br>24424<br>137 150 | 24425<br>24425<br>137 151 | 24426<br>24426<br>137 152 | 24427<br>24427<br>137 153 | 24428<br>24428<br>137 154 | 24429<br>24429<br>137 155 | 24430<br>24430<br>137 156 | 24431<br>24431<br>137 157 |
| 7− | 24432<br>24432<br>137 160 | 24433<br>24433<br>137 161 | 24434<br>24434<br>137 162 | 24435<br>24435<br>137 163 | 24436<br>24436<br>137 164 | 24437<br>24437<br>137 165 | 24438<br>24438<br>137 166 | 24439<br>24439<br>137 167 | 24440<br>24440<br>137 170 | 24441<br>24441<br>137 171 | 24442<br>24442<br>137 172 | 24443<br>24443<br>137 173 | 24444<br>24444<br>137 174 | 24445<br>24445<br>137 175 | 24446<br>24446<br>137 176 | 24447<br>24447<br>137 177 |
| 8− | 24448<br>24448<br>137 200 | 24449<br>24449<br>137 201 | 24450<br>24450<br>137 202 | 24451<br>24451<br>137 203 | 24452<br>24452<br>137 204 | 24453<br>24453<br>137 205 | 24454<br>24454<br>137 206 | 24455<br>24455<br>137 207 | 24456<br>24456<br>137 210 | 24457<br>24457<br>137 211 | 24458<br>24458<br>137 212 | 24459<br>24459<br>137 213 | 24460<br>24460<br>137 214 | 24461<br>24461<br>137 215 | 24462<br>24462<br>137 216 | 24463<br>24463<br>137 217 |
| 9− | 24464<br>24464<br>137 220 | 24465<br>24465<br>137 221 | 24466<br>24466<br>137 222 | 24467<br>24467<br>137 223 | 24468<br>24468<br>137 224 | 24469<br>24469<br>137 225 | 24470<br>24470<br>137 226 | 24471<br>24471<br>137 227 | 24472<br>24472<br>137 230 | 24473<br>24473<br>137 231 | 24474<br>24474<br>137 232 | 24475<br>24475<br>137 233 | 24476<br>24476<br>137 234 | 24477<br>24477<br>137 235 | 24478<br>24478<br>137 236 | 24479<br>24479<br>137 237 |
| A− | 24480<br>24480<br>137 240 | 24481<br>24481<br>137 241 | 24482<br>24482<br>137 242 | 24483<br>24483<br>137 243 | 24484<br>24484<br>137 244 | 24485<br>24485<br>137 245 | 24486<br>24486<br>137 246 | 24487<br>24487<br>137 247 | 24488<br>24488<br>137 250 | 24489<br>24489<br>137 251 | 24490<br>24490<br>137 252 | 24491<br>24491<br>137 253 | 24492<br>24492<br>137 254 | 24493<br>24493<br>137 255 | 24494<br>24494<br>137 256 | 24495<br>24495<br>137 257 |
| B− | 24496<br>24496<br>137 260 | 24497<br>24497<br>137 261 | 24498<br>24498<br>137 262 | 24499<br>24499<br>137 263 | 24500<br>24500<br>137 264 | 24501<br>24501<br>137 265 | 24502<br>24502<br>137 266 | 24503<br>24503<br>137 267 | 24504<br>24504<br>137 270 | 24505<br>24505<br>137 271 | 24506<br>24506<br>137 272 | 24507<br>24507<br>137 273 | 24508<br>24508<br>137 274 | 24509<br>24509<br>137 275 | 24510<br>24510<br>137 276 | 24511<br>24511<br>137 277 |
| C− | 24512<br>24512<br>137 300 | 24513<br>24513<br>137 301 | 24514<br>24514<br>137 302 | 24515<br>24515<br>137 303 | 24516<br>24516<br>137 304 | 24517<br>24517<br>137 305 | 24518<br>24518<br>137 306 | 24519<br>24519<br>137 307 | 24520<br>24520<br>137 310 | 24521<br>24521<br>137 311 | 24522<br>24522<br>137 312 | 24523<br>24523<br>137 313 | 24524<br>24524<br>137 314 | 24525<br>24525<br>137 315 | 24526<br>24526<br>137 316 | 24527<br>24527<br>137 317 |
| D− | 24528<br>24528<br>137 320 | 24529<br>24529<br>137 321 | 24530<br>24530<br>137 322 | 24531<br>24531<br>137 323 | 24532<br>24532<br>137 324 | 24533<br>24533<br>137 325 | 24534<br>24534<br>137 326 | 24535<br>24535<br>137 327 | 24536<br>24536<br>137 330 | 24537<br>24537<br>137 331 | 24538<br>24538<br>137 332 | 24539<br>24539<br>137 333 | 24540<br>24540<br>137 334 | 24541<br>24541<br>137 335 | 24542<br>24542<br>137 336 | 24543<br>24543<br>137 337 |
| E− | 24544<br>24544<br>137 340 | 24545<br>24545<br>137 341 | 24546<br>24546<br>137 342 | 24547<br>24547<br>137 343 | 24548<br>24548<br>137 344 | 24549<br>24549<br>137 345 | 24550<br>24550<br>137 346 | 24551<br>24551<br>137 347 | 24552<br>24552<br>137 350 | 24553<br>24553<br>137 351 | 24554<br>24554<br>137 352 | 24555<br>24555<br>137 353 | 24556<br>24556<br>137 354 | 24557<br>24557<br>137 355 | 24558<br>24558<br>137 356 | 24559<br>24559<br>137 357 |
| F− | 24560<br>24560<br>137 360 | 24561<br>24561<br>137 361 | 24562<br>24562<br>137 362 | 24563<br>24563<br>137 363 | 24564<br>24564<br>137 364 | 24565<br>24565<br>137 365 | 24566<br>24566<br>137 366 | 24567<br>24567<br>137 367 | 24568<br>24568<br>137 370 | 24569<br>24569<br>137 371 | 24570<br>24570<br>137 372 | 24571<br>24571<br>137 373 | 24572<br>24572<br>137 374 | 24573<br>24573<br>137 375 | 24574<br>24574<br>137 376 | 24575<br>24575<br>137 377 |

# FIRST HEX DIGIT



|  | −0 | −1 | −2 | −3 | −4 | −5 | −6 | −7 | −8 | −9 | −A | −B | −C | −D | −E | −F |
|---|---|---|---|---|---|---|---|---|---|---|---|---|---|---|---|---|
| **0−** | 24576<br>24576<br>140 000 | 24577<br>24577<br>140 001 | 24578<br>24578<br>140 002 | 24579<br>24579<br>140 003 | 24580<br>24580<br>140 004 | 24581<br>24581<br>140 005 | 24582<br>24582<br>140 006 | 24583<br>24583<br>140 007 | 24584<br>24584<br>140 010 | 24585<br>24585<br>140 011 | 24586<br>24586<br>140 012 | 24587<br>24587<br>140 013 | 24588<br>24588<br>140 014 | 24589<br>24589<br>140 015 | 24590<br>24590<br>140 016 | 24591<br>24591<br>140 017 |
| **1−** | 24592<br>24592<br>140 020 | 24593<br>24593<br>140 021 | 24594<br>24594<br>140 022 | 24595<br>24595<br>140 023 | 24596<br>24596<br>140 024 | 24597<br>24597<br>140 025 | 24598<br>24598<br>140 026 | 24599<br>24599<br>140 027 | 24600<br>24600<br>140 030 | 24601<br>24601<br>140 031 | 24602<br>24602<br>140 032 | 24603<br>24603<br>140 033 | 24604<br>24604<br>140 034 | 24605<br>24605<br>140 035 | 24606<br>24606<br>140 036 | 24607<br>24607<br>140 037 |
| **2−** | 24608<br>24608<br>140 040 | 24609<br>24609<br>140 041 | 24610<br>24610<br>140 042 | 24611<br>24611<br>140 043 | 24612<br>24612<br>140 044 | 24613<br>24613<br>140 045 | 24614<br>24614<br>140 046 | 24615<br>24615<br>140 047 | 24616<br>24616<br>140 050 | 24617<br>24617<br>140 051 | 24618<br>24618<br>140 052 | 24619<br>24619<br>140 053 | 24620<br>24620<br>140 054 | 24621<br>24621<br>140 055 | 24622<br>24622<br>140 056 | 24623<br>24623<br>140 057 |
| **3−** | 24624<br>24624<br>140 060 | 24625<br>24625<br>140 061 | 24626<br>24626<br>140 062 | 24627<br>24627<br>140 063 | 24628<br>24628<br>140 064 | 24629<br>24629<br>140 065 | 24630<br>24630<br>140 066 | 24631<br>24631<br>140 067 | 24632<br>24632<br>140 070 | 24633<br>24633<br>140 071 | 24634<br>24634<br>140 072 | 24635<br>24635<br>140 073 | 24636<br>24636<br>140 074 | 24637<br>24637<br>140 075 | 24638<br>24638<br>140 076 | 24639<br>24639<br>140 077 |
| **4−** | 24640<br>24640<br>140 100 | 24641<br>24641<br>140 101 | 24642<br>24642<br>140 102 | 24643<br>24643<br>140 103 | 24644<br>24644<br>140 104 | 24645<br>24645<br>140 105 | 24646<br>24646<br>140 106 | 24647<br>24647<br>140 107 | 24648<br>24648<br>140 110 | 24649<br>24649<br>140 111 | 24650<br>24650<br>140 112 | 24651<br>24651<br>140 113 | 24652<br>24652<br>140 114 | 24653<br>24653<br>140 115 | 24654<br>24654<br>140 116 | 24655<br>24655<br>140 117 |
| **5−** | 24656<br>24656<br>140 120 | 24657<br>24657<br>140 121 | 24658<br>24658<br>140 122 | 24659<br>24659<br>140 123 | 24660<br>24660<br>140 124 | 24661<br>24661<br>140 125 | 24662<br>24662<br>140 126 | 24663<br>24663<br>140 127 | 24664<br>24664<br>140 130 | 24665<br>24665<br>140 131 | 24666<br>24666<br>140 132 | 24667<br>24667<br>140 133 | 24668<br>24668<br>140 134 | 24669<br>24669<br>140 135 | 24670<br>24670<br>140 136 | 24671<br>24671<br>140 137 |
| **6−** | 24672<br>24672<br>140 140 | 24673<br>24673<br>140 141 | 24674<br>24674<br>140 142 | 24675<br>24675<br>140 143 | 24676<br>24676<br>140 144 | 24677<br>24677<br>140 145 | 24678<br>24678<br>140 146 | 24679<br>24679<br>140 147 | 24680<br>24680<br>140 150 | 24681<br>24681<br>140 151 | 24682<br>24682<br>140 152 | 24683<br>24683<br>140 153 | 24684<br>24684<br>140 154 | 24685<br>24685<br>140 155 | 24686<br>24686<br>140 156 | 24687<br>24687<br>140 157 |
| **7−** | 24688<br>24688<br>140 160 | 24689<br>24689<br>140 161 | 24690<br>24690<br>140 162 | 24691<br>24691<br>140 163 | 24692<br>24692<br>140 164 | 24693<br>24693<br>140 165 | 24694<br>24694<br>140 166 | 24695<br>24695<br>140 167 | 24696<br>24696<br>140 170 | 24697<br>24697<br>140 171 | 24698<br>24698<br>140 172 | 24699<br>24699<br>140 173 | 24700<br>24700<br>140 174 | 24701<br>24701<br>140 175 | 24702<br>24702<br>140 176 | 24703<br>24703<br>140 177 |
| **8−** | 24704<br>24704<br>140 200 | 24705<br>24705<br>140 201 | 24706<br>24706<br>140 202 | 24707<br>24707<br>140 203 | 24708<br>24708<br>140 204 | 24709<br>24709<br>140 205 | 24710<br>24710<br>140 206 | 24711<br>24711<br>140 207 | 24712<br>24712<br>140 210 | 24713<br>24713<br>140 211 | 24714<br>24714<br>140 212 | 24715<br>24715<br>140 213 | 24716<br>24716<br>140 214 | 24717<br>24717<br>140 215 | 24718<br>24718<br>140 216 | 24719<br>24719<br>140 217 |
| **9−** | 24720<br>24720<br>140 220 | 24721<br>24721<br>140 221 | 24722<br>24722<br>140 222 | 24723<br>24723<br>140 223 | 24724<br>24724<br>140 224 | 24725<br>24725<br>140 225 | 24726<br>24726<br>140 226 | 24727<br>24727<br>140 227 | 24728<br>24728<br>140 230 | 24729<br>24729<br>140 231 | 24730<br>24730<br>140 232 | 24731<br>24731<br>140 233 | 24732<br>24732<br>140 234 | 24733<br>24733<br>140 235 | 24734<br>24734<br>140 236 | 24735<br>24735<br>140 237 |
| **A−** | 24736<br>24736<br>140 240 | 24737<br>24737<br>140 241 | 24738<br>24738<br>140 242 | 24739<br>24739<br>140 243 | 24740<br>24740<br>140 244 | 24741<br>24741<br>140 245 | 24742<br>24742<br>140 246 | 24743<br>24743<br>140 247 | 24744<br>24744<br>140 250 | 24745<br>24745<br>140 251 | 24746<br>24746<br>140 252 | 24747<br>24747<br>140 253 | 24748<br>24748<br>140 254 | 24749<br>24749<br>140 255 | 24750<br>24750<br>140 256 | 24751<br>24751<br>140 257 |
| **B−** | 24752<br>24752<br>140 260 | 24753<br>24753<br>140 261 | 24754<br>24754<br>140 262 | 24755<br>24755<br>140 263 | 24756<br>24756<br>140 264 | 24757<br>24757<br>140 265 | 24758<br>24758<br>140 266 | 24759<br>24759<br>140 267 | 24760<br>24760<br>140 270 | 24761<br>24761<br>140 271 | 24762<br>24762<br>140 272 | 24763<br>24763<br>140 273 | 24764<br>24764<br>140 274 | 24765<br>24765<br>140 275 | 24766<br>24766<br>140 276 | 24767<br>24767<br>140 277 |
| **C−** | 24768<br>24768<br>140 300 | 24769<br>24769<br>140 301 | 24770<br>24770<br>140 302 | 24771<br>24771<br>140 303 | 24772<br>24772<br>140 304 | 24773<br>24773<br>140 305 | 24774<br>24774<br>140 306 | 24775<br>24775<br>140 307 | 24776<br>24776<br>140 310 | 24777<br>24777<br>140 311 | 24778<br>24778<br>140 312 | 24779<br>24779<br>140 313 | 24780<br>24780<br>140 314 | 24781<br>24781<br>140 315 | 24782<br>24782<br>140 316 | 24783<br>24783<br>140 317 |
| **D−** | 24784<br>24784<br>140 320 | 24785<br>24785<br>140 321 | 24786<br>24786<br>140 322 | 24787<br>24787<br>140 323 | 24788<br>24788<br>140 324 | 24789<br>24789<br>140 325 | 24790<br>24790<br>140 326 | 24791<br>24791<br>140 327 | 24792<br>24792<br>140 330 | 24793<br>24793<br>140 331 | 24794<br>24794<br>140 332 | 24795<br>24795<br>140 333 | 24796<br>24796<br>140 334 | 24797<br>24797<br>140 335 | 24798<br>24798<br>140 336 | 24799<br>24799<br>140 337 |
| **E−** | 24800<br>24800<br>140 340 | 24801<br>24801<br>140 341 | 24802<br>24802<br>140 342 | 24803<br>24803<br>140 343 | 24804<br>24804<br>140 344 | 24805<br>24805<br>140 345 | 24806<br>24806<br>140 346 | 24807<br>24807<br>140 347 | 24808<br>24808<br>140 350 | 24809<br>24809<br>140 351 | 24810<br>24810<br>140 352 | 24811<br>24811<br>140 353 | 24812<br>24812<br>140 354 | 24813<br>24813<br>140 355 | 24814<br>24814<br>140 356 | 24815<br>24815<br>140 357 |
| **F−** | 24816<br>24816<br>140 360 | 24817<br>24817<br>140 361 | 24818<br>24818<br>140 362 | 24819<br>24819<br>140 363 | 24820<br>24820<br>140 364 | 24821<br>24821<br>140 365 | 24822<br>24822<br>140 366 | 24823<br>24823<br>140 367 | 24824<br>24824<br>140 370 | 24825<br>24825<br>140 371 | 24826<br>24826<br>140 372 | 24827<br>24827<br>140 373 | 24828<br>24828<br>140 374 | 24829<br>24829<br>140 375 | 24830<br>24830<br>140 376 | 24831<br>24831<br>140 377 |

Row label: **SECOND HEX DIGIT**

Column annotations (right side): DECIMAL → , ⬤ DECIMAL → , OCTAL →

⬤ DECIMAL  `24576`   BINARY  `0110 0000`   DECIMAL  `24576`   HEXADECIMAL  ⬡ `60`   OCTAL  `140 000`

FOURTH HEX DIGIT →   ← THIRD HEX DIGIT

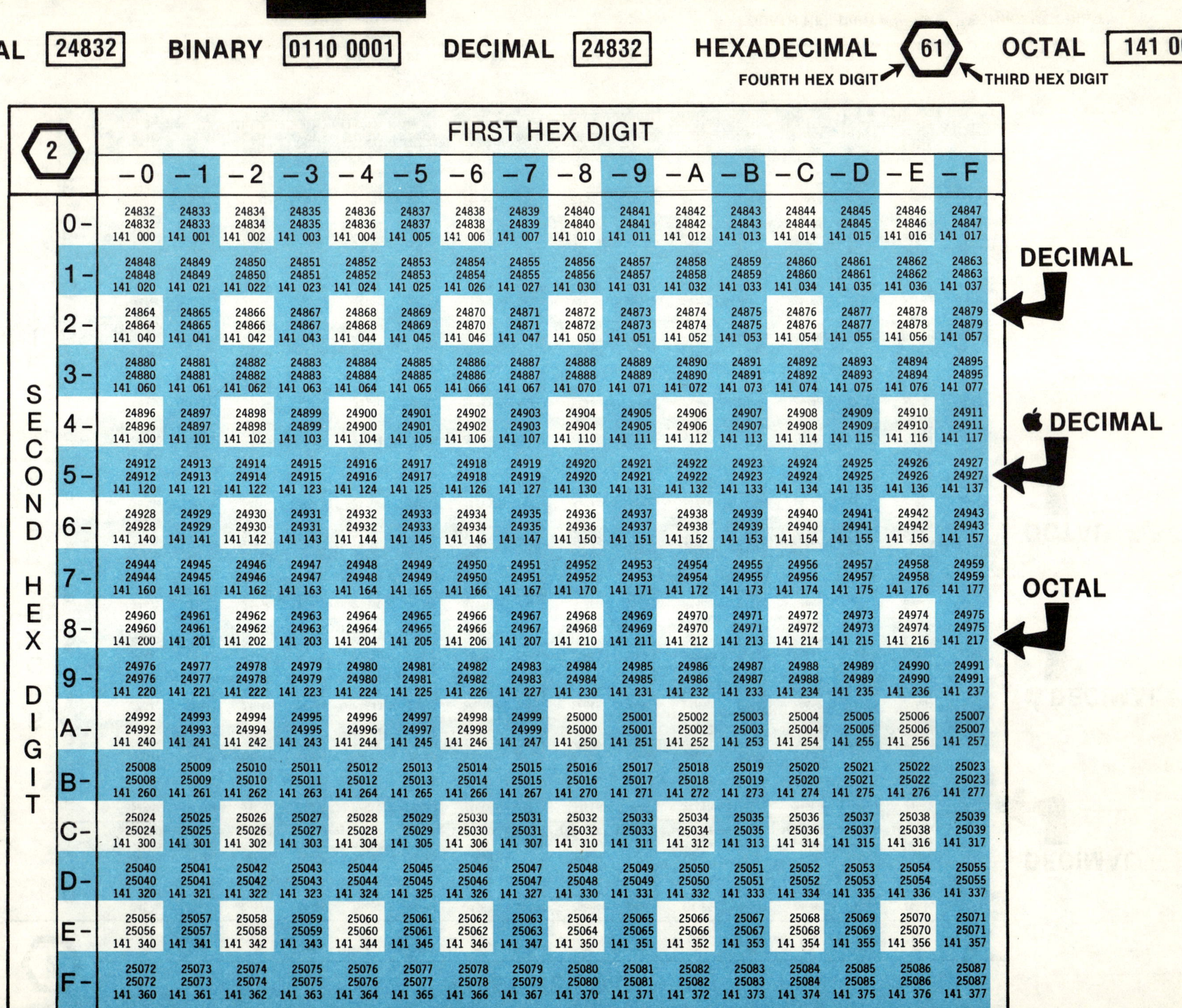

DECIMAL [24832]   BINARY [0110 0001]   DECIMAL [24832]   HEXADECIMAL ⬡61   OCTAL [141 000]

FOURTH HEX DIGIT → 61 ← THIRD HEX DIGIT

**FIRST HEX DIGIT** (columns); **SECOND HEX DIGIT** (rows). Each cell shows: decimal / decimal / octal.

⬡2

| | −0 | −1 | −2 | −3 | −4 | −5 | −6 | −7 | −8 | −9 | −A | −B | −C | −D | −E | −F |
|---|---|---|---|---|---|---|---|---|---|---|---|---|---|---|---|---|
| **0−** | 24832<br>24832<br>141 000 | 24833<br>24833<br>141 001 | 24834<br>24834<br>141 002 | 24835<br>24835<br>141 003 | 24836<br>24836<br>141 004 | 24837<br>24837<br>141 005 | 24838<br>24838<br>141 006 | 24839<br>24839<br>141 007 | 24840<br>24840<br>141 010 | 24841<br>24841<br>141 011 | 24842<br>24842<br>141 012 | 24843<br>24843<br>141 013 | 24844<br>24844<br>141 014 | 24845<br>24845<br>141 015 | 24846<br>24846<br>141 016 | 24847<br>24847<br>141 017 |
| **1−** | 24848<br>24848<br>141 020 | 24849<br>24849<br>141 021 | 24850<br>24850<br>141 022 | 24851<br>24851<br>141 023 | 24852<br>24852<br>141 024 | 24853<br>24853<br>141 025 | 24854<br>24854<br>141 026 | 24855<br>24855<br>141 027 | 24856<br>24856<br>141 030 | 24857<br>24857<br>141 031 | 24858<br>24858<br>141 032 | 24859<br>24859<br>141 033 | 24860<br>24860<br>141 034 | 24861<br>24861<br>141 035 | 24862<br>24862<br>141 036 | 24863<br>24863<br>141 037 |
| **2−** | 24864<br>24864<br>141 040 | 24865<br>24865<br>141 041 | 24866<br>24866<br>141 042 | 24867<br>24867<br>141 043 | 24868<br>24868<br>141 044 | 24869<br>24869<br>141 045 | 24870<br>24870<br>141 046 | 24871<br>24871<br>141 047 | 24872<br>24872<br>141 050 | 24873<br>24873<br>141 051 | 24874<br>24874<br>141 052 | 24875<br>24875<br>141 053 | 24876<br>24876<br>141 054 | 24877<br>24877<br>141 055 | 24878<br>24878<br>141 056 | 24879<br>24879<br>141 057 |
| **3−** | 24880<br>24880<br>141 060 | 24881<br>24881<br>141 061 | 24882<br>24882<br>141 062 | 24883<br>24883<br>141 063 | 24884<br>24884<br>141 064 | 24885<br>24885<br>141 065 | 24886<br>24886<br>141 066 | 24887<br>24887<br>141 067 | 24888<br>24888<br>141 070 | 24889<br>24889<br>141 071 | 24890<br>24890<br>141 072 | 24891<br>24891<br>141 073 | 24892<br>24892<br>141 074 | 24893<br>24893<br>141 075 | 24894<br>24894<br>141 076 | 24895<br>24895<br>141 077 |
| **4−** | 24896<br>24896<br>141 100 | 24897<br>24897<br>141 101 | 24898<br>24898<br>141 102 | 24899<br>24899<br>141 103 | 24900<br>24900<br>141 104 | 24901<br>24901<br>141 105 | 24902<br>24902<br>141 106 | 24903<br>24903<br>141 107 | 24904<br>24904<br>141 110 | 24905<br>24905<br>141 111 | 24906<br>24906<br>141 112 | 24907<br>24907<br>141 113 | 24908<br>24908<br>141 114 | 24909<br>24909<br>141 115 | 24910<br>24910<br>141 116 | 24911<br>24911<br>141 117 |
| **5−** | 24912<br>24912<br>141 120 | 24913<br>24913<br>141 121 | 24914<br>24914<br>141 122 | 24915<br>24915<br>141 123 | 24916<br>24916<br>141 124 | 24917<br>24917<br>141 125 | 24918<br>24918<br>141 126 | 24919<br>24919<br>141 127 | 24920<br>24920<br>141 130 | 24921<br>24921<br>141 131 | 24922<br>24922<br>141 132 | 24923<br>24923<br>141 133 | 24924<br>24924<br>141 134 | 24925<br>24925<br>141 135 | 24926<br>24926<br>141 136 | 24927<br>24927<br>141 137 |
| **6−** | 24928<br>24928<br>141 140 | 24929<br>24929<br>141 141 | 24930<br>24930<br>141 142 | 24931<br>24931<br>141 143 | 24932<br>24932<br>141 144 | 24933<br>24933<br>141 145 | 24934<br>24934<br>141 146 | 24935<br>24935<br>141 147 | 24936<br>24936<br>141 150 | 24937<br>24937<br>141 151 | 24938<br>24938<br>141 152 | 24939<br>24939<br>141 153 | 24940<br>24940<br>141 154 | 24941<br>24941<br>141 155 | 24942<br>24942<br>141 156 | 24943<br>24943<br>141 157 |
| **7−** | 24944<br>24944<br>141 160 | 24945<br>24945<br>141 161 | 24946<br>24946<br>141 162 | 24947<br>24947<br>141 163 | 24948<br>24948<br>141 164 | 24949<br>24949<br>141 165 | 24950<br>24950<br>141 166 | 24951<br>24951<br>141 167 | 24952<br>24952<br>141 170 | 24953<br>24953<br>141 171 | 24954<br>24954<br>141 172 | 24955<br>24955<br>141 173 | 24956<br>24956<br>141 174 | 24957<br>24957<br>141 175 | 24958<br>24958<br>141 176 | 24959<br>24959<br>141 177 |
| **8−** | 24960<br>24960<br>141 200 | 24961<br>24961<br>141 201 | 24962<br>24962<br>141 202 | 24963<br>24963<br>141 203 | 24964<br>24964<br>141 204 | 24965<br>24965<br>141 205 | 24966<br>24966<br>141 206 | 24967<br>24967<br>141 207 | 24968<br>24968<br>141 210 | 24969<br>24969<br>141 211 | 24970<br>24970<br>141 212 | 24971<br>24971<br>141 213 | 24972<br>24972<br>141 214 | 24973<br>24973<br>141 215 | 24974<br>24974<br>141 216 | 24975<br>24975<br>141 217 |
| **9−** | 24976<br>24976<br>141 220 | 24977<br>24977<br>141 221 | 24978<br>24978<br>141 222 | 24979<br>24979<br>141 223 | 24980<br>24980<br>141 224 | 24981<br>24981<br>141 225 | 24982<br>24982<br>141 226 | 24983<br>24983<br>141 227 | 24984<br>24984<br>141 230 | 24985<br>24985<br>141 231 | 24986<br>24986<br>141 232 | 24987<br>24987<br>141 233 | 24988<br>24988<br>141 234 | 24989<br>24989<br>141 235 | 24990<br>24990<br>141 236 | 24991<br>24991<br>141 237 |
| **A−** | 24992<br>24992<br>141 240 | 24993<br>24993<br>141 241 | 24994<br>24994<br>141 242 | 24995<br>24995<br>141 243 | 24996<br>24996<br>141 244 | 24997<br>24997<br>141 245 | 24998<br>24998<br>141 246 | 24999<br>24999<br>141 247 | 25000<br>25000<br>141 250 | 25001<br>25001<br>141 251 | 25002<br>25002<br>141 252 | 25003<br>25003<br>141 253 | 25004<br>25004<br>141 254 | 25005<br>25005<br>141 255 | 25006<br>25006<br>141 256 | 25007<br>25007<br>141 257 |
| **B−** | 25008<br>25008<br>141 260 | 25009<br>25009<br>141 261 | 25010<br>25010<br>141 262 | 25011<br>25011<br>141 263 | 25012<br>25012<br>141 264 | 25013<br>25013<br>141 265 | 25014<br>25014<br>141 266 | 25015<br>25015<br>141 267 | 25016<br>25016<br>141 270 | 25017<br>25017<br>141 271 | 25018<br>25018<br>141 272 | 25019<br>25019<br>141 273 | 25020<br>25020<br>141 274 | 25021<br>25021<br>141 275 | 25022<br>25022<br>141 276 | 25023<br>25023<br>141 277 |
| **C−** | 25024<br>25024<br>141 300 | 25025<br>25025<br>141 301 | 25026<br>25026<br>141 302 | 25027<br>25027<br>141 303 | 25028<br>25028<br>141 304 | 25029<br>25029<br>141 305 | 25030<br>25030<br>141 306 | 25031<br>25031<br>141 307 | 25032<br>25032<br>141 310 | 25033<br>25033<br>141 311 | 25034<br>25034<br>141 312 | 25035<br>25035<br>141 313 | 25036<br>25036<br>141 314 | 25037<br>25037<br>141 315 | 25038<br>25038<br>141 316 | 25039<br>25039<br>141 317 |
| **D−** | 25040<br>25040<br>141 320 | 25041<br>25041<br>141 321 | 25042<br>25042<br>141 322 | 25043<br>25043<br>141 323 | 25044<br>25044<br>141 324 | 25045<br>25045<br>141 325 | 25046<br>25046<br>141 326 | 25047<br>25047<br>141 327 | 25048<br>25048<br>141 330 | 25049<br>25049<br>141 331 | 25050<br>25050<br>141 332 | 25051<br>25051<br>141 333 | 25052<br>25052<br>141 334 | 25053<br>25053<br>141 335 | 25054<br>25054<br>141 336 | 25055<br>25055<br>141 337 |
| **E−** | 25056<br>25056<br>141 340 | 25057<br>25057<br>141 341 | 25058<br>25058<br>141 342 | 25059<br>25059<br>141 343 | 25060<br>25060<br>141 344 | 25061<br>25061<br>141 345 | 25062<br>25062<br>141 346 | 25063<br>25063<br>141 347 | 25064<br>25064<br>141 350 | 25065<br>25065<br>141 351 | 25066<br>25066<br>141 352 | 25067<br>25067<br>141 353 | 25068<br>25068<br>141 354 | 25069<br>25069<br>141 355 | 25070<br>25070<br>141 356 | 25071<br>25071<br>141 357 |
| **F−** | 25072<br>25072<br>141 360 | 25073<br>25073<br>141 361 | 25074<br>25074<br>141 362 | 25075<br>25075<br>141 363 | 25076<br>25076<br>141 364 | 25077<br>25077<br>141 365 | 25078<br>25078<br>141 366 | 25079<br>25079<br>141 367 | 25080<br>25080<br>141 370 | 25081<br>25081<br>141 371 | 25082<br>25082<br>141 372 | 25083<br>25083<br>141 373 | 25084<br>25084<br>141 374 | 25085<br>25085<br>141 375 | 25086<br>25086<br>141 376 | 25087<br>25087<br>141 377 |

| 2 | −0 | −1 | −2 | −3 | −4 | −5 | −6 | −7 | −8 | −9 | −A | −B | −C | −D | −E | −F |
|---|---|---|---|---|---|---|---|---|---|---|---|---|---|---|---|---|
| **0−** | 25088<br>25088<br>142 000 | 25089<br>25089<br>142 001 | 25090<br>25090<br>142 002 | 25091<br>25091<br>142 003 | 25092<br>25092<br>142 004 | 25093<br>25093<br>142 005 | 25094<br>25094<br>142 006 | 25095<br>25095<br>142 007 | 25096<br>25096<br>142 010 | 25097<br>25097<br>142 011 | 25098<br>25098<br>142 012 | 25099<br>25099<br>142 013 | 25100<br>25100<br>142 014 | 25101<br>25101<br>142 015 | 25102<br>25102<br>142 016 | 25103<br>25103<br>142 017 |
| **1−** | 25104<br>25104<br>142 020 | 25105<br>25105<br>142 021 | 25106<br>25106<br>142 022 | 25107<br>25107<br>142 023 | 25108<br>25108<br>142 024 | 25109<br>25109<br>142 025 | 25110<br>25110<br>142 026 | 25111<br>25111<br>142 027 | 25112<br>25112<br>142 030 | 25113<br>25113<br>142 031 | 25114<br>25114<br>142 032 | 25115<br>25115<br>142 033 | 25116<br>25116<br>142 034 | 25117<br>25117<br>142 035 | 25118<br>25118<br>142 036 | 25119<br>25119<br>142 037 |
| **2−** | 25120<br>25120<br>142 040 | 25121<br>25121<br>142 041 | 25122<br>25122<br>142 042 | 25123<br>25123<br>142 043 | 25124<br>25124<br>142 044 | 25125<br>25125<br>142 045 | 25126<br>25126<br>142 046 | 25127<br>25127<br>142 047 | 25128<br>25128<br>142 050 | 25129<br>25129<br>142 051 | 25130<br>25130<br>142 052 | 25131<br>25131<br>142 053 | 25132<br>25132<br>142 054 | 25133<br>25133<br>142 055 | 25134<br>25134<br>142 056 | 25135<br>25135<br>142 057 |
| **3−** | 25136<br>25136<br>142 060 | 25137<br>25137<br>142 061 | 25138<br>25138<br>142 062 | 25139<br>25139<br>142 063 | 25140<br>25140<br>142 064 | 25141<br>25141<br>142 065 | 25142<br>25142<br>142 066 | 25143<br>25143<br>142 067 | 25144<br>25144<br>142 070 | 25145<br>25145<br>142 071 | 25146<br>25146<br>142 072 | 25147<br>25147<br>142 073 | 25148<br>25148<br>142 074 | 25149<br>25149<br>142 075 | 25150<br>25150<br>142 076 | 25151<br>25151<br>142 077 |
| **4−** | 25152<br>25152<br>142 100 | 25153<br>25153<br>142 101 | 25154<br>25154<br>142 102 | 25155<br>25155<br>142 103 | 25156<br>25156<br>142 104 | 25157<br>25157<br>142 105 | 25158<br>25158<br>142 106 | 25159<br>25159<br>142 107 | 25160<br>25160<br>142 110 | 25161<br>25161<br>142 111 | 25162<br>25162<br>142 112 | 25163<br>25163<br>142 113 | 25164<br>25164<br>142 114 | 25165<br>25165<br>142 115 | 25166<br>25166<br>142 116 | 25167<br>25167<br>142 117 |
| **5−** | 25168<br>25168<br>142 120 | 25169<br>25169<br>142 121 | 25170<br>25170<br>142 122 | 25171<br>25171<br>142 123 | 25172<br>25172<br>142 124 | 25173<br>25173<br>142 125 | 25174<br>25174<br>142 126 | 25175<br>25175<br>142 127 | 25176<br>25176<br>142 130 | 25177<br>25177<br>142 131 | 25178<br>25178<br>142 132 | 25179<br>25179<br>142 133 | 25180<br>25180<br>142 134 | 25181<br>25181<br>142 135 | 25182<br>25182<br>142 136 | 25183<br>25183<br>142 137 |
| **6−** | 25184<br>25184<br>142 140 | 25185<br>25185<br>142 141 | 25186<br>25186<br>142 142 | 25187<br>25187<br>142 143 | 25188<br>25188<br>142 144 | 25189<br>25189<br>142 145 | 25190<br>25190<br>142 146 | 25191<br>25191<br>142 147 | 25192<br>25192<br>142 150 | 25193<br>25193<br>142 151 | 25194<br>25194<br>142 152 | 25195<br>25195<br>142 153 | 25196<br>25196<br>142 154 | 25197<br>25197<br>142 155 | 25198<br>25198<br>142 156 | 25199<br>25199<br>142 157 |
| **7−** | 25200<br>25200<br>142 160 | 25201<br>25201<br>142 161 | 25202<br>25202<br>142 162 | 25203<br>25203<br>142 163 | 25204<br>25204<br>142 164 | 25205<br>25205<br>142 165 | 25206<br>25206<br>142 166 | 25207<br>25207<br>142 167 | 25208<br>25208<br>142 170 | 25209<br>25209<br>142 171 | 25210<br>25210<br>142 172 | 25211<br>25211<br>142 173 | 25212<br>25212<br>142 174 | 25213<br>25213<br>142 175 | 25214<br>25214<br>142 176 | 25215<br>25215<br>142 177 |
| **8−** | 25216<br>25216<br>142 200 | 25217<br>25217<br>142 201 | 25218<br>25218<br>142 202 | 25219<br>25219<br>142 203 | 25220<br>25220<br>142 204 | 25221<br>25221<br>142 205 | 25222<br>25222<br>142 206 | 25223<br>25223<br>142 207 | 25224<br>25224<br>142 210 | 25225<br>25225<br>142 211 | 25226<br>25226<br>142 212 | 25227<br>25227<br>142 213 | 25228<br>25228<br>142 214 | 25229<br>25229<br>142 215 | 25230<br>25230<br>142 216 | 25231<br>25231<br>142 217 |
| **9−** | 25232<br>25232<br>142 220 | 25233<br>25233<br>142 221 | 25234<br>25234<br>142 222 | 25235<br>25235<br>142 223 | 25236<br>25236<br>142 224 | 25237<br>25237<br>142 225 | 25238<br>25238<br>142 226 | 25239<br>25239<br>142 227 | 25240<br>25240<br>142 230 | 25241<br>25241<br>142 231 | 25242<br>25242<br>142 232 | 25243<br>25243<br>142 233 | 25244<br>25244<br>142 234 | 25245<br>25245<br>142 235 | 25246<br>25246<br>142 236 | 25247<br>25247<br>142 237 |
| **A−** | 25248<br>25248<br>142 240 | 25249<br>25249<br>142 241 | 25250<br>25250<br>142 242 | 25251<br>25251<br>142 243 | 25252<br>25252<br>142 244 | 25253<br>25253<br>142 245 | 25254<br>25254<br>142 246 | 25255<br>25255<br>142 247 | 25256<br>25256<br>142 250 | 25257<br>25257<br>142 251 | 25258<br>25258<br>142 252 | 25259<br>25259<br>142 253 | 25260<br>25260<br>142 254 | 25261<br>25261<br>142 255 | 25262<br>25262<br>142 256 | 25263<br>25263<br>142 257 |
| **B−** | 25264<br>25264<br>142 260 | 25265<br>25265<br>142 261 | 25266<br>25266<br>142 262 | 25267<br>25267<br>142 263 | 25268<br>25268<br>142 264 | 25269<br>25269<br>142 265 | 25270<br>25270<br>142 266 | 25271<br>25271<br>142 267 | 25272<br>25272<br>142 270 | 25273<br>25273<br>142 271 | 25274<br>25274<br>142 272 | 25275<br>25275<br>142 273 | 25276<br>25276<br>142 274 | 25277<br>25277<br>142 275 | 25278<br>25278<br>142 276 | 25279<br>25279<br>142 277 |
| **C−** | 25280<br>25280<br>142 300 | 25281<br>25281<br>142 301 | 25282<br>25282<br>142 302 | 25283<br>25283<br>142 303 | 25284<br>25284<br>142 304 | 25285<br>25285<br>142 305 | 25286<br>25286<br>142 306 | 25287<br>25287<br>142 307 | 25288<br>25288<br>142 310 | 25289<br>25289<br>142 311 | 25290<br>25290<br>142 312 | 25291<br>25291<br>142 313 | 25292<br>25292<br>142 314 | 25293<br>25293<br>142 315 | 25294<br>25294<br>142 316 | 25295<br>25295<br>142 317 |
| **D−** | 25296<br>25296<br>142 320 | 25297<br>25297<br>142 321 | 25298<br>25298<br>142 322 | 25299<br>25299<br>142 323 | 25300<br>25300<br>142 324 | 25301<br>25301<br>142 325 | 25302<br>25302<br>142 326 | 25303<br>25303<br>142 327 | 25304<br>25304<br>142 330 | 25305<br>25305<br>142 331 | 25306<br>25306<br>142 332 | 25307<br>25307<br>142 333 | 25308<br>25308<br>142 334 | 25309<br>25309<br>142 335 | 25310<br>25310<br>142 336 | 25311<br>25311<br>142 337 |
| **E−** | 25312<br>25312<br>142 340 | 25313<br>25313<br>142 341 | 25314<br>25314<br>142 342 | 25315<br>25315<br>142 343 | 25316<br>25316<br>142 344 | 25317<br>25317<br>142 345 | 25318<br>25318<br>142 346 | 25319<br>25319<br>142 347 | 25320<br>25320<br>142 350 | 25321<br>25321<br>142 351 | 25322<br>25322<br>142 352 | 25323<br>25323<br>142 353 | 25324<br>25324<br>142 354 | 25325<br>25325<br>142 355 | 25326<br>25326<br>142 356 | 25327<br>25327<br>142 357 |
| **F−** | 25328<br>25328<br>142 360 | 25329<br>25329<br>142 361 | 25330<br>25330<br>142 362 | 25331<br>25331<br>142 363 | 25332<br>25332<br>142 364 | 25333<br>25333<br>142 365 | 25334<br>25334<br>142 366 | 25335<br>25335<br>142 367 | 25336<br>25336<br>142 370 | 25337<br>25337<br>142 371 | 25338<br>25338<br>142 372 | 25339<br>25339<br>142 373 | 25340<br>25340<br>142 374 | 25341<br>25341<br>142 375 | 25342<br>25342<br>142 376 | 25343<br>25343<br>142 377 |

SECOND HEX DIGIT

 DECIMAL →
 DECIMAL →
OCTAL →

**FIRST HEX DIGIT** (②)

| SECOND HEX DIGIT | −0 | −1 | −2 | −3 | −4 | −5 | −6 | −7 | −8 | −9 | −A | −B | −C | −D | −E | −F |
| --- | --- | --- | --- | --- | --- | --- | --- | --- | --- | --- | --- | --- | --- | --- | --- | --- |
| 0− | 25344<br>143 000 | 25345<br>143 001 | 25346<br>143 002 | 25347<br>143 003 | 25348<br>143 004 | 25349<br>143 005 | 25350<br>143 006 | 25351<br>143 007 | 25352<br>143 010 | 25353<br>143 011 | 25354<br>143 012 | 25355<br>143 013 | 25356<br>143 014 | 25357<br>143 015 | 25358<br>143 016 | 25359<br>143 017 |
| 1− | 25360<br>143 020 | 25361<br>143 021 | 25362<br>143 022 | 25363<br>143 023 | 25364<br>143 024 | 25365<br>143 025 | 25366<br>143 026 | 25367<br>143 027 | 25368<br>143 030 | 25369<br>143 031 | 25370<br>143 032 | 25371<br>143 033 | 25372<br>143 034 | 25373<br>143 035 | 25374<br>143 036 | 25375<br>143 037 |
| 2− | 25376<br>143 040 | 25377<br>143 041 | 25378<br>143 042 | 25379<br>143 043 | 25380<br>143 044 | 25381<br>143 045 | 25382<br>143 046 | 25383<br>143 047 | 25384<br>143 050 | 25385<br>143 051 | 25386<br>143 052 | 25387<br>143 053 | 25388<br>143 054 | 25389<br>143 055 | 25390<br>143 056 | 25391<br>143 057 |
| 3− | 25392<br>143 060 | 25393<br>143 061 | 25394<br>143 062 | 25395<br>143 063 | 25396<br>143 064 | 25397<br>143 065 | 25398<br>143 066 | 25399<br>143 067 | 25400<br>143 070 | 25401<br>143 071 | 25402<br>143 072 | 25403<br>143 073 | 25404<br>143 074 | 25405<br>143 075 | 25406<br>143 076 | 25407<br>143 077 |
| 4− | 25408<br>143 100 | 25409<br>143 101 | 25410<br>143 102 | 25411<br>143 103 | 25412<br>143 104 | 25413<br>143 105 | 25414<br>143 106 | 25415<br>143 107 | 25416<br>143 110 | 25417<br>143 111 | 25418<br>143 112 | 25419<br>143 113 | 25420<br>143 114 | 25421<br>143 115 | 25422<br>143 116 | 25423<br>143 117 |
| 5− | 25424<br>143 120 | 25425<br>143 121 | 25426<br>143 122 | 25427<br>143 123 | 25428<br>143 124 | 25429<br>143 125 | 25430<br>143 126 | 25431<br>143 127 | 25432<br>143 130 | 25433<br>143 131 | 25434<br>143 132 | 25435<br>143 133 | 25436<br>143 134 | 25437<br>143 135 | 25438<br>143 136 | 25439<br>143 137 |
| 6− | 25440<br>143 140 | 25441<br>143 141 | 25442<br>143 142 | 25443<br>143 143 | 25444<br>143 144 | 25445<br>143 145 | 25446<br>143 146 | 25447<br>143 147 | 25448<br>143 150 | 25449<br>143 151 | 25450<br>143 152 | 25451<br>143 153 | 25452<br>143 154 | 25453<br>143 155 | 25454<br>143 156 | 25455<br>143 157 |
| 7− | 25456<br>143 160 | 25457<br>143 161 | 25458<br>143 162 | 25459<br>143 163 | 25460<br>143 164 | 25461<br>143 165 | 25462<br>143 166 | 25463<br>143 167 | 25464<br>143 170 | 25465<br>143 171 | 25466<br>143 172 | 25467<br>143 173 | 25468<br>143 174 | 25469<br>143 175 | 25470<br>143 176 | 25471<br>143 177 |
| 8− | 25472<br>143 200 | 25473<br>143 201 | 25474<br>143 202 | 25475<br>143 203 | 25476<br>143 204 | 25477<br>143 205 | 25478<br>143 206 | 25479<br>143 207 | 25480<br>143 210 | 25481<br>143 211 | 25482<br>143 212 | 25483<br>143 213 | 25484<br>143 214 | 25485<br>143 215 | 25486<br>143 216 | 25487<br>143 217 |
| 9− | 25488<br>143 220 | 25489<br>143 221 | 25490<br>143 222 | 25491<br>143 223 | 25492<br>143 224 | 25493<br>143 225 | 25494<br>143 226 | 25495<br>143 227 | 25496<br>143 230 | 25497<br>143 231 | 25498<br>143 232 | 25499<br>143 233 | 25500<br>143 234 | 25501<br>143 235 | 25502<br>143 236 | 25503<br>143 237 |
| A− | 25504<br>143 240 | 25505<br>143 241 | 25506<br>143 242 | 25507<br>143 243 | 25508<br>143 244 | 25509<br>143 245 | 25510<br>143 246 | 25511<br>143 247 | 25512<br>143 250 | 25513<br>143 251 | 25514<br>143 252 | 25515<br>143 253 | 25516<br>143 254 | 25517<br>143 255 | 25518<br>143 256 | 25519<br>143 257 |
| B− | 25520<br>143 260 | 25521<br>143 261 | 25522<br>143 262 | 25523<br>143 263 | 25524<br>143 264 | 25525<br>143 265 | 25526<br>143 266 | 25527<br>143 267 | 25528<br>143 270 | 25529<br>143 271 | 25530<br>143 272 | 25531<br>143 273 | 25532<br>143 274 | 25533<br>143 275 | 25534<br>143 276 | 25535<br>143 277 |
| C− | 25536<br>143 300 | 25537<br>143 301 | 25538<br>143 302 | 25539<br>143 303 | 25540<br>143 304 | 25541<br>143 305 | 25542<br>143 306 | 25543<br>143 307 | 25544<br>143 310 | 25545<br>143 311 | 25546<br>143 312 | 25547<br>143 313 | 25548<br>143 314 | 25549<br>143 315 | 25550<br>143 316 | 25551<br>143 317 |
| D− | 25552<br>143 320 | 25553<br>143 321 | 25554<br>143 322 | 25555<br>143 323 | 25556<br>143 324 | 25557<br>143 325 | 25558<br>143 326 | 25559<br>143 327 | 25560<br>143 330 | 25561<br>143 331 | 25562<br>143 332 | 25563<br>143 333 | 25564<br>143 334 | 25565<br>143 335 | 25566<br>143 336 | 25567<br>143 337 |
| E− | 25568<br>143 340 | 25569<br>143 341 | 25570<br>143 342 | 25571<br>143 343 | 25572<br>143 344 | 25573<br>143 345 | 25574<br>143 346 | 25575<br>143 347 | 25576<br>143 350 | 25577<br>143 351 | 25578<br>143 352 | 25579<br>143 353 | 25580<br>143 354 | 25581<br>143 355 | 25582<br>143 356 | 25583<br>143 357 |
| F− | 25584<br>143 360 | 25585<br>143 361 | 25586<br>143 362 | 25587<br>143 363 | 25588<br>143 364 | 25589<br>143 365 | 25590<br>143 366 | 25591<br>143 367 | 25592<br>143 370 | 25593<br>143 371 | 25594<br>143 372 | 25595<br>143 373 | 25596<br>143 374 | 25597<br>143 375 | 25598<br>143 376 | 25599<br>143 377 |

| SECOND HEX DIGIT | −0 | −1 | −2 | −3 | −4 | −5 | −6 | −7 | −8 | −9 | −A | −B | −C | −D | −E | −F |
|---|---|---|---|---|---|---|---|---|---|---|---|---|---|---|---|---|
| 0− | 25600<br>144 000 | 25601<br>144 001 | 25602<br>144 002 | 25603<br>144 003 | 25604<br>144 004 | 25605<br>144 005 | 25606<br>144 006 | 25607<br>144 007 | 25608<br>144 010 | 25609<br>144 011 | 25610<br>144 012 | 25611<br>144 013 | 25612<br>144 014 | 25613<br>144 015 | 25614<br>144 016 | 25615<br>144 017 |
| 1− | 25616<br>144 020 | 25617<br>144 021 | 25618<br>144 022 | 25619<br>144 023 | 25620<br>144 024 | 25621<br>144 025 | 25622<br>144 026 | 25623<br>144 027 | 25624<br>144 030 | 25625<br>144 031 | 25626<br>144 032 | 25627<br>144 033 | 25628<br>144 034 | 25629<br>144 035 | 25630<br>144 036 | 25631<br>144 037 |
| 2− | 25632<br>144 040 | 25633<br>144 041 | 25634<br>144 042 | 25635<br>144 043 | 25636<br>144 044 | 25637<br>144 045 | 25638<br>144 046 | 25639<br>144 047 | 25640<br>144 050 | 25641<br>144 051 | 25642<br>144 052 | 25643<br>144 053 | 25644<br>144 054 | 25645<br>144 055 | 25646<br>144 056 | 25647<br>144 057 |
| 3− | 25648<br>144 060 | 25649<br>144 061 | 25650<br>144 062 | 25651<br>144 063 | 25652<br>144 064 | 25653<br>144 065 | 25654<br>144 066 | 25655<br>144 067 | 25656<br>144 070 | 25657<br>144 071 | 25658<br>144 072 | 25659<br>144 073 | 25660<br>144 074 | 25661<br>144 075 | 25662<br>144 076 | 25663<br>144 077 |
| 4− | 25664<br>144 100 | 25665<br>144 101 | 25666<br>144 102 | 25667<br>144 103 | 25668<br>144 104 | 25669<br>144 105 | 25670<br>144 106 | 25671<br>144 107 | 25672<br>144 110 | 25673<br>144 111 | 25674<br>144 112 | 25675<br>144 113 | 25676<br>144 114 | 25677<br>144 115 | 25678<br>144 116 | 25679<br>144 117 |
| 5− | 25680<br>144 120 | 25681<br>144 121 | 25682<br>144 122 | 25683<br>144 123 | 25684<br>144 124 | 25685<br>144 125 | 25686<br>144 126 | 25687<br>144 127 | 25688<br>144 130 | 25689<br>144 131 | 25690<br>144 132 | 25691<br>144 133 | 25692<br>144 134 | 25693<br>144 135 | 25694<br>144 136 | 25695<br>144 137 |
| 6− | 25696<br>144 140 | 25697<br>144 141 | 25698<br>144 142 | 25699<br>144 143 | 25700<br>144 144 | 25701<br>144 145 | 25702<br>144 146 | 25703<br>144 147 | 25704<br>144 150 | 25705<br>144 151 | 25706<br>144 152 | 25707<br>144 153 | 25708<br>144 154 | 25709<br>144 155 | 25710<br>144 156 | 25711<br>144 157 |
| 7− | 25712<br>144 160 | 25713<br>144 161 | 25714<br>144 162 | 25715<br>144 163 | 25716<br>144 164 | 25717<br>144 165 | 25718<br>144 166 | 25719<br>144 167 | 25720<br>144 170 | 25721<br>144 171 | 25722<br>144 172 | 25723<br>144 173 | 25724<br>144 174 | 25725<br>144 175 | 25726<br>144 176 | 25727<br>144 177 |
| 8− | 25728<br>144 200 | 25729<br>144 201 | 25730<br>144 202 | 25731<br>144 203 | 25732<br>144 204 | 25733<br>144 205 | 25734<br>144 206 | 25735<br>144 207 | 25736<br>144 210 | 25737<br>144 211 | 25738<br>144 212 | 25739<br>144 213 | 25740<br>144 214 | 25741<br>144 215 | 25742<br>144 216 | 25743<br>144 217 |
| 9− | 25744<br>144 220 | 25745<br>144 221 | 25746<br>144 222 | 25747<br>144 223 | 25748<br>144 224 | 25749<br>144 225 | 25750<br>144 226 | 25751<br>144 227 | 25752<br>144 230 | 25753<br>144 231 | 25754<br>144 232 | 25755<br>144 233 | 25756<br>144 234 | 25757<br>144 235 | 25758<br>144 236 | 25759<br>144 237 |
| A− | 25760<br>144 240 | 25761<br>144 241 | 25762<br>144 242 | 25763<br>144 243 | 25764<br>144 244 | 25765<br>144 245 | 25766<br>144 246 | 25767<br>144 247 | 25768<br>144 250 | 25769<br>144 251 | 25770<br>144 252 | 25771<br>144 253 | 25772<br>144 254 | 25773<br>144 255 | 25774<br>144 256 | 25775<br>144 257 |
| B− | 25776<br>144 260 | 25777<br>144 261 | 25778<br>144 262 | 25779<br>144 263 | 25780<br>144 264 | 25781<br>144 265 | 25782<br>144 266 | 25783<br>144 267 | 25784<br>144 270 | 25785<br>144 271 | 25786<br>144 272 | 25787<br>144 273 | 25788<br>144 274 | 25789<br>144 275 | 25790<br>144 276 | 25791<br>144 277 |
| C− | 25792<br>144 300 | 25793<br>144 301 | 25794<br>144 302 | 25795<br>144 303 | 25796<br>144 304 | 25797<br>144 305 | 25798<br>144 306 | 25799<br>144 307 | 25800<br>144 310 | 25801<br>144 311 | 25802<br>144 312 | 25803<br>144 313 | 25804<br>144 314 | 25805<br>144 315 | 25806<br>144 316 | 25807<br>144 317 |
| D− | 25808<br>144 320 | 25809<br>144 321 | 25810<br>144 322 | 25811<br>144 323 | 25812<br>144 324 | 25813<br>144 325 | 25814<br>144 326 | 25815<br>144 327 | 25816<br>144 330 | 25817<br>144 331 | 25818<br>144 332 | 25819<br>144 333 | 25820<br>144 334 | 25821<br>144 335 | 25822<br>144 336 | 25823<br>144 337 |
| E− | 25824<br>144 340 | 25825<br>144 341 | 25826<br>144 342 | 25827<br>144 343 | 25828<br>144 344 | 25829<br>144 345 | 25830<br>144 346 | 25831<br>144 347 | 25832<br>144 350 | 25833<br>144 351 | 25834<br>144 352 | 25835<br>144 353 | 25836<br>144 354 | 25837<br>144 355 | 25838<br>144 356 | 25839<br>144 357 |
| F− | 25840<br>144 360 | 25841<br>144 361 | 25842<br>144 362 | 25843<br>144 363 | 25844<br>144 364 | 25845<br>144 365 | 25846<br>144 366 | 25847<br>144 367 | 25848<br>144 370 | 25849<br>144 371 | 25850<br>144 372 | 25851<br>144 373 | 25852<br>144 374 | 25853<br>144 375 | 25854<br>144 376 | 25855<br>144 377 |

DECIMAL ←  DECIMAL ← OCTAL ←

 DECIMAL  25600     BINARY  0110 0100     DECIMAL  25600     HEXADECIMAL  ⬡ 64     OCTAL  144 000

FOURTH HEX DIGIT → ⬡ ← THIRD HEX DIGIT

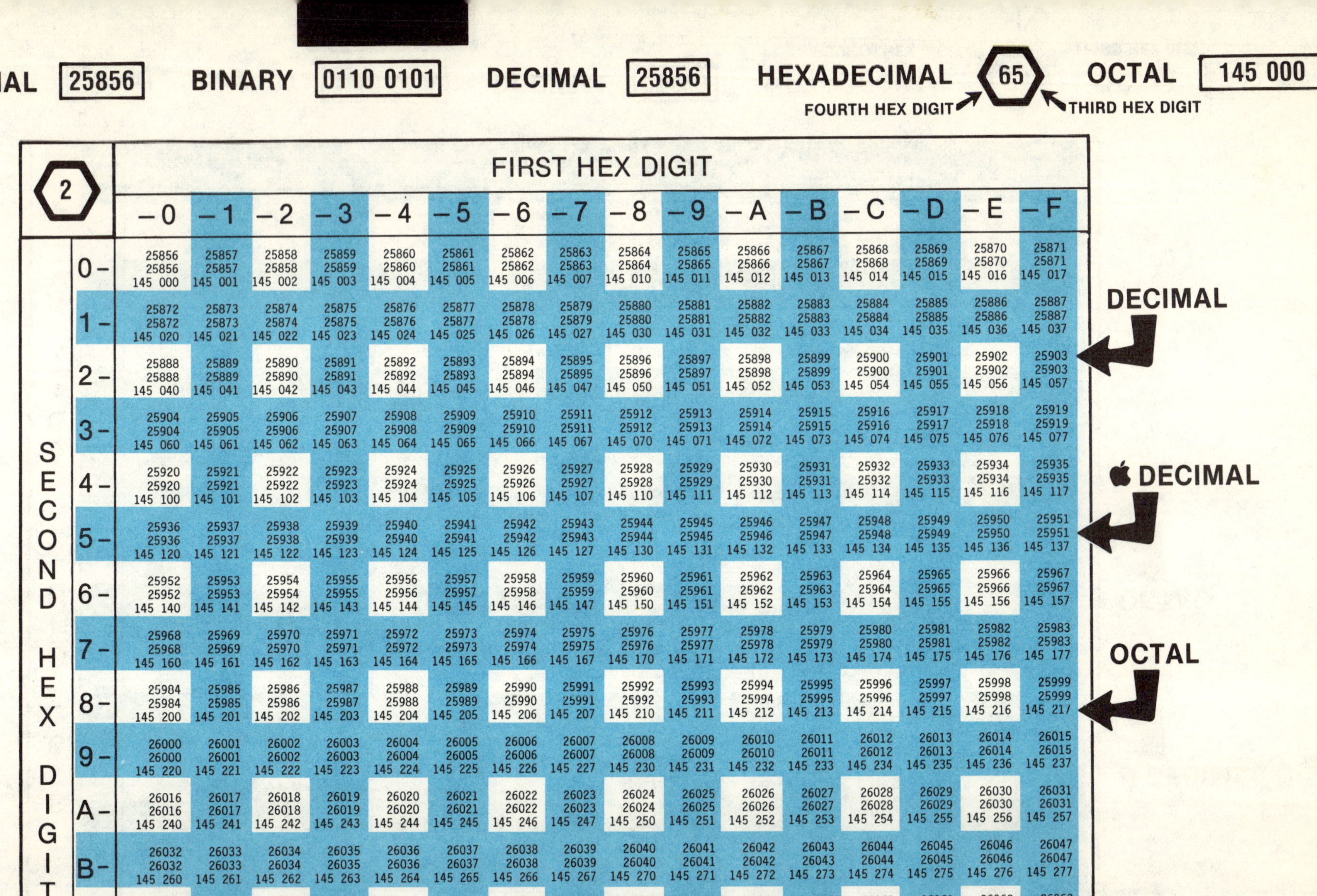

FIRST HEX DIGIT

| 2 / SECOND HEX DIGIT | −0 | −1 | −2 | −3 | −4 | −5 | −6 | −7 | −8 | −9 | −A | −B | −C | −D | −E | −F |
|---|---|---|---|---|---|---|---|---|---|---|---|---|---|---|---|---|
| 0− | 25856<br>25856<br>145 000 | 25857<br>25857<br>145 001 | 25858<br>25858<br>145 002 | 25859<br>25859<br>145 003 | 25860<br>25860<br>145 004 | 25861<br>25861<br>145 005 | 25862<br>25862<br>145 006 | 25863<br>25863<br>145 007 | 25864<br>25864<br>145 010 | 25865<br>25865<br>145 011 | 25866<br>25866<br>145 012 | 25867<br>25867<br>145 013 | 25868<br>25868<br>145 014 | 25869<br>25869<br>145 015 | 25870<br>25870<br>145 016 | 25871<br>25871<br>145 017 |
| 1− | 25872<br>25872<br>145 020 | 25873<br>25873<br>145 021 | 25874<br>25874<br>145 022 | 25875<br>25875<br>145 023 | 25876<br>25876<br>145 024 | 25877<br>25877<br>145 025 | 25878<br>25878<br>145 026 | 25879<br>25879<br>145 027 | 25880<br>25880<br>145 030 | 25881<br>25881<br>145 031 | 25882<br>25882<br>145 032 | 25883<br>25883<br>145 033 | 25884<br>25884<br>145 034 | 25885<br>25885<br>145 035 | 25886<br>25886<br>145 036 | 25887<br>25887<br>145 037 |
| 2− | 25888<br>25888<br>145 040 | 25889<br>25889<br>145 041 | 25890<br>25890<br>145 042 | 25891<br>25891<br>145 043 | 25892<br>25892<br>145 044 | 25893<br>25893<br>145 045 | 25894<br>25894<br>145 046 | 25895<br>25895<br>145 047 | 25896<br>25896<br>145 050 | 25897<br>25897<br>145 051 | 25898<br>25898<br>145 052 | 25899<br>25899<br>145 053 | 25900<br>25900<br>145 054 | 25901<br>25901<br>145 055 | 25902<br>25902<br>145 056 | 25903<br>25903<br>145 057 |
| 3− | 25904<br>25904<br>145 060 | 25905<br>25905<br>145 061 | 25906<br>25906<br>145 062 | 25907<br>25907<br>145 063 | 25908<br>25908<br>145 064 | 25909<br>25909<br>145 065 | 25910<br>25910<br>145 066 | 25911<br>25911<br>145 067 | 25912<br>25912<br>145 070 | 25913<br>25913<br>145 071 | 25914<br>25914<br>145 072 | 25915<br>25915<br>145 073 | 25916<br>25916<br>145 074 | 25917<br>25917<br>145 075 | 25918<br>25918<br>145 076 | 25919<br>25919<br>145 077 |
| 4− | 25920<br>25920<br>145 100 | 25921<br>25921<br>145 101 | 25922<br>25922<br>145 102 | 25923<br>25923<br>145 103 | 25924<br>25924<br>145 104 | 25925<br>25925<br>145 105 | 25926<br>25926<br>145 106 | 25927<br>25927<br>145 107 | 25928<br>25928<br>145 110 | 25929<br>25929<br>145 111 | 25930<br>25930<br>145 112 | 25931<br>25931<br>145 113 | 25932<br>25932<br>145 114 | 25933<br>25933<br>145 115 | 25934<br>25934<br>145 116 | 25935<br>25935<br>145 117 |
| 5− | 25936<br>25936<br>145 120 | 25937<br>25937<br>145 121 | 25938<br>25938<br>145 122 | 25939<br>25939<br>145 123 | 25940<br>25940<br>145 124 | 25941<br>25941<br>145 125 | 25942<br>25942<br>145 126 | 25943<br>25943<br>145 127 | 25944<br>25944<br>145 130 | 25945<br>25945<br>145 131 | 25946<br>25946<br>145 132 | 25947<br>25947<br>145 133 | 25948<br>25948<br>145 134 | 25949<br>25949<br>145 135 | 25950<br>25950<br>145 136 | 25951<br>25951<br>145 137 |
| 6− | 25952<br>25952<br>145 140 | 25953<br>25953<br>145 141 | 25954<br>25954<br>145 142 | 25955<br>25955<br>145 143 | 25956<br>25956<br>145 144 | 25957<br>25957<br>145 145 | 25958<br>25958<br>145 146 | 25959<br>25959<br>145 147 | 25960<br>25960<br>145 150 | 25961<br>25961<br>145 151 | 25962<br>25962<br>145 152 | 25963<br>25963<br>145 153 | 25964<br>25964<br>145 154 | 25965<br>25965<br>145 155 | 25966<br>25966<br>145 156 | 25967<br>25967<br>145 157 |
| 7− | 25968<br>25968<br>145 160 | 25969<br>25969<br>145 161 | 25970<br>25970<br>145 162 | 25971<br>25971<br>145 163 | 25972<br>25972<br>145 164 | 25973<br>25973<br>145 165 | 25974<br>25974<br>145 166 | 25975<br>25975<br>145 167 | 25976<br>25976<br>145 170 | 25977<br>25977<br>145 171 | 25978<br>25978<br>145 172 | 25979<br>25979<br>145 173 | 25980<br>25980<br>145 174 | 25981<br>25981<br>145 175 | 25982<br>25982<br>145 176 | 25983<br>25983<br>145 177 |
| 8− | 25984<br>25984<br>145 200 | 25985<br>25985<br>145 201 | 25986<br>25986<br>145 202 | 25987<br>25987<br>145 203 | 25988<br>25988<br>145 204 | 25989<br>25989<br>145 205 | 25990<br>25990<br>145 206 | 25991<br>25991<br>145 207 | 25992<br>25992<br>145 210 | 25993<br>25993<br>145 211 | 25994<br>25994<br>145 212 | 25995<br>25995<br>145 213 | 25996<br>25996<br>145 214 | 25997<br>25997<br>145 215 | 25998<br>25998<br>145 216 | 25999<br>25999<br>145 217 |
| 9− | 26000<br>26000<br>145 220 | 26001<br>26001<br>145 221 | 26002<br>26002<br>145 222 | 26003<br>26003<br>145 223 | 26004<br>26004<br>145 224 | 26005<br>26005<br>145 225 | 26006<br>26006<br>145 226 | 26007<br>26007<br>145 227 | 26008<br>26008<br>145 230 | 26009<br>26009<br>145 231 | 26010<br>26010<br>145 232 | 26011<br>26011<br>145 233 | 26012<br>26012<br>145 234 | 26013<br>26013<br>145 235 | 26014<br>26014<br>145 236 | 26015<br>26015<br>145 237 |
| A− | 26016<br>26016<br>145 240 | 26017<br>26017<br>145 241 | 26018<br>26018<br>145 242 | 26019<br>26019<br>145 243 | 26020<br>26020<br>145 244 | 26021<br>26021<br>145 245 | 26022<br>26022<br>145 246 | 26023<br>26023<br>145 247 | 26024<br>26024<br>145 250 | 26025<br>26025<br>145 251 | 26026<br>26026<br>145 252 | 26027<br>26027<br>145 253 | 26028<br>26028<br>145 254 | 26029<br>26029<br>145 255 | 26030<br>26030<br>145 256 | 26031<br>26031<br>145 257 |
| B− | 26032<br>26032<br>145 260 | 26033<br>26033<br>145 261 | 26034<br>26034<br>145 262 | 26035<br>26035<br>145 263 | 26036<br>26036<br>145 264 | 26037<br>26037<br>145 265 | 26038<br>26038<br>145 266 | 26039<br>26039<br>145 267 | 26040<br>26040<br>145 270 | 26041<br>26041<br>145 271 | 26042<br>26042<br>145 272 | 26043<br>26043<br>145 273 | 26044<br>26044<br>145 274 | 26045<br>26045<br>145 275 | 26046<br>26046<br>145 276 | 26047<br>26047<br>145 277 |
| C− | 26048<br>26048<br>145 300 | 26049<br>26049<br>145 301 | 26050<br>26050<br>145 302 | 26051<br>26051<br>145 303 | 26052<br>26052<br>145 304 | 26053<br>26053<br>145 305 | 26054<br>26054<br>145 306 | 26055<br>26055<br>145 307 | 26056<br>26056<br>145 310 | 26057<br>26057<br>145 311 | 26058<br>26058<br>145 312 | 26059<br>26059<br>145 313 | 26060<br>26060<br>145 314 | 26061<br>26061<br>145 315 | 26062<br>26062<br>145 316 | 26063<br>26063<br>145 317 |
| D− | 26064<br>26064<br>145 320 | 26065<br>26065<br>145 321 | 26066<br>26066<br>145 322 | 26067<br>26067<br>145 323 | 26068<br>26068<br>145 324 | 26069<br>26069<br>145 325 | 26070<br>26070<br>145 326 | 26071<br>26071<br>145 327 | 26072<br>26072<br>145 330 | 26073<br>26073<br>145 331 | 26074<br>26074<br>145 332 | 26075<br>26075<br>145 333 | 26076<br>26076<br>145 334 | 26077<br>26077<br>145 335 | 26078<br>26078<br>145 336 | 26079<br>26079<br>145 337 |
| E− | 26080<br>26080<br>145 340 | 26081<br>26081<br>145 341 | 26082<br>26082<br>145 342 | 26083<br>26083<br>145 343 | 26084<br>26084<br>145 344 | 26085<br>26085<br>145 345 | 26086<br>26086<br>145 346 | 26087<br>26087<br>145 347 | 26088<br>26088<br>145 350 | 26089<br>26089<br>145 351 | 26090<br>26090<br>145 352 | 26091<br>26091<br>145 353 | 26092<br>26092<br>145 354 | 26093<br>26093<br>145 355 | 26094<br>26094<br>145 356 | 26095<br>26095<br>145 357 |
| F− | 26096<br>26096<br>145 360 | 26097<br>26097<br>145 361 | 26098<br>26098<br>145 362 | 26099<br>26099<br>145 363 | 26100<br>26100<br>145 364 | 26101<br>26101<br>145 365 | 26102<br>26102<br>145 366 | 26103<br>26103<br>145 367 | 26104<br>26104<br>145 370 | 26105<br>26105<br>145 371 | 26106<br>26106<br>145 372 | 26107<br>26107<br>145 373 | 26108<br>26108<br>145 374 | 26109<br>26109<br>145 375 | 26110<br>26110<br>145 376 | 26111<br>26111<br>145 377 |

 DECIMAL 26368    BINARY 0110 0111    DECIMAL 26368    HEXADECIMAL 67    OCTAL 147 000

FOURTH HEX DIGIT    THIRD HEX DIGIT

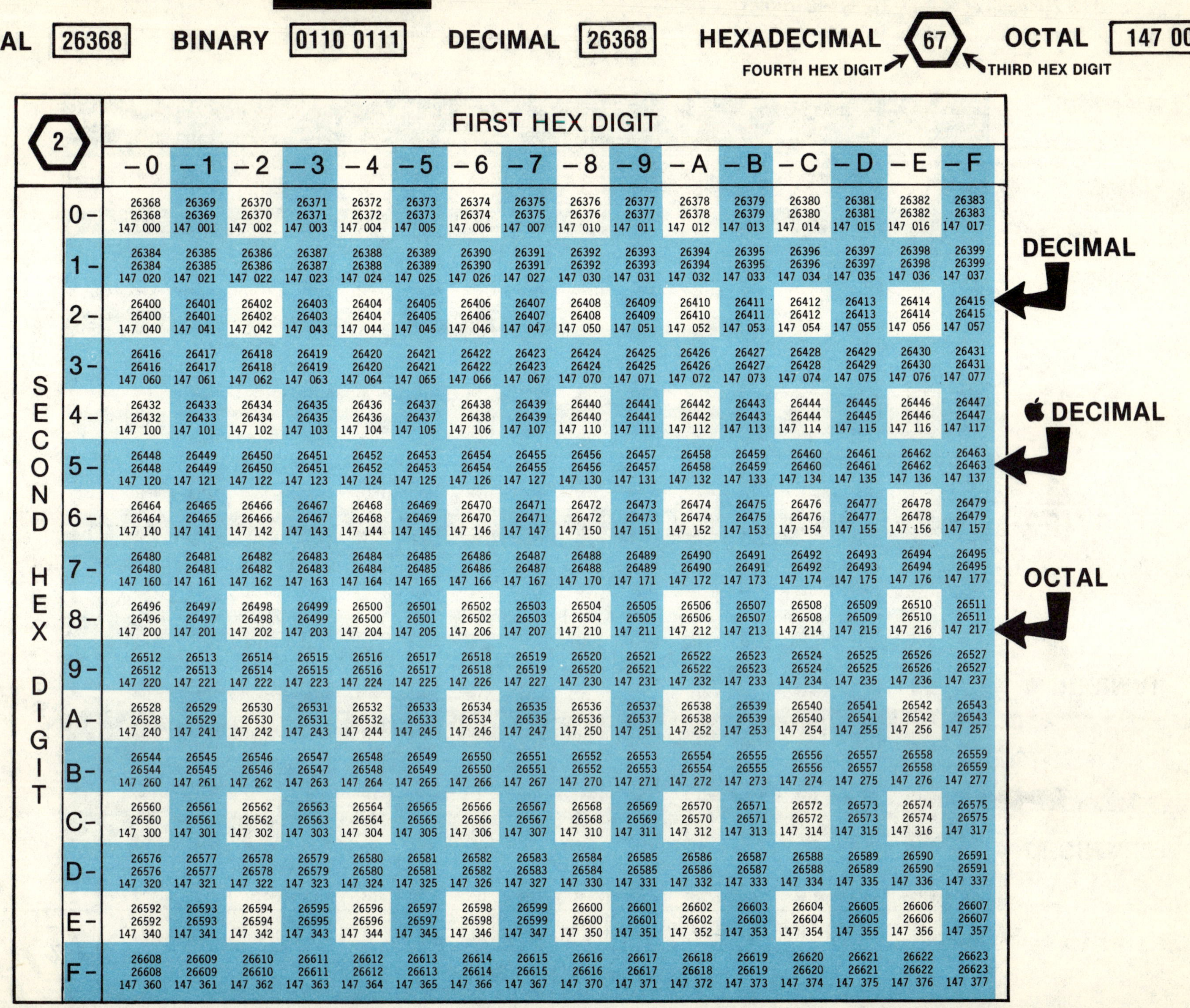

FIRST HEX DIGIT

| 2 / SECOND HEX DIGIT | -0 | -1 | -2 | -3 | -4 | -5 | -6 | -7 | -8 | -9 | -A | -B | -C | -D | -E | -F |
|---|---|---|---|---|---|---|---|---|---|---|---|---|---|---|---|---|
| 0- | 26368<br>147 000 | 26369<br>147 001 | 26370<br>147 002 | 26371<br>147 003 | 26372<br>147 004 | 26373<br>147 005 | 26374<br>147 006 | 26375<br>147 007 | 26376<br>147 010 | 26377<br>147 011 | 26378<br>147 012 | 26379<br>147 013 | 26380<br>147 014 | 26381<br>147 015 | 26382<br>147 016 | 26383<br>147 017 |
| 1- | 26384<br>147 020 | 26385<br>147 021 | 26386<br>147 022 | 26387<br>147 023 | 26388<br>147 024 | 26389<br>147 025 | 26390<br>147 026 | 26391<br>147 027 | 26392<br>147 030 | 26393<br>147 031 | 26394<br>147 032 | 26395<br>147 033 | 26396<br>147 034 | 26397<br>147 035 | 26398<br>147 036 | 26399<br>147 037 |
| 2- | 26400<br>147 040 | 26401<br>147 041 | 26402<br>147 042 | 26403<br>147 043 | 26404<br>147 044 | 26405<br>147 045 | 26406<br>147 046 | 26407<br>147 047 | 26408<br>147 050 | 26409<br>147 051 | 26410<br>147 052 | 26411<br>147 053 | 26412<br>147 054 | 26413<br>147 055 | 26414<br>147 056 | 26415<br>147 057 |
| 3- | 26416<br>147 060 | 26417<br>147 061 | 26418<br>147 062 | 26419<br>147 063 | 26420<br>147 064 | 26421<br>147 065 | 26422<br>147 066 | 26423<br>147 067 | 26424<br>147 070 | 26425<br>147 071 | 26426<br>147 072 | 26427<br>147 073 | 26428<br>147 074 | 26429<br>147 075 | 26430<br>147 076 | 26431<br>147 077 |
| 4- | 26432<br>147 100 | 26433<br>147 101 | 26434<br>147 102 | 26435<br>147 103 | 26436<br>147 104 | 26437<br>147 105 | 26438<br>147 106 | 26439<br>147 107 | 26440<br>147 110 | 26441<br>147 111 | 26442<br>147 112 | 26443<br>147 113 | 26444<br>147 114 | 26445<br>147 115 | 26446<br>147 116 | 26447<br>147 117 |
| 5- | 26448<br>147 120 | 26449<br>147 121 | 26450<br>147 122 | 26451<br>147 123 | 26452<br>147 124 | 26453<br>147 125 | 26454<br>147 126 | 26455<br>147 127 | 26456<br>147 130 | 26457<br>147 131 | 26458<br>147 132 | 26459<br>147 133 | 26460<br>147 134 | 26461<br>147 135 | 26462<br>147 136 | 26463<br>147 137 |
| 6- | 26464<br>147 140 | 26465<br>147 141 | 26466<br>147 142 | 26467<br>147 143 | 26468<br>147 144 | 26469<br>147 145 | 26470<br>147 146 | 26471<br>147 147 | 26472<br>147 150 | 26473<br>147 151 | 26474<br>147 152 | 26475<br>147 153 | 26476<br>147 154 | 26477<br>147 155 | 26478<br>147 156 | 26479<br>147 157 |
| 7- | 26480<br>147 160 | 26481<br>147 161 | 26482<br>147 162 | 26483<br>147 163 | 26484<br>147 164 | 26485<br>147 165 | 26486<br>147 166 | 26487<br>147 167 | 26488<br>147 170 | 26489<br>147 171 | 26490<br>147 172 | 26491<br>147 173 | 26492<br>147 174 | 26493<br>147 175 | 26494<br>147 176 | 26495<br>147 177 |
| 8- | 26496<br>147 200 | 26497<br>147 201 | 26498<br>147 202 | 26499<br>147 203 | 26500<br>147 204 | 26501<br>147 205 | 26502<br>147 206 | 26503<br>147 207 | 26504<br>147 210 | 26505<br>147 211 | 26506<br>147 212 | 26507<br>147 213 | 26508<br>147 214 | 26509<br>147 215 | 26510<br>147 216 | 26511<br>147 217 |
| 9- | 26512<br>147 220 | 26513<br>147 221 | 26514<br>147 222 | 26515<br>147 223 | 26516<br>147 224 | 26517<br>147 225 | 26518<br>147 226 | 26519<br>147 227 | 26520<br>147 230 | 26521<br>147 231 | 26522<br>147 232 | 26523<br>147 233 | 26524<br>147 234 | 26525<br>147 235 | 26526<br>147 236 | 26527<br>147 237 |
| A- | 26528<br>147 240 | 26529<br>147 241 | 26530<br>147 242 | 26531<br>147 243 | 26532<br>147 244 | 26533<br>147 245 | 26534<br>147 246 | 26535<br>147 247 | 26536<br>147 250 | 26537<br>147 251 | 26538<br>147 252 | 26539<br>147 253 | 26540<br>147 254 | 26541<br>147 255 | 26542<br>147 256 | 26543<br>147 257 |
| B- | 26544<br>147 260 | 26545<br>147 261 | 26546<br>147 262 | 26547<br>147 263 | 26548<br>147 264 | 26549<br>147 265 | 26550<br>147 266 | 26551<br>147 267 | 26552<br>147 270 | 26553<br>147 271 | 26554<br>147 272 | 26555<br>147 273 | 26556<br>147 274 | 26557<br>147 275 | 26558<br>147 276 | 26559<br>147 277 |
| C- | 26560<br>147 300 | 26561<br>147 301 | 26562<br>147 302 | 26563<br>147 303 | 26564<br>147 304 | 26565<br>147 305 | 26566<br>147 306 | 26567<br>147 307 | 26568<br>147 310 | 26569<br>147 311 | 26570<br>147 312 | 26571<br>147 313 | 26572<br>147 314 | 26573<br>147 315 | 26574<br>147 316 | 26575<br>147 317 |
| D- | 26576<br>147 320 | 26577<br>147 321 | 26578<br>147 322 | 26579<br>147 323 | 26580<br>147 324 | 26581<br>147 325 | 26582<br>147 326 | 26583<br>147 327 | 26584<br>147 330 | 26585<br>147 331 | 26586<br>147 332 | 26587<br>147 333 | 26588<br>147 334 | 26589<br>147 335 | 26590<br>147 336 | 26591<br>147 337 |
| E- | 26592<br>147 340 | 26593<br>147 341 | 26594<br>147 342 | 26595<br>147 343 | 26596<br>147 344 | 26597<br>147 345 | 26598<br>147 346 | 26599<br>147 347 | 26600<br>147 350 | 26601<br>147 351 | 26602<br>147 352 | 26603<br>147 353 | 26604<br>147 354 | 26605<br>147 355 | 26606<br>147 356 | 26607<br>147 357 |
| F- | 26608<br>147 360 | 26609<br>147 361 | 26610<br>147 362 | 26611<br>147 363 | 26612<br>147 364 | 26613<br>147 365 | 26614<br>147 366 | 26615<br>147 367 | 26616<br>147 370 | 26617<br>147 371 | 26618<br>147 372 | 26619<br>147 373 | 26620<br>147 374 | 26621<br>147 375 | 26622<br>147 376 | 26623<br>147 377 |

DECIMAL

 DECIMAL

OCTAL

| ⬡ 2 | −0 | −1 | −2 | −3 | −4 | −5 | −6 | −7 | −8 | −9 | −A | −B | −C | −D | −E | −F |
|---|---|---|---|---|---|---|---|---|---|---|---|---|---|---|---|---|
| 0- | 26624<br>26624<br>150 000 | 26625<br>26625<br>150 001 | 26626<br>26626<br>150 002 | 26627<br>26627<br>150 003 | 26628<br>26628<br>150 004 | 26629<br>26629<br>150 005 | 26630<br>26630<br>150 006 | 26631<br>26631<br>150 007 | 26632<br>26632<br>150 010 | 26633<br>26633<br>150 011 | 26634<br>26634<br>150 012 | 26635<br>26635<br>150 013 | 26636<br>26636<br>150 014 | 26637<br>26637<br>150 015 | 26638<br>26638<br>150 016 | 26639<br>26639<br>150 017 |
| 1- | 26640<br>26640<br>150 020 | 26641<br>26641<br>150 021 | 26642<br>26642<br>150 022 | 26643<br>26643<br>150 023 | 26644<br>26644<br>150 024 | 26645<br>26645<br>150 025 | 26646<br>26646<br>150 026 | 26647<br>26647<br>150 027 | 26648<br>26648<br>150 030 | 26649<br>26649<br>150 031 | 26650<br>26650<br>150 032 | 26651<br>26651<br>150 033 | 26652<br>26652<br>150 034 | 26653<br>26653<br>150 035 | 26654<br>26654<br>150 036 | 26655<br>26655<br>150 037 |
| 2- | 26656<br>26656<br>150 040 | 26657<br>26657<br>150 041 | 26658<br>26658<br>150 042 | 26659<br>26659<br>150 043 | 26660<br>26660<br>150 044 | 26661<br>26661<br>150 045 | 26662<br>26662<br>150 046 | 26663<br>26663<br>150 047 | 26664<br>26664<br>150 050 | 26665<br>26665<br>150 051 | 26666<br>26666<br>150 052 | 26667<br>26667<br>150 053 | 26668<br>26668<br>150 054 | 26669<br>26669<br>150 055 | 26670<br>26670<br>150 056 | 26671<br>26671<br>150 057 |
| 3- | 26672<br>26672<br>150 060 | 26673<br>26673<br>150 061 | 26674<br>26674<br>150 062 | 26675<br>26675<br>150 063 | 26676<br>26676<br>150 064 | 26677<br>26677<br>150 065 | 26678<br>26678<br>150 066 | 26679<br>26679<br>150 067 | 26680<br>26680<br>150 070 | 26681<br>26681<br>150 071 | 26682<br>26682<br>150 072 | 26683<br>26683<br>150 073 | 26684<br>26684<br>150 074 | 26685<br>26685<br>150 075 | 26686<br>26686<br>150 076 | 26687<br>26687<br>150 077 |
| 4- | 26688<br>26688<br>150 100 | 26689<br>26689<br>150 101 | 26690<br>26690<br>150 102 | 26691<br>26691<br>150 103 | 26692<br>26692<br>150 104 | 26693<br>26693<br>150 105 | 26694<br>26694<br>150 106 | 26695<br>26695<br>150 107 | 26696<br>26696<br>150 110 | 26697<br>26697<br>150 111 | 26698<br>26698<br>150 112 | 26699<br>26699<br>150 113 | 26700<br>26700<br>150 114 | 26701<br>26701<br>150 115 | 26702<br>26702<br>150 116 | 26703<br>26703<br>150 117 |
| 5- | 26704<br>26704<br>150 120 | 26705<br>26705<br>150 121 | 26706<br>26706<br>150 122 | 26707<br>26707<br>150 123 | 26708<br>26708<br>150 124 | 26709<br>26709<br>150 125 | 26710<br>26710<br>150 126 | 26711<br>26711<br>150 127 | 26712<br>26712<br>150 130 | 26713<br>26713<br>150 131 | 26714<br>26714<br>150 132 | 26715<br>26715<br>150 133 | 26716<br>26716<br>150 134 | 26717<br>26717<br>150 135 | 26718<br>26718<br>150 136 | 26719<br>26719<br>150 137 |
| 6- | 26720<br>26720<br>150 140 | 26721<br>26721<br>150 141 | 26722<br>26722<br>150 142 | 26723<br>26723<br>150 143 | 26724<br>26724<br>150 144 | 26725<br>26725<br>150 145 | 26726<br>26726<br>150 146 | 26727<br>26727<br>150 147 | 26728<br>26728<br>150 150 | 26729<br>26729<br>150 151 | 26730<br>26730<br>150 152 | 26731<br>26731<br>150 153 | 26732<br>26732<br>150 154 | 26733<br>26733<br>150 155 | 26734<br>26734<br>150 156 | 26735<br>26735<br>150 157 |
| 7- | 26736<br>26736<br>150 160 | 26737<br>26737<br>150 161 | 26738<br>26738<br>150 162 | 26739<br>26739<br>150 163 | 26740<br>26740<br>150 164 | 26741<br>26741<br>150 165 | 26742<br>26742<br>150 166 | 26743<br>26743<br>150 167 | 26744<br>26744<br>150 170 | 26745<br>26745<br>150 171 | 26746<br>26746<br>150 172 | 26747<br>26747<br>150 173 | 26748<br>26748<br>150 174 | 26749<br>26749<br>150 175 | 26750<br>26750<br>150 176 | 26751<br>26751<br>150 177 |
| 8- | 26752<br>26752<br>150 200 | 26753<br>26753<br>150 201 | 26754<br>26754<br>150 202 | 26755<br>26755<br>150 203 | 26756<br>26756<br>150 204 | 26757<br>26757<br>150 205 | 26758<br>26758<br>150 206 | 26759<br>26759<br>150 207 | 26760<br>26760<br>150 210 | 26761<br>26761<br>150 211 | 26762<br>26762<br>150 212 | 26763<br>26763<br>150 213 | 26764<br>26764<br>150 214 | 26765<br>26765<br>150 215 | 26766<br>26766<br>150 216 | 26767<br>26767<br>150 217 |
| 9- | 26768<br>26768<br>150 220 | 26769<br>26769<br>150 221 | 26770<br>26770<br>150 222 | 26771<br>26771<br>150 223 | 26772<br>26772<br>150 224 | 26773<br>26773<br>150 225 | 26774<br>26774<br>150 226 | 26775<br>26775<br>150 227 | 26776<br>26776<br>150 230 | 26777<br>26777<br>150 231 | 26778<br>26778<br>150 232 | 26779<br>26779<br>150 233 | 26780<br>26780<br>150 234 | 26781<br>26781<br>150 235 | 26782<br>26782<br>150 236 | 26783<br>26783<br>150 237 |
| A- | 26784<br>26784<br>150 240 | 26785<br>26785<br>150 241 | 26786<br>26786<br>150 242 | 26787<br>26787<br>150 243 | 26788<br>26788<br>150 244 | 26789<br>26789<br>150 245 | 26790<br>26790<br>150 246 | 26791<br>26791<br>150 247 | 26792<br>26792<br>150 250 | 26793<br>26793<br>150 251 | 26794<br>26794<br>150 252 | 26795<br>26795<br>150 253 | 26796<br>26796<br>150 254 | 26797<br>26797<br>150 255 | 26798<br>26798<br>150 256 | 26799<br>26799<br>150 257 |
| B- | 26800<br>26800<br>150 260 | 26801<br>26801<br>150 261 | 26802<br>26802<br>150 262 | 26803<br>26803<br>150 263 | 26804<br>26804<br>150 264 | 26805<br>26805<br>150 265 | 26806<br>26806<br>150 266 | 26807<br>26807<br>150 267 | 26808<br>26808<br>150 270 | 26809<br>26809<br>150 271 | 26810<br>26810<br>150 272 | 26811<br>26811<br>150 273 | 26812<br>26812<br>150 274 | 26813<br>26813<br>150 275 | 26814<br>26814<br>150 276 | 26815<br>26815<br>150 277 |
| C- | 26816<br>26816<br>150 300 | 26817<br>26817<br>150 301 | 26818<br>26818<br>150 302 | 26819<br>26819<br>150 303 | 26820<br>26820<br>150 304 | 26821<br>26821<br>150 305 | 26822<br>26822<br>150 306 | 26823<br>26823<br>150 307 | 26824<br>26824<br>150 310 | 26825<br>26825<br>150 311 | 26826<br>26826<br>150 312 | 26827<br>26827<br>150 313 | 26828<br>26828<br>150 314 | 26829<br>26829<br>150 315 | 26830<br>26830<br>150 316 | 26831<br>26831<br>150 317 |
| D- | 26832<br>26832<br>150 320 | 26833<br>26833<br>150 321 | 26834<br>26834<br>150 322 | 26835<br>26835<br>150 323 | 26836<br>26836<br>150 324 | 26837<br>26837<br>150 325 | 26838<br>26838<br>150 326 | 26839<br>26839<br>150 327 | 26840<br>26840<br>150 330 | 26841<br>26841<br>150 331 | 26842<br>26842<br>150 332 | 26843<br>26843<br>150 333 | 26844<br>26844<br>150 334 | 26845<br>26845<br>150 335 | 26846<br>26846<br>150 336 | 26847<br>26847<br>150 337 |
| E- | 26848<br>26848<br>150 340 | 26849<br>26849<br>150 341 | 26850<br>26850<br>150 342 | 26851<br>26851<br>150 343 | 26852<br>26852<br>150 344 | 26853<br>26853<br>150 345 | 26854<br>26854<br>150 346 | 26855<br>26855<br>150 347 | 26856<br>26856<br>150 350 | 26857<br>26857<br>150 351 | 26858<br>26858<br>150 352 | 26859<br>26859<br>150 353 | 26860<br>26860<br>150 354 | 26861<br>26861<br>150 355 | 26862<br>26862<br>150 356 | 26863<br>26863<br>150 357 |
| F- | 26864<br>26864<br>150 360 | 26865<br>26865<br>150 361 | 26866<br>26866<br>150 362 | 26867<br>26867<br>150 363 | 26868<br>26868<br>150 364 | 26869<br>26869<br>150 365 | 26870<br>26870<br>150 366 | 26871<br>26871<br>150 367 | 26872<br>26872<br>150 370 | 26873<br>26873<br>150 371 | 26874<br>26874<br>150 372 | 26875<br>26875<br>150 373 | 26876<br>26876<br>150 374 | 26877<br>26877<br>150 375 | 26878<br>26878<br>150 376 | 26879<br>26879<br>150 377 |

The leftmost column is labeled **SECOND HEX DIGIT**.

 DECIMAL | 26624    BINARY | 0110 1000    DECIMAL | 26624    HEXADECIMAL | ⬡ 68    OCTAL | 150 000

FOURTH HEX DIGIT →  ← THIRD HEX DIGIT

⟨2⟩

| SECOND HEX DIGIT \ FIRST HEX DIGIT | −0 | −1 | −2 | −3 | −4 | −5 | −6 | −7 | −8 | −9 | −A | −B | −C | −D | −E | −F |
|---|---|---|---|---|---|---|---|---|---|---|---|---|---|---|---|---|
| 0− | 26880<br>151 000 | 26881<br>151 001 | 26882<br>151 002 | 26883<br>151 003 | 26884<br>151 004 | 26885<br>151 005 | 26886<br>151 006 | 26887<br>151 007 | 26888<br>151 010 | 26889<br>151 011 | 26890<br>151 012 | 26891<br>151 013 | 26892<br>151 014 | 26893<br>151 015 | 26894<br>151 016 | 26895<br>151 017 |
| 1− | 26896<br>151 020 | 26897<br>151 021 | 26898<br>151 022 | 26899<br>151 023 | 26900<br>151 024 | 26901<br>151 025 | 26902<br>151 026 | 26903<br>151 027 | 26904<br>151 030 | 26905<br>151 031 | 26906<br>151 032 | 26907<br>151 033 | 26908<br>151 034 | 26909<br>151 035 | 26910<br>151 036 | 26911<br>151 037 |
| 2− | 26912<br>151 040 | 26913<br>151 041 | 26914<br>151 042 | 26915<br>151 043 | 26916<br>151 044 | 26917<br>151 045 | 26918<br>151 046 | 26919<br>151 047 | 26920<br>151 050 | 26921<br>151 051 | 26922<br>151 052 | 26923<br>151 053 | 26924<br>151 054 | 26925<br>151 055 | 26926<br>151 056 | 26927<br>151 057 |
| 3− | 26928<br>151 060 | 26929<br>151 061 | 26930<br>151 062 | 26931<br>151 063 | 26932<br>151 064 | 26933<br>151 065 | 26934<br>151 066 | 26935<br>151 067 | 26936<br>151 070 | 26937<br>151 071 | 26938<br>151 072 | 26939<br>151 073 | 26940<br>151 074 | 26941<br>151 075 | 26942<br>151 076 | 26943<br>151 077 |
| 4− | 26944<br>151 100 | 26945<br>151 101 | 26946<br>151 102 | 26947<br>151 103 | 26948<br>151 104 | 26949<br>151 105 | 26950<br>151 106 | 26951<br>151 107 | 26952<br>151 110 | 26953<br>151 111 | 26954<br>151 112 | 26955<br>151 113 | 26956<br>151 114 | 26957<br>151 115 | 26958<br>151 116 | 26959<br>151 117 |
| 5− | 26960<br>151 120 | 26961<br>151 121 | 26962<br>151 122 | 26963<br>151 123 | 26964<br>151 124 | 26965<br>151 125 | 26966<br>151 126 | 26967<br>151 127 | 26968<br>151 130 | 26969<br>151 131 | 26970<br>151 132 | 26971<br>151 133 | 26972<br>151 134 | 26973<br>151 135 | 26974<br>151 136 | 26975<br>151 137 |
| 6− | 26976<br>151 140 | 26977<br>151 141 | 26978<br>151 142 | 26979<br>151 143 | 26980<br>151 144 | 26981<br>151 145 | 26982<br>151 146 | 26983<br>151 147 | 26984<br>151 150 | 26985<br>151 151 | 26986<br>151 152 | 26987<br>151 153 | 26988<br>151 154 | 26989<br>151 155 | 26990<br>151 156 | 26991<br>151 157 |
| 7− | 26992<br>151 160 | 26993<br>151 161 | 26994<br>151 162 | 26995<br>151 163 | 26996<br>151 164 | 26997<br>151 165 | 26998<br>151 166 | 26999<br>151 167 | 27000<br>151 170 | 27001<br>151 171 | 27002<br>151 172 | 27003<br>151 173 | 27004<br>151 174 | 27005<br>151 175 | 27006<br>151 176 | 27007<br>151 177 |
| 8− | 27008<br>151 200 | 27009<br>151 201 | 27010<br>151 202 | 27011<br>151 203 | 27012<br>151 204 | 27013<br>151 205 | 27014<br>151 206 | 27015<br>151 207 | 27016<br>151 210 | 27017<br>151 211 | 27018<br>151 212 | 27019<br>151 213 | 27020<br>151 214 | 27021<br>151 215 | 27022<br>151 216 | 27023<br>151 217 |
| 9− | 27024<br>151 220 | 27025<br>151 221 | 27026<br>151 222 | 27027<br>151 223 | 27028<br>151 224 | 27029<br>151 225 | 27030<br>151 226 | 27031<br>151 227 | 27032<br>151 230 | 27033<br>151 231 | 27034<br>151 232 | 27035<br>151 233 | 27036<br>151 234 | 27037<br>151 235 | 27038<br>151 236 | 27039<br>151 237 |
| A− | 27040<br>151 240 | 27041<br>151 241 | 27042<br>151 242 | 27043<br>151 243 | 27044<br>151 244 | 27045<br>151 245 | 27046<br>151 246 | 27047<br>151 247 | 27048<br>151 250 | 27049<br>151 251 | 27050<br>151 252 | 27051<br>151 253 | 27052<br>151 254 | 27053<br>151 255 | 27054<br>151 256 | 27055<br>151 257 |
| B− | 27056<br>151 260 | 27057<br>151 261 | 27058<br>151 262 | 27059<br>151 263 | 27060<br>151 264 | 27061<br>151 265 | 27062<br>151 266 | 27063<br>151 267 | 27064<br>151 270 | 27065<br>151 271 | 27066<br>151 272 | 27067<br>151 273 | 27068<br>151 274 | 27069<br>151 275 | 27070<br>151 276 | 27071<br>151 277 |
| C− | 27072<br>151 300 | 27073<br>151 301 | 27074<br>151 302 | 27075<br>151 303 | 27076<br>151 304 | 27077<br>151 305 | 27078<br>151 306 | 27079<br>151 307 | 27080<br>151 310 | 27081<br>151 311 | 27082<br>151 312 | 27083<br>151 313 | 27084<br>151 314 | 27085<br>151 315 | 27086<br>151 316 | 27087<br>151 317 |
| D− | 27088<br>151 320 | 27089<br>151 321 | 27090<br>151 322 | 27091<br>151 323 | 27092<br>151 324 | 27093<br>151 325 | 27094<br>151 326 | 27095<br>151 327 | 27096<br>151 330 | 27097<br>151 331 | 27098<br>151 332 | 27099<br>151 333 | 27100<br>151 334 | 27101<br>151 335 | 27102<br>151 336 | 27103<br>151 337 |
| E− | 27104<br>151 340 | 27105<br>151 341 | 27106<br>151 342 | 27107<br>151 343 | 27108<br>151 344 | 27109<br>151 345 | 27110<br>151 346 | 27111<br>151 347 | 27112<br>151 350 | 27113<br>151 351 | 27114<br>151 352 | 27115<br>151 353 | 27116<br>151 354 | 27117<br>151 355 | 27118<br>151 356 | 27119<br>151 357 |
| F− | 27120<br>151 360 | 27121<br>151 361 | 27122<br>151 362 | 27123<br>151 363 | 27124<br>151 364 | 27125<br>151 365 | 27126<br>151 366 | 27127<br>151 367 | 27128<br>151 370 | 27129<br>151 371 | 27130<br>151 372 | 27131<br>151 373 | 27132<br>151 374 | 27133<br>151 375 | 27134<br>151 376 | 27135<br>151 377 |

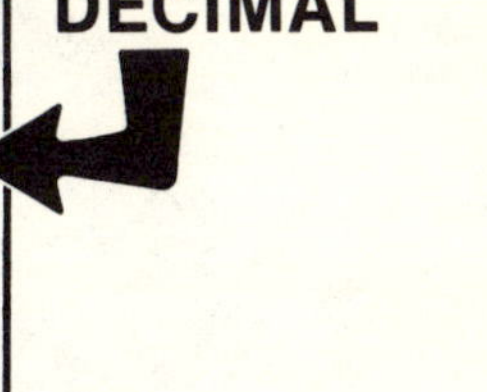

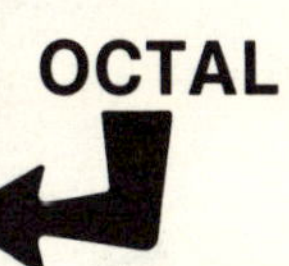

## ② FIRST HEX DIGIT

| SECOND HEX DIGIT | −0 | −1 | −2 | −3 | −4 | −5 | −6 | −7 | −8 | −9 | −A | −B | −C | −D | −E | −F |
|---|---|---|---|---|---|---|---|---|---|---|---|---|---|---|---|---|
| 0− | 27392<br>27392<br>153 000 | 27393<br>27393<br>153 001 | 27394<br>27394<br>153 002 | 27395<br>27395<br>153 003 | 27396<br>27396<br>153 004 | 27397<br>27397<br>153 005 | 27398<br>27398<br>153 006 | 27399<br>27399<br>153 007 | 27400<br>27400<br>153 010 | 27401<br>27401<br>153 011 | 27402<br>27402<br>153 012 | 27403<br>27403<br>153 013 | 27404<br>27404<br>153 014 | 27405<br>27405<br>153 015 | 27406<br>27406<br>153 016 | 27407<br>27407<br>153 017 |
| 1− | 27408<br>27408<br>153 020 | 27409<br>27409<br>153 021 | 27410<br>27410<br>153 022 | 27411<br>27411<br>153 023 | 27412<br>27412<br>153 024 | 27413<br>27413<br>153 025 | 27414<br>27414<br>153 026 | 27415<br>27415<br>153 027 | 27416<br>27416<br>153 030 | 27417<br>27417<br>153 031 | 27418<br>27418<br>153 032 | 27419<br>27419<br>153 033 | 27420<br>27420<br>153 034 | 27421<br>27421<br>153 035 | 27422<br>27422<br>153 036 | 27423<br>27423<br>153 037 |
| 2− | 27424<br>27424<br>153 040 | 27425<br>27425<br>153 041 | 27426<br>27426<br>153 042 | 27427<br>27427<br>153 043 | 27428<br>27428<br>153 044 | 27429<br>27429<br>153 045 | 27430<br>27430<br>153 046 | 27431<br>27431<br>153 047 | 27432<br>27432<br>153 050 | 27433<br>27433<br>153 051 | 27434<br>27434<br>153 052 | 27435<br>27435<br>153 053 | 27436<br>27436<br>153 054 | 27437<br>27437<br>153 055 | 27438<br>27438<br>153 056 | 27439<br>27439<br>153 057 |
| 3− | 27440<br>27440<br>153 060 | 27441<br>27441<br>153 061 | 27442<br>27442<br>153 062 | 27443<br>27443<br>153 063 | 27444<br>27444<br>153 064 | 27445<br>27445<br>153 065 | 27446<br>27446<br>153 066 | 27447<br>27447<br>153 067 | 27448<br>27448<br>153 070 | 27449<br>27449<br>153 071 | 27450<br>27450<br>153 072 | 27451<br>27451<br>153 073 | 27452<br>27452<br>153 074 | 27453<br>27453<br>153 075 | 27454<br>27454<br>153 076 | 27455<br>27455<br>153 077 |
| 4− | 27456<br>27456<br>153 100 | 27457<br>27457<br>153 101 | 27458<br>27458<br>153 102 | 27459<br>27459<br>153 103 | 27460<br>27460<br>153 104 | 27461<br>27461<br>153 105 | 27462<br>27462<br>153 106 | 27463<br>27463<br>153 107 | 27464<br>27464<br>153 110 | 27465<br>27465<br>153 111 | 27466<br>27466<br>153 112 | 27467<br>27467<br>153 113 | 27468<br>27468<br>153 114 | 27469<br>27469<br>153 115 | 27470<br>27470<br>153 116 | 27471<br>27471<br>153 117 |
| 5− | 27472<br>27472<br>153 120 | 27473<br>27473<br>153 121 | 27474<br>27474<br>153 122 | 27475<br>27475<br>153 123 | 27476<br>27476<br>153 124 | 27477<br>27477<br>153 125 | 27478<br>27478<br>153 126 | 27479<br>27479<br>153 127 | 27480<br>27480<br>153 130 | 27481<br>27481<br>153 131 | 27482<br>27482<br>153 132 | 27483<br>27483<br>153 133 | 27484<br>27484<br>153 134 | 27485<br>27485<br>153 135 | 27486<br>27486<br>153 136 | 27487<br>27487<br>153 137 |
| 6− | 27488<br>27488<br>153 140 | 27489<br>27489<br>153 141 | 27490<br>27490<br>153 142 | 27491<br>27491<br>153 143 | 27492<br>27492<br>153 144 | 27493<br>27493<br>153 145 | 27494<br>27494<br>153 146 | 27495<br>27495<br>153 147 | 27496<br>27496<br>153 150 | 27497<br>27497<br>153 151 | 27498<br>27498<br>153 152 | 27499<br>27499<br>153 153 | 27500<br>27500<br>153 154 | 27501<br>27501<br>153 155 | 27502<br>27502<br>153 156 | 27503<br>27503<br>153 157 |
| 7− | 27504<br>27504<br>153 160 | 27505<br>27505<br>153 161 | 27506<br>27506<br>153 162 | 27507<br>27507<br>153 163 | 27508<br>27508<br>153 164 | 27509<br>27509<br>153 165 | 27510<br>27510<br>153 166 | 27511<br>27511<br>153 167 | 27512<br>27512<br>153 170 | 27513<br>27513<br>153 171 | 27514<br>27514<br>153 172 | 27515<br>27515<br>153 173 | 27516<br>27516<br>153 174 | 27517<br>27517<br>153 175 | 27518<br>27518<br>153 176 | 27519<br>27519<br>153 177 |
| 8− | 27520<br>27520<br>153 200 | 27521<br>27521<br>153 201 | 27522<br>27522<br>153 202 | 27523<br>27523<br>153 203 | 27524<br>27524<br>153 204 | 27525<br>27525<br>153 205 | 27526<br>27526<br>153 206 | 27527<br>27527<br>153 207 | 27528<br>27528<br>153 210 | 27529<br>27529<br>153 211 | 27530<br>27530<br>153 212 | 27531<br>27531<br>153 213 | 27532<br>27532<br>153 214 | 27533<br>27533<br>153 215 | 27534<br>27534<br>153 216 | 27535<br>27535<br>153 217 |
| 9− | 27536<br>27536<br>153 220 | 27537<br>27537<br>153 221 | 27538<br>27538<br>153 222 | 27539<br>27539<br>153 223 | 27540<br>27540<br>153 224 | 27541<br>27541<br>153 225 | 27542<br>27542<br>153 226 | 27543<br>27543<br>153 227 | 27544<br>27544<br>153 230 | 27545<br>27545<br>153 231 | 27546<br>27546<br>153 232 | 27547<br>27547<br>153 233 | 27548<br>27548<br>153 234 | 27549<br>27549<br>153 235 | 27550<br>27550<br>153 236 | 27551<br>27551<br>153 237 |
| A− | 27552<br>27552<br>153 240 | 27553<br>27553<br>153 241 | 27554<br>27554<br>153 242 | 27555<br>27555<br>153 243 | 27556<br>27556<br>153 244 | 27557<br>27557<br>153 245 | 27558<br>27558<br>153 246 | 27559<br>27559<br>153 247 | 27560<br>27560<br>153 250 | 27561<br>27561<br>153 251 | 27562<br>27562<br>153 252 | 27563<br>27563<br>153 253 | 27564<br>27564<br>153 254 | 27565<br>27565<br>153 255 | 27566<br>27566<br>153 256 | 27567<br>27567<br>153 257 |
| B− | 27568<br>27568<br>153 260 | 27569<br>27569<br>153 261 | 27570<br>27570<br>153 262 | 27571<br>27571<br>153 263 | 27572<br>27572<br>153 264 | 27573<br>27573<br>153 265 | 27574<br>27574<br>153 266 | 27575<br>27575<br>153 267 | 27576<br>27576<br>153 270 | 27577<br>27577<br>153 271 | 27578<br>27578<br>153 272 | 27579<br>27579<br>153 273 | 27580<br>27580<br>153 274 | 27581<br>27581<br>153 275 | 27582<br>27582<br>153 276 | 27583<br>27583<br>153 277 |
| C− | 27584<br>27584<br>153 300 | 27585<br>27585<br>153 301 | 27586<br>27586<br>153 302 | 27587<br>27587<br>153 303 | 27588<br>27588<br>153 304 | 27589<br>27589<br>153 305 | 27590<br>27590<br>153 306 | 27591<br>27591<br>153 307 | 27592<br>27592<br>153 310 | 27593<br>27593<br>153 311 | 27594<br>27594<br>153 312 | 27595<br>27595<br>153 313 | 27596<br>27596<br>153 314 | 27597<br>27597<br>153 315 | 27598<br>27598<br>153 316 | 27599<br>27599<br>153 317 |
| D− | 27600<br>27600<br>153 320 | 27601<br>27601<br>153 321 | 27602<br>27602<br>153 322 | 27603<br>27603<br>153 323 | 27604<br>27604<br>153 324 | 27605<br>27605<br>153 325 | 27606<br>27606<br>153 326 | 27607<br>27607<br>153 327 | 27608<br>27608<br>153 330 | 27609<br>27609<br>153 331 | 27610<br>27610<br>153 332 | 27611<br>27611<br>153 333 | 27612<br>27612<br>153 334 | 27613<br>27613<br>153 335 | 27614<br>27614<br>153 336 | 27615<br>27615<br>153 337 |
| E− | 27616<br>27616<br>153 340 | 27617<br>27617<br>153 341 | 27618<br>27618<br>153 342 | 27619<br>27619<br>153 343 | 27620<br>27620<br>153 344 | 27621<br>27621<br>153 345 | 27622<br>27622<br>153 346 | 27623<br>27623<br>153 347 | 27624<br>27624<br>153 350 | 27625<br>27625<br>153 351 | 27626<br>27626<br>153 352 | 27627<br>27627<br>153 353 | 27628<br>27628<br>153 354 | 27629<br>27629<br>153 355 | 27630<br>27630<br>153 356 | 27631<br>27631<br>153 357 |
| F− | 27632<br>27632<br>153 360 | 27633<br>27633<br>153 361 | 27634<br>27634<br>153 362 | 27635<br>27635<br>153 363 | 27636<br>27636<br>153 364 | 27637<br>27637<br>153 365 | 27638<br>27638<br>153 366 | 27639<br>27639<br>153 367 | 27640<br>27640<br>153 370 | 27641<br>27641<br>153 371 | 27642<br>27642<br>153 372 | 27643<br>27643<br>153 373 | 27644<br>27644<br>153 374 | 27645<br>27645<br>153 375 | 27646<br>27646<br>153 376 | 27647<br>27647<br>153 377 |

DECIMAL ←

 DECIMAL ←

OCTAL ←

| SECOND HEX DIGIT | −0 | −1 | −2 | −3 | −4 | −5 | −6 | −7 | −8 | −9 | −A | −B | −C | −D | −E | −F |
|---|---|---|---|---|---|---|---|---|---|---|---|---|---|---|---|---|
| 0− | 27648<br>27648<br>154 000 | 27649<br>27649<br>154 001 | 27650<br>27650<br>154 002 | 27651<br>27651<br>154 003 | 27652<br>27652<br>154 004 | 27653<br>27653<br>154 005 | 27654<br>27654<br>154 006 | 27655<br>27655<br>154 007 | 27656<br>27656<br>154 010 | 27657<br>27657<br>154 011 | 27658<br>27658<br>154 012 | 27659<br>27659<br>154 013 | 27660<br>27660<br>154 014 | 27661<br>27661<br>154 015 | 27662<br>27662<br>154 016 | 27663<br>27663<br>154 017 |
| 1− | 27664<br>27664<br>154 020 | 27665<br>27665<br>154 021 | 27666<br>27666<br>154 022 | 27667<br>27667<br>154 023 | 27668<br>27668<br>154 024 | 27669<br>27669<br>154 025 | 27670<br>27670<br>154 026 | 27671<br>27671<br>154 027 | 27672<br>27672<br>154 030 | 27673<br>27673<br>154 031 | 27674<br>27674<br>154 032 | 27675<br>27675<br>154 033 | 27676<br>27676<br>154 034 | 27677<br>27677<br>154 035 | 27678<br>27678<br>154 036 | 27679<br>27679<br>154 037 |
| 2− | 27680<br>27680<br>154 040 | 27681<br>27681<br>154 041 | 27682<br>27682<br>154 042 | 27683<br>27683<br>154 043 | 27684<br>27684<br>154 044 | 27685<br>27685<br>154 045 | 27686<br>27686<br>154 046 | 27687<br>27687<br>154 047 | 27688<br>27688<br>154 050 | 27689<br>27689<br>154 051 | 27690<br>27690<br>154 052 | 27691<br>27691<br>154 053 | 27692<br>27692<br>154 054 | 27693<br>27693<br>154 055 | 27694<br>27694<br>154 056 | 27695<br>27695<br>154 057 |
| 3− | 27696<br>27696<br>154 060 | 27697<br>27697<br>154 061 | 27698<br>27698<br>154 062 | 27699<br>27699<br>154 063 | 27700<br>27700<br>154 064 | 27701<br>27701<br>154 065 | 27702<br>27702<br>154 066 | 27703<br>27703<br>154 067 | 27704<br>27704<br>154 070 | 27705<br>27705<br>154 071 | 27706<br>27706<br>154 072 | 27707<br>27707<br>154 073 | 27708<br>27708<br>154 074 | 27709<br>27709<br>154 075 | 27710<br>27710<br>154 076 | 27711<br>27711<br>154 077 |
| 4− | 27712<br>27712<br>154 100 | 27713<br>27713<br>154 101 | 27714<br>27714<br>154 102 | 27715<br>27715<br>154 103 | 27716<br>27716<br>154 104 | 27717<br>27717<br>154 105 | 27718<br>27718<br>154 106 | 27719<br>27719<br>154 107 | 27720<br>27720<br>154 110 | 27721<br>27721<br>154 111 | 27722<br>27722<br>154 112 | 27723<br>27723<br>154 113 | 27724<br>27724<br>154 114 | 27725<br>27725<br>154 115 | 27726<br>27726<br>154 116 | 27727<br>27727<br>154 117 |
| 5− | 27728<br>27728<br>154 120 | 27729<br>27729<br>154 121 | 27730<br>27730<br>154 122 | 27731<br>27731<br>154 123 | 27732<br>27732<br>154 124 | 27733<br>27733<br>154 125 | 27734<br>27734<br>154 126 | 27735<br>27735<br>154 127 | 27736<br>27736<br>154 130 | 27737<br>27737<br>154 131 | 27738<br>27738<br>154 132 | 27739<br>27739<br>154 133 | 27740<br>27740<br>154 134 | 27741<br>27741<br>154 135 | 27742<br>27742<br>154 136 | 27743<br>27743<br>154 137 |
| 6− | 27744<br>27744<br>154 140 | 27745<br>27745<br>154 141 | 27746<br>27746<br>154 142 | 27747<br>27747<br>154 143 | 27748<br>27748<br>154 144 | 27749<br>27749<br>154 145 | 27750<br>27750<br>154 146 | 27751<br>27751<br>154 147 | 27752<br>27752<br>154 150 | 27753<br>27753<br>154 151 | 27754<br>27754<br>154 152 | 27755<br>27755<br>154 153 | 27756<br>27756<br>154 154 | 27757<br>27757<br>154 155 | 27758<br>27758<br>154 156 | 27759<br>27759<br>154 157 |
| 7− | 27760<br>27760<br>154 160 | 27761<br>27761<br>154 161 | 27762<br>27762<br>154 162 | 27763<br>27763<br>154 163 | 27764<br>27764<br>154 164 | 27765<br>27765<br>154 165 | 27766<br>27766<br>154 166 | 27767<br>27767<br>154 167 | 27768<br>27768<br>154 170 | 27769<br>27769<br>154 171 | 27770<br>27770<br>154 172 | 27771<br>27771<br>154 173 | 27772<br>27772<br>154 174 | 27773<br>27773<br>154 175 | 27774<br>27774<br>154 176 | 27775<br>27775<br>154 177 |
| 8− | 27776<br>27776<br>154 200 | 27777<br>27777<br>154 201 | 27778<br>27778<br>154 202 | 27779<br>27779<br>154 203 | 27780<br>27780<br>154 204 | 27781<br>27781<br>154 205 | 27782<br>27782<br>154 206 | 27783<br>27783<br>154 207 | 27784<br>27784<br>154 210 | 27785<br>27785<br>154 211 | 27786<br>27786<br>154 212 | 27787<br>27787<br>154 213 | 27788<br>27788<br>154 214 | 27789<br>27789<br>154 215 | 27790<br>27790<br>154 216 | 27791<br>27791<br>154 217 |
| 9− | 27792<br>27792<br>154 220 | 27793<br>27793<br>154 221 | 27794<br>27794<br>154 222 | 27795<br>27795<br>154 223 | 27796<br>27796<br>154 224 | 27797<br>27797<br>154 225 | 27798<br>27798<br>154 226 | 27799<br>27799<br>154 227 | 27800<br>27800<br>154 230 | 27801<br>27801<br>154 231 | 27802<br>27802<br>154 232 | 27803<br>27803<br>154 233 | 27804<br>27804<br>154 234 | 27805<br>27805<br>154 235 | 27806<br>27806<br>154 236 | 27807<br>27807<br>154 237 |
| A− | 27808<br>27808<br>154 240 | 27809<br>27809<br>154 241 | 27810<br>27810<br>154 242 | 27811<br>27811<br>154 243 | 27812<br>27812<br>154 244 | 27813<br>27813<br>154 245 | 27814<br>27814<br>154 246 | 27815<br>27815<br>154 247 | 27816<br>27816<br>154 250 | 27817<br>27817<br>154 251 | 27818<br>27818<br>154 252 | 27819<br>27819<br>154 253 | 27820<br>27820<br>154 254 | 27821<br>27821<br>154 255 | 27822<br>27822<br>154 256 | 27823<br>27823<br>154 257 |
| B− | 27824<br>27824<br>154 260 | 27825<br>27825<br>154 261 | 27826<br>27826<br>154 262 | 27827<br>27827<br>154 263 | 27828<br>27828<br>154 264 | 27829<br>27829<br>154 265 | 27830<br>27830<br>154 266 | 27831<br>27831<br>154 267 | 27832<br>27832<br>154 270 | 27833<br>27833<br>154 271 | 27834<br>27834<br>154 272 | 27835<br>27835<br>154 273 | 27836<br>27836<br>154 274 | 27837<br>27837<br>154 275 | 27838<br>27838<br>154 276 | 27839<br>27839<br>154 277 |
| C− | 27840<br>27840<br>154 300 | 27841<br>27841<br>154 301 | 27842<br>27842<br>154 302 | 27843<br>27843<br>154 303 | 27844<br>27844<br>154 304 | 27845<br>27845<br>154 305 | 27846<br>27846<br>154 306 | 27847<br>27847<br>154 307 | 27848<br>27848<br>154 310 | 27849<br>27849<br>154 311 | 27850<br>27850<br>154 312 | 27851<br>27851<br>154 313 | 27852<br>27852<br>154 314 | 27853<br>27853<br>154 315 | 27854<br>27854<br>154 316 | 27855<br>27855<br>154 317 |
| D− | 27856<br>27856<br>154 320 | 27857<br>27857<br>154 321 | 27858<br>27858<br>154 322 | 27859<br>27859<br>154 323 | 27860<br>27860<br>154 324 | 27861<br>27861<br>154 325 | 27862<br>27862<br>154 326 | 27863<br>27863<br>154 327 | 27864<br>27864<br>154 330 | 27865<br>27865<br>154 331 | 27866<br>27866<br>154 332 | 27867<br>27867<br>154 333 | 27868<br>27868<br>154 334 | 27869<br>27869<br>154 335 | 27870<br>27870<br>154 336 | 27871<br>27871<br>154 337 |
| E− | 27872<br>27872<br>154 340 | 27873<br>27873<br>154 341 | 27874<br>27874<br>154 342 | 27875<br>27875<br>154 343 | 27876<br>27876<br>154 344 | 27877<br>27877<br>154 345 | 27878<br>27878<br>154 346 | 27879<br>27879<br>154 347 | 27880<br>27880<br>154 350 | 27881<br>27881<br>154 351 | 27882<br>27882<br>154 352 | 27883<br>27883<br>154 353 | 27884<br>27884<br>154 354 | 27885<br>27885<br>154 355 | 27886<br>27886<br>154 356 | 27887<br>27887<br>154 357 |
| F− | 27888<br>27888<br>154 360 | 27889<br>27889<br>154 361 | 27890<br>27890<br>154 362 | 27891<br>27891<br>154 363 | 27892<br>27892<br>154 364 | 27893<br>27893<br>154 365 | 27894<br>27894<br>154 366 | 27895<br>27895<br>154 367 | 27896<br>27896<br>154 370 | 27897<br>27897<br>154 371 | 27898<br>27898<br>154 372 | 27899<br>27899<br>154 373 | 27900<br>27900<br>154 374 | 27901<br>27901<br>154 375 | 27902<br>27902<br>154 376 | 27903<br>27903<br>154 377 |

DECIMAL

 DECIMAL

OCTAL

 DECIMAL [27648]  BINARY [0110 1100]  DECIMAL [27648]  HEXADECIMAL ⬡6C  OCTAL [154 000]

FOURTH HEX DIGIT → ⬡ ← THIRD HEX DIGIT

FIRST HEX DIGIT

(2)

SECOND HEX DIGIT

DECIMAL

DECIMAL

OCTAL

| SECOND \ FIRST | −0 | −1 | −2 | −3 | −4 | −5 | −6 | −7 | −8 | −9 | −A | −B | −C | −D | −E | −F |
|---|---|---|---|---|---|---|---|---|---|---|---|---|---|---|---|---|
| 0− | 27904 / 155 000 | 27905 / 155 001 | 27906 / 155 002 | 27907 / 155 003 | 27908 / 155 004 | 27909 / 155 005 | 27910 / 155 006 | 27911 / 155 007 | 27912 / 155 010 | 27913 / 155 011 | 27914 / 155 012 | 27915 / 155 013 | 27916 / 155 014 | 27917 / 155 015 | 27918 / 155 016 | 27919 / 155 017 |
| 1− | 27920 / 155 020 | 27921 / 155 021 | 27922 / 155 022 | 27923 / 155 023 | 27924 / 155 024 | 27925 / 155 025 | 27926 / 155 026 | 27927 / 155 027 | 27928 / 155 030 | 27929 / 155 031 | 27930 / 155 032 | 27931 / 155 033 | 27932 / 155 034 | 27933 / 155 035 | 27934 / 155 036 | 27935 / 155 037 |
| 2− | 27936 / 155 040 | 27937 / 155 041 | 27938 / 155 042 | 27939 / 155 043 | 27940 / 155 044 | 27941 / 155 045 | 27942 / 155 046 | 27943 / 155 047 | 27944 / 155 050 | 27945 / 155 051 | 27946 / 155 052 | 27947 / 155 053 | 27948 / 155 054 | 27949 / 155 055 | 27950 / 155 056 | 27951 / 155 057 |
| 3− | 27952 / 155 060 | 27953 / 155 061 | 27954 / 155 062 | 27955 / 155 063 | 27956 / 155 064 | 27957 / 155 065 | 27958 / 155 066 | 27959 / 155 067 | 27960 / 155 070 | 27961 / 155 071 | 27962 / 155 072 | 27963 / 155 073 | 27964 / 155 074 | 27965 / 155 075 | 27966 / 155 076 | 27967 / 155 077 |
| 4− | 27968 / 155 100 | 27969 / 155 101 | 27970 / 155 102 | 27971 / 155 103 | 27972 / 155 104 | 27973 / 155 105 | 27974 / 155 106 | 27975 / 155 107 | 27976 / 155 110 | 27977 / 155 111 | 27978 / 155 112 | 27979 / 155 113 | 27980 / 155 114 | 27981 / 155 115 | 27982 / 155 116 | 27983 / 155 117 |
| 5− | 27984 / 155 120 | 27985 / 155 121 | 27986 / 155 122 | 27987 / 155 123 | 27988 / 155 124 | 27989 / 155 125 | 27990 / 155 126 | 27991 / 155 127 | 27992 / 155 130 | 27993 / 155 131 | 27994 / 155 132 | 27995 / 155 133 | 27996 / 155 134 | 27997 / 155 135 | 27998 / 155 136 | 27999 / 155 137 |
| 6− | 28000 / 155 140 | 28001 / 155 141 | 28002 / 155 142 | 28003 / 155 143 | 28004 / 155 144 | 28005 / 155 145 | 28006 / 155 146 | 28007 / 155 147 | 28008 / 155 150 | 28009 / 155 151 | 28010 / 155 152 | 28011 / 155 153 | 28012 / 155 154 | 28013 / 155 155 | 28014 / 155 156 | 28015 / 155 157 |
| 7− | 28016 / 155 160 | 28017 / 155 161 | 28018 / 155 162 | 28019 / 155 163 | 28020 / 155 164 | 28021 / 155 165 | 28022 / 155 166 | 28023 / 155 167 | 28024 / 155 170 | 28025 / 155 171 | 28026 / 155 172 | 28027 / 155 173 | 28028 / 155 174 | 28029 / 155 175 | 28030 / 155 176 | 28031 / 155 177 |
| 8− | 28032 / 155 200 | 28033 / 155 201 | 28034 / 155 202 | 28035 / 155 203 | 28036 / 155 204 | 28037 / 155 205 | 28038 / 155 206 | 28039 / 155 207 | 28040 / 155 210 | 28041 / 155 211 | 28042 / 155 212 | 28043 / 155 213 | 28044 / 155 214 | 28045 / 155 215 | 28046 / 155 216 | 28047 / 155 217 |
| 9− | 28048 / 155 220 | 28049 / 155 221 | 28050 / 155 222 | 28051 / 155 223 | 28052 / 155 224 | 28053 / 155 225 | 28054 / 155 226 | 28055 / 155 227 | 28056 / 155 230 | 28057 / 155 231 | 28058 / 155 232 | 28059 / 155 233 | 28060 / 155 234 | 28061 / 155 235 | 28062 / 155 236 | 28063 / 155 237 |
| A− | 28064 / 155 240 | 28065 / 155 241 | 28066 / 155 242 | 28067 / 155 243 | 28068 / 155 244 | 28069 / 155 245 | 28070 / 155 246 | 28071 / 155 247 | 28072 / 155 250 | 28073 / 155 251 | 28074 / 155 252 | 28075 / 155 253 | 28076 / 155 254 | 28077 / 155 255 | 28078 / 155 256 | 28079 / 155 257 |
| B− | 28080 / 155 260 | 28081 / 155 261 | 28082 / 155 262 | 28083 / 155 263 | 28084 / 155 264 | 28085 / 155 265 | 28086 / 155 266 | 28087 / 155 267 | 28088 / 155 270 | 28089 / 155 271 | 28090 / 155 272 | 28091 / 155 273 | 28092 / 155 274 | 28093 / 155 275 | 28094 / 155 276 | 28095 / 155 277 |
| C− | 28096 / 155 300 | 28097 / 155 301 | 28098 / 155 302 | 28099 / 155 303 | 28100 / 155 304 | 28101 / 155 305 | 28102 / 155 306 | 28103 / 155 307 | 28104 / 155 310 | 28105 / 155 311 | 28106 / 155 312 | 28107 / 155 313 | 28108 / 155 314 | 28109 / 155 315 | 28110 / 155 316 | 28111 / 155 317 |
| D− | 28112 / 155 320 | 28113 / 155 321 | 28114 / 155 322 | 28115 / 155 323 | 28116 / 155 324 | 28117 / 155 325 | 28118 / 155 326 | 28119 / 155 327 | 28120 / 155 330 | 28121 / 155 331 | 28122 / 155 332 | 28123 / 155 333 | 28124 / 155 334 | 28125 / 155 335 | 28126 / 155 336 | 28127 / 155 337 |
| E− | 28128 / 155 340 | 28129 / 155 341 | 28130 / 155 342 | 28131 / 155 343 | 28132 / 155 344 | 28133 / 155 345 | 28134 / 155 346 | 28135 / 155 347 | 28136 / 155 350 | 28137 / 155 351 | 28138 / 155 352 | 28139 / 155 353 | 28140 / 155 354 | 28141 / 155 355 | 28142 / 155 356 | 28143 / 155 357 |
| F− | 28144 / 155 360 | 28145 / 155 361 | 28146 / 155 362 | 28147 / 155 363 | 28148 / 155 364 | 28149 / 155 365 | 28150 / 155 366 | 28151 / 155 367 | 28152 / 155 370 | 28153 / 155 371 | 28154 / 155 372 | 28155 / 155 373 | 28156 / 155 374 | 28157 / 155 375 | 28158 / 155 376 | 28159 / 155 377 |

# FIRST HEX DIGIT

Table 2

|  | −0 | −1 | −2 | −3 | −4 | −5 | −6 | −7 | −8 | −9 | −A | −B | −C | −D | −E | −F |
|---|---|---|---|---|---|---|---|---|---|---|---|---|---|---|---|---|
| **0−** | 28160<br>28160<br>156 000 | 28161<br>28161<br>156 001 | 28162<br>28162<br>156 002 | 28163<br>28163<br>156 003 | 28164<br>28164<br>156 004 | 28165<br>28165<br>156 005 | 28166<br>28166<br>156 006 | 28167<br>28167<br>156 007 | 28168<br>28168<br>156 010 | 28169<br>28169<br>156 011 | 28170<br>28170<br>156 012 | 28171<br>28171<br>156 013 | 28172<br>28172<br>156 014 | 28173<br>28173<br>156 015 | 28174<br>28174<br>156 016 | 28175<br>28175<br>156 017 |
| **1−** | 28176<br>28176<br>156 020 | 28177<br>28177<br>156 021 | 28178<br>28178<br>156 022 | 28179<br>28179<br>156 023 | 28180<br>28180<br>156 024 | 28181<br>28181<br>156 025 | 28182<br>28182<br>156 026 | 28183<br>28183<br>156 027 | 28184<br>28184<br>156 030 | 28185<br>28185<br>156 031 | 28186<br>28186<br>156 032 | 28187<br>28187<br>156 033 | 28188<br>28188<br>156 034 | 28189<br>28189<br>156 035 | 28190<br>28190<br>156 036 | 28191<br>28191<br>156 037 |
| **2−** | 28192<br>28192<br>156 040 | 28193<br>28193<br>156 041 | 28194<br>28194<br>156 042 | 28195<br>28195<br>156 043 | 28196<br>28196<br>156 044 | 28197<br>28197<br>156 045 | 28198<br>28198<br>156 046 | 28199<br>28199<br>156 047 | 28200<br>28200<br>156 050 | 28201<br>28201<br>156 051 | 28202<br>28202<br>156 052 | 28203<br>28203<br>156 053 | 28204<br>28204<br>156 054 | 28205<br>28205<br>156 055 | 28206<br>28206<br>156 056 | 28207<br>28207<br>156 057 |
| **3−** | 28208<br>28208<br>156 060 | 28209<br>28209<br>156 061 | 28210<br>28210<br>156 062 | 28211<br>28211<br>156 063 | 28212<br>28212<br>156 064 | 28213<br>28213<br>156 065 | 28214<br>28214<br>156 066 | 28215<br>28215<br>156 067 | 28216<br>28216<br>156 070 | 28217<br>28217<br>156 071 | 28218<br>28218<br>156 072 | 28219<br>28219<br>156 073 | 28220<br>28220<br>156 074 | 28221<br>28221<br>156 075 | 28222<br>28222<br>156 076 | 28223<br>28223<br>156 077 |
| **4−** | 28224<br>28224<br>156 100 | 28225<br>28225<br>156 101 | 28226<br>28226<br>156 102 | 28227<br>28227<br>156 103 | 28228<br>28228<br>156 104 | 28229<br>28229<br>156 105 | 28230<br>28230<br>156 106 | 28231<br>28231<br>156 107 | 28232<br>28232<br>156 110 | 28233<br>28233<br>156 111 | 28234<br>28234<br>156 112 | 28235<br>28235<br>156 113 | 28236<br>28236<br>156 114 | 28237<br>28237<br>156 115 | 28238<br>28238<br>156 116 | 28239<br>28239<br>156 117 |
| **5−** | 28240<br>28240<br>156 120 | 28241<br>28241<br>156 121 | 28242<br>28242<br>156 122 | 28243<br>28243<br>156 123 | 28244<br>28244<br>156 124 | 28245<br>28245<br>156 125 | 28246<br>28246<br>156 126 | 28247<br>28247<br>156 127 | 28248<br>28248<br>156 130 | 28249<br>28249<br>156 131 | 28250<br>28250<br>156 132 | 28251<br>28251<br>156 133 | 28252<br>28252<br>156 134 | 28253<br>28253<br>156 135 | 28254<br>28254<br>156 136 | 28255<br>28255<br>156 137 |
| **6−** | 28256<br>28256<br>156 140 | 28257<br>28257<br>156 141 | 28258<br>28258<br>156 142 | 28259<br>28259<br>156 143 | 28260<br>28260<br>156 144 | 28261<br>28261<br>156 145 | 28262<br>28262<br>156 146 | 28263<br>28263<br>156 147 | 28264<br>28264<br>156 150 | 28265<br>28265<br>156 151 | 28266<br>28266<br>156 152 | 28267<br>28267<br>156 153 | 28268<br>28268<br>156 154 | 28269<br>28269<br>156 155 | 28270<br>28270<br>156 156 | 28271<br>28271<br>156 157 |
| **7−** | 28272<br>28272<br>156 160 | 28273<br>28273<br>156 161 | 28274<br>28274<br>156 162 | 28275<br>28275<br>156 163 | 28276<br>28276<br>156 164 | 28277<br>28277<br>156 165 | 28278<br>28278<br>156 166 | 28279<br>28279<br>156 167 | 28280<br>28280<br>156 170 | 28281<br>28281<br>156 171 | 28282<br>28282<br>156 172 | 28283<br>28283<br>156 173 | 28284<br>28284<br>156 174 | 28285<br>28285<br>156 175 | 28286<br>28286<br>156 176 | 28287<br>28287<br>156 177 |
| **8−** | 28288<br>28288<br>156 200 | 28289<br>28289<br>156 201 | 28290<br>28290<br>156 202 | 28291<br>28291<br>156 203 | 28292<br>28292<br>156 204 | 28293<br>28293<br>156 205 | 28294<br>28294<br>156 206 | 28295<br>28295<br>156 207 | 28296<br>28296<br>156 210 | 28297<br>28297<br>156 211 | 28298<br>28298<br>156 212 | 28299<br>28299<br>156 213 | 28300<br>28300<br>156 214 | 28301<br>28301<br>156 215 | 28302<br>28302<br>156 216 | 28303<br>28303<br>156 217 |
| **9−** | 28304<br>28304<br>156 220 | 28305<br>28305<br>156 221 | 28306<br>28306<br>156 222 | 28307<br>28307<br>156 223 | 28308<br>28308<br>156 224 | 28309<br>28309<br>156 225 | 28310<br>28310<br>156 226 | 28311<br>28311<br>156 227 | 28312<br>28312<br>156 230 | 28313<br>28313<br>156 231 | 28314<br>28314<br>156 232 | 28315<br>28315<br>156 233 | 28316<br>28316<br>156 234 | 28317<br>28317<br>156 235 | 28318<br>28318<br>156 236 | 28319<br>28319<br>156 237 |
| **A−** | 28320<br>28320<br>156 240 | 28321<br>28321<br>156 241 | 28322<br>28322<br>156 242 | 28323<br>28323<br>156 243 | 28324<br>28324<br>156 244 | 28325<br>28325<br>156 245 | 28326<br>28326<br>156 246 | 28327<br>28327<br>156 247 | 28328<br>28328<br>156 250 | 28329<br>28329<br>156 251 | 28330<br>28330<br>156 252 | 28331<br>28331<br>156 253 | 28332<br>28332<br>156 254 | 28333<br>28333<br>156 255 | 28334<br>28334<br>156 256 | 28335<br>28335<br>156 257 |
| **B−** | 28336<br>28336<br>156 260 | 28337<br>28337<br>156 261 | 28338<br>28338<br>156 262 | 28339<br>28339<br>156 263 | 28340<br>28340<br>156 264 | 28341<br>28341<br>156 265 | 28342<br>28342<br>156 266 | 28343<br>28343<br>156 267 | 28344<br>28344<br>156 270 | 28345<br>28345<br>156 271 | 28346<br>28346<br>156 272 | 28347<br>28347<br>156 273 | 28348<br>28348<br>156 274 | 28349<br>28349<br>156 275 | 28350<br>28350<br>156 276 | 28351<br>28351<br>156 277 |
| **C−** | 28352<br>28352<br>156 300 | 28353<br>28353<br>156 301 | 28354<br>28354<br>156 302 | 28355<br>28355<br>156 303 | 28356<br>28356<br>156 304 | 28357<br>28357<br>156 305 | 28358<br>28358<br>156 306 | 28359<br>28359<br>156 307 | 28360<br>28360<br>156 310 | 28361<br>28361<br>156 311 | 28362<br>28362<br>156 312 | 28363<br>28363<br>156 313 | 28364<br>28364<br>156 314 | 28365<br>28365<br>156 315 | 28366<br>28366<br>156 316 | 28367<br>28367<br>156 317 |
| **D−** | 28368<br>28368<br>156 320 | 28369<br>28369<br>156 321 | 28370<br>28370<br>156 322 | 28371<br>28371<br>156 323 | 28372<br>28372<br>156 324 | 28373<br>28373<br>156 325 | 28374<br>28374<br>156 326 | 28375<br>28375<br>156 327 | 28376<br>28376<br>156 330 | 28377<br>28377<br>156 331 | 28378<br>28378<br>156 332 | 28379<br>28379<br>156 333 | 28380<br>28380<br>156 334 | 28381<br>28381<br>156 335 | 28382<br>28382<br>156 336 | 28383<br>28383<br>156 337 |
| **E−** | 28384<br>28384<br>156 340 | 28385<br>28385<br>156 341 | 28386<br>28386<br>156 342 | 28387<br>28387<br>156 343 | 28388<br>28388<br>156 344 | 28389<br>28389<br>156 345 | 28390<br>28390<br>156 346 | 28391<br>28391<br>156 347 | 28392<br>28392<br>156 350 | 28393<br>28393<br>156 351 | 28394<br>28394<br>156 352 | 28395<br>28395<br>156 353 | 28396<br>28396<br>156 354 | 28397<br>28397<br>156 355 | 28398<br>28398<br>156 356 | 28399<br>28399<br>156 357 |
| **F−** | 28400<br>28400<br>156 360 | 28401<br>28401<br>156 361 | 28402<br>28402<br>156 362 | 28403<br>28403<br>156 363 | 28404<br>28404<br>156 364 | 28405<br>28405<br>156 365 | 28406<br>28406<br>156 366 | 28407<br>28407<br>156 367 | 28408<br>28408<br>156 370 | 28409<br>28409<br>156 371 | 28410<br>28410<br>156 372 | 28411<br>28411<br>156 373 | 28412<br>28412<br>156 374 | 28413<br>28413<br>156 375 | 28414<br>28414<br>156 376 | 28415<br>28415<br>156 377 |

Row label: **SECOND HEX DIGIT**

DECIMAL →

 DECIMAL →

OCTAL →

 DECIMAL  28160    BINARY  0110 1110    DECIMAL  28160    HEXADECIMAL  6E    OCTAL  156 000

FOURTH HEX DIGIT → ← THIRD HEX DIGIT

# DECIMAL [28416]   BINARY [0110 1111]   DECIMAL [28416]   HEXADECIMAL ⬡6F   OCTAL [157 000]

FOURTH HEX DIGIT →   ← THIRD HEX DIGIT

DECIMAL

# DECIMAL

OCTAL

| ⬡2 | FIRST HEX DIGIT | | | | | | | | | | | | | | | |
|---|---|---|---|---|---|---|---|---|---|---|---|---|---|---|---|---|
| | −0 | −1 | −2 | −3 | −4 | −5 | −6 | −7 | −8 | −9 | −A | −B | −C | −D | −E | −F |
| 0− | 28416 28416 157 000 | 28417 28417 157 001 | 28418 28418 157 002 | 28419 28419 157 003 | 28420 28420 157 004 | 28421 28421 157 005 | 28422 28422 157 006 | 28423 28423 157 007 | 28424 28424 157 010 | 28425 28425 157 011 | 28426 28426 157 012 | 28427 28427 157 013 | 28428 28428 157 014 | 28429 28429 157 015 | 28430 28430 157 016 | 28431 28431 157 017 |
| 1− | 28432 28432 157 020 | 28433 28433 157 021 | 28434 28434 157 022 | 28435 28435 157 023 | 28436 28436 157 024 | 28437 28437 157 025 | 28438 28438 157 026 | 28439 28439 157 027 | 28440 28440 157 030 | 28441 28441 157 031 | 28442 28442 157 032 | 28443 28443 157 033 | 28444 28444 157 034 | 28445 28445 157 035 | 28446 28446 157 036 | 28447 28447 157 037 |
| 2− | 28448 28448 157 040 | 28449 28449 157 041 | 28450 28450 157 042 | 28451 28451 157 043 | 28452 28452 157 044 | 28453 28453 157 045 | 28454 28454 157 046 | 28455 28455 157 047 | 28456 28456 157 050 | 28457 28457 157 051 | 28458 28458 157 052 | 28459 28459 157 053 | 28460 28460 157 054 | 28461 28461 157 055 | 28462 28462 157 056 | 28463 28463 157 057 |
| 3− | 28464 28464 157 060 | 28465 28465 157 061 | 28466 28466 157 062 | 28467 28467 157 063 | 28468 28468 157 064 | 28469 28469 157 065 | 28470 28470 157 066 | 28471 28471 157 067 | 28472 28472 157 070 | 28473 28473 157 071 | 28474 28474 157 072 | 28475 28475 157 073 | 28476 28476 157 074 | 28477 28477 157 075 | 28478 28478 157 076 | 28479 28479 157 077 |
| 4− | 28480 28480 157 100 | 28481 28481 157 101 | 28482 28482 157 102 | 28483 28483 157 103 | 28484 28484 157 104 | 28485 28485 157 105 | 28486 28486 157 106 | 28487 28487 157 107 | 28488 28488 157 110 | 28489 28489 157 111 | 28490 28490 157 112 | 28491 28491 157 113 | 28492 28492 157 114 | 28493 28493 157 115 | 28494 28494 157 116 | 28495 28495 157 117 |
| 5− | 28496 28496 157 120 | 28497 28497 157 121 | 28498 28498 157 122 | 28499 28499 157 123 | 28500 28500 157 124 | 28501 28501 157 125 | 28502 28502 157 126 | 28503 28503 157 127 | 28504 28504 157 130 | 28505 28505 157 131 | 28506 28506 157 132 | 28507 28507 157 133 | 28508 28508 157 134 | 28509 28509 157 135 | 28510 28510 157 136 | 28511 28511 157 137 |
| 6− | 28512 28512 157 140 | 28513 28513 157 141 | 28514 28514 157 142 | 28515 28515 157 143 | 28516 28516 157 144 | 28517 28517 157 145 | 28518 28518 157 146 | 28519 28519 157 147 | 28520 28520 157 150 | 28521 28521 157 151 | 28522 28522 157 152 | 28523 28523 157 153 | 28524 28524 157 154 | 28525 28525 157 155 | 28526 28526 157 156 | 28527 28527 157 157 |
| 7− | 28528 28528 157 160 | 28529 28529 157 161 | 28530 28530 157 162 | 28531 28531 157 163 | 28532 28532 157 164 | 28533 28533 157 165 | 28534 28534 157 166 | 28535 28535 157 167 | 28536 28536 157 170 | 28537 28537 157 171 | 28538 28538 157 172 | 28539 28539 157 173 | 28540 28540 157 174 | 28541 28541 157 175 | 28542 28542 157 176 | 28543 28543 157 177 |
| 8− | 28544 28544 157 200 | 28545 28545 157 201 | 28546 28546 157 202 | 28547 28547 157 203 | 28548 28548 157 204 | 28549 28549 157 205 | 28550 28550 157 206 | 28551 28551 157 207 | 28552 28552 157 210 | 28553 28553 157 211 | 28554 28554 157 212 | 28555 28555 157 213 | 28556 28556 157 214 | 28557 28557 157 215 | 28558 28558 157 216 | 28559 28559 157 217 |
| 9− | 28560 28560 157 220 | 28561 28561 157 221 | 28562 28562 157 222 | 28563 28563 157 223 | 28564 28564 157 224 | 28565 28565 157 225 | 28566 28566 157 226 | 28567 28567 157 227 | 28568 28568 157 230 | 28569 28569 157 231 | 28570 28570 157 232 | 28571 28571 157 233 | 28572 28572 157 234 | 28573 28573 157 235 | 28574 28574 157 236 | 28575 28575 157 237 |
| A− | 28576 28576 157 240 | 28577 28577 157 241 | 28578 28578 157 242 | 28579 28579 157 243 | 28580 28580 157 244 | 28581 28581 157 245 | 28582 28582 157 246 | 28583 28583 157 247 | 28584 28584 157 250 | 28585 28585 157 251 | 28586 28586 157 252 | 28587 28587 157 253 | 28588 28588 157 254 | 28589 28589 157 255 | 28590 28590 157 256 | 28591 28591 157 257 |
| B− | 28592 28592 157 260 | 28593 28593 157 261 | 28594 28594 157 262 | 28595 28595 157 263 | 28596 28596 157 264 | 28597 28597 157 265 | 28598 28598 157 266 | 28599 28599 157 267 | 28600 28600 157 270 | 28601 28601 157 271 | 28602 28602 157 272 | 28603 28603 157 273 | 28604 28604 157 274 | 28605 28605 157 275 | 28606 28606 157 276 | 28607 28607 157 277 |
| C− | 28608 28608 157 300 | 28609 28609 157 301 | 28610 28610 157 302 | 28611 28611 157 303 | 28612 28612 157 304 | 28613 28613 157 305 | 28614 28614 157 306 | 28615 28615 157 307 | 28616 28616 157 310 | 28617 28617 157 311 | 28618 28618 157 312 | 28619 28619 157 313 | 28620 28620 157 314 | 28621 28621 157 315 | 28622 28622 157 316 | 28623 28623 157 317 |
| D− | 28624 28624 157 320 | 28625 28625 157 321 | 28626 28626 157 322 | 28627 28627 157 323 | 28628 28628 157 324 | 28629 28629 157 325 | 28630 28630 157 326 | 28631 28631 157 327 | 28632 28632 157 330 | 28633 28633 157 331 | 28634 28634 157 332 | 28635 28635 157 333 | 28636 28636 157 334 | 28637 28637 157 335 | 28638 28638 157 336 | 28639 28639 157 337 |
| E− | 28640 28640 157 340 | 28641 28641 157 341 | 28642 28642 157 342 | 28643 28643 157 343 | 28644 28644 157 344 | 28645 28645 157 345 | 28646 28646 157 346 | 28647 28647 157 347 | 28648 28648 157 350 | 28649 28649 157 351 | 28650 28650 157 352 | 28651 28651 157 353 | 28652 28652 157 354 | 28653 28653 157 355 | 28654 28654 157 356 | 28655 28655 157 357 |
| F− | 28656 28656 157 360 | 28657 28657 157 361 | 28658 28658 157 362 | 28659 28659 157 363 | 28660 28660 157 364 | 28661 28661 157 365 | 28662 28662 157 366 | 28663 28663 157 367 | 28664 28664 157 370 | 28665 28665 157 371 | 28666 28666 157 372 | 28667 28667 157 373 | 28668 28668 157 374 | 28669 28669 157 375 | 28670 28670 157 376 | 28671 28671 157 377 |

SECOND HEX DIGIT

# FIRST HEX DIGIT

| | −0 | −1 | −2 | −3 | −4 | −5 | −6 | −7 | −8 | −9 | −A | −B | −C | −D | −E | −F |
|---|---|---|---|---|---|---|---|---|---|---|---|---|---|---|---|---|
| **0-** | 28672<br>28672<br>160 000 | 28673<br>28673<br>160 001 | 28674<br>28674<br>160 002 | 28675<br>28675<br>160 003 | 28676<br>28676<br>160 004 | 28677<br>28677<br>160 005 | 28678<br>28678<br>160 006 | 28679<br>28679<br>160 007 | 28680<br>28680<br>160 010 | 28681<br>28681<br>160 011 | 28682<br>28682<br>160 012 | 28683<br>28683<br>160 013 | 28684<br>28684<br>160 014 | 28685<br>28685<br>160 015 | 28686<br>28686<br>160 016 | 28687<br>28687<br>160 017 |
| **1-** | 28688<br>28688<br>160 020 | 28689<br>28689<br>160 021 | 28690<br>28690<br>160 022 | 28691<br>28691<br>160 023 | 28692<br>28692<br>160 024 | 28693<br>28693<br>160 025 | 28694<br>28694<br>160 026 | 28695<br>28695<br>160 027 | 28696<br>28696<br>160 030 | 28697<br>28697<br>160 031 | 28698<br>28698<br>160 032 | 28699<br>28699<br>160 033 | 28700<br>28700<br>160·034 | 28701<br>28701<br>160 035 | 28702<br>28702<br>160 036 | 28703<br>28703<br>160 037 |
| **2-** | 28704<br>28704<br>160 040 | 28705<br>28705<br>160 041 | 28706<br>28706<br>160 042 | 28707<br>28707<br>160 043 | 28708<br>28708<br>160 044 | 28709<br>28709<br>160 045 | 28710<br>28710<br>160 046 | 28711<br>28711<br>160 047 | 28712<br>28712<br>160 050 | 28713<br>28713<br>160 051 | 28714<br>28714<br>160 052 | 28715<br>28715<br>160 053 | 28716<br>28716<br>160 054 | 28717<br>28717<br>160 055 | 28718<br>28718<br>160 056 | 28719<br>28719<br>160 057 |
| **3-** | 28720<br>28720<br>160 060 | 28721<br>28721<br>160 061 | 28722<br>28722<br>160 062 | 28723<br>28723<br>160 063 | 28724<br>28724<br>160 064 | 28725<br>28725<br>160 065 | 28726<br>28726<br>160 066 | 28727<br>28727<br>160 067 | 28728<br>28728<br>160 070 | 28729<br>28729<br>160 071 | 28730<br>28730<br>160 072 | 28731<br>28731<br>160 073 | 28732<br>28732<br>160 074 | 28733<br>28733<br>160 075 | 28734<br>28734<br>160 076 | 28735<br>28735<br>160 077 |
| **4-** | 28736<br>28736<br>160 100 | 28737<br>28737<br>160 101 | 28738<br>28738<br>160 102 | 28739<br>28739<br>160 103 | 28740<br>28740<br>160 104 | 28741<br>28741<br>160 105 | 28742<br>28742<br>160 106 | 28743<br>28743<br>160 107 | 28744<br>28744<br>160 110 | 28745<br>28745<br>160 111 | 28746<br>28746<br>160 112 | 28747<br>28747<br>160 113 | 28748<br>28748<br>160 114 | 28749<br>28749<br>160 115 | 28750<br>28750<br>160 116 | 28751<br>28751<br>160 117 |
| **5-** | 28752<br>28752<br>160 120 | 28753<br>28753<br>160 121 | 28754<br>28754<br>160 122 | 28755<br>28755<br>160 123 | 28756<br>28756<br>160 124 | 28757<br>28757<br>160 125 | 28758<br>28758<br>160 126 | 28759<br>28759<br>160 127 | 28760<br>28760<br>160 130 | 28761<br>28761<br>160 131 | 28762<br>28762<br>160 132 | 28763<br>28763<br>160 133 | 28764<br>28764<br>160 134 | 28765<br>28765<br>160 135 | 28766<br>28766<br>160 136 | 28767<br>28767<br>160 137 |
| **6-** | 28768<br>28768<br>160 140 | 28769<br>28769<br>160 141 | 28770<br>28770<br>160 142 | 28771<br>28771<br>160 143 | 28772<br>28772<br>160 144 | 28773<br>28773<br>160 145 | 28774<br>28774<br>160 146 | 28775<br>28775<br>160 147 | 28776<br>28776<br>160 150 | 28777<br>28777<br>160 151 | 28778<br>28778<br>160 152 | 28779<br>28779<br>160 153 | 28780<br>28780<br>160 154 | 28781<br>28781<br>160 155 | 28782<br>28782<br>160 156 | 28783<br>28783<br>160 157 |
| **7-** | 28784<br>28784<br>160 160 | 28785<br>28785<br>160 161 | 28786<br>28786<br>160 162 | 28787<br>28787<br>160 163 | 28788<br>28788<br>160 164 | 28789<br>28789<br>160 165 | 28790<br>28790<br>160 166 | 28791<br>28791<br>160 167 | 28792<br>28792<br>160 170 | 28793<br>28793<br>160 171 | 28794<br>28794<br>160 172 | 28795<br>28795<br>160 173 | 28796<br>28796<br>160 174 | 28797<br>28797<br>160 175 | 28798<br>28798<br>160 176 | 28799<br>28799<br>160 177 |
| **8-** | 28800<br>28800<br>160 200 | 28801<br>28801<br>160 201 | 28802<br>28802<br>160 202 | 28803<br>28803<br>160 203 | 28804<br>28804<br>160 204 | 28805<br>28805<br>160 205 | 28806<br>28806<br>160 206 | 28807<br>28807<br>160 207 | 28808<br>28808<br>160 210 | 28809<br>28809<br>160 211 | 28810<br>28810<br>160 212 | 28811<br>28811<br>160 213 | 28812<br>28812<br>160 214 | 28813<br>28813<br>160 215 | 28814<br>28814<br>160 216 | 28815<br>28815<br>160 217 |
| **9-** | 28816<br>28816<br>160 220 | 28817<br>28817<br>160 221 | 28818<br>28818<br>160 222 | 28819<br>28819<br>160 223 | 28820<br>28820<br>160 224 | 28821<br>28821<br>160 225 | 28822<br>28822<br>160 226 | 28823<br>28823<br>160 227 | 28824<br>28824<br>160 230 | 28825<br>28825<br>160 231 | 28826<br>28826<br>160 232 | 28827<br>28827<br>160 233 | 28828<br>28828<br>160 234 | 28829<br>28829<br>160 235 | 28830<br>28830<br>160 236 | 28831<br>28831<br>160 237 |
| **A-** | 28832<br>28832<br>160 240 | 28833<br>28833<br>160 241 | 28834<br>28834<br>160 242 | 28835<br>28835<br>160 243 | 28836<br>28836<br>160 244 | 28837<br>28837<br>160 245 | 28838<br>28838<br>160 246 | 28839<br>28839<br>160 247 | 28840<br>28840<br>160 250 | 28841<br>28841<br>160 251 | 28842<br>28842<br>160 252 | 28843<br>28843<br>160 253 | 28844<br>28844<br>160 254 | 28845<br>28845<br>160 255 | 28846<br>28846<br>160 256 | 28847<br>28847<br>160 257 |
| **B-** | 28848<br>28848<br>160 260 | 28849<br>28849<br>160 261 | 28850<br>28850<br>160 262 | 28851<br>28851<br>160 263 | 28852<br>28852<br>160 264 | 28853<br>28853<br>160 265 | 28854<br>28854<br>160 266 | 28855<br>28855<br>160 267 | 28856<br>28856<br>160 270 | 28857<br>28857<br>160 271 | 28858<br>28858<br>160 272 | 28859<br>28859<br>160 273 | 28860<br>28860<br>160 274 | 28861<br>28861<br>160 275 | 28862<br>28862<br>160 276 | 28863<br>28863<br>160 277 |
| **C-** | 28864<br>28864<br>160 300 | 28865<br>28865<br>160 301 | 28866<br>28866<br>160 302 | 28867<br>28867<br>160 303 | 28868<br>28868<br>160 304 | 28869<br>28869<br>160 305 | 28870<br>28870<br>160 306 | 28871<br>28871<br>160 307 | 28872<br>28872<br>160 310 | 28873<br>28873<br>160 311 | 28874<br>28874<br>160 312 | 28875<br>28875<br>160 313 | 28876<br>28876<br>160 314 | 28877<br>28877<br>160 315 | 28878<br>28878<br>160 316 | 28879<br>28879<br>160 317 |
| **D-** | 28880<br>28880<br>160 320 | 28881<br>28881<br>160 321 | 28882<br>28882<br>160 322 | 28883<br>28883<br>160 323 | 28884<br>28884<br>160 324 | 28885<br>28885<br>160 325 | 28886<br>28886<br>160 326 | 28887<br>28887<br>160 327 | 28888<br>28888<br>160 330 | 28889<br>28889<br>160 331 | 28890<br>28890<br>160 332 | 28891<br>28891<br>160 333 | 28892<br>28892<br>160 334 | 28893<br>28893<br>160 335 | 28894<br>28894<br>160 336 | 28895<br>28895<br>160 337 |
| **E-** | 28896<br>28896<br>160 340 | 28897<br>28897<br>160 341 | 28898<br>28898<br>160 342 | 28899<br>28899<br>160 343 | 28900<br>28900<br>160 344 | 28901<br>28901<br>160 345 | 28902<br>28902<br>160 346 | 28903<br>28903<br>160 347 | 28904<br>28904<br>160 350 | 28905<br>28905<br>160 351 | 28906<br>28906<br>160 352 | 28907<br>28907<br>160 353 | 28908<br>28908<br>160 354 | 28909<br>28909<br>160 355 | 28910<br>28910<br>160 356 | 28911<br>28911<br>160 357 |
| **F-** | 28912<br>28912<br>160 360 | 28913<br>28913<br>160 361 | 28914<br>28914<br>160 362 | 28915<br>28915<br>160 363 | 28916<br>28916<br>160 364 | 28917<br>28917<br>160 365 | 28918<br>28918<br>160 366 | 28919<br>28919<br>160 367 | 28920<br>28920<br>160 370 | 28921<br>28921<br>160 371 | 28922<br>28922<br>160 372 | 28923<br>28923<br>160 373 | 28924<br>28924<br>160 374 | 28925<br>28925<br>160 375 | 28926<br>28926<br>160 376 | 28927<br>28927<br>160 377 |

*(Row label: **SECOND HEX DIGIT**)*

Right-margin labels: **DECIMAL** ← · ⬥ **DECIMAL** ← · **OCTAL** ←

---

⬥ **DECIMAL** [ 28672 ]  **BINARY** [ 0111 0000 ]  **DECIMAL** [ 28672 ]  **HEXADECIMAL** ⬡ 70 ⬡  **OCTAL** [ 160 000 ]

FOURTH HEX DIGIT ↗ ↖ THIRD HEX DIGIT

 DECIMAL  28928     BINARY  0111 0001     DECIMAL  28928     HEXADECIMAL  (71)  OCTAL  161 000

FOURTH HEX DIGIT → (71) ← THIRD HEX DIGIT

| (2) | −0 | −1 | −2 | −3 | −4 | −5 | −6 | −7 | −8 | −9 | −A | −B | −C | −D | −E | −F |
|---|---|---|---|---|---|---|---|---|---|---|---|---|---|---|---|---|
| | | | | | | | | FIRST HEX DIGIT | | | | | | | | |
| 0− | 28928<br>28928<br>161 000 | 28929<br>28929<br>161 001 | 28930<br>28930<br>161 002 | 28931<br>28931<br>161 003 | 28932<br>28932<br>161 004 | 28933<br>28933<br>161 005 | 28934<br>28934<br>161 006 | 28935<br>28935<br>161 007 | 28936<br>28936<br>161 010 | 28937<br>28937<br>161 011 | 28938<br>28938<br>161 012 | 28939<br>28939<br>161 013 | 28940<br>28940<br>161 014 | 28941<br>28941<br>161 015 | 28942<br>28942<br>161 016 | 28943<br>28943<br>161 017 |
| 1− | 28944<br>28944<br>161 020 | 28945<br>28945<br>161 021 | 28946<br>28946<br>161 022 | 28947<br>28947<br>161 023 | 28948<br>28948<br>161 024 | 28949<br>28949<br>161 025 | 28950<br>28950<br>161 026 | 28951<br>28951<br>161 027 | 28952<br>28952<br>161 030 | 28953<br>28953<br>161 031 | 28954<br>28954<br>161 032 | 28955<br>28955<br>161 033 | 28956<br>28956<br>161 034 | 28957<br>28957<br>161 035 | 28958<br>28958<br>161 036 | 28959<br>28959<br>161 037 |
| 2− | 28960<br>28960<br>161 040 | 28961<br>28961<br>161 041 | 28962<br>28962<br>161 042 | 28963<br>28963<br>161 043 | 28964<br>28964<br>161 044 | 28965<br>28965<br>161 045 | 28966<br>28966<br>161 046 | 28967<br>28967<br>161 047 | 28968<br>28968<br>161 050 | 28969<br>28969<br>161 051 | 28970<br>28970<br>161 052 | 28971<br>28971<br>161 053 | 28972<br>28972<br>161 054 | 28973<br>28973<br>161 055 | 28974<br>28974<br>161 056 | 28975<br>28975<br>161 057 |
| 3− | 28976<br>28976<br>161 060 | 28977<br>28977<br>161 061 | 28978<br>28978<br>161 062 | 28979<br>28979<br>161 063 | 28980<br>28980<br>161 064 | 28981<br>28981<br>161 065 | 28982<br>28982<br>161 066 | 28983<br>28983<br>161 067 | 28984<br>28984<br>161 070 | 28985<br>28985<br>161 071 | 28986<br>28986<br>161 072 | 28987<br>28987<br>161 073 | 28988<br>28988<br>161 074 | 28989<br>28989<br>161 075 | 28990<br>28990<br>161 076 | 28991<br>28991<br>161 077 |
| 4− | 28992<br>28992<br>161 100 | 28993<br>28993<br>161 101 | 28994<br>28994<br>161 102 | 28995<br>28995<br>161 103 | 28996<br>28996<br>161 104 | 28997<br>28997<br>161 105 | 28998<br>28998<br>161 106 | 28999<br>28999<br>161 107 | 29000<br>29000<br>161 110 | 29001<br>29001<br>161 111 | 29002<br>29002<br>161 112 | 29003<br>29003<br>161 113 | 29004<br>29004<br>161 114 | 29005<br>29005<br>161 115 | 29006<br>29006<br>161 116 | 29007<br>29007<br>161 117 |
| 5− | 29008<br>29008<br>161 120 | 29009<br>29009<br>161 121 | 29010<br>29010<br>161 122 | 29011<br>29011<br>161 123 | 29012<br>29012<br>161 124 | 29013<br>29013<br>161 125 | 29014<br>29014<br>161 126 | 29015<br>29015<br>161 127 | 29016<br>29016<br>161 130 | 29017<br>29017<br>161 131 | 29018<br>29018<br>161 132 | 29019<br>29019<br>161 133 | 29020<br>29020<br>161 134 | 29021<br>29021<br>161 135 | 29022<br>29022<br>161 136 | 29023<br>29023<br>161 137 |
| 6− | 29024<br>29024<br>161 140 | 29025<br>29025<br>161 141 | 29026<br>29026<br>161 142 | 29027<br>29027<br>161 143 | 29028<br>29028<br>161 144 | 29029<br>29029<br>161 145 | 29030<br>29030<br>161 146 | 29031<br>29031<br>161 147 | 29032<br>29032<br>161 150 | 29033<br>29033<br>161 151 | 29034<br>29034<br>161 152 | 29035<br>29035<br>161 153 | 29036<br>29036<br>161 154 | 29037<br>29037<br>161 155 | 29038<br>29038<br>161 156 | 29039<br>29039<br>161 157 |
| 7− | 29040<br>29040<br>161 160 | 29041<br>29041<br>161 161 | 29042<br>29042<br>161 162 | 29043<br>29043<br>161 163 | 29044<br>29044<br>161 164 | 29045<br>29045<br>161 165 | 29046<br>29046<br>161 166 | 29047<br>29047<br>161 167 | 29048<br>29048<br>161 170 | 29049<br>29049<br>161 171 | 29050<br>29050<br>161 172 | 29051<br>29051<br>161 173 | 29052<br>29052<br>161 174 | 29053<br>29053<br>161 175 | 29054<br>29054<br>161 176 | 29055<br>29055<br>161 177 |
| 8− | 29056<br>29056<br>161 200 | 29057<br>29057<br>161 201 | 29058<br>29058<br>161 202 | 29059<br>29059<br>161 203 | 29060<br>29060<br>161 204 | 29061<br>29061<br>161 205 | 29062<br>29062<br>161 206 | 29063<br>29063<br>161 207 | 29064<br>29064<br>161 210 | 29065<br>29065<br>161 211 | 29066<br>29066<br>161 212 | 29067<br>29067<br>161 213 | 29068<br>29068<br>161 214 | 29069<br>29069<br>161 215 | 29070<br>29070<br>161 216 | 29071<br>29071<br>161 217 |
| 9− | 29072<br>29072<br>161 220 | 29073<br>29073<br>161 221 | 29074<br>29074<br>161 222 | 29075<br>29075<br>161 223 | 29076<br>29076<br>161 224 | 29077<br>29077<br>161 225 | 29078<br>29078<br>161 226 | 29079<br>29079<br>161 227 | 29080<br>29080<br>161 230 | 29081<br>29081<br>161 231 | 29082<br>29082<br>161 232 | 29083<br>29083<br>161 233 | 29084<br>29084<br>161 234 | 29085<br>29085<br>161 235 | 29086<br>29086<br>161 236 | 29087<br>29087<br>161 237 |
| A− | 29088<br>29088<br>161 240 | 29089<br>29089<br>161 241 | 29090<br>29090<br>161 242 | 29091<br>29091<br>161 243 | 29092<br>29092<br>161 244 | 29093<br>29093<br>161 245 | 29094<br>29094<br>161 246 | 29095<br>29095<br>161 247 | 29096<br>29096<br>161 250 | 29097<br>29097<br>161 251 | 29098<br>29098<br>161 252 | 29099<br>29099<br>161 253 | 29100<br>29100<br>161 254 | 29101<br>29101<br>161 255 | 29102<br>29102<br>161 256 | 29103<br>29103<br>161 257 |
| B− | 29104<br>29104<br>161 260 | 29105<br>29105<br>161 261 | 29106<br>29106<br>161 262 | 29107<br>29107<br>161 263 | 29108<br>29108<br>161 264 | 29109<br>29109<br>161 265 | 29110<br>29110<br>161 266 | 29111<br>29111<br>161 267 | 29112<br>29112<br>161 270 | 29113<br>29113<br>161 271 | 29114<br>29114<br>161 272 | 29115<br>29115<br>161 273 | 29116<br>29116<br>161 274 | 29117<br>29117<br>161 275 | 29118<br>29118<br>161 276 | 29119<br>29119<br>161 277 |
| C− | 29120<br>29120<br>161 300 | 29121<br>29121<br>161 301 | 29122<br>29122<br>161 302 | 29123<br>29123<br>161 303 | 29124<br>29124<br>161 304 | 29125<br>29125<br>161 305 | 29126<br>29126<br>161 306 | 29127<br>29127<br>161 307 | 29128<br>29128<br>161 310 | 29129<br>29129<br>161 311 | 29130<br>29130<br>161 312 | 29131<br>29131<br>161 313 | 29132<br>29132<br>161 314 | 29133<br>29133<br>161 315 | 29134<br>29134<br>161 316 | 29135<br>29135<br>161 317 |
| D− | 29136<br>29136<br>161 320 | 29137<br>29137<br>161 321 | 29138<br>29138<br>161 322 | 29139<br>29139<br>161 323 | 29140<br>29140<br>161 324 | 29141<br>29141<br>161 325 | 29142<br>29142<br>161 326 | 29143<br>29143<br>161 327 | 29144<br>29144<br>161 330 | 29145<br>29145<br>161 331 | 29146<br>29146<br>161 332 | 29147<br>29147<br>161 333 | 29148<br>29148<br>161 334 | 29149<br>29149<br>161 335 | 29150<br>29150<br>161 336 | 29151<br>29151<br>161 337 |
| E− | 29152<br>29152<br>161 340 | 29153<br>29153<br>161 341 | 29154<br>29154<br>161 342 | 29155<br>29155<br>161 343 | 29156<br>29156<br>161 344 | 29157<br>29157<br>161 345 | 29158<br>29158<br>161 346 | 29159<br>29159<br>161 347 | 29160<br>29160<br>161 350 | 29161<br>29161<br>161 351 | 29162<br>29162<br>161 352 | 29163<br>29163<br>161 353 | 29164<br>29164<br>161 354 | 29165<br>29165<br>161 355 | 29166<br>29166<br>161 356 | 29167<br>29167<br>161 357 |
| F− | 29168<br>29168<br>161 360 | 29169<br>29169<br>161 361 | 29170<br>29170<br>161 362 | 29171<br>29171<br>161 363 | 29172<br>29172<br>161 364 | 29173<br>29173<br>161 365 | 29174<br>29174<br>161 366 | 29175<br>29175<br>161 367 | 29176<br>29176<br>161 370 | 29177<br>29177<br>161 371 | 29178<br>29178<br>161 372 | 29179<br>29179<br>161 373 | 29180<br>29180<br>161 374 | 29181<br>29181<br>161 375 | 29182<br>29182<br>161 376 | 29183<br>29183<br>161 377 |

SECOND HEX DIGIT (row labels)

## ② FIRST HEX DIGIT

SECOND HEX DIGIT (rows) × FIRST HEX DIGIT (columns). Each cell lists DECIMAL, DECIMAL, OCTAL.

| | −0 | −1 | −2 | −3 | −4 | −5 | −6 | −7 | −8 | −9 | −A | −B | −C | −D | −E | −F |
|---|---|---|---|---|---|---|---|---|---|---|---|---|---|---|---|---|
| 0− | 29184<br>29184<br>162 000 | 29185<br>29185<br>162 001 | 29186<br>29186<br>162 002 | 29187<br>29187<br>162 003 | 29188<br>29188<br>162 004 | 29189<br>29189<br>162 005 | 29190<br>29190<br>162 006 | 29191<br>29191<br>162 007 | 29192<br>29192<br>162 010 | 29193<br>29193<br>162 011 | 29194<br>29194<br>162 012 | 29195<br>29195<br>162 013 | 29196<br>29196<br>162 014 | 29197<br>29197<br>162 015 | 29198<br>29198<br>162 016 | 29199<br>29199<br>162 017 |
| 1− | 29200<br>29200<br>162 020 | 29201<br>29201<br>162 021 | 29202<br>29202<br>162 022 | 29203<br>29203<br>162 023 | 29204<br>29204<br>162 024 | 29205<br>29205<br>162 025 | 29206<br>29206<br>162 026 | 29207<br>29207<br>162 027 | 29208<br>29208<br>162 030 | 29209<br>29209<br>162 031 | 29210<br>29210<br>162 032 | 29211<br>29211<br>162 033 | 29212<br>29212<br>162 034 | 29213<br>29213<br>162 035 | 29214<br>29214<br>162 036 | 29215<br>29215<br>162 037 |
| 2− | 29216<br>29216<br>162 040 | 29217<br>29217<br>162 041 | 29218<br>29218<br>162 042 | 29219<br>29219<br>162 043 | 29220<br>29220<br>162 044 | 29221<br>29221<br>162 045 | 29222<br>29222<br>162 046 | 29223<br>29223<br>162 047 | 29224<br>29224<br>162 050 | 29225<br>29225<br>162 051 | 29226<br>29226<br>162 052 | 29227<br>29227<br>162 053 | 29228<br>29228<br>162 054 | 29229<br>29229<br>162 055 | 29230<br>29230<br>162 056 | 29231<br>29231<br>162 057 |
| 3− | 29232<br>29232<br>162 060 | 29233<br>29233<br>162 061 | 29234<br>29234<br>162 062 | 29235<br>29235<br>162 063 | 29236<br>29236<br>162 064 | 29237<br>29237<br>162 065 | 29238<br>29238<br>162 066 | 29239<br>29239<br>162 067 | 29240<br>29240<br>162 070 | 29241<br>29241<br>162 071 | 29242<br>29242<br>162 072 | 29243<br>29243<br>162 073 | 29244<br>29244<br>162 074 | 29245<br>29245<br>162 075 | 29246<br>29246<br>162 076 | 29247<br>29247<br>162 077 |
| 4− | 29248<br>29248<br>162 100 | 29249<br>29249<br>162 101 | 29250<br>29250<br>162 102 | 29251<br>29251<br>162 103 | 29252<br>29252<br>162 104 | 29253<br>29253<br>162 105 | 29254<br>29254<br>162 106 | 29255<br>29255<br>162 107 | 29256<br>29256<br>162 110 | 29257<br>29257<br>162 111 | 29258<br>29258<br>162 112 | 29259<br>29259<br>162 113 | 29260<br>29260<br>162 114 | 29261<br>29261<br>162 115 | 29262<br>29262<br>162 116 | 29263<br>29263<br>162 117 |
| 5− | 29264<br>29264<br>162 120 | 29265<br>29265<br>162 121 | 29266<br>29266<br>162 122 | 29267<br>29267<br>162 123 | 29268<br>29268<br>162 124 | 29269<br>29269<br>162 125 | 29270<br>29270<br>162 126 | 29271<br>29271<br>162 127 | 29272<br>29272<br>162 130 | 29273<br>29273<br>162 131 | 29274<br>29274<br>162 132 | 29275<br>29275<br>162 133 | 29276<br>29276<br>162 134 | 29277<br>29277<br>162 135 | 29278<br>29278<br>162 136 | 29279<br>29279<br>162 137 |
| 6− | 29280<br>29280<br>162 140 | 29281<br>29281<br>162 141 | 29282<br>29282<br>162 142 | 29283<br>29283<br>162 143 | 29284<br>29284<br>162 144 | 29285<br>29285<br>162 145 | 29286<br>29286<br>162 146 | 29287<br>29287<br>162 147 | 29288<br>29288<br>162 150 | 29289<br>29289<br>162 151 | 29290<br>29290<br>162 152 | 29291<br>29291<br>162 153 | 29292<br>29292<br>162 154 | 29293<br>29293<br>162 155 | 29294<br>29294<br>162 156 | 29295<br>29295<br>162 157 |
| 7− | 29296<br>29296<br>162 160 | 29297<br>29297<br>162 161 | 29298<br>29298<br>162 162 | 29299<br>29299<br>162 163 | 29300<br>29300<br>162 164 | 29301<br>29301<br>162 165 | 29302<br>29302<br>162 166 | 29303<br>29303<br>162 167 | 29304<br>29304<br>162 170 | 29305<br>29305<br>162 171 | 29306<br>29306<br>162 172 | 29307<br>29307<br>162 173 | 29308<br>29308<br>162 174 | 29309<br>29309<br>162 175 | 29310<br>29310<br>162 176 | 29311<br>29311<br>162 177 |
| 8− | 29312<br>29312<br>162 200 | 29313<br>29313<br>162 201 | 29314<br>29314<br>162 202 | 29315<br>29315<br>162 203 | 29316<br>29316<br>162 204 | 29317<br>29317<br>162 205 | 29318<br>29318<br>162 206 | 29319<br>29319<br>162 207 | 29320<br>29320<br>162 210 | 29321<br>29321<br>162 211 | 29322<br>29322<br>162 212 | 29323<br>29323<br>162 213 | 29324<br>29324<br>162 214 | 29325<br>29325<br>162 215 | 29326<br>29326<br>162 216 | 29327<br>29327<br>162 217 |
| 9− | 29328<br>29328<br>162 220 | 29329<br>29329<br>162 221 | 29330<br>29330<br>162 222 | 29331<br>29331<br>162 223 | 29332<br>29332<br>162 224 | 29333<br>29333<br>162 225 | 29334<br>29334<br>162 226 | 29335<br>29335<br>162 227 | 29336<br>29336<br>162 230 | 29337<br>29337<br>162 231 | 29338<br>29338<br>162 232 | 29339<br>29339<br>162 233 | 29340<br>29340<br>162 234 | 29341<br>29341<br>162 235 | 29342<br>29342<br>162 236 | 29343<br>29343<br>162 237 |
| A− | 29344<br>29344<br>162 240 | 29345<br>29345<br>162 241 | 29346<br>29346<br>162 242 | 29347<br>29347<br>162 243 | 29348<br>29348<br>162 244 | 29349<br>29349<br>162 245 | 29350<br>29350<br>162 246 | 29351<br>29351<br>162 247 | 29352<br>29352<br>162 250 | 29353<br>29353<br>162 251 | 29354<br>29354<br>162 252 | 29355<br>29355<br>162 253 | 29356<br>29356<br>162 254 | 29357<br>29357<br>162 255 | 29358<br>29358<br>162 256 | 29359<br>29359<br>162 257 |
| B− | 29360<br>29360<br>162 260 | 29361<br>29361<br>162 261 | 29362<br>29362<br>162 262 | 29363<br>29363<br>162 263 | 29364<br>29364<br>162 264 | 29365<br>29365<br>162 265 | 29366<br>29366<br>162 266 | 29367<br>29367<br>162 267 | 29368<br>29368<br>162 270 | 29369<br>29369<br>162 271 | 29370<br>29370<br>162 272 | 29371<br>29371<br>162 273 | 29372<br>29372<br>162 274 | 29373<br>29373<br>162 275 | 29374<br>29374<br>162 276 | 29375<br>29375<br>162 277 |
| C− | 29376<br>29376<br>162 300 | 29377<br>29377<br>162 301 | 29378<br>29378<br>162 302 | 29379<br>29379<br>162 303 | 29380<br>29380<br>162 304 | 29381<br>29381<br>162 305 | 29382<br>29382<br>162 306 | 29383<br>29383<br>162 307 | 29384<br>29384<br>162 310 | 29385<br>29385<br>162 311 | 29386<br>29386<br>162 312 | 29387<br>29387<br>162 313 | 29388<br>29388<br>162 314 | 29389<br>29389<br>162 315 | 29390<br>29390<br>162 316 | 29391<br>29391<br>162 317 |
| D− | 29392<br>29392<br>162 320 | 29393<br>29393<br>162 321 | 29394<br>29394<br>162 322 | 29395<br>29395<br>162 323 | 29396<br>29396<br>162 324 | 29397<br>29397<br>162 325 | 29398<br>29398<br>162 326 | 29399<br>29399<br>162 327 | 29400<br>29400<br>162 330 | 29401<br>29401<br>162 331 | 29402<br>29402<br>162 332 | 29403<br>29403<br>162 333 | 29404<br>29404<br>162 334 | 29405<br>29405<br>162 335 | 29406<br>29406<br>162 336 | 29407<br>29407<br>162 337 |
| E− | 29408<br>29408<br>162 340 | 29409<br>29409<br>162 341 | 29410<br>29410<br>162 342 | 29411<br>29411<br>162 343 | 29412<br>29412<br>162 344 | 29413<br>29413<br>162 345 | 29414<br>29414<br>162 346 | 29415<br>29415<br>162 347 | 29416<br>29416<br>162 350 | 29417<br>29417<br>162 351 | 29418<br>29418<br>162 352 | 29419<br>29419<br>162 353 | 29420<br>29420<br>162 354 | 29421<br>29421<br>162 355 | 29422<br>29422<br>162 356 | 29423<br>29423<br>162 357 |
| F− | 29424<br>29424<br>162 360 | 29425<br>29425<br>162 361 | 29426<br>29426<br>162 362 | 29427<br>29427<br>162 363 | 29428<br>29428<br>162 364 | 29429<br>29429<br>162 365 | 29430<br>29430<br>162 366 | 29431<br>29431<br>162 367 | 29432<br>29432<br>162 370 | 29433<br>29433<br>162 371 | 29434<br>29434<br>162 372 | 29435<br>29435<br>162 373 | 29436<br>29436<br>162 374 | 29437<br>29437<br>162 375 | 29438<br>29438<br>162 376 | 29439<br>29439<br>162 377 |

DECIMAL

 DECIMAL

OCTAL

DECIMAL 29184  BINARY 0111 0010  DECIMAL 29184  HEXADECIMAL ⬡ 72  OCTAL 162 000

FOURTH HEX DIGIT   THIRD HEX DIGIT

⬡2

FIRST HEX DIGIT

SECOND HEX DIGIT

DECIMAL
🍎 DECIMAL
OCTAL

| | −0 | −1 | −2 | −3 | −4 | −5 | −6 | −7 | −8 | −9 | −A | −B | −C | −D | −E | −F |
|---|---|---|---|---|---|---|---|---|---|---|---|---|---|---|---|---|
| 0− | 29440<br>29440<br>163 000 | 29441<br>29441<br>163 001 | 29442<br>29442<br>163 002 | 29443<br>29443<br>163 003 | 29444<br>29444<br>163 004 | 29445<br>29445<br>163 005 | 29446<br>29446<br>163 006 | 29447<br>29447<br>163 007 | 29448<br>29448<br>163 010 | 29449<br>29449<br>163 011 | 29450<br>29450<br>163 012 | 29451<br>29451<br>163 013 | 29452<br>29452<br>163 014 | 29453<br>29453<br>163 015 | 29454<br>29454<br>163 016 | 29455<br>29455<br>163 017 |
| 1− | 29456<br>29456<br>163 020 | 29457<br>29457<br>163 021 | 29458<br>29458<br>163 022 | 29459<br>29459<br>163 023 | 29460<br>29460<br>163 024 | 29461<br>29461<br>163 025 | 29462<br>29462<br>163 026 | 29463<br>29463<br>163 027 | 29464<br>29464<br>163 030 | 29465<br>29465<br>163 031 | 29466<br>29466<br>163 032 | 29467<br>29467<br>163 033 | 29468<br>29468<br>163 034 | 29469<br>29469<br>163 035 | 29470<br>29470<br>163 036 | 29471<br>29471<br>163 037 |
| 2− | 29472<br>29472<br>163 040 | 29473<br>29473<br>163 041 | 29474<br>29474<br>163 042 | 29475<br>29475<br>163 043 | 29476<br>29476<br>163 044 | 29477<br>29477<br>163 045 | 29478<br>29478<br>163 046 | 29479<br>29479<br>163 047 | 29480<br>29480<br>163 050 | 29481<br>29481<br>163 051 | 29482<br>29482<br>163 052 | 29483<br>29483<br>163 053 | 29484<br>29484<br>163 054 | 29485<br>29485<br>163 055 | 29486<br>29486<br>163 056 | 29487<br>29487<br>163 057 |
| 3− | 29488<br>29488<br>163 060 | 29489<br>29489<br>163 061 | 29490<br>29490<br>163 062 | 29491<br>29491<br>163 063 | 29492<br>29492<br>163 064 | 29493<br>29493<br>163 065 | 29494<br>29494<br>163 066 | 29495<br>29495<br>163 067 | 29496<br>29496<br>163 070 | 29497<br>29497<br>163 071 | 29498<br>29498<br>163 072 | 29499<br>29499<br>163 073 | 29500<br>29500<br>163 074 | 29501<br>29501<br>163 075 | 29502<br>29502<br>163 076 | 29503<br>29503<br>163 077 |
| 4− | 29504<br>29504<br>163 100 | 29505<br>29505<br>163 101 | 29506<br>29506<br>163 102 | 29507<br>29507<br>163 103 | 29508<br>29508<br>163 104 | 29509<br>29509<br>163 105 | 29510<br>29510<br>163 106 | 29511<br>29511<br>163 107 | 29512<br>29512<br>163 110 | 29513<br>29513<br>163 111 | 29514<br>29514<br>163 112 | 29515<br>29515<br>163 113 | 29516<br>29516<br>163 114 | 29517<br>29517<br>163 115 | 29518<br>29518<br>163 116 | 29519<br>29519<br>163 117 |
| 5− | 29520<br>29520<br>163 120 | 29521<br>29521<br>163 121 | 29522<br>29522<br>163 122 | 29523<br>29523<br>163 123 | 29524<br>29524<br>163 124 | 29525<br>29525<br>163 125 | 29526<br>29526<br>163 126 | 29527<br>29527<br>163 127 | 29528<br>29528<br>163 130 | 29529<br>29529<br>163 131 | 29530<br>29530<br>163 132 | 29531<br>29531<br>163 133 | 29532<br>29532<br>163 134 | 29533<br>29533<br>163 135 | 29534<br>29534<br>163 136 | 29535<br>29535<br>163 137 |
| 6− | 29536<br>29536<br>163 140 | 29537<br>29537<br>163 141 | 29538<br>29538<br>163 142 | 29539<br>29539<br>163 143 | 29540<br>29540<br>163 144 | 29541<br>29541<br>163 145 | 29542<br>29542<br>163 146 | 29543<br>29543<br>163 147 | 29544<br>29544<br>163 150 | 29545<br>29545<br>163 151 | 29546<br>29546<br>163 152 | 29547<br>29547<br>163 153 | 29548<br>29548<br>163 154 | 29549<br>29549<br>163 155 | 29550<br>29550<br>163 156 | 29551<br>29551<br>163 157 |
| 7− | 29552<br>29552<br>163 160 | 29553<br>29553<br>163 161 | 29554<br>29554<br>163 162 | 29555<br>29555<br>163 163 | 29556<br>29556<br>163 164 | 29557<br>29557<br>163 165 | 29558<br>29558<br>163 166 | 29559<br>29559<br>163 167 | 29560<br>29560<br>163 170 | 29561<br>29561<br>163 171 | 29562<br>29562<br>163 172 | 29563<br>29563<br>163 173 | 29564<br>29564<br>163 174 | 29565<br>29565<br>163 175 | 29566<br>29566<br>163 176 | 29567<br>29567<br>163 177 |
| 8− | 29568<br>29568<br>163 200 | 29569<br>29569<br>163 201 | 29570<br>29570<br>163 202 | 295/1<br>29571<br>163 203 | 29572<br>29572<br>163 204 | 29573<br>29573<br>163 205 | 29574<br>29574<br>163 206 | 29575<br>29575<br>163 207 | 29576<br>29576<br>163 210 | 29577<br>29577<br>163 211 | 29578<br>29578<br>163 212 | 29579<br>29579<br>163 213 | 29580<br>29580<br>163 214 | 29581<br>29581<br>163 215 | 29582<br>29582<br>163 216 | 29583<br>29583<br>163 217 |
| 9− | 29584<br>29584<br>163 220 | 29585<br>29585<br>163 221 | 29586<br>29586<br>163 222 | 29587<br>29587<br>163 223 | 29588<br>29588<br>163 224 | 29589<br>29589<br>163 225 | 29590<br>29590<br>163 226 | 29591<br>29591<br>163 227 | 29592<br>29592<br>163 230 | 29593<br>29593<br>163 231 | 29594<br>29594<br>163 232 | 29595<br>29595<br>163 233 | 29596<br>29596<br>163 234 | 29597<br>29597<br>163 235 | 29598<br>29598<br>163 236 | 29599<br>29599<br>163 237 |
| A− | 29600<br>29600<br>163 240 | 29601<br>29601<br>163 241 | 29602<br>29602<br>163 242 | 29603<br>29603<br>163 243 | 29604<br>29604<br>163 244 | 29605<br>29605<br>163 245 | 29606<br>29606<br>163 246 | 29607<br>29607<br>163 247 | 29608<br>29608<br>163 250 | 29609<br>29609<br>163 251 | 29610<br>29610<br>163 252 | 29611<br>29611<br>163 253 | 29612<br>29612<br>163 254 | 29613<br>29613<br>163 255 | 29614<br>29614<br>163 256 | 29615<br>29615<br>163 257 |
| B− | 29616<br>29616<br>163 260 | 29617<br>29617<br>163 261 | 29618<br>29618<br>163 262 | 29619<br>29619<br>163 263 | 29620<br>29620<br>163 264 | 29621<br>29621<br>163 265 | 29622<br>29622<br>163 266 | 29623<br>29623<br>163 267 | 29624<br>29624<br>163 270 | 29625<br>29625<br>163 271 | 29626<br>29626<br>163 272 | 29627<br>29627<br>163 273 | 29628<br>29628<br>163 274 | 29629<br>29629<br>163 275 | 29630<br>29630<br>163 276 | 29631<br>29631<br>163 277 |
| C− | 29632<br>29632<br>163 300 | 29633<br>29633<br>163 301 | 29634<br>29634<br>163 302 | 29635<br>29635<br>163 303 | 29636<br>29636<br>163 304 | 29637<br>29637<br>163 305 | 29638<br>29638<br>163 306 | 29639<br>29639<br>163 307 | 29640<br>29640<br>163 310 | 29641<br>29641<br>163 311 | 29642<br>29642<br>163 312 | 29643<br>29643<br>163 313 | 29644<br>29644<br>163 314 | 29645<br>29645<br>163 315 | 29646<br>29646<br>163 316 | 29647<br>29647<br>163 317 |
| D− | 29648<br>29648<br>163 320 | 29649<br>29649<br>163 321 | 29650<br>29650<br>163 322 | 29651<br>29651<br>163 323 | 29652<br>29652<br>163 324 | 29653<br>29653<br>163 325 | 29654<br>29654<br>163 326 | 29655<br>29655<br>163 327 | 29656<br>29656<br>163 330 | 29657<br>29657<br>163 331 | 29658<br>29658<br>163 332 | 29659<br>29659<br>163 333 | 29660<br>29660<br>163 334 | 29661<br>29661<br>163 335 | 29662<br>29662<br>163 336 | 29663<br>29663<br>163 337 |
| E− | 29664<br>29664<br>163 340 | 29665<br>29665<br>163 341 | 29666<br>29666<br>163 342 | 29667<br>29667<br>163 343 | 29668<br>29668<br>163 344 | 29669<br>29669<br>163 345 | 29670<br>29670<br>163 346 | 29671<br>29671<br>163 347 | 29672<br>29672<br>163 350 | 29673<br>29673<br>163 351 | 29674<br>29674<br>163 352 | 29675<br>29675<br>163 353 | 29676<br>29676<br>163 354 | 29677<br>29677<br>163 355 | 29678<br>29678<br>163 356 | 29679<br>29679<br>163 357 |
| F− | 29680<br>29680<br>163 360 | 29681<br>29681<br>163 361 | 29682<br>29682<br>163 362 | 29683<br>29683<br>163 363 | 29684<br>29684<br>163 364 | 29685<br>29685<br>163 365 | 29686<br>29686<br>163 366 | 29687<br>29687<br>163 367 | 29688<br>29688<br>163 370 | 29689<br>29689<br>163 371 | 29690<br>29690<br>163 372 | 29691<br>29691<br>163 373 | 29692<br>29692<br>163 374 | 29693<br>29693<br>163 375 | 29694<br>29694<br>163 376 | 29695<br>29695<br>163 377 |

## FIRST HEX DIGIT

SECOND HEX DIGIT

| | −0 | −1 | −2 | −3 | −4 | −5 | −6 | −7 | −8 | −9 | −A | −B | −C | −D | −E | −F |
|---|---|---|---|---|---|---|---|---|---|---|---|---|---|---|---|---|
| **0-** | 29696<br>29696<br>164 000 | 29697<br>29697<br>164 001 | 29698<br>29698<br>164 002 | 29699<br>29699<br>164 003 | 29700<br>29700<br>164 004 | 29701<br>29701<br>164 005 | 29702<br>29702<br>164 006 | 29703<br>29703<br>164 007 | 29704<br>29704<br>164 010 | 29705<br>29705<br>164 011 | 29706<br>29706<br>164 012 | 29707<br>29707<br>164 013 | 29708<br>29708<br>164 014 | 29709<br>29709<br>164 015 | 29710<br>29710<br>164 016 | 29711<br>29711<br>164 017 |
| **1-** | 29712<br>29712<br>164 020 | 29713<br>29713<br>164 021 | 29714<br>29714<br>164 022 | 29715<br>29715<br>164 023 | 29716<br>29716<br>164 024 | 29717<br>29717<br>164 025 | 29718<br>29718<br>164 026 | 29719<br>29719<br>164 027 | 29720<br>29720<br>164 030 | 29721<br>29721<br>164 031 | 29722<br>29722<br>164 032 | 29723<br>29723<br>164 033 | 29724<br>29724<br>164 034 | 29725<br>29725<br>164 035 | 29726<br>29726<br>164 036 | 29727<br>29727<br>164 037 |
| **2-** | 29728<br>29728<br>164 040 | 29729<br>29729<br>164 041 | 29730<br>29730<br>164 042 | 29731<br>29731<br>164 043 | 29732<br>29732<br>164 044 | 29733<br>29733<br>164 045 | 29734<br>29734<br>164 046 | 29735<br>29735<br>164 047 | 29736<br>29736<br>164 050 | 29737<br>29737<br>164 051 | 29738<br>29738<br>164 052 | 29739<br>29739<br>164 053 | 29740<br>29740<br>164 054 | 29741<br>29741<br>164 055 | 29742<br>29742<br>164 056 | 29743<br>29743<br>164 057 |
| **3-** | 29744<br>29744<br>164 060 | 29745<br>29745<br>164 061 | 29746<br>29746<br>164 062 | 29747<br>29747<br>164 063 | 29748<br>29748<br>164 064 | 29749<br>29749<br>164 065 | 29750<br>29750<br>164 066 | 29751<br>29751<br>164 067 | 29752<br>29752<br>164 070 | 29753<br>29753<br>164 071 | 29754<br>29754<br>164 072 | 29755<br>29755<br>164 073 | 29756<br>29756<br>164 074 | 29757<br>29757<br>164 075 | 29758<br>29758<br>164 076 | 29759<br>29759<br>164 077 |
| **4-** | 29760<br>29760<br>164 100 | 29761<br>29761<br>164 101 | 29762<br>29762<br>164 102 | 29763<br>29763<br>164 103 | 29764<br>29764<br>164 104 | 29765<br>29765<br>164 105 | 29766<br>29766<br>164 106 | 29767<br>29767<br>164 107 | 29768<br>29768<br>164 110 | 29769<br>29769<br>164 111 | 29770<br>29770<br>164 112 | 29771<br>29771<br>164 113 | 29772<br>29772<br>164 114 | 29773<br>29773<br>164 115 | 29774<br>29774<br>164 116 | 29775<br>29775<br>164 117 |
| **5-** | 29776<br>29776<br>164 120 | 29777<br>29777<br>164 121 | 29778<br>29778<br>164 122 | 29779<br>29779<br>164 123 | 29780<br>29780<br>164 124 | 29781<br>29781<br>164 125 | 29782<br>29782<br>164 126 | 29783<br>29783<br>164 127 | 29784<br>29784<br>164 130 | 29785<br>29785<br>164 131 | 29786<br>29786<br>164 132 | 29787<br>29787<br>164 133 | 29788<br>29788<br>164 134 | 29789<br>29789<br>164 135 | 29790<br>29790<br>164 136 | 29791<br>29791<br>164 137 |
| **6-** | 29792<br>29792<br>164 140 | 29793<br>29793<br>164 141 | 29794<br>29794<br>164 142 | 29795<br>29795<br>164 143 | 29796<br>29796<br>164 144 | 29797<br>29797<br>164 145 | 29798<br>29798<br>164 146 | 29799<br>29799<br>164 147 | 29800<br>29800<br>164 150 | 29801<br>29801<br>164 151 | 29802<br>29802<br>164 152 | 29803<br>29803<br>164 153 | 29804<br>29804<br>164 154 | 29805<br>29805<br>164 155 | 29806<br>29806<br>164 156 | 29807<br>29807<br>164 157 |
| **7-** | 29808<br>29808<br>164 160 | 29809<br>29809<br>164 161 | 29810<br>29810<br>164 162 | 29811<br>29811<br>164 163 | 29812<br>29812<br>164 164 | 29813<br>29813<br>164 165 | 29814<br>29814<br>164 166 | 29815<br>29815<br>164 167 | 29816<br>29816<br>164 170 | 29817<br>29817<br>164 171 | 29818<br>29818<br>164 172 | 29819<br>29819<br>164 173 | 29820<br>29820<br>164 174 | 29821<br>29821<br>164 175 | 29822<br>29822<br>164 176 | 29823<br>29823<br>164 177 |
| **8-** | 29824<br>29824<br>164 200 | 29825<br>29825<br>164 201 | 29826<br>29826<br>164 202 | 29827<br>29827<br>164 203 | 29828<br>29828<br>164 204 | 29829<br>29829<br>164 205 | 29830<br>29830<br>164 206 | 29831<br>29831<br>164 207 | 29832<br>29832<br>164 210 | 29833<br>29833<br>164 211 | 29834<br>29834<br>164 212 | 29835<br>29835<br>164 213 | 29836<br>29836<br>164 214 | 29837<br>29837<br>164 215 | 29838<br>29838<br>164 216 | 29839<br>29839<br>164 217 |
| **9-** | 29840<br>29840<br>164 220 | 29841<br>29841<br>164 221 | 29842<br>29842<br>164 222 | 29843<br>29843<br>164 223 | 29844<br>29844<br>164 224 | 29845<br>29845<br>164 225 | 29846<br>29846<br>164 226 | 29847<br>29847<br>164 227 | 29848<br>29848<br>164 230 | 29849<br>29849<br>164 231 | 29850<br>29850<br>164 232 | 29851<br>29851<br>164 233 | 29852<br>29852<br>164 234 | 29853<br>29853<br>164 235 | 29854<br>29854<br>164 236 | 29855<br>29855<br>164 237 |
| **A-** | 29856<br>29856<br>164 240 | 29857<br>29857<br>164 241 | 29858<br>29858<br>164 242 | 29859<br>29859<br>164 243 | 29860<br>29860<br>164 244 | 29861<br>29861<br>164 245 | 29862<br>29862<br>164 246 | 29863<br>29863<br>164 247 | 29864<br>29864<br>164 250 | 29865<br>29865<br>164 251 | 29866<br>29866<br>164 252 | 29867<br>29867<br>164 253 | 29868<br>29868<br>164 254 | 29869<br>29869<br>164 255 | 29870<br>29870<br>164 256 | 29871<br>29871<br>164 257 |
| **B-** | 29872<br>29872<br>164 260 | 29873<br>29873<br>164 261 | 29874<br>29874<br>164 262 | 29875<br>29875<br>164 263 | 29876<br>29876<br>164 264 | 29877<br>29877<br>164 265 | 29878<br>29878<br>164 266 | 29879<br>29879<br>164 267 | 29880<br>29880<br>164 270 | 29881<br>29881<br>164 271 | 29882<br>29882<br>164 272 | 29883<br>29883<br>164 273 | 29884<br>29884<br>164 274 | 29885<br>29885<br>164 275 | 29886<br>29886<br>164 276 | 29887<br>29887<br>164 277 |
| **C-** | 29888<br>29888<br>164 300 | 29889<br>29889<br>164 301 | 29890<br>29890<br>164 302 | 29891<br>29891<br>164 303 | 29892<br>29892<br>164 304 | 29893<br>29893<br>164 305 | 29894<br>29894<br>164 306 | 29895<br>29895<br>164 307 | 29896<br>29896<br>164 310 | 29897<br>29897<br>164 311 | 29898<br>29898<br>164 312 | 29899<br>29899<br>164 313 | 29900<br>29900<br>164 314 | 29901<br>29901<br>164 315 | 29902<br>29902<br>164 316 | 29903<br>29903<br>164 317 |
| **D-** | 29904<br>29904<br>164 320 | 29905<br>29905<br>164 321 | 29906<br>29906<br>164 322 | 29907<br>29907<br>164 323 | 29908<br>29908<br>164 324 | 29909<br>29909<br>164 325 | 29910<br>29910<br>164 326 | 29911<br>29911<br>164 327 | 29912<br>29912<br>164 330 | 29913<br>29913<br>164 331 | 29914<br>29914<br>164 332 | 29915<br>29915<br>164 333 | 29916<br>29916<br>164 334 | 29917<br>29917<br>164 335 | 29918<br>29918<br>164 336 | 29919<br>29919<br>164 337 |
| **E-** | 29920<br>29920<br>164 340 | 29921<br>29921<br>164 341 | 29922<br>29922<br>164 342 | 29923<br>29923<br>164 343 | 29924<br>29924<br>164 344 | 29925<br>29925<br>164 345 | 29926<br>29926<br>164 346 | 29927<br>29927<br>164 347 | 29928<br>29928<br>164 350 | 29929<br>29929<br>164 351 | 29930<br>29930<br>164 352 | 29931<br>29931<br>164 353 | 29932<br>29932<br>164 354 | 29933<br>29933<br>164 355 | 29934<br>29934<br>164 356 | 29935<br>29935<br>164 357 |
| **F-** | 29936<br>29936<br>164 360 | 29937<br>29937<br>164 361 | 29938<br>29938<br>164 362 | 29939<br>29939<br>164 363 | 29940<br>29940<br>164 364 | 29941<br>29941<br>164 365 | 29942<br>29942<br>164 366 | 29943<br>29943<br>164 367 | 29944<br>29944<br>164 370 | 29945<br>29945<br>164 371 | 29946<br>29946<br>164 372 | 29947<br>29947<br>164 373 | 29948<br>29948<br>164 374 | 29949<br>29949<br>164 375 | 29950<br>29950<br>164 376 | 29951<br>29951<br>164 377 |

DECIMAL ← (arrow)

⬤ DECIMAL ← (arrow)

OCTAL ← (arrow)

⬤ DECIMAL  29696    BINARY  0111 0100    DECIMAL  29696    HEXADECIMAL  ⬡ 74    OCTAL  164 000

FOURTH HEX DIGIT →  ⬡  ← THIRD HEX DIGIT

FIRST HEX DIGIT — hexagon: 2

SECOND HEX DIGIT

| | −0 | −1 | −2 | −3 | −4 | −5 | −6 | −7 | −8 | −9 | −A | −B | −C | −D | −E | −F |
|---|---|---|---|---|---|---|---|---|---|---|---|---|---|---|---|---|
| 0− | 29952<br>29952<br>165 000 | 29953<br>29953<br>165 001 | 29954<br>29954<br>165 002 | 29955<br>29955<br>165 003 | 29956<br>29956<br>165 004 | 29957<br>29957<br>165 005 | 29958<br>29958<br>165 006 | 29959<br>29959<br>165 007 | 29960<br>29960<br>165 010 | 29961<br>29961<br>165 011 | 29962<br>29962<br>165 012 | 29963<br>29963<br>165 013 | 29964<br>29964<br>165 014 | 29965<br>29965<br>165 015 | 29966<br>29966<br>165 016 | 29967<br>29967<br>165 017 |
| 1− | 29968<br>29968<br>165 020 | 29969<br>29969<br>165 021 | 29970<br>29970<br>165 022 | 29971<br>29971<br>165 023 | 29972<br>29972<br>165 024 | 29973<br>29973<br>165 025 | 29974<br>29974<br>165 026 | 29975<br>29975<br>165 027 | 29976<br>29976<br>165 030 | 29977<br>29977<br>165 031 | 29978<br>29978<br>165 032 | 29979<br>29979<br>165 033 | 29980<br>29980<br>165 034 | 29981<br>29981<br>165 035 | 29982<br>29982<br>165 036 | 29983<br>29983<br>165 037 |
| 2− | 29984<br>29984<br>165 040 | 29985<br>29985<br>165 041 | 29986<br>29986<br>165 042 | 29987<br>29987<br>165 043 | 29988<br>29988<br>165 044 | 29989<br>29989<br>165 045 | 29990<br>29990<br>165 046 | 29991<br>29991<br>165 047 | 29992<br>29992<br>165 050 | 29993<br>29993<br>165 051 | 29994<br>29994<br>165 052 | 29995<br>29995<br>165 053 | 29996<br>29996<br>165 054 | 29997<br>29997<br>165 055 | 29998<br>29998<br>165 056 | 29999<br>29999<br>165 057 |
| 3− | 30000<br>30000<br>165 060 | 30001<br>30001<br>165 061 | 30002<br>30002<br>165 062 | 30003<br>30003<br>165 063 | 30004<br>30004<br>165 064 | 30005<br>30005<br>165 065 | 30006<br>30006<br>165 066 | 30007<br>30007<br>165 067 | 30008<br>30008<br>165 070 | 30009<br>30009<br>165 071 | 30010<br>30010<br>165 072 | 30011<br>30011<br>165 073 | 30012<br>30012<br>165 074 | 30013<br>30013<br>165 075 | 30014<br>30014<br>165 076 | 30015<br>30015<br>165 077 |
| 4− | 30016<br>30016<br>165 100 | 30017<br>30017<br>165 101 | 30018<br>30018<br>165 102 | 30019<br>30019<br>165 103 | 30020<br>30020<br>165 104 | 30021<br>30021<br>165 105 | 30022<br>30022<br>165 106 | 30023<br>30023<br>165 107 | 30024<br>30024<br>165 110 | 30025<br>30025<br>165 111 | 30026<br>30026<br>165 112 | 30027<br>30027<br>165 113 | 30028<br>30028<br>165 114 | 30029<br>30029<br>165 115 | 30030<br>30030<br>165 116 | 30031<br>30031<br>165 117 |
| 5− | 30032<br>30032<br>165 120 | 30033<br>30033<br>165 121 | 30034<br>30034<br>165 122 | 30035<br>30035<br>165 123 | 30036<br>30036<br>165 124 | 30037<br>30037<br>165 125 | 30038<br>30038<br>165 126 | 30039<br>30039<br>165 127 | 30040<br>30040<br>165 130 | 30041<br>30041<br>165 131 | 30042<br>30042<br>165 132 | 30043<br>30043<br>165 133 | 30044<br>30044<br>165 134 | 30045<br>30045<br>165 135 | 30046<br>30046<br>165 136 | 30047<br>30047<br>165 137 |
| 6− | 30048<br>30048<br>165 140 | 30049<br>30049<br>165 141 | 30050<br>30050<br>165 142 | 30051<br>30051<br>165 143 | 30052<br>30052<br>165 144 | 30053<br>30053<br>165 145 | 30054<br>30054<br>165 146 | 30055<br>30055<br>165 147 | 30056<br>30056<br>165 150 | 30057<br>30057<br>165 151 | 30058<br>30058<br>165 152 | 30059<br>30059<br>165 153 | 30060<br>30060<br>165 154 | 30061<br>30061<br>165 155 | 30062<br>30062<br>165 156 | 30063<br>30063<br>165 157 |
| 7− | 30064<br>30064<br>165 160 | 30065<br>30065<br>165 161 | 30066<br>30066<br>165 162 | 30067<br>30067<br>165 163 | 30068<br>30068<br>165 164 | 30069<br>30069<br>165 165 | 30070<br>30070<br>165 166 | 30071<br>30071<br>165 167 | 30072<br>30072<br>165 170 | 30073<br>30073<br>165 171 | 30074<br>30074<br>165 172 | 30075<br>30075<br>165 173 | 30076<br>30076<br>165 174 | 30077<br>30077<br>165 175 | 30078<br>30078<br>165 176 | 30079<br>30079<br>165 177 |
| 8− | 30080<br>30080<br>165 200 | 30081<br>30081<br>165 201 | 30082<br>30082<br>165 202 | 30083<br>30083<br>165 203 | 30084<br>30084<br>165 204 | 30085<br>30085<br>165 205 | 30086<br>30086<br>165 206 | 30087<br>30087<br>165 207 | 30088<br>30088<br>165 210 | 30089<br>30089<br>165 211 | 30090<br>30090<br>165 212 | 30091<br>30091<br>165 213 | 30092<br>30092<br>165 214 | 30093<br>30093<br>165 215 | 30094<br>30094<br>165 216 | 30095<br>30095<br>165 217 |
| 9− | 30096<br>30096<br>165 220 | 30097<br>30097<br>165 221 | 30098<br>30098<br>165 222 | 30099<br>30099<br>165 223 | 30100<br>30100<br>165 224 | 30101<br>30101<br>165 225 | 30102<br>30102<br>165 226 | 30103<br>30103<br>165 227 | 30104<br>30104<br>165 230 | 30105<br>30105<br>165 231 | 30106<br>30106<br>165 232 | 30107<br>30107<br>165 233 | 30108<br>30108<br>165 234 | 30109<br>30109<br>165 235 | 30110<br>30110<br>165 236 | 30111<br>30111<br>165 237 |
| A− | 30112<br>30112<br>165 240 | 30113<br>30113<br>165 241 | 30114<br>30114<br>165 242 | 30115<br>30115<br>165 243 | 30116<br>30116<br>165 244 | 30117<br>30117<br>165 245 | 30118<br>30118<br>165 246 | 30119<br>30119<br>165 247 | 30120<br>30120<br>165 250 | 30121<br>30121<br>165 251 | 30122<br>30122<br>165 252 | 30123<br>30123<br>165 253 | 30124<br>30124<br>165 254 | 30125<br>30125<br>165 255 | 30126<br>30126<br>165 256 | 30127<br>30127<br>165 257 |
| B− | 30128<br>30128<br>165 260 | 30129<br>30129<br>165 261 | 30130<br>30130<br>165 262 | 30131<br>30131<br>165 263 | 30132<br>30132<br>165 264 | 30133<br>30133<br>165 265 | 30134<br>30134<br>165 266 | 30135<br>30135<br>165 267 | 30136<br>30136<br>165 270 | 30137<br>30137<br>165 271 | 30138<br>30138<br>165 272 | 30139<br>30139<br>165 273 | 30140<br>30140<br>165 274 | 30141<br>30141<br>165 275 | 30142<br>30142<br>165 276 | 30143<br>30143<br>165 277 |
| C− | 30144<br>30144<br>165 300 | 30145<br>30145<br>165 301 | 30146<br>30146<br>165 302 | 30147<br>30147<br>165 303 | 30148<br>30148<br>165 304 | 30149<br>30149<br>165 305 | 30150<br>30150<br>165 306 | 30151<br>30151<br>165 307 | 30152<br>30152<br>165 310 | 30153<br>30153<br>165 311 | 30154<br>30154<br>165 312 | 30155<br>30155<br>165 313 | 30156<br>30156<br>165 314 | 30157<br>30157<br>165 315 | 30158<br>30158<br>165 316 | 30159<br>30159<br>165 317 |
| D− | 30160<br>30160<br>165 320 | 30161<br>30161<br>165 321 | 30162<br>30162<br>165 322 | 30163<br>30163<br>165 323 | 30164<br>30164<br>165 324 | 30165<br>30165<br>165 325 | 30166<br>30166<br>165 326 | 30167<br>30167<br>165 327 | 30168<br>30168<br>165 330 | 30169<br>30169<br>165 331 | 30170<br>30170<br>165 332 | 30171<br>30171<br>165 333 | 30172<br>30172<br>165 334 | 30173<br>30173<br>165 335 | 30174<br>30174<br>165 336 | 30175<br>30175<br>165 337 |
| E− | 30176<br>30176<br>165 340 | 30177<br>30177<br>165 341 | 30178<br>30178<br>165 342 | 30179<br>30179<br>165 343 | 30180<br>30180<br>165 344 | 30181<br>30181<br>165 345 | 30182<br>30182<br>165 346 | 30183<br>30183<br>165 347 | 30184<br>30184<br>165 350 | 30185<br>30185<br>165 351 | 30186<br>30186<br>165 352 | 30187<br>30187<br>165 353 | 30188<br>30188<br>165 354 | 30189<br>30189<br>165 355 | 30190<br>30190<br>165 356 | 30191<br>30191<br>165 357 |
| F− | 30192<br>30192<br>165 360 | 30193<br>30193<br>165 361 | 30194<br>30194<br>165 362 | 30195<br>30195<br>165 363 | 30196<br>30196<br>165 364 | 30197<br>30197<br>165 365 | 30198<br>30198<br>165 366 | 30199<br>30199<br>165 367 | 30200<br>30200<br>165 370 | 30201<br>30201<br>165 371 | 30202<br>30202<br>165 372 | 30203<br>30203<br>165 373 | 30204<br>30204<br>165 374 | 30205<br>30205<br>165 375 | 30206<br>30206<br>165 376 | 30207<br>30207<br>165 377 |

⬡ 2

# FIRST HEX DIGIT

|  | −0 | −1 | −2 | −3 | −4 | −5 | −6 | −7 | −8 | −9 | −A | −B | −C | −D | −E | −F |
|---|---|---|---|---|---|---|---|---|---|---|---|---|---|---|---|---|
| **0−** | 30208<br>30208<br>166 000 | 30209<br>30209<br>166 001 | 30210<br>30210<br>166 002 | 30211<br>30211<br>166 003 | 30212<br>30212<br>166 004 | 30213<br>30213<br>166 005 | 30214<br>30214<br>166 006 | 30215<br>30215<br>166 007 | 30216<br>30216<br>166 010 | 30217<br>30217<br>166 011 | 30218<br>30218<br>166 012 | 30219<br>30219<br>166 013 | 30220<br>30220<br>166 014 | 30221<br>30221<br>166 015 | 30222<br>30222<br>166 016 | 30223<br>30223<br>166 017 |
| **1−** | 30224<br>30224<br>166 020 | 30225<br>30225<br>166 021 | 30226<br>30226<br>166 022 | 30227<br>30227<br>166 023 | 30228<br>30228<br>166 024 | 30229<br>30229<br>166 025 | 30230<br>30230<br>166 026 | 30231<br>30231<br>166 027 | 30232<br>30232<br>166 030 | 30233<br>30233<br>166 031 | 30234<br>30234<br>166 032 | 30235<br>30235<br>166 033 | 30236<br>30236<br>166 034 | 30237<br>30237<br>166 035 | 30238<br>30238<br>166 036 | 30239<br>30239<br>166 037 |
| **2−** | 30240<br>30240<br>166 040 | 30241<br>30241<br>166 041 | 30242<br>30242<br>166 042 | 30243<br>30243<br>166 043 | 30244<br>30244<br>166 044 | 30245<br>30245<br>166 045 | 30246<br>30246<br>166 046 | 30247<br>30247<br>166 047 | 30248<br>30248<br>166 050 | 30249<br>30249<br>166 051 | 30250<br>30250<br>166 052 | 30251<br>30251<br>166 053 | 30252<br>30252<br>166 054 | 30253<br>30253<br>166 055 | 30254<br>30254<br>166 056 | 30255<br>30255<br>166 057 |
| **3−** | 30256<br>30256<br>166 060 | 30257<br>30257<br>166 061 | 30258<br>30258<br>166 062 | 30259<br>30259<br>166 063 | 30260<br>30260<br>166 064 | 30261<br>30261<br>166 065 | 30262<br>30262<br>166 066 | 30263<br>30263<br>166 067 | 30264<br>30264<br>166 070 | 30265<br>30265<br>166 071 | 30266<br>30266<br>166 072 | 30267<br>30267<br>166 073 | 30268<br>30268<br>166 074 | 30269<br>30269<br>166 075 | 30270<br>30270<br>166 076 | 30271<br>30271<br>166 077 |
| **4−** | 30272<br>30272<br>166 100 | 30273<br>30273<br>166 101 | 30274<br>30274<br>166 102 | 30275<br>30275<br>166 103 | 30276<br>30276<br>166 104 | 30277<br>30277<br>166 105 | 30278<br>30278<br>166 106 | 30279<br>30279<br>166 107 | 30280<br>30280<br>166 110 | 30281<br>30281<br>166 111 | 30282<br>30282<br>166 112 | 30283<br>30283<br>166 113 | 30284<br>30284<br>166 114 | 30285<br>30285<br>166 115 | 30286<br>30286<br>166 116 | 30287<br>30287<br>166 117 |
| **5−** | 30288<br>30288<br>166 120 | 30289<br>30289<br>166 121 | 30290<br>30290<br>166 122 | 30291<br>30291<br>166 123 | 30292<br>30292<br>166 124 | 30293<br>30293<br>166 125 | 30294<br>30294<br>166 126 | 30295<br>30295<br>166 127 | 30296<br>30296<br>166 130 | 30297<br>30297<br>166 131 | 30298<br>30298<br>166 132 | 30299<br>30299<br>166 133 | 30300<br>30300<br>166 134 | 30301<br>30301<br>166 135 | 30302<br>30302<br>166 136 | 30303<br>30303<br>166 137 |
| **6−** | 30304<br>30304<br>166 140 | 30305<br>30305<br>166 141 | 30306<br>30306<br>166 142 | 30307<br>30307<br>166 143 | 30308<br>30308<br>166 144 | 30309<br>30309<br>166 145 | 30310<br>30310<br>166 146 | 30311<br>30311<br>166 147 | 30312<br>30312<br>166 150 | 30313<br>30313<br>166 151 | 30314<br>30314<br>166 152 | 30315<br>30315<br>166 153 | 30316<br>30316<br>166 154 | 30317<br>30317<br>166 155 | 30318<br>30318<br>166 156 | 30319<br>30319<br>166 157 |
| **7−** | 30320<br>30320<br>166 160 | 30321<br>30321<br>166 161 | 30322<br>30322<br>166 162 | 30323<br>30323<br>166 163 | 30324<br>30324<br>166 164 | 30325<br>30325<br>166 165 | 30326<br>30326<br>166 166 | 30327<br>30327<br>166 167 | 30328<br>30328<br>166 170 | 30329<br>30329<br>166 171 | 30330<br>30330<br>166 172 | 30331<br>30331<br>166 173 | 30332<br>30332<br>166 174 | 30333<br>30333<br>166 175 | 30334<br>30334<br>166 176 | 30335<br>30335<br>166 177 |
| **8−** | 30336<br>30336<br>166 200 | 30337<br>30337<br>166 201 | 30338<br>30338<br>166 202 | 30339<br>30339<br>166 203 | 30340<br>30340<br>166 204 | 30341<br>30341<br>166 205 | 30342<br>30342<br>166 206 | 30343<br>30343<br>166 207 | 30344<br>30344<br>166 210 | 30345<br>30345<br>166 211 | 30346<br>30346<br>166 212 | 30347<br>30347<br>166 213 | 30348<br>30348<br>166 214 | 30349<br>30349<br>166 215 | 30350<br>30350<br>166 216 | 30351<br>30351<br>166 217 |
| **9−** | 30352<br>30352<br>166 220 | 30353<br>30353<br>166 221 | 30354<br>30354<br>166 222 | 30355<br>30355<br>166 223 | 30356<br>30356<br>166 224 | 30357<br>30357<br>166 225 | 30358<br>30358<br>166 226 | 30359<br>30359<br>166 227 | 30360<br>30360<br>166 230 | 30361<br>30361<br>166 231 | 30362<br>30362<br>166 232 | 30363<br>30363<br>166 233 | 30364<br>30364<br>166 234 | 30365<br>30365<br>166 235 | 30366<br>30366<br>166 236 | 30367<br>30367<br>166 237 |
| **A−** | 30368<br>30368<br>166 240 | 30369<br>30369<br>166 241 | 30370<br>30370<br>166 242 | 30371<br>30371<br>166 243 | 30372<br>30372<br>166 244 | 30373<br>30373<br>166 245 | 30374<br>30374<br>166 246 | 30375<br>30375<br>166 247 | 30376<br>30376<br>166 250 | 30377<br>30377<br>166 251 | 30378<br>30378<br>166 252 | 30379<br>30379<br>166 253 | 30380<br>30380<br>166 254 | 30381<br>30381<br>166 255 | 30382<br>30382<br>166 256 | 30383<br>30383<br>166 257 |
| **B−** | 30384<br>30384<br>166 260 | 30385<br>30385<br>166 261 | 30386<br>30386<br>166 262 | 30387<br>30387<br>166 263 | 30388<br>30388<br>166 264 | 30389<br>30389<br>166 265 | 30390<br>30390<br>166 266 | 30391<br>30391<br>166 267 | 30392<br>30392<br>166 270 | 30393<br>30393<br>166 271 | 30394<br>30394<br>166 272 | 30395<br>30395<br>166 273 | 30396<br>30396<br>166 274 | 30397<br>30397<br>166 275 | 30398<br>30398<br>166 276 | 30399<br>30399<br>166 277 |
| **C−** | 30400<br>30400<br>166 300 | 30401<br>30401<br>166 301 | 30402<br>30402<br>166 302 | 30403<br>30403<br>166 303 | 30404<br>30404<br>166 304 | 30405<br>30405<br>166 305 | 30406<br>30406<br>166 306 | 30407<br>30407<br>166 307 | 30408<br>30408<br>166 310 | 30409<br>30409<br>166 311 | 30410<br>30410<br>166 312 | 30411<br>30411<br>166 313 | 30412<br>30412<br>166 314 | 30413<br>30413<br>166 315 | 30414<br>30414<br>166 316 | 30415<br>30415<br>166 317 |
| **D−** | 30416<br>30416<br>166 320 | 30417<br>30417<br>166 321 | 30418<br>30418<br>166 322 | 30419<br>30419<br>166 323 | 30420<br>30420<br>166 324 | 30421<br>30421<br>166 325 | 30422<br>30422<br>166 326 | 30423<br>30423<br>166 327 | 30424<br>30424<br>166 330 | 30425<br>30425<br>166 331 | 30426<br>30426<br>166 332 | 30427<br>30427<br>166 333 | 30428<br>30428<br>166 334 | 30429<br>30429<br>166 335 | 30430<br>30430<br>166 336 | 30431<br>30431<br>166 337 |
| **E−** | 30432<br>30432<br>166 340 | 30433<br>30433<br>166 341 | 30434<br>30434<br>166 342 | 30435<br>30435<br>166 343 | 30436<br>30436<br>166 344 | 30437<br>30437<br>166 345 | 30438<br>30438<br>166 346 | 30439<br>30439<br>166 347 | 30440<br>30440<br>166 350 | 30441<br>30441<br>166 351 | 30442<br>30442<br>166 352 | 30443<br>30443<br>166 353 | 30444<br>30444<br>166 354 | 30445<br>30445<br>166 355 | 30446<br>30446<br>166 356 | 30447<br>30447<br>166 357 |
| **F−** | 30448<br>30448<br>166 360 | 30449<br>30449<br>166 361 | 30450<br>30450<br>166 362 | 30451<br>30451<br>166 363 | 30452<br>30452<br>166 364 | 30453<br>30453<br>166 365 | 30454<br>30454<br>166 366 | 30455<br>30455<br>166 367 | 30456<br>30456<br>166 370 | 30457<br>30457<br>166 371 | 30458<br>30458<br>166 372 | 30459<br>30459<br>166 373 | 30460<br>30460<br>166 374 | 30461<br>30461<br>166 375 | 30462<br>30462<br>166 376 | 30463<br>30463<br>166 377 |

Left margin: **SECOND HEX DIGIT**

Right margin: DECIMAL ← / ⬤ DECIMAL ← / OCTAL ←

⬤ DECIMAL  `30208`  BINARY  `0111 0110`  DECIMAL  `30208`  HEXADECIMAL ⬡ `76` OCTAL `166 000`

FOURTH HEX DIGIT ↗  ↖ THIRD HEX DIGIT

**FIRST HEX DIGIT**

Each cell shows the decimal value (top, repeated) and the octal value (bottom).

| ② | −0 | −1 | −2 | −3 | −4 | −5 | −6 | −7 | −8 | −9 | −A | −B | −C | −D | −E | −F |
|---|----|----|----|----|----|----|----|----|----|----|----|----|----|----|----|----|
| 0− | 30464 / 167 000 | 30465 / 167 001 | 30466 / 167 002 | 30467 / 167 003 | 30468 / 167 004 | 30469 / 167 005 | 30470 / 167 006 | 30471 / 167 007 | 30472 / 167 010 | 30473 / 167 011 | 30474 / 167 012 | 30475 / 167 013 | 30476 / 167 014 | 30477 / 167 015 | 30478 / 167 016 | 30479 / 167 017 |
| 1− | 30480 / 167 020 | 30481 / 167 021 | 30482 / 167 022 | 30483 / 167 023 | 30484 / 167 024 | 30485 / 167 025 | 30486 / 167 026 | 30487 / 167 027 | 30488 / 167 030 | 30489 / 167 031 | 30490 / 167 032 | 30491 / 167 033 | 30492 / 167 034 | 30493 / 167 035 | 30494 / 167 036 | 30495 / 167 037 |
| 2− | 30496 / 167 040 | 30497 / 167 041 | 30498 / 167 042 | 30499 / 167 043 | 30500 / 167 044 | 30501 / 167 045 | 30502 / 167 046 | 30503 / 167 047 | 30504 / 167 050 | 30505 / 167 051 | 30506 / 167 052 | 30507 / 167 053 | 30508 / 167 054 | 30509 / 167 055 | 30510 / 167 056 | 30511 / 167 057 |
| 3− | 30512 / 167 060 | 30513 / 167 061 | 30514 / 167 062 | 30515 / 167 063 | 30516 / 167 064 | 30517 / 167 065 | 30518 / 167 066 | 30519 / 167 067 | 30520 / 167 070 | 30521 / 167 071 | 30522 / 167 072 | 30523 / 167 073 | 30524 / 167 074 | 30525 / 167 075 | 30526 / 167 076 | 30527 / 167 077 |
| 4− | 30528 / 167 100 | 30529 / 167 101 | 30530 / 167 102 | 30531 / 167 103 | 30532 / 167 104 | 30533 / 167 105 | 30534 / 167 106 | 30535 / 167 107 | 30536 / 167 110 | 30537 / 167 111 | 30538 / 167 112 | 30539 / 167 113 | 30540 / 167 114 | 30541 / 167 115 | 30542 / 167 116 | 30543 / 167 117 |
| 5− | 30544 / 167 120 | 30545 / 167 121 | 30546 / 167 122 | 30547 / 167 123 | 30548 / 167 124 | 30549 / 167 125 | 30550 / 167 126 | 30551 / 167 127 | 30552 / 167 130 | 30553 / 167 131 | 30554 / 167 132 | 30555 / 167 133 | 30556 / 167 134 | 30557 / 167 135 | 30558 / 167 136 | 30559 / 167 137 |
| 6− | 30560 / 167 140 | 30561 / 167 141 | 30562 / 167 142 | 30563 / 167 143 | 30564 / 167 144 | 30565 / 167 145 | 30566 / 167 146 | 30567 / 167 147 | 30568 / 167 150 | 30569 / 167 151 | 30570 / 167 152 | 30571 / 167 153 | 30572 / 167 154 | 30573 / 167 155 | 30574 / 167 156 | 30575 / 167 157 |
| 7− | 30576 / 167 160 | 30577 / 167 161 | 30578 / 167 162 | 30579 / 167 163 | 30580 / 167 164 | 30581 / 167 165 | 30582 / 167 166 | 30583 / 167 167 | 30584 / 167 170 | 30585 / 167 171 | 30586 / 167 172 | 30587 / 167 173 | 30588 / 167 174 | 30589 / 167 175 | 30590 / 167 176 | 30591 / 167 177 |
| 8− | 30592 / 167 200 | 30593 / 167 201 | 30594 / 167 202 | 30595 / 167 203 | 30596 / 167 204 | 30597 / 167 205 | 30598 / 167 206 | 30599 / 167 207 | 30600 / 167 210 | 30601 / 167 211 | 30602 / 167 212 | 30603 / 167 213 | 30604 / 167 214 | 30605 / 167 215 | 30606 / 167 216 | 30607 / 167 217 |
| 9− | 30608 / 167 220 | 30609 / 167 221 | 30610 / 167 222 | 30611 / 167 223 | 30612 / 167 224 | 30613 / 167 225 | 30614 / 167 226 | 30615 / 167 227 | 30616 / 167 230 | 30617 / 167 231 | 30618 / 167 232 | 30619 / 167 233 | 30620 / 167 234 | 30621 / 167 235 | 30622 / 167 236 | 30623 / 167 237 |
| A− | 30624 / 167 240 | 30625 / 167 241 | 30626 / 167 242 | 30627 / 167 243 | 30628 / 167 244 | 30629 / 167 245 | 30630 / 167 246 | 30631 / 167 247 | 30632 / 167 250 | 30633 / 167 251 | 30634 / 167 252 | 30635 / 167 253 | 30636 / 167 254 | 30637 / 167 255 | 30638 / 167 256 | 30639 / 167 257 |
| B− | 30640 / 167 260 | 30641 / 167 261 | 30642 / 167 262 | 30643 / 167 263 | 30644 / 167 264 | 30645 / 167 265 | 30646 / 167 266 | 30647 / 167 267 | 30648 / 167 270 | 30649 / 167 271 | 30650 / 167 272 | 30651 / 167 273 | 30652 / 167 274 | 30653 / 167 275 | 30654 / 167 276 | 30655 / 167 277 |
| C− | 30656 / 167 300 | 30657 / 167 301 | 30658 / 167 302 | 30659 / 167 303 | 30660 / 167 304 | 30661 / 167 305 | 30662 / 167 306 | 30663 / 167 307 | 30664 / 167 310 | 30665 / 167 311 | 30666 / 167 312 | 30667 / 167 313 | 30668 / 167 314 | 30669 / 167 315 | 30670 / 167 316 | 30671 / 167 317 |
| D− | 30672 / 167 320 | 30673 / 167 321 | 30674 / 167 322 | 30675 / 167 323 | 30676 / 167 324 | 30677 / 167 325 | 30678 / 167 326 | 30679 / 167 327 | 30680 / 167 330 | 30681 / 167 331 | 30682 / 167 332 | 30683 / 167 333 | 30684 / 167 334 | 30685 / 167 335 | 30686 / 167 336 | 30687 / 167 337 |
| E− | 30688 / 167 340 | 30689 / 167 341 | 30690 / 167 342 | 30691 / 167 343 | 30692 / 167 344 | 30693 / 167 345 | 30694 / 167 346 | 30695 / 167 347 | 30696 / 167 350 | 30697 / 167 351 | 30698 / 167 352 | 30699 / 167 353 | 30700 / 167 354 | 30701 / 167 355 | 30702 / 167 356 | 30703 / 167 357 |
| F− | 30704 / 167 360 | 30705 / 167 361 | 30706 / 167 362 | 30707 / 167 363 | 30708 / 167 364 | 30709 / 167 365 | 30710 / 167 366 | 30711 / 167 367 | 30712 / 167 370 | 30713 / 167 371 | 30714 / 167 372 | 30715 / 167 373 | 30716 / 167 374 | 30717 / 167 375 | 30718 / 167 376 | 30719 / 167 377 |

SECOND HEX DIGIT

DECIMAL →   DECIMAL →   OCTAL →

## FIRST HEX DIGIT

(2) SECOND HEX DIGIT  — DECIMAL / DECIMAL / OCTAL

| | −0 | −1 | −2 | −3 | −4 | −5 | −6 | −7 | −8 | −9 | −A | −B | −C | −D | −E | −F |
|---|---|---|---|---|---|---|---|---|---|---|---|---|---|---|---|---|
| **0−** | 30720<br>30720<br>170 000 | 30721<br>30721<br>170 001 | 30722<br>30722<br>170 002 | 30723<br>30723<br>170 003 | 30724<br>30724<br>170 004 | 30725<br>30725<br>170 005 | 30726<br>30726<br>170 006 | 30727<br>30727<br>170 007 | 30728<br>30728<br>170 010 | 30729<br>30729<br>170 011 | 30730<br>30730<br>170 012 | 30731<br>30731<br>170 013 | 30732<br>30732<br>170 014 | 30733<br>30733<br>170 015 | 30734<br>30734<br>170 016 | 30735<br>30735<br>170 017 |
| **1−** | 30736<br>30736<br>170 020 | 30737<br>30737<br>170 021 | 30738<br>30738<br>170 022 | 30739<br>30739<br>170 023 | 30740<br>30740<br>170 024 | 30741<br>30741<br>170 025 | 30742<br>30742<br>170 026 | 30743<br>30743<br>170 027 | 30744<br>30744<br>170 030 | 30745<br>30745<br>170 031 | 30746<br>30746<br>170 032 | 30747<br>30747<br>170 033 | 30748<br>30748<br>170 034 | 30749<br>30749<br>170 035 | 30750<br>30750<br>170 036 | 30751<br>30751<br>170 037 |
| **2−** | 30752<br>30752<br>170 040 | 30753<br>30753<br>170 041 | 30754<br>30754<br>170 042 | 30755<br>30755<br>170 043 | 30756<br>30756<br>170 044 | 30757<br>30757<br>170 045 | 30758<br>30758<br>170 046 | 30759<br>30759<br>170 047 | 30760<br>30760<br>170 050 | 30761<br>30761<br>170 051 | 30762<br>30762<br>170 052 | 30763<br>30763<br>170 053 | 30764<br>30764<br>170 054 | 30765<br>30765<br>170 055 | 30766<br>30766<br>170 056 | 30767<br>30767<br>170 057 |
| **3−** | 30768<br>30768<br>170 060 | 30769<br>30769<br>170 061 | 30770<br>30770<br>170 062 | 30771<br>30771<br>170 063 | 30772<br>30772<br>170 064 | 30773<br>30773<br>170 065 | 30774<br>30774<br>170 066 | 30775<br>30775<br>170 067 | 30776<br>30776<br>170 070 | 30777<br>30777<br>170 071 | 30778<br>30778<br>170 072 | 30779<br>30779<br>170 073 | 30780<br>30780<br>170 074 | 30781<br>30781<br>170 075 | 30782<br>30782<br>170 076 | 30783<br>30783<br>170 077 |
| **4−** | 30784<br>30784<br>170 100 | 30785<br>30785<br>170 101 | 30786<br>30786<br>170 102 | 30787<br>30787<br>170 103 | 30788<br>30788<br>170 104 | 30789<br>30789<br>170 105 | 30790<br>30790<br>170 106 | 30791<br>30791<br>170 107 | 30792<br>30792<br>170 110 | 30793<br>30793<br>170 111 | 30794<br>30794<br>170 112 | 30795<br>30795<br>170 113 | 30796<br>30796<br>170 114 | 30797<br>30797<br>170 115 | 30798<br>30798<br>170 116 | 30799<br>30799<br>170 117 |
| **5−** | 30800<br>30800<br>170 120 | 30801<br>30801<br>170 121 | 30802<br>30802<br>170 122 | 30803<br>30803<br>170 123 | 30804<br>30804<br>170 124 | 30805<br>30805<br>170 125 | 30806<br>30806<br>170 126 | 30807<br>30807<br>170 127 | 30808<br>30808<br>170 130 | 30809<br>30809<br>170 131 | 30810<br>30810<br>170 132 | 30811<br>30811<br>170 133 | 30812<br>30812<br>170 134 | 30813<br>30813<br>170 135 | 30814<br>30814<br>170 136 | 30815<br>30815<br>170 137 |
| **6−** | 30816<br>30816<br>170 140 | 30817<br>30817<br>170 141 | 30818<br>30818<br>170 142 | 30819<br>30819<br>170 143 | 30820<br>30820<br>170 144 | 30821<br>30821<br>170 145 | 30822<br>30822<br>170 146 | 30823<br>30823<br>170 147 | 30824<br>30824<br>170 150 | 30825<br>30825<br>170 151 | 30826<br>30826<br>170 152 | 30827<br>30827<br>170 153 | 30828<br>30828<br>170 154 | 30829<br>30829<br>170 155 | 30830<br>30830<br>170 156 | 30831<br>30831<br>170 157 |
| **7−** | 30832<br>30832<br>170 160 | 30833<br>30833<br>170 161 | 30834<br>30834<br>170 162 | 30835<br>30835<br>170 163 | 30836<br>30836<br>170 164 | 30837<br>30837<br>170 165 | 30838<br>30838<br>170 166 | 30839<br>30839<br>170 167 | 30840<br>30840<br>170 170 | 30841<br>30841<br>170 171 | 30842<br>30842<br>170 172 | 30843<br>30843<br>170 173 | 30844<br>30844<br>170 174 | 30845<br>30845<br>170 175 | 30846<br>30846<br>170 176 | 30847<br>30847<br>170 177 |
| **8−** | 30848<br>30848<br>170 200 | 30849<br>30849<br>170 201 | 30850<br>30850<br>170 202 | 30851<br>30851<br>170 203 | 30852<br>30852<br>170 204 | 30853<br>30853<br>170 205 | 30854<br>30854<br>170 206 | 30855<br>30855<br>170 207 | 30856<br>30856<br>170 210 | 30857<br>30857<br>170 211 | 30858<br>30858<br>170 212 | 30859<br>30859<br>170 213 | 30860<br>30860<br>170 214 | 30861<br>30861<br>170 215 | 30862<br>30862<br>170 216 | 30863<br>30863<br>170 217 |
| **9−** | 30864<br>30864<br>170 220 | 30865<br>30865<br>170 221 | 30866<br>30866<br>170 222 | 30867<br>30867<br>170 223 | 30868<br>30868<br>170 224 | 30869<br>30869<br>170 225 | 30870<br>30870<br>170 226 | 30871<br>30871<br>170 227 | 30872<br>30872<br>170 230 | 30873<br>30873<br>170 231 | 30874<br>30874<br>170 232 | 30875<br>30875<br>170 233 | 30876<br>30876<br>170 234 | 30877<br>30877<br>170 235 | 30878<br>30878<br>170 236 | 30879<br>30879<br>170 237 |
| **A−** | 30880<br>30880<br>170 240 | 30881<br>30881<br>170 241 | 30882<br>30882<br>170 242 | 30883<br>30883<br>170 243 | 30884<br>30884<br>170 244 | 30885<br>30885<br>170 245 | 30886<br>30886<br>170 246 | 30887<br>30887<br>170 247 | 30888<br>30888<br>170 250 | 30889<br>30889<br>170 251 | 30890<br>30890<br>170 252 | 30891<br>30891<br>170 253 | 30892<br>30892<br>170 254 | 30893<br>30893<br>170 255 | 30894<br>30894<br>170 256 | 30895<br>30895<br>170 257 |
| **B−** | 30896<br>30896<br>170 260 | 30897<br>30897<br>170 261 | 30898<br>30898<br>170 262 | 30899<br>30899<br>170 263 | 30900<br>30900<br>170 264 | 30901<br>30901<br>170 265 | 30902<br>30902<br>170 266 | 30903<br>30903<br>170 267 | 30904<br>30904<br>170 270 | 30905<br>30905<br>170 271 | 30906<br>30906<br>170 272 | 30907<br>30907<br>170 273 | 30908<br>30908<br>170 274 | 30909<br>30909<br>170 275 | 30910<br>30910<br>170 276 | 30911<br>30911<br>170 277 |
| **C−** | 30912<br>30912<br>170 300 | 30913<br>30913<br>170 301 | 30914<br>30914<br>170 302 | 30915<br>30915<br>170 303 | 30916<br>30916<br>170 304 | 30917<br>30917<br>170 305 | 30918<br>30918<br>170 306 | 30919<br>30919<br>170 307 | 30920<br>30920<br>170 310 | 30921<br>30921<br>170 311 | 30922<br>30922<br>170 312 | 30923<br>30923<br>170 313 | 30924<br>30924<br>170 314 | 30925<br>30925<br>170 315 | 30926<br>30926<br>170 316 | 30927<br>30927<br>170 317 |
| **D−** | 30928<br>30928<br>170 320 | 30929<br>30929<br>170 321 | 30930<br>30930<br>170 322 | 30931<br>30931<br>170 323 | 30932<br>30932<br>170 324 | 30933<br>30933<br>170 325 | 30934<br>30934<br>170 326 | 30935<br>30935<br>170 327 | 30936<br>30936<br>170 330 | 30937<br>30937<br>170 331 | 30938<br>30938<br>170 332 | 30939<br>30939<br>170 333 | 30940<br>30940<br>170 334 | 30941<br>30941<br>170 335 | 30942<br>30942<br>170 336 | 30943<br>30943<br>170 337 |
| **E−** | 30944<br>30944<br>170 340 | 30945<br>30945<br>170 341 | 30946<br>30946<br>170 342 | 30947<br>30947<br>170 343 | 30948<br>30948<br>170 344 | 30949<br>30949<br>170 345 | 30950<br>30950<br>170 346 | 30951<br>30951<br>170 347 | 30952<br>30952<br>170 350 | 30953<br>30953<br>170 351 | 30954<br>30954<br>170 352 | 30955<br>30955<br>170 353 | 30956<br>30956<br>170 354 | 30957<br>30957<br>170 355 | 30958<br>30958<br>170 356 | 30959<br>30959<br>170 357 |
| **F−** | 30960<br>30960<br>170 360 | 30961<br>30961<br>170 361 | 30962<br>30962<br>170 362 | 30963<br>30963<br>170 363 | 30964<br>30964<br>170 364 | 30965<br>30965<br>170 365 | 30966<br>30966<br>170 366 | 30967<br>30967<br>170 367 | 30968<br>30968<br>170 370 | 30969<br>30969<br>170 371 | 30970<br>30970<br>170 372 | 30971<br>30971<br>170 373 | 30972<br>30972<br>170 374 | 30973<br>30973<br>170 375 | 30974<br>30974<br>170 376 | 30975<br>30975<br>170 377 |

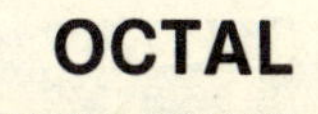

 DECIMAL 30720　BINARY 0111 1000　DECIMAL 30720　HEXADECIMAL (78) OCTAL 170 000

FOURTH HEX DIGIT → ← THIRD HEX DIGIT

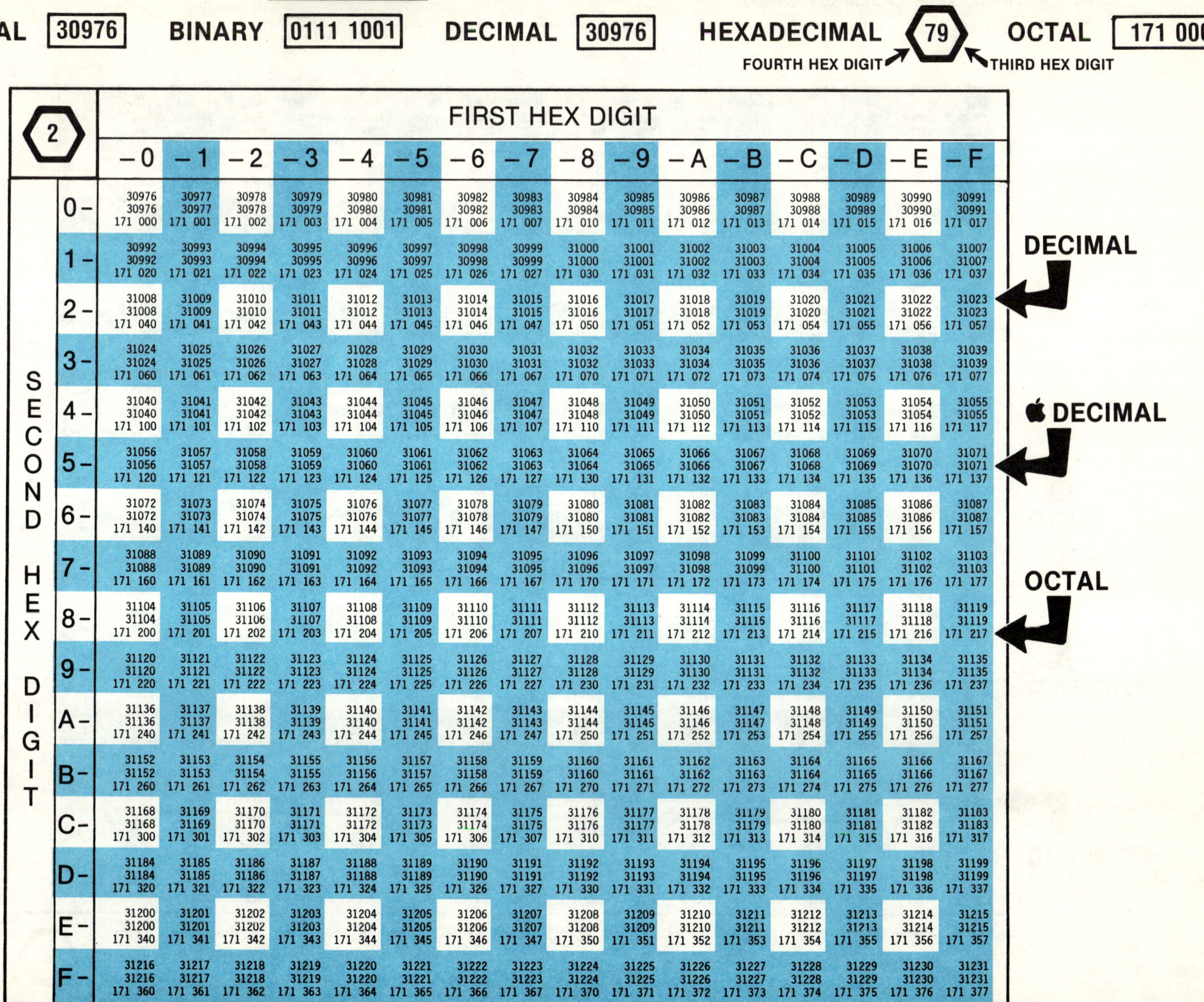



FIRST HEX DIGIT — 2

SECOND HEX DIGIT

| | −0 | −1 | −2 | −3 | −4 | −5 | −6 | −7 | −8 | −9 | −A | −B | −C | −D | −E | −F |
|---|---|---|---|---|---|---|---|---|---|---|---|---|---|---|---|---|
| 0− | 30976<br>30976<br>171 000 | 30977<br>30977<br>171 001 | 30978<br>30978<br>171 002 | 30979<br>30979<br>171 003 | 30980<br>30980<br>171 004 | 30981<br>30981<br>171 005 | 30982<br>30982<br>171 006 | 30983<br>30983<br>171 007 | 30984<br>30984<br>171 010 | 30985<br>30985<br>171 011 | 30986<br>30986<br>171 012 | 30987<br>30987<br>171 013 | 30988<br>30988<br>171 014 | 30989<br>30989<br>171 015 | 30990<br>30990<br>171 016 | 30991<br>30991<br>171 017 |
| 1− | 30992<br>30992<br>171 020 | 30993<br>30993<br>171 021 | 30994<br>30994<br>171 022 | 30995<br>30995<br>171 023 | 30996<br>30996<br>171 024 | 30997<br>30997<br>171 025 | 30998<br>30998<br>171 026 | 30999<br>30999<br>171 027 | 31000<br>31000<br>171 030 | 31001<br>31001<br>171 031 | 31002<br>31002<br>171 032 | 31003<br>31003<br>171 033 | 31004<br>31004<br>171 034 | 31005<br>31005<br>171 035 | 31006<br>31006<br>171 036 | 31007<br>31007<br>171 037 |
| 2− | 31008<br>31008<br>171 040 | 31009<br>31009<br>171 041 | 31010<br>31010<br>171 042 | 31011<br>31011<br>171 043 | 31012<br>31012<br>171 044 | 31013<br>31013<br>171 045 | 31014<br>31014<br>171 046 | 31015<br>31015<br>171 047 | 31016<br>31016<br>171 050 | 31017<br>31017<br>171 051 | 31018<br>31018<br>171 052 | 31019<br>31019<br>171 053 | 31020<br>31020<br>171 054 | 31021<br>31021<br>171 055 | 31022<br>31022<br>171 056 | 31023<br>31023<br>171 057 |
| 3− | 31024<br>31024<br>171 060 | 31025<br>31025<br>171 061 | 31026<br>31026<br>171 062 | 31027<br>31027<br>171 063 | 31028<br>31028<br>171 064 | 31029<br>31029<br>171 065 | 31030<br>31030<br>171 066 | 31031<br>31031<br>171 067 | 31032<br>31032<br>171 070 | 31033<br>31033<br>171 071 | 31034<br>31034<br>171 072 | 31035<br>31035<br>171 073 | 31036<br>31036<br>171 074 | 31037<br>31037<br>171 075 | 31038<br>31038<br>171 076 | 31039<br>31039<br>171 077 |
| 4− | 31040<br>31040<br>171 100 | 31041<br>31041<br>171 101 | 31042<br>31042<br>171 102 | 31043<br>31043<br>171 103 | 31044<br>31044<br>171 104 | 31045<br>31045<br>171 105 | 31046<br>31046<br>171 106 | 31047<br>31047<br>171 107 | 31048<br>31048<br>171 110 | 31049<br>31049<br>171 111 | 31050<br>31050<br>171 112 | 31051<br>31051<br>171 113 | 31052<br>31052<br>171 114 | 31053<br>31053<br>171 115 | 31054<br>31054<br>171 116 | 31055<br>31055<br>171 117 |
| 5− | 31056<br>31056<br>171 120 | 31057<br>31057<br>171 121 | 31058<br>31058<br>171 122 | 31059<br>31059<br>171 123 | 31060<br>31060<br>171 124 | 31061<br>31061<br>171 125 | 31062<br>31062<br>171 126 | 31063<br>31063<br>171 127 | 31064<br>31064<br>171 130 | 31065<br>31065<br>171 131 | 31066<br>31066<br>171 132 | 31067<br>31067<br>171 133 | 31068<br>31068<br>171 134 | 31069<br>31069<br>171 135 | 31070<br>31070<br>171 136 | 31071<br>31071<br>171 137 |
| 6− | 31072<br>31072<br>171 140 | 31073<br>31073<br>171 141 | 31074<br>31074<br>171 142 | 31075<br>31075<br>171 143 | 31076<br>31076<br>171 144 | 31077<br>31077<br>171 145 | 31078<br>31078<br>171 146 | 31079<br>31079<br>171 147 | 31080<br>31080<br>171 150 | 31081<br>31081<br>171 151 | 31082<br>31082<br>171 152 | 31083<br>31083<br>171 153 | 31084<br>31084<br>171 154 | 31085<br>31085<br>171 155 | 31086<br>31086<br>171 156 | 31087<br>31087<br>171 157 |
| 7− | 31088<br>31088<br>171 160 | 31089<br>31089<br>171 161 | 31090<br>31090<br>171 162 | 31091<br>31091<br>171 163 | 31092<br>31092<br>171 164 | 31093<br>31093<br>171 165 | 31094<br>31094<br>171 166 | 31095<br>31095<br>171 167 | 31096<br>31096<br>171 170 | 31097<br>31097<br>171 171 | 31098<br>31098<br>171 172 | 31099<br>31099<br>171 173 | 31100<br>31100<br>171 174 | 31101<br>31101<br>171 175 | 31102<br>31102<br>171 176 | 31103<br>31103<br>171 177 |
| 8− | 31104<br>31104<br>171 200 | 31105<br>31105<br>171 201 | 31106<br>31106<br>171 202 | 31107<br>31107<br>171 203 | 31108<br>31108<br>171 204 | 31109<br>31109<br>171 205 | 31110<br>31110<br>171 206 | 31111<br>31111<br>171 207 | 31112<br>31112<br>171 210 | 31113<br>31113<br>171 211 | 31114<br>31114<br>171 212 | 31115<br>31115<br>171 213 | 31116<br>31116<br>171 214 | 31117<br>31117<br>171 215 | 31118<br>31118<br>171 216 | 31119<br>31119<br>171 217 |
| 9− | 31120<br>31120<br>171 220 | 31121<br>31121<br>171 221 | 31122<br>31122<br>171 222 | 31123<br>31123<br>171 223 | 31124<br>31124<br>171 224 | 31125<br>31125<br>171 225 | 31126<br>31126<br>171 226 | 31127<br>31127<br>171 227 | 31128<br>31128<br>171 230 | 31129<br>31129<br>171 231 | 31130<br>31130<br>171 232 | 31131<br>31131<br>171 233 | 31132<br>31132<br>171 234 | 31133<br>31133<br>171 235 | 31134<br>31134<br>171 236 | 31135<br>31135<br>171 237 |
| A− | 31136<br>31136<br>171 240 | 31137<br>31137<br>171 241 | 31138<br>31138<br>171 242 | 31139<br>31139<br>171 243 | 31140<br>31140<br>171 244 | 31141<br>31141<br>171 245 | 31142<br>31142<br>171 246 | 31143<br>31143<br>171 247 | 31144<br>31144<br>171 250 | 31145<br>31145<br>171 251 | 31146<br>31146<br>171 252 | 31147<br>31147<br>171 253 | 31148<br>31148<br>171 254 | 31149<br>31149<br>171 255 | 31150<br>31150<br>171 256 | 31151<br>31151<br>171 257 |
| B− | 31152<br>31152<br>171 260 | 31153<br>31153<br>171 261 | 31154<br>31154<br>171 262 | 31155<br>31155<br>171 263 | 31156<br>31156<br>171 264 | 31157<br>31157<br>171 265 | 31158<br>31158<br>171 266 | 31159<br>31159<br>171 267 | 31160<br>31160<br>171 270 | 31161<br>31161<br>171 271 | 31162<br>31162<br>171 272 | 31163<br>31163<br>171 273 | 31164<br>31164<br>171 274 | 31165<br>31165<br>171 275 | 31166<br>31166<br>171 276 | 31167<br>31167<br>171 277 |
| C− | 31168<br>31168<br>171 300 | 31169<br>31169<br>171 301 | 31170<br>31170<br>171 302 | 31171<br>31171<br>171 303 | 31172<br>31172<br>171 304 | 31173<br>31173<br>171 305 | 31174<br>31174<br>171 306 | 31175<br>31175<br>171 307 | 31176<br>31176<br>171 310 | 31177<br>31177<br>171 311 | 31178<br>31178<br>171 312 | 31179<br>31179<br>171 313 | 31180<br>31180<br>171 314 | 31181<br>31181<br>171 315 | 31182<br>31182<br>171 316 | 31183<br>31183<br>171 317 |
| D− | 31184<br>31184<br>171 320 | 31185<br>31185<br>171 321 | 31186<br>31186<br>171 322 | 31187<br>31187<br>171 323 | 31188<br>31188<br>171 324 | 31189<br>31189<br>171 325 | 31190<br>31190<br>171 326 | 31191<br>31191<br>171 327 | 31192<br>31192<br>171 330 | 31193<br>31193<br>171 331 | 31194<br>31194<br>171 332 | 31195<br>31195<br>171 333 | 31196<br>31196<br>171 334 | 31197<br>31197<br>171 335 | 31198<br>31198<br>171 336 | 31199<br>31199<br>171 337 |
| E− | 31200<br>31200<br>171 340 | 31201<br>31201<br>171 341 | 31202<br>31202<br>171 342 | 31203<br>31203<br>171 343 | 31204<br>31204<br>171 344 | 31205<br>31205<br>171 345 | 31206<br>31206<br>171 346 | 31207<br>31207<br>171 347 | 31208<br>31208<br>171 350 | 31209<br>31209<br>171 351 | 31210<br>31210<br>171 352 | 31211<br>31211<br>171 353 | 31212<br>31212<br>171 354 | 31213<br>31213<br>171 355 | 31214<br>31214<br>171 356 | 31215<br>31215<br>171 357 |
| F− | 31216<br>31216<br>171 360 | 31217<br>31217<br>171 361 | 31218<br>31218<br>171 362 | 31219<br>31219<br>171 363 | 31220<br>31220<br>171 364 | 31221<br>31221<br>171 365 | 31222<br>31222<br>171 366 | 31223<br>31223<br>171 367 | 31224<br>31224<br>171 370 | 31225<br>31225<br>171 371 | 31226<br>31226<br>171 372 | 31227<br>31227<br>171 373 | 31228<br>31228<br>171 374 | 31229<br>31229<br>171 375 | 31230<br>31230<br>171 376 | 31231<br>31231<br>171 377 |

| SECOND HEX DIGIT | −0 | −1 | −2 | −3 | −4 | −5 | −6 | −7 | −8 | −9 | −A | −B | −C | −D | −E | −F |
|---|---|---|---|---|---|---|---|---|---|---|---|---|---|---|---|---|
| 0- | 31232<br>31232<br>172 000 | 31233<br>31233<br>172 001 | 31234<br>31234<br>172 002 | 31235<br>31235<br>172 003 | 31236<br>31236<br>172 004 | 31237<br>31237<br>172 005 | 31238<br>31238<br>172 006 | 31239<br>31239<br>172 007 | 31240<br>31240<br>172 010 | 31241<br>31241<br>172 011 | 31242<br>31242<br>172 012 | 31243<br>31243<br>172 013 | 31244<br>31244<br>172 014 | 31245<br>31245<br>172 015 | 31246<br>31246<br>172 016 | 31247<br>31247<br>172 017 |
| 1- | 31248<br>31248<br>172 020 | 31249<br>31249<br>172 021 | 31250<br>31250<br>172 022 | 31251<br>31251<br>172 023 | 31252<br>31252<br>172 024 | 31253<br>31253<br>172 025 | 31254<br>31254<br>172 026 | 31255<br>31255<br>172 027 | 31256<br>31256<br>172 030 | 31257<br>31257<br>172 031 | 31258<br>31258<br>172 032 | 31259<br>31259<br>172 033 | 31260<br>31260<br>172 034 | 31261<br>31261<br>172 035 | 31262<br>31262<br>172 036 | 31263<br>31263<br>172 037 |
| 2- | 31264<br>31264<br>172 040 | 31265<br>31265<br>172 041 | 31266<br>31266<br>172 042 | 31267<br>31267<br>172 043 | 31268<br>31268<br>172 044 | 31269<br>31269<br>172 045 | 31270<br>31270<br>172 046 | 31271<br>31271<br>172 047 | 31272<br>31272<br>172 050 | 31273<br>31273<br>172 051 | 31274<br>31274<br>172 052 | 31275<br>31275<br>172 053 | 31276<br>31276<br>172 054 | 31277<br>31277<br>172 055 | 31278<br>31278<br>172 056 | 31279<br>31279<br>172 057 |
| 3- | 31280<br>31280<br>172 060 | 31281<br>31281<br>172 061 | 31282<br>31282<br>172 062 | 31283<br>31283<br>172 063 | 31284<br>31284<br>172 064 | 31285<br>31285<br>172 065 | 31286<br>31286<br>172 066 | 31287<br>31287<br>172 067 | 31288<br>31288<br>172 070 | 31289<br>31289<br>172 071 | 31290<br>31290<br>172 072 | 31291<br>31291<br>172 073 | 31292<br>31292<br>172 074 | 31293<br>31293<br>172 075 | 31294<br>31294<br>172 076 | 31295<br>31295<br>172 077 |
| 4- | 31296<br>31296<br>172 100 | 31297<br>31297<br>172 101 | 31298<br>31298<br>172 102 | 31299<br>31299<br>172 103 | 31300<br>31300<br>172 104 | 31301<br>31301<br>172 105 | 31302<br>31302<br>172 106 | 31303<br>31303<br>172 107 | 31304<br>31304<br>172 110 | 31305<br>31305<br>172 111 | 31306<br>31306<br>172 112 | 31307<br>31307<br>172 113 | 31308<br>31308<br>172 114 | 31309<br>31309<br>172 115 | 31310<br>31310<br>172 116 | 31311<br>31311<br>172 117 |
| 5- | 31312<br>31312<br>172 120 | 31313<br>31313<br>172 121 | 31314<br>31314<br>172 122 | 31315<br>31315<br>172 123 | 31316<br>31316<br>172 124 | 31317<br>31317<br>172 125 | 31318<br>31318<br>172 126 | 31319<br>31319<br>172 127 | 31320<br>31320<br>172 130 | 31321<br>31321<br>172 131 | 31322<br>31322<br>172 132 | 31323<br>31323<br>172 133 | 31324<br>31324<br>172 134 | 31325<br>31325<br>172 135 | 31326<br>31326<br>172 136 | 31327<br>31327<br>172 137 |
| 6- | 31328<br>31328<br>172 140 | 31329<br>31329<br>172 141 | 31330<br>31330<br>172 142 | 31331<br>31331<br>172 143 | 31332<br>31332<br>172 144 | 31333<br>31333<br>172 145 | 31334<br>31334<br>172 146 | 31335<br>31335<br>172 147 | 31336<br>31336<br>172 150 | 31337<br>31337<br>172 151 | 31338<br>31338<br>172 152 | 31339<br>31339<br>172 153 | 31340<br>31340<br>172 154 | 31341<br>31341<br>172 155 | 31342<br>31342<br>172 156 | 31343<br>31343<br>172 157 |
| 7- | 31344<br>31344<br>172 160 | 31345<br>31345<br>172 161 | 31346<br>31346<br>172 162 | 31347<br>31347<br>172 163 | 31348<br>31348<br>172 164 | 31349<br>31349<br>172 165 | 31350<br>31350<br>172 166 | 31351<br>31351<br>172 167 | 31352<br>31352<br>172 170 | 31353<br>31353<br>172 171 | 31354<br>31354<br>172 172 | 31355<br>31355<br>172 173 | 31356<br>31356<br>172 174 | 31357<br>31357<br>172 175 | 31358<br>31358<br>172 176 | 31359<br>31359<br>172 177 |
| 8- | 31360<br>31360<br>172 200 | 31361<br>31361<br>172 201 | 31362<br>31362<br>172 202 | 31363<br>31363<br>172 203 | 31364<br>31364<br>172 204 | 31365<br>31365<br>172 205 | 31366<br>31366<br>172 206 | 31367<br>31367<br>172 207 | 31368<br>31368<br>172 210 | 31369<br>31369<br>172 211 | 31370<br>31370<br>172 212 | 31371<br>31371<br>172 213 | 31372<br>31372<br>172 214 | 31373<br>31373<br>172 215 | 31374<br>31374<br>172 216 | 31375<br>31375<br>172 217 |
| 9- | 31376<br>31376<br>172 220 | 31377<br>31377<br>172 221 | 31378<br>31378<br>172 222 | 31379<br>31379<br>172 223 | 31380<br>31380<br>172 224 | 31381<br>31381<br>172 225 | 31382<br>31382<br>172 226 | 31383<br>31383<br>172 227 | 31384<br>31384<br>172 230 | 31385<br>31385<br>172 231 | 31386<br>31386<br>172 232 | 31387<br>31387<br>172 233 | 31388<br>31388<br>172 234 | 31389<br>31389<br>172 235 | 31390<br>31390<br>172 236 | 31391<br>31391<br>172 237 |
| A- | 31392<br>31392<br>172 240 | 31393<br>31393<br>172 241 | 31394<br>31394<br>172 242 | 31395<br>31395<br>172 243 | 31396<br>31396<br>172 244 | 31397<br>31397<br>172 245 | 31398<br>31398<br>172 246 | 31399<br>31399<br>172 247 | 31400<br>31400<br>172 250 | 31401<br>31401<br>172 251 | 31402<br>31402<br>172 252 | 31403<br>31403<br>172 253 | 31404<br>31404<br>172 254 | 31405<br>31405<br>172 255 | 31406<br>31406<br>172 256 | 31407<br>31407<br>172 257 |
| B- | 31408<br>31408<br>172 260 | 31409<br>31409<br>172 261 | 31410<br>31410<br>172 262 | 31411<br>31411<br>172 263 | 31412<br>31412<br>172 264 | 31413<br>31413<br>172 265 | 31414<br>31414<br>172 266 | 31415<br>31415<br>172 267 | 31416<br>31416<br>172 270 | 31417<br>31417<br>172 271 | 31418<br>31418<br>172 272 | 31419<br>31419<br>172 273 | 31420<br>31420<br>172 274 | 31421<br>31421<br>172 275 | 31422<br>31422<br>172 276 | 31423<br>31423<br>172 277 |
| C- | 31424<br>31424<br>172 300 | 31425<br>31425<br>172 301 | 31426<br>31426<br>172 302 | 31427<br>31427<br>172 303 | 31428<br>31428<br>172 304 | 31429<br>31429<br>172 305 | 31430<br>31430<br>172 306 | 31431<br>31431<br>172 307 | 31432<br>31432<br>172 310 | 31433<br>31433<br>172 311 | 31434<br>31434<br>172 312 | 31435<br>31435<br>172 313 | 31436<br>31436<br>172 314 | 31437<br>31437<br>172 315 | 31438<br>31438<br>172 316 | 31439<br>31439<br>172 317 |
| D- | 31440<br>31440<br>172 320 | 31441<br>31441<br>172 321 | 31442<br>31442<br>172 322 | 31443<br>31443<br>172 323 | 31444<br>31444<br>172 324 | 31445<br>31445<br>172 325 | 31446<br>31446<br>172 326 | 31447<br>31447<br>172 327 | 31448<br>31448<br>172 330 | 31449<br>31449<br>172 331 | 31450<br>31450<br>172 332 | 31451<br>31451<br>172 333 | 31452<br>31452<br>172 334 | 31453<br>31453<br>172 335 | 31454<br>31454<br>172 336 | 31455<br>31455<br>172 337 |
| E- | 31456<br>31456<br>172 340 | 31457<br>31457<br>172 341 | 31458<br>31458<br>172 342 | 31459<br>31459<br>172 343 | 31460<br>31460<br>172 344 | 31461<br>31461<br>172 345 | 31462<br>31462<br>172 346 | 31463<br>31463<br>172 347 | 31464<br>31464<br>172 350 | 31465<br>31465<br>172 351 | 31466<br>31466<br>172 352 | 31467<br>31467<br>172 353 | 31468<br>31468<br>172 354 | 31469<br>31469<br>172 355 | 31470<br>31470<br>172 356 | 31471<br>31471<br>172 357 |
| F- | 31472<br>31472<br>172 360 | 31473<br>31473<br>172 361 | 31474<br>31474<br>172 362 | 31475<br>31475<br>172 363 | 31476<br>31476<br>172 364 | 31477<br>31477<br>172 365 | 31478<br>31478<br>172 366 | 31479<br>31479<br>172 367 | 31480<br>31480<br>172 370 | 31481<br>31481<br>172 371 | 31482<br>31482<br>172 372 | 31483<br>31483<br>172 373 | 31484<br>31484<br>172 374 | 31485<br>31485<br>172 375 | 31486<br>31486<br>172 376 | 31487<br>31487<br>172 377 |

DECIMAL

⬥ DECIMAL

OCTAL

⬥ DECIMAL  `31232`   BINARY  `0111 1010`   DECIMAL  `31232`   HEXADECIMAL  ⬡ `7A`   OCTAL  `172 000`

FOURTH HEX DIGIT → ⬡ ← THIRD HEX DIGIT

**FIRST HEX DIGIT** — (2)

SECOND HEX DIGIT (rows); arrows on right: DECIMAL, DECIMAL, OCTAL

| | −0 | −1 | −2 | −3 | −4 | −5 | −6 | −7 | −8 | −9 | −A | −B | −C | −D | −E | −F |
|---|---|---|---|---|---|---|---|---|---|---|---|---|---|---|---|---|
| 0- | 31488<br>31488<br>173 000 | 31489<br>31489<br>173 001 | 31490<br>31490<br>173 002 | 31491<br>31491<br>173 003 | 31492<br>31492<br>173 004 | 31493<br>31493<br>173 005 | 31494<br>31494<br>173 006 | 31495<br>31495<br>173 007 | 31496<br>31496<br>173 010 | 31497<br>31497<br>173 011 | 31498<br>31498<br>173 012 | 31499<br>31499<br>173 013 | 31500<br>31500<br>173 014 | 31501<br>31501<br>173 015 | 31502<br>31502<br>173 016 | 31503<br>31503<br>173 017 |
| 1- | 31504<br>31504<br>173 020 | 31505<br>31505<br>173 021 | 31506<br>31506<br>173 022 | 31507<br>31507<br>173 023 | 31508<br>31508<br>173 024 | 31509<br>31509<br>173 025 | 31510<br>31510<br>173 026 | 31511<br>31511<br>173 027 | 31512<br>31512<br>173 030 | 31513<br>31513<br>173 031 | 31514<br>31514<br>173 032 | 31515<br>31515<br>173 033 | 31516<br>31516<br>173 034 | 31517<br>31517<br>173 035 | 31518<br>31518<br>173 036 | 31519<br>31519<br>173 037 |
| 2- | 31520<br>31520<br>173 040 | 31521<br>31521<br>173 041 | 31522<br>31522<br>173 042 | 31523<br>31523<br>173 043 | 31524<br>31524<br>173 044 | 31525<br>31525<br>173 045 | 31526<br>31526<br>173 046 | 31527<br>31527<br>173 047 | 31528<br>31528<br>173 050 | 31529<br>31529<br>173 051 | 31530<br>31530<br>173 052 | 31531<br>31531<br>173 053 | 31532<br>31532<br>173 054 | 31533<br>31533<br>173 055 | 31534<br>31534<br>173 056 | 31535<br>31535<br>173 057 |
| 3- | 31536<br>31536<br>173 060 | 31537<br>31537<br>173 061 | 31538<br>31538<br>173 062 | 31539<br>31539<br>173 063 | 31540<br>31540<br>173 064 | 31541<br>31541<br>173 065 | 31542<br>31542<br>173 066 | 31543<br>31543<br>173 067 | 31544<br>31544<br>173 070 | 31545<br>31545<br>173 071 | 31546<br>31546<br>173 072 | 31547<br>31547<br>173 073 | 31548<br>31548<br>173 074 | 31549<br>31549<br>173 075 | 31550<br>31550<br>173 076 | 31551<br>31551<br>173 077 |
| 4- | 31552<br>31552<br>173 100 | 31553<br>31553<br>173 101 | 31554<br>31554<br>173 102 | 31555<br>31555<br>173 103 | 31556<br>31556<br>173 104 | 31557<br>31557<br>173 105 | 31558<br>31558<br>173 106 | 31559<br>31559<br>173 107 | 31560<br>31560<br>173 110 | 31561<br>31561<br>173 111 | 31562<br>31562<br>173 112 | 31563<br>31563<br>173 113 | 31564<br>31564<br>173 114 | 31565<br>31565<br>173 115 | 31566<br>31566<br>173 116 | 31567<br>31567<br>173 117 |
| 5- | 31568<br>31568<br>173 120 | 31569<br>31569<br>173 121 | 31570<br>31570<br>173 122 | 31571<br>31571<br>173 123 | 31572<br>31572<br>173 124 | 31573<br>31573<br>173 125 | 31574<br>31574<br>173 126 | 31575<br>31575<br>173 127 | 31576<br>31576<br>173 130 | 31577<br>31577<br>173 131 | 31578<br>31578<br>173 132 | 31579<br>31579<br>173 133 | 31580<br>31580<br>173 134 | 31581<br>31581<br>173 135 | 31582<br>31582<br>173 136 | 31583<br>31583<br>173 137 |
| 6- | 31584<br>31584<br>173 140 | 31585<br>31585<br>173 141 | 31586<br>31586<br>173 142 | 31587<br>31587<br>173 143 | 31588<br>31588<br>173 144 | 31589<br>31589<br>173 145 | 31590<br>31590<br>173 146 | 31591<br>31591<br>173 147 | 31592<br>31592<br>173 150 | 31593<br>31593<br>173 151 | 31594<br>31594<br>173 152 | 31595<br>31595<br>173 153 | 31596<br>31596<br>173 154 | 31597<br>31597<br>173 155 | 31598<br>31598<br>173 156 | 31599<br>31599<br>173 157 |
| 7- | 31600<br>31600<br>173 160 | 31601<br>31601<br>173 161 | 31602<br>31602<br>173 162 | 31603<br>31603<br>173 163 | 31604<br>31604<br>173 164 | 31605<br>31605<br>173 165 | 31606<br>31606<br>173 166 | 31607<br>31607<br>173 167 | 31608<br>31608<br>173 170 | 31609<br>31609<br>173 171 | 31610<br>31610<br>173 172 | 31611<br>31611<br>173 173 | 31612<br>31612<br>173 174 | 31613<br>31613<br>173 175 | 31614<br>31614<br>173 176 | 31615<br>31615<br>173 177 |
| 8- | 31616<br>31616<br>173 200 | 31617<br>31617<br>173 201 | 31618<br>31618<br>173 202 | 31619<br>31619<br>173 203 | 31620<br>31620<br>173 204 | 31621<br>31621<br>173 205 | 31622<br>31622<br>173 206 | 31623<br>31623<br>173 207 | 31624<br>31624<br>173 210 | 31625<br>31625<br>173 211 | 31626<br>31626<br>173 212 | 31627<br>31627<br>173 213 | 31628<br>31628<br>173 214 | 31629<br>31629<br>173 215 | 31630<br>31630<br>173 216 | 31631<br>31631<br>173 217 |
| 9- | 31632<br>31632<br>173 220 | 31633<br>31633<br>173 221 | 31634<br>31634<br>173 222 | 31635<br>31635<br>173 223 | 31636<br>31636<br>173 224 | 31637<br>31637<br>173 225 | 31638<br>31638<br>173 226 | 31639<br>31639<br>173 227 | 31640<br>31640<br>173 230 | 31641<br>31641<br>173 231 | 31642<br>31642<br>173 232 | 31643<br>31643<br>173 233 | 31644<br>31644<br>173 234 | 31645<br>31645<br>173 235 | 31646<br>31646<br>173 236 | 31647<br>31647<br>173 237 |
| A- | 31648<br>31648<br>173 240 | 31649<br>31649<br>173 241 | 31650<br>31650<br>173 242 | 31651<br>31651<br>173 243 | 31652<br>31652<br>173 244 | 31653<br>31653<br>173 245 | 31654<br>31654<br>173 246 | 31655<br>31655<br>173 247 | 31656<br>31656<br>173 250 | 31657<br>31657<br>173 251 | 31658<br>31658<br>173 252 | 31659<br>31659<br>173 253 | 31660<br>31660<br>173 254 | 31661<br>31661<br>173 255 | 31662<br>31662<br>173 256 | 31663<br>31663<br>173 257 |
| B- | 31664<br>31664<br>173 260 | 31665<br>31665<br>173 261 | 31666<br>31666<br>173 262 | 31667<br>31667<br>173 263 | 31668<br>31668<br>173 264 | 31669<br>31669<br>173 265 | 31670<br>31670<br>173 266 | 31671<br>31671<br>173 267 | 31672<br>31672<br>173 270 | 31673<br>31673<br>173 271 | 31674<br>31674<br>173 272 | 31675<br>31675<br>173 273 | 31676<br>31676<br>173 274 | 31677<br>31677<br>173 275 | 31678<br>31678<br>173 276 | 31679<br>31679<br>173 277 |
| C- | 31680<br>31680<br>173 300 | 31681<br>31681<br>173 301 | 31682<br>31682<br>173 302 | 31683<br>31683<br>173 303 | 31684<br>31684<br>173 304 | 31685<br>31685<br>173 305 | 31686<br>31686<br>173 306 | 31687<br>31687<br>173 307 | 31688<br>31688<br>173 310 | 31689<br>31689<br>173 311 | 31690<br>31690<br>173 312 | 31691<br>31691<br>173 313 | 31692<br>31692<br>173 314 | 31693<br>31693<br>173 315 | 31694<br>31694<br>173 316 | 31695<br>31695<br>173 317 |
| D- | 31696<br>31696<br>173 320 | 31697<br>31697<br>173 321 | 31698<br>31698<br>173 322 | 31699<br>31699<br>173 323 | 31700<br>31700<br>173 324 | 31701<br>31701<br>173 325 | 31702<br>31702<br>173 326 | 31703<br>31703<br>173 327 | 31704<br>31704<br>173 330 | 31705<br>31705<br>173 331 | 31706<br>31706<br>173 332 | 31707<br>31707<br>173 333 | 31708<br>31708<br>173 334 | 31709<br>31709<br>173 335 | 31710<br>31710<br>173 336 | 31711<br>31711<br>173 337 |
| E- | 31712<br>31712<br>173 340 | 31713<br>31713<br>173 341 | 31714<br>31714<br>173 342 | 31715<br>31715<br>173 343 | 31716<br>31716<br>173 344 | 31717<br>31717<br>173 345 | 31718<br>31718<br>173 346 | 31719<br>31719<br>173 347 | 31720<br>31720<br>173 350 | 31721<br>31721<br>173 351 | 31722<br>31722<br>173 352 | 31723<br>31723<br>173 353 | 31724<br>31724<br>173 354 | 31725<br>31725<br>173 355 | 31726<br>31726<br>173 356 | 31727<br>31727<br>173 357 |
| F- | 31728<br>31728<br>173 360 | 31729<br>31729<br>173 361 | 31730<br>31730<br>173 362 | 31731<br>31731<br>173 363 | 31732<br>31732<br>173 364 | 31733<br>31733<br>173 365 | 31734<br>31734<br>173 366 | 31735<br>31735<br>173 367 | 31736<br>31736<br>173 370 | 31737<br>31737<br>173 371 | 31738<br>31738<br>173 372 | 31739<br>31739<br>173 373 | 31740<br>31740<br>173 374 | 31741<br>31741<br>173 375 | 31742<br>31742<br>173 376 | 31743<br>31743<br>173 377 |

| SECOND HEX DIGIT | −0 | −1 | −2 | −3 | −4 | −5 | −6 | −7 | −8 | −9 | −A | −B | −C | −D | −E | −F |
|---|---|---|---|---|---|---|---|---|---|---|---|---|---|---|---|---|
| 0− | 31744<br>31744<br>174 000 | 31745<br>31745<br>174 001 | 31746<br>31746<br>174 002 | 31747<br>31747<br>174 003 | 31748<br>31748<br>174 004 | 31749<br>31749<br>174 005 | 31750<br>31750<br>174 006 | 31751<br>31751<br>174 007 | 31752<br>31752<br>174 010 | 31753<br>31753<br>174 011 | 31754<br>31754<br>174 012 | 31755<br>31755<br>174 013 | 31756<br>31756<br>174 014 | 31757<br>31757<br>174 015 | 31758<br>31758<br>174 016 | 31759<br>31759<br>174 017 |
| 1− | 31760<br>31760<br>174 020 | 31761<br>31761<br>174 021 | 31762<br>31762<br>174 022 | 31763<br>31763<br>174 023 | 31764<br>31764<br>174 024 | 31765<br>31765<br>174 025 | 31766<br>31766<br>174 026 | 31767<br>31767<br>174 027 | 31768<br>31768<br>174 030 | 31769<br>31769<br>174 031 | 31770<br>31770<br>174 032 | 31771<br>31771<br>174 033 | 31772<br>31772<br>174 034 | 31773<br>31773<br>174 035 | 31774<br>31774<br>174 036 | 31775<br>31775<br>174 037 |
| 2− | 31776<br>31776<br>174 040 | 31777<br>31777<br>174 041 | 31778<br>31778<br>174 042 | 31779<br>31779<br>174 043 | 31780<br>31780<br>174 044 | 31781<br>31781<br>174 045 | 31782<br>31782<br>174 046 | 31783<br>31783<br>174 047 | 31784<br>31784<br>174 050 | 31785<br>31785<br>174 051 | 31786<br>31786<br>174 052 | 31787<br>31787<br>174 053 | 31788<br>31788<br>174 054 | 31789<br>31789<br>174 055 | 31790<br>31790<br>174 056 | 31791<br>31791<br>174 057 |
| 3− | 31792<br>31792<br>174 060 | 31793<br>31793<br>174 061 | 31794<br>31794<br>174 062 | 31795<br>31795<br>174 063 | 31796<br>31796<br>174 064 | 31797<br>31797<br>174 065 | 31798<br>31798<br>174 066 | 31799<br>31799<br>174 067 | 31800<br>31800<br>174 070 | 31801<br>31801<br>174 071 | 31802<br>31802<br>174 072 | 31803<br>31803<br>174 073 | 31804<br>31804<br>174 074 | 31805<br>31805<br>174 075 | 31806<br>31806<br>174 076 | 31807<br>31807<br>174 077 |
| 4− | 31808<br>31808<br>174 100 | 31809<br>31809<br>174 101 | 31810<br>31810<br>174 102 | 31811<br>31811<br>174 103 | 31812<br>31812<br>174 104 | 31813<br>31813<br>174 105 | 31814<br>31814<br>174 106 | 31815<br>31815<br>174 107 | 31816<br>31816<br>174 110 | 31817<br>31817<br>174 111 | 31818<br>31818<br>174 112 | 31819<br>31819<br>174 113 | 31820<br>31820<br>174 114 | 31821<br>31821<br>174 115 | 31822<br>31822<br>174 116 | 31823<br>31823<br>174 117 |
| 5− | 31824<br>31824<br>174 120 | 31825<br>31825<br>174 121 | 31826<br>31826<br>174 122 | 31827<br>31827<br>174 123 | 31828<br>31828<br>174 124 | 31829<br>31829<br>174 125 | 31830<br>31830<br>174 126 | 31831<br>31831<br>174 127 | 31832<br>31832<br>174 130 | 31833<br>31833<br>174 131 | 31834<br>31834<br>174 132 | 31835<br>31835<br>174 133 | 31836<br>31836<br>174 134 | 31837<br>31837<br>174 135 | 31838<br>31838<br>174 136 | 31839<br>31839<br>174 137 |
| 6− | 31840<br>31840<br>174 140 | 31841<br>31841<br>174 141 | 31842<br>31842<br>174 142 | 31843<br>31843<br>174 143 | 31844<br>31844<br>174 144 | 31845<br>31845<br>174 145 | 31846<br>31846<br>174 146 | 31847<br>31847<br>174 147 | 31848<br>31848<br>174 150 | 31849<br>31849<br>174 151 | 31850<br>31850<br>174 152 | 31851<br>31851<br>174 153 | 31852<br>31852<br>174 154 | 31853<br>31853<br>174 155 | 31854<br>31854<br>174 156 | 31855<br>31855<br>174 157 |
| 7− | 31856<br>31856<br>174 160 | 31857<br>31857<br>174 161 | 31858<br>31858<br>174 162 | 31859<br>31859<br>174 163 | 31860<br>31860<br>174 164 | 31861<br>31861<br>174 165 | 31862<br>31862<br>174 166 | 31863<br>31863<br>174 167 | 31864<br>31864<br>174 170 | 31865<br>31865<br>174 171 | 31866<br>31866<br>174 172 | 31867<br>31867<br>174 173 | 31868<br>31868<br>174 174 | 31869<br>31869<br>174 175 | 31870<br>31870<br>174 176 | 31871<br>31871<br>174 177 |
| 8− | 31872<br>31872<br>174 200 | 31873<br>31873<br>174 201 | 31874<br>31874<br>174 202 | 31875<br>31875<br>174 203 | 31876<br>31876<br>174 204 | 31877<br>31877<br>174 205 | 31878<br>31878<br>174 206 | 31879<br>31879<br>174 207 | 31880<br>31880<br>174 210 | 31881<br>31881<br>174 211 | 31882<br>31882<br>174 212 | 31883<br>31883<br>174 213 | 31884<br>31884<br>174 214 | 31885<br>31885<br>174 215 | 31886<br>31886<br>174 216 | 31887<br>31887<br>174 217 |
| 9− | 31888<br>31888<br>174 220 | 31889<br>31889<br>174 221 | 31890<br>31890<br>174 222 | 31891<br>31891<br>174 223 | 31892<br>31892<br>174 224 | 31893<br>31893<br>174 225 | 31894<br>31894<br>174 226 | 31895<br>31895<br>174 227 | 31896<br>31896<br>174 230 | 31897<br>31897<br>174 231 | 31898<br>31898<br>174 232 | 31899<br>31899<br>174 233 | 31900<br>31900<br>174 234 | 31901<br>31901<br>174 235 | 31902<br>31902<br>174 236 | 31903<br>31903<br>174 237 |
| A− | 31904<br>31904<br>174 240 | 31905<br>31905<br>174 241 | 31906<br>31906<br>174 242 | 31907<br>31907<br>174 243 | 31908<br>31908<br>174 244 | 31909<br>31909<br>174 245 | 31910<br>31910<br>174 246 | 31911<br>31911<br>174 247 | 31912<br>31912<br>174 250 | 31913<br>31913<br>174 251 | 31914<br>31914<br>174 252 | 31915<br>31915<br>174 253 | 31916<br>31916<br>174 254 | 31917<br>31917<br>174 255 | 31918<br>31918<br>174 256 | 31919<br>31919<br>174 257 |
| B− | 31920<br>31920<br>174 260 | 31921<br>31921<br>174 261 | 31922<br>31922<br>174 262 | 31923<br>31923<br>174 263 | 31924<br>31924<br>174 264 | 31925<br>31925<br>174 265 | 31926<br>31926<br>174 266 | 31927<br>31927<br>174 267 | 31928<br>31928<br>174 270 | 31929<br>31929<br>174 271 | 31930<br>31930<br>174 272 | 31931<br>31931<br>174 273 | 31932<br>31932<br>174 274 | 31933<br>31933<br>174 275 | 31934<br>31934<br>174 276 | 31935<br>31935<br>174 277 |
| C− | 31936<br>31936<br>174 300 | 31937<br>31937<br>174 301 | 31938<br>31938<br>174 302 | 31939<br>31939<br>174 303 | 31940<br>31940<br>174 304 | 31941<br>31941<br>174 305 | 31942<br>31942<br>174 306 | 31943<br>31943<br>174 307 | 31944<br>31944<br>174 310 | 31945<br>31945<br>174 311 | 31946<br>31946<br>174 312 | 31947<br>31947<br>174 313 | 31948<br>31948<br>174 314 | 31949<br>31949<br>174 315 | 31950<br>31950<br>174 316 | 31951<br>31951<br>174 317 |
| D− | 31952<br>31952<br>174 320 | 31953<br>31953<br>174 321 | 31954<br>31954<br>174 322 | 31955<br>31955<br>174 323 | 31956<br>31956<br>174 324 | 31957<br>31957<br>174 325 | 31958<br>31958<br>174 326 | 31959<br>31959<br>174 327 | 31960<br>31960<br>174 330 | 31961<br>31961<br>174 331 | 31962<br>31962<br>174 332 | 31963<br>31963<br>174 333 | 31964<br>31964<br>174 334 | 31965<br>31965<br>174 335 | 31966<br>31966<br>174 336 | 31967<br>31967<br>174 337 |
| E− | 31968<br>31968<br>174 340 | 31969<br>31969<br>174 341 | 31970<br>31970<br>174 342 | 31971<br>31971<br>174 343 | 31972<br>31972<br>174 344 | 31973<br>31973<br>174 345 | 31974<br>31974<br>174 346 | 31975<br>31975<br>174 347 | 31976<br>31976<br>174 350 | 31977<br>31977<br>174 351 | 31978<br>31978<br>174 352 | 31979<br>31979<br>174 353 | 31980<br>31980<br>174 354 | 31981<br>31981<br>174 355 | 31982<br>31982<br>174 356 | 31983<br>31983<br>174 357 |
| F− | 31984<br>31984<br>174 360 | 31985<br>31985<br>174 361 | 31986<br>31986<br>174 362 | 31987<br>31987<br>174 363 | 31988<br>31988<br>174 364 | 31989<br>31989<br>174 365 | 31990<br>31990<br>174 366 | 31991<br>31991<br>174 367 | 31992<br>31992<br>174 370 | 31993<br>31993<br>174 371 | 31994<br>31994<br>174 372 | 31995<br>31995<br>174 373 | 31996<br>31996<br>174 374 | 31997<br>31997<br>174 375 | 31998<br>31998<br>174 376 | 31999<br>31999<br>174 377 |

 DECIMAL

 DECIMAL

OCTAL

 DECIMAL [ 31744 ]  BINARY [ 0111 1100 ]  DECIMAL [ 31744 ]  HEXADECIMAL ⬡ 7C  OCTAL [ 174 000 ]

FOURTH HEX DIGIT → 7C ← THIRD HEX DIGIT

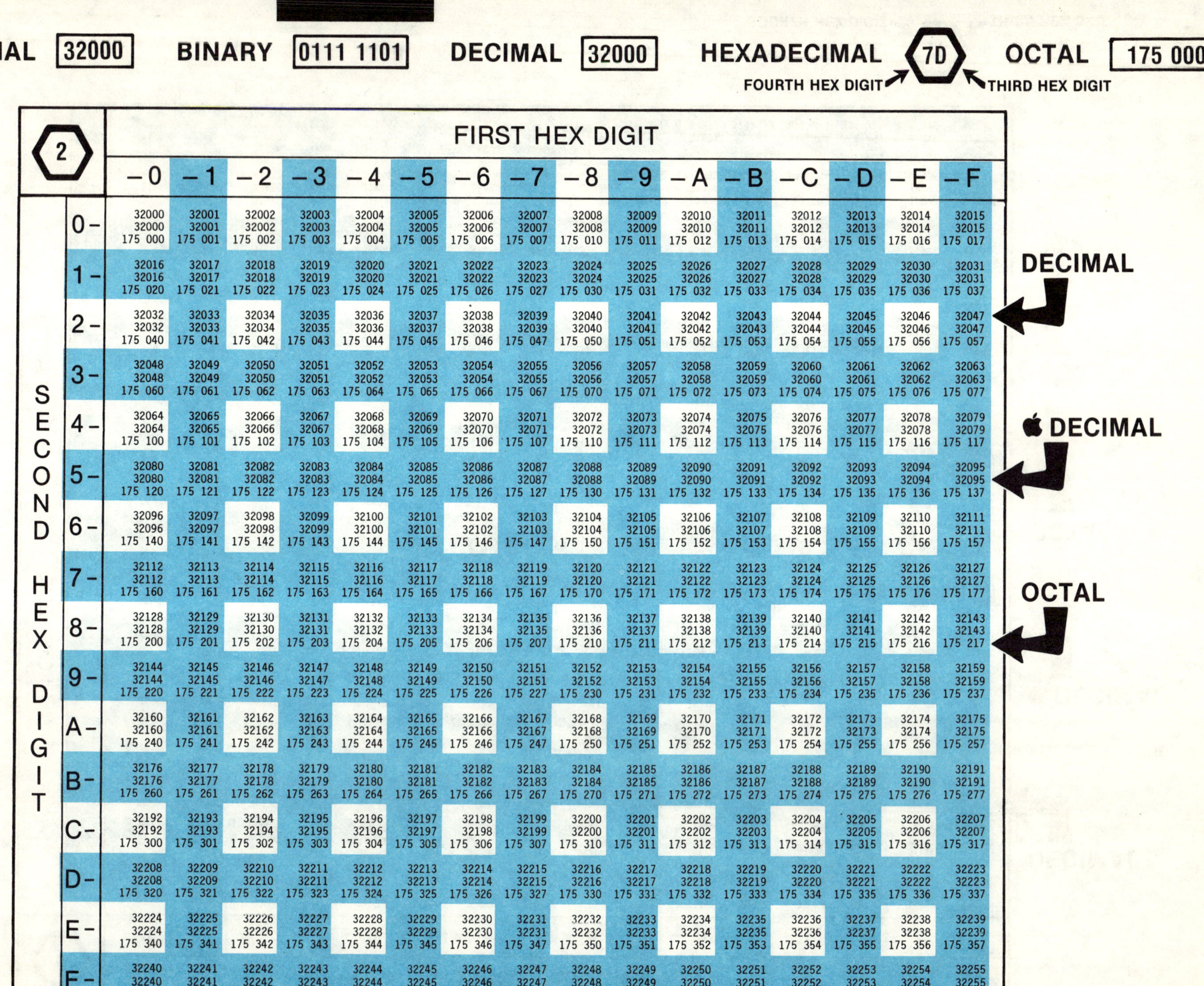


Each cell below lists, top to bottom: decimal, decimal, octal.

| 2 | FIRST HEX DIGIT | | | | | | | | | | | | | | | |
|---|---|---|---|---|---|---|---|---|---|---|---|---|---|---|---|---|
| SECOND HEX DIGIT | −0 | −1 | −2 | −3 | −4 | −5 | −6 | −7 | −8 | −9 | −A | −B | −C | −D | −E | −F |
| 0− | 32000 / 175 000 | 32001 / 175 001 | 32002 / 175 002 | 32003 / 175 003 | 32004 / 175 004 | 32005 / 175 005 | 32006 / 175 006 | 32007 / 175 007 | 32008 / 175 010 | 32009 / 175 011 | 32010 / 175 012 | 32011 / 175 013 | 32012 / 175 014 | 32013 / 175 015 | 32014 / 175 016 | 32015 / 175 017 |
| 1− | 32016 / 175 020 | 32017 / 175 021 | 32018 / 175 022 | 32019 / 175 023 | 32020 / 175 024 | 32021 / 175 025 | 32022 / 175 026 | 32023 / 175 027 | 32024 / 175 030 | 32025 / 175 031 | 32026 / 175 032 | 32027 / 175 033 | 32028 / 175 034 | 32029 / 175 035 | 32030 / 175 036 | 32031 / 175 037 |
| 2− | 32032 / 175 040 | 32033 / 175 041 | 32034 / 175 042 | 32035 / 175 043 | 32036 / 175 044 | 32037 / 175 045 | 32038 / 175 046 | 32039 / 175 047 | 32040 / 175 050 | 32041 / 175 051 | 32042 / 175 052 | 32043 / 175 053 | 32044 / 175 054 | 32045 / 175 055 | 32046 / 175 056 | 32047 / 175 057 |
| 3− | 32048 / 175 060 | 32049 / 175 061 | 32050 / 175 062 | 32051 / 175 063 | 32052 / 175 064 | 32053 / 175 065 | 32054 / 175 066 | 32055 / 175 067 | 32056 / 175 070 | 32057 / 175 071 | 32058 / 175 072 | 32059 / 175 073 | 32060 / 175 074 | 32061 / 175 075 | 32062 / 175 076 | 32063 / 175 077 |
| 4− | 32064 / 175 100 | 32065 / 175 101 | 32066 / 175 102 | 32067 / 175 103 | 32068 / 175 104 | 32069 / 175 105 | 32070 / 175 106 | 32071 / 175 107 | 32072 / 175 110 | 32073 / 175 111 | 32074 / 175 112 | 32075 / 175 113 | 32076 / 175 114 | 32077 / 175 115 | 32078 / 175 116 | 32079 / 175 117 |
| 5− | 32080 / 175 120 | 32081 / 175 121 | 32082 / 175 122 | 32083 / 175 123 | 32084 / 175 124 | 32085 / 175 125 | 32086 / 175 126 | 32087 / 175 127 | 32088 / 175 130 | 32089 / 175 131 | 32090 / 175 132 | 32091 / 175 133 | 32092 / 175 134 | 32093 / 175 135 | 32094 / 175 136 | 32095 / 175 137 |
| 6− | 32096 / 175 140 | 32097 / 175 141 | 32098 / 175 142 | 32099 / 175 143 | 32100 / 175 144 | 32101 / 175 145 | 32102 / 175 146 | 32103 / 175 147 | 32104 / 175 150 | 32105 / 175 151 | 32106 / 175 152 | 32107 / 175 153 | 32108 / 175 154 | 32109 / 175 155 | 32110 / 175 156 | 32111 / 175 157 |
| 7− | 32112 / 175 160 | 32113 / 175 161 | 32114 / 175 162 | 32115 / 175 163 | 32116 / 175 164 | 32117 / 175 165 | 32118 / 175 166 | 32119 / 175 167 | 32120 / 175 170 | 32121 / 175 171 | 32122 / 175 172 | 32123 / 175 173 | 32124 / 175 174 | 32125 / 175 175 | 32126 / 175 176 | 32127 / 175 177 |
| 8− | 32128 / 175 200 | 32129 / 175 201 | 32130 / 175 202 | 32131 / 175 203 | 32132 / 175 204 | 32133 / 175 205 | 32134 / 175 206 | 32135 / 175 207 | 32136 / 175 210 | 32137 / 175 211 | 32138 / 175 212 | 32139 / 175 213 | 32140 / 175 214 | 32141 / 175 215 | 32142 / 175 216 | 32143 / 175 217 |
| 9− | 32144 / 175 220 | 32145 / 175 221 | 32146 / 175 222 | 32147 / 175 223 | 32148 / 175 224 | 32149 / 175 225 | 32150 / 175 226 | 32151 / 175 227 | 32152 / 175 230 | 32153 / 175 231 | 32154 / 175 232 | 32155 / 175 233 | 32156 / 175 234 | 32157 / 175 235 | 32158 / 175 236 | 32159 / 175 237 |
| A− | 32160 / 175 240 | 32161 / 175 241 | 32162 / 175 242 | 32163 / 175 243 | 32164 / 175 244 | 32165 / 175 245 | 32166 / 175 246 | 32167 / 175 247 | 32168 / 175 250 | 32169 / 175 251 | 32170 / 175 252 | 32171 / 175 253 | 32172 / 175 254 | 32173 / 175 255 | 32174 / 175 256 | 32175 / 175 257 |
| B− | 32176 / 175 260 | 32177 / 175 261 | 32178 / 175 262 | 32179 / 175 263 | 32180 / 175 264 | 32181 / 175 265 | 32182 / 175 266 | 32183 / 175 267 | 32184 / 175 270 | 32185 / 175 271 | 32186 / 175 272 | 32187 / 175 273 | 32188 / 175 274 | 32189 / 175 275 | 32190 / 175 276 | 32191 / 175 277 |
| C− | 32192 / 175 300 | 32193 / 175 301 | 32194 / 175 302 | 32195 / 175 303 | 32196 / 175 304 | 32197 / 175 305 | 32198 / 175 306 | 32199 / 175 307 | 32200 / 175 310 | 32201 / 175 311 | 32202 / 175 312 | 32203 / 175 313 | 32204 / 175 314 | 32205 / 175 315 | 32206 / 175 316 | 32207 / 175 317 |
| D− | 32208 / 175 320 | 32209 / 175 321 | 32210 / 175 322 | 32211 / 175 323 | 32212 / 175 324 | 32213 / 175 325 | 32214 / 175 326 | 32215 / 175 327 | 32216 / 175 330 | 32217 / 175 331 | 32218 / 175 332 | 32219 / 175 333 | 32220 / 175 334 | 32221 / 175 335 | 32222 / 175 336 | 32223 / 175 337 |
| E− | 32224 / 175 340 | 32225 / 175 341 | 32226 / 175 342 | 32227 / 175 343 | 32228 / 175 344 | 32229 / 175 345 | 32230 / 175 346 | 32231 / 175 347 | 32232 / 175 350 | 32233 / 175 351 | 32234 / 175 352 | 32235 / 175 353 | 32236 / 175 354 | 32237 / 175 355 | 32238 / 175 356 | 32239 / 175 357 |
| F− | 32240 / 175 360 | 32241 / 175 361 | 32242 / 175 362 | 32243 / 175 363 | 32244 / 175 364 | 32245 / 175 365 | 32246 / 175 366 | 32247 / 175 367 | 32248 / 175 370 | 32249 / 175 371 | 32250 / 175 372 | 32251 / 175 373 | 32252 / 175 374 | 32253 / 175 375 | 32254 / 175 376 | 32255 / 175 377 |

## FIRST HEX DIGIT

| SECOND HEX DIGIT | −0 | −1 | −2 | −3 | −4 | −5 | −6 | −7 | −8 | −9 | −A | −B | −C | −D | −E | −F |
|---|---|---|---|---|---|---|---|---|---|---|---|---|---|---|---|---|
| 0− | 32256<br>32256<br>176 000 | 32257<br>32257<br>176 001 | 32258<br>32258<br>176 002 | 32259<br>32259<br>176 003 | 32260<br>32260<br>176 004 | 32261<br>32261<br>176 005 | 32262<br>32262<br>176 006 | 32263<br>32263<br>176 007 | 32264<br>32264<br>176 010 | 32265<br>32265<br>176 011 | 32266<br>32266<br>176 012 | 32267<br>32267<br>176 013 | 32268<br>32268<br>176 014 | 32269<br>32269<br>176 015 | 32270<br>32270<br>176 016 | 32271<br>32271<br>176 017 |
| 1− | 32272<br>32272<br>176 020 | 32273<br>32273<br>176 021 | 32274<br>32274<br>176 022 | 32275<br>32275<br>176 023 | 32276<br>32276<br>176 024 | 32277<br>32277<br>176 025 | 32278<br>32278<br>176 026 | 32279<br>32279<br>176 027 | 32280<br>32280<br>176 030 | 32281<br>32281<br>176 031 | 32282<br>32282<br>176 032 | 32283<br>32283<br>176 033 | 32284<br>32284<br>176 034 | 32285<br>32285<br>176 035 | 32286<br>32286<br>176 036 | 32287<br>32287<br>176 037 |
| 2− | 32288<br>32288<br>176 040 | 32289<br>32289<br>176 041 | 32290<br>32290<br>176 042 | 32291<br>32291<br>176 043 | 32292<br>32292<br>176 044 | 32293<br>32293<br>176 045 | 32294<br>32294<br>176 046 | 32295<br>32295<br>176 047 | 32296<br>32296<br>176 050 | 32297<br>32297<br>176 051 | 32298<br>32298<br>176 052 | 32299<br>32299<br>176 053 | 32300<br>32300<br>176 054 | 32301<br>32301<br>176 055 | 32302<br>32302<br>176 056 | 32303<br>32303<br>176 057 |
| 3− | 32304<br>32304<br>176 060 | 32305<br>32305<br>176 061 | 32306<br>32306<br>176 062 | 32307<br>32307<br>176 063 | 32308<br>32308<br>176 064 | 32309<br>32309<br>176 065 | 32310<br>32310<br>176 066 | 32311<br>32311<br>176 067 | 32312<br>32312<br>176 070 | 32313<br>32313<br>176 071 | 32314<br>32314<br>176 072 | 32315<br>32315<br>176 073 | 32316<br>32316<br>176 074 | 32317<br>32317<br>176 075 | 32318<br>32318<br>176 076 | 32319<br>32319<br>176 077 |
| 4− | 32320<br>32320<br>176 100 | 32321<br>32321<br>176 101 | 32322<br>32322<br>176 102 | 32323<br>32323<br>176 103 | 32324<br>32324<br>176 104 | 32325<br>32325<br>176 105 | 32326<br>32326<br>176 106 | 32327<br>32327<br>176 107 | 32328<br>32328<br>176 110 | 32329<br>32329<br>176 111 | 32330<br>32330<br>176 112 | 32331<br>32331<br>176 113 | 32332<br>32332<br>176 114 | 32333<br>32333<br>176 115 | 32334<br>32334<br>176 116 | 32335<br>32335<br>176 117 |
| 5− | 32336<br>32336<br>176 120 | 32337<br>32337<br>176 121 | 32338<br>32338<br>176 122 | 32339<br>32339<br>176 123 | 32340<br>32340<br>176 124 | 32341<br>32341<br>176 125 | 32342<br>32342<br>176 126 | 32343<br>32343<br>176 127 | 32344<br>32344<br>176 130 | 32345<br>32345<br>176 131 | 32346<br>32346<br>176 132 | 32347<br>32347<br>176 133 | 32348<br>32348<br>176 134 | 32349<br>32349<br>176 135 | 32350<br>32350<br>176 136 | 32351<br>32351<br>176 137 |
| 6− | 32352<br>32352<br>176 140 | 32353<br>32353<br>176 141 | 32354<br>32354<br>176 142 | 32355<br>32355<br>176 143 | 32356<br>32356<br>176 144 | 32357<br>32357<br>176 145 | 32358<br>32358<br>176 146 | 32359<br>32359<br>176 147 | 32360<br>32360<br>176 150 | 32361<br>32361<br>176 151 | 32362<br>32362<br>176 152 | 32363<br>32363<br>176 153 | 32364<br>32364<br>176 154 | 32365<br>32365<br>176 155 | 32366<br>32366<br>176 156 | 32367<br>32367<br>176 157 |
| 7− | 32368<br>32368<br>176 160 | 32369<br>32369<br>176 161 | 32370<br>32370<br>176 162 | 32371<br>32371<br>176 163 | 32372<br>32372<br>176 164 | 32373<br>32373<br>176 165 | 32374<br>32374<br>176 166 | 32375<br>32375<br>176 167 | 32376<br>32376<br>176 170 | 32377<br>32377<br>176 171 | 32378<br>32378<br>176 172 | 32379<br>32379<br>176 173 | 32380<br>32380<br>176 174 | 32381<br>32381<br>176 175 | 32382<br>32382<br>176 176 | 32383<br>32383<br>176 177 |
| 8− | 32384<br>32384<br>176 200 | 32385<br>32385<br>176 201 | 32386<br>32386<br>176 202 | 32387<br>32387<br>176 203 | 32388<br>32388<br>176 204 | 32389<br>32389<br>176 205 | 32390<br>32390<br>176 206 | 32391<br>32391<br>176 207 | 32392<br>32392<br>176 210 | 32393<br>32393<br>176 211 | 32394<br>32394<br>176 212 | 32395<br>32395<br>176 213 | 32396<br>32396<br>176 214 | 32397<br>32397<br>176 215 | 32398<br>32398<br>176 216 | 32399<br>32399<br>176 217 |
| 9− | 32400<br>32400<br>176 220 | 32401<br>32401<br>176 221 | 32402<br>32402<br>176 222 | 32403<br>32403<br>176 223 | 32404<br>32404<br>176 224 | 32405<br>32405<br>176 225 | 32406<br>32406<br>176 226 | 32407<br>32407<br>176 227 | 32408<br>32408<br>176 230 | 32409<br>32409<br>176 231 | 32410<br>32410<br>176 232 | 32411<br>32411<br>176 233 | 32412<br>32412<br>176 234 | 32413<br>32413<br>176 235 | 32414<br>32414<br>176 236 | 32415<br>32415<br>176 237 |
| A− | 32416<br>32416<br>176 240 | 32417<br>32417<br>176 241 | 32418<br>32418<br>176 242 | 32419<br>32419<br>176 243 | 32420<br>32420<br>176 244 | 32421<br>32421<br>176 245 | 32422<br>32422<br>176 246 | 32423<br>32423<br>176 247 | 32424<br>32424<br>176 250 | 32425<br>32425<br>176 251 | 32426<br>32426<br>176 252 | 32427<br>32427<br>176 253 | 32428<br>32428<br>176 254 | 32429<br>32429<br>176 255 | 32430<br>32430<br>176 256 | 32431<br>32431<br>176 257 |
| B− | 32432<br>32432<br>176 260 | 32433<br>32433<br>176 261 | 32434<br>32434<br>176 262 | 32435<br>32435<br>176 263 | 32436<br>32436<br>176 264 | 32437<br>32437<br>176 265 | 32438<br>32438<br>176 266 | 32439<br>32439<br>176 267 | 32440<br>32440<br>176 270 | 32441<br>32441<br>176 271 | 32442<br>32442<br>176 272 | 32443<br>32443<br>176 273 | 32444<br>32444<br>176 274 | 32445<br>32445<br>176 275 | 32446<br>32446<br>176 276 | 32447<br>32447<br>176 277 |
| C− | 32448<br>32448<br>176 300 | 32449<br>32449<br>176 301 | 32450<br>32450<br>176 302 | 32451<br>32451<br>176 303 | 32452<br>32452<br>176 304 | 32453<br>32453<br>176 305 | 32454<br>32454<br>176 306 | 32455<br>32455<br>176 307 | 32456<br>32456<br>176 310 | 32457<br>32457<br>176 311 | 32458<br>32458<br>176 312 | 32459<br>32459<br>176 313 | 32460<br>32460<br>176 314 | 32461<br>32461<br>176 315 | 32462<br>32462<br>176 316 | 32463<br>32463<br>176 317 |
| D− | 32464<br>32464<br>176 320 | 32465<br>32465<br>176 321 | 32466<br>32466<br>176 322 | 32467<br>32467<br>176 323 | 32468<br>32468<br>176 324 | 32469<br>32469<br>176 325 | 32470<br>32470<br>176 326 | 3247́1<br>32471<br>176 327 | 32472<br>32472<br>176 330 | 32473<br>32473<br>176 331 | 32474<br>32474<br>176 332 | 32475<br>32475<br>176 333 | 32476<br>32476<br>176 334 | 32477<br>32477<br>176 335 | 32478<br>32478<br>176 336 | 32479<br>32479<br>176 337 |
| E− | 32480<br>32480<br>176 340 | 32481<br>32481<br>176 341 | 32482<br>32482<br>176 342 | 32483<br>32483<br>176 343 | 32484<br>32484<br>176 344 | 32485<br>32485<br>176 345 | 32486<br>32486<br>176 346 | 32487<br>32487<br>176 347 | 32488<br>32488<br>176 350 | 32489<br>32489<br>176 351 | 32490<br>32490<br>176 352 | 32491<br>32491<br>176 353 | 32492<br>32492<br>176 354 | 32493<br>32493<br>176 355 | 32494<br>32494<br>176 356 | 32495<br>32495<br>176 357 |
| F− | 32496<br>32496<br>176 360 | 32497<br>32497<br>176 361 | 32498<br>32498<br>176 362 | 32499<br>32499<br>176 363 | 32500<br>32500<br>176 364 | 32501<br>32501<br>176 365 | 32502<br>32502<br>176 366 | 32503<br>32503<br>176 367 | 32504<br>32504<br>176 370 | 32505<br>32505<br>176 371 | 32506<br>32506<br>176 372 | 32507<br>32507<br>176 373 | 32508<br>32508<br>176 374 | 32509<br>32509<br>176 375 | 32510<br>32510<br>176 376 | 32511<br>32511<br>176 377 |

DECIMAL ⟵

⍟ DECIMAL ⟵

OCTAL ⟵

⍟ DECIMAL [ 32256 ]   BINARY [ 0111 1110 ]   DECIMAL [ 32256 ]   HEXADECIMAL ⟨7E⟩ OCTAL [ 176 000 ]

FOURTH HEX DIGIT ⟶   ⟵ THIRD HEX DIGIT

# ⌘ DECIMAL `32512`  BINARY `0111 1111`  DECIMAL `32512`  HEXADECIMAL `7F`  OCTAL `177 000`

FOURTH HEX DIGIT → 7F ← THIRD HEX DIGIT

**② FIRST HEX DIGIT**

DECIMAL / DECIMAL / OCTAL →

| SECOND HEX DIGIT | −0 | −1 | −2 | −3 | −4 | −5 | −6 | −7 | −8 | −9 | −A | −B | −C | −D | −E | −F |
|---|---|---|---|---|---|---|---|---|---|---|---|---|---|---|---|---|
| 0− | 32512<br>32512<br>177 000 | 32513<br>32513<br>177 001 | 32514<br>32514<br>177 002 | 32515<br>32515<br>177 003 | 32516<br>32516<br>177 004 | 32517<br>32517<br>177 005 | 32518<br>32518<br>177 006 | 32519<br>32519<br>177 007 | 32520<br>32520<br>177 010 | 32521<br>32521<br>177 011 | 32522<br>32522<br>177 012 | 32523<br>32523<br>177 013 | 32524<br>32524<br>177 014 | 32525<br>32525<br>177 015 | 32526<br>32526<br>177 016 | 32527<br>32527<br>177 017 |
| 1− | 32528<br>32528<br>177 020 | 32529<br>32529<br>177 021 | 32530<br>32530<br>177 022 | 32531<br>32531<br>177 023 | 32532<br>32532<br>177 024 | 32533<br>32533<br>177 025 | 32534<br>32534<br>177 026 | 32535<br>32535<br>177 027 | 32536<br>32536<br>177 030 | 32537<br>32537<br>177 031 | 32538<br>32538<br>177 032 | 32539<br>32539<br>177 033 | 32540<br>32540<br>177 034 | 32541<br>32541<br>177 035 | 32542<br>32542<br>177 036 | 32543<br>32543<br>177 037 |
| 2− | 32544<br>32544<br>177 040 | 32545<br>32545<br>177 041 | 32546<br>32546<br>177 042 | 32547<br>32547<br>177 043 | 32548<br>32548<br>177 044 | 32549<br>32549<br>177 045 | 32550<br>32550<br>177 046 | 32551<br>32551<br>177 047 | 32552<br>32552<br>177 050 | 32553<br>32553<br>177 051 | 32554<br>32554<br>177 052 | 32555<br>32555<br>177 053 | 32556<br>32556<br>177 054 | 32557<br>32557<br>177 055 | 32558<br>32558<br>177 056 | 32559<br>32559<br>177 057 |
| 3− | 32560<br>32560<br>177 060 | 32561<br>32561<br>177 061 | 32562<br>32562<br>177 062 | 32563<br>32563<br>177 063 | 32564<br>32564<br>177 064 | 32565<br>32565<br>177 065 | 32566<br>32566<br>177 066 | 32567<br>32567<br>177 067 | 32568<br>32568<br>177 070 | 32569<br>32569<br>177 071 | 32570<br>32570<br>177 072 | 32571<br>32571<br>177 073 | 32572<br>32572<br>177 074 | 32573<br>32573<br>177 075 | 32574<br>32574<br>177 076 | 32575<br>32575<br>177 077 |
| 4− | 32576<br>32576<br>177 100 | 32577<br>32577<br>177 101 | 32578<br>32578<br>177 102 | 32579<br>32579<br>177 103 | 32580<br>32580<br>177 104 | 32581<br>32581<br>177 105 | 32582<br>32582<br>177 106 | 32583<br>32583<br>177 107 | 32584<br>32584<br>177 110 | 32585<br>32585<br>177 111 | 32586<br>32586<br>177 112 | 32587<br>32587<br>177 113 | 32588<br>32588<br>177 114 | 32589<br>32589<br>177 115 | 32590<br>32590<br>177 116 | 32591<br>32591<br>177 117 |
| 5− | 32592<br>32592<br>177 120 | 32593<br>32593<br>177 121 | 32594<br>32594<br>177 122 | 32595<br>32595<br>177 123 | 32596<br>32596<br>177 124 | 32597<br>32597<br>177 125 | 32598<br>32598<br>177 126 | 32599<br>32599<br>177 127 | 32600<br>32600<br>177 130 | 32601<br>32601<br>177 131 | 32602<br>32602<br>177 132 | 32603<br>32603<br>177 133 | 32604<br>32604<br>177 134 | 32605<br>32605<br>177 135 | 32606<br>32606<br>177 136 | 32607<br>32607<br>177 137 |
| 6− | 32608<br>32608<br>177 140 | 32609<br>32609<br>177 141 | 32610<br>32610<br>177 142 | 32611<br>32611<br>177 143 | 32612<br>32612<br>177 144 | 32613<br>32613<br>177 145 | 32614<br>32614<br>177 146 | 32615<br>32615<br>177 147 | 32616<br>32616<br>177 150 | 32617<br>32617<br>177 151 | 32618<br>32618<br>177 152 | 32619<br>32619<br>177 153 | 32620<br>32620<br>177 154 | 32621<br>32621<br>177 155 | 32622<br>32622<br>177 156 | 32623<br>32623<br>177 157 |
| 7− | 32624<br>32624<br>177 160 | 32625<br>32625<br>177 161 | 32626<br>32626<br>177 162 | 32627<br>32627<br>177 163 | 32628<br>32628<br>177 164 | 32629<br>32629<br>177 165 | 32630<br>32630<br>177 166 | 32631<br>32631<br>177 167 | 32632<br>32632<br>177 170 | 32633<br>32633<br>177 171 | 32634<br>32634<br>177 172 | 32635<br>32635<br>177 173 | 32636<br>32636<br>177 174 | 32637<br>32637<br>177 175 | 32638<br>32638<br>177 176 | 32639<br>32639<br>177 177 |
| 8− | 32640<br>32640<br>177 200 | 32641<br>32641<br>177 201 | 32642<br>32642<br>177 202 | 32643<br>32643<br>177 203 | 32644<br>32644<br>177 204 | 32645<br>32645<br>177 205 | 32646<br>32646<br>177 206 | 32647<br>32647<br>177 207 | 32648<br>32648<br>177 210 | 32649<br>32649<br>177 211 | 32650<br>32650<br>177 212 | 32651<br>32651<br>177 213 | 32652<br>32652<br>177 214 | 32653<br>32653<br>177 215 | 32654<br>32654<br>177 216 | 32655<br>32655<br>177 217 |
| 9− | 32656<br>32656<br>177 220 | 32657<br>32657<br>177 221 | 32658<br>32658<br>177 222 | 32659<br>32659<br>177 223 | 32660<br>32660<br>177 224 | 32661<br>32661<br>177 225 | 32662<br>32662<br>177 226 | 32663<br>32663<br>177 227 | 32664<br>32664<br>177 230 | 32665<br>32665<br>177 231 | 32666<br>32666<br>177 232 | 32667<br>32667<br>177 233 | 32668<br>32668<br>177 234 | 32669<br>32669<br>177 235 | 32670<br>32670<br>177 236 | 32671<br>32671<br>177 237 |
| A− | 32672<br>32672<br>177 240 | 32673<br>32673<br>177 241 | 32674<br>32674<br>177 242 | 32675<br>32675<br>177 243 | 32676<br>32676<br>177 244 | 32677<br>32677<br>177 245 | 32678<br>32678<br>177 246 | 32679<br>32679<br>177 247 | 32680<br>32680<br>177 250 | 32681<br>32681<br>177 251 | 32682<br>32682<br>177 252 | 32683<br>32683<br>177 253 | 32684<br>32684<br>177 254 | 32685<br>32685<br>177 255 | 32686<br>32686<br>177 256 | 32687<br>32687<br>177 257 |
| B− | 32688<br>32688<br>177 260 | 32689<br>32689<br>177 261 | 32690<br>32690<br>177 262 | 32691<br>32691<br>177 263 | 32692<br>32692<br>177 264 | 32693<br>32693<br>177 265 | 32694<br>32694<br>177 266 | 32695<br>32695<br>177 267 | 32696<br>32696<br>177 270 | 32697<br>32697<br>177 271 | 32698<br>32698<br>177 272 | 32699<br>32699<br>177 273 | 32700<br>32700<br>177 274 | 32701<br>32701<br>177 275 | 32702<br>32702<br>177 276 | 32703<br>32703<br>177 277 |
| C− | 32704<br>32704<br>177 300 | 32705<br>32705<br>177 301 | 32706<br>32706<br>177 302 | 32707<br>32707<br>177 303 | 32708<br>32708<br>177 304 | 32709<br>32709<br>177 305 | 32710<br>32710<br>177 306 | 32711<br>32711<br>177 307 | 32712<br>32712<br>177 310 | 32713<br>32713<br>177 311 | 32714<br>32714<br>177 312 | 32715<br>32715<br>177 313 | 32716<br>32716<br>177 314 | 32717<br>32717<br>177 315 | 32718<br>32718<br>177 316 | 32719<br>32719<br>177 317 |
| D− | 32720<br>32720<br>177 320 | 32721<br>32721<br>177 321 | 32722<br>32722<br>177 322 | 32723<br>32723<br>177 323 | 32724<br>32724<br>177 324 | 32725<br>32725<br>177 325 | 32726<br>32726<br>177 326 | 32727<br>32727<br>177 327 | 32728<br>32728<br>177 330 | 32729<br>32729<br>177 331 | 32730<br>32730<br>177 332 | 32731<br>32731<br>177 333 | 32732<br>32732<br>177 334 | 32733<br>32733<br>177 335 | 32734<br>32734<br>177 336 | 32735<br>32735<br>177 337 |
| E− | 32736<br>32736<br>177 340 | 32737<br>32737<br>177 341 | 32738<br>32738<br>177 342 | 32739<br>32739<br>177 343 | 32740<br>32740<br>177 344 | 32741<br>32741<br>177 345 | 32742<br>32742<br>177 346 | 32743<br>32743<br>177 347 | 32744<br>32744<br>177 350 | 32745<br>32745<br>177 351 | 32746<br>32746<br>177 352 | 32747<br>32747<br>177 353 | 32748<br>32748<br>177 354 | 32749<br>32749<br>177 355 | 32750<br>32750<br>177 356 | 32751<br>32751<br>177 357 |
| F− | 32752<br>32752<br>177 360 | 32753<br>32753<br>177 361 | 32754<br>32754<br>177 362 | 32755<br>32755<br>177 363 | 32756<br>32756<br>177 364 | 32757<br>32757<br>177 365 | 32758<br>32758<br>177 366 | 32759<br>32759<br>177 367 | 32760<br>32760<br>177 370 | 32761<br>32761<br>177 371 | 32762<br>32762<br>177 372 | 32763<br>32763<br>177 373 | 32764<br>32764<br>177 374 | 32765<br>32765<br>177 375 | 32766<br>32766<br>177 376 | 32767<br>32767<br>177 377 |

DECIMAL → (row 1)  
⌘ DECIMAL → (row 4)  
OCTAL → (row 8)

| SECOND HEX DIGIT | −0 | −1 | −2 | −3 | −4 | −5 | −6 | −7 | −8 | −9 | −A | −B | −C | −D | −E | −F |
|---|---|---|---|---|---|---|---|---|---|---|---|---|---|---|---|---|
| **0-** | 32768<br>-32768<br>200 000 | 32769<br>-32767<br>200 001 | 32770<br>-32766<br>200 002 | 32771<br>-32765<br>200 003 | 32772<br>-32764<br>200 004 | 32773<br>-32763<br>200 005 | 32774<br>-32762<br>200 006 | 32775<br>-32761<br>200 007 | 32776<br>-32760<br>200 010 | 32777<br>-32759<br>200 011 | 32778<br>-32758<br>200 012 | 32779<br>-32757<br>200 013 | 32780<br>-32756<br>200 014 | 32781<br>-32755<br>200 015 | 32782<br>-32754<br>200 016 | 32783<br>-32753<br>200 017 |
| **1-** | 32784<br>-32752<br>200 020 | 32785<br>-32751<br>200 021 | 32786<br>-32750<br>200 022 | 32787<br>-32749<br>200 023 | 32788<br>-32748<br>200 024 | 32789<br>-32747<br>200 025 | 32790<br>-32746<br>200 026 | 32791<br>-32745<br>200 027 | 32792<br>-32744<br>200 030 | 32793<br>-32743<br>200 031 | 32794<br>-32742<br>200 032 | 32795<br>-32741<br>200 033 | 32796<br>-32740<br>200 034 | 32797<br>-32739<br>200 035 | 32798<br>-32738<br>200 036 | 32799<br>-32737<br>200 037 |
| **2-** | 32800<br>-32736<br>200 040 | 32801<br>-32735<br>200 041 | 32802<br>-32734<br>200 042 | 32803<br>-32733<br>200 043 | 32804<br>-32732<br>200 044 | 32805<br>-32731<br>200 045 | 32806<br>-32730<br>200 046 | 32807<br>-32729<br>200 047 | 32808<br>-32728<br>200 050 | 32809<br>-32727<br>200 051 | 32810<br>-32726<br>200 052 | 32811<br>-32725<br>200 053 | 32812<br>-32724<br>200 054 | 32813<br>-32723<br>200 055 | 32814<br>-32722<br>200 056 | 32815<br>-32721<br>200 057 |
| **3-** | 32816<br>-32720<br>200 060 | 32817<br>-32719<br>200 061 | 32818<br>-32718<br>200 062 | 32819<br>-32717<br>200 063 | 32820<br>-32716<br>200 064 | 32821<br>-32715<br>200 065 | 32822<br>-32714<br>200 066 | 32823<br>-32713<br>200 067 | 32824<br>-32712<br>200 070 | 32825<br>-32711<br>200 071 | 32826<br>-32710<br>200 072 | 32827<br>-32709<br>200 073 | 32828<br>-32708<br>200 074 | 32829<br>-32707<br>200 075 | 32830<br>-32706<br>200 076 | 32831<br>-32705<br>200 077 |
| **4-** | 32832<br>-32704<br>200 100 | 32833<br>-32703<br>200 101 | 32834<br>-32702<br>200 102 | 32835<br>-32701<br>200 103 | 32836<br>-32700<br>200 104 | 32837<br>-32699<br>200 105 | 32838<br>-32698<br>200 106 | 32839<br>-32697<br>200 107 | 32840<br>-32696<br>200 110 | 32841<br>-32695<br>200 111 | 32842<br>-32694<br>200 112 | 32843<br>-32693<br>200 113 | 32844<br>-32692<br>200 114 | 32845<br>-32691<br>200 115 | 32846<br>-32690<br>200 116 | 32847<br>-32689<br>200 117 |
| **5-** | 32848<br>-32688<br>200 120 | 32849<br>-32687<br>200 121 | 32850<br>-32686<br>200 122 | 32851<br>-32685<br>200 123 | 32852<br>-32684<br>200 124 | 32853<br>-32683<br>200 125 | 32854<br>-32682<br>200 126 | 32855<br>-32681<br>200 127 | 32856<br>-32680<br>200 130 | 32857<br>-32679<br>200 131 | 32858<br>-32678<br>200 132 | 32859<br>-32677<br>200 133 | 32860<br>-32676<br>200 134 | 32861<br>-32675<br>200 135 | 32862<br>-32674<br>200 136 | 32863<br>-32673<br>200 137 |
| **6-** | 32864<br>-32672<br>200 140 | 32865<br>-32671<br>200 141 | 32866<br>-32670<br>200 142 | 32867<br>-32669<br>200 143 | 32868<br>-32668<br>200 144 | 32869<br>-32667<br>200 145 | 32870<br>-32666<br>200 146 | 32871<br>-32665<br>200 147 | 32872<br>-32664<br>200 150 | 32873<br>-32663<br>200 151 | 32874<br>-32662<br>200 152 | 32875<br>-32661<br>200 153 | 32876<br>-32660<br>200 154 | 32877<br>-32659<br>200 155 | 32878<br>-32658<br>200 156 | 32879<br>-32657<br>200 157 |
| **7-** | 32880<br>-32656<br>200 160 | 32881<br>-32655<br>200 161 | 32882<br>-32654<br>200 162 | 32883<br>-32653<br>200 163 | 32884<br>-32652<br>200 164 | 32885<br>-32651<br>200 165 | 32886<br>-32650<br>200 166 | 32887<br>-32649<br>200 167 | 32888<br>-32648<br>200 170 | 32889<br>-32647<br>200 171 | 32890<br>-32646<br>200 172 | 32891<br>-32645<br>200 173 | 32892<br>-32644<br>200 174 | 32893<br>-32643<br>200 175 | 32894<br>-32642<br>200 176 | 32895<br>-32641<br>200 177 |
| **8-** | 32896<br>-32640<br>200 200 | 32897<br>-32639<br>200 201 | 32898<br>-32638<br>200 202 | 32899<br>-32637<br>200 203 | 32900<br>-32636<br>200 204 | 32901<br>-32635<br>200 205 | 32902<br>-32634<br>200 206 | 32903<br>-32633<br>200 207 | 32904<br>-32632<br>200 210 | 32905<br>-32631<br>200 211 | 32906<br>-32630<br>200 212 | 32907<br>-32629<br>200 213 | 32908<br>-32628<br>200 214 | 32909<br>-32627<br>200 215 | 32910<br>-32626<br>200 216 | 32911<br>-32625<br>200 217 |
| **9-** | 32912<br>-32624<br>200 220 | 32913<br>-32623<br>200 221 | 32914<br>-32622<br>200 222 | 32915<br>-32621<br>200 223 | 32916<br>-32620<br>200 224 | 32917<br>-32619<br>200 225 | 32918<br>-32618<br>200 226 | 32919<br>-32617<br>200 227 | 32920<br>-32616<br>200 230 | 32921<br>-32615<br>200 231 | 32922<br>-32614<br>200 232 | 32923<br>-32613<br>200 233 | 32924<br>-32612<br>200 234 | 32925<br>-32611<br>200 235 | 32926<br>-32610<br>200 236 | 32927<br>-32609<br>200 237 |
| **A-** | 32928<br>-32608<br>200 240 | 32929<br>-32607<br>200 241 | 32930<br>-32606<br>200 242 | 32931<br>-32605<br>200 243 | 32932<br>-32604<br>200 244 | 32933<br>-32603<br>200 245 | 32934<br>-32602<br>200 246 | 32935<br>-32601<br>200 247 | 32936<br>-32600<br>200 250 | 32937<br>-32599<br>200 251 | 32938<br>-32598<br>200 252 | 32939<br>-32597<br>200 253 | 32940<br>-32596<br>200 254 | 32941<br>-32595<br>200 255 | 32942<br>-32594<br>200 256 | 32943<br>-32593<br>200 257 |
| **B-** | 32944<br>-32592<br>200 260 | 32945<br>-32591<br>200 261 | 32946<br>-32590<br>200 262 | 32947<br>-32589<br>200 263 | 32948<br>-32588<br>200 264 | 32949<br>-32587<br>200 265 | 32950<br>-32586<br>200 266 | 32951<br>-32585<br>200 267 | 32952<br>-32584<br>200 270 | 32953<br>-32583<br>200 271 | 32954<br>-32582<br>200 272 | 32955<br>-32581<br>200 273 | 32956<br>-32580<br>200 274 | 32957<br>-32579<br>200 275 | 32958<br>-32578<br>200 276 | 32959<br>-32577<br>200 277 |
| **C-** | 32960<br>-32576<br>200 300 | 32961<br>-32575<br>200 301 | 32962<br>-32574<br>200 302 | 32963<br>-32573<br>200 303 | 32964<br>-32572<br>200 304 | 32965<br>-32571<br>200 305 | 32966<br>-32570<br>200 306 | 32967<br>-32569<br>200 307 | 32968<br>-32568<br>200 310 | 32969<br>-32567<br>200 311 | 32970<br>-32566<br>200 312 | 32971<br>-32565<br>200 313 | 32972<br>-32564<br>200 314 | 32973<br>-32563<br>200 315 | 32974<br>-32562<br>200 316 | 32975<br>-32561<br>200 317 |
| **D-** | 32976<br>-32560<br>200 320 | 32977<br>-32559<br>200 321 | 32978<br>-32558<br>200 322 | 32979<br>-32557<br>200 323 | 32980<br>-32556<br>200 324 | 32981<br>-32555<br>200 325 | 32982<br>-32554<br>200 326 | 32983<br>-32553<br>200 327 | 32984<br>-32552<br>200 330 | 32985<br>-32551<br>200 331 | 32986<br>-32550<br>200 332 | 32987<br>-32549<br>200 333 | 32988<br>-32548<br>200 334 | 32989<br>-32547<br>200 335 | 32990<br>-32546<br>200 336 | 32991<br>-32545<br>200 337 |
| **E-** | 32992<br>-32544<br>200 340 | 32993<br>-32543<br>200 341 | 32994<br>-32542<br>200 342 | 32995<br>-32541<br>200 343 | 32996<br>-32540<br>200 344 | 32997<br>-32539<br>200 345 | 32998<br>-32538<br>200 346 | 32999<br>-32537<br>200 347 | 33000<br>-32536<br>200 350 | 33001<br>-32535<br>200 351 | 33002<br>-32534<br>200 352 | 33003<br>-32533<br>200 353 | 33004<br>-32532<br>200 354 | 33005<br>-32531<br>200 355 | 33006<br>-32530<br>200 356 | 33007<br>-32529<br>200 357 |
| **F-** | 33008<br>-32528<br>200 360 | 33009<br>-32527<br>200 361 | 33010<br>-32526<br>200 362 | 33011<br>-32525<br>200 363 | 33012<br>-32524<br>200 364 | 33013<br>-32523<br>200 365 | 33014<br>-32522<br>200 366 | 33015<br>-32521<br>200 367 | 33016<br>-32520<br>200 370 | 33017<br>-32519<br>200 371 | 33018<br>-32518<br>200 372 | 33019<br>-32517<br>200 373 | 33020<br>-32516<br>200 374 | 33021<br>-32515<br>200 375 | 33022<br>-32514<br>200 376 | 33023<br>-32513<br>200 377 |

DECIMAL

 DECIMAL

OCTAL

 **DECIMAL** `-32768`  **BINARY** `1000 0000`  **DECIMAL** `32768`  **HEXADECIMAL** ⬡ 80  **OCTAL** `200 000`

FOURTH HEX DIGIT → ⬡ ← THIRD HEX DIGIT

**⌘ DECIMAL** | -32512    **BINARY** | 1000 0001    **DECIMAL** | 33024    **HEXADECIMAL** | 81    **OCTAL** | 201 000

FOURTH HEX DIGIT → ← THIRD HEX DIGIT

## FIRST HEX DIGIT

(2)

Each cell shows three values: decimal (positive) / decimal (negative) / octal.

| SECOND HEX DIGIT | -0 | -1 | -2 | -3 | -4 | -5 | -6 | -7 | -8 | -9 | -A | -B | -C | -D | -E | -F |
|---|---|---|---|---|---|---|---|---|---|---|---|---|---|---|---|---|
| 0- | 33024<br>-32512<br>201 000 | 33025<br>-32511<br>201 001 | 33026<br>-32510<br>201 002 | 33027<br>-32509<br>201 003 | 33028<br>-32508<br>201 004 | 33029<br>-32507<br>201 005 | 33030<br>-32506<br>201 006 | 33031<br>-32505<br>201 007 | 33032<br>-32504<br>201 010 | 33033<br>-32503<br>201 011 | 33034<br>-32502<br>201 012 | 33035<br>-32501<br>201 013 | 33036<br>-32500<br>201 014 | 33037<br>-32499<br>201 015 | 33038<br>-32498<br>201 016 | 33039<br>-32497<br>201 017 |
| 1- | 33040<br>-32496<br>201 020 | 33041<br>-32495<br>201 021 | 33042<br>-32494<br>201 022 | 33043<br>-32493<br>201 023 | 33044<br>-32492<br>201 024 | 33045<br>-32491<br>201 025 | 33046<br>-32490<br>201 026 | 33047<br>-32489<br>201 027 | 33048<br>-32488<br>201 030 | 33049<br>-32487<br>201 031 | 33050<br>-32486<br>201 032 | 33051<br>-32485<br>201 033 | 33052<br>-32484<br>201 034 | 33053<br>-32483<br>201 035 | 33054<br>-32482<br>201 036 | 33055<br>-32481<br>201 037 |
| 2- | 33056<br>-32480<br>201 040 | 33057<br>-32479<br>201 041 | 33058<br>-32478<br>201 042 | 33059<br>-32477<br>201 043 | 33060<br>-32476<br>201 044 | 33061<br>-32475<br>201 045 | 33062<br>-32474<br>201 046 | 33063<br>-32473<br>201 047 | 33064<br>-32472<br>201 050 | 33065<br>-32471<br>201 051 | 33066<br>-32470<br>201 052 | 33067<br>-32469<br>201 053 | 33068<br>-32468<br>201 054 | 33069<br>-32467<br>201 055 | 33070<br>-32466<br>201 056 | 33071<br>-32465<br>201 057 |
| 3- | 33072<br>-32464<br>201 060 | 33073<br>-32463<br>201 061 | 33074<br>-32462<br>201 062 | 33075<br>-32461<br>201 063 | 33076<br>-32460<br>201 064 | 33077<br>-32459<br>201 065 | 33078<br>-32458<br>201 066 | 33079<br>-32457<br>201 067 | 33080<br>-32456<br>201 070 | 33081<br>-32455<br>201 071 | 33082<br>-32454<br>201 072 | 33083<br>-32453<br>201 073 | 33084<br>-32452<br>201 074 | 33085<br>-32451<br>201 075 | 33086<br>-32450<br>201 076 | 33087<br>-32449<br>201 077 |
| 4- | 33088<br>-32448<br>201 100 | 33089<br>-32447<br>201 101 | 33090<br>-32446<br>201 102 | 33091<br>-32445<br>201 103 | 33092<br>-32444<br>201 104 | 33093<br>-32443<br>201 105 | 33094<br>-32442<br>201 106 | 33095<br>-32441<br>201 107 | 33096<br>-32440<br>201 110 | 33097<br>-32439<br>201 111 | 33098<br>-32438<br>201 112 | 33099<br>-32437<br>201 113 | 33100<br>-32436<br>201 114 | 33101<br>-32435<br>201 115 | 33102<br>-32434<br>201 116 | 33103<br>-32433<br>201 117 |
| 5- | 33104<br>-32432<br>201 120 | 33105<br>-32431<br>201 121 | 33106<br>-32430<br>201 122 | 33107<br>-32429<br>201 123 | 33108<br>-32428<br>201 124 | 33109<br>-32427<br>201 125 | 33110<br>-32426<br>201 126 | 33111<br>-32425<br>201 127 | 33112<br>-32424<br>201 130 | 33113<br>-32423<br>201 131 | 33114<br>-32422<br>201 132 | 33115<br>-32421<br>201 133 | 33116<br>-32420<br>201 134 | 33117<br>-32419<br>201 135 | 33118<br>-32418<br>201 136 | 33119<br>-32417<br>201 137 |
| 6- | 33120<br>-32416<br>201 140 | 33121<br>-32415<br>201 141 | 33122<br>-32414<br>201 142 | 33123<br>-32413<br>201 143 | 33124<br>-32412<br>201 144 | 33125<br>-32411<br>201 145 | 33126<br>-32410<br>201 146 | 33127<br>-32409<br>201 147 | 33128<br>-32408<br>201 150 | 33129<br>-32407<br>201 151 | 33130<br>-32406<br>201 152 | 33131<br>-32405<br>201 153 | 33132<br>-32404<br>201 154 | 33133<br>-32403<br>201 155 | 33134<br>-32402<br>201 156 | 33135<br>-32401<br>201 157 |
| 7- | 33136<br>-32400<br>201 160 | 33137<br>-32399<br>201 161 | 33138<br>-32398<br>201 162 | 33139<br>-32397<br>201 163 | 33140<br>-32396<br>201 164 | 33141<br>-32395<br>201 165 | 33142<br>-32394<br>201 166 | 33143<br>-32393<br>201 167 | 33144<br>-32392<br>201 170 | 33145<br>-32391<br>201 171 | 33146<br>-32390<br>201 172 | 33147<br>-32389<br>201 173 | 33148<br>-32388<br>201 174 | 33149<br>-32387<br>201 175 | 33150<br>-32386<br>201 176 | 33151<br>-32385<br>201 177 |
| 8- | 33152<br>-32384<br>201 200 | 33153<br>-32383<br>201 201 | 33154<br>-32382<br>201 202 | 33155<br>-32381<br>201 203 | 33156<br>-32380<br>201 204 | 33157<br>-32379<br>201 205 | 33158<br>-32378<br>201 206 | 33159<br>-32377<br>201 207 | 33160<br>-32376<br>201 210 | 33161<br>-32375<br>201 211 | 33162<br>-32374<br>201 212 | 33163<br>-32373<br>201 213 | 33164<br>-32372<br>201 214 | 33165<br>-32371<br>201 215 | 33166<br>-32370<br>201 216 | 33167<br>-32369<br>201 217 |
| 9- | 33168<br>-32368<br>201 220 | 33169<br>-32367<br>201 221 | 33170<br>-32366<br>201 222 | 33171<br>-32365<br>201 223 | 33172<br>-32364<br>201 224 | 33173<br>-32363<br>201 225 | 33174<br>-32362<br>201 226 | 33175<br>-32361<br>201 227 | 33176<br>-32360<br>201 230 | 33177<br>-32359<br>201 231 | 33178<br>-32358<br>201 232 | 33179<br>-32357<br>201 233 | 33180<br>-32356<br>201 234 | 33181<br>-32355<br>201 235 | 33182<br>-32354<br>201 236 | 33183<br>-32353<br>201 237 |
| A- | 33184<br>-32352<br>201 240 | 33185<br>-32351<br>201 241 | 33186<br>-32350<br>201 242 | 33187<br>-32349<br>201 243 | 33188<br>-32348<br>201 244 | 33189<br>-32347<br>201 245 | 33190<br>-32346<br>201 246 | 33191<br>-32345<br>201 247 | 33192<br>-32344<br>201 250 | 33193<br>-32343<br>201 251 | 33194<br>-32342<br>201 252 | 33195<br>-32341<br>201 253 | 33196<br>-32340<br>201 254 | 33197<br>-32339<br>201 255 | 33198<br>-32338<br>201 256 | 33199<br>-32337<br>201 257 |
| B- | 33200<br>-32336<br>201 260 | 33201<br>-32335<br>201 261 | 33202<br>-32334<br>201 262 | 33203<br>-32333<br>201 263 | 33204<br>-32332<br>201 264 | 33205<br>-32331<br>201 265 | 33206<br>-32330<br>201 266 | 33207<br>-32329<br>201 267 | 33208<br>-32328<br>201 270 | 33209<br>-32327<br>201 271 | 33210<br>-32326<br>201 272 | 33211<br>-32325<br>201 273 | 33212<br>-32324<br>201 274 | 33213<br>-32323<br>201 275 | 33214<br>-32322<br>201 276 | 33215<br>-32321<br>201 277 |
| C- | 33216<br>-32320<br>201 300 | 33217<br>-32319<br>201 301 | 33218<br>-32318<br>201 302 | 33219<br>-32317<br>201 303 | 33220<br>-32316<br>201 304 | 33221<br>-32315<br>201 305 | 33222<br>-32314<br>201 306 | 33223<br>-32313<br>201 307 | 33224<br>-32312<br>201 310 | 33225<br>-32311<br>201 311 | 33226<br>-32310<br>201 312 | 33227<br>-32309<br>201 313 | 33228<br>-32308<br>201 314 | 33229<br>-32307<br>201 315 | 33230<br>-32306<br>201 316 | 33231<br>-32305<br>201 317 |
| D- | 33232<br>-32304<br>201 320 | 33233<br>-32303<br>201 321 | 33234<br>-32302<br>201 322 | 33235<br>-32301<br>201 323 | 33236<br>-32300<br>201 324 | 33237<br>-32299<br>201 325 | 33238<br>-32298<br>201 326 | 33239<br>-32297<br>201 327 | 33240<br>-32296<br>201 330 | 33241<br>-32295<br>201 331 | 33242<br>-32294<br>201 332 | 33243<br>-32293<br>201 333 | 33244<br>-32292<br>201 334 | 33245<br>-32291<br>201 335 | 33246<br>-32290<br>201 336 | 33247<br>-32289<br>201 337 |
| E- | 33248<br>-32288<br>201 340 | 33249<br>-32287<br>201 341 | 33250<br>-32286<br>201 342 | 33251<br>-32285<br>201 343 | 33252<br>-32284<br>201 344 | 33253<br>-32283<br>201 345 | 33254<br>-32282<br>201 346 | 33255<br>-32281<br>201 347 | 33256<br>-32280<br>201 350 | 33257<br>-32279<br>201 351 | 33258<br>-32278<br>201 352 | 33259<br>-32277<br>201 353 | 33260<br>-32276<br>201 354 | 33261<br>-32275<br>201 355 | 33262<br>-32274<br>201 356 | 33263<br>-32273<br>201 357 |
| F- | 33264<br>-32272<br>201 360 | 33265<br>-32271<br>201 361 | 33266<br>-32270<br>201 362 | 33267<br>-32269<br>201 363 | 33268<br>-32268<br>201 364 | 33269<br>-32267<br>201 365 | 33270<br>-32266<br>201 366 | 33271<br>-32265<br>201 367 | 33272<br>-32264<br>201 370 | 33273<br>-32263<br>201 371 | 33274<br>-32262<br>201 372 | 33275<br>-32261<br>201 373 | 33276<br>-32260<br>201 374 | 33277<br>-32259<br>201 375 | 33278<br>-32258<br>201 376 | 33279<br>-32257<br>201 377 |

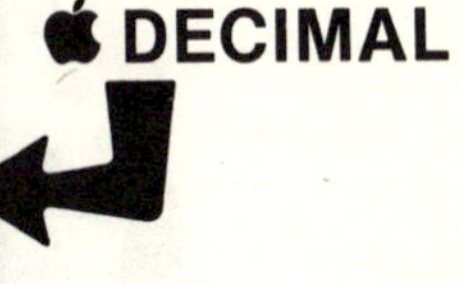

## FIRST HEX DIGIT

| SECOND HEX DIGIT | −0 | −1 | −2 | −3 | −4 | −5 | −6 | −7 | −8 | −9 | −A | −B | −C | −D | −E | −F |
|---|---|---|---|---|---|---|---|---|---|---|---|---|---|---|---|---|
| 0- | 33280<br>-32256<br>202 000 | 33281<br>-32255<br>202 001 | 33282<br>-32254<br>202 002 | 33283<br>-32253<br>202 003 | 33284<br>-32252<br>202 004 | 33285<br>-32251<br>202 005 | 33286<br>-32250<br>202 006 | 33287<br>-32249<br>202 007 | 33288<br>-32248<br>202 010 | 33289<br>-32247<br>202 011 | 33290<br>-32246<br>202 012 | 33291<br>-32245<br>202 013 | 33292<br>-32244<br>202 014 | 33293<br>-32243<br>202 015 | 33294<br>-32242<br>202 016 | 33295<br>-32241<br>202 017 |
| 1- | 33296<br>-32240<br>202 020 | 33297<br>-32239<br>202 021 | 33298<br>-32238<br>202 022 | 33299<br>-32237<br>202 023 | 33300<br>-32236<br>202 024 | 33301<br>-32235<br>202 025 | 33302<br>-32234<br>202 026 | 33303<br>-32233<br>202 027 | 33304<br>-32232<br>202 030 | 33305<br>-32231<br>202 031 | 33306<br>-32230<br>202 032 | 33307<br>-32229<br>202 033 | 33308<br>-32228<br>202 034 | 33309<br>-32227<br>202 035 | 33310<br>-32226<br>202 036 | 33311<br>-32225<br>202 037 |
| 2- | 33312<br>-32224<br>202 040 | 33313<br>-32223<br>202 041 | 33314<br>-32222<br>202 042 | 33315<br>-32221<br>202 043 | 33316<br>-32220<br>202 044 | 33317<br>-32219<br>202 045 | 33318<br>-32218<br>202 046 | 33319<br>-32217<br>202 047 | 33320<br>-32216<br>202 050 | 33321<br>-32215<br>202 051 | 33322<br>-32214<br>202 052 | 33323<br>-32213<br>202 053 | 33324<br>-32212<br>202 054 | 33325<br>-32211<br>202 055 | 33326<br>-32210<br>202 056 | 33327<br>-32209<br>202 057 |
| 3- | 33328<br>-32208<br>202 060 | 33329<br>-32207<br>202 061 | 33330<br>-32206<br>202 062 | 33331<br>-32205<br>202 063 | 33332<br>-32204<br>202 064 | 33333<br>-32203<br>202 065 | 33334<br>-32202<br>202 066 | 33335<br>-32201<br>202 067 | 33336<br>-32200<br>202 070 | 33337<br>-32199<br>202 071 | 33338<br>-32198<br>202 072 | 33339<br>-32197<br>202 073 | 33340<br>-32196<br>202 074 | 33341<br>-32195<br>202 075 | 33342<br>-32194<br>202 076 | 33343<br>-32193<br>202 077 |
| 4- | 33344<br>-32192<br>202 100 | 33345<br>-32191<br>202 101 | 33346<br>-32190<br>202 102 | 33347<br>-32189<br>202 103 | 33348<br>-32188<br>202 104 | 33349<br>-32187<br>202 105 | 33350<br>-32186<br>202 106 | 33351<br>-32185<br>202 107 | 33352<br>-32184<br>202 110 | 33353<br>-32183<br>202 111 | 33354<br>-32182<br>202 112 | 33355<br>-32181<br>202 113 | 33356<br>-32180<br>202 114 | 33357<br>-32179<br>202 115 | 33358<br>-32178<br>202 116 | 33359<br>-32177<br>202 117 |
| 5- | 33360<br>-32176<br>202 120 | 33361<br>-32175<br>202 121 | 33362<br>-32174<br>202 122 | 33363<br>-32173<br>202 123 | 33364<br>-32172<br>202 124 | 33365<br>-32171<br>202 125 | 33366<br>-32170<br>202 126 | 33367<br>-32169<br>202 127 | 33368<br>-32168<br>202 130 | 33369<br>-32167<br>202 131 | 33370<br>-32166<br>202 132 | 33371<br>-32165<br>202 133 | 33372<br>-32164<br>202 134 | 33373<br>-32163<br>202 135 | 33374<br>-32162<br>202 136 | 33375<br>-32161<br>202 137 |
| 6- | 33376<br>-32160<br>202 140 | 33377<br>-32159<br>202 141 | 33378<br>-32158<br>202 142 | 33379<br>-32157<br>202 143 | 33380<br>-32156<br>202 144 | 33381<br>-32155<br>202 145 | 33382<br>-32154<br>202 146 | 33383<br>-32153<br>202 147 | 33384<br>-32152<br>202 150 | 33385<br>-32151<br>202 151 | 33386<br>-32150<br>202 152 | 33387<br>-32149<br>202 153 | 33388<br>-32148<br>202 154 | 33389<br>-32147<br>202 155 | 33390<br>-32146<br>202 156 | 33391<br>-32145<br>202 157 |
| 7- | 33392<br>-32144<br>202 160 | 33393<br>-32143<br>202 161 | 33394<br>-32142<br>202 162 | 33395<br>-32141<br>202 163 | 33396<br>-32140<br>202 164 | 33397<br>-32139<br>202 165 | 33398<br>-32138<br>202 166 | 33399<br>-32137<br>202 167 | 33400<br>-32136<br>202 170 | 33401<br>-32135<br>202 171 | 33402<br>-32134<br>202 172 | 33403<br>-32133<br>202 173 | 33404<br>-32132<br>202 174 | 33405<br>-32131<br>202 175 | 33406<br>-32130<br>202 176 | 33407<br>-32129<br>202 177 |
| 8- | 33408<br>-32128<br>202 200 | 33409<br>-32127<br>202 201 | 33410<br>-32126<br>202 202 | 33411<br>-32125<br>202 203 | 33412<br>-32124<br>202 204 | 33413<br>-32123<br>202 205 | 33414<br>-32122<br>202 206 | 33415<br>-32121<br>202 207 | 33416<br>-32120<br>202 210 | 33417<br>-32119<br>202 211 | 33418<br>-32118<br>202 212 | 33419<br>-32117<br>202 213 | 33420<br>-32116<br>202 214 | 33421<br>-32115<br>202 215 | 33422<br>-32114<br>202 216 | 33423<br>-32113<br>202 217 |
| 9- | 33424<br>-32112<br>202 220 | 33425<br>-32111<br>202 221 | 33426<br>-32110<br>202 222 | 33427<br>-32109<br>202 223 | 33428<br>-32108<br>202 224 | 33429<br>-32107<br>202 225 | 33430<br>-32106<br>202 226 | 33431<br>-32105<br>202 227 | 33432<br>-32104<br>202 230 | 33433<br>-32103<br>202 231 | 33434<br>-32102<br>202 232 | 33435<br>-32101<br>202 233 | 33436<br>-32100<br>202 234 | 33437<br>-32099<br>202 235 | 33438<br>-32098<br>202 236 | 33439<br>-32097<br>202 237 |
| A- | 33440<br>-32096<br>202 240 | 33441<br>-32095<br>202 241 | 33442<br>-32094<br>202 242 | 33443<br>-32093<br>202 243 | 33444<br>-32092<br>202 244 | 33445<br>-32091<br>202 245 | 33446<br>-32090<br>202 246 | 33447<br>-32089<br>202 247 | 33448<br>-32088<br>202 250 | 33449<br>-32087<br>202 251 | 33450<br>-32086<br>202 252 | 33451<br>-32085<br>202 253 | 33452<br>-32084<br>202 254 | 33453<br>-32083<br>202 255 | 33454<br>-32082<br>202 256 | 33455<br>-32081<br>202 257 |
| B- | 33456<br>-32080<br>202 260 | 33457<br>-32079<br>202 261 | 33458<br>-32078<br>202 262 | 33459<br>-32077<br>202 263 | 33460<br>-32076<br>202 264 | 33461<br>-32075<br>202 265 | 33462<br>-32074<br>202 266 | 33463<br>-32073<br>202 267 | 33464<br>-32072<br>202 270 | 33465<br>-32071<br>202 271 | 33466<br>-32070<br>202 272 | 33467<br>-32069<br>202 273 | 33468<br>-32068<br>202 274 | 33469<br>-32067<br>202 275 | 33470<br>-32066<br>202 276 | 33471<br>-32065<br>202 277 |
| C- | 33472<br>-32064<br>202 300 | 33473<br>-32063<br>202 301 | 33474<br>-32062<br>202 302 | 33475<br>-32061<br>202 303 | 33476<br>-32060<br>202 304 | 33477<br>-32059<br>202 305 | 33478<br>-32058<br>202 306 | 33479<br>-32057<br>202 307 | 33480<br>-32056<br>202 310 | 33481<br>-32055<br>202 311 | 33482<br>-32054<br>202 312 | 33483<br>-32053<br>202 313 | 33484<br>-32052<br>202 314 | 33485<br>-32051<br>202 315 | 33486<br>-32050<br>202 316 | 33487<br>-32049<br>202 317 |
| D- | 33488<br>-32048<br>202 320 | 33489<br>-32047<br>202 321 | 33490<br>-32046<br>202 322 | 33491<br>-32045<br>202 323 | 33492<br>-32044<br>202 324 | 33493<br>-32043<br>202 325 | 33494<br>-32042<br>202 326 | 33495<br>-32041<br>202 327 | 33496<br>-32040<br>202 330 | 33497<br>-32039<br>202 331 | 33498<br>-32038<br>202 332 | 33499<br>-32037<br>202 333 | 33500<br>-32036<br>202 334 | 33501<br>-32035<br>202 335 | 33502<br>-32034<br>202 336 | 33503<br>-32033<br>202 337 |
| E- | 33504<br>-32032<br>202 340 | 33505<br>-32031<br>202 341 | 33506<br>-32030<br>202 342 | 33507<br>-32029<br>202 343 | 33508<br>-32028<br>202 344 | 33509<br>-32027<br>202 345 | 33510<br>-32026<br>202 346 | 33511<br>-32025<br>202 347 | 33512<br>-32024<br>202 350 | 33513<br>-32023<br>202 351 | 33514<br>-32022<br>202 352 | 33515<br>-32021<br>202 353 | 33516<br>-32020<br>202 354 | 33517<br>-32019<br>202 355 | 33518<br>-32018<br>202 356 | 33519<br>-32017<br>202 357 |
| F- | 33520<br>-32016<br>202 360 | 33521<br>-32015<br>202 361 | 33522<br>-32014<br>202 362 | 33523<br>-32013<br>202 363 | 33524<br>-32012<br>202 364 | 33525<br>-32011<br>202 365 | 33526<br>-32010<br>202 366 | 33527<br>-32009<br>202 367 | 33528<br>-32008<br>202 370 | 33529<br>-32007<br>202 371 | 33530<br>-32006<br>202 372 | 33531<br>-32005<br>202 373 | 33532<br>-32004<br>202 374 | 33533<br>-32003<br>202 375 | 33534<br>-32002<br>202 376 | 33535<br>-32001<br>202 377 |

SECOND HEX DIGIT

DECIMAL

 DECIMAL

OCTAL

 DECIMAL  -32256   BINARY  1000 0010   DECIMAL  33280   HEXADECIMAL  82  OCTAL  202 000

FOURTH HEX DIGIT → ← THIRD HEX DIGIT

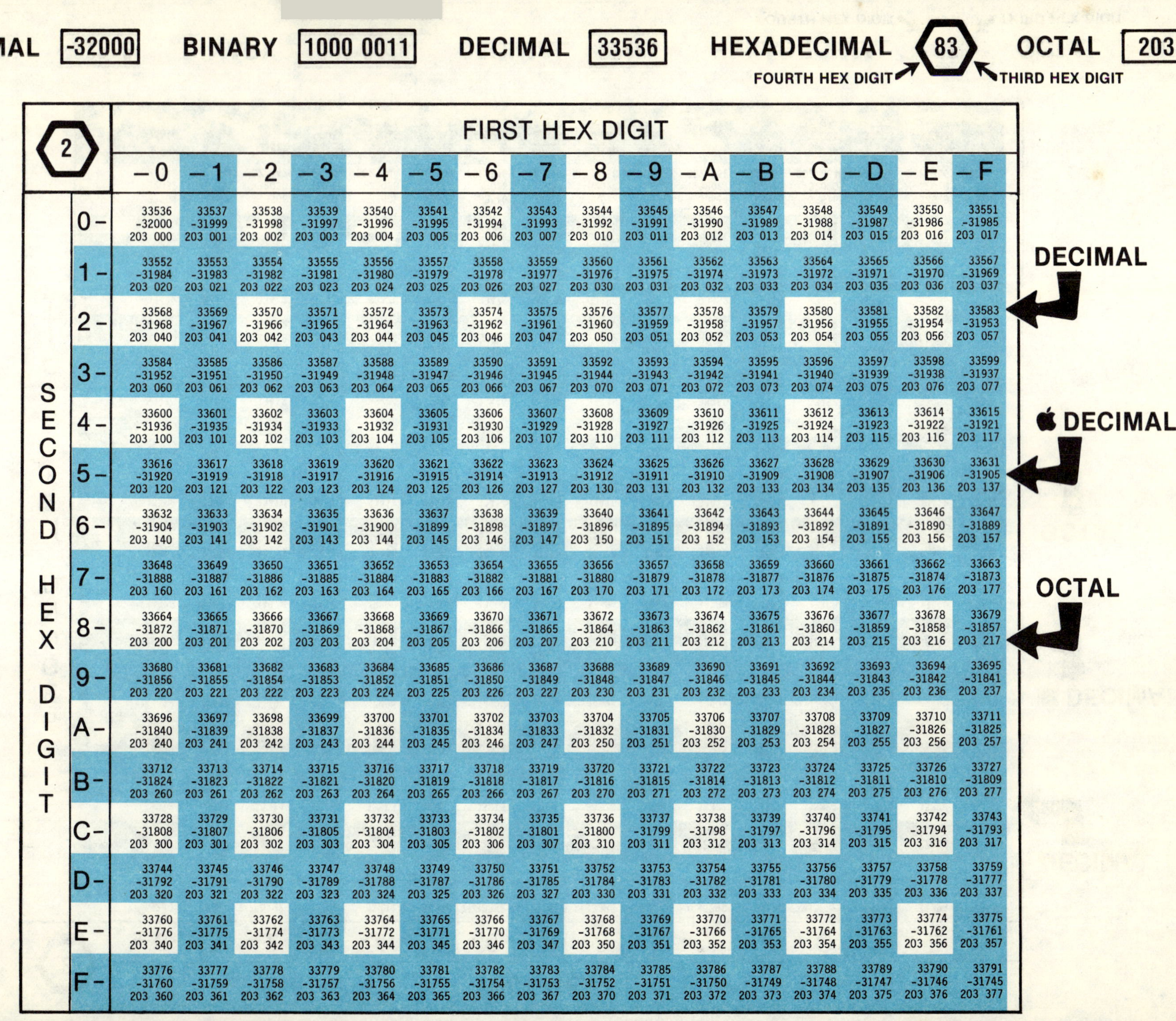



**FIRST HEX DIGIT** (hexagon: 2) — rows: **SECOND HEX DIGIT**

Each cell: decimal / negative decimal / octal.

| | −0 | −1 | −2 | −3 | −4 | −5 | −6 | −7 | −8 | −9 | −A | −B | −C | −D | −E | −F |
|---|---|---|---|---|---|---|---|---|---|---|---|---|---|---|---|---|
| 0− | 33536<br>−32000<br>203 000 | 33537<br>−31999<br>203 001 | 33538<br>−31998<br>203 002 | 33539<br>−31997<br>203 003 | 33540<br>−31996<br>203 004 | 33541<br>−31995<br>203 005 | 33542<br>−31994<br>203 006 | 33543<br>−31993<br>203 007 | 33544<br>−31992<br>203 010 | 33545<br>−31991<br>203 011 | 33546<br>−31990<br>203 012 | 33547<br>−31989<br>203 013 | 33548<br>−31988<br>203 014 | 33549<br>−31987<br>203 015 | 33550<br>−31986<br>203 016 | 33551<br>−31985<br>203 017 |
| 1− | 33552<br>−31984<br>203 020 | 33553<br>−31983<br>203 021 | 33554<br>−31982<br>203 022 | 33555<br>−31981<br>203 023 | 33556<br>−31980<br>203 024 | 33557<br>−31979<br>203 025 | 33558<br>−31978<br>203 026 | 33559<br>−31977<br>203 027 | 33560<br>−31976<br>203 030 | 33561<br>−31975<br>203 031 | 33562<br>−31974<br>203 032 | 33563<br>−31973<br>203 033 | 33564<br>−31972<br>203 034 | 33565<br>−31971<br>203 035 | 33566<br>−31970<br>203 036 | 33567<br>−31969<br>203 037 |
| 2− | 33568<br>−31968<br>203 040 | 33569<br>−31967<br>203 041 | 33570<br>−31966<br>203 042 | 33571<br>−31965<br>203 043 | 33572<br>−31964<br>203 044 | 33573<br>−31963<br>203 045 | 33574<br>−31962<br>203 046 | 33575<br>−31961<br>203 047 | 33576<br>−31960<br>203 050 | 33577<br>−31959<br>203 051 | 33578<br>−31958<br>203 052 | 33579<br>−31957<br>203 053 | 33580<br>−31956<br>203 054 | 33581<br>−31955<br>203 055 | 33582<br>−31954<br>203 056 | 33583<br>−31953<br>203 057 |
| 3− | 33584<br>−31952<br>203 060 | 33585<br>−31951<br>203 061 | 33586<br>−31950<br>203 062 | 33587<br>−31949<br>203 063 | 33588<br>−31948<br>203 064 | 33589<br>−31947<br>203 065 | 33590<br>−31946<br>203 066 | 33591<br>−31945<br>203 067 | 33592<br>−31944<br>203 070 | 33593<br>−31943<br>203 071 | 33594<br>−31942<br>203 072 | 33595<br>−31941<br>203 073 | 33596<br>−31940<br>203 074 | 33597<br>−31939<br>203 075 | 33598<br>−31938<br>203 076 | 33599<br>−31937<br>203 077 |
| 4− | 33600<br>−31936<br>203 100 | 33601<br>−31935<br>203 101 | 33602<br>−31934<br>203 102 | 33603<br>−31933<br>203 103 | 33604<br>−31932<br>203 104 | 33605<br>−31931<br>203 105 | 33606<br>−31930<br>203 106 | 33607<br>−31929<br>203 107 | 33608<br>−31928<br>203 110 | 33609<br>−31927<br>203 111 | 33610<br>−31926<br>203 112 | 33611<br>−31925<br>203 113 | 33612<br>−31924<br>203 114 | 33613<br>−31923<br>203 115 | 33614<br>−31922<br>203 116 | 33615<br>−31921<br>203 117 |
| 5− | 33616<br>−31920<br>203 120 | 33617<br>−31919<br>203 121 | 33618<br>−31918<br>203 122 | 33619<br>−31917<br>203 123 | 33620<br>−31916<br>203 124 | 33621<br>−31915<br>203 125 | 33622<br>−31914<br>203 126 | 33623<br>−31913<br>203 127 | 33624<br>−31912<br>203 130 | 33625<br>−31911<br>203 131 | 33626<br>−31910<br>203 132 | 33627<br>−31909<br>203 133 | 33628<br>−31908<br>203 134 | 33629<br>−31907<br>203 135 | 33630<br>−31906<br>203 136 | 33631<br>−31905<br>203 137 |
| 6− | 33632<br>−31904<br>203 140 | 33633<br>−31903<br>203 141 | 33634<br>−31902<br>203 142 | 33635<br>−31901<br>203 143 | 33636<br>−31900<br>203 144 | 33637<br>−31899<br>203 145 | 33638<br>−31898<br>203 146 | 33639<br>−31897<br>203 147 | 33640<br>−31896<br>203 150 | 33641<br>−31895<br>203 151 | 33642<br>−31894<br>203 152 | 33643<br>−31893<br>203 153 | 33644<br>−31892<br>203 154 | 33645<br>−31891<br>203 155 | 33646<br>−31890<br>203 156 | 33647<br>−31889<br>203 157 |
| 7− | 33648<br>−31888<br>203 160 | 33649<br>−31887<br>203 161 | 33650<br>−31886<br>203 162 | 33651<br>−31885<br>203 163 | 33652<br>−31884<br>203 164 | 33653<br>−31883<br>203 165 | 33654<br>−31882<br>203 166 | 33655<br>−31881<br>203 167 | 33656<br>−31880<br>203 170 | 33657<br>−31879<br>203 171 | 33658<br>−31878<br>203 172 | 33659<br>−31877<br>203 173 | 33660<br>−31876<br>203 174 | 33661<br>−31875<br>203 175 | 33662<br>−31874<br>203 176 | 33663<br>−31873<br>203 177 |
| 8− | 33664<br>−31872<br>203 200 | 33665<br>−31871<br>203 201 | 33666<br>−31870<br>203 202 | 33667<br>−31869<br>203 203 | 33668<br>−31868<br>203 204 | 33669<br>−31867<br>203 205 | 33670<br>−31866<br>203 206 | 33671<br>−31865<br>203 207 | 33672<br>−31864<br>203 210 | 33673<br>−31863<br>203 211 | 33674<br>−31862<br>203 212 | 33675<br>−31861<br>203 213 | 33676<br>−31860<br>203 214 | 33677<br>−31859<br>203 215 | 33678<br>−31858<br>203 216 | 33679<br>−31857<br>203 217 |
| 9− | 33680<br>−31856<br>203 220 | 33681<br>−31855<br>203 221 | 33682<br>−31854<br>203 222 | 33683<br>−31853<br>203 223 | 33684<br>−31852<br>203 224 | 33685<br>−31851<br>203 225 | 33686<br>−31850<br>203 226 | 33687<br>−31849<br>203 227 | 33688<br>−31848<br>203 230 | 33689<br>−31847<br>203 231 | 33690<br>−31846<br>203 232 | 33691<br>−31845<br>203 233 | 33692<br>−31844<br>203 234 | 33693<br>−31843<br>203 235 | 33694<br>−31842<br>203 236 | 33695<br>−31841<br>203 237 |
| A− | 33696<br>−31840<br>203 240 | 33697<br>−31839<br>203 241 | 33698<br>−31838<br>203 242 | 33699<br>−31837<br>203 243 | 33700<br>−31836<br>203 244 | 33701<br>−31835<br>203 245 | 33702<br>−31834<br>203 246 | 33703<br>−31833<br>203 247 | 33704<br>−31832<br>203 250 | 33705<br>−31831<br>203 251 | 33706<br>−31830<br>203 252 | 33707<br>−31829<br>203 253 | 33708<br>−31828<br>203 254 | 33709<br>−31827<br>203 255 | 33710<br>−31826<br>203 256 | 33711<br>−31825<br>203 257 |
| B− | 33712<br>−31824<br>203 260 | 33713<br>−31823<br>203 261 | 33714<br>−31822<br>203 262 | 33715<br>−31821<br>203 263 | 33716<br>−31820<br>203 264 | 33717<br>−31819<br>203 265 | 33718<br>−31818<br>203 266 | 33719<br>−31817<br>203 267 | 33720<br>−31816<br>203 270 | 33721<br>−31815<br>203 271 | 33722<br>−31814<br>203 272 | 33723<br>−31813<br>203 273 | 33724<br>−31812<br>203 274 | 33725<br>−31811<br>203 275 | 33726<br>−31810<br>203 276 | 33727<br>−31809<br>203 277 |
| C− | 33728<br>−31808<br>203 300 | 33729<br>−31807<br>203 301 | 33730<br>−31806<br>203 302 | 33731<br>−31805<br>203 303 | 33732<br>−31804<br>203 304 | 33733<br>−31803<br>203 305 | 33734<br>−31802<br>203 306 | 33735<br>−31801<br>203 307 | 33736<br>−31800<br>203 310 | 33737<br>−31799<br>203 311 | 33738<br>−31798<br>203 312 | 33739<br>−31797<br>203 313 | 33740<br>−31796<br>203 314 | 33741<br>−31795<br>203 315 | 33742<br>−31794<br>203 316 | 33743<br>−31793<br>203 317 |
| D− | 33744<br>−31792<br>203 320 | 33745<br>−31791<br>203 321 | 33746<br>−31790<br>203 322 | 33747<br>−31789<br>203 323 | 33748<br>−31788<br>203 324 | 33749<br>−31787<br>203 325 | 33750<br>−31786<br>203 326 | 33751<br>−31785<br>203 327 | 33752<br>−31784<br>203 330 | 33753<br>−31783<br>203 331 | 33754<br>−31782<br>203 332 | 33755<br>−31781<br>203 333 | 33756<br>−31780<br>203 334 | 33757<br>−31779<br>203 335 | 33758<br>−31778<br>203 336 | 33759<br>−31777<br>203 337 |
| E− | 33760<br>−31776<br>203 340 | 33761<br>−31775<br>203 341 | 33762<br>−31774<br>203 342 | 33763<br>−31773<br>203 343 | 33764<br>−31772<br>203 344 | 33765<br>−31771<br>203 345 | 33766<br>−31770<br>203 346 | 33767<br>−31769<br>203 347 | 33768<br>−31768<br>203 350 | 33769<br>−31767<br>203 351 | 33770<br>−31766<br>203 352 | 33771<br>−31765<br>203 353 | 33772<br>−31764<br>203 354 | 33773<br>−31763<br>203 355 | 33774<br>−31762<br>203 356 | 33775<br>−31761<br>203 357 |
| F− | 33776<br>−31760<br>203 360 | 33777<br>−31759<br>203 361 | 33778<br>−31758<br>203 362 | 33779<br>−31757<br>203 363 | 33780<br>−31756<br>203 364 | 33781<br>−31755<br>203 365 | 33782<br>−31754<br>203 366 | 33783<br>−31753<br>203 367 | 33784<br>−31752<br>203 370 | 33785<br>−31751<br>203 371 | 33786<br>−31750<br>203 372 | 33787<br>−31749<br>203 373 | 33788<br>−31748<br>203 374 | 33789<br>−31747<br>203 375 | 33790<br>−31746<br>203 376 | 33791<br>−31745<br>203 377 |

| SECOND HEX DIGIT | −0 | −1 | −2 | −3 | −4 | −5 | −6 | −7 | −8 | −9 | −A | −B | −C | −D | −E | −F |
|---|---|---|---|---|---|---|---|---|---|---|---|---|---|---|---|---|
| **0-** | 33792<br>−31744<br>204 000 | 33793<br>−31743<br>204 001 | 33794<br>−31742<br>204 002 | 33795<br>−31741<br>204 003 | 33796<br>−31740<br>204 004 | 33797<br>−31739<br>204 005 | 33798<br>−31738<br>204 006 | 33799<br>−31737<br>204 007 | 33800<br>−31736<br>204 010 | 33801<br>−31735<br>204 011 | 33802<br>−31734<br>204 012 | 33803<br>−31733<br>204 013 | 33804<br>−31732<br>204 014 | 33805<br>−31731<br>204 015 | 33806<br>−31730<br>204 016 | 33807<br>−31729<br>204 017 |
| **1-** | 33808<br>−31728<br>204 020 | 33809<br>−31727<br>204 021 | 33810<br>−31726<br>204 022 | 33811<br>−31725<br>204 023 | 33812<br>−31724<br>204 024 | 33813<br>−31723<br>204 025 | 33814<br>−31722<br>204 026 | 33815<br>−31721<br>204 027 | 33816<br>−31720<br>204 030 | 33817<br>−31719<br>204 031 | 33818<br>−31718<br>204 032 | 33819<br>−31717<br>204 033 | 33820<br>−31716<br>204 034 | 33821<br>−31715<br>204 035 | 33822<br>−31714<br>204 036 | 33823<br>−31713<br>204 037 |
| **2-** | 33824<br>−31712<br>204 040 | 33825<br>−31711<br>204 041 | 33826<br>−31710<br>204 042 | 33827<br>−31709<br>204 043 | 33828<br>−31708<br>204 044 | 33829<br>−31707<br>204 045 | 33830<br>−31706<br>204 046 | 33831<br>−31705<br>204 047 | 33832<br>−31704<br>204 050 | 33833<br>−31703<br>204 051 | 33834<br>−31702<br>204 052 | 33835<br>−31701<br>204 053 | 33836<br>−31700<br>204 054 | 33837<br>−31699<br>204 055 | 33838<br>−31698<br>204 056 | 33839<br>−31697<br>204 057 |
| **3-** | 33840<br>−31696<br>204 060 | 33841<br>−31695<br>204 061 | 33842<br>−31694<br>204 062 | 33843<br>−31693<br>204 063 | 33844<br>−31692<br>204 064 | 33845<br>−31691<br>204 065 | 33846<br>−31690<br>204 066 | 33847<br>−31689<br>204 067 | 33848<br>−31688<br>204 070 | 33849<br>−31687<br>204 071 | 33850<br>−31686<br>204 072 | 33851<br>−31685<br>204 073 | 33852<br>−31684<br>204 074 | 33853<br>−31683<br>204 075 | 33854<br>−31682<br>204 076 | 33855<br>−31681<br>204 077 |
| **4-** | 33856<br>−31680<br>204 100 | 33857<br>−31679<br>204 101 | 33858<br>−31678<br>204 102 | 33859<br>−31677<br>204 103 | 33860<br>−31676<br>204 104 | 33861<br>−31675<br>204 105 | 33862<br>−31674<br>204 106 | 33863<br>−31673<br>204 107 | 33864<br>−31672<br>204 110 | 33865<br>−31671<br>204 111 | 33866<br>−31670<br>204 112 | 33867<br>−31669<br>204 113 | 33868<br>−31668<br>204 114 | 33869<br>−31667<br>204 115 | 33870<br>−31666<br>204 116 | 33871<br>−31665<br>204 117 |
| **5-** | 33872<br>−31664<br>204 120 | 33873<br>−31663<br>204 121 | 33874<br>−31662<br>204 122 | 33875<br>−31661<br>204 123 | 33876<br>−31660<br>204 124 | 33877<br>−31659<br>204 125 | 33878<br>−31658<br>204 126 | 33879<br>−31657<br>204 127 | 33880<br>−31656<br>204 130 | 33881<br>−31655<br>204 131 | 33882<br>−31654<br>204 132 | 33883<br>−31653<br>204 133 | 33884<br>−31652<br>204 134 | 33885<br>−31651<br>204 135 | 33886<br>−31650<br>204 136 | 33887<br>−31649<br>204 137 |
| **6-** | 33888<br>−31648<br>204 140 | 33889<br>−31647<br>204 141 | 33890<br>−31646<br>204 142 | 33891<br>−31645<br>204 143 | 33892<br>−31644<br>204 144 | 33893<br>−31643<br>204 145 | 33894<br>−31642<br>204 146 | 33895<br>−31641<br>204 147 | 33896<br>−31640<br>204 150 | 33897<br>−31639<br>204 151 | 33898<br>−31638<br>204 152 | 33899<br>−31637<br>204 153 | 33900<br>−31636<br>204 154 | 33901<br>−31635<br>204 155 | 33902<br>−31634<br>204 156 | 33903<br>−31633<br>204 157 |
| **7-** | 33904<br>−31632<br>204 160 | 33905<br>−31631<br>204 161 | 33906<br>−31630<br>204 162 | 33907<br>−31629<br>204 163 | 33908<br>−31628<br>204 164 | 33909<br>−31627<br>204 165 | 33910<br>−31626<br>204 166 | 33911<br>−31625<br>204 167 | 33912<br>−31624<br>204 170 | 33913<br>−31623<br>204 171 | 33914<br>−31622<br>204 172 | 33915<br>−31621<br>204 173 | 33916<br>−31620<br>204 174 | 33917<br>−31619<br>204 175 | 33918<br>−31618<br>204 176 | 33919<br>−31617<br>204 177 |
| **8-** | 33920<br>−31616<br>204 200 | 33921<br>−31615<br>204 201 | 33922<br>−31614<br>204 202 | 33923<br>−31613<br>204 203 | 33924<br>−31612<br>204 204 | 33925<br>−31611<br>204 205 | 33926<br>−31610<br>204 206 | 33927<br>−31609<br>204 207 | 33928<br>−31608<br>204 210 | 33929<br>−31607<br>204 211 | 33930<br>−31606<br>204 212 | 33931<br>−31605<br>204 213 | 33932<br>−31604<br>204 214 | 33933<br>−31603<br>204 215 | 33934<br>−31602<br>204 216 | 33935<br>−31601<br>204 217 |
| **9-** | 33936<br>−31600<br>204 220 | 33937<br>−31599<br>204 221 | 33938<br>−31598<br>204 222 | 33939<br>−31597<br>204 223 | 33940<br>−31596<br>204 224 | 33941<br>−31595<br>204 225 | 33942<br>−31594<br>204 226 | 33943<br>−31593<br>204 227 | 33944<br>−31592<br>204 230 | 33945<br>−31591<br>204 231 | 33946<br>−31590<br>204 232 | 33947<br>−31589<br>204 233 | 33948<br>−31588<br>204 234 | 33949<br>−31587<br>204 235 | 33950<br>−31586<br>204 236 | 33951<br>−31585<br>204 237 |
| **A-** | 33952<br>−31584<br>204 240 | 33953<br>−31583<br>204 241 | 33954<br>−31582<br>204 242 | 33955<br>−31581<br>204 243 | 33956<br>−31580<br>204 244 | 33957<br>−31579<br>204 245 | 33958<br>−31578<br>204 246 | 33959<br>−31577<br>204 247 | 33960<br>−31576<br>204 250 | 33961<br>−31575<br>204 251 | 33962<br>−31574<br>204 252 | 33963<br>−31573<br>204 253 | 33964<br>−31572<br>204 254 | 33965<br>−31571<br>204 255 | 33966<br>−31570<br>204 256 | 33967<br>−31569<br>204 257 |
| **B-** | 33968<br>−31568<br>204 260 | 33969<br>−31567<br>204 261 | 33970<br>−31566<br>204 262 | 33971<br>−31565<br>204 263 | 33972<br>−31564<br>204 264 | 33973<br>−31563<br>204 265 | 33974<br>−31562<br>204 266 | 33975<br>−31561<br>204 267 | 33976<br>−31560<br>204 270 | 33977<br>−31559<br>204 271 | 33978<br>−31558<br>204 272 | 33979<br>−31557<br>204 273 | 33980<br>−31556<br>204 274 | 33981<br>−31555<br>204 275 | 33982<br>−31554<br>204 276 | 33983<br>−31553<br>204 277 |
| **C-** | 33984<br>−31552<br>204 300 | 33985<br>−31551<br>204 301 | 33986<br>−31550<br>204 302 | 33987<br>−31549<br>204 303 | 33988<br>−31548<br>204 304 | 33989<br>−31547<br>204 305 | 33990<br>−31546<br>204 306 | 33991<br>−31545<br>204 307 | 33992<br>−31544<br>204 310 | 33993<br>−31543<br>204 311 | 33994<br>−31542<br>204 312 | 33995<br>−31541<br>204 313 | 33996<br>−31540<br>204 314 | 33997<br>−31539<br>204 315 | 33998<br>−31538<br>204 316 | 33999<br>−31537<br>204 317 |
| **D-** | 34000<br>−31536<br>204 320 | 34001<br>−31535<br>204 321 | 34002<br>−31534<br>204 322 | 34003<br>−31533<br>204 323 | 34004<br>−31532<br>204 324 | 34005<br>−31531<br>204 325 | 34006<br>−31530<br>204 326 | 34007<br>−31529<br>204 327 | 34008<br>−31528<br>204 330 | 34009<br>−31527<br>204 331 | 34010<br>−31526<br>204 332 | 34011<br>−31525<br>204 333 | 34012<br>−31524<br>204 334 | 34013<br>−31523<br>204 335 | 34014<br>−31522<br>204 336 | 34015<br>−31521<br>204 337 |
| **E-** | 34016<br>−31520<br>204 340 | 34017<br>−31519<br>204 341 | 34018<br>−31518<br>204 342 | 34019<br>−31517<br>204 343 | 34020<br>−31516<br>204 344 | 34021<br>−31515<br>204 345 | 34022<br>−31514<br>204 346 | 34023<br>−31513<br>204 347 | 34024<br>−31512<br>204 350 | 34025<br>−31511<br>204 351 | 34026<br>−31510<br>204 352 | 34027<br>−31509<br>204 353 | 34028<br>−31508<br>204 354 | 34029<br>−31507<br>204 355 | 34030<br>−31506<br>204 356 | 34031<br>−31505<br>204 357 |
| **F-** | 34032<br>−31504<br>204 360 | 34033<br>−31503<br>204 361 | 34034<br>−31502<br>204 362 | 34035<br>−31501<br>204 363 | 34036<br>−31500<br>204 364 | 34037<br>−31499<br>204 365 | 34038<br>−31498<br>204 366 | 34039<br>−31497<br>204 367 | 34040<br>−31496<br>204 370 | 34041<br>−31495<br>204 371 | 34042<br>−31494<br>204 372 | 34043<br>−31493<br>204 373 | 34044<br>−31492<br>204 374 | 34045<br>−31491<br>204 375 | 34046<br>−31490<br>204 376 | 34047<br>−31489<br>204 377 |

DECIMAL → (first hex digit row)  DECIMAL → (Apple decimal)  OCTAL →

 DECIMAL −31744  BINARY 1000 0100  DECIMAL 33792  HEXADECIMAL 84  OCTAL 204 000

FOURTH HEX DIGIT → ⬧ ← THIRD HEX DIGIT

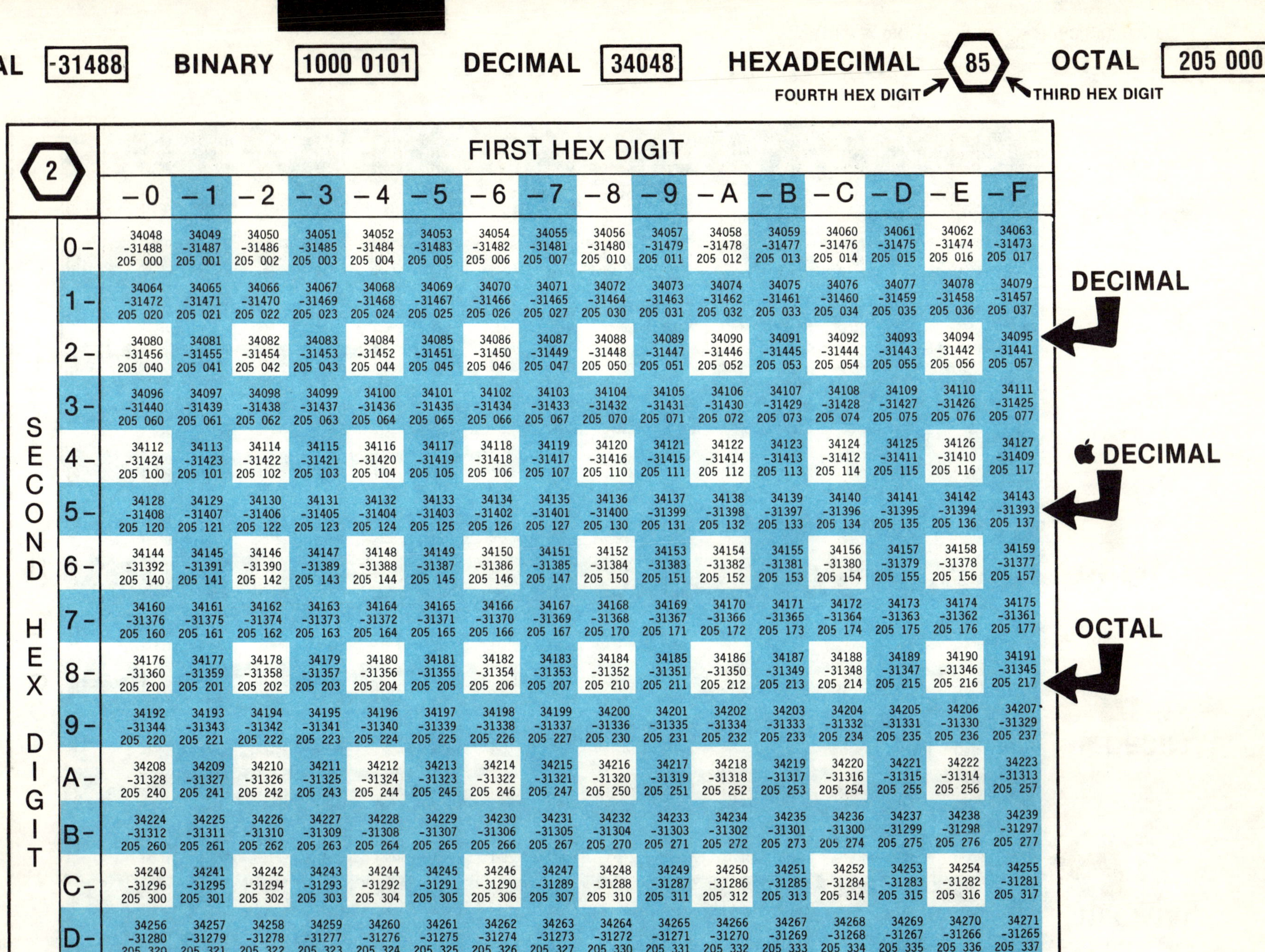



### FIRST HEX DIGIT

| 2 | −0 | −1 | −2 | −3 | −4 | −5 | −6 | −7 | −8 | −9 | −A | −B | −C | −D | −E | −F |
|---|---|---|---|---|---|---|---|---|---|---|---|---|---|---|---|---|
| **0−** | 34048<br>−31488<br>205 000 | 34049<br>−31487<br>205 001 | 34050<br>−31486<br>205 002 | 34051<br>−31485<br>205 003 | 34052<br>−31484<br>205 004 | 34053<br>−31483<br>205 005 | 34054<br>−31482<br>205 006 | 34055<br>−31481<br>205 007 | 34056<br>−31480<br>205 010 | 34057<br>−31479<br>205 011 | 34058<br>−31478<br>205 012 | 34059<br>−31477<br>205 013 | 34060<br>−31476<br>205 014 | 34061<br>−31475<br>205 015 | 34062<br>−31474<br>205 016 | 34063<br>−31473<br>205 017 |
| **1−** | 34064<br>−31472<br>205 020 | 34065<br>−31471<br>205 021 | 34066<br>−31470<br>205 022 | 34067<br>−31469<br>205 023 | 34068<br>−31468<br>205 024 | 34069<br>−31467<br>205 025 | 34070<br>−31466<br>205 026 | 34071<br>−31465<br>205 027 | 34072<br>−31464<br>205 030 | 34073<br>−31463<br>205 031 | 34074<br>−31462<br>205 032 | 34075<br>−31461<br>205 033 | 34076<br>−31460<br>205 034 | 34077<br>−31459<br>205 035 | 34078<br>−31458<br>205 036 | 34079<br>−31457<br>205 037 |
| **2−** | 34080<br>−31456<br>205 040 | 34081<br>−31455<br>205 041 | 34082<br>−31454<br>205 042 | 34083<br>−31453<br>205 043 | 34084<br>−31452<br>205 044 | 34085<br>−31451<br>205 045 | 34086<br>−31450<br>205 046 | 34087<br>−31449<br>205 047 | 34088<br>−31448<br>205 050 | 34089<br>−31447<br>205 051 | 34090<br>−31446<br>205 052 | 34091<br>−31445<br>205 053 | 34092<br>−31444<br>205 054 | 34093<br>−31443<br>205 055 | 34094<br>−31442<br>205 056 | 34095<br>−31441<br>205 057 |
| **3−** | 34096<br>−31440<br>205 060 | 34097<br>−31439<br>205 061 | 34098<br>−31438<br>205 062 | 34099<br>−31437<br>205 063 | 34100<br>−31436<br>205 064 | 34101<br>−31435<br>205 065 | 34102<br>−31434<br>205 066 | 34103<br>−31433<br>205 067 | 34104<br>−31432<br>205 070 | 34105<br>−31431<br>205 071 | 34106<br>−31430<br>205 072 | 34107<br>−31429<br>205 073 | 34108<br>−31428<br>205 074 | 34109<br>−31427<br>205 075 | 34110<br>−31426<br>205 076 | 34111<br>−31425<br>205 077 |
| **4−** | 34112<br>−31424<br>205 100 | 34113<br>−31423<br>205 101 | 34114<br>−31422<br>205 102 | 34115<br>−31421<br>205 103 | 34116<br>−31420<br>205 104 | 34117<br>−31419<br>205 105 | 34118<br>−31418<br>205 106 | 34119<br>−31417<br>205 107 | 34120<br>−31416<br>205 110 | 34121<br>−31415<br>205 111 | 34122<br>−31414<br>205 112 | 34123<br>−31413<br>205 113 | 34124<br>−31412<br>205 114 | 34125<br>−31411<br>205 115 | 34126<br>−31410<br>205 116 | 34127<br>−31409<br>205 117 |
| **5−** | 34128<br>−31408<br>205 120 | 34129<br>−31407<br>205 121 | 34130<br>−31406<br>205 122 | 34131<br>−31405<br>205 123 | 34132<br>−31404<br>205 124 | 34133<br>−31403<br>205 125 | 34134<br>−31402<br>205 126 | 34135<br>−31401<br>205 127 | 34136<br>−31400<br>205 130 | 34137<br>−31399<br>205 131 | 34138<br>−31398<br>205 132 | 34139<br>−31397<br>205 133 | 34140<br>−31396<br>205 134 | 34141<br>−31395<br>205 135 | 34142<br>−31394<br>205 136 | 34143<br>−31393<br>205 137 |
| **6−** | 34144<br>−31392<br>205 140 | 34145<br>−31391<br>205 141 | 34146<br>−31390<br>205 142 | 34147<br>−31389<br>205 143 | 34148<br>−31388<br>205 144 | 34149<br>−31387<br>205 145 | 34150<br>−31386<br>205 146 | 34151<br>−31385<br>205 147 | 34152<br>−31384<br>205 150 | 34153<br>−31383<br>205 151 | 34154<br>−31382<br>205 152 | 34155<br>−31381<br>205 153 | 34156<br>−31380<br>205 154 | 34157<br>−31379<br>205 155 | 34158<br>−31378<br>205 156 | 34159<br>−31377<br>205 157 |
| **7−** | 34160<br>−31376<br>205 160 | 34161<br>−31375<br>205 161 | 34162<br>−31374<br>205 162 | 34163<br>−31373<br>205 163 | 34164<br>−31372<br>205 164 | 34165<br>−31371<br>205 165 | 34166<br>−31370<br>205 166 | 34167<br>−31369<br>205 167 | 34168<br>−31368<br>205 170 | 34169<br>−31367<br>205 171 | 34170<br>−31366<br>205 172 | 34171<br>−31365<br>205 173 | 34172<br>−31364<br>205 174 | 34173<br>−31363<br>205 175 | 34174<br>−31362<br>205 176 | 34175<br>−31361<br>205 177 |
| **8−** | 34176<br>−31360<br>205 200 | 34177<br>−31359<br>205 201 | 34178<br>−31358<br>205 202 | 34179<br>−31357<br>205 203 | 34180<br>−31356<br>205 204 | 34181<br>−31355<br>205 205 | 34182<br>−31354<br>205 206 | 34183<br>−31353<br>205 207 | 34184<br>−31352<br>205 210 | 34185<br>−31351<br>205 211 | 34186<br>−31350<br>205 212 | 34187<br>−31349<br>205 213 | 34188<br>−31348<br>205 214 | 34189<br>−31347<br>205 215 | 34190<br>−31346<br>205 216 | 34191<br>−31345<br>205 217 |
| **9−** | 34192<br>−31344<br>205 220 | 34193<br>−31343<br>205 221 | 34194<br>−31342<br>205 222 | 34195<br>−31341<br>205 223 | 34196<br>−31340<br>205 224 | 34197<br>−31339<br>205 225 | 34198<br>−31338<br>205 226 | 34199<br>−31337<br>205 227 | 34200<br>−31336<br>205 230 | 34201<br>−31335<br>205 231 | 34202<br>−31334<br>205 232 | 34203<br>−31333<br>205 233 | 34204<br>−31332<br>205 234 | 34205<br>−31331<br>205 235 | 34206<br>−31330<br>205 236 | 34207<br>−31329<br>205 237 |
| **A−** | 34208<br>−31328<br>205 240 | 34209<br>−31327<br>205 241 | 34210<br>−31326<br>205 242 | 34211<br>−31325<br>205 243 | 34212<br>−31324<br>205 244 | 34213<br>−31323<br>205 245 | 34214<br>−31322<br>205 246 | 34215<br>−31321<br>205 247 | 34216<br>−31320<br>205 250 | 34217<br>−31319<br>205 251 | 34218<br>−31318<br>205 252 | 34219<br>−31317<br>205 253 | 34220<br>−31316<br>205 254 | 34221<br>−31315<br>205 255 | 34222<br>−31314<br>205 256 | 34223<br>−31313<br>205 257 |
| **B−** | 34224<br>−31312<br>205 260 | 34225<br>−31311<br>205 261 | 34226<br>−31310<br>205 262 | 34227<br>−31309<br>205 263 | 34228<br>−31308<br>205 264 | 34229<br>−31307<br>205 265 | 34230<br>−31306<br>205 266 | 34231<br>−31305<br>205 267 | 34232<br>−31304<br>205 270 | 34233<br>−31303<br>205 271 | 34234<br>−31302<br>205 272 | 34235<br>−31301<br>205 273 | 34236<br>−31300<br>205 274 | 34237<br>−31299<br>205 275 | 34238<br>−31298<br>205 276 | 34239<br>−31297<br>205 277 |
| **C−** | 34240<br>−31296<br>205 300 | 34241<br>−31295<br>205 301 | 34242<br>−31294<br>205 302 | 34243<br>−31293<br>205 303 | 34244<br>−31292<br>205 304 | 34245<br>−31291<br>205 305 | 34246<br>−31290<br>205 306 | 34247<br>−31289<br>205 307 | 34248<br>−31288<br>205 310 | 34249<br>−31287<br>205 311 | 34250<br>−31286<br>205 312 | 34251<br>−31285<br>205 313 | 34252<br>−31284<br>205 314 | 34253<br>−31283<br>205 315 | 34254<br>−31282<br>205 316 | 34255<br>−31281<br>205 317 |
| **D−** | 34256<br>−31280<br>205 320 | 34257<br>−31279<br>205 321 | 34258<br>−31278<br>205 322 | 34259<br>−31277<br>205 323 | 34260<br>−31276<br>205 324 | 34261<br>−31275<br>205 325 | 34262<br>−31274<br>205 326 | 34263<br>−31273<br>205 327 | 34264<br>−31272<br>205 330 | 34265<br>−31271<br>205 331 | 34266<br>−31270<br>205 332 | 34267<br>−31269<br>205 333 | 34268<br>−31268<br>205 334 | 34269<br>−31267<br>205 335 | 34270<br>−31266<br>205 336 | 34271<br>−31265<br>205 337 |
| **E−** | 34272<br>−31264<br>205 340 | 34273<br>−31263<br>205 341 | 34274<br>−31262<br>205 342 | 34275<br>−31261<br>205 343 | 34276<br>−31260<br>205 344 | 34277<br>−31259<br>205 345 | 34278<br>−31258<br>205 346 | 34279<br>−31257<br>205 347 | 34280<br>−31256<br>205 350 | 34281<br>−31255<br>205 351 | 34282<br>−31254<br>205 352 | 34283<br>−31253<br>205 353 | 34284<br>−31252<br>205 354 | 34285<br>−31251<br>205 355 | 34286<br>−31250<br>205 356 | 34287<br>−31249<br>205 357 |
| **F−** | 34288<br>−31248<br>205 360 | 34289<br>−31247<br>205 361 | 34290<br>−31246<br>205 362 | 34291<br>−31245<br>205 363 | 34292<br>−31244<br>205 364 | 34293<br>−31243<br>205 365 | 34294<br>−31242<br>205 366 | 34295<br>−31241<br>205 367 | 34296<br>−31240<br>205 370 | 34297<br>−31239<br>205 371 | 34298<br>−31238<br>205 372 | 34299<br>−31237<br>205 373 | 34300<br>−31236<br>205 374 | 34301<br>−31235<br>205 375 | 34302<br>−31234<br>205 376 | 34303<br>−31233<br>205 377 |

*SECOND HEX DIGIT* (row labels)

# FIRST HEX DIGIT

⬡ 2

| SECOND HEX DIGIT | –0 | –1 | –2 | –3 | –4 | –5 | –6 | –7 | –8 | –9 | –A | –B | –C | –D | –E | –F |
|---|---|---|---|---|---|---|---|---|---|---|---|---|---|---|---|---|
| **0–** | 34304<br>-31232<br>206 000 | 34305<br>-31231<br>206 001 | 34306<br>-31230<br>206 002 | 34307<br>-31229<br>206 003 | 34308<br>-31228<br>206 004 | 34309<br>-31227<br>206 005 | 34310<br>-31226<br>206 006 | 34311<br>-31225<br>206 007 | 34312<br>-31224<br>206 010 | 34313<br>-31223<br>206 011 | 34314<br>-31222<br>206 012 | 34315<br>-31221<br>206 013 | 34316<br>-31220<br>206 014 | 34317<br>-31219<br>206 015 | 34318<br>-31218<br>206 016 | 34319<br>-31217<br>206 017 |
| **1–** | 34320<br>-31216<br>206 020 | 34321<br>-31215<br>206 021 | 34322<br>-31214<br>206 022 | 34323<br>-31213<br>206 023 | 34324<br>-31212<br>206 024 | 34325<br>-31211<br>206 025 | 34326<br>-31210<br>206 026 | 34327<br>-31209<br>206 027 | 34328<br>-31208<br>206 030 | 34329<br>-31207<br>206 031 | 34330<br>-31206<br>206 032 | 34331<br>-31205<br>206 033 | 34332<br>-31204<br>206 034 | 34333<br>-31203<br>206 035 | 34334<br>-31202<br>206 036 | 34335<br>-31201<br>206 037 |
| **2–** | 34336<br>-31200<br>206 040 | 34337<br>-31199<br>206 041 | 34338<br>-31198<br>206 042 | 34339<br>-31197<br>206 043 | 34340<br>-31196<br>206 044 | 34341<br>-31195<br>206 045 | 34342<br>-31194<br>206 046 | 34343<br>-31193<br>206 047 | 34344<br>-31192<br>206 050 | 34345<br>-31191<br>206 051 | 34346<br>-31190<br>206 052 | 34347<br>-31189<br>206 053 | 34348<br>-31188<br>206 054 | 34349<br>-31187<br>206 055 | 34350<br>-31186<br>206 056 | 34351<br>-31185<br>206 057 |
| **3–** | 34352<br>-31184<br>206 060 | 34353<br>-31183<br>206 061 | 34354<br>-31182<br>206 062 | 34355<br>-31181<br>206 063 | 34356<br>-31180<br>206 064 | 34357<br>-31179<br>206 065 | 34358<br>-31178<br>206 066 | 34359<br>-31177<br>206 067 | 34360<br>-31176<br>206 070 | 34361<br>-31175<br>206 071 | 34362<br>-31174<br>206 072 | 34363<br>-31173<br>206 073 | 34364<br>-31172<br>206 074 | 34365<br>-31171<br>206 075 | 34366<br>-31170<br>206 076 | 34367<br>-31169<br>206 077 |
| **4–** | 34368<br>-31168<br>206 100 | 34369<br>-31167<br>206 101 | 34370<br>-31166<br>206 102 | 34371<br>-31165<br>206 103 | 34372<br>-31164<br>206 104 | 34373<br>-31163<br>206 105 | 34374<br>-31162<br>206 106 | 34375<br>-31161<br>206 107 | 34376<br>-31160<br>206 110 | 34377<br>-31159<br>206 111 | 34378<br>-31158<br>206 112 | 34379<br>-31157<br>206 113 | 34380<br>-31156<br>206 114 | 34381<br>-31155<br>206 115 | 34382<br>-31154<br>206 116 | 34383<br>-31153<br>206 117 |
| **5–** | 34384<br>-31152<br>206 120 | 34385<br>-31151<br>206 121 | 34386<br>-31150<br>206 122 | 34387<br>-31149<br>206 123 | 34388<br>-31148<br>206 124 | 34389<br>-31147<br>206 125 | 34390<br>-31146<br>206 126 | 34391<br>-31145<br>206 127 | 34392<br>-31144<br>206 130 | 34393<br>-31143<br>206 131 | 34394<br>-31142<br>206 132 | 34395<br>-31141<br>206 133 | 34396<br>-31140<br>206 134 | 34397<br>-31139<br>206 135 | 34398<br>-31138<br>206 136 | 34399<br>-31137<br>206 137 |
| **6–** | 34400<br>-31136<br>206 140 | 34401<br>-31135<br>206 141 | 34402<br>-31134<br>206 142 | 34403<br>-31133<br>206 143 | 34404<br>-31132<br>206 144 | 34405<br>-31131<br>206 145 | 34406<br>-31130<br>206 146 | 34407<br>-31129<br>206 147 | 34408<br>-31128<br>206 150 | 34409<br>-31127<br>206 151 | 34410<br>-31126<br>206 152 | 34411<br>-31125<br>206 153 | 34412<br>-31124<br>206 154 | 34413<br>-31123<br>206 155 | 34414<br>-31122<br>206 156 | 34415<br>-31121<br>206 157 |
| **7–** | 34416<br>-31120<br>206 160 | 34417<br>-31119<br>206 161 | 34418<br>-31118<br>206 162 | 34419<br>-31117<br>206 163 | 34420<br>-31116<br>206 164 | 34421<br>-31115<br>206 165 | 34422<br>-31114<br>206 166 | 34423<br>-31113<br>206 167 | 34424<br>-31112<br>206 170 | 34425<br>-31111<br>206 171 | 34426<br>-31110<br>206 172 | 34427<br>-31109<br>206 173 | 34428<br>-31108<br>206 174 | 34429<br>-31107<br>206 175 | 34430<br>-31106<br>206 176 | 34431<br>-31105<br>206 177 |
| **8–** | 34432<br>-31104<br>206 200 | 34433<br>-31103<br>206 201 | 34434<br>-31102<br>206 202 | 34435<br>-31101<br>206 203 | 34436<br>-31100<br>206 204 | 34437<br>-31099<br>206 205 | 34438<br>-31098<br>206 206 | 34439<br>-31097<br>206 207 | 34440<br>-31096<br>206 210 | 34441<br>-31095<br>206 211 | 34442<br>-31094<br>206 212 | 34443<br>-31093<br>206 213 | 34444<br>-31092<br>206 214 | 34445<br>-31091<br>206 215 | 34446<br>-31090<br>206 216 | 34447<br>-31089<br>206 217 |
| **9–** | 34448<br>-31088<br>206 220 | 34449<br>-31087<br>206 221 | 34450<br>-31086<br>206 222 | 34451<br>-31085<br>206 223 | 34452<br>-31084<br>206 224 | 34453<br>-31083<br>206 225 | 34454<br>-31082<br>206 226 | 34455<br>-31081<br>206 227 | 34456<br>-31080<br>206 230 | 34457<br>-31079<br>206 231 | 34458<br>-31078<br>206 232 | 34459<br>-31077<br>206 233 | 34460<br>-31076<br>206 234 | 34461<br>-31075<br>206 235 | 34462<br>-31074<br>206 236 | 34463<br>-31073<br>206 237 |
| **A–** | 34464<br>-31072<br>206 240 | 34465<br>-31071<br>206 241 | 34466<br>-31070<br>206 242 | 34467<br>-31069<br>206 243 | 34468<br>-31068<br>206 244 | 34469<br>-31067<br>206 245 | 34470<br>-31066<br>206 246 | 34471<br>-31065<br>206 247 | 34472<br>-31064<br>206 250 | 34473<br>-31063<br>206 251 | 34474<br>-31062<br>206 252 | 34475<br>-31061<br>206 253 | 34476<br>-31060<br>206 254 | 34477<br>-31059<br>206 255 | 34478<br>-31058<br>206 256 | 34479<br>-31057<br>206 257 |
| **B–** | 34480<br>-31056<br>206 260 | 34481<br>-31055<br>206 261 | 34482<br>-31054<br>206 262 | 34483<br>-31053<br>206 263 | 34484<br>-31052<br>206 264 | 34485<br>-31051<br>206 265 | 34486<br>-31050<br>206 266 | 34487<br>-31049<br>206 267 | 34488<br>-31048<br>206 270 | 34489<br>-31047<br>206 271 | 34490<br>-31046<br>206 272 | 34491<br>-31045<br>206 273 | 34492<br>-31044<br>206 274 | 34493<br>-31043<br>206 275 | 34494<br>-31042<br>206 276 | 34495<br>-31041<br>206 277 |
| **C–** | 34496<br>-31040<br>206 300 | 34497<br>-31039<br>206 301 | 34498<br>-31038<br>206 302 | 34499<br>-31037<br>206 303 | 34500<br>-31036<br>206 304 | 34501<br>-31035<br>206 305 | 34502<br>-31034<br>206 306 | 34503<br>-31033<br>206 307 | 34504<br>-31032<br>206 310 | 34505<br>-31031<br>206 311 | 34506<br>-31030<br>206 312 | 34507<br>-31029<br>206 313 | 34508<br>-31028<br>206 314 | 34509<br>-31027<br>206 315 | 34510<br>-31026<br>206 316 | 34511<br>-31025<br>206 317 |
| **D–** | 34512<br>-31024<br>206 320 | 34513<br>-31023<br>206 321 | 34514<br>-31022<br>206 322 | 34515<br>-31021<br>206 323 | 34516<br>-31020<br>206 324 | 34517<br>-31019<br>206 325 | 34518<br>-31018<br>206 326 | 34519<br>-31017<br>206 327 | 34520<br>-31016<br>206 330 | 34521<br>-31015<br>206 331 | 34522<br>-31014<br>206 332 | 34523<br>-31013<br>206 333 | 34524<br>-31012<br>206 334 | 34525<br>-31011<br>206 335 | 34526<br>-31010<br>206 336 | 34527<br>-31009<br>206 337 |
| **E–** | 34528<br>-31008<br>206 340 | 34529<br>-31007<br>206 341 | 34530<br>-31006<br>206 342 | 34531<br>-31005<br>206 343 | 34532<br>-31004<br>206 344 | 34533<br>-31003<br>206 345 | 34534<br>-31002<br>206 346 | 34535<br>-31001<br>206 347 | 34536<br>-31000<br>206 350 | 34537<br>-30999<br>206 351 | 34538<br>-30998<br>206 352 | 34539<br>-30997<br>206 353 | 34540<br>-30996<br>206 354 | 34541<br>-30995<br>206 355 | 34542<br>-30994<br>206 356 | 34543<br>-30993<br>206 357 |
| **F–** | 34544<br>-30992<br>206 360 | 34545<br>-30991<br>206 361 | 34546<br>-30990<br>206 362 | 34547<br>-30989<br>206 363 | 34548<br>-30988<br>206 364 | 34549<br>-30987<br>206 365 | 34550<br>-30986<br>206 366 | 34551<br>-30985<br>206 367 | 34552<br>-30984<br>206 370 | 34553<br>-30983<br>206 371 | 34554<br>-30982<br>206 372 | 34555<br>-30981<br>206 373 | 34556<br>-30980<br>206 374 | 34557<br>-30979<br>206 375 | 34558<br>-30978<br>206 376 | 34559<br>-30977<br>206 377 |

**DECIMAL** ← (top)
 **DECIMAL** ← (⬤)
**OCTAL** ← (bottom)

⬤ DECIMAL `-31232`  **BINARY** `1000 0110`  **DECIMAL** `34304`  **HEXADECIMAL** ⬡ `86`  **OCTAL** `206 000`

FOURTH HEX DIGIT → ⬡ ← THIRD HEX DIGIT

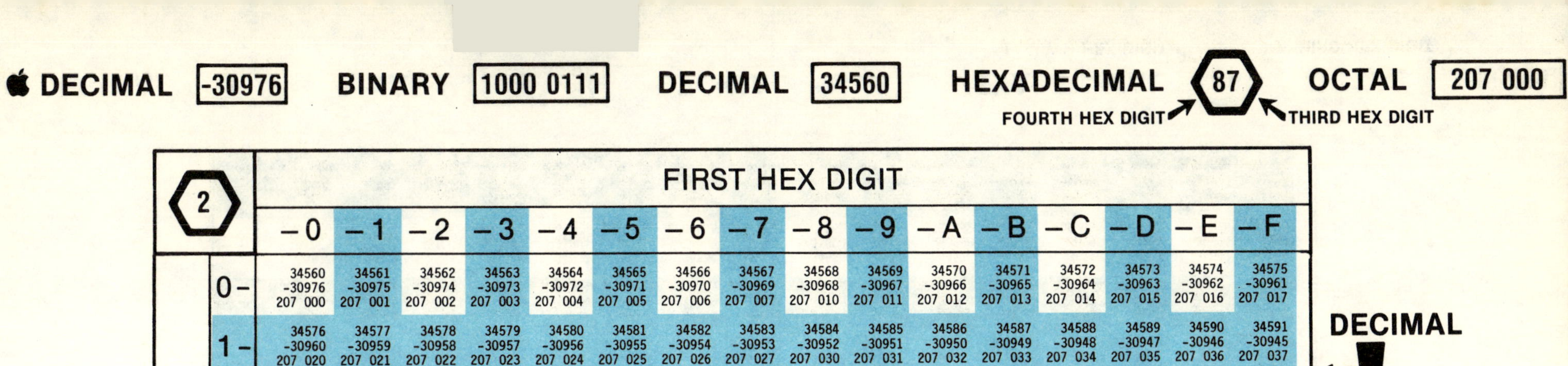

 DECIMAL `-30976`   BINARY `1000 0111`   DECIMAL `34560`   HEXADECIMAL ⬡ `87`   OCTAL `207 000`

FOURTH HEX DIGIT → 8   THIRD HEX DIGIT → 7

| ⬡ 2 | −0 | −1 | −2 | −3 | −4 | −5 | −6 | −7 | −8 | −9 | −A | −B | −C | −D | −E | −F |
|---|---|---|---|---|---|---|---|---|---|---|---|---|---|---|---|---|
| **FIRST HEX DIGIT** | | | | | | | | | | | | | | | | |
| 0- | 34560<br>-30976<br>207 000 | 34561<br>-30975<br>207 001 | 34562<br>-30974<br>207 002 | 34563<br>-30973<br>207 003 | 34564<br>-30972<br>207 004 | 34565<br>-30971<br>207 005 | 34566<br>-30970<br>207 006 | 34567<br>-30969<br>207 007 | 34568<br>-30968<br>207 010 | 34569<br>-30967<br>207 011 | 34570<br>-30966<br>207 012 | 34571<br>-30965<br>207 013 | 34572<br>-30964<br>207 014 | 34573<br>-30963<br>207 015 | 34574<br>-30962<br>207 016 | 34575<br>-30961<br>207 017 |
| 1- | 34576<br>-30960<br>207 020 | 34577<br>-30959<br>207 021 | 34578<br>-30958<br>207 022 | 34579<br>-30957<br>207 023 | 34580<br>-30956<br>207 024 | 34581<br>-30955<br>207 025 | 34582<br>-30954<br>207 026 | 34583<br>-30953<br>207 027 | 34584<br>-30952<br>207 030 | 34585<br>-30951<br>207 031 | 34586<br>-30950<br>207 032 | 34587<br>-30949<br>207 033 | 34588<br>-30948<br>207 034 | 34589<br>-30947<br>207 035 | 34590<br>-30946<br>207 036 | 34591<br>-30945<br>207 037 |
| 2- | 34592<br>-30944<br>207 040 | 34593<br>-30943<br>207 041 | 34594<br>-30942<br>207 042 | 34595<br>-30941<br>207 043 | 34596<br>-30940<br>207 044 | 34597<br>-30939<br>207 045 | 34598<br>-30938<br>207 046 | 34599<br>-30937<br>207 047 | 34600<br>-30936<br>207 050 | 34601<br>-30935<br>207 051 | 34602<br>-30934<br>207 052 | 34603<br>-30933<br>207 053 | 34604<br>-30932<br>207 054 | 34605<br>-30931<br>207 055 | 34606<br>-30930<br>207 056 | 34607<br>-30929<br>207 057 |
| 3- | 34608<br>-30928<br>207 060 | 34609<br>-30927<br>207 061 | 34610<br>-30926<br>207 062 | 34611<br>-30925<br>207 063 | 34612<br>-30924<br>207 064 | 34613<br>-30923<br>207 065 | 34614<br>-30922<br>207 066 | 34615<br>-30921<br>207 067 | 34616<br>-30920<br>207 070 | 34617<br>-30919<br>207 071 | 34618<br>-30918<br>207 072 | 34619<br>-30917<br>207 073 | 34620<br>-30916<br>207 074 | 34621<br>-30915<br>207 075 | 34622<br>-30914<br>207 076 | 34623<br>-30913<br>207 077 |
| 4- | 34624<br>-30912<br>207 100 | 34625<br>-30911<br>207 101 | 34626<br>-30910<br>207 102 | 34627<br>-30909<br>207 103 | 34628<br>-30908<br>207 104 | 34629<br>-30907<br>207 105 | 34630<br>-30906<br>207 106 | 34631<br>-30905<br>207 107 | 34632<br>-30904<br>207 110 | 34633<br>-30903<br>207 111 | 34634<br>-30902<br>207 112 | 34635<br>-30901<br>207 113 | 34636<br>-30900<br>207 114 | 34637<br>-30899<br>207 115 | 34638<br>-30898<br>207 116 | 34639<br>-30897<br>207 117 |
| 5- | 34640<br>-30896<br>207 120 | 34641<br>-30895<br>207 121 | 34642<br>-30894<br>207 122 | 34643<br>-30893<br>207 123 | 34644<br>-30892<br>207 124 | 34645<br>-30891<br>207 125 | 34646<br>-30890<br>207 126 | 34647<br>-30889<br>207 127 | 34648<br>-30888<br>207 130 | 34649<br>-30887<br>207 131 | 34650<br>-30886<br>207 132 | 34651<br>-30885<br>207 133 | 34652<br>-30884<br>207 134 | 34653<br>-30883<br>207 135 | 34654<br>-30882<br>207 136 | 34655<br>-30881<br>207 137 |
| 6- | 34656<br>-30880<br>207 140 | 34657<br>-30879<br>207 141 | 34658<br>-30878<br>207 142 | 34659<br>-30877<br>207 143 | 34660<br>-30876<br>207 144 | 34661<br>-30875<br>207 145 | 34662<br>-30874<br>207 146 | 34663<br>-30873<br>207 147 | 34664<br>-30872<br>207 150 | 34665<br>-30871<br>207 151 | 34666<br>-30870<br>207 152 | 34667<br>-30869<br>207 153 | 34668<br>-30868<br>207 154 | 34669<br>-30867<br>207 155 | 34670<br>-30866<br>207 156 | 34671<br>-30865<br>207 157 |
| 7- | 34672<br>-30864<br>207 160 | 34673<br>-30863<br>207 161 | 34674<br>-30862<br>207 162 | 34675<br>-30861<br>207 163 | 34676<br>-30860<br>207 164 | 34677<br>-30859<br>207 165 | 34678<br>-30858<br>207 166 | 34679<br>-30857<br>207 167 | 34680<br>-30856<br>207 170 | 34681<br>-30855<br>207 171 | 34682<br>-30854<br>207 172 | 34683<br>-30853<br>207 173 | 34684<br>-30852<br>207 174 | 34685<br>-30851<br>207 175 | 34686<br>-30850<br>207 176 | 34687<br>-30849<br>207 177 |
| 8- | 34688<br>-30848<br>207 200 | 34689<br>-30847<br>207 201 | 34690<br>-30846<br>207 202 | 34691<br>-30845<br>207 203 | 34692<br>-30844<br>207 204 | 34693<br>-30843<br>207 205 | 34694<br>-30842<br>207 206 | 34695<br>-30841<br>207 207 | 34696<br>-30840<br>207 210 | 34697<br>-30839<br>207 211 | 34698<br>-30838<br>207 212 | 34699<br>-30837<br>207 213 | 34700<br>-30836<br>207 214 | 34701<br>-30835<br>207 215 | 34702<br>-30834<br>207 216 | 34703<br>-30833<br>207 217 |
| 9- | 34704<br>-30832<br>207 220 | 34705<br>-30831<br>207 221 | 34706<br>-30830<br>207 222 | 34707<br>-30829<br>207 223 | 34708<br>-30828<br>207 224 | 34709<br>-30827<br>207 225 | 34710<br>-30826<br>207 226 | 34711<br>-30825<br>207 227 | 34712<br>-30824<br>207 230 | 34713<br>-30823<br>207 231 | 34714<br>-30822<br>207 232 | 34715<br>-30821<br>207 233 | 34716<br>-30820<br>207 234 | 34717<br>-30819<br>207 235 | 34718<br>-30818<br>207 236 | 34719<br>-30817<br>207 237 |
| A- | 34720<br>-30816<br>207 240 | 34721<br>-30815<br>207 241 | 34722<br>-30814<br>207 242 | 34723<br>-30813<br>207 243 | 34724<br>-30812<br>207 244 | 34725<br>-30811<br>207 245 | 34726<br>-30810<br>207 246 | 34727<br>-30809<br>207 247 | 34728<br>-30808<br>207 250 | 34729<br>-30807<br>207 251 | 34730<br>-30806<br>207 252 | 34731<br>-30805<br>207 253 | 34732<br>-30804<br>207 254 | 34733<br>-30803<br>207 255 | 34734<br>-30802<br>207 256 | 34735<br>-30801<br>207 257 |
| B- | 34736<br>-30800<br>207 260 | 34737<br>-30799<br>207 261 | 34738<br>-30798<br>207 262 | 34739<br>-30797<br>207 263 | 34740<br>-30796<br>207 264 | 34741<br>-30795<br>207 265 | 34742<br>-30794<br>207 266 | 34743<br>-30793<br>207 267 | 34744<br>-30792<br>207 270 | 34745<br>-30791<br>207 271 | 34746<br>-30790<br>207 272 | 34747<br>-30789<br>207 273 | 34748<br>-30788<br>207 274 | 34749<br>-30787<br>207 275 | 34750<br>-30786<br>207 276 | 34751<br>-30785<br>207 277 |
| C- | 34752<br>-30784<br>207 300 | 34753<br>-30783<br>207 301 | 34754<br>-30782<br>207 302 | 34755<br>-30781<br>207 303 | 34756<br>-30780<br>207 304 | 34757<br>-30779<br>207 305 | 34758<br>-30778<br>207 306 | 34759<br>-30777<br>207 307 | 34760<br>-30776<br>207 310 | 34761<br>-30775<br>207 311 | 34762<br>-30774<br>207 312 | 34763<br>-30773<br>207 313 | 34764<br>-30772<br>207 314 | 34765<br>-30771<br>207 315 | 34766<br>-30770<br>207 316 | 34767<br>-30769<br>207 317 |
| D- | 34768<br>-30768<br>207 320 | 34769<br>-30767<br>207 321 | 34770<br>-30766<br>207 322 | 34771<br>-30765<br>207 323 | 34772<br>-30764<br>207 324 | 34773<br>-30763<br>207 325 | 34774<br>-30762<br>207 326 | 34775<br>-30761<br>207 327 | 34776<br>-30760<br>207 330 | 34777<br>-30759<br>207 331 | 34778<br>-30758<br>207 332 | 34779<br>-30757<br>207 333 | 34780<br>-30756<br>207 334 | 34781<br>-30755<br>207 335 | 34782<br>-30754<br>207 336 | 34783<br>-30753<br>207 337 |
| E- | 34784<br>-30752<br>207 340 | 34785<br>-30751<br>207 341 | 34786<br>-30750<br>207 342 | 34787<br>-30749<br>207 343 | 34788<br>-30748<br>207 344 | 34789<br>-30747<br>207 345 | 34790<br>-30746<br>207 346 | 34791<br>-30745<br>207 347 | 34792<br>-30744<br>207 350 | 34793<br>-30743<br>207 351 | 34794<br>-30742<br>207 352 | 34795<br>-30741<br>207 353 | 34796<br>-30740<br>207 354 | 34797<br>-30739<br>207 355 | 34798<br>-30738<br>207 356 | 34799<br>-30737<br>207 357 |
| F- | 34800<br>-30736<br>207 360 | 34801<br>-30735<br>207 361 | 34802<br>-30734<br>207 362 | 34803<br>-30733<br>207 363 | 34804<br>-30732<br>207 364 | 34805<br>-30731<br>207 365 | 34806<br>-30730<br>207 366 | 34807<br>-30729<br>207 367 | 34808<br>-30728<br>207 370 | 34809<br>-30727<br>207 371 | 34810<br>-30726<br>207 372 | 34811<br>-30725<br>207 373 | 34812<br>-30724<br>207 374 | 34813<br>-30723<br>207 375 | 34814<br>-30722<br>207 376 | 34815<br>-30721<br>207 377 |

Left margin label: **SECOND HEX DIGIT**

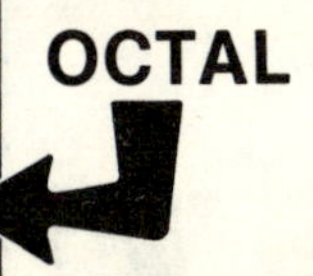

## FIRST HEX DIGIT

| (2) | −0 | −1 | −2 | −3 | −4 | −5 | −6 | −7 | −8 | −9 | −A | −B | −C | −D | −E | −F |
|---|---|---|---|---|---|---|---|---|---|---|---|---|---|---|---|---|
| **0−** | 34816<br>-30720<br>210 000 | 34817<br>-30719<br>210 001 | 34818<br>-30718<br>210 002 | 34819<br>-30717<br>210 003 | 34820<br>-30716<br>210 004 | 34821<br>-30715<br>210 005 | 34822<br>-30714<br>210 006 | 34823<br>-30713<br>210 007 | 34824<br>-30712<br>210 010 | 34825<br>-30711<br>210 011 | 34826<br>-30710<br>210 012 | 34827<br>-30709<br>210 013 | 34828<br>-30708<br>210 014 | 34829<br>-30707<br>210 015 | 34830<br>-30706<br>210 016 | 34831<br>-30705<br>210 017 |
| **1−** | 34832<br>-30704<br>210 020 | 34833<br>-30703<br>210 021 | 34834<br>-30702<br>210 022 | 34835<br>-30701<br>210 023 | 34836<br>-30700<br>210 024 | 34837<br>-30699<br>210 025 | 34838<br>-30698<br>210 026 | 34839<br>-30697<br>210 027 | 34840<br>-30696<br>210 030 | 34841<br>-30695<br>210 031 | 34842<br>-30694<br>210 032 | 34843<br>-30693<br>210 033 | 34844<br>-30692<br>210 034 | 34845<br>-30691<br>210 035 | 34846<br>-30690<br>210 036 | 34847<br>-30689<br>210 037 |
| **2−** | 34848<br>-30688<br>210 040 | 34849<br>-30687<br>210 041 | 34850<br>-30686<br>210 042 | 34851<br>-30685<br>210 043 | 34852<br>-30684<br>210 044 | 34853<br>-30683<br>210 045 | 34854<br>-30682<br>210 046 | 34855<br>-30681<br>210 047 | 34856<br>-30680<br>210 050 | 34857<br>-30679<br>210 051 | 34858<br>-30678<br>210 052 | 34859<br>-30677<br>210 053 | 34860<br>-30676<br>210 054 | 34861<br>-30675<br>210 055 | 34862<br>-30674<br>210 056 | 34863<br>-30673<br>210 057 |
| **3−** | 34864<br>-30672<br>210 060 | 34865<br>-30671<br>210 061 | 34866<br>-30670<br>210 062 | 34867<br>-30669<br>210 063 | 34868<br>-30668<br>210 064 | 34869<br>-30667<br>210 065 | 34870<br>-30666<br>210 066 | 34871<br>-30665<br>210 067 | 34872<br>-30664<br>210 070 | 34873<br>-30663<br>210 071 | 34874<br>-30662<br>210 072 | 34875<br>-30661<br>210 073 | 34876<br>-30660<br>210 074 | 34877<br>-30659<br>210 075 | 34878<br>-30658<br>210 076 | 34879<br>-30657<br>210 077 |
| **4−** | 34880<br>-30656<br>210 100 | 34881<br>-30655<br>210 101 | 34882<br>-30654<br>210 102 | 34883<br>-30653<br>210 103 | 34884<br>-30652<br>210 104 | 34885<br>-30651<br>210 105 | 34886<br>-30650<br>210 106 | 34887<br>-30649<br>210 107 | 34888<br>-30648<br>210 110 | 34889<br>-30647<br>210 111 | 34890<br>-30646<br>210 112 | 34891<br>-30645<br>210 113 | 34892<br>-30644<br>210 114 | 34893<br>-30643<br>210 115 | 34894<br>-30642<br>210 116 | 34895<br>-30641<br>210 117 |
| **5−** | 34896<br>-30640<br>210 120 | 34897<br>-30639<br>210 121 | 34898<br>-30638<br>210 122 | 34899<br>-30637<br>210 123 | 34900<br>-30636<br>210 124 | 34901<br>-30635<br>210 125 | 34902<br>-30634<br>210 126 | 34903<br>-30633<br>210 127 | 34904<br>-30632<br>210 130 | 34905<br>-30631<br>210 131 | 34906<br>-30630<br>210 132 | 34907<br>-30629<br>210 133 | 34908<br>-30628<br>210 134 | 34909<br>-30627<br>210 135 | 34910<br>-30626<br>210 136 | 34911<br>-30625<br>210 137 |
| **6−** | 34912<br>-30624<br>210 140 | 34913<br>-30623<br>210 141 | 34914<br>-30622<br>210 142 | 34915<br>-30621<br>210 143 | 34916<br>-30620<br>210 144 | 34917<br>-30619<br>210 145 | 34918<br>-30618<br>210 146 | 34919<br>-30617<br>210 147 | 34920<br>-30616<br>210 150 | 34921<br>-30615<br>210 151 | 34922<br>-30614<br>210 152 | 34923<br>-30613<br>210 153 | 34924<br>-30612<br>210 154 | 34925<br>-30611<br>210 155 | 34926<br>-30610<br>210 156 | 34927<br>-30609<br>210 157 |
| **7−** | 34928<br>-30608<br>210 160 | 34929<br>-30607<br>210 161 | 34930<br>-30606<br>210 162 | 34931<br>-30605<br>210 163 | 34932<br>-30604<br>210 164 | 34933<br>-30603<br>210 165 | 34934<br>-30602<br>210 166 | 34935<br>-30601<br>210 167 | 34936<br>-30600<br>210 170 | 34937<br>-30599<br>210 171 | 34938<br>-30598<br>210 172 | 34939<br>-30597<br>210 173 | 34940<br>-30596<br>210 174 | 34941<br>-30595<br>210 175 | 34942<br>-30594<br>210 176 | 34943<br>-30593<br>210 177 |
| **8−** | 34944<br>-30592<br>210 200 | 34945<br>-30591<br>210 201 | 34946<br>-30590<br>210 202 | 34947<br>-30589<br>210 203 | 34948<br>-30588<br>210 204 | 34949<br>-30587<br>210 205 | 34950<br>-30586<br>210 206 | 34951<br>-30585<br>210 207 | 34952<br>-30584<br>210 210 | 34953<br>-30583<br>210 211 | 34954<br>-30582<br>210 212 | 34955<br>-30581<br>210 213 | 34956<br>-30580<br>210 214 | 34957<br>-30579<br>210 215 | 34958<br>-30578<br>210 216 | 34959<br>-30577<br>210 217 |
| **9−** | 34960<br>-30576<br>210 220 | 34961<br>-30575<br>210 221 | 34962<br>-30574<br>210 222 | 34963<br>-30573<br>210 223 | 34964<br>-30572<br>210 224 | 34965<br>-30571<br>210 225 | 34966<br>-30570<br>210 226 | 34967<br>-30569<br>210 227 | 34968<br>-30568<br>210 230 | 34969<br>-30567<br>210 231 | 34970<br>-30566<br>210 232 | 34971<br>-30565<br>210 233 | 34972<br>-30564<br>210 234 | 34973<br>-30563<br>210 235 | 34974<br>-30562<br>210 236 | 34975<br>-30561<br>210 237 |
| **A−** | 34976<br>-30560<br>210 240 | 34977<br>-30559<br>210 241 | 34978<br>-30558<br>210 242 | 34979<br>-30557<br>210 243 | 34980<br>-30556<br>210 244 | 34981<br>-30555<br>210 245 | 34982<br>-30554<br>210 246 | 34983<br>-30553<br>210 247 | 34984<br>-30552<br>210 250 | 34985<br>-30551<br>210 251 | 34986<br>-30550<br>210 252 | 34987<br>-30549<br>210 253 | 34988<br>-30548<br>210 254 | 34989<br>-30547<br>210 255 | 34990<br>-30546<br>210 256 | 34991<br>-30545<br>210 257 |
| **B−** | 34992<br>-30544<br>210 260 | 34993<br>-30543<br>210 261 | 34994<br>-30542<br>210 262 | 34995<br>-30541<br>210 263 | 34996<br>-30540<br>210 264 | 34997<br>-30539<br>210 265 | 34998<br>-30538<br>210 266 | 34999<br>-30537<br>210 267 | 35000<br>-30536<br>210 270 | 35001<br>-30535<br>210 271 | 35002<br>-30534<br>210 272 | 35003<br>-30533<br>210 273 | 35004<br>-30532<br>210 274 | 35005<br>-30531<br>210 275 | 35006<br>-30530<br>210 276 | 35007<br>-30529<br>210 277 |
| **C−** | 35008<br>-30528<br>210 300 | 35009<br>-30527<br>210 301 | 35010<br>-30526<br>210 302 | 35011<br>-30525<br>210 303 | 35012<br>-30524<br>210 304 | 35013<br>-30523<br>210 305 | 35014<br>-30522<br>210 306 | 35015<br>-30521<br>210 307 | 35016<br>-30520<br>210 310 | 35017<br>-30519<br>210 311 | 35018<br>-30518<br>210 312 | 35019<br>-30517<br>210 313 | 35020<br>-30516<br>210 314 | 35021<br>-30515<br>210 315 | 35022<br>-30514<br>210 316 | 35023<br>-30513<br>210 317 |
| **D−** | 35024<br>-30512<br>210 320 | 35025<br>-30511<br>210 321 | 35026<br>-30510<br>210 322 | 35027<br>-30509<br>210 323 | 35028<br>-30508<br>210 324 | 35029<br>-30507<br>210 325 | 35030<br>-30506<br>210 326 | 35031<br>-30505<br>210 327 | 35032<br>-30504<br>210 330 | 35033<br>-30503<br>210 331 | 35034<br>-30502<br>210 332 | 35035<br>-30501<br>210 333 | 35036<br>-30500<br>210 334 | 35037<br>-30499<br>210 335 | 35038<br>-30498<br>210 336 | 35039<br>-30497<br>210 337 |
| **E−** | 35040<br>-30496<br>210 340 | 35041<br>-30495<br>210 341 | 35042<br>-30494<br>210 342 | 35043<br>-30493<br>210 343 | 35044<br>-30492<br>210 344 | 35045<br>-30491<br>210 345 | 35046<br>-30490<br>210 346 | 35047<br>-30489<br>210 347 | 35048<br>-30488<br>210 350 | 35049<br>-30487<br>210 351 | 35050<br>-30486<br>210 352 | 35051<br>-30485<br>210 353 | 35052<br>-30484<br>210 354 | 35053<br>-30483<br>210 355 | 35054<br>-30482<br>210 356 | 35055<br>-30481<br>210 357 |
| **F−** | 35056<br>-30480<br>210 360 | 35057<br>-30479<br>210 361 | 35058<br>-30478<br>210 362 | 35059<br>-30477<br>210 363 | 35060<br>-30476<br>210 364 | 35061<br>-30475<br>210 365 | 35062<br>-30474<br>210 366 | 35063<br>-30473<br>210 367 | 35064<br>-30472<br>210 370 | 35065<br>-30471<br>210 371 | 35066<br>-30470<br>210 372 | 35067<br>-30469<br>210 373 | 35068<br>-30468<br>210 374 | 35069<br>-30467<br>210 375 | 35070<br>-30466<br>210 376 | 35071<br>-30465<br>210 377 |

SECOND HEX DIGIT (row labels at left)

DECIMAL →
 DECIMAL →
OCTAL →

 DECIMAL [ -30720 ]   BINARY [ 1000 1000 ]   DECIMAL [ 34816 ]   HEXADECIMAL (88)   OCTAL [ 210 000 ]

FOURTH HEX DIGIT → ← THIRD HEX DIGIT

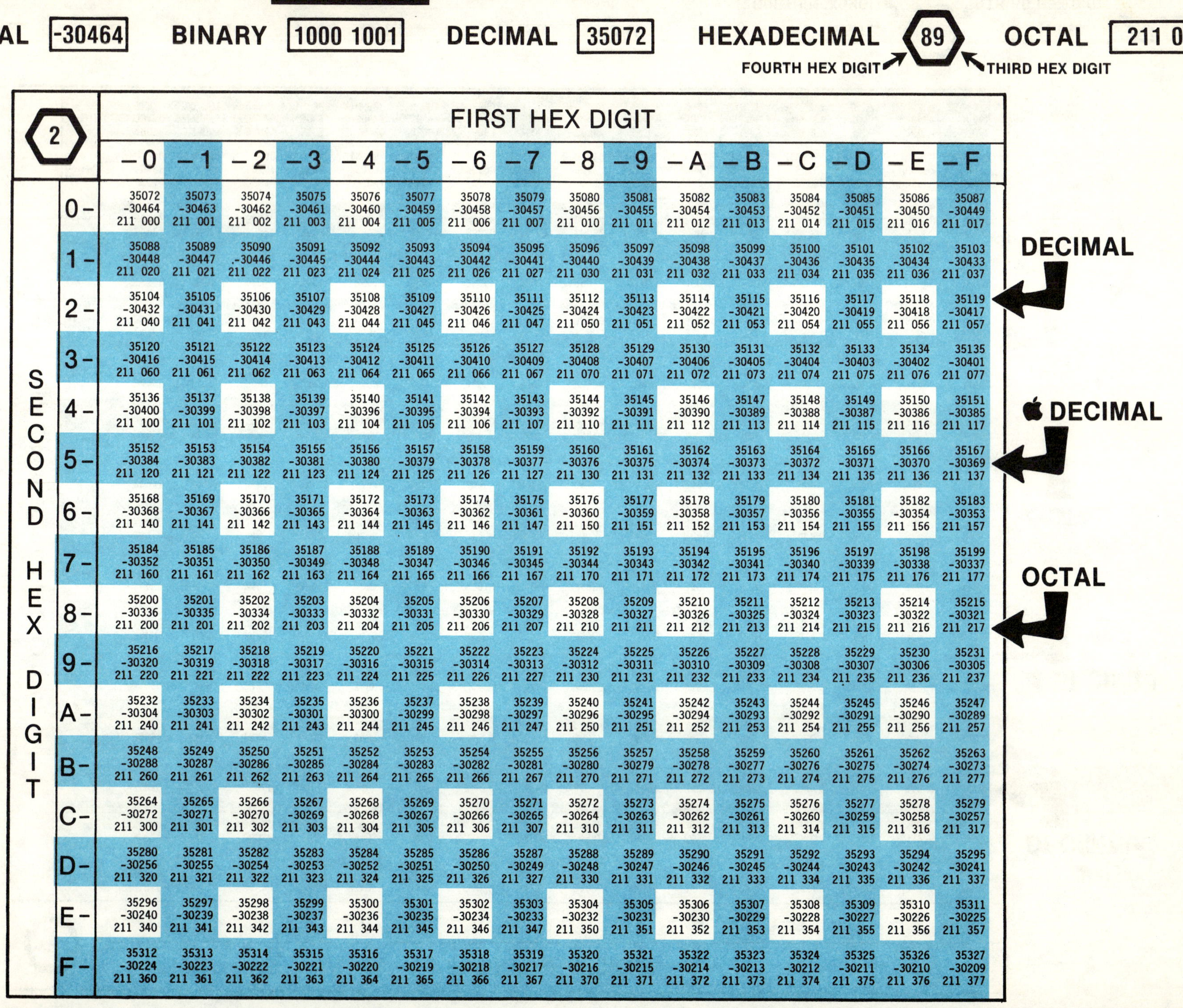

DECIMAL [-30464]  BINARY [1000 1001]  DECIMAL [35072]  HEXADECIMAL ⬡89  OCTAL [211 000]

FOURTH HEX DIGIT → ← THIRD HEX DIGIT

⬡2 — SECOND HEX DIGIT / FIRST HEX DIGIT

| 2 | −0 | −1 | −2 | −3 | −4 | −5 | −6 | −7 | −8 | −9 | −A | −B | −C | −D | −E | −F |
|---|---|---|---|---|---|---|---|---|---|---|---|---|---|---|---|---|
| 0− | 35072<br>-30464<br>211 000 | 35073<br>-30463<br>211 001 | 35074<br>-30462<br>211 002 | 35075<br>-30461<br>211 003 | 35076<br>-30460<br>211 004 | 35077<br>-30459<br>211 005 | 35078<br>-30458<br>211 006 | 35079<br>-30457<br>211 007 | 35080<br>-30456<br>211 010 | 35081<br>-30455<br>211 011 | 35082<br>-30454<br>211 012 | 35083<br>-30453<br>211 013 | 35084<br>-30452<br>211 014 | 35085<br>-30451<br>211 015 | 35086<br>-30450<br>211 016 | 35087<br>-30449<br>211 017 |
| 1− | 35088<br>-30448<br>211 020 | 35089<br>-30447<br>211 021 | 35090<br>-30446<br>211 022 | 35091<br>-30445<br>211 023 | 35092<br>-30444<br>211 024 | 35093<br>-30443<br>211 025 | 35094<br>-30442<br>211 026 | 35095<br>-30441<br>211 027 | 35096<br>-30440<br>211 030 | 35097<br>-30439<br>211 031 | 35098<br>-30438<br>211 032 | 35099<br>-30437<br>211 033 | 35100<br>-30436<br>211 034 | 35101<br>-30435<br>211 035 | 35102<br>-30434<br>211 036 | 35103<br>-30433<br>211 037 |
| 2− | 35104<br>-30432<br>211 040 | 35105<br>-30431<br>211 041 | 35106<br>-30430<br>211 042 | 35107<br>-30429<br>211 043 | 35108<br>-30428<br>211 044 | 35109<br>-30427<br>211 045 | 35110<br>-30426<br>211 046 | 35111<br>-30425<br>211 047 | 35112<br>-30424<br>211 050 | 35113<br>-30423<br>211 051 | 35114<br>-30422<br>211 052 | 35115<br>-30421<br>211 053 | 35116<br>-30420<br>211 054 | 35117<br>-30419<br>211 055 | 35118<br>-30418<br>211 056 | 35119<br>-30417<br>211 057 |
| 3− | 35120<br>-30416<br>211 060 | 35121<br>-30415<br>211 061 | 35122<br>-30414<br>211 062 | 35123<br>-30413<br>211 063 | 35124<br>-30412<br>211 064 | 35125<br>-30411<br>211 065 | 35126<br>-30410<br>211 066 | 35127<br>-30409<br>211 067 | 35128<br>-30408<br>211 070 | 35129<br>-30407<br>211 071 | 35130<br>-30406<br>211 072 | 35131<br>-30405<br>211 073 | 35132<br>-30404<br>211 074 | 35133<br>-30403<br>211 075 | 35134<br>-30402<br>211 076 | 35135<br>-30401<br>211 077 |
| 4− | 35136<br>-30400<br>211 100 | 35137<br>-30399<br>211 101 | 35138<br>-30398<br>211 102 | 35139<br>-30397<br>211 103 | 35140<br>-30396<br>211 104 | 35141<br>-30395<br>211 105 | 35142<br>-30394<br>211 106 | 35143<br>-30393<br>211 107 | 35144<br>-30392<br>211 110 | 35145<br>-30391<br>211 111 | 35146<br>-30390<br>211 112 | 35147<br>-30389<br>211 113 | 35148<br>-30388<br>211 114 | 35149<br>-30387<br>211 115 | 35150<br>-30386<br>211 116 | 35151<br>-30385<br>211 117 |
| 5− | 35152<br>-30384<br>211 120 | 35153<br>-30383<br>211 121 | 35154<br>-30382<br>211 122 | 35155<br>-30381<br>211 123 | 35156<br>-30380<br>211 124 | 35157<br>-30379<br>211 125 | 35158<br>-30378<br>211 126 | 35159<br>-30377<br>211 127 | 35160<br>-30376<br>211 130 | 35161<br>-30375<br>211 131 | 35162<br>-30374<br>211 132 | 35163<br>-30373<br>211 133 | 35164<br>-30372<br>211 134 | 35165<br>-30371<br>211 135 | 35166<br>-30370<br>211 136 | 35167<br>-30369<br>211 137 |
| 6− | 35168<br>-30368<br>211 140 | 35169<br>-30367<br>211 141 | 35170<br>-30366<br>211 142 | 35171<br>-30365<br>211 143 | 35172<br>-30364<br>211 144 | 35173<br>-30363<br>211 145 | 35174<br>-30362<br>211 146 | 35175<br>-30361<br>211 147 | 35176<br>-30360<br>211 150 | 35177<br>-30359<br>211 151 | 35178<br>-30358<br>211 152 | 35179<br>-30357<br>211 153 | 35180<br>-30356<br>211 154 | 35181<br>-30355<br>211 155 | 35182<br>-30354<br>211 156 | 35183<br>-30353<br>211 157 |
| 7− | 35184<br>-30352<br>211 160 | 35185<br>-30351<br>211 161 | 35186<br>-30350<br>211 162 | 35187<br>-30349<br>211 163 | 35188<br>-30348<br>211 164 | 35189<br>-30347<br>211 165 | 35190<br>-30346<br>211 166 | 35191<br>-30345<br>211 167 | 35192<br>-30344<br>211 170 | 35193<br>-30343<br>211 171 | 35194<br>-30342<br>211 172 | 35195<br>-30341<br>211 173 | 35196<br>-30340<br>211 174 | 35197<br>-30339<br>211 175 | 35198<br>-30338<br>211 176 | 35199<br>-30337<br>211 177 |
| 8− | 35200<br>-30336<br>211 200 | 35201<br>-30335<br>211 201 | 35202<br>-30334<br>211 202 | 35203<br>-30333<br>211 203 | 35204<br>-30332<br>211 204 | 35205<br>-30331<br>211 205 | 35206<br>-30330<br>211 206 | 35207<br>-30329<br>211 207 | 35208<br>-30328<br>211 210 | 35209<br>-30327<br>211 211 | 35210<br>-30326<br>211 212 | 35211<br>-30325<br>211 213 | 35212<br>-30324<br>211 214 | 35213<br>-30323<br>211 215 | 35214<br>-30322<br>211 216 | 35215<br>-30321<br>211 217 |
| 9− | 35216<br>-30320<br>211 220 | 35217<br>-30319<br>211 221 | 35218<br>-30318<br>211 222 | 35219<br>-30317<br>211 223 | 35220<br>-30316<br>211 224 | 35221<br>-30315<br>211 225 | 35222<br>-30314<br>211 226 | 35223<br>-30313<br>211 227 | 35224<br>-30312<br>211 230 | 35225<br>-30311<br>211 231 | 35226<br>-30310<br>211 232 | 35227<br>-30309<br>211 233 | 35228<br>-30308<br>211 234 | 35229<br>-30307<br>211 235 | 35230<br>-30306<br>211 236 | 35231<br>-30305<br>211 237 |
| A− | 35232<br>-30304<br>211 240 | 35233<br>-30303<br>211 241 | 35234<br>-30302<br>211 242 | 35235<br>-30301<br>211 243 | 35236<br>-30300<br>211 244 | 35237<br>-30299<br>211 245 | 35238<br>-30298<br>211 246 | 35239<br>-30297<br>211 247 | 35240<br>-30296<br>211 250 | 35241<br>-30295<br>211 251 | 35242<br>-30294<br>211 252 | 35243<br>-30293<br>211 253 | 35244<br>-30292<br>211 254 | 35245<br>-30291<br>211 255 | 35246<br>-30290<br>211 256 | 35247<br>-30289<br>211 257 |
| B− | 35248<br>-30288<br>211 260 | 35249<br>-30287<br>211 261 | 35250<br>-30286<br>211 262 | 35251<br>-30285<br>211 263 | 35252<br>-30284<br>211 264 | 35253<br>-30283<br>211 265 | 35254<br>-30282<br>211 266 | 35255<br>-30281<br>211 267 | 35256<br>-30280<br>211 270 | 35257<br>-30279<br>211 271 | 35258<br>-30278<br>211 272 | 35259<br>-30277<br>211 273 | 35260<br>-30276<br>211 274 | 35261<br>-30275<br>211 275 | 35262<br>-30274<br>211 276 | 35263<br>-30273<br>211 277 |
| C− | 35264<br>-30272<br>211 300 | 35265<br>-30271<br>211 301 | 35266<br>-30270<br>211 302 | 35267<br>-30269<br>211 303 | 35268<br>-30268<br>211 304 | 35269<br>-30267<br>211 305 | 35270<br>-30266<br>211 306 | 35271<br>-30265<br>211 307 | 35272<br>-30264<br>211 310 | 35273<br>-30263<br>211 311 | 35274<br>-30262<br>211 312 | 35275<br>-30261<br>211 313 | 35276<br>-30260<br>211 314 | 35277<br>-30259<br>211 315 | 35278<br>-30258<br>211 316 | 35279<br>-30257<br>211 317 |
| D− | 35280<br>-30256<br>211 320 | 35281<br>-30255<br>211 321 | 35282<br>-30254<br>211 322 | 35283<br>-30253<br>211 323 | 35284<br>-30252<br>211 324 | 35285<br>-30251<br>211 325 | 35286<br>-30250<br>211 326 | 35287<br>-30249<br>211 327 | 35288<br>-30248<br>211 330 | 35289<br>-30247<br>211 331 | 35290<br>-30246<br>211 332 | 35291<br>-30245<br>211 333 | 35292<br>-30244<br>211 334 | 35293<br>-30243<br>211 335 | 35294<br>-30242<br>211 336 | 35295<br>-30241<br>211 337 |
| E− | 35296<br>-30240<br>211 340 | 35297<br>-30239<br>211 341 | 35298<br>-30238<br>211 342 | 35299<br>-30237<br>211 343 | 35300<br>-30236<br>211 344 | 35301<br>-30235<br>211 345 | 35302<br>-30234<br>211 346 | 35303<br>-30233<br>211 347 | 35304<br>-30232<br>211 350 | 35305<br>-30231<br>211 351 | 35306<br>-30230<br>211 352 | 35307<br>-30229<br>211 353 | 35308<br>-30228<br>211 354 | 35309<br>-30227<br>211 355 | 35310<br>-30226<br>211 356 | 35311<br>-30225<br>211 357 |
| F− | 35312<br>-30224<br>211 360 | 35313<br>-30223<br>211 361 | 35314<br>-30222<br>211 362 | 35315<br>-30221<br>211 363 | 35316<br>-30220<br>211 364 | 35317<br>-30219<br>211 365 | 35318<br>-30218<br>211 366 | 35319<br>-30217<br>211 367 | 35320<br>-30216<br>211 370 | 35321<br>-30215<br>211 371 | 35322<br>-30214<br>211 372 | 35323<br>-30213<br>211 373 | 35324<br>-30212<br>211 374 | 35325<br>-30211<br>211 375 | 35326<br>-30210<br>211 376 | 35327<br>-30209<br>211 377 |

<table>
<thead>
<tr><th>⬡ 2</th><th colspan="16">FIRST HEX DIGIT</th></tr>
<tr><th></th><th>−0</th><th>−1</th><th>−2</th><th>−3</th><th>−4</th><th>−5</th><th>−6</th><th>−7</th><th>−8</th><th>−9</th><th>−A</th><th>−B</th><th>−C</th><th>−D</th><th>−E</th><th>−F</th></tr>
</thead>
<tbody>
<tr><td>0−</td><td>35328<br>-30208<br>212 000</td><td>35329<br>-30207<br>212 001</td><td>35330<br>-30206<br>212 002</td><td>35331<br>-30205<br>212 003</td><td>35332<br>-30204<br>212 004</td><td>35333<br>-30203<br>212 005</td><td>35334<br>-30202<br>212 006</td><td>35335<br>-30201<br>212 007</td><td>35336<br>-30200<br>212 010</td><td>35337<br>-30199<br>212 011</td><td>35338<br>-30198<br>212 012</td><td>35339<br>-30197<br>212 013</td><td>35340<br>-30196<br>212 014</td><td>35341<br>-30195<br>212 015</td><td>35342<br>-30194<br>212 016</td><td>35343<br>-30193<br>212 017</td></tr>
<tr><td>1−</td><td>35344<br>-30192<br>212 020</td><td>35345<br>-30191<br>212 021</td><td>35346<br>-30190<br>212 022</td><td>35347<br>-30189<br>212 023</td><td>35348<br>-30188<br>212 024</td><td>35349<br>-30187<br>212 025</td><td>35350<br>-30186<br>212 026</td><td>35351<br>-30185<br>212 027</td><td>35352<br>-30184<br>212 030</td><td>35353<br>-30183<br>212 031</td><td>35354<br>-30182<br>212 032</td><td>35355<br>-30181<br>212 033</td><td>35356<br>-30180<br>212 034</td><td>35357<br>-30179<br>212 035</td><td>35358<br>-30178<br>212 036</td><td>35359<br>-30177<br>212 037</td></tr>
<tr><td>2−</td><td>35360<br>-30176<br>212 040</td><td>35361<br>-30175<br>212 041</td><td>35362<br>-30174<br>212 042</td><td>35363<br>-30173<br>212 043</td><td>35364<br>-30172<br>212 044</td><td>35365<br>-30171<br>212 045</td><td>35366<br>-30170<br>212 046</td><td>35367<br>-30169<br>212 047</td><td>35368<br>-30168<br>212 050</td><td>35369<br>-30167<br>212 051</td><td>35370<br>-30166<br>212 052</td><td>35371<br>-30165<br>212 053</td><td>35372<br>-30164<br>212 054</td><td>35373<br>-30163<br>212 055</td><td>35374<br>-30162<br>212 056</td><td>35375<br>-30161<br>212 057</td></tr>
<tr><td>3−</td><td>35376<br>-30160<br>212 060</td><td>35377<br>-30159<br>212 061</td><td>35378<br>-30158<br>212 062</td><td>35379<br>-30157<br>212 063</td><td>35380<br>-30156<br>212 064</td><td>35381<br>-30155<br>212 065</td><td>35382<br>-30154<br>212 066</td><td>35383<br>-30153<br>212 067</td><td>35384<br>-30152<br>212 070</td><td>35385<br>-30151<br>212 071</td><td>35386<br>-30150<br>212 072</td><td>35387<br>-30149<br>212 073</td><td>35388<br>-30148<br>212 074</td><td>35389<br>-30147<br>212 075</td><td>35390<br>-30146<br>212 076</td><td>35391<br>-30145<br>212 077</td></tr>
<tr><td>4−</td><td>35392<br>-30144<br>212 100</td><td>35393<br>-30143<br>212 101</td><td>35394<br>-30142<br>212 102</td><td>35395<br>-30141<br>212 103</td><td>35396<br>-30140<br>212 104</td><td>35397<br>-30139<br>212 105</td><td>35398<br>-30138<br>212 106</td><td>35399<br>-30137<br>212 107</td><td>35400<br>-30136<br>212 110</td><td>35401<br>-30135<br>212 111</td><td>35402<br>-30134<br>212 112</td><td>35403<br>-30133<br>212 113</td><td>35404<br>-30132<br>212 114</td><td>35405<br>-30131<br>212 115</td><td>35406<br>-30130<br>212 116</td><td>35407<br>-30129<br>212 117</td></tr>
<tr><td>5−</td><td>35408<br>-30128<br>212 120</td><td>35409<br>-30127<br>212 121</td><td>35410<br>-30126<br>212 122</td><td>35411<br>-30125<br>212 123</td><td>35412<br>-30124<br>212 124</td><td>35413<br>-30123<br>212 125</td><td>35414<br>-30122<br>212 126</td><td>35415<br>-30121<br>212 127</td><td>35416<br>-30120<br>212 130</td><td>35417<br>-30119<br>212 131</td><td>35418<br>-30118<br>212 132</td><td>35419<br>-30117<br>212 133</td><td>35420<br>-30116<br>212 134</td><td>35421<br>-30115<br>212 135</td><td>35422<br>-30114<br>212 136</td><td>35423<br>-30113<br>212 137</td></tr>
<tr><td>6−</td><td>35424<br>-30112<br>212 140</td><td>35425<br>-30111<br>212 141</td><td>35426<br>-30110<br>212 142</td><td>35427<br>-30109<br>212 143</td><td>35428<br>-30108<br>212 144</td><td>35429<br>-30107<br>212 145</td><td>35430<br>-30106<br>212 146</td><td>35431<br>-30105<br>212 147</td><td>35432<br>-30104<br>212 150</td><td>35433<br>-30103<br>212 151</td><td>35434<br>-30102<br>212 152</td><td>35435<br>-30101<br>212 153</td><td>35436<br>-30100<br>212 154</td><td>35437<br>-30099<br>212 155</td><td>35438<br>-30098<br>212 156</td><td>35439<br>-30097<br>212 157</td></tr>
<tr><td>7−</td><td>35440<br>-30096<br>212 160</td><td>35441<br>-30095<br>212 161</td><td>35442<br>-30094<br>212 162</td><td>35443<br>-30093<br>212 163</td><td>35444<br>-30092<br>212 164</td><td>35445<br>-30091<br>212 165</td><td>35446<br>-30090<br>212 166</td><td>35447<br>-30089<br>212 167</td><td>35448<br>-30088<br>212 170</td><td>35449<br>-30087<br>212 171</td><td>35450<br>-30086<br>212 172</td><td>35451<br>-30085<br>212 173</td><td>35452<br>-30084<br>212 174</td><td>35453<br>-30083<br>212 175</td><td>35454<br>-30082<br>212 176</td><td>35455<br>-30081<br>212 177</td></tr>
<tr><td>8−</td><td>35456<br>-30080<br>212 200</td><td>35457<br>-30079<br>212 201</td><td>35458<br>-30078<br>212 202</td><td>35459<br>-30077<br>212 203</td><td>35460<br>-30076<br>212 204</td><td>35461<br>-30075<br>212 205</td><td>35462<br>-30074<br>212 206</td><td>35463<br>-30073<br>212 207</td><td>35464<br>-30072<br>212 210</td><td>35465<br>-30071<br>212 211</td><td>35466<br>-30070<br>212 212</td><td>35467<br>-30069<br>212 213</td><td>35468<br>-30068<br>212 214</td><td>35469<br>-30067<br>212 215</td><td>35470<br>-30066<br>212 216</td><td>35471<br>-30065<br>212 217</td></tr>
<tr><td>9−</td><td>35472<br>-30064<br>212 220</td><td>35473<br>-30063<br>212 221</td><td>35474<br>-30062<br>212 222</td><td>35475<br>-30061<br>212 223</td><td>35476<br>-30060<br>212 224</td><td>35477<br>-30059<br>212 225</td><td>35478<br>-30058<br>212 226</td><td>35479<br>-30057<br>212 227</td><td>35480<br>-30056<br>212 230</td><td>35481<br>-30055<br>212 231</td><td>35482<br>-30054<br>212 232</td><td>35483<br>-30053<br>212 233</td><td>35484<br>-30052<br>212 234</td><td>35485<br>-30051<br>212 235</td><td>35486<br>-30050<br>212 236</td><td>35487<br>-30049<br>212 237</td></tr>
<tr><td>A−</td><td>35488<br>-30048<br>212 240</td><td>35489<br>-30047<br>212 241</td><td>35490<br>-30046<br>212 242</td><td>35491<br>-30045<br>212 243</td><td>35492<br>-30044<br>212 244</td><td>35493<br>-30043<br>212 245</td><td>35494<br>-30042<br>212 246</td><td>35495<br>-30041<br>212 247</td><td>35496<br>-30040<br>212 250</td><td>35497<br>-30039<br>212 251</td><td>35498<br>-30038<br>212 252</td><td>35499<br>-30037<br>212 253</td><td>35500<br>-30036<br>212 254</td><td>35501<br>-30035<br>212 255</td><td>35502<br>-30034<br>212 256</td><td>35503<br>-30033<br>212 257</td></tr>
<tr><td>B−</td><td>35504<br>-30032<br>212 260</td><td>35505<br>-30031<br>212 261</td><td>35506<br>-30030<br>212 262</td><td>35507<br>-30029<br>212 263</td><td>35508<br>-30028<br>212 264</td><td>35509<br>-30027<br>212 265</td><td>35510<br>-30026<br>212 266</td><td>35511<br>-30025<br>212 267</td><td>35512<br>-30024<br>212 270</td><td>35513<br>-30023<br>212 271</td><td>35514<br>-30022<br>212 272</td><td>35515<br>-30021<br>212 273</td><td>35516<br>-30020<br>212 274</td><td>35517<br>-30019<br>212 275</td><td>35518<br>-30018<br>212 276</td><td>35519<br>-30017<br>212 277</td></tr>
<tr><td>C−</td><td>35520<br>-30016<br>212 300</td><td>35521<br>-30015<br>212 301</td><td>35522<br>-30014<br>212 302</td><td>35523<br>-30013<br>212 303</td><td>35524<br>-30012<br>212 304</td><td>35525<br>-30011<br>212 305</td><td>35526<br>-30010<br>212 306</td><td>35527<br>-30009<br>212 307</td><td>35528<br>-30008<br>212 310</td><td>35529<br>-30007<br>212 311</td><td>35530<br>-30006<br>212 312</td><td>35531<br>-30005<br>212 313</td><td>35532<br>-30004<br>212 314</td><td>35533<br>-30003<br>212 315</td><td>35534<br>-30002<br>212 316</td><td>35535<br>-30001<br>212 317</td></tr>
<tr><td>D−</td><td>35536<br>-30000<br>212 320</td><td>35537<br>-29999<br>212 321</td><td>35538<br>-29998<br>212 322</td><td>35539<br>-29997<br>212 323</td><td>35540<br>-29996<br>212 324</td><td>35541<br>-29995<br>212 325</td><td>35542<br>-29994<br>212 326</td><td>35543<br>-29993<br>212 327</td><td>35544<br>-29992<br>212 330</td><td>35545<br>-29991<br>212 331</td><td>35546<br>-29990<br>212 332</td><td>35547<br>-29989<br>212 333</td><td>35548<br>-29988<br>212 334</td><td>35549<br>-29987<br>212 335</td><td>35550<br>-29986<br>212 336</td><td>35551<br>-29985<br>212 337</td></tr>
<tr><td>E−</td><td>35552<br>-29984<br>212 340</td><td>35553<br>-29983<br>212 341</td><td>35554<br>-29982<br>212 342</td><td>35555<br>-29981<br>212 343</td><td>35556<br>-29980<br>212 344</td><td>35557<br>-29979<br>212 345</td><td>35558<br>-29978<br>212 346</td><td>35559<br>-29977<br>212 347</td><td>35560<br>-29976<br>212 350</td><td>35561<br>-29975<br>212 351</td><td>35562<br>-29974<br>212 352</td><td>35563<br>-29973<br>212 353</td><td>35564<br>-29972<br>212 354</td><td>35565<br>-29971<br>212 355</td><td>35566<br>-29970<br>212 356</td><td>35567<br>-29969<br>212 357</td></tr>
<tr><td>F−</td><td>35568<br>-29968<br>212 360</td><td>35569<br>-29967<br>212 361</td><td>35570<br>-29966<br>212 362</td><td>35571<br>-29965<br>212 363</td><td>35572<br>-29964<br>212 364</td><td>35573<br>-29963<br>212 365</td><td>35574<br>-29962<br>212 366</td><td>35575<br>-29961<br>212 367</td><td>35576<br>-29960<br>212 370</td><td>35577<br>-29959<br>212 371</td><td>35578<br>-29958<br>212 372</td><td>35579<br>-29957<br>212 373</td><td>35580<br>-29956<br>212 374</td><td>35581<br>-29955<br>212 375</td><td>35582<br>-29954<br>212 376</td><td>35583<br>-29953<br>212 377</td></tr>
</tbody>
</table>

SECOND HEX DIGIT (row labels, top to bottom)

DECIMAL → (points to the top decimal value in each cell)

⌘ DECIMAL → (points to the middle negative decimal value in each cell)

OCTAL → (points to the bottom octal value in each cell)

---

⌘ DECIMAL  `-30208`  BINARY  `1000 1010`  DECIMAL  `35328`  HEXADECIMAL  ⬡ `8A`  OCTAL  `212 000`

FOURTH HEX DIGIT →  ⬡  ← THIRD HEX DIGIT

DECIMAL `-29952`  BINARY `1000 1011`  DECIMAL `35584`  HEXADECIMAL (8B)  OCTAL `213 000`

FOURTH HEX DIGIT → (8B) ← THIRD HEX DIGIT

(2)

## FIRST HEX DIGIT

| | −0 | −1 | −2 | −3 | −4 | −5 | −6 | −7 | −8 | −9 | −A | −B | −C | −D | −E | −F |
|---|---|---|---|---|---|---|---|---|---|---|---|---|---|---|---|---|
| 0− | 35584<br>-29952<br>213 000 | 35585<br>-29951<br>213 001 | 35586<br>-29950<br>213 002 | 35587<br>-29949<br>213 003 | 35588<br>-29948<br>213 004 | 35589<br>-29947<br>213 005 | 35590<br>-29946<br>213 006 | 35591<br>-29945<br>213 007 | 35592<br>-29944<br>213 010 | 35593<br>-29943<br>213 011 | 35594<br>-29942<br>213 012 | 35595<br>-29941<br>213 013 | 35596<br>-29940<br>213 014 | 35597<br>-29939<br>213 015 | 35598<br>-29938<br>213 016 | 35599<br>-29937<br>213 017 |
| 1− | 35600<br>-29936<br>213 020 | 35601<br>-29935<br>213 021 | 35602<br>-29934<br>213 022 | 35603<br>-29933<br>213 023 | 35604<br>-29932<br>213 024 | 35605<br>-29931<br>213 025 | 35606<br>-29930<br>213 026 | 35607<br>-29929<br>213 027 | 35608<br>-29928<br>213 030 | 35609<br>-29927<br>213 031 | 35610<br>-29926<br>213 032 | 35611<br>-29925<br>213 033 | 35612<br>-29924<br>213 034 | 35613<br>-29923<br>213 035 | 35614<br>-29922<br>213 036 | 35615<br>-29921<br>213 037 |
| 2− | 35616<br>-29920<br>213 040 | 35617<br>-29919<br>213 041 | 35618<br>-29918<br>213 042 | 35619<br>-29917<br>213 043 | 35620<br>-29916<br>213 044 | 35621<br>-29915<br>213 045 | 35622<br>-29914<br>213 046 | 35623<br>-29913<br>213 047 | 35624<br>-29912<br>213 050 | 35625<br>-29911<br>213 051 | 35626<br>-29910<br>213 052 | 35627<br>-29909<br>213 053 | 35628<br>-29908<br>213 054 | 35629<br>-29907<br>213 055 | 35630<br>-29906<br>213 056 | 35631<br>-29905<br>213 057 |
| 3− | 35632<br>-29904<br>213 060 | 35633<br>-29903<br>213 061 | 35634<br>-29902<br>213 062 | 35635<br>-29901<br>213 063 | 35636<br>-29900<br>213 064 | 35637<br>-29899<br>213 065 | 35638<br>-29898<br>213 066 | 35639<br>-29897<br>213 067 | 35640<br>-29896<br>213 070 | 35641<br>-29895<br>213 071 | 35642<br>-29894<br>213 072 | 35643<br>-29893<br>213 073 | 35644<br>-29892<br>213 074 | 35645<br>-29891<br>213 075 | 35646<br>-29890<br>213 076 | 35647<br>-29889<br>213 077 |
| 4− | 35648<br>-29888<br>213 100 | 35649<br>-29887<br>213 101 | 35650<br>-29886<br>213 102 | 35651<br>-29885<br>213 103 | 35652<br>-29884<br>213 104 | 35653<br>-29883<br>213 105 | 35654<br>-29882<br>213 106 | 35655<br>-29881<br>213 107 | 35656<br>-29880<br>213 110 | 35657<br>-29879<br>213 111 | 35658<br>-29878<br>213 112 | 35659<br>-29877<br>213 113 | 35660<br>-29876<br>213 114 | 35661<br>-29875<br>213 115 | 35662<br>-29874<br>213 116 | 35663<br>-29873<br>213 117 |
| 5− | 35664<br>-29872<br>213 120 | 35665<br>-29871<br>213 121 | 35666<br>-29870<br>213 122 | 35667<br>-29869<br>213 123 | 35668<br>-29868<br>213 124 | 35669<br>-29867<br>213 125 | 35670<br>-29866<br>213 126 | 35671<br>-29865<br>213 127 | 35672<br>-29864<br>213 130 | 35673<br>-29863<br>213 131 | 35674<br>-29862<br>213 132 | 35675<br>-29861<br>213 133 | 35676<br>-29860<br>213 134 | 35677<br>-29859<br>213 135 | 35678<br>-29858<br>213 136 | 35679<br>-29857<br>213 137 |
| 6− | 35680<br>-29856<br>213 140 | 35681<br>-29855<br>213 141 | 35682<br>-29854<br>213 142 | 35683<br>-29853<br>213 143 | 35684<br>-29852<br>213 144 | 35685<br>-29851<br>213 145 | 35686<br>-29850<br>213 146 | 35687<br>-29849<br>213 147 | 35688<br>-29848<br>213 150 | 35689<br>-29847<br>213 151 | 35690<br>-29846<br>213 152 | 35691<br>-29845<br>213 153 | 35692<br>-29844<br>213 154 | 35693<br>-29843<br>213 155 | 35694<br>-29842<br>213 156 | 35695<br>-29841<br>213 157 |
| 7− | 35696<br>-29840<br>213 160 | 35697<br>-29839<br>213 161 | 35698<br>-29838<br>213 162 | 35699<br>-29837<br>213 163 | 35700<br>-29836<br>213 164 | 35701<br>-29835<br>213 165 | 35702<br>-29834<br>213 166 | 35703<br>-29833<br>213 167 | 35704<br>-29832<br>213 170 | 35705<br>-29831<br>213 171 | 35706<br>-29830<br>213 172 | 35707<br>-29829<br>213 173 | 35708<br>-29828<br>213 174 | 35709<br>-29827<br>213 175 | 35710<br>-29826<br>213 176 | 35711<br>-29825<br>213 177 |
| 8− | 35712<br>-29824<br>213 200 | 35713<br>-29823<br>213 201 | 35714<br>-29822<br>213 202 | 35715<br>-29821<br>213 203 | 35716<br>-29820<br>213 204 | 35717<br>-29819<br>213 205 | 35718<br>-29818<br>213 206 | 35719<br>-29817<br>213 207 | 35720<br>-29816<br>213 210 | 35721<br>-29815<br>213 211 | 35722<br>-29814<br>213 212 | 35723<br>-29813<br>213 213 | 35724<br>-29812<br>213 214 | 35725<br>-29811<br>213 215 | 35726<br>-29810<br>213 216 | 35727<br>-29809<br>213 217 |
| 9− | 35728<br>-29808<br>213 220 | 35729<br>-29807<br>213 221 | 35730<br>-29806<br>213 222 | 35731<br>-29805<br>213 223 | 35732<br>-29804<br>213 224 | 35733<br>-29803<br>213 225 | 35734<br>-29802<br>213 226 | 35735<br>-29801<br>213 227 | 35736<br>-29800<br>213 230 | 35737<br>-29799<br>213 231 | 35738<br>-29798<br>213 232 | 35739<br>-29797<br>213 233 | 35740<br>-29796<br>213 234 | 35741<br>-29795<br>213 235 | 35742<br>-29794<br>213 236 | 35743<br>-29793<br>213 237 |
| A− | 35744<br>-29792<br>213 240 | 35745<br>-29791<br>213 241 | 35746<br>-29790<br>213 242 | 35747<br>-29789<br>213 243 | 35748<br>-29788<br>213 244 | 35749<br>-29787<br>213 245 | 35750<br>-29786<br>213 246 | 35751<br>-29785<br>213 247 | 35752<br>-29784<br>213 250 | 35753<br>-29783<br>213 251 | 35754<br>-29782<br>213 252 | 35755<br>-29781<br>213 253 | 35756<br>-29780<br>213 254 | 35757<br>-29779<br>213 255 | 35758<br>-29778<br>213 256 | 35759<br>-29777<br>213 257 |
| B− | 35760<br>-29776<br>213 260 | 35761<br>-29775<br>213 261 | 35762<br>-29774<br>213 262 | 35763<br>-29773<br>213 263 | 35764<br>-29772<br>213 264 | 35765<br>-29771<br>213 265 | 35766<br>-29770<br>213 266 | 35767<br>-29769<br>213 267 | 35768<br>-29768<br>213 270 | 35769<br>-29767<br>213 271 | 35770<br>-29766<br>213 272 | 35771<br>-29765<br>213 273 | 35772<br>-29764<br>213 274 | 35773<br>-29763<br>213 275 | 35774<br>-29762<br>213 276 | 35775<br>-29761<br>213 277 |
| C− | 35776<br>-29760<br>213 300 | 35777<br>-29759<br>213 301 | 35778<br>-29758<br>213 302 | 35779<br>-29757<br>213 303 | 35780<br>-29756<br>213 304 | 35781<br>-29755<br>213 305 | 35782<br>-29754<br>213 306 | 35783<br>-29753<br>213 307 | 35784<br>-29752<br>213 310 | 35785<br>-29751<br>213 311 | 35786<br>-29750<br>213 312 | 35787<br>-29749<br>213 313 | 35788<br>-29748<br>213 314 | 35789<br>-29747<br>213 315 | 35790<br>-29746<br>213 316 | 35791<br>-29745<br>213 317 |
| D− | 35792<br>-29744<br>213 320 | 35793<br>-29743<br>213 321 | 35794<br>-29742<br>213 322 | 35795<br>-29741<br>213 323 | 35796<br>-29740<br>213 324 | 35797<br>-29739<br>213 325 | 35798<br>-29738<br>213 326 | 35799<br>-29737<br>213 327 | 35800<br>-29736<br>213 330 | 35801<br>-29735<br>213 331 | 35802<br>-29734<br>213 332 | 35803<br>-29733<br>213 333 | 35804<br>-29732<br>213 334 | 35805<br>-29731<br>213 335 | 35806<br>-29730<br>213 336 | 35807<br>-29729<br>213 337 |
| E− | 35808<br>-29728<br>213 340 | 35809<br>-29727<br>213 341 | 35810<br>-29726<br>213 342 | 35811<br>-29725<br>213 343 | 35812<br>-29724<br>213 344 | 35813<br>-29723<br>213 345 | 35814<br>-29722<br>213 346 | 35815<br>-29721<br>213 347 | 35816<br>-29720<br>213 350 | 35817<br>-29719<br>213 351 | 35818<br>-29718<br>213 352 | 35819<br>-29717<br>213 353 | 35820<br>-29716<br>213 354 | 35821<br>-29715<br>213 355 | 35822<br>-29714<br>213 356 | 35823<br>-29713<br>213 357 |
| F− | 35824<br>-29712<br>213 360 | 35825<br>-29711<br>213 361 | 35826<br>-29710<br>213 362 | 35827<br>-29709<br>213 363 | 35828<br>-29708<br>213 364 | 35829<br>-29707<br>213 365 | 35830<br>-29706<br>213 366 | 35831<br>-29705<br>213 367 | 35832<br>-29704<br>213 370 | 35833<br>-29703<br>213 371 | 35834<br>-29702<br>213 372 | 35835<br>-29701<br>213 373 | 35836<br>-29700<br>213 374 | 35837<br>-29699<br>213 375 | 35838<br>-29698<br>213 376 | 35839<br>-29697<br>213 377 |

SECOND HEX DIGIT (row labels, left side)

DECIMAL · DECIMAL · OCTAL (right-side labels)

| SECOND HEX DIGIT | −0 | −1 | −2 | −3 | −4 | −5 | −6 | −7 | −8 | −9 | −A | −B | −C | −D | −E | −F |
|---|---|---|---|---|---|---|---|---|---|---|---|---|---|---|---|---|
| 0- | 35840<br>-29696<br>214 000 | 35841<br>-29695<br>214 001 | 35842<br>-29694<br>214 002 | 35843<br>-29693<br>214 003 | 35844<br>-29692<br>214 004 | 35845<br>-29691<br>214 005 | 35846<br>-29690<br>214 006 | 35847<br>-29689<br>214 007 | 35848<br>-29688<br>214 010 | 35849<br>-29687<br>214 011 | 35850<br>-29686<br>214 012 | 35851<br>-29685<br>214 013 | 35852<br>-29684<br>214 014 | 35853<br>-29683<br>214 015 | 35854<br>-29682<br>214 016 | 35855<br>-29681<br>214 017 |
| 1- | 35856<br>-29680<br>214 020 | 35857<br>-29679<br>214 021 | 35858<br>-29678<br>214 022 | 35859<br>-29677<br>214 023 | 35860<br>-29676<br>214 024 | 35861<br>-29675<br>214 025 | 35862<br>-29674<br>214 026 | 35863<br>-29673<br>214 027 | 35864<br>-29672<br>214 030 | 35865<br>-29671<br>214 031 | 35866<br>-29670<br>214 032 | 35867<br>-29669<br>214 033 | 35868<br>-29668<br>214 034 | 35869<br>-29667<br>214 035 | 35870<br>-29666<br>214 036 | 35871<br>-29665<br>214 037 |
| 2- | 35872<br>-29664<br>214 040 | 35873<br>-29663<br>214 041 | 35874<br>-29662<br>214 042 | 35875<br>-29661<br>214 043 | 35876<br>-29660<br>214 044 | 35877<br>-29659<br>214 045 | 35878<br>-29658<br>214 046 | 35879<br>-29657<br>214 047 | 35880<br>-29656<br>214 050 | 35881<br>-29655<br>214 051 | 35882<br>-29654<br>214 052 | 35883<br>-29653<br>214 053 | 35884<br>-29652<br>214 054 | 35885<br>-29651<br>214 055 | 35886<br>-29650<br>214 056 | 35887<br>-29649<br>214 057 |
| 3- | 35888<br>-29648<br>214 060 | 35889<br>-29647<br>214 061 | 35890<br>-29646<br>214 062 | 35891<br>-29645<br>214 063 | 35892<br>-29644<br>214 064 | 35893<br>-29643<br>214 065 | 35894<br>-29642<br>214 066 | 35895<br>-29641<br>214 067 | 35896<br>-29640<br>214 070 | 35897<br>-29639<br>214 071 | 35898<br>-29638<br>214 072 | 35899<br>-29637<br>214 073 | 35900<br>-29636<br>214 074 | 35901<br>-29635<br>214 075 | 35902<br>-29634<br>214 076 | 35903<br>-29633<br>214 077 |
| 4- | 35904<br>-29632<br>214 100 | 35905<br>-29631<br>214 101 | 35906<br>-29630<br>214 102 | 35907<br>-29629<br>214 103 | 35908<br>-29628<br>214 104 | 35909<br>-29627<br>214 105 | 35910<br>-29626<br>214 106 | 35911<br>-29625<br>214 107 | 35912<br>-29624<br>214 110 | 35913<br>-29623<br>214 111 | 35914<br>-29622<br>214 112 | 35915<br>-29621<br>214 113 | 35916<br>-29620<br>214 114 | 35917<br>-29619<br>214 115 | 35918<br>-29618<br>214 116 | 35919<br>-29617<br>214 117 |
| 5- | 35920<br>-29616<br>214 120 | 35921<br>-29615<br>214 121 | 35922<br>-29614<br>214 122 | 35923<br>-29613<br>214 123 | 35924<br>-29612<br>214 124 | 35925<br>-29611<br>214 125 | 35926<br>-29610<br>214 126 | 35927<br>-29609<br>214 127 | 35928<br>-29608<br>214 130 | 35929<br>-29607<br>214 131 | 35930<br>-29606<br>214 132 | 35931<br>-29605<br>214 133 | 35932<br>-29604<br>214 134 | 35933<br>-29603<br>214 135 | 35934<br>-29602<br>214 136 | 35935<br>-29601<br>214 137 |
| 6- | 35936<br>-29600<br>214 140 | 35937<br>-29599<br>214 141 | 35938<br>-29598<br>214 142 | 35939<br>-29597<br>214 143 | 35940<br>-29596<br>214 144 | 35941<br>-29595<br>214 145 | 35942<br>-29594<br>214 146 | 35943<br>-29593<br>214 147 | 35944<br>-29592<br>214 150 | 35945<br>-29591<br>214 151 | 35946<br>-29590<br>214 152 | 35947<br>-29589<br>214 153 | 35948<br>-29588<br>214 154 | 35949<br>-29587<br>214 155 | 35950<br>-29586<br>214 156 | 35951<br>-29585<br>214 157 |
| 7- | 35952<br>-29584<br>214 160 | 35953<br>-29583<br>214 161 | 35954<br>-29582<br>214 162 | 35955<br>-29581<br>214 163 | 35956<br>-29580<br>214 164 | 35957<br>-29579<br>214 165 | 35958<br>-29578<br>214 166 | 35959<br>-29577<br>214 167 | 35960<br>-29576<br>214 170 | 35961<br>-29575<br>214 171 | 35962<br>-29574<br>214 172 | 35963<br>-29573<br>214 173 | 35964<br>-29572<br>214 174 | 35965<br>-29571<br>214 175 | 35966<br>-29570<br>214 176 | 35967<br>-29569<br>214 177 |
| 8- | 35968<br>-29568<br>214 200 | 35969<br>-29567<br>214 201 | 35970<br>-29566<br>214 202 | 35971<br>-29565<br>214 203 | 35972<br>-29564<br>214 204 | 35973<br>-29563<br>214 205 | 35974<br>-29562<br>214 206 | 35975<br>-29561<br>214 207 | 35976<br>-29560<br>214 210 | 35977<br>-29559<br>214 211 | 35978<br>-29558<br>214 212 | 35979<br>-29557<br>214 213 | 35980<br>-29556<br>214 214 | 35981<br>-29555<br>214 215 | 35982<br>-29554<br>214 216 | 35983<br>-29553<br>214 217 |
| 9- | 35984<br>-29552<br>214 220 | 35985<br>-29551<br>214 221 | 35986<br>-29550<br>214 222 | 35987<br>-29549<br>214 223 | 35988<br>-29548<br>214 224 | 35989<br>-29547<br>214 225 | 35990<br>-29546<br>214 226 | 35991<br>-29545<br>214 227 | 35992<br>-29544<br>214 230 | 35993<br>-29543<br>214 231 | 35994<br>-29542<br>214 232 | 35995<br>-29541<br>214 233 | 35996<br>-29540<br>214 234 | 35997<br>-29539<br>214 235 | 35998<br>-29538<br>214 236 | 35999<br>-29537<br>214 237 |
| A- | 36000<br>-29536<br>214 240 | 36001<br>-29535<br>214 241 | 36002<br>-29534<br>214 242 | 36003<br>-29533<br>214 243 | 36004<br>-29532<br>214 244 | 36005<br>-29531<br>214 245 | 36006<br>-29530<br>214 246 | 36007<br>-29529<br>214 247 | 36008<br>-29528<br>214 250 | 36009<br>-29527<br>214 251 | 36010<br>-29526<br>214 252 | 36011<br>-29525<br>214 253 | 36012<br>-29524<br>214 254 | 36013<br>-29523<br>214 255 | 36014<br>-29522<br>214 256 | 36015<br>-29521<br>214 257 |
| B- | 36016<br>-29520<br>214 260 | 36017<br>-29519<br>214 261 | 36018<br>-29518<br>214 262 | 36019<br>-29517<br>214 263 | 36020<br>-29516<br>214 264 | 36021<br>-29515<br>214 265 | 36022<br>-29514<br>214 266 | 36023<br>-29513<br>214 267 | 36024<br>-29512<br>214 270 | 36025<br>-29511<br>214 271 | 36026<br>-29510<br>214 272 | 36027<br>-29509<br>214 273 | 36028<br>-29508<br>214 274 | 36029<br>-29507<br>214 275 | 36030<br>-29506<br>214 276 | 36031<br>-29505<br>214 277 |
| C- | 36032<br>-29504<br>214 300 | 36033<br>-29503<br>214 301 | 36034<br>-29502<br>214 302 | 36035<br>-29501<br>214 303 | 36036<br>-29500<br>214 304 | 36037<br>-29499<br>214 305 | 36038<br>-29498<br>214 306 | 36039<br>-29497<br>214 307 | 36040<br>-29496<br>214 310 | 36041<br>-29495<br>214 311 | 36042<br>-29494<br>214 312 | 36043<br>-29493<br>214 313 | 36044<br>-29492<br>214 314 | 36045<br>-29491<br>214 315 | 36046<br>-29490<br>214 316 | 36047<br>-29489<br>214 317 |
| D- | 36048<br>-29488<br>214 320 | 36049<br>-29487<br>214 321 | 36050<br>-29486<br>214 322 | 36051<br>-29485<br>214 323 | 36052<br>-29484<br>214 324 | 36053<br>-29483<br>214 325 | 36054<br>-29482<br>214 326 | 36055<br>-29481<br>214 327 | 36056<br>-29480<br>214 330 | 36057<br>-29479<br>214 331 | 36058<br>-29478<br>214 332 | 36059<br>-29477<br>214 333 | 36060<br>-29476<br>214 334 | 36061<br>-29475<br>214 335 | 36062<br>-29474<br>214 336 | 36063<br>-29473<br>214 337 |
| E- | 36064<br>-29472<br>214 340 | 36065<br>-29471<br>214 341 | 36066<br>-29470<br>214 342 | 36067<br>-29469<br>214 343 | 36068<br>-29468<br>214 344 | 36069<br>-29467<br>214 345 | 36070<br>-29466<br>214 346 | 36071<br>-29465<br>214 347 | 36072<br>-29464<br>214 350 | 36073<br>-29463<br>214 351 | 36074<br>-29462<br>214 352 | 36075<br>-29461<br>214 353 | 36076<br>-29460<br>214 354 | 36077<br>-29459<br>214 355 | 36078<br>-29458<br>214 356 | 36079<br>-29457<br>214 357 |
| F- | 36080<br>-29456<br>214 360 | 36081<br>-29455<br>214 361 | 36082<br>-29454<br>214 362 | 36083<br>-29453<br>214 363 | 36084<br>-29452<br>214 364 | 36085<br>-29451<br>214 365 | 36086<br>-29450<br>214 366 | 36087<br>-29449<br>214 367 | 36088<br>-29448<br>214 370 | 36089<br>-29447<br>214 371 | 36090<br>-29446<br>214 372 | 36091<br>-29445<br>214 373 | 36092<br>-29444<br>214 374 | 36093<br>-29443<br>214 375 | 36094<br>-29442<br>214 376 | 36095<br>-29441<br>214 377 |

DECIMAL → (right margin)
DECIMAL → (right margin)
OCTAL → (right margin)

 DECIMAL `-29696`   BINARY `1000 1100`   DECIMAL `35840`   HEXADECIMAL 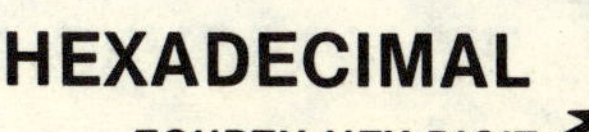  `8C`   OCTAL `214 000`

FOURTH HEX DIGIT → 8C ← THIRD HEX DIGIT

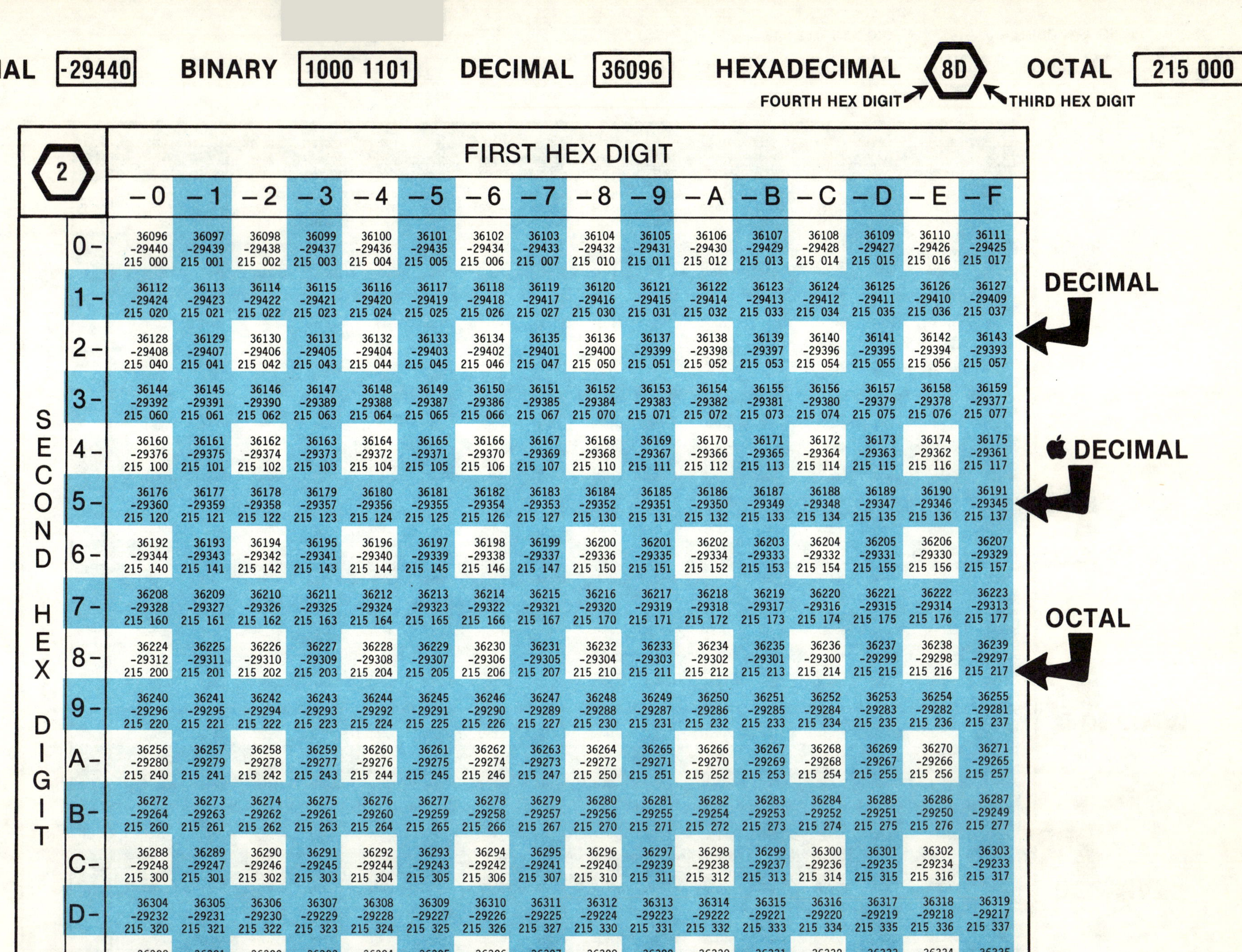



FIRST HEX DIGIT

| (2) | −0 | −1 | −2 | −3 | −4 | −5 | −6 | −7 | −8 | −9 | −A | −B | −C | −D | −E | −F |
|---|---|---|---|---|---|---|---|---|---|---|---|---|---|---|---|---|
| 0− | 36096<br>−29440<br>215 000 | 36097<br>−29439<br>215 001 | 36098<br>−29438<br>215 002 | 36099<br>−29437<br>215 003 | 36100<br>−29436<br>215 004 | 36101<br>−29435<br>215 005 | 36102<br>−29434<br>215 006 | 36103<br>−29433<br>215 007 | 36104<br>−29432<br>215 010 | 36105<br>−29431<br>215 011 | 36106<br>−29430<br>215 012 | 36107<br>−29429<br>215 013 | 36108<br>−29428<br>215 014 | 36109<br>−29427<br>215 015 | 36110<br>−29426<br>215 016 | 36111<br>−29425<br>215 017 |
| 1− | 36112<br>−29424<br>215 020 | 36113<br>−29423<br>215 021 | 36114<br>−29422<br>215 022 | 36115<br>−29421<br>215 023 | 36116<br>−29420<br>215 024 | 36117<br>−29419<br>215 025 | 36118<br>−29418<br>215 026 | 36119<br>−29417<br>215 027 | 36120<br>−29416<br>215 030 | 36121<br>−29415<br>215 031 | 36122<br>−29414<br>215 032 | 36123<br>−29413<br>215 033 | 36124<br>−29412<br>215 034 | 36125<br>−29411<br>215 035 | 36126<br>−29410<br>215 036 | 36127<br>−29409<br>215 037 |
| 2− | 36128<br>−29408<br>215 040 | 36129<br>−29407<br>215 041 | 36130<br>−29406<br>215 042 | 36131<br>−29405<br>215 043 | 36132<br>−29404<br>215 044 | 36133<br>−29403<br>215 045 | 36134<br>−29402<br>215 046 | 36135<br>−29401<br>215 047 | 36136<br>−29400<br>215 050 | 36137<br>−29399<br>215 051 | 36138<br>−29398<br>215 052 | 36139<br>−29397<br>215 053 | 36140<br>−29396<br>215 054 | 36141<br>−29395<br>215 055 | 36142<br>−29394<br>215 056 | 36143<br>−29393<br>215 057 |
| 3− | 36144<br>−29392<br>215 060 | 36145<br>−29391<br>215 061 | 36146<br>−29390<br>215 062 | 36147<br>−29389<br>215 063 | 36148<br>−29388<br>215 064 | 36149<br>−29387<br>215 065 | 36150<br>−29386<br>215 066 | 36151<br>−29385<br>215 067 | 36152<br>−29384<br>215 070 | 36153<br>−29383<br>215 071 | 36154<br>−29382<br>215 072 | 36155<br>−29381<br>215 073 | 36156<br>−29380<br>215 074 | 36157<br>−29379<br>215 075 | 36158<br>−29378<br>215 076 | 36159<br>−29377<br>215 077 |
| 4− | 36160<br>−29376<br>215 100 | 36161<br>−29375<br>215 101 | 36162<br>−29374<br>215 102 | 36163<br>−29373<br>215 103 | 36164<br>−29372<br>215 104 | 36165<br>−29371<br>215 105 | 36166<br>−29370<br>215 106 | 36167<br>−29369<br>215 107 | 36168<br>−29368<br>215 110 | 36169<br>−29367<br>215 111 | 36170<br>−29366<br>215 112 | 36171<br>−29365<br>215 113 | 36172<br>−29364<br>215 114 | 36173<br>−29363<br>215 115 | 36174<br>−29362<br>215 116 | 36175<br>−29361<br>215 117 |
| 5− | 36176<br>−29360<br>215 120 | 36177<br>−29359<br>215 121 | 36178<br>−29358<br>215 122 | 36179<br>−29357<br>215 123 | 36180<br>−29356<br>215 124 | 36181<br>−29355<br>215 125 | 36182<br>−29354<br>215 126 | 36183<br>−29353<br>215 127 | 36184<br>−29352<br>215 130 | 36185<br>−29351<br>215 131 | 36186<br>−29350<br>215 132 | 36187<br>−29349<br>215 133 | 36188<br>−29348<br>215 134 | 36189<br>−29347<br>215 135 | 36190<br>−29346<br>215 136 | 36191<br>−29345<br>215 137 |
| 6− | 36192<br>−29344<br>215 140 | 36193<br>−29343<br>215 141 | 36194<br>−29342<br>215 142 | 36195<br>−29341<br>215 143 | 36196<br>−29340<br>215 144 | 36197<br>−29339<br>215 145 | 36198<br>−29338<br>215 146 | 36199<br>−29337<br>215 147 | 36200<br>−29336<br>215 150 | 36201<br>−29335<br>215 151 | 36202<br>−29334<br>215 152 | 36203<br>−29333<br>215 153 | 36204<br>−29332<br>215 154 | 36205<br>−29331<br>215 155 | 36206<br>−29330<br>215 156 | 36207<br>−29329<br>215 157 |
| 7− | 36208<br>−29328<br>215 160 | 36209<br>−29327<br>215 161 | 36210<br>−29326<br>215 162 | 36211<br>−29325<br>215 163 | 36212<br>−29324<br>215 164 | 36213<br>−29323<br>215 165 | 36214<br>−29322<br>215 166 | 36215<br>−29321<br>215 167 | 36216<br>−29320<br>215 170 | 36217<br>−29319<br>215 171 | 36218<br>−29318<br>215 172 | 36219<br>−29317<br>215 173 | 36220<br>−29316<br>215 174 | 36221<br>−29315<br>215 175 | 36222<br>−29314<br>215 176 | 36223<br>−29313<br>215 177 |
| 8− | 36224<br>−29312<br>215 200 | 36225<br>−29311<br>215 201 | 36226<br>−29310<br>215 202 | 36227<br>−29309<br>215 203 | 36228<br>−29308<br>215 204 | 36229<br>−29307<br>215 205 | 36230<br>−29306<br>215 206 | 36231<br>−29305<br>215 207 | 36232<br>−29304<br>215 210 | 36233<br>−29303<br>215 211 | 36234<br>−29302<br>215 212 | 36235<br>−29301<br>215 213 | 36236<br>−29300<br>215 214 | 36237<br>−29299<br>215 215 | 36238<br>−29298<br>215 216 | 36239<br>−29297<br>215 217 |
| 9− | 36240<br>−29296<br>215 220 | 36241<br>−29295<br>215 221 | 36242<br>−29294<br>215 222 | 36243<br>−29293<br>215 223 | 36244<br>−29292<br>215 224 | 36245<br>−29291<br>215 225 | 36246<br>−29290<br>215 226 | 36247<br>−29289<br>215 227 | 36248<br>−29288<br>215 230 | 36249<br>−29287<br>215 231 | 36250<br>−29286<br>215 232 | 36251<br>−29285<br>215 233 | 36252<br>−29284<br>215 234 | 36253<br>−29283<br>215 235 | 36254<br>−29282<br>215 236 | 36255<br>−29281<br>215 237 |
| A− | 36256<br>−29280<br>215 240 | 36257<br>−29279<br>215 241 | 36258<br>−29278<br>215 242 | 36259<br>−29277<br>215 243 | 36260<br>−29276<br>215 244 | 36261<br>−29275<br>215 245 | 36262<br>−29274<br>215 246 | 36263<br>−29273<br>215 247 | 36264<br>−29272<br>215 250 | 36265<br>−29271<br>215 251 | 36266<br>−29270<br>215 252 | 36267<br>−29269<br>215 253 | 36268<br>−29268<br>215 254 | 36269<br>−29267<br>215 255 | 36270<br>−29266<br>215 256 | 36271<br>−29265<br>215 257 |
| B− | 36272<br>−29264<br>215 260 | 36273<br>−29263<br>215 261 | 36274<br>−29262<br>215 262 | 36275<br>−29261<br>215 263 | 36276<br>−29260<br>215 264 | 36277<br>−29259<br>215 265 | 36278<br>−29258<br>215 266 | 36279<br>−29257<br>215 267 | 36280<br>−29256<br>215 270 | 36281<br>−29255<br>215 271 | 36282<br>−29254<br>215 272 | 36283<br>−29253<br>215 273 | 36284<br>−29252<br>215 274 | 36285<br>−29251<br>215 275 | 36286<br>−29250<br>215 276 | 36287<br>−29249<br>215 277 |
| C− | 36288<br>−29248<br>215 300 | 36289<br>−29247<br>215 301 | 36290<br>−29246<br>215 302 | 36291<br>−29245<br>215 303 | 36292<br>−29244<br>215 304 | 36293<br>−29243<br>215 305 | 36294<br>−29242<br>215 306 | 36295<br>−29241<br>215 307 | 36296<br>−29240<br>215 310 | 36297<br>−29239<br>215 311 | 36298<br>−29238<br>215 312 | 36299<br>−29237<br>215 313 | 36300<br>−29236<br>215 314 | 36301<br>−29235<br>215 315 | 36302<br>−29234<br>215 316 | 36303<br>−29233<br>215 317 |
| D− | 36304<br>−29232<br>215 320 | 36305<br>−29231<br>215 321 | 36306<br>−29230<br>215 322 | 36307<br>−29229<br>215 323 | 36308<br>−29228<br>215 324 | 36309<br>−29227<br>215 325 | 36310<br>−29226<br>215 326 | 36311<br>−29225<br>215 327 | 36312<br>−29224<br>215 330 | 36313<br>−29223<br>215 331 | 36314<br>−29222<br>215 332 | 36315<br>−29221<br>215 333 | 36316<br>−29220<br>215 334 | 36317<br>−29219<br>215 335 | 36318<br>−29218<br>215 336 | 36319<br>−29217<br>215 337 |
| E− | 36320<br>−29216<br>215 340 | 36321<br>−29215<br>215 341 | 36322<br>−29214<br>215 342 | 36323<br>−29213<br>215 343 | 36324<br>−29212<br>215 344 | 36325<br>−29211<br>215 345 | 36326<br>−29210<br>215 346 | 36327<br>−29209<br>215 347 | 36328<br>−29208<br>215 350 | 36329<br>−29207<br>215 351 | 36330<br>−29206<br>215 352 | 36331<br>−29205<br>215 353 | 36332<br>−29204<br>215 354 | 36333<br>−29203<br>215 355 | 36334<br>−29202<br>215 356 | 36335<br>−29201<br>215 357 |
| F− | 36336<br>−29200<br>215 360 | 36337<br>−29199<br>215 361 | 36338<br>−29198<br>215 362 | 36339<br>−29197<br>215 363 | 36340<br>−29196<br>215 364 | 36341<br>−29195<br>215 365 | 36342<br>−29194<br>215 366 | 36343<br>−29193<br>215 367 | 36344<br>−29192<br>215 370 | 36345<br>−29191<br>215 371 | 36346<br>−29190<br>215 372 | 36347<br>−29189<br>215 373 | 36348<br>−29188<br>215 374 | 36349<br>−29187<br>215 375 | 36350<br>−29186<br>215 376 | 36351<br>−29185<br>215 377 |

SECOND HEX DIGIT (row labels, left side)

## FIRST HEX DIGIT

**② SECOND HEX DIGIT**

Each cell lists: DECIMAL (top) / DECIMAL negative (middle) / OCTAL (bottom).

| | −0 | −1 | −2 | −3 | −4 | −5 | −6 | −7 | −8 | −9 | −A | −B | −C | −D | −E | −F |
|---|---|---|---|---|---|---|---|---|---|---|---|---|---|---|---|---|
| **0−** | 36352<br>−29184<br>216 000 | 36353<br>−29183<br>216 001 | 36354<br>−29182<br>216 002 | 36355<br>−29181<br>216 003 | 36356<br>−29180<br>216 004 | 36357<br>−29179<br>216 005 | 36358<br>−29178<br>216 006 | 36359<br>−29177<br>216 007 | 36360<br>−29176<br>216 010 | 36361<br>−29175<br>216 011 | 36362<br>−29174<br>216 012 | 36363<br>−29173<br>216 013 | 36364<br>−29172<br>216 014 | 36365<br>−29171<br>216 015 | 36366<br>−29170<br>216 016 | 36367<br>−29169<br>216 017 |
| **1−** | 36368<br>−29168<br>216 020 | 36369<br>−29167<br>216 021 | 36370<br>−29166<br>216 022 | 36371<br>−29165<br>216 023 | 36372<br>−29164<br>216 024 | 36373<br>−29163<br>216 025 | 36374<br>−29162<br>216 026 | 36375<br>−29161<br>216 027 | 36376<br>−29160<br>216 030 | 36377<br>−29159<br>216 031 | 36378<br>−29158<br>216 032 | 36379<br>−29157<br>216 033 | 36380<br>−29156<br>216 034 | 36381<br>−29155<br>216 035 | 36382<br>−29154<br>216 036 | 36383<br>−29153<br>216 037 |
| **2−** | 36384<br>−29152<br>216 040 | 36385<br>−29151<br>216 041 | 36386<br>−29150<br>216 042 | 36387<br>−29149<br>216 043 | 36388<br>−29148<br>216 044 | 36389<br>−29147<br>216 045 | 36390<br>−29146<br>216 046 | 36391<br>−29145<br>216 047 | 36392<br>−29144<br>216 050 | 36393<br>−29143<br>216 051 | 36394<br>−29142<br>216 052 | 36395<br>−29141<br>216 053 | 36396<br>−29140<br>216 054 | 36397<br>−29139<br>216 055 | 36398<br>−29138<br>216 056 | 36399<br>−29137<br>216 057 |
| **3−** | 36400<br>−29136<br>216 060 | 36401<br>−29135<br>216 061 | 36402<br>−29134<br>216 062 | 36403<br>−29133<br>216 063 | 36404<br>−29132<br>216 064 | 36405<br>−29131<br>216 065 | 36406<br>−29130<br>216 066 | 36407<br>−29129<br>216 067 | 36408<br>−29128<br>216 070 | 36409<br>−29127<br>216 071 | 36410<br>−29126<br>216 072 | 36411<br>−29125<br>216 073 | 36412<br>−29124<br>216 074 | 36413<br>−29123<br>216 075 | 36414<br>−29122<br>216 076 | 36415<br>−29121<br>216 077 |
| **4−** | 36416<br>−29120<br>216 100 | 36417<br>−29119<br>216 101 | 36418<br>−29118<br>216 102 | 36419<br>−29117<br>216 103 | 36420<br>−29116<br>216 104 | 36421<br>−29115<br>216 105 | 36422<br>−29114<br>216 106 | 36423<br>−29113<br>216 107 | 36424<br>−29112<br>216 110 | 36425<br>−29111<br>216 111 | 36426<br>−29110<br>216 112 | 36427<br>−29109<br>216 113 | 36428<br>−29108<br>216 114 | 36429<br>−29107<br>216 115 | 36430<br>−29106<br>216 116 | 36431<br>−29105<br>216 117 |
| **5−** | 36432<br>−29104<br>216 120 | 36433<br>−29103<br>216 121 | 36434<br>−29102<br>216 122 | 36435<br>−29101<br>216 123 | 36436<br>−29100<br>216 124 | 36437<br>−29099<br>216 125 | 36438<br>−29098<br>216 126 | 36439<br>−29097<br>216 127 | 36440<br>−29096<br>216 130 | 36441<br>−29095<br>216 131 | 36442<br>−29094<br>216 132 | 36443<br>−29093<br>216 133 | 36444<br>−29092<br>216 134 | 36445<br>−29091<br>216 135 | 36446<br>−29090<br>216 136 | 36447<br>−29089<br>216 137 |
| **6−** | 36448<br>−29088<br>216 140 | 36449<br>−29087<br>216 141 | 36450<br>−29086<br>216 142 | 36451<br>−29085<br>216 143 | 36452<br>−29084<br>216 144 | 36453<br>−29083<br>216 145 | 36454<br>−29082<br>216 146 | 36455<br>−29081<br>216 147 | 36456<br>−29080<br>216 150 | 36457<br>−29079<br>216 151 | 36458<br>−29078<br>216 152 | 36459<br>−29077<br>216 153 | 36460<br>−29076<br>216 154 | 36461<br>−29075<br>216 155 | 36462<br>−29074<br>216 156 | 36463<br>−29073<br>216 157 |
| **7−** | 36464<br>−29072<br>216 160 | 36465<br>−29071<br>216 161 | 36466<br>−29070<br>216 162 | 36467<br>−29069<br>216 163 | 36468<br>−29068<br>216 164 | 36469<br>−29067<br>216 165 | 36470<br>−29066<br>216 166 | 36471<br>−29065<br>216 167 | 36472<br>−29064<br>216 170 | 36473<br>−29063<br>216 171 | 36474<br>−29062<br>216 172 | 36475<br>−29061<br>216 173 | 36476<br>−29060<br>216 174 | 36477<br>−29059<br>216 175 | 36478<br>−29058<br>216 176 | 36479<br>−29057<br>216 177 |
| **8−** | 36480<br>−29056<br>216 200 | 36481<br>−29055<br>216 201 | 36482<br>−29054<br>216 202 | 36483<br>−29053<br>216 203 | 36484<br>−29052<br>216 204 | 36485<br>−29051<br>216 205 | 36486<br>−29050<br>216 206 | 36487<br>−29049<br>216 207 | 36488<br>−29048<br>216 210 | 36489<br>−29047<br>216 211 | 36490<br>−29046<br>216 212 | 36491<br>−29045<br>216 213 | 36492<br>−29044<br>216 214 | 36493<br>−29043<br>216 215 | 36494<br>−29042<br>216 216 | 36495<br>−29041<br>216 217 |
| **9−** | 36496<br>−29040<br>216 220 | 36497<br>−29039<br>216 221 | 36498<br>−29038<br>216 222 | 36499<br>−29037<br>216 223 | 36500<br>−29036<br>216 224 | 36501<br>−29035<br>216 225 | 36502<br>−29034<br>216 226 | 36503<br>−29033<br>216 227 | 36504<br>−29032<br>216 230 | 36505<br>−29031<br>216 231 | 36506<br>−29030<br>216 232 | 36507<br>−29029<br>216 233 | 36508<br>−29028<br>216 234 | 36509<br>−29027<br>216 235 | 36510<br>−29026<br>216 236 | 36511<br>−29025<br>216 237 |
| **A−** | 36512<br>−29024<br>216 240 | 36513<br>−29023<br>216 241 | 36514<br>−29022<br>216 242 | 36515<br>−29021<br>216 243 | 36516<br>−29020<br>216 244 | 36517<br>−29019<br>216 245 | 36518<br>−29018<br>216 246 | 36519<br>−29017<br>216 247 | 36520<br>−29016<br>216 250 | 36521<br>−29015<br>216 251 | 36522<br>−29014<br>216 252 | 36523<br>−29013<br>216 253 | 36524<br>−29012<br>216 254 | 36525<br>−29011<br>216 255 | 36526<br>−29010<br>216 256 | 36527<br>−29009<br>216 257 |
| **B−** | 36528<br>−29008<br>216 260 | 36529<br>−29007<br>216 261 | 36530<br>−29006<br>216 262 | 36531<br>−29005<br>216 263 | 36532<br>−29004<br>216 264 | 36533<br>−29003<br>216 265 | 36534<br>−29002<br>216 266 | 36535<br>−29001<br>216 267 | 36536<br>−29000<br>216 270 | 36537<br>−28999<br>216 271 | 36538<br>−28998<br>216 272 | 36539<br>−28997<br>216 273 | 36540<br>−28996<br>216 274 | 36541<br>−28995<br>216 275 | 36542<br>−28994<br>216 276 | 36543<br>−28993<br>216 277 |
| **C−** | 36544<br>−28992<br>216 300 | 36545<br>−28991<br>216 301 | 36546<br>−28990<br>216 302 | 36547<br>−28989<br>216 303 | 36548<br>−28988<br>216 304 | 36549<br>−28987<br>216 305 | 36550<br>−28986<br>216 306 | 36551<br>−28985<br>216 307 | 36552<br>−28984<br>216 310 | 36553<br>−28983<br>216 311 | 36554<br>−28982<br>216 312 | 36555<br>−28981<br>216 313 | 36556<br>−28980<br>216 314 | 36557<br>−28979<br>216 315 | 36558<br>−28978<br>216 316 | 36559<br>−28977<br>216 317 |
| **D−** | 36560<br>−28976<br>216 320 | 36561<br>−28975<br>216 321 | 36562<br>−28974<br>216 322 | 36563<br>−28973<br>216 323 | 36564<br>−28972<br>216 324 | 36565<br>−28971<br>216 325 | 36566<br>−28970<br>216 326 | 36567<br>−28969<br>216 327 | 36568<br>−28968<br>216 330 | 36569<br>−28967<br>216 331 | 36570<br>−28966<br>216 332 | 36571<br>−28965<br>216 333 | 36572<br>−28964<br>216 334 | 36573<br>−28963<br>216 335 | 36574<br>−28962<br>216 336 | 36575<br>−28961<br>216 337 |
| **E−** | 36576<br>−28960<br>216 340 | 36577<br>−28959<br>216 341 | 36578<br>−28958<br>216 342 | 36579<br>−28957<br>216 343 | 36580<br>−28956<br>216 344 | 36581<br>−28955<br>216 345 | 36582<br>−28954<br>216 346 | 36583<br>−28953<br>216 347 | 36584<br>−28952<br>216 350 | 36585<br>−28951<br>216 351 | 36586<br>−28950<br>216 352 | 36587<br>−28949<br>216 353 | 36588<br>−28948<br>216 354 | 36589<br>−28947<br>216 355 | 36590<br>−28946<br>216 356 | 36591<br>−28945<br>216 357 |
| **F−** | 36592<br>−28944<br>216 360 | 36593<br>−28943<br>216 361 | 36594<br>−28942<br>216 362 | 36595<br>−28941<br>216 363 | 36596<br>−28940<br>216 364 | 36597<br>−28939<br>216 365 | 36598<br>−28938<br>216 366 | 36599<br>−28937<br>216 367 | 36600<br>−28936<br>216 370 | 36601<br>−28935<br>216 371 | 36602<br>−28934<br>216 372 | 36603<br>−28933<br>216 373 | 36604<br>−28932<br>216 374 | 36605<br>−28931<br>216 375 | 36606<br>−28930<br>216 376 | 36607<br>−28929<br>216 377 |

DECIMAL ←

 DECIMAL ←

OCTAL ←

 DECIMAL  −29184   BINARY  1000 1110   DECIMAL  36352   HEXADECIMAL  ⬡ 8E   OCTAL  216 000

FOURTH HEX DIGIT → ⬡ ← THIRD HEX DIGIT

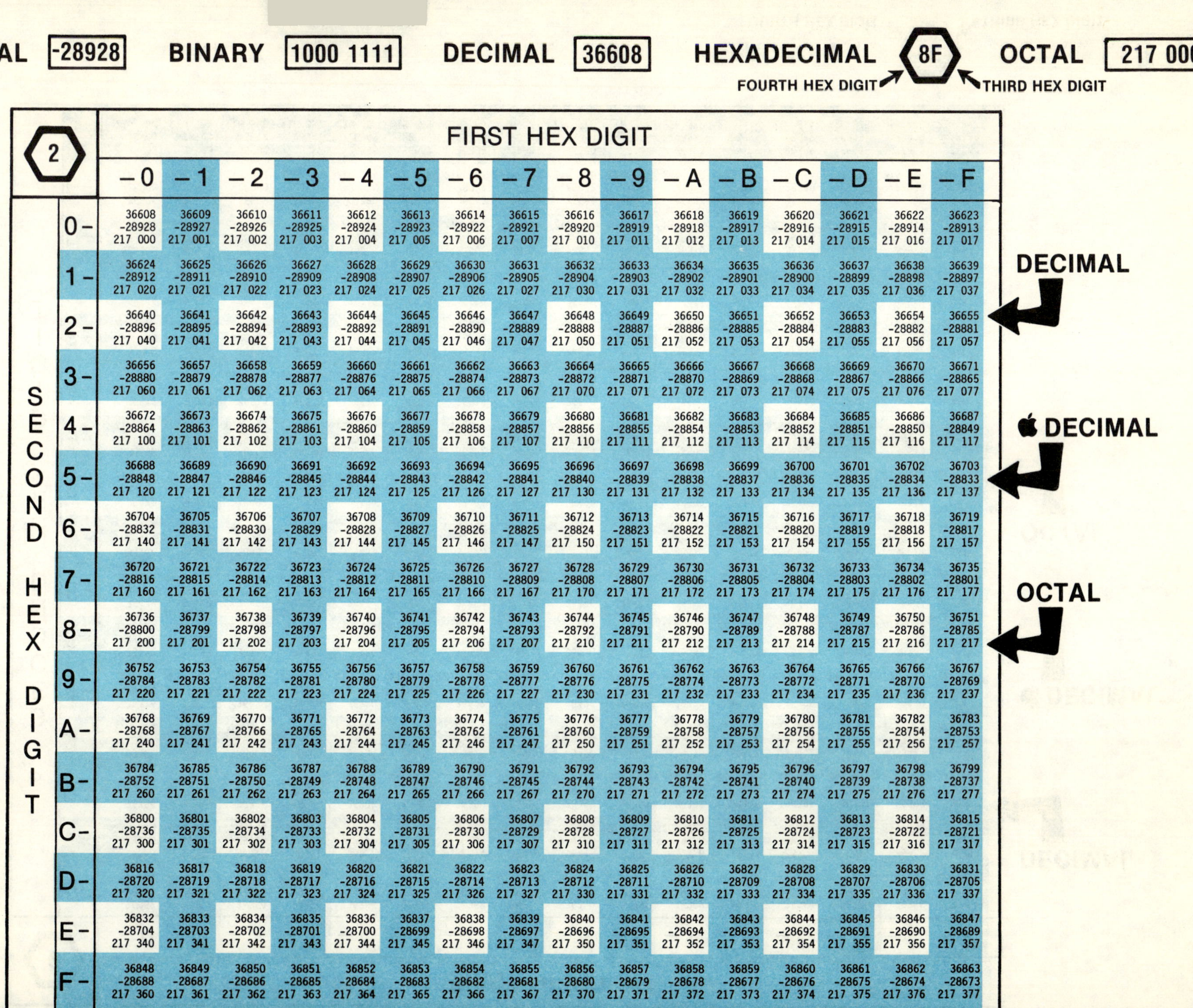

 DECIMAL `-28928`  BINARY `1000 1111`  DECIMAL `36608`  HEXADECIMAL ⬡ `8F`  OCTAL `217 000`

FOURTH HEX DIGIT → ⬡ ← THIRD HEX DIGIT

⬡ 2

| SECOND HEX DIGIT | FIRST HEX DIGIT | | | | | | | | | | | | | | | |
|---|---|---|---|---|---|---|---|---|---|---|---|---|---|---|---|---|
| | −0 | −1 | −2 | −3 | −4 | −5 | −6 | −7 | −8 | −9 | −A | −B | −C | −D | −E | −F |
| 0− | 36608<br>−28928<br>217 000 | 36609<br>−28927<br>217 001 | 36610<br>−28926<br>217 002 | 36611<br>−28925<br>217 003 | 36612<br>−28924<br>217 004 | 36613<br>−28923<br>217 005 | 36614<br>−28922<br>217 006 | 36615<br>−28921<br>217 007 | 36616<br>−28920<br>217 010 | 36617<br>−28919<br>217 011 | 36618<br>−28918<br>217 012 | 36619<br>−28917<br>217 013 | 36620<br>−28916<br>217 014 | 36621<br>−28915<br>217 015 | 36622<br>−28914<br>217 016 | 36623<br>−28913<br>217 017 |
| 1− | 36624<br>−28912<br>217 020 | 36625<br>−28911<br>217 021 | 36626<br>−28910<br>217 022 | 36627<br>−28909<br>217 023 | 36628<br>−28908<br>217 024 | 36629<br>−28907<br>217 025 | 36630<br>−28906<br>217 026 | 36631<br>−28905<br>217 027 | 36632<br>−28904<br>217 030 | 36633<br>−28903<br>217 031 | 36634<br>−28902<br>217 032 | 36635<br>−28901<br>217 033 | 36636<br>−28900<br>217 034 | 36637<br>−28899<br>217 035 | 36638<br>−28898<br>217 036 | 36639<br>−28897<br>217 037 |
| 2− | 36640<br>−28896<br>217 040 | 36641<br>−28895<br>217 041 | 36642<br>−28894<br>217 042 | 36643<br>−28893<br>217 043 | 36644<br>−28892<br>217 044 | 36645<br>−28891<br>217 045 | 36646<br>−28890<br>217 046 | 36647<br>−28889<br>217 047 | 36648<br>−28888<br>217 050 | 36649<br>−28887<br>217 051 | 36650<br>−28886<br>217 052 | 36651<br>−28885<br>217 053 | 36652<br>−28884<br>217 054 | 36653<br>−28883<br>217 055 | 36654<br>−28882<br>217 056 | 36655<br>−28881<br>217 057 |
| 3− | 36656<br>−28880<br>217 060 | 36657<br>−28879<br>217 061 | 36658<br>−28878<br>217 062 | 36659<br>−28877<br>217 063 | 36660<br>−28876<br>217 064 | 36661<br>−28875<br>217 065 | 36662<br>−28874<br>217 066 | 36663<br>−28873<br>217 067 | 36664<br>−28872<br>217 070 | 36665<br>−28871<br>217 071 | 36666<br>−28870<br>217 072 | 36667<br>−28869<br>217 073 | 36668<br>−28868<br>217 074 | 36669<br>−28867<br>217 075 | 36670<br>−28866<br>217 076 | 36671<br>−28865<br>217 077 |
| 4− | 36672<br>−28864<br>217 100 | 36673<br>−28863<br>217 101 | 36674<br>−28862<br>217 102 | 36675<br>−28861<br>217 103 | 36676<br>−28860<br>217 104 | 36677<br>−28859<br>217 105 | 36678<br>−28858<br>217 106 | 36679<br>−28857<br>217 107 | 36680<br>−28856<br>217 110 | 36681<br>−28855<br>217 111 | 36682<br>−28854<br>217 112 | 36683<br>−28853<br>217 113 | 36684<br>−28852<br>217 114 | 36685<br>−28851<br>217 115 | 36686<br>−28850<br>217 116 | 36687<br>−28849<br>217 117 |
| 5− | 36688<br>−28848<br>217 120 | 36689<br>−28847<br>217 121 | 36690<br>−28846<br>217 122 | 36691<br>−28845<br>217 123 | 36692<br>−28844<br>217 124 | 36693<br>−28843<br>217 125 | 36694<br>−28842<br>217 126 | 36695<br>−28841<br>217 127 | 36696<br>−28840<br>217 130 | 36697<br>−28839<br>217 131 | 36698<br>−28838<br>217 132 | 36699<br>−28837<br>217 133 | 36700<br>−28836<br>217 134 | 36701<br>−28835<br>217 135 | 36702<br>−28834<br>217 136 | 36703<br>−28833<br>217 137 |
| 6− | 36704<br>−28832<br>217 140 | 36705<br>−28831<br>217 141 | 36706<br>−28830<br>217 142 | 36707<br>−28829<br>217 143 | 36708<br>−28828<br>217 144 | 36709<br>−28827<br>217 145 | 36710<br>−28826<br>217 146 | 36711<br>−28825<br>217 147 | 36712<br>−28824<br>217 150 | 36713<br>−28823<br>217 151 | 36714<br>−28822<br>217 152 | 36715<br>−28821<br>217 153 | 36716<br>−28820<br>217 154 | 36717<br>−28819<br>217 155 | 36718<br>−28818<br>217 156 | 36719<br>−28817<br>217 157 |
| 7− | 36720<br>−28816<br>217 160 | 36721<br>−28815<br>217 161 | 36722<br>−28814<br>217 162 | 36723<br>−28813<br>217 163 | 36724<br>−28812<br>217 164 | 36725<br>−28811<br>217 165 | 36726<br>−28810<br>217 166 | 36727<br>−28809<br>217 167 | 36728<br>−28808<br>217 170 | 36729<br>−28807<br>217 171 | 36730<br>−28806<br>217 172 | 36731<br>−28805<br>217 173 | 36732<br>−28804<br>217 174 | 36733<br>−28803<br>217 175 | 36734<br>−28802<br>217 176 | 36735<br>−28801<br>217 177 |
| 8− | 36736<br>−28800<br>217 200 | 36737<br>−28799<br>217 201 | 36738<br>−28798<br>217 202 | 36739<br>−28797<br>217 203 | 36740<br>−28796<br>217 204 | 36741<br>−28795<br>217 205 | 36742<br>−28794<br>217 206 | 36743<br>−28793<br>217 207 | 36744<br>−28792<br>217 210 | 36745<br>−28791<br>217 211 | 36746<br>−28790<br>217 212 | 36747<br>−28789<br>217 213 | 36748<br>−28788<br>217 214 | 36749<br>−28787<br>217 215 | 36750<br>−28786<br>217 216 | 36751<br>−28785<br>217 217 |
| 9− | 36752<br>−28784<br>217 220 | 36753<br>−28783<br>217 221 | 36754<br>−28782<br>217 222 | 36755<br>−28781<br>217 223 | 36756<br>−28780<br>217 224 | 36757<br>−28779<br>217 225 | 36758<br>−28778<br>217 226 | 36759<br>−28777<br>217 227 | 36760<br>−28776<br>217 230 | 36761<br>−28775<br>217 231 | 36762<br>−28774<br>217 232 | 36763<br>−28773<br>217 233 | 36764<br>−28772<br>217 234 | 36765<br>−28771<br>217 235 | 36766<br>−28770<br>217 236 | 36767<br>−28769<br>217 237 |
| A− | 36768<br>−28768<br>217 240 | 36769<br>−28767<br>217 241 | 36770<br>−28766<br>217 242 | 36771<br>−28765<br>217 243 | 36772<br>−28764<br>217 244 | 36773<br>−28763<br>217 245 | 36774<br>−28762<br>217 246 | 36775<br>−28761<br>217 247 | 36776<br>−28760<br>217 250 | 36777<br>−28759<br>217 251 | 36778<br>−28758<br>217 252 | 36779<br>−28757<br>217 253 | 36780<br>−28756<br>217 254 | 36781<br>−28755<br>217 255 | 36782<br>−28754<br>217 256 | 36783<br>−28753<br>217 257 |
| B− | 36784<br>−28752<br>217 260 | 36785<br>−28751<br>217 261 | 36786<br>−28750<br>217 262 | 36787<br>−28749<br>217 263 | 36788<br>−28748<br>217 264 | 36789<br>−28747<br>217 265 | 36790<br>−28746<br>217 266 | 36791<br>−28745<br>217 267 | 36792<br>−28744<br>217 270 | 36793<br>−28743<br>217 271 | 36794<br>−28742<br>217 272 | 36795<br>−28741<br>217 273 | 36796<br>−28740<br>217 274 | 36797<br>−28739<br>217 275 | 36798<br>−28738<br>217 276 | 36799<br>−28737<br>217 277 |
| C− | 36800<br>−28736<br>217 300 | 36801<br>−28735<br>217 301 | 36802<br>−28734<br>217 302 | 36803<br>−28733<br>217 303 | 36804<br>−28732<br>217 304 | 36805<br>−28731<br>217 305 | 36806<br>−28730<br>217 306 | 36807<br>−28729<br>217 307 | 36808<br>−28728<br>217 310 | 36809<br>−28727<br>217 311 | 36810<br>−28726<br>217 312 | 36811<br>−28725<br>217 313 | 36812<br>−28724<br>217 314 | 36813<br>−28723<br>217 315 | 36814<br>−28722<br>217 316 | 36815<br>−28721<br>217 317 |
| D− | 36816<br>−28720<br>217 320 | 36817<br>−28719<br>217 321 | 36818<br>−28718<br>217 322 | 36819<br>−28717<br>217 323 | 36820<br>−28716<br>217 324 | 36821<br>−28715<br>217 325 | 36822<br>−28714<br>217 326 | 36823<br>−28713<br>217 327 | 36824<br>−28712<br>217 330 | 36825<br>−28711<br>217 331 | 36826<br>−28710<br>217 332 | 36827<br>−28709<br>217 333 | 36828<br>−28708<br>217 334 | 36829<br>−28707<br>217 335 | 36830<br>−28706<br>217 336 | 36831<br>−28705<br>217 337 |
| E− | 36832<br>−28704<br>217 340 | 36833<br>−28703<br>217 341 | 36834<br>−28702<br>217 342 | 36835<br>−28701<br>217 343 | 36836<br>−28700<br>217 344 | 36837<br>−28699<br>217 345 | 36838<br>−28698<br>217 346 | 36839<br>−28697<br>217 347 | 36840<br>−28696<br>217 350 | 36841<br>−28695<br>217 351 | 36842<br>−28694<br>217 352 | 36843<br>−28693<br>217 353 | 36844<br>−28692<br>217 354 | 36845<br>−28691<br>217 355 | 36846<br>−28690<br>217 356 | 36847<br>−28689<br>217 357 |
| F− | 36848<br>−28688<br>217 360 | 36849<br>−28687<br>217 361 | 36850<br>−28686<br>217 362 | 36851<br>−28685<br>217 363 | 36852<br>−28684<br>217 364 | 36853<br>−28683<br>217 365 | 36854<br>−28682<br>217 366 | 36855<br>−28681<br>217 367 | 36856<br>−28680<br>217 370 | 36857<br>−28679<br>217 371 | 36858<br>−28678<br>217 372 | 36859<br>−28677<br>217 373 | 36860<br>−28676<br>217 374 | 36861<br>−28675<br>217 375 | 36862<br>−28674<br>217 376 | 36863<br>−28673<br>217 377 |

| SECOND HEX DIGIT | −0 | −1 | −2 | −3 | −4 | −5 | −6 | −7 | −8 | −9 | −A | −B | −C | −D | −E | −F |
|---|---|---|---|---|---|---|---|---|---|---|---|---|---|---|---|---|
| 0- | 36864<br>-28672<br>220 000 | 36865<br>-28671<br>220 001 | 36866<br>-28670<br>220 002 | 36867<br>-28669<br>220 003 | 36868<br>-28668<br>220 004 | 36869<br>-28667<br>220 005 | 36870<br>-28666<br>220 006 | 36871<br>-28665<br>220 007 | 36872<br>-28664<br>220 010 | 36873<br>-28663<br>220 011 | 36874<br>-28662<br>220 012 | 36875<br>-28661<br>220 013 | 36876<br>-28660<br>220 014 | 36877<br>-28659<br>220 015 | 36878<br>-28658<br>220 016 | 36879<br>-28657<br>220 017 |
| 1- | 36880<br>-28656<br>220 020 | 36881<br>-28655<br>220 021 | 36882<br>-28654<br>220 022 | 36883<br>-28653<br>220 023 | 36884<br>-28652<br>220 024 | 36885<br>-28651<br>220 025 | 36886<br>-28650<br>220 026 | 36887<br>-28649<br>220 027 | 36888<br>-28648<br>220 030 | 36889<br>-28647<br>220 031 | 36890<br>-28646<br>220 032 | 36891<br>-28645<br>220 033 | 36892<br>-28644<br>220 034 | 36893<br>-28643<br>220 035 | 36894<br>-28642<br>220 036 | 36895<br>-28641<br>220 037 |
| 2- | 36896<br>-28640<br>220 040 | 36897<br>-28639<br>220 041 | 36898<br>-28638<br>220 042 | 36899<br>-28637<br>220 043 | 36900<br>-28636<br>220 044 | 36901<br>-28635<br>220 045 | 36902<br>-28634<br>220 046 | 36903<br>-28633<br>220 047 | 36904<br>-28632<br>220 050 | 36905<br>-28631<br>220 051 | 36906<br>-28630<br>220 052 | 36907<br>-28629<br>220 053 | 36908<br>-28628<br>220 054 | 36909<br>-28627<br>220 055 | 36910<br>-28626<br>220 056 | 36911<br>-28625<br>220 057 |
| 3- | 36912<br>-28624<br>220 060 | 36913<br>-28623<br>220 061 | 36914<br>-28622<br>220 062 | 36915<br>-28621<br>220 063 | 36916<br>-28620<br>220 064 | 36917<br>-28619<br>220 065 | 36918<br>-28618<br>220 066 | 36919<br>-28617<br>220 067 | 36920<br>-28616<br>220 070 | 36921<br>-28615<br>220 071 | 36922<br>-28614<br>220 072 | 36923<br>-28613<br>220 073 | 36924<br>-28612<br>220 074 | 36925<br>-28611<br>220 075 | 36926<br>-28610<br>220 076 | 36927<br>-28609<br>220 077 |
| 4- | 36928<br>-28608<br>220 100 | 36929<br>-28607<br>220 101 | 36930<br>-28606<br>220 102 | 36931<br>-28605<br>220 103 | 36932<br>-28604<br>220 104 | 36933<br>-28603<br>220 105 | 36934<br>-28602<br>220 106 | 36935<br>-28601<br>220 107 | 36936<br>-28600<br>220 110 | 36937<br>-28599<br>220 111 | 36938<br>-28598<br>220 112 | 36939<br>-28597<br>220 113 | 36940<br>-28596<br>220 114 | 36941<br>-28595<br>220 115 | 36942<br>-28594<br>220 116 | 36943<br>-28593<br>220 117 |
| 5- | 36944<br>-28592<br>220 120 | 36945<br>-28591<br>220 121 | 36946<br>-28590<br>220 122 | 36947<br>-28589<br>220 123 | 36948<br>-28588<br>220 124 | 36949<br>-28587<br>220 125 | 36950<br>-28586<br>220 126 | 36951<br>-28585<br>220 127 | 36952<br>-28584<br>220 130 | 36953<br>-28583<br>220 131 | 36954<br>-28582<br>220 132 | 36955<br>-28581<br>220 133 | 36956<br>-28580<br>220 134 | 36957<br>-28579<br>220 135 | 36958<br>-28578<br>220 136 | 36959<br>-28577<br>220 137 |
| 6- | 36960<br>-28576<br>220 140 | 36961<br>-28575<br>220 141 | 36962<br>-28574<br>220 142 | 36963<br>-28573<br>220 143 | 36964<br>-28572<br>220 144 | 36965<br>-28571<br>220 145 | 36966<br>-28570<br>220 146 | 36967<br>-28569<br>220 147 | 36968<br>-28568<br>220 150 | 36969<br>-28567<br>220 151 | 36970<br>-28566<br>220 152 | 36971<br>-28565<br>220 153 | 36972<br>-28564<br>220 154 | 36973<br>-28563<br>220 155 | 36974<br>-28562<br>220 156 | 36975<br>-28561<br>220 157 |
| 7- | 36976<br>-28560<br>220 160 | 36977<br>-28559<br>220 161 | 36978<br>-28558<br>220 162 | 36979<br>-28557<br>220 163 | 36980<br>-28556<br>220 164 | 36981<br>-28555<br>220 165 | 36982<br>-28554<br>220 166 | 36983<br>-28553<br>220 167 | 36984<br>-28552<br>220 170 | 36985<br>-28551<br>220 171 | 36986<br>-28550<br>220 172 | 36987<br>-28549<br>220 173 | 36988<br>-28548<br>220 174 | 36989<br>-28547<br>220 175 | 36990<br>-28546<br>220 176 | 36991<br>-28545<br>220 177 |
| 8- | 36992<br>-28544<br>220 200 | 36993<br>-28543<br>220 201 | 36994<br>-28542<br>220 202 | 36995<br>-28541<br>220 203 | 36996<br>-28540<br>220 204 | 36997<br>-28539<br>220 205 | 36998<br>-28538<br>220 206 | 36999<br>-28537<br>220 207 | 37000<br>-28536<br>220 210 | 37001<br>-28535<br>220 211 | 37002<br>-28534<br>220 212 | 37003<br>-28533<br>220 213 | 37004<br>-28532<br>220 214 | 37005<br>-28531<br>220 215 | 37006<br>-28530<br>220 216 | 37007<br>-28529<br>220 217 |
| 9- | 37008<br>-28528<br>220 220 | 37009<br>-28527<br>220 221 | 37010<br>-28526<br>220 222 | 37011<br>-28525<br>220 223 | 37012<br>-28524<br>220 224 | 37013<br>-28523<br>220 225 | 37014<br>-28522<br>220 226 | 37015<br>-28521<br>220 227 | 37016<br>-28520<br>220 230 | 37017<br>-28519<br>220 231 | 37018<br>-28518<br>220 232 | 37019<br>-28517<br>220 233 | 37020<br>-28516<br>220 234 | 37021<br>-28515<br>220 235 | 37022<br>-28514<br>220 236 | 37023<br>-28513<br>220 237 |
| A- | 37024<br>-28512<br>220 240 | 37025<br>-28511<br>220 241 | 37026<br>-28510<br>220 242 | 37027<br>-28509<br>220 243 | 37028<br>-28508<br>220 244 | 37029<br>-28507<br>220 245 | 37030<br>-28506<br>220 246 | 37031<br>-28505<br>220 247 | 37032<br>-28504<br>220 250 | 37033<br>-28503<br>220 251 | 37034<br>-28502<br>220 252 | 37035<br>-28501<br>220 253 | 37036<br>-28500<br>220 254 | 37037<br>-28499<br>220 255 | 37038<br>-28498<br>220 256 | 37039<br>-28497<br>220 257 |
| B- | 37040<br>-28496<br>220 260 | 37041<br>-28495<br>220 261 | 37042<br>-28494<br>220 262 | 37043<br>-28493<br>220 263 | 37044<br>-28492<br>220 264 | 37045<br>-28491<br>220 265 | 37046<br>-28490<br>220 266 | 37047<br>-28489<br>220 267 | 37048<br>-28488<br>220 270 | 37049<br>-28487<br>220 271 | 37050<br>-28486<br>220 272 | 37051<br>-28485<br>220 273 | 37052<br>-28484<br>220 274 | 37053<br>-28483<br>220 275 | 37054<br>-28482<br>220 276 | 37055<br>-28481<br>220 277 |
| C- | 37056<br>-28480<br>220 300 | 37057<br>-28479<br>220 301 | 37058<br>-28478<br>220 302 | 37059<br>-28477<br>220 303 | 37060<br>-28476<br>220 304 | 37061<br>-28475<br>220 305 | 37062<br>-28474<br>220 306 | 37063<br>-28473<br>220 307 | 37064<br>-28472<br>220 310 | 37065<br>-28471<br>220 311 | 37066<br>-28470<br>220 312 | 37067<br>-28469<br>220 313 | 37068<br>-28468<br>220 314 | 37069<br>-28467<br>220 315 | 37070<br>-28466<br>220 316 | 37071<br>-28465<br>220 317 |
| D- | 37072<br>-28464<br>220 320 | 37073<br>-28463<br>220 321 | 37074<br>-28462<br>220 322 | 37075<br>-28461<br>220 323 | 37076<br>-28460<br>220 324 | 37077<br>-28459<br>220 325 | 37078<br>-28458<br>220 326 | 37079<br>-28457<br>220 327 | 37080<br>-28456<br>220 330 | 37081<br>-28455<br>220 331 | 37082<br>-28454<br>220 332 | 37083<br>-28453<br>220 333 | 37084<br>-28452<br>220 334 | 37085<br>-28451<br>220 335 | 37086<br>-28450<br>220 336 | 37087<br>-28449<br>220 337 |
| E- | 37088<br>-28448<br>220 340 | 37089<br>-28447<br>220 341 | 37090<br>-28446<br>220 342 | 37091<br>-28445<br>220 343 | 37092<br>-28444<br>220 344 | 37093<br>-28443<br>220 345 | 37094<br>-28442<br>220 346 | 37095<br>-28441<br>220 347 | 37096<br>-28440<br>220 350 | 37097<br>-28439<br>220 351 | 37098<br>-28438<br>220 352 | 37099<br>-28437<br>220 353 | 37100<br>-28436<br>220 354 | 37101<br>-28435<br>220 355 | 37102<br>-28434<br>220 356 | 37103<br>-28433<br>220 357 |
| F- | 37104<br>-28432<br>220 360 | 37105<br>-28431<br>220 361 | 37106<br>-28430<br>220 362 | 37107<br>-28429<br>220 363 | 37108<br>-28428<br>220 364 | 37109<br>-28427<br>220 365 | 37110<br>-28426<br>220 366 | 37111<br>-28425<br>220 367 | 37112<br>-28424<br>220 370 | 37113<br>-28423<br>220 371 | 37114<br>-28422<br>220 372 | 37115<br>-28421<br>220 373 | 37116<br>-28420<br>220 374 | 37117<br>-28419<br>220 375 | 37118<br>-28418<br>220 376 | 37119<br>-28417<br>220 377 |

DECIMAL → 36911

 DECIMAL → 36959 (⌘ DECIMAL)

OCTAL → 220 217

 DECIMAL  -28672   BINARY  1001 0000   DECIMAL  36864   HEXADECIMAL  ⬡ 90   OCTAL  220 000

FOURTH HEX DIGIT → ⬡ ← THIRD HEX DIGIT

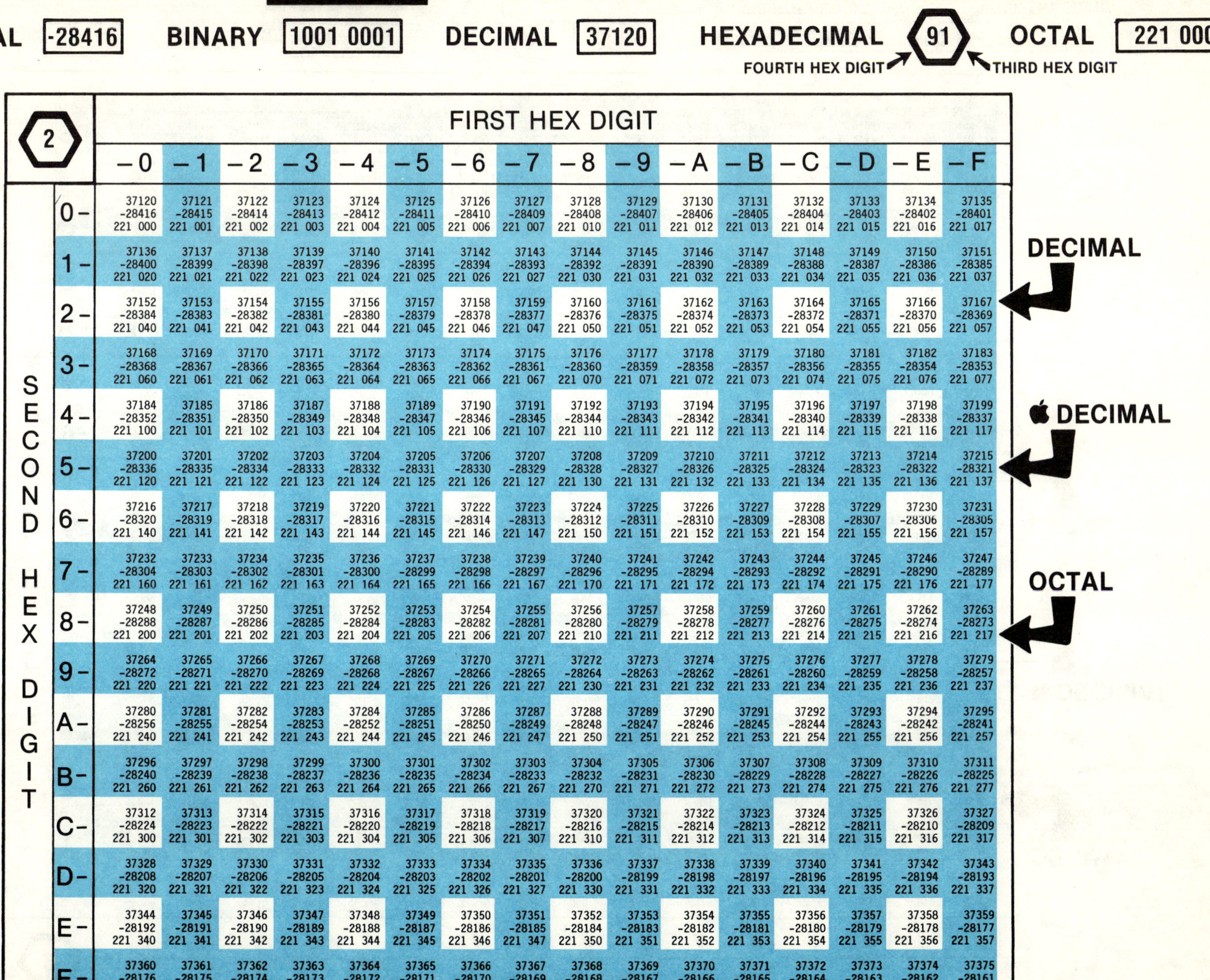



**FIRST HEX DIGIT** (top) / **SECOND HEX DIGIT** (left); selector: 2

| | −0 | −1 | −2 | −3 | −4 | −5 | −6 | −7 | −8 | −9 | −A | −B | −C | −D | −E | −F |
|---|---|---|---|---|---|---|---|---|---|---|---|---|---|---|---|---|
| 0− | 37120<br>−28416<br>221 000 | 37121<br>−28415<br>221 001 | 37122<br>−28414<br>221 002 | 37123<br>−28413<br>221 003 | 37124<br>−28412<br>221 004 | 37125<br>−28411<br>221 005 | 37126<br>−28410<br>221 006 | 37127<br>−28409<br>221 007 | 37128<br>−28408<br>221 010 | 37129<br>−28407<br>221 011 | 37130<br>−28406<br>221 012 | 37131<br>−28405<br>221 013 | 37132<br>−28404<br>221 014 | 37133<br>−28403<br>221 015 | 37134<br>−28402<br>221 016 | 37135<br>−28401<br>221 017 |
| 1− | 37136<br>−28400<br>221 020 | 37137<br>−28399<br>221 021 | 37138<br>−28398<br>221 022 | 37139<br>−28397<br>221 023 | 37140<br>−28396<br>221 024 | 37141<br>−28395<br>221 025 | 37142<br>−28394<br>221 026 | 37143<br>−28393<br>221 027 | 37144<br>−28392<br>221 030 | 37145<br>−28391<br>221 031 | 37146<br>−28390<br>221 032 | 37147<br>−28389<br>221 033 | 37148<br>−28388<br>221 034 | 37149<br>−28387<br>221 035 | 37150<br>−28386<br>221 036 | 37151<br>−28385<br>221 037 |
| 2− | 37152<br>−28384<br>221 040 | 37153<br>−28383<br>221 041 | 37154<br>−28382<br>221 042 | 37155<br>−28381<br>221 043 | 37156<br>−28380<br>221 044 | 37157<br>−28379<br>221 045 | 37158<br>−28378<br>221 046 | 37159<br>−28377<br>221 047 | 37160<br>−28376<br>221 050 | 37161<br>−28375<br>221 051 | 37162<br>−28374<br>221 052 | 37163<br>−28373<br>221 053 | 37164<br>−28372<br>221 054 | 37165<br>−28371<br>221 055 | 37166<br>−28370<br>221 056 | 37167<br>−28369<br>221 057 |
| 3− | 37168<br>−28368<br>221 060 | 37169<br>−28367<br>221 061 | 37170<br>−28366<br>221 062 | 37171<br>−28365<br>221 063 | 37172<br>−28364<br>221 064 | 37173<br>−28363<br>221 065 | 37174<br>−28362<br>221 066 | 37175<br>−28361<br>221 067 | 37176<br>−28360<br>221 070 | 37177<br>−28359<br>221 071 | 37178<br>−28358<br>221 072 | 37179<br>−28357<br>221 073 | 37180<br>−28356<br>221 074 | 37181<br>−28355<br>221 075 | 37182<br>−28354<br>221 076 | 37183<br>−28353<br>221 077 |
| 4− | 37184<br>−28352<br>221 100 | 37185<br>−28351<br>221 101 | 37186<br>−28350<br>221 102 | 37187<br>−28349<br>221 103 | 37188<br>−28348<br>221 104 | 37189<br>−28347<br>221 105 | 37190<br>−28346<br>221 106 | 37191<br>−28345<br>221 107 | 37192<br>−28344<br>221 110 | 37193<br>−28343<br>221 111 | 37194<br>−28342<br>221 112 | 37195<br>−28341<br>221 113 | 37196<br>−28340<br>221 114 | 37197<br>−28339<br>221 115 | 37198<br>−28338<br>221 116 | 37199<br>−28337<br>221 117 |
| 5− | 37200<br>−28336<br>221 120 | 37201<br>−28335<br>221 121 | 37202<br>−28334<br>221 122 | 37203<br>−28333<br>221 123 | 37204<br>−28332<br>221 124 | 37205<br>−28331<br>221 125 | 37206<br>−28330<br>221 126 | 37207<br>−28329<br>221 127 | 37208<br>−28328<br>221 130 | 37209<br>−28327<br>221 131 | 37210<br>−28326<br>221 132 | 37211<br>−28325<br>221 133 | 37212<br>−28324<br>221 134 | 37213<br>−28323<br>221 135 | 37214<br>−28322<br>221 136 | 37215<br>−28321<br>221 137 |
| 6− | 37216<br>−28320<br>221 140 | 37217<br>−28319<br>221 141 | 37218<br>−28318<br>221 142 | 37219<br>−28317<br>221 143 | 37220<br>−28316<br>221 144 | 37221<br>−28315<br>221 145 | 37222<br>−28314<br>221 146 | 37223<br>−28313<br>221 147 | 37224<br>−28312<br>221 150 | 37225<br>−28311<br>221 151 | 37226<br>−28310<br>221 152 | 37227<br>−28309<br>221 153 | 37228<br>−28308<br>221 154 | 37229<br>−28307<br>221 155 | 37230<br>−28306<br>221 156 | 37231<br>−28305<br>221 157 |
| 7− | 37232<br>−28304<br>221 160 | 37233<br>−28303<br>221 161 | 37234<br>−28302<br>221 162 | 37235<br>−28301<br>221 163 | 37236<br>−28300<br>221 164 | 37237<br>−28299<br>221 165 | 37238<br>−28298<br>221 166 | 37239<br>−28297<br>221 167 | 37240<br>−28296<br>221 170 | 37241<br>−28295<br>221 171 | 37242<br>−28294<br>221 172 | 37243<br>−28293<br>221 173 | 37244<br>−28292<br>221 174 | 37245<br>−28291<br>221 175 | 37246<br>−28290<br>221 176 | 37247<br>−28289<br>221 177 |
| 8− | 37248<br>−28288<br>221 200 | 37249<br>−28287<br>221 201 | 37250<br>−28286<br>221 202 | 37251<br>−28285<br>221 203 | 37252<br>−28284<br>221 204 | 37253<br>−28283<br>221 205 | 37254<br>−28282<br>221 206 | 37255<br>−28281<br>221 207 | 37256<br>−28280<br>221 210 | 37257<br>−28279<br>221 211 | 37258<br>−28278<br>221 212 | 37259<br>−28277<br>221 213 | 37260<br>−28276<br>221 214 | 37261<br>−28275<br>221 215 | 37262<br>−28274<br>221 216 | 37263<br>−28273<br>221 217 |
| 9− | 37264<br>−28272<br>221 220 | 37265<br>−28271<br>221 221 | 37266<br>−28270<br>221 222 | 37267<br>−28269<br>221 223 | 37268<br>−28268<br>221 224 | 37269<br>−28267<br>221 225 | 37270<br>−28266<br>221 226 | 37271<br>−28265<br>221 227 | 37272<br>−28264<br>221 230 | 37273<br>−28263<br>221 231 | 37274<br>−28262<br>221 232 | 37275<br>−28261<br>221 233 | 37276<br>−28260<br>221 234 | 37277<br>−28259<br>221 235 | 37278<br>−28258<br>221 236 | 37279<br>−28257<br>221 237 |
| A− | 37280<br>−28256<br>221 240 | 37281<br>−28255<br>221 241 | 37282<br>−28254<br>221 242 | 37283<br>−28253<br>221 243 | 37284<br>−28252<br>221 244 | 37285<br>−28251<br>221 245 | 37286<br>−28250<br>221 246 | 37287<br>−28249<br>221 247 | 37288<br>−28248<br>221 250 | 37289<br>−28247<br>221 251 | 37290<br>−28246<br>221 252 | 37291<br>−28245<br>221 253 | 37292<br>−28244<br>221 254 | 37293<br>−28243<br>221 255 | 37294<br>−28242<br>221 256 | 37295<br>−28241<br>221 257 |
| B− | 37296<br>−28240<br>221 260 | 37297<br>−28239<br>221 261 | 37298<br>−28238<br>221 262 | 37299<br>−28237<br>221 263 | 37300<br>−28236<br>221 264 | 37301<br>−28235<br>221 265 | 37302<br>−28234<br>221 266 | 37303<br>−28233<br>221 267 | 37304<br>−28232<br>221 270 | 37305<br>−28231<br>221 271 | 37306<br>−28230<br>221 272 | 37307<br>−28229<br>221 273 | 37308<br>−28228<br>221 274 | 37309<br>−28227<br>221 275 | 37310<br>−28226<br>221 276 | 37311<br>−28225<br>221 277 |
| C− | 37312<br>−28224<br>221 300 | 37313<br>−28223<br>221 301 | 37314<br>−28222<br>221 302 | 37315<br>−28221<br>221 303 | 37316<br>−28220<br>221 304 | 37317<br>−28219<br>221 305 | 37318<br>−28218<br>221 306 | 37319<br>−28217<br>221 307 | 37320<br>−28216<br>221 310 | 37321<br>−28215<br>221 311 | 37322<br>−28214<br>221 312 | 37323<br>−28213<br>221 313 | 37324<br>−28212<br>221 314 | 37325<br>−28211<br>221 315 | 37326<br>−28210<br>221 316 | 37327<br>−28209<br>221 317 |
| D− | 37328<br>−28208<br>221 320 | 37329<br>−28207<br>221 321 | 37330<br>−28206<br>221 322 | 37331<br>−28205<br>221 323 | 37332<br>−28204<br>221 324 | 37333<br>−28203<br>221 325 | 37334<br>−28202<br>221 326 | 37335<br>−28201<br>221 327 | 37336<br>−28200<br>221 330 | 37337<br>−28199<br>221 331 | 37338<br>−28198<br>221 332 | 37339<br>−28197<br>221 333 | 37340<br>−28196<br>221 334 | 37341<br>−28195<br>221 335 | 37342<br>−28194<br>221 336 | 37343<br>−28193<br>221 337 |
| E− | 37344<br>−28192<br>221 340 | 37345<br>−28191<br>221 341 | 37346<br>−28190<br>221 342 | 37347<br>−28189<br>221 343 | 37348<br>−28188<br>221 344 | 37349<br>−28187<br>221 345 | 37350<br>−28186<br>221 346 | 37351<br>−28185<br>221 347 | 37352<br>−28184<br>221 350 | 37353<br>−28183<br>221 351 | 37354<br>−28182<br>221 352 | 37355<br>−28181<br>221 353 | 37356<br>−28180<br>221 354 | 37357<br>−28179<br>221 355 | 37358<br>−28178<br>221 356 | 37359<br>−28177<br>221 357 |
| F− | 37360<br>−28176<br>221 360 | 37361<br>−28175<br>221 361 | 37362<br>−28174<br>221 362 | 37363<br>−28173<br>221 363 | 37364<br>−28172<br>221 364 | 37365<br>−28171<br>221 365 | 37366<br>−28170<br>221 366 | 37367<br>−28169<br>221 367 | 37368<br>−28168<br>221 370 | 37369<br>−28167<br>221 371 | 37370<br>−28166<br>221 372 | 37371<br>−28165<br>221 373 | 37372<br>−28164<br>221 374 | 37373<br>−28163<br>221 375 | 37374<br>−28162<br>221 376 | 37375<br>−28161<br>221 377 |

**(2)**

| SECOND HEX DIGIT | −0 | −1 | −2 | −3 | −4 | −5 | −6 | −7 | −8 | −9 | −A | −B | −C | −D | −E | −F |
|---|---|---|---|---|---|---|---|---|---|---|---|---|---|---|---|---|
| **0−** | 37376<br>−28160<br>222 000 | 37377<br>−28159<br>222 001 | 37378<br>−28158<br>222 002 | 37379<br>−28157<br>222 003 | 37380<br>−28156<br>222 004 | 37381<br>−28155<br>222 005 | 37382<br>−28154<br>222 006 | 37383<br>−28153<br>222 007 | 37384<br>−28152<br>222 010 | 37385<br>−28151<br>222 011 | 37386<br>−28150<br>222 012 | 37387<br>−28149<br>222 013 | 37388<br>−28148<br>222 014 | 37389<br>−28147<br>222 015 | 37390<br>−28146<br>222 016 | 37391<br>−28145<br>222 017 |
| **1−** | 37392<br>−28144<br>222 020 | 37393<br>−28143<br>222 021 | 37394<br>−28142<br>222 022 | 37395<br>−28141<br>222 023 | 37396<br>−28140<br>222 024 | 37397<br>−28139<br>222 025 | 37398<br>−28138<br>222 026 | 37399<br>−28137<br>222 027 | 37400<br>−28136<br>222 030 | 37401<br>−28135<br>222 031 | 37402<br>−28134<br>222 032 | 37403<br>−28133<br>222 033 | 37404<br>−28132<br>222 034 | 37405<br>−28131<br>222 035 | 37406<br>−28130<br>222 036 | 37407<br>−28129<br>222 037 |
| **2−** | 37408<br>−28128<br>222 040 | 37409<br>−28127<br>222 041 | 37410<br>−28126<br>222 042 | 37411<br>−28125<br>222 043 | 37412<br>−28124<br>222 044 | 37413<br>−28123<br>222 045 | 37414<br>−28122<br>222 046 | 37415<br>−28121<br>222 047 | 37416<br>−28120<br>222 050 | 37417<br>−28119<br>222 051 | 37418<br>−28118<br>222 052 | 37419<br>−28117<br>222 053 | 37420<br>−28116<br>222 054 | 37421<br>−28115<br>222 055 | 37422<br>−28114<br>222 056 | 37423<br>−28113<br>222 057 |
| **3−** | 37424<br>−28112<br>222 060 | 37425<br>−28111<br>222 061 | 37426<br>−28110<br>222 062 | 37427<br>−28109<br>222 063 | 37428<br>−28108<br>222 064 | 37429<br>−28107<br>222 065 | 37430<br>−28106<br>222 066 | 37431<br>−28105<br>222 067 | 37432<br>−28104<br>222 070 | 37433<br>−28103<br>222 071 | 37434<br>−28102<br>222 072 | 37435<br>−28101<br>222 073 | 37436<br>−28100<br>222 074 | 37437<br>−28099<br>222 075 | 37438<br>−28098<br>222 076 | 37439<br>−28097<br>222 077 |
| **4−** | 37440<br>−28096<br>222 100 | 37441<br>−28095<br>222 101 | 37442<br>−28094<br>222 102 | 37443<br>−28093<br>222 103 | 37444<br>−28092<br>222 104 | 37445<br>−28091<br>222 105 | 37446<br>−28090<br>222 106 | 37447<br>−28089<br>222 107 | 37448<br>−28088<br>222 110 | 37449<br>−28087<br>222 111 | 37450<br>−28086<br>222 112 | 37451<br>−28085<br>222 113 | 37452<br>−28084<br>222 114 | 37453<br>−28083<br>222 115 | 37454<br>−28082<br>222 116 | 37455<br>−28081<br>222 117 |
| **5−** | 37456<br>−28080<br>222 120 | 37457<br>−28079<br>222 121 | 37458<br>−28078<br>222 122 | 37459<br>−28077<br>222 123 | 37460<br>−28076<br>222 124 | 37461<br>−28075<br>222 125 | 37462<br>−28074<br>222 126 | 37463<br>−28073<br>222 127 | 37464<br>−28072<br>222 130 | 37465<br>−28071<br>222 131 | 37466<br>−28070<br>222 132 | 37467<br>−28069<br>222 133 | 37468<br>−28068<br>222 134 | 37469<br>−28067<br>222 135 | 37470<br>−28066<br>222 136 | 37471<br>−28065<br>222 137 |
| **6−** | 37472<br>−28064<br>222 140 | 37473<br>−28063<br>222 141 | 37474<br>−28062<br>222 142 | 37475<br>−28061<br>222 143 | 37476<br>−28060<br>222 144 | 37477<br>−28059<br>222 145 | 37478<br>−28058<br>222 146 | 37479<br>−28057<br>222 147 | 37480<br>−28056<br>222 150 | 37481<br>−28055<br>222 151 | 37482<br>−28054<br>222 152 | 37483<br>−28053<br>222 153 | 37484<br>−28052<br>222 154 | 37485<br>−28051<br>222 155 | 37486<br>−28050<br>222 156 | 37487<br>−28049<br>222 157 |
| **7−** | 37488<br>−28048<br>222 160 | 37489<br>−28047<br>222 161 | 37490<br>−28046<br>222 162 | 37491<br>−28045<br>222 163 | 37492<br>−28044<br>222 164 | 37493<br>−28043<br>222 165 | 37494<br>−28042<br>222 166 | 37495<br>−28041<br>222 167 | 37496<br>−28040<br>222 170 | 37497<br>−28039<br>222 171 | 37498<br>−28038<br>222 172 | 37499<br>−28037<br>222 173 | 37500<br>−28036<br>222 174 | 37501<br>−28035<br>222 175 | 37502<br>−28034<br>222 176 | 37503<br>−28033<br>222 177 |
| **8−** | 37504<br>−28032<br>222 200 | 37505<br>−28031<br>222 201 | 37506<br>−28030<br>222 202 | 37507<br>−28029<br>222 203 | 37508<br>−28028<br>222 204 | 37509<br>−28027<br>222 205 | 37510<br>−28026<br>222 206 | 37511<br>−28025<br>222 207 | 37512<br>−28024<br>222 210 | 37513<br>−28023<br>222 211 | 37514<br>−28022<br>222 212 | 37515<br>−28021<br>222 213 | 37516<br>−28020<br>222 214 | 37517<br>−28019<br>222 215 | 37518<br>−28018<br>222 216 | 37519<br>−28017<br>222 217 |
| **9−** | 37520<br>−28016<br>222 220 | 37521<br>−28015<br>222 221 | 37522<br>−28014<br>222 222 | 37523<br>−28013<br>222 223 | 37524<br>−28012<br>222 224 | 37525<br>−28011<br>222 225 | 37526<br>−28010<br>222 226 | 37527<br>−28009<br>222 227 | 37528<br>−28008<br>222 230 | 37529<br>−28007<br>222 231 | 37530<br>−28006<br>222 232 | 37531<br>−28005<br>222 233 | 37532<br>−28004<br>222 234 | 37533<br>−28003<br>222 235 | 37534<br>−28002<br>222 236 | 37535<br>−28001<br>222 237 |
| **A−** | 37536<br>−28000<br>222 240 | 37537<br>−27999<br>222 241 | 37538<br>−27998<br>222 242 | 37539<br>−27997<br>222 243 | 37540<br>−27996<br>222 244 | 37541<br>−27995<br>222 245 | 37542<br>−27994<br>222 246 | 37543<br>−27993<br>222 247 | 37544<br>−27992<br>222 250 | 37545<br>−27991<br>222 251 | 37546<br>−27990<br>222 252 | 37547<br>−27989<br>222 253 | 37548<br>−27988<br>222 254 | 37549<br>−27987<br>222 255 | 37550<br>−27986<br>222 256 | 37551<br>−27985<br>222 257 |
| **B−** | 37552<br>−27984<br>222 260 | 37553<br>−27983<br>222 261 | 37554<br>−27982<br>222 262 | 37555<br>−27981<br>222 263 | 37556<br>−27980<br>222 264 | 37557<br>−27979<br>222 265 | 37558<br>−27978<br>222 266 | 37559<br>−27977<br>222 267 | 37560<br>−27976<br>222 270 | 37561<br>−27975<br>222 271 | 37562<br>−27974<br>222 272 | 37563<br>−27973<br>222 273 | 37564<br>−27972<br>222 274 | 37565<br>−27971<br>222 275 | 37566<br>−27970<br>222 276 | 37567<br>−27969<br>222 277 |
| **C−** | 37568<br>−27968<br>222 300 | 37569<br>−27967<br>222 301 | 37570<br>−27966<br>222 302 | 37571<br>−27965<br>222 303 | 37572<br>−27964<br>222 304 | 37573<br>−27963<br>222 305 | 37574<br>−27962<br>222 306 | 37575<br>−27961<br>222 307 | 37576<br>−27960<br>222 310 | 37577<br>−27959<br>222 311 | 37578<br>−27958<br>222 312 | 37579<br>−27957<br>222 313 | 37580<br>−27956<br>222 314 | 37581<br>−27955<br>222 315 | 37582<br>−27954<br>222 316 | 37583<br>−27953<br>222 317 |
| **D−** | 37584<br>−27952<br>222 320 | 37585<br>−27951<br>222 321 | 37586<br>−27950<br>222 322 | 37587<br>−27949<br>222 323 | 37588<br>−27948<br>222 324 | 37589<br>−27947<br>222 325 | 37590<br>−27946<br>222 326 | 37591<br>−27945<br>222 327 | 37592<br>−27944<br>222 330 | 37593<br>−27943<br>222 331 | 37594<br>−27942<br>222 332 | 37595<br>−27941<br>222 333 | 37596<br>−27940<br>222 334 | 37597<br>−27939<br>222 335 | 37598<br>−27938<br>222 336 | 37599<br>−27937<br>222 337 |
| **E−** | 37600<br>−27936<br>222 340 | 37601<br>−27935<br>222 341 | 37602<br>−27934<br>222 342 | 37603<br>−27933<br>222 343 | 37604<br>−27932<br>222 344 | 37605<br>−27931<br>222 345 | 37606<br>−27930<br>222 346 | 37607<br>−27929<br>222 347 | 37608<br>−27928<br>222 350 | 37609<br>−27927<br>222 351 | 37610<br>−27926<br>222 352 | 37611<br>−27925<br>222 353 | 37612<br>−27924<br>222 354 | 37613<br>−27923<br>222 355 | 37614<br>−27922<br>222 356 | 37615<br>−27921<br>222 357 |
| **F−** | 37616<br>−27920<br>222 360 | 37617<br>−27919<br>222 361 | 37618<br>−27918<br>222 362 | 37619<br>−27917<br>222 363 | 37620<br>−27916<br>222 364 | 37621<br>−27915<br>222 365 | 37622<br>−27914<br>222 366 | 37623<br>−27913<br>222 367 | 37624<br>−27912<br>222 370 | 37625<br>−27911<br>222 371 | 37626<br>−27910<br>222 372 | 37627<br>−27909<br>222 373 | 37628<br>−27908<br>222 374 | 37629<br>−27907<br>222 375 | 37630<br>−27906<br>222 376 | 37631<br>−27905<br>222 377 |

DECIMAL

⌘ DECIMAL

OCTAL

⌘ DECIMAL **−28160**  BINARY **1001 0010**  DECIMAL **37376**  HEXADECIMAL **(92)**  OCTAL **222 000**

FOURTH HEX DIGIT → ← THIRD HEX DIGIT

FIRST HEX DIGIT

| 2 | -0 | -1 | -2 | -3 | -4 | -5 | -6 | -7 | -8 | -9 | -A | -B | -C | -D | -E | -F |
|---|---|---|---|---|---|---|---|---|---|---|---|---|---|---|---|---|
| 0- | 37632<br>-27904<br>223 000 | 37633<br>-27903<br>223 001 | 37634<br>-27902<br>223 002 | 37635<br>-27901<br>223 003 | 37636<br>-27900<br>223 004 | 37637<br>-27899<br>223 005 | 37638<br>-27898<br>223 006 | 37639<br>-27897<br>223 007 | 37640<br>-27896<br>223 010 | 37641<br>-27895<br>223 011 | 37642<br>-27894<br>223 012 | 37643<br>-27893<br>223 013 | 37644<br>-27892<br>223 014 | 37645<br>-27891<br>223 015 | 37646<br>-27890<br>223 016 | 37647<br>-27889<br>223 017 |
| 1- | 37648<br>-27888<br>223 020 | 37649<br>-27887<br>223 021 | 37650<br>-27886<br>223 022 | 37651<br>-27885<br>223 023 | 37652<br>-27884<br>223 024 | 37653<br>-27883<br>223 025 | 37654<br>-27882<br>223 026 | 37655<br>-27881<br>223 027 | 37656<br>-27880<br>223 030 | 37657<br>-27879<br>223 031 | 37658<br>-27878<br>223 032 | 37659<br>-27877<br>223 033 | 37660<br>-27876<br>223 034 | 37661<br>-27875<br>223 035 | 37662<br>-27874<br>223 036 | 37663<br>-27873<br>223 037 |
| 2- | 37664<br>-27872<br>223 040 | 37665<br>-27871<br>223 041 | 37666<br>-27870<br>223 042 | 37667<br>-27869<br>223 043 | 37668<br>-27868<br>223 044 | 37669<br>-27867<br>223 045 | 37670<br>-27866<br>223 046 | 37671<br>-27865<br>223 047 | 37672<br>-27864<br>223 050 | 37673<br>-27863<br>223 051 | 37674<br>-27862<br>223 052 | 37675<br>-27861<br>223 053 | 37676<br>-27860<br>223 054 | 37677<br>-27859<br>223 055 | 37678<br>-27858<br>223 056 | 37679<br>-27857<br>223 057 |
| 3- | 37680<br>-27856<br>223 060 | 37681<br>-27855<br>223 061 | 37682<br>-27854<br>223 062 | 37683<br>-27853<br>223 063 | 37684<br>-27852<br>223 064 | 37685<br>-27851<br>223 065 | 37686<br>-27850<br>223 066 | 37687<br>-27849<br>223 067 | 37688<br>-27848<br>223 070 | 37689<br>-27847<br>223 071 | 37690<br>-27846<br>223 072 | 37691<br>-27845<br>223 073 | 37692<br>-27844<br>223 074 | 37693<br>-27843<br>223 075 | 37694<br>-27842<br>223 076 | 37695<br>-27841<br>223 077 |
| 4- | 37696<br>-27840<br>223 100 | 37697<br>-27839<br>223 101 | 37698<br>-27838<br>223 102 | 37699<br>-27837<br>223 103 | 37700<br>-27836<br>223 104 | 37701<br>-27835<br>223 105 | 37702<br>-27834<br>223 106 | 37703<br>-27833<br>223 107 | 37704<br>-27832<br>223 110 | 37705<br>-27831<br>223 111 | 37706<br>-27830<br>223 112 | 37707<br>-27829<br>223 113 | 37708<br>-27828<br>223 114 | 37709<br>-27827<br>223 115 | 37710<br>-27826<br>223 116 | 37711<br>-27825<br>223 117 |
| 5- | 37712<br>-27824<br>223 120 | 37713<br>-27823<br>223 121 | 37714<br>-27822<br>223 122 | 37715<br>-27821<br>223 123 | 37716<br>-27820<br>223 124 | 37717<br>-27819<br>223 125 | 37718<br>-27818<br>223 126 | 37719<br>-27817<br>223 127 | 37720<br>-27816<br>223 130 | 37721<br>-27815<br>223 131 | 37722<br>-27814<br>223 132 | 37723<br>-27813<br>223 133 | 37724<br>-27812<br>223 134 | 37725<br>-27811<br>223 135 | 37726<br>-27810<br>223 136 | 37727<br>-27809<br>223 137 |
| 6- | 37728<br>-27808<br>223 140 | 37729<br>-27807<br>223 141 | 37730<br>-27806<br>223 142 | 37731<br>-27805<br>223 143 | 37732<br>-27804<br>223 144 | 37733<br>-27803<br>223 145 | 37734<br>-27802<br>223 146 | 37735<br>-27801<br>223 147 | 37736<br>-27800<br>223 150 | 37737<br>-27799<br>223 151 | 37738<br>-27798<br>223 152 | 37739<br>-27797<br>223 153 | 37740<br>-27796<br>223 154 | 37741<br>-27795<br>223 155 | 37742<br>-27794<br>223 156 | 37743<br>-27793<br>223 157 |
| 7- | 37744<br>-27792<br>223 160 | 37745<br>-27791<br>223 161 | 37746<br>-27790<br>223 162 | 37747<br>-27789<br>223 163 | 37748<br>-27788<br>223 164 | 37749<br>-27787<br>223 165 | 37750<br>-27786<br>223 166 | 37751<br>-27785<br>223 167 | 37752<br>-27784<br>223 170 | 37753<br>-27783<br>223 171 | 37754<br>-27782<br>223 172 | 37755<br>-27781<br>223 173 | 37756<br>-27780<br>223 174 | 37757<br>-27779<br>223 175 | 37758<br>-27778<br>223 176 | 37759<br>-27777<br>223 177 |
| 8- | 37760<br>-27776<br>223 200 | 37761<br>-27775<br>223 201 | 37762<br>-27774<br>223 202 | 37763<br>-27773<br>223 203 | 37764<br>-27772<br>223 204 | 37765<br>-27771<br>223 205 | 37766<br>-27770<br>223 206 | 37767<br>-27769<br>223 207 | 37768<br>-27768<br>223 210 | 37769<br>-27767<br>223 211 | 37770<br>-27766<br>223 212 | 37771<br>-27765<br>223 213 | 37772<br>-27764<br>223 214 | 37773<br>-27763<br>223 215 | 37774<br>-27762<br>223 216 | 37775<br>-27761<br>223 217 |
| 9- | 37776<br>-27760<br>223 220 | 37777<br>-27759<br>223 221 | 37778<br>-27758<br>223 222 | 37779<br>-27757<br>223 223 | 37780<br>-27756<br>223 224 | 37781<br>-27755<br>223 225 | 37782<br>-27754<br>223 226 | 37783<br>-27753<br>223 227 | 37784<br>-27752<br>223 230 | 37785<br>-27751<br>223 231 | 37786<br>-27750<br>223 232 | 37787<br>-27749<br>223 233 | 37788<br>-27748<br>223 234 | 37789<br>-27747<br>223 235 | 37790<br>-27746<br>223 236 | 37791<br>-27745<br>223 237 |
| A- | 37792<br>-27744<br>223 240 | 37793<br>-27743<br>223 241 | 37794<br>-27742<br>223 242 | 37795<br>-27741<br>223 243 | 37796<br>-27740<br>223 244 | 37797<br>-27739<br>223 245 | 37798<br>-27738<br>223 246 | 37799<br>-27737<br>223 247 | 37800<br>-27736<br>223 250 | 37801<br>-27735<br>223 251 | 37802<br>-27734<br>223 252 | 37803<br>-27733<br>223 253 | 37804<br>-27732<br>223 254 | 37805<br>-27731<br>223 255 | 37806<br>-27730<br>223 256 | 37807<br>-27729<br>223 257 |
| B- | 37808<br>-27728<br>223 260 | 37809<br>-27727<br>223 261 | 37810<br>-27726<br>223 262 | 37811<br>-27725<br>223 263 | 37812<br>-27724<br>223 264 | 37813<br>-27723<br>223 265 | 37814<br>-27722<br>223 266 | 37815<br>-27721<br>223 267 | 37816<br>-27720<br>223 270 | 37817<br>-27719<br>223 271 | 37818<br>-27718<br>223 272 | 37819<br>-27717<br>223 273 | 37820<br>-27716<br>223 274 | 37821<br>-27715<br>223 275 | 37822<br>-27714<br>223 276 | 37823<br>-27713<br>223 277 |
| C- | 37824<br>-27712<br>223 300 | 37825<br>-27711<br>223 301 | 37826<br>-27710<br>223 302 | 37827<br>-27709<br>223 303 | 37828<br>-27708<br>223 304 | 37829<br>-27707<br>223 305 | 37830<br>-27706<br>223 306 | 37831<br>-27705<br>223 307 | 37832<br>-27704<br>223 310 | 37833<br>-27703<br>223 311 | 37834<br>-27702<br>223 312 | 37835<br>-27701<br>223 313 | 37836<br>-27700<br>223 314 | 37837<br>-27699<br>223 315 | 37838<br>-27698<br>223 316 | 37839<br>-27697<br>223 317 |
| D- | 37840<br>-27696<br>223 320 | 37841<br>-27695<br>223 321 | 37842<br>-27694<br>223 322 | 37843<br>-27693<br>223 323 | 37844<br>-27692<br>223 324 | 37845<br>-27691<br>223 325 | 37846<br>-27690<br>223 326 | 37847<br>-27689<br>223 327 | 37848<br>-27688<br>223 330 | 37849<br>-27687<br>223 331 | 37850<br>-27686<br>223 332 | 37851<br>-27685<br>223 333 | 37852<br>-27684<br>223 334 | 37853<br>-27683<br>223 335 | 37854<br>-27682<br>223 336 | 37855<br>-27681<br>223 337 |
| E- | 37856<br>-27680<br>223 340 | 37857<br>-27679<br>223 341 | 37858<br>-27678<br>223 342 | 37859<br>-27677<br>223 343 | 37860<br>-27676<br>223 344 | 37861<br>-27675<br>223 345 | 37862<br>-27674<br>223 346 | 37863<br>-27673<br>223 347 | 37864<br>-27672<br>223 350 | 37865<br>-27671<br>223 351 | 37866<br>-27670<br>223 352 | 37867<br>-27669<br>223 353 | 37868<br>-27668<br>223 354 | 37869<br>-27667<br>223 355 | 37870<br>-27666<br>223 356 | 37871<br>-27665<br>223 357 |
| F- | 37872<br>-27664<br>223 360 | 37873<br>-27663<br>223 361 | 37874<br>-27662<br>223 362 | 37875<br>-27661<br>223 363 | 37876<br>-27660<br>223 364 | 37877<br>-27659<br>223 365 | 37878<br>-27658<br>223 366 | 37879<br>-27657<br>223 367 | 37880<br>-27656<br>223 370 | 37881<br>-27655<br>223 371 | 37882<br>-27654<br>223 372 | 37883<br>-27653<br>223 373 | 37884<br>-27652<br>223 374 | 37885<br>-27651<br>223 375 | 37886<br>-27650<br>223 376 | 37887<br>-27649<br>223 377 |

SECOND HEX DIGIT (row labels at left)

DECIMAL / DECIMAL / OCTAL (row guides at right)

(2) **FIRST HEX DIGIT**

 **DECIMAL** (top), **DECIMAL** (Apple, middle, negative), **OCTAL** (bottom).

| SECOND HEX DIGIT | −0 | −1 | −2 | −3 | −4 | −5 | −6 | −7 | −8 | −9 | −A | −B | −C | −D | −E | −F |
|---|---|---|---|---|---|---|---|---|---|---|---|---|---|---|---|---|
| **0−** | 37888<br>−27648<br>224 000 | 37889<br>−27647<br>224 001 | 37890<br>−27646<br>224 002 | 37891<br>−27645<br>224 003 | 37892<br>−27644<br>224 004 | 37893<br>−27643<br>224 005 | 37894<br>−27642<br>224 006 | 37895<br>−27641<br>224 007 | 37896<br>−27640<br>224 010 | 37897<br>−27639<br>224 011 | 37898<br>−27638<br>224 012 | 37899<br>−27637<br>224 013 | 37900<br>−27636<br>224 014 | 37901<br>−27635<br>224 015 | 37902<br>−27634<br>224 016 | 37903<br>−27633<br>224 017 |
| **1−** | 37904<br>−27632<br>224 020 | 37905<br>−27631<br>224 021 | 37906<br>−27630<br>224 022 | 37907<br>−27629<br>224 023 | 37908<br>−27628<br>224 024 | 37909<br>−27627<br>224 025 | 37910<br>−27626<br>224 026 | 37911<br>−27625<br>224 027 | 37912<br>−27624<br>224 030 | 37913<br>−27623<br>224 031 | 37914<br>−27622<br>224 032 | 37915<br>−27621<br>224 033 | 37916<br>−27620<br>224 034 | 37917<br>−27619<br>224 035 | 37918<br>−27618<br>224 036 | 37919<br>−27617<br>224 037 |
| **2−** | 37920<br>−27616<br>224 040 | 37921<br>−27615<br>224 041 | 37922<br>−27614<br>224 042 | 37923<br>−27613<br>224 043 | 37924<br>−27612<br>224 044 | 37925<br>−27611<br>224 045 | 37926<br>−27610<br>224 046 | 37927<br>−27609<br>224 047 | 37928<br>−27608<br>224 050 | 37929<br>−27607<br>224 051 | 37930<br>−27606<br>224 052 | 37931<br>−27605<br>224 053 | 37932<br>−27604<br>224 054 | 37933<br>−27603<br>224 055 | 37934<br>−27602<br>224 056 | 37935<br>−27601<br>224 057 |
| **3−** | 37936<br>−27600<br>224 060 | 37937<br>−27599<br>224 061 | 37938<br>−27598<br>224 062 | 37939<br>−27597<br>224 063 | 37940<br>−27596<br>224 064 | 37941<br>−27595<br>224 065 | 37942<br>−27594<br>224 066 | 37943<br>−27593<br>224 067 | 37944<br>−27592<br>224 070 | 37945<br>−27591<br>224 071 | 37946<br>−27590<br>224 072 | 37947<br>−27589<br>224 073 | 37948<br>−27588<br>224 074 | 37949<br>−27587<br>224 075 | 37950<br>−27586<br>224 076 | 37951<br>−27585<br>224 077 |
| **4−** | 37952<br>−27584<br>224 100 | 37953<br>−27583<br>224 101 | 37954<br>−27582<br>224 102 | 37955<br>−27581<br>224 103 | 37956<br>−27580<br>224 104 | 37957<br>−27579<br>224 105 | 37958<br>−27578<br>224 106 | 37959<br>−27577<br>224 107 | 37960<br>−27576<br>224 110 | 37961<br>−27575<br>224 111 | 37962<br>−27574<br>224 112 | 37963<br>−27573<br>224 113 | 37964<br>−27572<br>224 114 | 37965<br>−27571<br>224 115 | 37966<br>−27570<br>224 116 | 37967<br>−27569<br>224 117 |
| **5−** | 37968<br>−27568<br>224 120 | 37969<br>−27567<br>224 121 | 37970<br>−27566<br>224 122 | 37971<br>−27565<br>224 123 | 37972<br>−27564<br>224 124 | 37973<br>−27563<br>224 125 | 37974<br>−27562<br>224 126 | 37975<br>−27561<br>224 127 | 37976<br>−27560<br>224 130 | 37977<br>−27559<br>224 131 | 37978<br>−27558<br>224 132 | 37979<br>−27557<br>224 133 | 37980<br>−27556<br>224 134 | 37981<br>−27555<br>224 135 | 37982<br>−27554<br>224 136 | 37983<br>−27553<br>224 137 |
| **6−** | 37984<br>−27552<br>224 140 | 37985<br>−27551<br>224 141 | 37986<br>−27550<br>224 142 | 37987<br>−27549<br>224 143 | 37988<br>−27548<br>224 144 | 37989<br>−27547<br>224 145 | 37990<br>−27546<br>224 146 | 37991<br>−27545<br>224 147 | 37992<br>−27544<br>224 150 | 37993<br>−27543<br>224 151 | 37994<br>−27542<br>224 152 | 37995<br>−27541<br>224 153 | 37996<br>−27540<br>224 154 | 37997<br>−27539<br>224 155 | 37998<br>−27538<br>224 156 | 37999<br>−27537<br>224 157 |
| **7−** | 38000<br>−27536<br>224 160 | 38001<br>−27535<br>224 161 | 38002<br>−27534<br>224 162 | 38003<br>−27533<br>224 163 | 38004<br>−27532<br>224 164 | 38005<br>−27531<br>224 165 | 38006<br>−27530<br>224 166 | 38007<br>−27529<br>224 167 | 38008<br>−27528<br>224 170 | 38009<br>−27527<br>224 171 | 38010<br>−27526<br>224 172 | 38011<br>−27525<br>224 173 | 38012<br>−27524<br>224 174 | 38013<br>−27523<br>224 175 | 38014<br>−27522<br>224 176 | 38015<br>−27521<br>224 177 |
| **8−** | 38016<br>−27520<br>224 200 | 38017<br>−27519<br>224 201 | 38018<br>−27518<br>224 202 | 38019<br>−27517<br>224 203 | 38020<br>−27516<br>224 204 | 38021<br>−27515<br>224 205 | 38022<br>−27514<br>224 206 | 38023<br>−27513<br>224 207 | 38024<br>−27512<br>224 210 | 38025<br>−27511<br>224 211 | 38026<br>−27510<br>224 212 | 38027<br>−27509<br>224 213 | 38028<br>−27508<br>224 214 | 38029<br>−27507<br>224 215 | 38030<br>−27506<br>224 216 | 38031<br>−27505<br>224 217 |
| **9−** | 38032<br>−27504<br>224 220 | 38033<br>−27503<br>224 221 | 38034<br>−27502<br>224 222 | 38035<br>−27501<br>224 223 | 38036<br>−27500<br>224 224 | 38037<br>−27499<br>224 225 | 38038<br>−27498<br>224 226 | 38039<br>−27497<br>224 227 | 38040<br>−27496<br>224 230 | 38041<br>−27495<br>224 231 | 38042<br>−27494<br>224 232 | 38043<br>−27493<br>224 233 | 38044<br>−27492<br>224 234 | 38045<br>−27491<br>224 235 | 38046<br>−27490<br>224 236 | 38047<br>−27489<br>224 237 |
| **A−** | 38048<br>−27488<br>224 240 | 38049<br>−27487<br>224 241 | 38050<br>−27486<br>224 242 | 38051<br>−27485<br>224 243 | 38052<br>−27484<br>224 244 | 38053<br>−27483<br>224 245 | 38054<br>−27482<br>224 246 | 38055<br>−27481<br>224 247 | 38056<br>−27480<br>224 250 | 38057<br>−27479<br>224 251 | 38058<br>−27478<br>224 252 | 38059<br>−27477<br>224 253 | 38060<br>−27476<br>224 254 | 38061<br>−27475<br>224 255 | 38062<br>−27474<br>224 256 | 38063<br>−27473<br>224 257 |
| **B−** | 38064<br>−27472<br>224 260 | 38065<br>−27471<br>224 261 | 38066<br>−27470<br>224 262 | 38067<br>−27469<br>224 263 | 38068<br>−27468<br>224 264 | 38069<br>−27467<br>224 265 | 38070<br>−27466<br>224 266 | 38071<br>−27465<br>224 267 | 38072<br>−27464<br>224 270 | 38073<br>−27463<br>224 271 | 38074<br>−27462<br>224 272 | 38075<br>−27461<br>224 273 | 38076<br>−27460<br>224 274 | 38077<br>−27459<br>224 275 | 38078<br>−27458<br>224 276 | 38079<br>−27457<br>224 277 |
| **C−** | 38080<br>−27456<br>224 300 | 38081<br>−27455<br>224 301 | 38082<br>−27454<br>224 302 | 38083<br>−27453<br>224 303 | 38084<br>−27452<br>224 304 | 38085<br>−27451<br>224 305 | 38086<br>−27450<br>224 306 | 38087<br>−27449<br>224 307 | 38088<br>−27448<br>224 310 | 38089<br>−27447<br>224 311 | 38090<br>−27446<br>224 312 | 38091<br>−27445<br>224 313 | 38092<br>−27444<br>224 314 | 38093<br>−27443<br>224 315 | 38094<br>−27442<br>224 316 | 38095<br>−27441<br>224 317 |
| **D−** | 38096<br>−27440<br>224 320 | 38097<br>−27439<br>224 321 | 38098<br>−27438<br>224 322 | 38099<br>−27437<br>224 323 | 38100<br>−27436<br>224 324 | 38101<br>−27435<br>224 325 | 38102<br>−27434<br>224 326 | 38103<br>−27433<br>224 327 | 38104<br>−27432<br>224 330 | 38105<br>−27431<br>224 331 | 38106<br>−27430<br>224 332 | 38107<br>−27429<br>224 333 | 38108<br>−27428<br>224 334 | 38109<br>−27427<br>224 335 | 38110<br>−27426<br>224 336 | 38111<br>−27425<br>224 337 |
| **E−** | 38112<br>−27424<br>224 340 | 38113<br>−27423<br>224 341 | 38114<br>−27422<br>224 342 | 38115<br>−27421<br>224 343 | 38116<br>−27420<br>224 344 | 38117<br>−27419<br>224 345 | 38118<br>−27418<br>224 346 | 38119<br>−27417<br>224 347 | 38120<br>−27416<br>224 350 | 38121<br>−27415<br>224 351 | 38122<br>−27414<br>224 352 | 38123<br>−27413<br>224 353 | 38124<br>−27412<br>224 354 | 38125<br>−27411<br>224 355 | 38126<br>−27410<br>224 356 | 38127<br>−27409<br>224 357 |
| **F−** | 38128<br>−27408<br>224 360 | 38129<br>−27407<br>224 361 | 38130<br>−27406<br>224 362 | 38131<br>−27405<br>224 363 | 38132<br>−27404<br>224 364 | 38133<br>−27403<br>224 365 | 38134<br>−27402<br>224 366 | 38135<br>−27401<br>224 367 | 38136<br>−27400<br>224 370 | 38137<br>−27399<br>224 371 | 38138<br>−27398<br>224 372 | 38139<br>−27397<br>224 373 | 38140<br>−27396<br>224 374 | 38141<br>−27395<br>224 375 | 38142<br>−27394<br>224 376 | 38143<br>−27393<br>224 377 |

SECOND HEX DIGIT

DECIMAL →    DECIMAL →    OCTAL →

**DECIMAL** −27648    **BINARY** 1001 0100    **DECIMAL** 37888    **HEXADECIMAL** (94)    **OCTAL** 224 000

FOURTH HEX DIGIT →   ← THIRD HEX DIGIT

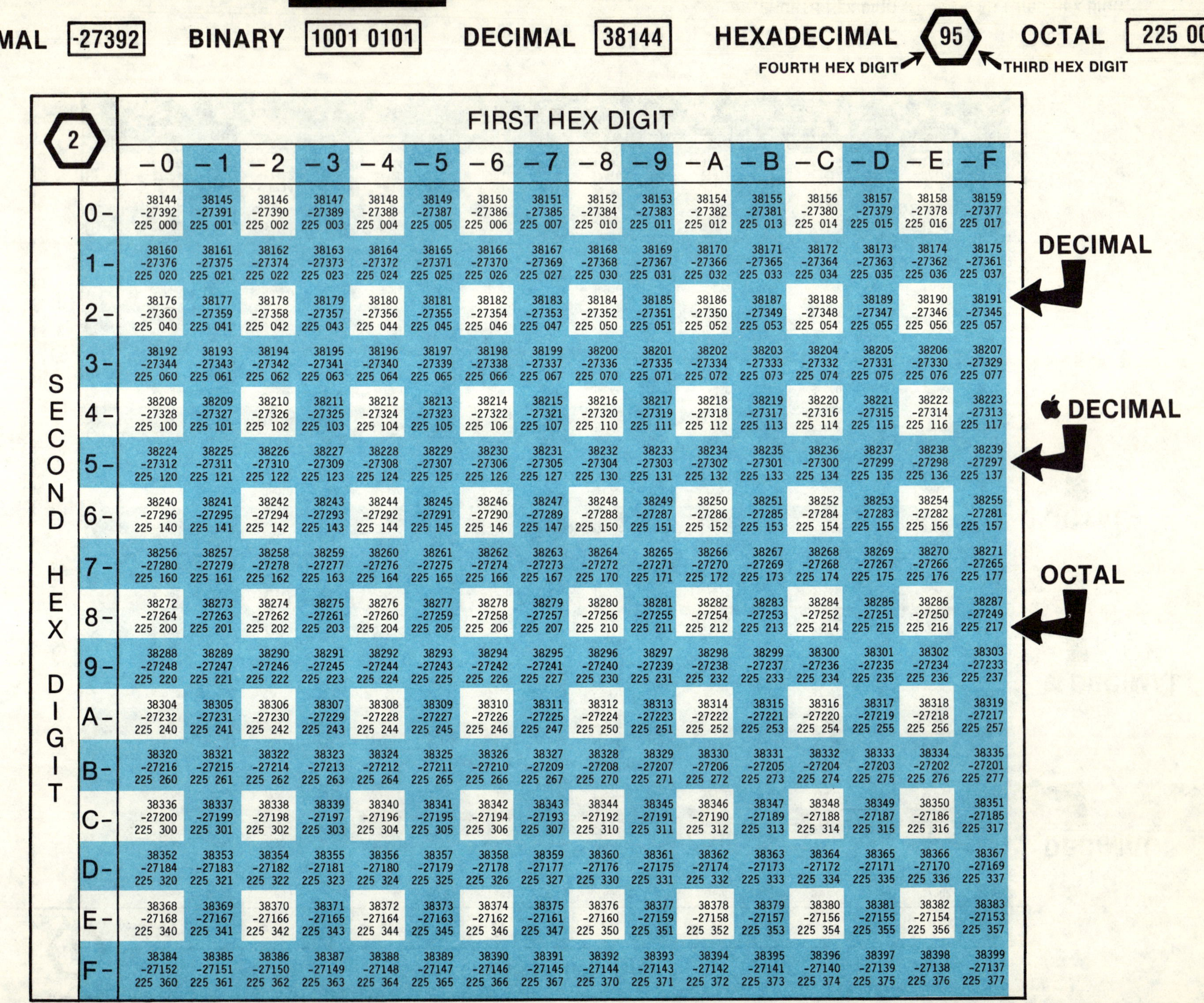

**②**

|  | −0 | −1 | −2 | −3 | −4 | −5 | −6 | −7 | −8 | −9 | −A | −B | −C | −D | −E | −F |
|---|---|---|---|---|---|---|---|---|---|---|---|---|---|---|---|---|
| **0−** | 38144<br>−27392<br>225 000 | 38145<br>−27391<br>225 001 | 38146<br>−27390<br>225 002 | 38147<br>−27389<br>225 003 | 38148<br>−27388<br>225 004 | 38149<br>−27387<br>225 005 | 38150<br>−27386<br>225 006 | 38151<br>−27385<br>225 007 | 38152<br>−27384<br>225 010 | 38153<br>−27383<br>225 011 | 38154<br>−27382<br>225 012 | 38155<br>−27381<br>225 013 | 38156<br>−27380<br>225 014 | 38157<br>−27379<br>225 015 | 38158<br>−27378<br>225 016 | 38159<br>−27377<br>225 017 |
| **1−** | 38160<br>−27376<br>225 020 | 38161<br>−27375<br>225 021 | 38162<br>−27374<br>225 022 | 38163<br>−27373<br>225 023 | 38164<br>−27372<br>225 024 | 38165<br>−27371<br>225 025 | 38166<br>−27370<br>225 026 | 38167<br>−27369<br>225 027 | 38168<br>−27368<br>225 030 | 38169<br>−27367<br>225 031 | 38170<br>−27366<br>225 032 | 38171<br>−27365<br>225 033 | 38172<br>−27364<br>225 034 | 38173<br>−27363<br>225 035 | 38174<br>−27362<br>225 036 | 38175<br>−27361<br>225 037 |
| **2−** | 38176<br>−27360<br>225 040 | 38177<br>−27359<br>225 041 | 38178<br>−27358<br>225 042 | 38179<br>−27357<br>225 043 | 38180<br>−27356<br>225 044 | 38181<br>−27355<br>225 045 | 38182<br>−27354<br>225 046 | 38183<br>−27353<br>225 047 | 38184<br>−27352<br>225 050 | 38185<br>−27351<br>225 051 | 38186<br>−27350<br>225 052 | 38187<br>−27349<br>225 053 | 38188<br>−27348<br>225 054 | 38189<br>−27347<br>225 055 | 38190<br>−27346<br>225 056 | 38191<br>−27345<br>225 057 |
| **3−** | 38192<br>−27344<br>225 060 | 38193<br>−27343<br>225 061 | 38194<br>−27342<br>225 062 | 38195<br>−27341<br>225 063 | 38196<br>−27340<br>225 064 | 38197<br>−27339<br>225 065 | 38198<br>−27338<br>225 066 | 38199<br>−27337<br>225 067 | 38200<br>−27336<br>225 070 | 38201<br>−27335<br>225 071 | 38202<br>−27334<br>225 072 | 38203<br>−27333<br>225 073 | 38204<br>−27332<br>225 074 | 38205<br>−27331<br>225 075 | 38206<br>−27330<br>225 076 | 38207<br>−27329<br>225 077 |
| **4−** | 38208<br>−27328<br>225 100 | 38209<br>−27327<br>225 101 | 38210<br>−27326<br>225 102 | 38211<br>−27325<br>225 103 | 38212<br>−27324<br>225 104 | 38213<br>−27323<br>225 105 | 38214<br>−27322<br>225 106 | 38215<br>−27321<br>225 107 | 38216<br>−27320<br>225 110 | 38217<br>−27319<br>225 111 | 38218<br>−27318<br>225 112 | 38219<br>−27317<br>225 113 | 38220<br>−27316<br>225 114 | 38221<br>−27315<br>225 115 | 38222<br>−27314<br>225 116 | 38223<br>−27313<br>225 117 |
| **5−** | 38224<br>−27312<br>225 120 | 38225<br>−27311<br>225 121 | 38226<br>−27310<br>225 122 | 38227<br>−27309<br>225 123 | 38228<br>−27308<br>225 124 | 38229<br>−27307<br>225 125 | 38230<br>−27306<br>225 126 | 38231<br>−27305<br>225 127 | 38232<br>−27304<br>225 130 | 38233<br>−27303<br>225 131 | 38234<br>−27302<br>225 132 | 38235<br>−27301<br>225 133 | 38236<br>−27300<br>225 134 | 38237<br>−27299<br>225 135 | 38238<br>−27298<br>225 136 | 38239<br>−27297<br>225 137 |
| **6−** | 38240<br>−27296<br>225 140 | 38241<br>−27295<br>225 141 | 38242<br>−27294<br>225 142 | 38243<br>−27293<br>225 143 | 38244<br>−27292<br>225 144 | 38245<br>−27291<br>225 145 | 38246<br>−27290<br>225 146 | 38247<br>−27289<br>225 147 | 38248<br>−27288<br>225 150 | 38249<br>−27287<br>225 151 | 38250<br>−27286<br>225 152 | 38251<br>−27285<br>225 153 | 38252<br>−27284<br>225 154 | 38253<br>−27283<br>225 155 | 38254<br>−27282<br>225 156 | 38255<br>−27281<br>225 157 |
| **7−** | 38256<br>−27280<br>225 160 | 38257<br>−27279<br>225 161 | 38258<br>−27278<br>225 162 | 38259<br>−27277<br>225 163 | 38260<br>−27276<br>225 164 | 38261<br>−27275<br>225 165 | 38262<br>−27274<br>225 166 | 38263<br>−27273<br>225 167 | 38264<br>−27272<br>225 170 | 38265<br>−27271<br>225 171 | 38266<br>−27270<br>225 172 | 38267<br>−27269<br>225 173 | 38268<br>−27268<br>225 174 | 38269<br>−27267<br>225 175 | 38270<br>−27266<br>225 176 | 38271<br>−27265<br>225 177 |
| **8−** | 38272<br>−27264<br>225 200 | 38273<br>−27263<br>225 201 | 38274<br>−27262<br>225 202 | 38275<br>−27261<br>225 203 | 38276<br>−27260<br>225 204 | 38277<br>−27259<br>225 205 | 38278<br>−27258<br>225 206 | 38279<br>−27257<br>225 207 | 38280<br>−27256<br>225 210 | 38281<br>−27255<br>225 211 | 38282<br>−27254<br>225 212 | 38283<br>−27253<br>225 213 | 38284<br>−27252<br>225 214 | 38285<br>−27251<br>225 215 | 38286<br>−27250<br>225 216 | 38287<br>−27249<br>225 217 |
| **9−** | 38288<br>−27248<br>225 220 | 38289<br>−27247<br>225 221 | 38290<br>−27246<br>225 222 | 38291<br>−27245<br>225 223 | 38292<br>−27244<br>225 224 | 38293<br>−27243<br>225 225 | 38294<br>−27242<br>225 226 | 38295<br>−27241<br>225 227 | 38296<br>−27240<br>225 230 | 38297<br>−27239<br>225 231 | 38298<br>−27238<br>225 232 | 38299<br>−27237<br>225 233 | 38300<br>−27236<br>225 234 | 38301<br>−27235<br>225 235 | 38302<br>−27234<br>225 236 | 38303<br>−27233<br>225 237 |
| **A−** | 38304<br>−27232<br>225 240 | 38305<br>−27231<br>225 241 | 38306<br>−27230<br>225 242 | 38307<br>−27229<br>225 243 | 38308<br>−27228<br>225 244 | 38309<br>−27227<br>225 245 | 38310<br>−27226<br>225 246 | 38311<br>−27225<br>225 247 | 38312<br>−27224<br>225 250 | 38313<br>−27223<br>225 251 | 38314<br>−27222<br>225 252 | 38315<br>−27221<br>225 253 | 38316<br>−27220<br>225 254 | 38317<br>−27219<br>225 255 | 38318<br>−27218<br>225 256 | 38319<br>−27217<br>225 257 |
| **B−** | 38320<br>−27216<br>225 260 | 38321<br>−27215<br>225 261 | 38322<br>−27214<br>225 262 | 38323<br>−27213<br>225 263 | 38324<br>−27212<br>225 264 | 38325<br>−27211<br>225 265 | 38326<br>−27210<br>225 266 | 38327<br>−27209<br>225 267 | 38328<br>−27208<br>225 270 | 38329<br>−27207<br>225 271 | 38330<br>−27206<br>225 272 | 38331<br>−27205<br>225 273 | 38332<br>−27204<br>225 274 | 38333<br>−27203<br>225 275 | 38334<br>−27202<br>225 276 | 38335<br>−27201<br>225 277 |
| **C−** | 38336<br>−27200<br>225 300 | 38337<br>−27199<br>225 301 | 38338<br>−27198<br>225 302 | 38339<br>−27197<br>225 303 | 38340<br>−27196<br>225 304 | 38341<br>−27195<br>225 305 | 38342<br>−27194<br>225 306 | 38343<br>−27193<br>225 307 | 38344<br>−27192<br>225 310 | 38345<br>−27191<br>225 311 | 38346<br>−27190<br>225 312 | 38347<br>−27189<br>225 313 | 38348<br>−27188<br>225 314 | 38349<br>−27187<br>225 315 | 38350<br>−27186<br>225 316 | 38351<br>−27185<br>225 317 |
| **D−** | 38352<br>−27184<br>225 320 | 38353<br>−27183<br>225 321 | 38354<br>−27182<br>225 322 | 38355<br>−27181<br>225 323 | 38356<br>−27180<br>225 324 | 38357<br>−27179<br>225 325 | 38358<br>−27178<br>225 326 | 38359<br>−27177<br>225 327 | 38360<br>−27176<br>225 330 | 38361<br>−27175<br>225 331 | 38362<br>−27174<br>225 332 | 38363<br>−27173<br>225 333 | 38364<br>−27172<br>225 334 | 38365<br>−27171<br>225 335 | 38366<br>−27170<br>225 336 | 38367<br>−27169<br>225 337 |
| **E−** | 38368<br>−27168<br>225 340 | 38369<br>−27167<br>225 341 | 38370<br>−27166<br>225 342 | 38371<br>−27165<br>225 343 | 38372<br>−27164<br>225 344 | 38373<br>−27163<br>225 345 | 38374<br>−27162<br>225 346 | 38375<br>−27161<br>225 347 | 38376<br>−27160<br>225 350 | 38377<br>−27159<br>225 351 | 38378<br>−27158<br>225 352 | 38379<br>−27157<br>225 353 | 38380<br>−27156<br>225 354 | 38381<br>−27155<br>225 355 | 38382<br>−27154<br>225 356 | 38383<br>−27153<br>225 357 |
| **F−** | 38384<br>−27152<br>225 360 | 38385<br>−27151<br>225 361 | 38386<br>−27150<br>225 362 | 38387<br>−27149<br>225 363 | 38388<br>−27148<br>225 364 | 38389<br>−27147<br>225 365 | 38390<br>−27146<br>225 366 | 38391<br>−27145<br>225 367 | 38392<br>−27144<br>225 370 | 38393<br>−27143<br>225 371 | 38394<br>−27142<br>225 372 | 38395<br>−27141<br>225 373 | 38396<br>−27140<br>225 374 | 38397<br>−27139<br>225 375 | 38398<br>−27138<br>225 376 | 38399<br>−27137<br>225 377 |

# FIRST HEX DIGIT

**② SECOND HEX DIGIT**

| | −0 | −1 | −2 | −3 | −4 | −5 | −6 | −7 | −8 | −9 | −A | −B | −C | −D | −E | −F |
|---|---|---|---|---|---|---|---|---|---|---|---|---|---|---|---|---|
| **0−** | 38400<br>−27136<br>226 000 | 38401<br>−27135<br>226 001 | 38402<br>−27134<br>226 002 | 38403<br>−27133<br>226 003 | 38404<br>−27132<br>226 004 | 38405<br>−27131<br>226 005 | 38406<br>−27130<br>226 006 | 38407<br>−27129<br>226 007 | 38408<br>−27128<br>226 010 | 38409<br>−27127<br>226 011 | 38410<br>−27126<br>226 012 | 38411<br>−27125<br>226 013 | 38412<br>−27124<br>226 014 | 38413<br>−27123<br>226 015 | 38414<br>−27122<br>226 016 | 38415<br>−27121<br>226 017 |
| **1−** | 38416<br>−27120<br>226 020 | 38417<br>−27119<br>226 021 | 38418<br>−27118<br>226 022 | 38419<br>−27117<br>226 023 | 38420<br>−27116<br>226 024 | 38421<br>−27115<br>226 025 | 38422<br>−27114<br>226 026 | 38423<br>−27113<br>226 027 | 38424<br>−27112<br>226 030 | 38425<br>−27111<br>226 031 | 38426<br>−27110<br>226 032 | 38427<br>−27109<br>226 033 | 38428<br>−27108<br>226 034 | 38429<br>−27107<br>226 035 | 38430<br>−27106<br>226 036 | 38431<br>−27105<br>226 037 |
| **2−** | 38432<br>−27104<br>226 040 | 38433<br>−27103<br>226 041 | 38434<br>−27102<br>226 042 | 38435<br>−27101<br>226 043 | 38436<br>−27100<br>226 044 | 38437<br>−27099<br>226 045 | 38438<br>−27098<br>226 046 | 38439<br>−27097<br>226 047 | 38440<br>−27096<br>226 050 | 38441<br>−27095<br>226 051 | 38442<br>−27094<br>226 052 | 38443<br>−27093<br>226 053 | 38444<br>−27092<br>226 054 | 38445<br>−27091<br>226 055 | 38446<br>−27090<br>226 056 | 38447<br>−27089<br>226 057 |
| **3−** | 38448<br>−27088<br>226 060 | 38449<br>−27087<br>226 061 | 38450<br>−27086<br>226 062 | 38451<br>−27085<br>226 063 | 38452<br>−27084<br>226 064 | 38453<br>−27083<br>226 065 | 38454<br>−27082<br>226 066 | 38455<br>−27081<br>226 067 | 38456<br>−27080<br>226 070 | 38457<br>−27079<br>226 071 | 38458<br>−27078<br>226 072 | 38459<br>−27077<br>226 073 | 38460<br>−27076<br>226 074 | 38461<br>−27075<br>226 075 | 38462<br>−27074<br>226 076 | 38463<br>−27073<br>226 077 |
| **4−** | 38464<br>−27072<br>226 100 | 38465<br>−27071<br>226 101 | 38466<br>−27070<br>226 102 | 38467<br>−27069<br>226 103 | 38468<br>−27068<br>226 104 | 38469<br>−27067<br>226 105 | 38470<br>−27066<br>226 106 | 38471<br>−27065<br>226 107 | 38472<br>−27064<br>226 110 | 38473<br>−27063<br>226 111 | 38474<br>−27062<br>226 112 | 38475<br>−27061<br>226 113 | 38476<br>−27060<br>226 114 | 38477<br>−27059<br>226 115 | 38478<br>−27058<br>226 116 | 38479<br>−27057<br>226 117 |
| **5−** | 38480<br>−27056<br>226 120 | 38481<br>−27055<br>226 121 | 38482<br>−27054<br>226 122 | 38483<br>−27053<br>226 123 | 38484<br>−27052<br>226 124 | 38485<br>−27051<br>226 125 | 38486<br>−27050<br>226 126 | 38487<br>−27049<br>226 127 | 38488<br>−27048<br>226 130 | 38489<br>−27047<br>226 131 | 38490<br>−27046<br>226 132 | 38491<br>−27045<br>226 133 | 38492<br>−27044<br>226 134 | 38493<br>−27043<br>226 135 | 38494<br>−27042<br>226 136 | 38495<br>−27041<br>226 137 |
| **6−** | 38496<br>−27040<br>226 140 | 38497<br>−27039<br>226 141 | 38498<br>−27038<br>226 142 | 38499<br>−27037<br>226 143 | 38500<br>−27036<br>226 144 | 38501<br>−27035<br>226 145 | 38502<br>−27034<br>226 146 | 38503<br>−27033<br>226 147 | 38504<br>−27032<br>226 150 | 38505<br>−27031<br>226 151 | 38506<br>−27030<br>226 152 | 38507<br>−27029<br>226 153 | 38508<br>−27028<br>226 154 | 38509<br>−27027<br>226 155 | 38510<br>−27026<br>226 156 | 38511<br>−27025<br>226 157 |
| **7−** | 38512<br>−27024<br>226 160 | 38513<br>−27023<br>226 161 | 38514<br>−27022<br>226 162 | 38515<br>−27021<br>226 163 | 38516<br>−27020<br>226 164 | 38517<br>−27019<br>226 165 | 38518<br>−27018<br>226 166 | 38519<br>−27017<br>226 167 | 38520<br>−27016<br>226 170 | 38521<br>−27015<br>226 171 | 38522<br>−27014<br>226 172 | 38523<br>−27013<br>226 173 | 38524<br>−27012<br>226 174 | 38525<br>−27011<br>226 175 | 38526<br>−27010<br>226 176 | 38527<br>−27009<br>226 177 |
| **8−** | 38528<br>−27008<br>226 200 | 38529<br>−27007<br>226 201 | 38530<br>−27006<br>226 202 | 38531<br>−27005<br>226 203 | 38532<br>−27004<br>226 204 | 38533<br>−27003<br>226 205 | 38534<br>−27002<br>226 206 | 38535<br>−27001<br>226 207 | 38536<br>−27000<br>226 210 | 38537<br>−26999<br>226 211 | 38538<br>−26998<br>226 212 | 38539<br>−26997<br>226 213 | 38540<br>−26996<br>226 214 | 38541<br>−26995<br>226 215 | 38542<br>−26994<br>226 216 | 38543<br>−26993<br>226 217 |
| **9−** | 38544<br>−26992<br>226 220 | 38545<br>−26991<br>226 221 | 38546<br>−26990<br>226 222 | 38547<br>−26989<br>226 223 | 38548<br>−26988<br>226 224 | 38549<br>−26987<br>226 225 | 38550<br>−26986<br>226 226 | 38551<br>−26985<br>226 227 | 38552<br>−26984<br>226 230 | 38553<br>−26983<br>226 231 | 38554<br>−26982<br>226 232 | 38555<br>−26981<br>226 233 | 38556<br>−26980<br>226 234 | 38557<br>−26979<br>226 235 | 38558<br>−26978<br>226 236 | 38559<br>−26977<br>226 237 |
| **A−** | 38560<br>−26976<br>226 240 | 38561<br>−26975<br>226 241 | 38562<br>−26974<br>226 242 | 38563<br>−26973<br>226 243 | 38564<br>−26972<br>226 244 | 38565<br>−26971<br>226 245 | 38566<br>−26970<br>226 246 | 38567<br>−26969<br>226 247 | 38568<br>−26968<br>226 250 | 38569<br>−26967<br>226 251 | 38570<br>−26966<br>226 252 | 38571<br>−26965<br>226 253 | 38572<br>−26964<br>226 254 | 38573<br>−26963<br>226 255 | 38574<br>−26962<br>226 256 | 38575<br>−26961<br>226 257 |
| **B−** | 38576<br>−26960<br>226 260 | 38577<br>−26959<br>226 261 | 38578<br>−26958<br>226 262 | 38579<br>−26957<br>226 263 | 38580<br>−26956<br>226 264 | 38581<br>−26955<br>226 265 | 38582<br>−26954<br>226 266 | 38583<br>−26953<br>226 267 | 38584<br>−26952<br>226 270 | 38585<br>−26951<br>226 271 | 38586<br>−26950<br>226 272 | 38587<br>−26949<br>226 273 | 38588<br>−26948<br>226 274 | 38589<br>−26947<br>226 275 | 38590<br>−26946<br>226 276 | 38591<br>−26945<br>226 277 |
| **C−** | 38592<br>−26944<br>226 300 | 38593<br>−26943<br>226 301 | 38594<br>−26942<br>226 302 | 38595<br>−26941<br>226 303 | 38596<br>−26940<br>226 304 | 38597<br>−26939<br>226 305 | 38598<br>−26938<br>226 306 | 38599<br>−26937<br>226 307 | 38600<br>−26936<br>226 310 | 38601<br>−26935<br>226 311 | 38602<br>−26934<br>226 312 | 38603<br>−26933<br>226 313 | 38604<br>−26932<br>226 314 | 38605<br>−26931<br>226 315 | 38606<br>−26930<br>226 316 | 38607<br>−26929<br>226 317 |
| **D−** | 38608<br>−26928<br>226 320 | 38609<br>−26927<br>226 321 | 38610<br>−26926<br>226 322 | 38611<br>−26925<br>226 323 | 38612<br>−26924<br>226 324 | 38613<br>−26923<br>226 325 | 38614<br>−26922<br>226 326 | 38615<br>−26921<br>226 327 | 38616<br>−26920<br>226 330 | 38617<br>−26919<br>226 331 | 38618<br>−26918<br>226 332 | 38619<br>−26917<br>226 333 | 38620<br>−26916<br>226 334 | 38621<br>−26915<br>226 335 | 38622<br>−26914<br>226 336 | 38623<br>−26913<br>226 337 |
| **E−** | 38624<br>−26912<br>226 340 | 38625<br>−26911<br>226 341 | 38626<br>−26910<br>226 342 | 38627<br>−26909<br>226 343 | 38628<br>−26908<br>226 344 | 38629<br>−26907<br>226 345 | 38630<br>−26906<br>226 346 | 38631<br>−26905<br>226 347 | 38632<br>−26904<br>226 350 | 38633<br>−26903<br>226 351 | 38634<br>−26902<br>226 352 | 38635<br>−26901<br>226 353 | 38636<br>−26900<br>226 354 | 38637<br>−26899<br>226 355 | 38638<br>−26898<br>226 356 | 38639<br>−26897<br>226 357 |
| **F−** | 38640<br>−26896<br>226 360 | 38641<br>−26895<br>226 361 | 38642<br>−26894<br>226 362 | 38643<br>−26893<br>226 363 | 38644<br>−26892<br>226 364 | 38645<br>−26891<br>226 365 | 38646<br>−26890<br>226 366 | 38647<br>−26889<br>226 367 | 38648<br>−26888<br>226 370 | 38649<br>−26887<br>226 371 | 38650<br>−26886<br>226 372 | 38651<br>−26885<br>226 373 | 38652<br>−26884<br>226 374 | 38653<br>−26883<br>226 375 | 38654<br>−26882<br>226 376 | 38655<br>−26881<br>226 377 |

DECIMAL

 DECIMAL

OCTAL

 DECIMAL −27136  BINARY 1001 0110  DECIMAL 38400  HEXADECIMAL ⬡96  OCTAL 226 000

FOURTH HEX DIGIT → ⬡ ← THIRD HEX DIGIT

 DECIMAL [-26880]  BINARY [1001 0111]  DECIMAL [38656]  HEXADECIMAL (97)  OCTAL [227 000]

FOURTH HEX DIGIT → 97 ← THIRD HEX DIGIT

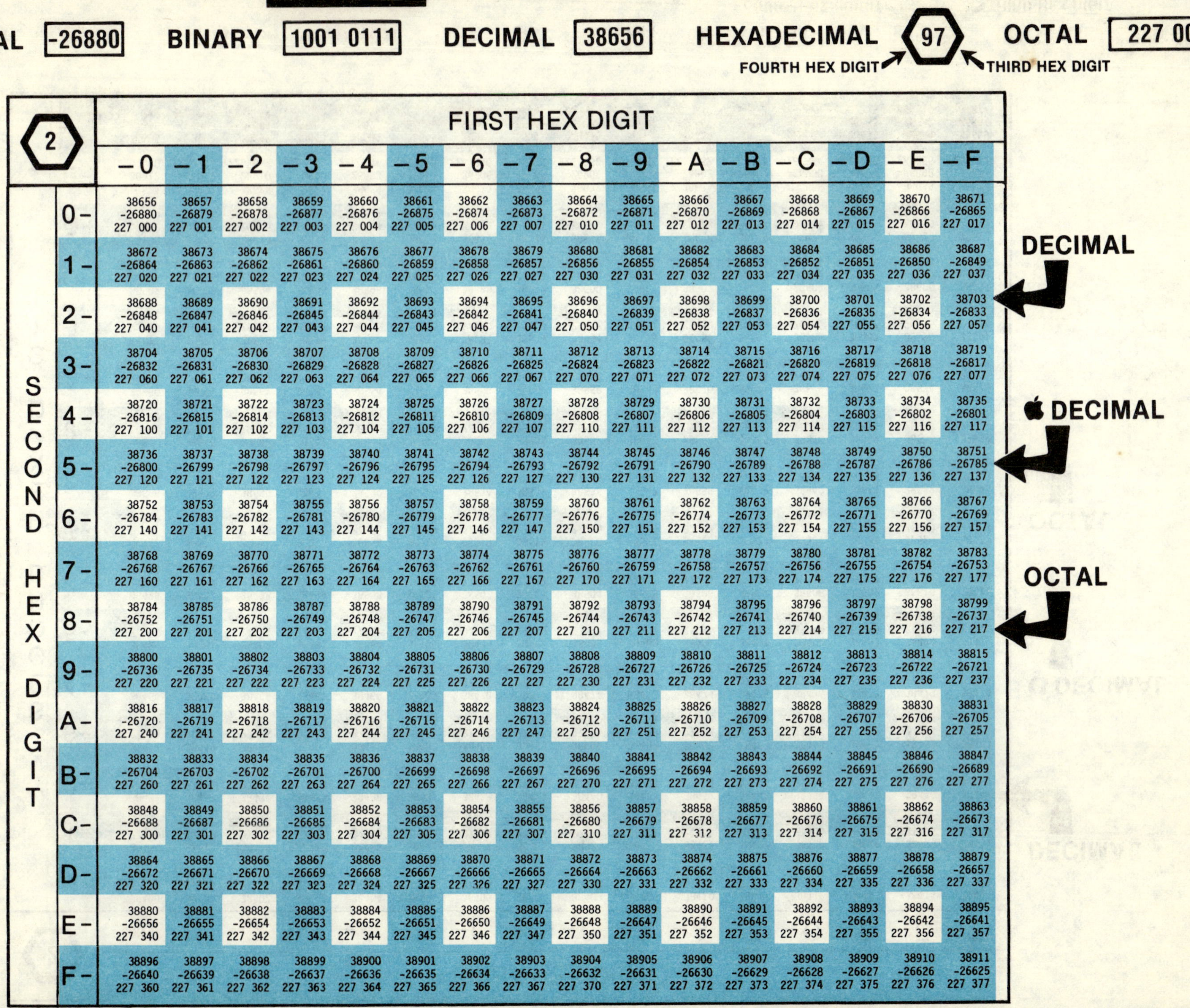



2 — FIRST HEX DIGIT / SECOND HEX DIGIT

| | −0 | −1 | −2 | −3 | −4 | −5 | −6 | −7 | −8 | −9 | −A | −B | −C | −D | −E | −F |
|---|---|---|---|---|---|---|---|---|---|---|---|---|---|---|---|---|
| 0− | 38656<br>−26880<br>227 000 | 38657<br>−26879<br>227 001 | 38658<br>−26878<br>227 002 | 38659<br>−26877<br>227 003 | 38660<br>−26876<br>227 004 | 38661<br>−26875<br>227 005 | 38662<br>−26874<br>227 006 | 38663<br>−26873<br>227 007 | 38664<br>−26872<br>227 010 | 38665<br>−26871<br>227 011 | 38666<br>−26870<br>227 012 | 38667<br>−26869<br>227 013 | 38668<br>−26868<br>227 014 | 38669<br>−26867<br>227 015 | 38670<br>−26866<br>227 016 | 38671<br>−26865<br>227 017 |
| 1− | 38672<br>−26864<br>227 020 | 38673<br>−26863<br>227 021 | 38674<br>−26862<br>227 022 | 38675<br>−26861<br>227 023 | 38676<br>−26860<br>227 024 | 38677<br>−26859<br>227 025 | 38678<br>−26858<br>227 026 | 38679<br>−26857<br>227 027 | 38680<br>−26856<br>227 030 | 38681<br>−26855<br>227 031 | 38682<br>−26854<br>227 032 | 38683<br>−26853<br>227 033 | 38684<br>−26852<br>227 034 | 38685<br>−26851<br>227 035 | 38686<br>−26850<br>227 036 | 38687<br>−26849<br>227 037 |
| 2− | 38688<br>−26848<br>227 040 | 38689<br>−26847<br>227 041 | 38690<br>−26846<br>227 042 | 38691<br>−26845<br>227 043 | 38692<br>−26844<br>227 044 | 38693<br>−26843<br>227 045 | 38694<br>−26842<br>227 046 | 38695<br>−26841<br>227 047 | 38696<br>−26840<br>227 050 | 38697<br>−26839<br>227 051 | 38698<br>−26838<br>227 052 | 38699<br>−26837<br>227 053 | 38700<br>−26836<br>227 054 | 38701<br>−26835<br>227 055 | 38702<br>−26834<br>227 056 | 38703<br>−26833<br>227 057 |
| 3− | 38704<br>−26832<br>227 060 | 38705<br>−26831<br>227 061 | 38706<br>−26830<br>227 062 | 38707<br>−26829<br>227 063 | 38708<br>−26828<br>227 064 | 38709<br>−26827<br>227 065 | 38710<br>−26826<br>227 066 | 38711<br>−26825<br>227 067 | 38712<br>−26824<br>227 070 | 38713<br>−26823<br>227 071 | 38714<br>−26822<br>227 072 | 38715<br>−26821<br>227 073 | 38716<br>−26820<br>227 074 | 38717<br>−26819<br>227 075 | 38718<br>−26818<br>227 076 | 38719<br>−26817<br>227 077 |
| 4− | 38720<br>−26816<br>227 100 | 38721<br>−26815<br>227 101 | 38722<br>−26814<br>227 102 | 38723<br>−26813<br>227 103 | 38724<br>−26812<br>227 104 | 38725<br>−26811<br>227 105 | 38726<br>−26810<br>227 106 | 38727<br>−26809<br>227 107 | 38728<br>−26808<br>227 110 | 38729<br>−26807<br>227 111 | 38730<br>−26806<br>227 112 | 38731<br>−26805<br>227 113 | 38732<br>−26804<br>227 114 | 38733<br>−26803<br>227 115 | 38734<br>−26802<br>227 116 | 38735<br>−26801<br>227 117 |
| 5− | 38736<br>−26800<br>227 120 | 38737<br>−26799<br>227 121 | 38738<br>−26798<br>227 122 | 38739<br>−26797<br>227 123 | 38740<br>−26796<br>227 124 | 38741<br>−26795<br>227 125 | 38742<br>−26794<br>227 126 | 38743<br>−26793<br>227 127 | 38744<br>−26792<br>227 130 | 38745<br>−26791<br>227 131 | 38746<br>−26790<br>227 132 | 38747<br>−26789<br>227 133 | 38748<br>−26788<br>227 134 | 38749<br>−26787<br>227 135 | 38750<br>−26786<br>227 136 | 38751<br>−26785<br>227 137 |
| 6− | 38752<br>−26784<br>227 140 | 38753<br>−26783<br>227 141 | 38754<br>−26782<br>227 142 | 38755<br>−26781<br>227 143 | 38756<br>−26780<br>227 144 | 38757<br>−26779<br>227 145 | 38758<br>−26778<br>227 146 | 38759<br>−26777<br>227 147 | 38760<br>−26776<br>227 150 | 38761<br>−26775<br>227 151 | 38762<br>−26774<br>227 152 | 38763<br>−26773<br>227 153 | 38764<br>−26772<br>227 154 | 38765<br>−26771<br>227 155 | 38766<br>−26770<br>227 156 | 38767<br>−26769<br>227 157 |
| 7− | 38768<br>−26768<br>227 160 | 38769<br>−26767<br>227 161 | 38770<br>−26766<br>227 162 | 38771<br>−26765<br>227 163 | 38772<br>−26764<br>227 164 | 38773<br>−26763<br>227 165 | 38774<br>−26762<br>227 166 | 38775<br>−26761<br>227 167 | 38776<br>−26760<br>227 170 | 38777<br>−26759<br>227 171 | 38778<br>−26758<br>227 172 | 38779<br>−26757<br>227 173 | 38780<br>−26756<br>227 174 | 38781<br>−26755<br>227 175 | 38782<br>−26754<br>227 176 | 38783<br>−26753<br>227 177 |
| 8− | 38784<br>−26752<br>227 200 | 38785<br>−26751<br>227 201 | 38786<br>−26750<br>227 202 | 38787<br>−26749<br>227 203 | 38788<br>−26748<br>227 204 | 38789<br>−26747<br>227 205 | 38790<br>−26746<br>227 206 | 38791<br>−26745<br>227 207 | 38792<br>−26744<br>227 210 | 38793<br>−26743<br>227 211 | 38794<br>−26742<br>227 212 | 38795<br>−26741<br>227 213 | 38796<br>−26740<br>227 214 | 38797<br>−26739<br>227 215 | 38798<br>−26738<br>227 216 | 38799<br>−26737<br>227 217 |
| 9− | 38800<br>−26736<br>227 220 | 38801<br>−26735<br>227 221 | 38802<br>−26734<br>227 222 | 38803<br>−26733<br>227 223 | 38804<br>−26732<br>227 224 | 38805<br>−26731<br>227 225 | 38806<br>−26730<br>227 226 | 38807<br>−26729<br>227 227 | 38808<br>−26728<br>227 230 | 38809<br>−26727<br>227 231 | 38810<br>−26726<br>227 232 | 38811<br>−26725<br>227 233 | 38812<br>−26724<br>227 234 | 38813<br>−26723<br>227 235 | 38814<br>−26722<br>227 236 | 38815<br>−26721<br>227 237 |
| A− | 38816<br>−26720<br>227 240 | 38817<br>−26719<br>227 241 | 38818<br>−26718<br>227 242 | 38819<br>−26717<br>227 243 | 38820<br>−26716<br>227 244 | 38821<br>−26715<br>227 245 | 38822<br>−26714<br>227 246 | 38823<br>−26713<br>227 247 | 38824<br>−26712<br>227 250 | 38825<br>−26711<br>227 251 | 38826<br>−26710<br>227 252 | 38827<br>−26709<br>227 253 | 38828<br>−26708<br>227 254 | 38829<br>−26707<br>227 255 | 38830<br>−26706<br>227 256 | 38831<br>−26705<br>227 257 |
| B− | 38832<br>−26704<br>227 260 | 38833<br>−26703<br>227 261 | 38834<br>−26702<br>227 262 | 38835<br>−26701<br>227 263 | 38836<br>−26700<br>227 264 | 38837<br>−26699<br>227 265 | 38838<br>−26698<br>227 266 | 38839<br>−26697<br>227 267 | 38840<br>−26696<br>227 270 | 38841<br>−26695<br>227 271 | 38842<br>−26694<br>227 272 | 38843<br>−26693<br>227 273 | 38844<br>−26692<br>227 274 | 38845<br>−26691<br>227 275 | 38846<br>−26690<br>227 276 | 38847<br>−26689<br>227 277 |
| C− | 38848<br>−26688<br>227 300 | 38849<br>−26687<br>227 301 | 38850<br>−26686<br>227 302 | 38851<br>−26685<br>227 303 | 38852<br>−26684<br>227 304 | 38853<br>−26683<br>227 305 | 38854<br>−26682<br>227 306 | 38855<br>−26681<br>227 307 | 38856<br>−26680<br>227 310 | 38857<br>−26679<br>227 311 | 38858<br>−26678<br>227 312 | 38859<br>−26677<br>227 313 | 38860<br>−26676<br>227 314 | 38861<br>−26675<br>227 315 | 38862<br>−26674<br>227 316 | 38863<br>−26673<br>227 317 |
| D− | 38864<br>−26672<br>227 320 | 38865<br>−26671<br>227 321 | 38866<br>−26670<br>227 322 | 38867<br>−26669<br>227 323 | 38868<br>−26668<br>227 324 | 38869<br>−26667<br>227 325 | 38870<br>−26666<br>227 326 | 38871<br>−26665<br>227 327 | 38872<br>−26664<br>227 330 | 38873<br>−26663<br>227 331 | 38874<br>−26662<br>227 332 | 38875<br>−26661<br>227 333 | 38876<br>−26660<br>227 334 | 38877<br>−26659<br>227 335 | 38878<br>−26658<br>227 336 | 38879<br>−26657<br>227 337 |
| E− | 38880<br>−26656<br>227 340 | 38881<br>−26655<br>227 341 | 38882<br>−26654<br>227 342 | 38883<br>−26653<br>227 343 | 38884<br>−26652<br>227 344 | 38885<br>−26651<br>227 345 | 38886<br>−26650<br>227 346 | 38887<br>−26649<br>227 347 | 38888<br>−26648<br>227 350 | 38889<br>−26647<br>227 351 | 38890<br>−26646<br>227 352 | 38891<br>−26645<br>227 353 | 38892<br>−26644<br>227 354 | 38893<br>−26643<br>227 355 | 38894<br>−26642<br>227 356 | 38895<br>−26641<br>227 357 |
| F− | 38896<br>−26640<br>227 360 | 38897<br>−26639<br>227 361 | 38898<br>−26638<br>227 362 | 38899<br>−26637<br>227 363 | 38900<br>−26636<br>227 364 | 38901<br>−26635<br>227 365 | 38902<br>−26634<br>227 366 | 38903<br>−26633<br>227 367 | 38904<br>−26632<br>227 370 | 38905<br>−26631<br>227 371 | 38906<br>−26630<br>227 372 | 38907<br>−26629<br>227 373 | 38908<br>−26628<br>227 374 | 38909<br>−26627<br>227 375 | 38910<br>−26626<br>227 376 | 38911<br>−26625<br>227 377 |

|  | FIRST HEX DIGIT | | | | | | | | | | | | | | | |
|---|---|---|---|---|---|---|---|---|---|---|---|---|---|---|---|---|
| **SECOND HEX DIGIT** | **−0** | **−1** | **−2** | **−3** | **−4** | **−5** | **−6** | **−7** | **−8** | **−9** | **−A** | **−B** | **−C** | **−D** | **−E** | **−F** |
| **0−** | 38912<br>−26624<br>230 000 | 38913<br>−26623<br>230 001 | 38914<br>−26622<br>230 002 | 38915<br>−26621<br>230 003 | 38916<br>−26620<br>230 004 | 38917<br>−26619<br>230 005 | 38918<br>−26618<br>230 006 | 38919<br>−26617<br>230 007 | 38920<br>−26616<br>230 010 | 38921<br>−26615<br>230 011 | 38922<br>−26614<br>230 012 | 38923<br>−26613<br>230 013 | 38924<br>−26612<br>230 014 | 38925<br>−26611<br>230 015 | 38926<br>−26610<br>230 016 | 38927<br>−26609<br>230 017 |
| **1−** | 38928<br>−26608<br>230 020 | 38929<br>−26607<br>230 021 | 38930<br>−26606<br>230 022 | 38931<br>−26605<br>230 023 | 38932<br>−26604<br>230 024 | 38933<br>−26603<br>230 025 | 38934<br>−26602<br>230 026 | 38935<br>−26601<br>230 027 | 38936<br>−26600<br>230 030 | 38937<br>−26599<br>230 031 | 38938<br>−26598<br>230 032 | 38939<br>−26597<br>230 033 | 38940<br>−26596<br>230 034 | 38941<br>−26595<br>230 035 | 38942<br>−26594<br>230 036 | 38943<br>−26593<br>230 037 |
| **2−** | 38944<br>−26592<br>230 040 | 38945<br>−26591<br>230 041 | 38946<br>−26590<br>230 042 | 38947<br>−26589<br>230 043 | 38948<br>−26588<br>230 044 | 38949<br>−26587<br>230 045 | 38950<br>−26586<br>230 046 | 38951<br>−26585<br>230 047 | 38952<br>−26584<br>230 050 | 38953<br>−26583<br>230 051 | 38954<br>−26582<br>230 052 | 38955<br>−26581<br>230 053 | 38956<br>−26580<br>230 054 | 38957<br>−26579<br>230 055 | 38958<br>−26578<br>230 056 | 38959<br>−26577<br>230 057 |
| **3−** | 38960<br>−26576<br>230 060 | 38961<br>−26575<br>230 061 | 38962<br>−26574<br>230 062 | 38963<br>−26573<br>230 063 | 38964<br>−26572<br>230 064 | 38965<br>−26571<br>230 065 | 38966<br>−26570<br>230 066 | 38967<br>−26569<br>230 067 | 38968<br>−26568<br>230 070 | 38969<br>−26567<br>230 071 | 38970<br>−26566<br>230 072 | 38971<br>−26565<br>230 073 | 38972<br>−26564<br>230 074 | 38973<br>−26563<br>230 075 | 38974<br>−26562<br>230 076 | 38975<br>−26561<br>230 077 |
| **4−** | 38976<br>−26560<br>230 100 | 38977<br>−26559<br>230 101 | 38978<br>−26558<br>230 102 | 38979<br>−26557<br>230 103 | 38980<br>−26556<br>230 104 | 38981<br>−26555<br>230 105 | 38982<br>−26554<br>230 106 | 38983<br>−26553<br>230 107 | 38984<br>−26552<br>230 110 | 38985<br>−26551<br>230 111 | 38986<br>−26550<br>230 112 | 38987<br>−26549<br>230 113 | 38988<br>−26548<br>230 114 | 38989<br>−26547<br>230 115 | 38990<br>−26546<br>230 116 | 38991<br>−26545<br>230 117 |
| **5−** | 38992<br>−26544<br>230 120 | 38993<br>−26543<br>230 121 | 38994<br>−26542<br>230 122 | 38995<br>−26541<br>230 123 | 38996<br>−26540<br>230 124 | 38997<br>−26539<br>230 125 | 38998<br>−26538<br>230 126 | 38999<br>−26537<br>230 127 | 39000<br>−26536<br>230 130 | 39001<br>−26535<br>230 131 | 39002<br>−26534<br>230 132 | 39003<br>−26533<br>230 133 | 39004<br>−26532<br>230 134 | 39005<br>−26531<br>230 135 | 39006<br>−26530<br>230 136 | 39007<br>−26529<br>230 137 |
| **6−** | 39008<br>−26528<br>230 140 | 39009<br>−26527<br>230 141 | 39010<br>−26526<br>230 142 | 39011<br>−26525<br>230 143 | 39012<br>−26524<br>230 144 | 39013<br>−26523<br>230 145 | 39014<br>−26522<br>230 146 | 39015<br>−26521<br>230 147 | 39016<br>−26520<br>230 150 | 39017<br>−26519<br>230 151 | 39018<br>−26518<br>230 152 | 39019<br>−26517<br>230 153 | 39020<br>−26516<br>230 154 | 39021<br>−26515<br>230 155 | 39022<br>−26514<br>230 156 | 39023<br>−26513<br>230 157 |
| **7−** | 39024<br>−26512<br>230 160 | 39025<br>−26511<br>230 161 | 39026<br>−26510<br>230 162 | 39027<br>−26509<br>230 163 | 39028<br>−26508<br>230 164 | 39029<br>−26507<br>230 165 | 39030<br>−26506<br>230 166 | 39031<br>−26505<br>230 167 | 39032<br>−26504<br>230 170 | 39033<br>−26503<br>230 171 | 39034<br>−26502<br>230 172 | 39035<br>−26501<br>230 173 | 39036<br>−26500<br>230 174 | 39037<br>−26499<br>230 175 | 39038<br>−26498<br>230 176 | 39039<br>−26497<br>230 177 |
| **8−** | 39040<br>−26496<br>230 200 | 39041<br>−26495<br>230 201 | 39042<br>−26494<br>230 202 | 39043<br>−26493<br>230 203 | 39044<br>−26492<br>230 204 | 39045<br>−26491<br>230 205 | 39046<br>−26490<br>230 206 | 39047<br>−26489<br>230 207 | 39048<br>−26488<br>230 210 | 39049<br>−26487<br>230 211 | 39050<br>−26486<br>230 212 | 39051<br>−26485<br>230 213 | 39052<br>−26484<br>230 214 | 39053<br>−26483<br>230 215 | 39054<br>−26482<br>230 216 | 39055<br>−26481<br>230 217 |
| **9−** | 39056<br>−26480<br>230 220 | 39057<br>−26479<br>230 221 | 39058<br>−26478<br>230 222 | 39059<br>−26477<br>230 223 | 39060<br>−26476<br>230 224 | 39061<br>−26475<br>230 225 | 39062<br>−26474<br>230 226 | 39063<br>−26473<br>230 227 | 39064<br>−26472<br>230 230 | 39065<br>−26471<br>230 231 | 39066<br>−26470<br>230 232 | 39067<br>−26469<br>230 233 | 39068<br>−26468<br>230 234 | 39069<br>−26467<br>230 235 | 39070<br>−26466<br>230 236 | 39071<br>−26465<br>230 237 |
| **A−** | 39072<br>−26464<br>230 240 | 39073<br>−26463<br>230 241 | 39074<br>−26462<br>230 242 | 39075<br>−26461<br>230 243 | 39076<br>−26460<br>230 244 | 39077<br>−26459<br>230 245 | 39078<br>−26458<br>230 246 | 39079<br>−26457<br>230 247 | 39080<br>−26456<br>230 250 | 39081<br>−26455<br>230 251 | 39082<br>−26454<br>230 252 | 39083<br>−26453<br>230 253 | 39084<br>−26452<br>230 254 | 39085<br>−26451<br>230 255 | 39086<br>−26450<br>230 256 | 39087<br>−26449<br>230 257 |
| **B−** | 39088<br>−26448<br>230 260 | 39089<br>−26447<br>230 261 | 39090<br>−26446<br>230 262 | 39091<br>−26445<br>230 263 | 39092<br>−26444<br>230 264 | 39093<br>−26443<br>230 265 | 39094<br>−26442<br>230 266 | 39095<br>−26441<br>230 267 | 39096<br>−26440<br>230 270 | 39097<br>−26439<br>230 271 | 39098<br>−26438<br>230 272 | 39099<br>−26437<br>230 273 | 39100<br>−26436<br>230 274 | 39101<br>−26435<br>230 275 | 39102<br>−26434<br>230 276 | 39103<br>−26433<br>230 277 |
| **C−** | 39104<br>−26432<br>230 300 | 39105<br>−26431<br>230 301 | 39106<br>−26430<br>230 302 | 39107<br>−26429<br>230 303 | 39108<br>−26428<br>230 304 | 39109<br>−26427<br>230 305 | 39110<br>−26426<br>230 306 | 39111<br>−26425<br>230 307 | 39112<br>−26424<br>230 310 | 39113<br>−26423<br>230 311 | 39114<br>−26422<br>230 312 | 39115<br>−26421<br>230 313 | 39116<br>−26420<br>230 314 | 39117<br>−26419<br>230 315 | 39118<br>−26418<br>230 316 | 39119<br>−26417<br>230 317 |
| **D−** | 39120<br>−26416<br>230 320 | 39121<br>−26415<br>230 321 | 39122<br>−26414<br>230 322 | 39123<br>−26413<br>230 323 | 39124<br>−26412<br>230 324 | 39125<br>−26411<br>230 325 | 39126<br>−26410<br>230 326 | 39127<br>−26409<br>230 327 | 39128<br>−26408<br>230 330 | 39129<br>−26407<br>230 331 | 39130<br>−26406<br>230 332 | 39131<br>−26405<br>230 333 | 39132<br>−26404<br>230 334 | 39133<br>−26403<br>230 335 | 39134<br>−26402<br>230 336 | 39135<br>−26401<br>230 337 |
| **E−** | 39136<br>−26400<br>230 340 | 39137<br>−26399<br>230 341 | 39138<br>−26398<br>230 342 | 39139<br>−26397<br>230 343 | 39140<br>−26396<br>230 344 | 39141<br>−26395<br>230 345 | 39142<br>−26394<br>230 346 | 39143<br>−26393<br>230 347 | 39144<br>−26392<br>230 350 | 39145<br>−26391<br>230 351 | 39146<br>−26390<br>230 352 | 39147<br>−26389<br>230 353 | 39148<br>−26388<br>230 354 | 39149<br>−26387<br>230 355 | 39150<br>−26386<br>230 356 | 39151<br>−26385<br>230 357 |
| **F−** | 39152<br>−26384<br>230 360 | 39153<br>−26383<br>230 361 | 39154<br>−26382<br>230 362 | 39155<br>−26381<br>230 363 | 39156<br>−26380<br>230 364 | 39157<br>−26379<br>230 365 | 39158<br>−26378<br>230 366 | 39159<br>−26377<br>230 367 | 39160<br>−26376<br>230 370 | 39161<br>−26375<br>230 371 | 39162<br>−26374<br>230 372 | 39163<br>−26373<br>230 373 | 39164<br>−26372<br>230 374 | 39165<br>−26371<br>230 375 | 39166<br>−26370<br>230 376 | 39167<br>−26369<br>230 377 |

**DECIMAL**

 **DECIMAL**

**OCTAL**

 **DECIMAL** | −26624    **BINARY** | 1001 1000    **DECIMAL** | 38912    **HEXADECIMAL** ⬡98 **OCTAL** | 230 000

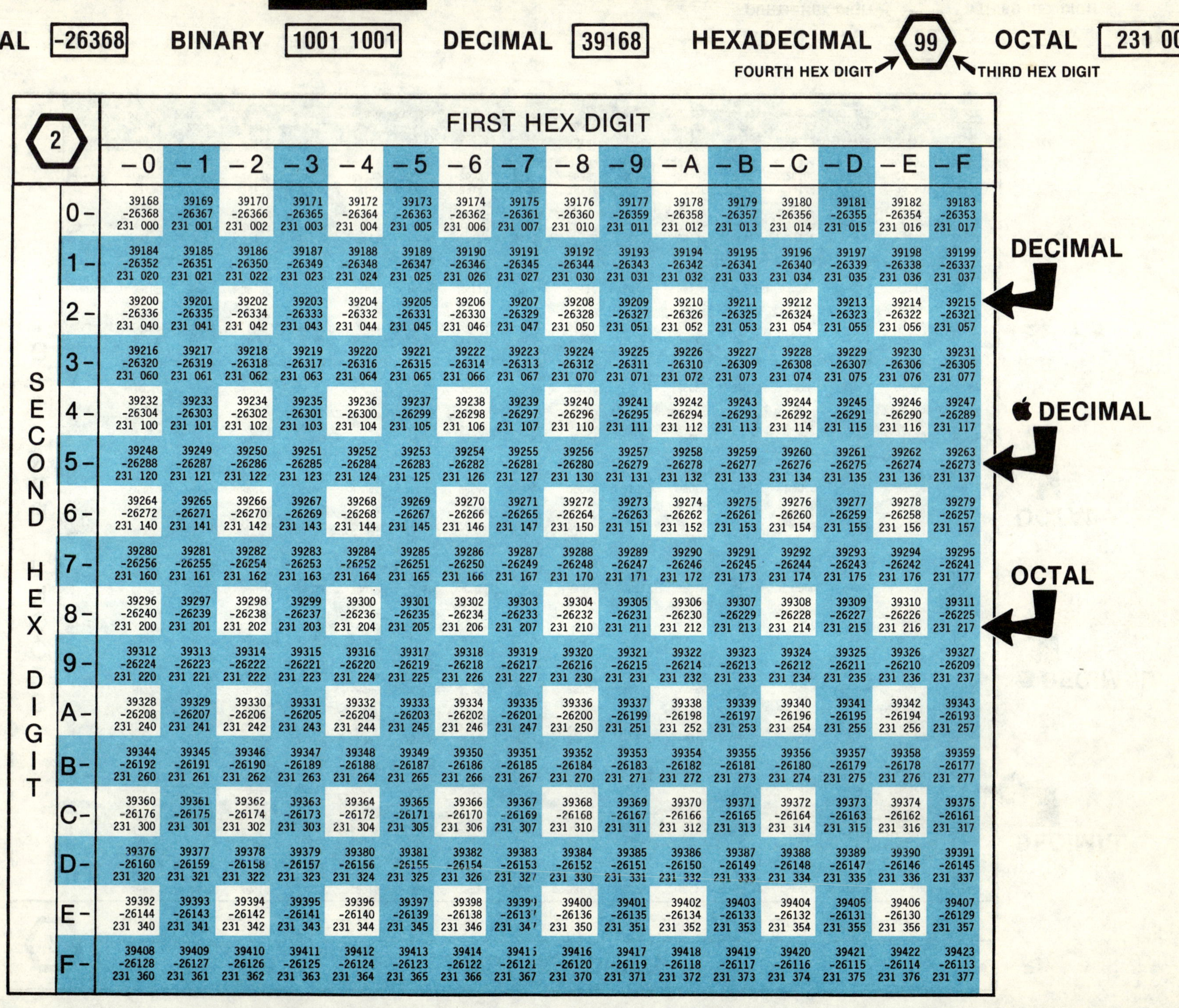

 DECIMAL -26368   BINARY 1001 1001   DECIMAL 39168   HEXADECIMAL 99   OCTAL 231 000

FOURTH HEX DIGIT → 99 ← THIRD HEX DIGIT

2 — FIRST HEX DIGIT

| SECOND HEX DIGIT | −0 | −1 | −2 | −3 | −4 | −5 | −6 | −7 | −8 | −9 | −A | −B | −C | −D | −E | −F |
|---|---|---|---|---|---|---|---|---|---|---|---|---|---|---|---|---|
| 0- | 39168<br>-26368<br>231 000 | 39169<br>-26367<br>231 001 | 39170<br>-26366<br>231 002 | 39171<br>-26365<br>231 003 | 39172<br>-26364<br>231 004 | 39173<br>-26363<br>231 005 | 39174<br>-26362<br>231 006 | 39175<br>-26361<br>231 007 | 39176<br>-26360<br>231 010 | 39177<br>-26359<br>231 011 | 39178<br>-26358<br>231 012 | 39179<br>-26357<br>231 013 | 39180<br>-26356<br>231 014 | 39181<br>-26355<br>231 015 | 39182<br>-26354<br>231 016 | 39183<br>-26353<br>231 017 |
| 1- | 39184<br>-26352<br>231 020 | 39185<br>-26351<br>231 021 | 39186<br>-26350<br>231 022 | 39187<br>-26349<br>231 023 | 39188<br>-26348<br>231 024 | 39189<br>-26347<br>231 025 | 39190<br>-26346<br>231 026 | 39191<br>-26345<br>231 027 | 39192<br>-26344<br>231 030 | 39193<br>-26343<br>231 031 | 39194<br>-26342<br>231 032 | 39195<br>-26341<br>231 033 | 39196<br>-26340<br>231 034 | 39197<br>-26339<br>231 035 | 39198<br>-26338<br>231 036 | 39199<br>-26337<br>231 037 |
| 2- | 39200<br>-26336<br>231 040 | 39201<br>-26335<br>231 041 | 39202<br>-26334<br>231 042 | 39203<br>-26333<br>231 043 | 39204<br>-26332<br>231 044 | 39205<br>-26331<br>231 045 | 39206<br>-26330<br>231 046 | 39207<br>-26329<br>231 047 | 39208<br>-26328<br>231 050 | 39209<br>-26327<br>231 051 | 39210<br>-26326<br>231 052 | 39211<br>-26325<br>231 053 | 39212<br>-26324<br>231 054 | 39213<br>-26323<br>231 055 | 39214<br>-26322<br>231 056 | 39215<br>-26321<br>231 057 |
| 3- | 39216<br>-26320<br>231 060 | 39217<br>-26319<br>231 061 | 39218<br>-26318<br>231 062 | 39219<br>-26317<br>231 063 | 39220<br>-26316<br>231 064 | 39221<br>-26315<br>231 065 | 39222<br>-26314<br>231 066 | 39223<br>-26313<br>231 067 | 39224<br>-26312<br>231 070 | 39225<br>-26311<br>231 071 | 39226<br>-26310<br>231 072 | 39227<br>-26309<br>231 073 | 39228<br>-26308<br>231 074 | 39229<br>-26307<br>231 075 | 39230<br>-26306<br>231 076 | 39231<br>-26305<br>231 077 |
| 4- | 39232<br>-26304<br>231 100 | 39233<br>-26303<br>231 101 | 39234<br>-26302<br>231 102 | 39235<br>-26301<br>231 103 | 39236<br>-26300<br>231 104 | 39237<br>-26299<br>231 105 | 39238<br>-26298<br>231 106 | 39239<br>-26297<br>231 107 | 39240<br>-26296<br>231 110 | 39241<br>-26295<br>231 111 | 39242<br>-26294<br>231 112 | 39243<br>-26293<br>231 113 | 39244<br>-26292<br>231 114 | 39245<br>-26291<br>231 115 | 39246<br>-26290<br>231 116 | 39247<br>-26289<br>231 117 |
| 5- | 39248<br>-26288<br>231 120 | 39249<br>-26287<br>231 121 | 39250<br>-26286<br>231 122 | 39251<br>-26285<br>231 123 | 39252<br>-26284<br>231 124 | 39253<br>-26283<br>231 125 | 39254<br>-26282<br>231 126 | 39255<br>-26281<br>231 127 | 39256<br>-26280<br>231 130 | 39257<br>-26279<br>231 131 | 39258<br>-26278<br>231 132 | 39259<br>-26277<br>231 133 | 39260<br>-26276<br>231 134 | 39261<br>-26275<br>231 135 | 39262<br>-26274<br>231 136 | 39263<br>-26273<br>231 137 |
| 6- | 39264<br>-26272<br>231 140 | 39265<br>-26271<br>231 141 | 39266<br>-26270<br>231 142 | 39267<br>-26269<br>231 143 | 39268<br>-26268<br>231 144 | 39269<br>-26267<br>231 145 | 39270<br>-26266<br>231 146 | 39271<br>-26265<br>231 147 | 39272<br>-26264<br>231 150 | 39273<br>-26263<br>231 151 | 39274<br>-26262<br>231 152 | 39275<br>-26261<br>231 153 | 39276<br>-26260<br>231 154 | 39277<br>-26259<br>231 155 | 39278<br>-26258<br>231 156 | 39279<br>-26257<br>231 157 |
| 7- | 39280<br>-26256<br>231 160 | 39281<br>-26255<br>231 161 | 39282<br>-26254<br>231 162 | 39283<br>-26253<br>231 163 | 39284<br>-26252<br>231 164 | 39285<br>-26251<br>231 165 | 39286<br>-26250<br>231 166 | 39287<br>-26249<br>231 167 | 39288<br>-26248<br>231 170 | 39289<br>-26247<br>231 171 | 39290<br>-26246<br>231 172 | 39291<br>-26245<br>231 173 | 39292<br>-26244<br>231 174 | 39293<br>-26243<br>231 175 | 39294<br>-26242<br>231 176 | 39295<br>-26241<br>231 177 |
| 8- | 39296<br>-26240<br>231 200 | 39297<br>-26239<br>231 201 | 39298<br>-26238<br>231 202 | 39299<br>-26237<br>231 203 | 39300<br>-26236<br>231 204 | 39301<br>-26235<br>231 205 | 39302<br>-26234<br>231 206 | 39303<br>-26233<br>231 207 | 39304<br>-26232<br>231 210 | 39305<br>-26231<br>231 211 | 39306<br>-26230<br>231 212 | 39307<br>-26229<br>231 213 | 39308<br>-26228<br>231 214 | 39309<br>-26227<br>231 215 | 39310<br>-26226<br>231 216 | 39311<br>-26225<br>231 217 |
| 9- | 39312<br>-26224<br>231 220 | 39313<br>-26223<br>231 221 | 39314<br>-26222<br>231 222 | 39315<br>-26221<br>231 223 | 39316<br>-26220<br>231 224 | 39317<br>-26219<br>231 225 | 39318<br>-26218<br>231 226 | 39319<br>-26217<br>231 227 | 39320<br>-26216<br>231 230 | 39321<br>-26215<br>231 231 | 39322<br>-26214<br>231 232 | 39323<br>-26213<br>231 233 | 39324<br>-26212<br>231 234 | 39325<br>-26211<br>231 235 | 39326<br>-26210<br>231 236 | 39327<br>-26209<br>231 237 |
| A- | 39328<br>-26208<br>231 240 | 39329<br>-26207<br>231 241 | 39330<br>-26206<br>231 242 | 39331<br>-26205<br>231 243 | 39332<br>-26204<br>231 244 | 39333<br>-26203<br>231 245 | 39334<br>-26202<br>231 246 | 39335<br>-26201<br>231 247 | 39336<br>-26200<br>231 250 | 39337<br>-26199<br>231 251 | 39338<br>-26198<br>231 252 | 39339<br>-26197<br>231 253 | 39340<br>-26196<br>231 254 | 39341<br>-26195<br>231 255 | 39342<br>-26194<br>231 256 | 39343<br>-26193<br>231 257 |
| B- | 39344<br>-26192<br>231 260 | 39345<br>-26191<br>231 261 | 39346<br>-26190<br>231 262 | 39347<br>-26189<br>231 263 | 39348<br>-26188<br>231 264 | 39349<br>-26187<br>231 265 | 39350<br>-26186<br>231 266 | 39351<br>-26185<br>231 267 | 39352<br>-26184<br>231 270 | 39353<br>-26183<br>231 271 | 39354<br>-26182<br>231 272 | 39355<br>-26181<br>231 273 | 39356<br>-26180<br>231 274 | 39357<br>-26179<br>231 275 | 39358<br>-26178<br>231 276 | 39359<br>-26177<br>231 277 |
| C- | 39360<br>-26176<br>231 300 | 39361<br>-26175<br>231 301 | 39362<br>-26174<br>231 302 | 39363<br>-26173<br>231 303 | 39364<br>-26172<br>231 304 | 39365<br>-26171<br>231 305 | 39366<br>-26170<br>231 306 | 39367<br>-26169<br>231 307 | 39368<br>-26168<br>231 310 | 39369<br>-26167<br>231 311 | 39370<br>-26166<br>231 312 | 39371<br>-26165<br>231 313 | 39372<br>-26164<br>231 314 | 39373<br>-26163<br>231 315 | 39374<br>-26162<br>231 316 | 39375<br>-26161<br>231 317 |
| D- | 39376<br>-26160<br>231 320 | 39377<br>-26159<br>231 321 | 39378<br>-26158<br>231 322 | 39379<br>-26157<br>231 323 | 39380<br>-26156<br>231 324 | 39381<br>-26155<br>231 325 | 39382<br>-26154<br>231 326 | 39383<br>-26153<br>231 327 | 39384<br>-26152<br>231 330 | 39385<br>-26151<br>231 331 | 39386<br>-26150<br>231 332 | 39387<br>-26149<br>231 333 | 39388<br>-26148<br>231 334 | 39389<br>-26147<br>231 335 | 39390<br>-26146<br>231 336 | 39391<br>-26145<br>231 337 |
| E- | 39392<br>-26144<br>231 340 | 39393<br>-26143<br>231 341 | 39394<br>-26142<br>231 342 | 39395<br>-26141<br>231 343 | 39396<br>-26140<br>231 344 | 39397<br>-26139<br>231 345 | 39398<br>-26138<br>231 346 | 39399<br>-26137<br>231 347 | 39400<br>-26136<br>231 350 | 39401<br>-26135<br>231 351 | 39402<br>-26134<br>231 352 | 39403<br>-26133<br>231 353 | 39404<br>-26132<br>231 354 | 39405<br>-26131<br>231 355 | 39406<br>-26130<br>231 356 | 39407<br>-26129<br>231 357 |
| F- | 39408<br>-26128<br>231 360 | 39409<br>-26127<br>231 361 | 39410<br>-26126<br>231 362 | 39411<br>-26125<br>231 363 | 39412<br>-26124<br>231 364 | 39413<br>-26123<br>231 365 | 39414<br>-26122<br>231 366 | 39415<br>-26121<br>231 367 | 39416<br>-26120<br>231 370 | 39417<br>-26119<br>231 371 | 39418<br>-26118<br>231 372 | 39419<br>-26117<br>231 373 | 39420<br>-26116<br>231 374 | 39421<br>-26115<br>231 375 | 39422<br>-26114<br>231 376 | 39423<br>-26113<br>231 377 |

# 2

## FIRST HEX DIGIT

SECOND HEX DIGIT

| | −0 | −1 | −2 | −3 | −4 | −5 | −6 | −7 | −8 | −9 | −A | −B | −C | −D | −E | −F |
|---|---|---|---|---|---|---|---|---|---|---|---|---|---|---|---|---|
| 0− | 39424<br>-26112<br>232 000 | 39425<br>-26111<br>232 001 | 39426<br>-26110<br>232 002 | 39427<br>-26109<br>232 003 | 39428<br>-26108<br>232 004 | 39429<br>-26107<br>232 005 | 39430<br>-26106<br>232 006 | 39431<br>-26105<br>232 007 | 39432<br>-26104<br>232 010 | 39433<br>-26103<br>232 011 | 39434<br>-26102<br>232 012 | 39435<br>-26101<br>232 013 | 39436<br>-26100<br>232 014 | 39437<br>-26099<br>232 015 | 39438<br>-26098<br>232 016 | 39439<br>-26097<br>232 017 |
| 1− | 39440<br>-26096<br>232 020 | 39441<br>-26095<br>232 021 | 39442<br>-26094<br>232 022 | 39443<br>-26093<br>232 023 | 39444<br>-26092<br>232 024 | 39445<br>-26091<br>232 025 | 39446<br>-26090<br>232 026 | 39447<br>-26089<br>232 027 | 39448<br>-26088<br>232 030 | 39449<br>-26087<br>232 031 | 39450<br>-26086<br>232 032 | 39451<br>-26085<br>232 033 | 39452<br>-26084<br>232 034 | 39453<br>-26083<br>232 035 | 39454<br>-26082<br>232 036 | 39455<br>-26081<br>232 037 |
| 2− | 39456<br>-26080<br>232 040 | 39457<br>-26079<br>232 041 | 39458<br>-26078<br>232 042 | 39459<br>-26077<br>232 043 | 39460<br>-26076<br>232 044 | 39461<br>-26075<br>232 045 | 39462<br>-26074<br>232 046 | 39463<br>-26073<br>232 047 | 39464<br>-26072<br>232 050 | 39465<br>-26071<br>232 051 | 39466<br>-26070<br>232 052 | 39467<br>-26069<br>232 053 | 39468<br>-26068<br>232 054 | 39469<br>-26067<br>232 055 | 39470<br>-26066<br>232 056 | 39471<br>-26065<br>232 057 |
| 3− | 39472<br>-26064<br>232 060 | 39473<br>-26063<br>232 061 | 39474<br>-26062<br>232 062 | 39475<br>-26061<br>232 063 | 39476<br>-26060<br>232 064 | 39477<br>-26059<br>232 065 | 39478<br>-26058<br>232 066 | 39479<br>-26057<br>232 067 | 39480<br>-26056<br>232 070 | 39481<br>-26055<br>232 071 | 39482<br>-26054<br>232 072 | 39483<br>-26053<br>232 073 | 39484<br>-26052<br>232 074 | 39485<br>-26051<br>232 075 | 39486<br>-26050<br>232 076 | 39487<br>-26049<br>232 077 |
| 4− | 39488<br>-26048<br>232 100 | 39489<br>-26047<br>232 101 | 39490<br>-26046<br>232 102 | 39491<br>-26045<br>232 103 | 39492<br>-26044<br>232 104 | 39493<br>-26043<br>232 105 | 39494<br>-26042<br>232 106 | 39495<br>-26041<br>232 107 | 39496<br>-26040<br>232 110 | 39497<br>-26039<br>232 111 | 39498<br>-26038<br>232 112 | 39499<br>-26037<br>232 113 | 39500<br>-26036<br>232 114 | 39501<br>-26035<br>232 115 | 39502<br>-26034<br>232 116 | 39503<br>-26033<br>232 117 |
| 5− | 39504<br>-26032<br>232 120 | 39505<br>-26031<br>232 121 | 39506<br>-26030<br>232 122 | 39507<br>-26029<br>232 123 | 39508<br>-26028<br>232 124 | 39509<br>-26027<br>232 125 | 39510<br>-26026<br>232 126 | 39511<br>-26025<br>232 127 | 39512<br>-26024<br>232 130 | 39513<br>-26023<br>232 131 | 39514<br>-26022<br>232 132 | 39515<br>-26021<br>232 133 | 39516<br>-26020<br>232 134 | 39517<br>-26019<br>232 135 | 39518<br>-26018<br>232 136 | 39519<br>-26017<br>232 137 |
| 6− | 39520<br>-26016<br>232 140 | 39521<br>-26015<br>232 141 | 39522<br>-26014<br>232 142 | 39523<br>-26013<br>232 143 | 39524<br>-26012<br>232 144 | 39525<br>-26011<br>232 145 | 39526<br>-26010<br>232 146 | 39527<br>-26009<br>232 147 | 39528<br>-26008<br>232 150 | 39529<br>-26007<br>232 151 | 39530<br>-26006<br>232 152 | 39531<br>-26005<br>232 153 | 39532<br>-26004<br>232 154 | 39533<br>-26003<br>232 155 | 39534<br>-26002<br>232 156 | 39535<br>-26001<br>232 157 |
| 7− | 39536<br>-26000<br>232 160 | 39537<br>-25999<br>232 161 | 39538<br>-25998<br>232 162 | 39539<br>-25997<br>232 163 | 39540<br>-25996<br>232 164 | 39541<br>-25995<br>232 165 | 39542<br>-25994<br>232 166 | 39543<br>-25993<br>232 167 | 39544<br>-25992<br>232 170 | 39545<br>-25991<br>232 171 | 39546<br>-25990<br>232 172 | 39547<br>-25989<br>232 173 | 39548<br>-25988<br>232 174 | 39549<br>-25987<br>232 175 | 39550<br>-25986<br>232 176 | 39551<br>-25985<br>232 177 |
| 8− | 39552<br>-25984<br>232 200 | 39553<br>-25983<br>232 201 | 39554<br>-25982<br>232 202 | 39555<br>-25981<br>232 203 | 39556<br>-25980<br>232 204 | 39557<br>-25979<br>232 205 | 39558<br>-25978<br>232 206 | 39559<br>-25977<br>232 207 | 39560<br>-25976<br>232 210 | 39561<br>-25975<br>232 211 | 39562<br>-25974<br>232 212 | 39563<br>-25973<br>232 213 | 39564<br>-25972<br>232 214 | 39565<br>-25971<br>232 215 | 39566<br>-25970<br>232 216 | 39567<br>-25969<br>232 217 |
| 9− | 39568<br>-25968<br>232 220 | 39569<br>-25967<br>232 221 | 39570<br>-25966<br>232 222 | 39571<br>-25965<br>232 223 | 39572<br>-25964<br>232 224 | 39573<br>-25963<br>232 225 | 39574<br>-25962<br>232 226 | 39575<br>-25961<br>232 227 | 39576<br>-25960<br>232 230 | 39577<br>-25959<br>232 231 | 39578<br>-25958<br>232 232 | 39579<br>-25957<br>232 233 | 39580<br>-25956<br>232 234 | 39581<br>-25955<br>232 235 | 39582<br>-25954<br>232 236 | 39583<br>-25953<br>232 237 |
| A− | 39584<br>-25952<br>232 240 | 39585<br>-25951<br>232 241 | 39586<br>-25950<br>232 242 | 39587<br>-25949<br>232 243 | 39588<br>-25948<br>232 244 | 39589<br>-25947<br>232 245 | 39590<br>-25946<br>232 246 | 39591<br>-25945<br>232 247 | 39592<br>-25944<br>232 250 | 39593<br>-25943<br>232 251 | 39594<br>-25942<br>232 252 | 39595<br>-25941<br>232 253 | 39596<br>-25940<br>232 254 | 39597<br>-25939<br>232 255 | 39598<br>-25938<br>232 256 | 39599<br>-25937<br>232 257 |
| B− | 39600<br>-25936<br>232 260 | 39601<br>-25935<br>232 261 | 39602<br>-25934<br>232 262 | 39603<br>-25933<br>232 263 | 39604<br>-25932<br>232 264 | 39605<br>-25931<br>232 265 | 39606<br>-25930<br>232 266 | 39607<br>-25929<br>232 267 | 39608<br>-25928<br>232 270 | 39609<br>-25927<br>232 271 | 39610<br>-25926<br>232 272 | 39611<br>-25925<br>232 273 | 39612<br>-25924<br>232 274 | 39613<br>-25923<br>232 275 | 39614<br>-25922<br>232 276 | 39615<br>-25921<br>232 277 |
| C− | 39616<br>-25920<br>232 300 | 39617<br>-25919<br>232 301 | 39618<br>-25918<br>232 302 | 39619<br>-25917<br>232 303 | 39620<br>-25916<br>232 304 | 39621<br>-25915<br>232 305 | 39622<br>-25914<br>232 306 | 39623<br>-25913<br>232 307 | 39624<br>-25912<br>232 310 | 39625<br>-25911<br>232 311 | 39626<br>-25910<br>232 312 | 39627<br>-25909<br>232 313 | 39628<br>-25908<br>232 314 | 39629<br>-25907<br>232 315 | 39630<br>-25906<br>232 316 | 39631<br>-25905<br>232 317 |
| D− | 39632<br>-25904<br>232 320 | 39633<br>-25903<br>232 321 | 39634<br>-25902<br>232 322 | 39635<br>-25901<br>232 323 | 39636<br>-25900<br>232 324 | 39637<br>-25899<br>232 325 | 39638<br>-25898<br>232 326 | 39639<br>-25897<br>232 327 | 39640<br>-25896<br>232 330 | 39641<br>-25895<br>232 331 | 39642<br>-25894<br>232 332 | 39643<br>-25893<br>232 333 | 39644<br>-25892<br>232 334 | 39645<br>-25891<br>232 335 | 39646<br>-25890<br>232 336 | 39647<br>-25889<br>232 337 |
| E− | 39648<br>-25888<br>232 340 | 39649<br>-25887<br>232 341 | 39650<br>-25886<br>232 342 | 39651<br>-25885<br>232 343 | 39652<br>-25884<br>232 344 | 39653<br>-25883<br>232 345 | 39654<br>-25882<br>232 346 | 39655<br>-25881<br>232 347 | 39656<br>-25880<br>232 350 | 39657<br>-25879<br>232 351 | 39658<br>-25878<br>232 352 | 39659<br>-25877<br>232 353 | 39660<br>-25876<br>232 354 | 39661<br>-25875<br>232 355 | 39662<br>-25874<br>232 356 | 39663<br>-25873<br>232 357 |
| F− | 39664<br>-25872<br>232 360 | 39665<br>-25871<br>232 361 | 39666<br>-25870<br>232 362 | 39667<br>-25869<br>232 363 | 39668<br>-25868<br>232 364 | 39669<br>-25867<br>232 365 | 39670<br>-25866<br>232 366 | 39671<br>-25865<br>232 367 | 39672<br>-25864<br>232 370 | 39673<br>-25863<br>232 371 | 39674<br>-25862<br>232 372 | 39675<br>-25861<br>232 373 | 39676<br>-25860<br>232 374 | 39677<br>-25859<br>232 375 | 39678<br>-25858<br>232 376 | 39679<br>-25857<br>232 377 |

DECIMAL

 DECIMAL

OCTAL

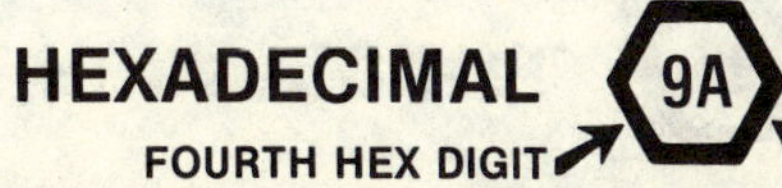

 DECIMAL -26112 BINARY 1001 1010 DECIMAL 39424 HEXADECIMAL 9A OCTAL 232 000

FOURTH HEX DIGIT — THIRD HEX DIGIT

| 2 | FIRST HEX DIGIT | | | | | | | | | | | | | | | |
|---|−0|−1|−2|−3|−4|−5|−6|−7|−8|−9|−A|−B|−C|−D|−E|−F|
| 0− | 39680<br>-25856<br>233 000 | 39681<br>-25855<br>233 001 | 39682<br>-25854<br>233 002 | 39683<br>-25853<br>233 003 | 39684<br>-25852<br>233 004 | 39685<br>-25851<br>233 005 | 39686<br>-25850<br>233 006 | 39687<br>-25849<br>233 007 | 39688<br>-25848<br>233 010 | 39689<br>-25847<br>233 011 | 39690<br>-25846<br>233 012 | 39691<br>-25845<br>233 013 | 39692<br>-25844<br>233 014 | 39693<br>-25843<br>233 015 | 39694<br>-25842<br>233 016 | 39695<br>-25841<br>233 017 |
| 1− | 39696<br>-25840<br>233 020 | 39697<br>-25839<br>233 021 | 39698<br>-25838<br>233 022 | 39699<br>-25837<br>233 023 | 39700<br>-25836<br>233 024 | 39701<br>-25835<br>233 025 | 39702<br>-25834<br>233 026 | 39703<br>-25833<br>233 027 | 39704<br>-25832<br>233 030 | 39705<br>-25831<br>233 031 | 39706<br>-25830<br>233 032 | 39707<br>-25829<br>233 033 | 39708<br>-25828<br>233 034 | 39709<br>-25827<br>233 035 | 39710<br>-25826<br>233 036 | 39711<br>-25825<br>233 037 |
| 2− | 39712<br>-25824<br>233 040 | 39713<br>-25823<br>233 041 | 39714<br>-25822<br>233 042 | 39715<br>-25821<br>233 043 | 39716<br>-25820<br>233 044 | 39717<br>-25819<br>233 045 | 39718<br>-25818<br>233 046 | 39719<br>-25817<br>233 047 | 39720<br>-25816<br>233 050 | 39721<br>-25815<br>233 051 | 39722<br>-25814<br>233 052 | 39723<br>-25813<br>233 053 | 39724<br>-25812<br>233 054 | 39725<br>-25811<br>233 055 | 39726<br>-25810<br>233 056 | 39727<br>-25809<br>233 057 |
| 3− | 39728<br>-25808<br>233 060 | 39729<br>-25807<br>233 061 | 39730<br>-25806<br>233 062 | 39731<br>-25805<br>233 063 | 39732<br>-25804<br>233 064 | 39733<br>-25803<br>233 065 | 39734<br>-25802<br>233 066 | 39735<br>-25801<br>233 067 | 39736<br>-25800<br>233 070 | 39737<br>-25799<br>233 071 | 39738<br>-25798<br>233 072 | 39739<br>-25797<br>233 073 | 39740<br>-25796<br>233 074 | 39741<br>-25795<br>233 075 | 39742<br>-25794<br>233 076 | 39743<br>-25793<br>233 077 |
| 4− | 39744<br>-25792<br>233 100 | 39745<br>-25791<br>233 101 | 39746<br>-25790<br>233 102 | 39747<br>-25789<br>233 103 | 39748<br>-25788<br>233 104 | 39749<br>-25787<br>233 105 | 39750<br>-25786<br>233 106 | 39751<br>-25785<br>233 107 | 39752<br>-25784<br>233 110 | 39753<br>-25783<br>233 111 | 39754<br>-25782<br>233 112 | 39755<br>-25781<br>233 113 | 39756<br>-25780<br>233 114 | 39757<br>-25779<br>233 115 | 39758<br>-25778<br>233 116 | 39759<br>-25777<br>233 117 |
| 5− | 39760<br>-25776<br>233 120 | 39761<br>-25775<br>233 121 | 39762<br>-25774<br>233 122 | 39763<br>-25773<br>233 123 | 39764<br>-25772<br>233 124 | 39765<br>-25771<br>233 125 | 39766<br>-25770<br>233 126 | 39767<br>-25769<br>233 127 | 39768<br>-25768<br>233 130 | 39769<br>-25767<br>233 131 | 39770<br>-25766<br>233 132 | 39771<br>-25765<br>233 133 | 39772<br>-25764<br>233 134 | 39773<br>-25763<br>233 135 | 39774<br>-25762<br>233 136 | 39775<br>-25761<br>233 137 |
| 6− | 39776<br>-25760<br>233 140 | 39777<br>-25759<br>233 141 | 39778<br>-25758<br>233 142 | 39779<br>-25757<br>233 143 | 39780<br>-25756<br>233 144 | 39781<br>-25755<br>233 145 | 39782<br>-25754<br>233 146 | 39783<br>-25753<br>233 147 | 39784<br>-25752<br>233 150 | 39785<br>-25751<br>233 151 | 39786<br>-25750<br>233 152 | 39787<br>-25749<br>233 153 | 39788<br>-25748<br>233 154 | 39789<br>-25747<br>233 155 | 39790<br>-25746<br>233 156 | 39791<br>-25745<br>233 157 |
| 7− | 39792<br>-25744<br>233 160 | 39793<br>-25743<br>233 161 | 39794<br>-25742<br>233 162 | 39795<br>-25741<br>233 163 | 39796<br>-25740<br>233 164 | 39797<br>-25739<br>233 165 | 39798<br>-25738<br>233 166 | 39799<br>-25737<br>233 167 | 39800<br>-25736<br>233 170 | 39801<br>-25735<br>233 171 | 39802<br>-25734<br>233 172 | 39803<br>-25733<br>233 173 | 39804<br>-25732<br>233 174 | 39805<br>-25731<br>233 175 | 39806<br>-25730<br>233 176 | 39807<br>-25729<br>233 177 |
| 8− | 39808<br>-25728<br>233 200 | 39809<br>-25727<br>233 201 | 39810<br>-25726<br>233 202 | 39811<br>-25725<br>233 203 | 39812<br>-25724<br>233 204 | 39813<br>-25723<br>233 205 | 39814<br>-25722<br>233 206 | 39815<br>-25721<br>233 207 | 39816<br>-25720<br>233 210 | 39817<br>-25719<br>233 211 | 39818<br>-25718<br>233 212 | 39819<br>-25717<br>233 213 | 39820<br>-25716<br>233 214 | 39821<br>-25715<br>233 215 | 39822<br>-25714<br>233 216 | 39823<br>-25713<br>233 217 |
| 9− | 39824<br>-25712<br>233 220 | 39825<br>-25711<br>233 221 | 39826<br>-25710<br>233 222 | 39827<br>-25709<br>233 223 | 39828<br>-25708<br>233 224 | 39829<br>-25707<br>233 225 | 39830<br>-25706<br>233 226 | 39831<br>-25705<br>233 227 | 39832<br>-25704<br>233 230 | 39833<br>-25703<br>233 231 | 39834<br>-25702<br>233 232 | 39835<br>-25701<br>233 233 | 39836<br>-25700<br>233 234 | 39837<br>-25699<br>233 235 | 39838<br>-25698<br>233 236 | 39839<br>-25697<br>233 237 |
| A− | 39840<br>-25696<br>233 240 | 39841<br>-25695<br>233 241 | 39842<br>-25694<br>233 242 | 39843<br>-25693<br>233 243 | 39844<br>-25692<br>233 244 | 39845<br>-25691<br>233 245 | 39846<br>-25690<br>233 246 | 39847<br>-25689<br>233 247 | 39848<br>-25688<br>233 250 | 39849<br>-25687<br>233 251 | 39850<br>-25686<br>233 252 | 39851<br>-25685<br>233 253 | 39852<br>-25684<br>233 254 | 39853<br>-25683<br>233 255 | 39854<br>-25682<br>233 256 | 39855<br>-25681<br>233 257 |
| B− | 39856<br>-25680<br>233 260 | 39857<br>-25679<br>233 261 | 39858<br>-25678<br>233 262 | 39859<br>-25677<br>233 263 | 39860<br>-25676<br>233 264 | 39861<br>-25675<br>233 265 | 39862<br>-25674<br>233 266 | 39863<br>-25673<br>233 267 | 39864<br>-25672<br>233 270 | 39865<br>-25671<br>233 271 | 39866<br>-25670<br>233 272 | 39867<br>-25669<br>233 273 | 39868<br>-25668<br>233 274 | 39869<br>-25667<br>233 275 | 39870<br>-25666<br>233 276 | 39871<br>-25665<br>233 277 |
| C− | 39872<br>-25664<br>233 300 | 39873<br>-25663<br>233 301 | 39874<br>-25662<br>233 302 | 39875<br>-25661<br>233 303 | 39876<br>-25660<br>233 304 | 39877<br>-25659<br>233 305 | 39878<br>-25658<br>233 306 | 39879<br>-25657<br>233 307 | 39880<br>-25656<br>233 310 | 39881<br>-25655<br>233 311 | 39882<br>-25654<br>233 312 | 39883<br>-25653<br>233 313 | 39884<br>-25652<br>233 314 | 39885<br>-25651<br>233 315 | 39886<br>-25650<br>233 316 | 39887<br>-25649<br>233 317 |
| D− | 39888<br>-25648<br>233 320 | 39889<br>-25647<br>233 321 | 39890<br>-25646<br>233 322 | 39891<br>-25645<br>233 323 | 39892<br>-25644<br>233 324 | 39893<br>-25643<br>233 325 | 39894<br>-25642<br>233 326 | 39895<br>-25641<br>233 327 | 39896<br>-25640<br>233 330 | 39897<br>-25639<br>233 331 | 39898<br>-25638<br>233 332 | 39899<br>-25637<br>233 333 | 39900<br>-25636<br>233 334 | 39901<br>-25635<br>233 335 | 39902<br>-25634<br>233 336 | 39903<br>-25633<br>233 337 |
| E− | 39904<br>-25632<br>233 340 | 39905<br>-25631<br>233 341 | 39906<br>-25630<br>233 342 | 39907<br>-25629<br>233 343 | 39908<br>-25628<br>233 344 | 39909<br>-25627<br>233 345 | 39910<br>-25626<br>233 346 | 39911<br>-25625<br>233 347 | 39912<br>-25624<br>233 350 | 39913<br>-25623<br>233 351 | 39914<br>-25622<br>233 352 | 39915<br>-25621<br>233 353 | 39916<br>-25620<br>233 354 | 39917<br>-25619<br>233 355 | 39918<br>-25618<br>233 356 | 39919<br>-25617<br>233 357 |
| F− | 39920<br>-25616<br>233 360 | 39921<br>-25615<br>233 361 | 39922<br>-25614<br>233 362 | 39923<br>-25613<br>233 363 | 39924<br>-25612<br>233 364 | 39925<br>-25611<br>233 365 | 39926<br>-25610<br>233 366 | 39927<br>-25609<br>233 367 | 39928<br>-25608<br>233 370 | 39929<br>-25607<br>233 371 | 39930<br>-25606<br>233 372 | 39931<br>-25605<br>233 373 | 39932<br>-25604<br>233 374 | 39933<br>-25603<br>233 375 | 39934<br>-25602<br>233 376 | 39935<br>-25601<br>233 377 |

SECOND HEX DIGIT

## FIRST HEX DIGIT

DECIMAL / ★ DECIMAL / OCTAL

| SECOND HEX DIGIT | −0 | −1 | −2 | −3 | −4 | −5 | −6 | −7 | −8 | −9 | −A | −B | −C | −D | −E | −F |
|---|---|---|---|---|---|---|---|---|---|---|---|---|---|---|---|---|
| **0−** | 39936<br>−25600<br>234 000 | 39937<br>−25599<br>234 001 | 39938<br>−25598<br>234 002 | 39939<br>−25597<br>234 003 | 39940<br>−25596<br>234 004 | 39941<br>−25595<br>234 005 | 39942<br>−25594<br>234 006 | 39943<br>−25593<br>234 007 | 39944<br>−25592<br>234 010 | 39945<br>−25591<br>234 011 | 39946<br>−25590<br>234 012 | 39947<br>−25589<br>234 013 | 39948<br>−25588<br>234 014 | 39949<br>−25587<br>234 015 | 39950<br>−25586<br>234 016 | 39951<br>−25585<br>234 017 |
| **1−** | 39952<br>−25584<br>234 020 | 39953<br>−25583<br>234 021 | 39954<br>−25582<br>234 022 | 39955<br>−25581<br>234 023 | 39956<br>−25580<br>234 024 | 39957<br>−25579<br>234 025 | 39958<br>−25578<br>234 026 | 39959<br>−25577<br>234 027 | 39960<br>−25576<br>234 030 | 39961<br>−25575<br>234 031 | 39962<br>−25574<br>234 032 | 39963<br>−25573<br>234 033 | 39964<br>−25572<br>234 034 | 39965<br>−25571<br>234 035 | 39966<br>−25570<br>234 036 | 39967<br>−25569<br>234 037 |
| **2−** | 39968<br>−25568<br>234 040 | 39969<br>−25567<br>234 041 | 39970<br>−25566<br>234 042 | 39971<br>−25565<br>234 043 | 39972<br>−25564<br>234 044 | 39973<br>−25563<br>234 045 | 39974<br>−25562<br>234 046 | 39975<br>−25561<br>234 047 | 39976<br>−25560<br>234 050 | 39977<br>−25559<br>234 051 | 39978<br>−25558<br>234 052 | 39979<br>−25557<br>234 053 | 39980<br>−25556<br>234 054 | 39981<br>−25555<br>234 055 | 39982<br>−25554<br>234 056 | 39983<br>−25553<br>234 057 |
| **3−** | 39984<br>−25552<br>234 060 | 39985<br>−25551<br>234 061 | 39986<br>−25550<br>234 062 | 39987<br>−25549<br>234 063 | 39988<br>−25548<br>234 064 | 39989<br>−25547<br>234 065 | 39990<br>−25546<br>234 066 | 39991<br>−25545<br>234 067 | 39992<br>−25544<br>234 070 | 39993<br>−25543<br>234 071 | 39994<br>−25542<br>234 072 | 39995<br>−25541<br>234 073 | 39996<br>−25540<br>234 074 | 39997<br>−25539<br>234 075 | 39998<br>−25538<br>234 076 | 39999<br>−25537<br>234 077 |
| **4−** | 40000<br>−25536<br>234 100 | 40001<br>−25535<br>234 101 | 40002<br>−25534<br>234 102 | 40003<br>−25533<br>234 103 | 40004<br>−25532<br>234 104 | 40005<br>−25531<br>234 105 | 40006<br>−25530<br>234 106 | 40007<br>−25529<br>234 107 | 40008<br>−25528<br>234 110 | 40009<br>−25527<br>234 111 | 40010<br>−25526<br>234 112 | 40011<br>−25525<br>234 113 | 40012<br>−25524<br>234 114 | 40013<br>−25523<br>234 115 | 40014<br>−25522<br>234 116 | 40015<br>−25521<br>234 117 |
| **5−** | 40016<br>−25520<br>234 120 | 40017<br>−25519<br>234 121 | 40018<br>−25518<br>234 122 | 40019<br>−25517<br>234 123 | 40020<br>−25516<br>234 124 | 40021<br>−25515<br>234 125 | 40022<br>−25514<br>234 126 | 40023<br>−25513<br>234 127 | 40024<br>−25512<br>234 130 | 40025<br>−25511<br>234 131 | 40026<br>−25510<br>234 132 | 40027<br>−25509<br>234 133 | 40028<br>−25508<br>234 134 | 40029<br>−25507<br>234 135 | 40030<br>−25506<br>234 136 | 40031<br>−25505<br>234 137 |
| **6−** | 40032<br>−25504<br>234 140 | 40033<br>−25503<br>234 141 | 40034<br>−25502<br>234 142 | 40035<br>−25501<br>234 143 | 40036<br>−25500<br>234 144 | 40037<br>−25499<br>234 145 | 40038<br>−25498<br>234 146 | 40039<br>−25497<br>234 147 | 40040<br>−25496<br>234 150 | 40041<br>−25495<br>234 151 | 40042<br>−25494<br>234 152 | 40043<br>−25493<br>234 153 | 40044<br>−25492<br>234 154 | 40045<br>−25491<br>234 155 | 40046<br>−25490<br>234 156 | 40047<br>−25489<br>234 157 |
| **7−** | 40048<br>−25488<br>234 160 | 40049<br>−25487<br>234 161 | 40050<br>−25486<br>234 162 | 40051<br>−25485<br>234 163 | 40052<br>−25484<br>234 164 | 40053<br>−25483<br>234 165 | 40054<br>−25482<br>234 166 | 40055<br>−25481<br>234 167 | 40056<br>−25480<br>234 170 | 40057<br>−25479<br>234 171 | 40058<br>−25478<br>234 172 | 40059<br>−25477<br>234 173 | 40060<br>−25476<br>234 174 | 40061<br>−25475<br>234 175 | 40062<br>−25474<br>234 176 | 40063<br>−25473<br>234 177 |
| **8−** | 40064<br>−25472<br>234 200 | 40065<br>−25471<br>234 201 | 40066<br>−25470<br>234 202 | 40067<br>−25469<br>234 203 | 40068<br>−25468<br>234 204 | 40069<br>−25467<br>234 205 | 40070<br>−25466<br>234 206 | 40071<br>−25465<br>234 207 | 40072<br>−25464<br>234 210 | 40073<br>−25463<br>234 211 | 40074<br>−25462<br>234 212 | 40075<br>−25461<br>234 213 | 40076<br>−25460<br>234 214 | 40077<br>−25459<br>234 215 | 40078<br>−25458<br>234 216 | 40079<br>−25457<br>234 217 |
| **9−** | 40080<br>−25456<br>234 220 | 40081<br>−25455<br>234 221 | 40082<br>−25454<br>234 222 | 40083<br>−25453<br>234 223 | 40084<br>−25452<br>234 224 | 40085<br>−25451<br>234 225 | 40086<br>−25450<br>234 226 | 40087<br>−25449<br>234 227 | 40088<br>−25448<br>234 230 | 40089<br>−25447<br>234 231 | 40090<br>−25446<br>234 232 | 40091<br>−25445<br>234 233 | 40092<br>−25444<br>234 234 | 40093<br>−25443<br>234 235 | 40094<br>−25442<br>234 236 | 40095<br>−25441<br>234 237 |
| **A−** | 40096<br>−25440<br>234 240 | 40097<br>−25439<br>234 241 | 40098<br>−25438<br>234 242 | 40099<br>−25437<br>234 243 | 40100<br>−25436<br>234 244 | 40101<br>−25435<br>234 245 | 40102<br>−25434<br>234 246 | 40103<br>−25433<br>234 247 | 40104<br>−25432<br>234 250 | 40105<br>−25431<br>234 251 | 40106<br>−25430<br>234 252 | 40107<br>−25429<br>234 253 | 40108<br>−25428<br>234 254 | 40109<br>−25427<br>234 255 | 40110<br>−25426<br>234 256 | 40111<br>−25425<br>234 257 |
| **B−** | 40112<br>−25424<br>234 260 | 40113<br>−25423<br>234 261 | 40114<br>−25422<br>234 262 | 40115<br>−25421<br>234 263 | 40116<br>−25420<br>234 264 | 40117<br>−25419<br>234 265 | 40118<br>−25418<br>234 266 | 40119<br>−25417<br>234 267 | 40120<br>−25416<br>234 270 | 40121<br>−25415<br>234 271 | 40122<br>−25414<br>234 272 | 40123<br>−25413<br>234 273 | 40124<br>−25412<br>234 274 | 40125<br>−25411<br>234 275 | 40126<br>−25410<br>234 276 | 40127<br>−25409<br>234 277 |
| **C−** | 40128<br>−25408<br>234 300 | 40129<br>−25407<br>234 301 | 40130<br>−25406<br>234 302 | 40131<br>−25405<br>234 303 | 40132<br>−25404<br>234 304 | 40133<br>−25403<br>234 305 | 40134<br>−25402<br>234 306 | 40135<br>−25401<br>234 307 | 40136<br>−25400<br>234 310 | 40137<br>−25399<br>234 311 | 40138<br>−25398<br>234 312 | 40139<br>−25397<br>234 313 | 40140<br>−25396<br>234 314 | 40141<br>−25395<br>234 315 | 40142<br>−25394<br>234 316 | 40143<br>−25393<br>234 317 |
| **D−** | 40144<br>−25392<br>234 320 | 40145<br>−25391<br>234 321 | 40146<br>−25390<br>234 322 | 40147<br>−25389<br>234 323 | 40148<br>−25388<br>234 324 | 40149<br>−25387<br>234 325 | 40150<br>−25386<br>234 326 | 40151<br>−25385<br>234 327 | 40152<br>−25384<br>234 330 | 40153<br>−25383<br>234 331 | 40154<br>−25382<br>234 332 | 40155<br>−25381<br>234 333 | 40156<br>−25380<br>234 334 | 40157<br>−25379<br>234 335 | 40158<br>−25378<br>234 336 | 40159<br>−25377<br>234 337 |
| **E−** | 40160<br>−25376<br>234 340 | 40161<br>−25375<br>234 341 | 40162<br>−25374<br>234 342 | 40163<br>−25373<br>234 343 | 40164<br>−25372<br>234 344 | 40165<br>−25371<br>234 345 | 40166<br>−25370<br>234 346 | 40167<br>−25369<br>234 347 | 40168<br>−25368<br>234 350 | 40169<br>−25367<br>234 351 | 40170<br>−25366<br>234 352 | 40171<br>−25365<br>234 353 | 40172<br>−25364<br>234 354 | 40173<br>−25363<br>234 355 | 40174<br>−25362<br>234 356 | 40175<br>−25361<br>234 357 |
| **F−** | 40176<br>−25360<br>234 360 | 40177<br>−25359<br>234 361 | 40178<br>−25358<br>234 362 | 40179<br>−25357<br>234 363 | 40180<br>−25356<br>234 364 | 40181<br>−25355<br>234 365 | 40182<br>−25354<br>234 366 | 40183<br>−25353<br>234 367 | 40184<br>−25352<br>234 370 | 40185<br>−25351<br>234 371 | 40186<br>−25350<br>234 372 | 40187<br>−25349<br>234 373 | 40188<br>−25348<br>234 374 | 40189<br>−25347<br>234 375 | 40190<br>−25346<br>234 376 | 40191<br>−25345<br>234 377 |

 **DECIMAL** −25600   **BINARY** 1001 1100   **DECIMAL** 39936   **HEXADECIMAL** 9C   **OCTAL** 234 000

FOURTH HEX DIGIT → ← THIRD HEX DIGIT

[redacted]

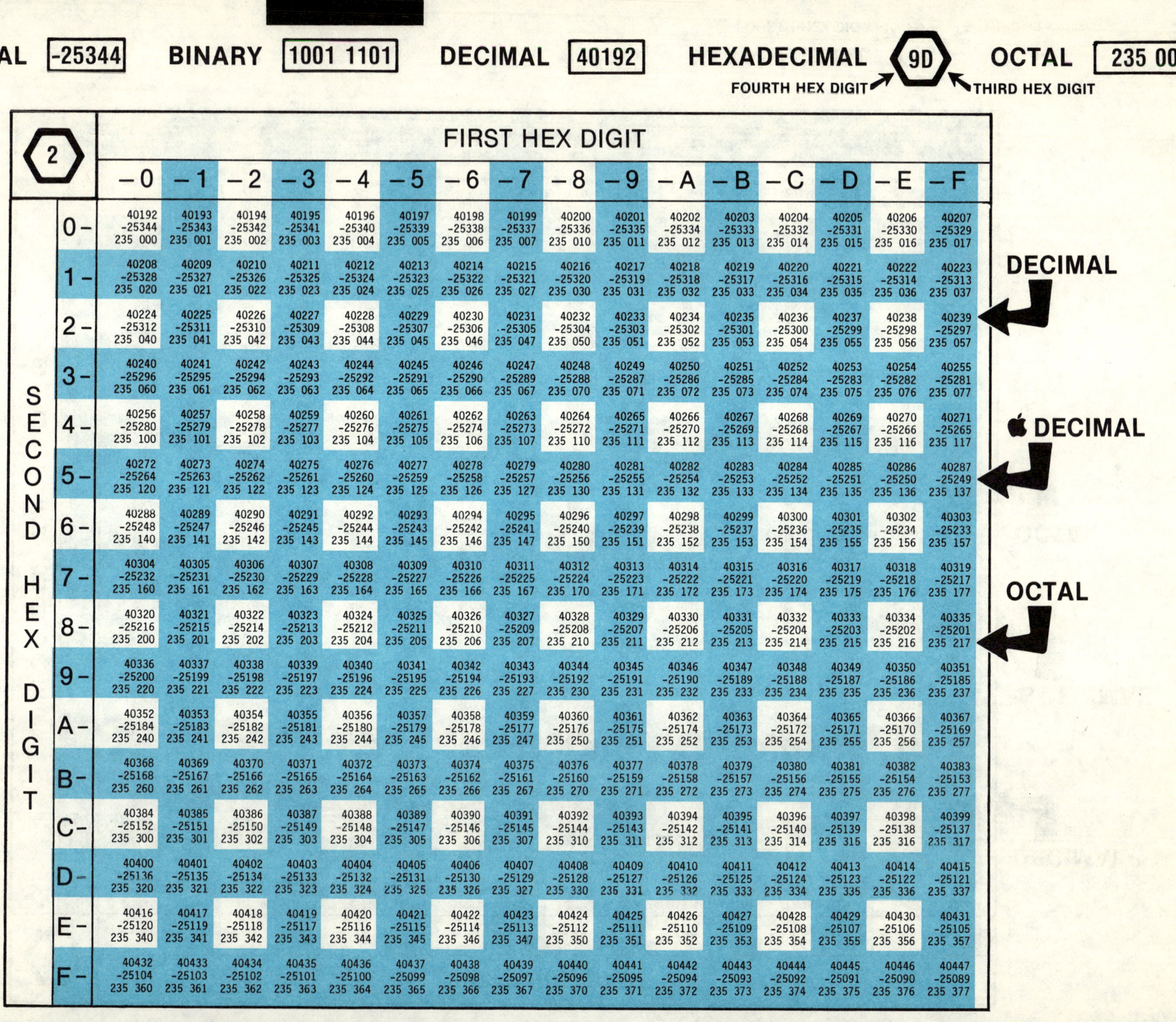

DECIMAL -25344 | BINARY 1001 1101 | DECIMAL 40192 | HEXADECIMAL 9D | OCTAL 235 000

FOURTH HEX DIGIT ↗ 9D ↖ THIRD HEX DIGIT

2

| SECOND HEX DIGIT \ FIRST HEX DIGIT | –0 | –1 | –2 | –3 | –4 | –5 | –6 | –7 | –8 | –9 | –A | –B | –C | –D | –E | –F |
|---|---|---|---|---|---|---|---|---|---|---|---|---|---|---|---|---|
| 0– | 40192<br>-25344<br>235 000 | 40193<br>-25343<br>235 001 | 40194<br>-25342<br>235 002 | 40195<br>-25341<br>235 003 | 40196<br>-25340<br>235 004 | 40197<br>-25339<br>235 005 | 40198<br>-25338<br>235 006 | 40199<br>-25337<br>235 007 | 40200<br>-25336<br>235 010 | 40201<br>-25335<br>235 011 | 40202<br>-25334<br>235 012 | 40203<br>-25333<br>235 013 | 40204<br>-25332<br>235 014 | 40205<br>-25331<br>235 015 | 40206<br>-25330<br>235 016 | 40207<br>-25329<br>235 017 |
| 1– | 40208<br>-25328<br>235 020 | 40209<br>-25327<br>235 021 | 40210<br>-25326<br>235 022 | 40211<br>-25325<br>235 023 | 40212<br>-25324<br>235 024 | 40213<br>-25323<br>235 025 | 40214<br>-25322<br>235 026 | 40215<br>-25321<br>235 027 | 40216<br>-25320<br>235 030 | 40217<br>-25319<br>235 031 | 40218<br>-25318<br>235 032 | 40219<br>-25317<br>235 033 | 40220<br>-25316<br>235 034 | 40221<br>-25315<br>235 035 | 40222<br>-25314<br>235 036 | 40223<br>-25313<br>235 037 |
| 2– | 40224<br>-25312<br>235 040 | 40225<br>-25311<br>235 041 | 40226<br>-25310<br>235 042 | 40227<br>-25309<br>235 043 | 40228<br>-25308<br>235 044 | 40229<br>-25307<br>235 045 | 40230<br>-25306<br>235 046 | 40231<br>-25305<br>235 047 | 40232<br>-25304<br>235 050 | 40233<br>-25303<br>235 051 | 40234<br>-25302<br>235 052 | 40235<br>-25301<br>235 053 | 40236<br>-25300<br>235 054 | 40237<br>-25299<br>235 055 | 40238<br>-25298<br>235 056 | 40239<br>-25297<br>235 057 |
| 3– | 40240<br>-25296<br>235 060 | 40241<br>-25295<br>235 061 | 40242<br>-25294<br>235 062 | 40243<br>-25293<br>235 063 | 40244<br>-25292<br>235 064 | 40245<br>-25291<br>235 065 | 40246<br>-25290<br>235 066 | 40247<br>-25289<br>235 067 | 40248<br>-25288<br>235 070 | 40249<br>-25287<br>235 071 | 40250<br>-25286<br>235 072 | 40251<br>-25285<br>235 073 | 40252<br>-25284<br>235 074 | 40253<br>-25283<br>235 075 | 40254<br>-25282<br>235 076 | 40255<br>-25281<br>235 077 |
| 4– | 40256<br>-25280<br>235 100 | 40257<br>-25279<br>235 101 | 40258<br>-25278<br>235 102 | 40259<br>-25277<br>235 103 | 40260<br>-25276<br>235 104 | 40261<br>-25275<br>235 105 | 40262<br>-25274<br>235 106 | 40263<br>-25273<br>235 107 | 40264<br>-25272<br>235 110 | 40265<br>-25271<br>235 111 | 40266<br>-25270<br>235 112 | 40267<br>-25269<br>235 113 | 40268<br>-25268<br>235 114 | 40269<br>-25267<br>235 115 | 40270<br>-25266<br>235 116 | 40271<br>-25265<br>235 117 |
| 5– | 40272<br>-25264<br>235 120 | 40273<br>-25263<br>235 121 | 40274<br>-25262<br>235 122 | 40275<br>-25261<br>235 123 | 40276<br>-25260<br>235 124 | 40277<br>-25259<br>235 125 | 40278<br>-25258<br>235 126 | 40279<br>-25257<br>235 127 | 40280<br>-25256<br>235 130 | 40281<br>-25255<br>235 131 | 40282<br>-25254<br>235 132 | 40283<br>-25253<br>235 133 | 40284<br>-25252<br>235 134 | 40285<br>-25251<br>235 135 | 40286<br>-25250<br>235 136 | 40287<br>-25249<br>235 137 |
| 6– | 40288<br>-25248<br>235 140 | 40289<br>-25247<br>235 141 | 40290<br>-25246<br>235 142 | 40291<br>-25245<br>235 143 | 40292<br>-25244<br>235 144 | 40293<br>-25243<br>235 145 | 40294<br>-25242<br>235 146 | 40295<br>-25241<br>235 147 | 40296<br>-25240<br>235 150 | 40297<br>-25239<br>235 151 | 40298<br>-25238<br>235 152 | 40299<br>-25237<br>235 153 | 40300<br>-25236<br>235 154 | 40301<br>-25235<br>235 155 | 40302<br>-25234<br>235 156 | 40303<br>-25233<br>235 157 |
| 7– | 40304<br>-25232<br>235 160 | 40305<br>-25231<br>235 161 | 40306<br>-25230<br>235 162 | 40307<br>-25229<br>235 163 | 40308<br>-25228<br>235 164 | 40309<br>-25227<br>235 165 | 40310<br>-25226<br>235 166 | 40311<br>-25225<br>235 167 | 40312<br>-25224<br>235 170 | 40313<br>-25223<br>235 171 | 40314<br>-25222<br>235 172 | 40315<br>-25221<br>235 173 | 40316<br>-25220<br>235 174 | 40317<br>-25219<br>235 175 | 40318<br>-25218<br>235 176 | 40319<br>-25217<br>235 177 |
| 8– | 40320<br>-25216<br>235 200 | 40321<br>-25215<br>235 201 | 40322<br>-25214<br>235 202 | 40323<br>-25213<br>235 203 | 40324<br>-25212<br>235 204 | 40325<br>-25211<br>235 205 | 40326<br>-25210<br>235 206 | 40327<br>-25209<br>235 207 | 40328<br>-25208<br>235 210 | 40329<br>-25207<br>235 211 | 40330<br>-25206<br>235 212 | 40331<br>-25205<br>235 213 | 40332<br>-25204<br>235 214 | 40333<br>-25203<br>235 215 | 40334<br>-25202<br>235 216 | 40335<br>-25201<br>235 217 |
| 9– | 40336<br>-25200<br>235 220 | 40337<br>-25199<br>235 221 | 40338<br>-25198<br>235 222 | 40339<br>-25197<br>235 223 | 40340<br>-25196<br>235 224 | 40341<br>-25195<br>235 225 | 40342<br>-25194<br>235 226 | 40343<br>-25193<br>235 227 | 40344<br>-25192<br>235 230 | 40345<br>-25191<br>235 231 | 40346<br>-25190<br>235 232 | 40347<br>-25189<br>235 233 | 40348<br>-25188<br>235 234 | 40349<br>-25187<br>235 235 | 40350<br>-25186<br>235 236 | 40351<br>-25185<br>235 237 |
| A– | 40352<br>-25184<br>235 240 | 40353<br>-25183<br>235 241 | 40354<br>-25182<br>235 242 | 40355<br>-25181<br>235 243 | 40356<br>-25180<br>235 244 | 40357<br>-25179<br>235 245 | 40358<br>-25178<br>235 246 | 40359<br>-25177<br>235 247 | 40360<br>-25176<br>235 250 | 40361<br>-25175<br>235 251 | 40362<br>-25174<br>235 252 | 40363<br>-25173<br>235 253 | 40364<br>-25172<br>235 254 | 40365<br>-25171<br>235 255 | 40366<br>-25170<br>235 256 | 40367<br>-25169<br>235 257 |
| B– | 40368<br>-25168<br>235 260 | 40369<br>-25167<br>235 261 | 40370<br>-25166<br>235 262 | 40371<br>-25165<br>235 263 | 40372<br>-25164<br>235 264 | 40373<br>-25163<br>235 265 | 40374<br>-25162<br>235 266 | 40375<br>-25161<br>235 267 | 40376<br>-25160<br>235 270 | 40377<br>-25159<br>235 271 | 40378<br>-25158<br>235 272 | 40379<br>-25157<br>235 273 | 40380<br>-25156<br>235 274 | 40381<br>-25155<br>235 275 | 40382<br>-25154<br>235 276 | 40383<br>-25153<br>235 277 |
| C– | 40384<br>-25152<br>235 300 | 40385<br>-25151<br>235 301 | 40386<br>-25150<br>235 302 | 40387<br>-25149<br>235 303 | 40388<br>-25148<br>235 304 | 40389<br>-25147<br>235 305 | 40390<br>-25146<br>235 306 | 40391<br>-25145<br>235 307 | 40392<br>-25144<br>235 310 | 40393<br>-25143<br>235 311 | 40394<br>-25142<br>235 312 | 40395<br>-25141<br>235 313 | 40396<br>-25140<br>235 314 | 40397<br>-25139<br>235 315 | 40398<br>-25138<br>235 316 | 40399<br>-25137<br>235 317 |
| D– | 40400<br>-25136<br>235 320 | 40401<br>-25135<br>235 321 | 40402<br>-25134<br>235 322 | 40403<br>-25133<br>235 323 | 40404<br>-25132<br>235 324 | 40405<br>-25131<br>235 325 | 40406<br>-25130<br>235 326 | 40407<br>-25129<br>235 327 | 40408<br>-25128<br>235 330 | 40409<br>-25127<br>235 331 | 40410<br>-25126<br>235 332 | 40411<br>-25125<br>235 333 | 40412<br>-25124<br>235 334 | 40413<br>-25123<br>235 335 | 40414<br>-25122<br>235 336 | 40415<br>-25121<br>235 337 |
| E– | 40416<br>-25120<br>235 340 | 40417<br>-25119<br>235 341 | 40418<br>-25118<br>235 342 | 40419<br>-25117<br>235 343 | 40420<br>-25116<br>235 344 | 40421<br>-25115<br>235 345 | 40422<br>-25114<br>235 346 | 40423<br>-25113<br>235 347 | 40424<br>-25112<br>235 350 | 40425<br>-25111<br>235 351 | 40426<br>-25110<br>235 352 | 40427<br>-25109<br>235 353 | 40428<br>-25108<br>235 354 | 40429<br>-25107<br>235 355 | 40430<br>-25106<br>235 356 | 40431<br>-25105<br>235 357 |
| F– | 40432<br>-25104<br>235 360 | 40433<br>-25103<br>235 361 | 40434<br>-25102<br>235 362 | 40435<br>-25101<br>235 363 | 40436<br>-25100<br>235 364 | 40437<br>-25099<br>235 365 | 40438<br>-25098<br>235 366 | 40439<br>-25097<br>235 367 | 40440<br>-25096<br>235 370 | 40441<br>-25095<br>235 371 | 40442<br>-25094<br>235 372 | 40443<br>-25093<br>235 373 | 40444<br>-25092<br>235 374 | 40445<br>-25091<br>235 375 | 40446<br>-25090<br>235 376 | 40447<br>-25089<br>235 377 |

DECIMAL ←

DECIMAL ←

OCTAL ←

# FIRST HEX DIGIT

Hex conversion table (2). Each cell: DECIMAL (top), ⌘ DECIMAL (middle), OCTAL (bottom).

| SECOND HEX DIGIT | −0 | −1 | −2 | −3 | −4 | −5 | −6 | −7 | −8 | −9 | −A | −B | −C | −D | −E | −F |
|---|---|---|---|---|---|---|---|---|---|---|---|---|---|---|---|---|
| 0− | 40448<br>−25088<br>236 000 | 40449<br>−25087<br>236 001 | 40450<br>−25086<br>236 002 | 40451<br>−25085<br>236 003 | 40452<br>−25084<br>236 004 | 40453<br>−25083<br>236 005 | 40454<br>−25082<br>236 006 | 40455<br>−25081<br>236 007 | 40456<br>−25080<br>236 010 | 40457<br>−25079<br>236 011 | 40458<br>−25078<br>236 012 | 40459<br>−25077<br>236 013 | 40460<br>−25076<br>236 014 | 40461<br>−25075<br>236 015 | 40462<br>−25074<br>236 016 | 40463<br>−25073<br>236 017 |
| 1− | 40464<br>−25072<br>236 020 | 40465<br>−25071<br>236 021 | 40466<br>−25070<br>236 022 | 40467<br>−25069<br>236 023 | 40468<br>−25068<br>236 024 | 40469<br>−25067<br>236 025 | 40470<br>−25066<br>236 026 | 40471<br>−25065<br>236 027 | 40472<br>−25064<br>236 030 | 40473<br>−25063<br>236 031 | 40474<br>−25062<br>236 032 | 40475<br>−25061<br>236 033 | 40476<br>−25060<br>236 034 | 40477<br>−25059<br>236 035 | 40478<br>−25058<br>236 036 | 40479<br>−25057<br>236 037 |
| 2− | 40480<br>−25056<br>236 040 | 40481<br>−25055<br>236 041 | 40482<br>−25054<br>236 042 | 40483<br>−25053<br>236 043 | 40484<br>−25052<br>236 044 | 40485<br>−25051<br>236 045 | 40486<br>−25050<br>236 046 | 40487<br>−25049<br>236 047 | 40488<br>−25048<br>236 050 | 40489<br>−25047<br>236 051 | 40490<br>−25046<br>236 052 | 40491<br>−25045<br>236 053 | 40492<br>−25044<br>236 054 | 40493<br>−25043<br>236 055 | 40494<br>−25042<br>236 056 | 40495<br>−25041<br>236 057 |
| 3− | 40496<br>−25040<br>236 060 | 40497<br>−25039<br>236 061 | 40498<br>−25038<br>236 062 | 40499<br>−25037<br>236 063 | 40500<br>−25036<br>236 064 | 40501<br>−25035<br>236 065 | 40502<br>−25034<br>236 066 | 40503<br>−25033<br>236 067 | 40504<br>−25032<br>236 070 | 40505<br>−25031<br>236 071 | 40506<br>−25030<br>236 072 | 40507<br>−25029<br>236 073 | 40508<br>−25028<br>236 074 | 40509<br>−25027<br>236 075 | 40510<br>−25026<br>236 076 | 40511<br>−25025<br>236 077 |
| 4− | 40512<br>−25024<br>236 100 | 40513<br>−25023<br>236 101 | 40514<br>−25022<br>236 102 | 40515<br>−25021<br>236 103 | 40516<br>−25020<br>236 104 | 40517<br>−25019<br>236 105 | 40518<br>−25018<br>236 106 | 40519<br>−25017<br>236 107 | 40520<br>−25016<br>236 110 | 40521<br>−25015<br>236 111 | 40522<br>−25014<br>236 112 | 40523<br>−25013<br>236 113 | 40524<br>−25012<br>236 114 | 40525<br>−25011<br>236 115 | 40526<br>−25010<br>236 116 | 40527<br>−25009<br>236 117 |
| 5− | 40528<br>−25008<br>236 120 | 40529<br>−25007<br>236 121 | 40530<br>−25006<br>236 122 | 40531<br>−25005<br>236 123 | 40532<br>−25004<br>236 124 | 40533<br>−25003<br>236 125 | 40534<br>−25002<br>236 126 | 40535<br>−25001<br>236 127 | 40536<br>−25000<br>236 130 | 40537<br>−24999<br>236 131 | 40538<br>−24998<br>236 132 | 40539<br>−24997<br>236 133 | 40540<br>−24996<br>236 134 | 40541<br>−24995<br>236 135 | 40542<br>−24994<br>236 136 | 40543<br>−24993<br>236 137 |
| 6− | 40544<br>−24992<br>236 140 | 40545<br>−24991<br>236 141 | 40546<br>−24990<br>236 142 | 40547<br>−24989<br>236 143 | 40548<br>−24988<br>236 144 | 40549<br>−24987<br>236 145 | 40550<br>−24986<br>236 146 | 40551<br>−24985<br>236 147 | 40552<br>−24984<br>236 150 | 40553<br>−24983<br>236 151 | 40554<br>−24982<br>236 152 | 40555<br>−24981<br>236 153 | 40556<br>−24980<br>236 154 | 40557<br>−24979<br>236 155 | 40558<br>−24978<br>236 156 | 40559<br>−24977<br>236 157 |
| 7− | 40560<br>−24976<br>236 160 | 40561<br>−24975<br>236 161 | 40562<br>−24974<br>236 162 | 40563<br>−24973<br>236 163 | 40564<br>−24972<br>236 164 | 40565<br>−24971<br>236 165 | 40566<br>−24970<br>236 166 | 40567<br>−24969<br>236 167 | 40568<br>−24968<br>236 170 | 40569<br>−24967<br>236 171 | 40570<br>−24966<br>236 172 | 40571<br>−24965<br>236 173 | 40572<br>−24964<br>236 174 | 40573<br>−24963<br>236 175 | 40574<br>−24962<br>236 176 | 40575<br>−24961<br>236 177 |
| 8− | 40576<br>−24960<br>236 200 | 40577<br>−24959<br>236 201 | 40578<br>−24958<br>236 202 | 40579<br>−24957<br>236 203 | 40580<br>−24956<br>236 204 | 40581<br>−24955<br>236 205 | 40582<br>−24954<br>236 206 | 40583<br>−24953<br>236 207 | 40584<br>−24952<br>236 210 | 40585<br>−24951<br>236 211 | 40586<br>−24950<br>236 212 | 40587<br>−24949<br>236 213 | 40588<br>−24948<br>236 214 | 40589<br>−24947<br>236 215 | 40590<br>−24946<br>236 216 | 40591<br>−24945<br>236 217 |
| 9− | 40592<br>−24944<br>236 220 | 40593<br>−24943<br>236 221 | 40594<br>−24942<br>236 222 | 40595<br>−24941<br>236 223 | 40596<br>−24940<br>236 224 | 40597<br>−24939<br>236 225 | 40598<br>−24938<br>236 226 | 40599<br>−24937<br>236 227 | 40600<br>−24936<br>236 230 | 40601<br>−24935<br>236 231 | 40602<br>−24934<br>236 232 | 40603<br>−24933<br>236 233 | 40604<br>−24932<br>236 234 | 40605<br>−24931<br>236 235 | 40606<br>−24930<br>236 236 | 40607<br>−24929<br>236 237 |
| A− | 40608<br>−24928<br>236 240 | 40609<br>−24927<br>236 241 | 40610<br>−24926<br>236 242 | 40611<br>−24925<br>236 243 | 40612<br>−24924<br>236 244 | 40613<br>−24923<br>236 245 | 40614<br>−24922<br>236 246 | 40615<br>−24921<br>236 247 | 40616<br>−24920<br>236 250 | 40617<br>−24919<br>236 251 | 40618<br>−24918<br>236 252 | 40619<br>−24917<br>236 253 | 40620<br>−24916<br>236 254 | 40621<br>−24915<br>236 255 | 40622<br>−24914<br>236 256 | 40623<br>−24913<br>236 257 |
| B− | 40624<br>−24912<br>236 260 | 40625<br>−24911<br>236 261 | 40626<br>−24910<br>236 262 | 40627<br>−24909<br>236 263 | 40628<br>−24908<br>236 264 | 40629<br>−24907<br>236 265 | 40630<br>−24906<br>236 266 | 40631<br>−24905<br>236 267 | 40632<br>−24904<br>236 270 | 40633<br>−24903<br>236 271 | 40634<br>−24902<br>236 272 | 40635<br>−24901<br>236 273 | 40636<br>−24900<br>236 274 | 40637<br>−24899<br>236 275 | 40638<br>−24898<br>236 276 | 40639<br>−24897<br>236 277 |
| C− | 40640<br>−24896<br>236 300 | 40641<br>−24895<br>236 301 | 40642<br>−24894<br>236 302 | 40643<br>−24893<br>236 303 | 40644<br>−24892<br>236 304 | 40645<br>−24891<br>236 305 | 40646<br>−24890<br>236 306 | 40647<br>−24889<br>236 307 | 40648<br>−24888<br>236 310 | 40649<br>−24887<br>236 311 | 40650<br>−24886<br>236 312 | 40651<br>−24885<br>236 313 | 40652<br>−24884<br>236 314 | 40653<br>−24883<br>236 315 | 40654<br>−24882<br>236 316 | 40655<br>−24881<br>236 317 |
| D− | 40656<br>−24880<br>236 320 | 40657<br>−24879<br>236 321 | 40658<br>−24878<br>236 322 | 40659<br>−24877<br>236 323 | 40660<br>−24876<br>236 324 | 40661<br>−24875<br>236 325 | 40662<br>−24874<br>236 326 | 40663<br>−24873<br>236 327 | 40664<br>−24872<br>236 330 | 40665<br>−24871<br>236 331 | 40666<br>−24870<br>236 332 | 40667<br>−24869<br>236 333 | 40668<br>−24868<br>236 334 | 40669<br>−24867<br>236 335 | 40670<br>−24866<br>236 336 | 40671<br>−24865<br>236 337 |
| E− | 40672<br>−24864<br>236 340 | 40673<br>−24863<br>236 341 | 40674<br>−24862<br>236 342 | 40675<br>−24861<br>236 343 | 40676<br>−24860<br>236 344 | 40677<br>−24859<br>236 345 | 40678<br>−24858<br>236 346 | 40679<br>−24857<br>236 347 | 40680<br>−24856<br>236 350 | 40681<br>−24855<br>236 351 | 40682<br>−24854<br>236 352 | 40683<br>−24853<br>236 353 | 40684<br>−24852<br>236 354 | 40685<br>−24851<br>236 355 | 40686<br>−24850<br>236 356 | 40687<br>−24849<br>236 357 |
| F− | 40688<br>−24848<br>236 360 | 40689<br>−24847<br>236 361 | 40690<br>−24846<br>236 362 | 40691<br>−24845<br>236 363 | 40692<br>−24844<br>236 364 | 40693<br>−24843<br>236 365 | 40694<br>−24842<br>236 366 | 40695<br>−24841<br>236 367 | 40696<br>−24840<br>236 370 | 40697<br>−24839<br>236 371 | 40698<br>−24838<br>236 372 | 40699<br>−24837<br>236 373 | 40700<br>−24836<br>236 374 | 40701<br>−24835<br>236 375 | 40702<br>−24834<br>236 376 | 40703<br>−24833<br>236 377 |


⌘ DECIMAL `−25088`   BINARY `1001 1110`   DECIMAL `40448`   HEXADECIMAL ⬡ `9E`   OCTAL `236 000`

FOURTH HEX DIGIT → ← THIRD HEX DIGIT

## FIRST HEX DIGIT

⬡ 2

Each cell lists: decimal / negative decimal / octal.

| SECOND HEX DIGIT | −0 | −1 | −2 | −3 | −4 | −5 | −6 | −7 | −8 | −9 | −A | −B | −C | −D | −E | −F |
|---|---|---|---|---|---|---|---|---|---|---|---|---|---|---|---|---|
| 0− | 40704<br>−24832<br>237 000 | 40705<br>−24831<br>237 001 | 40706<br>−24830<br>237 002 | 40707<br>−24829<br>237 003 | 40708<br>−24828<br>237 004 | 40709<br>−24827<br>237 005 | 40710<br>−24826<br>237 006 | 40711<br>−24825<br>237 007 | 40712<br>−24824<br>237 010 | 40713<br>−24823<br>237 011 | 40714<br>−24822<br>237 012 | 40715<br>−24821<br>237 013 | 40716<br>−24820<br>237 014 | 40717<br>−24819<br>237 015 | 40718<br>−24818<br>237 016 | 40719<br>−24817<br>237 017 |
| 1− | 40720<br>−24816<br>237 020 | 40721<br>−24815<br>237 021 | 40722<br>−24814<br>237 022 | 40723<br>−24813<br>237 023 | 40724<br>−24812<br>237 024 | 40725<br>−24811<br>237 025 | 40726<br>−24810<br>237 026 | 40727<br>−24809<br>237 027 | 40728<br>−24808<br>237 030 | 40729<br>−24807<br>237 031 | 40730<br>−24806<br>237 032 | 40731<br>−24805<br>237 033 | 40732<br>−24804<br>237 034 | 40733<br>−24803<br>237 035 | 40734<br>−24802<br>237 036 | 40735<br>−24801<br>237 037 |
| 2− | 40736<br>−24800<br>237 040 | 40737<br>−24799<br>237 041 | 40738<br>−24798<br>237 042 | 40739<br>−24797<br>237 043 | 40740<br>−24796<br>237 044 | 40741<br>−24795<br>237 045 | 40742<br>−24794<br>237 046 | 40743<br>−24793<br>237 047 | 40744<br>−24792<br>237 050 | 40745<br>−24791<br>237 051 | 40746<br>−24790<br>237 052 | 40747<br>−24789<br>237 053 | 40748<br>−24788<br>237 054 | 40749<br>−24787<br>237 055 | 40750<br>−24786<br>237 056 | 40751<br>−24785<br>237 057 |
| 3− | 40752<br>−24784<br>237 060 | 40753<br>−24783<br>237 061 | 40754<br>−24782<br>237 062 | 40755<br>−24781<br>237 063 | 40756<br>−24780<br>237 064 | 40757<br>−24779<br>237 065 | 40758<br>−24778<br>237 066 | 40759<br>−24777<br>237 067 | 40760<br>−24776<br>237 070 | 40761<br>−24775<br>237 071 | 40762<br>−24774<br>237 072 | 40763<br>−24773<br>237 073 | 40764<br>−24772<br>237 074 | 40765<br>−24771<br>237 075 | 40766<br>−24770<br>237 076 | 40767<br>−24769<br>237 077 |
| 4− | 40768<br>−24768<br>237 100 | 40769<br>−24767<br>237 101 | 40770<br>−24766<br>237 102 | 40771<br>−24765<br>237 103 | 40772<br>−24764<br>237 104 | 40773<br>−24763<br>237 105 | 40774<br>−24762<br>237 106 | 40775<br>−24761<br>237 107 | 40776<br>−24760<br>237 110 | 40777<br>−24759<br>237 111 | 40778<br>−24758<br>237 112 | 40779<br>−24757<br>237 113 | 40780<br>−24756<br>237 114 | 40781<br>−24755<br>237 115 | 40782<br>−24754<br>237 116 | 40783<br>−24753<br>237 117 |
| 5− | 40784<br>−24752<br>237 120 | 40785<br>−24751<br>237 121 | 40786<br>−24750<br>237 122 | 40787<br>−24749<br>237 123 | 40788<br>−24748<br>237 124 | 40789<br>−24747<br>237 125 | 40790<br>−24746<br>237 126 | 40791<br>−24745<br>237 127 | 40792<br>−24744<br>237 130 | 40793<br>−24743<br>237 131 | 40794<br>−24742<br>237 132 | 40795<br>−24741<br>237 133 | 40796<br>−24740<br>237 134 | 40797<br>−24739<br>237 135 | 40798<br>−24738<br>237 136 | 40799<br>−24737<br>237 137 |
| 6− | 40800<br>−24736<br>237 140 | 40801<br>−24735<br>237 141 | 40802<br>−24734<br>237 142 | 40803<br>−24733<br>237 143 | 40804<br>−24732<br>237 144 | 40805<br>−24731<br>237 145 | 40806<br>−24730<br>237 146 | 40807<br>−24729<br>237 147 | 40808<br>−24728<br>237 150 | 40809<br>−24727<br>237 151 | 40810<br>−24726<br>237 152 | 40811<br>−24725<br>237 153 | 40812<br>−24724<br>237 154 | 40813<br>−24723<br>237 155 | 40814<br>−24722<br>237 156 | 40815<br>−24721<br>237 157 |
| 7− | 40816<br>−24720<br>237 160 | 40817<br>−24719<br>237 161 | 40818<br>−24718<br>237 162 | 40819<br>−24717<br>237 163 | 40820<br>−24716<br>237 164 | 40821<br>−24715<br>237 165 | 40822<br>−24714<br>237 166 | 40823<br>−24713<br>237 167 | 40824<br>−24712<br>237 170 | 40825<br>−24711<br>237 171 | 40826<br>−24710<br>237 172 | 40827<br>−24709<br>237 173 | 40828<br>−24708<br>237 174 | 40829<br>−24707<br>237 175 | 40830<br>−24706<br>237 176 | 40831<br>−24705<br>237 177 |
| 8− | 40832<br>−24704<br>237 200 | 40833<br>−24703<br>237 201 | 40834<br>−24702<br>237 202 | 40835<br>−24701<br>237 203 | 40836<br>−24700<br>237 204 | 40837<br>−24699<br>237 205 | 40838<br>−24698<br>237 206 | 40839<br>−24697<br>237 207 | 40840<br>−24696<br>237 210 | 40841<br>−24695<br>237 211 | 40842<br>−24694<br>237 212 | 40843<br>−24693<br>237 213 | 40844<br>−24692<br>237 214 | 40845<br>−24691<br>237 215 | 40846<br>−24690<br>237 216 | 40847<br>−24689<br>237 217 |
| 9− | 40848<br>−24688<br>237 220 | 40849<br>−24687<br>237 221 | 40850<br>−24686<br>237 222 | 40851<br>−24685<br>237 223 | 40852<br>−24684<br>237 224 | 40853<br>−24683<br>237 225 | 40854<br>−24682<br>237 226 | 40855<br>−24681<br>237 227 | 40856<br>−24680<br>237 230 | 40857<br>−24679<br>237 231 | 40858<br>−24678<br>237 232 | 40859<br>−24677<br>237 233 | 40860<br>−24676<br>237 234 | 40861<br>−24675<br>237 235 | 40862<br>−24674<br>237 236 | 40863<br>−24673<br>237 237 |
| A− | 40864<br>−24672<br>237 240 | 40865<br>−24671<br>237 241 | 40866<br>−24670<br>237 242 | 40867<br>−24669<br>237 243 | 40868<br>−24668<br>237 244 | 40869<br>−24667<br>237 245 | 40870<br>−24666<br>237 246 | 40871<br>−24665<br>237 247 | 40872<br>−24664<br>237 250 | 40873<br>−24663<br>237 251 | 40874<br>−24662<br>237 252 | 40875<br>−24661<br>237 253 | 40876<br>−24660<br>237 254 | 40877<br>−24659<br>237 255 | 40878<br>−24658<br>237 256 | 40879<br>−24657<br>237 257 |
| B− | 40880<br>−24656<br>237 260 | 40881<br>−24655<br>237 261 | 40882<br>−24654<br>237 262 | 40883<br>−24653<br>237 263 | 40884<br>−24652<br>237 264 | 40885<br>−24651<br>237 265 | 40886<br>−24650<br>237 266 | 40887<br>−24649<br>237 267 | 40888<br>−24648<br>237 270 | 40889<br>−24647<br>237 271 | 40890<br>−24646<br>237 272 | 40891<br>−24645<br>237 273 | 40892<br>−24644<br>237 274 | 40893<br>−24643<br>237 275 | 40894<br>−24642<br>237 276 | 40895<br>−24641<br>237 277 |
| C− | 40896<br>−24640<br>237 300 | 40897<br>−24639<br>237 301 | 40898<br>−24638<br>237 302 | 40899<br>−24637<br>237 303 | 40900<br>−24636<br>237 304 | 40901<br>−24635<br>237 305 | 40902<br>−24634<br>237 306 | 40903<br>−24633<br>237 307 | 40904<br>−24632<br>237 310 | 40905<br>−24631<br>237 311 | 40906<br>−24630<br>237 312 | 40907<br>−24629<br>237 313 | 40908<br>−24628<br>237 314 | 40909<br>−24627<br>237 315 | 40910<br>−24626<br>237 316 | 40911<br>−24625<br>237 317 |
| D− | 40912<br>−24624<br>237 320 | 40913<br>−24623<br>237 321 | 40914<br>−24622<br>237 322 | 40915<br>−24621<br>237 323 | 40916<br>−24620<br>237 324 | 40917<br>−24619<br>237 325 | 40918<br>−24618<br>237 326 | 40919<br>−24617<br>237 327 | 40920<br>−24616<br>237 330 | 40921<br>−24615<br>237 331 | 40922<br>−24614<br>237 332 | 40923<br>−24613<br>237 333 | 40924<br>−24612<br>237 334 | 40925<br>−24611<br>237 335 | 40926<br>−24610<br>237 336 | 40927<br>−24609<br>237 337 |
| E− | 40928<br>−24608<br>237 340 | 40929<br>−24607<br>237 341 | 40930<br>−24606<br>237 342 | 40931<br>−24605<br>237 343 | 40932<br>−24604<br>237 344 | 40933<br>−24603<br>237 345 | 40934<br>−24602<br>237 346 | 40935<br>−24601<br>237 347 | 40936<br>−24600<br>237 350 | 40937<br>−24599<br>237 351 | 40938<br>−24598<br>237 352 | 40939<br>−24597<br>237 353 | 40940<br>−24596<br>237 354 | 40941<br>−24595<br>237 355 | 40942<br>−24594<br>237 356 | 40943<br>−24593<br>237 357 |
| F− | 40944<br>−24592<br>237 360 | 40945<br>−24591<br>237 361 | 40946<br>−24590<br>237 362 | 40947<br>−24589<br>237 363 | 40948<br>−24588<br>237 364 | 40949<br>−24587<br>237 365 | 40950<br>−24586<br>237 366 | 40951<br>−24585<br>237 367 | 40952<br>−24584<br>237 370 | 40953<br>−24583<br>237 371 | 40954<br>−24582<br>237 372 | 40955<br>−24581<br>237 373 | 40956<br>−24580<br>237 374 | 40957<br>−24579<br>237 375 | 40958<br>−24578<br>237 376 | 40959<br>−24577<br>237 377 |

DECIMAL →

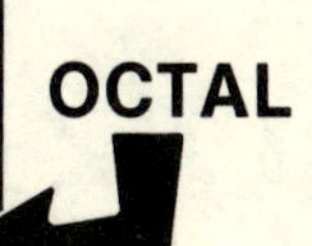 DECIMAL →

OCTAL →

| SECOND HEX DIGIT | −0 | −1 | −2 | −3 | −4 | −5 | −6 | −7 | −8 | −9 | −A | −B | −C | −D | −E | −F |
|---|---|---|---|---|---|---|---|---|---|---|---|---|---|---|---|---|
| 0− | 40960<br>−24576<br>240 000 | 40961<br>−24575<br>240 001 | 40962<br>−24574<br>240 002 | 40963<br>−24573<br>240 003 | 40964<br>−24572<br>240 004 | 40965<br>−24571<br>240 005 | 40966<br>−24570<br>240 006 | 40967<br>−24569<br>240 007 | 40968<br>−24568<br>240 010 | 40969<br>−24567<br>240 011 | 40970<br>−24566<br>240 012 | 40971<br>−24565<br>240 013 | 40972<br>−24564<br>240 014 | 40973<br>−24563<br>240 015 | 40974<br>−24562<br>240 016 | 40975<br>−24561<br>240 017 |
| 1− | 40976<br>−24560<br>240 020 | 40977<br>−24559<br>240 021 | 40978<br>−24558<br>240 022 | 40979<br>−24557<br>240 023 | 40980<br>−24556<br>240 024 | 40981<br>−24555<br>240 025 | 40982<br>−24554<br>240 026 | 40983<br>−24553<br>240 027 | 40984<br>−24552<br>240 030 | 40985<br>−24551<br>240 031 | 40986<br>−24550<br>240 032 | 40987<br>−24549<br>240 033 | 40988<br>−24548<br>240 034 | 40989<br>−24547<br>240 035 | 40990<br>−24546<br>240 036 | 40991<br>−24545<br>240 037 |
| 2− | 40992<br>−24544<br>240 040 | 40993<br>−24543<br>240 041 | 40994<br>−24542<br>240 042 | 40995<br>−24541<br>240 043 | 40996<br>−24540<br>240 044 | 40997<br>−24539<br>240 045 | 40998<br>−24538<br>240 046 | 40999<br>−24537<br>240 047 | 41000<br>−24536<br>240 050 | 41001<br>−24535<br>240 051 | 41002<br>−24534<br>240 052 | 41003<br>−24533<br>240 053 | 41004<br>−24532<br>240 054 | 41005<br>−24531<br>240 055 | 41006<br>−24530<br>240 056 | 41007<br>−24529<br>240 057 |
| 3− | 41008<br>−24528<br>240 060 | 41009<br>−24527<br>240 061 | 41010<br>−24526<br>240 062 | 41011<br>−24525<br>240 063 | 41012<br>−24524<br>240 064 | 41013<br>−24523<br>240 065 | 41014<br>−24522<br>240 066 | 41015<br>−24521<br>240 067 | 41016<br>−24520<br>240 070 | 41017<br>−24519<br>240 071 | 41018<br>−24518<br>240 072 | 41019<br>−24517<br>240 073 | 41020<br>−24516<br>240 074 | 41021<br>−24515<br>240 075 | 41022<br>−24514<br>240 076 | 41023<br>−24513<br>240 077 |
| 4− | 41024<br>−24512<br>240 100 | 41025<br>−24511<br>240 101 | 41026<br>−24510<br>240 102 | 41027<br>−24509<br>240 103 | 41028<br>−24508<br>240 104 | 41029<br>−24507<br>240 105 | 41030<br>−24506<br>240 106 | 41031<br>−24505<br>240 107 | 41032<br>−24504<br>240 110 | 41033<br>−24503<br>240 111 | 41034<br>−24502<br>240 112 | 41035<br>−24501<br>240 113 | 41036<br>−24500<br>240 114 | 41037<br>−24499<br>240 115 | 41038<br>−24498<br>240 116 | 41039<br>−24497<br>240 117 |
| 5− | 41040<br>−24496<br>240 120 | 41041<br>−24495<br>240 121 | 41042<br>−24494<br>240 122 | 41043<br>−24493<br>240 123 | 41044<br>−24492<br>240 124 | 41045<br>−24491<br>240 125 | 41046<br>−24490<br>240 126 | 41047<br>−24489<br>240 127 | 41048<br>−24488<br>240 130 | 41049<br>−24487<br>240 131 | 41050<br>−24486<br>240 132 | 41051<br>−24485<br>240 133 | 41052<br>−24484<br>240 134 | 41053<br>−24483<br>240 135 | 41054<br>−24482<br>240 136 | 41055<br>−24481<br>240 137 |
| 6− | 41056<br>−24480<br>240 140 | 41057<br>−24479<br>240 141 | 41058<br>−24478<br>240 142 | 41059<br>−24477<br>240 143 | 41060<br>−24476<br>240 144 | 41061<br>−24475<br>240 145 | 41062<br>−24474<br>240 146 | 41063<br>−24473<br>240 147 | 41064<br>−24472<br>240 150 | 41065<br>−24471<br>240 151 | 41066<br>−24470<br>240 152 | 41067<br>−24469<br>240 153 | 41068<br>−24468<br>240 154 | 41069<br>−24467<br>240 155 | 41070<br>−24466<br>240 156 | 41071<br>−24465<br>240 157 |
| 7− | 41072<br>−24464<br>240 160 | 41073<br>−24463<br>240 161 | 41074<br>−24462<br>240 162 | 41075<br>−24461<br>240 163 | 41076<br>−24460<br>240 164 | 41077<br>−24459<br>240 165 | 41078<br>−24458<br>240 166 | 41079<br>−24457<br>240 167 | 41080<br>−24456<br>240 170 | 41081<br>−24455<br>240 171 | 41082<br>−24454<br>240 172 | 41083<br>−24453<br>240 173 | 41084<br>−24452<br>240 174 | 41085<br>−24451<br>240 175 | 41086<br>−24450<br>240 176 | 41087<br>−24449<br>240 177 |
| 8− | 41088<br>−24448<br>240 200 | 41089<br>−24447<br>240 201 | 41090<br>−24446<br>240 202 | 41091<br>−24445<br>240 203 | 41092<br>−24444<br>240 204 | 41093<br>−24443<br>240 205 | 41094<br>−24442<br>240 206 | 41095<br>−24441<br>240 207 | 41096<br>−24440<br>240 210 | 41097<br>−24439<br>240 211 | 41098<br>−24438<br>240 212 | 41099<br>−24437<br>240 213 | 41100<br>−24436<br>240 214 | 41101<br>−24435<br>240 215 | 41102<br>−24434<br>240 216 | 41103<br>−24433<br>240 217 |
| 9− | 41104<br>−24432<br>240 220 | 41105<br>−24431<br>240 221 | 41106<br>−24430<br>240 222 | 41107<br>−24429<br>240 223 | 41108<br>−24428<br>240 224 | 41109<br>−24427<br>240 225 | 41110<br>−24426<br>240 226 | 41111<br>−24425<br>240 227 | 41112<br>−24424<br>240 230 | 41113<br>−24423<br>240 231 | 41114<br>−24422<br>240 232 | 41115<br>−24421<br>240 233 | 41116<br>−24420<br>240 234 | 41117<br>−24419<br>240 235 | 41118<br>−24418<br>240 236 | 41119<br>−24417<br>240 237 |
| A− | 41120<br>−24416<br>240 240 | 41121<br>−24415<br>240 241 | 41122<br>−24414<br>240 242 | 41123<br>−24413<br>240 243 | 41124<br>−24412<br>240 244 | 41125<br>−24411<br>240 245 | 41126<br>−24410<br>240 246 | 41127<br>−24409<br>240 247 | 41128<br>−24408<br>240 250 | 41129<br>−24407<br>240 251 | 41130<br>−24406<br>240 252 | 41131<br>−24405<br>240 253 | 41132<br>−24404<br>240 254 | 41133<br>−24403<br>240 255 | 41134<br>−24402<br>240 256 | 41135<br>−24401<br>240 257 |
| B− | 41136<br>−24400<br>240 260 | 41137<br>−24399<br>240 261 | 41138<br>−24398<br>240 262 | 41139<br>−24397<br>240 263 | 41140<br>−24396<br>240 264 | 41141<br>−24395<br>240 265 | 41142<br>−24394<br>240 266 | 41143<br>−24393<br>240 267 | 41144<br>−24392<br>240 270 | 41145<br>−24391<br>240 271 | 41146<br>−24390<br>240 272 | 41147<br>−24389<br>240 273 | 41148<br>−24388<br>240 274 | 41149<br>−24387<br>240 275 | 41150<br>−24386<br>240 276 | 41151<br>−24385<br>240 277 |
| C− | 41152<br>−24384<br>240 300 | 41153<br>−24383<br>240 301 | 41154<br>−24382<br>240 302 | 41155<br>−24381<br>240 303 | 41156<br>−24380<br>240 304 | 41157<br>−24379<br>240 305 | 41158<br>−24378<br>240 306 | 41159<br>−24377<br>240 307 | 41160<br>−24376<br>240 310 | 41161<br>−24375<br>240 311 | 41162<br>−24374<br>240 312 | 41163<br>−24373<br>240 313 | 41164<br>−24372<br>240 314 | 41165<br>−24371<br>240 315 | 41166<br>−24370<br>240 316 | 41167<br>−24369<br>240 317 |
| D− | 41168<br>−24368<br>240 320 | 41169<br>−24367<br>240 321 | 41170<br>−24366<br>240 322 | 41171<br>−24365<br>240 323 | 41172<br>−24364<br>240 324 | 41173<br>−24363<br>240 325 | 41174<br>−24362<br>240 326 | 41175<br>−24361<br>240 327 | 41176<br>−24360<br>240 330 | 41177<br>−24359<br>240 331 | 41178<br>−24358<br>240 332 | 41179<br>−24357<br>240 333 | 41180<br>−24356<br>240 334 | 41181<br>−24355<br>240 335 | 41182<br>−24354<br>240 336 | 41183<br>−24353<br>240 337 |
| E− | 41184<br>−24352<br>240 340 | 41185<br>−24351<br>240 341 | 41186<br>−24350<br>240 342 | 41187<br>−24349<br>240 343 | 41188<br>−24348<br>240 344 | 41189<br>−24347<br>240 345 | 41190<br>−24346<br>240 346 | 41191<br>−24345<br>240 347 | 41192<br>−24344<br>240 350 | 41193<br>−24343<br>240 351 | 41194<br>−24342<br>240 352 | 41195<br>−24341<br>240 353 | 41196<br>−24340<br>240 354 | 41197<br>−24339<br>240 355 | 41198<br>−24338<br>240 356 | 41199<br>−24337<br>240 357 |
| F− | 41200<br>−24336<br>240 360 | 41201<br>−24335<br>240 361 | 41202<br>−24334<br>240 362 | 41203<br>−24333<br>240 363 | 41204<br>−24332<br>240 364 | 41205<br>−24331<br>240 365 | 41206<br>−24330<br>240 366 | 41207<br>−24329<br>240 367 | 41208<br>−24328<br>240 370 | 41209<br>−24327<br>240 371 | 41210<br>−24326<br>240 372 | 41211<br>−24325<br>240 373 | 41212<br>−24324<br>240 374 | 41213<br>−24323<br>240 375 | 41214<br>−24322<br>240 376 | 41215<br>−24321<br>240 377 |

**DECIMAL** → (right margin)

 **DECIMAL**

**OCTAL** →

 DECIMAL  −24576    BINARY  1010 0000    DECIMAL  40960    HEXADECIMAL  ⬡ A0    OCTAL  240 000

FOURTH HEX DIGIT ↗   ↖ THIRD HEX DIGIT

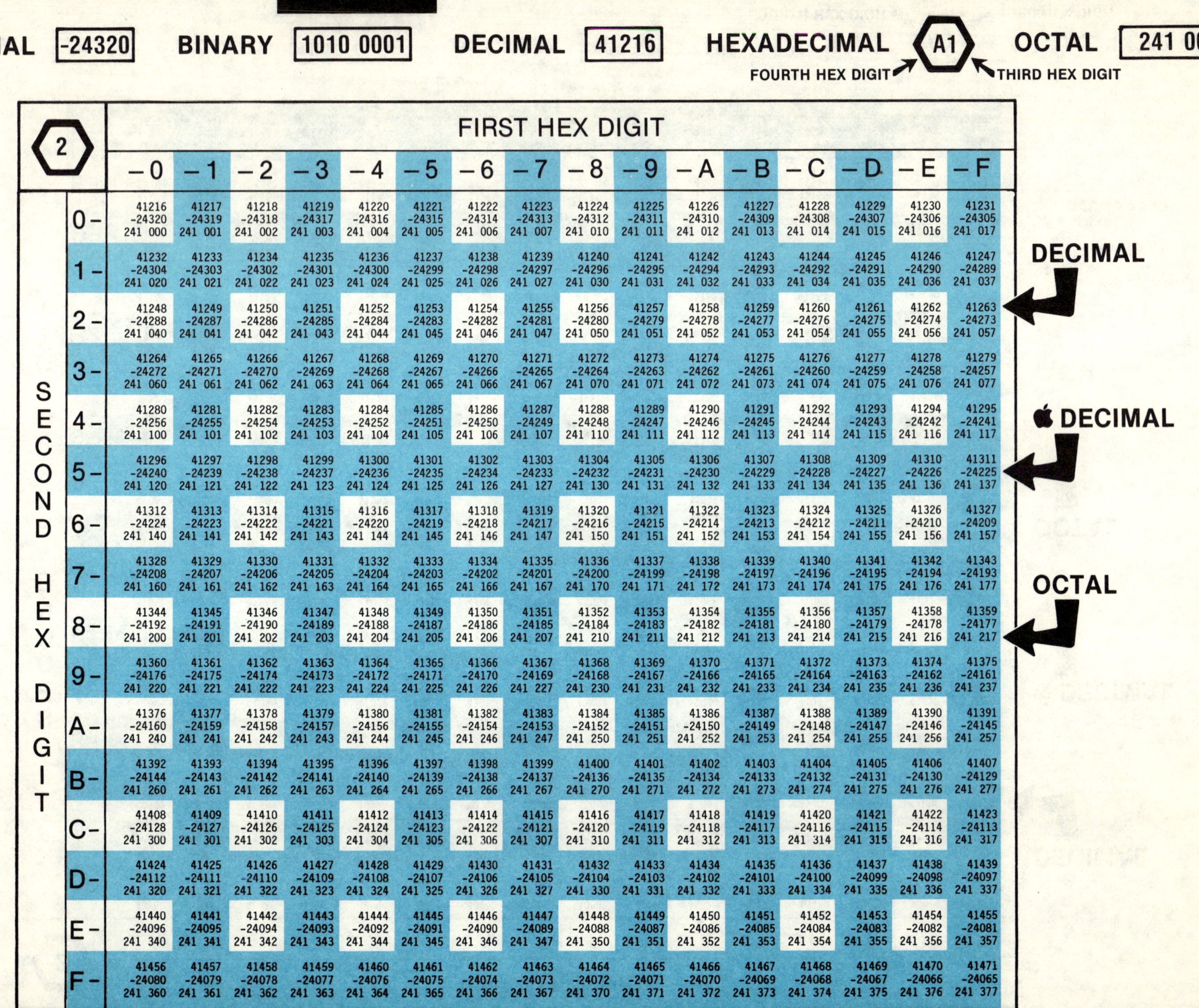

 DECIMAL -24320    BINARY 1010 0001    DECIMAL 41216    HEXADECIMAL A1    OCTAL 241 000

FOURTH HEX DIGIT → A1 ← THIRD HEX DIGIT

② FIRST HEX DIGIT / SECOND HEX DIGIT

Each cell lists: decimal (positive) / decimal (negative) / octal.

| 2 | −0 | −1 | −2 | −3 | −4 | −5 | −6 | −7 | −8 | −9 | −A | −B | −C | −D | −E | −F |
|---|---|---|---|---|---|---|---|---|---|---|---|---|---|---|---|---|
| 0− | 41216<br>−24320<br>241 000 | 41217<br>−24319<br>241 001 | 41218<br>−24318<br>241 002 | 41219<br>−24317<br>241 003 | 41220<br>−24316<br>241 004 | 41221<br>−24315<br>241 005 | 41222<br>−24314<br>241 006 | 41223<br>−24313<br>241 007 | 41224<br>−24312<br>241 010 | 41225<br>−24311<br>241 011 | 41226<br>−24310<br>241 012 | 41227<br>−24309<br>241 013 | 41228<br>−24308<br>241 014 | 41229<br>−24307<br>241 015 | 41230<br>−24306<br>241 016 | 41231<br>−24305<br>241 017 |
| 1− | 41232<br>−24304<br>241 020 | 41233<br>−24303<br>241 021 | 41234<br>−24302<br>241 022 | 41235<br>−24301<br>241 023 | 41236<br>−24300<br>241 024 | 41237<br>−24299<br>241 025 | 41238<br>−24298<br>241 026 | 41239<br>−24297<br>241 027 | 41240<br>−24296<br>241 030 | 41241<br>−24295<br>241 031 | 41242<br>−24294<br>241 032 | 41243<br>−24293<br>241 033 | 41244<br>−24292<br>241 034 | 41245<br>−24291<br>241 035 | 41246<br>−24290<br>241 036 | 41247<br>−24289<br>241 037 |
| 2− | 41248<br>−24288<br>241 040 | 41249<br>−24287<br>241 041 | 41250<br>−24286<br>241 042 | 41251<br>−24285<br>241 043 | 41252<br>−24284<br>241 044 | 41253<br>−24283<br>241 045 | 41254<br>−24282<br>241 046 | 41255<br>−24281<br>241 047 | 41256<br>−24280<br>241 050 | 41257<br>−24279<br>241 051 | 41258<br>−24278<br>241 052 | 41259<br>−24277<br>241 053 | 41260<br>−24276<br>241 054 | 41261<br>−24275<br>241 055 | 41262<br>−24274<br>241 056 | 41263<br>−24273<br>241 057 |
| 3− | 41264<br>−24272<br>241 060 | 41265<br>−24271<br>241 061 | 41266<br>−24270<br>241 062 | 41267<br>−24269<br>241 063 | 41268<br>−24268<br>241 064 | 41269<br>−24267<br>241 065 | 41270<br>−24266<br>241 066 | 41271<br>−24265<br>241 067 | 41272<br>−24264<br>241 070 | 41273<br>−24263<br>241 071 | 41274<br>−24262<br>241 072 | 41275<br>−24261<br>241 073 | 41276<br>−24260<br>241 074 | 41277<br>−24259<br>241 075 | 41278<br>−24258<br>241 076 | 41279<br>−24257<br>241 077 |
| 4− | 41280<br>−24256<br>241 100 | 41281<br>−24255<br>241 101 | 41282<br>−24254<br>241 102 | 41283<br>−24253<br>241 103 | 41284<br>−24252<br>241 104 | 41285<br>−24251<br>241 105 | 41286<br>−24250<br>241 106 | 41287<br>−24249<br>241 107 | 41288<br>−24248<br>241 110 | 41289<br>−24247<br>241 111 | 41290<br>−24246<br>241 112 | 41291<br>−24245<br>241 113 | 41292<br>−24244<br>241 114 | 41293<br>−24243<br>241 115 | 41294<br>−24242<br>241 116 | 41295<br>−24241<br>241 117 |
| 5− | 41296<br>−24240<br>241 120 | 41297<br>−24239<br>241 121 | 41298<br>−24238<br>241 122 | 41299<br>−24237<br>241 123 | 41300<br>−24236<br>241 124 | 41301<br>−24235<br>241 125 | 41302<br>−24234<br>241 126 | 41303<br>−24233<br>241 127 | 41304<br>−24232<br>241 130 | 41305<br>−24231<br>241 131 | 41306<br>−24230<br>241 132 | 41307<br>−24229<br>241 133 | 41308<br>−24228<br>241 134 | 41309<br>−24227<br>241 135 | 41310<br>−24226<br>241 136 | 41311<br>−24225<br>241 137 |
| 6− | 41312<br>−24224<br>241 140 | 41313<br>−24223<br>241 141 | 41314<br>−24222<br>241 142 | 41315<br>−24221<br>241 143 | 41316<br>−24220<br>241 144 | 41317<br>−24219<br>241 145 | 41318<br>−24218<br>241 146 | 41319<br>−24217<br>241 147 | 41320<br>−24216<br>241 150 | 41321<br>−24215<br>241 151 | 41322<br>−24214<br>241 152 | 41323<br>−24213<br>241 153 | 41324<br>−24212<br>241 154 | 41325<br>−24211<br>241 155 | 41326<br>−24210<br>241 156 | 41327<br>−24209<br>241 157 |
| 7− | 41328<br>−24208<br>241 160 | 41329<br>−24207<br>241 161 | 41330<br>−24206<br>241 162 | 41331<br>−24205<br>241 163 | 41332<br>−24204<br>241 164 | 41333<br>−24203<br>241 165 | 41334<br>−24202<br>241 166 | 41335<br>−24201<br>241 167 | 41336<br>−24200<br>241 170 | 41337<br>−24199<br>241 171 | 41338<br>−24198<br>241 172 | 41339<br>−24197<br>241 173 | 41340<br>−24196<br>241 174 | 41341<br>−24195<br>241 175 | 41342<br>−24194<br>241 176 | 41343<br>−24193<br>241 177 |
| 8− | 41344<br>−24192<br>241 200 | 41345<br>−24191<br>241 201 | 41346<br>−24190<br>241 202 | 41347<br>−24189<br>241 203 | 41348<br>−24188<br>241 204 | 41349<br>−24187<br>241 205 | 41350<br>−24186<br>241 206 | 41351<br>−24185<br>241 207 | 41352<br>−24184<br>241 210 | 41353<br>−24183<br>241 211 | 41354<br>−24182<br>241 212 | 41355<br>−24181<br>241 213 | 41356<br>−24180<br>241 214 | 41357<br>−24179<br>241 215 | 41358<br>−24178<br>241 216 | 41359<br>−24177<br>241 217 |
| 9− | 41360<br>−24176<br>241 220 | 41361<br>−24175<br>241 221 | 41362<br>−24174<br>241 222 | 41363<br>−24173<br>241 223 | 41364<br>−24172<br>241 224 | 41365<br>−24171<br>241 225 | 41366<br>−24170<br>241 226 | 41367<br>−24169<br>241 227 | 41368<br>−24168<br>241 230 | 41369<br>−24167<br>241 231 | 41370<br>−24166<br>241 232 | 41371<br>−24165<br>241 233 | 41372<br>−24164<br>241 234 | 41373<br>−24163<br>241 235 | 41374<br>−24162<br>241 236 | 41375<br>−24161<br>241 237 |
| A− | 41376<br>−24160<br>241 240 | 41377<br>−24159<br>241 241 | 41378<br>−24158<br>241 242 | 41379<br>−24157<br>241 243 | 41380<br>−24156<br>241 244 | 41381<br>−24155<br>241 245 | 41382<br>−24154<br>241 246 | 41383<br>−24153<br>241 247 | 41384<br>−24152<br>241 250 | 41385<br>−24151<br>241 251 | 41386<br>−24150<br>241 252 | 41387<br>−24149<br>241 253 | 41388<br>−24148<br>241 254 | 41389<br>−24147<br>241 255 | 41390<br>−24146<br>241 256 | 41391<br>−24145<br>241 257 |
| B− | 41392<br>−24144<br>241 260 | 41393<br>−24143<br>241 261 | 41394<br>−24142<br>241 262 | 41395<br>−24141<br>241 263 | 41396<br>−24140<br>241 264 | 41397<br>−24139<br>241 265 | 41398<br>−24138<br>241 266 | 41399<br>−24137<br>241 267 | 41400<br>−24136<br>241 270 | 41401<br>−24135<br>241 271 | 41402<br>−24134<br>241 272 | 41403<br>−24133<br>241 273 | 41404<br>−24132<br>241 274 | 41405<br>−24131<br>241 275 | 41406<br>−24130<br>241 276 | 41407<br>−24129<br>241 277 |
| C− | 41408<br>−24128<br>241 300 | 41409<br>−24127<br>241 301 | 41410<br>−24126<br>241 302 | 41411<br>−24125<br>241 303 | 41412<br>−24124<br>241 304 | 41413<br>−24123<br>241 305 | 41414<br>−24122<br>241 306 | 41415<br>−24121<br>241 307 | 41416<br>−24120<br>241 310 | 41417<br>−24119<br>241 311 | 41418<br>−24118<br>241 312 | 41419<br>−24117<br>241 313 | 41420<br>−24116<br>241 314 | 41421<br>−24115<br>241 315 | 41422<br>−24114<br>241 316 | 41423<br>−24113<br>241 317 |
| D− | 41424<br>−24112<br>241 320 | 41425<br>−24111<br>241 321 | 41426<br>−24110<br>241 322 | 41427<br>−24109<br>241 323 | 41428<br>−24108<br>241 324 | 41429<br>−24107<br>241 325 | 41430<br>−24106<br>241 326 | 41431<br>−24105<br>241 327 | 41432<br>−24104<br>241 330 | 41433<br>−24103<br>241 331 | 41434<br>−24102<br>241 332 | 41435<br>−24101<br>241 333 | 41436<br>−24100<br>241 334 | 41437<br>−24099<br>241 335 | 41438<br>−24098<br>241 336 | 41439<br>−24097<br>241 337 |
| E− | 41440<br>−24096<br>241 340 | 41441<br>−24095<br>241 341 | 41442<br>−24094<br>241 342 | 41443<br>−24093<br>241 343 | 41444<br>−24092<br>241 344 | 41445<br>−24091<br>241 345 | 41446<br>−24090<br>241 346 | 41447<br>−24089<br>241 347 | 41448<br>−24088<br>241 350 | 41449<br>−24087<br>241 351 | 41450<br>−24086<br>241 352 | 41451<br>−24085<br>241 353 | 41452<br>−24084<br>241 354 | 41453<br>−24083<br>241 355 | 41454<br>−24082<br>241 356 | 41455<br>−24081<br>241 357 |
| F− | 41456<br>−24080<br>241 360 | 41457<br>−24079<br>241 361 | 41458<br>−24078<br>241 362 | 41459<br>−24077<br>241 363 | 41460<br>−24076<br>241 364 | 41461<br>−24075<br>241 365 | 41462<br>−24074<br>241 366 | 41463<br>−24073<br>241 367 | 41464<br>−24072<br>241 370 | 41465<br>−24071<br>241 371 | 41466<br>−24070<br>241 372 | 41467<br>−24069<br>241 373 | 41468<br>−24068<br>241 374 | 41469<br>−24067<br>241 375 | 41470<br>−24066<br>241 376 | 41471<br>−24065<br>241 377 |

## FIRST HEX DIGIT

Table 2 — Conversion: each cell shows DECIMAL (top), 🍎 DECIMAL (middle), OCTAL (bottom).

| SECOND HEX DIGIT | −0 | −1 | −2 | −3 | −4 | −5 | −6 | −7 | −8 | −9 | −A | −B | −C | −D | −E | −F |
|---|---|---|---|---|---|---|---|---|---|---|---|---|---|---|---|---|
| 0− | 41472<br>−24064<br>242 000 | 41473<br>−24063<br>242 001 | 41474<br>−24062<br>242 002 | 41475<br>−24061<br>242 003 | 41476<br>−24060<br>242 004 | 41477<br>−24059<br>242 005 | 41478<br>−24058<br>242 006 | 41479<br>−24057<br>242 007 | 41480<br>−24056<br>242 010 | 41481<br>−24055<br>242 011 | 41482<br>−24054<br>242 012 | 41483<br>−24053<br>242 013 | 41484<br>−24052<br>242 014 | 41485<br>−24051<br>242 015 | 41486<br>−24050<br>242 016 | 41487<br>−24049<br>242 017 |
| 1− | 41488<br>−24048<br>242 020 | 41489<br>−24047<br>242 021 | 41490<br>−24046<br>242 022 | 41491<br>−24045<br>242 023 | 41492<br>−24044<br>242 024 | 41493<br>−24043<br>242 025 | 41494<br>−24042<br>242 026 | 41495<br>−24041<br>242 027 | 41496<br>−24040<br>242 030 | 41497<br>−24039<br>242 031 | 41498<br>−24038<br>242 032 | 41499<br>−24037<br>242 033 | 41500<br>−24036<br>242 034 | 41501<br>−24035<br>242 035 | 41502<br>−24034<br>242 036 | 41503<br>−24033<br>242 037 |
| 2− | 41504<br>−24032<br>242 040 | 41505<br>−24031<br>242 041 | 41506<br>−24030<br>242 042 | 41507<br>−24029<br>242 043 | 41508<br>−24028<br>242 044 | 41509<br>−24027<br>242 045 | 41510<br>−24026<br>242 046 | 41511<br>−24025<br>242 047 | 41512<br>−24024<br>242 050 | 41513<br>−24023<br>242 051 | 41514<br>−24022<br>242 052 | 41515<br>−24021<br>242 053 | 41516<br>−24020<br>242 054 | 41517<br>−24019<br>242 055 | 41518<br>−24018<br>242 056 | 41519<br>−24017<br>242 057 |
| 3− | 41520<br>−24016<br>242 060 | 41521<br>−24015<br>242 061 | 41522<br>−24014<br>242 062 | 41523<br>−24013<br>242 063 | 41524<br>−24012<br>242 064 | 41525<br>−24011<br>242 065 | 41526<br>−24010<br>242 066 | 41527<br>−24009<br>242 067 | 41528<br>−24008<br>242 070 | 41529<br>−24007<br>242 071 | 41530<br>−24006<br>242 072 | 41531<br>−24005<br>242 073 | 41532<br>−24004<br>242 074 | 41533<br>−24003<br>242 075 | 41534<br>−24002<br>242 076 | 41535<br>−24001<br>242 077 |
| 4− | 41536<br>−24000<br>242 100 | 41537<br>−23999<br>242 101 | 41538<br>−23998<br>242 102 | 41539<br>−23997<br>242 103 | 41540<br>−23996<br>242 104 | 41541<br>−23995<br>242 105 | 41542<br>−23994<br>242 106 | 41543<br>−23993<br>242 107 | 41544<br>−23992<br>242 110 | 41545<br>−23991<br>242 111 | 41546<br>−23990<br>242 112 | 41547<br>−23989<br>242 113 | 41548<br>−23988<br>242 114 | 41549<br>−23987<br>242 115 | 41550<br>−23986<br>242 116 | 41551<br>−23985<br>242 117 |
| 5− | 41552<br>−23984<br>242 120 | 41553<br>−23983<br>242 121 | 41554<br>−23982<br>242 122 | 41555<br>−23981<br>242 123 | 41556<br>−23980<br>242 124 | 41557<br>−23979<br>242 125 | 41558<br>−23978<br>242 126 | 41559<br>−23977<br>242 127 | 41560<br>−23976<br>242 130 | 41561<br>−23975<br>242 131 | 41562<br>−23974<br>242 132 | 41563<br>−23973<br>242 133 | 41564<br>−23972<br>242 134 | 41565<br>−23971<br>242 135 | 41566<br>−23970<br>242 136 | 41567<br>−23969<br>242 137 |
| 6− | 41568<br>−23968<br>242 140 | 41569<br>−23967<br>242 141 | 41570<br>−23966<br>242 142 | 41571<br>−23965<br>242 143 | 41572<br>−23964<br>242 144 | 41573<br>−23963<br>242 145 | 41574<br>−23962<br>242 146 | 41575<br>−23961<br>242 147 | 41576<br>−23960<br>242 150 | 41577<br>−23959<br>242 151 | 41578<br>−23958<br>242 152 | 41579<br>−23957<br>242 153 | 41580<br>−23956<br>242 154 | 41581<br>−23955<br>242 155 | 41582<br>−23954<br>242 156 | 41583<br>−23953<br>242 157 |
| 7− | 41584<br>−23952<br>242 160 | 41585<br>−23951<br>242 161 | 41586<br>−23950<br>242 162 | 41587<br>−23949<br>242 163 | 41588<br>−23948<br>242 164 | 41589<br>−23947<br>242 165 | 41590<br>−23946<br>242 166 | 41591<br>−23945<br>242 167 | 41592<br>−23944<br>242 170 | 41593<br>−23943<br>242 171 | 41594<br>−23942<br>242 172 | 41595<br>−23941<br>242 173 | 41596<br>−23940<br>242 174 | 41597<br>−23939<br>242 175 | 41598<br>−23938<br>242 176 | 41599<br>−23937<br>242 177 |
| 8− | 41600<br>−23936<br>242 200 | 41601<br>−23935<br>242 201 | 41602<br>−23934<br>242 202 | 41603<br>−23933<br>242 203 | 41604<br>−23932<br>242 204 | 41605<br>−23931<br>242 205 | 41606<br>−23930<br>242 206 | 41607<br>−23929<br>242 207 | 41608<br>−23928<br>242 210 | 41609<br>−23927<br>242 211 | 41610<br>−23926<br>242 212 | 41611<br>−23925<br>242 213 | 41612<br>−23924<br>242 214 | 41613<br>−23923<br>242 215 | 41614<br>−23922<br>242 216 | 41615<br>−23921<br>242 217 |
| 9− | 41616<br>−23920<br>242 220 | 41617<br>−23919<br>242 221 | 41618<br>−23918<br>242 222 | 41619<br>−23917<br>242 223 | 41620<br>−23916<br>242 224 | 41621<br>−23915<br>242 225 | 41622<br>−23914<br>242 226 | 41623<br>−23913<br>242 227 | 41624<br>−23912<br>242 230 | 41625<br>−23911<br>242 231 | 41626<br>−23910<br>242 232 | 41627<br>−23909<br>242 233 | 41628<br>−23908<br>242 234 | 41629<br>−23907<br>242 235 | 41630<br>−23906<br>242 236 | 41631<br>−23905<br>242 237 |
| A− | 41632<br>−23904<br>242 240 | 41633<br>−23903<br>242 241 | 41634<br>−23902<br>242 242 | 41635<br>−23901<br>242 243 | 41636<br>−23900<br>242 244 | 41637<br>−23899<br>242 245 | 41638<br>−23898<br>242 246 | 41639<br>−23897<br>242 247 | 41640<br>−23896<br>242 250 | 41641<br>−23895<br>242 251 | 41642<br>−23894<br>242 252 | 41643<br>−23893<br>242 253 | 41644<br>−23892<br>242 254 | 41645<br>−23891<br>242 255 | 41646<br>−23890<br>242 256 | 41647<br>−23889<br>242 257 |
| B− | 41648<br>−23888<br>242 260 | 41649<br>−23887<br>242 261 | 41650<br>−23886<br>242 262 | 41651<br>−23885<br>242 263 | 41652<br>−23884<br>242 264 | 41653<br>−23883<br>242 265 | 41654<br>−23882<br>242 266 | 41655<br>−23881<br>242 267 | 41656<br>−23880<br>242 270 | 41657<br>−23879<br>242 271 | 41658<br>−23878<br>242 272 | 41659<br>−23877<br>242 273 | 41660<br>−23876<br>242 274 | 41661<br>−23875<br>242 275 | 41662<br>−23874<br>242 276 | 41663<br>−23873<br>242 277 |
| C− | 41664<br>−23872<br>242 300 | 41665<br>−23871<br>242 301 | 41666<br>−23870<br>242 302 | 41667<br>−23869<br>242 303 | 41668<br>−23868<br>242 304 | 41669<br>−23867<br>242 305 | 41670<br>−23866<br>242 306 | 41671<br>−23865<br>242 307 | 41672<br>−23864<br>242 310 | 41673<br>−23863<br>242 311 | 41674<br>−23862<br>242 312 | 41675<br>−23861<br>242 313 | 41676<br>−23860<br>242 314 | 41677<br>−23859<br>242 315 | 41678<br>−23858<br>242 316 | 41679<br>−23857<br>242 317 |
| D− | 41680<br>−23856<br>242 320 | 41681<br>−23855<br>242 321 | 41682<br>−23854<br>242 322 | 41683<br>−23853<br>242 323 | 41684<br>−23852<br>242 324 | 41685<br>−23851<br>242 325 | 41686<br>−23850<br>242 326 | 41687<br>−23849<br>242 327 | 41688<br>−23848<br>242 330 | 41689<br>−23847<br>242 331 | 41690<br>−23846<br>242 332 | 41691<br>−23845<br>242 333 | 41692<br>−23844<br>242 334 | 41693<br>−23843<br>242 335 | 41694<br>−23842<br>242 336 | 41695<br>−23841<br>242 337 |
| E− | 41696<br>−23840<br>242 340 | 41697<br>−23839<br>242 341 | 41698<br>−23838<br>242 342 | 41699<br>−23837<br>242 343 | 41700<br>−23836<br>242 344 | 41701<br>−23835<br>242 345 | 41702<br>−23834<br>242 346 | 41703<br>−23833<br>242 347 | 41704<br>−23832<br>242 350 | 41705<br>−23831<br>242 351 | 41706<br>−23830<br>242 352 | 41707<br>−23829<br>242 353 | 41708<br>−23828<br>242 354 | 41709<br>−23827<br>242 355 | 41710<br>−23826<br>242 356 | 41711<br>−23825<br>242 357 |
| F− | 41712<br>−23824<br>242 360 | 41713<br>−23823<br>242 361 | 41714<br>−23822<br>242 362 | 41715<br>−23821<br>242 363 | 41716<br>−23820<br>242 364 | 41717<br>−23819<br>242 365 | 41718<br>−23818<br>242 366 | 41719<br>−23817<br>242 367 | 41720<br>−23816<br>242 370 | 41721<br>−23815<br>242 371 | 41722<br>−23814<br>242 372 | 41723<br>−23813<br>242 373 | 41724<br>−23812<br>242 374 | 41725<br>−23811<br>242 375 | 41726<br>−23810<br>242 376 | 41727<br>−23809<br>242 377 |

Legend markers at right: **DECIMAL**, 🍎 **DECIMAL**, **OCTAL**

🍎 DECIMAL `−24064`  BINARY `1010 0010`  DECIMAL `41472`  HEXADECIMAL  (A2)  OCTAL `242 000`

FOURTH HEX DIGIT →  ← THIRD HEX DIGIT

DECIMAL -23808    BINARY 1010 0011    DECIMAL 41728    HEXADECIMAL A3    OCTAL 243 000

FOURTH HEX DIGIT → A3 ← THIRD HEX DIGIT

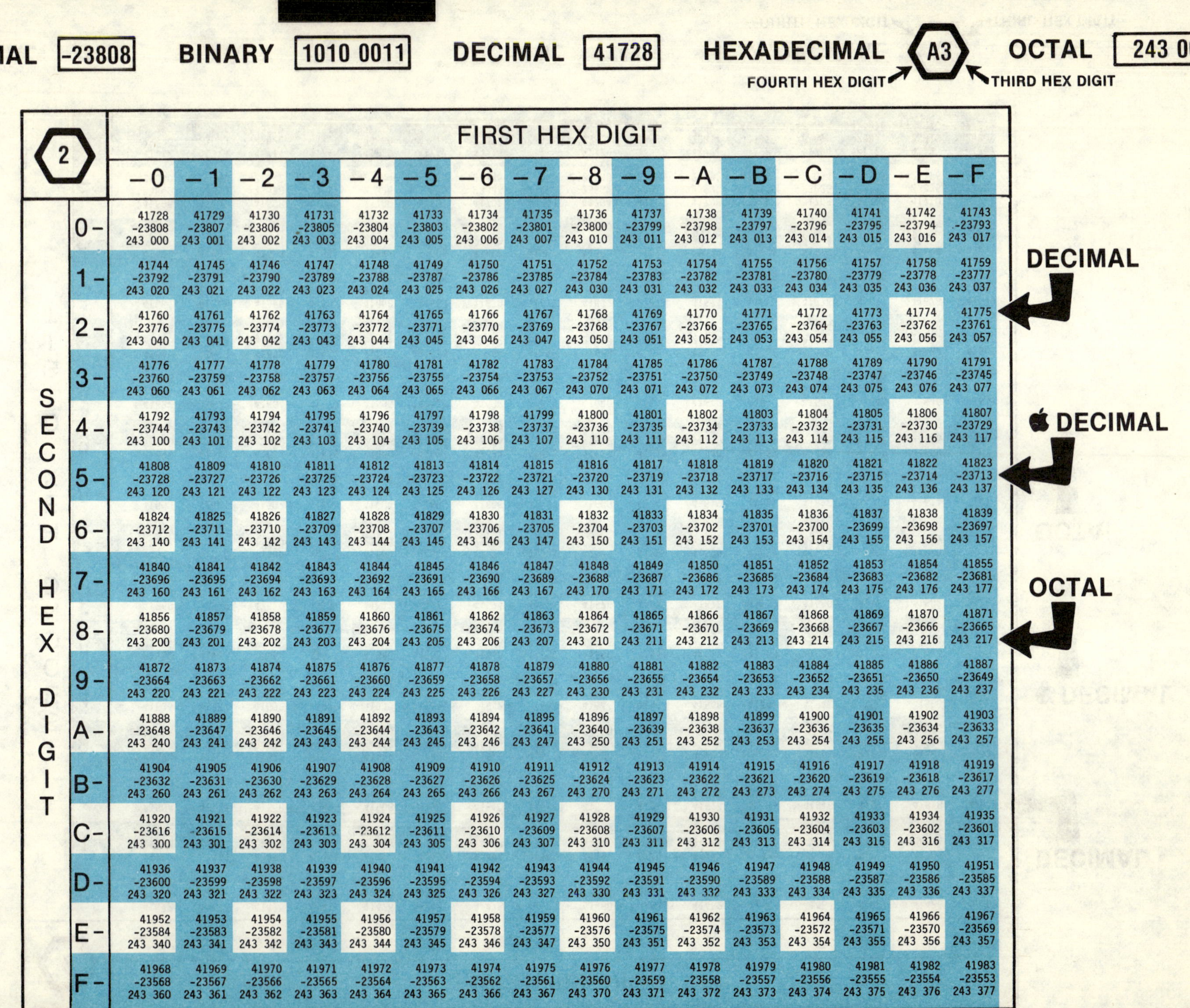

FIRST HEX DIGIT (columns) / SECOND HEX DIGIT (rows). Each cell lists: decimal (unsigned), decimal (signed), octal.

| 2 | −0 | −1 | −2 | −3 | −4 | −5 | −6 | −7 | −8 | −9 | −A | −B | −C | −D | −E | −F |
|---|---|---|---|---|---|---|---|---|---|---|---|---|---|---|---|---|
| 0− | 41728<br>−23808<br>243 000 | 41729<br>−23807<br>243 001 | 41730<br>−23806<br>243 002 | 41731<br>−23805<br>243 003 | 41732<br>−23804<br>243 004 | 41733<br>−23803<br>243 005 | 41734<br>−23802<br>243 006 | 41735<br>−23801<br>243 007 | 41736<br>−23800<br>243 010 | 41737<br>−23799<br>243 011 | 41738<br>−23798<br>243 012 | 41739<br>−23797<br>243 013 | 41740<br>−23796<br>243 014 | 41741<br>−23795<br>243 015 | 41742<br>−23794<br>243 016 | 41743<br>−23793<br>243 017 |
| 1− | 41744<br>−23792<br>243 020 | 41745<br>−23791<br>243 021 | 41746<br>−23790<br>243 022 | 41747<br>−23789<br>243 023 | 41748<br>−23788<br>243 024 | 41749<br>−23787<br>243 025 | 41750<br>−23786<br>243 026 | 41751<br>−23785<br>243 027 | 41752<br>−23784<br>243 030 | 41753<br>−23783<br>243 031 | 41754<br>−23782<br>243 032 | 41755<br>−23781<br>243 033 | 41756<br>−23780<br>243 034 | 41757<br>−23779<br>243 035 | 41758<br>−23778<br>243 036 | 41759<br>−23777<br>243 037 |
| 2− | 41760<br>−23776<br>243 040 | 41761<br>−23775<br>243 041 | 41762<br>−23774<br>243 042 | 41763<br>−23773<br>243 043 | 41764<br>−23772<br>243 044 | 41765<br>−23771<br>243 045 | 41766<br>−23770<br>243 046 | 41767<br>−23769<br>243 047 | 41768<br>−23768<br>243 050 | 41769<br>−23767<br>243 051 | 41770<br>−23766<br>243 052 | 41771<br>−23765<br>243 053 | 41772<br>−23764<br>243 054 | 41773<br>−23763<br>243 055 | 41774<br>−23762<br>243 056 | 41775<br>−23761<br>243 057 |
| 3− | 41776<br>−23760<br>243 060 | 41777<br>−23759<br>243 061 | 41778<br>−23758<br>243 062 | 41779<br>−23757<br>243 063 | 41780<br>−23756<br>243 064 | 41781<br>−23755<br>243 065 | 41782<br>−23754<br>243 066 | 41783<br>−23753<br>243 067 | 41784<br>−23752<br>243 070 | 41785<br>−23751<br>243 071 | 41786<br>−23750<br>243 072 | 41787<br>−23749<br>243 073 | 41788<br>−23748<br>243 074 | 41789<br>−23747<br>243 075 | 41790<br>−23746<br>243 076 | 41791<br>−23745<br>243 077 |
| 4− | 41792<br>−23744<br>243 100 | 41793<br>−23743<br>243 101 | 41794<br>−23742<br>243 102 | 41795<br>−23741<br>243 103 | 41796<br>−23740<br>243 104 | 41797<br>−23739<br>243 105 | 41798<br>−23738<br>243 106 | 41799<br>−23737<br>243 107 | 41800<br>−23736<br>243 110 | 41801<br>−23735<br>243 111 | 41802<br>−23734<br>243 112 | 41803<br>−23733<br>243 113 | 41804<br>−23732<br>243 114 | 41805<br>−23731<br>243 115 | 41806<br>−23730<br>243 116 | 41807<br>−23729<br>243 117 |
| 5− | 41808<br>−23728<br>243 120 | 41809<br>−23727<br>243 121 | 41810<br>−23726<br>243 122 | 41811<br>−23725<br>243 123 | 41812<br>−23724<br>243 124 | 41813<br>−23723<br>243 125 | 41814<br>−23722<br>243 126 | 41815<br>−23721<br>243 127 | 41816<br>−23720<br>243 130 | 41817<br>−23719<br>243 131 | 41818<br>−23718<br>243 132 | 41819<br>−23717<br>243 133 | 41820<br>−23716<br>243 134 | 41821<br>−23715<br>243 135 | 41822<br>−23714<br>243 136 | 41823<br>−23713<br>243 137 |
| 6− | 41824<br>−23712<br>243 140 | 41825<br>−23711<br>243 141 | 41826<br>−23710<br>243 142 | 41827<br>−23709<br>243 143 | 41828<br>−23708<br>243 144 | 41829<br>−23707<br>243 145 | 41830<br>−23706<br>243 146 | 41831<br>−23705<br>243 147 | 41832<br>−23704<br>243 150 | 41833<br>−23703<br>243 151 | 41834<br>−23702<br>243 152 | 41835<br>−23701<br>243 153 | 41836<br>−23700<br>243 154 | 41837<br>−23699<br>243 155 | 41838<br>−23698<br>243 156 | 41839<br>−23697<br>243 157 |
| 7− | 41840<br>−23696<br>243 160 | 41841<br>−23695<br>243 161 | 41842<br>−23694<br>243 162 | 41843<br>−23693<br>243 163 | 41844<br>−23692<br>243 164 | 41845<br>−23691<br>243 165 | 41846<br>−23690<br>243 166 | 41847<br>−23689<br>243 167 | 41848<br>−23688<br>243 170 | 41849<br>−23687<br>243 171 | 41850<br>−23686<br>243 172 | 41851<br>−23685<br>243 173 | 41852<br>−23684<br>243 174 | 41853<br>−23683<br>243 175 | 41854<br>−23682<br>243 176 | 41855<br>−23681<br>243 177 |
| 8− | 41856<br>−23680<br>243 200 | 41857<br>−23679<br>243 201 | 41858<br>−23678<br>243 202 | 41859<br>−23677<br>243 203 | 41860<br>−23676<br>243 204 | 41861<br>−23675<br>243 205 | 41862<br>−23674<br>243 206 | 41863<br>−23673<br>243 207 | 41864<br>−23672<br>243 210 | 41865<br>−23671<br>243 211 | 41866<br>−23670<br>243 212 | 41867<br>−23669<br>243 213 | 41868<br>−23668<br>243 214 | 41869<br>−23667<br>243 215 | 41870<br>−23666<br>243 216 | 41871<br>−23665<br>243 217 |
| 9− | 41872<br>−23664<br>243 220 | 41873<br>−23663<br>243 221 | 41874<br>−23662<br>243 222 | 41875<br>−23661<br>243 223 | 41876<br>−23660<br>243 224 | 41877<br>−23659<br>243 225 | 41878<br>−23658<br>243 226 | 41879<br>−23657<br>243 227 | 41880<br>−23656<br>243 230 | 41881<br>−23655<br>243 231 | 41882<br>−23654<br>243 232 | 41883<br>−23653<br>243 233 | 41884<br>−23652<br>243 234 | 41885<br>−23651<br>243 235 | 41886<br>−23650<br>243 236 | 41887<br>−23649<br>243 237 |
| A− | 41888<br>−23648<br>243 240 | 41889<br>−23647<br>243 241 | 41890<br>−23646<br>243 242 | 41891<br>−23645<br>243 243 | 41892<br>−23644<br>243 244 | 41893<br>−23643<br>243 245 | 41894<br>−23642<br>243 246 | 41895<br>−23641<br>243 247 | 41896<br>−23640<br>243 250 | 41897<br>−23639<br>243 251 | 41898<br>−23638<br>243 252 | 41899<br>−23637<br>243 253 | 41900<br>−23636<br>243 254 | 41901<br>−23635<br>243 255 | 41902<br>−23634<br>243 256 | 41903<br>−23633<br>243 257 |
| B− | 41904<br>−23632<br>243 260 | 41905<br>−23631<br>243 261 | 41906<br>−23630<br>243 262 | 41907<br>−23629<br>243 263 | 41908<br>−23628<br>243 264 | 41909<br>−23627<br>243 265 | 41910<br>−23626<br>243 266 | 41911<br>−23625<br>243 267 | 41912<br>−23624<br>243 270 | 41913<br>−23623<br>243 271 | 41914<br>−23622<br>243 272 | 41915<br>−23621<br>243 273 | 41916<br>−23620<br>243 274 | 41917<br>−23619<br>243 275 | 41918<br>−23618<br>243 276 | 41919<br>−23617<br>243 277 |
| C− | 41920<br>−23616<br>243 300 | 41921<br>−23615<br>243 301 | 41922<br>−23614<br>243 302 | 41923<br>−23613<br>243 303 | 41924<br>−23612<br>243 304 | 41925<br>−23611<br>243 305 | 41926<br>−23610<br>243 306 | 41927<br>−23609<br>243 307 | 41928<br>−23608<br>243 310 | 41929<br>−23607<br>243 311 | 41930<br>−23606<br>243 312 | 41931<br>−23605<br>243 313 | 41932<br>−23604<br>243 314 | 41933<br>−23603<br>243 315 | 41934<br>−23602<br>243 316 | 41935<br>−23601<br>243 317 |
| D− | 41936<br>−23600<br>243 320 | 41937<br>−23599<br>243 321 | 41938<br>−23598<br>243 322 | 41939<br>−23597<br>243 323 | 41940<br>−23596<br>243 324 | 41941<br>−23595<br>243 325 | 41942<br>−23594<br>243 326 | 41943<br>−23593<br>243 327 | 41944<br>−23592<br>243 330 | 41945<br>−23591<br>243 331 | 41946<br>−23590<br>243 332 | 41947<br>−23589<br>243 333 | 41948<br>−23588<br>243 334 | 41949<br>−23587<br>243 335 | 41950<br>−23586<br>243 336 | 41951<br>−23585<br>243 337 |
| E− | 41952<br>−23584<br>243 340 | 41953<br>−23583<br>243 341 | 41954<br>−23582<br>243 342 | 41955<br>−23581<br>243 343 | 41956<br>−23580<br>243 344 | 41957<br>−23579<br>243 345 | 41958<br>−23578<br>243 346 | 41959<br>−23577<br>243 347 | 41960<br>−23576<br>243 350 | 41961<br>−23575<br>243 351 | 41962<br>−23574<br>243 352 | 41963<br>−23573<br>243 353 | 41964<br>−23572<br>243 354 | 41965<br>−23571<br>243 355 | 41966<br>−23570<br>243 356 | 41967<br>−23569<br>243 357 |
| F− | 41968<br>−23568<br>243 360 | 41969<br>−23567<br>243 361 | 41970<br>−23566<br>243 362 | 41971<br>−23565<br>243 363 | 41972<br>−23564<br>243 364 | 41973<br>−23563<br>243 365 | 41974<br>−23562<br>243 366 | 41975<br>−23561<br>243 367 | 41976<br>−23560<br>243 370 | 41977<br>−23559<br>243 371 | 41978<br>−23558<br>243 372 | 41979<br>−23557<br>243 373 | 41980<br>−23556<br>243 374 | 41981<br>−23555<br>243 375 | 41982<br>−23554<br>243 376 | 41983<br>−23553<br>243 377 |

## FIRST HEX DIGIT

| SECOND HEX DIGIT | −0 | −1 | −2 | −3 | −4 | −5 | −6 | −7 | −8 | −9 | −A | −B | −C | −D | −E | −F |
|---|---|---|---|---|---|---|---|---|---|---|---|---|---|---|---|---|
| **0−** | 41984<br>−23552<br>244 000 | 41985<br>−23551<br>244 001 | 41986<br>−23550<br>244 002 | 41987<br>−23549<br>244 003 | 41988<br>−23548<br>244 004 | 41989<br>−23547<br>244 005 | 41990<br>−23546<br>244 006 | 41991<br>−23545<br>244 007 | 41992<br>−23544<br>244 010 | 41993<br>−23543<br>244 011 | 41994<br>−23542<br>244 012 | 41995<br>−23541<br>244 013 | 41996<br>−23540<br>244 014 | 41997<br>−23539<br>244 015 | 41998<br>−23538<br>244 016 | 41999<br>−23537<br>244 017 |
| **1−** | 42000<br>−23536<br>244 020 | 42001<br>−23535<br>244 021 | 42002<br>−23534<br>244 022 | 42003<br>−23533<br>244 023 | 42004<br>−23532<br>244 024 | 42005<br>−23531<br>244 025 | 42006<br>−23530<br>244 026 | 42007<br>−23529<br>244 027 | 42008<br>−23528<br>244 030 | 42009<br>−23527<br>244 031 | 42010<br>−23526<br>244 032 | 42011<br>−23525<br>244 033 | 42012<br>−23524<br>244 034 | 42013<br>−23523<br>244 035 | 42014<br>−23522<br>244 036 | 42015<br>−23521<br>244 037 |
| **2−** | 42016<br>−23520<br>244 040 | 42017<br>−23519<br>244 041 | 42018<br>−23518<br>244 042 | 42019<br>−23517<br>244 043 | 42020<br>−23516<br>244 044 | 42021<br>−23515<br>244 045 | 42022<br>−23514<br>244 046 | 42023<br>−23513<br>244 047 | 42024<br>−23512<br>244 050 | 42025<br>−23511<br>244 051 | 42026<br>−23510<br>244 052 | 42027<br>−23509<br>244 053 | 42028<br>−23508<br>244 054 | 42029<br>−23507<br>244 055 | 42030<br>−23506<br>244 056 | 42031<br>−23505<br>244 057 |
| **3−** | 42032<br>−23504<br>244 060 | 42033<br>−23503<br>244 061 | 42034<br>−23502<br>244 062 | 42035<br>−23501<br>244 063 | 42036<br>−23500<br>244 064 | 42037<br>−23499<br>244 065 | 42038<br>−23498<br>244 066 | 42039<br>−23497<br>244 067 | 42040<br>−23496<br>244 070 | 42041<br>−23495<br>244 071 | 42042<br>−23494<br>244 072 | 42043<br>−23493<br>244 073 | 42044<br>−23492<br>244 074 | 42045<br>−23491<br>244 075 | 42046<br>−23490<br>244 076 | 42047<br>−23489<br>244 077 |
| **4−** | 42048<br>−23488<br>244 100 | 42049<br>−23487<br>244 101 | 42050<br>−23486<br>244 102 | 42051<br>−23485<br>244 103 | 42052<br>−23484<br>244 104 | 42053<br>−23483<br>244 105 | 42054<br>−23482<br>244 106 | 42055<br>−23481<br>244 107 | 42056<br>−23480<br>244 110 | 42057<br>−23479<br>244 111 | 42058<br>−23478<br>244 112 | 42059<br>−23477<br>244 113 | 42060<br>−23476<br>244 114 | 42061<br>−23475<br>244 115 | 42062<br>−23474<br>244 116 | 42063<br>−23473<br>244 117 |
| **5−** | 42064<br>−23472<br>244 120 | 42065<br>−23471<br>244 121 | 42066<br>−23470<br>244 122 | 42067<br>−23469<br>244 123 | 42068<br>−23468<br>244 124 | 42069<br>−23467<br>244 125 | 42070<br>−23466<br>244 126 | 42071<br>−23465<br>244 127 | 42072<br>−23464<br>244 130 | 42073<br>−23463<br>244 131 | 42074<br>−23462<br>244 132 | 42075<br>−23461<br>244 133 | 42076<br>−23460<br>244 134 | 42077<br>−23459<br>244 135 | 42078<br>−23458<br>244 136 | 42079<br>−23457<br>244 137 |
| **6−** | 42080<br>−23456<br>244 140 | 42081<br>−23455<br>244 141 | 42082<br>−23454<br>244 142 | 42083<br>−23453<br>244 143 | 42084<br>−23452<br>244 144 | 42085<br>−23451<br>244 145 | 42086<br>−23450<br>244 146 | 42087<br>−23449<br>244 147 | 42088<br>−23448<br>244 150 | 42089<br>−23447<br>244 151 | 42090<br>−23446<br>244 152 | 42091<br>−23445<br>244 153 | 42092<br>−23444<br>244 154 | 42093<br>−23443<br>244 155 | 42094<br>−23442<br>244 156 | 42095<br>−23441<br>244 157 |
| **7−** | 42096<br>−23440<br>244 160 | 42097<br>−23439<br>244 161 | 42098<br>−23438<br>244 162 | 42099<br>−23437<br>244 163 | 42100<br>−23436<br>244 164 | 42101<br>−23435<br>244 165 | 42102<br>−23434<br>244 166 | 42103<br>−23433<br>244 167 | 42104<br>−23432<br>244 170 | 42105<br>−23431<br>244 171 | 42106<br>−23430<br>244 172 | 42107<br>−23429<br>244 173 | 42108<br>−23428<br>244 174 | 42109<br>−23427<br>244 175 | 42110<br>−23426<br>244 176 | 42111<br>−23425<br>244 177 |
| **8−** | 42112<br>−23424<br>244 200 | 42113<br>−23423<br>244 201 | 42114<br>−23422<br>244 202 | 42115<br>−23421<br>244 203 | 42116<br>−23420<br>244 204 | 42117<br>−23419<br>244 205 | 42118<br>−23418<br>244 206 | 42119<br>−23417<br>244 207 | 42120<br>−23416<br>244 210 | 42121<br>−23415<br>244 211 | 42122<br>−23414<br>244 212 | 42123<br>−23413<br>244 213 | 42124<br>−23412<br>244 214 | 42125<br>−23411<br>244 215 | 42126<br>−23410<br>244 216 | 42127<br>−23409<br>244 217 |
| **9−** | 42128<br>−23408<br>244 220 | 42129<br>−23407<br>244 221 | 42130<br>−23406<br>244 222 | 42131<br>−23405<br>244 223 | 42132<br>−23404<br>244 224 | 42133<br>−23403<br>244 225 | 42134<br>−23402<br>244 226 | 42135<br>−23401<br>244 227 | 42136<br>−23400<br>244 230 | 42137<br>−23399<br>244 231 | 42138<br>−23398<br>244 232 | 42139<br>−23397<br>244 233 | 42140<br>−23396<br>244 234 | 42141<br>−23395<br>244 235 | 42142<br>−23394<br>244 236 | 42143<br>−23393<br>244 237 |
| **A−** | 42144<br>−23392<br>244 240 | 42145<br>−23391<br>244 241 | 42146<br>−23390<br>244 242 | 42147<br>−23389<br>244 243 | 42148<br>−23388<br>244 244 | 42149<br>−23387<br>244 245 | 42150<br>−23386<br>244 246 | 42151<br>−23385<br>244 247 | 42152<br>−23384<br>244 250 | 42153<br>−23383<br>244 251 | 42154<br>−23382<br>244 252 | 42155<br>−23381<br>244 253 | 42156<br>−23380<br>244 254 | 42157<br>−23379<br>244 255 | 42158<br>−23378<br>244 256 | 42159<br>−23377<br>244 257 |
| **B−** | 42160<br>−23376<br>244 260 | 42161<br>−23375<br>244 261 | 42162<br>−23374<br>244 262 | 42163<br>−23373<br>244 263 | 42164<br>−23372<br>244 264 | 42165<br>−23371<br>244 265 | 42166<br>−23370<br>244 266 | 42167<br>−23369<br>244 267 | 42168<br>−23368<br>244 270 | 42169<br>−23367<br>244 271 | 42170<br>−23366<br>244 272 | 42171<br>−23365<br>244 273 | 42172<br>−23364<br>244 274 | 42173<br>−23363<br>244 275 | 42174<br>−23362<br>244 276 | 42175<br>−23361<br>244 277 |
| **C−** | 42176<br>−23360<br>244 300 | 42177<br>−23359<br>244 301 | 42178<br>−23358<br>244 302 | 42179<br>−23357<br>244 303 | 42180<br>−23356<br>244 304 | 42181<br>−23355<br>244 305 | 42182<br>−23354<br>244 306 | 42183<br>−23353<br>244 307 | 42184<br>−23352<br>244 310 | 42185<br>−23351<br>244 311 | 42186<br>−23350<br>244 312 | 42187<br>−23349<br>244 313 | 42188<br>−23348<br>244 314 | 42189<br>−23347<br>244 315 | 42190<br>−23346<br>244 316 | 42191<br>−23345<br>244 317 |
| **D−** | 42192<br>−23344<br>244 320 | 42193<br>−23343<br>244 321 | 42194<br>−23342<br>244 322 | 42195<br>−23341<br>244 323 | 42196<br>−23340<br>244 324 | 42197<br>−23339<br>244 325 | 42198<br>−23338<br>244 326 | 42199<br>−23337<br>244 327 | 42200<br>−23336<br>244 330 | 42201<br>−23335<br>244 331 | 42202<br>−23334<br>244 332 | 42203<br>−23333<br>244 333 | 42204<br>−23332<br>244 334 | 42205<br>−23331<br>244 335 | 42206<br>−23330<br>244 336 | 42207<br>−23329<br>244 337 |
| **E−** | 42208<br>−23328<br>244 340 | 42209<br>−23327<br>244 341 | 42210<br>−23326<br>244 342 | 42211<br>−23325<br>244 343 | 42212<br>−23324<br>244 344 | 42213<br>−23323<br>244 345 | 42214<br>−23322<br>244 346 | 42215<br>−23321<br>244 347 | 42216<br>−23320<br>244 350 | 42217<br>−23319<br>244 351 | 42218<br>−23318<br>244 352 | 42219<br>−23317<br>244 353 | 42220<br>−23316<br>244 354 | 42221<br>−23315<br>244 355 | 42222<br>−23314<br>244 356 | 42223<br>−23313<br>244 357 |
| **F−** | 42224<br>−23312<br>244 360 | 42225<br>−23311<br>244 361 | 42226<br>−23310<br>244 362 | 42227<br>−23309<br>244 363 | 42228<br>−23308<br>244 364 | 42229<br>−23307<br>244 365 | 42230<br>−23306<br>244 366 | 42231<br>−23305<br>244 367 | 42232<br>−23304<br>244 370 | 42233<br>−23303<br>244 371 | 42234<br>−23302<br>244 372 | 42235<br>−23301<br>244 373 | 42236<br>−23300<br>244 374 | 42237<br>−23299<br>244 375 | 42238<br>−23298<br>244 376 | 42239<br>−23297<br>244 377 |

**DECIMAL** →

 **DECIMAL** →

**OCTAL** →

 **DECIMAL** −23552  **BINARY** 1010 0100  **DECIMAL** 41984  **HEXADECIMAL** ⬡ A4  **OCTAL** 244 000

FOURTH HEX DIGIT → A4 ← THIRD HEX DIGIT

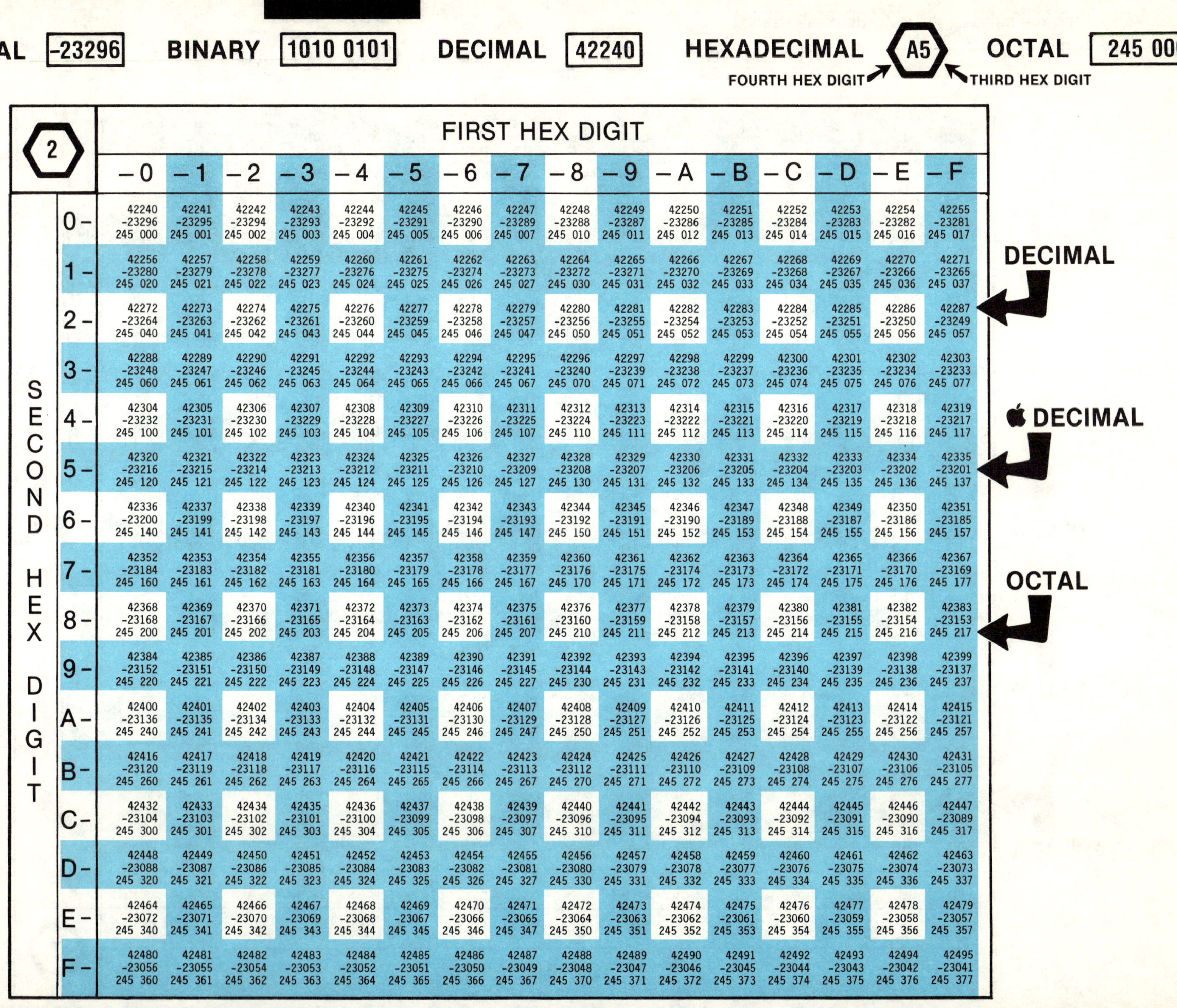


| 2 | −0 | −1 | −2 | −3 | −4 | −5 | −6 | −7 | −8 | −9 | −A | −B | −C | −D | −E | −F |
|---|---|---|---|---|---|---|---|---|---|---|---|---|---|---|---|---|
| 0− | 42240 −23296 245 000 | 42241 −23295 245 001 | 42242 −23294 245 002 | 42243 −23293 245 003 | 42244 −23292 245 004 | 42245 −23291 245 005 | 42246 −23290 245 006 | 42247 −23289 245 007 | 42248 −23288 245 010 | 42249 −23287 245 011 | 42250 −23286 245 012 | 42251 −23285 245 013 | 42252 −23284 245 014 | 42253 −23283 245 015 | 42254 −23282 245 016 | 42255 −23281 245 017 |
| 1− | 42256 −23280 245 020 | 42257 −23279 245 021 | 42258 −23278 245 022 | 42259 −23277 245 023 | 42260 −23276 245 024 | 42261 −23275 245 025 | 42262 −23274 245 026 | 42263 −23273 245 027 | 42264 −23272 245 030 | 42265 −23271 245 031 | 42266 −23270 245 032 | 42267 −23269 245 033 | 42268 −23268 245 034 | 42269 −23267 245 035 | 42270 −23266 245 036 | 42271 −23265 245 037 |
| 2− | 42272 −23264 245 040 | 42273 −23263 245 041 | 42274 −23262 245 042 | 42275 −23261 245 043 | 42276 −23260 245 044 | 42277 −23259 245 045 | 42278 −23258 245 046 | 42279 −23257 245 047 | 42280 −23256 245 050 | 42281 −23255 245 051 | 42282 −23254 245 052 | 42283 −23253 245 053 | 42284 −23252 245 054 | 42285 −23251 245 055 | 42286 −23250 245 056 | 42287 −23249 245 057 |
| 3− | 42288 −23248 245 060 | 42289 −23247 245 061 | 42290 −23246 245 062 | 42291 −23245 245 063 | 42292 −23244 245 064 | 42293 −23243 245 065 | 42294 −23242 245 066 | 42295 −23241 245 067 | 42296 −23240 245 070 | 42297 −23239 245 071 | 42298 −23238 245 072 | 42299 −23237 245 073 | 42300 −23236 245 074 | 42301 −23235 245 075 | 42302 −23234 245 076 | 42303 −23233 245 077 |
| 4− | 42304 −23232 245 100 | 42305 −23231 245 101 | 42306 −23230 245 102 | 42307 −23229 245 103 | 42308 −23228 245 104 | 42309 −23227 245 105 | 42310 −23226 245 106 | 42311 −23225 245 107 | 42312 −23224 245 110 | 42313 −23223 245 111 | 42314 −23222 245 112 | 42315 −23221 245 113 | 42316 −23220 245 114 | 42317 −23219 245 115 | 42318 −23218 245 116 | 42319 −23217 245 117 |
| 5− | 42320 −23216 245 120 | 42321 −23215 245 121 | 42322 −23214 245 122 | 42323 −23213 245 123 | 42324 −23212 245 124 | 42325 −23211 245 125 | 42326 −23210 245 126 | 42327 −23209 245 127 | 42328 −23208 245 130 | 42329 −23207 245 131 | 42330 −23206 245 132 | 42331 −23205 245 133 | 42332 −23204 245 134 | 42333 −23203 245 135 | 42334 −23202 245 136 | 42335 −23201 245 137 |
| 6− | 42336 −23200 245 140 | 42337 −23199 245 141 | 42338 −23198 245 142 | 42339 −23197 245 143 | 42340 −23196 245 144 | 42341 −23195 245 145 | 42342 −23194 245 146 | 42343 −23193 245 147 | 42344 −23192 245 150 | 42345 −23191 245 151 | 42346 −23190 245 152 | 42347 −23189 245 153 | 42348 −23188 245 154 | 42349 −23187 245 155 | 42350 −23186 245 156 | 42351 −23185 245 157 |
| 7− | 42352 −23184 245 160 | 42353 −23183 245 161 | 42354 −23182 245 162 | 42355 −23181 245 163 | 42356 −23180 245 164 | 42357 −23179 245 165 | 42358 −23178 245 166 | 42359 −23177 245 167 | 42360 −23176 245 170 | 42361 −23175 245 171 | 42362 −23174 245 172 | 42363 −23173 245 173 | 42364 −23172 245 174 | 42365 −23171 245 175 | 42366 −23170 245 176 | 42367 −23169 245 177 |
| 8− | 42368 −23168 245 200 | 42369 −23167 245 201 | 42370 −23166 245 202 | 42371 −23165 245 203 | 42372 −23164 245 204 | 42373 −23163 245 205 | 42374 −23162 245 206 | 42375 −23161 245 207 | 42376 −23160 245 210 | 42377 −23159 245 211 | 42378 −23158 245 212 | 42379 −23157 245 213 | 42380 −23156 245 214 | 42381 −23155 245 215 | 42382 −23154 245 216 | 42383 −23153 245 217 |
| 9− | 42384 −23152 245 220 | 42385 −23151 245 221 | 42386 −23150 245 222 | 42387 −23149 245 223 | 42388 −23148 245 224 | 42389 −23147 245 225 | 42390 −23146 245 226 | 42391 −23145 245 227 | 42392 −23144 245 230 | 42393 −23143 245 231 | 42394 −23142 245 232 | 42395 −23141 245 233 | 42396 −23140 245 234 | 42397 −23139 245 235 | 42398 −23138 245 236 | 42399 −23137 245 237 |
| A− | 42400 −23136 245 240 | 42401 −23135 245 241 | 42402 −23134 245 242 | 42403 −23133 245 243 | 42404 −23132 245 244 | 42405 −23131 245 245 | 42406 −23130 245 246 | 42407 −23129 245 247 | 42408 −23128 245 250 | 42409 −23127 245 251 | 42410 −23126 245 252 | 42411 −23125 245 253 | 42412 −23124 245 254 | 42413 −23123 245 255 | 42414 −23122 245 256 | 42415 −23121 245 257 |
| B− | 42416 −23120 245 260 | 42417 −23119 245 261 | 42418 −23118 245 262 | 42419 −23117 245 263 | 42420 −23116 245 264 | 42421 −23115 245 265 | 42422 −23114 245 266 | 42423 −23113 245 267 | 42424 −23112 245 270 | 42425 −23111 245 271 | 42426 −23110 245 272 | 42427 −23109 245 273 | 42428 −23108 245 274 | 42429 −23107 245 275 | 42430 −23106 245 276 | 42431 −23105 245 277 |
| C− | 42432 −23104 245 300 | 42433 −23103 245 301 | 42434 −23102 245 302 | 42435 −23101 245 303 | 42436 −23100 245 304 | 42437 −23099 245 305 | 42438 −23098 245 306 | 42439 −23097 245 307 | 42440 −23096 245 310 | 42441 −23095 245 311 | 42442 −23094 245 312 | 42443 −23093 245 313 | 42444 −23092 245 314 | 42445 −23091 245 315 | 42446 −23090 245 316 | 42447 −23089 245 317 |
| D− | 42448 −23088 245 320 | 42449 −23087 245 321 | 42450 −23086 245 322 | 42451 −23085 245 323 | 42452 −23084 245 324 | 42453 −23083 245 325 | 42454 −23082 245 326 | 42455 −23081 245 327 | 42456 −23080 245 330 | 42457 −23079 245 331 | 42458 −23078 245 332 | 42459 −23077 245 333 | 42460 −23076 245 334 | 42461 −23075 245 335 | 42462 −23074 245 336 | 42463 −23073 245 337 |
| E− | 42464 −23072 245 340 | 42465 −23071 245 341 | 42466 −23070 245 342 | 42467 −23069 245 343 | 42468 −23068 245 344 | 42469 −23067 245 345 | 42470 −23066 245 346 | 42471 −23065 245 347 | 42472 −23064 245 350 | 42473 −23063 245 351 | 42474 −23062 245 352 | 42475 −23061 245 353 | 42476 −23060 245 354 | 42477 −23059 245 355 | 42478 −23058 245 356 | 42479 −23057 245 357 |
| F− | 42480 −23056 245 360 | 42481 −23055 245 361 | 42482 −23054 245 362 | 42483 −23053 245 363 | 42484 −23052 245 364 | 42485 −23051 245 365 | 42486 −23050 245 366 | 42487 −23049 245 367 | 42488 −23048 245 370 | 42489 −23047 245 371 | 42490 −23046 245 372 | 42491 −23045 245 373 | 42492 −23044 245 374 | 42493 −23043 245 375 | 42494 −23042 245 376 | 42495 −23041 245 377 |

SECOND HEX DIGIT

| | −0 | −1 | −2 | −3 | −4 | −5 | −6 | −7 | −8 | −9 | −A | −B | −C | −D | −E | −F |
|---|---|---|---|---|---|---|---|---|---|---|---|---|---|---|---|---|
| **0−** | 42496<br>−23040<br>246 000 | 42497<br>−23039<br>246 001 | 42498<br>−23038<br>246 002 | 42499<br>−23037<br>246 003 | 42500<br>−23036<br>246 004 | 42501<br>−23035<br>246 005 | 42502<br>−23034<br>246 006 | 42503<br>−23033<br>246 007 | 42504<br>−23032<br>246 010 | 42505<br>−23031<br>246 011 | 42506<br>−23030<br>246 012 | 42507<br>−23029<br>246 013 | 42508<br>−23028<br>246 014 | 42509<br>−23027<br>246 015 | 42510<br>−23026<br>246 016 | 42511<br>−23025<br>246 017 |
| **1−** | 42512<br>−23024<br>246 020 | 42513<br>−23023<br>246 021 | 42514<br>−23022<br>246 022 | 42515<br>−23021<br>246 023 | 42516<br>−23020<br>246 024 | 42517<br>−23019<br>246 025 | 42518<br>−23018<br>246 026 | 42519<br>−23017<br>246 027 | 42520<br>−23016<br>246 030 | 42521<br>−23015<br>246 031 | 42522<br>−23014<br>246 032 | 42523<br>−23013<br>246 033 | 42524<br>−23012<br>246 034 | 42525<br>−23011<br>246 035 | 42526<br>−23010<br>246 036 | 42527<br>−23009<br>246 037 |
| **2−** | 42528<br>−23008<br>246 040 | 42529<br>−23007<br>246 041 | 42530<br>−23006<br>246 042 | 42531<br>−23005<br>246 043 | 42532<br>−23004<br>246 044 | 42533<br>−23003<br>246 045 | 42534<br>−23002<br>246 046 | 42535<br>−23001<br>246 047 | 42536<br>−23000<br>246 050 | 42537<br>−22999<br>246 051 | 42538<br>−22998<br>246 052 | 42539<br>−22997<br>246 053 | 42540<br>−22996<br>246 054 | 42541<br>−22995<br>246 055 | 42542<br>−22994<br>246 056 | 42543<br>−22993<br>246 057 |
| **3−** | 42544<br>−22992<br>246 060 | 42545<br>−22991<br>246 061 | 42546<br>−22990<br>246 062 | 42547<br>−22989<br>246 063 | 42548<br>−22988<br>246 064 | 42549<br>−22987<br>246 065 | 42550<br>−22986<br>246 066 | 42551<br>−22985<br>246 067 | 42552<br>−22984<br>246 070 | 42553<br>−22983<br>246 071 | 42554<br>−22982<br>246 072 | 42555<br>−22981<br>246 073 | 42556<br>−22980<br>246 074 | 42557<br>−22979<br>246 075 | 42558<br>−22978<br>246 076 | 42559<br>−22977<br>246 077 |
| **4−** | 42560<br>−22976<br>246 100 | 42561<br>−22975<br>246 101 | 42562<br>−22974<br>246 102 | 42563<br>−22973<br>246 103 | 42564<br>−22972<br>246 104 | 42565<br>−22971<br>246 105 | 42566<br>−22970<br>246 106 | 42567<br>−22969<br>246 107 | 42568<br>−22968<br>246 110 | 42569<br>−22967<br>246 111 | 42570<br>−22966<br>246 112 | 42571<br>−22965<br>246 113 | 42572<br>−22964<br>246 114 | 42573<br>−22963<br>246 115 | 42574<br>−22962<br>246 116 | 42575<br>−22961<br>246 117 |
| **5−** | 42576<br>−22960<br>246 120 | 42577<br>−22959<br>246 121 | 42578<br>−22958<br>246 122 | 42579<br>−22957<br>246 123 | 42580<br>−22956<br>246 124 | 42581<br>−22955<br>246 125 | 42582<br>−22954<br>246 126 | 42583<br>−22953<br>246 127 | 42584<br>−22952<br>246 130 | 42585<br>−22951<br>246 131 | 42586<br>−22950<br>246 132 | 42587<br>−22949<br>246 133 | 42588<br>−22948<br>246 134 | 42589<br>−22947<br>246 135 | 42590<br>−22946<br>246 136 | 42591<br>−22945<br>246 137 |
| **6−** | 42592<br>−22944<br>246 140 | 42593<br>−22943<br>246 141 | 42594<br>−22942<br>246 142 | 42595<br>−22941<br>246 143 | 42596<br>−22940<br>246 144 | 42597<br>−22939<br>246 145 | 42598<br>−22938<br>246 146 | 42599<br>−22937<br>246 147 | 42600<br>−22936<br>246 150 | 42601<br>−22935<br>246 151 | 42602<br>−22934<br>246 152 | 42603<br>−22933<br>246 153 | 42604<br>−22932<br>246 154 | 42605<br>−22931<br>246 155 | 42606<br>−22930<br>246 156 | 42607<br>−22929<br>246 157 |
| **7−** | 42608<br>−22928<br>246 160 | 42609<br>−22927<br>246 161 | 42610<br>−22926<br>246 162 | 42611<br>−22925<br>246 163 | 42612<br>−22924<br>246 164 | 42613<br>−22923<br>246 165 | 42614<br>−22922<br>246 166 | 42615<br>−22921<br>246 167 | 42616<br>−22920<br>246 170 | 42617<br>−22919<br>246 171 | 42618<br>−22918<br>246 172 | 42619<br>−22917<br>246 173 | 42620<br>−22916<br>246 174 | 42621<br>−22915<br>246 175 | 42622<br>−22914<br>246 176 | 42623<br>−22913<br>246 177 |
| **8−** | 42624<br>−22912<br>246 200 | 42625<br>−22911<br>246 201 | 42626<br>−22910<br>246 202 | 42627<br>−22909<br>246 203 | 42628<br>−22908<br>246 204 | 42629<br>−22907<br>246 205 | 42630<br>−22906<br>246 206 | 42631<br>−22905<br>246 207 | 42632<br>−22904<br>246 210 | 42633<br>−22903<br>246 211 | 42634<br>−22902<br>246 212 | 42635<br>−22901<br>246 213 | 42636<br>−22900<br>246 214 | 42637<br>−22899<br>246 215 | 42638<br>−22898<br>246 216 | 42639<br>−22897<br>246 217 |
| **9−** | 42640<br>−22896<br>246 220 | 42641<br>−22895<br>246 221 | 42642<br>−22894<br>246 222 | 42643<br>−22893<br>246 223 | 42644<br>−22892<br>246 224 | 42645<br>−22891<br>246 225 | 42646<br>−22890<br>246 226 | 42647<br>−22889<br>246 227 | 42648<br>−22888<br>246 230 | 42649<br>−22887<br>246 231 | 42650<br>−22886<br>246 232 | 42651<br>−22885<br>246 233 | 42652<br>−22884<br>246 234 | 42653<br>−22883<br>246 235 | 42654<br>−22882<br>246 236 | 42655<br>−22881<br>246 237 |
| **A−** | 42656<br>−22880<br>246 240 | 42657<br>−22879<br>246 241 | 42658<br>−22878<br>246 242 | 42659<br>−22877<br>246 243 | 42660<br>−22876<br>246 244 | 42661<br>−22875<br>246 245 | 42662<br>−22874<br>246 246 | 42663<br>−22873<br>246 247 | 42664<br>−22872<br>246 250 | 42665<br>−22871<br>246 251 | 42666<br>−22870<br>246 252 | 42667<br>−22869<br>246 253 | 42668<br>−22868<br>246 254 | 42669<br>−22867<br>246 255 | 42670<br>−22866<br>246 256 | 42671<br>−22865<br>246 257 |
| **B−** | 42672<br>−22864<br>246 260 | 42673<br>−22863<br>246 261 | 42674<br>−22862<br>246 262 | 42675<br>−22861<br>246 263 | 42676<br>−22860<br>246 264 | 42677<br>−22859<br>246 265 | 42678<br>−22858<br>246 266 | 42679<br>−22857<br>246 267 | 42680<br>−22856<br>246 270 | 42681<br>−22855<br>246 271 | 42682<br>−22854<br>246 272 | 42683<br>−22853<br>246 273 | 42684<br>−22852<br>246 274 | 42685<br>−22851<br>246 275 | 42686<br>−22850<br>246 276 | 42687<br>−22849<br>246 277 |
| **C−** | 42688<br>−22848<br>246 300 | 42689<br>−22847<br>246 301 | 42690<br>−22846<br>246 302 | 42691<br>−22845<br>246 303 | 42692<br>−22844<br>246 304 | 42693<br>−22843<br>246 305 | 42694<br>−22842<br>246 306 | 42695<br>−22841<br>246 307 | 42696<br>−22840<br>246 310 | 42697<br>−22839<br>246 311 | 42698<br>−22838<br>246 312 | 42699<br>−22837<br>246 313 | 42700<br>−22836<br>246 314 | 42701<br>−22835<br>246 315 | 42702<br>−22834<br>246 316 | 42703<br>−22833<br>246 317 |
| **D−** | 42704<br>−22832<br>246 320 | 42705<br>−22831<br>246 321 | 42706<br>−22830<br>246 322 | 42707<br>−22829<br>246 323 | 42708<br>−22828<br>246 324 | 42709<br>−22827<br>246 325 | 42710<br>−22826<br>246 326 | 42711<br>−22825<br>246 327 | 42712<br>−22824<br>246 330 | 42713<br>−22823<br>246 331 | 42714<br>−22822<br>246 332 | 42715<br>−22821<br>246 333 | 42716<br>−22820<br>246 334 | 42717<br>−22819<br>246 335 | 42718<br>−22818<br>246 336 | 42719<br>−22817<br>246 337 |
| **E−** | 42720<br>−22816<br>246 340 | 42721<br>−22815<br>246 341 | 42722<br>−22814<br>246 342 | 42723<br>−22813<br>246 343 | 42724<br>−22812<br>246 344 | 42725<br>−22811<br>246 345 | 42726<br>−22810<br>246 346 | 42727<br>−22809<br>246 347 | 42728<br>−22808<br>246 350 | 42729<br>−22807<br>246 351 | 42730<br>−22806<br>246 352 | 42731<br>−22805<br>246 353 | 42732<br>−22804<br>246 354 | 42733<br>−22803<br>246 355 | 42734<br>−22802<br>246 356 | 42735<br>−22801<br>246 357 |
| **F−** | 42736<br>−22800<br>246 360 | 42737<br>−22799<br>246 361 | 42738<br>−22798<br>246 362 | 42739<br>−22797<br>246 363 | 42740<br>−22796<br>246 364 | 42741<br>−22795<br>246 365 | 42742<br>−22794<br>246 366 | 42743<br>−22793<br>246 367 | 42744<br>−22792<br>246 370 | 42745<br>−22791<br>246 371 | 42746<br>−22790<br>246 372 | 42747<br>−22789<br>246 373 | 42748<br>−22788<br>246 374 | 42749<br>−22787<br>246 375 | 42750<br>−22786<br>246 376 | 42751<br>−22785<br>246 377 |

DECIMAL → (42543)

 DECIMAL → (42591)

OCTAL → (246 217)

 DECIMAL −23040    BINARY 1010 0110    DECIMAL 42496    HEXADECIMAL  A6    OCTAL 246 000

FOURTH HEX DIGIT →    ← THIRD HEX DIGIT

 DECIMAL -22784    BINARY 1010 0111    DECIMAL 42752    HEXADECIMAL A7    OCTAL 247 000

FOURTH HEX DIGIT → A7 ← THIRD HEX DIGIT

**② — FIRST HEX DIGIT / SECOND HEX DIGIT**

Each cell lists: decimal (positive) / decimal (negative) / octal.

| SECOND HEX DIGIT | −0 | −1 | −2 | −3 | −4 | −5 | −6 | −7 | −8 | −9 | −A | −B | −C | −D | −E | −F |
|---|---|---|---|---|---|---|---|---|---|---|---|---|---|---|---|---|
| 0− | 42752<br>−22784<br>247 000 | 42753<br>−22783<br>247 001 | 42754<br>−22782<br>247 002 | 42755<br>−22781<br>247 003 | 42756<br>−22780<br>247 004 | 42757<br>−22779<br>247 005 | 42758<br>−22778<br>247 006 | 42759<br>−22777<br>247 007 | 42760<br>−22776<br>247 010 | 42761<br>−22775<br>247 011 | 42762<br>−22774<br>247 012 | 42763<br>−22773<br>247 013 | 42764<br>−22772<br>247 014 | 42765<br>−22771<br>247 015 | 42766<br>−22770<br>247 016 | 42767<br>−22769<br>247 017 |
| 1− | 42768<br>−22768<br>247 020 | 42769<br>−22767<br>247 021 | 42770<br>−22766<br>247 022 | 42771<br>−22765<br>247 023 | 42772<br>−22764<br>247 024 | 42773<br>−22763<br>247 025 | 42774<br>−22762<br>247 026 | 42775<br>−22761<br>247 027 | 42776<br>−22760<br>247 030 | 42777<br>−22759<br>247 031 | 42778<br>−22758<br>247 032 | 42779<br>−22757<br>247 033 | 42780<br>−22756<br>247 034 | 42781<br>−22755<br>247 035 | 42782<br>−22754<br>247 036 | 42783<br>−22753<br>247 037 |
| 2− | 42784<br>−22752<br>247 040 | 42785<br>−22751<br>247 041 | 42786<br>−22750<br>247 042 | 42787<br>−22749<br>247 043 | 42788<br>−22748<br>247 044 | 42789<br>−22747<br>247 045 | 42790<br>−22746<br>247 046 | 42791<br>−22745<br>247 047 | 42792<br>−22744<br>247 050 | 42793<br>−22743<br>247 051 | 42794<br>−22742<br>247 052 | 42795<br>−22741<br>247 053 | 42796<br>−22740<br>247 054 | 42797<br>−22739<br>247 055 | 42798<br>−22738<br>247 056 | 42799<br>−22737<br>247 057 |
| 3− | 42800<br>−22736<br>247 060 | 42801<br>−22735<br>247 061 | 42802<br>−22734<br>247 062 | 42803<br>−22733<br>247 063 | 42804<br>−22732<br>247 064 | 42805<br>−22731<br>247 065 | 42806<br>−22730<br>247 066 | 42807<br>−22729<br>247 067 | 42808<br>−22728<br>247 070 | 42809<br>−22727<br>247 071 | 42810<br>−22726<br>247 072 | 42811<br>−22725<br>247 073 | 42812<br>−22724<br>247 074 | 42813<br>−22723<br>247 075 | 42814<br>−22722<br>247 076 | 42815<br>−22721<br>247 077 |
| 4− | 42816<br>−22720<br>247 100 | 42817<br>−22719<br>247 101 | 42818<br>−22718<br>247 102 | 42819<br>−22717<br>247 103 | 42820<br>−22716<br>247 104 | 42821<br>−22715<br>247 105 | 42822<br>−22714<br>247 106 | 42823<br>−22713<br>247 107 | 42824<br>−22712<br>247 110 | 42825<br>−22711<br>247 111 | 42826<br>−22710<br>247 112 | 42827<br>−22709<br>247 113 | 42828<br>−22708<br>247 114 | 42829<br>−22707<br>247 115 | 42830<br>−22706<br>247 116 | 42831<br>−22705<br>247 117 |
| 5− | 42832<br>−22704<br>247 120 | 42833<br>−22703<br>247 121 | 42834<br>−22702<br>247 122 | 42835<br>−22701<br>247 123 | 42836<br>−22700<br>247 124 | 42837<br>−22699<br>247 125 | 42838<br>−22698<br>247 126 | 42839<br>−22697<br>247 127 | 42840<br>−22696<br>247 130 | 42841<br>−22695<br>247 131 | 42842<br>−22694<br>247 132 | 42843<br>−22693<br>247 133 | 42844<br>−22692<br>247 134 | 42845<br>−22691<br>247 135 | 42846<br>−22690<br>247 136 | 42847<br>−22689<br>247 137 |
| 6− | 42848<br>−22688<br>247 140 | 42849<br>−22687<br>247 141 | 42850<br>−22686<br>247 142 | 42851<br>−22685<br>247 143 | 42852<br>−22684<br>247 144 | 42853<br>−22683<br>247 145 | 42854<br>−22682<br>247 146 | 42855<br>−22681<br>247 147 | 42856<br>−22680<br>247 150 | 42857<br>−22679<br>247 151 | 42858<br>−22678<br>247 152 | 42859<br>−22677<br>247 153 | 42860<br>−22676<br>247 154 | 42861<br>−22675<br>247 155 | 42862<br>−22674<br>247 156 | 42863<br>−22673<br>247 157 |
| 7− | 42864<br>−22672<br>247 160 | 42865<br>−22671<br>247 161 | 42866<br>−22670<br>247 162 | 42867<br>−22669<br>247 163 | 42868<br>−22668<br>247 164 | 42869<br>−22667<br>247 165 | 42870<br>−22666<br>247 166 | 42871<br>−22665<br>247 167 | 42872<br>−22664<br>247 170 | 42873<br>−22663<br>247 171 | 42874<br>−22662<br>247 172 | 42875<br>−22661<br>247 173 | 42876<br>−22660<br>247 174 | 42877<br>−22659<br>247 175 | 42878<br>−22658<br>247 176 | 42879<br>−22657<br>247 177 |
| 8− | 42880<br>−22656<br>247 200 | 42881<br>−22655<br>247 201 | 42882<br>−22654<br>247 202 | 42883<br>−22653<br>247 203 | 42884<br>−22652<br>247 204 | 42885<br>−22651<br>247 205 | 42886<br>−22650<br>247 206 | 42887<br>−22649<br>247 207 | 42888<br>−22648<br>247 210 | 42889<br>−22647<br>247 211 | 42890<br>−22646<br>247 212 | 42891<br>−22645<br>247 213 | 42892<br>−22644<br>247 214 | 42893<br>−22643<br>247 215 | 42894<br>−22642<br>247 216 | 42895<br>−22641<br>247 217 |
| 9− | 42896<br>−22640<br>247 220 | 42897<br>−22639<br>247 221 | 42898<br>−22638<br>247 222 | 42899<br>−22637<br>247 223 | 42900<br>−22636<br>247 224 | 42901<br>−22635<br>247 225 | 42902<br>−22634<br>247 226 | 42903<br>−22633<br>247 227 | 42904<br>−22632<br>247 230 | 42905<br>−22631<br>247 231 | 42906<br>−22630<br>247 232 | 42907<br>−22629<br>247 233 | 42908<br>−22628<br>247 234 | 42909<br>−22627<br>247 235 | 42910<br>−22626<br>247 236 | 42911<br>−22625<br>247 237 |
| A− | 42912<br>−22624<br>247 240 | 42913<br>−22623<br>247 241 | 42914<br>−22622<br>247 242 | 42915<br>−22621<br>247 243 | 42916<br>−22620<br>247 244 | 42917<br>−22619<br>247 245 | 42918<br>−22618<br>247 246 | 42919<br>−22617<br>247 247 | 42920<br>−22616<br>247 250 | 42921<br>−22615<br>247 251 | 42922<br>−22614<br>247 252 | 42923<br>−22613<br>247 253 | 42924<br>−22612<br>247 254 | 42925<br>−22611<br>247 255 | 42926<br>−22610<br>247 256 | 42927<br>−22609<br>247 257 |
| B− | 42928<br>−22608<br>247 260 | 42929<br>−22607<br>247 261 | 42930<br>−22606<br>247 262 | 42931<br>−22605<br>247 263 | 42932<br>−22604<br>247 264 | 42933<br>−22603<br>247 265 | 42934<br>−22602<br>247 266 | 42935<br>−22601<br>247 267 | 42936<br>−22600<br>247 270 | 42937<br>−22599<br>247 271 | 42938<br>−22598<br>247 272 | 42939<br>−22597<br>247 273 | 42940<br>−22596<br>247 274 | 42941<br>−22595<br>247 275 | 42942<br>−22594<br>247 276 | 42943<br>−22593<br>247 277 |
| C− | 42944<br>−22592<br>247 300 | 42945<br>−22591<br>247 301 | 42946<br>−22590<br>247 302 | 42947<br>−22589<br>247 303 | 42948<br>−22588<br>247 304 | 42949<br>−22587<br>247 305 | 42950<br>−22586<br>247 306 | 42951<br>−22585<br>247 307 | 42952<br>−22584<br>247 310 | 42953<br>−22583<br>247 311 | 42954<br>−22582<br>247 312 | 42955<br>−22581<br>247 313 | 42956<br>−22580<br>247 314 | 42957<br>−22579<br>247 315 | 42958<br>−22578<br>247 316 | 42959<br>−22577<br>247 317 |
| D− | 42960<br>−22576<br>247 320 | 42961<br>−22575<br>247 321 | 42962<br>−22574<br>247 322 | 42963<br>−22573<br>247 323 | 42964<br>−22572<br>247 324 | 42965<br>−22571<br>247 325 | 42966<br>−22570<br>247 326 | 42967<br>−22569<br>247 327 | 42968<br>−22568<br>247 330 | 42969<br>−22567<br>247 331 | 42970<br>−22566<br>247 332 | 42971<br>−22565<br>247 333 | 42972<br>−22564<br>247 334 | 42973<br>−22563<br>247 335 | 42974<br>−22562<br>247 336 | 42975<br>−22561<br>247 337 |
| E− | 42976<br>−22560<br>247 340 | 42977<br>−22559<br>247 341 | 42978<br>−22558<br>247 342 | 42979<br>−22557<br>247 343 | 42980<br>−22556<br>247 344 | 42981<br>−22555<br>247 345 | 42982<br>−22554<br>247 346 | 42983<br>−22553<br>247 347 | 42984<br>−22552<br>247 350 | 42985<br>−22551<br>247 351 | 42986<br>−22550<br>247 352 | 42987<br>−22549<br>247 353 | 42988<br>−22548<br>247 354 | 42989<br>−22547<br>247 355 | 42990<br>−22546<br>247 356 | 42991<br>−22545<br>247 357 |
| F− | 42992<br>−22544<br>247 360 | 42993<br>−22543<br>247 361 | 42994<br>−22542<br>247 362 | 42995<br>−22541<br>247 363 | 42996<br>−22540<br>247 364 | 42997<br>−22539<br>247 365 | 42998<br>−22538<br>247 366 | 42999<br>−22537<br>247 367 | 43000<br>−22536<br>247 370 | 43001<br>−22535<br>247 371 | 43002<br>−22534<br>247 372 | 43003<br>−22533<br>247 373 | 43004<br>−22532<br>247 374 | 43005<br>−22531<br>247 375 | 43006<br>−22530<br>247 376 | 43007<br>−22529<br>247 377 |

DECIMAL ←  ● DECIMAL ←  OCTAL ←

# FIRST HEX DIGIT

**(2)**

Each cell shows: DECIMAL (top), DECIMAL (middle), OCTAL (bottom).

| SECOND HEX DIGIT | −0 | −1 | −2 | −3 | −4 | −5 | −6 | −7 | −8 | −9 | −A | −B | −C | −D | −E | −F |
|---|---|---|---|---|---|---|---|---|---|---|---|---|---|---|---|---|
| 0- | 43008<br>-22528<br>250 000 | 43009<br>-22527<br>250 001 | 43010<br>-22526<br>250 002 | 43011<br>-22525<br>250 003 | 43012<br>-22524<br>250 004 | 43013<br>-22523<br>250 005 | 43014<br>-22522<br>250 006 | 43015<br>-22521<br>250 007 | 43016<br>-22520<br>250 010 | 43017<br>-22519<br>250 011 | 43018<br>-22518<br>250 012 | 43019<br>-22517<br>250 013 | 43020<br>-22516<br>250 014 | 43021<br>-22515<br>250 015 | 43022<br>-22514<br>250 016 | 43023<br>-22513<br>250 017 |
| 1- | 43024<br>-22512<br>250 020 | 43025<br>-22511<br>250 021 | 43026<br>-22510<br>250 022 | 43027<br>-22509<br>250 023 | 43028<br>-22508<br>250 024 | 43029<br>-22507<br>250 025 | 43030<br>-22506<br>250 026 | 43031<br>-22505<br>250 027 | 43032<br>-22504<br>250 030 | 43033<br>-22503<br>250 031 | 43034<br>-22502<br>250 032 | 43035<br>-22501<br>250 033 | 43036<br>-22500<br>250 034 | 43037<br>-22499<br>250 035 | 43038<br>-22498<br>250 036 | 43039<br>-22497<br>250 037 |
| 2- | 43040<br>-22496<br>250 040 | 43041<br>-22495<br>250 041 | 43042<br>-22494<br>250 042 | 43043<br>-22493<br>250 043 | 43044<br>-22492<br>250 044 | 43045<br>-22491<br>250 045 | 43046<br>-22490<br>250 046 | 43047<br>-22489<br>250 047 | 43048<br>-22488<br>250 050 | 43049<br>-22487<br>250 051 | 43050<br>-22486<br>250 052 | 43051<br>-22485<br>250 053 | 43052<br>-22484<br>250 054 | 43053<br>-22483<br>250 055 | 43054<br>-22482<br>250 056 | 43055<br>-22481<br>250 057 |
| 3- | 43056<br>-22480<br>250 060 | 43057<br>-22479<br>250 061 | 43058<br>-22478<br>250 062 | 43059<br>-22477<br>250 063 | 43060<br>-22476<br>250 064 | 43061<br>-22475<br>250 065 | 43062<br>-22474<br>250 066 | 43063<br>-22473<br>250 067 | 43064<br>-22472<br>250 070 | 43065<br>-22471<br>250 071 | 43066<br>-22470<br>250 072 | 43067<br>-22469<br>250 073 | 43068<br>-22468<br>250 074 | 43069<br>-22467<br>250 075 | 43070<br>-22466<br>250 076 | 43071<br>-22465<br>250 077 |
| 4- | 43072<br>-22464<br>250 100 | 43073<br>-22463<br>250 101 | 43074<br>-22462<br>250 102 | 43075<br>-22461<br>250 103 | 43076<br>-22460<br>250 104 | 43077<br>-22459<br>250 105 | 43078<br>-22458<br>250 106 | 43079<br>-22457<br>250 107 | 43080<br>-22456<br>250 110 | 43081<br>-22455<br>250 111 | 43082<br>-22454<br>250 112 | 43083<br>-22453<br>250 113 | 43084<br>-22452<br>250 114 | 43085<br>-22451<br>250 115 | 43086<br>-22450<br>250 116 | 43087<br>-22449<br>250 117 |
| 5- | 43088<br>-22448<br>250 120 | 43089<br>-22447<br>250 121 | 43090<br>-22446<br>250 122 | 43091<br>-22445<br>250 123 | 43092<br>-22444<br>250 124 | 43093<br>-22443<br>250 125 | 43094<br>-22442<br>250 126 | 43095<br>-22441<br>250 127 | 43096<br>-22440<br>250 130 | 43097<br>-22439<br>250 131 | 43098<br>-22438<br>250 132 | 43099<br>-22437<br>250 133 | 43100<br>-22436<br>250 134 | 43101<br>-22435<br>250 135 | 43102<br>-22434<br>250 136 | 43103<br>-22433<br>250 137 |
| 6- | 43104<br>-22432<br>250 140 | 43105<br>-22431<br>250 141 | 43106<br>-22430<br>250 142 | 43107<br>-22429<br>250 143 | 43108<br>-22428<br>250 144 | 43109<br>-22427<br>250 145 | 43110<br>-22426<br>250 146 | 43111<br>-22425<br>250 147 | 43112<br>-22424<br>250 150 | 43113<br>-22423<br>250 151 | 43114<br>-22422<br>250 152 | 43115<br>-22421<br>250 153 | 43116<br>-22420<br>250 154 | 43117<br>-22419<br>250 155 | 43118<br>-22418<br>250 156 | 43119<br>-22417<br>250 157 |
| 7- | 43120<br>-22416<br>250 160 | 43121<br>-22415<br>250 161 | 43122<br>-22414<br>250 162 | 43123<br>-22413<br>250 163 | 43124<br>-22412<br>250 164 | 43125<br>-22411<br>250 165 | 43126<br>-22410<br>250 166 | 43127<br>-22409<br>250 167 | 43128<br>-22408<br>250 170 | 43129<br>-22407<br>250 171 | 43130<br>-22406<br>250 172 | 43131<br>-22405<br>250 173 | 43132<br>-22404<br>250 174 | 43133<br>-22403<br>250 175 | 43134<br>-22402<br>250 176 | 43135<br>-22401<br>250 177 |
| 8- | 43136<br>-22400<br>250 200 | 43137<br>-22399<br>250 201 | 43138<br>-22398<br>250 202 | 43139<br>-22397<br>250 203 | 43140<br>-22396<br>250 204 | 43141<br>-22395<br>250 205 | 43142<br>-22394<br>250 206 | 43143<br>-22393<br>250 207 | 43144<br>-22392<br>250 210 | 43145<br>-22391<br>250 211 | 43146<br>-22390<br>250 212 | 43147<br>-22389<br>250 213 | 43148<br>-22388<br>250 214 | 43149<br>-22387<br>250 215 | 43150<br>-22386<br>250 216 | 43151<br>-22385<br>250 217 |
| 9- | 43152<br>-22384<br>250 220 | 43153<br>-22383<br>250 221 | 43154<br>-22382<br>250 222 | 43155<br>-22381<br>250 223 | 43156<br>-22380<br>250 224 | 43157<br>-22379<br>250 225 | 43158<br>-22378<br>250 226 | 43159<br>-22377<br>250 227 | 43160<br>-22376<br>250 230 | 43161<br>-22375<br>250 231 | 43162<br>-22374<br>250 232 | 43163<br>-22373<br>250 233 | 43164<br>-22372<br>250 234 | 43165<br>-22371<br>250 235 | 43166<br>-22370<br>250 236 | 43167<br>-22369<br>250 237 |
| A- | 43168<br>-22368<br>250 240 | 43169<br>-22367<br>250 241 | 43170<br>-22366<br>250 242 | 43171<br>-22365<br>250 243 | 43172<br>-22364<br>250 244 | 43173<br>-22363<br>250 245 | 43174<br>-22362<br>250 246 | 43175<br>-22361<br>250 247 | 43176<br>-22360<br>250 250 | 43177<br>-22359<br>250 251 | 43178<br>-22358<br>250 252 | 43179<br>-22357<br>250 253 | 43180<br>-22356<br>250 254 | 43181<br>-22355<br>250 255 | 43182<br>-22354<br>250 256 | 43183<br>-22353<br>250 257 |
| B- | 43184<br>-22352<br>250 260 | 43185<br>-22351<br>250 261 | 43186<br>-22350<br>250 262 | 43187<br>-22349<br>250 263 | 43188<br>-22348<br>250 264 | 43189<br>-22347<br>250 265 | 43190<br>-22346<br>250 266 | 43191<br>-22345<br>250 267 | 43192<br>-22344<br>250 270 | 43193<br>-22343<br>250 271 | 43194<br>-22342<br>250 272 | 43195<br>-22341<br>250 273 | 43196<br>-22340<br>250 274 | 43197<br>-22339<br>250 275 | 43198<br>-22338<br>250 276 | 43199<br>-22337<br>250 277 |
| C- | 43200<br>-22336<br>250 300 | 43201<br>-22335<br>250 301 | 43202<br>-22334<br>250 302 | 43203<br>-22333<br>250 303 | 43204<br>-22332<br>250 304 | 43205<br>-22331<br>250 305 | 43206<br>-22330<br>250 306 | 43207<br>-22329<br>250 307 | 43208<br>-22328<br>250 310 | 43209<br>-22327<br>250 311 | 43210<br>-22326<br>250 312 | 43211<br>-22325<br>250 313 | 43212<br>-22324<br>250 314 | 43213<br>-22323<br>250 315 | 43214<br>-22322<br>250 316 | 43215<br>-22321<br>250 317 |
| D- | 43216<br>-22320<br>250 320 | 43217<br>-22319<br>250 321 | 43218<br>-22318<br>250 322 | 43219<br>-22317<br>250 323 | 43220<br>-22316<br>250 324 | 43221<br>-22315<br>250 325 | 43222<br>-22314<br>250 326 | 43223<br>-22313<br>250 327 | 43224<br>-22312<br>250 330 | 43225<br>-22311<br>250 331 | 43226<br>-22310<br>250 332 | 43227<br>-22309<br>250 333 | 43228<br>-22308<br>250 334 | 43229<br>-22307<br>250 335 | 43230<br>-22306<br>250 336 | 43231<br>-22305<br>250 337 |
| E- | 43232<br>-22304<br>250 340 | 43233<br>-22303<br>250 341 | 43234<br>-22302<br>250 342 | 43235<br>-22301<br>250 343 | 43236<br>-22300<br>250 344 | 43237<br>-22299<br>250 345 | 43238<br>-22298<br>250 346 | 43239<br>-22297<br>250 347 | 43240<br>-22296<br>250 350 | 43241<br>-22295<br>250 351 | 43242<br>-22294<br>250 352 | 43243<br>-22293<br>250 353 | 43244<br>-22292<br>250 354 | 43245<br>-22291<br>250 355 | 43246<br>-22290<br>250 356 | 43247<br>-22289<br>250 357 |
| F- | 43248<br>-22288<br>250 360 | 43249<br>-22287<br>250 361 | 43250<br>-22286<br>250 362 | 43251<br>-22285<br>250 363 | 43252<br>-22284<br>250 364 | 43253<br>-22283<br>250 365 | 43254<br>-22282<br>250 366 | 43255<br>-22281<br>250 367 | 43256<br>-22280<br>250 370 | 43257<br>-22279<br>250 371 | 43258<br>-22278<br>250 372 | 43259<br>-22277<br>250 373 | 43260<br>-22276<br>250 374 | 43261<br>-22275<br>250 375 | 43262<br>-22274<br>250 376 | 43263<br>-22273<br>250 377 |

DECIMAL ⬅

 DECIMAL ⬅

OCTAL ⬅

 DECIMAL | -22528 |  BINARY | 1010 1000 |  DECIMAL | 43008 |  HEXADECIMAL ⬡ A8  OCTAL | 250 000

FOURTH HEX DIGIT → ⬡ ← THIRD HEX DIGIT

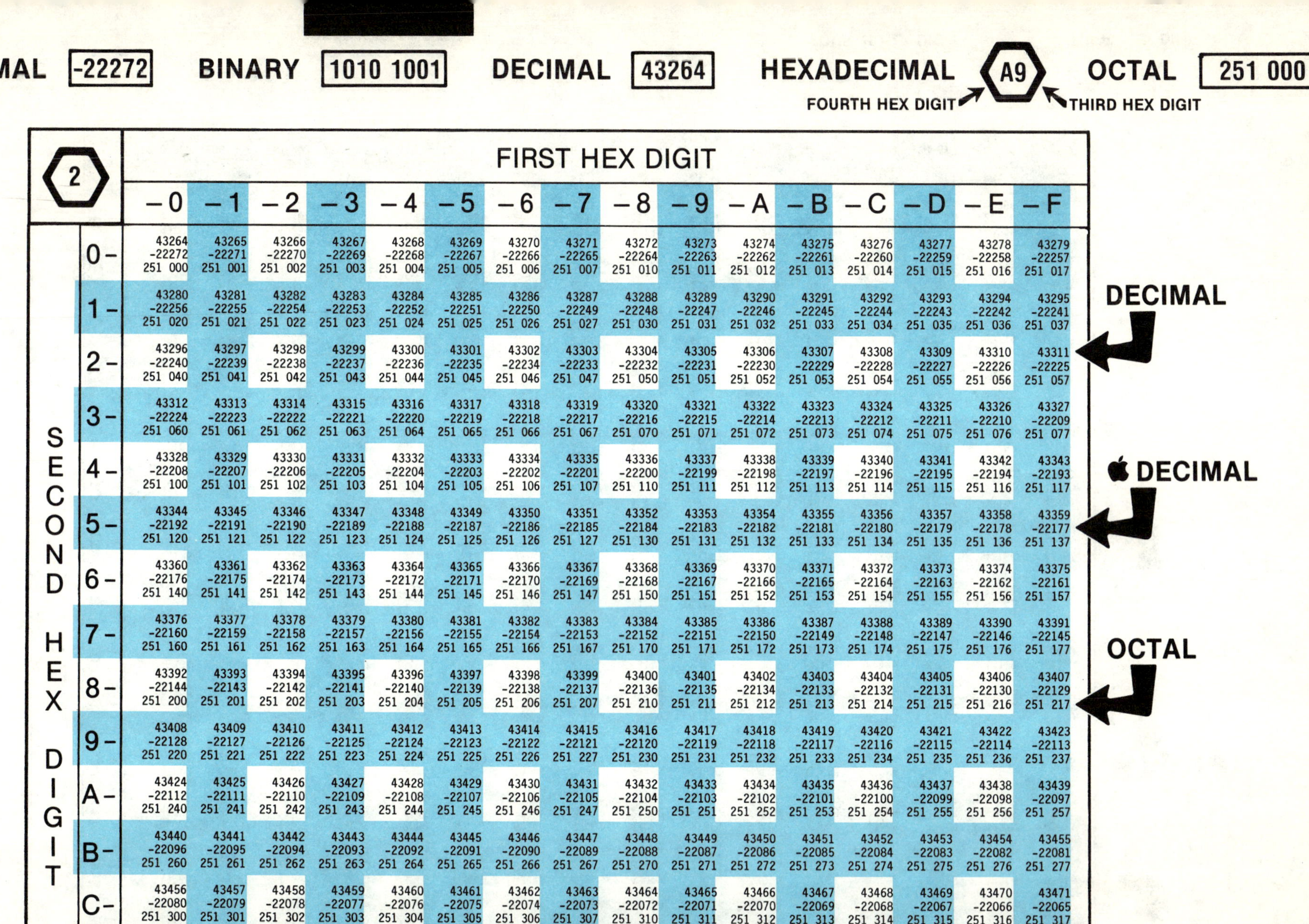

 DECIMAL `-22272`   BINARY `1010 1001`   DECIMAL `43264`   HEXADECIMAL `A9`   OCTAL `251 000`

FOURTH HEX DIGIT → A9 ← THIRD HEX DIGIT

FIRST HEX DIGIT

| `2` | | −0 | −1 | −2 | −3 | −4 | −5 | −6 | −7 | −8 | −9 | −A | −B | −C | −D | −E | −F |
|---|---|---|---|---|---|---|---|---|---|---|---|---|---|---|---|---|---|
| **S** | 0− | 43264<br>−22272<br>251 000 | 43265<br>−22271<br>251 001 | 43266<br>−22270<br>251 002 | 43267<br>−22269<br>251 003 | 43268<br>−22268<br>251 004 | 43269<br>−22267<br>251 005 | 43270<br>−22266<br>251 006 | 43271<br>−22265<br>251 007 | 43272<br>−22264<br>251 010 | 43273<br>−22263<br>251 011 | 43274<br>−22262<br>251 012 | 43275<br>−22261<br>251 013 | 43276<br>−22260<br>251 014 | 43277<br>−22259<br>251 015 | 43278<br>−22258<br>251 016 | 43279<br>−22257<br>251 017 |
| **E** | 1− | 43280<br>−22256<br>251 020 | 43281<br>−22255<br>251 021 | 43282<br>−22254<br>251 022 | 43283<br>−22253<br>251 023 | 43284<br>−22252<br>251 024 | 43285<br>−22251<br>251 025 | 43286<br>−22250<br>251 026 | 43287<br>−22249<br>251 027 | 43288<br>−22248<br>251 030 | 43289<br>−22247<br>251 031 | 43290<br>−22246<br>251 032 | 43291<br>−22245<br>251 033 | 43292<br>−22244<br>251 034 | 43293<br>−22243<br>251 035 | 43294<br>−22242<br>251 036 | 43295<br>−22241<br>251 037 |
| **C** | 2− | 43296<br>−22240<br>251 040 | 43297<br>−22239<br>251 041 | 43298<br>−22238<br>251 042 | 43299<br>−22237<br>251 043 | 43300<br>−22236<br>251 044 | 43301<br>−22235<br>251 045 | 43302<br>−22234<br>251 046 | 43303<br>−22233<br>251 047 | 43304<br>−22232<br>251 050 | 43305<br>−22231<br>251 051 | 43306<br>−22230<br>251 052 | 43307<br>−22229<br>251 053 | 43308<br>−22228<br>251 054 | 43309<br>−22227<br>251 055 | 43310<br>−22226<br>251 056 | 43311<br>−22225<br>251 057 |
| **O** | 3− | 43312<br>−22224<br>251 060 | 43313<br>−22223<br>251 061 | 43314<br>−22222<br>251 062 | 43315<br>−22221<br>251 063 | 43316<br>−22220<br>251 064 | 43317<br>−22219<br>251 065 | 43318<br>−22218<br>251 066 | 43319<br>−22217<br>251 067 | 43320<br>−22216<br>251 070 | 43321<br>−22215<br>251 071 | 43322<br>−22214<br>251 072 | 43323<br>−22213<br>251 073 | 43324<br>−22212<br>251 074 | 43325<br>−22211<br>251 075 | 43326<br>−22210<br>251 076 | 43327<br>−22209<br>251 077 |
| **N** | 4− | 43328<br>−22208<br>251 100 | 43329<br>−22207<br>251 101 | 43330<br>−22206<br>251 102 | 43331<br>−22205<br>251 103 | 43332<br>−22204<br>251 104 | 43333<br>−22203<br>251 105 | 43334<br>−22202<br>251 106 | 43335<br>−22201<br>251 107 | 43336<br>−22200<br>251 110 | 43337<br>−22199<br>251 111 | 43338<br>−22198<br>251 112 | 43339<br>−22197<br>251 113 | 43340<br>−22196<br>251 114 | 43341<br>−22195<br>251 115 | 43342<br>−22194<br>251 116 | 43343<br>−22193<br>251 117 |
| **D** | 5− | 43344<br>−22192<br>251 120 | 43345<br>−22191<br>251 121 | 43346<br>−22190<br>251 122 | 43347<br>−22189<br>251 123 | 43348<br>−22188<br>251 124 | 43349<br>−22187<br>251 125 | 43350<br>−22186<br>251 126 | 43351<br>−22185<br>251 127 | 43352<br>−22184<br>251 130 | 43353<br>−22183<br>251 131 | 43354<br>−22182<br>251 132 | 43355<br>−22181<br>251 133 | 43356<br>−22180<br>251 134 | 43357<br>−22179<br>251 135 | 43358<br>−22178<br>251 136 | 43359<br>−22177<br>251 137 |
| | 6− | 43360<br>−22176<br>251 140 | 43361<br>−22175<br>251 141 | 43362<br>−22174<br>251 142 | 43363<br>−22173<br>251 143 | 43364<br>−22172<br>251 144 | 43365<br>−22171<br>251 145 | 43366<br>−22170<br>251 146 | 43367<br>−22169<br>251 147 | 43368<br>−22168<br>251 150 | 43369<br>−22167<br>251 151 | 43370<br>−22166<br>251 152 | 43371<br>−22165<br>251 153 | 43372<br>−22164<br>251 154 | 43373<br>−22163<br>251 155 | 43374<br>−22162<br>251 156 | 43375<br>−22161<br>251 157 |
| **H** | 7− | 43376<br>−22160<br>251 160 | 43377<br>−22159<br>251 161 | 43378<br>−22158<br>251 162 | 43379<br>−22157<br>251 163 | 43380<br>−22156<br>251 164 | 43381<br>−22155<br>251 165 | 43382<br>−22154<br>251 166 | 43383<br>−22153<br>251 167 | 43384<br>−22152<br>251 170 | 43385<br>−22151<br>251 171 | 43386<br>−22150<br>251 172 | 43387<br>−22149<br>251 173 | 43388<br>−22148<br>251 174 | 43389<br>−22147<br>251 175 | 43390<br>−22146<br>251 176 | 43391<br>−22145<br>251 177 |
| **E** | 8− | 43392<br>−22144<br>251 200 | 43393<br>−22143<br>251 201 | 43394<br>−22142<br>251 202 | 43395<br>−22141<br>251 203 | 43396<br>−22140<br>251 204 | 43397<br>−22139<br>251 205 | 43398<br>−22138<br>251 206 | 43399<br>−22137<br>251 207 | 43400<br>−22136<br>251 210 | 43401<br>−22135<br>251 211 | 43402<br>−22134<br>251 212 | 43403<br>−22133<br>251 213 | 43404<br>−22132<br>251 214 | 43405<br>−22131<br>251 215 | 43406<br>−22130<br>251 216 | 43407<br>−22129<br>251 217 |
| **X** | 9− | 43408<br>−22128<br>251 220 | 43409<br>−22127<br>251 221 | 43410<br>−22126<br>251 222 | 43411<br>−22125<br>251 223 | 43412<br>−22124<br>251 224 | 43413<br>−22123<br>251 225 | 43414<br>−22122<br>251 226 | 43415<br>−22121<br>251 227 | 43416<br>−22120<br>251 230 | 43417<br>−22119<br>251 231 | 43418<br>−22118<br>251 232 | 43419<br>−22117<br>251 233 | 43420<br>−22116<br>251 234 | 43421<br>−22115<br>251 235 | 43422<br>−22114<br>251 236 | 43423<br>−22113<br>251 237 |
| | A− | 43424<br>−22112<br>251 240 | 43425<br>−22111<br>251 241 | 43426<br>−22110<br>251 242 | 43427<br>−22109<br>251 243 | 43428<br>−22108<br>251 244 | 43429<br>−22107<br>251 245 | 43430<br>−22106<br>251 246 | 43431<br>−22105<br>251 247 | 43432<br>−22104<br>251 250 | 43433<br>−22103<br>251 251 | 43434<br>−22102<br>251 252 | 43435<br>−22101<br>251 253 | 43436<br>−22100<br>251 254 | 43437<br>−22099<br>251 255 | 43438<br>−22098<br>251 256 | 43439<br>−22097<br>251 257 |
| **D** | B− | 43440<br>−22096<br>251 260 | 43441<br>−22095<br>251 261 | 43442<br>−22094<br>251 262 | 43443<br>−22093<br>251 263 | 43444<br>−22092<br>251 264 | 43445<br>−22091<br>251 265 | 43446<br>−22090<br>251 266 | 43447<br>−22089<br>251 267 | 43448<br>−22088<br>251 270 | 43449<br>−22087<br>251 271 | 43450<br>−22086<br>251 272 | 43451<br>−22085<br>251 273 | 43452<br>−22084<br>251 274 | 43453<br>−22083<br>251 275 | 43454<br>−22082<br>251 276 | 43455<br>−22081<br>251 277 |
| **I** | C− | 43456<br>−22080<br>251 300 | 43457<br>−22079<br>251 301 | 43458<br>−22078<br>251 302 | 43459<br>−22077<br>251 303 | 43460<br>−22076<br>251 304 | 43461<br>−22075<br>251 305 | 43462<br>−22074<br>251 306 | 43463<br>−22073<br>251 307 | 43464<br>−22072<br>251 310 | 43465<br>−22071<br>251 311 | 43466<br>−22070<br>251 312 | 43467<br>−22069<br>251 313 | 43468<br>−22068<br>251 314 | 43469<br>−22067<br>251 315 | 43470<br>−22066<br>251 316 | 43471<br>−22065<br>251 317 |
| **G** | D− | 43472<br>−22064<br>251 320 | 43473<br>−22063<br>251 321 | 43474<br>−22062<br>251 322 | 43475<br>−22061<br>251 323 | 43476<br>−22060<br>251 324 | 43477<br>−22059<br>251 325 | 43478<br>−22058<br>251 326 | 43479<br>−22057<br>251 327 | 43480<br>−22056<br>251 330 | 43481<br>−22055<br>251 331 | 43482<br>−22054<br>251 332 | 43483<br>−22053<br>251 333 | 43484<br>−22052<br>251 334 | 43485<br>−22051<br>251 335 | 43486<br>−22050<br>251 336 | 43487<br>−22049<br>251 337 |
| **I** | E− | 43488<br>−22048<br>251 340 | 43489<br>−22047<br>251 341 | 43490<br>−22046<br>251 342 | 43491<br>−22045<br>251 343 | 43492<br>−22044<br>251 344 | 43493<br>−22043<br>251 345 | 43494<br>−22042<br>251 346 | 43495<br>−22041<br>251 347 | 43496<br>−22040<br>251 350 | 43497<br>−22039<br>251 351 | 43498<br>−22038<br>251 352 | 43499<br>−22037<br>251 353 | 43500<br>−22036<br>251 354 | 43501<br>−22035<br>251 355 | 43502<br>−22034<br>251 356 | 43503<br>−22033<br>251 357 |
| **T** | F− | 43504<br>−22032<br>251 360 | 43505<br>−22031<br>251 361 | 43506<br>−22030<br>251 362 | 43507<br>−22029<br>251 363 | 43508<br>−22028<br>251 364 | 43509<br>−22027<br>251 365 | 43510<br>−22026<br>251 366 | 43511<br>−22025<br>251 367 | 43512<br>−22024<br>251 370 | 43513<br>−22023<br>251 371 | 43514<br>−22022<br>251 372 | 43515<br>−22021<br>251 373 | 43516<br>−22020<br>251 374 | 43517<br>−22019<br>251 375 | 43518<br>−22018<br>251 376 | 43519<br>−22017<br>251 377 |

SECOND HEX DIGIT

## FIRST HEX DIGIT

| | −0 | −1 | −2 | −3 | −4 | −5 | −6 | −7 | −8 | −9 | −A | −B | −C | −D | −E | −F |
|---|---|---|---|---|---|---|---|---|---|---|---|---|---|---|---|---|
| **0−** | 43520<br>−22016<br>252 000 | 43521<br>−22015<br>252 001 | 43522<br>−22014<br>252 002 | 43523<br>−22013<br>252 003 | 43524<br>−22012<br>252 004 | 43525<br>−22011<br>252 005 | 43526<br>−22010<br>252 006 | 43527<br>−22009<br>252 007 | 43528<br>−22008<br>252 010 | 43529<br>−22007<br>252 011 | 43530<br>−22006<br>252 012 | 43531<br>−22005<br>252 013 | 43532<br>−22004<br>252 014 | 43533<br>−22003<br>252 015 | 43534<br>−22002<br>252 016 | 43535<br>−22001<br>252 017 |
| **1−** | 43536<br>−22000<br>252 020 | 43537<br>−21999<br>252 021 | 43538<br>−21998<br>252 022 | 43539<br>−21997<br>252 023 | 43540<br>−21996<br>252 024 | 43541<br>−21995<br>252 025 | 43542<br>−21994<br>252 026 | 43543<br>−21993<br>252 027 | 43544<br>−21992<br>252 030 | 43545<br>−21991<br>252 031 | 43546<br>−21990<br>252 032 | 43547<br>−21989<br>252 033 | 43548<br>−21988<br>252 034 | 43549<br>−21987<br>252 035 | 43550<br>−21986<br>252 036 | 43551<br>−21985<br>252 037 |
| **2−** | 43552<br>−21984<br>252 040 | 43553<br>−21983<br>252 041 | 43554<br>−21982<br>252 042 | 43555<br>−21981<br>252 043 | 43556<br>−21980<br>252 044 | 43557<br>−21979<br>252 045 | 43558<br>−21978<br>252 046 | 43559<br>−21977<br>252 047 | 43560<br>−21976<br>252 050 | 43561<br>−21975<br>252 051 | 43562<br>−21974<br>252 052 | 43563<br>−21973<br>252 053 | 43564<br>−21972<br>252 054 | 43565<br>−21971<br>252 055 | 43566<br>−21970<br>252 056 | 43567<br>−21969<br>252 057 |
| **3−** | 43568<br>−21968<br>252 060 | 43569<br>−21967<br>252 061 | 43570<br>−21966<br>252 062 | 43571<br>−21965<br>252 063 | 43572<br>−21964<br>252 064 | 43573<br>−21963<br>252 065 | 43574<br>−21962<br>252 066 | 43575<br>−21961<br>252 067 | 43576<br>−21960<br>252 070 | 43577<br>−21959<br>252 071 | 43578<br>−21958<br>252 072 | 43579<br>−21957<br>252 073 | 43580<br>−21956<br>252 074 | 43581<br>−21955<br>252 075 | 43582<br>−21954<br>252 076 | 43583<br>−21953<br>252 077 |
| **4−** | 43584<br>−21952<br>252 100 | 43585<br>−21951<br>252 101 | 43586<br>−21950<br>252 102 | 43587<br>−21949<br>252 103 | 43588<br>−21948<br>252 104 | 43589<br>−21947<br>252 105 | 43590<br>−21946<br>252 106 | 43591<br>−21945<br>252 107 | 43592<br>−21944<br>252 110 | 43593<br>−21943<br>252 111 | 43594<br>−21942<br>252 112 | 43595<br>−21941<br>252 113 | 43596<br>−21940<br>252 114 | 43597<br>−21939<br>252 115 | 43598<br>−21938<br>252 116 | 43599<br>−21937<br>252 117 |
| **5−** | 43600<br>−21936<br>252 120 | 43601<br>−21935<br>252 121 | 43602<br>−21934<br>252 122 | 43603<br>−21933<br>252 123 | 43604<br>−21932<br>252 124 | 43605<br>−21931<br>252 125 | 43606<br>−21930<br>252 126 | 43607<br>−21929<br>252 127 | 43608<br>−21928<br>252 130 | 43609<br>−21927<br>252 131 | 43610<br>−21926<br>252 132 | 43611<br>−21925<br>252 133 | 43612<br>−21924<br>252 134 | 43613<br>−21923<br>252 135 | 43614<br>−21922<br>252 136 | 43615<br>−21921<br>252 137 |
| **6−** | 43616<br>−21920<br>252 140 | 43617<br>−21919<br>252 141 | 43618<br>−21918<br>252 142 | 43619<br>−21917<br>252 143 | 43620<br>−21916<br>252 144 | 43621<br>−21915<br>252 145 | 43622<br>−21914<br>252 146 | 43623<br>−21913<br>252 147 | 43624<br>−21912<br>252 150 | 43625<br>−21911<br>252 151 | 43626<br>−21910<br>252 152 | 43627<br>−21909<br>252 153 | 43628<br>−21908<br>252 154 | 43629<br>−21907<br>252 155 | 43630<br>−21906<br>252 156 | 43631<br>−21905<br>252 157 |
| **7−** | 43632<br>−21904<br>252 160 | 43633<br>−21903<br>252 161 | 43634<br>−21902<br>252 162 | 43635<br>−21901<br>252 163 | 43636<br>−21900<br>252 164 | 43637<br>−21899<br>252 165 | 43638<br>−21898<br>252 166 | 43639<br>−21897<br>252 167 | 43640<br>−21896<br>252 170 | 43641<br>−21895<br>252 171 | 43642<br>−21894<br>252 172 | 43643<br>−21893<br>252 173 | 43644<br>−21892<br>252 174 | 43645<br>−21891<br>252 175 | 43646<br>−21890<br>252 176 | 43647<br>−21889<br>252 177 |
| **8−** | 43648<br>−21888<br>252 200 | 43649<br>−21887<br>252 201 | 43650<br>−21886<br>252 202 | 43651<br>−21885<br>252 203 | 43652<br>−21884<br>252 204 | 43653<br>−21883<br>252 205 | 43654<br>−21882<br>252 206 | 43655<br>−21881<br>252 207 | 43656<br>−21880<br>252 210 | 43657<br>−21879<br>252 211 | 43658<br>−21878<br>252 212 | 43659<br>−21877<br>252 213 | 43660<br>−21876<br>252 214 | 43661<br>−21875<br>252 215 | 43662<br>−21874<br>252 216 | 43663<br>−21873<br>252 217 |
| **9−** | 43664<br>−21872<br>252 220 | 43665<br>−21871<br>252 221 | 43666<br>−21870<br>252 222 | 43667<br>−21869<br>252 223 | 43668<br>−21868<br>252 224 | 43669<br>−21867<br>252 225 | 43670<br>−21866<br>252 226 | 43671<br>−21865<br>252 227 | 43672<br>−21864<br>252 230 | 43673<br>−21863<br>252 231 | 43674<br>−21862<br>252 232 | 43675<br>−21861<br>252 233 | 43676<br>−21860<br>252 234 | 43677<br>−21859<br>252 235 | 43678<br>−21858<br>252 236 | 43679<br>−21857<br>252 237 |
| **A−** | 43680<br>−21856<br>252 240 | 43681<br>−21855<br>252 241 | 43682<br>−21854<br>252 242 | 43683<br>−21853<br>252 243 | 43684<br>−21852<br>252 244 | 43685<br>−21851<br>252 245 | 43686<br>−21850<br>252 246 | 43687<br>−21849<br>252 247 | 43688<br>−21848<br>252 250 | 43689<br>−21847<br>252 251 | 43690<br>−21846<br>252 252 | 43691<br>−21845<br>252 253 | 43692<br>−21844<br>252 254 | 43693<br>−21843<br>252 255 | 43694<br>−21842<br>252 256 | 43695<br>−21841<br>252 257 |
| **B−** | 43696<br>−21840<br>252 260 | 43697<br>−21839<br>252 261 | 43698<br>−21838<br>252 262 | 43699<br>−21837<br>252 263 | 43700<br>−21836<br>252 264 | 43701<br>−21835<br>252 265 | 43702<br>−21834<br>252 266 | 43703<br>−21833<br>252 267 | 43704<br>−21832<br>252 270 | 43705<br>−21831<br>252 271 | 43706<br>−21830<br>252 272 | 43707<br>−21829<br>252 273 | 43708<br>−21828<br>252 274 | 43709<br>−21827<br>252 275 | 43710<br>−21826<br>252 276 | 43711<br>−21825<br>252 277 |
| **C−** | 43712<br>−21824<br>252 300 | 43713<br>−21823<br>252 301 | 43714<br>−21822<br>252 302 | 43715<br>−21821<br>252 303 | 43716<br>−21820<br>252 304 | 43717<br>−21819<br>252 305 | 43718<br>−21818<br>252 306 | 43719<br>−21817<br>252 307 | 43720<br>−21816<br>252 310 | 43721<br>−21815<br>252 311 | 43722<br>−21814<br>252 312 | 43723<br>−21813<br>252 313 | 43724<br>−21812<br>252 314 | 43725<br>−21811<br>252 315 | 43726<br>−21810<br>252 316 | 43727<br>−21809<br>252 317 |
| **D−** | 43728<br>−21808<br>252 320 | 43729<br>−21807<br>252 321 | 43730<br>−21806<br>252 322 | 43731<br>−21805<br>252 323 | 43732<br>−21804<br>252 324 | 43733<br>−21803<br>252 325 | 43734<br>−21802<br>252 326 | 43735<br>−21801<br>252 327 | 43736<br>−21800<br>252 330 | 43737<br>−21799<br>252 331 | 43738<br>−21798<br>252 332 | 43739<br>−21797<br>252 333 | 43740<br>−21796<br>252 334 | 43741<br>−21795<br>252 335 | 43742<br>−21794<br>252 336 | 43743<br>−21793<br>252 337 |
| **E−** | 43744<br>−21792<br>252 340 | 43745<br>−21791<br>252 341 | 43746<br>−21790<br>252 342 | 43747<br>−21789<br>252 343 | 43748<br>−21788<br>252 344 | 43749<br>−21787<br>252 345 | 43750<br>−21786<br>252 346 | 43751<br>−21785<br>252 347 | 43752<br>−21784<br>252 350 | 43753<br>−21783<br>252 351 | 43754<br>−21782<br>252 352 | 43755<br>−21781<br>252 353 | 43756<br>−21780<br>252 354 | 43757<br>−21779<br>252 355 | 43758<br>−21778<br>252 356 | 43759<br>−21777<br>252 357 |
| **F−** | 43760<br>−21776<br>252 360 | 43761<br>−21775<br>252 361 | 43762<br>−21774<br>252 362 | 43763<br>−21773<br>252 363 | 43764<br>−21772<br>252 364 | 43765<br>−21771<br>252 365 | 43766<br>−21770<br>252 366 | 43767<br>−21769<br>252 367 | 43768<br>−21768<br>252 370 | 43769<br>−21767<br>252 371 | 43770<br>−21766<br>252 372 | 43771<br>−21765<br>252 373 | 43772<br>−21764<br>252 374 | 43773<br>−21763<br>252 375 | 43774<br>−21762<br>252 376 | 43775<br>−21761<br>252 377 |

**SECOND HEX DIGIT** (row labels) — **DECIMAL** / ⬤ **DECIMAL** / **OCTAL**

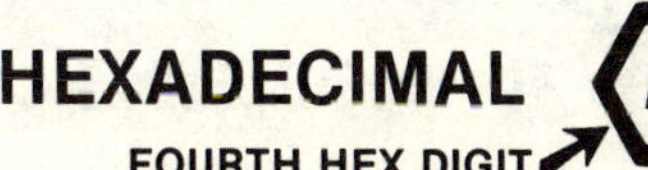


⬤ DECIMAL `−22016`　　BINARY `1010 1010`　　DECIMAL `43520`　　HEXADECIMAL ⬡ **AA**　　OCTAL `252 000`

FOURTH HEX DIGIT →　　← THIRD HEX DIGIT

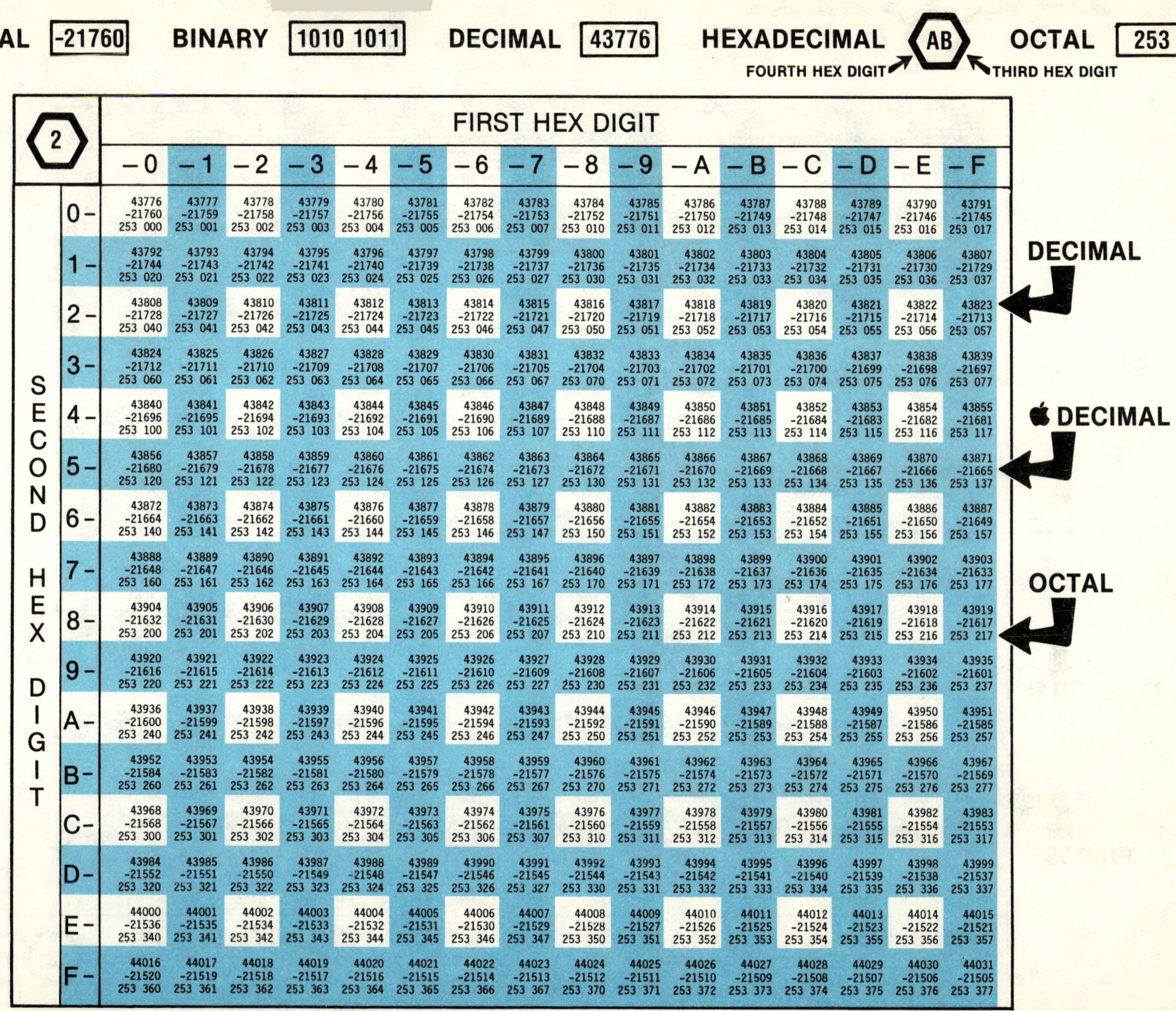



FIRST HEX DIGIT — 2

| SECOND HEX DIGIT | −0 | −1 | −2 | −3 | −4 | −5 | −6 | −7 | −8 | −9 | −A | −B | −C | −D | −E | −F |
|---|---|---|---|---|---|---|---|---|---|---|---|---|---|---|---|---|
| 0− | 43776<br>-21760<br>253 000 | 43777<br>-21759<br>253 001 | 43778<br>-21758<br>253 002 | 43779<br>-21757<br>253 003 | 43780<br>-21756<br>253 004 | 43781<br>-21755<br>253 005 | 43782<br>-21754<br>253 006 | 43783<br>-21753<br>253 007 | 43784<br>-21752<br>253 010 | 43785<br>-21751<br>253 011 | 43786<br>-21750<br>253 012 | 43787<br>-21749<br>253 013 | 43788<br>-21748<br>253 014 | 43789<br>-21747<br>253 015 | 43790<br>-21746<br>253 016 | 43791<br>-21745<br>253 017 |
| 1− | 43792<br>-21744<br>253 020 | 43793<br>-21743<br>253 021 | 43794<br>-21742<br>253 022 | 43795<br>-21741<br>253 023 | 43796<br>-21740<br>253 024 | 43797<br>-21739<br>253 025 | 43798<br>-21738<br>253 026 | 43799<br>-21737<br>253 027 | 43800<br>-21736<br>253 030 | 43801<br>-21735<br>253 031 | 43802<br>-21734<br>253 032 | 43803<br>-21733<br>253 033 | 43804<br>-21732<br>253 034 | 43805<br>-21731<br>253 035 | 43806<br>-21730<br>253 036 | 43807<br>-21729<br>253 037 |
| 2− | 43808<br>-21728<br>253 040 | 43809<br>-21727<br>253 041 | 43810<br>-21726<br>253 042 | 43811<br>-21725<br>253 043 | 43812<br>-21724<br>253 044 | 43813<br>-21723<br>253 045 | 43814<br>-21722<br>253 046 | 43815<br>-21721<br>253 047 | 43816<br>-21720<br>253 050 | 43817<br>-21719<br>253 051 | 43818<br>-21718<br>253 052 | 43819<br>-21717<br>253 053 | 43820<br>-21716<br>253 054 | 43821<br>-21715<br>253 055 | 43822<br>-21714<br>253 056 | 43823<br>-21713<br>253 057 |
| 3− | 43824<br>-21712<br>253 060 | 43825<br>-21711<br>253 061 | 43826<br>-21710<br>253 062 | 43827<br>-21709<br>253 063 | 43828<br>-21708<br>253 064 | 43829<br>-21707<br>253 065 | 43830<br>-21706<br>253 066 | 43831<br>-21705<br>253 067 | 43832<br>-21704<br>253 070 | 43833<br>-21703<br>253 071 | 43834<br>-21702<br>253 072 | 43835<br>-21701<br>253 073 | 43836<br>-21700<br>253 074 | 43837<br>-21699<br>253 075 | 43838<br>-21698<br>253 076 | 43839<br>-21697<br>253 077 |
| 4− | 43840<br>-21696<br>253 100 | 43841<br>-21695<br>253 101 | 43842<br>-21694<br>253 102 | 43843<br>-21693<br>253 103 | 43844<br>-21692<br>253 104 | 43845<br>-21691<br>253 105 | 43846<br>-21690<br>253 106 | 43847<br>-21689<br>253 107 | 43848<br>-21688<br>253 110 | 43849<br>-21687<br>253 111 | 43850<br>-21686<br>253 112 | 43851<br>-21685<br>253 113 | 43852<br>-21684<br>253 114 | 43853<br>-21683<br>253 115 | 43854<br>-21682<br>253 116 | 43855<br>-21681<br>253 117 |
| 5− | 43856<br>-21680<br>253 120 | 43857<br>-21679<br>253 121 | 43858<br>-21678<br>253 122 | 43859<br>-21677<br>253 123 | 43860<br>-21676<br>253 124 | 43861<br>-21675<br>253 125 | 43862<br>-21674<br>253 126 | 43863<br>-21673<br>253 127 | 43864<br>-21672<br>253 130 | 43865<br>-21671<br>253 131 | 43866<br>-21670<br>253 132 | 43867<br>-21669<br>253 133 | 43868<br>-21668<br>253 134 | 43869<br>-21667<br>253 135 | 43870<br>-21666<br>253 136 | 43871<br>-21665<br>253 137 |
| 6− | 43872<br>-21664<br>253 140 | 43873<br>-21663<br>253 141 | 43874<br>-21662<br>253 142 | 43875<br>-21661<br>253 143 | 43876<br>-21660<br>253 144 | 43877<br>-21659<br>253 145 | 43878<br>-21658<br>253 146 | 43879<br>-21657<br>253 147 | 43880<br>-21656<br>253 150 | 43881<br>-21655<br>253 151 | 43882<br>-21654<br>253 152 | 43883<br>-21653<br>253 153 | 43884<br>-21652<br>253 154 | 43885<br>-21651<br>253 155 | 43886<br>-21650<br>253 156 | 43887<br>-21649<br>253 157 |
| 7− | 43888<br>-21648<br>253 160 | 43889<br>-21647<br>253 161 | 43890<br>-21646<br>253 162 | 43891<br>-21645<br>253 163 | 43892<br>-21644<br>253 164 | 43893<br>-21643<br>253 165 | 43894<br>-21642<br>253 166 | 43895<br>-21641<br>253 167 | 43896<br>-21640<br>253 170 | 43897<br>-21639<br>253 171 | 43898<br>-21638<br>253 172 | 43899<br>-21637<br>253 173 | 43900<br>-21636<br>253 174 | 43901<br>-21635<br>253 175 | 43902<br>-21634<br>253 176 | 43903<br>-21633<br>253 177 |
| 8− | 43904<br>-21632<br>253 200 | 43905<br>-21631<br>253 201 | 43906<br>-21630<br>253 202 | 43907<br>-21629<br>253 203 | 43908<br>-21628<br>253 204 | 43909<br>-21627<br>253 205 | 43910<br>-21626<br>253 206 | 43911<br>-21625<br>253 207 | 43912<br>-21624<br>253 210 | 43913<br>-21623<br>253 211 | 43914<br>-21622<br>253 212 | 43915<br>-21621<br>253 213 | 43916<br>-21620<br>253 214 | 43917<br>-21619<br>253 215 | 43918<br>-21618<br>253 216 | 43919<br>-21617<br>253 217 |
| 9− | 43920<br>-21616<br>253 220 | 43921<br>-21615<br>253 221 | 43922<br>-21614<br>253 222 | 43923<br>-21613<br>253 223 | 43924<br>-21612<br>253 224 | 43925<br>-21611<br>253 225 | 43926<br>-21610<br>253 226 | 43927<br>-21609<br>253 227 | 43928<br>-21608<br>253 230 | 43929<br>-21607<br>253 231 | 43930<br>-21606<br>253 232 | 43931<br>-21605<br>253 233 | 43932<br>-21604<br>253 234 | 43933<br>-21603<br>253 235 | 43934<br>-21602<br>253 236 | 43935<br>-21601<br>253 237 |
| A− | 43936<br>-21600<br>253 240 | 43937<br>-21599<br>253 241 | 43938<br>-21598<br>253 242 | 43939<br>-21597<br>253 243 | 43940<br>-21596<br>253 244 | 43941<br>-21595<br>253 245 | 43942<br>-21594<br>253 246 | 43943<br>-21593<br>253 247 | 43944<br>-21592<br>253 250 | 43945<br>-21591<br>253 251 | 43946<br>-21590<br>253 252 | 43947<br>-21589<br>253 253 | 43948<br>-21588<br>253 254 | 43949<br>-21587<br>253 255 | 43950<br>-21586<br>253 256 | 43951<br>-21585<br>253 257 |
| B− | 43952<br>-21584<br>253 260 | 43953<br>-21583<br>253 261 | 43954<br>-21582<br>253 262 | 43955<br>-21581<br>253 263 | 43956<br>-21580<br>253 264 | 43957<br>-21579<br>253 265 | 43958<br>-21578<br>253 266 | 43959<br>-21577<br>253 267 | 43960<br>-21576<br>253 270 | 43961<br>-21575<br>253 271 | 43962<br>-21574<br>253 272 | 43963<br>-21573<br>253 273 | 43964<br>-21572<br>253 274 | 43965<br>-21571<br>253 275 | 43966<br>-21570<br>253 276 | 43967<br>-21569<br>253 277 |
| C− | 43968<br>-21568<br>253 300 | 43969<br>-21567<br>253 301 | 43970<br>-21566<br>253 302 | 43971<br>-21565<br>253 303 | 43972<br>-21564<br>253 304 | 43973<br>-21563<br>253 305 | 43974<br>-21562<br>253 306 | 43975<br>-21561<br>253 307 | 43976<br>-21560<br>253 310 | 43977<br>-21559<br>253 311 | 43978<br>-21558<br>253 312 | 43979<br>-21557<br>253 313 | 43980<br>-21556<br>253 314 | 43981<br>-21555<br>253 315 | 43982<br>-21554<br>253 316 | 43983<br>-21553<br>253 317 |
| D− | 43984<br>-21552<br>253 320 | 43985<br>-21551<br>253 321 | 43986<br>-21550<br>253 322 | 43987<br>-21549<br>253 323 | 43988<br>-21548<br>253 324 | 43989<br>-21547<br>253 325 | 43990<br>-21546<br>253 326 | 43991<br>-21545<br>253 327 | 43992<br>-21544<br>253 330 | 43993<br>-21543<br>253 331 | 43994<br>-21542<br>253 332 | 43995<br>-21541<br>253 333 | 43996<br>-21540<br>253 334 | 43997<br>-21539<br>253 335 | 43998<br>-21538<br>253 336 | 43999<br>-21537<br>253 337 |
| E− | 44000<br>-21536<br>253 340 | 44001<br>-21535<br>253 341 | 44002<br>-21534<br>253 342 | 44003<br>-21533<br>253 343 | 44004<br>-21532<br>253 344 | 44005<br>-21531<br>253 345 | 44006<br>-21530<br>253 346 | 44007<br>-21529<br>253 347 | 44008<br>-21528<br>253 350 | 44009<br>-21527<br>253 351 | 44010<br>-21526<br>253 352 | 44011<br>-21525<br>253 353 | 44012<br>-21524<br>253 354 | 44013<br>-21523<br>253 355 | 44014<br>-21522<br>253 356 | 44015<br>-21521<br>253 357 |
| F− | 44016<br>-21520<br>253 360 | 44017<br>-21519<br>253 361 | 44018<br>-21518<br>253 362 | 44019<br>-21517<br>253 363 | 44020<br>-21516<br>253 364 | 44021<br>-21515<br>253 365 | 44022<br>-21514<br>253 366 | 44023<br>-21513<br>253 367 | 44024<br>-21512<br>253 370 | 44025<br>-21511<br>253 371 | 44026<br>-21510<br>253 372 | 44027<br>-21509<br>253 373 | 44028<br>-21508<br>253 374 | 44029<br>-21507<br>253 375 | 44030<br>-21506<br>253 376 | 44031<br>-21505<br>253 377 |

**② — SECOND HEX DIGIT / FIRST HEX DIGIT**

| | −0 | −1 | −2 | −3 | −4 | −5 | −6 | −7 | −8 | −9 | −A | −B | −C | −D | −E | −F |
|---|---|---|---|---|---|---|---|---|---|---|---|---|---|---|---|---|
| **0-** | 44032<br>-21504<br>254 000 | 44033<br>-21503<br>254 001 | 44034<br>-21502<br>254 002 | 44035<br>-21501<br>254 003 | 44036<br>-21500<br>254 004 | 44037<br>-21499<br>254 005 | 44038<br>-21498<br>254 006 | 44039<br>-21497<br>254 007 | 44040<br>-21496<br>254 010 | 44041<br>-21495<br>254 011 | 44042<br>-21494<br>254 012 | 44043<br>-21493<br>254 013 | 44044<br>-21492<br>254 014 | 44045<br>-21491<br>254 015 | 44046<br>-21490<br>254 016 | 44047<br>-21489<br>254 017 |
| **1-** | 44048<br>-21488<br>254 020 | 44049<br>-21487<br>254 021 | 44050<br>-21486<br>254 022 | 44051<br>-21485<br>254 023 | 44052<br>-21484<br>254 024 | 44053<br>-21483<br>254 025 | 44054<br>-21482<br>254 026 | 44055<br>-21481<br>254 027 | 44056<br>-21480<br>254 030 | 44057<br>-21479<br>254 031 | 44058<br>-21478<br>254 032 | 44059<br>-21477<br>254 033 | 44060<br>-21476<br>254 034 | 44061<br>-21475<br>254 035 | 44062<br>-21474<br>254 036 | 44063<br>-21473<br>254 037 |
| **2-** | 44064<br>-21472<br>254 040 | 44065<br>-21471<br>254 041 | 44066<br>-21470<br>254 042 | 44067<br>-21469<br>254 043 | 44068<br>-21468<br>254 044 | 44069<br>-21467<br>254 045 | 44070<br>-21466<br>254 046 | 44071<br>-21465<br>254 047 | 44072<br>-21464<br>254 050 | 44073<br>-21463<br>254 051 | 44074<br>-21462<br>254 052 | 44075<br>-21461<br>254 053 | 44076<br>-21460<br>254 054 | 44077<br>-21459<br>254 055 | 44078<br>-21458<br>254 056 | 44079<br>-21457<br>254 057 |
| **3-** | 44080<br>-21456<br>254 060 | 44081<br>-21455<br>254 061 | 44082<br>-21454<br>254 062 | 44083<br>-21453<br>254 063 | 44084<br>-21452<br>254 064 | 44085<br>-21451<br>254 065 | 44086<br>-21450<br>254 066 | 44087<br>-21449<br>254 067 | 44088<br>-21448<br>254 070 | 44089<br>-21447<br>254 071 | 44090<br>-21446<br>254 072 | 44091<br>-21445<br>254 073 | 44092<br>-21444<br>254 074 | 44093<br>-21443<br>254 075 | 44094<br>-21442<br>254 076 | 44095<br>-21441<br>254 077 |
| **4-** | 44096<br>-21440<br>254 100 | 44097<br>-21439<br>254 101 | 44098<br>-21438<br>254 102 | 44099<br>-21437<br>254 103 | 44100<br>-21436<br>254 104 | 44101<br>-21435<br>254 105 | 44102<br>-21434<br>254 106 | 44103<br>-21433<br>254 107 | 44104<br>-21432<br>254 110 | 44105<br>-21431<br>254 111 | 44106<br>-21430<br>254 112 | 44107<br>-21429<br>254 113 | 44108<br>-21428<br>254 114 | 44109<br>-21427<br>254 115 | 44110<br>-21426<br>254 116 | 44111<br>-21425<br>254 117 |
| **5-** | 44112<br>-21424<br>254 120 | 44113<br>-21423<br>254 121 | 44114<br>-21422<br>254 122 | 44115<br>-21421<br>254 123 | 44116<br>-21420<br>254 124 | 44117<br>-21419<br>254 125 | 44118<br>-21418<br>254 126 | 44119<br>-21417<br>254 127 | 44120<br>-21416<br>254 130 | 44121<br>-21415<br>254 131 | 44122<br>-21414<br>254 132 | 44123<br>-21413<br>254 133 | 44124<br>-21412<br>254 134 | 44125<br>-21411<br>254 135 | 44126<br>-21410<br>254 136 | 44127<br>-21409<br>254 137 |
| **6-** | 44128<br>-21408<br>254 140 | 44129<br>-21407<br>254 141 | 44130<br>-21406<br>254 142 | 44131<br>-21405<br>254 143 | 44132<br>-21404<br>254 144 | 44133<br>-21403<br>254 145 | 44134<br>-21402<br>254 146 | 44135<br>-21401<br>254 147 | 44136<br>-21400<br>254 150 | 44137<br>-21399<br>254 151 | 44138<br>-21398<br>254 152 | 44139<br>-21397<br>254 153 | 44140<br>-21396<br>254 154 | 44141<br>-21395<br>254 155 | 44142<br>-21394<br>254 156 | 44143<br>-21393<br>254 157 |
| **7-** | 44144<br>-21392<br>254 160 | 44145<br>-21391<br>254 161 | 44146<br>-21390<br>254 162 | 44147<br>-21389<br>254 163 | 44148<br>-21388<br>254 164 | 44149<br>-21387<br>254 165 | 44150<br>-21386<br>254 166 | 44151<br>-21385<br>254 167 | 44152<br>-21384<br>254 170 | 44153<br>-21383<br>254 171 | 44154<br>-21382<br>254 172 | 44155<br>-21381<br>254 173 | 44156<br>-21380<br>254 174 | 44157<br>-21379<br>254 175 | 44158<br>-21378<br>254 176 | 44159<br>-21377<br>254 177 |
| **8-** | 44160<br>-21376<br>254 200 | 44161<br>-21375<br>254 201 | 44162<br>-21374<br>254 202 | 44163<br>-21373<br>254 203 | 44164<br>-21372<br>254 204 | 44165<br>-21371<br>254 205 | 44166<br>-21370<br>254 206 | 44167<br>-21369<br>254 207 | 44168<br>-21368<br>254 210 | 44169<br>-21367<br>254 211 | 44170<br>-21366<br>254 212 | 44171<br>-21365<br>254 213 | 44172<br>-21364<br>254 214 | 44173<br>-21363<br>254 215 | 44174<br>-21362<br>254 216 | 44175<br>-21361<br>254 217 |
| **9-** | 44176<br>-21360<br>254 220 | 44177<br>-21359<br>254 221 | 44178<br>-21358<br>254 222 | 44179<br>-21357<br>254 223 | 44180<br>-21356<br>254 224 | 44181<br>-21355<br>254 225 | 44182<br>-21354<br>254 226 | 44183<br>-21353<br>254 227 | 44184<br>-21352<br>254 230 | 44185<br>-21351<br>254 231 | 44186<br>-21350<br>254 232 | 44187<br>-21349<br>254 233 | 44188<br>-21348<br>254 234 | 44189<br>-21347<br>254 235 | 44190<br>-21346<br>254 236 | 44191<br>-21345<br>254 237 |
| **A-** | 44192<br>-21344<br>254 240 | 44193<br>-21343<br>254 241 | 44194<br>-21342<br>254 242 | 44195<br>-21341<br>254 243 | 44196<br>-21340<br>254 244 | 44197<br>-21339<br>254 245 | 44198<br>-21338<br>254 246 | 44199<br>-21337<br>254 247 | 44200<br>-21336<br>254 250 | 44201<br>-21335<br>254 251 | 44202<br>-21334<br>254 252 | 44203<br>-21333<br>254 253 | 44204<br>-21332<br>254 254 | 44205<br>-21331<br>254 255 | 44206<br>-21330<br>254 256 | 44207<br>-21329<br>254 257 |
| **B-** | 44208<br>-21328<br>254 260 | 44209<br>-21327<br>254 261 | 44210<br>-21326<br>254 262 | 44211<br>-21325<br>254 263 | 44212<br>-21324<br>254 264 | 44213<br>-21323<br>254 265 | 44214<br>-21322<br>254 266 | 44215<br>-21321<br>254 267 | 44216<br>-21320<br>254 270 | 44217<br>-21319<br>254 271 | 44218<br>-21318<br>254 272 | 44219<br>-21317<br>254 273 | 44220<br>-21316<br>254 274 | 44221<br>-21315<br>254 275 | 44222<br>-21314<br>254 276 | 44223<br>-21313<br>254 277 |
| **C-** | 44224<br>-21312<br>254 300 | 44225<br>-21311<br>254 301 | 44226<br>-21310<br>254 302 | 44227<br>-21309<br>254 303 | 44228<br>-21308<br>254 304 | 44229<br>-21307<br>254 305 | 44230<br>-21306<br>254 306 | 44231<br>-21305<br>254 307 | 44232<br>-21304<br>254 310 | 44233<br>-21303<br>254 311 | 44234<br>-21302<br>254 312 | 44235<br>-21301<br>254 313 | 44236<br>-21300<br>254 314 | 44237<br>-21299<br>254 315 | 44238<br>-21298<br>254 316 | 44239<br>-21297<br>254 317 |
| **D-** | 44240<br>-21296<br>254 320 | 44241<br>-21295<br>254 321 | 44242<br>-21294<br>254 322 | 44243<br>-21293<br>254 323 | 44244<br>-21292<br>254 324 | 44245<br>-21291<br>254 325 | 44246<br>-21290<br>254 326 | 44247<br>-21289<br>254 327 | 44248<br>-21288<br>254 330 | 44249<br>-21287<br>254 331 | 44250<br>-21286<br>254 332 | 44251<br>-21285<br>254 333 | 44252<br>-21284<br>254 334 | 44253<br>-21283<br>254 335 | 44254<br>-21282<br>254 336 | 44255<br>-21281<br>254 337 |
| **E-** | 44256<br>-21280<br>254 340 | 44257<br>-21279<br>254 341 | 44258<br>-21278<br>254 342 | 44259<br>-21277<br>254 343 | 44260<br>-21276<br>254 344 | 44261<br>-21275<br>254 345 | 44262<br>-21274<br>254 346 | 44263<br>-21273<br>254 347 | 44264<br>-21272<br>254 350 | 44265<br>-21271<br>254 351 | 44266<br>-21270<br>254 352 | 44267<br>-21269<br>254 353 | 44268<br>-21268<br>254 354 | 44269<br>-21267<br>254 355 | 44270<br>-21266<br>254 356 | 44271<br>-21265<br>254 357 |
| **F-** | 44272<br>-21264<br>254 360 | 44273<br>-21263<br>254 361 | 44274<br>-21262<br>254 362 | 44275<br>-21261<br>254 363 | 44276<br>-21260<br>254 364 | 44277<br>-21259<br>254 365 | 44278<br>-21258<br>254 366 | 44279<br>-21257<br>254 367 | 44280<br>-21256<br>254 370 | 44281<br>-21255<br>254 371 | 44282<br>-21254<br>254 372 | 44283<br>-21253<br>254 373 | 44284<br>-21252<br>254 374 | 44285<br>-21251<br>254 375 | 44286<br>-21250<br>254 376 | 44287<br>-21249<br>254 377 |

DECIMAL → (row 1)  
 DECIMAL → (row 4)  
OCTAL → (row 8)

SECOND HEX DIGIT

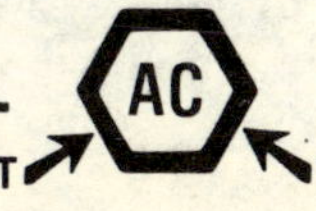 DECIMAL  −21504   BINARY  1010 1100   DECIMAL  44032   HEXADECIMAL  (AC)   OCTAL  254 000

FOURTH HEX DIGIT →   ← THIRD HEX DIGIT

 DECIMAL `-21248`   BINARY `1010 1101`   DECIMAL `44288`   HEXADECIMAL (AD)   OCTAL `255 000`

FOURTH HEX DIGIT → (AD) ← THIRD HEX DIGIT

| ② | FIRST HEX DIGIT | | | | | | | | | | | | | | | |
|---|---|---|---|---|---|---|---|---|---|---|---|---|---|---|---|---|
| SECOND HEX DIGIT | −0 | −1 | −2 | −3 | −4 | −5 | −6 | −7 | −8 | −9 | −A | −B | −C | −D | −E | −F |
| 0− | 44288<br>−21248<br>255 000 | 44289<br>−21247<br>255 001 | 44290<br>−21246<br>255 002 | 44291<br>−21245<br>255 003 | 44292<br>−21244<br>255 004 | 44293<br>−21243<br>255 005 | 44294<br>−21242<br>255 006 | 44295<br>−21241<br>255 007 | 44296<br>−21240<br>255 010 | 44297<br>−21239<br>255 011 | 44298<br>−21238<br>255 012 | 44299<br>−21237<br>255 013 | 44300<br>−21236<br>255 014 | 44301<br>−21235<br>255 015 | 44302<br>−21234<br>255 016 | 44303<br>−21233<br>255 017 |
| 1− | 44304<br>−21232<br>255 020 | 44305<br>−21231<br>255 021 | 44306<br>−21230<br>255 022 | 44307<br>−21229<br>255 023 | 44308<br>−21228<br>255 024 | 44309<br>−21227<br>255 025 | 44310<br>−21226<br>255 026 | 44311<br>−21225<br>255 027 | 44312<br>−21224<br>255 030 | 44313<br>−21223<br>255 031 | 44314<br>−21222<br>255 032 | 44315<br>−21221<br>255 033 | 44316<br>−21220<br>255 034 | 44317<br>−21219<br>255 035 | 44318<br>−21218<br>255 036 | 44319<br>−21217<br>255 037 |
| 2− | 44320<br>−21216<br>255 040 | 44321<br>−21215<br>255 041 | 44322<br>−21214<br>255 042 | 44323<br>−21213<br>255 043 | 44324<br>−21212<br>255 044 | 44325<br>−21211<br>255 045 | 44326<br>−21210<br>255 046 | 44327<br>−21209<br>255 047 | 44328<br>−21208<br>255 050 | 44329<br>−21207<br>255 051 | 44330<br>−21206<br>255 052 | 44331<br>−21205<br>255 053 | 44332<br>−21204<br>255 054 | 44333<br>−21203<br>255 055 | 44334<br>−21202<br>255 056 | 44335<br>−21201<br>255 057 |
| 3− | 44336<br>−21200<br>255 060 | 44337<br>−21199<br>255 061 | 44338<br>−21198<br>255 062 | 44339<br>−21197<br>255 063 | 44340<br>−21196<br>255 064 | 44341<br>−21195<br>255 065 | 44342<br>−21194<br>255 066 | 44343<br>−21193<br>255 067 | 44344<br>−21192<br>255 070 | 44345<br>−21191<br>255 071 | 44346<br>−21190<br>255 072 | 44347<br>−21189<br>255 073 | 44348<br>−21188<br>255 074 | 44349<br>−21187<br>255 075 | 44350<br>−21186<br>255 076 | 44351<br>−21185<br>255 077 |
| 4− | 44352<br>−21184<br>255 100 | 44353<br>−21183<br>255 101 | 44354<br>−21182<br>255 102 | 44355<br>−21181<br>255 103 | 44356<br>−21180<br>255 104 | 44357<br>−21179<br>255 105 | 44358<br>−21178<br>255 106 | 44359<br>−21177<br>255 107 | 44360<br>−21176<br>255 110 | 44361<br>−21175<br>255 111 | 44362<br>−21174<br>255 112 | 44363<br>−21173<br>255 113 | 44364<br>−21172<br>255 114 | 44365<br>−21171<br>255 115 | 44366<br>−21170<br>255 116 | 44367<br>−21169<br>255 117 |
| 5− | 44368<br>−21168<br>255 120 | 44369<br>−21167<br>255 121 | 44370<br>−21166<br>255 122 | 44371<br>−21165<br>255 123 | 44372<br>−21164<br>255 124 | 44373<br>−21163<br>255 125 | 44374<br>−21162<br>255 126 | 44375<br>−21161<br>255 127 | 44376<br>−21160<br>255 130 | 44377<br>−21159<br>255 131 | 44378<br>−21158<br>255 132 | 44379<br>−21157<br>255 133 | 44380<br>−21156<br>255 134 | 44381<br>−21155<br>255 135 | 44382<br>−21154<br>255 136 | 44383<br>−21153<br>255 137 |
| 6− | 44384<br>−21152<br>255 140 | 44385<br>−21151<br>255 141 | 44386<br>−21150<br>255 142 | 44387<br>−21149<br>255 143 | 44388<br>−21148<br>255 144 | 44389<br>−21147<br>255 145 | 44390<br>−21146<br>255 146 | 44391<br>−21145<br>255 147 | 44392<br>−21144<br>255 150 | 44393<br>−21143<br>255 151 | 44394<br>−21142<br>255 152 | 44395<br>−21141<br>255 153 | 44396<br>−21140<br>255 154 | 44397<br>−21139<br>255 155 | 44398<br>−21138<br>255 156 | 44399<br>−21137<br>255 157 |
| 7− | 44400<br>−21136<br>255 160 | 44401<br>−21135<br>255 161 | 44402<br>−21134<br>255 162 | 44403<br>−21133<br>255 163 | 44404<br>−21132<br>255 164 | 44405<br>−21131<br>255 165 | 44406<br>−21130<br>255 166 | 44407<br>−21129<br>255 167 | 44408<br>−21128<br>255 170 | 44409<br>−21127<br>255 171 | 44410<br>−21126<br>255 172 | 44411<br>−21125<br>255 173 | 44412<br>−21124<br>255 174 | 44413<br>−21123<br>255 175 | 44414<br>−21122<br>255 176 | 44415<br>−21121<br>255 177 |
| 8− | 44416<br>−21120<br>255 200 | 44417<br>−21119<br>255 201 | 44418<br>−21118<br>255 202 | 44419<br>−21117<br>255 203 | 44420<br>−21116<br>255 204 | 44421<br>−21115<br>255 205 | 44422<br>−21114<br>255 206 | 44423<br>−21113<br>255 207 | 44424<br>−21112<br>255 210 | 44425<br>−21111<br>255 211 | 44426<br>−21110<br>255 212 | 44427<br>−21109<br>255 213 | 44428<br>−21108<br>255 214 | 44429<br>−21107<br>255 215 | 44430<br>−21106<br>255 216 | 44431<br>−21105<br>255 217 |
| 9− | 44432<br>−21104<br>255 220 | 44433<br>−21103<br>255 221 | 44434<br>−21102<br>255 222 | 44435<br>−21101<br>255 223 | 44436<br>−21100<br>255 224 | 44437<br>−21099<br>255 225 | 44438<br>−21098<br>255 226 | 44439<br>−21097<br>255 227 | 44440<br>−21096<br>255 230 | 44441<br>−21095<br>255 231 | 44442<br>−21094<br>255 232 | 44443<br>−21093<br>255 233 | 44444<br>−21092<br>255 234 | 44445<br>−21091<br>255 235 | 44446<br>−21090<br>255 236 | 44447<br>−21089<br>255 237 |
| A− | 44448<br>−21088<br>255 240 | 44449<br>−21087<br>255 241 | 44450<br>−21086<br>255 242 | 44451<br>−21085<br>255 243 | 44452<br>−21084<br>255 244 | 44453<br>−21083<br>255 245 | 44454<br>−21082<br>255 246 | 44455<br>−21081<br>255 247 | 44456<br>−21080<br>255 250 | 44457<br>−21079<br>255 251 | 44458<br>−21078<br>255 252 | 44459<br>−21077<br>255 253 | 44460<br>−21076<br>255 254 | 44461<br>−21075<br>255 255 | 44462<br>−21074<br>255 256 | 44463<br>−21073<br>255 257 |
| B− | 44464<br>−21072<br>255 260 | 44465<br>−21071<br>255 261 | 44466<br>−21070<br>255 262 | 44467<br>−21069<br>255 263 | 44468<br>−21068<br>255 264 | 44469<br>−21067<br>255 265 | 44470<br>−21066<br>255 266 | 44471<br>−21065<br>255 267 | 44472<br>−21064<br>255 270 | 44473<br>−21063<br>255 271 | 44474<br>−21062<br>255 272 | 44475<br>−21061<br>255 273 | 44476<br>−21060<br>255 274 | 44477<br>−21059<br>255 275 | 44478<br>−21058<br>255 276 | 44479<br>−21057<br>255 277 |
| C− | 44480<br>−21056<br>255 300 | 44481<br>−21055<br>255 301 | 44482<br>−21054<br>255 302 | 44483<br>−21053<br>255 303 | 44484<br>−21052<br>255 304 | 44485<br>−21051<br>255 305 | 44486<br>−21050<br>255 306 | 44487<br>−21049<br>255 307 | 44488<br>−21048<br>255 310 | 44489<br>−21047<br>255 311 | 44490<br>−21046<br>255 312 | 44491<br>−21045<br>255 313 | 44492<br>−21044<br>255 314 | 44493<br>−21043<br>255 315 | 44494<br>−21042<br>255 316 | 44495<br>−21041<br>255 317 |
| D− | 44496<br>−21040<br>255 320 | 44497<br>−21039<br>255 321 | 44498<br>−21038<br>255 322 | 44499<br>−21037<br>255 323 | 44500<br>−21036<br>255 324 | 44501<br>−21035<br>255 325 | 44502<br>−21034<br>255 326 | 44503<br>−21033<br>255 327 | 44504<br>−21032<br>255 330 | 44505<br>−21031<br>255 331 | 44506<br>−21030<br>255 332 | 44507<br>−21029<br>255 333 | 44508<br>−21028<br>255 334 | 44509<br>−21027<br>255 335 | 44510<br>−21026<br>255 336 | 44511<br>−21025<br>255 337 |
| E− | 44512<br>−21024<br>255 340 | 44513<br>−21023<br>255 341 | 44514<br>−21022<br>255 342 | 44515<br>−21021<br>255 343 | 44516<br>−21020<br>255 344 | 44517<br>−21019<br>255 345 | 44518<br>−21018<br>255 346 | 44519<br>−21017<br>255 347 | 44520<br>−21016<br>255 350 | 44521<br>−21015<br>255 351 | 44522<br>−21014<br>255 352 | 44523<br>−21013<br>255 353 | 44524<br>−21012<br>255 354 | 44525<br>−21011<br>255 355 | 44526<br>−21010<br>255 356 | 44527<br>−21009<br>255 357 |
| F− | 44528<br>−21008<br>255 360 | 44529<br>−21007<br>255 361 | 44530<br>−21006<br>255 362 | 44531<br>−21005<br>255 363 | 44532<br>−21004<br>255 364 | 44533<br>−21003<br>255 365 | 44534<br>−21002<br>255 366 | 44535<br>−21001<br>255 367 | 44536<br>−21000<br>255 370 | 44537<br>−20999<br>255 371 | 44538<br>−20998<br>255 372 | 44539<br>−20997<br>255 373 | 44540<br>−20996<br>255 374 | 44541<br>−20995<br>255 375 | 44542<br>−20994<br>255 376 | 44543<br>−20993<br>255 377 |

DECIMAL ←

 DECIMAL ←

OCTAL ←

# FIRST HEX DIGIT

| SECOND HEX DIGIT | -0 | -1 | -2 | -3 | -4 | -5 | -6 | -7 | -8 | -9 | -A | -B | -C | -D | -E | -F |
|---|---|---|---|---|---|---|---|---|---|---|---|---|---|---|---|---|
| 0- | 44544<br>-20992<br>256 000 | 44545<br>-20991<br>256 001 | 44546<br>-20990<br>256 002 | 44547<br>-20989<br>256 003 | 44548<br>-20988<br>256 004 | 44549<br>-20987<br>256 005 | 44550<br>-20986<br>256 006 | 44551<br>-20985<br>256 007 | 44552<br>-20984<br>256 010 | 44553<br>-20983<br>256 011 | 44554<br>-20982<br>256 012 | 44555<br>-20981<br>256 013 | 44556<br>-20980<br>256 014 | 44557<br>-20979<br>256 015 | 44558<br>-20978<br>256 016 | 44559<br>-20977<br>256 017 |
| 1- | 44560<br>-20976<br>256 020 | 44561<br>-20975<br>256 021 | 44562<br>-20974<br>256 022 | 44563<br>-20973<br>256 023 | 44564<br>-20972<br>256 024 | 44565<br>-20971<br>256 025 | 44566<br>-20970<br>256 026 | 44567<br>-20969<br>256 027 | 44568<br>-20968<br>256 030 | 44569<br>-20967<br>256 031 | 44570<br>-20966<br>256 032 | 44571<br>-20965<br>256 033 | 44572<br>-20964<br>256 034 | 44573<br>-20963<br>256 035 | 44574<br>-20962<br>256 036 | 44575<br>-20961<br>256 037 |
| 2- | 44576<br>-20960<br>256 040 | 44577<br>-20959<br>256 041 | 44578<br>-20958<br>256 042 | 44579<br>-20957<br>256 043 | 44580<br>-20956<br>256 044 | 44581<br>-20955<br>256 045 | 44582<br>-20954<br>256 046 | 44583<br>-20953<br>256 047 | 44584<br>-20952<br>256 050 | 44585<br>-20951<br>256 051 | 44586<br>-20950<br>256 052 | 44587<br>-20949<br>256 053 | 44588<br>-20948<br>256 054 | 44589<br>-20947<br>256 055 | 44590<br>-20946<br>256 056 | 44591<br>-20945<br>256 057 |
| 3- | 44592<br>-20944<br>256 060 | 44593<br>-20943<br>256 061 | 44594<br>-20942<br>256 062 | 44595<br>-20941<br>256 063 | 44596<br>-20940<br>256 064 | 44597<br>-20939<br>256 065 | 44598<br>-20938<br>256 066 | 44599<br>-20937<br>256 067 | 44600<br>-20936<br>256 070 | 44601<br>-20935<br>256 071 | 44602<br>-20934<br>256 072 | 44603<br>-20933<br>256 073 | 44604<br>-20932<br>256 074 | 44605<br>-20931<br>256 075 | 44606<br>-20930<br>256 076 | 44607<br>-20929<br>256 077 |
| 4- | 44608<br>-20928<br>256 100 | 44609<br>-20927<br>256 101 | 44610<br>-20926<br>256 102 | 44611<br>-20925<br>256 103 | 44612<br>-20924<br>256 104 | 44613<br>-20923<br>256 105 | 44614<br>-20922<br>256 106 | 44615<br>-20921<br>256 107 | 44616<br>-20920<br>256 110 | 44617<br>-20919<br>256 111 | 44618<br>-20918<br>256 112 | 44619<br>-20917<br>256 113 | 44620<br>-20916<br>256 114 | 44621<br>-20915<br>256 115 | 44622<br>-20914<br>256 116 | 44623<br>-20913<br>256 117 |
| 5- | 44624<br>-20912<br>256 120 | 44625<br>-20911<br>256 121 | 44626<br>-20910<br>256 122 | 44627<br>-20909<br>256 123 | 44628<br>-20908<br>256 124 | 44629<br>-20907<br>256 125 | 44630<br>-20906<br>256 126 | 44631<br>-20905<br>256 127 | 44632<br>-20904<br>256 130 | 44633<br>-20903<br>256 131 | 44634<br>-20902<br>256 132 | 44635<br>-20901<br>256 133 | 44636<br>-20900<br>256 134 | 44637<br>-20899<br>256 135 | 44638<br>-20898<br>256 136 | 44639<br>-20897<br>256 137 |
| 6- | 44640<br>-20896<br>256 140 | 44641<br>-20895<br>256 141 | 44642<br>-20894<br>256 142 | 44643<br>-20893<br>256 143 | 44644<br>-20892<br>256 144 | 44645<br>-20891<br>256 145 | 44646<br>-20890<br>256 146 | 44647<br>-20889<br>256 147 | 44648<br>-20888<br>256 150 | 44649<br>-20887<br>256 151 | 44650<br>-20886<br>256 152 | 44651<br>-20885<br>256 153 | 44652<br>-20884<br>256 154 | 44653<br>-20883<br>256 155 | 44654<br>-20882<br>256 156 | 44655<br>-20881<br>256 157 |
| 7- | 44656<br>-20880<br>256 160 | 44657<br>-20879<br>256 161 | 44658<br>-20878<br>256 162 | 44659<br>-20877<br>256 163 | 44660<br>-20876<br>256 164 | 44661<br>-20875<br>256 165 | 44662<br>-20874<br>256 166 | 44663<br>-20873<br>256 167 | 44664<br>-20872<br>256 170 | 44665<br>-20871<br>256 171 | 44666<br>-20870<br>256 172 | 44667<br>-20869<br>256 173 | 44668<br>-20868<br>256 174 | 44669<br>-20867<br>256 175 | 44670<br>-20866<br>256 176 | 44671<br>-20865<br>256 177 |
| 8- | 44672<br>-20864<br>256 200 | 44673<br>-20863<br>256 201 | 44674<br>-20862<br>256 202 | 44675<br>-20861<br>256 203 | 44676<br>-20860<br>256 204 | 44677<br>-20859<br>256 205 | 44678<br>-20858<br>256 206 | 44679<br>-20857<br>256 207 | 44680<br>-20856<br>256 210 | 44681<br>-20855<br>256 211 | 44682<br>-20854<br>256 212 | 44683<br>-20853<br>256 213 | 44684<br>-20852<br>256 214 | 44685<br>-20851<br>256 215 | 44686<br>-20850<br>256 216 | 44687<br>-20849<br>256 217 |
| 9- | 44688<br>-20848<br>256 220 | 44689<br>-20847<br>256 221 | 44690<br>-20846<br>256 222 | 44691<br>-20845<br>256 223 | 44692<br>-20844<br>256 224 | 44693<br>-20843<br>256 225 | 44694<br>-20842<br>256 226 | 44695<br>-20841<br>256 227 | 44696<br>-20840<br>256 230 | 44697<br>-20839<br>256 231 | 44698<br>-20838<br>256 232 | 44699<br>-20837<br>256 233 | 44700<br>-20836<br>256 234 | 44701<br>-20835<br>256 235 | 44702<br>-20834<br>256 236 | 44703<br>-20833<br>256 237 |
| A- | 44704<br>-20832<br>256 240 | 44705<br>-20831<br>256 241 | 44706<br>-20830<br>256 242 | 44707<br>-20829<br>256 243 | 44708<br>-20828<br>256 244 | 44709<br>-20827<br>256 245 | 44710<br>-20826<br>256 246 | 44711<br>-20825<br>256 247 | 44712<br>-20824<br>256 250 | 44713<br>-20823<br>256 251 | 44714<br>-20822<br>256 252 | 44715<br>-20821<br>256 253 | 44716<br>-20820<br>256 254 | 44717<br>-20819<br>256 255 | 44718<br>-20818<br>256 256 | 44719<br>-20817<br>256 257 |
| B- | 44720<br>-20816<br>256 260 | 44721<br>-20815<br>256 261 | 44722<br>-20814<br>256 262 | 44723<br>-20813<br>256 263 | 44724<br>-20812<br>256 264 | 44725<br>-20811<br>256 265 | 44726<br>-20810<br>256 266 | 44727<br>-20809<br>256 267 | 44728<br>-20808<br>256 270 | 44729<br>-20807<br>256 271 | 44730<br>-20806<br>256 272 | 44731<br>-20805<br>256 273 | 44732<br>-20804<br>256 274 | 44733<br>-20803<br>256 275 | 44734<br>-20802<br>256 276 | 44735<br>-20801<br>256 277 |
| C- | 44736<br>-20800<br>256 300 | 44737<br>-20799<br>256 301 | 44738<br>-20798<br>256 302 | 44739<br>-20797<br>256 303 | 44740<br>-20796<br>256 304 | 44741<br>-20795<br>256 305 | 44742<br>-20794<br>256 306 | 44743<br>-20793<br>256 307 | 44744<br>-20792<br>256 310 | 44745<br>-20791<br>256 311 | 44746<br>-20790<br>256 312 | 44747<br>-20789<br>256 313 | 44748<br>-20788<br>256 314 | 44749<br>-20787<br>256 315 | 44750<br>-20786<br>256 316 | 44751<br>-20785<br>256 317 |
| D- | 44752<br>-20784<br>256 320 | 44753<br>-20783<br>256 321 | 44754<br>-20782<br>256 322 | 44755<br>-20781<br>256 323 | 44756<br>-20780<br>256 324 | 44757<br>-20779<br>256 325 | 44758<br>-20778<br>256 326 | 44759<br>-20777<br>256 327 | 44760<br>-20776<br>256 330 | 44761<br>-20775<br>256 331 | 44762<br>-20774<br>256 332 | 44763<br>-20773<br>256 333 | 44764<br>-20772<br>256 334 | 44765<br>-20771<br>256 335 | 44766<br>-20770<br>256 336 | 44767<br>-20769<br>256 337 |
| E- | 44768<br>-20768<br>256 340 | 44769<br>-20767<br>256 341 | 44770<br>-20766<br>256 342 | 44771<br>-20765<br>256 343 | 44772<br>-20764<br>256 344 | 44773<br>-20763<br>256 345 | 44774<br>-20762<br>256 346 | 44775<br>-20761<br>256 347 | 44776<br>-20760<br>256 350 | 44777<br>-20759<br>256 351 | 44778<br>-20758<br>256 352 | 44779<br>-20757<br>256 353 | 44780<br>-20756<br>256 354 | 44781<br>-20755<br>256 355 | 44782<br>-20754<br>256 356 | 44783<br>-20753<br>256 357 |
| F- | 44784<br>-20752<br>256 360 | 44785<br>-20751<br>256 361 | 44786<br>-20750<br>256 362 | 44787<br>-20749<br>256 363 | 44788<br>-20748<br>256 364 | 44789<br>-20747<br>256 365 | 44790<br>-20746<br>256 366 | 44791<br>-20745<br>256 367 | 44792<br>-20744<br>256 370 | 44793<br>-20743<br>256 371 | 44794<br>-20742<br>256 372 | 44795<br>-20741<br>256 373 | 44796<br>-20740<br>256 374 | 44797<br>-20739<br>256 375 | 44798<br>-20738<br>256 376 | 44799<br>-20737<br>256 377 |

DECIMAL   DECIMAL   OCTAL

 DECIMAL  `-20992`    BINARY  `1010 1110`    DECIMAL  `44544`    HEXADECIMAL  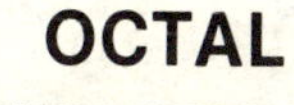  `AE`  OCTAL  `256 000`

FOURTH HEX DIGIT →   ← THIRD HEX DIGIT

**FIRST HEX DIGIT** (②) — each cell: decimal / signed decimal / octal. Arrows mark: DECIMAL,  DECIMAL, OCTAL. Rows = SECOND HEX DIGIT.

| | −0 | −1 | −2 | −3 | −4 | −5 | −6 | −7 | −8 | −9 | −A | −B | −C | −D | −E | −F |
|---|---|---|---|---|---|---|---|---|---|---|---|---|---|---|---|---|
| 0− | 44800<br>−20736<br>257 000 | 44801<br>−20735<br>257 001 | 44802<br>−20734<br>257 002 | 44803<br>−20733<br>257 003 | 44804<br>−20732<br>257 004 | 44805<br>−20731<br>257 005 | 44806<br>−20730<br>257 006 | 44807<br>−20729<br>257 007 | 44808<br>−20728<br>257 010 | 44809<br>−20727<br>257 011 | 44810<br>−20726<br>257 012 | 44811<br>−20725<br>257 013 | 44812<br>−20724<br>257 014 | 44813<br>−20723<br>257 015 | 44814<br>−20722<br>257 016 | 44815<br>−20721<br>257 017 |
| 1− | 44816<br>−20720<br>257 020 | 44817<br>−20719<br>257 021 | 44818<br>−20718<br>257 022 | 44819<br>−20717<br>257 023 | 44820<br>−20716<br>257 024 | 44821<br>−20715<br>257 025 | 44822<br>−20714<br>257 026 | 44823<br>−20713<br>257 027 | 44824<br>−20712<br>257 030 | 44825<br>−20711<br>257 031 | 44826<br>−20710<br>257 032 | 44827<br>−20709<br>257 033 | 44828<br>−20708<br>257 034 | 44829<br>−20707<br>257 035 | 44830<br>−20706<br>257 036 | 44831<br>−20705<br>257 037 |
| 2− | 44832<br>−20704<br>257 040 | 44833<br>−20703<br>257 041 | 44834<br>−20702<br>257 042 | 44835<br>−20701<br>257 043 | 44836<br>−20700<br>257 044 | 44837<br>−20699<br>257 045 | 44838<br>−20698<br>257 046 | 44839<br>−20697<br>257 047 | 44840<br>−20696<br>257 050 | 44841<br>−20695<br>257 051 | 44842<br>−20694<br>257 052 | 44843<br>−20693<br>257 053 | 44844<br>−20692<br>257 054 | 44845<br>−20691<br>257 055 | 44846<br>−20690<br>257 056 | 44847<br>−20689<br>257 057 |
| 3− | 44848<br>−20688<br>257 060 | 44849<br>−20687<br>257 061 | 44850<br>−20686<br>257 062 | 44851<br>−20685<br>257 063 | 44852<br>−20684<br>257 064 | 44853<br>−20683<br>257 065 | 44854<br>−20682<br>257 066 | 44855<br>−20681<br>257 067 | 44856<br>−20680<br>257 070 | 44857<br>−20679<br>257 071 | 44858<br>−20678<br>257 072 | 44859<br>−20677<br>257 073 | 44860<br>−20676<br>257 074 | 44861<br>−20675<br>257 075 | 44862<br>−20674<br>257 076 | 44863<br>−20673<br>257 077 |
| 4− | 44864<br>−20672<br>257 100 | 44865<br>−20671<br>257 101 | 44866<br>−20670<br>257 102 | 44867<br>−20669<br>257 103 | 44868<br>−20668<br>257 104 | 44869<br>−20667<br>257 105 | 44870<br>−20666<br>257 106 | 44871<br>−20665<br>257 107 | 44872<br>−20664<br>257 110 | 44873<br>−20663<br>257 111 | 44874<br>−20662<br>257 112 | 44875<br>−20661<br>257 113 | 44876<br>−20660<br>257 114 | 44877<br>−20659<br>257 115 | 44878<br>−20658<br>257 116 | 44879<br>−20657<br>257 117 |
| 5− | 44880<br>−20656<br>257 120 | 44881<br>−20655<br>257 121 | 44882<br>−20654<br>257 122 | 44883<br>−20653<br>257 123 | 44884<br>−20652<br>257 124 | 44885<br>−20651<br>257 125 | 44886<br>−20650<br>257 126 | 44887<br>−20649<br>257 127 | 44888<br>−20648<br>257 130 | 44889<br>−20647<br>257 131 | 44890<br>−20646<br>257 132 | 44891<br>−20645<br>257 133 | 44892<br>−20644<br>257 134 | 44893<br>−20643<br>257 135 | 44894<br>−20642<br>257 136 | 44895<br>−20641<br>257 137 |
| 6− | 44896<br>−20640<br>257 140 | 44897<br>−20639<br>257 141 | 44898<br>−20638<br>257 142 | 44899<br>−20637<br>257 143 | 44900<br>−20636<br>257 144 | 44901<br>−20635<br>257 145 | 44902<br>−20634<br>257 146 | 44903<br>−20633<br>257 147 | 44904<br>−20632<br>257 150 | 44905<br>−20631<br>257 151 | 44906<br>−20630<br>257 152 | 44907<br>−20629<br>257 153 | 44908<br>−20628<br>257 154 | 44909<br>−20627<br>257 155 | 44910<br>−20626<br>257 156 | 44911<br>−20625<br>257 157 |
| 7− | 44912<br>−20624<br>257 160 | 44913<br>−20623<br>257 161 | 44914<br>−20622<br>257 162 | 44915<br>−20621<br>257 163 | 44916<br>−20620<br>257 164 | 44917<br>−20619<br>257 165 | 44918<br>−20618<br>257 166 | 44919<br>−20617<br>257 167 | 44920<br>−20616<br>257 170 | 44921<br>−20615<br>257 171 | 44922<br>−20614<br>257 172 | 44923<br>−20613<br>257 173 | 44924<br>−20612<br>257 174 | 44925<br>−20611<br>257 175 | 44926<br>−20610<br>257 176 | 44927<br>−20609<br>257 177 |
| 8− | 44928<br>−20608<br>257 200 | 44929<br>−20607<br>257 201 | 44930<br>−20606<br>257 202 | 44931<br>−20605<br>257 203 | 44932<br>−20604<br>257 204 | 44933<br>−20603<br>257 205 | 44934<br>−20602<br>257 206 | 44935<br>−20601<br>257 207 | 44936<br>−20600<br>257 210 | 44937<br>−20599<br>257 211 | 44938<br>−20598<br>257 212 | 44939<br>−20597<br>257 213 | 44940<br>−20596<br>257 214 | 44941<br>−20595<br>257 215 | 44942<br>−20594<br>257 216 | 44943<br>−20593<br>257 217 |
| 9− | 44944<br>−20592<br>257 220 | 44945<br>−20591<br>257 221 | 44946<br>−20590<br>257 222 | 44947<br>−20589<br>257 223 | 44948<br>−20588<br>257 224 | 44949<br>−20587<br>257 225 | 44950<br>−20586<br>257 226 | 44951<br>−20585<br>257 227 | 44952<br>−20584<br>257 230 | 44953<br>−20583<br>257 231 | 44954<br>−20582<br>257 232 | 44955<br>−20581<br>257 233 | 44956<br>−20580<br>257 234 | 44957<br>−20579<br>257 235 | 44958<br>−20578<br>257 236 | 44959<br>−20577<br>257 237 |
| A− | 44960<br>−20576<br>257 240 | 44961<br>−20575<br>257 241 | 44962<br>−20574<br>257 242 | 44963<br>−20573<br>257 243 | 44964<br>−20572<br>257 244 | 44965<br>−20571<br>257 245 | 44966<br>−20570<br>257 246 | 44967<br>−20569<br>257 247 | 44968<br>−20568<br>257 250 | 44969<br>−20567<br>257 251 | 44970<br>−20566<br>257 252 | 44971<br>−20565<br>257 253 | 44972<br>−20564<br>257 254 | 44973<br>−20563<br>257 255 | 44974<br>−20562<br>257 256 | 44975<br>−20561<br>257 257 |
| B− | 44976<br>−20560<br>257 260 | 44977<br>−20559<br>257 261 | 44978<br>−20558<br>257 262 | 44979<br>−20557<br>257 263 | 44980<br>−20556<br>257 264 | 44981<br>−20555<br>257 265 | 44982<br>−20554<br>257 266 | 44983<br>−20553<br>257 267 | 44984<br>−20552<br>257 270 | 44985<br>−20551<br>257 271 | 44986<br>−20550<br>257 272 | 44987<br>−20549<br>257 273 | 44988<br>−20548<br>257 274 | 44989<br>−20547<br>257 275 | 44990<br>−20546<br>257 276 | 44991<br>−20545<br>257 277 |
| C− | 44992<br>−20544<br>257 300 | 44993<br>−20543<br>257 301 | 44994<br>−20542<br>257 302 | 44995<br>−20541<br>257 303 | 44996<br>−20540<br>257 304 | 44997<br>−20539<br>257 305 | 44998<br>−20538<br>257 306 | 44999<br>−20537<br>257 307 | 45000<br>−20536<br>257 310 | 45001<br>−20535<br>257 311 | 45002<br>−20534<br>257 312 | 45003<br>−20533<br>257 313 | 45004<br>−20532<br>257 314 | 45005<br>−20531<br>257 315 | 45006<br>−20530<br>257 316 | 45007<br>−20529<br>257 317 |
| D− | 45008<br>−20528<br>257 320 | 45009<br>−20527<br>257 321 | 45010<br>−20526<br>257 322 | 45011<br>−20525<br>257 323 | 45012<br>−20524<br>257 324 | 45013<br>−20523<br>257 325 | 45014<br>−20522<br>257 326 | 45015<br>−20521<br>257 327 | 45016<br>−20520<br>257 330 | 45017<br>−20519<br>257 331 | 45018<br>−20518<br>257 332 | 45019<br>−20517<br>257 333 | 45020<br>−20516<br>257 334 | 45021<br>−20515<br>257 335 | 45022<br>−20514<br>257 336 | 45023<br>−20513<br>257 337 |
| E− | 45024<br>−20512<br>257 340 | 45025<br>−20511<br>257 341 | 45026<br>−20510<br>257 342 | 45027<br>−20509<br>257 343 | 45028<br>−20508<br>257 344 | 45029<br>−20507<br>257 345 | 45030<br>−20506<br>257 346 | 45031<br>−20505<br>257 347 | 45032<br>−20504<br>257 350 | 45033<br>−20503<br>257 351 | 45034<br>−20502<br>257 352 | 45035<br>−20501<br>257 353 | 45036<br>−20500<br>257 354 | 45037<br>−20499<br>257 355 | 45038<br>−20498<br>257 356 | 45039<br>−20497<br>257 357 |
| F− | 45040<br>−20496<br>257 360 | 45041<br>−20495<br>257 361 | 45042<br>−20494<br>257 362 | 45043<br>−20493<br>257 363 | 45044<br>−20492<br>257 364 | 45045<br>−20491<br>257 365 | 45046<br>−20490<br>257 366 | 45047<br>−20489<br>257 367 | 45048<br>−20488<br>257 370 | 45049<br>−20487<br>257 371 | 45050<br>−20486<br>257 372 | 45051<br>−20485<br>257 373 | 45052<br>−20484<br>257 374 | 45053<br>−20483<br>257 375 | 45054<br>−20482<br>257 376 | 45055<br>−20481<br>257 377 |

# FIRST HEX DIGIT

| 2 | | −0 | −1 | −2 | −3 | −4 | −5 | −6 | −7 | −8 | −9 | −A | −B | −C | −D | −E | −F |
|---|---|---|---|---|---|---|---|---|---|---|---|---|---|---|---|---|---|
| **S** | **0-** | 45056<br>−20480<br>260 000 | 45057<br>−20479<br>260 001 | 45058<br>−20478<br>260 002 | 45059<br>−20477<br>260 003 | 45060<br>−20476<br>260 004 | 45061<br>−20475<br>260 005 | 45062<br>−20474<br>260 006 | 45063<br>−20473<br>260 007 | 45064<br>−20472<br>260 010 | 45065<br>−20471<br>260 011 | 45066<br>−20470<br>260 012 | 45067<br>−20469<br>260 013 | 45068<br>−20468<br>260 014 | 45069<br>−20467<br>260 015 | 45070<br>−20466<br>260 016 | 45071<br>−20465<br>260 017 |
| **E** | **1-** | 45072<br>−20464<br>260 020 | 45073<br>−20463<br>260 021 | 45074<br>−20462<br>260 022 | 45075<br>−20461<br>260 023 | 45076<br>−20460<br>260 024 | 45077<br>−20459<br>260 025 | 45078<br>−20458<br>260 026 | 45079<br>−20457<br>260 027 | 45080<br>−20456<br>260 030 | 45081<br>−20455<br>260 031 | 45082<br>−20454<br>260 032 | 45083<br>−20453<br>260 033 | 45084<br>−20452<br>260 034 | 45085<br>−20451<br>260 035 | 45086<br>−20450<br>260 036 | 45087<br>−20449<br>260 037 |
| **C** | **2-** | 45088<br>−20448<br>260 040 | 45089<br>−20447<br>260 041 | 45090<br>−20446<br>260 042 | 45091<br>−20445<br>260 043 | 45092<br>−20444<br>260 044 | 45093<br>−20443<br>260 045 | 45094<br>−20442<br>260 046 | 45095<br>−20441<br>260 047 | 45096<br>−20440<br>260 050 | 45097<br>−20439<br>260 051 | 45098<br>−20438<br>260 052 | 45099<br>−20437<br>260 053 | 45100<br>−20436<br>260 054 | 45101<br>−20435<br>260 055 | 45102<br>−20434<br>260 056 | 45103<br>−20433<br>260 057 |
| **O** | **3-** | 45104<br>−20432<br>260 060 | 45105<br>−20431<br>260 061 | 45106<br>−20430<br>260 062 | 45107<br>−20429<br>260 063 | 45108<br>−20428<br>260 064 | 45109<br>−20427<br>260 065 | 45110<br>−20426<br>260 066 | 45111<br>−20425<br>260 067 | 45112<br>−20424<br>260 070 | 45113<br>−20423<br>260 071 | 45114<br>−20422<br>260 072 | 45115<br>−20421<br>260 073 | 45116<br>−20420<br>260 074 | 45117<br>−20419<br>260 075 | 45118<br>−20418<br>260 076 | 45119<br>−20417<br>260 077 |
| **N** | **4-** | 45120<br>−20416<br>260 100 | 45121<br>−20415<br>260 101 | 45122<br>−20414<br>260 102 | 45123<br>−20413<br>260 103 | 45124<br>−20412<br>260 104 | 45125<br>−20411<br>260 105 | 45126<br>−20410<br>260 106 | 45127<br>−20409<br>260 107 | 45128<br>−20408<br>260 110 | 45129<br>−20407<br>260 111 | 45130<br>−20406<br>260 112 | 45131<br>−20405<br>260 113 | 45132<br>−20404<br>260 114 | 45133<br>−20403<br>260 115 | 45134<br>−20402<br>260 116 | 45135<br>−20401<br>260 117 |
| **D** | **5-** | 45136<br>−20400<br>260 120 | 45137<br>−20399<br>260 121 | 45138<br>−20398<br>260 122 | 45139<br>−20397<br>260 123 | 45140<br>−20396<br>260 124 | 45141<br>−20395<br>260 125 | 45142<br>−20394<br>260 126 | 45143<br>−20393<br>260 127 | 45144<br>−20392<br>260 130 | 45145<br>−20391<br>260 131 | 45146<br>−20390<br>260 132 | 45147<br>−20389<br>260 133 | 45148<br>−20388<br>260 134 | 45149<br>−20387<br>260 135 | 45150<br>−20386<br>260 136 | 45151<br>−20385<br>260 137 |
| | **6-** | 45152<br>−20384<br>260 140 | 45153<br>−20383<br>260 141 | 45154<br>−20382<br>260 142 | 45155<br>−20381<br>260 143 | 45156<br>−20380<br>260 144 | 45157<br>−20379<br>260 145 | 45158<br>−20378<br>260 146 | 45159<br>−20377<br>260 147 | 45160<br>−20376<br>260 150 | 45161<br>−20375<br>260 151 | 45162<br>−20374<br>260 152 | 45163<br>−20373<br>260 153 | 45164<br>−20372<br>260 154 | 45165<br>−20371<br>260 155 | 45166<br>−20370<br>260 156 | 45167<br>−20369<br>260 157 |
| **H** | **7-** | 45168<br>−20368<br>260 160 | 45169<br>−20367<br>260 161 | 45170<br>−20366<br>260 162 | 45171<br>−20365<br>260 163 | 45172<br>−20364<br>260 164 | 45173<br>−20363<br>260 165 | 45174<br>−20362<br>260 166 | 45175<br>−20361<br>260 167 | 45176<br>−20360<br>260 170 | 45177<br>−20359<br>260 171 | 45178<br>−20358<br>260 172 | 45179<br>−20357<br>260 173 | 45180<br>−20356<br>260 174 | 45181<br>−20355<br>260 175 | 45182<br>−20354<br>260 176 | 45183<br>−20353<br>260 177 |
| **E** | **8-** | 45184<br>−20352<br>260 200 | 45185<br>−20351<br>260 201 | 45186<br>−20350<br>260 202 | 45187<br>−20349<br>260 203 | 45188<br>−20348<br>260 204 | 45189<br>−20347<br>260 205 | 45190<br>−20346<br>260 206 | 45191<br>−20345<br>260 207 | 45192<br>−20344<br>260 210 | 45193<br>−20343<br>260 211 | 45194<br>−20342<br>260 212 | 45195<br>−20341<br>260 213 | 45196<br>−20340<br>260 214 | 45197<br>−20339<br>260 215 | 45198<br>−20338<br>260 216 | 45199<br>−20337<br>260 217 |
| **X** | **9-** | 45200<br>−20336<br>260 220 | 45201<br>−20335<br>260 221 | 45202<br>−20334<br>260 222 | 45203<br>−20333<br>260 223 | 45204<br>−20332<br>260 224 | 45205<br>−20331<br>260 225 | 45206<br>−20330<br>260 226 | 45207<br>−20329<br>260 227 | 45208<br>−20328<br>260 230 | 45209<br>−20327<br>260 231 | 45210<br>−20326<br>260 232 | 45211<br>−20325<br>260 233 | 45212<br>−20324<br>260 234 | 45213<br>−20323<br>260 235 | 45214<br>−20322<br>260 236 | 45215<br>−20321<br>260 237 |
| | **A-** | 45216<br>−20320<br>260 240 | 45217<br>−20319<br>260 241 | 45218<br>−20318<br>260 242 | 45219<br>−20317<br>260 243 | 45220<br>−20316<br>260 244 | 45221<br>−20315<br>260 245 | 45222<br>−20314<br>260 246 | 45223<br>−20313<br>260 247 | 45224<br>−20312<br>260 250 | 45225<br>−20311<br>260 251 | 45226<br>−20310<br>260 252 | 45227<br>−20309<br>260 253 | 45228<br>−20308<br>260 254 | 45229<br>−20307<br>260 255 | 45230<br>−20306<br>260 256 | 45231<br>−20305<br>260 257 |
| **D** | **B-** | 45232<br>−20304<br>260 260 | 45233<br>−20303<br>260 261 | 45234<br>−20302<br>260 262 | 45235<br>−20301<br>260 263 | 45236<br>−20300<br>260 264 | 45237<br>−20299<br>260 265 | 45238<br>−20298<br>260 266 | 45239<br>−20297<br>260 267 | 45240<br>−20296<br>260 270 | 45241<br>−20295<br>260 271 | 45242<br>−20294<br>260 272 | 45243<br>−20293<br>260 273 | 45244<br>−20292<br>260 274 | 45245<br>−20291<br>260 275 | 45246<br>−20290<br>260 276 | 45247<br>−20289<br>260 277 |
| **I** | **C-** | 45248<br>−20288<br>260 300 | 45249<br>−20287<br>260 301 | 45250<br>−20286<br>260 302 | 45251<br>−20285<br>260 303 | 45252<br>−20284<br>260 304 | 45253<br>−20283<br>260 305 | 45254<br>−20282<br>260 306 | 45255<br>−20281<br>260 307 | 45256<br>−20280<br>260 310 | 45257<br>−20279<br>260 311 | 45258<br>−20278<br>260 312 | 45259<br>−20277<br>260 313 | 45260<br>−20276<br>260 314 | 45261<br>−20275<br>260 315 | 45262<br>−20274<br>260 316 | 45263<br>−20273<br>260 317 |
| **G** | **D-** | 45264<br>−20272<br>260 320 | 45265<br>−20271<br>260 321 | 45266<br>−20270<br>260 322 | 45267<br>−20269<br>260 323 | 45268<br>−20268<br>260 324 | 45269<br>−20267<br>260 325 | 45270<br>−20266<br>260 326 | 45271<br>−20265<br>260 327 | 45272<br>−20264<br>260 330 | 45273<br>−20263<br>260 331 | 45274<br>−20262<br>260 332 | 45275<br>−20261<br>260 333 | 45276<br>−20260<br>260 334 | 45277<br>−20259<br>260 335 | 45278<br>−20258<br>260 336 | 45279<br>−20257<br>260 337 |
| **I** | **E-** | 45280<br>−20256<br>260 340 | 45281<br>−20255<br>260 341 | 45282<br>−20254<br>260 342 | 45283<br>−20253<br>260 343 | 45284<br>−20252<br>260 344 | 45285<br>−20251<br>260 345 | 45286<br>−20250<br>260 346 | 45287<br>−20249<br>260 347 | 45288<br>−20248<br>260 350 | 45289<br>−20247<br>260 351 | 45290<br>−20246<br>260 352 | 45291<br>−20245<br>260 353 | 45292<br>−20244<br>260 354 | 45293<br>−20243<br>260 355 | 45294<br>−20242<br>260 356 | 45295<br>−20241<br>260 357 |
| **T** | **F-** | 45296<br>−20240<br>260 360 | 45297<br>−20239<br>260 361 | 45298<br>−20238<br>260 362 | 45299<br>−20237<br>260 363 | 45300<br>−20236<br>260 364 | 45301<br>−20235<br>260 365 | 45302<br>−20234<br>260 366 | 45303<br>−20233<br>260 367 | 45304<br>−20232<br>260 370 | 45305<br>−20231<br>260 371 | 45306<br>−20230<br>260 372 | 45307<br>−20229<br>260 373 | 45308<br>−20228<br>260 374 | 45309<br>−20227<br>260 375 | 45310<br>−20226<br>260 376 | 45311<br>−20225<br>260 377 |

SECOND HEX DIGIT

DECIMAL    ⌘ DECIMAL    OCTAL

---

⌘ DECIMAL `−20480`     **BINARY** `1011 0000`     **DECIMAL** `45056`     **HEXADECIMAL** (B0) **OCTAL** `260 000`

FOURTH HEX DIGIT → ← THIRD HEX DIGIT

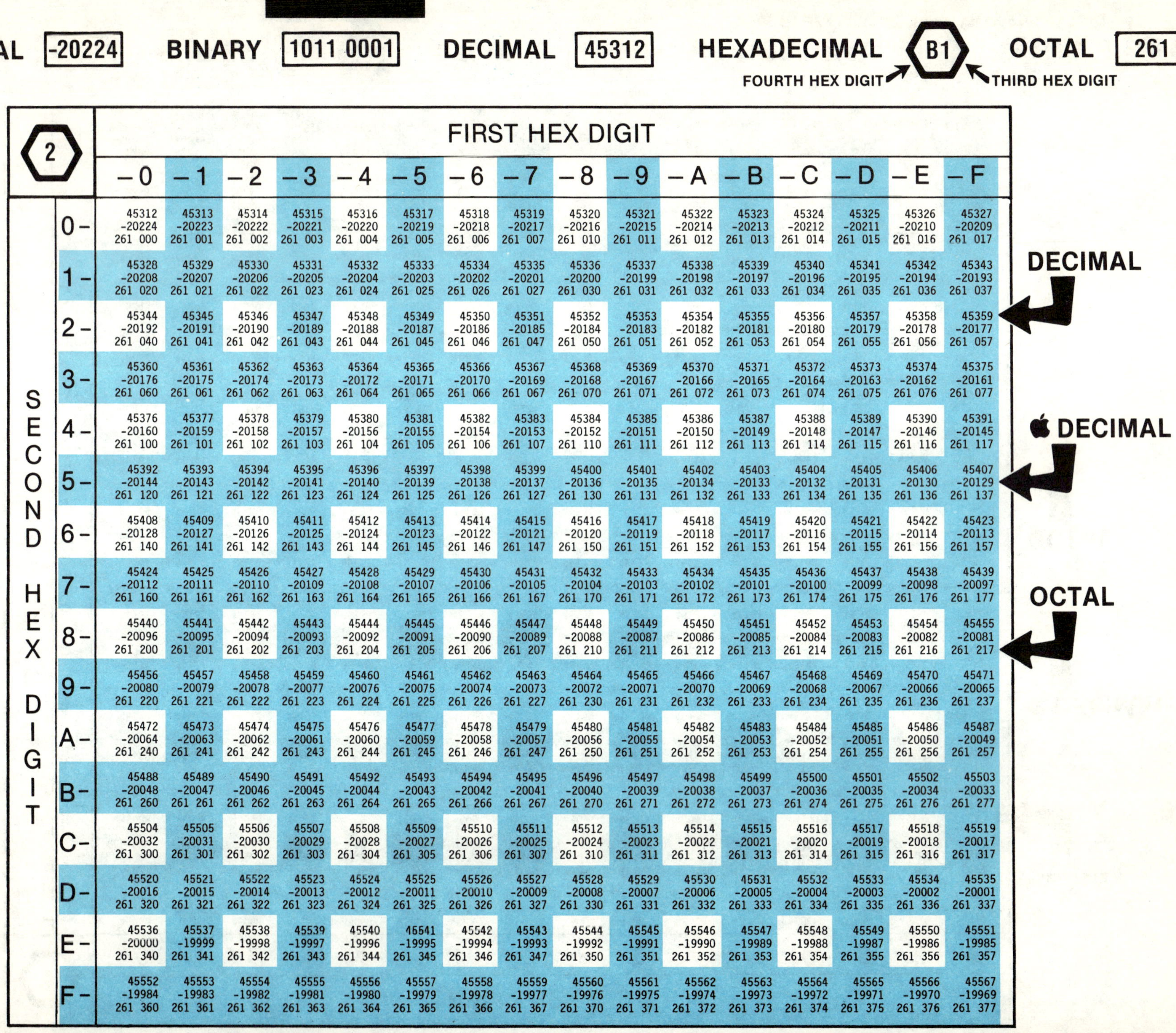

DECIMAL `-20224`  BINARY `1011 0001`  DECIMAL `45312`  HEXADECIMAL (B1) OCTAL `261 000`

FOURTH HEX DIGIT → B1 ← THIRD HEX DIGIT

(2)

| SECOND HEX DIGIT | FIRST HEX DIGIT −0 | −1 | −2 | −3 | −4 | −5 | −6 | −7 | −8 | −9 | −A | −B | −C | −D | −E | −F |
|---|---|---|---|---|---|---|---|---|---|---|---|---|---|---|---|---|
| 0- | 45312<br>-20224<br>261 000 | 45313<br>-20223<br>261 001 | 45314<br>-20222<br>261 002 | 45315<br>-20221<br>261 003 | 45316<br>-20220<br>261 004 | 45317<br>-20219<br>261 005 | 45318<br>-20218<br>261 006 | 45319<br>-20217<br>261 007 | 45320<br>-20216<br>261 010 | 45321<br>-20215<br>261 011 | 45322<br>-20214<br>261 012 | 45323<br>-20213<br>261 013 | 45324<br>-20212<br>261 014 | 45325<br>-20211<br>261 015 | 45326<br>-20210<br>261 016 | 45327<br>-20209<br>261 017 |
| 1- | 45328<br>-20208<br>261 020 | 45329<br>-20207<br>261 021 | 45330<br>-20206<br>261 022 | 45331<br>-20205<br>261 023 | 45332<br>-20204<br>261 024 | 45333<br>-20203<br>261 025 | 45334<br>-20202<br>261 026 | 45335<br>-20201<br>261 027 | 45336<br>-20200<br>261 030 | 45337<br>-20199<br>261 031 | 45338<br>-20198<br>261 032 | 45339<br>-20197<br>261 033 | 45340<br>-20196<br>261 034 | 45341<br>-20195<br>261 035 | 45342<br>-20194<br>261 036 | 45343<br>-20193<br>261 037 |
| 2- | 45344<br>-20192<br>261 040 | 45345<br>-20191<br>261 041 | 45346<br>-20190<br>261 042 | 45347<br>-20189<br>261 043 | 45348<br>-20188<br>261 044 | 45349<br>-20187<br>261 045 | 45350<br>-20186<br>261 046 | 45351<br>-20185<br>261 047 | 45352<br>-20184<br>261 050 | 45353<br>-20183<br>261 051 | 45354<br>-20182<br>261 052 | 45355<br>-20181<br>261 053 | 45356<br>-20180<br>261 054 | 45357<br>-20179<br>261 055 | 45358<br>-20178<br>261 056 | 45359<br>-20177<br>261 057 |
| 3- | 45360<br>-20176<br>261 060 | 45361<br>-20175<br>261 061 | 45362<br>-20174<br>261 062 | 45363<br>-20173<br>261 063 | 45364<br>-20172<br>261 064 | 45365<br>-20171<br>261 065 | 45366<br>-20170<br>261 066 | 45367<br>-20169<br>261 067 | 45368<br>-20168<br>261 070 | 45369<br>-20167<br>261 071 | 45370<br>-20166<br>261 072 | 45371<br>-20165<br>261 073 | 45372<br>-20164<br>261 074 | 45373<br>-20163<br>261 075 | 45374<br>-20162<br>261 076 | 45375<br>-20161<br>261 077 |
| 4- | 45376<br>-20160<br>261 100 | 45377<br>-20159<br>261 101 | 45378<br>-20158<br>261 102 | 45379<br>-20157<br>261 103 | 45380<br>-20156<br>261 104 | 45381<br>-20155<br>261 105 | 45382<br>-20154<br>261 106 | 45383<br>-20153<br>261 107 | 45384<br>-20152<br>261 110 | 45385<br>-20151<br>261 111 | 45386<br>-20150<br>261 112 | 45387<br>-20149<br>261 113 | 45388<br>-20148<br>261 114 | 45389<br>-20147<br>261 115 | 45390<br>-20146<br>261 116 | 45391<br>-20145<br>261 117 |
| 5- | 45392<br>-20144<br>261 120 | 45393<br>-20143<br>261 121 | 45394<br>-20142<br>261 122 | 45395<br>-20141<br>261 123 | 45396<br>-20140<br>261 124 | 45397<br>-20139<br>261 125 | 45398<br>-20138<br>261 126 | 45399<br>-20137<br>261 127 | 45400<br>-20136<br>261 130 | 45401<br>-20135<br>261 131 | 45402<br>-20134<br>261 132 | 45403<br>-20133<br>261 133 | 45404<br>-20132<br>261 134 | 45405<br>-20131<br>261 135 | 45406<br>-20130<br>261 136 | 45407<br>-20129<br>261 137 |
| 6- | 45408<br>-20128<br>261 140 | 45409<br>-20127<br>261 141 | 45410<br>-20126<br>261 142 | 45411<br>-20125<br>261 143 | 45412<br>-20124<br>261 144 | 45413<br>-20123<br>261 145 | 45414<br>-20122<br>261 146 | 45415<br>-20121<br>261 147 | 45416<br>-20120<br>261 150 | 45417<br>-20119<br>261 151 | 45418<br>-20118<br>261 152 | 45419<br>-20117<br>261 153 | 45420<br>-20116<br>261 154 | 45421<br>-20115<br>261 155 | 45422<br>-20114<br>261 156 | 45423<br>-20113<br>261 157 |
| 7- | 45424<br>-20112<br>261 160 | 45425<br>-20111<br>261 161 | 45426<br>-20110<br>261 162 | 45427<br>-20109<br>261 163 | 45428<br>-20108<br>261 164 | 45429<br>-20107<br>261 165 | 45430<br>-20106<br>261 166 | 45431<br>-20105<br>261 167 | 45432<br>-20104<br>261 170 | 45433<br>-20103<br>261 171 | 45434<br>-20102<br>261 172 | 45435<br>-20101<br>261 173 | 45436<br>-20100<br>261 174 | 45437<br>-20099<br>261 175 | 45438<br>-20098<br>261 176 | 45439<br>-20097<br>261 177 |
| 8- | 45440<br>-20096<br>261 200 | 45441<br>-20095<br>261 201 | 45442<br>-20094<br>261 202 | 45443<br>-20093<br>261 203 | 45444<br>-20092<br>261 204 | 45445<br>-20091<br>261 205 | 45446<br>-20090<br>261 206 | 45447<br>-20089<br>261 207 | 45448<br>-20088<br>261 210 | 45449<br>-20087<br>261 211 | 45450<br>-20086<br>261 212 | 45451<br>-20085<br>261 213 | 45452<br>-20084<br>261 214 | 45453<br>-20083<br>261 215 | 45454<br>-20082<br>261 216 | 45455<br>-20081<br>261 217 |
| 9- | 45456<br>-20080<br>261 220 | 45457<br>-20079<br>261 221 | 45458<br>-20078<br>261 222 | 45459<br>-20077<br>261 223 | 45460<br>-20076<br>261 224 | 45461<br>-20075<br>261 225 | 45462<br>-20074<br>261 226 | 45463<br>-20073<br>261 227 | 45464<br>-20072<br>261 230 | 45465<br>-20071<br>261 231 | 45466<br>-20070<br>261 232 | 45467<br>-20069<br>261 233 | 45468<br>-20068<br>261 234 | 45469<br>-20067<br>261 235 | 45470<br>-20066<br>261 236 | 45471<br>-20065<br>261 237 |
| A- | 45472<br>-20064<br>261 240 | 45473<br>-20063<br>261 241 | 45474<br>-20062<br>261 242 | 45475<br>-20061<br>261 243 | 45476<br>-20060<br>261 244 | 45477<br>-20059<br>261 245 | 45478<br>-20058<br>261 246 | 45479<br>-20057<br>261 247 | 45480<br>-20056<br>261 250 | 45481<br>-20055<br>261 251 | 45482<br>-20054<br>261 252 | 45483<br>-20053<br>261 253 | 45484<br>-20052<br>261 254 | 45485<br>-20051<br>261 255 | 45486<br>-20050<br>261 256 | 45487<br>-20049<br>261 257 |
| B- | 45488<br>-20048<br>261 260 | 45489<br>-20047<br>261 261 | 45490<br>-20046<br>261 262 | 45491<br>-20045<br>261 263 | 45492<br>-20044<br>261 264 | 45493<br>-20043<br>261 265 | 45494<br>-20042<br>261 266 | 45495<br>-20041<br>261 267 | 45496<br>-20040<br>261 270 | 45497<br>-20039<br>261 271 | 45498<br>-20038<br>261 272 | 45499<br>-20037<br>261 273 | 45500<br>-20036<br>261 274 | 45501<br>-20035<br>261 275 | 45502<br>-20034<br>261 276 | 45503<br>-20033<br>261 277 |
| C- | 45504<br>-20032<br>261 300 | 45505<br>-20031<br>261 301 | 45506<br>-20030<br>261 302 | 45507<br>-20029<br>261 303 | 45508<br>-20028<br>261 304 | 45509<br>-20027<br>261 305 | 45510<br>-20026<br>261 306 | 45511<br>-20025<br>261 307 | 45512<br>-20024<br>261 310 | 45513<br>-20023<br>261 311 | 45514<br>-20022<br>261 312 | 45515<br>-20021<br>261 313 | 45516<br>-20020<br>261 314 | 45517<br>-20019<br>261 315 | 45518<br>-20018<br>261 316 | 45519<br>-20017<br>261 317 |
| D- | 45520<br>-20016<br>261 320 | 45521<br>-20015<br>261 321 | 45522<br>-20014<br>261 322 | 45523<br>-20013<br>261 323 | 45524<br>-20012<br>261 324 | 45525<br>-20011<br>261 325 | 45526<br>-20010<br>261 326 | 45527<br>-20009<br>261 327 | 45528<br>-20008<br>261 330 | 45529<br>-20007<br>261 331 | 45530<br>-20006<br>261 332 | 45531<br>-20005<br>261 333 | 45532<br>-20004<br>261 334 | 45533<br>-20003<br>261 335 | 45534<br>-20002<br>261 336 | 45535<br>-20001<br>261 337 |
| E- | 45536<br>-20000<br>261 340 | 45537<br>-19999<br>261 341 | 45538<br>-19998<br>261 342 | 45539<br>-19997<br>261 343 | 45540<br>-19996<br>261 344 | 45541<br>-19995<br>261 345 | 45542<br>-19994<br>261 346 | 45543<br>-19993<br>261 347 | 45544<br>-19992<br>261 350 | 45545<br>-19991<br>261 351 | 45546<br>-19990<br>261 352 | 45547<br>-19989<br>261 353 | 45548<br>-19988<br>261 354 | 45549<br>-19987<br>261 355 | 45550<br>-19986<br>261 356 | 45551<br>-19985<br>261 357 |
| F- | 45552<br>-19984<br>261 360 | 45553<br>-19983<br>261 361 | 45554<br>-19982<br>261 362 | 45555<br>-19981<br>261 363 | 45556<br>-19980<br>261 364 | 45557<br>-19979<br>261 365 | 45558<br>-19978<br>261 366 | 45559<br>-19977<br>261 367 | 45560<br>-19976<br>261 370 | 45561<br>-19975<br>261 371 | 45562<br>-19974<br>261 372 | 45563<br>-19973<br>261 373 | 45564<br>-19972<br>261 374 | 45565<br>-19971<br>261 375 | 45566<br>-19970<br>261 376 | 45567<br>-19969<br>261 377 |

## FIRST HEX DIGIT — ②

SECOND HEX DIGIT (rows) × FIRST HEX DIGIT (columns). Each cell: decimal / decimal (negative) / octal.

| | −0 | −1 | −2 | −3 | −4 | −5 | −6 | −7 | −8 | −9 | −A | −B | −C | −D | −E | −F |
|---|---|---|---|---|---|---|---|---|---|---|---|---|---|---|---|---|
| **0-** | 45568<br>-19968<br>262 000 | 45569<br>-19967<br>262 001 | 45570<br>-19966<br>262 002 | 45571<br>-19965<br>262 003 | 45572<br>-19964<br>262 004 | 45573<br>-19963<br>262 005 | 45574<br>-19962<br>262 006 | 45575<br>-19961<br>262 007 | 45576<br>-19960<br>262 010 | 45577<br>-19959<br>262 011 | 45578<br>-19958<br>262 012 | 45579<br>-19957<br>262 013 | 45580<br>-19956<br>262 014 | 45581<br>-19955<br>262 015 | 45582<br>-19954<br>262 016 | 45583<br>-19953<br>262 017 |
| **1-** | 45584<br>-19952<br>262 020 | 45585<br>-19951<br>262 021 | 45586<br>-19950<br>262 022 | 45587<br>-19949<br>262 023 | 45588<br>-19948<br>262 024 | 45589<br>-19947<br>262 025 | 45590<br>-19946<br>262 026 | 45591<br>-19945<br>262 027 | 45592<br>-19944<br>262 030 | 45593<br>-19943<br>262 031 | 45594<br>-19942<br>262 032 | 45595<br>-19941<br>262 033 | 45596<br>-19940<br>262 034 | 45597<br>-19939<br>262 035 | 45598<br>-19938<br>262 036 | 45599<br>-19937<br>262 037 |
| **2-** | 45600<br>-19936<br>262 040 | 45601<br>-19935<br>262 041 | 45602<br>-19934<br>262 042 | 45603<br>-19933<br>262 043 | 45604<br>-19932<br>262 044 | 45605<br>-19931<br>262 045 | 45606<br>-19930<br>262 046 | 45607<br>-19929<br>262 047 | 45608<br>-19928<br>262 050 | 45609<br>-19927<br>262 051 | 45610<br>-19926<br>262 052 | 45611<br>-19925<br>262 053 | 45612<br>-19924<br>262 054 | 45613<br>-19923<br>262 055 | 45614<br>-19922<br>262 056 | 45615<br>-19921<br>262 057 |
| **3-** | 45616<br>-19920<br>262 060 | 45617<br>-19919<br>262 061 | 45618<br>-19918<br>262 062 | 45619<br>-19917<br>262 063 | 45620<br>-19916<br>262 064 | 45621<br>-19915<br>262 065 | 45622<br>-19914<br>262 066 | 45623<br>-19913<br>262 067 | 45624<br>-19912<br>262 070 | 45625<br>-19911<br>262 071 | 45626<br>-19910<br>262 072 | 45627<br>-19909<br>262 073 | 45628<br>-19908<br>262 074 | 45629<br>-19907<br>262 075 | 45630<br>-19906<br>262 076 | 45631<br>-19905<br>262 077 |
| **4-** | 45632<br>-19904<br>262 100 | 45633<br>-19903<br>262 101 | 45634<br>-19902<br>262 102 | 45635<br>-19901<br>262 103 | 45636<br>-19900<br>262 104 | 45637<br>-19899<br>262 105 | 45638<br>-19898<br>262 106 | 45639<br>-19897<br>262 107 | 45640<br>-19896<br>262 110 | 45641<br>-19895<br>262 111 | 45642<br>-19894<br>262 112 | 45643<br>-19893<br>262 113 | 45644<br>-19892<br>262 114 | 45645<br>-19891<br>262 115 | 45646<br>-19890<br>262 116 | 45647<br>-19889<br>262 117 |
| **5-** | 45648<br>-19888<br>262 120 | 45649<br>-19887<br>262 121 | 45650<br>-19886<br>262 122 | 45651<br>-19885<br>262 123 | 45652<br>-19884<br>262 124 | 45653<br>-19883<br>262 125 | 45654<br>-19882<br>262 126 | 45655<br>-19881<br>262 127 | 45656<br>-19880<br>262 130 | 45657<br>-19879<br>262 131 | 45658<br>-19878<br>262 132 | 45659<br>-19877<br>262 133 | 45660<br>-19876<br>262 134 | 45661<br>-19875<br>262 135 | 45662<br>-19874<br>262 136 | 45663<br>-19873<br>262 137 |
| **6-** | 45664<br>-19872<br>262 140 | 45665<br>-19871<br>262 141 | 45666<br>-19870<br>262 142 | 45667<br>-19869<br>262 143 | 45668<br>-19868<br>262 144 | 45669<br>-19867<br>262 145 | 45670<br>-19866<br>262 146 | 45671<br>-19865<br>262 147 | 45672<br>-19864<br>262 150 | 45673<br>-19863<br>262 151 | 45674<br>-19862<br>262 152 | 45675<br>-19861<br>262 153 | 45676<br>-19860<br>262 154 | 45677<br>-19859<br>262 155 | 45678<br>-19858<br>262 156 | 45679<br>-19857<br>262 157 |
| **7-** | 45680<br>-19856<br>262 160 | 45681<br>-19855<br>262 161 | 45682<br>-19854<br>262 162 | 45683<br>-19853<br>262 163 | 45684<br>-19852<br>262 164 | 45685<br>-19851<br>262 165 | 45686<br>-19850<br>262 166 | 45687<br>-19849<br>262 167 | 45688<br>-19848<br>262 170 | 45689<br>-19847<br>262 171 | 45690<br>-19846<br>262 172 | 45691<br>-19845<br>262 173 | 45692<br>-19844<br>262 174 | 45693<br>-19843<br>262 175 | 45694<br>-19842<br>262 176 | 45695<br>-19841<br>262 177 |
| **8-** | 45696<br>-19840<br>262 200 | 45697<br>-19839<br>262 201 | 45698<br>-19838<br>262 202 | 45699<br>-19837<br>262 203 | 45700<br>-19836<br>262 204 | 45701<br>-19835<br>262 205 | 45702<br>-19834<br>262 206 | 45703<br>-19833<br>262 207 | 45704<br>-19832<br>262 210 | 45705<br>-19831<br>262 211 | 45706<br>-19830<br>262 212 | 45707<br>-19829<br>262 213 | 45708<br>-19828<br>262 214 | 45709<br>-19827<br>262 215 | 45710<br>-19826<br>262 216 | 45711<br>-19825<br>262 217 |
| **9-** | 45712<br>-19824<br>262 220 | 45713<br>-19823<br>262 221 | 45714<br>-19822<br>262 222 | 45715<br>-19821<br>262 223 | 45716<br>-19820<br>262 224 | 45717<br>-19819<br>262 225 | 45718<br>-19818<br>262 226 | 45719<br>-19817<br>262 227 | 45720<br>-19816<br>262 230 | 45721<br>-19815<br>262 231 | 45722<br>-19814<br>262 232 | 45723<br>-19813<br>262 233 | 45724<br>-19812<br>262 234 | 45725<br>-19811<br>262 235 | 45726<br>-19810<br>262 236 | 45727<br>-19809<br>262 237 |
| **A-** | 45728<br>-19808<br>262 240 | 45729<br>-19807<br>262 241 | 45730<br>-19806<br>262 242 | 45731<br>-19805<br>262 243 | 45732<br>-19804<br>262 244 | 45733<br>-19803<br>262 245 | 45734<br>-19802<br>262 246 | 45735<br>-19801<br>262 247 | 45736<br>-19800<br>262 250 | 45737<br>-19799<br>262 251 | 45738<br>-19798<br>262 252 | 45739<br>-19797<br>262 253 | 45740<br>-19796<br>262 254 | 45741<br>-19795<br>262 255 | 45742<br>-19794<br>262 256 | 45743<br>-19793<br>262 257 |
| **B-** | 45744<br>-19792<br>262 260 | 45745<br>-19791<br>262 261 | 45746<br>-19790<br>262 262 | 45747<br>-19789<br>262 263 | 45748<br>-19788<br>262 264 | 45749<br>-19787<br>262 265 | 45750<br>-19786<br>262 266 | 45751<br>-19785<br>262 267 | 45752<br>-19784<br>262 270 | 45753<br>-19783<br>262 271 | 45754<br>-19782<br>262 272 | 45755<br>-19781<br>262 273 | 45756<br>-19780<br>262 274 | 45757<br>-19779<br>262 275 | 45758<br>-19778<br>262 276 | 45759<br>-19777<br>262 277 |
| **C-** | 45760<br>-19776<br>262 300 | 45761<br>-19775<br>262 301 | 45762<br>-19774<br>262 302 | 45763<br>-19773<br>262 303 | 45764<br>-19772<br>262 304 | 45765<br>-19771<br>262 305 | 45766<br>-19770<br>262 306 | 45767<br>-19769<br>262 307 | 45768<br>-19768<br>262 310 | 45769<br>-19767<br>262 311 | 45770<br>-19766<br>262 312 | 45771<br>-19765<br>262 313 | 45772<br>-19764<br>262 314 | 45773<br>-19763<br>262 315 | 45774<br>-19762<br>262 316 | 45775<br>-19761<br>262 317 |
| **D-** | 45776<br>-19760<br>262 320 | 45777<br>-19759<br>262 321 | 45778<br>-19758<br>262 322 | 45779<br>-19757<br>262 323 | 45780<br>-19756<br>262 324 | 45781<br>-19755<br>262 325 | 45782<br>-19754<br>262 326 | 45783<br>-19753<br>262 327 | 45784<br>-19752<br>262 330 | 45785<br>-19751<br>262 331 | 45786<br>-19750<br>262 332 | 45787<br>-19749<br>262 333 | 45788<br>-19748<br>262 334 | 45789<br>-19747<br>262 335 | 45790<br>-19746<br>262 336 | 45791<br>-19745<br>262 337 |
| **E-** | 45792<br>-19744<br>262 340 | 45793<br>-19743<br>262 341 | 45794<br>-19742<br>262 342 | 45795<br>-19741<br>262 343 | 45796<br>-19740<br>262 344 | 45797<br>-19739<br>262 345 | 45798<br>-19738<br>262 346 | 45799<br>-19737<br>262 347 | 45800<br>-19736<br>262 350 | 45801<br>-19735<br>262 351 | 45802<br>-19734<br>262 352 | 45803<br>-19733<br>262 353 | 45804<br>-19732<br>262 354 | 45805<br>-19731<br>262 355 | 45806<br>-19730<br>262 356 | 45807<br>-19729<br>262 357 |
| **F-** | 45808<br>-19728<br>262 360 | 45809<br>-19727<br>262 361 | 45810<br>-19726<br>262 362 | 45811<br>-19725<br>262 363 | 45812<br>-19724<br>262 364 | 45813<br>-19723<br>262 365 | 45814<br>-19722<br>262 366 | 45815<br>-19721<br>262 367 | 45816<br>-19720<br>262 370 | 45817<br>-19719<br>262 371 | 45818<br>-19718<br>262 372 | 45819<br>-19717<br>262 373 | 45820<br>-19716<br>262 374 | 45821<br>-19715<br>262 375 | 45822<br>-19714<br>262 376 | 45823<br>-19713<br>262 377 |

Right-margin labels: DECIMAL · DECIMAL · OCTAL. Left margin: SECOND HEX DIGIT.

---

 DECIMAL  `-19968`   BINARY  `1011 0010`   DECIMAL  `45568`   HEXADECIMAL  ⬡ **B2**   OCTAL  `262 000`

FOURTH HEX DIGIT → B2 ← THIRD HEX DIGIT

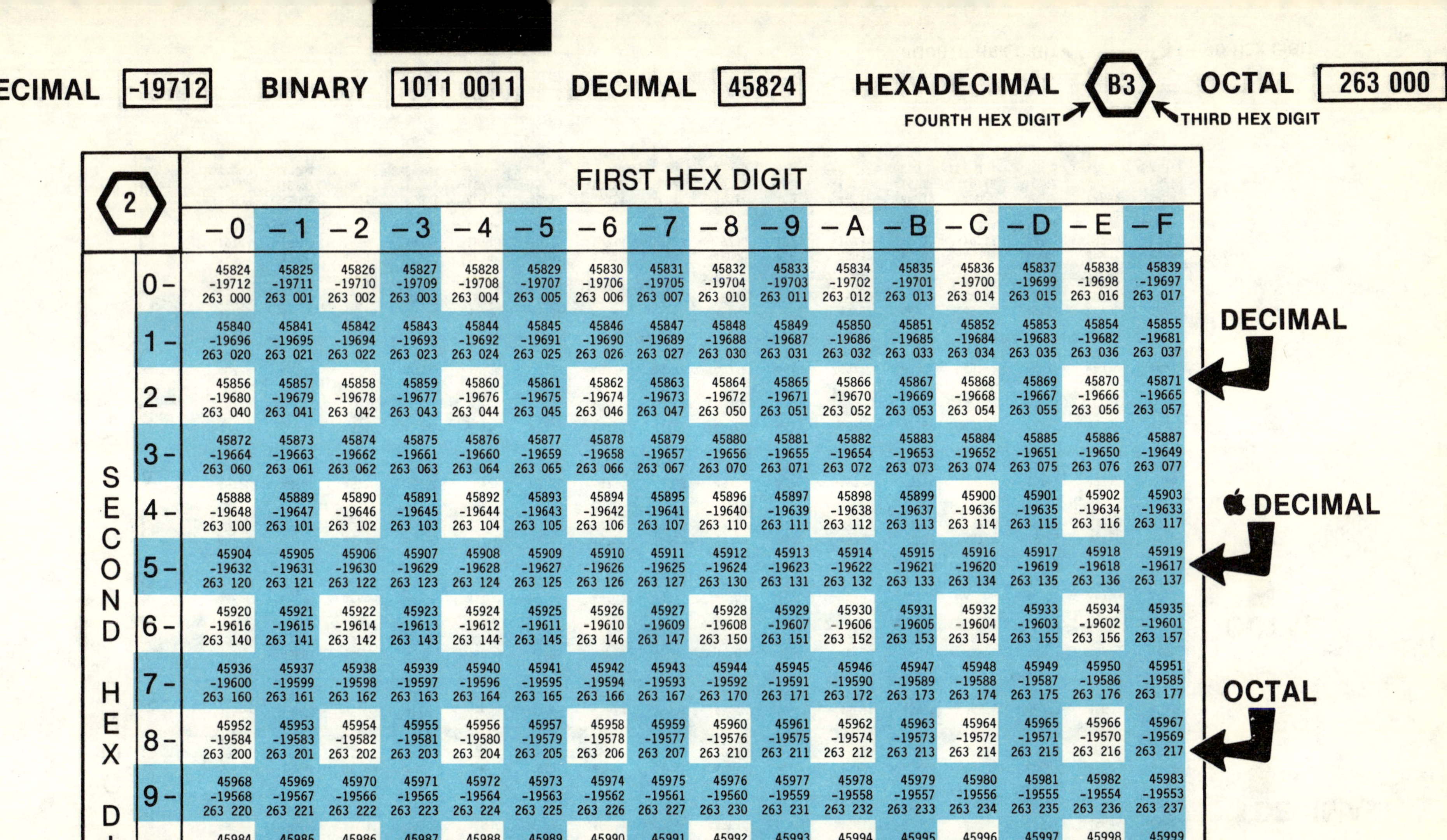

FIRST HEX DIGIT

| ② | −0 | −1 | −2 | −3 | −4 | −5 | −6 | −7 | −8 | −9 | −A | −B | −C | −D | −E | −F |
|---|---|---|---|---|---|---|---|---|---|---|---|---|---|---|---|---|
| 0− | 45824<br>-19712<br>263 000 | 45825<br>-19711<br>263 001 | 45826<br>-19710<br>263 002 | 45827<br>-19709<br>263 003 | 45828<br>-19708<br>263 004 | 45829<br>-19707<br>263 005 | 45830<br>-19706<br>263 006 | 45831<br>-19705<br>263 007 | 45832<br>-19704<br>263 010 | 45833<br>-19703<br>263 011 | 45834<br>-19702<br>263 012 | 45835<br>-19701<br>263 013 | 45836<br>-19700<br>263 014 | 45837<br>-19699<br>263 015 | 45838<br>-19698<br>263 016 | 45839<br>-19697<br>263 017 |
| 1− | 45840<br>-19696<br>263 020 | 45841<br>-19695<br>263 021 | 45842<br>-19694<br>263 022 | 45843<br>-19693<br>263 023 | 45844<br>-19692<br>263 024 | 45845<br>-19691<br>263 025 | 45846<br>-19690<br>263 026 | 45847<br>-19689<br>263 027 | 45848<br>-19688<br>263 030 | 45849<br>-19687<br>263 031 | 45850<br>-19686<br>263 032 | 45851<br>-19685<br>263 033 | 45852<br>-19684<br>263 034 | 45853<br>-19683<br>263 035 | 45854<br>-19682<br>263 036 | 45855<br>-19681<br>263 037 |
| 2− | 45856<br>-19680<br>263 040 | 45857<br>-19679<br>263 041 | 45858<br>-19678<br>263 042 | 45859<br>-19677<br>263 043 | 45860<br>-19676<br>263 044 | 45861<br>-19675<br>263 045 | 45862<br>-19674<br>263 046 | 45863<br>-19673<br>263 047 | 45864<br>-19672<br>263 050 | 45865<br>-19671<br>263 051 | 45866<br>-19670<br>263 052 | 45867<br>-19669<br>263 053 | 45868<br>-19668<br>263 054 | 45869<br>-19667<br>263 055 | 45870<br>-19666<br>263 056 | 45871<br>-19665<br>263 057 |
| 3− | 45872<br>-19664<br>263 060 | 45873<br>-19663<br>263 061 | 45874<br>-19662<br>263 062 | 45875<br>-19661<br>263 063 | 45876<br>-19660<br>263 064 | 45877<br>-19659<br>263 065 | 45878<br>-19658<br>263 066 | 45879<br>-19657<br>263 067 | 45880<br>-19656<br>263 070 | 45881<br>-19655<br>263 071 | 45882<br>-19654<br>263 072 | 45883<br>-19653<br>263 073 | 45884<br>-19652<br>263 074 | 45885<br>-19651<br>263 075 | 45886<br>-19650<br>263 076 | 45887<br>-19649<br>263 077 |
| 4− | 45888<br>-19648<br>263 100 | 45889<br>-19647<br>263 101 | 45890<br>-19646<br>263 102 | 45891<br>-19645<br>263 103 | 45892<br>-19644<br>263 104 | 45893<br>-19643<br>263 105 | 45894<br>-19642<br>263 106 | 45895<br>-19641<br>263 107 | 45896<br>-19640<br>263 110 | 45897<br>-19639<br>263 111 | 45898<br>-19638<br>263 112 | 45899<br>-19637<br>263 113 | 45900<br>-19636<br>263 114 | 45901<br>-19635<br>263 115 | 45902<br>-19634<br>263 116 | 45903<br>-19633<br>263 117 |
| 5− | 45904<br>-19632<br>263 120 | 45905<br>-19631<br>263 121 | 45906<br>-19630<br>263 122 | 45907<br>-19629<br>263 123 | 45908<br>-19628<br>263 124 | 45909<br>-19627<br>263 125 | 45910<br>-19626<br>263 126 | 45911<br>-19625<br>263 127 | 45912<br>-19624<br>263 130 | 45913<br>-19623<br>263 131 | 45914<br>-19622<br>263 132 | 45915<br>-19621<br>263 133 | 45916<br>-19620<br>263 134 | 45917<br>-19619<br>263 135 | 45918<br>-19618<br>263 136 | 45919<br>-19617<br>263 137 |
| 6− | 45920<br>-19616<br>263 140 | 45921<br>-19615<br>263 141 | 45922<br>-19614<br>263 142 | 45923<br>-19613<br>263 143 | 45924<br>-19612<br>263 144 | 45925<br>-19611<br>263 145 | 45926<br>-19610<br>263 146 | 45927<br>-19609<br>263 147 | 45928<br>-19608<br>263 150 | 45929<br>-19607<br>263 151 | 45930<br>-19606<br>263 152 | 45931<br>-19605<br>263 153 | 45932<br>-19604<br>263 154 | 45933<br>-19603<br>263 155 | 45934<br>-19602<br>263 156 | 45935<br>-19601<br>263 157 |
| 7− | 45936<br>-19600<br>263 160 | 45937<br>-19599<br>263 161 | 45938<br>-19598<br>263 162 | 45939<br>-19597<br>263 163 | 45940<br>-19596<br>263 164 | 45941<br>-19595<br>263 165 | 45942<br>-19594<br>263 166 | 45943<br>-19593<br>263 167 | 45944<br>-19592<br>263 170 | 45945<br>-19591<br>263 171 | 45946<br>-19590<br>263 172 | 45947<br>-19589<br>263 173 | 45948<br>-19588<br>263 174 | 45949<br>-19587<br>263 175 | 45950<br>-19586<br>263 176 | 45951<br>-19585<br>263 177 |
| 8− | 45952<br>-19584<br>263 200 | 45953<br>-19583<br>263 201 | 45954<br>-19582<br>263 202 | 45955<br>-19581<br>263 203 | 45956<br>-19580<br>263 204 | 45957<br>-19579<br>263 205 | 45958<br>-19578<br>263 206 | 45959<br>-19577<br>263 207 | 45960<br>-19576<br>263 210 | 45961<br>-19575<br>263 211 | 45962<br>-19574<br>263 212 | 45963<br>-19573<br>263 213 | 45964<br>-19572<br>263 214 | 45965<br>-19571<br>263 215 | 45966<br>-19570<br>263 216 | 45967<br>-19569<br>263 217 |
| 9− | 45968<br>-19568<br>263 220 | 45969<br>-19567<br>263 221 | 45970<br>-19566<br>263 222 | 45971<br>-19565<br>263 223 | 45972<br>-19564<br>263 224 | 45973<br>-19563<br>263 225 | 45974<br>-19562<br>263 226 | 45975<br>-19561<br>263 227 | 45976<br>-19560<br>263 230 | 45977<br>-19559<br>263 231 | 45978<br>-19558<br>263 232 | 45979<br>-19557<br>263 233 | 45980<br>-19556<br>263 234 | 45981<br>-19555<br>263 235 | 45982<br>-19554<br>263 236 | 45983<br>-19553<br>263 237 |
| A− | 45984<br>-19552<br>263 240 | 45985<br>-19551<br>263 241 | 45986<br>-19550<br>263 242 | 45987<br>-19549<br>263 243 | 45988<br>-19548<br>263 244 | 45989<br>-19547<br>263 245 | 45990<br>-19546<br>263 246 | 45991<br>-19545<br>263 247 | 45992<br>-19544<br>263 250 | 45993<br>-19543<br>263 251 | 45994<br>-19542<br>263 252 | 45995<br>-19541<br>263 253 | 45996<br>-19540<br>263 254 | 45997<br>-19539<br>263 255 | 45998<br>-19538<br>263 256 | 45999<br>-19537<br>263 257 |
| B− | 46000<br>-19536<br>263 260 | 46001<br>-19535<br>263 261 | 46002<br>-19534<br>263 262 | 46003<br>-19533<br>263 263 | 46004<br>-19532<br>263 264 | 46005<br>-19531<br>263 265 | 46006<br>-19530<br>263 266 | 46007<br>-19529<br>263 267 | 46008<br>-19528<br>263 270 | 46009<br>-19527<br>263 271 | 46010<br>-19526<br>263 272 | 46011<br>-19525<br>263 273 | 46012<br>-19524<br>263 274 | 46013<br>-19523<br>263 275 | 46014<br>-19522<br>263 276 | 46015<br>-19521<br>263 277 |
| C− | 46016<br>-19520<br>263 300 | 46017<br>-19519<br>263 301 | 46018<br>-19518<br>263 302 | 46019<br>-19517<br>263 303 | 46020<br>-19516<br>263 304 | 46021<br>-19515<br>263 305 | 46022<br>-19514<br>263 306 | 46023<br>-19513<br>263 307 | 46024<br>-19512<br>263 310 | 46025<br>-19511<br>263 311 | 46026<br>-19510<br>263 312 | 46027<br>-19509<br>263 313 | 46028<br>-19508<br>263 314 | 46029<br>-19507<br>263 315 | 46030<br>-19506<br>263 316 | 46031<br>-19505<br>263 317 |
| D− | 46032<br>-19504<br>263 320 | 46033<br>-19503<br>263 321 | 46034<br>-19502<br>263 322 | 46035<br>-19501<br>263 323 | 46036<br>-19500<br>263 324 | 46037<br>-19499<br>263 325 | 46038<br>-19498<br>263 326 | 46039<br>-19497<br>263 327 | 46040<br>-19496<br>263 330 | 46041<br>-19495<br>263 331 | 46042<br>-19494<br>263 332 | 46043<br>-19493<br>263 333 | 46044<br>-19492<br>263 334 | 46045<br>-19491<br>263 335 | 46046<br>-19490<br>263 336 | 46047<br>-19489<br>263 337 |
| E− | 46048<br>-19488<br>263 340 | 46049<br>-19487<br>263 341 | 46050<br>-19486<br>263 342 | 46051<br>-19485<br>263 343 | 46052<br>-19484<br>263 344 | 46053<br>-19483<br>263 345 | 46054<br>-19482<br>263 346 | 46055<br>-19481<br>263 347 | 46056<br>-19480<br>263 350 | 46057<br>-19479<br>263 351 | 46058<br>-19478<br>263 352 | 46059<br>-19477<br>263 353 | 46060<br>-19476<br>263 354 | 46061<br>-19475<br>263 355 | 46062<br>-19474<br>263 356 | 46063<br>-19473<br>263 357 |
| F− | 46064<br>-19472<br>263 360 | 46065<br>-19471<br>263 361 | 46066<br>-19470<br>263 362 | 46067<br>-19469<br>263 363 | 46068<br>-19468<br>263 364 | 46069<br>-19467<br>263 365 | 46070<br>-19466<br>263 366 | 46071<br>-19465<br>263 367 | 46072<br>-19464<br>263 370 | 46073<br>-19463<br>263 371 | 46074<br>-19462<br>263 372 | 46075<br>-19461<br>263 373 | 46076<br>-19460<br>263 374 | 46077<br>-19459<br>263 375 | 46078<br>-19458<br>263 376 | 46079<br>-19457<br>263 377 |

SECOND HEX DIGIT

DECIMAL → ← DECIMAL → OCTAL →

## FIRST HEX DIGIT

Columns: −0 … −7

| SECOND HEX DIGIT | −0 | −1 | −2 | −3 | −4 | −5 | −6 | −7 |
|---|---|---|---|---|---|---|---|---|
| 0- | 46080<br>-19456<br>264 000 | 46081<br>-19455<br>264 001 | 46082<br>-19454<br>264 002 | 46083<br>-19453<br>264 003 | 46084<br>-19452<br>264 004 | 46085<br>-19451<br>264 005 | 46086<br>-19450<br>264 006 | 46087<br>-19449<br>264 007 |
| 1- | 46096<br>-19440<br>264 020 | 46097<br>-19439<br>264 021 | 46098<br>-19438<br>264 022 | 46099<br>-19437<br>264 023 | 46100<br>-19436<br>264 024 | 46101<br>-19435<br>264 025 | 46102<br>-19434<br>264 026 | 46103<br>-19433<br>264 027 |
| 2- | 46112<br>-19424<br>264 040 | 46113<br>-19423<br>264 041 | 46114<br>-19422<br>264 042 | 46115<br>-19421<br>264 043 | 46116<br>-19420<br>264 044 | 46117<br>-19419<br>264 045 | 46118<br>-19418<br>264 046 | 46119<br>-19417<br>264 047 |
| 3- | 46128<br>-19408<br>264 060 | 46129<br>-19407<br>264 061 | 46130<br>-19406<br>264 062 | 46131<br>-19405<br>264 063 | 46132<br>-19404<br>264 064 | 46133<br>-19403<br>264 065 | 46134<br>-19402<br>264 066 | 46135<br>-19401<br>264 067 |
| 4- | 46144<br>-19392<br>264 100 | 46145<br>-19391<br>264 101 | 46146<br>-19390<br>264 102 | 46147<br>-19389<br>264 103 | 46148<br>-19388<br>264 104 | 46149<br>-19387<br>264 105 | 46150<br>-19386<br>264 106 | 46151<br>-19385<br>264 107 |
| 5- | 46160<br>-19376<br>264 120 | 46161<br>-19375<br>264 121 | 46162<br>-19374<br>264 122 | 46163<br>-19373<br>264 123 | 46164<br>-19372<br>264 124 | 46165<br>-19371<br>264 125 | 46166<br>-19370<br>264 126 | 46167<br>-19369<br>264 127 |
| 6- | 46176<br>-19360<br>264 140 | 46177<br>-19359<br>264 141 | 46178<br>-19358<br>264 142 | 46179<br>-19357<br>264 143 | 46180<br>-19356<br>264 144 | 46181<br>-19355<br>264 145 | 46182<br>-19354<br>264 146 | 46183<br>-19353<br>264 147 |
| 7- | 46192<br>-19344<br>264 160 | 46193<br>-19343<br>264 161 | 46194<br>-19342<br>264 162 | 46195<br>-19341<br>264 163 | 46196<br>-19340<br>264 164 | 46197<br>-19339<br>264 165 | 46198<br>-19338<br>264 166 | 46199<br>-19337<br>264 167 |
| 8- | 46208<br>-19328<br>264 200 | 46209<br>-19327<br>264 201 | 46210<br>-19326<br>264 202 | 46211<br>-19325<br>264 203 | 46212<br>-19324<br>264 204 | 46213<br>-19323<br>264 205 | 46214<br>-19322<br>264 206 | 46215<br>-19321<br>264 207 |
| 9- | 46224<br>-19312<br>264 220 | 46225<br>-19311<br>264 221 | 46226<br>-19310<br>264 222 | 46227<br>-19309<br>264 223 | 46228<br>-19308<br>264 224 | 46229<br>-19307<br>264 225 | 46230<br>-19306<br>264 226 | 46231<br>-19305<br>264 227 |
| A- | 46240<br>-19296<br>264 240 | 46241<br>-19295<br>264 241 | 46242<br>-19294<br>264 242 | 46243<br>-19293<br>264 243 | 46244<br>-19292<br>264 244 | 46245<br>-19291<br>264 245 | 46246<br>-19290<br>264 246 | 46247<br>-19289<br>264 247 |
| B- | 46256<br>-19280<br>264 260 | 46257<br>-19279<br>264 261 | 46258<br>-19278<br>264 262 | 46259<br>-19277<br>264 263 | 46260<br>-19276<br>264 264 | 46261<br>-19275<br>264 265 | 46262<br>-19274<br>264 266 | 46263<br>-19273<br>264 267 |
| C- | 46272<br>-19264<br>264 300 | 46273<br>-19263<br>264 301 | 46274<br>-19262<br>264 302 | 46275<br>-19261<br>264 303 | 46276<br>-19260<br>264 304 | 46277<br>-19259<br>264 305 | 46278<br>-19258<br>264 306 | 46279<br>-19257<br>264 307 |
| D- | 46288<br>-19248<br>264 320 | 46289<br>-19247<br>264 321 | 46290<br>-19246<br>264 322 | 46291<br>-19245<br>264 323 | 46292<br>-19244<br>264 324 | 46293<br>-19243<br>264 325 | 46294<br>-19242<br>264 326 | 46295<br>-19241<br>264 327 |
| E- | 46304<br>-19232<br>264 340 | 46305<br>-19231<br>264 341 | 46306<br>-19230<br>264 342 | 46307<br>-19229<br>264 343 | 46308<br>-19228<br>264 344 | 46309<br>-19227<br>264 345 | 46310<br>-19226<br>264 346 | 46311<br>-19225<br>264 347 |
| F- | 46320<br>-19216<br>264 360 | 46321<br>-19215<br>264 361 | 46322<br>-19214<br>264 362 | 46323<br>-19213<br>264 363 | 46324<br>-19212<br>264 364 | 46325<br>-19211<br>264 365 | 46326<br>-19210<br>264 366 | 46327<br>-19209<br>264 367 |

Columns: −8 … −F

| SECOND HEX DIGIT | −8 | −9 | −A | −B | −C | −D | −E | −F |
|---|---|---|---|---|---|---|---|---|
| 0- | 46088<br>-19448<br>264 010 | 46089<br>-19447<br>264 011 | 46090<br>-19446<br>264 012 | 46091<br>-19445<br>264 013 | 46092<br>-19444<br>264 014 | 46093<br>-19443<br>264 015 | 46094<br>-19442<br>264 016 | 46095<br>-19441<br>264 017 |
| 1- | 46104<br>-19432<br>264 030 | 46105<br>-19431<br>264 031 | 46106<br>-19430<br>264 032 | 46107<br>-19429<br>264 033 | 46108<br>-19428<br>264 034 | 46109<br>-19427<br>264 035 | 46110<br>-19426<br>264 036 | 46111<br>-19425<br>264 037 |
| 2- | 46120<br>-19416<br>264 050 | 46121<br>-19415<br>264 051 | 46122<br>-19414<br>264 052 | 46123<br>-19413<br>264 053 | 46124<br>-19412<br>264 054 | 46125<br>-19411<br>264 055 | 46126<br>-19410<br>264 056 | 46127<br>-19409<br>264 057 |
| 3- | 46136<br>-19400<br>264 070 | 46137<br>-19399<br>264 071 | 46138<br>-19398<br>264 072 | 46139<br>-19397<br>264 073 | 46140<br>-19396<br>264 074 | 46141<br>-19395<br>264 075 | 46142<br>-19394<br>264 076 | 46143<br>-19393<br>264 077 |
| 4- | 46152<br>-19384<br>264 110 | 46153<br>-19383<br>264 111 | 46154<br>-19382<br>264 112 | 46155<br>-19381<br>264 113 | 46156<br>-19380<br>264 114 | 46157<br>-19379<br>264 115 | 46158<br>-19378<br>264 116 | 46159<br>-19377<br>264 117 |
| 5- | 46168<br>-19368<br>264 130 | 46169<br>-19367<br>264 131 | 46170<br>-19366<br>264 132 | 46171<br>-19365<br>264 133 | 46172<br>-19364<br>264 134 | 46173<br>-19363<br>264 135 | 46174<br>-19362<br>264 136 | 46175<br>-19361<br>264 137 |
| 6- | 46184<br>-19352<br>264 150 | 46185<br>-19351<br>264 151 | 46186<br>-19350<br>264 152 | 46187<br>-19349<br>264 153 | 46188<br>-19348<br>264 154 | 46189<br>-19347<br>264 155 | 46190<br>-19346<br>264 156 | 46191<br>-19345<br>264 157 |
| 7- | 46200<br>-19336<br>264 170 | 46201<br>-19335<br>264 171 | 46202<br>-19334<br>264 172 | 46203<br>-19333<br>264 173 | 46204<br>-19332<br>264 174 | 46205<br>-19331<br>264 175 | 46206<br>-19330<br>264 176 | 46207<br>-19329<br>264 177 |
| 8- | 46216<br>-19320<br>264 210 | 46217<br>-19319<br>264 211 | 46218<br>-19318<br>264 212 | 46219<br>-19317<br>264 213 | 46220<br>-19316<br>264 214 | 46221<br>-19315<br>264 215 | 46222<br>-19314<br>264 216 | 46223<br>-19313<br>264 217 |
| 9- | 46232<br>-19304<br>264 230 | 46233<br>-19303<br>264 231 | 46234<br>-19302<br>264 232 | 46235<br>-19301<br>264 233 | 46236<br>-19300<br>264 234 | 46237<br>-19299<br>264 235 | 46238<br>-19298<br>264 236 | 46239<br>-19297<br>264 237 |
| A- | 46248<br>-19288<br>264 250 | 46249<br>-19287<br>264 251 | 46250<br>-19286<br>264 252 | 46251<br>-19285<br>264 253 | 46252<br>-19284<br>264 254 | 46253<br>-19283<br>264 255 | 46254<br>-19282<br>264 256 | 46255<br>-19281<br>264 257 |
| B- | 46264<br>-19272<br>264 270 | 46265<br>-19271<br>264 271 | 46266<br>-19270<br>264 272 | 46267<br>-19269<br>264 273 | 46268<br>-19268<br>264 274 | 46269<br>-19267<br>264 275 | 46270<br>-19266<br>264 276 | 46271<br>-19265<br>264 277 |
| C- | 46280<br>-19256<br>264 310 | 46281<br>-19255<br>264 311 | 46282<br>-19254<br>264 312 | 46283<br>-19253<br>264 313 | 46284<br>-19252<br>264 314 | 46285<br>-19251<br>264 315 | 46286<br>-19250<br>264 316 | 46287<br>-19249<br>264 317 |
| D- | 46296<br>-19240<br>264 330 | 46297<br>-19239<br>264 331 | 46298<br>-19238<br>264 332 | 46299<br>-19237<br>264 333 | 46300<br>-19236<br>264 334 | 46301<br>-19235<br>264 335 | 46302<br>-19234<br>264 336 | 46303<br>-19233<br>264 337 |
| E- | 46312<br>-19224<br>264 350 | 46313<br>-19223<br>264 351 | 46314<br>-19222<br>264 352 | 46315<br>-19221<br>264 353 | 46316<br>-19220<br>264 354 | 46317<br>-19219<br>264 355 | 46318<br>-19218<br>264 356 | 46319<br>-19217<br>264 357 |
| F- | 46328<br>-19208<br>264 370 | 46329<br>-19207<br>264 371 | 46330<br>-19206<br>264 372 | 46331<br>-19205<br>264 373 | 46332<br>-19204<br>264 374 | 46333<br>-19203<br>264 375 | 46334<br>-19202<br>264 376 | 46335<br>-19201<br>264 377 |

DECIMAL

 DECIMAL

OCTAL

| ⬥ DECIMAL | -19456 | BINARY | 1011 0100 | DECIMAL | 46080 | HEXADECIMAL | B4 | OCTAL | 264 000 |
|---|---|---|---|---|---|---|---|---|---|

FOURTH HEX DIGIT → ⬡ ← THIRD HEX DIGIT

 DECIMAL [-19200]　BINARY [1011 0101]　DECIMAL [46336]　HEXADECIMAL (B5) OCTAL [265 000]

FOURTH HEX DIGIT → (B5) ← THIRD HEX DIGIT

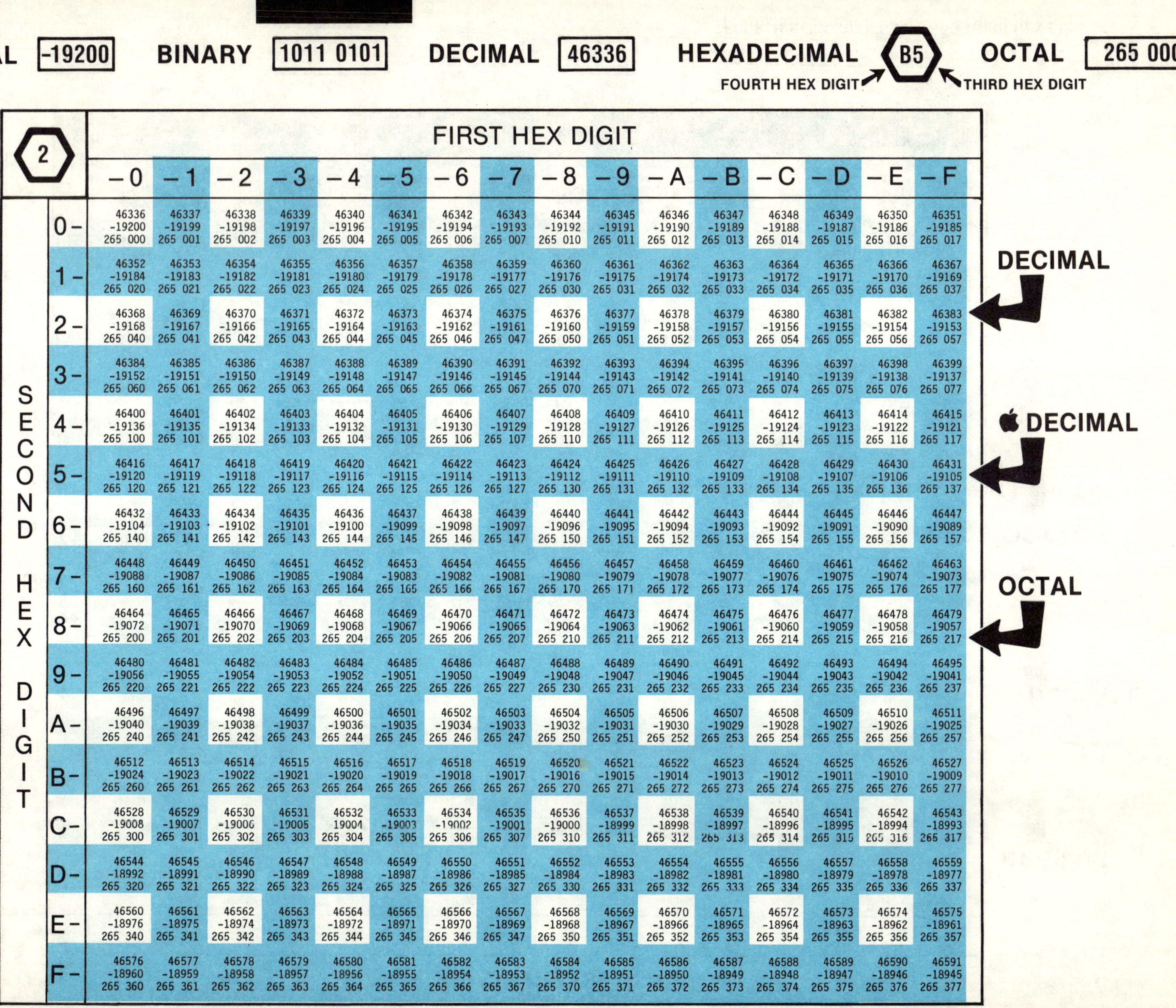

## FIRST HEX DIGIT

(2) — SECOND HEX DIGIT (rows) × FIRST HEX DIGIT (columns). Each cell: decimal / negative decimal / octal.

| 2 | −0 | −1 | −2 | −3 | −4 | −5 | −6 | −7 | −8 | −9 | −A | −B | −C | −D | −E | −F |
|---|---|---|---|---|---|---|---|---|---|---|---|---|---|---|---|---|
| 0− | 46336<br>-19200<br>265 000 | 46337<br>-19199<br>265 001 | 46338<br>-19198<br>265 002 | 46339<br>-19197<br>265 003 | 46340<br>-19196<br>265 004 | 46341<br>-19195<br>265 005 | 46342<br>-19194<br>265 006 | 46343<br>-19193<br>265 007 | 46344<br>-19192<br>265 010 | 46345<br>-19191<br>265 011 | 46346<br>-19190<br>265 012 | 46347<br>-19189<br>265 013 | 46348<br>-19188<br>265 014 | 46349<br>-19187<br>265 015 | 46350<br>-19186<br>265 016 | 46351<br>-19185<br>265 017 |
| 1− | 46352<br>-19184<br>265 020 | 46353<br>-19183<br>265 021 | 46354<br>-19182<br>265 022 | 46355<br>-19181<br>265 023 | 46356<br>-19180<br>265 024 | 46357<br>-19179<br>265 025 | 46358<br>-19178<br>265 026 | 46359<br>-19177<br>265 027 | 46360<br>-19176<br>265 030 | 46361<br>-19175<br>265 031 | 46362<br>-19174<br>265 032 | 46363<br>-19173<br>265 033 | 46364<br>-19172<br>265 034 | 46365<br>-19171<br>265 035 | 46366<br>-19170<br>265 036 | 46367<br>-19169<br>265 037 |
| 2− | 46368<br>-19168<br>265 040 | 46369<br>-19167<br>265 041 | 46370<br>-19166<br>265 042 | 46371<br>-19165<br>265 043 | 46372<br>-19164<br>265 044 | 46373<br>-19163<br>265 045 | 46374<br>-19162<br>265 046 | 46375<br>-19161<br>265 047 | 46376<br>-19160<br>265 050 | 46377<br>-19159<br>265 051 | 46378<br>-19158<br>265 052 | 46379<br>-19157<br>265 053 | 46380<br>-19156<br>265 054 | 46381<br>-19155<br>265 055 | 46382<br>-19154<br>265 056 | 46383<br>-19153<br>265 057 |
| 3− | 46384<br>-19152<br>265 060 | 46385<br>-19151<br>265 061 | 46386<br>-19150<br>265 062 | 46387<br>-19149<br>265 063 | 46388<br>-19148<br>265 064 | 46389<br>-19147<br>265 065 | 46390<br>-19146<br>265 066 | 46391<br>-19145<br>265 067 | 46392<br>-19144<br>265 070 | 46393<br>-19143<br>265 071 | 46394<br>-19142<br>265 072 | 46395<br>-19141<br>265 073 | 46396<br>-19140<br>265 074 | 46397<br>-19139<br>265 075 | 46398<br>-19138<br>265 076 | 46399<br>-19137<br>265 077 |
| 4− | 46400<br>-19136<br>265 100 | 46401<br>-19135<br>265 101 | 46402<br>-19134<br>265 102 | 46403<br>-19133<br>265 103 | 46404<br>-19132<br>265 104 | 46405<br>-19131<br>265 105 | 46406<br>-19130<br>265 106 | 46407<br>-19129<br>265 107 | 46408<br>-19128<br>265 110 | 46409<br>-19127<br>265 111 | 46410<br>-19126<br>265 112 | 46411<br>-19125<br>265 113 | 46412<br>-19124<br>265 114 | 46413<br>-19123<br>265 115 | 46414<br>-19122<br>265 116 | 46415<br>-19121<br>265 117 |
| 5− | 46416<br>-19120<br>265 120 | 46417<br>-19119<br>265 121 | 46418<br>-19118<br>265 122 | 46419<br>-19117<br>265 123 | 46420<br>-19116<br>265 124 | 46421<br>-19115<br>265 125 | 46422<br>-19114<br>265 126 | 46423<br>-19113<br>265 127 | 46424<br>-19112<br>265 130 | 46425<br>-19111<br>265 131 | 46426<br>-19110<br>265 132 | 46427<br>-19109<br>265 133 | 46428<br>-19108<br>265 134 | 46429<br>-19107<br>265 135 | 46430<br>-19106<br>265 136 | 46431<br>-19105<br>265 137 |
| 6− | 46432<br>-19104<br>265 140 | 46433<br>-19103<br>265 141 | 46434<br>-19102<br>265 142 | 46435<br>-19101<br>265 143 | 46436<br>-19100<br>265 144 | 46437<br>-19099<br>265 145 | 46438<br>-19098<br>265 146 | 46439<br>-19097<br>265 147 | 46440<br>-19096<br>265 150 | 46441<br>-19095<br>265 151 | 46442<br>-19094<br>265 152 | 46443<br>-19093<br>265 153 | 46444<br>-19092<br>265 154 | 46445<br>-19091<br>265 155 | 46446<br>-19090<br>265 156 | 46447<br>-19089<br>265 157 |
| 7− | 46448<br>-19088<br>265 160 | 46449<br>-19087<br>265 161 | 46450<br>-19086<br>265 162 | 46451<br>-19085<br>265 163 | 46452<br>-19084<br>265 164 | 46453<br>-19083<br>265 165 | 46454<br>-19082<br>265 166 | 46455<br>-19081<br>265 167 | 46456<br>-19080<br>265 170 | 46457<br>-19079<br>265 171 | 46458<br>-19078<br>265 172 | 46459<br>-19077<br>265 173 | 46460<br>-19076<br>265 174 | 46461<br>-19075<br>265 175 | 46462<br>-19074<br>265 176 | 46463<br>-19073<br>265 177 |
| 8− | 46464<br>-19072<br>265 200 | 46465<br>-19071<br>265 201 | 46466<br>-19070<br>265 202 | 46467<br>-19069<br>265 203 | 46468<br>-19068<br>265 204 | 46469<br>-19067<br>265 205 | 46470<br>-19066<br>265 206 | 46471<br>-19065<br>265 207 | 46472<br>-19064<br>265 210 | 46473<br>-19063<br>265 211 | 46474<br>-19062<br>265 212 | 46475<br>-19061<br>265 213 | 46476<br>-19060<br>265 214 | 46477<br>-19059<br>265 215 | 46478<br>-19058<br>265 216 | 46479<br>-19057<br>265 217 |
| 9− | 46480<br>-19056<br>265 220 | 46481<br>-19055<br>265 221 | 46482<br>-19054<br>265 222 | 46483<br>-19053<br>265 223 | 46484<br>-19052<br>265 224 | 46485<br>-19051<br>265 225 | 46486<br>-19050<br>265 226 | 46487<br>-19049<br>265 227 | 46488<br>-19048<br>265 230 | 46489<br>-19047<br>265 231 | 46490<br>-19046<br>265 232 | 46491<br>-19045<br>265 233 | 46492<br>-19044<br>265 234 | 46493<br>-19043<br>265 235 | 46494<br>-19042<br>265 236 | 46495<br>-19041<br>265 237 |
| A− | 46496<br>-19040<br>265 240 | 46497<br>-19039<br>265 241 | 46498<br>-19038<br>265 242 | 46499<br>-19037<br>265 243 | 46500<br>-19036<br>265 244 | 46501<br>-19035<br>265 245 | 46502<br>-19034<br>265 246 | 46503<br>-19033<br>265 247 | 46504<br>-19032<br>265 250 | 46505<br>-19031<br>265 251 | 46506<br>-19030<br>265 252 | 46507<br>-19029<br>265 253 | 46508<br>-19028<br>265 254 | 46509<br>-19027<br>265 255 | 46510<br>-19026<br>265 256 | 46511<br>-19025<br>265 257 |
| B− | 46512<br>-19024<br>265 260 | 46513<br>-19023<br>265 261 | 46514<br>-19022<br>265 262 | 46515<br>-19021<br>265 263 | 46516<br>-19020<br>265 264 | 46517<br>-19019<br>265 265 | 46518<br>-19018<br>265 266 | 46519<br>-19017<br>265 267 | 46520<br>-19016<br>265 270 | 46521<br>-19015<br>265 271 | 46522<br>-19014<br>265 272 | 46523<br>-19013<br>265 273 | 46524<br>-19012<br>265 274 | 46525<br>-19011<br>265 275 | 46526<br>-19010<br>265 276 | 46527<br>-19009<br>265 277 |
| C− | 46528<br>-19008<br>265 300 | 46529<br>-19007<br>265 301 | 46530<br>-19006<br>265 302 | 46531<br>-19005<br>265 303 | 46532<br>-19004<br>265 304 | 46533<br>-19003<br>265 305 | 46534<br>-19002<br>265 306 | 46535<br>-19001<br>265 307 | 46536<br>-19000<br>265 310 | 46537<br>-18999<br>265 311 | 46538<br>-18998<br>265 312 | 46539<br>-18997<br>265 313 | 46540<br>-18996<br>265 314 | 46541<br>-18995<br>265 315 | 46542<br>-18994<br>265 316 | 46543<br>-18993<br>265 317 |
| D− | 46544<br>-18992<br>265 320 | 46545<br>-18991<br>265 321 | 46546<br>-18990<br>265 322 | 46547<br>-18989<br>265 323 | 46548<br>-18988<br>265 324 | 46549<br>-18987<br>265 325 | 46550<br>-18986<br>265 326 | 46551<br>-18985<br>265 327 | 46552<br>-18984<br>265 330 | 46553<br>-18983<br>265 331 | 46554<br>-18982<br>265 332 | 46555<br>-18981<br>265 333 | 46556<br>-18980<br>265 334 | 46557<br>-18979<br>265 335 | 46558<br>-18978<br>265 336 | 46559<br>-18977<br>265 337 |
| E− | 46560<br>-18976<br>265 340 | 46561<br>-18975<br>265 341 | 46562<br>-18974<br>265 342 | 46563<br>-18973<br>265 343 | 46564<br>-18972<br>265 344 | 46565<br>-18971<br>265 345 | 46566<br>-18970<br>265 346 | 46567<br>-18969<br>265 347 | 46568<br>-18968<br>265 350 | 46569<br>-18967<br>265 351 | 46570<br>-18966<br>265 352 | 46571<br>-18965<br>265 353 | 46572<br>-18964<br>265 354 | 46573<br>-18963<br>265 355 | 46574<br>-18962<br>265 356 | 46575<br>-18961<br>265 357 |
| F− | 46576<br>-18960<br>265 360 | 46577<br>-18959<br>265 361 | 46578<br>-18958<br>265 362 | 46579<br>-18957<br>265 363 | 46580<br>-18956<br>265 364 | 46581<br>-18955<br>265 365 | 46582<br>-18954<br>265 366 | 46583<br>-18953<br>265 367 | 46584<br>-18952<br>265 370 | 46585<br>-18951<br>265 371 | 46586<br>-18950<br>265 372 | 46587<br>-18949<br>265 373 | 46588<br>-18948<br>265 374 | 46589<br>-18947<br>265 375 | 46590<br>-18946<br>265 376 | 46591<br>-18945<br>265 377 |

| SECOND HEX DIGIT | −0 | −1 | −2 | −3 | −4 | −5 | −6 | −7 | −8 | −9 | −A | −B | −C | −D | −E | −F |
|---|---|---|---|---|---|---|---|---|---|---|---|---|---|---|---|---|
| 0− | 46592<br>−18944<br>266 000 | 46593<br>−18943<br>266 001 | 46594<br>−18942<br>266 002 | 46595<br>−18941<br>266 003 | 46596<br>−18940<br>266 004 | 46597<br>−18939<br>266 005 | 46598<br>−18938<br>266 006 | 46599<br>−18937<br>266 007 | 46600<br>−18936<br>266 010 | 46601<br>−18935<br>266 011 | 46602<br>−18934<br>266 012 | 46603<br>−18933<br>266 013 | 46604<br>−18932<br>266 014 | 46605<br>−18931<br>266 015 | 46606<br>−18930<br>266 016 | 46607<br>−18929<br>266 017 |
| 1− | 46608<br>−18928<br>266 020 | 46609<br>−18927<br>266 021 | 46610<br>−18926<br>266 022 | 46611<br>−18925<br>266 023 | 46612<br>−18924<br>266 024 | 46613<br>−18923<br>266 025 | 46614<br>−18922<br>266 026 | 46615<br>−18921<br>266 027 | 46616<br>−18920<br>266 030 | 46617<br>−18919<br>266 031 | 46618<br>−18918<br>266 032 | 46619<br>−18917<br>266 033 | 46620<br>−18916<br>266 034 | 46621<br>−18915<br>266 035 | 46622<br>−18914<br>266 036 | 46623<br>−18913<br>266 037 |
| 2− | 46624<br>−18912<br>266 040 | 46625<br>−18911<br>266 041 | 46626<br>−18910<br>266 042 | 46627<br>−18909<br>266 043 | 46628<br>−18908<br>266 044 | 46629<br>−18907<br>266 045 | 46630<br>−18906<br>266 046 | 46631<br>−18905<br>266 047 | 46632<br>−18904<br>266 050 | 46633<br>−18903<br>266 051 | 46634<br>−18902<br>266 052 | 46635<br>−18901<br>266 053 | 46636<br>−18900<br>266 054 | 46637<br>−18899<br>266 055 | 46638<br>−18898<br>266 056 | 46639<br>−18897<br>266 057 |
| 3− | 46640<br>−18896<br>266 060 | 46641<br>−18895<br>266 061 | 46642<br>−18894<br>266 062 | 46643<br>−18893<br>266 063 | 46644<br>−18892<br>266 064 | 46645<br>−18891<br>266 065 | 46646<br>−18890<br>266 066 | 46647<br>−18889<br>266 067 | 46648<br>−18888<br>266 070 | 46649<br>−18887<br>266 071 | 46650<br>−18886<br>266 072 | 46651<br>−18885<br>266 073 | 46652<br>−18884<br>266 074 | 46653<br>−18883<br>266 075 | 46654<br>−18882<br>266 076 | 46655<br>−18881<br>266 077 |
| 4− | 46656<br>−18880<br>266 100 | 46657<br>−18879<br>266 101 | 46658<br>−18878<br>266 102 | 46659<br>−18877<br>266 103 | 46660<br>−18876<br>266 104 | 46661<br>−18875<br>266 105 | 46662<br>−18874<br>266 106 | 46663<br>−18873<br>266 107 | 46664<br>−18872<br>266 110 | 46665<br>−18871<br>266 111 | 46666<br>−18870<br>266 112 | 46667<br>−18869<br>266 113 | 46668<br>−18868<br>266 114 | 46669<br>−18867<br>266 115 | 46670<br>−18866<br>266 116 | 46671<br>−18865<br>266 117 |
| 5− | 46672<br>−18864<br>266 120 | 46673<br>−18863<br>266 121 | 46674<br>−18862<br>266 122 | 46675<br>−18861<br>266 123 | 46676<br>−18860<br>266 124 | 46677<br>−18859<br>266 125 | 46678<br>−18858<br>266 126 | 46679<br>−18857<br>266 127 | 46680<br>−18856<br>266 130 | 46681<br>−18855<br>266 131 | 46682<br>−18854<br>266 132 | 46683<br>−18853<br>266 133 | 46684<br>−18852<br>266 134 | 46685<br>−18851<br>266 135 | 46686<br>−18850<br>266 136 | 46687<br>−18849<br>266 137 |
| 6− | 46688<br>−18848<br>266 140 | 46689<br>−18847<br>266 141 | 46690<br>−18846<br>266 142 | 46691<br>−18845<br>266 143 | 46692<br>−18844<br>266 144 | 46693<br>−18843<br>266 145 | 46694<br>−18842<br>266 146 | 46695<br>−18841<br>266 147 | 46696<br>−18840<br>266 150 | 46697<br>−18839<br>266 151 | 46698<br>−18838<br>266 152 | 46699<br>−18837<br>266 153 | 46700<br>−18836<br>266 154 | 46701<br>−18835<br>266 155 | 46702<br>−18834<br>266 156 | 46703<br>−18833<br>266 157 |
| 7− | 46704<br>−18832<br>266 160 | 46705<br>−18831<br>266 161 | 46706<br>−18830<br>266 162 | 46707<br>−18829<br>266 163 | 46708<br>−18828<br>266 164 | 46709<br>−18827<br>266 165 | 46710<br>−18826<br>266 166 | 46711<br>−18825<br>266 167 | 46712<br>−18824<br>266 170 | 46713<br>−18823<br>266 171 | 46714<br>−18822<br>266 172 | 46715<br>−18821<br>266 173 | 46716<br>−18820<br>266 174 | 46717<br>−18819<br>266 175 | 46718<br>−18818<br>266 176 | 46719<br>−18817<br>266 177 |
| 8− | 46720<br>−18816<br>266 200 | 46721<br>−18815<br>266 201 | 46722<br>−18814<br>266 202 | 46723<br>−18813<br>266 203 | 46724<br>−18812<br>266 204 | 46725<br>−18811<br>266 205 | 46726<br>−18810<br>266 206 | 46727<br>−18809<br>266 207 | 46728<br>−18808<br>266 210 | 46729<br>−18807<br>266 211 | 46730<br>−18806<br>266 212 | 46731<br>−18805<br>266 213 | 46732<br>−18804<br>266 214 | 46733<br>−18803<br>266 215 | 46734<br>−18802<br>266 216 | 46735<br>−18801<br>266 217 |
| 9− | 46736<br>−18800<br>266 220 | 46737<br>−18799<br>266 221 | 46738<br>−18798<br>266 222 | 46739<br>−18797<br>266 223 | 46740<br>−18796<br>266 224 | 46741<br>−18795<br>266 225 | 46742<br>−18794<br>266 226 | 46743<br>−18793<br>266 227 | 46744<br>−18792<br>266 230 | 46745<br>−18791<br>266 231 | 46746<br>−18790<br>266 232 | 46747<br>−18789<br>266 233 | 46748<br>−18788<br>266 234 | 46749<br>−18787<br>266 235 | 46750<br>−18786<br>266 236 | 46751<br>−18785<br>266 237 |
| A− | 46752<br>−18784<br>266 240 | 46753<br>−18783<br>266 241 | 46754<br>−18782<br>266 242 | 46755<br>−18781<br>266 243 | 46756<br>−18780<br>266 244 | 46757<br>−18779<br>266 245 | 46758<br>−18778<br>266 246 | 46759<br>−18777<br>266 247 | 46760<br>−18776<br>266 250 | 46761<br>−18775<br>266 251 | 46762<br>−18774<br>266 252 | 46763<br>−18773<br>266 253 | 46764<br>−18772<br>266 254 | 46765<br>−18771<br>266 255 | 46766<br>−18770<br>266 256 | 46767<br>−18769<br>266 257 |
| B− | 46768<br>−18768<br>266 260 | 46769<br>−18767<br>266 261 | 46770<br>−18766<br>266 262 | 46771<br>−18765<br>266 263 | 46772<br>−18764<br>266 264 | 46773<br>−18763<br>266 265 | 46774<br>−18762<br>266 266 | 46775<br>−18761<br>266 267 | 46776<br>−18760<br>266 270 | 46777<br>−18759<br>266 271 | 46778<br>−18758<br>266 272 | 46779<br>−18757<br>266 273 | 46780<br>−18756<br>266 274 | 46781<br>−18755<br>266 275 | 46782<br>−18754<br>266 276 | 46783<br>−18753<br>266 277 |
| C− | 46784<br>−18752<br>266 300 | 46785<br>−18751<br>266 301 | 46786<br>−18750<br>266 302 | 46787<br>−18749<br>266 303 | 46788<br>−18748<br>266 304 | 46789<br>−18747<br>266 305 | 46790<br>−18746<br>266 306 | 46791<br>−18745<br>266 307 | 46792<br>−18744<br>266 310 | 46793<br>−18743<br>266 311 | 46794<br>−18742<br>266 312 | 46795<br>−18741<br>266 313 | 46796<br>−18740<br>266 314 | 46797<br>−18739<br>266 315 | 46798<br>−18738<br>266 316 | 46799<br>−18737<br>266 317 |
| D− | 46800<br>−18736<br>266 320 | 46801<br>−18735<br>266 321 | 46802<br>−18734<br>266 322 | 46803<br>−18733<br>266 323 | 46804<br>−18732<br>266 324 | 46805<br>−18731<br>266 325 | 46806<br>−18730<br>266 326 | 46807<br>−18729<br>266 327 | 46808<br>−18728<br>266 330 | 46809<br>−18727<br>266 331 | 46810<br>−18726<br>266 332 | 46811<br>−18725<br>266 333 | 46812<br>−18724<br>266 334 | 46813<br>−18723<br>266 335 | 46814<br>−18722<br>266 336 | 46815<br>−18721<br>266 337 |
| E− | 46816<br>−18720<br>266 340 | 46817<br>−18719<br>266 341 | 46818<br>−18718<br>266 342 | 46819<br>−18717<br>266 343 | 46820<br>−18716<br>266 344 | 46821<br>−18715<br>266 345 | 46822<br>−18714<br>266 346 | 46823<br>−18713<br>266 347 | 46824<br>−18712<br>266 350 | 46825<br>−18711<br>266 351 | 46826<br>−18710<br>266 352 | 46827<br>−18709<br>266 353 | 46828<br>−18708<br>266 354 | 46829<br>−18707<br>266 355 | 46830<br>−18706<br>266 356 | 46831<br>−18705<br>266 357 |
| F− | 46832<br>−18704<br>266 360 | 46833<br>−18703<br>266 361 | 46834<br>−18702<br>266 362 | 46835<br>−18701<br>266 363 | 46836<br>−18700<br>266 364 | 46837<br>−18699<br>266 365 | 46838<br>−18698<br>266 366 | 46839<br>−18697<br>266 367 | 46840<br>−18696<br>266 370 | 46841<br>−18695<br>266 371 | 46842<br>−18694<br>266 372 | 46843<br>−18693<br>266 373 | 46844<br>−18692<br>266 374 | 46845<br>−18691<br>266 375 | 46846<br>−18690<br>266 376 | 46847<br>−18689<br>266 377 |

DECIMAL ←
 DECIMAL ←
OCTAL ←

 DECIMAL [ −18944 ]   BINARY [ 1011 0110 ]   DECIMAL [ 46592 ]   HEXADECIMAL ⬡ B6   OCTAL [ 266 000 ]

FOURTH HEX DIGIT →   ← THIRD HEX DIGIT

**FIRST HEX DIGIT**

(2)

| SECOND HEX DIGIT | −0 | −1 | −2 | −3 | −4 | −5 | −6 | −7 | −8 | −9 | −A | −B | −C | −D | −E | −F |
|---|---|---|---|---|---|---|---|---|---|---|---|---|---|---|---|---|
| 0− | 46848<br>-18688<br>267 000 | 46849<br>-18687<br>267 001 | 46850<br>-18686<br>267 002 | 46851<br>-18685<br>267 003 | 46852<br>-18684<br>267 004 | 46853<br>-18683<br>267 005 | 46854<br>-18682<br>267 006 | 46855<br>-18681<br>267 007 | 46856<br>-18680<br>267 010 | 46857<br>-18679<br>267 011 | 46858<br>-18678<br>267 012 | 46859<br>-18677<br>267 013 | 46860<br>-18676<br>267 014 | 46861<br>-18675<br>267 015 | 46862<br>-18674<br>267 016 | 46863<br>-18673<br>267 017 |
| 1− | 46864<br>-18672<br>267 020 | 46865<br>-18671<br>267 021 | 46866<br>-18670<br>267 022 | 46867<br>-18669<br>267 023 | 46868<br>-18668<br>267 024 | 46869<br>-18667<br>267 025 | 46870<br>-18666<br>267 026 | 46871<br>-18665<br>267 027 | 46872<br>-18664<br>267 030 | 46873<br>-18663<br>267 031 | 46874<br>-18662<br>267 032 | 46875<br>-18661<br>267 033 | 46876<br>-18660<br>267 034 | 46877<br>-18659<br>267 035 | 46878<br>-18658<br>267 036 | 46879<br>-18657<br>267 037 |
| 2− | 46880<br>-18656<br>267 040 | 46881<br>-18655<br>267 041 | 46882<br>-18654<br>267 042 | 46883<br>-18653<br>267 043 | 46884<br>-18652<br>267 044 | 46885<br>-18651<br>267 045 | 46886<br>-18650<br>267 046 | 46887<br>-18649<br>267 047 | 46888<br>-18648<br>267 050 | 46889<br>-18647<br>267 051 | 46890<br>-18646<br>267 052 | 46891<br>-18645<br>267 053 | 46892<br>-18644<br>267 054 | 46893<br>-18643<br>267 055 | 46894<br>-18642<br>267 056 | 46895<br>-18641<br>267 057 |
| 3− | 46896<br>-18640<br>267 060 | 46897<br>-18639<br>267 061 | 46898<br>-18638<br>267 062 | 46899<br>-18637<br>267 063 | 46900<br>-18636<br>267 064 | 46901<br>-18635<br>267 065 | 46902<br>-18634<br>267 066 | 46903<br>-18633<br>267 067 | 46904<br>-18632<br>267 070 | 46905<br>-18631<br>267 071 | 46906<br>-18630<br>267 072 | 46907<br>-18629<br>267 073 | 46908<br>-18628<br>267 074 | 46909<br>-18627<br>267 075 | 46910<br>-18626<br>267 076 | 46911<br>-18625<br>267 077 |
| 4− | 46912<br>-18624<br>267 100 | 46913<br>-18623<br>267 101 | 46914<br>-18622<br>267 102 | 46915<br>-18621<br>267 103 | 46916<br>-18620<br>267 104 | 46917<br>-18619<br>267 105 | 46918<br>-18618<br>267 106 | 46919<br>-18617<br>267 107 | 46920<br>-18616<br>267 110 | 46921<br>-18615<br>267 111 | 46922<br>-18614<br>267 112 | 46923<br>-18613<br>267 113 | 46924<br>-18612<br>267 114 | 46925<br>-18611<br>267 115 | 46926<br>-18610<br>267 116 | 46927<br>-18609<br>267 117 |
| 5− | 46928<br>-18608<br>267 120 | 46929<br>-18607<br>267 121 | 46930<br>-18606<br>267 122 | 46931<br>-18605<br>267 123 | 46932<br>-18604<br>267 124 | 46933<br>-18603<br>267 125 | 46934<br>-18602<br>267 126 | 46935<br>-18601<br>267 127 | 46936<br>-18600<br>267 130 | 46937<br>-18599<br>267 131 | 46938<br>-18598<br>267 132 | 46939<br>-18597<br>267 133 | 46940<br>-18596<br>267 134 | 46941<br>-18595<br>267 135 | 46942<br>-18594<br>267 136 | 46943<br>-18593<br>267 137 |
| 6− | 46944<br>-18592<br>267 140 | 46945<br>-18591<br>267 141 | 46946<br>-18590<br>267 142 | 46947<br>-18589<br>267 143 | 46948<br>-18588<br>267 144 | 46949<br>-18587<br>267 145 | 46950<br>-18586<br>267 146 | 46951<br>-18585<br>267 147 | 46952<br>-18584<br>267 150 | 46953<br>-18583<br>267 151 | 46954<br>-18582<br>267 152 | 46955<br>-18581<br>267 153 | 46956<br>-18580<br>267 154 | 46957<br>-18579<br>267 155 | 46958<br>-18578<br>267 156 | 46959<br>-18577<br>267 157 |
| 7− | 46960<br>-18576<br>267 160 | 46961<br>-18575<br>267 161 | 46962<br>-18574<br>267 162 | 46963<br>-18573<br>267 163 | 46964<br>-18572<br>267 164 | 46965<br>-18571<br>267 165 | 46966<br>-18570<br>267 166 | 46967<br>-18569<br>267 167 | 46968<br>-18568<br>267 170 | 46969<br>-18567<br>267 171 | 46970<br>-18566<br>267 172 | 46971<br>-18565<br>267 173 | 46972<br>-18564<br>267 174 | 46973<br>-18563<br>267 175 | 46974<br>-18562<br>267 176 | 46975<br>-18561<br>267 177 |
| 8− | 46976<br>-18560<br>267 200 | 46977<br>-18559<br>267 201 | 46978<br>-18558<br>267 202 | 46979<br>-18557<br>267 203 | 46980<br>-18556<br>267 204 | 46981<br>-18555<br>267 205 | 46982<br>-18554<br>267 206 | 46983<br>-18553<br>267 207 | 46984<br>-18552<br>267 210 | 46985<br>-18551<br>267 211 | 46986<br>-18550<br>267 212 | 46987<br>-18549<br>267 213 | 46988<br>-18548<br>267 214 | 46989<br>-18547<br>267 215 | 46990<br>-18546<br>267 216 | 46991<br>-18545<br>267 217 |
| 9− | 46992<br>-18544<br>267 220 | 46993<br>-18543<br>267 221 | 46994<br>-18542<br>267 222 | 46995<br>-18541<br>267 223 | 46996<br>-18540<br>267 224 | 46997<br>-18539<br>267 225 | 46998<br>-18538<br>267 226 | 46999<br>-18537<br>267 227 | 47000<br>-18536<br>267 230 | 47001<br>-18535<br>267 231 | 47002<br>-18534<br>267 232 | 47003<br>-18533<br>267 233 | 47004<br>-18532<br>267 234 | 47005<br>-18531<br>267 235 | 47006<br>-18530<br>267 236 | 47007<br>-18529<br>267 237 |
| A− | 47008<br>-18528<br>267 240 | 47009<br>-18527<br>267 241 | 47010<br>-18526<br>267 242 | 47011<br>-18525<br>267 243 | 47012<br>-18524<br>267 244 | 47013<br>-18523<br>267 245 | 47014<br>-18522<br>267 246 | 47015<br>-18521<br>267 247 | 47016<br>-18520<br>267 250 | 47017<br>-18519<br>267 251 | 47018<br>-18518<br>267 252 | 47019<br>-18517<br>267 253 | 47020<br>-18516<br>267 254 | 47021<br>-18515<br>267 255 | 47022<br>-18514<br>267 256 | 47023<br>-18513<br>267 257 |
| B− | 47024<br>-18512<br>267 260 | 47025<br>-18511<br>267 261 | 47026<br>-18510<br>267 262 | 47027<br>-18509<br>267 263 | 47028<br>-18508<br>267 264 | 47029<br>-18507<br>267 265 | 47030<br>-18506<br>267 266 | 47031<br>-18505<br>267 267 | 47032<br>-18504<br>267 270 | 47033<br>-18503<br>267 271 | 47034<br>-18502<br>267 272 | 47035<br>-18501<br>267 273 | 47036<br>-18500<br>267 274 | 47037<br>-18499<br>267 275 | 47038<br>-18498<br>267 276 | 47039<br>-18497<br>267 277 |
| C− | 47040<br>-18496<br>267 300 | 47041<br>-18495<br>267 301 | 47042<br>-18494<br>267 302 | 47043<br>-18493<br>267 303 | 47044<br>-18492<br>267 304 | 47045<br>-18491<br>267 305 | 47046<br>-18490<br>267 306 | 47047<br>-18489<br>267 307 | 47048<br>-18488<br>267 310 | 47049<br>-18487<br>267 311 | 47050<br>-18486<br>267 312 | 47051<br>-18485<br>267 313 | 47052<br>-18484<br>267 314 | 47053<br>-18483<br>267 315 | 47054<br>-18482<br>267 316 | 47055<br>-18481<br>267 317 |
| D− | 47056<br>-18480<br>267 320 | 47057<br>-18479<br>267 321 | 47058<br>-18478<br>267 322 | 47059<br>-18477<br>267 323 | 47060<br>-18476<br>267 324 | 47061<br>-18475<br>267 325 | 47062<br>-18474<br>267 326 | 47063<br>-18473<br>267 327 | 47064<br>-18472<br>267 330 | 47065<br>-18471<br>267 331 | 47066<br>-18470<br>267 332 | 47067<br>-18469<br>267 333 | 47068<br>-18468<br>267 334 | 47069<br>-18467<br>267 335 | 47070<br>-18466<br>267 336 | 47071<br>-18465<br>267 337 |
| E− | 47072<br>-18464<br>267 340 | 47073<br>-18463<br>267 341 | 47074<br>-18462<br>267 342 | 47075<br>-18461<br>267 343 | 47076<br>-18460<br>267 344 | 47077<br>-18459<br>267 345 | 47078<br>-18458<br>267 346 | 47079<br>-18457<br>267 347 | 47080<br>-18456<br>267 350 | 47081<br>-18455<br>267 351 | 47082<br>-18454<br>267 352 | 47083<br>-18453<br>267 353 | 47084<br>-18452<br>267 354 | 47085<br>-18451<br>267 355 | 47086<br>-18450<br>267 356 | 47087<br>-18449<br>267 357 |
| F− | 47088<br>-18448<br>267 360 | 47089<br>-18447<br>267 361 | 47090<br>-18446<br>267 362 | 47091<br>-18445<br>267 363 | 47092<br>-18444<br>267 364 | 47093<br>-18443<br>267 365 | 47094<br>-18442<br>267 366 | 47095<br>-18441<br>267 367 | 47096<br>-18440<br>267 370 | 47097<br>-18439<br>267 371 | 47098<br>-18438<br>267 372 | 47099<br>-18437<br>267 373 | 47100<br>-18436<br>267 374 | 47101<br>-18435<br>267 375 | 47102<br>-18434<br>267 376 | 47103<br>-18433<br>267 377 |

| SECOND HEX DIGIT | −0 | −1 | −2 | −3 | −4 | −5 | −6 | −7 | −8 | −9 | −A | −B | −C | −D | −E | −F |
|---|---|---|---|---|---|---|---|---|---|---|---|---|---|---|---|---|
| 0− | 47104<br>−18432<br>270 000 | 47105<br>−18431<br>270 001 | 47106<br>−18430<br>270 002 | 47107<br>−18429<br>270 003 | 47108<br>−18428<br>270 004 | 47109<br>−18427<br>270 005 | 47110<br>−18426<br>270 006 | 47111<br>−18425<br>270 007 | 47112<br>−18424<br>270 010 | 47113<br>−18423<br>270 011 | 47114<br>−18422<br>270 012 | 47115<br>−18421<br>270 013 | 47116<br>−18420<br>270 014 | 47117<br>−18419<br>270 015 | 47118<br>−18418<br>270 016 | 47119<br>−18417<br>270 017 |
| 1− | 47120<br>−18416<br>270 020 | 47121<br>−18415<br>270 021 | 47122<br>−18414<br>270 022 | 47123<br>−18413<br>270 023 | 47124<br>−18412<br>270 024 | 47125<br>−18411<br>270 025 | 47126<br>−18410<br>270 026 | 47127<br>−18409<br>270 027 | 47128<br>−18408<br>270 030 | 47129<br>−18407<br>270 031 | 47130<br>−18406<br>270 032 | 47131<br>−18405<br>270 033 | 47132<br>−18404<br>270 034 | 47133<br>−18403<br>270 035 | 47134<br>−18402<br>270 036 | 47135<br>−18401<br>270 037 |
| 2− | 47136<br>−18400<br>270 040 | 47137<br>−18399<br>270 041 | 47138<br>−18398<br>270 042 | 47139<br>−18397<br>270 043 | 47140<br>−18396<br>270 044 | 47141<br>−18395<br>270 045 | 47142<br>−18394<br>270 046 | 47143<br>−18393<br>270 047 | 47144<br>−18392<br>270 050 | 47145<br>−18391<br>270 051 | 47146<br>−18390<br>270 052 | 47147<br>−18389<br>270 053 | 47148<br>−18388<br>270 054 | 47149<br>−18387<br>270 055 | 47150<br>−18386<br>270 056 | 47151<br>−18385<br>270 057 |
| 3− | 47152<br>−18384<br>270 060 | 47153<br>−18383<br>270 061 | 47154<br>−18382<br>270 062 | 47155<br>−18381<br>270 063 | 47156<br>−18380<br>270 064 | 47157<br>−18379<br>270 065 | 47158<br>−18378<br>270 066 | 47159<br>−18377<br>270 067 | 47160<br>−18376<br>270 070 | 47161<br>−18375<br>270 071 | 47162<br>−18374<br>270 072 | 47163<br>−18373<br>270 073 | 47164<br>−18372<br>270 074 | 47165<br>−18371<br>270 075 | 47166<br>−18370<br>270 076 | 47167<br>−18369<br>270 077 |
| 4− | 47168<br>−18368<br>270 100 | 47169<br>−18367<br>270 101 | 47170<br>−18366<br>270 102 | 47171<br>−18365<br>270 103 | 47172<br>−18364<br>270 104 | 47173<br>−18363<br>270 105 | 47174<br>−18362<br>270 106 | 47175<br>−18361<br>270 107 | 47176<br>−18360<br>270 110 | 47177<br>−18359<br>270 111 | 47178<br>−18358<br>270 112 | 47179<br>−18357<br>270 113 | 47180<br>−18356<br>270 114 | 47181<br>−18355<br>270 115 | 47182<br>−18354<br>270 116 | 47183<br>−18353<br>270 117 |
| 5− | 47184<br>−18352<br>270 120 | 47185<br>−18351<br>270 121 | 47186<br>−18350<br>270 122 | 47187<br>−18349<br>270 123 | 47188<br>−18348<br>270 124 | 47189<br>−18347<br>270 125 | 47190<br>−18346<br>270 126 | 47191<br>−18345<br>270 127 | 47192<br>−18344<br>270 130 | 47193<br>−18343<br>270 131 | 47194<br>−18342<br>270 132 | 47195<br>−18341<br>270 133 | 47196<br>−18340<br>270 134 | 47197<br>−18339<br>270 135 | 47198<br>−18338<br>270 136 | 47199<br>−18337<br>270 137 |
| 6− | 47200<br>−18336<br>270 140 | 47201<br>−18335<br>270 141 | 47202<br>−18334<br>270 142 | 47203<br>−18333<br>270 143 | 47204<br>−18332<br>270 144 | 47205<br>−18331<br>270 145 | 47206<br>−18330<br>270 146 | 47207<br>−18329<br>270 147 | 47208<br>−18328<br>270 150 | 47209<br>−18327<br>270 151 | 47210<br>−18326<br>270 152 | 47211<br>−18325<br>270 153 | 47212<br>−18324<br>270 154 | 47213<br>−18323<br>270 155 | 47214<br>−18322<br>270 156 | 47215<br>−18321<br>270 157 |
| 7− | 47216<br>−18320<br>270 160 | 47217<br>−18319<br>270 161 | 47218<br>−18318<br>270 162 | 47219<br>−18317<br>270 163 | 47220<br>−18316<br>270 164 | 47221<br>−18315<br>270 165 | 47222<br>−18314<br>270 166 | 47223<br>−18313<br>270 167 | 47224<br>−18312<br>270 170 | 47225<br>−18311<br>270 171 | 47226<br>−18310<br>270 172 | 47227<br>−18309<br>270 173 | 47228<br>−18308<br>270 174 | 47229<br>−18307<br>270 175 | 47230<br>−18306<br>270 176 | 47231<br>−18305<br>270 177 |
| 8− | 47232<br>−18304<br>270 200 | 47233<br>−18303<br>270 201 | 47234<br>−18302<br>270 202 | 47235<br>−18301<br>270 203 | 47236<br>−18300<br>270 204 | 47237<br>−18299<br>270 205 | 47238<br>−18298<br>270 206 | 47239<br>−18297<br>270 207 | 47240<br>−18296<br>270 210 | 47241<br>−18295<br>270 211 | 47242<br>−18294<br>270 212 | 47243<br>−18293<br>270 213 | 47244<br>−18292<br>270 214 | 47245<br>−18291<br>270 215 | 47246<br>−18290<br>270 216 | 47247<br>−18289<br>270 217 |
| 9− | 47248<br>−18288<br>270 220 | 47249<br>−18287<br>270 221 | 47250<br>−18286<br>270 222 | 47251<br>−18285<br>270 223 | 47252<br>−18284<br>270 224 | 47253<br>−18283<br>270 225 | 47254<br>−18282<br>270 226 | 47255<br>−18281<br>270 227 | 47256<br>−18280<br>270 230 | 47257<br>−18279<br>270 231 | 47258<br>−18278<br>270 232 | 47259<br>−18277<br>270 233 | 47260<br>−18276<br>270 234 | 47261<br>−18275<br>270 235 | 47262<br>−18274<br>270 236 | 47263<br>−18273<br>270 237 |
| A− | 47264<br>−18272<br>270 240 | 47265<br>−18271<br>270 241 | 47266<br>−18270<br>270 242 | 47267<br>−18269<br>270 243 | 47268<br>−18268<br>270 244 | 47269<br>−18267<br>270 245 | 47270<br>−18266<br>270 246 | 47271<br>−18265<br>270 247 | 47272<br>−18264<br>270 250 | 47273<br>−18263<br>270 251 | 47274<br>−18262<br>270 252 | 47275<br>−18261<br>270 253 | 47276<br>−18260<br>270 254 | 47277<br>−18259<br>270 255 | 47278<br>−18258<br>270 256 | 47279<br>−18257<br>270 257 |
| B− | 47280<br>−18256<br>270 260 | 47281<br>−18255<br>270 261 | 47282<br>−18254<br>270 262 | 47283<br>−18253<br>270 263 | 47284<br>−18252<br>270 264 | 47285<br>−18251<br>270 265 | 47286<br>−18250<br>270 266 | 47287<br>−18249<br>270 267 | 47288<br>−18248<br>270 270 | 47289<br>−18247<br>270 271 | 47290<br>−18246<br>270 272 | 47291<br>−18245<br>270 273 | 47292<br>−18244<br>270 274 | 47293<br>−18243<br>270 275 | 47294<br>−18242<br>270 276 | 47295<br>−18241<br>270 277 |
| C− | 47296<br>−18240<br>270 300 | 47297<br>−18239<br>270 301 | 47298<br>−18238<br>270 302 | 47299<br>−18237<br>270 303 | 47300<br>−18236<br>270 304 | 47301<br>−18235<br>270 305 | 47302<br>−18234<br>270 306 | 47303<br>−18233<br>270 307 | 47304<br>−18232<br>270 310 | 47305<br>−18231<br>270 311 | 47306<br>−18230<br>270 312 | 47307<br>−18229<br>270 313 | 47308<br>−18228<br>270 314 | 47309<br>−18227<br>270 315 | 47310<br>−18226<br>270 316 | 47311<br>−18225<br>270 317 |
| D− | 47312<br>−18224<br>270 320 | 47313<br>−18223<br>270 321 | 47314<br>−18222<br>270 322 | 47315<br>−18221<br>270 323 | 47316<br>−18220<br>270 324 | 47317<br>−18219<br>270 325 | 47318<br>−18218<br>270 326 | 47319<br>−18217<br>270 327 | 47320<br>−18216<br>270 330 | 47321<br>−18215<br>270 331 | 47322<br>−18214<br>270 332 | 47323<br>−18213<br>270 333 | 47324<br>−18212<br>270 334 | 47325<br>−18211<br>270 335 | 47326<br>−18210<br>270 336 | 47327<br>−18209<br>270 337 |
| E− | 47328<br>−18208<br>270 340 | 47329<br>−18207<br>270 341 | 47330<br>−18206<br>270 342 | 47331<br>−18205<br>270 343 | 47332<br>−18204<br>270 344 | 47333<br>−18203<br>270 345 | 47334<br>−18202<br>270 346 | 47335<br>−18201<br>270 347 | 47336<br>−18200<br>270 350 | 47337<br>−18199<br>270 351 | 47338<br>−18198<br>270 352 | 47339<br>−18197<br>270 353 | 47340<br>−18196<br>270 354 | 47341<br>−18195<br>270 355 | 47342<br>−18194<br>270 356 | 47343<br>−18193<br>270 357 |
| F− | 47344<br>−18192<br>270 360 | 47345<br>−18191<br>270 361 | 47346<br>−18190<br>270 362 | 47347<br>−18189<br>270 363 | 47348<br>−18188<br>270 364 | 47349<br>−18187<br>270 365 | 47350<br>−18186<br>270 366 | 47351<br>−18185<br>270 367 | 47352<br>−18184<br>270 370 | 47353<br>−18183<br>270 371 | 47354<br>−18182<br>270 372 | 47355<br>−18181<br>270 373 | 47356<br>−18180<br>270 374 | 47357<br>−18179<br>270 375 | 47358<br>−18178<br>270 376 | 47359<br>−18177<br>270 377 |

Arrows at right: **DECIMAL**, **DECIMAL**, **OCTAL**

 DECIMAL  −18432    BINARY  1011 1000    DECIMAL  47104    HEXADECIMAL  B8    OCTAL  270 000

FOURTH HEX DIGIT → B8 ← THIRD HEX DIGIT

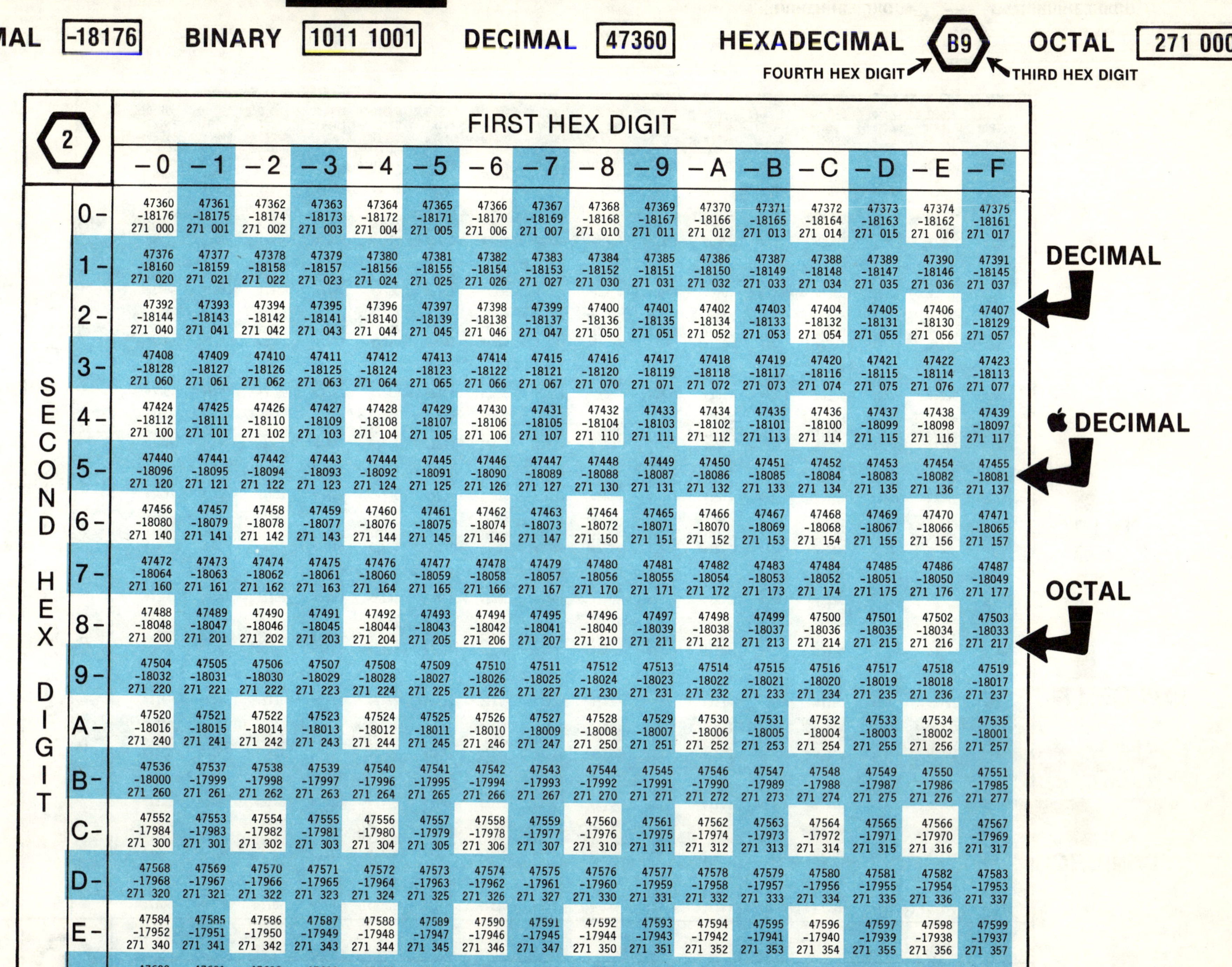

**DECIMAL** -18176 **BINARY** 1011 1001 **DECIMAL** 47360 **HEXADECIMAL** B9 **OCTAL** 271 000

FOURTH HEX DIGIT — THIRD HEX DIGIT

2

FIRST HEX DIGIT

SECOND HEX DIGIT

DECIMAL

 DECIMAL

OCTAL

| | –0 | –1 | –2 | –3 | –4 | –5 | –6 | –7 | –8 | –9 | –A | –B | –C | –D | –E | –F |
|---|---|---|---|---|---|---|---|---|---|---|---|---|---|---|---|---|
| 0– | 47360<br>-18176<br>271 000 | 47361<br>-18175<br>271 001 | 47362<br>-18174<br>271 002 | 47363<br>-18173<br>271 003 | 47364<br>-18172<br>271 004 | 47365<br>-18171<br>271 005 | 47366<br>-18170<br>271 006 | 47367<br>-18169<br>271 007 | 47368<br>-18168<br>271 010 | 47369<br>-18167<br>271 011 | 47370<br>-18166<br>271 012 | 47371<br>-18165<br>271 013 | 47372<br>-18164<br>271 014 | 47373<br>-18163<br>271 015 | 47374<br>-18162<br>271 016 | 47375<br>-18161<br>271 017 |
| 1– | 47376<br>-18160<br>271 020 | 47377<br>-18159<br>271 021 | 47378<br>-18158<br>271 022 | 47379<br>-18157<br>271 023 | 47380<br>-18156<br>271 024 | 47381<br>-18155<br>271 025 | 47382<br>-18154<br>271 026 | 47383<br>-18153<br>271 027 | 47384<br>-18152<br>271 030 | 47385<br>-18151<br>271 031 | 47386<br>-18150<br>271 032 | 47387<br>-18149<br>271 033 | 47388<br>-18148<br>271 034 | 47389<br>-18147<br>271 035 | 47390<br>-18146<br>271 036 | 47391<br>-18145<br>271 037 |
| 2– | 47392<br>-18144<br>271 040 | 47393<br>-18143<br>271 041 | 47394<br>-18142<br>271 042 | 47395<br>-18141<br>271 043 | 47396<br>-18140<br>271 044 | 47397<br>-18139<br>271 045 | 47398<br>-18138<br>271 046 | 47399<br>-18137<br>271 047 | 47400<br>-18136<br>271 050 | 47401<br>-18135<br>271 051 | 47402<br>-18134<br>271 052 | 47403<br>-18133<br>271 053 | 47404<br>-18132<br>271 054 | 47405<br>-18131<br>271 055 | 47406<br>-18130<br>271 056 | 47407<br>-18129<br>271 057 |
| 3– | 47408<br>-18128<br>271 060 | 47409<br>-18127<br>271 061 | 47410<br>-18126<br>271 062 | 47411<br>-18125<br>271 063 | 47412<br>-18124<br>271 064 | 47413<br>-18123<br>271 065 | 47414<br>-18122<br>271 066 | 47415<br>-18121<br>271 067 | 47416<br>-18120<br>271 070 | 47417<br>-18119<br>271 071 | 47418<br>-18118<br>271 072 | 47419<br>-18117<br>271 073 | 47420<br>-18116<br>271 074 | 47421<br>-18115<br>271 075 | 47422<br>-18114<br>271 076 | 47423<br>-18113<br>271 077 |
| 4– | 47424<br>-18112<br>271 100 | 47425<br>-18111<br>271 101 | 47426<br>-18110<br>271 102 | 47427<br>-18109<br>271 103 | 47428<br>-18108<br>271 104 | 47429<br>-18107<br>271 105 | 47430<br>-18106<br>271 106 | 47431<br>-18105<br>271 107 | 47432<br>-18104<br>271 110 | 47433<br>-18103<br>271 111 | 47434<br>-18102<br>271 112 | 47435<br>-18101<br>271 113 | 47436<br>-18100<br>271 114 | 47437<br>-18099<br>271 115 | 47438<br>-18098<br>271 116 | 47439<br>-18097<br>271 117 |
| 5– | 47440<br>-18096<br>271 120 | 47441<br>-18095<br>271 121 | 47442<br>-18094<br>271 122 | 47443<br>-18093<br>271 123 | 47444<br>-18092<br>271 124 | 47445<br>-18091<br>271 125 | 47446<br>-18090<br>271 126 | 47447<br>-18089<br>271 127 | 47448<br>-18088<br>271 130 | 47449<br>-18087<br>271 131 | 47450<br>-18086<br>271 132 | 47451<br>-18085<br>271 133 | 47452<br>-18084<br>271 134 | 47453<br>-18083<br>271 135 | 47454<br>-18082<br>271 136 | 47455<br>-18081<br>271 137 |
| 6– | 47456<br>-18080<br>271 140 | 47457<br>-18079<br>271 141 | 47458<br>-18078<br>271 142 | 47459<br>-18077<br>271 143 | 47460<br>-18076<br>271 144 | 47461<br>-18075<br>271 145 | 47462<br>-18074<br>271 146 | 47463<br>-18073<br>271 147 | 47464<br>-18072<br>271 150 | 47465<br>-18071<br>271 151 | 47466<br>-18070<br>271 152 | 47467<br>-18069<br>271 153 | 47468<br>-18068<br>271 154 | 47469<br>-18067<br>271 155 | 47470<br>-18066<br>271 156 | 47471<br>-18065<br>271 157 |
| 7– | 47472<br>-18064<br>271 160 | 47473<br>-18063<br>271 161 | 47474<br>-18062<br>271 162 | 47475<br>-18061<br>271 163 | 47476<br>-18060<br>271 164 | 47477<br>-18059<br>271 165 | 47478<br>-18058<br>271 166 | 47479<br>-18057<br>271 167 | 47480<br>-18056<br>271 170 | 47481<br>-18055<br>271 171 | 47482<br>-18054<br>271 172 | 47483<br>-18053<br>271 173 | 47484<br>-18052<br>271 174 | 47485<br>-18051<br>271 175 | 47486<br>-18050<br>271 176 | 47487<br>-18049<br>271 177 |
| 8– | 47488<br>-18048<br>271 200 | 47489<br>-18047<br>271 201 | 47490<br>-18046<br>271 202 | 47491<br>-18045<br>271 203 | 47492<br>-18044<br>271 204 | 47493<br>-18043<br>271 205 | 47494<br>-18042<br>271 206 | 47495<br>-18041<br>271 207 | 47496<br>-18040<br>271 210 | 47497<br>-18039<br>271 211 | 47498<br>-18038<br>271 212 | 47499<br>-18037<br>271 213 | 47500<br>-18036<br>271 214 | 47501<br>-18035<br>271 215 | 47502<br>-18034<br>271 216 | 47503<br>-18033<br>271 217 |
| 9– | 47504<br>-18032<br>271 220 | 47505<br>-18031<br>271 221 | 47506<br>-18030<br>271 222 | 47507<br>-18029<br>271 223 | 47508<br>-18028<br>271 224 | 47509<br>-18027<br>271 225 | 47510<br>-18026<br>271 226 | 47511<br>-18025<br>271 227 | 47512<br>-18024<br>271 230 | 47513<br>-18023<br>271 231 | 47514<br>-18022<br>271 232 | 47515<br>-18021<br>271 233 | 47516<br>-18020<br>271 234 | 47517<br>-18019<br>271 235 | 47518<br>-18018<br>271 236 | 47519<br>-18017<br>271 237 |
| A– | 47520<br>-18016<br>271 240 | 47521<br>-18015<br>271 241 | 47522<br>-18014<br>271 242 | 47523<br>-18013<br>271 243 | 47524<br>-18012<br>271 244 | 47525<br>-18011<br>271 245 | 47526<br>-18010<br>271 246 | 47527<br>-18009<br>271 247 | 47528<br>-18008<br>271 250 | 47529<br>-18007<br>271 251 | 47530<br>-18006<br>271 252 | 47531<br>-18005<br>271 253 | 47532<br>-18004<br>271 254 | 47533<br>-18003<br>271 255 | 47534<br>-18002<br>271 256 | 47535<br>-18001<br>271 257 |
| B– | 47536<br>-18000<br>271 260 | 47537<br>-17999<br>271 261 | 47538<br>-17998<br>271 262 | 47539<br>-17997<br>271 263 | 47540<br>-17996<br>271 264 | 47541<br>-17995<br>271 265 | 47542<br>-17994<br>271 266 | 47543<br>-17993<br>271 267 | 47544<br>-17992<br>271 270 | 47545<br>-17991<br>271 271 | 47546<br>-17990<br>271 272 | 47547<br>-17989<br>271 273 | 47548<br>-17988<br>271 274 | 47549<br>-17987<br>271 275 | 47550<br>-17986<br>271 276 | 47551<br>-17985<br>271 277 |
| C– | 47552<br>-17984<br>271 300 | 47553<br>-17983<br>271 301 | 47554<br>-17982<br>271 302 | 47555<br>-17981<br>271 303 | 47556<br>-17980<br>271 304 | 47557<br>-17979<br>271 305 | 47558<br>-17978<br>271 306 | 47559<br>-17977<br>271 307 | 47560<br>-17976<br>271 310 | 47561<br>-17975<br>271 311 | 47562<br>-17974<br>271 312 | 47563<br>-17973<br>271 313 | 47564<br>-17972<br>271 314 | 47565<br>-17971<br>271 315 | 47566<br>-17970<br>271 316 | 47567<br>-17969<br>271 317 |
| D– | 47568<br>-17968<br>271 320 | 47569<br>-17967<br>271 321 | 47570<br>-17966<br>271 322 | 47571<br>-17965<br>271 323 | 47572<br>-17964<br>271 324 | 47573<br>-17963<br>271 325 | 47574<br>-17962<br>271 326 | 47575<br>-17961<br>271 327 | 47576<br>-17960<br>271 330 | 47577<br>-17959<br>271 331 | 47578<br>-17958<br>271 332 | 47579<br>-17957<br>271 333 | 47580<br>-17956<br>271 334 | 47581<br>-17955<br>271 335 | 47582<br>-17954<br>271 336 | 47583<br>-17953<br>271 337 |
| E– | 47584<br>-17952<br>271 340 | 47585<br>-17951<br>271 341 | 47586<br>-17950<br>271 342 | 47587<br>-17949<br>271 343 | 47588<br>-17948<br>271 344 | 47589<br>-17947<br>271 345 | 47590<br>-17946<br>271 346 | 47591<br>-17945<br>271 347 | 47592<br>-17944<br>271 350 | 47593<br>-17943<br>271 351 | 47594<br>-17942<br>271 352 | 47595<br>-17941<br>271 353 | 47596<br>-17940<br>271 354 | 47597<br>-17939<br>271 355 | 47598<br>-17938<br>271 356 | 47599<br>-17937<br>271 357 |
| F– | 47600<br>-17936<br>271 360 | 47601<br>-17935<br>271 361 | 47602<br>-17934<br>271 362 | 47603<br>-17933<br>271 363 | 47604<br>-17932<br>271 364 | 47605<br>-17931<br>271 365 | 47606<br>-17930<br>271 366 | 47607<br>-17929<br>271 367 | 47608<br>-17928<br>271 370 | 47609<br>-17927<br>271 371 | 47610<br>-17926<br>271 372 | 47611<br>-17925<br>271 373 | 47612<br>-17924<br>271 374 | 47613<br>-17923<br>271 375 | 47614<br>-17922<br>271 376 | 47615<br>-17921<br>271 377 |

## FIRST HEX DIGIT

(2)

| SECOND HEX DIGIT | −0 | −1 | −2 | −3 | −4 | −5 | −6 | −7 | −8 | −9 | −A | −B | −C | −D | −E | −F |
|---|---|---|---|---|---|---|---|---|---|---|---|---|---|---|---|---|
| 0- | 47616<br>-17920<br>272 000 | 47617<br>-17919<br>272 001 | 47618<br>-17918<br>272 002 | 47619<br>-17917<br>272 003 | 47620<br>-17916<br>272 004 | 47621<br>-17915<br>272 005 | 47622<br>-17914<br>272 006 | 47623<br>-17913<br>272 007 | 47624<br>-17912<br>272 010 | 47625<br>-17911<br>272 011 | 47626<br>-17910<br>272 012 | 47627<br>-17909<br>272 013 | 47628<br>-17908<br>272 014 | 47629<br>-17907<br>272 015 | 47630<br>-17906<br>272 016 | 47631<br>-17905<br>272 017 |
| 1- | 47632<br>-17904<br>272 020 | 47633<br>-17903<br>272 021 | 47634<br>-17902<br>272 022 | 47635<br>-17901<br>272 023 | 47636<br>-17900<br>272 024 | 47637<br>-17899<br>272 025 | 47638<br>-17898<br>272 026 | 47639<br>-17897<br>272 027 | 47640<br>-17896<br>272 030 | 47641<br>-17895<br>272 031 | 47642<br>-17894<br>272 032 | 47643<br>-17893<br>272 033 | 47644<br>-17892<br>272 034 | 47645<br>-17891<br>272 035 | 47646<br>-17890<br>272 036 | 47647<br>-17889<br>272 037 |
| 2- | 47648<br>-17888<br>272 040 | 47649<br>-17887<br>272 041 | 47650<br>-17886<br>272 042 | 47651<br>-17885<br>272 043 | 47652<br>-17884<br>272 044 | 47653<br>-17883<br>272 045 | 47654<br>-17882<br>272 046 | 47655<br>-17881<br>272 047 | 47656<br>-17880<br>272 050 | 47657<br>-17879<br>272 051 | 47658<br>-17878<br>272 052 | 47659<br>-17877<br>272 053 | 47660<br>-17876<br>272 054 | 47661<br>-17875<br>272 055 | 47662<br>-17874<br>272 056 | 47663<br>-17873<br>272 057 |
| 3- | 47664<br>-17872<br>272 060 | 47665<br>-17871<br>272 061 | 47666<br>-17870<br>272 062 | 47667<br>-17869<br>272 063 | 47668<br>-17868<br>272 064 | 47669<br>-17867<br>272 065 | 47670<br>-17866<br>272 066 | 47671<br>-17865<br>272 067 | 47672<br>-17864<br>272 070 | 47673<br>-17863<br>272 071 | 47674<br>-17862<br>272 072 | 47675<br>-17861<br>272 073 | 47676<br>-17860<br>272 074 | 47677<br>-17859<br>272 075 | 47678<br>-17858<br>272 076 | 47679<br>-17857<br>272 077 |
| 4- | 47680<br>-17856<br>272 100 | 47681<br>-17855<br>272 101 | 47682<br>-17854<br>272 102 | 47683<br>-17853<br>272 103 | 47684<br>-17852<br>272 104 | 47685<br>-17851<br>272 105 | 47686<br>-17850<br>272 106 | 47687<br>-17849<br>272 107 | 47688<br>-17848<br>272 110 | 47689<br>-17847<br>272 111 | 47690<br>-17846<br>272 112 | 47691<br>-17845<br>272 113 | 47692<br>-17844<br>272 114 | 47693<br>-17843<br>272 115 | 47694<br>-17842<br>272 116 | 47695<br>-17841<br>272 117 |
| 5- | 47696<br>-17840<br>272 120 | 47697<br>-17839<br>272 121 | 47698<br>-17838<br>272 122 | 47699<br>-17837<br>272 123 | 47700<br>-17836<br>272 124 | 47701<br>-17835<br>272 125 | 47702<br>-17834<br>272 126 | 47703<br>-17833<br>272 127 | 47704<br>-17832<br>272 130 | 47705<br>-17831<br>272 131 | 47706<br>-17830<br>272 132 | 47707<br>-17829<br>272 133 | 47708<br>-17828<br>272 134 | 47709<br>-17827<br>272 135 | 47710<br>-17826<br>272 136 | 47711<br>-17825<br>272 137 |
| 6- | 47712<br>-17824<br>272 140 | 47713<br>-17823<br>272 141 | 47714<br>-17822<br>272 142 | 47715<br>-17821<br>272 143 | 47716<br>-17820<br>272 144 | 47717<br>-17819<br>272 145 | 47718<br>-17818<br>272 146 | 47719<br>-17817<br>272 147 | 47720<br>-17816<br>272 150 | 47721<br>-17815<br>272 151 | 47722<br>-17814<br>272 152 | 47723<br>-17813<br>272 153 | 47724<br>-17812<br>272 154 | 47725<br>-17811<br>272 155 | 47726<br>-17810<br>272 156 | 47727<br>-17809<br>272 157 |
| 7- | 47728<br>-17808<br>272 160 | 47729<br>-17807<br>272 161 | 47730<br>-17806<br>272 162 | 47731<br>-17805<br>272 163 | 47732<br>-17804<br>272 164 | 47733<br>-17803<br>272 165 | 47734<br>-17802<br>272 166 | 47735<br>-17801<br>272 167 | 47736<br>-17800<br>272 170 | 47737<br>-17799<br>272 171 | 47738<br>-17798<br>272 172 | 47739<br>-17797<br>272 173 | 47740<br>-17796<br>272 174 | 47741<br>-17795<br>272 175 | 47742<br>-17794<br>272 176 | 47743<br>-17793<br>272 177 |
| 8- | 47744<br>-17792<br>272 200 | 47745<br>-17791<br>272 201 | 47746<br>-17790<br>272 202 | 47747<br>-17789<br>272 203 | 47748<br>-17788<br>272 204 | 47749<br>-17787<br>272 205 | 47750<br>-17786<br>272 206 | 47751<br>-17785<br>272 207 | 47752<br>-17784<br>272 210 | 47753<br>-17783<br>272 211 | 47754<br>-17782<br>272 212 | 47755<br>-17781<br>272 213 | 47756<br>-17780<br>272 214 | 47757<br>-17779<br>272 215 | 47758<br>-17778<br>272 216 | 47759<br>-17777<br>272 217 |
| 9- | 47760<br>-17776<br>272 220 | 47761<br>-17775<br>272 221 | 47762<br>-17774<br>272 222 | 47763<br>-17773<br>272 223 | 47764<br>-17772<br>272 224 | 47765<br>-17771<br>272 225 | 47766<br>-17770<br>272 226 | 47767<br>-17769<br>272 227 | 47768<br>-17768<br>272 230 | 47769<br>-17767<br>272 231 | 47770<br>-17766<br>272 232 | 47771<br>-17765<br>272 233 | 47772<br>-17764<br>272 234 | 47773<br>-17763<br>272 235 | 47774<br>-17762<br>272 236 | 47775<br>-17761<br>272 237 |
| A- | 47776<br>-17760<br>272 240 | 47777<br>-17759<br>272 241 | 47778<br>-17758<br>272 242 | 47779<br>-17757<br>272 243 | 47780<br>-17756<br>272 244 | 47781<br>-17755<br>272 245 | 47782<br>-17754<br>272 246 | 47783<br>-17753<br>272 247 | 47784<br>-17752<br>272 250 | 47785<br>-17751<br>272 251 | 47786<br>-17750<br>272 252 | 47787<br>-17749<br>272 253 | 47788<br>-17748<br>272 254 | 47789<br>-17747<br>272 255 | 47790<br>-17746<br>272 256 | 47791<br>-17745<br>272 257 |
| B- | 47792<br>-17744<br>272 260 | 47793<br>-17743<br>272 261 | 47794<br>-17742<br>272 262 | 47795<br>-17741<br>272 263 | 47796<br>-17740<br>272 264 | 47797<br>-17739<br>272 265 | 47798<br>-17738<br>272 266 | 47799<br>-17737<br>272 267 | 47800<br>-17736<br>272 270 | 47801<br>-17735<br>272 271 | 47802<br>-17734<br>272 272 | 47803<br>-17733<br>272 273 | 47804<br>-17732<br>272 274 | 47805<br>-17731<br>272 275 | 47806<br>-17730<br>272 276 | 47807<br>-17729<br>272 277 |
| C- | 47808<br>-17728<br>272 300 | 47809<br>-17727<br>272 301 | 47810<br>-17726<br>272 302 | 47811<br>-17725<br>272 303 | 47812<br>-17724<br>272 304 | 47813<br>-17723<br>272 305 | 47814<br>-17722<br>272 306 | 47815<br>-17721<br>272 307 | 47816<br>-17720<br>272 310 | 47817<br>-17719<br>272 311 | 47818<br>-17718<br>272 312 | 47819<br>-17717<br>272 313 | 47820<br>-17716<br>272 314 | 47821<br>-17715<br>272 315 | 47822<br>-17714<br>272 316 | 47823<br>-17713<br>272 317 |
| D- | 47824<br>-17712<br>272 320 | 47825<br>-17711<br>272 321 | 47826<br>-17710<br>272 322 | 47827<br>-17709<br>272 323 | 47828<br>-17708<br>272 324 | 47829<br>-17707<br>272 325 | 47830<br>-17706<br>272 326 | 47831<br>-17705<br>272 327 | 47832<br>-17704<br>272 330 | 47833<br>-17703<br>272 331 | 47834<br>-17702<br>272 332 | 47835<br>-17701<br>272 333 | 47836<br>-17700<br>272 334 | 47837<br>-17699<br>272 335 | 47838<br>-17698<br>272 336 | 47839<br>-17697<br>272 337 |
| E- | 47840<br>-17696<br>272 340 | 47841<br>-17695<br>272 341 | 47842<br>-17694<br>272 342 | 47843<br>-17693<br>272 343 | 47844<br>-17692<br>272 344 | 47845<br>-17691<br>272 345 | 47846<br>-17690<br>272 346 | 47847<br>-17689<br>272 347 | 47848<br>-17688<br>272 350 | 47849<br>-17687<br>272 351 | 47850<br>-17686<br>272 352 | 47851<br>-17685<br>272 353 | 47852<br>-17684<br>272 354 | 47853<br>-17683<br>272 355 | 47854<br>-17682<br>272 356 | 47855<br>-17681<br>272 357 |
| F- | 47856<br>-17680<br>272 360 | 47857<br>-17679<br>272 361 | 47858<br>-17678<br>272 362 | 47859<br>-17677<br>272 363 | 47860<br>-17676<br>272 364 | 47861<br>-17675<br>272 365 | 47862<br>-17674<br>272 366 | 47863<br>-17673<br>272 367 | 47864<br>-17672<br>272 370 | 47865<br>-17671<br>272 371 | 47866<br>-17670<br>272 372 | 47867<br>-17669<br>272 373 | 47868<br>-17668<br>272 374 | 47869<br>-17667<br>272 375 | 47870<br>-17666<br>272 376 | 47871<br>-17665<br>272 377 |

DECIMAL ←

 DECIMAL ←

OCTAL ←

 DECIMAL  -17920    BINARY  1011 1010    DECIMAL  47616    HEXADECIMAL  BA    OCTAL  272 000

FOURTH HEX DIGIT → BA ← THIRD HEX DIGIT

| 2 | FIRST HEX DIGIT | | | | | | | | | | | | | | | |
|---|---|---|---|---|---|---|---|---|---|---|---|---|---|---|---|---|
| SECOND HEX DIGIT | −0 | −1 | −2 | −3 | −4 | −5 | −6 | −7 | −8 | −9 | −A | −B | −C | −D | −E | −F |
| 0− | 47872<br>−17664<br>273 000 | 47873<br>−17663<br>273 001 | 47874<br>−17662<br>273 002 | 47875<br>−17661<br>273 003 | 47876<br>−17660<br>273 004 | 47877<br>−17659<br>273 005 | 47878<br>−17658<br>273 006 | 47879<br>−17657<br>273 007 | 47880<br>−17656<br>273 010 | 47881<br>−17655<br>273 011 | 47882<br>−17654<br>273 012 | 47883<br>−17653<br>273 013 | 47884<br>−17652<br>273 014 | 47885<br>−17651<br>273 015 | 47886<br>−17650<br>273 016 | 47887<br>−17649<br>273 017 |
| 1− | 47888<br>−17648<br>273 020 | 47889<br>−17647<br>273 021 | 47890<br>−17646<br>273 022 | 47891<br>−17645<br>273 023 | 47892<br>−17644<br>273 024 | 47893<br>−17643<br>273 025 | 47894<br>−17642<br>273 026 | 47895<br>−17641<br>273 027 | 47896<br>−17640<br>273 030 | 47897<br>−17639<br>273 031 | 47898<br>−17638<br>273 032 | 47899<br>−17637<br>273 033 | 47900<br>−17636<br>273 034 | 47901<br>−17635<br>273 035 | 47902<br>−17634<br>273 036 | 47903<br>−17633<br>273 037 |
| 2− | 47904<br>−17632<br>273 040 | 47905<br>−17631<br>273 041 | 47906<br>−17630<br>273 042 | 47907<br>−17629<br>273 043 | 47908<br>−17628<br>273 044 | 47909<br>−17627<br>273 045 | 47910<br>−17626<br>273 046 | 47911<br>−17625<br>273 047 | 47912<br>−17624<br>273 050 | 47913<br>−17623<br>273 051 | 47914<br>−17622<br>273 052 | 47915<br>−17621<br>273 053 | 47916<br>−17620<br>273 054 | 47917<br>−17619<br>273 055 | 47918<br>−17618<br>273 056 | 47919<br>−17617<br>273 057 |
| 3− | 47920<br>−17616<br>273 060 | 47921<br>−17615<br>273 061 | 47922<br>−17614<br>273 062 | 47923<br>−17613<br>273 063 | 47924<br>−17612<br>273 064 | 47925<br>−17611<br>273 065 | 47926<br>−17610<br>273 066 | 47927<br>−17609<br>273 067 | 47928<br>−17608<br>273 070 | 47929<br>−17607<br>273 071 | 47930<br>−17606<br>273 072 | 47931<br>−17605<br>273 073 | 47932<br>−17604<br>273 074 | 47933<br>−17603<br>273 075 | 47934<br>−17602<br>273 076 | 47935<br>−17601<br>273 077 |
| 4− | 47936<br>−17600<br>273 100 | 47937<br>−17599<br>273 101 | 47938<br>−17598<br>273 102 | 47939<br>−17597<br>273 103 | 47940<br>−17596<br>273 104 | 47941<br>−17595<br>273 105 | 47942<br>−17594<br>273 106 | 47943<br>−17593<br>273 107 | 47944<br>−17592<br>273 110 | 47945<br>−17591<br>273 111 | 47946<br>−17590<br>273 112 | 47947<br>−17589<br>273 113 | 47948<br>−17588<br>273 114 | 47949<br>−17587<br>273 115 | 47950<br>−17586<br>273 116 | 47951<br>−17585<br>273 117 |
| 5− | 47952<br>−17584<br>273 120 | 47953<br>−17583<br>273 121 | 47954<br>−17582<br>273 122 | 47955<br>−17581<br>273 123 | 47956<br>−17580<br>273 124 | 47957<br>−17579<br>273 125 | 47958<br>−17578<br>273 126 | 47959<br>−17577<br>273 127 | 47960<br>−17576<br>273 130 | 47961<br>−17575<br>273 131 | 47962<br>−17574<br>273 132 | 47963<br>−17573<br>273 133 | 47964<br>−17572<br>273 134 | 47965<br>−17571<br>273 135 | 47966<br>−17570<br>273 136 | 47967<br>−17569<br>273 137 |
| 6− | 47968<br>−17568<br>273 140 | 47969<br>−17567<br>273 141 | 47970<br>−17566<br>273 142 | 47971<br>−17565<br>273 143 | 47972<br>−17564<br>273 144 | 47973<br>−17563<br>273 145 | 47974<br>−17562<br>273 146 | 47975<br>−17561<br>273 147 | 47976<br>−17560<br>273 150 | 47977<br>−17559<br>273 151 | 47978<br>−17558<br>273 152 | 47979<br>−17557<br>273 153 | 47980<br>−17556<br>273 154 | 47981<br>−17555<br>273 155 | 47982<br>−17554<br>273 156 | 47983<br>−17553<br>273 157 |
| 7− | 47984<br>−17552<br>273 160 | 47985<br>−17551<br>273 161 | 47986<br>−17550<br>273 162 | 47987<br>−17549<br>273 163 | 47988<br>−17548<br>273 164 | 47989<br>−17547<br>273 165 | 47990<br>−17546<br>273 166 | 47991<br>−17545<br>273 167 | 47992<br>−17544<br>273 170 | 47993<br>−17543<br>273 171 | 47994<br>−17542<br>273 172 | 47995<br>−17541<br>273 173 | 47996<br>−17540<br>273 174 | 47997<br>−17539<br>273 175 | 47998<br>−17538<br>273 176 | 47999<br>−17537<br>273 177 |
| 8− | 48000<br>−17536<br>273 200 | 48001<br>−17535<br>273 201 | 48002<br>−17534<br>273 202 | 48003<br>−17533<br>273 203 | 48004<br>−17532<br>273 204 | 48005<br>−17531<br>273 205 | 48006<br>−17530<br>273 206 | 48007<br>−17529<br>273 207 | 48008<br>−17528<br>273 210 | 48009<br>−17527<br>273 211 | 48010<br>−17526<br>273 212 | 48011<br>−17525<br>273 213 | 48012<br>−17524<br>273 214 | 48013<br>−17523<br>273 215 | 48014<br>−17522<br>273 216 | 48015<br>−17521<br>273 217 |
| 9− | 48016<br>−17520<br>273 220 | 48017<br>−17519<br>273 221 | 48018<br>−17518<br>273 222 | 48019<br>−17517<br>273 223 | 48020<br>−17516<br>273 224 | 48021<br>−17515<br>273 225 | 48022<br>−17514<br>273 226 | 48023<br>−17513<br>273 227 | 48024<br>−17512<br>273 230 | 48025<br>−17511<br>273 231 | 48026<br>−17510<br>273 232 | 48027<br>−17509<br>273 233 | 48028<br>−17508<br>273 234 | 48029<br>−17507<br>273 235 | 48030<br>−17506<br>273 236 | 48031<br>−17505<br>273 237 |
| A− | 48032<br>−17504<br>273 240 | 48033<br>−17503<br>273 241 | 48034<br>−17502<br>273 242 | 48035<br>−17501<br>273 243 | 48036<br>−17500<br>273 244 | 48037<br>−17499<br>273 245 | 48038<br>−17498<br>273 246 | 48039<br>−17497<br>273 247 | 48040<br>−17496<br>273 250 | 48041<br>−17495<br>273 251 | 48042<br>−17494<br>273 252 | 48043<br>−17493<br>273 253 | 48044<br>−17492<br>273 254 | 48045<br>−17491<br>273 255 | 48046<br>−17490<br>273 256 | 48047<br>−17489<br>273 257 |
| B− | 48048<br>−17488<br>273 260 | 48049<br>−17487<br>273 261 | 48050<br>−17486<br>273 262 | 48051<br>−17485<br>273 263 | 48052<br>−17484<br>273 264 | 48053<br>−17483<br>273 265 | 48054<br>−17482<br>273 266 | 48055<br>−17481<br>273 267 | 48056<br>−17480<br>273 270 | 48057<br>−17479<br>273 271 | 48058<br>−17478<br>273 272 | 48059<br>−17477<br>273 273 | 48060<br>−17476<br>273 274 | 48061<br>−17475<br>273 275 | 48062<br>−17474<br>273 276 | 48063<br>−17473<br>273 277 |
| C− | 48064<br>−17472<br>273 300 | 48065<br>−17471<br>273 301 | 48066<br>−17470<br>273 302 | 48067<br>−17469<br>273 303 | 48068<br>−17468<br>273 304 | 48069<br>−17467<br>273 305 | 48070<br>−17466<br>273 306 | 48071<br>−17465<br>273 307 | 48072<br>−17464<br>273 310 | 48073<br>−17463<br>273 311 | 48074<br>−17462<br>273 312 | 48075<br>−17461<br>273 313 | 48076<br>−17460<br>273 314 | 48077<br>−17459<br>273 315 | 48078<br>−17458<br>273 316 | 48079<br>−17457<br>273 317 |
| D− | 48080<br>−17456<br>273 320 | 48081<br>−17455<br>273 321 | 48082<br>−17454<br>273 322 | 48083<br>−17453<br>273 323 | 48084<br>−17452<br>273 324 | 48085<br>−17451<br>273 325 | 48086<br>−17450<br>273 326 | 48087<br>−17449<br>273 327 | 48088<br>−17448<br>273 330 | 48089<br>−17447<br>273 331 | 48090<br>−17446<br>273 332 | 48091<br>−17445<br>273 333 | 48092<br>−17444<br>273 334 | 48093<br>−17443<br>273 335 | 48094<br>−17442<br>273 336 | 48095<br>−17441<br>273 337 |
| E− | 48096<br>−17440<br>273 340 | 48097<br>−17439<br>273 341 | 48098<br>−17438<br>273 342 | 48099<br>−17437<br>273 343 | 48100<br>−17436<br>273 344 | 48101<br>−17435<br>273 345 | 48102<br>−17434<br>273 346 | 48103<br>−17433<br>273 347 | 48104<br>−17432<br>273 350 | 48105<br>−17431<br>273 351 | 48106<br>−17430<br>273 352 | 48107<br>−17429<br>273 353 | 48108<br>−17428<br>273 354 | 48109<br>−17427<br>273 355 | 48110<br>−17426<br>273 356 | 48111<br>−17425<br>273 357 |
| F− | 48112<br>−17424<br>273 360 | 48113<br>−17423<br>273 361 | 48114<br>−17422<br>273 362 | 48115<br>−17421<br>273 363 | 48116<br>−17420<br>273 364 | 48117<br>−17419<br>273 365 | 48118<br>−17418<br>273 366 | 48119<br>−17417<br>273 367 | 48120<br>−17416<br>273 370 | 48121<br>−17415<br>273 371 | 48122<br>−17414<br>273 372 | 48123<br>−17413<br>273 373 | 48124<br>−17412<br>273 374 | 48125<br>−17411<br>273 375 | 48126<br>−17410<br>273 376 | 48127<br>−17409<br>273 377 |

| ② | −0 | −1 | −2 | −3 | −4 | −5 | −6 | −7 | −8 | −9 | −A | −B | −C | −D | −E | −F |
|---|---|---|---|---|---|---|---|---|---|---|---|---|---|---|---|---|
| **0−** | 48128<br>−17408<br>274 000 | 48129<br>−17407<br>274 001 | 48130<br>−17406<br>274 002 | 48131<br>−17405<br>274 003 | 48132<br>−17404<br>274 004 | 48133<br>−17403<br>274 005 | 48134<br>−17402<br>274 006 | 48135<br>−17401<br>274 007 | 48136<br>−17400<br>274 010 | 48137<br>−17399<br>274 011 | 48138<br>−17398<br>274 012 | 48139<br>−17397<br>274 013 | 48140<br>−17396<br>274 014 | 48141<br>−17395<br>274 015 | 48142<br>−17394<br>274 016 | 48143<br>−17393<br>274 017 |
| **1−** | 48144<br>−17392<br>274 020 | 48145<br>−17391<br>274 021 | 48146<br>−17390<br>274 022 | 48147<br>−17389<br>274 023 | 48148<br>−17388<br>274 024 | 48149<br>−17387<br>274 025 | 48150<br>−17386<br>274 026 | 48151<br>−17385<br>274 027 | 48152<br>−17384<br>274 030 | 48153<br>−17383<br>274 031 | 48154<br>−17382<br>274 032 | 48155<br>−17381<br>274 033 | 48156<br>−17380<br>274 034 | 48157<br>−17379<br>274 035 | 48158<br>−17378<br>274 036 | 48159<br>−17377<br>274 037 |
| **2−** | 48160<br>−17376<br>274 040 | 48161<br>−17375<br>274 041 | 48162<br>−17374<br>274 042 | 48163<br>−17373<br>274 043 | 48164<br>−17372<br>274 044 | 48165<br>−17371<br>274 045 | 48166<br>−17370<br>274 046 | 48167<br>−17369<br>274 047 | 48168<br>−17368<br>274 050 | 48169<br>−17367<br>274 051 | 48170<br>−17366<br>274 052 | 48171<br>−17365<br>274 053 | 48172<br>−17364<br>274 054 | 48173<br>−17363<br>274 055 | 48174<br>−17362<br>274 056 | 48175<br>−17361<br>274 057 |
| **3−** | 48176<br>−17360<br>274 060 | 48177<br>−17359<br>274 061 | 48178<br>−17358<br>274 062 | 48179<br>−17357<br>274 063 | 48180<br>−17356<br>274 064 | 48181<br>−17355<br>274 065 | 48182<br>−17354<br>274 066 | 48183<br>−17353<br>274 067 | 48184<br>−17352<br>274 070 | 48185<br>−17351<br>274 071 | 48186<br>−17350<br>274 072 | 48187<br>−17349<br>274 073 | 48188<br>−17348<br>274 074 | 48189<br>−17347<br>274 075 | 48190<br>−17346<br>274 076 | 48191<br>−17345<br>274 077 |
| **4−** | 48192<br>−17344<br>274 100 | 48193<br>−17343<br>274 101 | 48194<br>−17342<br>274 102 | 48195<br>−17341<br>274 103 | 48196<br>−17340<br>274 104 | 48197<br>−17339<br>274 105 | 48198<br>−17338<br>274 106 | 48199<br>−17337<br>274 107 | 48200<br>−17336<br>274 110 | 48201<br>−17335<br>274 111 | 48202<br>−17334<br>274 112 | 48203<br>−17333<br>274 113 | 48204<br>−17332<br>274 114 | 48205<br>−17331<br>274 115 | 48206<br>−17330<br>274 116 | 48207<br>−17329<br>274 117 |
| **5−** | 48208<br>−17328<br>274 120 | 48209<br>−17327<br>274 121 | 48210<br>−17326<br>274 122 | 48211<br>−17325<br>274 123 | 48212<br>−17324<br>274 124 | 48213<br>−17323<br>274 125 | 48214<br>−17322<br>274 126 | 48215<br>−17321<br>274 127 | 48216<br>−17320<br>274 130 | 48217<br>−17319<br>274 131 | 48218<br>−17318<br>274 132 | 48219<br>−17317<br>274 133 | 48220<br>−17316<br>274 134 | 48221<br>−17315<br>274 135 | 48222<br>−17314<br>274 136 | 48223<br>−17313<br>274 137 |
| **6−** | 48224<br>−17312<br>274 140 | 48225<br>−17311<br>274 141 | 48226<br>−17310<br>274 142 | 48227<br>−17309<br>274 143 | 48228<br>−17308<br>274 144 | 48229<br>−17307<br>274 145 | 48230<br>−17306<br>274 146 | 48231<br>−17305<br>274 147 | 48232<br>−17304<br>274 150 | 48233<br>−17303<br>274 151 | 48234<br>−17302<br>274 152 | 48235<br>−17301<br>274 153 | 48236<br>−17300<br>274 154 | 48237<br>−17299<br>274 155 | 48238<br>−17298<br>274 156 | 48239<br>−17297<br>274 157 |
| **7−** | 48240<br>−17296<br>274 160 | 48241<br>−17295<br>274 161 | 48242<br>−17294<br>274 162 | 48243<br>−17293<br>274 163 | 48244<br>−17292<br>274 164 | 48245<br>−17291<br>274 165 | 48246<br>−17290<br>274 166 | 48247<br>−17289<br>274 167 | 48248<br>−17288<br>274 170 | 48249<br>−17287<br>274 171 | 48250<br>−17286<br>274 172 | 48251<br>−17285<br>274 173 | 48252<br>−17284<br>274 174 | 48253<br>−17283<br>274 175 | 48254<br>−17282<br>274 176 | 48255<br>−17281<br>274 177 |
| **8−** | 48256<br>−17280<br>274 200 | 48257<br>−17279<br>274 201 | 48258<br>−17278<br>274 202 | 48259<br>−17277<br>274 203 | 48260<br>−17276<br>274 204 | 48261<br>−17275<br>274 205 | 48262<br>−17274<br>274 206 | 48263<br>−17273<br>274 207 | 48264<br>−17272<br>274 210 | 48265<br>−17271<br>274 211 | 48266<br>−17270<br>274 212 | 48267<br>−17269<br>274 213 | 48268<br>−17268<br>274 214 | 48269<br>−17267<br>274 215 | 48270<br>−17266<br>274 216 | 48271<br>−17265<br>274 217 |
| **9−** | 48272<br>−17264<br>274 220 | 48273<br>−17263<br>274 221 | 48274<br>−17262<br>274 222 | 48275<br>−17261<br>274 223 | 48276<br>−17260<br>274 224 | 48277<br>−17259<br>274 225 | 48278<br>−17258<br>274 226 | 48279<br>−17257<br>274 227 | 48280<br>−17256<br>274 230 | 48281<br>−17255<br>274 231 | 48282<br>−17254<br>274 232 | 48283<br>−17253<br>274 233 | 48284<br>−17252<br>274 234 | 48285<br>−17251<br>274 235 | 48286<br>−17250<br>274 236 | 48287<br>−17249<br>274 237 |
| **A−** | 48288<br>−17248<br>274 240 | 48289<br>−17247<br>274 241 | 48290<br>−17246<br>274 242 | 48291<br>−17245<br>274 243 | 48292<br>−17244<br>274 244 | 48293<br>−17243<br>274 245 | 48294<br>−17242<br>274 246 | 48295<br>−17241<br>274 247 | 48296<br>−17240<br>274 250 | 48297<br>−17239<br>274 251 | 48298<br>−17238<br>274 252 | 48299<br>−17237<br>274 253 | 48300<br>−17236<br>274 254 | 48301<br>−17235<br>274 255 | 48302<br>−17234<br>274 256 | 48303<br>−17233<br>274 257 |
| **B−** | 48304<br>−17232<br>274 260 | 48305<br>−17231<br>274 261 | 48306<br>−17230<br>274 262 | 48307<br>−17229<br>274 263 | 48308<br>−17228<br>274 264 | 48309<br>−17227<br>274 265 | 48310<br>−17226<br>274 266 | 48311<br>−17225<br>274 267 | 48312<br>−17224<br>274 270 | 48313<br>−17223<br>274 271 | 48314<br>−17222<br>274 272 | 48315<br>−17221<br>274 273 | 48316<br>−17220<br>274 274 | 48317<br>−17219<br>274 275 | 48318<br>−17218<br>274 276 | 48319<br>−17217<br>274 277 |
| **C−** | 48320<br>−17216<br>274 300 | 48321<br>−17215<br>274 301 | 48322<br>−17214<br>274 302 | 48323<br>−17213<br>274 303 | 48324<br>−17212<br>274 304 | 48325<br>−17211<br>274 305 | 48326<br>−17210<br>274 306 | 48327<br>−17209<br>274 307 | 48328<br>−17208<br>274 310 | 48329<br>−17207<br>274 311 | 48330<br>−17206<br>274 312 | 48331<br>−17205<br>274 313 | 48332<br>−17204<br>274 314 | 48333<br>−17203<br>274 315 | 48334<br>−17202<br>274 316 | 48335<br>−17201<br>274 317 |
| **D−** | 48336<br>−17200<br>274 320 | 48337<br>−17199<br>274 321 | 48338<br>−17198<br>274 322 | 48339<br>−17197<br>274 323 | 48340<br>−17196<br>274 324 | 48341<br>−17195<br>274 325 | 48342<br>−17194<br>274 326 | 48343<br>−17193<br>274 327 | 48344<br>−17192<br>274 330 | 48345<br>−17191<br>274 331 | 48346<br>−17190<br>274 332 | 48347<br>−17189<br>274 333 | 48348<br>−17188<br>274 334 | 48349<br>−17187<br>274 335 | 48350<br>−17186<br>274 336 | 48351<br>−17185<br>274 337 |
| **E−** | 48352<br>−17184<br>274 340 | 48353<br>−17183<br>274 341 | 48354<br>−17182<br>274 342 | 48355<br>−17181<br>274 343 | 48356<br>−17180<br>274 344 | 48357<br>−17179<br>274 345 | 48358<br>−17178<br>274 346 | 48359<br>−17177<br>274 347 | 48360<br>−17176<br>274 350 | 48361<br>−17175<br>274 351 | 48362<br>−17174<br>274 352 | 48363<br>−17173<br>274 353 | 48364<br>−17172<br>274 354 | 48365<br>−17171<br>274 355 | 48366<br>−17170<br>274 356 | 48367<br>−17169<br>274 357 |
| **F−** | 48368<br>−17168<br>274 360 | 48369<br>−17167<br>274 361 | 48370<br>−17166<br>274 362 | 48371<br>−17165<br>274 363 | 48372<br>−17164<br>274 364 | 48373<br>−17163<br>274 365 | 48374<br>−17162<br>274 366 | 48375<br>−17161<br>274 367 | 48376<br>−17160<br>274 370 | 48377<br>−17159<br>274 371 | 48378<br>−17158<br>274 372 | 48379<br>−17157<br>274 373 | 48380<br>−17156<br>274 374 | 48381<br>−17155<br>274 375 | 48382<br>−17154<br>274 376 | 48383<br>−17153<br>274 377 |

**SECOND HEX DIGIT**

DECIMAL

 DECIMAL

OCTAL

 DECIMAL −17408  BINARY 1011 1100  DECIMAL 48128  HEXADECIMAL BC OCTAL 274 000

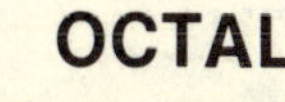

FOURTH HEX DIGIT → BC ← THIRD HEX DIGIT

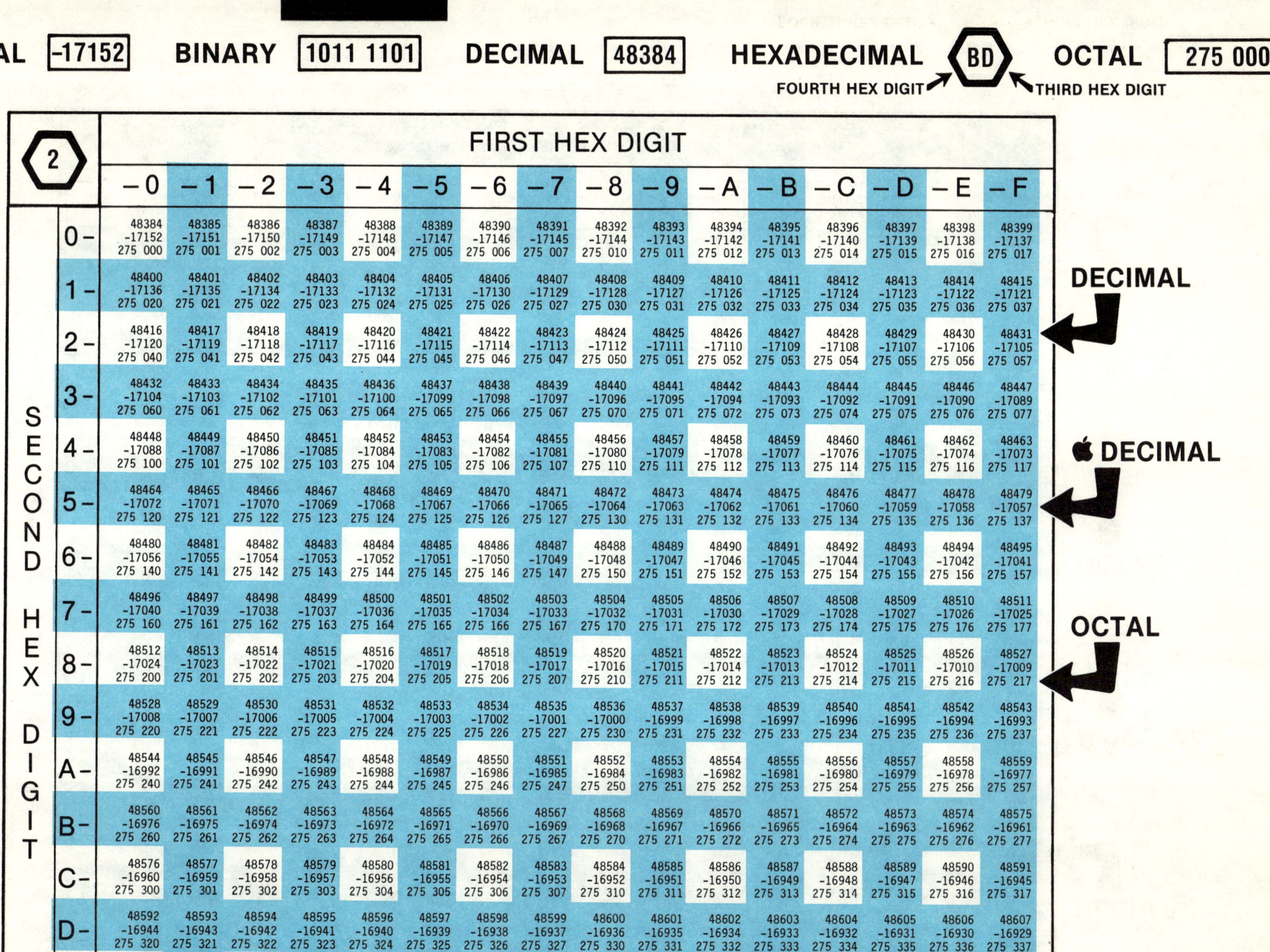

FIRST HEX DIGIT — 2

| SECOND HEX DIGIT | −0 | −1 | −2 | −3 | −4 | −5 | −6 | −7 | −8 | −9 | −A | −B | −C | −D | −E | −F |
|---|---|---|---|---|---|---|---|---|---|---|---|---|---|---|---|---|
| 0− | 48384<br>−17152<br>275 000 | 48385<br>−17151<br>275 001 | 48386<br>−17150<br>275 002 | 48387<br>−17149<br>275 003 | 48388<br>−17148<br>275 004 | 48389<br>−17147<br>275 005 | 48390<br>−17146<br>275 006 | 48391<br>−17145<br>275 007 | 48392<br>−17144<br>275 010 | 48393<br>−17143<br>275 011 | 48394<br>−17142<br>275 012 | 48395<br>−17141<br>275 013 | 48396<br>−17140<br>275 014 | 48397<br>−17139<br>275 015 | 48398<br>−17138<br>275 016 | 48399<br>−17137<br>275 017 |
| 1− | 48400<br>−17136<br>275 020 | 48401<br>−17135<br>275 021 | 48402<br>−17134<br>275 022 | 48403<br>−17133<br>275 023 | 48404<br>−17132<br>275 024 | 48405<br>−17131<br>275 025 | 48406<br>−17130<br>275 026 | 48407<br>−17129<br>275 027 | 48408<br>−17128<br>275 030 | 48409<br>−17127<br>275 031 | 48410<br>−17126<br>275 032 | 48411<br>−17125<br>275 033 | 48412<br>−17124<br>275 034 | 48413<br>−17123<br>275 035 | 48414<br>−17122<br>275 036 | 48415<br>−17121<br>275 037 |
| 2− | 48416<br>−17120<br>275 040 | 48417<br>−17119<br>275 041 | 48418<br>−17118<br>275 042 | 48419<br>−17117<br>275 043 | 48420<br>−17116<br>275 044 | 48421<br>−17115<br>275 045 | 48422<br>−17114<br>275 046 | 48423<br>−17113<br>275 047 | 48424<br>−17112<br>275 050 | 48425<br>−17111<br>275 051 | 48426<br>−17110<br>275 052 | 48427<br>−17109<br>275 053 | 48428<br>−17108<br>275 054 | 48429<br>−17107<br>275 055 | 48430<br>−17106<br>275 056 | 48431<br>−17105<br>275 057 |
| 3− | 48432<br>−17104<br>275 060 | 48433<br>−17103<br>275 061 | 48434<br>−17102<br>275 062 | 48435<br>−17101<br>275 063 | 48436<br>−17100<br>275 064 | 48437<br>−17099<br>275 065 | 48438<br>−17098<br>275 066 | 48439<br>−17097<br>275 067 | 48440<br>−17096<br>275 070 | 48441<br>−17095<br>275 071 | 48442<br>−17094<br>275 072 | 48443<br>−17093<br>275 073 | 48444<br>−17092<br>275 074 | 48445<br>−17091<br>275 075 | 48446<br>−17090<br>275 076 | 48447<br>−17089<br>275 077 |
| 4− | 48448<br>−17088<br>275 100 | 48449<br>−17087<br>275 101 | 48450<br>−17086<br>275 102 | 48451<br>−17085<br>275 103 | 48452<br>−17084<br>275 104 | 48453<br>−17083<br>275 105 | 48454<br>−17082<br>275 106 | 48455<br>−17081<br>275 107 | 48456<br>−17080<br>275 110 | 48457<br>−17079<br>275 111 | 48458<br>−17078<br>275 112 | 48459<br>−17077<br>275 113 | 48460<br>−17076<br>275 114 | 48461<br>−17075<br>275 115 | 48462<br>−17074<br>275 116 | 48463<br>−17073<br>275 117 |
| 5− | 48464<br>−17072<br>275 120 | 48465<br>−17071<br>275 121 | 48466<br>−17070<br>275 122 | 48467<br>−17069<br>275 123 | 48468<br>−17068<br>275 124 | 48469<br>−17067<br>275 125 | 48470<br>−17066<br>275 126 | 48471<br>−17065<br>275 127 | 48472<br>−17064<br>275 130 | 48473<br>−17063<br>275 131 | 48474<br>−17062<br>275 132 | 48475<br>−17061<br>275 133 | 48476<br>−17060<br>275 134 | 48477<br>−17059<br>275 135 | 48478<br>−17058<br>275 136 | 48479<br>−17057<br>275 137 |
| 6− | 48480<br>−17056<br>275 140 | 48481<br>−17055<br>275 141 | 48482<br>−17054<br>275 142 | 48483<br>−17053<br>275 143 | 48484<br>−17052<br>275 144 | 48485<br>−17051<br>275 145 | 48486<br>−17050<br>275 146 | 48487<br>−17049<br>275 147 | 48488<br>−17048<br>275 150 | 48489<br>−17047<br>275 151 | 48490<br>−17046<br>275 152 | 48491<br>−17045<br>275 153 | 48492<br>−17044<br>275 154 | 48493<br>−17043<br>275 155 | 48494<br>−17042<br>275 156 | 48495<br>−17041<br>275 157 |
| 7− | 48496<br>−17040<br>275 160 | 48497<br>−17039<br>275 161 | 48498<br>−17038<br>275 162 | 48499<br>−17037<br>275 163 | 48500<br>−17036<br>275 164 | 48501<br>−17035<br>275 165 | 48502<br>−17034<br>275 166 | 48503<br>−17033<br>275 167 | 48504<br>−17032<br>275 170 | 48505<br>−17031<br>275 171 | 48506<br>−17030<br>275 172 | 48507<br>−17029<br>275 173 | 48508<br>−17028<br>275 174 | 48509<br>−17027<br>275 175 | 48510<br>−17026<br>275 176 | 48511<br>−17025<br>275 177 |
| 8− | 48512<br>−17024<br>275 200 | 48513<br>−17023<br>275 201 | 48514<br>−17022<br>275 202 | 48515<br>−17021<br>275 203 | 48516<br>−17020<br>275 204 | 48517<br>−17019<br>275 205 | 48518<br>−17018<br>275 206 | 48519<br>−17017<br>275 207 | 48520<br>−17016<br>275 210 | 48521<br>−17015<br>275 211 | 48522<br>−17014<br>275 212 | 48523<br>−17013<br>275 213 | 48524<br>−17012<br>275 214 | 48525<br>−17011<br>275 215 | 48526<br>−17010<br>275 216 | 48527<br>−17009<br>275 217 |
| 9− | 48528<br>−17008<br>275 220 | 48529<br>−17007<br>275 221 | 48530<br>−17006<br>275 222 | 48531<br>−17005<br>275 223 | 48532<br>−17004<br>275 224 | 48533<br>−17003<br>275 225 | 48534<br>−17002<br>275 226 | 48535<br>−17001<br>275 227 | 48536<br>−17000<br>275 230 | 48537<br>−16999<br>275 231 | 48538<br>−16998<br>275 232 | 48539<br>−16997<br>275 233 | 48540<br>−16996<br>275 234 | 48541<br>−16995<br>275 235 | 48542<br>−16994<br>275 236 | 48543<br>−16993<br>275 237 |
| A− | 48544<br>−16992<br>275 240 | 48545<br>−16991<br>275 241 | 48546<br>−16990<br>275 242 | 48547<br>−16989<br>275 243 | 48548<br>−16988<br>275 244 | 48549<br>−16987<br>275 245 | 48550<br>−16986<br>275 246 | 48551<br>−16985<br>275 247 | 48552<br>−16984<br>275 250 | 48553<br>−16983<br>275 251 | 48554<br>−16982<br>275 252 | 48555<br>−16981<br>275 253 | 48556<br>−16980<br>275 254 | 48557<br>−16979<br>275 255 | 48558<br>−16978<br>275 256 | 48559<br>−16977<br>275 257 |
| B− | 48560<br>−16976<br>275 260 | 48561<br>−16975<br>275 261 | 48562<br>−16974<br>275 262 | 48563<br>−16973<br>275 263 | 48564<br>−16972<br>275 264 | 48565<br>−16971<br>275 265 | 48566<br>−16970<br>275 266 | 48567<br>−16969<br>275 267 | 48568<br>−16968<br>275 270 | 48569<br>−16967<br>275 271 | 48570<br>−16966<br>275 272 | 48571<br>−16965<br>275 273 | 48572<br>−16964<br>275 274 | 48573<br>−16963<br>275 275 | 48574<br>−16962<br>275 276 | 48575<br>−16961<br>275 277 |
| C− | 48576<br>−16960<br>275 300 | 48577<br>−16959<br>275 301 | 48578<br>−16958<br>275 302 | 48579<br>−16957<br>275 303 | 48580<br>−16956<br>275 304 | 48581<br>−16955<br>275 305 | 48582<br>−16954<br>275 306 | 48583<br>−16953<br>275 307 | 48584<br>−16952<br>275 310 | 48585<br>−16951<br>275 311 | 48586<br>−16950<br>275 312 | 48587<br>−16949<br>275 313 | 48588<br>−16948<br>275 314 | 48589<br>−16947<br>275 315 | 48590<br>−16946<br>275 316 | 48591<br>−16945<br>275 317 |
| D− | 48592<br>−16944<br>275 320 | 48593<br>−16943<br>275 321 | 48594<br>−16942<br>275 322 | 48595<br>−16941<br>275 323 | 48596<br>−16940<br>275 324 | 48597<br>−16939<br>275 325 | 48598<br>−16938<br>275 326 | 48599<br>−16937<br>275 327 | 48600<br>−16936<br>275 330 | 48601<br>−16935<br>275 331 | 48602<br>−16934<br>275 332 | 48603<br>−16933<br>275 333 | 48604<br>−16932<br>275 334 | 48605<br>−16931<br>275 335 | 48606<br>−16930<br>275 336 | 48607<br>−16929<br>275 337 |
| E− | 48608<br>−16928<br>275 340 | 48609<br>−16927<br>275 341 | 48610<br>−16926<br>275 342 | 48611<br>−16925<br>275 343 | 48612<br>−16924<br>275 344 | 48613<br>−16923<br>275 345 | 48614<br>−16922<br>275 346 | 48615<br>−16921<br>275 347 | 48616<br>−16920<br>275 350 | 48617<br>−16919<br>275 351 | 48618<br>−16918<br>275 352 | 48619<br>−16917<br>275 353 | 48620<br>−16916<br>275 354 | 48621<br>−16915<br>275 355 | 48622<br>−16914<br>275 356 | 48623<br>−16913<br>275 357 |
| F− | 48624<br>−16912<br>275 360 | 48625<br>−16911<br>275 361 | 48626<br>−16910<br>275 362 | 48627<br>−16909<br>275 363 | 48628<br>−16908<br>275 364 | 48629<br>−16907<br>275 365 | 48630<br>−16906<br>275 366 | 48631<br>−16905<br>275 367 | 48632<br>−16904<br>275 370 | 48633<br>−16903<br>275 371 | 48634<br>−16902<br>275 372 | 48635<br>−16901<br>275 373 | 48636<br>−16900<br>275 374 | 48637<br>−16899<br>275 375 | 48638<br>−16898<br>275 376 | 48639<br>−16897<br>275 377 |

# FIRST HEX DIGIT

Hexagon label: **2**

Legend (right side): **DECIMAL** / **DECIMAL** / **OCTAL**

SECOND HEX DIGIT (rows) × FIRST HEX DIGIT (columns). Each cell: decimal (top), Apple decimal (middle), octal (bottom).

| | −0 | −1 | −2 | −3 | −4 | −5 | −6 | −7 | −8 | −9 | −A | −B | −C | −D | −E | −F |
|---|---|---|---|---|---|---|---|---|---|---|---|---|---|---|---|---|
| **0−** | 48640<br>−16896<br>276 000 | 48641<br>−16895<br>276 001 | 48642<br>−16894<br>276 002 | 48643<br>−16893<br>276 003 | 48644<br>−16892<br>276 004 | 48645<br>−16891<br>276 005 | 48646<br>−16890<br>276 006 | 48647<br>−16889<br>276 007 | 48648<br>−16888<br>276 010 | 48649<br>−16887<br>276 011 | 48650<br>−16886<br>276 012 | 48651<br>−16885<br>276 013 | 48652<br>−16884<br>276 014 | 48653<br>−16883<br>276 015 | 48654<br>−16882<br>276 016 | 48655<br>−16881<br>276 017 |
| **1−** | 48656<br>−16880<br>276 020 | 48657<br>−16879<br>276 021 | 48658<br>−16878<br>276 022 | 48659<br>−16877<br>276 023 | 48660<br>−16876<br>276 024 | 48661<br>−16875<br>276 025 | 48662<br>−16874<br>276 026 | 48663<br>−16873<br>276 027 | 48664<br>−16872<br>276 030 | 48665<br>−16871<br>276 031 | 48666<br>−16870<br>276 032 | 48667<br>−16869<br>276 033 | 48668<br>−16868<br>276 034 | 48669<br>−16867<br>276 035 | 48670<br>−16866<br>276 036 | 48671<br>−16865<br>276 037 |
| **2−** | 48672<br>−16864<br>276 040 | 48673<br>−16863<br>276 041 | 48674<br>−16862<br>276 042 | 48675<br>−16861<br>276 043 | 48676<br>−16860<br>276 044 | 48677<br>−16859<br>276 045 | 48678<br>−16858<br>276 046 | 48679<br>−16857<br>276 047 | 48680<br>−16856<br>276 050 | 48681<br>−16855<br>276 051 | 48682<br>−16854<br>276 052 | 48683<br>−16853<br>276 053 | 48684<br>−16852<br>276 054 | 48685<br>−16851<br>276 055 | 48686<br>−16850<br>276 056 | 48687<br>−16849<br>276 057 |
| **3−** | 48688<br>−16848<br>276 060 | 48689<br>−16847<br>276 061 | 48690<br>−16846<br>276 062 | 48691<br>−16845<br>276 063 | 48692<br>−16844<br>276 064 | 48693<br>−16843<br>276 065 | 48694<br>−16842<br>276 066 | 48695<br>−16841<br>276 067 | 48696<br>−16840<br>276 070 | 48697<br>−16839<br>276 071 | 48698<br>−16838<br>276 072 | 48699<br>−16837<br>276 073 | 48700<br>−16836<br>276 074 | 48701<br>−16835<br>276 075 | 48702<br>−16834<br>276 076 | 48703<br>−16833<br>276 077 |
| **4−** | 48704<br>−16832<br>276 100 | 48705<br>−16831<br>276 101 | 48706<br>−16830<br>276 102 | 48707<br>−16829<br>276 103 | 48708<br>−16828<br>276 104 | 48709<br>−16827<br>276 105 | 48710<br>−16826<br>276 106 | 48711<br>−16825<br>276 107 | 48712<br>−16824<br>276 110 | 48713<br>−16823<br>276 111 | 48714<br>−16822<br>276 112 | 48715<br>−16821<br>276 113 | 48716<br>−16820<br>276 114 | 48717<br>−16819<br>276 115 | 48718<br>−16818<br>276 116 | 48719<br>−16817<br>276 117 |
| **5−** | 48720<br>−16816<br>276 120 | 48721<br>−16815<br>276 121 | 48722<br>−16814<br>276 122 | 48723<br>−16813<br>276 123 | 48724<br>−16812<br>276 124 | 48725<br>−16811<br>276 125 | 48726<br>−16810<br>276 126 | 48727<br>−16809<br>276 127 | 48728<br>−16808<br>276 130 | 48729<br>−16807<br>276 131 | 48730<br>−16806<br>276 132 | 48731<br>−16805<br>276 133 | 48732<br>−16804<br>276 134 | 48733<br>−16803<br>276 135 | 48734<br>−16802<br>276 136 | 48735<br>−16801<br>276 137 |
| **6−** | 48736<br>−16800<br>276 140 | 48737<br>−16799<br>276 141 | 48738<br>−16798<br>276 142 | 48739<br>−16797<br>276 143 | 48740<br>−16796<br>276 144 | 48741<br>−16795<br>276 145 | 48742<br>−16794<br>276 146 | 48743<br>−16793<br>276 147 | 48744<br>−16792<br>276 150 | 48745<br>−16791<br>276 151 | 48746<br>−16790<br>276 152 | 48747<br>−16789<br>276 153 | 48748<br>−16788<br>276 154 | 48749<br>−16787<br>276 155 | 48750<br>−16786<br>276 156 | 48751<br>−16785<br>276 157 |
| **7−** | 48752<br>−16784<br>276 160 | 48753<br>−16783<br>276 161 | 48754<br>−16782<br>276 162 | 48755<br>−16781<br>276 163 | 48756<br>−16780<br>276 164 | 48757<br>−16779<br>276 165 | 48758<br>−16778<br>276 166 | 48759<br>−16777<br>276 167 | 48760<br>−16776<br>276 170 | 48761<br>−16775<br>276 171 | 48762<br>−16774<br>276 172 | 48763<br>−16773<br>276 173 | 48764<br>−16772<br>276 174 | 48765<br>−16771<br>276 175 | 48766<br>−16770<br>276 176 | 48767<br>−16769<br>276 177 |
| **8−** | 48768<br>−16768<br>276 200 | 48769<br>−16767<br>276 201 | 48770<br>−16766<br>276 202 | 48771<br>−16765<br>276 203 | 48772<br>−16764<br>276 204 | 48773<br>−16763<br>276 205 | 48774<br>−16762<br>276 206 | 48775<br>−16761<br>276 207 | 48776<br>−16760<br>276 210 | 48777<br>−16759<br>276 211 | 48778<br>−16758<br>276 212 | 48779<br>−16757<br>276 213 | 48780<br>−16756<br>276 214 | 48781<br>−16755<br>276 215 | 48782<br>−16754<br>276 216 | 48783<br>−16753<br>276 217 |
| **9−** | 48784<br>−16752<br>276 220 | 48785<br>−16751<br>276 221 | 48786<br>−16750<br>276 222 | 48787<br>−16749<br>276 223 | 48788<br>−16748<br>276 224 | 48789<br>−16747<br>276 225 | 48790<br>−16746<br>276 226 | 48791<br>−16745<br>276 227 | 48792<br>−16744<br>276 230 | 48793<br>−16743<br>276 231 | 48794<br>−16742<br>276 232 | 48795<br>−16741<br>276 233 | 48796<br>−16740<br>276 234 | 48797<br>−16739<br>276 235 | 48798<br>−16738<br>276 236 | 48799<br>−16737<br>276 237 |
| **A−** | 48800<br>−16736<br>276 240 | 48801<br>−16735<br>276 241 | 48802<br>−16734<br>276 242 | 48803<br>−16733<br>276 243 | 48804<br>−16732<br>276 244 | 48805<br>−16731<br>276 245 | 48806<br>−16730<br>276 246 | 48807<br>−16729<br>276 247 | 48808<br>−16728<br>276 250 | 48809<br>−16727<br>276 251 | 48810<br>−16726<br>276 252 | 48811<br>−16725<br>276 253 | 48812<br>−16724<br>276 254 | 48813<br>−16723<br>276 255 | 48814<br>−16722<br>276 256 | 48815<br>−16721<br>276 257 |
| **B−** | 48816<br>−16720<br>276 260 | 48817<br>−16719<br>276 261 | 48818<br>−16718<br>276 262 | 48819<br>−16717<br>276 263 | 48820<br>−16716<br>276 264 | 48821<br>−16715<br>276 265 | 48822<br>−16714<br>276 266 | 48823<br>−16713<br>276 267 | 48824<br>−16712<br>276 270 | 48825<br>−16711<br>276 271 | 48826<br>−16710<br>276 272 | 48827<br>−16709<br>276 273 | 48828<br>−16708<br>276 274 | 48829<br>−16707<br>276 275 | 48830<br>−16706<br>276 276 | 48831<br>−16705<br>276 277 |
| **C−** | 48832<br>−16704<br>276 300 | 48833<br>−16703<br>276 301 | 48834<br>−16702<br>276 302 | 48835<br>−16701<br>276 303 | 48836<br>−16700<br>276 304 | 48837<br>−16699<br>276 305 | 48838<br>−16698<br>276 306 | 48839<br>−16697<br>276 307 | 48840<br>−16696<br>276 310 | 48841<br>−16695<br>276 311 | 48842<br>−16694<br>276 312 | 48843<br>−16693<br>276 313 | 48844<br>−16692<br>276 314 | 48845<br>−16691<br>276 315 | 48846<br>−16690<br>276 316 | 48847<br>−16689<br>276 317 |
| **D−** | 48848<br>−16688<br>276 320 | 48849<br>−16687<br>276 321 | 48850<br>−16686<br>276 322 | 48851<br>−16685<br>276 323 | 48852<br>−16684<br>276 324 | 48853<br>−16683<br>276 325 | 48854<br>−16682<br>276 326 | 40055<br>−16681<br>276 327 | 48856<br>−16680<br>276 330 | 48857<br>−16679<br>276 331 | 48858<br>−16678<br>276 332 | 48859<br>−16677<br>276 333 | 48860<br>−16676<br>276 334 | 48861<br>−16675<br>276 335 | 48862<br>−16674<br>276 336 | 48863<br>−16673<br>276 337 |
| **E−** | 48864<br>−16672<br>276 340 | 48865<br>−16671<br>276 341 | 48866<br>−16670<br>276 342 | 48867<br>−16669<br>276 343 | 48868<br>−16668<br>276 344 | 48869<br>−16667<br>276 345 | 48870<br>−16666<br>276 346 | 48871<br>−16665<br>276 347 | 48872<br>−16664<br>276 350 | 48873<br>−16663<br>276 351 | 48874<br>−16662<br>276 352 | 48875<br>−16661<br>276 353 | 48876<br>−16660<br>276 354 | 48877<br>−16659<br>276 355 | 48878<br>−16658<br>276 356 | 48879<br>−16657<br>276 357 |
| **F−** | 48880<br>−16656<br>276 360 | 48881<br>−16655<br>276 361 | 48882<br>−16654<br>276 362 | 48883<br>−16653<br>276 363 | 48884<br>−16652<br>276 364 | 48885<br>−16651<br>276 365 | 48886<br>−16650<br>276 366 | 48887<br>−16649<br>276 367 | 48888<br>−16648<br>276 370 | 48889<br>−16647<br>276 371 | 48890<br>−16646<br>276 372 | 48891<br>−16645<br>276 373 | 48892<br>−16644<br>276 374 | 48893<br>−16643<br>276 375 | 48894<br>−16642<br>276 376 | 48895<br>−16641<br>276 377 |

 **DECIMAL** `−16896`  **BINARY** `1011 1110`  **DECIMAL** `48640`  **HEXADECIMAL** **BE**  **OCTAL** `276 000`

FOURTH HEX DIGIT → **BE** ← THIRD HEX DIGIT

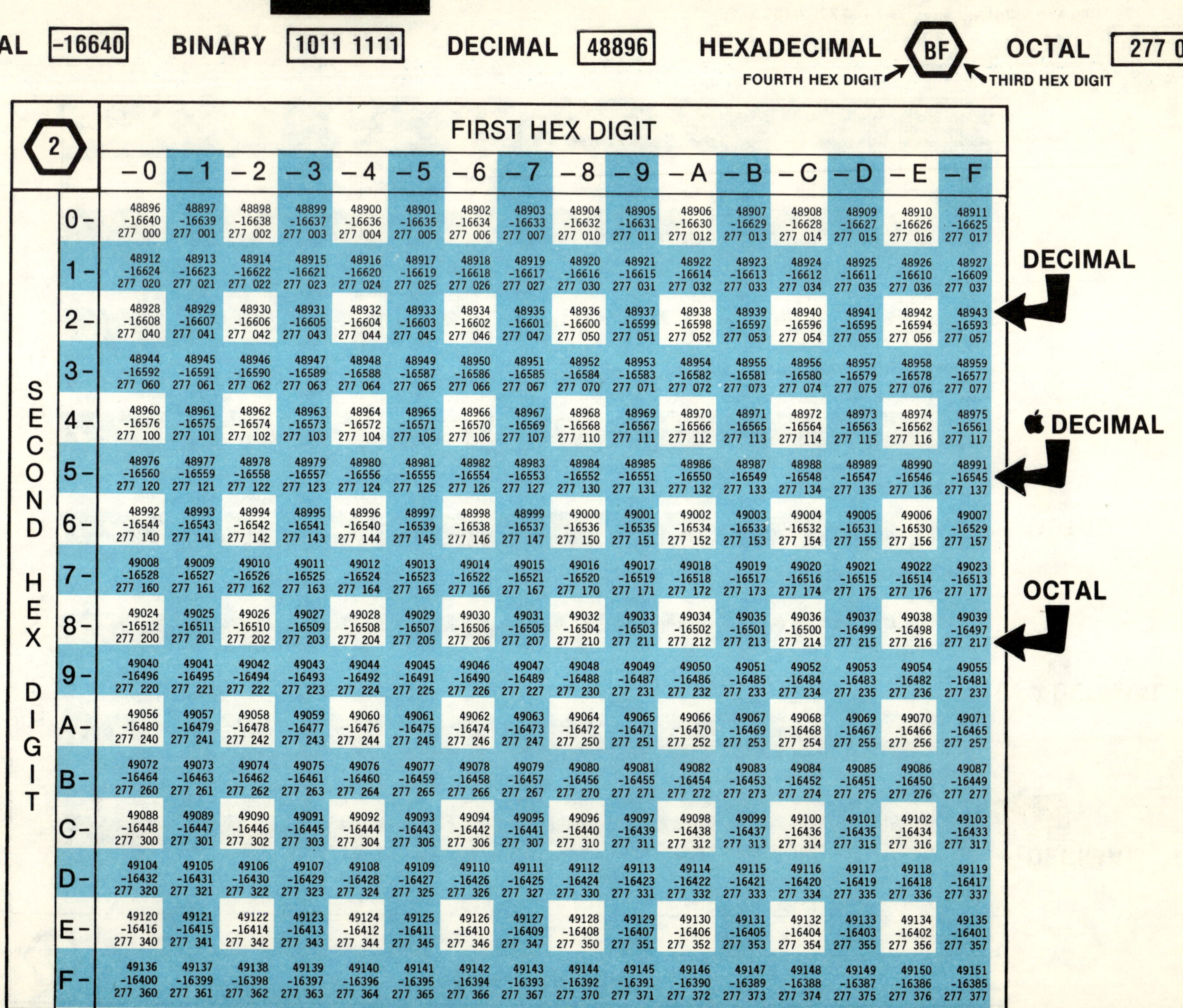



FIRST HEX DIGIT

| 2 | −0 | −1 | −2 | −3 | −4 | −5 | −6 | −7 | −8 | −9 | −A | −B | −C | −D | −E | −F |
|---|---|---|---|---|---|---|---|---|---|---|---|---|---|---|---|---|
| 0− | 48896<br>−16640<br>277 000 | 48897<br>−16639<br>277 001 | 48898<br>−16638<br>277 002 | 48899<br>−16637<br>277 003 | 48900<br>−16636<br>277 004 | 48901<br>−16635<br>277 005 | 48902<br>−16634<br>277 006 | 48903<br>−16633<br>277 007 | 48904<br>−16632<br>277 010 | 48905<br>−16631<br>277 011 | 48906<br>−16630<br>277 012 | 48907<br>−16629<br>277 013 | 48908<br>−16628<br>277 014 | 48909<br>−16627<br>277 015 | 48910<br>−16626<br>277 016 | 48911<br>−16625<br>277 017 |
| 1− | 48912<br>−16624<br>277 020 | 48913<br>−16623<br>277 021 | 48914<br>−16622<br>277 022 | 48915<br>−16621<br>277 023 | 48916<br>−16620<br>277 024 | 48917<br>−16619<br>277 025 | 48918<br>−16618<br>277 026 | 48919<br>−16617<br>277 027 | 48920<br>−16616<br>277 030 | 48921<br>−16615<br>277 031 | 48922<br>−16614<br>277 032 | 48923<br>−16613<br>277 033 | 48924<br>−16612<br>277 034 | 48925<br>−16611<br>277 035 | 48926<br>−16610<br>277 036 | 48927<br>−16609<br>277 037 |
| 2− | 48928<br>−16608<br>277 040 | 48929<br>−16607<br>277 041 | 48930<br>−16606<br>277 042 | 48931<br>−16605<br>277 043 | 48932<br>−16604<br>277 044 | 48933<br>−16603<br>277 045 | 48934<br>−16602<br>277 046 | 48935<br>−16601<br>277 047 | 48936<br>−16600<br>277 050 | 48937<br>−16599<br>277 051 | 48938<br>−16598<br>277 052 | 48939<br>−16597<br>277 053 | 48940<br>−16596<br>277 054 | 48941<br>−16595<br>277 055 | 48942<br>−16594<br>277 056 | 48943<br>−16593<br>277 057 |
| 3− | 48944<br>−16592<br>277 060 | 48945<br>−16591<br>277 061 | 48946<br>−16590<br>277 062 | 48947<br>−16589<br>277 063 | 48948<br>−16588<br>277 064 | 48949<br>−16587<br>277 065 | 48950<br>−16586<br>277 066 | 48951<br>−16585<br>277 067 | 48952<br>−16584<br>277 070 | 48953<br>−16583<br>277 071 | 48954<br>−16582<br>277 072 | 48955<br>−16581<br>277 073 | 48956<br>−16580<br>277 074 | 48957<br>−16579<br>277 075 | 48958<br>−16578<br>277 076 | 48959<br>−16577<br>277 077 |
| 4− | 48960<br>−16576<br>277 100 | 48961<br>−16575<br>277 101 | 48962<br>−16574<br>277 102 | 48963<br>−16573<br>277 103 | 48964<br>−16572<br>277 104 | 48965<br>−16571<br>277 105 | 48966<br>−16570<br>277 106 | 48967<br>−16569<br>277 107 | 48968<br>−16568<br>277 110 | 48969<br>−16567<br>277 111 | 48970<br>−16566<br>277 112 | 48971<br>−16565<br>277 113 | 48972<br>−16564<br>277 114 | 48973<br>−16563<br>277 115 | 48974<br>−16562<br>277 116 | 48975<br>−16561<br>277 117 |
| 5− | 48976<br>−16560<br>277 120 | 48977<br>−16559<br>277 121 | 48978<br>−16558<br>277 122 | 48979<br>−16557<br>277 123 | 48980<br>−16556<br>277 124 | 48981<br>−16555<br>277 125 | 48982<br>−16554<br>277 126 | 48983<br>−16553<br>277 127 | 48984<br>−16552<br>277 130 | 48985<br>−16551<br>277 131 | 48986<br>−16550<br>277 132 | 48987<br>−16549<br>277 133 | 48988<br>−16548<br>277 134 | 48989<br>−16547<br>277 135 | 48990<br>−16546<br>277 136 | 48991<br>−16545<br>277 137 |
| 6− | 48992<br>−16544<br>277 140 | 48993<br>−16543<br>277 141 | 48994<br>−16542<br>277 142 | 48995<br>−16541<br>277 143 | 48996<br>−16540<br>277 144 | 48997<br>−16539<br>277 145 | 48998<br>−16538<br>277 146 | 48999<br>−16537<br>277 147 | 49000<br>−16536<br>277 150 | 49001<br>−16535<br>277 151 | 49002<br>−16534<br>277 152 | 49003<br>−16533<br>277 153 | 49004<br>−16532<br>277 154 | 49005<br>−16531<br>277 155 | 49006<br>−16530<br>277 156 | 49007<br>−16529<br>277 157 |
| 7− | 49008<br>−16528<br>277 160 | 49009<br>−16527<br>277 161 | 49010<br>−16526<br>277 162 | 49011<br>−16525<br>277 163 | 49012<br>−16524<br>277 164 | 49013<br>−16523<br>277 165 | 49014<br>−16522<br>277 166 | 49015<br>−16521<br>277 167 | 49016<br>−16520<br>277 170 | 49017<br>−16519<br>277 171 | 49018<br>−16518<br>277 172 | 49019<br>−16517<br>277 173 | 49020<br>−16516<br>277 174 | 49021<br>−16515<br>277 175 | 49022<br>−16514<br>277 176 | 49023<br>−16513<br>277 177 |
| 8− | 49024<br>−16512<br>277 200 | 49025<br>−16511<br>277 201 | 49026<br>−16510<br>277 202 | 49027<br>−16509<br>277 203 | 49028<br>−16508<br>277 204 | 49029<br>−16507<br>277 205 | 49030<br>−16506<br>277 206 | 49031<br>−16505<br>277 207 | 49032<br>−16504<br>277 210 | 49033<br>−16503<br>277 211 | 49034<br>−16502<br>277 212 | 49035<br>−16501<br>277 213 | 49036<br>−16500<br>277 214 | 49037<br>−16499<br>277 215 | 49038<br>−16498<br>277 216 | 49039<br>−16497<br>277 217 |
| 9− | 49040<br>−16496<br>277 220 | 49041<br>−16495<br>277 221 | 49042<br>−16494<br>277 222 | 49043<br>−16493<br>277 223 | 49044<br>−16492<br>277 224 | 49045<br>−16491<br>277 225 | 49046<br>−16490<br>277 226 | 49047<br>−16489<br>277 227 | 49048<br>−16488<br>277 230 | 49049<br>−16487<br>277 231 | 49050<br>−16486<br>277 232 | 49051<br>−16485<br>277 233 | 49052<br>−16484<br>277 234 | 49053<br>−16483<br>277 235 | 49054<br>−16482<br>277 236 | 49055<br>−16481<br>277 237 |
| A− | 49056<br>−16480<br>277 240 | 49057<br>−16479<br>277 241 | 49058<br>−16478<br>277 242 | 49059<br>−16477<br>277 243 | 49060<br>−16476<br>277 244 | 49061<br>−16475<br>277 245 | 49062<br>−16474<br>277 246 | 49063<br>−16473<br>277 247 | 49064<br>−16472<br>277 250 | 49065<br>−16471<br>277 251 | 49066<br>−16470<br>277 252 | 49067<br>−16469<br>277 253 | 49068<br>−16468<br>277 254 | 49069<br>−16467<br>277 255 | 49070<br>−16466<br>277 256 | 49071<br>−16465<br>277 257 |
| B− | 49072<br>−16464<br>277 260 | 49073<br>−16463<br>277 261 | 49074<br>−16462<br>277 262 | 49075<br>−16461<br>277 263 | 49076<br>−16460<br>277 264 | 49077<br>−16459<br>277 265 | 49078<br>−16458<br>277 266 | 49079<br>−16457<br>277 267 | 49080<br>−16456<br>277 270 | 49081<br>−16455<br>277 271 | 49082<br>−16454<br>277 272 | 49083<br>−16453<br>277 273 | 49084<br>−16452<br>277 274 | 49085<br>−16451<br>277 275 | 49086<br>−16450<br>277 276 | 49087<br>−16449<br>277 277 |
| C− | 49088<br>−16448<br>277 300 | 49089<br>−16447<br>277 301 | 49090<br>−16446<br>277 302 | 49091<br>−16445<br>277 303 | 49092<br>−16444<br>277 304 | 49093<br>−16443<br>277 305 | 49094<br>−16442<br>277 306 | 49095<br>−16441<br>277 307 | 49096<br>−16440<br>277 310 | 49097<br>−16439<br>277 311 | 49098<br>−16438<br>277 312 | 49099<br>−16437<br>277 313 | 49100<br>−16436<br>277 314 | 49101<br>−16435<br>277 315 | 49102<br>−16434<br>277 316 | 49103<br>−16433<br>277 317 |
| D− | 49104<br>−16432<br>277 320 | 49105<br>−16431<br>277 321 | 49106<br>−16430<br>277 322 | 49107<br>−16429<br>277 323 | 49108<br>−16428<br>277 324 | 49109<br>−16427<br>277 325 | 49110<br>−16426<br>277 326 | 49111<br>−16425<br>277 327 | 49112<br>−16424<br>277 330 | 49113<br>−16423<br>277 331 | 49114<br>−16422<br>277 332 | 49115<br>−16421<br>277 333 | 49116<br>−16420<br>277 334 | 49117<br>−16419<br>277 335 | 49118<br>−16418<br>277 336 | 49119<br>−16417<br>277 337 |
| E− | 49120<br>−16416<br>277 340 | 49121<br>−16415<br>277 341 | 49122<br>−16414<br>277 342 | 49123<br>−16413<br>277 343 | 49124<br>−16412<br>277 344 | 49125<br>−16411<br>277 345 | 49126<br>−16410<br>277 346 | 49127<br>−16409<br>277 347 | 49128<br>−16408<br>277 350 | 49129<br>−16407<br>277 351 | 49130<br>−16406<br>277 352 | 49131<br>−16405<br>277 353 | 49132<br>−16404<br>277 354 | 49133<br>−16403<br>277 355 | 49134<br>−16402<br>277 356 | 49135<br>−16401<br>277 357 |
| F− | 49136<br>−16400<br>277 360 | 49137<br>−16399<br>277 361 | 49138<br>−16398<br>277 362 | 49139<br>−16397<br>277 363 | 49140<br>−16396<br>277 364 | 49141<br>−16395<br>277 365 | 49142<br>−16394<br>277 366 | 49143<br>−16393<br>277 367 | 49144<br>−16392<br>277 370 | 49145<br>−16391<br>277 371 | 49146<br>−16390<br>277 372 | 49147<br>−16389<br>277 373 | 49148<br>−16388<br>277 374 | 49149<br>−16387<br>277 375 | 49150<br>−16386<br>277 376 | 49151<br>−16385<br>277 377 |

| 2 | FIRST HEX DIGIT | | | | | | | | | | | | | | | |
|---|---|---|---|---|---|---|---|---|---|---|---|---|---|---|---|---|
| SECOND HEX DIGIT | −0 | −1 | −2 | −3 | −4 | −5 | −6 | −7 | −8 | −9 | −A | −B | −C | −D | −E | −F |
| 0− | 49152<br>-16384<br>300 000 | 49153<br>-16383<br>300 001 | 49154<br>-16382<br>300 002 | 49155<br>-16381<br>300 003 | 49156<br>-16380<br>300 004 | 49157<br>-16379<br>300 005 | 49158<br>-16378<br>300 006 | 49159<br>-16377<br>300 007 | 49160<br>-16376<br>300 010 | 49161<br>-16375<br>300 011 | 49162<br>-16374<br>300 012 | 49163<br>-16373<br>300 013 | 49164<br>-16372<br>300 014 | 49165<br>-16371<br>300 015 | 49166<br>-16370<br>300 016 | 49167<br>-16369<br>300 017 |
| 1− | 49168<br>-16368<br>300 020 | 49169<br>-16367<br>300 021 | 49170<br>-16366<br>300 022 | 49171<br>-16365<br>300 023 | 49172<br>-16364<br>300 024 | 49173<br>-16363<br>300 025 | 49174<br>-16362<br>300 026 | 49175<br>-16361<br>300 027 | 49176<br>-16360<br>300 030 | 49177<br>-16359<br>300 031 | 49178<br>-16358<br>300 032 | 49179<br>-16357<br>300 033 | 49180<br>-16356<br>300 034 | 49181<br>-16355<br>300 035 | 49182<br>-16354<br>300 036 | 49183<br>-16353<br>300 037 |
| 2− | 49184<br>-16352<br>300 040 | 49185<br>-16351<br>300 041 | 49186<br>-16350<br>300 042 | 49187<br>-16349<br>300 043 | 49188<br>-16348<br>300 044 | 49189<br>-16347<br>300 045 | 49190<br>-16346<br>300 046 | 49191<br>-16345<br>300 047 | 49192<br>-16344<br>300 050 | 49193<br>-16343<br>300 051 | 49194<br>-16342<br>300 052 | 49195<br>-16341<br>300 053 | 49196<br>-16340<br>300 054 | 49197<br>-16339<br>300 055 | 49198<br>-16338<br>300 056 | 49199<br>-16337<br>300 057 |
| 3− | 49200<br>-16336<br>300 060 | 49201<br>-16335<br>300 061 | 49202<br>-16334<br>300 062 | 49203<br>-16333<br>300 063 | 49204<br>-16332<br>300 064 | 49205<br>-16331<br>300 065 | 49206<br>-16330<br>300 066 | 49207<br>-16329<br>300 067 | 49208<br>-16328<br>300 070 | 49209<br>-16327<br>300 071 | 49210<br>-16326<br>300 072 | 49211<br>-16325<br>300 073 | 49212<br>-16324<br>300 074 | 49213<br>-16323<br>300 075 | 49214<br>-16322<br>300 076 | 49215<br>-16321<br>300 077 |
| 4− | 49216<br>-16320<br>300 100 | 49217<br>-16319<br>300 101 | 49218<br>-16318<br>300 102 | 49219<br>-16317<br>300 103 | 49220<br>-16316<br>300 104 | 49221<br>-16315<br>300 105 | 49222<br>-16314<br>300 106 | 49223<br>-16313<br>300 107 | 49224<br>-16312<br>300 110 | 49225<br>-16311<br>300 111 | 49226<br>-16310<br>300 112 | 49227<br>-16309<br>300 113 | 49228<br>-16308<br>300 114 | 49229<br>-16307<br>300 115 | 49230<br>-16306<br>300 116 | 49231<br>-16305<br>300 117 |
| 5− | 49232<br>-16304<br>300 120 | 49233<br>-16303<br>300 121 | 49234<br>-16302<br>300 122 | 49235<br>-16301<br>300 123 | 49236<br>-16300<br>300 124 | 49237<br>-16299<br>300 125 | 49238<br>-16298<br>300 126 | 49239<br>-16297<br>300 127 | 49240<br>-16296<br>300 130 | 49241<br>-16295<br>300 131 | 49242<br>-16294<br>300 132 | 49243<br>-16293<br>300 133 | 49244<br>-16292<br>300 134 | 49245<br>-16291<br>300 135 | 49246<br>-16290<br>300 136 | 49247<br>-16289<br>300 137 |
| 6− | 49248<br>-16288<br>300 140 | 49249<br>-16287<br>300 141 | 49250<br>-16286<br>300 142 | 49251<br>-16285<br>300 143 | 49252<br>-16284<br>300 144 | 49253<br>-16283<br>300 145 | 49254<br>-16282<br>300 146 | 49255<br>-16281<br>300 147 | 49256<br>-16280<br>300 150 | 49257<br>-16279<br>300 151 | 49258<br>-16278<br>300 152 | 49259<br>-16277<br>300 153 | 49260<br>-16276<br>300 154 | 49261<br>-16275<br>300 155 | 49262<br>-16274<br>300 156 | 49263<br>-16273<br>300 157 |
| 7− | 49264<br>-16272<br>300 160 | 49265<br>-16271<br>300 161 | 49266<br>-16270<br>300 162 | 49267<br>-16269<br>300 163 | 49268<br>-16268<br>300 164 | 49269<br>-16267<br>300 165 | 49270<br>-16266<br>300 166 | 49271<br>-16265<br>300 167 | 49272<br>-16264<br>300 170 | 49273<br>-16263<br>300 171 | 49274<br>-16262<br>300 172 | 49275<br>-16261<br>300 173 | 49276<br>-16260<br>300 174 | 49277<br>-16259<br>300 175 | 49278<br>-16258<br>300 176 | 49279<br>-16257<br>300 177 |
| 8− | 49280<br>-16256<br>300 200 | 49281<br>-16255<br>300 201 | 49282<br>-16254<br>300 202 | 49283<br>-16253<br>300 203 | 49284<br>-16252<br>300 204 | 49285<br>-16251<br>300 205 | 49286<br>-16250<br>300 206 | 49287<br>-16249<br>300 207 | 49288<br>-16248<br>300 210 | 49289<br>-16247<br>300 211 | 49290<br>-16246<br>300 212 | 49291<br>-16245<br>300 213 | 49292<br>-16244<br>300 214 | 49293<br>-16243<br>300 215 | 49294<br>-16242<br>300 216 | 49295<br>-16241<br>300 217 |
| 9− | 49296<br>-16240<br>300 220 | 49297<br>-16239<br>300 221 | 49298<br>-16238<br>300 222 | 49299<br>-16237<br>300 223 | 49300<br>-16236<br>300 224 | 49301<br>-16235<br>300 225 | 49302<br>-16234<br>300 226 | 49303<br>-16233<br>300 227 | 49304<br>-16232<br>300 230 | 49305<br>-16231<br>300 231 | 49306<br>-16230<br>300 232 | 49307<br>-16229<br>300 233 | 49308<br>-16228<br>300 234 | 49309<br>-16227<br>300 235 | 49310<br>-16226<br>300 236 | 49311<br>-16225<br>300 237 |
| A− | 49312<br>-16224<br>300 240 | 49313<br>-16223<br>300 241 | 49314<br>-16222<br>300 242 | 49315<br>-16221<br>300 243 | 49316<br>-16220<br>300 244 | 49317<br>-16219<br>300 245 | 49318<br>-16218<br>300 246 | 49319<br>-16217<br>300 247 | 49320<br>-16216<br>300 250 | 49321<br>-16215<br>300 251 | 49322<br>-16214<br>300 252 | 49323<br>-16213<br>300 253 | 49324<br>-16212<br>300 254 | 49325<br>-16211<br>300 255 | 49326<br>-16210<br>300 256 | 49327<br>-16209<br>300 257 |
| B− | 49328<br>-16208<br>300 260 | 49329<br>-16207<br>300 261 | 49330<br>-16206<br>300 262 | 49331<br>-16205<br>300 263 | 49332<br>-16204<br>300 264 | 49333<br>-16203<br>300 265 | 49334<br>-16202<br>300 266 | 49335<br>-16201<br>300 267 | 49336<br>-16200<br>300 270 | 49337<br>-16199<br>300 271 | 49338<br>-16198<br>300 272 | 49339<br>-16197<br>300 273 | 49340<br>-16196<br>300 274 | 49341<br>-16195<br>300 275 | 49342<br>-16194<br>300 276 | 49343<br>-16193<br>300 277 |
| C− | 49344<br>-16192<br>300 300 | 49345<br>-16191<br>300 301 | 49346<br>-16190<br>300 302 | 49347<br>-16189<br>300 303 | 49348<br>-16188<br>300 304 | 49349<br>-16187<br>300 305 | 49350<br>-16186<br>300 306 | 49351<br>-16185<br>300 307 | 49352<br>-16184<br>300 310 | 49353<br>-16183<br>300 311 | 49354<br>-16182<br>300 312 | 49355<br>-16181<br>300 313 | 49356<br>-16180<br>300 314 | 49357<br>-16179<br>300 315 | 49358<br>-16178<br>300 316 | 49359<br>-16177<br>300 317 |
| D− | 49360<br>-16176<br>300 320 | 49361<br>-16175<br>300 321 | 49362<br>-16174<br>300 322 | 49363<br>-16173<br>300 323 | 49364<br>-16172<br>300 324 | 49365<br>-16171<br>300 325 | 49366<br>-16170<br>300 326 | 49367<br>-16169<br>300 327 | 49368<br>-16168<br>300 330 | 49369<br>-16167<br>300 331 | 49370<br>-16166<br>300 332 | 49371<br>-16165<br>300 333 | 49372<br>-16164<br>300 334 | 49373<br>-16163<br>300 335 | 49374<br>-16162<br>300 336 | 49375<br>-16161<br>300 337 |
| E− | 49376<br>-16160<br>300 340 | 49377<br>-16159<br>300 341 | 49378<br>-16158<br>300 342 | 49379<br>-16157<br>300 343 | 49380<br>-16156<br>300 344 | 49381<br>-16155<br>300 345 | 49382<br>-16154<br>300 346 | 49383<br>-16153<br>300 347 | 49384<br>-16152<br>300 350 | 49385<br>-16151<br>300 351 | 49386<br>-16150<br>300 352 | 49387<br>-16149<br>300 353 | 49388<br>-16148<br>300 354 | 49389<br>-16147<br>300 355 | 49390<br>-16146<br>300 356 | 49391<br>-16145<br>300 357 |
| F− | 49392<br>-16144<br>300 360 | 49393<br>-16143<br>300 361 | 49394<br>-16142<br>300 362 | 49395<br>-16141<br>300 363 | 49396<br>-16140<br>300 364 | 49397<br>-16139<br>300 365 | 49398<br>-16138<br>300 366 | 49399<br>-16137<br>300 367 | 49400<br>-16136<br>300 370 | 49401<br>-16135<br>300 371 | 49402<br>-16134<br>300 372 | 49403<br>-16133<br>300 373 | 49404<br>-16132<br>300 374 | 49405<br>-16131<br>300 375 | 49406<br>-16130<br>300 376 | 49407<br>-16129<br>300 377 |

**DECIMAL** (first line in each box)

**DECIMAL** (second line in each box)

**OCTAL** (third line in each box)

**DECIMAL** -16384 **BINARY** 1100 0000 **DECIMAL** 49152 **HEXADECIMAL** C0 **OCTAL** 300 000

FOURTH HEX DIGIT (C) THIRD HEX DIGIT (0)

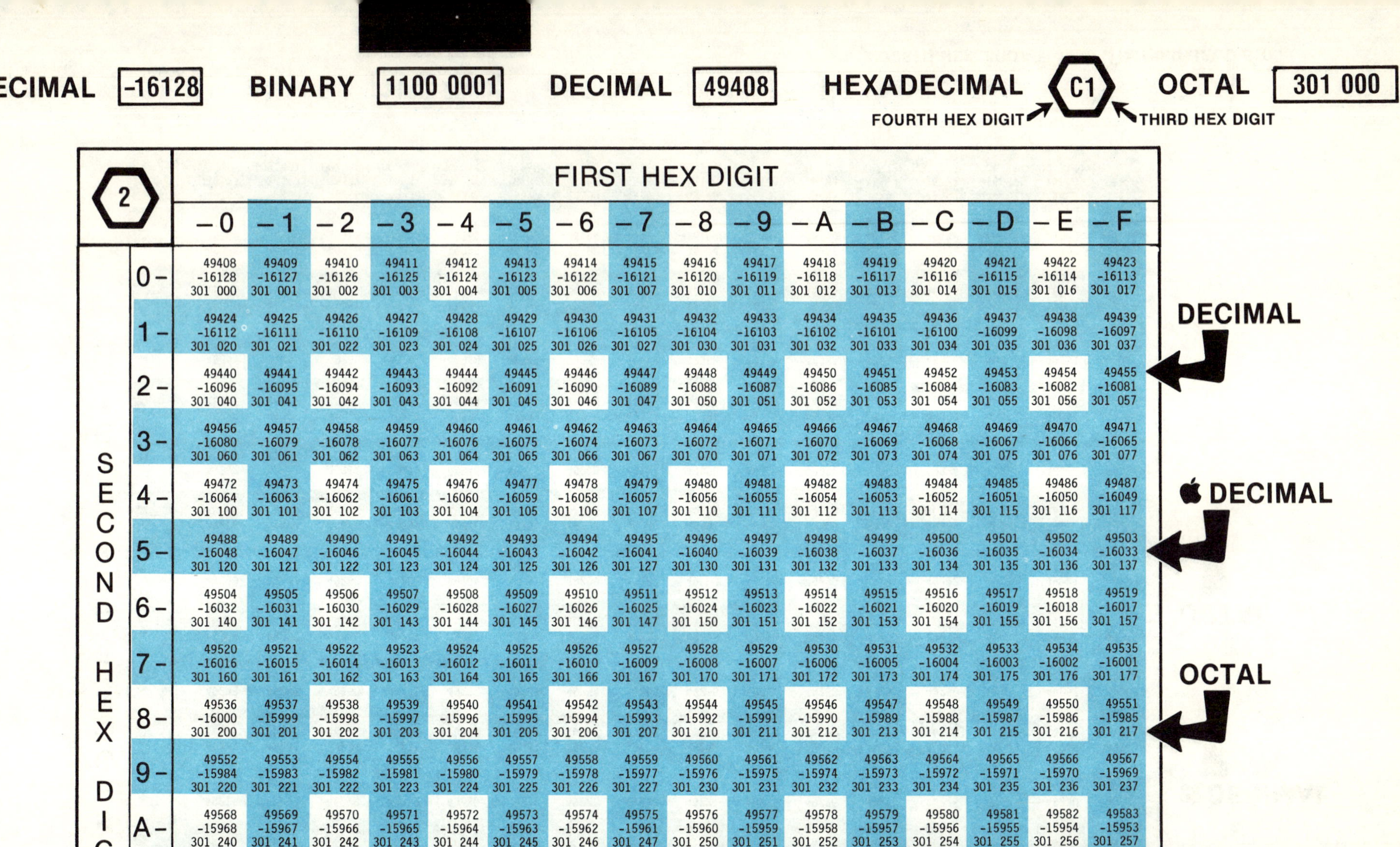

**FIRST HEX DIGIT** (hexagon 2) / **SECOND HEX DIGIT**

| | −0 | −1 | −2 | −3 | −4 | −5 | −6 | −7 | −8 | −9 | −A | −B | −C | −D | −E | −F |
|---|---|---|---|---|---|---|---|---|---|---|---|---|---|---|---|---|
| 0− | 49408<br>−16128<br>301 000 | 49409<br>−16127<br>301 001 | 49410<br>−16126<br>301 002 | 49411<br>−16125<br>301 003 | 49412<br>−16124<br>301 004 | 49413<br>−16123<br>301 005 | 49414<br>−16122<br>301 006 | 49415<br>−16121<br>301 007 | 49416<br>−16120<br>301 010 | 49417<br>−16119<br>301 011 | 49418<br>−16118<br>301 012 | 49419<br>−16117<br>301 013 | 49420<br>−16116<br>301 014 | 49421<br>−16115<br>301 015 | 49422<br>−16114<br>301 016 | 49423<br>−16113<br>301 017 |
| 1− | 49424<br>−16112<br>301 020 | 49425<br>−16111<br>301 021 | 49426<br>−16110<br>301 022 | 49427<br>−16109<br>301 023 | 49428<br>−16108<br>301 024 | 49429<br>−16107<br>301 025 | 49430<br>−16106<br>301 026 | 49431<br>−16105<br>301 027 | 49432<br>−16104<br>301 030 | 49433<br>−16103<br>301 031 | 49434<br>−16102<br>301 032 | 49435<br>−16101<br>301 033 | 49436<br>−16100<br>301 034 | 49437<br>−16099<br>301 035 | 49438<br>−16098<br>301 036 | 49439<br>−16097<br>301 037 |
| 2− | 49440<br>−16096<br>301 040 | 49441<br>−16095<br>301 041 | 49442<br>−16094<br>301 042 | 49443<br>−16093<br>301 043 | 49444<br>−16092<br>301 044 | 49445<br>−16091<br>301 045 | 49446<br>−16090<br>301 046 | 49447<br>−16089<br>301 047 | 49448<br>−16088<br>301 050 | 49449<br>−16087<br>301 051 | 49450<br>−16086<br>301 052 | 49451<br>−16085<br>301 053 | 49452<br>−16084<br>301 054 | 49453<br>−16083<br>301 055 | 49454<br>−16082<br>301 056 | 49455<br>−16081<br>301 057 |
| 3− | 49456<br>−16080<br>301 060 | 49457<br>−16079<br>301 061 | 49458<br>−16078<br>301 062 | 49459<br>−16077<br>301 063 | 49460<br>−16076<br>301 064 | 49461<br>−16075<br>301 065 | 49462<br>−16074<br>301 066 | 49463<br>−16073<br>301 067 | 49464<br>−16072<br>301 070 | 49465<br>−16071<br>301 071 | 49466<br>−16070<br>301 072 | 49467<br>−16069<br>301 073 | 49468<br>−16068<br>301 074 | 49469<br>−16067<br>301 075 | 49470<br>−16066<br>301 076 | 49471<br>−16065<br>301 077 |
| 4− | 49472<br>−16064<br>301 100 | 49473<br>−16063<br>301 101 | 49474<br>−16062<br>301 102 | 49475<br>−16061<br>301 103 | 49476<br>−16060<br>301 104 | 49477<br>−16059<br>301 105 | 49478<br>−16058<br>301 106 | 49479<br>−16057<br>301 107 | 49480<br>−16056<br>301 110 | 49481<br>−16055<br>301 111 | 49482<br>−16054<br>301 112 | 49483<br>−16053<br>301 113 | 49484<br>−16052<br>301 114 | 49485<br>−16051<br>301 115 | 49486<br>−16050<br>301 116 | 49487<br>−16049<br>301 117 |
| 5− | 49488<br>−16048<br>301 120 | 49489<br>−16047<br>301 121 | 49490<br>−16046<br>301 122 | 49491<br>−16045<br>301 123 | 49492<br>−16044<br>301 124 | 49493<br>−16043<br>301 125 | 49494<br>−16042<br>301 126 | 49495<br>−16041<br>301 127 | 49496<br>−16040<br>301 130 | 49497<br>−16039<br>301 131 | 49498<br>−16038<br>301 132 | 49499<br>−16037<br>301 133 | 49500<br>−16036<br>301 134 | 49501<br>−16035<br>301 135 | 49502<br>−16034<br>301 136 | 49503<br>−16033<br>301 137 |
| 6− | 49504<br>−16032<br>301 140 | 49505<br>−16031<br>301 141 | 49506<br>−16030<br>301 142 | 49507<br>−16029<br>301 143 | 49508<br>−16028<br>301 144 | 49509<br>−16027<br>301 145 | 49510<br>−16026<br>301 146 | 49511<br>−16025<br>301 147 | 49512<br>−16024<br>301 150 | 49513<br>−16023<br>301 151 | 49514<br>−16022<br>301 152 | 49515<br>−16021<br>301 153 | 49516<br>−16020<br>301 154 | 49517<br>−16019<br>301 155 | 49518<br>−16018<br>301 156 | 49519<br>−16017<br>301 157 |
| 7− | 49520<br>−16016<br>301 160 | 49521<br>−16015<br>301 161 | 49522<br>−16014<br>301 162 | 49523<br>−16013<br>301 163 | 49524<br>−16012<br>301 164 | 49525<br>−16011<br>301 165 | 49526<br>−16010<br>301 166 | 49527<br>−16009<br>301 167 | 49528<br>−16008<br>301 170 | 49529<br>−16007<br>301 171 | 49530<br>−16006<br>301 172 | 49531<br>−16005<br>301 173 | 49532<br>−16004<br>301 174 | 49533<br>−16003<br>301 175 | 49534<br>−16002<br>301 176 | 49535<br>−16001<br>301 177 |
| 8− | 49536<br>−16000<br>301 200 | 49537<br>−15999<br>301 201 | 49538<br>−15998<br>301 202 | 49539<br>−15997<br>301 203 | 49540<br>−15996<br>301 204 | 49541<br>−15995<br>301 205 | 49542<br>−15994<br>301 206 | 49543<br>−15993<br>301 207 | 49544<br>−15992<br>301 210 | 49545<br>−15991<br>301 211 | 49546<br>−15990<br>301 212 | 49547<br>−15989<br>301 213 | 49548<br>−15988<br>301 214 | 49549<br>−15987<br>301 215 | 49550<br>−15986<br>301 216 | 49551<br>−15985<br>301 217 |
| 9− | 49552<br>−15984<br>301 220 | 49553<br>−15983<br>301 221 | 49554<br>−15982<br>301 222 | 49555<br>−15981<br>301 223 | 49556<br>−15980<br>301 224 | 49557<br>−15979<br>301 225 | 49558<br>−15978<br>301 226 | 49559<br>−15977<br>301 227 | 49560<br>−15976<br>301 230 | 49561<br>−15975<br>301 231 | 49562<br>−15974<br>301 232 | 49563<br>−15973<br>301 233 | 49564<br>−15972<br>301 234 | 49565<br>−15971<br>301 235 | 49566<br>−15970<br>301 236 | 49567<br>−15969<br>301 237 |
| A− | 49568<br>−15968<br>301 240 | 49569<br>−15967<br>301 241 | 49570<br>−15966<br>301 242 | 49571<br>−15965<br>301 243 | 49572<br>−15964<br>301 244 | 49573<br>−15963<br>301 245 | 49574<br>−15962<br>301 246 | 49575<br>−15961<br>301 247 | 49576<br>−15960<br>301 250 | 49577<br>−15959<br>301 251 | 49578<br>−15958<br>301 252 | 49579<br>−15957<br>301 253 | 49580<br>−15956<br>301 254 | 49581<br>−15955<br>301 255 | 49582<br>−15954<br>301 256 | 49583<br>−15953<br>301 257 |
| B− | 49584<br>−15952<br>301 260 | 49585<br>−15951<br>301 261 | 49586<br>−15950<br>301 262 | 49587<br>−15949<br>301 263 | 49588<br>−15948<br>301 264 | 49589<br>−15947<br>301 265 | 49590<br>−15946<br>301 266 | 49591<br>−15945<br>301 267 | 49592<br>−15944<br>301 270 | 49593<br>−15943<br>301 271 | 49594<br>−15942<br>301 272 | 49595<br>−15941<br>301 273 | 49596<br>−15940<br>301 274 | 49597<br>−15939<br>301 275 | 49598<br>−15938<br>301 276 | 49599<br>−15937<br>301 277 |
| C− | 49600<br>−15936<br>301 300 | 49601<br>−15935<br>301 301 | 49602<br>−15934<br>301 302 | 49603<br>−15933<br>301 303 | 49604<br>−15932<br>301 304 | 49605<br>−15931<br>301 305 | 49606<br>−15930<br>301 306 | 49607<br>−15929<br>301 307 | 49608<br>−15928<br>301 310 | 49609<br>−15927<br>301 311 | 49610<br>−15926<br>301 312 | 49611<br>−15925<br>301 313 | 49612<br>−15924<br>301 314 | 49613<br>−15923<br>301 315 | 49614<br>−15922<br>301 316 | 49615<br>−15921<br>301 317 |
| D− | 49616<br>−15920<br>301 320 | 49617<br>−15919<br>301 321 | 49618<br>−15918<br>301 322 | 49619<br>−15917<br>301 323 | 49620<br>−15916<br>301 324 | 49621<br>−15915<br>301 325 | 49622<br>−15914<br>301 326 | 49623<br>−15913<br>301 327 | 49624<br>−15912<br>301 330 | 49625<br>−15911<br>301 331 | 49626<br>−15910<br>301 332 | 49627<br>−15909<br>301 333 | 49628<br>−15908<br>301 334 | 49629<br>−15907<br>301 335 | 49630<br>−15906<br>301 336 | 49631<br>−15905<br>301 337 |
| E− | 49632<br>−15904<br>301 340 | 49633<br>−15903<br>301 341 | 49634<br>−15902<br>301 342 | 49635<br>−15901<br>301 343 | 49636<br>−15900<br>301 344 | 49637<br>−15899<br>301 345 | 49638<br>−15898<br>301 346 | 49639<br>−15897<br>301 347 | 49640<br>−15896<br>301 350 | 49641<br>−15895<br>301 351 | 49642<br>−15894<br>301 352 | 49643<br>−15893<br>301 353 | 49644<br>−15892<br>301 354 | 49645<br>−15891<br>301 355 | 49646<br>−15890<br>301 356 | 49647<br>−15889<br>301 357 |
| F− | 49648<br>−15888<br>301 360 | 49649<br>−15887<br>301 361 | 49650<br>−15886<br>301 362 | 49651<br>−15885<br>301 363 | 49652<br>−15884<br>301 364 | 49653<br>−15883<br>301 365 | 49654<br>−15882<br>301 366 | 49655<br>−15881<br>301 367 | 49656<br>−15880<br>301 370 | 49657<br>−15879<br>301 371 | 49658<br>−15878<br>301 372 | 49659<br>−15877<br>301 373 | 49660<br>−15876<br>301 374 | 49661<br>−15875<br>301 375 | 49662<br>−15874<br>301 376 | 49663<br>−15873<br>301 377 |

Each cell lists three values: **DECIMAL** (top), ** DECIMAL** (negative, middle), **OCTAL** (bottom).

| SECOND HEX DIGIT | −0 | −1 | −2 | −3 | −4 | −5 | −6 | −7 | −8 | −9 | −A | −B | −C | −D | −E | −F |
|---|---|---|---|---|---|---|---|---|---|---|---|---|---|---|---|---|
| 0− | 49664<br>−15872<br>302 000 | 49665<br>−15871<br>302 001 | 49666<br>−15870<br>302 002 | 49667<br>−15869<br>302 003 | 49668<br>−15868<br>302 004 | 49669<br>−15867<br>302 005 | 49670<br>−15866<br>302 006 | 49671<br>−15865<br>302 007 | 49672<br>−15864<br>302 010 | 49673<br>−15863<br>302 011 | 49674<br>−15862<br>302 012 | 49675<br>−15861<br>302 013 | 49676<br>−15860<br>302 014 | 49677<br>−15859<br>302 015 | 49678<br>−15858<br>302 016 | 49679<br>−15857<br>302 017 |
| 1− | 49680<br>−15856<br>302 020 | 49681<br>−15855<br>302 021 | 49682<br>−15854<br>302 022 | 49683<br>−15853<br>302 023 | 49684<br>−15852<br>302 024 | 49685<br>−15851<br>302 025 | 49686<br>−15850<br>302 026 | 49687<br>−15849<br>302 027 | 49688<br>−15848<br>302 030 | 49689<br>−15847<br>302 031 | 49690<br>−15846<br>302 032 | 49691<br>−15845<br>302 033 | 49692<br>−15844<br>302 034 | 49693<br>−15843<br>302 035 | 49694<br>−15842<br>302 036 | 49695<br>−15841<br>302 037 |
| 2− | 49696<br>−15840<br>302 040 | 49697<br>−15839<br>302 041 | 49698<br>−15838<br>302 042 | 49699<br>−15837<br>302 043 | 49700<br>−15836<br>302 044 | 49701<br>−15835<br>302 045 | 49702<br>−15834<br>302 046 | 49703<br>−15833<br>302 047 | 49704<br>−15832<br>302 050 | 49705<br>−15831<br>302 051 | 49706<br>−15830<br>302 052 | 49707<br>−15829<br>302 053 | 49708<br>−15828<br>302 054 | 49709<br>−15827<br>302 055 | 49710<br>−15826<br>302 056 | 49711<br>−15825<br>302 057 |
| 3− | 49712<br>−15824<br>302 060 | 49713<br>−15823<br>302 061 | 49714<br>−15822<br>302 062 | 49715<br>−15821<br>302 063 | 49716<br>−15820<br>302 064 | 49717<br>−15819<br>302 065 | 49718<br>−15818<br>302 066 | 49719<br>−15817<br>302 067 | 49720<br>−15816<br>302 070 | 49721<br>−15815<br>302 071 | 49722<br>−15814<br>302 072 | 49723<br>−15813<br>302 073 | 49724<br>−15812<br>302 074 | 49725<br>−15811<br>302 075 | 49726<br>−15810<br>302 076 | 49727<br>−15809<br>302 077 |
| 4− | 49728<br>−15808<br>302 100 | 49729<br>−15807<br>302 101 | 49730<br>−15806<br>302 102 | 49731<br>−15805<br>302 103 | 49732<br>−15804<br>302 104 | 49733<br>−15803<br>302 105 | 49734<br>−15802<br>302 106 | 49735<br>−15801<br>302 107 | 49736<br>−15800<br>302 110 | 49737<br>−15799<br>302 111 | 49738<br>−15798<br>302 112 | 49739<br>−15797<br>302 113 | 49740<br>−15796<br>302 114 | 49741<br>−15795<br>302 115 | 49742<br>−15794<br>302 116 | 49743<br>−15793<br>302 117 |
| 5− | 49744<br>−15792<br>302 120 | 49745<br>−15791<br>302 121 | 49746<br>−15790<br>302 122 | 49747<br>−15789<br>302 123 | 49748<br>−15788<br>302 124 | 49749<br>−15787<br>302 125 | 49750<br>−15786<br>302 126 | 49751<br>−15785<br>302 127 | 49752<br>−15784<br>302 130 | 49753<br>−15783<br>302 131 | 49754<br>−15782<br>302 132 | 49755<br>−15781<br>302 133 | 49756<br>−15780<br>302 134 | 49757<br>−15779<br>302 135 | 49758<br>−15778<br>302 136 | 49759<br>−15777<br>302 137 |
| 6− | 49760<br>−15776<br>302 140 | 49761<br>−15775<br>302 141 | 49762<br>−15774<br>302 142 | 49763<br>−15773<br>302 143 | 49764<br>−15772<br>302 144 | 49765<br>−15771<br>302 145 | 49766<br>−15770<br>302 146 | 49767<br>−15769<br>302 147 | 49768<br>−15768<br>302 150 | 49769<br>−15767<br>302 151 | 49770<br>−15766<br>302 152 | 49771<br>−15765<br>302 153 | 49772<br>−15764<br>302 154 | 49773<br>−15763<br>302 155 | 49774<br>−15762<br>302 156 | 49775<br>−15761<br>302 157 |
| 7− | 49776<br>−15760<br>302 160 | 49777<br>−15759<br>302 161 | 49778<br>−15758<br>302 162 | 49779<br>−15757<br>302 163 | 49780<br>−15756<br>302 164 | 49781<br>−15755<br>302 165 | 49782<br>−15754<br>302 166 | 49783<br>−15753<br>302 167 | 49784<br>−15752<br>302 170 | 49785<br>−15751<br>302 171 | 49786<br>−15750<br>302 172 | 49787<br>−15749<br>302 173 | 49788<br>−15748<br>302 174 | 49789<br>−15747<br>302 175 | 49790<br>−15746<br>302 176 | 49791<br>−15745<br>302 177 |
| 8− | 49792<br>−15744<br>302 200 | 49793<br>−15743<br>302 201 | 49794<br>−15742<br>302 202 | 49795<br>−15741<br>302 203 | 49796<br>−15740<br>302 204 | 49797<br>−15739<br>302 205 | 49798<br>−15738<br>302 206 | 49799<br>−15737<br>302 207 | 49800<br>−15736<br>302 210 | 49801<br>−15735<br>302 211 | 49802<br>−15734<br>302 212 | 49803<br>−15733<br>302 213 | 49804<br>−15732<br>302 214 | 49805<br>−15731<br>302 215 | 49806<br>−15730<br>302 216 | 49807<br>−15729<br>302 217 |
| 9− | 49808<br>−15728<br>302 220 | 49809<br>−15727<br>302 221 | 49810<br>−15726<br>302 222 | 49811<br>−15725<br>302 223 | 49812<br>−15724<br>302 224 | 49813<br>−15723<br>302 225 | 49814<br>−15722<br>302 226 | 49815<br>−15721<br>302 227 | 49816<br>−15720<br>302 230 | 49817<br>−15719<br>302 231 | 49818<br>−15718<br>302 232 | 49819<br>−15717<br>302 233 | 49820<br>−15716<br>302 234 | 49821<br>−15715<br>302 235 | 49822<br>−15714<br>302 236 | 49823<br>−15713<br>302 237 |
| A− | 49824<br>−15712<br>302 240 | 49825<br>−15711<br>302 241 | 49826<br>−15710<br>302 242 | 49827<br>−15709<br>302 243 | 49828<br>−15708<br>302 244 | 49829<br>−15707<br>302 245 | 49830<br>−15706<br>302 246 | 49831<br>−15705<br>302 247 | 49832<br>−15704<br>302 250 | 49833<br>−15703<br>302 251 | 49834<br>−15702<br>302 252 | 49835<br>−15701<br>302 253 | 49836<br>−15700<br>302 254 | 49837<br>−15699<br>302 255 | 49838<br>−15698<br>302 256 | 49839<br>−15697<br>302 257 |
| B− | 49840<br>−15696<br>302 260 | 49841<br>−15695<br>302 261 | 49842<br>−15694<br>302 262 | 49843<br>−15693<br>302 263 | 49844<br>−15692<br>302 264 | 49845<br>−15691<br>302 265 | 49846<br>−15690<br>302 266 | 49847<br>−15689<br>302 267 | 49848<br>−15688<br>302 270 | 49849<br>−15687<br>302 271 | 49850<br>−15686<br>302 272 | 49851<br>−15685<br>302 273 | 49852<br>−15684<br>302 274 | 49853<br>−15683<br>302 275 | 49854<br>−15682<br>302 276 | 49855<br>−15681<br>302 277 |
| C− | 49856<br>−15680<br>302 300 | 49857<br>−15679<br>302 301 | 49858<br>−15678<br>302 302 | 49859<br>−15677<br>302 303 | 49860<br>−15676<br>302 304 | 49861<br>−15675<br>302 305 | 49862<br>−15674<br>302 306 | 49863<br>−15673<br>302 307 | 49864<br>−15672<br>302 310 | 49865<br>−15671<br>302 311 | 49866<br>−15670<br>302 312 | 49867<br>−15669<br>302 313 | 49868<br>−15668<br>302 314 | 49869<br>−15667<br>302 315 | 49870<br>−15666<br>302 316 | 49871<br>−15665<br>302 317 |
| D− | 49872<br>−15664<br>302 320 | 49873<br>−15663<br>302 321 | 49874<br>−15662<br>302 322 | 49875<br>−15661<br>302 323 | 49876<br>−15660<br>302 324 | 49877<br>−15659<br>302 325 | 49878<br>−15658<br>302 326 | 49879<br>−15657<br>302 327 | 49880<br>−15656<br>302 330 | 49881<br>−15655<br>302 331 | 49882<br>−15654<br>302 332 | 49883<br>−15653<br>302 333 | 49884<br>−15652<br>302 334 | 49885<br>−15651<br>302 335 | 49886<br>−15650<br>302 336 | 49887<br>−15649<br>302 337 |
| E− | 49888<br>−15648<br>302 340 | 49889<br>−15647<br>302 341 | 49890<br>−15646<br>302 342 | 49891<br>−15645<br>302 343 | 49892<br>−15644<br>302 344 | 49893<br>−15643<br>302 345 | 49894<br>−15642<br>302 346 | 49895<br>−15641<br>302 347 | 49896<br>−15640<br>302 350 | 49897<br>−15639<br>302 351 | 49898<br>−15638<br>302 352 | 49899<br>−15637<br>302 353 | 49900<br>−15636<br>302 354 | 49901<br>−15635<br>302 355 | 49902<br>−15634<br>302 356 | 49903<br>−15633<br>302 357 |
| F− | 49904<br>−15632<br>302 360 | 49905<br>−15631<br>302 361 | 49906<br>−15630<br>302 362 | 49907<br>−15629<br>302 363 | 49908<br>−15628<br>302 364 | 49909<br>−15627<br>302 365 | 49910<br>−15626<br>302 366 | 49911<br>−15625<br>302 367 | 49912<br>−15624<br>302 370 | 49913<br>−15623<br>302 371 | 49914<br>−15622<br>302 372 | 49915<br>−15621<br>302 373 | 49916<br>−15620<br>302 374 | 49917<br>−15619<br>302 375 | 49918<br>−15618<br>302 376 | 49919<br>−15617<br>302 377 |

DECIMAL ←

 DECIMAL ←

OCTAL ←

 DECIMAL  −15872    BINARY  1100 0010    DECIMAL  49664    HEXADECIMAL  ② C2    OCTAL  302 000

## FIRST HEX DIGIT

| ⬡2 | −0 | −1 | −2 | −3 | −4 | −5 | −6 | −7 | −8 | −9 | −A | −B | −C | −D | −E | −F |
|---|---|---|---|---|---|---|---|---|---|---|---|---|---|---|---|---|
| **0−** | 49920<br>-15616<br>303 000 | 49921<br>-15615<br>303 001 | 49922<br>-15614<br>303 002 | 49923<br>-15613<br>303 003 | 49924<br>-15612<br>303 004 | 49925<br>-15611<br>303 005 | 49926<br>-15610<br>303 006 | 49927<br>-15609<br>303 007 | 49928<br>-15608<br>303 010 | 49929<br>-15607<br>303 011 | 49930<br>-15606<br>303 012 | 49931<br>-15605<br>303 013 | 49932<br>-15604<br>303 014 | 49933<br>-15603<br>303 015 | 49934<br>-15602<br>303 016 | 49935<br>-15601<br>303 017 |
| **1−** | 49936<br>-15600<br>303 020 | 49937<br>-15599<br>303 021 | 49938<br>-15598<br>303 022 | 49939<br>-15597<br>303 023 | 49940<br>-15596<br>303 024 | 49941<br>-15595<br>303 025 | 49942<br>-15594<br>303 026 | 49943<br>-15593<br>303 027 | 49944<br>-15592<br>303 030 | 49945<br>-15591<br>303 031 | 49946<br>-15590<br>303 032 | 49947<br>-15589<br>303 033 | 49948<br>-15588<br>303 034 | 49949<br>-15587<br>303 035 | 49950<br>-15586<br>303 036 | 49951<br>-15585<br>303 037 |
| **2−** | 49952<br>-15584<br>303 040 | 49953<br>-15583<br>303 041 | 49954<br>-15582<br>303 042 | 49955<br>-15581<br>303 043 | 49956<br>-15580<br>303 044 | 49957<br>-15579<br>303 045 | 49958<br>-15578<br>303 046 | 49959<br>-15577<br>303 047 | 49960<br>-15576<br>303 050 | 49961<br>-15575<br>303 051 | 49962<br>-15574<br>303 052 | 49963<br>-15573<br>303 053 | 49964<br>-15572<br>303 054 | 49965<br>-15571<br>303 055 | 49966<br>-15570<br>303 056 | 49967<br>-15569<br>303 057 |
| **3−** | 49968<br>-15568<br>303 060 | 49969<br>-15567<br>303 061 | 49970<br>-15566<br>303 062 | 49971<br>-15565<br>303 063 | 49972<br>-15564<br>303 064 | 49973<br>-15563<br>303 065 | 49974<br>-15562<br>303 066 | 49975<br>-15561<br>303 067 | 49976<br>-15560<br>303 070 | 49977<br>-15559<br>303 071 | 49978<br>-15558<br>303 072 | 49979<br>-15557<br>303 073 | 49980<br>-15556<br>303 074 | 49981<br>-15555<br>303 075 | 49982<br>-15554<br>303 076 | 49983<br>-15553<br>303 077 |
| **4−** | 49984<br>-15552<br>303 100 | 49985<br>-15551<br>303 101 | 49986<br>-15550<br>303 102 | 49987<br>-15549<br>303 103 | 49988<br>-15548<br>303 104 | 49989<br>-15547<br>303 105 | 49990<br>-15546<br>303 106 | 49991<br>-15545<br>303 107 | 49992<br>-15544<br>303 110 | 49993<br>-15543<br>303 111 | 49994<br>-15542<br>303 112 | 49995<br>-15541<br>303 113 | 49996<br>-15540<br>303 114 | 49997<br>-15539<br>303 115 | 49998<br>-15538<br>303 116 | 49999<br>-15537<br>303 117 |
| **5−** | 50000<br>-15536<br>303 120 | 50001<br>-15535<br>303 121 | 50002<br>-15534<br>303 122 | 50003<br>-15533<br>303 123 | 50004<br>-15532<br>303 124 | 50005<br>-15531<br>303 125 | 50006<br>-15530<br>303 126 | 50007<br>-15529<br>303 127 | 50008<br>-15528<br>303 130 | 50009<br>-15527<br>303 131 | 50010<br>-15526<br>303 132 | 50011<br>-15525<br>303 133 | 50012<br>-15524<br>303 134 | 50013<br>-15523<br>303 135 | 50014<br>-15522<br>303 136 | 50015<br>-15521<br>303 137 |
| **6−** | 50016<br>-15520<br>303 140 | 50017<br>-15519<br>303 141 | 50018<br>-15518<br>303 142 | 50019<br>-15517<br>303 143 | 50020<br>-15516<br>303 144 | 50021<br>-15515<br>303 145 | 50022<br>-15514<br>303 146 | 50023<br>-15513<br>303 147 | 50024<br>-15512<br>303 150 | 50025<br>-15511<br>303 151 | 50026<br>-15510<br>303 152 | 50027<br>-15509<br>303 153 | 50028<br>-15508<br>303 154 | 50029<br>-15507<br>303 155 | 50030<br>-15506<br>303 156 | 50031<br>-15505<br>303 157 |
| **7−** | 50032<br>-15504<br>303 160 | 50033<br>-15503<br>303 161 | 50034<br>-15502<br>303 162 | 50035<br>-15501<br>303 163 | 50036<br>-15500<br>303 164 | 50037<br>-15499<br>303 165 | 50038<br>-15498<br>303 166 | 50039<br>-15497<br>303 167 | 50040<br>-15496<br>303 170 | 50041<br>-15495<br>303 171 | 50042<br>-15494<br>303 172 | 50043<br>-15493<br>303 173 | 50044<br>-15492<br>303 174 | 50045<br>-15491<br>303 175 | 50046<br>-15490<br>303 176 | 50047<br>-15489<br>303 177 |
| **8−** | 50048<br>-15488<br>303 200 | 50049<br>-15487<br>303 201 | 50050<br>-15486<br>303 202 | 50051<br>-15485<br>303 203 | 50052<br>-15484<br>303 204 | 50053<br>-15483<br>303 205 | 50054<br>-15482<br>303 206 | 50055<br>-15481<br>303 207 | 50056<br>-15480<br>303 210 | 50057<br>-15479<br>303 211 | 50058<br>-15478<br>303 212 | 50059<br>-15477<br>303 213 | 50060<br>-15476<br>303 214 | 50061<br>-15475<br>303 215 | 50062<br>-15474<br>303 216 | 50063<br>-15473<br>303 217 |
| **9−** | 50064<br>-15472<br>303 220 | 50065<br>-15471<br>303 221 | 50066<br>-15470<br>303 222 | 50067<br>-15469<br>303 223 | 50068<br>-15468<br>303 224 | 50069<br>-15467<br>303 225 | 50070<br>-15466<br>303 226 | 50071<br>-15465<br>303 227 | 50072<br>-15464<br>303 230 | 50073<br>-15463<br>303 231 | 50074<br>-15462<br>303 232 | 50075<br>-15461<br>303 233 | 50076<br>-15460<br>303 234 | 50077<br>-15459<br>303 235 | 50078<br>-15458<br>303 236 | 50079<br>-15457<br>303 237 |
| **A−** | 50080<br>-15456<br>303 240 | 50081<br>-15455<br>303 241 | 50082<br>-15454<br>303 242 | 50083<br>-15453<br>303 243 | 50084<br>-15452<br>303 244 | 50085<br>-15451<br>303 245 | 50086<br>-15450<br>303 246 | 50087<br>-15449<br>303 247 | 50088<br>-15448<br>303 250 | 50089<br>-15447<br>303 251 | 50090<br>-15446<br>303 252 | 50091<br>-15445<br>303 253 | 50092<br>-15444<br>303 254 | 50093<br>-15443<br>303 255 | 50094<br>-15442<br>303 256 | 50095<br>-15441<br>303 257 |
| **B−** | 50096<br>-15440<br>303 260 | 50097<br>-15439<br>303 261 | 50098<br>-15438<br>303 262 | 50099<br>-15437<br>303 263 | 50100<br>-15436<br>303 264 | 50101<br>-15435<br>303 265 | 50102<br>-15434<br>303 266 | 50103<br>-15433<br>303 267 | 50104<br>-15432<br>303 270 | 50105<br>-15431<br>303 271 | 50106<br>-15430<br>303 272 | 50107<br>-15429<br>303 273 | 50108<br>-15428<br>303 274 | 50109<br>-15427<br>303 275 | 50110<br>-15426<br>303 276 | 50111<br>-15425<br>303 277 |
| **C−** | 50112<br>-15424<br>303 300 | 50113<br>-15423<br>303 301 | 50114<br>-15422<br>303 302 | 50115<br>-15421<br>303 303 | 50116<br>-15420<br>303 304 | 50117<br>-15419<br>303 305 | 50118<br>-15418<br>303 306 | 50119<br>-15417<br>303 307 | 50120<br>-15416<br>303 310 | 50121<br>-15415<br>303 311 | 50122<br>-15414<br>303 312 | 50123<br>-15413<br>303 313 | 50124<br>-15412<br>303 314 | 50125<br>-15411<br>303 315 | 50126<br>-15410<br>303 316 | 50127<br>-15409<br>303 317 |
| **D−** | 50128<br>-15408<br>303 320 | 50129<br>-15407<br>303 321 | 50130<br>-15406<br>303 322 | 50131<br>-15405<br>303 323 | 50132<br>-15404<br>303 324 | 50133<br>-15403<br>303 325 | 50134<br>-15402<br>303 326 | 50135<br>-15401<br>303 327 | 50136<br>-15400<br>303 330 | 50137<br>-15399<br>303 331 | 50138<br>-15398<br>303 332 | 50139<br>-15397<br>303 333 | 50140<br>-15396<br>303 334 | 50141<br>-15395<br>303 335 | 50142<br>-15394<br>303 336 | 50143<br>-15393<br>303 337 |
| **E−** | 50144<br>-15392<br>303 340 | 50145<br>-15391<br>303 341 | 50146<br>-15390<br>303 342 | 50147<br>-15389<br>303 343 | 50148<br>-15388<br>303 344 | 50149<br>-15387<br>303 345 | 50150<br>-15386<br>303 346 | 50151<br>-15385<br>303 347 | 50152<br>-15384<br>303 350 | 50153<br>-15383<br>303 351 | 50154<br>-15382<br>303 352 | 50155<br>-15381<br>303 353 | 50156<br>-15380<br>303 354 | 50157<br>-15379<br>303 355 | 50158<br>-15378<br>303 356 | 50159<br>-15377<br>303 357 |
| **F−** | 50160<br>-15376<br>303 360 | 50161<br>-15375<br>303 361 | 50162<br>-15374<br>303 362 | 50163<br>-15373<br>303 363 | 50164<br>-15372<br>303 364 | 50165<br>-15371<br>303 365 | 50166<br>-15370<br>303 366 | 50167<br>-15369<br>303 367 | 50168<br>-15368<br>303 370 | 50169<br>-15367<br>303 371 | 50170<br>-15366<br>303 372 | 50171<br>-15365<br>303 373 | 50172<br>-15364<br>303 374 | 50173<br>-15363<br>303 375 | 50174<br>-15362<br>303 376 | 50175<br>-15361<br>303 377 |

SECOND HEX DIGIT

DECIMAL  
◆ DECIMAL  
OCTAL

⬡ 2

## FIRST HEX DIGIT

| SECOND HEX DIGIT | −0 | −1 | −2 | −3 | −4 | −5 | −6 | −7 | −8 | −9 | −A | −B | −C | −D | −E | −F |
|---|---|---|---|---|---|---|---|---|---|---|---|---|---|---|---|---|
| **0−** | 50176<br>−15360<br>304 000 | 50177<br>−15359<br>304 001 | 50178<br>−15358<br>304 002 | 50179<br>−15357<br>304 003 | 50180<br>−15356<br>304 004 | 50181<br>−15355<br>304 005 | 50182<br>−15354<br>304 006 | 50183<br>−15353<br>304 007 | 50184<br>−15352<br>304 010 | 50185<br>−15351<br>304 011 | 50186<br>−15350<br>304 012 | 50187<br>−15349<br>304 013 | 50188<br>−15348<br>304 014 | 50189<br>−15347<br>304 015 | 50190<br>−15346<br>304 016 | 50191<br>−15345<br>304 017 |
| **1−** | 50192<br>−15344<br>304 020 | 50193<br>−15343<br>304 021 | 50194<br>−15342<br>304 022 | 50195<br>−15341<br>304 023 | 50196<br>−15340<br>304 024 | 50197<br>−15339<br>304 025 | 50198<br>−15338<br>304 026 | 50199<br>−15337<br>304 027 | 50200<br>−15336<br>304 030 | 50201<br>−15335<br>304 031 | 50202<br>−15334<br>304 032 | 50203<br>−15333<br>304 033 | 50204<br>−15332<br>304 034 | 50205<br>−15331<br>304 035 | 50206<br>−15330<br>304 036 | 50207<br>−15329<br>304 037 |
| **2−** | 50208<br>−15328<br>304 040 | 50209<br>−15327<br>304 041 | 50210<br>−15326<br>304 042 | 50211<br>−15325<br>304 043 | 50212<br>−15324<br>304 044 | 50213<br>−15323<br>304 045 | 50214<br>−15322<br>304 046 | 50215<br>−15321<br>304 047 | 50216<br>−15320<br>304 050 | 50217<br>−15319<br>304 051 | 50218<br>−15318<br>304 052 | 50219<br>−15317<br>304 053 | 50220<br>−15316<br>304 054 | 50221<br>−15315<br>304 055 | 50222<br>−15314<br>304 056 | 50223<br>−15313<br>304 057 |
| **3−** | 50224<br>−15312<br>304 060 | 50225<br>−15311<br>304 061 | 50226<br>−15310<br>304 062 | 50227<br>−15309<br>304 063 | 50228<br>−15308<br>304 064 | 50229<br>−15307<br>304 065 | 50230<br>−15306<br>304 066 | 50231<br>−15305<br>304 067 | 50232<br>−15304<br>304 070 | 50233<br>−15303<br>304 071 | 50234<br>−15302<br>304 072 | 50235<br>−15301<br>304 073 | 50236<br>−15300<br>304 074 | 50237<br>−15299<br>304 075 | 50238<br>−15298<br>304 076 | 50239<br>−15297<br>304 077 |
| **4−** | 50240<br>−15296<br>304 100 | 50241<br>−15295<br>304 101 | 50242<br>−15294<br>304 102 | 50243<br>−15293<br>304 103 | 50244<br>−15292<br>304 104 | 50245<br>−15291<br>304 105 | 50246<br>−15290<br>304 106 | 50247<br>−15289<br>304 107 | 50248<br>−15288<br>304 110 | 50249<br>−15287<br>304 111 | 50250<br>−15286<br>304 112 | 50251<br>−15285<br>304 113 | 50252<br>−15284<br>304 114 | 50253<br>−15283<br>304 115 | 50254<br>−15282<br>304 116 | 50255<br>−15281<br>304 117 |
| **5−** | 50256<br>−15280<br>304 120 | 50257<br>−15279<br>304 121 | 50258<br>−15278<br>304 122 | 50259<br>−15277<br>304 123 | 50260<br>−15276<br>304 124 | 50261<br>−15275<br>304 125 | 50262<br>−15274<br>304 126 | 50263<br>−15273<br>304 127 | 50264<br>−15272<br>304 130 | 50265<br>−15271<br>304 131 | 50266<br>−15270<br>304 132 | 50267<br>−15269<br>304 133 | 50268<br>−15268<br>304 134 | 50269<br>−15267<br>304 135 | 50270<br>−15266<br>304 136 | 50271<br>−15265<br>304 137 |
| **6−** | 50272<br>−15264<br>304 140 | 50273<br>−15263<br>304 141 | 50274<br>−15262<br>304 142 | 50275<br>−15261<br>304 143 | 50276<br>−15260<br>304 144 | 50277<br>−15259<br>304 145 | 50278<br>−15258<br>304 146 | 50279<br>−15257<br>304 147 | 50280<br>−15256<br>304 150 | 50281<br>−15255<br>304 151 | 50282<br>−15254<br>304 152 | 50283<br>−15253<br>304 153 | 50284<br>−15252<br>304 154 | 50285<br>−15251<br>304 155 | 50286<br>−15250<br>304 156 | 50287<br>−15249<br>304 157 |
| **7−** | 50288<br>−15248<br>304 160 | 50289<br>−15247<br>304 161 | 50290<br>−15246<br>304 162 | 50291<br>−15245<br>304 163 | 50292<br>−15244<br>304 164 | 50293<br>−15243<br>304 165 | 50294<br>−15242<br>304 166 | 50295<br>−15241<br>304 167 | 50296<br>−15240<br>304 170 | 50297<br>−15239<br>304 171 | 50298<br>−15238<br>304 172 | 50299<br>−15237<br>304 173 | 50300<br>−15236<br>304 174 | 50301<br>−15235<br>304 175 | 50302<br>−15234<br>304 176 | 50303<br>−15233<br>304 177 |
| **8−** | 50304<br>−15232<br>304 200 | 50305<br>−15231<br>304 201 | 50306<br>−15230<br>304 202 | 50307<br>−15229<br>304 203 | 50308<br>−15228<br>304 204 | 50309<br>−15227<br>304 205 | 50310<br>−15226<br>304 206 | 50311<br>−15225<br>304 207 | 50312<br>−15224<br>304 210 | 50313<br>−15223<br>304 211 | 50314<br>−15222<br>304 212 | 50315<br>−15221<br>304 213 | 50316<br>−15220<br>304 214 | 50317<br>−15219<br>304 215 | 50318<br>−15218<br>304 216 | 50319<br>−15217<br>304 217 |
| **9−** | 50320<br>−15216<br>304 220 | 50321<br>−15215<br>304 221 | 50322<br>−15214<br>304 222 | 50323<br>−15213<br>304 223 | 50324<br>−15212<br>304 224 | 50325<br>−15211<br>304 225 | 50326<br>−15210<br>304 226 | 50327<br>−15209<br>304 227 | 50328<br>−15208<br>304 230 | 50329<br>−15207<br>304 231 | 50330<br>−15206<br>304 232 | 50331<br>−15205<br>304 233 | 50332<br>−15204<br>304 234 | 50333<br>−15203<br>304 235 | 50334<br>−15202<br>304 236 | 50335<br>−15201<br>304 237 |
| **A−** | 50336<br>−15200<br>304 240 | 50337<br>−15199<br>304 241 | 50338<br>−15198<br>304 242 | 50339<br>−15197<br>304 243 | 50340<br>−15196<br>304 244 | 50341<br>−15195<br>304 245 | 50342<br>−15194<br>304 246 | 50343<br>−15193<br>304 247 | 50344<br>−15192<br>304 250 | 50345<br>−15191<br>304 251 | 50346<br>−15190<br>304 252 | 50347<br>−15189<br>304 253 | 50348<br>−15188<br>304 254 | 50349<br>−15187<br>304 255 | 50350<br>−15186<br>304 256 | 50351<br>−15185<br>304 257 |
| **B−** | 50352<br>−15184<br>304 260 | 50353<br>−15183<br>304 261 | 50354<br>−15182<br>304 262 | 50355<br>−15181<br>304 263 | 50356<br>−15180<br>304 264 | 50357<br>−15179<br>304 265 | 50358<br>−15178<br>304 266 | 50359<br>−15177<br>304 267 | 50360<br>−15176<br>304 270 | 50361<br>−15175<br>304 271 | 50362<br>−15174<br>304 272 | 50363<br>−15173<br>304 273 | 50364<br>−15172<br>304 274 | 50365<br>−15171<br>304 275 | 50366<br>−15170<br>304 276 | 50367<br>−15169<br>304 277 |
| **C−** | 50368<br>−15168<br>304 300 | 50369<br>−15167<br>304 301 | 50370<br>−15166<br>304 302 | 50371<br>−15165<br>304 303 | 50372<br>−15164<br>304 304 | 50373<br>−15163<br>304 305 | 50374<br>−15162<br>304 306 | 50375<br>−15161<br>304 307 | 50376<br>−15160<br>304 310 | 50377<br>−15159<br>304 311 | 50378<br>−15158<br>304 312 | 50379<br>−15157<br>304 313 | 50380<br>−15156<br>304 314 | 50381<br>−15155<br>304 315 | 50382<br>−15154<br>304 316 | 50383<br>−15153<br>304 317 |
| **D−** | 50384<br>−15152<br>304 320 | 50385<br>−15151<br>304 321 | 50386<br>−15150<br>304 322 | 50387<br>−15149<br>304 323 | 50388<br>−15148<br>304 324 | 50389<br>−15147<br>304 325 | 50390<br>−15146<br>304 326 | 50391<br>−15145<br>304 327 | 50392<br>−15144<br>304 330 | 50393<br>−15143<br>304 331 | 50394<br>−15142<br>304 332 | 50395<br>−15141<br>304 333 | 50396<br>−15140<br>304 334 | 50397<br>−15139<br>304 335 | 50398<br>−15138<br>304 336 | 50399<br>−15137<br>304 337 |
| **E−** | 50400<br>−15136<br>304 340 | 50401<br>−15135<br>304 341 | 50402<br>−15134<br>304 342 | 50403<br>−15133<br>304 343 | 50404<br>−15132<br>304 344 | 50405<br>−15131<br>304 345 | 50406<br>−15130<br>304 346 | 50407<br>−15129<br>304 347 | 50408<br>−15128<br>304 350 | 50409<br>−15127<br>304 351 | 50410<br>−15126<br>304 352 | 50411<br>−15125<br>304 353 | 50412<br>−15124<br>304 354 | 50413<br>−15123<br>304 355 | 50414<br>−15122<br>304 356 | 50415<br>−15121<br>304 357 |
| **F−** | 50416<br>−15120<br>304 360 | 50417<br>−15119<br>304 361 | 50418<br>−15118<br>304 362 | 50419<br>−15117<br>304 363 | 50420<br>−15116<br>304 364 | 50421<br>−15115<br>304 365 | 50422<br>−15114<br>304 366 | 50423<br>−15113<br>304 367 | 50424<br>−15112<br>304 370 | 50425<br>−15111<br>304 371 | 50426<br>−15110<br>304 372 | 50427<br>−15109<br>304 373 | 50428<br>−15108<br>304 374 | 50429<br>−15107<br>304 375 | 50430<br>−15106<br>304 376 | 50431<br>−15105<br>304 377 |

**DECIMAL** ← (2−)

⌘ **DECIMAL** ← (4−)

← (5−)

**OCTAL** ← (8−)

---

 **DECIMAL** [ −15360 ]  **BINARY** [ 1100 0100 ]  **DECIMAL** [ 50176 ]  **HEXADECIMAL** ⬡ C4  **OCTAL** [ 304 000 ]

FOURTH HEX DIGIT →  ← THIRD HEX DIGIT

🍎 DECIMAL [ -15104 ]    BINARY [ 1100 0101 ]    DECIMAL [ 50432 ]    HEXADECIMAL (C5) OCTAL [ 305 000 ]

FOURTH HEX DIGIT → ← THIRD HEX DIGIT

**SECOND HEX DIGIT** (rows) × **FIRST HEX DIGIT** (columns). Each cell: decimal (top) / negative decimal (middle) / octal (bottom).

| (2) | −0 | −1 | −2 | −3 | −4 | −5 | −6 | −7 | −8 | −9 | −A | −B | −C | −D | −E | −F |
|---|---|---|---|---|---|---|---|---|---|---|---|---|---|---|---|---|
| 0− | 50432<br>-15104<br>305 000 | 50433<br>-15103<br>305 001 | 50434<br>-15102<br>305 002 | 50435<br>-15101<br>305 003 | 50436<br>-15100<br>305 004 | 50437<br>-15099<br>305 005 | 50438<br>-15098<br>305 006 | 50439<br>-15097<br>305 007 | 50440<br>-15096<br>305 010 | 50441<br>-15095<br>305 011 | 50442<br>-15094<br>305 012 | 50443<br>-15093<br>305 013 | 50444<br>-15092<br>305 014 | 50445<br>-15091<br>305 015 | 50446<br>-15090<br>305 016 | 50447<br>-15089<br>305 017 |
| 1− | 50448<br>-15088<br>305 020 | 50449<br>-15087<br>305 021 | 50450<br>-15086<br>305 022 | 50451<br>-15085<br>305 023 | 50452<br>-15084<br>305 024 | 50453<br>-15083<br>305 025 | 50454<br>-15082<br>305 026 | 50455<br>-15081<br>305 027 | 50456<br>-15080<br>305 030 | 50457<br>-15079<br>305 031 | 50458<br>-15078<br>305 032 | 50459<br>-15077<br>305 033 | 50460<br>-15076<br>305 034 | 50461<br>-15075<br>305 035 | 50462<br>-15074<br>305 036 | 50463<br>-15073<br>305 037 |
| 2− | 50464<br>-15072<br>305 040 | 50465<br>-15071<br>305 041 | 50466<br>-15070<br>305 042 | 50467<br>-15069<br>305 043 | 50468<br>-15068<br>305 044 | 50469<br>-15067<br>305 045 | 50470<br>-15066<br>305 046 | 50471<br>-15065<br>305 047 | 50472<br>-15064<br>305 050 | 50473<br>-15063<br>305 051 | 50474<br>-15062<br>305 052 | 50475<br>-15061<br>305 053 | 50476<br>-15060<br>305 054 | 50477<br>-15059<br>305 055 | 50478<br>-15058<br>305 056 | 50479<br>-15057<br>305 057 |
| 3− | 50480<br>-15056<br>305 060 | 50481<br>-15055<br>305 061 | 50482<br>-15054<br>305 062 | 50483<br>-15053<br>305 063 | 50484<br>-15052<br>305 064 | 50485<br>-15051<br>305 065 | 50486<br>-15050<br>305 066 | 50487<br>-15049<br>305 067 | 50488<br>-15048<br>305 070 | 50489<br>-15047<br>305 071 | 50490<br>-15046<br>305 072 | 50491<br>-15045<br>305 073 | 50492<br>-15044<br>305 074 | 50493<br>-15043<br>305 075 | 50494<br>-15042<br>305 076 | 50495<br>-15041<br>305 077 |
| 4− | 50496<br>-15040<br>305 100 | 50497<br>-15039<br>305 101 | 50498<br>-15038<br>305 102 | 50499<br>-15037<br>305 103 | 50500<br>-15036<br>305 104 | 50501<br>-15035<br>305 105 | 50502<br>-15034<br>305 106 | 50503<br>-15033<br>305 107 | 50504<br>-15032<br>305 110 | 50505<br>-15031<br>305 111 | 50506<br>-15030<br>305 112 | 50507<br>-15029<br>305 113 | 50508<br>-15028<br>305 114 | 50509<br>-15027<br>305 115 | 50510<br>-15026<br>305 116 | 50511<br>-15025<br>305 117 |
| 5− | 50512<br>-15024<br>305 120 | 50513<br>-15023<br>305 121 | 50514<br>-15022<br>305 122 | 50515<br>-15021<br>305 123 | 50516<br>-15020<br>305 124 | 50517<br>-15019<br>305 125 | 50518<br>-15018<br>305 126 | 50519<br>-15017<br>305 127 | 50520<br>-15016<br>305 130 | 50521<br>-15015<br>305 131 | 50522<br>-15014<br>305 132 | 50523<br>-15013<br>305 133 | 50524<br>-15012<br>305 134 | 50525<br>-15011<br>305 135 | 50526<br>-15010<br>305 136 | 50527<br>-15009<br>305 137 |
| 6− | 50528<br>-15008<br>305 140 | 50529<br>-15007<br>305 141 | 50530<br>-15006<br>305 142 | 50531<br>-15005<br>305 143 | 50532<br>-15004<br>305 144 | 50533<br>-15003<br>305 145 | 50534<br>-15002<br>305 146 | 50535<br>-15001<br>305 147 | 50536<br>-15000<br>305 150 | 50537<br>-14999<br>305 151 | 50538<br>-14998<br>305 152 | 50539<br>-14997<br>305 153 | 50540<br>-14996<br>305 154 | 50541<br>-14995<br>305 155 | 50542<br>-14994<br>305 156 | 50543<br>-14993<br>305 157 |
| 7− | 50544<br>-14992<br>305 160 | 50545<br>-14991<br>305 161 | 50546<br>-14990<br>305 162 | 50547<br>-14989<br>305 163 | 50548<br>-14988<br>305 164 | 50549<br>-14987<br>305 165 | 50550<br>-14986<br>305 166 | 50551<br>-14985<br>305 167 | 50552<br>-14984<br>305 170 | 50553<br>-14983<br>305 171 | 50554<br>-14982<br>305 172 | 50555<br>-14981<br>305 173 | 50556<br>-14980<br>305 174 | 50557<br>-14979<br>305 175 | 50558<br>-14978<br>305 176 | 50559<br>-14977<br>305 177 |
| 8− | 50560<br>-14976<br>305 200 | 50561<br>-14975<br>305 201 | 50562<br>-14974<br>305 202 | 50563<br>-14973<br>305 203 | 50564<br>-14972<br>305 204 | 50565<br>-14971<br>305 205 | 50566<br>-14970<br>305 206 | 50567<br>-14969<br>305 207 | 50568<br>-14968<br>305 210 | 50569<br>-14967<br>305 211 | 50570<br>-14966<br>305 212 | 50571<br>-14965<br>305 213 | 50572<br>-14964<br>305 214 | 50573<br>-14963<br>305 215 | 50574<br>-14962<br>305 216 | 50575<br>-14961<br>305 217 |
| 9− | 50576<br>-14960<br>305 220 | 50577<br>-14959<br>305 221 | 50578<br>-14958<br>305 222 | 50579<br>-14957<br>305 223 | 50580<br>-14956<br>305 224 | 50581<br>-14955<br>305 225 | 50582<br>-14954<br>305 226 | 50583<br>-14953<br>305 227 | 50584<br>-14952<br>305 230 | 50585<br>-14951<br>305 231 | 50586<br>-14950<br>305 232 | 50587<br>-14949<br>305 233 | 50588<br>-14948<br>305 234 | 50589<br>-14947<br>305 235 | 50590<br>-14946<br>305 236 | 50591<br>-14945<br>305 237 |
| A− | 50592<br>-14944<br>305 240 | 50593<br>-14943<br>305 241 | 50594<br>-14942<br>305 242 | 50595<br>-14941<br>305 243 | 50596<br>-14940<br>305 244 | 50597<br>-14939<br>305 245 | 50598<br>-14938<br>305 246 | 50599<br>-14937<br>305 247 | 50600<br>-14936<br>305 250 | 50601<br>-14935<br>305 251 | 50602<br>-14934<br>305 252 | 50603<br>-14933<br>305 253 | 50604<br>-14932<br>305 254 | 50605<br>-14931<br>305 255 | 50606<br>-14930<br>305 256 | 50607<br>-14929<br>305 257 |
| B− | 50608<br>-14928<br>305 260 | 50609<br>-14927<br>305 261 | 50610<br>-14926<br>305 262 | 50611<br>-14925<br>305 263 | 50612<br>-14924<br>305 264 | 50613<br>-14923<br>305 265 | 50614<br>-14922<br>305 266 | 50615<br>-14921<br>305 267 | 50616<br>-14920<br>305 270 | 50617<br>-14919<br>305 271 | 50618<br>-14918<br>305 272 | 50619<br>-14917<br>305 273 | 50620<br>-14916<br>305 274 | 50621<br>-14915<br>305 275 | 50622<br>-14914<br>305 276 | 50623<br>-14913<br>305 277 |
| C− | 50624<br>-14912<br>305 300 | 50625<br>-14911<br>305 301 | 50626<br>-14910<br>305 302 | 50627<br>-14909<br>305 303 | 50628<br>-14908<br>305 304 | 50629<br>-14907<br>305 305 | 50630<br>-14906<br>305 306 | 50631<br>-14905<br>305 307 | 50632<br>-14904<br>305 310 | 50633<br>-14903<br>305 311 | 50634<br>-14902<br>305 312 | 50635<br>-14901<br>305 313 | 50636<br>-14900<br>305 314 | 50637<br>-14899<br>305 315 | 50638<br>-14898<br>305 316 | 50639<br>-14897<br>305 317 |
| D− | 50640<br>-14896<br>305 320 | 50641<br>-14895<br>305 321 | 50642<br>-14894<br>305 322 | 50643<br>-14893<br>305 323 | 50644<br>-14892<br>305 324 | 50645<br>-14891<br>305 325 | 50646<br>-14890<br>305 326 | 50647<br>-14889<br>305 327 | 50648<br>-14888<br>305 330 | 50649<br>-14887<br>305 331 | 50650<br>-14886<br>305 332 | 50651<br>-14885<br>305 333 | 50652<br>-14884<br>305 334 | 50653<br>-14883<br>305 335 | 50654<br>-14882<br>305 336 | 50655<br>-14881<br>305 337 |
| E− | 50656<br>-14880<br>305 340 | 50657<br>-14879<br>305 341 | 50658<br>-14878<br>305 342 | 50659<br>-14877<br>305 343 | 50660<br>-14876<br>305 344 | 50661<br>-14875<br>305 345 | 50662<br>-14874<br>305 346 | 50663<br>-14873<br>305 347 | 50664<br>-14872<br>305 350 | 50665<br>-14871<br>305 351 | 50666<br>-14870<br>305 352 | 50667<br>-14869<br>305 353 | 50668<br>-14868<br>305 354 | 50669<br>-14867<br>305 355 | 50670<br>-14866<br>305 356 | 50671<br>-14865<br>305 357 |
| F− | 50672<br>-14864<br>305 360 | 50673<br>-14863<br>305 361 | 50674<br>-14862<br>305 362 | 50675<br>-14861<br>305 363 | 50676<br>-14860<br>305 364 | 50677<br>-14859<br>305 365 | 50678<br>-14858<br>305 366 | 50679<br>-14857<br>305 367 | 50680<br>-14856<br>305 370 | 50681<br>-14855<br>305 371 | 50682<br>-14854<br>305 372 | 50683<br>-14853<br>305 373 | 50684<br>-14852<br>305 374 | 50685<br>-14851<br>305 375 | 50686<br>-14850<br>305 376 | 50687<br>-14849<br>305 377 |

DECIMAL — 🍎 DECIMAL — OCTAL

| SECOND HEX DIGIT | -0 | -1 | -2 | -3 | -4 | -5 | -6 | -7 | -8 | -9 | -A | -B | -C | -D | -E | -F |
|---|---|---|---|---|---|---|---|---|---|---|---|---|---|---|---|---|
| 0- | 50688<br>-14848<br>306 000 | 50689<br>-14847<br>306 001 | 50690<br>-14846<br>306 002 | 50691<br>-14845<br>306 003 | 50692<br>-14844<br>306 004 | 50693<br>-14843<br>306 005 | 50694<br>-14842<br>306 006 | 50695<br>-14841<br>306 007 | 50696<br>-14840<br>306 010 | 50697<br>-14839<br>306 011 | 50698<br>-14838<br>306 012 | 50699<br>-14837<br>306 013 | 50700<br>-14836<br>306 014 | 50701<br>-14835<br>306 015 | 50702<br>-14834<br>306 016 | 50703<br>-14833<br>306 017 |
| 1- | 50704<br>-14832<br>306 020 | 50705<br>-14831<br>306 021 | 50706<br>-14830<br>306 022 | 50707<br>-14829<br>306 023 | 50708<br>-14828<br>306 024 | 50709<br>-14827<br>306 025 | 50710<br>-14826<br>306 026 | 50711<br>-14825<br>306 027 | 50712<br>-14824<br>306 030 | 50713<br>-14823<br>306 031 | 50714<br>-14822<br>306 032 | 50715<br>-14821<br>306 033 | 50716<br>-14820<br>306 034 | 50717<br>-14819<br>306 035 | 50718<br>-14818<br>306 036 | 50719<br>-14817<br>306 037 |
| 2- | 50720<br>-14816<br>306 040 | 50721<br>-14815<br>306 041 | 50722<br>-14814<br>306 042 | 50723<br>-14813<br>306 043 | 50724<br>-14812<br>306 044 | 50725<br>-14811<br>306 045 | 50726<br>-14810<br>306 046 | 50727<br>-14809<br>306 047 | 50728<br>-14808<br>306 050 | 50729<br>-14807<br>306 051 | 50730<br>-14806<br>306 052 | 50731<br>-14805<br>306 053 | 50732<br>-14804<br>306 054 | 50733<br>-14803<br>306 055 | 50734<br>-14802<br>306 056 | 50735<br>-14801<br>306 057 |
| 3- | 50736<br>-14800<br>306 060 | 50737<br>-14799<br>306 061 | 50738<br>-14798<br>306 062 | 50739<br>-14797<br>306 063 | 50740<br>-14796<br>306 064 | 50741<br>-14795<br>306 065 | 50742<br>-14794<br>306 066 | 50743<br>-14793<br>306 067 | 50744<br>-14792<br>306 070 | 50745<br>-14791<br>306 071 | 50746<br>-14790<br>306 072 | 50747<br>-14789<br>306 073 | 50748<br>-14788<br>306 074 | 50749<br>-14787<br>306 075 | 50750<br>-14786<br>306 076 | 50751<br>-14785<br>306 077 |
| 4- | 50752<br>-14784<br>306 100 | 50753<br>-14783<br>306 101 | 50754<br>-14782<br>306 102 | 50755<br>-14781<br>306 103 | 50756<br>-14780<br>306 104 | 50757<br>-14779<br>306 105 | 50758<br>-14778<br>306 106 | 50759<br>-14777<br>306 107 | 50760<br>-14776<br>306 110 | 50761<br>-14775<br>306 111 | 50762<br>-14774<br>306 112 | 50763<br>-14773<br>306 113 | 50764<br>-14772<br>306 114 | 50765<br>-14771<br>306 115 | 50766<br>-14770<br>306 116 | 50767<br>-14769<br>306 117 |
| 5- | 50768<br>-14768<br>306 120 | 50769<br>-14767<br>306 121 | 50770<br>-14766<br>306 122 | 50771<br>-14765<br>306 123 | 50772<br>-14764<br>306 124 | 50773<br>-14763<br>306 125 | 50774<br>-14762<br>306 126 | 50775<br>-14761<br>306 127 | 50776<br>-14760<br>306 130 | 50777<br>-14759<br>306 131 | 50778<br>-14758<br>306 132 | 50779<br>-14757<br>306 133 | 50780<br>-14756<br>306 134 | 50781<br>-14755<br>306 135 | 50782<br>-14754<br>306 136 | 50783<br>-14753<br>306 137 |
| 6- | 50784<br>-14752<br>306 140 | 50785<br>-14751<br>306 141 | 50786<br>-14750<br>306 142 | 50787<br>-14749<br>306 143 | 50788<br>-14748<br>306 144 | 50789<br>-14747<br>306 145 | 50790<br>-14746<br>306 146 | 50791<br>-14745<br>306 147 | 50792<br>-14744<br>306 150 | 50793<br>-14743<br>306 151 | 50794<br>-14742<br>306 152 | 50795<br>-14741<br>306 153 | 50796<br>-14740<br>306 154 | 50797<br>-14739<br>306 155 | 50798<br>-14738<br>306 156 | 50799<br>-14737<br>306 157 |
| 7- | 50800<br>-14736<br>306 160 | 50801<br>-14735<br>306 161 | 50802<br>-14734<br>306 162 | 50803<br>-14733<br>306 163 | 50804<br>-14732<br>306 164 | 50805<br>-14731<br>306 165 | 50806<br>-14730<br>306 166 | 50807<br>-14729<br>306 167 | 50808<br>-14728<br>306 170 | 50809<br>-14727<br>306 171 | 50810<br>-14726<br>306 172 | 50811<br>-14725<br>306 173 | 50812<br>-14724<br>306 174 | 50813<br>-14723<br>306 175 | 50814<br>-14722<br>306 176 | 50815<br>-14721<br>306 177 |
| 8- | 50816<br>-14720<br>306 200 | 50817<br>-14719<br>306 201 | 50818<br>-14718<br>306 202 | 50819<br>-14717<br>306 203 | 50820<br>-14716<br>306 204 | 50821<br>-14715<br>306 205 | 50822<br>-14714<br>306 206 | 50823<br>-14713<br>306 207 | 50824<br>-14712<br>306 210 | 50825<br>-14711<br>306 211 | 50826<br>-14710<br>306 212 | 50827<br>-14709<br>306 213 | 50828<br>-14708<br>306 214 | 50829<br>-14707<br>306 215 | 50830<br>-14706<br>306 216 | 50831<br>-14705<br>306 217 |
| 9- | 50832<br>-14704<br>306 220 | 50833<br>-14703<br>306 221 | 50834<br>-14702<br>306 222 | 50835<br>-14701<br>306 223 | 50836<br>-14700<br>306 224 | 50837<br>-14699<br>306 225 | 50838<br>-14698<br>306 226 | 50839<br>-14697<br>306 227 | 50840<br>-14696<br>306 230 | 50841<br>-14695<br>306 231 | 50842<br>-14694<br>306 232 | 50843<br>-14693<br>306 233 | 50844<br>-14692<br>306 234 | 50845<br>-14691<br>306 235 | 50846<br>-14690<br>306 236 | 50847<br>-14689<br>306 237 |
| A- | 50848<br>-14688<br>306 240 | 50849<br>-14687<br>306 241 | 50850<br>-14686<br>306 242 | 50851<br>-14685<br>306 243 | 50852<br>-14684<br>306 244 | 50853<br>-14683<br>306 245 | 50854<br>-14682<br>306 246 | 50855<br>-14681<br>306 247 | 50856<br>-14680<br>306 250 | 50857<br>-14679<br>306 251 | 50858<br>-14678<br>306 252 | 50859<br>-14677<br>306 253 | 50860<br>-14676<br>306 254 | 50861<br>-14675<br>306 255 | 50862<br>-14674<br>306 256 | 50863<br>-14673<br>306 257 |
| B- | 50864<br>-14672<br>306 260 | 50865<br>-14671<br>306 261 | 50866<br>-14670<br>306 262 | 50867<br>-14669<br>306 263 | 50868<br>-14668<br>306 264 | 50869<br>-14667<br>306 265 | 50870<br>-14666<br>306 266 | 50871<br>-14665<br>306 267 | 50872<br>-14664<br>306 270 | 50873<br>-14663<br>306 271 | 50874<br>-14662<br>306 272 | 50875<br>-14661<br>306 273 | 50876<br>-14660<br>306 274 | 50877<br>-14659<br>306 275 | 50878<br>-14658<br>306 276 | 50879<br>-14657<br>306 277 |
| C- | 50880<br>-14656<br>306 300 | 50881<br>-14655<br>306 301 | 50882<br>-14654<br>306 302 | 50883<br>-14653<br>306 303 | 50884<br>-14652<br>306 304 | 50885<br>-14651<br>306 305 | 50886<br>-14650<br>306 306 | 50887<br>-14649<br>306 307 | 50888<br>-14648<br>306 310 | 50889<br>-14647<br>306 311 | 50890<br>-14646<br>306 312 | 50891<br>-14645<br>306 313 | 50892<br>-14644<br>306 314 | 50893<br>-14643<br>306 315 | 50894<br>-14642<br>306 316 | 50895<br>-14641<br>306 317 |
| D- | 50896<br>-14640<br>306 320 | 50897<br>-14639<br>306 321 | 50898<br>-14638<br>306 322 | 50899<br>-14637<br>306 323 | 50900<br>-14636<br>306 324 | 50901<br>-14635<br>306 325 | 50902<br>-14634<br>306 326 | 50903<br>-14633<br>306 327 | 50904<br>-14632<br>306 330 | 50905<br>-14631<br>306 331 | 50906<br>-14630<br>306 332 | 50907<br>-14629<br>306 333 | 50908<br>-14628<br>306 334 | 50909<br>-14627<br>306 335 | 50910<br>-14626<br>306 336 | 50911<br>-14625<br>306 337 |
| E- | 50912<br>-14624<br>306 340 | 50913<br>-14623<br>306 341 | 50914<br>-14622<br>306 342 | 50915<br>-14621<br>306 343 | 50916<br>-14620<br>306 344 | 50917<br>-14619<br>306 345 | 50918<br>-14618<br>306 346 | 50919<br>-14617<br>306 347 | 50920<br>-14616<br>306 350 | 50921<br>-14615<br>306 351 | 50922<br>-14614<br>306 352 | 50923<br>-14613<br>306 353 | 50924<br>-14612<br>306 354 | 50925<br>-14611<br>306 355 | 50926<br>-14610<br>306 356 | 50927<br>-14609<br>306 357 |
| F- | 50928<br>-14608<br>306 360 | 50929<br>-14607<br>306 361 | 50930<br>-14606<br>306 362 | 50931<br>-14605<br>306 363 | 50932<br>-14604<br>306 364 | 50933<br>-14603<br>306 365 | 50934<br>-14602<br>306 366 | 50935<br>-14601<br>306 367 | 50936<br>-14600<br>306 370 | 50937<br>-14599<br>306 371 | 50938<br>-14598<br>306 372 | 50939<br>-14597<br>306 373 | 50940<br>-14596<br>306 374 | 50941<br>-14595<br>306 375 | 50942<br>-14594<br>306 376 | 50943<br>-14593<br>306 377 |

DECIMAL

 DECIMAL

OCTAL

 DECIMAL  -14848   BINARY  1100 0110   DECIMAL  50688   HEXADECIMAL  ⬡ C6   OCTAL  306 000

FOURTH HEX DIGIT →   ← THIRD HEX DIGIT

DECIMAL -14592    BINARY 1100 0111    DECIMAL 50944    HEXADECIMAL C7    OCTAL 307 000

FOURTH HEX DIGIT → | ← THIRD HEX DIGIT

| 2 | FIRST HEX DIGIT | | | | | | | | | | | | | | | |
|---|---|---|---|---|---|---|---|---|---|---|---|---|---|---|---|---|
| SECOND HEX DIGIT | −0 | −1 | −2 | −3 | −4 | −5 | −6 | −7 | −8 | −9 | −A | −B | −C | −D | −E | −F |
| 0− | 50944<br>−14592<br>307 000 | 50945<br>−14591<br>307 001 | 50946<br>−14590<br>307 002 | 50947<br>−14589<br>307 003 | 50948<br>−14588<br>307 004 | 50949<br>−14587<br>307 005 | 50950<br>−14586<br>307 006 | 50951<br>−14585<br>307 007 | 50952<br>−14584<br>307 010 | 50953<br>−14583<br>307 011 | 50954<br>−14582<br>307 012 | 50955<br>−14581<br>307 013 | 50956<br>−14580<br>307 014 | 50957<br>−14579<br>307 015 | 50958<br>−14578<br>307 016 | 50959<br>−14577<br>307 017 |
| 1− | 50960<br>−14576<br>307 020 | 50961<br>−14575<br>307 021 | 50962<br>−14574<br>307 022 | 50963<br>−14573<br>307 023 | 50964<br>−14572<br>307 024 | 50965<br>−14571<br>307 025 | 50966<br>−14570<br>307 026 | 50967<br>−14569<br>307 027 | 50968<br>−14568<br>307 030 | 50969<br>−14567<br>307 031 | 50970<br>−14566<br>307 032 | 50971<br>−14565<br>307 033 | 50972<br>−14564<br>307 034 | 50973<br>−14563<br>307 035 | 50974<br>−14562<br>307 036 | 50975<br>−14561<br>307 037 |
| 2− | 50976<br>−14560<br>307 040 | 50977<br>−14559<br>307 041 | 50978<br>−14558<br>307 042 | 50979<br>−14557<br>307 043 | 50980<br>−14556<br>307 044 | 50981<br>−14555<br>307 045 | 50982<br>−14554<br>307 046 | 50983<br>−14553<br>307 047 | 50984<br>−14552<br>307 050 | 50985<br>−14551<br>307 051 | 50986<br>−14550<br>307 052 | 50987<br>−14549<br>307 053 | 50988<br>−14548<br>307 054 | 50989<br>−14547<br>307 055 | 50990<br>−14546<br>307 056 | 50991<br>−14545<br>307 057 |
| 3− | 50992<br>−14544<br>307 060 | 50993<br>−14543<br>307 061 | 50994<br>−14542<br>307 062 | 50995<br>−14541<br>307 063 | 50996<br>−14540<br>307 064 | 50997<br>−14539<br>307 065 | 50998<br>−14538<br>307 066 | 50999<br>−14537<br>307 067 | 51000<br>−14536<br>307 070 | 51001<br>−14535<br>307 071 | 51002<br>−14534<br>307 072 | 51003<br>−14533<br>307 073 | 51004<br>−14532<br>307 074 | 51005<br>−14531<br>307 075 | 51006<br>−14530<br>307 076 | 51007<br>−14529<br>307 077 |
| 4− | 51008<br>−14528<br>307 100 | 51009<br>−14527<br>307 101 | 51010<br>−14526<br>307 102 | 51011<br>−14525<br>307 103 | 51012<br>−14524<br>307 104 | 51013<br>−14523<br>307 105 | 51014<br>−14522<br>307 106 | 51015<br>−14521<br>307 107 | 51016<br>−14520<br>307 110 | 51017<br>−14519<br>307 111 | 51018<br>−14518<br>307 112 | 51019<br>−14517<br>307 113 | 51020<br>−14516<br>307 114 | 51021<br>−14515<br>307 115 | 51022<br>−14514<br>307 116 | 51023<br>−14513<br>307 117 |
| 5− | 51024<br>−14512<br>307 120 | 51025<br>−14511<br>307 121 | 51026<br>−14510<br>307 122 | 51027<br>−14509<br>307 123 | 51028<br>−14508<br>307 124 | 51029<br>−14507<br>307 125 | 51030<br>−14506<br>307 126 | 51031<br>−14505<br>307 127 | 51032<br>−14504<br>307 130 | 51033<br>−14503<br>307 131 | 51034<br>−14502<br>307 132 | 51035<br>−14501<br>307 133 | 51036<br>−14500<br>307 134 | 51037<br>−14499<br>307 135 | 51038<br>−14498<br>307 136 | 51039<br>−14497<br>307 137 |
| 6− | 51040<br>−14496<br>307 140 | 51041<br>−14495<br>307 141 | 51042<br>−14494<br>307 142 | 51043<br>−14493<br>307 143 | 51044<br>−14492<br>307 144 | 51045<br>−14491<br>307 145 | 51046<br>−14490<br>307 146 | 51047<br>−14489<br>307 147 | 51048<br>−14488<br>307 150 | 51049<br>−14487<br>307 151 | 51050<br>−14486<br>307 152 | 51051<br>−14485<br>307 153 | 51052<br>−14484<br>307 154 | 51053<br>−14483<br>307 155 | 51054<br>−14482<br>307 156 | 51055<br>−14481<br>307 157 |
| 7− | 51056<br>−14480<br>307 160 | 51057<br>−14479<br>307 161 | 51058<br>−14478<br>307 162 | 51059<br>−14477<br>307 163 | 51060<br>−14476<br>307 164 | 51061<br>−14475<br>307 165 | 51062<br>−14474<br>307 166 | 51063<br>−14473<br>307 167 | 51064<br>−14472<br>307 170 | 51065<br>−14471<br>307 171 | 51066<br>−14470<br>307 172 | 51067<br>−14469<br>307 173 | 51068<br>−14468<br>307 174 | 51069<br>−14467<br>307 175 | 51070<br>−14466<br>307 176 | 51071<br>−14465<br>307 177 |
| 8− | 51072<br>−14464<br>307 200 | 51073<br>−14463<br>307 201 | 51074<br>−14462<br>307 202 | 51075<br>−14461<br>307 203 | 51076<br>−14460<br>307 204 | 51077<br>−14459<br>307 205 | 51078<br>−14458<br>307 206 | 51079<br>−14457<br>307 207 | 51080<br>−14456<br>307 210 | 51081<br>−14455<br>307 211 | 51082<br>−14454<br>307 212 | 51083<br>−14453<br>307 213 | 51084<br>−14452<br>307 214 | 51085<br>−14451<br>307 215 | 51086<br>−14450<br>307 216 | 51087<br>−14449<br>307 217 |
| 9− | 51088<br>−14448<br>307 220 | 51089<br>−14447<br>307 221 | 51090<br>−14446<br>307 222 | 51091<br>−14445<br>307 223 | 51092<br>−14444<br>307 224 | 51093<br>−14443<br>307 225 | 51094<br>−14442<br>307 226 | 51095<br>−14441<br>307 227 | 51096<br>−14440<br>307 230 | 51097<br>−14439<br>307 231 | 51098<br>−14438<br>307 232 | 51099<br>−14437<br>307 233 | 51100<br>−14436<br>307 234 | 51101<br>−14435<br>307 235 | 51102<br>−14434<br>307 236 | 51103<br>−14433<br>307 237 |
| A− | 51104<br>−14432<br>307 240 | 51105<br>−14431<br>307 241 | 51106<br>−14430<br>307 242 | 51107<br>−14429<br>307 243 | 51108<br>−14428<br>307 244 | 51109<br>−14427<br>307 245 | 51110<br>−14426<br>307 246 | 51111<br>−14425<br>307 247 | 51112<br>−14424<br>307 250 | 51113<br>−14423<br>307 251 | 51114<br>−14422<br>307 252 | 51115<br>−14421<br>307 253 | 51116<br>−14420<br>307 254 | 51117<br>−14419<br>307 255 | 51118<br>−14418<br>307 256 | 51119<br>−14417<br>307 257 |
| B− | 51120<br>−14416<br>307 260 | 51121<br>−14415<br>307 261 | 51122<br>−14414<br>307 262 | 51123<br>−14413<br>307 263 | 51124<br>−14412<br>307 264 | 51125<br>−14411<br>307 265 | 51126<br>−14410<br>307 266 | 51127<br>−14409<br>307 267 | 51128<br>−14408<br>307 270 | 51129<br>−14407<br>307 271 | 51130<br>−14406<br>307 272 | 51131<br>−14405<br>307 273 | 51132<br>−14404<br>307 274 | 51133<br>−14403<br>307 275 | 51134<br>−14402<br>307 276 | 51135<br>−14401<br>307 277 |
| C− | 51136<br>−14400<br>307 300 | 51137<br>−14399<br>307 301 | 51138<br>−14398<br>307 302 | 51139<br>−14397<br>307 303 | 51140<br>−14396<br>307 304 | 51141<br>−14395<br>307 305 | 51142<br>−14394<br>307 306 | 51143<br>−14393<br>307 307 | 51144<br>−14392<br>307 310 | 51145<br>−14391<br>307 311 | 51146<br>−14390<br>307 312 | 51147<br>−14389<br>307 313 | 51148<br>−14388<br>307 314 | 51149<br>−14387<br>307 315 | 51150<br>−14386<br>307 316 | 51151<br>−14385<br>307 317 |
| D− | 51152<br>−14384<br>307 320 | 51153<br>−14383<br>307 321 | 51154<br>−14382<br>307 322 | 51155<br>−14381<br>307 323 | 51156<br>−14380<br>307 324 | 51157<br>−14379<br>307 325 | 51158<br>−14378<br>307 326 | 51159<br>−14377<br>307 327 | 51160<br>−14376<br>307 330 | 51161<br>−14375<br>307 331 | 51162<br>−14374<br>307 332 | 51163<br>−14373<br>307 333 | 51164<br>−14372<br>307 334 | 51165<br>−14371<br>307 335 | 51166<br>−14370<br>307 336 | 51167<br>−14369<br>307 337 |
| E− | 51168<br>−14368<br>307 340 | 51169<br>−14367<br>307 341 | 51170<br>−14366<br>307 342 | 51171<br>−14365<br>307 343 | 51172<br>−14364<br>307 344 | 51173<br>−14363<br>307 345 | 51174<br>−14362<br>307 346 | 51175<br>−14361<br>307 347 | 51176<br>−14360<br>307 350 | 51177<br>−14359<br>307 351 | 51178<br>−14358<br>307 352 | 51179<br>−14357<br>307 353 | 51180<br>−14356<br>307 354 | 51181<br>−14355<br>307 355 | 51182<br>−14354<br>307 356 | 51183<br>−14353<br>307 357 |
| F− | 51184<br>−14352<br>307 360 | 51185<br>−14351<br>307 361 | 51186<br>−14350<br>307 362 | 51187<br>−14349<br>307 363 | 51188<br>−14348<br>307 364 | 51189<br>−14347<br>307 365 | 51190<br>−14346<br>307 366 | 51191<br>−14345<br>307 367 | 51192<br>−14344<br>307 370 | 51193<br>−14343<br>307 371 | 51194<br>−14342<br>307 372 | 51195<br>−14341<br>307 373 | 51196<br>−14340<br>307 374 | 51197<br>−14339<br>307 375 | 51198<br>−14338<br>307 376 | 51199<br>−14337<br>307 377 |

DECIMAL    DECIMAL    OCTAL

| 2 | −0 | −1 | −2 | −3 | −4 | −5 | −6 | −7 | −8 | −9 | −A | −B | −C | −D | −E | −F |
|---|---|---|---|---|---|---|---|---|---|---|---|---|---|---|---|---|
| **0−** | 51200<br>−14336<br>310 000 | 51201<br>−14335<br>310 001 | 51202<br>−14334<br>310 002 | 51203<br>−14333<br>310 003 | 51204<br>−14332<br>310 004 | 51205<br>−14331<br>310 005 | 51206<br>−14330<br>310 006 | 51207<br>−14329<br>310 007 | 51208<br>−14328<br>310 010 | 51209<br>−14327<br>310 011 | 51210<br>−14326<br>310 012 | 51211<br>−14325<br>310 013 | 51212<br>−14324<br>310 014 | 51213<br>−14323<br>310 015 | 51214<br>−14322<br>310 016 | 51215<br>−14321<br>310 017 |
| **1−** | 51216<br>−14320<br>310 020 | 51217<br>−14319<br>310 021 | 51218<br>−14318<br>310 022 | 51219<br>−14317<br>310 023 | 51220<br>−14316<br>310 024 | 51221<br>−14315<br>310 025 | 51222<br>−14314<br>310 026 | 51223<br>−14313<br>310 027 | 51224<br>−14312<br>310 030 | 51225<br>−14311<br>310 031 | 51226<br>−14310<br>310 032 | 51227<br>−14309<br>310 033 | 51228<br>−14308<br>310 034 | 51229<br>−14307<br>310 035 | 51230<br>−14306<br>310 036 | 51231<br>−14305<br>310 037 |
| **2−** | 51232<br>−14304<br>310 040 | 51233<br>−14303<br>310 041 | 51234<br>−14302<br>310 042 | 51235<br>−14301<br>310 043 | 51236<br>−14300<br>310 044 | 51237<br>−14299<br>310 045 | 51238<br>−14298<br>310 046 | 51239<br>−14297<br>310 047 | 51240<br>−14296<br>310 050 | 51241<br>−14295<br>310 051 | 51242<br>−14294<br>310 052 | 51243<br>−14293<br>310 053 | 51244<br>−14292<br>310 054 | 51245<br>−14291<br>310 055 | 51246<br>−14290<br>310 056 | 51247<br>−14289<br>310 057 |
| **3−** | 51248<br>−14288<br>310 060 | 51249<br>−14287<br>310 061 | 51250<br>−14286<br>310 062 | 51251<br>−14285<br>310 063 | 51252<br>−14284<br>310 064 | 51253<br>−14283<br>310 065 | 51254<br>−14282<br>310 066 | 51255<br>−14281<br>310 067 | 51256<br>−14280<br>310 070 | 51257<br>−14279<br>310 071 | 51258<br>−14278<br>310 072 | 51259<br>−14277<br>310 073 | 51260<br>−14276<br>310 074 | 51261<br>−14275<br>310 075 | 51262<br>−14274<br>310 076 | 51263<br>−14273<br>310 077 |
| **4−** | 51264<br>−14272<br>310 100 | 51265<br>−14271<br>310 101 | 51266<br>−14270<br>310 102 | 51267<br>−14269<br>310 103 | 51268<br>−14268<br>310 104 | 51269<br>−14267<br>310 105 | 51270<br>−14266<br>310 106 | 51271<br>−14265<br>310 107 | 51272<br>−14264<br>310 110 | 51273<br>−14263<br>310 111 | 51274<br>−14262<br>310 112 | 51275<br>−14261<br>310 113 | 51276<br>−14260<br>310 114 | 51277<br>−14259<br>310 115 | 51278<br>−14258<br>310 116 | 51279<br>−14257<br>310 117 |
| **5−** | 51280<br>−14256<br>310 120 | 51281<br>−14255<br>310 121 | 51282<br>−14254<br>310 122 | 51283<br>−14253<br>310 123 | 51284<br>−14252<br>310 124 | 51285<br>−14251<br>310 125 | 51286<br>−14250<br>310 126 | 51287<br>−14249<br>310 127 | 51288<br>−14248<br>310 130 | 51289<br>−14247<br>310 131 | 51290<br>−14246<br>310 132 | 51291<br>−14245<br>310 133 | 51292<br>−14244<br>310 134 | 51293<br>−14243<br>310 135 | 51294<br>−14242<br>310 136 | 51295<br>−14241<br>310 137 |
| **6−** | 51296<br>−14240<br>310 140 | 51297<br>−14239<br>310 141 | 51298<br>−14238<br>310 142 | 51299<br>−14237<br>310 143 | 51300<br>−14236<br>310 144 | 51301<br>−14235<br>310 145 | 51302<br>−14234<br>310 146 | 51303<br>−14233<br>310 147 | 51304<br>−14232<br>310 150 | 51305<br>−14231<br>310 151 | 51306<br>−14230<br>310 152 | 51307<br>−14229<br>310 153 | 51308<br>−14228<br>310 154 | 51309<br>−14227<br>310 155 | 51310<br>−14226<br>310 156 | 51311<br>−14225<br>310 157 |
| **7−** | 51312<br>−14224<br>310 160 | 51313<br>−14223<br>310 161 | 51314<br>−14222<br>310 162 | 51315<br>−14221<br>310 163 | 51316<br>−14220<br>310 164 | 51317<br>−14219<br>310 165 | 51318<br>−14218<br>310 166 | 51319<br>−14217<br>310 167 | 51320<br>−14216<br>310 170 | 51321<br>−14215<br>310 171 | 51322<br>−14214<br>310 172 | 51323<br>−14213<br>310 173 | 51324<br>−14212<br>310 174 | 51325<br>−14211<br>310 175 | 51326<br>−14210<br>310 176 | 51327<br>−14209<br>310 177 |
| **8−** | 51328<br>−14208<br>310 200 | 51329<br>−14207<br>310 201 | 51330<br>−14206<br>310 202 | 51331<br>−14205<br>310 203 | 51332<br>−14204<br>310 204 | 51333<br>−14203<br>310 205 | 51334<br>−14202<br>310 206 | 51335<br>−14201<br>310 207 | 51336<br>−14200<br>310 210 | 51337<br>−14199<br>310 211 | 51338<br>−14198<br>310 212 | 51339<br>−14197<br>310 213 | 51340<br>−14196<br>310 214 | 51341<br>−14195<br>310 215 | 51342<br>−14194<br>310 216 | 51343<br>−14193<br>310 217 |
| **9−** | 51344<br>−14192<br>310 220 | 51345<br>−14191<br>310 221 | 51346<br>−14190<br>310 222 | 51347<br>−14189<br>310 223 | 51348<br>−14188<br>310 224 | 51349<br>−14187<br>310 225 | 51350<br>−14186<br>310 226 | 51351<br>−14185<br>310 227 | 51352<br>−14184<br>310 230 | 51353<br>−14183<br>310 231 | 51354<br>−14182<br>310 232 | 51355<br>−14181<br>310 233 | 51356<br>−14180<br>310 234 | 51357<br>−14179<br>310 235 | 51358<br>−14178<br>310 236 | 51359<br>−14177<br>310 237 |
| **A−** | 51360<br>−14176<br>310 240 | 51361<br>−14175<br>310 241 | 51362<br>−14174<br>310 242 | 51363<br>−14173<br>310 243 | 51364<br>−14172<br>310 244 | 51365<br>−14171<br>310 245 | 51366<br>−14170<br>310 246 | 51367<br>−14169<br>310 247 | 51368<br>−14168<br>310 250 | 51369<br>−14167<br>310 251 | 51370<br>−14166<br>310 252 | 51371<br>−14165<br>310 253 | 51372<br>−14164<br>310 254 | 51373<br>−14163<br>310 255 | 51374<br>−14162<br>310 256 | 51375<br>−14161<br>310 257 |
| **B−** | 51376<br>−14160<br>310 260 | 51377<br>−14159<br>310 261 | 51378<br>−14158<br>310 262 | 51379<br>−14157<br>310 263 | 51380<br>−14156<br>310 264 | 51381<br>−14155<br>310 265 | 51382<br>−14154<br>310 266 | 51383<br>−14153<br>310 267 | 51384<br>−14152<br>310 270 | 51385<br>−14151<br>310 271 | 51386<br>−14150<br>310 272 | 51387<br>−14149<br>310 273 | 51388<br>−14148<br>310 274 | 51389<br>−14147<br>310 275 | 51390<br>−14146<br>310 276 | 51391<br>−14145<br>310 277 |
| **C−** | 51392<br>−14144<br>310 300 | 51393<br>−14143<br>310 301 | 51394<br>−14142<br>310 302 | 51395<br>−14141<br>310 303 | 51396<br>−14140<br>310 304 | 51397<br>−14139<br>310 305 | 51398<br>−14138<br>310 306 | 51399<br>−14137<br>310 307 | 51400<br>−14136<br>310 310 | 51401<br>−14135<br>310 311 | 51402<br>−14134<br>310 312 | 51403<br>−14133<br>310 313 | 51404<br>−14132<br>310 314 | 51405<br>−14131<br>310 315 | 51406<br>−14130<br>310 316 | 51407<br>−14129<br>310 317 |
| **D−** | 51408<br>−14128<br>310 320 | 51409<br>−14127<br>310 321 | 51410<br>−14126<br>310 322 | 51411<br>−14125<br>310 323 | 51412<br>−14124<br>310 324 | 51413<br>−14123<br>310 325 | 51414<br>−14122<br>310 326 | 51415<br>−14121<br>310 327 | 51416<br>−14120<br>310 330 | 51417<br>−14119<br>310 331 | 51418<br>−14118<br>310 332 | 51419<br>−14117<br>310 333 | 51420<br>−14116<br>310 334 | 51421<br>−14115<br>310 335 | 51422<br>−14114<br>310 336 | 51423<br>−14113<br>310 337 |
| **E−** | 51424<br>−14112<br>310 340 | 51425<br>−14111<br>310 341 | 51426<br>−14110<br>310 342 | 51427<br>−14109<br>310 343 | 51428<br>−14108<br>310 344 | 51429<br>−14107<br>310 345 | 51430<br>−14106<br>310 346 | 51431<br>−14105<br>310 347 | 51432<br>−14104<br>310 350 | 51433<br>−14103<br>310 351 | 51434<br>−14102<br>310 352 | 51435<br>−14101<br>310 353 | 51436<br>−14100<br>310 354 | 51437<br>−14099<br>310 355 | 51438<br>−14098<br>310 356 | 51439<br>−14097<br>310 357 |
| **F−** | 51440<br>−14096<br>310 360 | 51441<br>−14095<br>310 361 | 51442<br>−14094<br>310 362 | 51443<br>−14093<br>310 363 | 51444<br>−14092<br>310 364 | 51445<br>−14091<br>310 365 | 51446<br>−14090<br>310 366 | 51447<br>−14089<br>310 367 | 51448<br>−14088<br>310 370 | 51449<br>−14087<br>310 371 | 51450<br>−14086<br>310 372 | 51451<br>−14085<br>310 373 | 51452<br>−14084<br>310 374 | 51453<br>−14083<br>310 375 | 51454<br>−14082<br>310 376 | 51455<br>−14081<br>310 377 |

Row label (left side): **SECOND HEX DIGIT**

Right-side legend: **DECIGIT** DECIMAL · ⌘ DECIMAL · OCTAL

⌘ DECIMAL  | −14336 |   BINARY  | 1100 1000 |   DECIMAL  | 51200 |   HEXADECIMAL

HEXADECIMAL  C8   OCTAL  | 310 000 |

FOURTH HEX DIGIT →   ← THIRD HEX DIGIT

| 2 | −0 | −1 | −2 | −3 | −4 | −5 | −6 | −7 | −8 | −9 | −A | −B | −C | −D | −E | −F |
|---|---|---|---|---|---|---|---|---|---|---|---|---|---|---|---|---|
| 0− | 51456<br>−14080<br>311 000 | 51457<br>−14079<br>311 001 | 51458<br>−14078<br>311 002 | 51459<br>−14077<br>311 003 | 51460<br>−14076<br>311 004 | 51461<br>−14075<br>311 005 | 51462<br>−14074<br>311 006 | 51463<br>−14073<br>311 007 | 51464<br>−14072<br>311 010 | 51465<br>−14071<br>311 011 | 51466<br>−14070<br>311 012 | 51467<br>−14069<br>311 013 | 51468<br>−14068<br>311 014 | 51469<br>−14067<br>311 015 | 51470<br>−14066<br>311 016 | 51471<br>−14065<br>311 017 |
| 1− | 51472<br>−14064<br>311 020 | 51473<br>−14063<br>311 021 | 51474<br>−14062<br>311 022 | 51475<br>−14061<br>311 023 | 51476<br>−14060<br>311 024 | 51477<br>−14059<br>311 025 | 51478<br>−14058<br>311 026 | 51479<br>−14057<br>311 027 | 51480<br>−14056<br>311 030 | 51481<br>−14055<br>311 031 | 51482<br>−14054<br>311 032 | 51483<br>−14053<br>311 033 | 51484<br>−14052<br>311 034 | 51485<br>−14051<br>311 035 | 51486<br>−14050<br>311 036 | 51487<br>−14049<br>311 037 |
| 2− | 51488<br>−14048<br>311 040 | 51489<br>−14047<br>311 041 | 51490<br>−14046<br>311 042 | 51491<br>−14045<br>311 043 | 51492<br>−14044<br>311 044 | 51493<br>−14043<br>311 045 | 51494<br>−14042<br>311 046 | 51495<br>−14041<br>311 047 | 51496<br>−14040<br>311 050 | 51497<br>−14039<br>311 051 | 51498<br>−14038<br>311 052 | 51499<br>−14037<br>311 053 | 51500<br>−14036<br>311 054 | 51501<br>−14035<br>311 055 | 51502<br>−14034<br>311 056 | 51503<br>−14033<br>311 057 |
| 3− | 51504<br>−14032<br>311 060 | 51505<br>−14031<br>311 061 | 51506<br>−14030<br>311 062 | 51507<br>−14029<br>311 063 | 51508<br>−14028<br>311 064 | 51509<br>−14027<br>311 065 | 51510<br>−14026<br>311 066 | 51511<br>−14025<br>311 067 | 51512<br>−14024<br>311 070 | 51513<br>−14023<br>311 071 | 51514<br>−14022<br>311 072 | 51515<br>−14021<br>311 073 | 51516<br>−14020<br>311 074 | 51517<br>−14019<br>311 075 | 51518<br>−14018<br>311 076 | 51519<br>−14017<br>311 077 |
| 4− | 51520<br>−14016<br>311 100 | 51521<br>−14015<br>311 101 | 51522<br>−14014<br>311 102 | 51523<br>−14013<br>311 103 | 51524<br>−14012<br>311 104 | 51525<br>−14011<br>311 105 | 51526<br>−14010<br>311 106 | 51527<br>−14009<br>311 107 | 51528<br>−14008<br>311 110 | 51529<br>−14007<br>311 111 | 51530<br>−14006<br>311 112 | 51531<br>−14005<br>311 113 | 51532<br>−14004<br>311 114 | 51533<br>−14003<br>311 115 | 51534<br>−14002<br>311 116 | 51535<br>−14001<br>311 117 |
| 5− | 51536<br>−14000<br>311 120 | 51537<br>−13999<br>311 121 | 51538<br>−13998<br>311 122 | 51539<br>−13997<br>311 123 | 51540<br>−13996<br>311 124 | 51541<br>−13995<br>311 125 | 51542<br>−13994<br>311 126 | 51543<br>−13993<br>311 127 | 51544<br>−13992<br>311 130 | 51545<br>−13991<br>311 131 | 51546<br>−13990<br>311 132 | 51547<br>−13989<br>311 133 | 51548<br>−13988<br>311 134 | 51549<br>−13987<br>311 135 | 51550<br>−13986<br>311 136 | 51551<br>−13985<br>311 137 |
| 6− | 51552<br>−13984<br>311 140 | 51553<br>−13983<br>311 141 | 51554<br>−13982<br>311 142 | 51555<br>−13981<br>311 143 | 51556<br>−13980<br>311 144 | 51557<br>−13979<br>311 145 | 51558<br>−13978<br>311 146 | 51559<br>−13977<br>311 147 | 51560<br>−13976<br>311 150 | 51561<br>−13975<br>311 151 | 51562<br>−13974<br>311 152 | 51563<br>−13973<br>311 153 | 51564<br>−13972<br>311 154 | 51565<br>−13971<br>311 155 | 51566<br>−13970<br>311 156 | 51567<br>−13969<br>311 157 |
| 7− | 51568<br>−13968<br>311 160 | 51569<br>−13967<br>311 161 | 51570<br>−13966<br>311 162 | 51571<br>−13965<br>311 163 | 51572<br>−13964<br>311 164 | 51573<br>−13963<br>311 165 | 51574<br>−13962<br>311 166 | 51575<br>−13961<br>311 167 | 51576<br>−13960<br>311 170 | 51577<br>−13959<br>311 171 | 51578<br>−13958<br>311 172 | 51579<br>−13957<br>311 173 | 51580<br>−13956<br>311 174 | 51581<br>−13955<br>311 175 | 51582<br>−13954<br>311 176 | 51583<br>−13953<br>311 177 |
| 8− | 51584<br>−13952<br>311 200 | 51585<br>−13951<br>311 201 | 51586<br>−13950<br>311 202 | 51587<br>−13949<br>311 203 | 51588<br>−13948<br>311 204 | 51589<br>−13947<br>311 205 | 51590<br>−13946<br>311 206 | 51591<br>−13945<br>311 207 | 51592<br>−13944<br>311 210 | 51593<br>−13943<br>311 211 | 51594<br>−13942<br>311 212 | 51595<br>−13941<br>311 213 | 51596<br>−13940<br>311 214 | 51597<br>−13939<br>311 215 | 51598<br>−13938<br>311 216 | 51599<br>−13937<br>311 217 |
| 9− | 51600<br>−13936<br>311 220 | 51601<br>−13935<br>311 221 | 51602<br>−13934<br>311 222 | 51603<br>−13933<br>311 223 | 51604<br>−13932<br>311 224 | 51605<br>−13931<br>311 225 | 51606<br>−13930<br>311 226 | 51607<br>−13929<br>311 227 | 51608<br>−13928<br>311 230 | 51609<br>−13927<br>311 231 | 51610<br>−13926<br>311 232 | 51611<br>−13925<br>311 233 | 51612<br>−13924<br>311 234 | 51613<br>−13923<br>311 235 | 51614<br>−13922<br>311 236 | 51615<br>−13921<br>311 237 |
| A− | 51616<br>−13920<br>311 240 | 51617<br>−13919<br>311 241 | 51618<br>−13918<br>311 242 | 51619<br>−13917<br>311 243 | 51620<br>−13916<br>311 244 | 51621<br>−13915<br>311 245 | 51622<br>−13914<br>311 246 | 51623<br>−13913<br>311 247 | 51624<br>−13912<br>311 250 | 51625<br>−13911<br>311 251 | 51626<br>−13910<br>311 252 | 51627<br>−13909<br>311 253 | 51628<br>−13908<br>311 254 | 51629<br>−13907<br>311 255 | 51630<br>−13906<br>311 256 | 51631<br>−13905<br>311 257 |
| B− | 51632<br>−13904<br>311 260 | 51633<br>−13903<br>311 261 | 51634<br>−13902<br>311 262 | 51635<br>−13901<br>311 263 | 51636<br>−13900<br>311 264 | 51637<br>−13899<br>311 265 | 51638<br>−13898<br>311 266 | 51639<br>−13897<br>311 267 | 51640<br>−13896<br>311 270 | 51641<br>−13895<br>311 271 | 51642<br>−13894<br>311 272 | 51643<br>−13893<br>311 273 | 51644<br>−13892<br>311 274 | 51645<br>−13891<br>311 275 | 51646<br>−13890<br>311 276 | 51647<br>−13889<br>311 277 |
| C− | 51648<br>−13888<br>311 300 | 51649<br>−13887<br>311 301 | 51650<br>−13886<br>311 302 | 51651<br>−13885<br>311 303 | 51652<br>−13884<br>311 304 | 51653<br>−13883<br>311 305 | 51654<br>−13882<br>311 306 | 51655<br>−13881<br>311 307 | 51656<br>−13880<br>311 310 | 51657<br>−13879<br>311 311 | 51658<br>−13878<br>311 312 | 51659<br>−13877<br>311 313 | 51660<br>−13876<br>311 314 | 51661<br>−13875<br>311 315 | 51662<br>−13874<br>311 316 | 51663<br>−13873<br>311 317 |
| D− | 51664<br>−13872<br>311 320 | 51665<br>−13871<br>311 321 | 51666<br>−13870<br>311 322 | 51667<br>−13869<br>311 323 | 51668<br>−13868<br>311 324 | 51669<br>−13867<br>311 325 | 51670<br>−13866<br>311 326 | 51671<br>−13865<br>311 327 | 51672<br>−13864<br>311 330 | 51673<br>−13863<br>311 331 | 51674<br>−13862<br>311 332 | 51675<br>−13861<br>311 333 | 51676<br>−13860<br>311 334 | 51677<br>−13859<br>311 335 | 51678<br>−13858<br>311 336 | 51679<br>−13857<br>311 337 |
| E− | 51680<br>−13856<br>311 340 | 51681<br>−13855<br>311 341 | 51682<br>−13854<br>311 342 | 51683<br>−13853<br>311 343 | 51684<br>−13852<br>311 344 | 51685<br>−13851<br>311 345 | 51686<br>−13850<br>311 346 | 51687<br>−13849<br>311 347 | 51688<br>−13848<br>311 350 | 51689<br>−13847<br>311 351 | 51690<br>−13846<br>311 352 | 51691<br>−13845<br>311 353 | 51692<br>−13844<br>311 354 | 51693<br>−13843<br>311 355 | 51694<br>−13842<br>311 356 | 51695<br>−13841<br>311 357 |
| F− | 51696<br>−13840<br>311 360 | 51697<br>−13839<br>311 361 | 51698<br>−13838<br>311 362 | 51699<br>−13837<br>311 363 | 51700<br>−13836<br>311 364 | 51701<br>−13835<br>311 365 | 51702<br>−13834<br>311 366 | 51703<br>−13833<br>311 367 | 51704<br>−13832<br>311 370 | 51705<br>−13831<br>311 371 | 51706<br>−13830<br>311 372 | 51707<br>−13829<br>311 373 | 51708<br>−13828<br>311 374 | 51709<br>−13827<br>311 375 | 51710<br>−13826<br>311 376 | 51711<br>−13825<br>311 377 |

## FIRST HEX DIGIT

|  | −0 | −1 | −2 | −3 | −4 | −5 | −6 | −7 | −8 | −9 | −A | −B | −C | −D | −E | −F |
|---|---|---|---|---|---|---|---|---|---|---|---|---|---|---|---|---|
| **0-** | 51712<br>-13824<br>312 000 | 51713<br>-13823<br>312 001 | 51714<br>-13822<br>312 002 | 51715<br>-13821<br>312 003 | 51716<br>-13820<br>312 004 | 51717<br>-13819<br>312 005 | 51718<br>-13818<br>312 006 | 51719<br>-13817<br>312 007 | 51720<br>-13816<br>312 010 | 51721<br>-13815<br>312 011 | 51722<br>-13814<br>312 012 | 51723<br>-13813<br>312 013 | 51724<br>-13812<br>312 014 | 51725<br>-13811<br>312 015 | 51726<br>-13810<br>312 016 | 51727<br>-13809<br>312 017 |
| **1-** | 51728<br>-13808<br>312 020 | 51729<br>-13807<br>312 021 | 51730<br>-13806<br>312 022 | 51731<br>-13805<br>312 023 | 51732<br>-13804<br>312 024 | 51733<br>-13803<br>312 025 | 51734<br>-13802<br>312 026 | 51735<br>-13801<br>312 027 | 51736<br>-13800<br>312 030 | 51737<br>-13799<br>312 031 | 51738<br>-13798<br>312 032 | 51739<br>-13797<br>312 033 | 51740<br>-13796<br>312 034 | 51741<br>-13795<br>312 035 | 51742<br>-13794<br>312 036 | 51743<br>-13793<br>312 037 |
| **2-** | 51744<br>-13792<br>312 040 | 51745<br>-13791<br>312 041 | 51746<br>-13790<br>312 042 | 51747<br>-13789<br>312 043 | 51748<br>-13788<br>312 044 | 51749<br>-13787<br>312 045 | 51750<br>-13786<br>312 046 | 51751<br>-13785<br>312 047 | 51752<br>-13784<br>312 050 | 51753<br>-13783<br>312 051 | 51754<br>-13782<br>312 052 | 51755<br>-13781<br>312 053 | 51756<br>-13780<br>312 054 | 51757<br>-13779<br>312 055 | 51758<br>-13778<br>312 056 | 51759<br>-13777<br>312 057 |
| **3-** | 51760<br>-13776<br>312 060 | 51761<br>-13775<br>312 061 | 51762<br>-13774<br>312 062 | 51763<br>-13773<br>312 063 | 51764<br>-13772<br>312 064 | 51765<br>-13771<br>312 065 | 51766<br>-13770<br>312 066 | 51767<br>-13769<br>312 067 | 51768<br>-13768<br>312 070 | 51769<br>-13767<br>312 071 | 51770<br>-13766<br>312 072 | 51771<br>-13765<br>312 073 | 51772<br>-13764<br>312 074 | 51773<br>-13763<br>312 075 | 51774<br>-13762<br>312 076 | 51775<br>-13761<br>312 077 |
| **4-** | 51776<br>-13760<br>312 100 | 51777<br>-13759<br>312 101 | 51778<br>-13758<br>312 102 | 51779<br>-13757<br>312 103 | 51780<br>-13756<br>312 104 | 51781<br>-13755<br>312 105 | 51782<br>-13754<br>312 106 | 51783<br>-13753<br>312 107 | 51784<br>-13752<br>312 110 | 51785<br>-13751<br>312 111 | 51786<br>-13750<br>312 112 | 51787<br>-13749<br>312 113 | 51788<br>-13748<br>312 114 | 51789<br>-13747<br>312 115 | 51790<br>-13746<br>312 116 | 51791<br>-13745<br>312 117 |
| **5-** | 51792<br>-13744<br>312 120 | 51793<br>-13743<br>312 121 | 51794<br>-13742<br>312 122 | 51795<br>-13741<br>312 123 | 51796<br>-13740<br>312 124 | 51797<br>-13739<br>312 125 | 51798<br>-13738<br>312 126 | 51799<br>-13737<br>312 127 | 51800<br>-13736<br>312 130 | 51801<br>-13735<br>312 131 | 51802<br>-13734<br>312 132 | 51803<br>-13733<br>312 133 | 51804<br>-13732<br>312 134 | 51805<br>-13731<br>312 135 | 51806<br>-13730<br>312 136 | 51807<br>-13729<br>312 137 |
| **6-** | 51808<br>-13728<br>312 140 | 51809<br>-13727<br>312 141 | 51810<br>-13726<br>312 142 | 51811<br>-13725<br>312 143 | 51812<br>-13724<br>312 144 | 51813<br>-13723<br>312 145 | 51814<br>-13722<br>312 146 | 51815<br>-13721<br>312 147 | 51816<br>-13720<br>312 150 | 51817<br>-13719<br>312 151 | 51818<br>-13718<br>312 152 | 51819<br>-13717<br>312 153 | 51820<br>-13716<br>312 154 | 51821<br>-13715<br>312 155 | 51822<br>-13714<br>312 156 | 51823<br>-13713<br>312 157 |
| **7-** | 51824<br>-13712<br>312 160 | 51825<br>-13711<br>312 161 | 51826<br>-13710<br>312 162 | 51827<br>-13709<br>312 163 | 51828<br>-13708<br>312 164 | 51829<br>-13707<br>312 165 | 51830<br>-13706<br>312 166 | 51831<br>-13705<br>312 167 | 51832<br>-13704<br>312 170 | 51833<br>-13703<br>312 171 | 51834<br>-13702<br>312 172 | 51835<br>-13701<br>312 173 | 51836<br>-13700<br>312 174 | 51837<br>-13699<br>312 175 | 51838<br>-13698<br>312 176 | 51839<br>-13697<br>312 177 |
| **8-** | 51840<br>-13696<br>312 200 | 51841<br>-13695<br>312 201 | 51842<br>-13694<br>312 202 | 51843<br>-13693<br>312 203 | 51844<br>-13692<br>312 204 | 51845<br>-13691<br>312 205 | 51846<br>-13690<br>312 206 | 51847<br>-13689<br>312 207 | 51848<br>-13688<br>312 210 | 51849<br>-13687<br>312 211 | 51850<br>-13686<br>312 212 | 51851<br>-13685<br>312 213 | 51852<br>-13684<br>312 214 | 51853<br>-13683<br>312 215 | 51854<br>-13682<br>312 216 | 51855<br>-13681<br>312 217 |
| **9-** | 51856<br>-13680<br>312 220 | 51857<br>-13679<br>312 221 | 51858<br>-13678<br>312 222 | 51859<br>-13677<br>312 223 | 51860<br>-13676<br>312 224 | 51861<br>-13675<br>312 225 | 51862<br>-13674<br>312 226 | 51863<br>-13673<br>312 227 | 51864<br>-13672<br>312 230 | 51865<br>-13671<br>312 231 | 51866<br>-13670<br>312 232 | 51867<br>-13669<br>312 233 | 51868<br>-13668<br>312 234 | 51869<br>-13667<br>312 235 | 51870<br>-13666<br>312 236 | 51871<br>-13665<br>312 237 |
| **A-** | 51872<br>-13664<br>312 240 | 51873<br>-13663<br>312 241 | 51874<br>-13662<br>312 242 | 51875<br>-13661<br>312 243 | 51876<br>-13660<br>312 244 | 51877<br>-13659<br>312 245 | 51878<br>-13658<br>312 246 | 51879<br>-13657<br>312 247 | 51880<br>-13656<br>312 250 | 51881<br>-13655<br>312 251 | 51882<br>-13654<br>312 252 | 51883<br>-13653<br>312 253 | 51884<br>-13652<br>312 254 | 51885<br>-13651<br>312 255 | 51886<br>-13650<br>312 256 | 51887<br>-13649<br>312 257 |
| **B-** | 51888<br>-13648<br>312 260 | 51889<br>-13647<br>312 261 | 51890<br>-13646<br>312 262 | 51891<br>-13645<br>312 263 | 51892<br>-13644<br>312 264 | 51893<br>-13643<br>312 265 | 51894<br>-13642<br>312 266 | 51895<br>-13641<br>312 267 | 51896<br>-13640<br>312 270 | 51897<br>-13639<br>312 271 | 51898<br>-13638<br>312 272 | 51899<br>-13637<br>312 273 | 51900<br>-13636<br>312 274 | 51901<br>-13635<br>312 275 | 51902<br>-13634<br>312 276 | 51903<br>-13633<br>312 277 |
| **C-** | 51904<br>-13632<br>312 300 | 51905<br>-13631<br>312 301 | 51906<br>-13630<br>312 302 | 51907<br>-13629<br>312 303 | 51908<br>-13628<br>312 304 | 51909<br>-13627<br>312 305 | 51910<br>-13626<br>312 306 | 51911<br>-13625<br>312 307 | 51912<br>-13624<br>312 310 | 51913<br>-13623<br>312 311 | 51914<br>-13622<br>312 312 | 51915<br>-13621<br>312 313 | 51916<br>-13620<br>312 314 | 51917<br>-13619<br>312 315 | 51918<br>-13618<br>312 316 | 51919<br>-13617<br>312 317 |
| **D-** | 51920<br>-13616<br>312 320 | 51921<br>-13615<br>312 321 | 51922<br>-13614<br>312 322 | 51923<br>-13613<br>312 323 | 51924<br>-13612<br>312 324 | 51925<br>-13611<br>312 325 | 51926<br>-13610<br>312 326 | 51927<br>-13609<br>312 327 | 51928<br>-13608<br>312 330 | 51929<br>-13607<br>312 331 | 51930<br>-13606<br>312 332 | 51931<br>-13605<br>312 333 | 51932<br>-13604<br>312 334 | 51933<br>-13603<br>312 335 | 51934<br>-13602<br>312 336 | 51935<br>-13601<br>312 337 |
| **E-** | 51936<br>-13600<br>312 340 | 51937<br>-13599<br>312 341 | 51938<br>-13598<br>312 342 | 51939<br>-13597<br>312 343 | 51940<br>-13596<br>312 344 | 51941<br>-13595<br>312 345 | 51942<br>-13594<br>312 346 | 51943<br>-13593<br>312 347 | 51944<br>-13592<br>312 350 | 51945<br>-13591<br>312 351 | 51946<br>-13590<br>312 352 | 51947<br>-13589<br>312 353 | 51948<br>-13588<br>312 354 | 51949<br>-13587<br>312 355 | 51950<br>-13586<br>312 356 | 51951<br>-13585<br>312 357 |
| **F-** | 51952<br>-13584<br>312 360 | 51953<br>-13583<br>312 361 | 51954<br>-13582<br>312 362 | 51955<br>-13581<br>312 363 | 51956<br>-13580<br>312 364 | 51957<br>-13579<br>312 365 | 51958<br>-13578<br>312 366 | 51959<br>-13577<br>312 367 | 51960<br>-13576<br>312 370 | 51961<br>-13575<br>312 371 | 51962<br>-13574<br>312 372 | 51963<br>-13573<br>312 373 | 51964<br>-13572<br>312 374 | 51965<br>-13571<br>312 375 | 51966<br>-13570<br>312 376 | 51967<br>-13569<br>312 377 |

SECOND HEX DIGIT (row labels, left side)

🍎 DECIMAL → (rows)

OCTAL →

---

🍎 DECIMAL  | -13824 |   BINARY  | 1100 1010 |   DECIMAL  | 51712 |   HEXADECIMAL  ⬡ CA  OCTAL  | 312 000 |

FOURTH HEX DIGIT → ⬡ ← THIRD HEX DIGIT

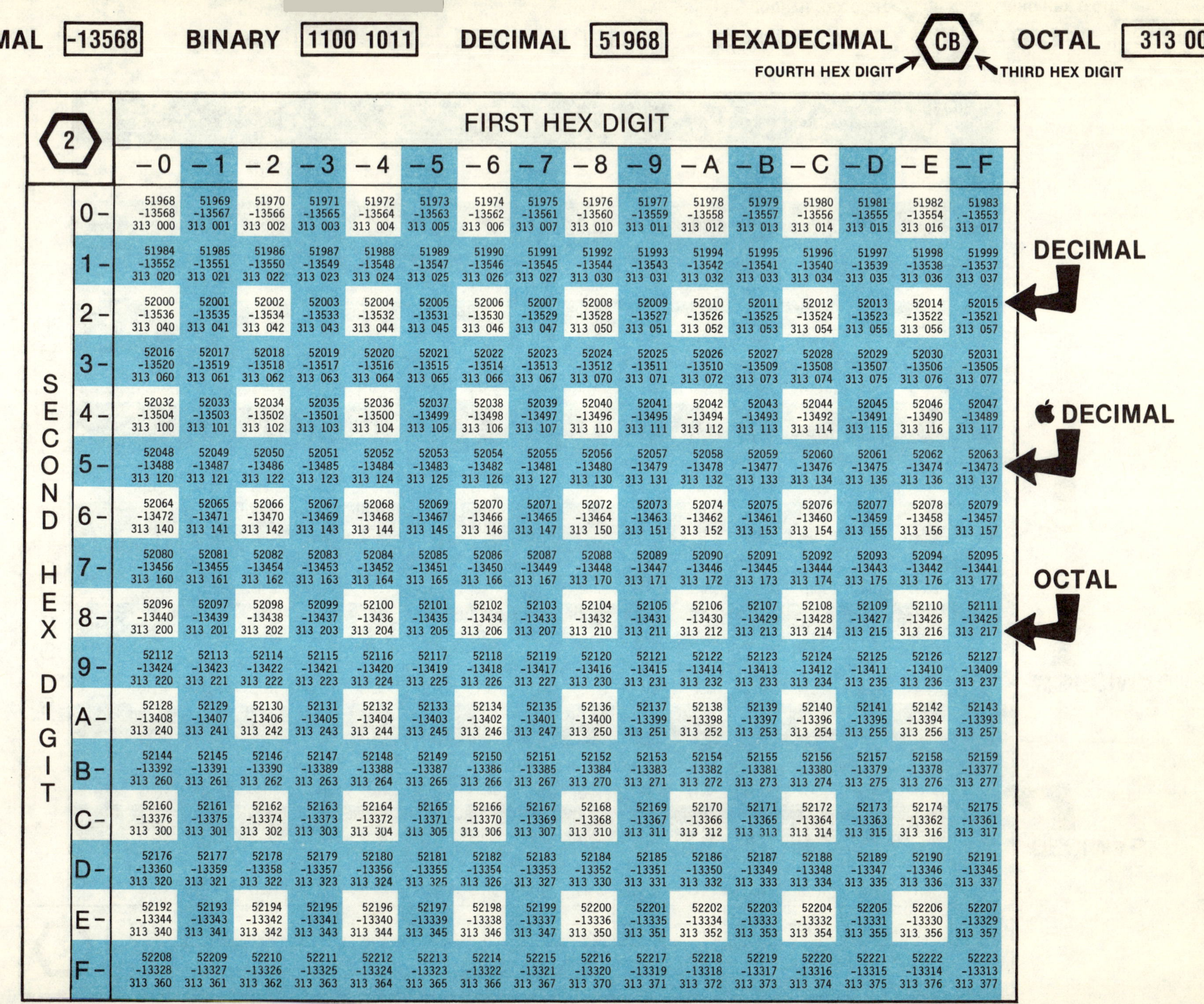



| 2 | −0 | −1 | −2 | −3 | −4 | −5 | −6 | −7 | −8 | −9 | −A | −B | −C | −D | −E | −F |
|---|---|---|---|---|---|---|---|---|---|---|---|---|---|---|---|---|
| **FIRST HEX DIGIT** | | | | | | | | | | | | | | | | |
| 0− | 51968<br>-13568<br>313 000 | 51969<br>-13567<br>313 001 | 51970<br>-13566<br>313 002 | 51971<br>-13565<br>313 003 | 51972<br>-13564<br>313 004 | 51973<br>-13563<br>313 005 | 51974<br>-13562<br>313 006 | 51975<br>-13561<br>313 007 | 51976<br>-13560<br>313 010 | 51977<br>-13559<br>313 011 | 51978<br>-13558<br>313 012 | 51979<br>-13557<br>313 013 | 51980<br>-13556<br>313 014 | 51981<br>-13555<br>313 015 | 51982<br>-13554<br>313 016 | 51983<br>-13553<br>313 017 |
| 1− | 51984<br>-13552<br>313 020 | 51985<br>-13551<br>313 021 | 51986<br>-13550<br>313 022 | 51987<br>-13549<br>313 023 | 51988<br>-13548<br>313 024 | 51989<br>-13547<br>313 025 | 51990<br>-13546<br>313 026 | 51991<br>-13545<br>313 027 | 51992<br>-13544<br>313 030 | 51993<br>-13543<br>313 031 | 51994<br>-13542<br>313 032 | 51995<br>-13541<br>313 033 | 51996<br>-13540<br>313 034 | 51997<br>-13539<br>313 035 | 51998<br>-13538<br>313 036 | 51999<br>-13537<br>313 037 |
| 2− | 52000<br>-13536<br>313 040 | 52001<br>-13535<br>313 041 | 52002<br>-13534<br>313 042 | 52003<br>-13533<br>313 043 | 52004<br>-13532<br>313 044 | 52005<br>-13531<br>313 045 | 52006<br>-13530<br>313 046 | 52007<br>-13529<br>313 047 | 52008<br>-13528<br>313 050 | 52009<br>-13527<br>313 051 | 52010<br>-13526<br>313 052 | 52011<br>-13525<br>313 053 | 52012<br>-13524<br>313 054 | 52013<br>-13523<br>313 055 | 52014<br>-13522<br>313 056 | 52015<br>-13521<br>313 057 |
| 3− | 52016<br>-13520<br>313 060 | 52017<br>-13519<br>313 061 | 52018<br>-13518<br>313 062 | 52019<br>-13517<br>313 063 | 52020<br>-13516<br>313 064 | 52021<br>-13515<br>313 065 | 52022<br>-13514<br>313 066 | 52023<br>-13513<br>313 067 | 52024<br>-13512<br>313 070 | 52025<br>-13511<br>313 071 | 52026<br>-13510<br>313 072 | 52027<br>-13509<br>313 073 | 52028<br>-13508<br>313 074 | 52029<br>-13507<br>313 075 | 52030<br>-13506<br>313 076 | 52031<br>-13505<br>313 077 |
| 4− | 52032<br>-13504<br>313 100 | 52033<br>-13503<br>313 101 | 52034<br>-13502<br>313 102 | 52035<br>-13501<br>313 103 | 52036<br>-13500<br>313 104 | 52037<br>-13499<br>313 105 | 52038<br>-13498<br>313 106 | 52039<br>-13497<br>313 107 | 52040<br>-13496<br>313 110 | 52041<br>-13495<br>313 111 | 52042<br>-13494<br>313 112 | 52043<br>-13493<br>313 113 | 52044<br>-13492<br>313 114 | 52045<br>-13491<br>313 115 | 52046<br>-13490<br>313 116 | 52047<br>-13489<br>313 117 |
| 5− | 52048<br>-13488<br>313 120 | 52049<br>-13487<br>313 121 | 52050<br>-13486<br>313 122 | 52051<br>-13485<br>313 123 | 52052<br>-13484<br>313 124 | 52053<br>-13483<br>313 125 | 52054<br>-13482<br>313 126 | 52055<br>-13481<br>313 127 | 52056<br>-13480<br>313 130 | 52057<br>-13479<br>313 131 | 52058<br>-13478<br>313 132 | 52059<br>-13477<br>313 133 | 52060<br>-13476<br>313 134 | 52061<br>-13475<br>313 135 | 52062<br>-13474<br>313 136 | 52063<br>-13473<br>313 137 |
| 6− | 52064<br>-13472<br>313 140 | 52065<br>-13471<br>313 141 | 52066<br>-13470<br>313 142 | 52067<br>-13469<br>313 143 | 52068<br>-13468<br>313 144 | 52069<br>-13467<br>313 145 | 52070<br>-13466<br>313 146 | 52071<br>-13465<br>313 147 | 52072<br>-13464<br>313 150 | 52073<br>-13463<br>313 151 | 52074<br>-13462<br>313 152 | 52075<br>-13461<br>313 153 | 52076<br>-13460<br>313 154 | 52077<br>-13459<br>313 155 | 52078<br>-13458<br>313 156 | 52079<br>-13457<br>313 157 |
| 7− | 52080<br>-13456<br>313 160 | 52081<br>-13455<br>313 161 | 52082<br>-13454<br>313 162 | 52083<br>-13453<br>313 163 | 52084<br>-13452<br>313 164 | 52085<br>-13451<br>313 165 | 52086<br>-13450<br>313 166 | 52087<br>-13449<br>313 167 | 52088<br>-13448<br>313 170 | 52089<br>-13447<br>313 171 | 52090<br>-13446<br>313 172 | 52091<br>-13445<br>313 173 | 52092<br>-13444<br>313 174 | 52093<br>-13443<br>313 175 | 52094<br>-13442<br>313 176 | 52095<br>-13441<br>313 177 |
| 8− | 52096<br>-13440<br>313 200 | 52097<br>-13439<br>313 201 | 52098<br>-13438<br>313 202 | 52099<br>-13437<br>313 203 | 52100<br>-13436<br>313 204 | 52101<br>-13435<br>313 205 | 52102<br>-13434<br>313 206 | 52103<br>-13433<br>313 207 | 52104<br>-13432<br>313 210 | 52105<br>-13431<br>313 211 | 52106<br>-13430<br>313 212 | 52107<br>-13429<br>313 213 | 52108<br>-13428<br>313 214 | 52109<br>-13427<br>313 215 | 52110<br>-13426<br>313 216 | 52111<br>-13425<br>313 217 |
| 9− | 52112<br>-13424<br>313 220 | 52113<br>-13423<br>313 221 | 52114<br>-13422<br>313 222 | 52115<br>-13421<br>313 223 | 52116<br>-13420<br>313 224 | 52117<br>-13419<br>313 225 | 52118<br>-13418<br>313 226 | 52119<br>-13417<br>313 227 | 52120<br>-13416<br>313 230 | 52121<br>-13415<br>313 231 | 52122<br>-13414<br>313 232 | 52123<br>-13413<br>313 233 | 52124<br>-13412<br>313 234 | 52125<br>-13411<br>313 235 | 52126<br>-13410<br>313 236 | 52127<br>-13409<br>313 237 |
| A− | 52128<br>-13408<br>313 240 | 52129<br>-13407<br>313 241 | 52130<br>-13406<br>313 242 | 52131<br>-13405<br>313 243 | 52132<br>-13404<br>313 244 | 52133<br>-13403<br>313 245 | 52134<br>-13402<br>313 246 | 52135<br>-13401<br>313 247 | 52136<br>-13400<br>313 250 | 52137<br>-13399<br>313 251 | 52138<br>-13398<br>313 252 | 52139<br>-13397<br>313 253 | 52140<br>-13396<br>313 254 | 52141<br>-13395<br>313 255 | 52142<br>-13394<br>313 256 | 52143<br>-13393<br>313 257 |
| B− | 52144<br>-13392<br>313 260 | 52145<br>-13391<br>313 261 | 52146<br>-13390<br>313 262 | 52147<br>-13389<br>313 263 | 52148<br>-13388<br>313 264 | 52149<br>-13387<br>313 265 | 52150<br>-13386<br>313 266 | 52151<br>-13385<br>313 267 | 52152<br>-13384<br>313 270 | 52153<br>-13383<br>313 271 | 52154<br>-13382<br>313 272 | 52155<br>-13381<br>313 273 | 52156<br>-13380<br>313 274 | 52157<br>-13379<br>313 275 | 52158<br>-13378<br>313 276 | 52159<br>-13377<br>313 277 |
| C− | 52160<br>-13376<br>313 300 | 52161<br>-13375<br>313 301 | 52162<br>-13374<br>313 302 | 52163<br>-13373<br>313 303 | 52164<br>-13372<br>313 304 | 52165<br>-13371<br>313 305 | 52166<br>-13370<br>313 306 | 52167<br>-13369<br>313 307 | 52168<br>-13368<br>313 310 | 52169<br>-13367<br>313 311 | 52170<br>-13366<br>313 312 | 52171<br>-13365<br>313 313 | 52172<br>-13364<br>313 314 | 52173<br>-13363<br>313 315 | 52174<br>-13362<br>313 316 | 52175<br>-13361<br>313 317 |
| D− | 52176<br>-13360<br>313 320 | 52177<br>-13359<br>313 321 | 52178<br>-13358<br>313 322 | 52179<br>-13357<br>313 323 | 52180<br>-13356<br>313 324 | 52181<br>-13355<br>313 325 | 52182<br>-13354<br>313 326 | 52183<br>-13353<br>313 327 | 52184<br>-13352<br>313 330 | 52185<br>-13351<br>313 331 | 52186<br>-13350<br>313 332 | 52187<br>-13349<br>313 333 | 52188<br>-13348<br>313 334 | 52189<br>-13347<br>313 335 | 52190<br>-13346<br>313 336 | 52191<br>-13345<br>313 337 |
| E− | 52192<br>-13344<br>313 340 | 52193<br>-13343<br>313 341 | 52194<br>-13342<br>313 342 | 52195<br>-13341<br>313 343 | 52196<br>-13340<br>313 344 | 52197<br>-13339<br>313 345 | 52198<br>-13338<br>313 346 | 52199<br>-13337<br>313 347 | 52200<br>-13336<br>313 350 | 52201<br>-13335<br>313 351 | 52202<br>-13334<br>313 352 | 52203<br>-13333<br>313 353 | 52204<br>-13332<br>313 354 | 52205<br>-13331<br>313 355 | 52206<br>-13330<br>313 356 | 52207<br>-13329<br>313 357 |
| F− | 52208<br>-13328<br>313 360 | 52209<br>-13327<br>313 361 | 52210<br>-13326<br>313 362 | 52211<br>-13325<br>313 363 | 52212<br>-13324<br>313 364 | 52213<br>-13323<br>313 365 | 52214<br>-13322<br>313 366 | 52215<br>-13321<br>313 367 | 52216<br>-13320<br>313 370 | 52217<br>-13319<br>313 371 | 52218<br>-13318<br>313 372 | 52219<br>-13317<br>313 373 | 52220<br>-13316<br>313 374 | 52221<br>-13315<br>313 375 | 52222<br>-13314<br>313 376 | 52223<br>-13313<br>313 377 |

**(2)** FIRST HEX DIGIT

SECOND HEX DIGIT

| | −0 | −1 | −2 | −3 | −4 | −5 | −6 | −7 | −8 | −9 | −A | −B | −C | −D | −E | −F |
|---|---|---|---|---|---|---|---|---|---|---|---|---|---|---|---|---|
| 0− | 52224<br>−13312<br>314 000 | 52225<br>−13311<br>314 001 | 52226<br>−13310<br>314 002 | 52227<br>−13309<br>314 003 | 52228<br>−13308<br>314 004 | 52229<br>−13307<br>314 005 | 52230<br>−13306<br>314 006 | 52231<br>−13305<br>314 007 | 52232<br>−13304<br>314 010 | 52233<br>−13303<br>314 011 | 52234<br>−13302<br>314 012 | 52235<br>−13301<br>314 013 | 52236<br>−13300<br>314 014 | 52237<br>−13299<br>314 015 | 52238<br>−13298<br>314 016 | 52239<br>−13297<br>314 017 |
| 1− | 52240<br>−13296<br>314 020 | 52241<br>−13295<br>314 021 | 52242<br>−13294<br>314 022 | 52243<br>−13293<br>314 023 | 52244<br>−13292<br>314 024 | 52245<br>−13291<br>314 025 | 52246<br>−13290<br>314 026 | 52247<br>−13289<br>314 027 | 52248<br>−13288<br>314 030 | 52249<br>−13287<br>314 031 | 52250<br>−13286<br>314 032 | 52251<br>−13285<br>314 033 | 52252<br>−13284<br>314 034 | 52253<br>−13283<br>314 035 | 52254<br>−13282<br>314 036 | 52255<br>−13281<br>314 037 |
| 2− | 52256<br>−13280<br>314 040 | 52257<br>−13279<br>314 041 | 52258<br>−13278<br>314 042 | 52259<br>−13277<br>314 043 | 52260<br>−13276<br>314 044 | 52261<br>−13275<br>314 045 | 52262<br>−13274<br>314 046 | 52263<br>−13273<br>314 047 | 52264<br>−13272<br>314 050 | 52265<br>−13271<br>314 051 | 52266<br>−13270<br>314 052 | 52267<br>−13269<br>314 053 | 52268<br>−13268<br>314 054 | 52269<br>−13267<br>314 055 | 52270<br>−13266<br>314 056 | 52271<br>−13265<br>314 057 |
| 3− | 52272<br>−13264<br>314 060 | 52273<br>−13263<br>314 061 | 52274<br>−13262<br>314 062 | 52275<br>−13261<br>314 063 | 52276<br>−13260<br>314 064 | 52277<br>−13259<br>314 065 | 52278<br>−13258<br>314 066 | 52279<br>−13257<br>314 067 | 52280<br>−13256<br>314 070 | 52281<br>−13255<br>314 071 | 52282<br>−13254<br>314 072 | 52283<br>−13253<br>314 073 | 52284<br>−13252<br>314 074 | 52285<br>−13251<br>314 075 | 52286<br>−13250<br>314 076 | 52287<br>−13249<br>314 077 |
| 4− | 52288<br>−13248<br>314 100 | 52289<br>−13247<br>314 101 | 52290<br>−13246<br>314 102 | 52291<br>−13245<br>314 103 | 52292<br>−13244<br>314 104 | 52293<br>−13243<br>314 105 | 52294<br>−13242<br>314 106 | 52295<br>−13241<br>314 107 | 52296<br>−13240<br>314 110 | 52297<br>−13239<br>314 111 | 52298<br>−13238<br>314 112 | 52299<br>−13237<br>314 113 | 52300<br>−13236<br>314 114 | 52301<br>−13235<br>314 115 | 52302<br>−13234<br>314 116 | 52303<br>−13233<br>314 117 |
| 5− | 52304<br>−13232<br>314 120 | 52305<br>−13231<br>314 121 | 52306<br>−13230<br>314 122 | 52307<br>−13229<br>314 123 | 52308<br>−13228<br>314 124 | 52309<br>−13227<br>314 125 | 52310<br>−13226<br>314 126 | 52311<br>−13225<br>314 127 | 52312<br>−13224<br>314 130 | 52313<br>−13223<br>314 131 | 52314<br>−13222<br>314 132 | 52315<br>−13221<br>314 133 | 52316<br>−13220<br>314 134 | 52317<br>−13219<br>314 135 | 52318<br>−13218<br>314 136 | 52319<br>−13217<br>314 137 |
| 6− | 52320<br>−13216<br>314 140 | 52321<br>−13215<br>314 141 | 52322<br>−13214<br>314 142 | 52323<br>−13213<br>314 143 | 52324<br>−13212<br>314 144 | 52325<br>−13211<br>314 145 | 52326<br>−13210<br>314 146 | 52327<br>−13209<br>314 147 | 52328<br>−13208<br>314 150 | 52329<br>−13207<br>314 151 | 52330<br>−13206<br>314 152 | 52331<br>−13205<br>314 153 | 52332<br>−13204<br>314 154 | 52333<br>−13203<br>314 155 | 52334<br>−13202<br>314 156 | 52335<br>−13201<br>314 157 |
| 7− | 52336<br>−13200<br>314 160 | 52337<br>−13199<br>314 161 | 52338<br>−13198<br>314 162 | 52339<br>−13197<br>314 163 | 52340<br>−13196<br>314 164 | 52341<br>−13195<br>314 165 | 52342<br>−13194<br>314 166 | 52343<br>−13193<br>314 167 | 52344<br>−13192<br>314 170 | 52345<br>−13191<br>314 171 | 52346<br>−13190<br>314 172 | 52347<br>−13189<br>314 173 | 52348<br>−13188<br>314 174 | 52349<br>−13187<br>314 175 | 52350<br>−13186<br>314 176 | 52351<br>−13185<br>314 177 |
| 8− | 52352<br>−13184<br>314 200 | 52353<br>−13183<br>314 201 | 52354<br>−13182<br>314 202 | 52355<br>−13181<br>314 203 | 52356<br>−13180<br>314 204 | 52357<br>−13179<br>314 205 | 52358<br>−13178<br>314 206 | 52359<br>−13177<br>314 207 | 52360<br>−13176<br>314 210 | 52361<br>−13175<br>314 211 | 52362<br>−13174<br>314 212 | 52363<br>−13173<br>314 213 | 52364<br>−13172<br>314 214 | 52365<br>−13171<br>314 215 | 52366<br>−13170<br>314 216 | 52367<br>−13169<br>314 217 |
| 9− | 52368<br>−13168<br>314 220 | 52369<br>−13167<br>314 221 | 52370<br>−13166<br>314 222 | 52371<br>−13165<br>314 223 | 52372<br>−13164<br>314 224 | 52373<br>−13163<br>314 225 | 52374<br>−13162<br>314 226 | 52375<br>−13161<br>314 227 | 52376<br>−13160<br>314 230 | 52377<br>−13159<br>314 231 | 52378<br>−13158<br>314 232 | 52379<br>−13157<br>314 233 | 52380<br>−13156<br>314 234 | 52381<br>−13155<br>314 235 | 52382<br>−13154<br>314 236 | 52383<br>−13153<br>314 237 |
| A− | 52384<br>−13152<br>314 240 | 52385<br>−13151<br>314 241 | 52386<br>−13150<br>314 242 | 52387<br>−13149<br>314 243 | 52388<br>−13148<br>314 244 | 52389<br>−13147<br>314 245 | 52390<br>−13146<br>314 246 | 52391<br>−13145<br>314 247 | 52392<br>−13144<br>314 250 | 52393<br>−13143<br>314 251 | 52394<br>−13142<br>314 252 | 52395<br>−13141<br>314 253 | 52396<br>−13140<br>314 254 | 52397<br>−13139<br>314 255 | 52398<br>−13138<br>314 256 | 52399<br>−13137<br>314 257 |
| B− | 52400<br>−13136<br>314 260 | 52401<br>−13135<br>314 261 | 52402<br>−13134<br>314 262 | 52403<br>−13133<br>314 263 | 52404<br>−13132<br>314 264 | 52405<br>−13131<br>314 265 | 52406<br>−13130<br>314 266 | 52407<br>−13129<br>314 267 | 52408<br>−13128<br>314 270 | 52409<br>−13127<br>314 271 | 52410<br>−13126<br>314 272 | 52411<br>−13125<br>314 273 | 52412<br>−13124<br>314 274 | 52413<br>−13123<br>314 275 | 52414<br>−13122<br>314 276 | 52415<br>−13121<br>314 277 |
| C− | 52416<br>−13120<br>314 300 | 52417<br>−13119<br>314 301 | 52418<br>−13118<br>314 302 | 52419<br>−13117<br>314 303 | 52420<br>−13116<br>314 304 | 52421<br>−13115<br>314 305 | 52422<br>−13114<br>314 306 | 52423<br>−13113<br>314 307 | 52424<br>−13112<br>314 310 | 52425<br>−13111<br>314 311 | 52426<br>−13110<br>314 312 | 52427<br>−13109<br>314 313 | 52428<br>−13108<br>314 314 | 52429<br>−13107<br>314 315 | 52430<br>−13106<br>314 316 | 52431<br>−13105<br>314 317 |
| D− | 52432<br>−13104<br>314 320 | 52433<br>−13103<br>314 321 | 52434<br>−13102<br>314 322 | 52435<br>−13101<br>314 323 | 52436<br>−13100<br>314 324 | 52437<br>−13099<br>314 325 | 52438<br>−13098<br>314 326 | 52439<br>−13097<br>314 327 | 52440<br>−13096<br>314 330 | 52441<br>−13095<br>314 331 | 52442<br>−13094<br>314 332 | 52443<br>−13093<br>314 333 | 52444<br>−13092<br>314 334 | 52445<br>−13091<br>314 335 | 52446<br>−13090<br>314 336 | 52447<br>−13089<br>314 337 |
| E− | 52448<br>−13088<br>314 340 | 52449<br>−13087<br>314 341 | 52450<br>−13086<br>314 342 | 52451<br>−13085<br>314 343 | 52452<br>−13084<br>314 344 | 52453<br>−13083<br>314 345 | 52454<br>−13082<br>314 346 | 52455<br>−13081<br>314 347 | 52456<br>−13080<br>314 350 | 52457<br>−13079<br>314 351 | 52458<br>−13078<br>314 352 | 52459<br>−13077<br>314 353 | 52460<br>−13076<br>314 354 | 52461<br>−13075<br>314 355 | 52462<br>−13074<br>314 356 | 52463<br>−13073<br>314 357 |
| F− | 52464<br>−13072<br>314 360 | 52465<br>−13071<br>314 361 | 52466<br>−13070<br>314 362 | 52467<br>−13069<br>314 363 | 52468<br>−13068<br>314 364 | 52469<br>−13067<br>314 365 | 52470<br>−13066<br>314 366 | 52471<br>−13065<br>314 367 | 52472<br>−13064<br>314 370 | 52473<br>−13063<br>314 371 | 52474<br>−13062<br>314 372 | 52475<br>−13061<br>314 373 | 52476<br>−13060<br>314 374 | 52477<br>−13059<br>314 375 | 52478<br>−13058<br>314 376 | 52479<br>−13057<br>314 377 |

DECIMAL ← (top right arrow)

 DECIMAL ← (Apple icon, middle right arrow)

OCTAL ← (bottom right arrow)

 DECIMAL  −13312   BINARY  1100 1100   DECIMAL  52224   HEXADECIMAL  (CC)  OCTAL  314 000

FOURTH HEX DIGIT →   ← THIRD HEX DIGIT

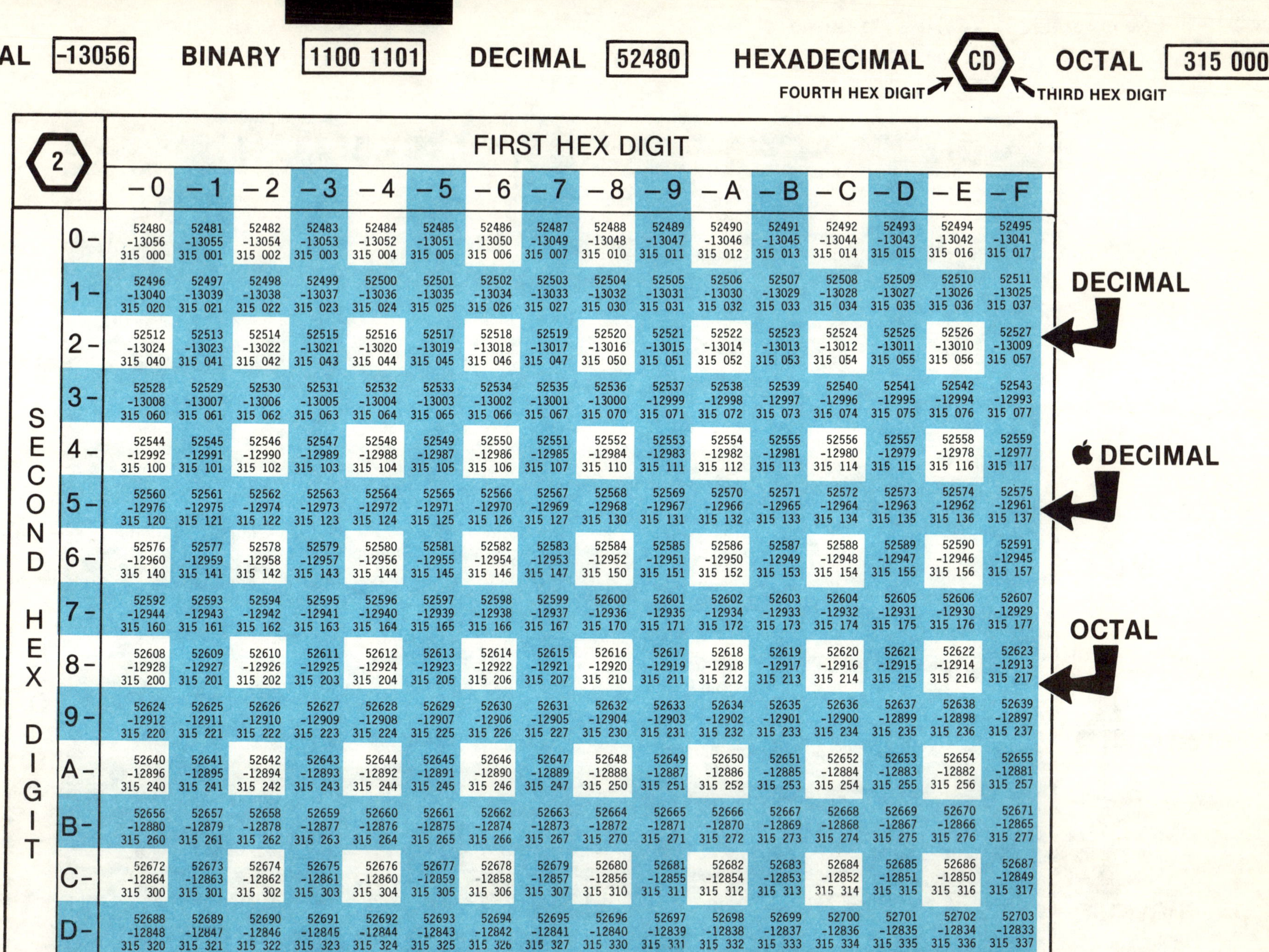



FIRST HEX DIGIT — SECOND HEX DIGIT

| ② | −0 | −1 | −2 | −3 | −4 | −5 | −6 | −7 | −8 | −9 | −A | −B | −C | −D | −E | −F |
|---|---|---|---|---|---|---|---|---|---|---|---|---|---|---|---|---|
| **0−** | 52480<br>-13056<br>315 000 | 52481<br>-13055<br>315 001 | 52482<br>-13054<br>315 002 | 52483<br>-13053<br>315 003 | 52484<br>-13052<br>315 004 | 52485<br>-13051<br>315 005 | 52486<br>-13050<br>315 006 | 52487<br>-13049<br>315 007 | 52488<br>-13048<br>315 010 | 52489<br>-13047<br>315 011 | 52490<br>-13046<br>315 012 | 52491<br>-13045<br>315 013 | 52492<br>-13044<br>315 014 | 52493<br>-13043<br>315 015 | 52494<br>-13042<br>315 016 | 52495<br>-13041<br>315 017 |
| **1−** | 52496<br>-13040<br>315 020 | 52497<br>-13039<br>315 021 | 52498<br>-13038<br>315 022 | 52499<br>-13037<br>315 023 | 52500<br>-13036<br>315 024 | 52501<br>-13035<br>315 025 | 52502<br>-13034<br>315 026 | 52503<br>-13033<br>315 027 | 52504<br>-13032<br>315 030 | 52505<br>-13031<br>315 031 | 52506<br>-13030<br>315 032 | 52507<br>-13029<br>315 033 | 52508<br>-13028<br>315 034 | 52509<br>-13027<br>315 035 | 52510<br>-13026<br>315 036 | 52511<br>-13025<br>315 037 |
| **2−** | 52512<br>-13024<br>315 040 | 52513<br>-13023<br>315 041 | 52514<br>-13022<br>315 042 | 52515<br>-13021<br>315 043 | 52516<br>-13020<br>315 044 | 52517<br>-13019<br>315 045 | 52518<br>-13018<br>315 046 | 52519<br>-13017<br>315 047 | 52520<br>-13016<br>315 050 | 52521<br>-13015<br>315 051 | 52522<br>-13014<br>315 052 | 52523<br>-13013<br>315 053 | 52524<br>-13012<br>315 054 | 52525<br>-13011<br>315 055 | 52526<br>-13010<br>315 056 | 52527<br>-13009<br>315 057 |
| **3−** | 52528<br>-13008<br>315 060 | 52529<br>-13007<br>315 061 | 52530<br>-13006<br>315 062 | 52531<br>-13005<br>315 063 | 52532<br>-13004<br>315 064 | 52533<br>-13003<br>315 065 | 52534<br>-13002<br>315 066 | 52535<br>-13001<br>315 067 | 52536<br>-13000<br>315 070 | 52537<br>-12999<br>315 071 | 52538<br>-12998<br>315 072 | 52539<br>-12997<br>315 073 | 52540<br>-12996<br>315 074 | 52541<br>-12995<br>315 075 | 52542<br>-12994<br>315 076 | 52543<br>-12993<br>315 077 |
| **4−** | 52544<br>-12992<br>315 100 | 52545<br>-12991<br>315 101 | 52546<br>-12990<br>315 102 | 52547<br>-12989<br>315 103 | 52548<br>-12988<br>315 104 | 52549<br>-12987<br>315 105 | 52550<br>-12986<br>315 106 | 52551<br>-12985<br>315 107 | 52552<br>-12984<br>315 110 | 52553<br>-12983<br>315 111 | 52554<br>-12982<br>315 112 | 52555<br>-12981<br>315 113 | 52556<br>-12980<br>315 114 | 52557<br>-12979<br>315 115 | 52558<br>-12978<br>315 116 | 52559<br>-12977<br>315 117 |
| **5−** | 52560<br>-12976<br>315 120 | 52561<br>-12975<br>315 121 | 52562<br>-12974<br>315 122 | 52563<br>-12973<br>315 123 | 52564<br>-12972<br>315 124 | 52565<br>-12971<br>315 125 | 52566<br>-12970<br>315 126 | 52567<br>-12969<br>315 127 | 52568<br>-12968<br>315 130 | 52569<br>-12967<br>315 131 | 52570<br>-12966<br>315 132 | 52571<br>-12965<br>315 133 | 52572<br>-12964<br>315 134 | 52573<br>-12963<br>315 135 | 52574<br>-12962<br>315 136 | 52575<br>-12961<br>315 137 |
| **6−** | 52576<br>-12960<br>315 140 | 52577<br>-12959<br>315 141 | 52578<br>-12958<br>315 142 | 52579<br>-12957<br>315 143 | 52580<br>-12956<br>315 144 | 52581<br>-12955<br>315 145 | 52582<br>-12954<br>315 146 | 52583<br>-12953<br>315 147 | 52584<br>-12952<br>315 150 | 52585<br>-12951<br>315 151 | 52586<br>-12950<br>315 152 | 52587<br>-12949<br>315 153 | 52588<br>-12948<br>315 154 | 52589<br>-12947<br>315 155 | 52590<br>-12946<br>315 156 | 52591<br>-12945<br>315 157 |
| **7−** | 52592<br>-12944<br>315 160 | 52593<br>-12943<br>315 161 | 52594<br>-12942<br>315 162 | 52595<br>-12941<br>315 163 | 52596<br>-12940<br>315 164 | 52597<br>-12939<br>315 165 | 52598<br>-12938<br>315 166 | 52599<br>-12937<br>315 167 | 52600<br>-12936<br>315 170 | 52601<br>-12935<br>315 171 | 52602<br>-12934<br>315 172 | 52603<br>-12933<br>315 173 | 52604<br>-12932<br>315 174 | 52605<br>-12931<br>315 175 | 52606<br>-12930<br>315 176 | 52607<br>-12929<br>315 177 |
| **8−** | 52608<br>-12928<br>315 200 | 52609<br>-12927<br>315 201 | 52610<br>-12926<br>315 202 | 52611<br>-12925<br>315 203 | 52612<br>-12924<br>315 204 | 52613<br>-12923<br>315 205 | 52614<br>-12922<br>315 206 | 52615<br>-12921<br>315 207 | 52616<br>-12920<br>315 210 | 52617<br>-12919<br>315 211 | 52618<br>-12918<br>315 212 | 52619<br>-12917<br>315 213 | 52620<br>-12916<br>315 214 | 52621<br>-12915<br>315 215 | 52622<br>-12914<br>315 216 | 52623<br>-12913<br>315 217 |
| **9−** | 52624<br>-12912<br>315 220 | 52625<br>-12911<br>315 221 | 52626<br>-12910<br>315 222 | 52627<br>-12909<br>315 223 | 52628<br>-12908<br>315 224 | 52629<br>-12907<br>315 225 | 52630<br>-12906<br>315 226 | 52631<br>-12905<br>315 227 | 52632<br>-12904<br>315 230 | 52633<br>-12903<br>315 231 | 52634<br>-12902<br>315 232 | 52635<br>-12901<br>315 233 | 52636<br>-12900<br>315 234 | 52637<br>-12899<br>315 235 | 52638<br>-12898<br>315 236 | 52639<br>-12897<br>315 237 |
| **A−** | 52640<br>-12896<br>315 240 | 52641<br>-12895<br>315 241 | 52642<br>-12894<br>315 242 | 52643<br>-12893<br>315 243 | 52644<br>-12892<br>315 244 | 52645<br>-12891<br>315 245 | 52646<br>-12890<br>315 246 | 52647<br>-12889<br>315 247 | 52648<br>-12888<br>315 250 | 52649<br>-12887<br>315 251 | 52650<br>-12886<br>315 252 | 52651<br>-12885<br>315 253 | 52652<br>-12884<br>315 254 | 52653<br>-12883<br>315 255 | 52654<br>-12882<br>315 256 | 52655<br>-12881<br>315 257 |
| **B−** | 52656<br>-12880<br>315 260 | 52657<br>-12879<br>315 261 | 52658<br>-12878<br>315 262 | 52659<br>-12877<br>315 263 | 52660<br>-12876<br>315 264 | 52661<br>-12875<br>315 265 | 52662<br>-12874<br>315 266 | 52663<br>-12873<br>315 267 | 52664<br>-12872<br>315 270 | 52665<br>-12871<br>315 271 | 52666<br>-12870<br>315 272 | 52667<br>-12869<br>315 273 | 52668<br>-12868<br>315 274 | 52669<br>-12867<br>315 275 | 52670<br>-12866<br>315 276 | 52671<br>-12865<br>315 277 |
| **C−** | 52672<br>-12864<br>315 300 | 52673<br>-12863<br>315 301 | 52674<br>-12862<br>315 302 | 52675<br>-12861<br>315 303 | 52676<br>-12860<br>315 304 | 52677<br>-12859<br>315 305 | 52678<br>-12858<br>315 306 | 52679<br>-12857<br>315 307 | 52680<br>-12856<br>315 310 | 52681<br>-12855<br>315 311 | 52682<br>-12854<br>315 312 | 52683<br>-12853<br>315 313 | 52684<br>-12852<br>315 314 | 52685<br>-12851<br>315 315 | 52686<br>-12850<br>315 316 | 52687<br>-12849<br>315 317 |
| **D−** | 52688<br>-12848<br>315 320 | 52689<br>-12847<br>315 321 | 52690<br>-12846<br>315 322 | 52691<br>-12845<br>315 323 | 52692<br>-12844<br>315 324 | 52693<br>-12843<br>315 325 | 52694<br>-12842<br>315 326 | 52695<br>-12841<br>315 327 | 52696<br>-12840<br>315 330 | 52697<br>-12839<br>315 331 | 52698<br>-12838<br>315 332 | 52699<br>-12837<br>315 333 | 52700<br>-12836<br>315 334 | 52701<br>-12835<br>315 335 | 52702<br>-12834<br>315 336 | 52703<br>-12833<br>315 337 |
| **E−** | 52704<br>-12832<br>315 340 | 52705<br>-12831<br>315 341 | 52706<br>-12830<br>315 342 | 52707<br>-12829<br>315 343 | 52708<br>-12828<br>315 344 | 52709<br>-12827<br>315 345 | 52710<br>-12826<br>315 346 | 52711<br>-12825<br>315 347 | 52712<br>-12824<br>315 350 | 52713<br>-12823<br>315 351 | 52714<br>-12822<br>315 352 | 52715<br>-12821<br>315 353 | 52716<br>-12820<br>315 354 | 52717<br>-12819<br>315 355 | 52718<br>-12818<br>315 356 | 52719<br>-12817<br>315 357 |
| **F−** | 52720<br>-12816<br>315 360 | 52721<br>-12815<br>315 361 | 52722<br>-12814<br>315 362 | 52723<br>-12813<br>315 363 | 52724<br>-12812<br>315 364 | 52725<br>-12811<br>315 365 | 52726<br>-12810<br>315 366 | 52727<br>-12809<br>315 367 | 52728<br>-12808<br>315 370 | 52729<br>-12807<br>315 371 | 52730<br>-12806<br>315 372 | 52731<br>-12805<br>315 373 | 52732<br>-12804<br>315 374 | 52733<br>-12803<br>315 375 | 52734<br>-12802<br>315 376 | 52735<br>-12801<br>315 377 |

# FIRST HEX DIGIT · SECOND HEX DIGIT

Each cell lists: DECIMAL (top), DECIMAL signed (middle), OCTAL (bottom).

| | −0 | −1 | −2 | −3 | −4 | −5 | −6 | −7 | −8 | −9 | −A | −B | −C | −D | −E | −F |
|---|---|---|---|---|---|---|---|---|---|---|---|---|---|---|---|---|
| **0−** | 52736<br>−12800<br>316 000 | 52737<br>−12799<br>316 001 | 52738<br>−12798<br>316 002 | 52739<br>−12797<br>316 003 | 52740<br>−12796<br>316 004 | 52741<br>−12795<br>316 005 | 52742<br>−12794<br>316 006 | 52743<br>−12793<br>316 007 | 52744<br>−12792<br>316 010 | 52745<br>−12791<br>316 011 | 52746<br>−12790<br>316 012 | 52747<br>−12789<br>316 013 | 52748<br>−12788<br>316 014 | 52749<br>−12787<br>316 015 | 52750<br>−12786<br>316 016 | 52751<br>−12785<br>316 017 |
| **1−** | 52752<br>−12784<br>316 020 | 52753<br>−12783<br>316 021 | 52754<br>−12782<br>316 022 | 52755<br>−12781<br>316 023 | 52756<br>−12780<br>316 024 | 52757<br>−12779<br>316 025 | 52758<br>−12778<br>316 026 | 52759<br>−12777<br>316 027 | 52760<br>−12776<br>316 030 | 52761<br>−12775<br>316 031 | 52762<br>−12774<br>316 032 | 52763<br>−12773<br>316 033 | 52764<br>−12772<br>316 034 | 52765<br>−12771<br>316 035 | 52766<br>−12770<br>316 036 | 52767<br>−12769<br>316 037 |
| **2−** | 52768<br>−12768<br>316 040 | 52769<br>−12767<br>316 041 | 52770<br>−12766<br>316 042 | 52771<br>−12765<br>316 043 | 52772<br>−12764<br>316 044 | 52773<br>−12763<br>316 045 | 52774<br>−12762<br>316 046 | 52775<br>−12761<br>316 047 | 52776<br>−12760<br>316 050 | 52777<br>−12759<br>316 051 | 52778<br>−12758<br>316 052 | 52779<br>−12757<br>316 053 | 52780<br>−12756<br>316 054 | 52781<br>−12755<br>316 055 | 52782<br>−12754<br>316 056 | 52783<br>−12753<br>316 057 |
| **3−** | 52784<br>−12752<br>316 060 | 52785<br>−12751<br>316 061 | 52786<br>−12750<br>316 062 | 52787<br>−12749<br>316 063 | 52788<br>−12748<br>316 064 | 52789<br>−12747<br>316 065 | 52790<br>−12746<br>316 066 | 52791<br>−12745<br>316 067 | 52792<br>−12744<br>316 070 | 52793<br>−12743<br>316 071 | 52794<br>−12742<br>316 072 | 52795<br>−12741<br>316 073 | 52796<br>−12740<br>316 074 | 52797<br>−12739<br>316 075 | 52798<br>−12738<br>316 076 | 52799<br>−12737<br>316 077 |
| **4−** | 52800<br>−12736<br>316 100 | 52801<br>−12735<br>316 101 | 52802<br>−12734<br>316 102 | 52803<br>−12733<br>316 103 | 52804<br>−12732<br>316 104 | 52805<br>−12731<br>316 105 | 52806<br>−12730<br>316 106 | 52807<br>−12729<br>316 107 | 52808<br>−12728<br>316 110 | 52809<br>−12727<br>316 111 | 52810<br>−12726<br>316 112 | 52811<br>−12725<br>316 113 | 52812<br>−12724<br>316 114 | 52813<br>−12723<br>316 115 | 52814<br>−12722<br>316 116 | 52815<br>−12721<br>316 117 |
| **5−** | 52816<br>−12720<br>316 120 | 52817<br>−12719<br>316 121 | 52818<br>−12718<br>316 122 | 52819<br>−12717<br>316 123 | 52820<br>−12716<br>316 124 | 52821<br>−12715<br>316 125 | 52822<br>−12714<br>316 126 | 52823<br>−12713<br>316 127 | 52824<br>−12712<br>316 130 | 52825<br>−12711<br>316 131 | 52826<br>−12710<br>316 132 | 52827<br>−12709<br>316 133 | 52828<br>−12708<br>316 134 | 52829<br>−12707<br>316 135 | 52830<br>−12706<br>316 136 | 52831<br>−12705<br>316 137 |
| **6−** | 52832<br>−12704<br>316 140 | 52833<br>−12703<br>316 141 | 52834<br>−12702<br>316 142 | 52835<br>−12701<br>316 143 | 52836<br>−12700<br>316 144 | 52837<br>−12699<br>316 145 | 52838<br>−12698<br>316 146 | 52839<br>−12697<br>316 147 | 52840<br>−12696<br>316 150 | 52841<br>−12695<br>316 151 | 52842<br>−12694<br>316 152 | 52843<br>−12693<br>316 153 | 52844<br>−12692<br>316 154 | 52845<br>−12691<br>316 155 | 52846<br>−12690<br>316 156 | 52847<br>−12689<br>316 157 |
| **7−** | 52848<br>−12688<br>316 160 | 52849<br>−12687<br>316 161 | 52850<br>−12686<br>316 162 | 52851<br>−12685<br>316 163 | 52852<br>−12684<br>316 164 | 52853<br>−12683<br>316 165 | 52854<br>−12682<br>316 166 | 52855<br>−12681<br>316 167 | 52856<br>−12680<br>316 170 | 52857<br>−12679<br>316 171 | 52858<br>−12678<br>316 172 | 52859<br>−12677<br>316 173 | 52860<br>−12676<br>316 174 | 52861<br>−12675<br>316 175 | 52862<br>−12674<br>316 176 | 52863<br>−12673<br>316 177 |
| **8−** | 52864<br>−12672<br>316 200 | 52865<br>−12671<br>316 201 | 52866<br>−12670<br>316 202 | 52867<br>−12669<br>316 203 | 52868<br>−12668<br>316 204 | 52869<br>−12667<br>316 205 | 52870<br>−12666<br>316 206 | 52871<br>−12665<br>316 207 | 52872<br>−12664<br>316 210 | 52873<br>−12663<br>316 211 | 52874<br>−12662<br>316 212 | 52875<br>−12661<br>316 213 | 52876<br>−12660<br>316 214 | 52877<br>−12659<br>316 215 | 52878<br>−12658<br>316 216 | 52879<br>−12657<br>316 217 |
| **9−** | 52880<br>−12656<br>316 220 | 52881<br>−12655<br>316 221 | 52882<br>−12654<br>316 222 | 52883<br>−12653<br>316 223 | 52884<br>−12652<br>316 224 | 52885<br>−12651<br>316 225 | 52886<br>−12650<br>316 226 | 52887<br>−12649<br>316 227 | 52888<br>−12648<br>316 230 | 52889<br>−12647<br>316 231 | 52890<br>−12646<br>316 232 | 52891<br>−12645<br>316 233 | 52892<br>−12644<br>316 234 | 52893<br>−12643<br>316 235 | 52894<br>−12642<br>316 236 | 52895<br>−12641<br>316 237 |
| **A−** | 52896<br>−12640<br>316 240 | 52897<br>−12639<br>316 241 | 52898<br>−12638<br>316 242 | 52899<br>−12637<br>316 243 | 52900<br>−12636<br>316 244 | 52901<br>−12635<br>316 245 | 52902<br>−12634<br>316 246 | 52903<br>−12633<br>316 247 | 52904<br>−12632<br>316 250 | 52905<br>−12631<br>316 251 | 52906<br>−12630<br>316 252 | 52907<br>−12629<br>316 253 | 52908<br>−12628<br>316 254 | 52909<br>−12627<br>316 255 | 52910<br>−12626<br>316 256 | 52911<br>−12625<br>316 257 |
| **B−** | 52912<br>−12624<br>316 260 | 52913<br>−12623<br>316 261 | 52914<br>−12622<br>316 262 | 52915<br>−12621<br>316 263 | 52916<br>−12620<br>316 264 | 52917<br>−12619<br>316 265 | 52918<br>−12618<br>316 266 | 52919<br>−12617<br>316 267 | 52920<br>−12616<br>316 270 | 52921<br>−12615<br>316 271 | 52922<br>−12614<br>316 272 | 52923<br>−12613<br>316 273 | 52924<br>−12612<br>316 274 | 52925<br>−12611<br>316 275 | 52926<br>−12610<br>316 276 | 52927<br>−12609<br>316 277 |
| **C−** | 52928<br>−12608<br>316 300 | 52929<br>−12607<br>316 301 | 52930<br>−12606<br>316 302 | 52931<br>−12605<br>316 303 | 52932<br>−12604<br>316 304 | 52933<br>−12603<br>316 305 | 52934<br>−12602<br>316 306 | 52935<br>−12601<br>316 307 | 52936<br>−12600<br>316 310 | 52937<br>−12599<br>316 311 | 52938<br>−12598<br>316 312 | 52939<br>−12597<br>316 313 | 52940<br>−12596<br>316 314 | 52941<br>−12595<br>316 315 | 52942<br>−12594<br>316 316 | 52943<br>−12593<br>316 317 |
| **D−** | 52944<br>−12592<br>316 320 | 52945<br>−12591<br>316 321 | 52946<br>−12590<br>316 322 | 52947<br>−12589<br>316 323 | 52948<br>−12588<br>316 324 | 52949<br>−12587<br>316 325 | 52950<br>−12586<br>316 326 | 52951<br>−12585<br>316 327 | 52952<br>−12584<br>316 330 | 52953<br>−12583<br>316 331 | 52954<br>−12582<br>316 332 | 52955<br>−12581<br>316 333 | 52956<br>−12580<br>316 334 | 52957<br>−12579<br>316 335 | 52958<br>−12578<br>316 336 | 52959<br>−12577<br>316 337 |
| **E−** | 52960<br>−12576<br>316 340 | 52961<br>−12575<br>316 341 | 52962<br>−12574<br>316 342 | 52963<br>−12573<br>316 343 | 52964<br>−12572<br>316 344 | 52965<br>−12571<br>316 345 | 52966<br>−12570<br>316 346 | 52967<br>−12569<br>316 347 | 52968<br>−12568<br>316 350 | 52969<br>−12567<br>316 351 | 52970<br>−12566<br>316 352 | 52971<br>−12565<br>316 353 | 52972<br>−12564<br>316 354 | 52973<br>−12563<br>316 355 | 52974<br>−12562<br>316 356 | 52975<br>−12561<br>316 357 |
| **F−** | 52976<br>−12560<br>316 360 | 52977<br>−12559<br>316 361 | 52978<br>−12558<br>316 362 | 52979<br>−12557<br>316 363 | 52980<br>−12556<br>316 364 | 52981<br>−12555<br>316 365 | 52982<br>−12554<br>316 366 | 52983<br>−12553<br>316 367 | 52984<br>−12552<br>316 370 | 52985<br>−12551<br>316 371 | 52986<br>−12550<br>316 372 | 52987<br>−12549<br>316 373 | 52988<br>−12548<br>316 374 | 52989<br>−12547<br>316 375 | 52990<br>−12546<br>316 376 | 52991<br>−12545<br>316 377 |

DECIMAL (right margin)

**SECOND HEX DIGIT** (left margin)

OCTAL

 DECIMAL  −12800   BINARY  1100 1110   DECIMAL  52736   HEXADECIMAL  (CE)  OCTAL  316 000

FOURTH HEX DIGIT →  ← THIRD HEX DIGIT

DECIMAL [-12544]   BINARY [1100 1111]   DECIMAL [52992]   HEXADECIMAL ⬡CF OCTAL [317 000]

FOURTH HEX DIGIT → ⬡CF ← THIRD HEX DIGIT

⬡2 — FIRST HEX DIGIT

| SECOND HEX DIGIT | −0 | −1 | −2 | −3 | −4 | −5 | −6 | −7 | −8 | −9 | −A | −B | −C | −D | −E | −F |
|---|---|---|---|---|---|---|---|---|---|---|---|---|---|---|---|---|
| 0− | 52992<br>−12544<br>317 000 | 52993<br>−12543<br>317 001 | 52994<br>−12542<br>317 002 | 52995<br>−12541<br>317 003 | 52996<br>−12540<br>317 004 | 52997<br>−12539<br>317 005 | 52998<br>−12538<br>317 006 | 52999<br>−12537<br>317 007 | 53000<br>−12536<br>317 010 | 53001<br>−12535<br>317 011 | 53002<br>−12534<br>317 012 | 53003<br>−12533<br>317 013 | 53004<br>−12532<br>317 014 | 53005<br>−12531<br>317 015 | 53006<br>−12530<br>317 016 | 53007<br>−12529<br>317 017 |
| 1− | 53008<br>−12528<br>317 020 | 53009<br>−12527<br>317 021 | 53010<br>−12526<br>317 022 | 53011<br>−12525<br>317 023 | 53012<br>−12524<br>317 024 | 53013<br>−12523<br>317 025 | 53014<br>−12522<br>317 026 | 53015<br>−12521<br>317 027 | 53016<br>−12520<br>317 030 | 53017<br>−12519<br>317 031 | 53018<br>−12518<br>317 032 | 53019<br>−12517<br>317 033 | 53020<br>−12516<br>317 034 | 53021<br>−12515<br>317 035 | 53022<br>−12514<br>317 036 | 53023<br>−12513<br>317 037 |
| 2− | 53024<br>−12512<br>317 040 | 53025<br>−12511<br>317 041 | 53026<br>−12510<br>317 042 | 53027<br>−12509<br>317 043 | 53028<br>−12508<br>317 044 | 53029<br>−12507<br>317 045 | 53030<br>−12506<br>317 046 | 53031<br>−12505<br>317 047 | 53032<br>−12504<br>317 050 | 53033<br>−12503<br>317 051 | 53034<br>−12502<br>317 052 | 53035<br>−12501<br>317 053 | 53036<br>−12500<br>317 054 | 53037<br>−12499<br>317 055 | 53038<br>−12498<br>317 056 | 53039<br>−12497<br>317 057 |
| 3− | 53040<br>−12496<br>317 060 | 53041<br>−12495<br>317 061 | 53042<br>−12494<br>317 062 | 53043<br>−12493<br>317 063 | 53044<br>−12492<br>317 064 | 53045<br>−12491<br>317 065 | 53046<br>−12490<br>317 066 | 53047<br>−12489<br>317 067 | 53048<br>−12488<br>317 070 | 53049<br>−12487<br>317 071 | 53050<br>−12486<br>317 072 | 53051<br>−12485<br>317 073 | 53052<br>−12484<br>317 074 | 53053<br>−12483<br>317 075 | 53054<br>−12482<br>317 076 | 53055<br>−12481<br>317 077 |
| 4− | 53056<br>−12480<br>317 100 | 53057<br>−12479<br>317 101 | 53058<br>−12478<br>317 102 | 53059<br>−12477<br>317 103 | 53060<br>−12476<br>317 104 | 53061<br>−12475<br>317 105 | 53062<br>−12474<br>317 106 | 53063<br>−12473<br>317 107 | 53064<br>−12472<br>317 110 | 53065<br>−12471<br>317 111 | 53066<br>−12470<br>317 112 | 53067<br>−12469<br>317 113 | 53068<br>−12468<br>317 114 | 53069<br>−12467<br>317 115 | 53070<br>−12466<br>317 116 | 53071<br>−12465<br>317 117 |
| 5− | 53072<br>−12464<br>317 120 | 53073<br>−12463<br>317 121 | 53074<br>−12462<br>317 122 | 53075<br>−12461<br>317 123 | 53076<br>−12460<br>317 124 | 53077<br>−12459<br>317 125 | 53078<br>−12458<br>317 126 | 53079<br>−12457<br>317 127 | 53080<br>−12456<br>317 130 | 53081<br>−12455<br>317 131 | 53082<br>−12454<br>317 132 | 53083<br>−12453<br>317 133 | 53084<br>−12452<br>317 134 | 53085<br>−12451<br>317 135 | 53086<br>−12450<br>317 136 | 53087<br>−12449<br>317 137 |
| 6− | 53088<br>−12448<br>317 140 | 53089<br>−12447<br>317 141 | 53090<br>−12446<br>317 142 | 53091<br>−12445<br>317 143 | 53092<br>−12444<br>317 144 | 53093<br>−12443<br>317 145 | 53094<br>−12442<br>317 146 | 53095<br>−12441<br>317 147 | 53096<br>−12440<br>317 150 | 53097<br>−12439<br>317 151 | 53098<br>−12438<br>317 152 | 53099<br>−12437<br>317 153 | 53100<br>−12436<br>317 154 | 53101<br>−12435<br>317 155 | 53102<br>−12434<br>317 156 | 53103<br>−12433<br>317 157 |
| 7− | 53104<br>−12432<br>317 160 | 53105<br>−12431<br>317 161 | 53106<br>−12430<br>317 162 | 53107<br>−12429<br>317 163 | 53108<br>−12428<br>317 164 | 53109<br>−12427<br>317 165 | 53110<br>−12426<br>317 166 | 53111<br>−12425<br>317 167 | 53112<br>−12424<br>317 170 | 53113<br>−12423<br>317 171 | 53114<br>−12422<br>317 172 | 53115<br>−12421<br>317 173 | 53116<br>−12420<br>317 174 | 53117<br>−12419<br>317 175 | 53118<br>−12418<br>317 176 | 53119<br>−12417<br>317 177 |
| 8− | 53120<br>−12416<br>317 200 | 53121<br>−12415<br>317 201 | 53122<br>−12414<br>317 202 | 53123<br>−12413<br>317 203 | 53124<br>−12412<br>317 204 | 53125<br>−12411<br>317 205 | 53126<br>−12410<br>317 206 | 53127<br>−12409<br>317 207 | 53128<br>−12408<br>317 210 | 53129<br>−12407<br>317 211 | 53130<br>−12406<br>317 212 | 53131<br>−12405<br>317 213 | 53132<br>−12404<br>317 214 | 53133<br>−12403<br>317 215 | 53134<br>−12402<br>317 216 | 53135<br>−12401<br>317 217 |
| 9− | 53136<br>−12400<br>317 220 | 53137<br>−12399<br>317 221 | 53138<br>−12398<br>317 222 | 53139<br>−12397<br>317 223 | 53140<br>−12396<br>317 224 | 53141<br>−12395<br>317 225 | 53142<br>−12394<br>317 226 | 53143<br>−12393<br>317 227 | 53144<br>−12392<br>317 230 | 53145<br>−12391<br>317 231 | 53146<br>−12390<br>317 232 | 53147<br>−12389<br>317 233 | 53148<br>−12388<br>317 234 | 53149<br>−12387<br>317 235 | 53150<br>−12386<br>317 236 | 53151<br>−12385<br>317 237 |
| A− | 53152<br>−12384<br>317 240 | 53153<br>−12383<br>317 241 | 53154<br>−12382<br>317 242 | 53155<br>−12381<br>317 243 | 53156<br>−12380<br>317 244 | 53157<br>−12379<br>317 245 | 53158<br>−12378<br>317 246 | 53159<br>−12377<br>317 247 | 53160<br>−12376<br>317 250 | 53161<br>−12375<br>317 251 | 53162<br>−12374<br>317 252 | 53163<br>−12373<br>317 253 | 53164<br>−12372<br>317 254 | 53165<br>−12371<br>317 255 | 53166<br>−12370<br>317 256 | 53167<br>−12369<br>317 257 |
| B− | 53168<br>−12368<br>317 260 | 53169<br>−12367<br>317 261 | 53170<br>−12366<br>317 262 | 53171<br>−12365<br>317 263 | 53172<br>−12364<br>317 264 | 53173<br>−12363<br>317 265 | 53174<br>−12362<br>317 266 | 53175<br>−12361<br>317 267 | 53176<br>−12360<br>317 270 | 53177<br>−12359<br>317 271 | 53178<br>−12358<br>317 272 | 53179<br>−12357<br>317 273 | 53180<br>−12356<br>317 274 | 53181<br>−12355<br>317 275 | 53182<br>−12354<br>317 276 | 53183<br>−12353<br>317 277 |
| C− | 53184<br>−12352<br>317 300 | 53185<br>−12351<br>317 301 | 53186<br>−12350<br>317 302 | 53187<br>−12349<br>317 303 | 53188<br>−12348<br>317 304 | 53189<br>−12347<br>317 305 | 53190<br>−12346<br>317 306 | 53191<br>−12345<br>317 307 | 53192<br>−12344<br>317 310 | 53193<br>−12343<br>317 311 | 53194<br>−12342<br>317 312 | 53195<br>−12341<br>317 313 | 53196<br>−12340<br>317 314 | 53197<br>−12339<br>317 315 | 53198<br>−12338<br>317 316 | 53199<br>−12337<br>317 317 |
| D− | 53200<br>−12336<br>317 320 | 53201<br>−12335<br>317 321 | 53202<br>−12334<br>317 322 | 53203<br>−12333<br>317 323 | 53204<br>−12332<br>317 324 | 53205<br>−12331<br>317 325 | 53206<br>−12330<br>317 326 | 53207<br>−12329<br>317 327 | 53208<br>−12328<br>317 330 | 53209<br>−12327<br>317 331 | 53210<br>−12326<br>317 332 | 53211<br>−12325<br>317 333 | 53212<br>−12324<br>317 334 | 53213<br>−12323<br>317 335 | 53214<br>−12322<br>317 336 | 53215<br>−12321<br>317 337 |
| E− | 53216<br>−12320<br>317 340 | 53217<br>−12319<br>317 341 | 53218<br>−12318<br>317 342 | 53219<br>−12317<br>317 343 | 53220<br>−12316<br>317 344 | 53221<br>−12315<br>317 345 | 53222<br>−12314<br>317 346 | 53223<br>−12313<br>317 347 | 53224<br>−12312<br>317 350 | 53225<br>−12311<br>317 351 | 53226<br>−12310<br>317 352 | 53227<br>−12309<br>317 353 | 53228<br>−12308<br>317 354 | 53229<br>−12307<br>317 355 | 53230<br>−12306<br>317 356 | 53231<br>−12305<br>317 357 |
| F− | 53232<br>−12304<br>317 360 | 53233<br>−12303<br>317 361 | 53234<br>−12302<br>317 362 | 53235<br>−12301<br>317 363 | 53236<br>−12300<br>317 364 | 53237<br>−12299<br>317 365 | 53238<br>−12298<br>317 366 | 53239<br>−12297<br>317 367 | 53240<br>−12296<br>317 370 | 53241<br>−12295<br>317 371 | 53242<br>−12294<br>317 372 | 53243<br>−12293<br>317 373 | 53244<br>−12292<br>317 374 | 53245<br>−12291<br>317 375 | 53246<br>−12290<br>317 376 | 53247<br>−12289<br>317 377 |

DECIMAL ←

⬆ DECIMAL ←

OCTAL ←

| SECOND HEX DIGIT | −0 | −1 | −2 | −3 | −4 | −5 | −6 | −7 | −8 | −9 | −A | −B | −C | −D | −E | −F |
|---|---|---|---|---|---|---|---|---|---|---|---|---|---|---|---|---|
| **0−** | 53248<br>−12288<br>320 000 | 53249<br>−12287<br>320 001 | 53250<br>−12286<br>320 002 | 53251<br>−12285<br>320 003 | 53252<br>−12284<br>320 004 | 53253<br>−12283<br>320 005 | 53254<br>−12282<br>320 006 | 53255<br>−12281<br>320 007 | 53256<br>−12280<br>320 010 | 53257<br>−12279<br>320 011 | 53258<br>−12278<br>320 012 | 53259<br>−12277<br>320 013 | 53260<br>−12276<br>320 014 | 53261<br>−12275<br>320 015 | 53262<br>−12274<br>320 016 | 53263<br>−12273<br>320 017 |
| **1−** | 53264<br>−12272<br>320 020 | 53265<br>−12271<br>320 021 | 53266<br>−12270<br>320 022 | 53267<br>−12269<br>320 023 | 53268<br>−12268<br>320 024 | 53269<br>−12267<br>320 025 | 53270<br>−12266<br>320 026 | 53271<br>−12265<br>320 027 | 53272<br>−12264<br>320 030 | 53273<br>−12263<br>320 031 | 53274<br>−12262<br>320 032 | 53275<br>−12261<br>320 033 | 53276<br>−12260<br>320 034 | 53277<br>−12259<br>320 035 | 53278<br>−12258<br>320 036 | 53279<br>−12257<br>320 037 |
| **2−** | 53280<br>−12256<br>320 040 | 53281<br>−12255<br>320 041 | 53282<br>−12254<br>320 042 | 53283<br>−12253<br>320 043 | 53284<br>−12252<br>320 044 | 53285<br>−12251<br>320 045 | 53286<br>−12250<br>320 046 | 53287<br>−12249<br>320 047 | 53288<br>−12248<br>320 050 | 53289<br>−12247<br>320 051 | 53290<br>−12246<br>320 052 | 53291<br>−12245<br>320 053 | 53292<br>−12244<br>320 054 | 53293<br>−12243<br>320 055 | 53294<br>−12242<br>320 056 | 53295<br>−12241<br>320 057 |
| **3−** | 53296<br>−12240<br>320 060 | 53297<br>−12239<br>320 061 | 53298<br>−12238<br>320 062 | 53299<br>−12237<br>320 063 | 53300<br>−12236<br>320 064 | 53301<br>−12235<br>320 065 | 53302<br>−12234<br>320 066 | 53303<br>−12233<br>320 067 | 53304<br>−12232<br>320 070 | 53305<br>−12231<br>320 071 | 53306<br>−12230<br>320 072 | 53307<br>−12229<br>320 073 | 53308<br>−12228<br>320 074 | 53309<br>−12227<br>320 075 | 53310<br>−12226<br>320 076 | 53311<br>−12225<br>320 077 |
| **4−** | 53312<br>−12224<br>320 100 | 53313<br>−12223<br>320 101 | 53314<br>−12222<br>320 102 | 53315<br>−12221<br>320 103 | 53316<br>−12220<br>320 104 | 53317<br>−12219<br>320 105 | 53318<br>−12218<br>320 106 | 53319<br>−12217<br>320 107 | 53320<br>−12216<br>320 110 | 53321<br>−12215<br>320 111 | 53322<br>−12214<br>320 112 | 53323<br>−12213<br>320 113 | 53324<br>−12212<br>320 114 | 53325<br>−12211<br>320 115 | 53326<br>−12210<br>320 116 | 53327<br>−12209<br>320 117 |
| **5−** | 53328<br>−12208<br>320 120 | 53329<br>−12207<br>320 121 | 53330<br>−12206<br>320 122 | 53331<br>−12205<br>320 123 | 53332<br>−12204<br>320 124 | 53333<br>−12203<br>320 125 | 53334<br>−12202<br>320 126 | 53335<br>−12201<br>320 127 | 53336<br>−12200<br>320 130 | 53337<br>−12199<br>320 131 | 53338<br>−12198<br>320 132 | 53339<br>−12197<br>320 133 | 53340<br>−12196<br>320 134 | 53341<br>−12195<br>320 135 | 53342<br>−12194<br>320 136 | 53343<br>−12193<br>320 137 |
| **6−** | 53344<br>−12192<br>320 140 | 53345<br>−12191<br>320 141 | 53346<br>−12190<br>320 142 | 53347<br>−12189<br>320 143 | 53348<br>−12188<br>320 144 | 53349<br>−12187<br>320 145 | 53350<br>−12186<br>320 146 | 53351<br>−12185<br>320 147 | 53352<br>−12184<br>320 150 | 53353<br>−12183<br>320 151 | 53354<br>−12182<br>320 152 | 53355<br>−12181<br>320 153 | 53356<br>−12180<br>320 154 | 53357<br>−12179<br>320 155 | 53358<br>−12178<br>320 156 | 53359<br>−12177<br>320 157 |
| **7−** | 53360<br>−12176<br>320 160 | 53361<br>−12175<br>320 161 | 53362<br>−12174<br>320 162 | 53363<br>−12173<br>320 163 | 53364<br>−12172<br>320 164 | 53365<br>−12171<br>320 165 | 53366<br>−12170<br>320 166 | 53367<br>−12169<br>320 167 | 53368<br>−12168<br>320 170 | 53369<br>−12167<br>320 171 | 53370<br>−12166<br>320 172 | 53371<br>−12165<br>320 173 | 53372<br>−12164<br>320 174 | 53373<br>−12163<br>320 175 | 53374<br>−12162<br>320 176 | 53375<br>−12161<br>320 177 |
| **8−** | 53376<br>−12160<br>320 200 | 53377<br>−12159<br>320 201 | 53378<br>−12158<br>320 202 | 53379<br>−12157<br>320 203 | 53380<br>−12156<br>320 204 | 53381<br>−12155<br>320 205 | 53382<br>−12154<br>320 206 | 53383<br>−12153<br>320 207 | 53384<br>−12152<br>320 210 | 53385<br>−12151<br>320 211 | 53386<br>−12150<br>320 212 | 53387<br>−12149<br>320 213 | 53388<br>−12148<br>320 214 | 53389<br>−12147<br>320 215 | 53390<br>−12146<br>320 216 | 53391<br>−12145<br>320 217 |
| **9−** | 53392<br>−12144<br>320 220 | 53393<br>−12143<br>320 221 | 53394<br>−12142<br>320 222 | 53395<br>−12141<br>320 223 | 53396<br>−12140<br>320 224 | 53397<br>−12139<br>320 225 | 53398<br>−12138<br>320 226 | 53399<br>−12137<br>320 227 | 53400<br>−12136<br>320 230 | 53401<br>−12135<br>320 231 | 53402<br>−12134<br>320 232 | 53403<br>−12133<br>320 233 | 53404<br>−12132<br>320 234 | 53405<br>−12131<br>320 235 | 53406<br>−12130<br>320 236 | 53407<br>−12129<br>320 237 |
| **A−** | 53408<br>−12128<br>320 240 | 53409<br>−12127<br>320 241 | 53410<br>−12126<br>320 242 | 53411<br>−12125<br>320 243 | 53412<br>−12124<br>320 244 | 53413<br>−12123<br>320 245 | 53414<br>−12122<br>320 246 | 53415<br>−12121<br>320 247 | 53416<br>−12120<br>320 250 | 53417<br>−12119<br>320 251 | 53418<br>−12118<br>320 252 | 53419<br>−12117<br>320 253 | 53420<br>−12116<br>320 254 | 53421<br>−12115<br>320 255 | 53422<br>−12114<br>320 256 | 53423<br>−12113<br>320 257 |
| **B−** | 53424<br>−12112<br>320 260 | 53425<br>−12111<br>320 261 | 53426<br>−12110<br>320 262 | 53427<br>−12109<br>320 263 | 53428<br>−12108<br>320 264 | 53429<br>−12107<br>320 265 | 53430<br>−12106<br>320 266 | 53431<br>−12105<br>320 267 | 53432<br>−12104<br>320 270 | 53433<br>−12103<br>320 271 | 53434<br>−12102<br>320 272 | 53435<br>−12101<br>320 273 | 53436<br>−12100<br>320 274 | 53437<br>−12099<br>320 275 | 53438<br>−12098<br>320 276 | 53439<br>−12097<br>320 277 |
| **C−** | 53440<br>−12096<br>320 300 | 53441<br>−12095<br>320 301 | 53442<br>−12094<br>320 302 | 53443<br>−12093<br>320 303 | 53444<br>−12092<br>320 304 | 53445<br>−12091<br>320 305 | 53446<br>−12090<br>320 306 | 53447<br>−12089<br>320 307 | 53448<br>−12088<br>320 310 | 53449<br>−12087<br>320 311 | 53450<br>−12086<br>320 312 | 53451<br>−12085<br>320 313 | 53452<br>−12084<br>320 314 | 53453<br>−12083<br>320 315 | 53454<br>−12082<br>320 316 | 53455<br>−12081<br>320 317 |
| **D−** | 53456<br>−12080<br>320 320 | 53457<br>−12079<br>320 321 | 53458<br>−12078<br>320 322 | 53459<br>−12077<br>320 323 | 53460<br>−12076<br>320 324 | 53461<br>−12075<br>320 325 | 53462<br>−12074<br>320 326 | 53463<br>−12073<br>320 327 | 53464<br>−12072<br>320 330 | 53465<br>−12071<br>320 331 | 53466<br>−12070<br>320 332 | 53467<br>−12069<br>320 333 | 53468<br>−12068<br>320 334 | 53469<br>−12067<br>320 335 | 53470<br>−12066<br>320 336 | 53471<br>−12065<br>320 337 |
| **E−** | 53472<br>−12064<br>320 340 | 53473<br>−12063<br>320 341 | 53474<br>−12062<br>320 342 | 53475<br>−12061<br>320 343 | 53476<br>−12060<br>320 344 | 53477<br>−12059<br>320 345 | 53478<br>−12058<br>320 346 | 53479<br>−12057<br>320 347 | 53480<br>−12056<br>320 350 | 53481<br>−12055<br>320 351 | 53482<br>−12054<br>320 352 | 53483<br>−12053<br>320 353 | 53484<br>−12052<br>320 354 | 53485<br>−12051<br>320 355 | 53486<br>−12050<br>320 356 | 53487<br>−12049<br>320 357 |
| **F−** | 53488<br>−12048<br>320 360 | 53489<br>−12047<br>320 361 | 53490<br>−12046<br>320 362 | 53491<br>−12045<br>320 363 | 53492<br>−12044<br>320 364 | 53493<br>−12043<br>320 365 | 53494<br>−12042<br>320 366 | 53495<br>−12041<br>320 367 | 53496<br>−12040<br>320 370 | 53497<br>−12039<br>320 371 | 53498<br>−12038<br>320 372 | 53499<br>−12037<br>320 373 | 53500<br>−12036<br>320 374 | 53501<br>−12035<br>320 375 | 53502<br>−12034<br>320 376 | 53503<br>−12033<br>320 377 |

Legend (right side): DECIMAL · DECIMAL · OCTAL

 DECIMAL `-12288`   BINARY `1101 0000`   DECIMAL `53248`   HEXADECIMAL ⬡ **D0**   OCTAL `320 000`

FOURTH HEX DIGIT → ⬡ ← THIRD HEX DIGIT

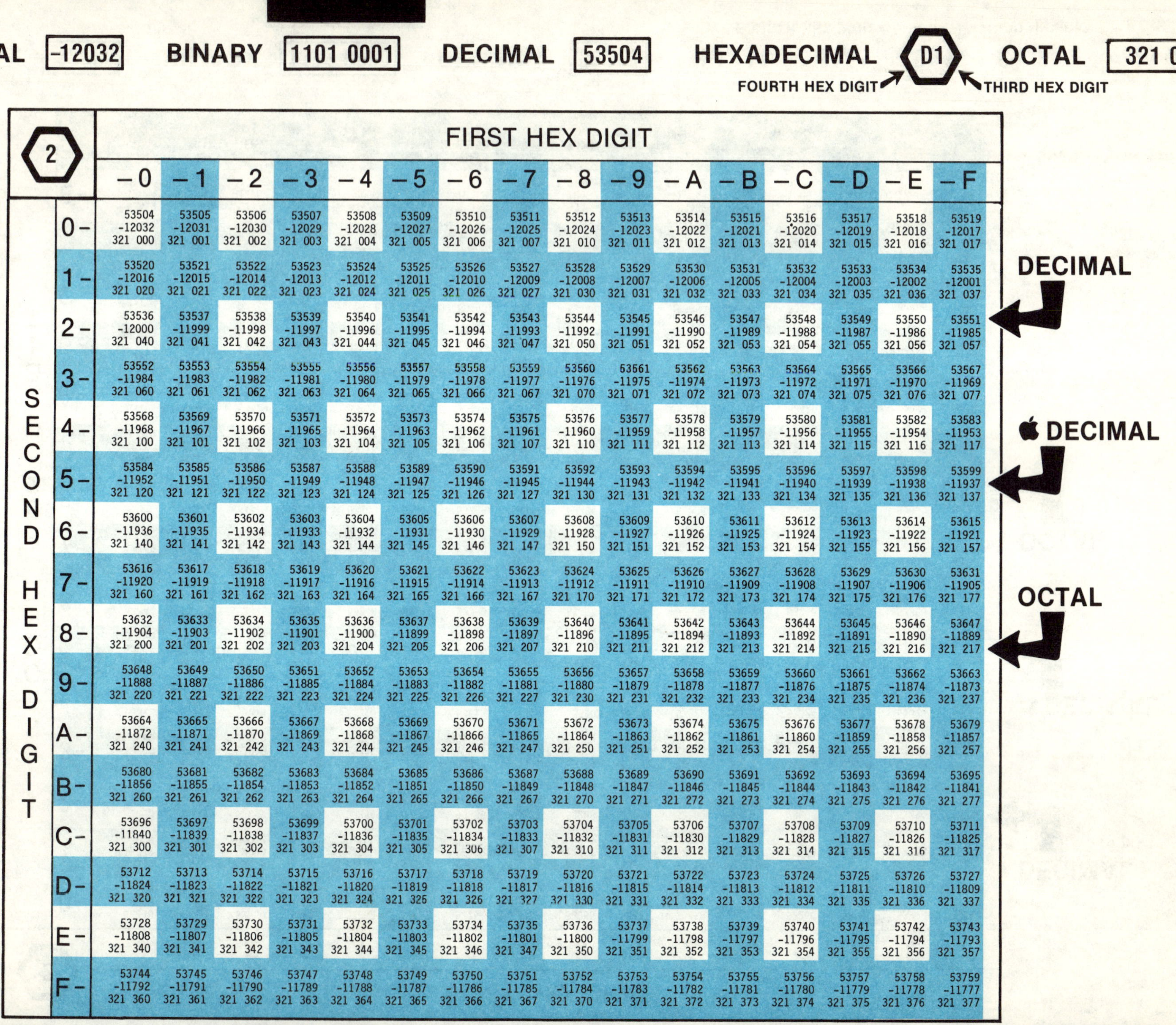

 DECIMAL [−12032]   BINARY [1101 0001]   DECIMAL [53504]   HEXADECIMAL ⬡D1   OCTAL [321 000]
FOURTH HEX DIGIT → D1 ← THIRD HEX DIGIT

⬡2  — SECOND HEX DIGIT (rows) / FIRST HEX DIGIT (columns)

| | −0 | −1 | −2 | −3 | −4 | −5 | −6 | −7 | −8 | −9 | −A | −B | −C | −D | −E | −F |
|---|---|---|---|---|---|---|---|---|---|---|---|---|---|---|---|---|
| 0− | 53504<br>−12032<br>321 000 | 53505<br>−12031<br>321 001 | 53506<br>−12030<br>321 002 | 53507<br>−12029<br>321 003 | 53508<br>−12028<br>321 004 | 53509<br>−12027<br>321 005 | 53510<br>−12026<br>321 006 | 53511<br>−12025<br>321 007 | 53512<br>−12024<br>321 010 | 53513<br>−12023<br>321 011 | 53514<br>−12022<br>321 012 | 53515<br>−12021<br>321 013 | 53516<br>−12020<br>321 014 | 53517<br>−12019<br>321 015 | 53518<br>−12018<br>321 016 | 53519<br>−12017<br>321 017 |
| 1− | 53520<br>−12016<br>321 020 | 53521<br>−12015<br>321 021 | 53522<br>−12014<br>321 022 | 53523<br>−12013<br>321 023 | 53524<br>−12012<br>321 024 | 53525<br>−12011<br>321 025 | 53526<br>−12010<br>321 026 | 53527<br>−12009<br>321 027 | 53528<br>−12008<br>321 030 | 53529<br>−12007<br>321 031 | 53530<br>−12006<br>321 032 | 53531<br>−12005<br>321 033 | 53532<br>−12004<br>321 034 | 53533<br>−12003<br>321 035 | 53534<br>−12002<br>321 036 | 53535<br>−12001<br>321 037 |
| 2− | 53536<br>−12000<br>321 040 | 53537<br>−11999<br>321 041 | 53538<br>−11998<br>321 042 | 53539<br>−11997<br>321 043 | 53540<br>−11996<br>321 044 | 53541<br>−11995<br>321 045 | 53542<br>−11994<br>321 046 | 53543<br>−11993<br>321 047 | 53544<br>−11992<br>321 050 | 53545<br>−11991<br>321 051 | 53546<br>−11990<br>321 052 | 53547<br>−11989<br>321 053 | 53548<br>−11988<br>321 054 | 53549<br>−11987<br>321 055 | 53550<br>−11986<br>321 056 | 53551<br>−11985<br>321 057 |
| 3− | 53552<br>−11984<br>321 060 | 53553<br>−11983<br>321 061 | 53554<br>−11982<br>321 062 | 53555<br>−11981<br>321 063 | 53556<br>−11980<br>321 064 | 53557<br>−11979<br>321 065 | 53558<br>−11978<br>321 066 | 53559<br>−11977<br>321 067 | 53560<br>−11976<br>321 070 | 53561<br>−11975<br>321 071 | 53562<br>−11974<br>321 072 | 53563<br>−11973<br>321 073 | 53564<br>−11972<br>321 074 | 53565<br>−11971<br>321 075 | 53566<br>−11970<br>321 076 | 53567<br>−11969<br>321 077 |
| 4− | 53568<br>−11968<br>321 100 | 53569<br>−11967<br>321 101 | 53570<br>−11966<br>321 102 | 53571<br>−11965<br>321 103 | 53572<br>−11964<br>321 104 | 53573<br>−11963<br>321 105 | 53574<br>−11962<br>321 106 | 53575<br>−11961<br>321 107 | 53576<br>−11960<br>321 110 | 53577<br>−11959<br>321 111 | 53578<br>−11958<br>321 112 | 53579<br>−11957<br>321 113 | 53580<br>−11956<br>321 114 | 53581<br>−11955<br>321 115 | 53582<br>−11954<br>321 116 | 53583<br>−11953<br>321 117 |
| 5− | 53584<br>−11952<br>321 120 | 53585<br>−11951<br>321 121 | 53586<br>−11950<br>321 122 | 53587<br>−11949<br>321 123 | 53588<br>−11948<br>321 124 | 53589<br>−11947<br>321 125 | 53590<br>−11946<br>321 126 | 53591<br>−11945<br>321 127 | 53592<br>−11944<br>321 130 | 53593<br>−11943<br>321 131 | 53594<br>−11942<br>321 132 | 53595<br>−11941<br>321 133 | 53596<br>−11940<br>321 134 | 53597<br>−11939<br>321 135 | 53598<br>−11938<br>321 136 | 53599<br>−11937<br>321 137 |
| 6− | 53600<br>−11936<br>321 140 | 53601<br>−11935<br>321 141 | 53602<br>−11934<br>321 142 | 53603<br>−11933<br>321 143 | 53604<br>−11932<br>321 144 | 53605<br>−11931<br>321 145 | 53606<br>−11930<br>321 146 | 53607<br>−11929<br>321 147 | 53608<br>−11928<br>321 150 | 53609<br>−11927<br>321 151 | 53610<br>−11926<br>321 152 | 53611<br>−11925<br>321 153 | 53612<br>−11924<br>321 154 | 53613<br>−11923<br>321 155 | 53614<br>−11922<br>321 156 | 53615<br>−11921<br>321 157 |
| 7− | 53616<br>−11920<br>321 160 | 53617<br>−11919<br>321 161 | 53618<br>−11918<br>321 162 | 53619<br>−11917<br>321 163 | 53620<br>−11916<br>321 164 | 53621<br>−11915<br>321 165 | 53622<br>−11914<br>321 166 | 53623<br>−11913<br>321 167 | 53624<br>−11912<br>321 170 | 53625<br>−11911<br>321 171 | 53626<br>−11910<br>321 172 | 53627<br>−11909<br>321 173 | 53628<br>−11908<br>321 174 | 53629<br>−11907<br>321 175 | 53630<br>−11906<br>321 176 | 53631<br>−11905<br>321 177 |
| 8− | 53632<br>−11904<br>321 200 | 53633<br>−11903<br>321 201 | 53634<br>−11902<br>321 202 | 53635<br>−11901<br>321 203 | 53636<br>−11900<br>321 204 | 53637<br>−11899<br>321 205 | 53638<br>−11898<br>321 206 | 53639<br>−11897<br>321 207 | 53640<br>−11896<br>321 210 | 53641<br>−11895<br>321 211 | 53642<br>−11894<br>321 212 | 53643<br>−11893<br>321 213 | 53644<br>−11892<br>321 214 | 53645<br>−11891<br>321 215 | 53646<br>−11890<br>321 216 | 53647<br>−11889<br>321 217 |
| 9− | 53648<br>−11888<br>321 220 | 53649<br>−11887<br>321 221 | 53650<br>−11886<br>321 222 | 53651<br>−11885<br>321 223 | 53652<br>−11884<br>321 224 | 53653<br>−11883<br>321 225 | 53654<br>−11882<br>321 226 | 53655<br>−11881<br>321 227 | 53656<br>−11880<br>321 230 | 53657<br>−11879<br>321 231 | 53658<br>−11878<br>321 232 | 53659<br>−11877<br>321 233 | 53660<br>−11876<br>321 234 | 53661<br>−11875<br>321 235 | 53662<br>−11874<br>321 236 | 53663<br>−11873<br>321 237 |
| A− | 53664<br>−11872<br>321 240 | 53665<br>−11871<br>321 241 | 53666<br>−11870<br>321 242 | 53667<br>−11869<br>321 243 | 53668<br>−11868<br>321 244 | 53669<br>−11867<br>321 245 | 53670<br>−11866<br>321 246 | 53671<br>−11865<br>321 247 | 53672<br>−11864<br>321 250 | 53673<br>−11863<br>321 251 | 53674<br>−11862<br>321 252 | 53675<br>−11861<br>321 253 | 53676<br>−11860<br>321 254 | 53677<br>−11859<br>321 255 | 53678<br>−11858<br>321 256 | 53679<br>−11857<br>321 257 |
| B− | 53680<br>−11856<br>321 260 | 53681<br>−11855<br>321 261 | 53682<br>−11854<br>321 262 | 53683<br>−11853<br>321 263 | 53684<br>−11852<br>321 264 | 53685<br>−11851<br>321 265 | 53686<br>−11850<br>321 266 | 53687<br>−11849<br>321 267 | 53688<br>−11848<br>321 270 | 53689<br>−11847<br>321 271 | 53690<br>−11846<br>321 272 | 53691<br>−11845<br>321 273 | 53692<br>−11844<br>321 274 | 53693<br>−11843<br>321 275 | 53694<br>−11842<br>321 276 | 53695<br>−11841<br>321 277 |
| C− | 53696<br>−11840<br>321 300 | 53697<br>−11839<br>321 301 | 53698<br>−11838<br>321 302 | 53699<br>−11837<br>321 303 | 53700<br>−11836<br>321 304 | 53701<br>−11835<br>321 305 | 53702<br>−11834<br>321 306 | 53703<br>−11833<br>321 307 | 53704<br>−11832<br>321 310 | 53705<br>−11831<br>321 311 | 53706<br>−11830<br>321 312 | 53707<br>−11829<br>321 313 | 53708<br>−11828<br>321 314 | 53709<br>−11827<br>321 315 | 53710<br>−11826<br>321 316 | 53711<br>−11825<br>321 317 |
| D− | 53712<br>−11824<br>321 320 | 53713<br>−11823<br>321 321 | 53714<br>−11822<br>321 322 | 53715<br>−11821<br>321 323 | 53716<br>−11820<br>321 324 | 53717<br>−11819<br>321 325 | 53718<br>−11818<br>321 326 | 53719<br>−11817<br>321 327 | 53720<br>−11816<br>321 330 | 53721<br>−11815<br>321 331 | 53722<br>−11814<br>321 332 | 53723<br>−11813<br>321 333 | 53724<br>−11812<br>321 334 | 53725<br>−11811<br>321 335 | 53726<br>−11810<br>321 336 | 53727<br>−11809<br>321 337 |
| E− | 53728<br>−11808<br>321 340 | 53729<br>−11807<br>321 341 | 53730<br>−11806<br>321 342 | 53731<br>−11805<br>321 343 | 53732<br>−11804<br>321 344 | 53733<br>−11803<br>321 345 | 53734<br>−11802<br>321 346 | 53735<br>−11801<br>321 347 | 53736<br>−11800<br>321 350 | 53737<br>−11799<br>321 351 | 53738<br>−11798<br>321 352 | 53739<br>−11797<br>321 353 | 53740<br>−11796<br>321 354 | 53741<br>−11795<br>321 355 | 53742<br>−11794<br>321 356 | 53743<br>−11793<br>321 357 |
| F− | 53744<br>−11792<br>321 360 | 53745<br>−11791<br>321 361 | 53746<br>−11790<br>321 362 | 53747<br>−11789<br>321 363 | 53748<br>−11788<br>321 364 | 53749<br>−11787<br>321 365 | 53750<br>−11786<br>321 366 | 53751<br>−11785<br>321 367 | 53752<br>−11784<br>321 370 | 53753<br>−11783<br>321 371 | 53754<br>−11782<br>321 372 | 53755<br>−11781<br>321 373 | 53756<br>−11780<br>321 374 | 53757<br>−11779<br>321 375 | 53758<br>−11778<br>321 376 | 53759<br>−11777<br>321 377 |

## FIRST HEX DIGIT

| | −0 | −1 | −2 | −3 | −4 | −5 | −6 | −7 | −8 | −9 | −A | −B | −C | −D | −E | −F |
|---|---|---|---|---|---|---|---|---|---|---|---|---|---|---|---|---|
| **0-** | 53760<br>-11776<br>322 000 | 53761<br>-11775<br>322 001 | 53762<br>-11774<br>322 002 | 53763<br>-11773<br>322 003 | 53764<br>-11772<br>322 004 | 53765<br>-11771<br>322 005 | 53766<br>-11770<br>322 006 | 53767<br>-11769<br>322 007 | 53768<br>-11768<br>322 010 | 53769<br>-11767<br>322 011 | 53770<br>-11766<br>322 012 | 53771<br>-11765<br>322 013 | 53772<br>-11764<br>322 014 | 53773<br>-11763<br>322 015 | 53774<br>-11762<br>322 016 | 53775<br>-11761<br>322 017 |
| **1-** | 53776<br>-11760<br>322 020 | 53777<br>-11759<br>322 021 | 53778<br>-11758<br>322 022 | 53779<br>-11757<br>322 023 | 53780<br>-11756<br>322 024 | 53781<br>-11755<br>322 025 | 53782<br>-11754<br>322 026 | 53783<br>-11753<br>322 027 | 53784<br>-11752<br>322 030 | 53785<br>-11751<br>322 031 | 53786<br>-11750<br>322 032 | 53787<br>-11749<br>322 033 | 53788<br>-11748<br>322 034 | 53789<br>-11747<br>322 035 | 53790<br>-11746<br>322 036 | 53791<br>-11745<br>322 037 |
| **2-** | 53792<br>-11744<br>322 040 | 53793<br>-11743<br>322 041 | 53794<br>-11742<br>322 042 | 53795<br>-11741<br>322 043 | 53796<br>-11740<br>322 044 | 53797<br>-11739<br>322 045 | 53798<br>-11738<br>322 046 | 53799<br>-11737<br>322 047 | 53800<br>-11736<br>322 050 | 53801<br>-11735<br>322 051 | 53802<br>-11734<br>322 052 | 53803<br>-11733<br>322 053 | 53804<br>-11732<br>322 054 | 53805<br>-11731<br>322 055 | 53806<br>-11730<br>322 056 | 53807<br>-11729<br>322 057 |
| **3-** | 53808<br>-11728<br>322 060 | 53809<br>-11727<br>322 061 | 53810<br>-11726<br>322 062 | 53811<br>-11725<br>322 063 | 53812<br>-11724<br>322 064 | 53813<br>-11723<br>322 065 | 53814<br>-11722<br>322 066 | 53815<br>-11721<br>322 067 | 53816<br>-11720<br>322 070 | 53817<br>-11719<br>322 071 | 53818<br>-11718<br>322 072 | 53819<br>-11717<br>322 073 | 53820<br>-11716<br>322 074 | 53821<br>-11715<br>322 075 | 53822<br>-11714<br>322 076 | 53823<br>-11713<br>322 077 |
| **4-** | 53824<br>-11712<br>322 100 | 53825<br>-11711<br>322 101 | 53826<br>-11710<br>322 102 | 53827<br>-11709<br>322 103 | 53828<br>-11708<br>322 104 | 53829<br>-11707<br>322 105 | 53830<br>-11706<br>322 106 | 53831<br>-11705<br>322 107 | 53832<br>-11704<br>322 110 | 53833<br>-11703<br>322 111 | 53834<br>-11702<br>322 112 | 53835<br>-11701<br>322 113 | 53836<br>-11700<br>322 114 | 53837<br>-11699<br>322 115 | 53838<br>-11698<br>322 116 | 53839<br>-11697<br>322 117 |
| **5-** | 53840<br>-11696<br>322 120 | 53841<br>-11695<br>322 121 | 53842<br>-11694<br>322 122 | 53843<br>-11693<br>322 123 | 53844<br>-11692<br>322 124 | 53845<br>-11691<br>322 125 | 53846<br>-11690<br>322 126 | 53847<br>-11689<br>322 127 | 53848<br>-11688<br>322 130 | 53849<br>-11687<br>322 131 | 53850<br>-11686<br>322 132 | 53851<br>-11685<br>322 133 | 53852<br>-11684<br>322 134 | 53853<br>-11683<br>322 135 | 53854<br>-11682<br>322 136 | 53855<br>-11681<br>322 137 |
| **6-** | 53856<br>-11680<br>322 140 | 53857<br>-11679<br>322 141 | 53858<br>-11678<br>322 142 | 53859<br>-11677<br>322 143 | 53860<br>-11676<br>322 144 | 53861<br>-11675<br>322 145 | 53862<br>-11674<br>322 146 | 53863<br>-11673<br>322 147 | 53864<br>-11672<br>322 150 | 53865<br>-11671<br>322 151 | 53866<br>-11670<br>322 152 | 53867<br>-11669<br>322 153 | 53868<br>-11668<br>322 154 | 53869<br>-11667<br>322 155 | 53870<br>-11666<br>322 156 | 53871<br>-11665<br>322 157 |
| **7-** | 53872<br>-11664<br>322 160 | 53873<br>-11663<br>322 161 | 53874<br>-11662<br>322 162 | 53875<br>-11661<br>322 163 | 53876<br>-11660<br>322 164 | 53877<br>-11659<br>322 165 | 53878<br>-11658<br>322 166 | 53879<br>-11657<br>322 167 | 53880<br>-11656<br>322 170 | 53881<br>-11655<br>322 171 | 53882<br>-11654<br>322 172 | 53883<br>-11653<br>322 173 | 53884<br>-11652<br>322 174 | 53885<br>-11651<br>322 175 | 53886<br>-11650<br>322 176 | 53887<br>-11649<br>322 177 |
| **8-** | 53888<br>-11648<br>322 200 | 53889<br>-11647<br>322 201 | 53890<br>-11646<br>322 202 | 53891<br>-11645<br>322 203 | 53892<br>-11644<br>322 204 | 53893<br>-11643<br>322 205 | 53894<br>-11642<br>322 206 | 53895<br>-11641<br>322 207 | 53896<br>-11640<br>322 210 | 53897<br>-11639<br>322 211 | 53898<br>-11638<br>322 212 | 53899<br>-11637<br>322 213 | 53900<br>-11636<br>322 214 | 53901<br>-11635<br>322 215 | 53902<br>-11634<br>322 216 | 53903<br>-11633<br>322 217 |
| **9-** | 53904<br>-11632<br>322 220 | 53905<br>-11631<br>322 221 | 53906<br>-11630<br>322 222 | 53907<br>-11629<br>322 223 | 53908<br>-11628<br>322 224 | 53909<br>-11627<br>322 225 | 53910<br>-11626<br>322 226 | 53911<br>-11625<br>322 227 | 53912<br>-11624<br>322 230 | 53913<br>-11623<br>322 231 | 53914<br>-11622<br>322 232 | 53915<br>-11621<br>322 233 | 53916<br>-11620<br>322 234 | 53917<br>-11619<br>322 235 | 53918<br>-11618<br>322 236 | 53919<br>-11617<br>322 237 |
| **A-** | 53920<br>-11616<br>322 240 | 53921<br>-11615<br>322 241 | 53922<br>-11614<br>322 242 | 53923<br>-11613<br>322 243 | 53924<br>-11612<br>322 244 | 53925<br>-11611<br>322 245 | 53926<br>-11610<br>322 246 | 53927<br>-11609<br>322 247 | 53928<br>-11608<br>322 250 | 53929<br>-11607<br>322 251 | 53930<br>-11606<br>322 252 | 53931<br>-11605<br>322 253 | 53932<br>-11604<br>322 254 | 53933<br>-11603<br>322 255 | 53934<br>-11602<br>322 256 | 53935<br>-11601<br>322 257 |
| **B-** | 53936<br>-11600<br>322 260 | 53937<br>-11599<br>322 261 | 53938<br>-11598<br>322 262 | 53939<br>-11597<br>322 263 | 53940<br>-11596<br>322 264 | 53941<br>-11595<br>322 265 | 53942<br>-11594<br>322 266 | 53943<br>-11593<br>322 267 | 53944<br>-11592<br>322 270 | 53945<br>-11591<br>322 271 | 53946<br>-11590<br>322 272 | 53947<br>-11589<br>322 273 | 53948<br>-11588<br>322 274 | 53949<br>-11587<br>322 275 | 53950<br>-11586<br>322 276 | 53951<br>-11585<br>322 277 |
| **C-** | 53952<br>-11584<br>322 300 | 53953<br>-11583<br>322 301 | 53954<br>-11582<br>322 302 | 53955<br>-11581<br>322 303 | 53956<br>-11580<br>322 304 | 53957<br>-11579<br>322 305 | 53958<br>-11578<br>322 306 | 53959<br>-11577<br>322 307 | 53960<br>-11576<br>322 310 | 53961<br>-11575<br>322 311 | 53962<br>-11574<br>322 312 | 53963<br>-11573<br>322 313 | 53964<br>-11572<br>322 314 | 53965<br>-11571<br>322 315 | 53966<br>-11570<br>322 316 | 53967<br>-11569<br>322 317 |
| **D-** | 53968<br>-11568<br>322 320 | 53969<br>-11567<br>322 321 | 53970<br>-11566<br>322 322 | 53971<br>-11565<br>322 323 | 53972<br>-11564<br>322 324 | 53973<br>-11563<br>322 325 | 53974<br>-11562<br>322 326 | 53975<br>-11561<br>322 327 | 53976<br>-11560<br>322 330 | 53977<br>-11559<br>322 331 | 53978<br>-11558<br>322 332 | 53979<br>-11557<br>322 333 | 53980<br>-11556<br>322 334 | 53981<br>-11555<br>322 335 | 53982<br>-11554<br>322 336 | 53983<br>-11553<br>322 337 |
| **E-** | 53984<br>-11552<br>322 340 | 53985<br>-11551<br>322 341 | 53986<br>-11550<br>322 342 | 53987<br>-11549<br>322 343 | 53988<br>-11548<br>322 344 | 53989<br>-11547<br>322 345 | 53990<br>-11546<br>322 346 | 53991<br>-11545<br>322 347 | 53992<br>-11544<br>322 350 | 53993<br>-11543<br>322 351 | 53994<br>-11542<br>322 352 | 53995<br>-11541<br>322 353 | 53996<br>-11540<br>322 354 | 53997<br>-11539<br>322 355 | 53998<br>-11538<br>322 356 | 53999<br>-11537<br>322 357 |
| **F-** | 54000<br>-11536<br>322 360 | 54001<br>-11535<br>322 361 | 54002<br>-11534<br>322 362 | 54003<br>-11533<br>322 363 | 54004<br>-11532<br>322 364 | 54005<br>-11531<br>322 365 | 54006<br>-11530<br>322 366 | 54007<br>-11529<br>322 367 | 54008<br>-11528<br>322 370 | 54009<br>-11527<br>322 371 | 54010<br>-11526<br>322 372 | 54011<br>-11525<br>322 373 | 54012<br>-11524<br>322 374 | 54013<br>-11523<br>322 375 | 54014<br>-11522<br>322 376 | 54015<br>-11521<br>322 377 |

Left axis: **SECOND HEX DIGIT**

Right-side labels: DECIMAL, ⬤ DECIMAL, OCTAL

⬤ DECIMAL  `-11776`   BINARY  `1101 0010`   DECIMAL  `53760`   HEXADECIMAL  ⬡ D2   OCTAL  `322 000`

FOURTH HEX DIGIT → ⬡ ← THIRD HEX DIGIT

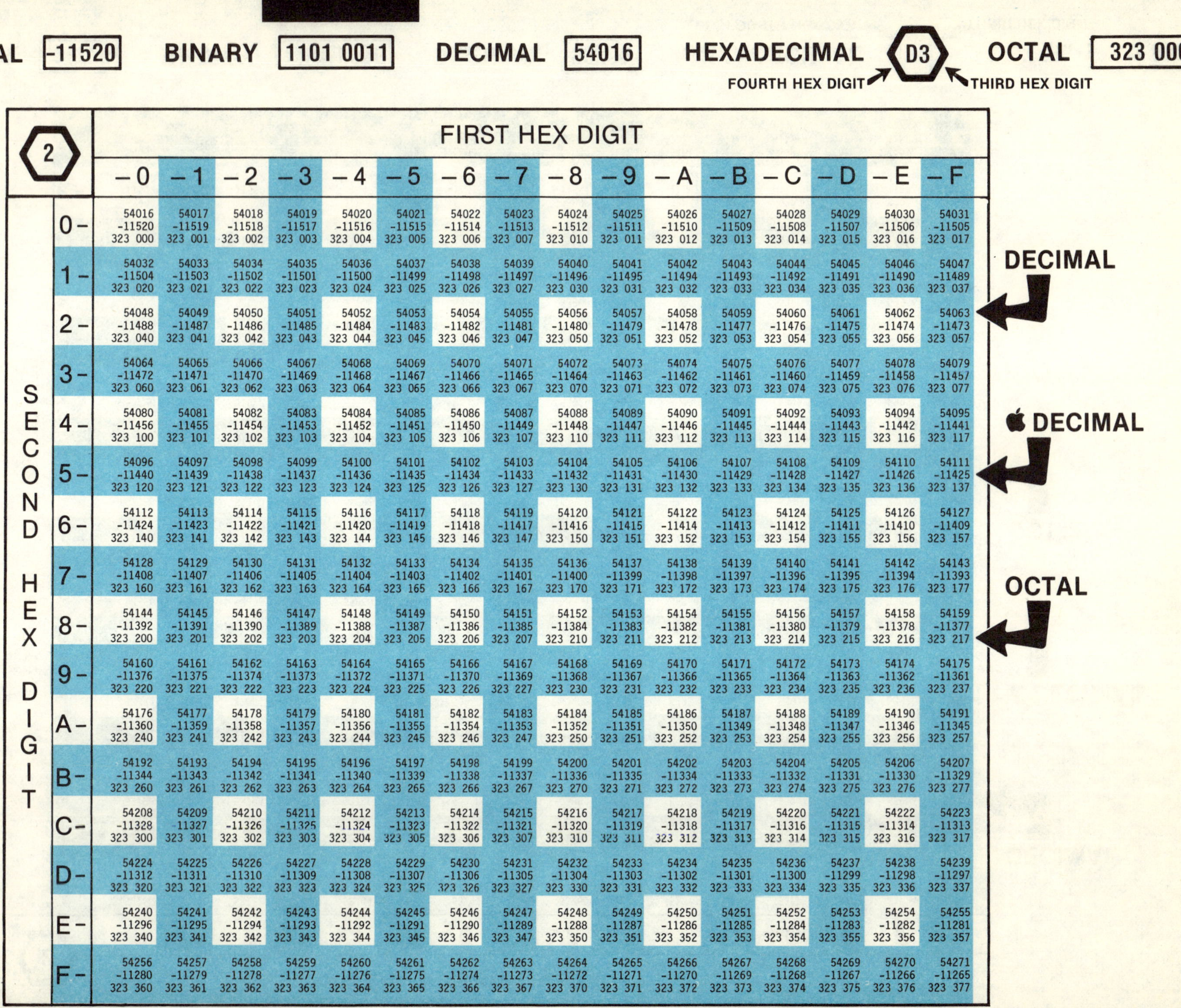

🍎 DECIMAL `-11520`   BINARY `1101 0011`   DECIMAL `54016`   HEXADECIMAL (D3)   OCTAL `323 000`

FOURTH HEX DIGIT → ◆ ← THIRD HEX DIGIT

**FIRST HEX DIGIT**

| (2) | −0 | −1 | −2 | −3 | −4 | −5 | −6 | −7 | −8 | −9 | −A | −B | −C | −D | −E | −F |
|---|---|---|---|---|---|---|---|---|---|---|---|---|---|---|---|---|
| **0−** | 54016<br>-11520<br>323 000 | 54017<br>-11519<br>323 001 | 54018<br>-11518<br>323 002 | 54019<br>-11517<br>323 003 | 54020<br>-11516<br>323 004 | 54021<br>-11515<br>323 005 | 54022<br>-11514<br>323 006 | 54023<br>-11513<br>323 007 | 54024<br>-11512<br>323 010 | 54025<br>-11511<br>323 011 | 54026<br>-11510<br>323 012 | 54027<br>-11509<br>323 013 | 54028<br>-11508<br>323 014 | 54029<br>-11507<br>323 015 | 54030<br>-11506<br>323 016 | 54031<br>-11505<br>323 017 |
| **1−** | 54032<br>-11504<br>323 020 | 54033<br>-11503<br>323 021 | 54034<br>-11502<br>323 022 | 54035<br>-11501<br>323 023 | 54036<br>-11500<br>323 024 | 54037<br>-11499<br>323 025 | 54038<br>-11498<br>323 026 | 54039<br>-11497<br>323 027 | 54040<br>-11496<br>323 030 | 54041<br>-11495<br>323 031 | 54042<br>-11494<br>323 032 | 54043<br>-11493<br>323 033 | 54044<br>-11492<br>323 034 | 54045<br>-11491<br>323 035 | 54046<br>-11490<br>323 036 | 54047<br>-11489<br>323 037 |
| **2−** | 54048<br>-11488<br>323 040 | 54049<br>-11487<br>323 041 | 54050<br>-11486<br>323 042 | 54051<br>-11485<br>323 043 | 54052<br>-11484<br>323 044 | 54053<br>-11483<br>323 045 | 54054<br>-11482<br>323 046 | 54055<br>-11481<br>323 047 | 54056<br>-11480<br>323 050 | 54057<br>-11479<br>323 051 | 54058<br>-11478<br>323 052 | 54059<br>-11477<br>323 053 | 54060<br>-11476<br>323 054 | 54061<br>-11475<br>323 055 | 54062<br>-11474<br>323 056 | 54063<br>-11473<br>323 057 |
| **3−** | 54064<br>-11472<br>323 060 | 54065<br>-11471<br>323 061 | 54066<br>-11470<br>323 062 | 54067<br>-11469<br>323 063 | 54068<br>-11468<br>323 064 | 54069<br>-11467<br>323 065 | 54070<br>-11466<br>323 066 | 54071<br>-11465<br>323 067 | 54072<br>-11464<br>323 070 | 54073<br>-11463<br>323 071 | 54074<br>-11462<br>323 072 | 54075<br>-11461<br>323 073 | 54076<br>-11460<br>323 074 | 54077<br>-11459<br>323 075 | 54078<br>-11458<br>323 076 | 54079<br>-11457<br>323 077 |
| **4−** | 54080<br>-11456<br>323 100 | 54081<br>-11455<br>323 101 | 54082<br>-11454<br>323 102 | 54083<br>-11453<br>323 103 | 54084<br>-11452<br>323 104 | 54085<br>-11451<br>323 105 | 54086<br>-11450<br>323 106 | 54087<br>-11449<br>323 107 | 54088<br>-11448<br>323 110 | 54089<br>-11447<br>323 111 | 54090<br>-11446<br>323 112 | 54091<br>-11445<br>323 113 | 54092<br>-11444<br>323 114 | 54093<br>-11443<br>323 115 | 54094<br>-11442<br>323 116 | 54095<br>-11441<br>323 117 |
| **5−** | 54096<br>-11440<br>323 120 | 54097<br>-11439<br>323 121 | 54098<br>-11438<br>323 122 | 54099<br>-11437<br>323 123 | 54100<br>-11436<br>323 124 | 54101<br>-11435<br>323 125 | 54102<br>-11434<br>323 126 | 54103<br>-11433<br>323 127 | 54104<br>-11432<br>323 130 | 54105<br>-11431<br>323 131 | 54106<br>-11430<br>323 132 | 54107<br>-11429<br>323 133 | 54108<br>-11428<br>323 134 | 54109<br>-11427<br>323 135 | 54110<br>-11426<br>323 136 | 54111<br>-11425<br>323 137 |
| **6−** | 54112<br>-11424<br>323 140 | 54113<br>-11423<br>323 141 | 54114<br>-11422<br>323 142 | 54115<br>-11421<br>323 143 | 54116<br>-11420<br>323 144 | 54117<br>-11419<br>323 145 | 54118<br>-11418<br>323 146 | 54119<br>-11417<br>323 147 | 54120<br>-11416<br>323 150 | 54121<br>-11415<br>323 151 | 54122<br>-11414<br>323 152 | 54123<br>-11413<br>323 153 | 54124<br>-11412<br>323 154 | 54125<br>-11411<br>323 155 | 54126<br>-11410<br>323 156 | 54127<br>-11409<br>323 157 |
| **7−** | 54128<br>-11408<br>323 160 | 54129<br>-11407<br>323 161 | 54130<br>-11406<br>323 162 | 54131<br>-11405<br>323 163 | 54132<br>-11404<br>323 164 | 54133<br>-11403<br>323 165 | 54134<br>-11402<br>323 166 | 54135<br>-11401<br>323 167 | 54136<br>-11400<br>323 170 | 54137<br>-11399<br>323 171 | 54138<br>-11398<br>323 172 | 54139<br>-11397<br>323 173 | 54140<br>-11396<br>323 174 | 54141<br>-11395<br>323 175 | 54142<br>-11394<br>323 176 | 54143<br>-11393<br>323 177 |
| **8−** | 54144<br>-11392<br>323 200 | 54145<br>-11391<br>323 201 | 54146<br>-11390<br>323 202 | 54147<br>-11389<br>323 203 | 54148<br>-11388<br>323 204 | 54149<br>-11387<br>323 205 | 54150<br>-11386<br>323 206 | 54151<br>-11385<br>323 207 | 54152<br>-11384<br>323 210 | 54153<br>-11383<br>323 211 | 54154<br>-11382<br>323 212 | 54155<br>-11381<br>323 213 | 54156<br>-11380<br>323 214 | 54157<br>-11379<br>323 215 | 54158<br>-11378<br>323 216 | 54159<br>-11377<br>323 217 |
| **9−** | 54160<br>-11376<br>323 220 | 54161<br>-11375<br>323 221 | 54162<br>-11374<br>323 222 | 54163<br>-11373<br>323 223 | 54164<br>-11372<br>323 224 | 54165<br>-11371<br>323 225 | 54166<br>-11370<br>323 226 | 54167<br>-11369<br>323 227 | 54168<br>-11368<br>323 230 | 54169<br>-11367<br>323 231 | 54170<br>-11366<br>323 232 | 54171<br>-11365<br>323 233 | 54172<br>-11364<br>323 234 | 54173<br>-11363<br>323 235 | 54174<br>-11362<br>323 236 | 54175<br>-11361<br>323 237 |
| **A−** | 54176<br>-11360<br>323 240 | 54177<br>-11359<br>323 241 | 54178<br>-11358<br>323 242 | 54179<br>-11357<br>323 243 | 54180<br>-11356<br>323 244 | 54181<br>-11355<br>323 245 | 54182<br>-11354<br>323 246 | 54183<br>-11353<br>323 247 | 54184<br>-11352<br>323 250 | 54185<br>-11351<br>323 251 | 54186<br>-11350<br>323 252 | 54187<br>-11349<br>323 253 | 54188<br>-11348<br>323 254 | 54189<br>-11347<br>323 255 | 54190<br>-11346<br>323 256 | 54191<br>-11345<br>323 257 |
| **B−** | 54192<br>-11344<br>323 260 | 54193<br>-11343<br>323 261 | 54194<br>-11342<br>323 262 | 54195<br>-11341<br>323 263 | 54196<br>-11340<br>323 264 | 54197<br>-11339<br>323 265 | 54198<br>-11338<br>323 266 | 54199<br>-11337<br>323 267 | 54200<br>-11336<br>323 270 | 54201<br>-11335<br>323 271 | 54202<br>-11334<br>323 272 | 54203<br>-11333<br>323 273 | 54204<br>-11332<br>323 274 | 54205<br>-11331<br>323 275 | 54206<br>-11330<br>323 276 | 54207<br>-11329<br>323 277 |
| **C−** | 54208<br>-11328<br>323 300 | 54209<br>-11327<br>323 301 | 54210<br>-11326<br>323 302 | 54211<br>-11325<br>323 303 | 54212<br>-11324<br>323 304 | 54213<br>-11323<br>323 305 | 54214<br>-11322<br>323 306 | 54215<br>-11321<br>323 307 | 54216<br>-11320<br>323 310 | 54217<br>-11319<br>323 311 | 54218<br>-11318<br>323 312 | 54219<br>-11317<br>323 313 | 54220<br>-11316<br>323 314 | 54221<br>-11315<br>323 315 | 54222<br>-11314<br>323 316 | 54223<br>-11313<br>323 317 |
| **D−** | 54224<br>-11312<br>323 320 | 54225<br>-11311<br>323 321 | 54226<br>-11310<br>323 322 | 54227<br>-11309<br>323 323 | 54228<br>-11308<br>323 324 | 54229<br>-11307<br>323 325 | 54230<br>-11306<br>323 326 | 54231<br>-11305<br>323 327 | 54232<br>-11304<br>323 330 | 54233<br>-11303<br>323 331 | 54234<br>-11302<br>323 332 | 54235<br>-11301<br>323 333 | 54236<br>-11300<br>323 334 | 54237<br>-11299<br>323 335 | 54238<br>-11298<br>323 336 | 54239<br>-11297<br>323 337 |
| **E−** | 54240<br>-11296<br>323 340 | 54241<br>-11295<br>323 341 | 54242<br>-11294<br>323 342 | 54243<br>-11293<br>323 343 | 54244<br>-11292<br>323 344 | 54245<br>-11291<br>323 345 | 54246<br>-11290<br>323 346 | 54247<br>-11289<br>323 347 | 54248<br>-11288<br>323 350 | 54249<br>-11287<br>323 351 | 54250<br>-11286<br>323 352 | 54251<br>-11285<br>323 353 | 54252<br>-11284<br>323 354 | 54253<br>-11283<br>323 355 | 54254<br>-11282<br>323 356 | 54255<br>-11281<br>323 357 |
| **F−** | 54256<br>-11280<br>323 360 | 54257<br>-11279<br>323 361 | 54258<br>-11278<br>323 362 | 54259<br>-11277<br>323 363 | 54260<br>-11276<br>323 364 | 54261<br>-11275<br>323 365 | 54262<br>-11274<br>323 366 | 54263<br>-11273<br>323 367 | 54264<br>-11272<br>323 370 | 54265<br>-11271<br>323 371 | 54266<br>-11270<br>323 372 | 54267<br>-11269<br>323 373 | 54268<br>-11268<br>323 374 | 54269<br>-11267<br>323 375 | 54270<br>-11266<br>323 376 | 54271<br>-11265<br>323 377 |

<table>
<tr><td rowspan="2">2</td><td colspan="16" align="center">FIRST HEX DIGIT</td></tr>
<tr><td>−0</td><td>−1</td><td>−2</td><td>−3</td><td>−4</td><td>−5</td><td>−6</td><td>−7</td><td>−8</td><td>−9</td><td>−A</td><td>−B</td><td>−C</td><td>−D</td><td>−E</td><td>−F</td></tr>
<tr><td>0−</td>
<td>54272<br>-11264<br>324 000</td><td>54273<br>-11263<br>324 001</td><td>54274<br>-11262<br>324 002</td><td>54275<br>-11261<br>324 003</td><td>54276<br>-11260<br>324 004</td><td>54277<br>-11259<br>324 005</td><td>54278<br>-11258<br>324 006</td><td>54279<br>-11257<br>324 007</td><td>54280<br>-11256<br>324 010</td><td>54281<br>-11255<br>324 011</td><td>54282<br>-11254<br>324 012</td><td>54283<br>-11253<br>324 013</td><td>54284<br>-11252<br>324 014</td><td>54285<br>-11251<br>324 015</td><td>54286<br>-11250<br>324 016</td><td>54287<br>-11249<br>324 017</td></tr>
<tr><td>1−</td>
<td>54288<br>-11248<br>324 020</td><td>54289<br>-11247<br>324 021</td><td>54290<br>-11246<br>324 022</td><td>54291<br>-11245<br>324 023</td><td>54292<br>-11244<br>324 024</td><td>54293<br>-11243<br>324 025</td><td>54294<br>-11242<br>324 026</td><td>54295<br>-11241<br>324 027</td><td>54296<br>-11240<br>324 030</td><td>54297<br>-11239<br>324 031</td><td>54298<br>-11238<br>324 032</td><td>54299<br>-11237<br>324 033</td><td>54300<br>-11236<br>324 034</td><td>54301<br>-11235<br>324 035</td><td>54302<br>-11234<br>324 036</td><td>54303<br>-11233<br>324 037</td></tr>
<tr><td>2−</td>
<td>54304<br>-11232<br>324 040</td><td>54305<br>-11231<br>324 041</td><td>54306<br>-11230<br>324 042</td><td>54307<br>-11229<br>324 043</td><td>54308<br>-11228<br>324 044</td><td>54309<br>-11227<br>324 045</td><td>54310<br>-11226<br>324 046</td><td>54311<br>-11225<br>324 047</td><td>54312<br>-11224<br>324 050</td><td>54313<br>-11223<br>324 051</td><td>54314<br>-11222<br>324 052</td><td>54315<br>-11221<br>324 053</td><td>54316<br>-11220<br>324 054</td><td>54317<br>-11219<br>324 055</td><td>54318<br>-11218<br>324 056</td><td>54319<br>-11217<br>324 057</td></tr>
<tr><td>3−</td>
<td>54320<br>-11216<br>324 060</td><td>54321<br>-11215<br>324 061</td><td>54322<br>-11214<br>324 062</td><td>54323<br>-11213<br>324 063</td><td>54324<br>-11212<br>324 064</td><td>54325<br>-11211<br>324 065</td><td>54326<br>-11210<br>324 066</td><td>54327<br>-11209<br>324 067</td><td>54328<br>-11208<br>324 070</td><td>54329<br>-11207<br>324 071</td><td>54330<br>-11206<br>324 072</td><td>54331<br>-11205<br>324 073</td><td>54332<br>-11204<br>324 074</td><td>54333<br>-11203<br>324 075</td><td>54334<br>-11202<br>324 076</td><td>54335<br>-11201<br>324 077</td></tr>
<tr><td>4−</td>
<td>54336<br>-11200<br>324 100</td><td>54337<br>-11199<br>324 101</td><td>54338<br>-11198<br>324 102</td><td>54339<br>-11197<br>324 103</td><td>54340<br>-11196<br>324 104</td><td>54341<br>-11195<br>324 105</td><td>54342<br>-11194<br>324 106</td><td>54343<br>-11193<br>324 107</td><td>54344<br>-11192<br>324 110</td><td>54345<br>-11191<br>324 111</td><td>54346<br>-11190<br>324 112</td><td>54347<br>-11189<br>324 113</td><td>54348<br>-11188<br>324 114</td><td>54349<br>-11187<br>324 115</td><td>54350<br>-11186<br>324 116</td><td>54351<br>-11185<br>324 117</td></tr>
<tr><td>5−</td>
<td>54352<br>-11184<br>324 120</td><td>54353<br>-11183<br>324 121</td><td>54354<br>-11182<br>324 122</td><td>54355<br>-11181<br>324 123</td><td>54356<br>-11180<br>324 124</td><td>54357<br>-11179<br>324 125</td><td>54358<br>-11178<br>324 126</td><td>54359<br>-11177<br>324 127</td><td>54360<br>-11176<br>324 130</td><td>54361<br>-11175<br>324 131</td><td>54362<br>-11174<br>324 132</td><td>54363<br>-11173<br>324 133</td><td>54364<br>-11172<br>324 134</td><td>54365<br>-11171<br>324 135</td><td>54366<br>-11170<br>324 136</td><td>54367<br>-11169<br>324 137</td></tr>
<tr><td>6−</td>
<td>54368<br>-11168<br>324 140</td><td>54369<br>-11167<br>324 141</td><td>54370<br>-11166<br>324 142</td><td>54371<br>-11165<br>324 143</td><td>54372<br>-11164<br>324 144</td><td>54373<br>-11163<br>324 145</td><td>54374<br>-11162<br>324 146</td><td>54375<br>-11161<br>324 147</td><td>54376<br>-11160<br>324 150</td><td>54377<br>-11159<br>324 151</td><td>54378<br>-11158<br>324 152</td><td>54379<br>-11157<br>324 153</td><td>54380<br>-11156<br>324 154</td><td>54381<br>-11155<br>324 155</td><td>54382<br>-11154<br>324 156</td><td>54383<br>-11153<br>324 157</td></tr>
<tr><td>7−</td>
<td>54384<br>-11152<br>324 160</td><td>54385<br>-11151<br>324 161</td><td>54386<br>-11150<br>324 162</td><td>54387<br>-11149<br>324 163</td><td>54388<br>-11148<br>324 164</td><td>54389<br>-11147<br>324 165</td><td>54390<br>-11146<br>324 166</td><td>54391<br>-11145<br>324 167</td><td>54392<br>-11144<br>324 170</td><td>54393<br>-11143<br>324 171</td><td>54394<br>-11142<br>324 172</td><td>54395<br>-11141<br>324 173</td><td>54396<br>-11140<br>324 174</td><td>54397<br>-11139<br>324 175</td><td>54398<br>-11138<br>324 176</td><td>54399<br>-11137<br>324 177</td></tr>
<tr><td>8−</td>
<td>54400<br>-11136<br>324 200</td><td>54401<br>-11135<br>324 201</td><td>54402<br>-11134<br>324 202</td><td>54403<br>-11133<br>324 203</td><td>54404<br>-11132<br>324 204</td><td>54405<br>-11131<br>324 205</td><td>54406<br>-11130<br>324 206</td><td>54407<br>-11129<br>324 207</td><td>54408<br>-11128<br>324 210</td><td>54409<br>-11127<br>324 211</td><td>54410<br>-11126<br>324 212</td><td>54411<br>-11125<br>324 213</td><td>54412<br>-11124<br>324 214</td><td>54413<br>-11123<br>324 215</td><td>54414<br>-11122<br>324 216</td><td>54415<br>-11121<br>324 217</td></tr>
<tr><td>9−</td>
<td>54416<br>-11120<br>324 220</td><td>54417<br>-11119<br>324 221</td><td>54418<br>-11118<br>324 222</td><td>54419<br>-11117<br>324 223</td><td>54420<br>-11116<br>324 224</td><td>54421<br>-11115<br>324 225</td><td>54422<br>-11114<br>324 226</td><td>54423<br>-11113<br>324 227</td><td>54424<br>-11112<br>324 230</td><td>54425<br>-11111<br>324 231</td><td>54426<br>-11110<br>324 232</td><td>54427<br>-11109<br>324 233</td><td>54428<br>-11108<br>324 234</td><td>54429<br>-11107<br>324 235</td><td>54430<br>-11106<br>324 236</td><td>54431<br>-11105<br>324 237</td></tr>
<tr><td>A−</td>
<td>54432<br>-11104<br>324 240</td><td>54433<br>-11103<br>324 241</td><td>54434<br>-11102<br>324 242</td><td>54435<br>-11101<br>324 243</td><td>54436<br>-11100<br>324 244</td><td>54437<br>-11099<br>324 245</td><td>54438<br>-11098<br>324 246</td><td>54439<br>-11097<br>324 247</td><td>54440<br>-11096<br>324 250</td><td>54441<br>-11095<br>324 251</td><td>54442<br>-11094<br>324 252</td><td>54443<br>-11093<br>324 253</td><td>54444<br>-11092<br>324 254</td><td>54445<br>-11091<br>324 255</td><td>54446<br>-11090<br>324 256</td><td>54447<br>-11089<br>324 257</td></tr>
<tr><td>B−</td>
<td>54448<br>-11088<br>324 260</td><td>54449<br>-11087<br>324 261</td><td>54450<br>-11086<br>324 262</td><td>54451<br>-11085<br>324 263</td><td>54452<br>-11084<br>324 264</td><td>54453<br>-11083<br>324 265</td><td>54454<br>-11082<br>324 266</td><td>54455<br>-11081<br>324 267</td><td>54456<br>-11080<br>324 270</td><td>54457<br>-11079<br>324 271</td><td>54458<br>-11078<br>324 272</td><td>54459<br>-11077<br>324 273</td><td>54460<br>-11076<br>324 274</td><td>54461<br>-11075<br>324 275</td><td>54462<br>-11074<br>324 276</td><td>54463<br>-11073<br>324 277</td></tr>
<tr><td>C−</td>
<td>54464<br>-11072<br>324 300</td><td>54465<br>-11071<br>324 301</td><td>54466<br>-11070<br>324 302</td><td>54467<br>-11069<br>324 303</td><td>54468<br>-11068<br>324 304</td><td>54469<br>-11067<br>324 305</td><td>54470<br>-11066<br>324 306</td><td>54471<br>-11065<br>324 307</td><td>54472<br>-11064<br>324 310</td><td>54473<br>-11063<br>324 311</td><td>54474<br>-11062<br>324 312</td><td>54475<br>-11061<br>324 313</td><td>54476<br>-11060<br>324 314</td><td>54477<br>-11059<br>324 315</td><td>54478<br>-11058<br>324 316</td><td>54479<br>-11057<br>324 317</td></tr>
<tr><td>D−</td>
<td>54480<br>-11056<br>324 320</td><td>54481<br>-11055<br>324 321</td><td>54482<br>-11054<br>324 322</td><td>54483<br>-11053<br>324 323</td><td>54484<br>-11052<br>324 324</td><td>54485<br>-11051<br>324 325</td><td>54486<br>-11050<br>324 326</td><td>54487<br>-11049<br>324 327</td><td>54488<br>-11048<br>324 330</td><td>54489<br>-11047<br>324 331</td><td>54490<br>-11046<br>324 332</td><td>54491<br>-11045<br>324 333</td><td>54492<br>-11044<br>324 334</td><td>54493<br>-11043<br>324 335</td><td>54494<br>-11042<br>324 336</td><td>54495<br>-11041<br>324 337</td></tr>
<tr><td>E−</td>
<td>54496<br>-11040<br>324 340</td><td>54497<br>-11039<br>324 341</td><td>54498<br>-11038<br>324 342</td><td>54499<br>-11037<br>324 343</td><td>54500<br>-11036<br>324 344</td><td>54501<br>-11035<br>324 345</td><td>54502<br>-11034<br>324 346</td><td>54503<br>-11033<br>324 347</td><td>54504<br>-11032<br>324 350</td><td>54505<br>-11031<br>324 351</td><td>54506<br>-11030<br>324 352</td><td>54507<br>-11029<br>324 353</td><td>54508<br>-11028<br>324 354</td><td>54509<br>-11027<br>324 355</td><td>54510<br>-11026<br>324 356</td><td>54511<br>-11025<br>324 357</td></tr>
<tr><td>F−</td>
<td>54512<br>-11024<br>324 360</td><td>54513<br>-11023<br>324 361</td><td>54514<br>-11022<br>324 362</td><td>54515<br>-11021<br>324 363</td><td>54516<br>-11020<br>324 364</td><td>54517<br>-11019<br>324 365</td><td>54518<br>-11018<br>324 366</td><td>54519<br>-11017<br>324 367</td><td>54520<br>-11016<br>324 370</td><td>54521<br>-11015<br>324 371</td><td>54522<br>-11014<br>324 372</td><td>54523<br>-11013<br>324 373</td><td>54524<br>-11012<br>324 374</td><td>54525<br>-11011<br>324 375</td><td>54526<br>-11010<br>324 376</td><td>54527<br>-11009<br>324 377</td></tr>
</table>

*(Left margin label, vertical: SECOND HEX DIGIT)*

Right-side labels: DECIMAL → ; DECIMAL → ; OCTAL →

DECIMAL -11008 | BINARY 1101 0101 | DECIMAL 54528 | HEXADECIMAL D5 | OCTAL 325 000

FOURTH HEX DIGIT · THIRD HEX DIGIT

2

FIRST HEX DIGIT — SECOND HEX DIGIT

Each cell lists: decimal (positive) / decimal (negative) / octal.

| SECOND | −0 | −1 | −2 | −3 | −4 | −5 | −6 | −7 | −8 | −9 | −A | −B | −C | −D | −E | −F |
|---|---|---|---|---|---|---|---|---|---|---|---|---|---|---|---|---|
| 0− | 54528<br>−11008<br>325 000 | 54529<br>−11007<br>325 001 | 54530<br>−11006<br>325 002 | 54531<br>−11005<br>325 003 | 54532<br>−11004<br>325 004 | 54533<br>−11003<br>325 005 | 54534<br>−11002<br>325 006 | 54535<br>−11001<br>325 007 | 54536<br>−11000<br>325 010 | 54537<br>−10999<br>325 011 | 54538<br>−10998<br>325 012 | 54539<br>−10997<br>325 013 | 54540<br>−10996<br>325 014 | 54541<br>−10995<br>325 015 | 54542<br>−10994<br>325 016 | 54543<br>−10993<br>325 017 |
| 1− | 54544<br>−10992<br>325 020 | 54545<br>−10991<br>325 021 | 54546<br>−10990<br>325 022 | 54547<br>−10989<br>325 023 | 54548<br>−10988<br>325 024 | 54549<br>−10987<br>325 025 | 54550<br>−10986<br>325 026 | 54551<br>−10985<br>325 027 | 54552<br>−10984<br>325 030 | 54553<br>−10983<br>325 031 | 54554<br>−10982<br>325 032 | 54555<br>−10981<br>325 033 | 54556<br>−10980<br>325 034 | 54557<br>−10979<br>325 035 | 54558<br>−10978<br>325 036 | 54559<br>−10977<br>325 037 |
| 2− | 54560<br>−10976<br>325 040 | 54561<br>−10975<br>325 041 | 54562<br>−10974<br>325 042 | 54563<br>−10973<br>325 043 | 54564<br>−10972<br>325 044 | 54565<br>−10971<br>325 045 | 54566<br>−10970<br>325 046 | 54567<br>−10969<br>325 047 | 54568<br>−10968<br>325 050 | 54569<br>−10967<br>325 051 | 54570<br>−10966<br>325 052 | 54571<br>−10965<br>325 053 | 54572<br>−10964<br>325 054 | 54573<br>−10963<br>325 055 | 54574<br>−10962<br>325 056 | 54575<br>−10961<br>325 057 |
| 3− | 54576<br>−10960<br>325 060 | 54577<br>−10959<br>325 061 | 54578<br>−10958<br>325 062 | 54579<br>−10957<br>325 063 | 54580<br>−10956<br>325 064 | 54581<br>−10955<br>325 065 | 54582<br>−10954<br>325 066 | 54583<br>−10953<br>325 067 | 54584<br>−10952<br>325 070 | 54585<br>−10951<br>325 071 | 54586<br>−10950<br>325 072 | 54587<br>−10949<br>325 073 | 54588<br>−10948<br>325 074 | 54589<br>−10947<br>325 075 | 54590<br>−10946<br>325 076 | 54591<br>−10945<br>325 077 |
| 4− | 54592<br>−10944<br>325 100 | 54593<br>−10943<br>325 101 | 54594<br>−10942<br>325 102 | 54595<br>−10941<br>325 103 | 54596<br>−10940<br>325 104 | 54597<br>−10939<br>325 105 | 54598<br>−10938<br>325 106 | 54599<br>−10937<br>325 107 | 54600<br>−10936<br>325 110 | 54601<br>−10935<br>325 111 | 54602<br>−10934<br>325 112 | 54603<br>−10933<br>325 113 | 54604<br>−10932<br>325 114 | 54605<br>−10931<br>325 115 | 54606<br>−10930<br>325 116 | 54607<br>−10929<br>325 117 |
| 5− | 54608<br>−10928<br>325 120 | 54609<br>−10927<br>325 121 | 54610<br>−10926<br>325 122 | 54611<br>−10925<br>325 123 | 54612<br>−10924<br>325 124 | 54613<br>−10923<br>325 125 | 54614<br>−10922<br>325 126 | 54615<br>−10921<br>325 127 | 54616<br>−10920<br>325 130 | 54617<br>−10919<br>325 131 | 54618<br>−10918<br>325 132 | 54619<br>−10917<br>325 133 | 54620<br>−10916<br>325 134 | 54621<br>−10915<br>325 135 | 54622<br>−10914<br>325 136 | 54623<br>−10913<br>325 137 |
| 6− | 54624<br>−10912<br>325 140 | 54625<br>−10911<br>325 141 | 54626<br>−10910<br>325 142 | 54627<br>−10909<br>325 143 | 54628<br>−10908<br>325 144 | 54629<br>−10907<br>325 145 | 54630<br>−10906<br>325 146 | 54631<br>−10905<br>325 147 | 54632<br>−10904<br>325 150 | 54633<br>−10903<br>325 151 | 54634<br>−10902<br>325 152 | 54635<br>−10901<br>325 153 | 54636<br>−10900<br>325 154 | 54637<br>−10899<br>325 155 | 54638<br>−10898<br>325 156 | 54639<br>−10897<br>325 157 |
| 7− | 54640<br>−10896<br>325 160 | 54641<br>−10895<br>325 161 | 54642<br>−10894<br>325 162 | 54643<br>−10893<br>325 163 | 54644<br>−10892<br>325 164 | 54645<br>−10891<br>325 165 | 54646<br>−10890<br>325 166 | 54647<br>−10889<br>325 167 | 54648<br>−10888<br>325 170 | 54649<br>−10887<br>325 171 | 54650<br>−10886<br>325 172 | 54651<br>−10885<br>325 173 | 54652<br>−10884<br>325 174 | 54653<br>−10883<br>325 175 | 54654<br>−10882<br>325 176 | 54655<br>−10881<br>325 177 |
| 8− | 54656<br>−10880<br>325 200 | 54657<br>−10879<br>325 201 | 54658<br>−10878<br>325 202 | 54659<br>−10877<br>325 203 | 54660<br>−10876<br>325 204 | 54661<br>−10875<br>325 205 | 54662<br>−10874<br>325 206 | 54663<br>−10873<br>325 207 | 54664<br>−10872<br>325 210 | 54665<br>−10871<br>325 211 | 54666<br>−10870<br>325 212 | 54667<br>−10869<br>325 213 | 54668<br>−10868<br>325 214 | 54669<br>−10867<br>325 215 | 54670<br>−10866<br>325 216 | 54671<br>−10865<br>325 217 |
| 9− | 54672<br>−10864<br>325 220 | 54673<br>−10863<br>325 221 | 54674<br>−10862<br>325 222 | 54675<br>−10861<br>325 223 | 54676<br>−10860<br>325 224 | 54677<br>−10859<br>325 225 | 54678<br>−10858<br>325 226 | 54679<br>−10857<br>325 227 | 54680<br>−10856<br>325 230 | 54681<br>−10855<br>325 231 | 54682<br>−10854<br>325 232 | 54683<br>−10853<br>325 233 | 54684<br>−10852<br>325 234 | 54685<br>−10851<br>325 235 | 54686<br>−10850<br>325 236 | 54687<br>−10849<br>325 237 |
| A− | 54688<br>−10848<br>325 240 | 54689<br>−10847<br>325 241 | 54690<br>−10846<br>325 242 | 54691<br>−10845<br>325 243 | 54692<br>−10844<br>325 244 | 54693<br>−10843<br>325 245 | 54694<br>−10842<br>325 246 | 54695<br>−10841<br>325 247 | 54696<br>−10840<br>325 250 | 54697<br>−10839<br>325 251 | 54698<br>−10838<br>325 252 | 54699<br>−10837<br>325 253 | 54700<br>−10836<br>325 254 | 54701<br>−10835<br>325 255 | 54702<br>−10834<br>325 256 | 54703<br>−10833<br>325 257 |
| B− | 54704<br>−10832<br>325 260 | 54705<br>−10831<br>325 261 | 54706<br>−10830<br>325 262 | 54707<br>−10829<br>325 263 | 54708<br>−10828<br>325 264 | 54709<br>−10827<br>325 265 | 54710<br>−10826<br>325 266 | 54711<br>−10825<br>325 267 | 54712<br>−10824<br>325 270 | 54713<br>−10823<br>325 271 | 54714<br>−10822<br>325 272 | 54715<br>−10821<br>325 273 | 54716<br>−10820<br>325 274 | 54717<br>−10819<br>325 275 | 54718<br>−10818<br>325 276 | 54719<br>−10817<br>325 277 |
| C− | 54720<br>−10816<br>325 300 | 54721<br>−10815<br>325 301 | 54722<br>−10814<br>325 302 | 54723<br>−10813<br>325 303 | 54724<br>−10812<br>325 304 | 54725<br>−10811<br>325 305 | 54726<br>−10810<br>325 306 | 54727<br>−10809<br>325 307 | 54728<br>−10808<br>325 310 | 54729<br>−10807<br>325 311 | 54730<br>−10806<br>325 312 | 54731<br>−10805<br>325 313 | 54732<br>−10804<br>325 314 | 54733<br>−10803<br>325 315 | 54734<br>−10802<br>325 316 | 54735<br>−10801<br>325 317 |
| D− | 54736<br>−10800<br>325 320 | 54737<br>−10799<br>325 321 | 54738<br>−10798<br>325 322 | 54739<br>−10797<br>325 323 | 54740<br>−10796<br>325 324 | 54741<br>−10795<br>325 325 | 54742<br>−10794<br>325 326 | 54743<br>−10793<br>325 327 | 54744<br>−10792<br>325 330 | 54745<br>−10791<br>325 331 | 54746<br>−10790<br>325 332 | 54747<br>−10789<br>325 333 | 54748<br>−10788<br>325 334 | 54749<br>−10787<br>325 335 | 54750<br>−10786<br>325 336 | 54751<br>−10785<br>325 337 |
| E− | 54752<br>−10784<br>325 340 | 54753<br>−10783<br>325 341 | 54754<br>−10782<br>325 342 | 54755<br>−10781<br>325 343 | 54756<br>−10780<br>325 344 | 54757<br>−10779<br>325 345 | 54758<br>−10778<br>325 346 | 54759<br>−10777<br>325 347 | 54760<br>−10776<br>325 350 | 54761<br>−10775<br>325 351 | 54762<br>−10774<br>325 352 | 54763<br>−10773<br>325 353 | 54764<br>−10772<br>325 354 | 54765<br>−10771<br>325 355 | 54766<br>−10770<br>325 356 | 54767<br>−10769<br>325 357 |
| F− | 54768<br>−10768<br>325 360 | 54769<br>−10767<br>325 361 | 54770<br>−10766<br>325 362 | 54771<br>−10765<br>325 363 | 54772<br>−10764<br>325 364 | 54773<br>−10763<br>325 365 | 54774<br>−10762<br>325 366 | 54775<br>−10761<br>325 367 | 54776<br>−10760<br>325 370 | 54777<br>−10759<br>325 371 | 54778<br>−10758<br>325 372 | 54779<br>−10757<br>325 373 | 54780<br>−10756<br>325 374 | 54781<br>−10755<br>325 375 | 54782<br>−10754<br>325 376 | 54783<br>−10753<br>325 377 |

DECIMAL →

 DECIMAL →

OCTAL →

# FIRST HEX DIGIT

**② SECOND HEX DIGIT**

| | −0 | −1 | −2 | −3 | −4 | −5 | −6 | −7 | −8 | −9 | −A | −B | −C | −D | −E | −F |
|---|---|---|---|---|---|---|---|---|---|---|---|---|---|---|---|---|
| **0−** | 54784<br>−10752<br>326 000 | 54785<br>−10751<br>326 001 | 54786<br>−10750<br>326 002 | 54787<br>−10749<br>326 003 | 54788<br>−10748<br>326 004 | 54789<br>−10747<br>326 005 | 54790<br>−10746<br>326 006 | 54791<br>−10745<br>326 007 | 54792<br>−10744<br>326 010 | 54793<br>−10743<br>326 011 | 54794<br>−10742<br>326 012 | 54795<br>−10741<br>326 013 | 54796<br>−10740<br>326 014 | 54797<br>−10739<br>326 015 | 54798<br>−10738<br>326 016 | 54799<br>−10737<br>326 017 |
| **1−** | 54800<br>−10736<br>326 020 | 54801<br>−10735<br>326 021 | 54802<br>−10734<br>326 022 | 54803<br>−10733<br>326 023 | 54804<br>−10732<br>326 024 | 54805<br>−10731<br>326 025 | 54806<br>−10730<br>326 026 | 54807<br>−10729<br>326 027 | 54808<br>−10728<br>326 030 | 54809<br>−10727<br>326 031 | 54810<br>−10726<br>326 032 | 54811<br>−10725<br>326 033 | 54812<br>−10724<br>326 034 | 54813<br>−10723<br>326 035 | 54814<br>−10722<br>326 036 | 54815<br>−10721<br>326 037 |
| **2−** | 54816<br>−10720<br>326 040 | 54817<br>−10719<br>326 041 | 54818<br>−10718<br>326 042 | 54819<br>−10717<br>326 043 | 54820<br>−10716<br>326 044 | 54821<br>−10715<br>326 045 | 54822<br>−10714<br>326 046 | 54823<br>−10713<br>326 047 | 54824<br>−10712<br>326 050 | 54825<br>−10711<br>326 051 | 54826<br>−10710<br>326 052 | 54827<br>−10709<br>326 053 | 54828<br>−10708<br>326 054 | 54829<br>−10707<br>326 055 | 54830<br>−10706<br>326 056 | 54831<br>−10705<br>326 057 |
| **3−** | 54832<br>−10704<br>326 060 | 54833<br>−10703<br>326 061 | 54834<br>−10702<br>326 062 | 54835<br>−10701<br>326 063 | 54836<br>−10700<br>326 064 | 54837<br>−10699<br>326 065 | 54838<br>−10698<br>326 066 | 54839<br>−10697<br>326 067 | 54840<br>−10696<br>326 070 | 54841<br>−10695<br>326 071 | 54842<br>−10694<br>326 072 | 54843<br>−10693<br>326 073 | 54844<br>−10692<br>326 074 | 54845<br>−10691<br>326 075 | 54846<br>−10690<br>326 076 | 54847<br>−10689<br>326 077 |
| **4−** | 54848<br>−10688<br>326 100 | 54849<br>−10687<br>326 101 | 54850<br>−10686<br>326 102 | 54851<br>−10685<br>326 103 | 54852<br>−10684<br>326 104 | 54853<br>−10683<br>326 105 | 54854<br>−10682<br>326 106 | 54855<br>−10681<br>326 107 | 54856<br>−10680<br>326 110 | 54857<br>−10679<br>326 111 | 54858<br>−10678<br>326 112 | 54859<br>−10677<br>326 113 | 54860<br>−10676<br>326 114 | 54861<br>−10675<br>326 115 | 54862<br>−10674<br>326 116 | 54863<br>−10673<br>326 117 |
| **5−** | 54864<br>−10672<br>326 120 | 54865<br>−10671<br>326 121 | 54866<br>−10670<br>326 122 | 54867<br>−10669<br>326 123 | 54868<br>−10668<br>326 124 | 54869<br>−10667<br>326 125 | 54870<br>−10666<br>326 126 | 54871<br>−10665<br>326 127 | 54872<br>−10664<br>326 130 | 54873<br>−10663<br>326 131 | 54874<br>−10662<br>326 132 | 54875<br>−10661<br>326 133 | 54876<br>−10660<br>326 134 | 54877<br>−10659<br>326 135 | 54878<br>−10658<br>326 136 | 54879<br>−10657<br>326 137 |
| **6−** | 54880<br>−10656<br>326 140 | 54881<br>−10655<br>326 141 | 54882<br>−10654<br>326 142 | 54883<br>−10653<br>326 143 | 54884<br>−10652<br>326 144 | 54885<br>−10651<br>326 145 | 54886<br>−10650<br>326 146 | 54887<br>−10649<br>326 147 | 54888<br>−10648<br>326 150 | 54889<br>−10647<br>326 151 | 54890<br>−10646<br>326 152 | 54891<br>−10645<br>326 153 | 54892<br>−10644<br>326 154 | 54893<br>−10643<br>326 155 | 54894<br>−10642<br>326 156 | 54895<br>−10641<br>326 157 |
| **7−** | 54896<br>−10640<br>326 160 | 54897<br>−10639<br>326 161 | 54898<br>−10638<br>326 162 | 54899<br>−10637<br>326 163 | 54900<br>−10636<br>326 164 | 54901<br>−10635<br>326 165 | 54902<br>−10634<br>326 166 | 54903<br>−10633<br>326 167 | 54904<br>−10632<br>326 170 | 54905<br>−10631<br>326 171 | 54906<br>−10630<br>326 172 | 54907<br>−10629<br>326 173 | 54908<br>−10628<br>326 174 | 54909<br>−10627<br>326 175 | 54910<br>−10626<br>326 176 | 54911<br>−10625<br>326 177 |
| **8−** | 54912<br>−10624<br>326 200 | 54913<br>−10623<br>326 201 | 54914<br>−10622<br>326 202 | 54915<br>−10621<br>326 203 | 54916<br>−10620<br>326 204 | 54917<br>−10619<br>326 205 | 54918<br>−10618<br>326 206 | 54919<br>−10617<br>326 207 | 54920<br>−10616<br>326 210 | 54921<br>−10615<br>326 211 | 54922<br>−10614<br>326 212 | 54923<br>−10613<br>326 213 | 54924<br>−10612<br>326 214 | 54925<br>−10611<br>326 215 | 54926<br>−10610<br>326 216 | 54927<br>−10609<br>326 217 |
| **9−** | 54928<br>−10608<br>326 220 | 54929<br>−10607<br>326 221 | 54930<br>−10606<br>326 222 | 54931<br>−10605<br>326 223 | 54932<br>−10604<br>326 224 | 54933<br>−10603<br>326 225 | 54934<br>−10602<br>326 226 | 54935<br>−10601<br>326 227 | 54936<br>−10600<br>326 230 | 54937<br>−10599<br>326 231 | 54938<br>−10598<br>326 232 | 54939<br>−10597<br>326 233 | 54940<br>−10596<br>326 234 | 54941<br>−10595<br>326 235 | 54942<br>−10594<br>326 236 | 54943<br>−10593<br>326 237 |
| **A−** | 54944<br>−10592<br>326 240 | 54945<br>−10591<br>326 241 | 54946<br>−10590<br>326 242 | 54947<br>−10589<br>326 243 | 54948<br>−10588<br>326 244 | 54949<br>−10587<br>326 245 | 54950<br>−10586<br>326 246 | 54951<br>−10585<br>326 247 | 54952<br>−10584<br>326 250 | 54953<br>−10583<br>326 251 | 54954<br>−10582<br>326 252 | 54955<br>−10581<br>326 253 | 54956<br>−10580<br>326 254 | 54957<br>−10579<br>326 255 | 54958<br>−10578<br>326 256 | 54959<br>−10577<br>326 257 |
| **B−** | 54960<br>−10576<br>326 260 | 54961<br>−10575<br>326 261 | 54962<br>−10574<br>326 262 | 54963<br>−10573<br>326 263 | 54964<br>−10572<br>326 264 | 54965<br>−10571<br>326 265 | 54966<br>−10570<br>326 266 | 54967<br>−10569<br>326 267 | 54968<br>−10568<br>326 270 | 54969<br>−10567<br>326 271 | 54970<br>−10566<br>326 272 | 54971<br>−10565<br>326 273 | 54972<br>−10564<br>326 274 | 54973<br>−10563<br>326 275 | 54974<br>−10562<br>326 276 | 54975<br>−10561<br>326 277 |
| **C−** | 54976<br>−10560<br>326 300 | 54977<br>−10559<br>326 301 | 54978<br>−10558<br>326 302 | 54979<br>−10557<br>326 303 | 54980<br>−10556<br>326 304 | 54981<br>−10555<br>326 305 | 54982<br>−10554<br>326 306 | 54983<br>−10553<br>326 307 | 54984<br>−10552<br>326 310 | 54985<br>−10551<br>326 311 | 54986<br>−10550<br>326 312 | 54987<br>−10549<br>326 313 | 54988<br>−10548<br>326 314 | 54989<br>−10547<br>326 315 | 54990<br>−10546<br>326 316 | 54991<br>−10545<br>326 317 |
| **D−** | 54992<br>−10544<br>326 320 | 54993<br>−10543<br>326 321 | 54994<br>−10542<br>326 322 | 54995<br>−10541<br>326 323 | 54996<br>−10540<br>326 324 | 54997<br>−10539<br>326 325 | 54998<br>−10538<br>326 326 | 54999<br>−10537<br>326 327 | 55000<br>−10536<br>326 330 | 55001<br>−10535<br>326 331 | 55002<br>−10534<br>326 332 | 55003<br>−10533<br>326 333 | 55004<br>−10532<br>326 334 | 55005<br>−10531<br>326 335 | 55006<br>−10530<br>326 336 | 55007<br>−10529<br>326 337 |
| **E−** | 55008<br>−10528<br>326 340 | 55009<br>−10527<br>326 341 | 55010<br>−10526<br>326 342 | 55011<br>−10525<br>326 343 | 55012<br>−10524<br>326 344 | 55013<br>−10523<br>326 345 | 55014<br>−10522<br>326 346 | 55015<br>−10521<br>326 347 | 55016<br>−10520<br>326 350 | 55017<br>−10519<br>326 351 | 55018<br>−10518<br>326 352 | 55019<br>−10517<br>326 353 | 55020<br>−10516<br>326 354 | 55021<br>−10515<br>326 355 | 55022<br>−10514<br>326 356 | 55023<br>−10513<br>326 357 |
| **F−** | 55024<br>−10512<br>326 360 | 55025<br>−10511<br>326 361 | 55026<br>−10510<br>326 362 | 55027<br>−10509<br>326 363 | 55028<br>−10508<br>326 364 | 55029<br>−10507<br>326 365 | 55030<br>−10506<br>326 366 | 55031<br>−10505<br>326 367 | 55032<br>−10504<br>326 370 | 55033<br>−10503<br>326 371 | 55034<br>−10502<br>326 372 | 55035<br>−10501<br>326 373 | 55036<br>−10500<br>326 374 | 55037<br>−10499<br>326 375 | 55038<br>−10498<br>326 376 | 55039<br>−10497<br>326 377 |

**DECIMAL** ←
🍎 **DECIMAL** ←
**OCTAL** ←

---

🍎 DECIMAL  `−10752`    BINARY  `1101 0110`    DECIMAL  `54784`    HEXADECIMAL  ⬡ **D6**    OCTAL  `326 000`

FOURTH HEX DIGIT ↗ ↖ THIRD HEX DIGIT

FIRST HEX DIGIT — hexagon ②

| SECOND HEX DIGIT | -0 | -1 | -2 | -3 | -4 | -5 | -6 | -7 | -8 | -9 | -A | -B | -C | -D | -E | -F |
|---|---|---|---|---|---|---|---|---|---|---|---|---|---|---|---|---|
| 0- | 55040<br>-10496<br>327 000 | 55041<br>-10495<br>327 001 | 55042<br>-10494<br>327 002 | 55043<br>-10493<br>327 003 | 55044<br>-10492<br>327 004 | 55045<br>-10491<br>327 005 | 55046<br>-10490<br>327 006 | 55047<br>-10489<br>327 007 | 55048<br>-10488<br>327 010 | 55049<br>-10487<br>327 011 | 55050<br>-10486<br>327 012 | 55051<br>-10485<br>327 013 | 55052<br>-10484<br>327 014 | 55053<br>-10483<br>327 015 | 55054<br>-10482<br>327 016 | 55055<br>-10481<br>327 017 |
| 1- | 55056<br>-10480<br>327 020 | 55057<br>-10479<br>327 021 | 55058<br>-10478<br>327 022 | 55059<br>-10477<br>327 023 | 55060<br>-10476<br>327 024 | 55061<br>-10475<br>327 025 | 55062<br>-10474<br>327 026 | 55063<br>-10473<br>327 027 | 55064<br>-10472<br>327 030 | 55065<br>-10471<br>327 031 | 55066<br>-10470<br>327 032 | 55067<br>-10469<br>327 033 | 55068<br>-10468<br>327 034 | 55069<br>-10467<br>327 035 | 55070<br>-10466<br>327 036 | 55071<br>-10465<br>327 037 |
| 2- | 55072<br>-10464<br>327 040 | 55073<br>-10463<br>327 041 | 55074<br>-10462<br>327 042 | 55075<br>-10461<br>327 043 | 55076<br>-10460<br>327 044 | 55077<br>-10459<br>327 045 | 55078<br>-10458<br>327 046 | 55079<br>-10457<br>327 047 | 55080<br>-10456<br>327 050 | 55081<br>-10455<br>327 051 | 55082<br>-10454<br>327 052 | 55083<br>-10453<br>327 053 | 55084<br>-10452<br>327 054 | 55085<br>-10451<br>327 055 | 55086<br>-10450<br>327 056 | 55087<br>-10449<br>327 057 |
| 3- | 55088<br>-10448<br>327 060 | 55089<br>-10447<br>327 061 | 55090<br>-10446<br>327 062 | 55091<br>-10445<br>327 063 | 55092<br>-10444<br>327 064 | 55093<br>-10443<br>327 065 | 55094<br>-10442<br>327 066 | 55095<br>-10441<br>327 067 | 55096<br>-10440<br>327 070 | 55097<br>-10439<br>327 071 | 55098<br>-10438<br>327 072 | 55099<br>-10437<br>327 073 | 55100<br>-10436<br>327 074 | 55101<br>-10435<br>327 075 | 55102<br>-10434<br>327 076 | 55103<br>-10433<br>327 077 |
| 4- | 55104<br>-10432<br>327 100 | 55105<br>-10431<br>327 101 | 55106<br>-10430<br>327 102 | 55107<br>-10429<br>327 103 | 55108<br>-10428<br>327 104 | 55109<br>-10427<br>327 105 | 55110<br>-10426<br>327 106 | 55111<br>-10425<br>327 107 | 55112<br>-10424<br>327 110 | 55113<br>-10423<br>327 111 | 55114<br>-10422<br>327 112 | 55115<br>-10421<br>327 113 | 55116<br>-10420<br>327 114 | 55117<br>-10419<br>327 115 | 55118<br>-10418<br>327 116 | 55119<br>-10417<br>327 117 |
| 5- | 55120<br>-10416<br>327 120 | 55121<br>-10415<br>327 121 | 55122<br>-10414<br>327 122 | 55123<br>-10413<br>327 123 | 55124<br>-10412<br>327 124 | 55125<br>-10411<br>327 125 | 55126<br>-10410<br>327 126 | 55127<br>-10409<br>327 127 | 55128<br>-10408<br>327 130 | 55129<br>-10407<br>327 131 | 55130<br>-10406<br>327 132 | 55131<br>-10405<br>327 133 | 55132<br>-10404<br>327 134 | 55133<br>-10403<br>327 135 | 55134<br>-10402<br>327 136 | 55135<br>-10401<br>327 137 |
| 6- | 55136<br>-10400<br>327 140 | 55137<br>-10399<br>327 141 | 55138<br>-10398<br>327 142 | 55139<br>-10397<br>327 143 | 55140<br>-10396<br>327 144 | 55141<br>-10395<br>327 145 | 55142<br>-10394<br>327 146 | 55143<br>-10393<br>327 147 | 55144<br>-10392<br>327 150 | 55145<br>-10391<br>327 151 | 55146<br>-10390<br>327 152 | 55147<br>-10389<br>327 153 | 55148<br>-10388<br>327 154 | 55149<br>-10387<br>327 155 | 55150<br>-10386<br>327 156 | 55151<br>-10385<br>327 157 |
| 7- | 55152<br>-10384<br>327 160 | 55153<br>-10383<br>327 161 | 55154<br>-10382<br>327 162 | 55155<br>-10381<br>327 163 | 55156<br>-10380<br>327 164 | 55157<br>-10379<br>327 165 | 55158<br>-10378<br>327 166 | 55159<br>-10377<br>327 167 | 55160<br>-10376<br>327 170 | 55161<br>-10375<br>327 171 | 55162<br>-10374<br>327 172 | 55163<br>-10373<br>327 173 | 55164<br>-10372<br>327 174 | 55165<br>-10371<br>327 175 | 55166<br>-10370<br>327 176 | 55167<br>-10369<br>327 177 |
| 8- | 55168<br>-10368<br>327 200 | 55169<br>-10367<br>327 201 | 55170<br>-10366<br>327 202 | 55171<br>-10365<br>327 203 | 55172<br>-10364<br>327 204 | 55173<br>-10363<br>327 205 | 55174<br>-10362<br>327 206 | 55175<br>-10361<br>327 207 | 55176<br>-10360<br>327 210 | 55177<br>-10359<br>327 211 | 55178<br>-10358<br>327 212 | 55179<br>-10357<br>327 213 | 55180<br>-10356<br>327 214 | 55181<br>-10355<br>327 215 | 55182<br>-10354<br>327 216 | 55183<br>-10353<br>327 217 |
| 9- | 55184<br>-10352<br>327 220 | 55185<br>-10351<br>327 221 | 55186<br>-10350<br>327 222 | 55187<br>-10349<br>327 223 | 55188<br>-10348<br>327 224 | 55189<br>-10347<br>327 225 | 55190<br>-10346<br>327 226 | 55191<br>-10345<br>327 227 | 55192<br>-10344<br>327 230 | 55193<br>-10343<br>327 231 | 55194<br>-10342<br>327 232 | 55195<br>-10341<br>327 233 | 55196<br>-10340<br>327 234 | 55197<br>-10339<br>327 235 | 55198<br>-10338<br>327 236 | 55199<br>-10337<br>327 237 |
| A- | 55200<br>-10336<br>327 240 | 55201<br>-10335<br>327 241 | 55202<br>-10334<br>327 242 | 55203<br>-10333<br>327 243 | 55204<br>-10332<br>327 244 | 55205<br>-10331<br>327 245 | 55206<br>-10330<br>327 246 | 55207<br>-10329<br>327 247 | 55208<br>-10328<br>327 250 | 55209<br>-10327<br>327 251 | 55210<br>-10326<br>327 252 | 55211<br>-10325<br>327 253 | 55212<br>-10324<br>327 254 | 55213<br>-10323<br>327 255 | 55214<br>-10322<br>327 256 | 55215<br>-10321<br>327 257 |
| B- | 55216<br>-10320<br>327 260 | 55217<br>-10319<br>327 261 | 55218<br>-10318<br>327 262 | 55219<br>-10317<br>327 263 | 55220<br>-10316<br>327 264 | 55221<br>-10315<br>327 265 | 55222<br>-10314<br>327 266 | 55223<br>-10313<br>327 267 | 55224<br>-10312<br>327 270 | 55225<br>-10311<br>327 271 | 55226<br>-10310<br>327 272 | 55227<br>-10309<br>327 273 | 55228<br>-10308<br>327 274 | 55229<br>-10307<br>327 275 | 55230<br>-10306<br>327 276 | 55231<br>-10305<br>327 277 |
| C- | 55232<br>-10304<br>327 300 | 55233<br>-10303<br>327 301 | 55234<br>-10302<br>327 302 | 55235<br>-10301<br>327 303 | 55236<br>-10300<br>327 304 | 55237<br>-10299<br>327 305 | 55238<br>-10298<br>327 306 | 55239<br>-10297<br>327 307 | 55240<br>-10296<br>327 310 | 55241<br>-10295<br>327 311 | 55242<br>-10294<br>327 312 | 55243<br>-10293<br>327 313 | 55244<br>-10292<br>327 314 | 55245<br>-10291<br>327 315 | 55246<br>-10290<br>327 316 | 55247<br>-10289<br>327 317 |
| D- | 55248<br>-10288<br>327 320 | 55249<br>-10287<br>327 321 | 55250<br>-10286<br>327 322 | 55251<br>-10285<br>327 323 | 55252<br>-10284<br>327 324 | 55253<br>-10283<br>327 325 | 55254<br>-10282<br>327 326 | 55255<br>-10281<br>327 327 | 55256<br>-10280<br>327 330 | 55257<br>-10279<br>327 331 | 55258<br>-10278<br>327 332 | 55259<br>-10277<br>327 333 | 55260<br>-10276<br>327 334 | 55261<br>-10275<br>327 335 | 55262<br>-10274<br>327 336 | 55263<br>-10273<br>327 337 |
| E- | 55264<br>-10272<br>327 340 | 55265<br>-10271<br>327 341 | 55266<br>-10270<br>327 342 | 55267<br>-10269<br>327 343 | 55268<br>-10268<br>327 344 | 55269<br>-10267<br>327 345 | 55270<br>-10266<br>327 346 | 55271<br>-10265<br>327 347 | 55272<br>-10264<br>327 350 | 55273<br>-10263<br>327 351 | 55274<br>-10262<br>327 352 | 55275<br>-10261<br>327 353 | 55276<br>-10260<br>327 354 | 55277<br>-10259<br>327 355 | 55278<br>-10258<br>327 356 | 55279<br>-10257<br>327 357 |
| F- | 55280<br>-10256<br>327 360 | 55281<br>-10255<br>327 361 | 55282<br>-10254<br>327 362 | 55283<br>-10253<br>327 363 | 55284<br>-10252<br>327 364 | 55285<br>-10251<br>327 365 | 55286<br>-10250<br>327 366 | 55287<br>-10249<br>327 367 | 55288<br>-10248<br>327 370 | 55289<br>-10247<br>327 371 | 55290<br>-10246<br>327 372 | 55291<br>-10245<br>327 373 | 55292<br>-10244<br>327 374 | 55293<br>-10243<br>327 375 | 55294<br>-10242<br>327 376 | 55295<br>-10241<br>327 377 |

# FIRST HEX DIGIT (Table 2)

Each cell: decimal (top) / signed decimal (middle) / octal (bottom). Rows = SECOND HEX DIGIT.

| | −0 | −1 | −2 | −3 | −4 | −5 | −6 | −7 | −8 | −9 | −A | −B | −C | −D | −E | −F |
|---|---|---|---|---|---|---|---|---|---|---|---|---|---|---|---|---|
| **0−** | 55296<br>-10240<br>330 000 | 55297<br>-10239<br>330 001 | 55298<br>-10238<br>330 002 | 55299<br>-10237<br>330 003 | 55300<br>-10236<br>330 004 | 55301<br>-10235<br>330 005 | 55302<br>-10234<br>330 006 | 55303<br>-10233<br>330 007 | 55304<br>-10232<br>330 010 | 55305<br>-10231<br>330 011 | 55306<br>-10230<br>330 012 | 55307<br>-10229<br>330 013 | 55308<br>-10228<br>330 014 | 55309<br>-10227<br>330 015 | 55310<br>-10226<br>330 016 | 55311<br>-10225<br>330 017 |
| **1−** | 55312<br>-10224<br>330 020 | 55313<br>-10223<br>330 021 | 55314<br>-10222<br>330 022 | 55315<br>-10221<br>330 023 | 55316<br>-10220<br>330 024 | 55317<br>-10219<br>330 025 | 55318<br>-10218<br>330 026 | 55319<br>-10217<br>330 027 | 55320<br>-10216<br>330 030 | 55321<br>-10215<br>330 031 | 55322<br>-10214<br>330 032 | 55323<br>-10213<br>330 033 | 55324<br>-10212<br>330 034 | 55325<br>-10211<br>330 035 | 55326<br>-10210<br>330 036 | 55327<br>-10209<br>330 037 |
| **2−** | 55328<br>-10208<br>330 040 | 55329<br>-10207<br>330 041 | 55330<br>-10206<br>330 042 | 55331<br>-10205<br>330 043 | 55332<br>-10204<br>330 044 | 55333<br>-10203<br>330 045 | 55334<br>-10202<br>330 046 | 55335<br>-10201<br>330 047 | 55336<br>-10200<br>330 050 | 55337<br>-10199<br>330 051 | 55338<br>-10198<br>330 052 | 55339<br>-10197<br>330 053 | 55340<br>-10196<br>330 054 | 55341<br>-10195<br>330 055 | 55342<br>-10194<br>330 056 | 55343<br>-10193<br>330 057 |
| **3−** | 55344<br>-10192<br>330 060 | 55345<br>-10191<br>330 061 | 55346<br>-10190<br>330 062 | 55347<br>-10189<br>330 063 | 55348<br>-10188<br>330 064 | 55349<br>-10187<br>330 065 | 55350<br>-10186<br>330 066 | 55351<br>-10185<br>330 067 | 55352<br>-10184<br>330 070 | 55353<br>-10183<br>330 071 | 55354<br>-10182<br>330 072 | 55355<br>-10181<br>330 073 | 55356<br>-10180<br>330 074 | 55357<br>-10179<br>330 075 | 55358<br>-10178<br>330 076 | 55359<br>-10177<br>330 077 |
| **4−** | 55360<br>-10176<br>330 100 | 55361<br>-10175<br>330 101 | 55362<br>-10174<br>330 102 | 55363<br>-10173<br>330 103 | 55364<br>-10172<br>330 104 | 55365<br>-10171<br>330 105 | 55366<br>-10170<br>330 106 | 55367<br>-10169<br>330 107 | 55368<br>-10168<br>330 110 | 55369<br>-10167<br>330 111 | 55370<br>-10166<br>330 112 | 55371<br>-10165<br>330 113 | 55372<br>-10164<br>330 114 | 55373<br>-10163<br>330 115 | 55374<br>-10162<br>330 116 | 55375<br>-10161<br>330 117 |
| **5−** | 55376<br>-10160<br>330 120 | 55377<br>-10159<br>330 121 | 55378<br>-10158<br>330 122 | 55379<br>-10157<br>330 123 | 55380<br>-10156<br>330 124 | 55381<br>-10155<br>330 125 | 55382<br>-10154<br>330 126 | 55383<br>-10153<br>330 127 | 55384<br>-10152<br>330 130 | 55385<br>-10151<br>330 131 | 55386<br>-10150<br>330 132 | 55387<br>-10149<br>330 133 | 55388<br>-10148<br>330 134 | 55389<br>-10147<br>330 135 | 55390<br>-10146<br>330 136 | 55391<br>-10145<br>330 137 |
| **6−** | 55392<br>-10144<br>330 140 | 55393<br>-10143<br>330 141 | 55394<br>-10142<br>330 142 | 55395<br>-10141<br>330 143 | 55396<br>-10140<br>330 144 | 55397<br>-10139<br>330 145 | 55398<br>-10138<br>330 146 | 55399<br>-10137<br>330 147 | 55400<br>-10136<br>330 150 | 55401<br>-10135<br>330 151 | 55402<br>-10134<br>330 152 | 55403<br>-10133<br>330 153 | 55404<br>-10132<br>330 154 | 55405<br>-10131<br>330 155 | 55406<br>-10130<br>330 156 | 55407<br>-10129<br>330 157 |
| **7−** | 55408<br>-10128<br>330 160 | 55409<br>-10127<br>330 161 | 55410<br>-10126<br>330 162 | 55411<br>-10125<br>330 163 | 55412<br>-10124<br>330 164 | 55413<br>-10123<br>330 165 | 55414<br>-10122<br>330 166 | 55415<br>-10121<br>330 167 | 55416<br>-10120<br>330 170 | 55417<br>-10119<br>330 171 | 55418<br>-10118<br>330 172 | 55419<br>-10117<br>330 173 | 55420<br>-10116<br>330 174 | 55421<br>-10115<br>330 175 | 55422<br>-10114<br>330 176 | 55423<br>-10113<br>330 177 |
| **8−** | 55424<br>-10112<br>330 200 | 55425<br>-10111<br>330 201 | 55426<br>-10110<br>330 202 | 55427<br>-10109<br>330 203 | 55428<br>-10108<br>330 204 | 55429<br>-10107<br>330 205 | 55430<br>-10106<br>330 206 | 55431<br>-10105<br>330 207 | 55432<br>-10104<br>330 210 | 55433<br>-10103<br>330 211 | 55434<br>-10102<br>330 212 | 55435<br>-10101<br>330 213 | 55436<br>-10100<br>330 214 | 55437<br>-10099<br>330 215 | 55438<br>-10098<br>330 216 | 55439<br>-10097<br>330 217 |
| **9−** | 55440<br>-10096<br>330 220 | 55441<br>-10095<br>330 221 | 55442<br>-10094<br>330 222 | 55443<br>-10093<br>330 223 | 55444<br>-10092<br>330 224 | 55445<br>-10091<br>330 225 | 55446<br>-10090<br>330 226 | 55447<br>-10089<br>330 227 | 55448<br>-10088<br>330 230 | 55449<br>-10087<br>330 231 | 55450<br>-10086<br>330 232 | 55451<br>-10085<br>330 233 | 55452<br>-10084<br>330 234 | 55453<br>-10083<br>330 235 | 55454<br>-10082<br>330 236 | 55455<br>-10081<br>330 237 |
| **A−** | 55456<br>-10080<br>330 240 | 55457<br>-10079<br>330 241 | 55458<br>-10078<br>330 242 | 55459<br>-10077<br>330 243 | 55460<br>-10076<br>330 244 | 55461<br>-10075<br>330 245 | 55462<br>-10074<br>330 246 | 55463<br>-10073<br>330 247 | 55464<br>-10072<br>330 250 | 55465<br>-10071<br>330 251 | 55466<br>-10070<br>330 252 | 55467<br>-10069<br>330 253 | 55468<br>-10068<br>330 254 | 55469<br>-10067<br>330 255 | 55470<br>-10066<br>330 256 | 55471<br>-10065<br>330 257 |
| **B−** | 55472<br>-10064<br>330 260 | 55473<br>-10063<br>330 261 | 55474<br>-10062<br>330 262 | 55475<br>-10061<br>330 263 | 55476<br>-10060<br>330 264 | 55477<br>-10059<br>330 265 | 55478<br>-10058<br>330 266 | 55479<br>-10057<br>330 267 | 55480<br>-10056<br>330 270 | 55481<br>-10055<br>330 271 | 55482<br>-10054<br>330 272 | 55483<br>-10053<br>330 273 | 55484<br>-10052<br>330 274 | 55485<br>-10051<br>330 275 | 55486<br>-10050<br>330 276 | 55487<br>-10049<br>330 277 |
| **C−** | 55488<br>-10048<br>330 300 | 55489<br>-10047<br>330 301 | 55490<br>-10046<br>330 302 | 55491<br>-10045<br>330 303 | 55492<br>-10044<br>330 304 | 55493<br>-10043<br>330 305 | 55494<br>-10042<br>330 306 | 55495<br>-10041<br>330 307 | 55496<br>-10040<br>330 310 | 55497<br>-10039<br>330 311 | 55498<br>-10038<br>330 312 | 55499<br>-10037<br>330 313 | 55500<br>-10036<br>330 314 | 55501<br>-10035<br>330 315 | 55502<br>-10034<br>330 316 | 55503<br>-10033<br>330 317 |
| **D−** | 55504<br>-10032<br>330 320 | 55505<br>-10031<br>330 321 | 55506<br>-10030<br>330 322 | 55507<br>-10029<br>330 323 | 55508<br>-10028<br>330 324 | 55509<br>-10027<br>330 325 | 55510<br>-10026<br>330 326 | 55511<br>-10025<br>330 327 | 55512<br>-10024<br>330 330 | 55513<br>-10023<br>330 331 | 55514<br>-10022<br>330 332 | 55515<br>-10021<br>330 333 | 55516<br>-10020<br>330 334 | 55517<br>-10019<br>330 335 | 55518<br>-10018<br>330 336 | 55519<br>-10017<br>330 337 |
| **E−** | 55520<br>-10016<br>330 340 | 55521<br>-10015<br>330 341 | 55522<br>-10014<br>330 342 | 55523<br>-10013<br>330 343 | 55524<br>-10012<br>330 344 | 55525<br>-10011<br>330 345 | 55526<br>-10010<br>330 346 | 55527<br>-10009<br>330 347 | 55528<br>-10008<br>330 350 | 55529<br>-10007<br>330 351 | 55530<br>-10006<br>330 352 | 55531<br>-10005<br>330 353 | 55532<br>-10004<br>330 354 | 55533<br>-10003<br>330 355 | 55534<br>-10002<br>330 356 | 55535<br>-10001<br>330 357 |
| **F−** | 55536<br>-10000<br>330 360 | 55537<br>-9999<br>330 361 | 55538<br>-9998<br>330 362 | 55539<br>-9997<br>330 363 | 55540<br>-9996<br>330 364 | 55541<br>-9995<br>330 365 | 55542<br>-9994<br>330 366 | 55543<br>-9993<br>330 367 | 55544<br>-9992<br>330 370 | 55545<br>-9991<br>330 371 | 55546<br>-9990<br>330 372 | 55547<br>-9989<br>330 373 | 55548<br>-9988<br>330 374 | 55549<br>-9987<br>330 375 | 55550<br>-9986<br>330 376 | 55551<br>-9985<br>330 377 |

DECIMAL

 DECIMAL

OCTAL

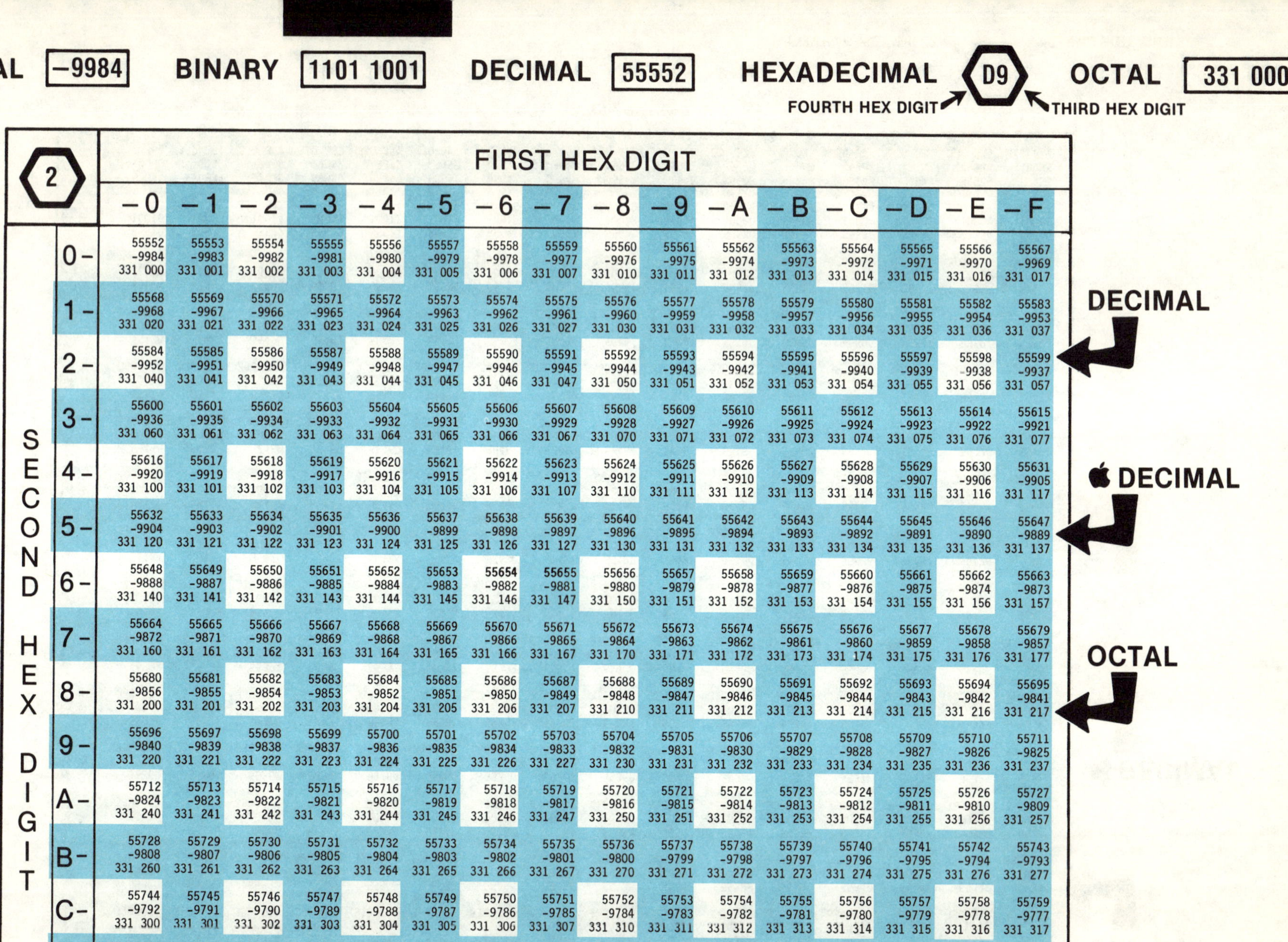

DECIMAL `−9984`   BINARY `1101 1001`   DECIMAL `55552`   HEXADECIMAL ⬡ D9   OCTAL `331 000`

FOURTH HEX DIGIT → ⬡ ← THIRD HEX DIGIT

⬡ 2

| SECOND HEX DIGIT \ FIRST HEX DIGIT | −0 | −1 | −2 | −3 | −4 | −5 | −6 | −7 | −8 | −9 | −A | −B | −C | −D | −E | −F |
|---|---|---|---|---|---|---|---|---|---|---|---|---|---|---|---|---|
| 0− | 55552<br>−9984<br>331 000 | 55553<br>−9983<br>331 001 | 55554<br>−9982<br>331 002 | 55555<br>−9981<br>331 003 | 55556<br>−9980<br>331 004 | 55557<br>−9979<br>331 005 | 55558<br>−9978<br>331 006 | 55559<br>−9977<br>331 007 | 55560<br>−9976<br>331 010 | 55561<br>−9975<br>331 011 | 55562<br>−9974<br>331 012 | 55563<br>−9973<br>331 013 | 55564<br>−9972<br>331 014 | 55565<br>−9971<br>331 015 | 55566<br>−9970<br>331 016 | 55567<br>−9969<br>331 017 |
| 1− | 55568<br>−9968<br>331 020 | 55569<br>−9967<br>331 021 | 55570<br>−9966<br>331 022 | 55571<br>−9965<br>331 023 | 55572<br>−9964<br>331 024 | 55573<br>−9963<br>331 025 | 55574<br>−9962<br>331 026 | 55575<br>−9961<br>331 027 | 55576<br>−9960<br>331 030 | 55577<br>−9959<br>331 031 | 55578<br>−9958<br>331 032 | 55579<br>−9957<br>331 033 | 55580<br>−9956<br>331 034 | 55581<br>−9955<br>331 035 | 55582<br>−9954<br>331 036 | 55583<br>−9953<br>331 037 |
| 2− | 55584<br>−9952<br>331 040 | 55585<br>−9951<br>331 041 | 55586<br>−9950<br>331 042 | 55587<br>−9949<br>331 043 | 55588<br>−9948<br>331 044 | 55589<br>−9947<br>331 045 | 55590<br>−9946<br>331 046 | 55591<br>−9945<br>331 047 | 55592<br>−9944<br>331 050 | 55593<br>−9943<br>331 051 | 55594<br>−9942<br>331 052 | 55595<br>−9941<br>331 053 | 55596<br>−9940<br>331 054 | 55597<br>−9939<br>331 055 | 55598<br>−9938<br>331 056 | 55599<br>−9937<br>331 057 |
| 3− | 55600<br>−9936<br>331 060 | 55601<br>−9935<br>331 061 | 55602<br>−9934<br>331 062 | 55603<br>−9933<br>331 063 | 55604<br>−9932<br>331 064 | 55605<br>−9931<br>331 065 | 55606<br>−9930<br>331 066 | 55607<br>−9929<br>331 067 | 55608<br>−9928<br>331 070 | 55609<br>−9927<br>331 071 | 55610<br>−9926<br>331 072 | 55611<br>−9925<br>331 073 | 55612<br>−9924<br>331 074 | 55613<br>−9923<br>331 075 | 55614<br>−9922<br>331 076 | 55615<br>−9921<br>331 077 |
| 4− | 55616<br>−9920<br>331 100 | 55617<br>−9919<br>331 101 | 55618<br>−9918<br>331 102 | 55619<br>−9917<br>331 103 | 55620<br>−9916<br>331 104 | 55621<br>−9915<br>331 105 | 55622<br>−9914<br>331 106 | 55623<br>−9913<br>331 107 | 55624<br>−9912<br>331 110 | 55625<br>−9911<br>331 111 | 55626<br>−9910<br>331 112 | 55627<br>−9909<br>331 113 | 55628<br>−9908<br>331 114 | 55629<br>−9907<br>331 115 | 55630<br>−9906<br>331 116 | 55631<br>−9905<br>331 117 |
| 5− | 55632<br>−9904<br>331 120 | 55633<br>−9903<br>331 121 | 55634<br>−9902<br>331 122 | 55635<br>−9901<br>331 123 | 55636<br>−9900<br>331 124 | 55637<br>−9899<br>331 125 | 55638<br>−9898<br>331 126 | 55639<br>−9897<br>331 127 | 55640<br>−9896<br>331 130 | 55641<br>−9895<br>331 131 | 55642<br>−9894<br>331 132 | 55643<br>−9893<br>331 133 | 55644<br>−9892<br>331 134 | 55645<br>−9891<br>331 135 | 55646<br>−9890<br>331 136 | 55647<br>−9889<br>331 137 |
| 6− | 55648<br>−9888<br>331 140 | 55649<br>−9887<br>331 141 | 55650<br>−9886<br>331 142 | 55651<br>−9885<br>331 143 | 55652<br>−9884<br>331 144 | 55653<br>−9883<br>331 145 | 55654<br>−9882<br>331 146 | 55655<br>−9881<br>331 147 | 55656<br>−9880<br>331 150 | 55657<br>−9879<br>331 151 | 55658<br>−9878<br>331 152 | 55659<br>−9877<br>331 153 | 55660<br>−9876<br>331 154 | 55661<br>−9875<br>331 155 | 55662<br>−9874<br>331 156 | 55663<br>−9873<br>331 157 |
| 7− | 55664<br>−9872<br>331 160 | 55665<br>−9871<br>331 161 | 55666<br>−9870<br>331 162 | 55667<br>−9869<br>331 163 | 55668<br>−9868<br>331 164 | 55669<br>−9867<br>331 165 | 55670<br>−9866<br>331 166 | 55671<br>−9865<br>331 167 | 55672<br>−9864<br>331 170 | 55673<br>−9863<br>331 171 | 55674<br>−9862<br>331 172 | 55675<br>−9861<br>331 173 | 55676<br>−9860<br>331 174 | 55677<br>−9859<br>331 175 | 55678<br>−9858<br>331 176 | 55679<br>−9857<br>331 177 |
| 8− | 55680<br>−9856<br>331 200 | 55681<br>−9855<br>331 201 | 55682<br>−9854<br>331 202 | 55683<br>−9853<br>331 203 | 55684<br>−9852<br>331 204 | 55685<br>−9851<br>331 205 | 55686<br>−9850<br>331 206 | 55687<br>−9849<br>331 207 | 55688<br>−9848<br>331 210 | 55689<br>−9847<br>331 211 | 55690<br>−9846<br>331 212 | 55691<br>−9845<br>331 213 | 55692<br>−9844<br>331 214 | 55693<br>−9843<br>331 215 | 55694<br>−9842<br>331 216 | 55695<br>−9841<br>331 217 |
| 9− | 55696<br>−9840<br>331 220 | 55697<br>−9839<br>331 221 | 55698<br>−9838<br>331 222 | 55699<br>−9837<br>331 223 | 55700<br>−9836<br>331 224 | 55701<br>−9835<br>331 225 | 55702<br>−9834<br>331 226 | 55703<br>−9833<br>331 227 | 55704<br>−9832<br>331 230 | 55705<br>−9831<br>331 231 | 55706<br>−9830<br>331 232 | 55707<br>−9829<br>331 233 | 55708<br>−9828<br>331 234 | 55709<br>−9827<br>331 235 | 55710<br>−9826<br>331 236 | 55711<br>−9825<br>331 237 |
| A− | 55712<br>−9824<br>331 240 | 55713<br>−9823<br>331 241 | 55714<br>−9822<br>331 242 | 55715<br>−9821<br>331 243 | 55716<br>−9820<br>331 244 | 55717<br>−9819<br>331 245 | 55718<br>−9818<br>331 246 | 55719<br>−9817<br>331 247 | 55720<br>−9816<br>331 250 | 55721<br>−9815<br>331 251 | 55722<br>−9814<br>331 252 | 55723<br>−9813<br>331 253 | 55724<br>−9812<br>331 254 | 55725<br>−9811<br>331 255 | 55726<br>−9810<br>331 256 | 55727<br>−9809<br>331 257 |
| B− | 55728<br>−9808<br>331 260 | 55729<br>−9807<br>331 261 | 55730<br>−9806<br>331 262 | 55731<br>−9805<br>331 263 | 55732<br>−9804<br>331 264 | 55733<br>−9803<br>331 265 | 55734<br>−9802<br>331 266 | 55735<br>−9801<br>331 267 | 55736<br>−9800<br>331 270 | 55737<br>−9799<br>331 271 | 55738<br>−9798<br>331 272 | 55739<br>−9797<br>331 273 | 55740<br>−9796<br>331 274 | 55741<br>−9795<br>331 275 | 55742<br>−9794<br>331 276 | 55743<br>−9793<br>331 277 |
| C− | 55744<br>−9792<br>331 300 | 55745<br>−9791<br>331 301 | 55746<br>−9790<br>331 302 | 55747<br>−9789<br>331 303 | 55748<br>−9788<br>331 304 | 55749<br>−9787<br>331 305 | 55750<br>−9786<br>331 306 | 55751<br>−9785<br>331 307 | 55752<br>−9784<br>331 310 | 55753<br>−9783<br>331 311 | 55754<br>−9782<br>331 312 | 55755<br>−9781<br>331 313 | 55756<br>−9780<br>331 314 | 55757<br>−9779<br>331 315 | 55758<br>−9778<br>331 316 | 55759<br>−9777<br>331 317 |
| D− | 55760<br>−9776<br>331 320 | 55761<br>−9775<br>331 321 | 55762<br>−9774<br>331 322 | 55763<br>−9773<br>331 323 | 55764<br>−9772<br>331 324 | 55765<br>−9771<br>331 325 | 55766<br>−9770<br>331 326 | 55767<br>−9769<br>331 327 | 55768<br>−9768<br>331 330 | 55769<br>−9767<br>331 331 | 55770<br>−9766<br>331 332 | 55771<br>−9765<br>331 333 | 55772<br>−9764<br>331 334 | 55773<br>−9763<br>331 335 | 55774<br>−9762<br>331 336 | 55775<br>−9761<br>331 337 |
| E− | 55776<br>−9760<br>331 340 | 55777<br>−9759<br>331 341 | 55778<br>−9758<br>331 342 | 55779<br>−9757<br>331 343 | 55780<br>−9756<br>331 344 | 55781<br>−9755<br>331 345 | 55782<br>−9754<br>331 346 | 55783<br>−9753<br>331 347 | 55784<br>−9752<br>331 350 | 55785<br>−9751<br>331 351 | 55786<br>−9750<br>331 352 | 55787<br>−9749<br>331 353 | 55788<br>−9748<br>331 354 | 55789<br>−9747<br>331 355 | 55790<br>−9746<br>331 356 | 55791<br>−9745<br>331 357 |
| F− | 55792<br>−9744<br>331 360 | 55793<br>−9743<br>331 361 | 55794<br>−9742<br>331 362 | 55795<br>−9741<br>331 363 | 55796<br>−9740<br>331 364 | 55797<br>−9739<br>331 365 | 55798<br>−9738<br>331 366 | 55799<br>−9737<br>331 367 | 55800<br>−9736<br>331 370 | 55801<br>−9735<br>331 371 | 55802<br>−9734<br>331 372 | 55803<br>−9733<br>331 373 | 55804<br>−9732<br>331 374 | 55805<br>−9731<br>331 375 | 55806<br>−9730<br>331 376 | 55807<br>−9729<br>331 377 |

②

| SECOND HEX DIGIT | -0 | -1 | -2 | -3 | -4 | -5 | -6 | -7 | -8 | -9 | -A | -B | -C | -D | -E | -F |
|---|---|---|---|---|---|---|---|---|---|---|---|---|---|---|---|---|
| **0-** | 55808<br>-9728<br>332 000 | 55809<br>-9727<br>332 001 | 55810<br>-9726<br>332 002 | 55811<br>-9725<br>332 003 | 55812<br>-9724<br>332 004 | 55813<br>-9723<br>332 005 | 55814<br>-9722<br>332 006 | 55815<br>-9721<br>332 007 | 55816<br>-9720<br>332 010 | 55817<br>-9719<br>332 011 | 55818<br>-9718<br>332 012 | 55819<br>-9717<br>332 013 | 55820<br>-9716<br>332 014 | 55821<br>-9715<br>332 015 | 55822<br>-9714<br>332 016 | 55823<br>-9713<br>332 017 |
| **1-** | 55824<br>-9712<br>332 020 | 55825<br>-9711<br>332 021 | 55826<br>-9710<br>332 022 | 55827<br>-9709<br>332 023 | 55828<br>-9708<br>332 024 | 55829<br>-9707<br>332 025 | 55830<br>-9706<br>332 026 | 55831<br>-9705<br>332 027 | 55832<br>-9704<br>332 030 | 55833<br>-9703<br>332 031 | 55834<br>-9702<br>332 032 | 55835<br>-9701<br>332 033 | 55836<br>-9700<br>332 034 | 55837<br>-9699<br>332 035 | 55838<br>-9698<br>332 036 | 55839<br>-9697<br>332 037 |
| **2-** | 55840<br>-9696<br>332 040 | 55841<br>-9695<br>332 041 | 55842<br>-9694<br>332 042 | 55843<br>-9693<br>332 043 | 55844<br>-9692<br>332 044 | 55845<br>-9691<br>332 045 | 55846<br>-9690<br>332 046 | 55847<br>-9689<br>332 047 | 55848<br>-9688<br>332 050 | 55849<br>-9687<br>332 051 | 55850<br>-9686<br>332 052 | 55851<br>-9685<br>332 053 | 55852<br>-9684<br>332 054 | 55853<br>-9683<br>332 055 | 55854<br>-9682<br>332 056 | 55855<br>-9681<br>332 057 |
| **3-** | 55856<br>-9680<br>332 060 | 55857<br>-9679<br>332 061 | 55858<br>-9678<br>332 062 | 55859<br>-9677<br>332 063 | 55860<br>-9676<br>332 064 | 55861<br>-9675<br>332 065 | 55862<br>-9674<br>332 066 | 55863<br>-9673<br>332 067 | 55864<br>-9672<br>332 070 | 55865<br>-9671<br>332 071 | 55866<br>-9670<br>332 072 | 55867<br>-9669<br>332 073 | 55868<br>-9668<br>332 074 | 55869<br>-9667<br>332 075 | 55870<br>-9666<br>332 076 | 55871<br>-9665<br>332 077 |
| **4-** | 55872<br>-9664<br>332 100 | 55873<br>-9663<br>332 101 | 55874<br>-9662<br>332 102 | 55875<br>-9661<br>332 103 | 55876<br>-9660<br>332 104 | 55877<br>-9659<br>332 105 | 55878<br>-9658<br>332 106 | 55879<br>-9657<br>332 107 | 55880<br>-9656<br>332 110 | 55881<br>-9655<br>332 111 | 55882<br>-9654<br>332 112 | 55883<br>-9653<br>332 113 | 55884<br>-9652<br>332 114 | 55885<br>-9651<br>332 115 | 55886<br>-9650<br>332 116 | 55887<br>-9649<br>332 117 |
| **5-** | 55888<br>-9648<br>332 120 | 55889<br>-9647<br>332 121 | 55890<br>-9646<br>332 122 | 55891<br>-9645<br>332 123 | 55892<br>-9644<br>332 124 | 55893<br>-9643<br>332 125 | 55894<br>-9642<br>332 126 | 55895<br>-9641<br>332 127 | 55896<br>-9640<br>332 130 | 55897<br>-9639<br>332 131 | 55898<br>-9638<br>332 132 | 55899<br>-9637<br>332 133 | 55900<br>-9636<br>332 134 | 55901<br>-9635<br>332 135 | 55902<br>-9634<br>332 136 | 55903<br>-9633<br>332 137 |
| **6-** | 55904<br>-9632<br>332 140 | 55905<br>-9631<br>332 141 | 55906<br>-9630<br>332 142 | 55907<br>-9629<br>332 143 | 55908<br>-9628<br>332 144 | 55909<br>-9627<br>332 145 | 55910<br>-9626<br>332 146 | 55911<br>-9625<br>332 147 | 55912<br>-9624<br>332 150 | 55913<br>-9623<br>332 151 | 55914<br>-9622<br>332 152 | 55915<br>-9621<br>332 153 | 55916<br>-9620<br>332 154 | 55917<br>-9619<br>332 155 | 55918<br>-9618<br>332 156 | 55919<br>-9617<br>332 157 |
| **7-** | 55920<br>-9616<br>332 160 | 55921<br>-9615<br>332 161 | 55922<br>-9614<br>332 162 | 55923<br>-9613<br>332 163 | 55924<br>-9612<br>332 164 | 55925<br>-9611<br>332 165 | 55926<br>-9610<br>332 166 | 55927<br>-9609<br>332 167 | 55928<br>-9608<br>332 170 | 55929<br>-9607<br>332 171 | 55930<br>-9606<br>332 172 | 55931<br>-9605<br>332 173 | 55932<br>-9604<br>332 174 | 55933<br>-9603<br>332 175 | 55934<br>-9602<br>332 176 | 55935<br>-9601<br>332 177 |
| **8-** | 55936<br>-9600<br>332 200 | 55937<br>-9599<br>332 201 | 55938<br>-9598<br>332 202 | 55939<br>-9597<br>332 203 | 55940<br>-9596<br>332 204 | 55941<br>-9595<br>332 205 | 55942<br>-9594<br>332 206 | 55943<br>-9593<br>332 207 | 55944<br>-9592<br>332 210 | 55945<br>-9591<br>332 211 | 55946<br>-9590<br>332 212 | 55947<br>-9589<br>332 213 | 55948<br>-9588<br>332 214 | 55949<br>-9587<br>332 215 | 55950<br>-9586<br>332 216 | 55951<br>-9585<br>332 217 |
| **9-** | 55952<br>-9584<br>332 220 | 55953<br>-9583<br>332 221 | 55954<br>-9582<br>332 222 | 55955<br>-9581<br>332 223 | 55956<br>-9580<br>332 224 | 55957<br>-9579<br>332 225 | 55958<br>-9578<br>332 226 | 55959<br>-9577<br>332 227 | 55960<br>-9576<br>332 230 | 55961<br>-9575<br>332 231 | 55962<br>-9574<br>332 232 | 55963<br>-9573<br>332 233 | 55964<br>-9572<br>332 234 | 55965<br>-9571<br>332 235 | 55966<br>-9570<br>332 236 | 55967<br>-9569<br>332 237 |
| **A-** | 55968<br>-9568<br>332 240 | 55969<br>-9567<br>332 241 | 55970<br>-9566<br>332 242 | 55971<br>-9565<br>332 243 | 55972<br>-9564<br>332 244 | 55973<br>-9563<br>332 245 | 55974<br>-9562<br>332 246 | 55975<br>-9561<br>332 247 | 55976<br>-9560<br>332 250 | 55977<br>-9559<br>332 251 | 55978<br>-9558<br>332 252 | 55979<br>-9557<br>332 253 | 55980<br>-9556<br>332 254 | 55981<br>-9555<br>332 255 | 55982<br>-9554<br>332 256 | 55983<br>-9553<br>332 257 |
| **B-** | 55984<br>-9552<br>332 260 | 55985<br>-9551<br>332 261 | 55986<br>-9550<br>332 262 | 55987<br>-9549<br>332 263 | 55988<br>-9548<br>332 264 | 55989<br>-9547<br>332 265 | 55990<br>-9546<br>332 266 | 55991<br>-9545<br>332 267 | 55992<br>-9544<br>332 270 | 55993<br>-9543<br>332 271 | 55994<br>-9542<br>332 272 | 55995<br>-9541<br>332 273 | 55996<br>-9540<br>332 274 | 55997<br>-9539<br>332 275 | 55998<br>-9538<br>332 276 | 55999<br>-9537<br>332 277 |
| **C-** | 56000<br>-9536<br>332 300 | 56001<br>-9535<br>332 301 | 56002<br>-9534<br>332 302 | 56003<br>-9533<br>332 303 | 56004<br>-9532<br>332 304 | 56005<br>-9531<br>332 305 | 56006<br>-9530<br>332 306 | 56007<br>-9529<br>332 307 | 56008<br>-9528<br>332 310 | 56009<br>-9527<br>332 311 | 56010<br>-9526<br>332 312 | 56011<br>-9525<br>332 313 | 56012<br>-9524<br>332 314 | 56013<br>-9523<br>332 315 | 56014<br>-9522<br>332 316 | 56015<br>-9521<br>332 317 |
| **D-** | 56016<br>-9520<br>332 320 | 56017<br>-9519<br>332 321 | 56018<br>-9518<br>332 322 | 56019<br>-9517<br>332 323 | 56020<br>-9516<br>332 324 | 56021<br>-9515<br>332 325 | 56022<br>-9514<br>332 326 | 56023<br>-9513<br>332 327 | 56024<br>-9512<br>332 330 | 56025<br>-9511<br>332 331 | 56026<br>-9510<br>332 332 | 56027<br>-9509<br>332 333 | 56028<br>-9508<br>332 334 | 56029<br>-9507<br>332 335 | 56030<br>-9506<br>332 336 | 56031<br>-9505<br>332 337 |
| **E-** | 56032<br>-9504<br>332 340 | 56033<br>-9503<br>332 341 | 56034<br>-9502<br>332 342 | 56035<br>-9501<br>332 343 | 56036<br>-9500<br>332 344 | 56037<br>-9499<br>332 345 | 56038<br>-9498<br>332 346 | 56039<br>-9497<br>332 347 | 56040<br>-9496<br>332 350 | 56041<br>-9495<br>332 351 | 56042<br>-9494<br>332 352 | 56043<br>-9493<br>332 353 | 56044<br>-9492<br>332 354 | 56045<br>-9491<br>332 355 | 56046<br>-9490<br>332 356 | 56047<br>-9489<br>332 357 |
| **F-** | 56048<br>-9488<br>332 360 | 56049<br>-9487<br>332 361 | 56050<br>-9486<br>332 362 | 56051<br>-9485<br>332 363 | 56052<br>-9484<br>332 364 | 56053<br>-9483<br>332 365 | 56054<br>-9482<br>332 366 | 56055<br>-9481<br>332 367 | 56056<br>-9480<br>332 370 | 56057<br>-9479<br>332 371 | 56058<br>-9478<br>332 372 | 56059<br>-9477<br>332 373 | 56060<br>-9476<br>332 374 | 56061<br>-9475<br>332 375 | 56062<br>-9474<br>332 376 | 56063<br>-9473<br>332 377 |

**DECIMAL** ←

 **DECIMAL** ←

**OCTAL** ←

 **DECIMAL** | -9728 |  **BINARY** | 1101 1010 |  **DECIMAL** | 55808 |  **HEXADECIMAL** ⬡ DA  **OCTAL** | 332 000 |

FOURTH HEX DIGIT → ← THIRD HEX DIGIT

 DECIMAL $\boxed{-9472}$  BINARY $\boxed{1101\ 1011}$  DECIMAL $\boxed{56064}$  HEXADECIMAL ⬡DB  OCTAL $\boxed{333\ 000}$

FOURTH HEX DIGIT → ⬡ ← THIRD HEX DIGIT

⬡2  — FIRST HEX DIGIT

Each cell is shown as: decimal (positive) / decimal (negative) / octal.

| SECOND HEX DIGIT | −0 | −1 | −2 | −3 | −4 | −5 | −6 | −7 | −8 | −9 | −A | −B | −C | −D | −E | −F |
|---|---|---|---|---|---|---|---|---|---|---|---|---|---|---|---|---|
| 0− | 56064<br>−9472<br>333 000 | 56065<br>−9471<br>333 001 | 56066<br>−9470<br>333 002 | 56067<br>−9469<br>333 003 | 56068<br>−9468<br>333 004 | 56069<br>−9467<br>333 005 | 56070<br>−9466<br>333 006 | 56071<br>−9465<br>333 007 | 56072<br>−9464<br>333 010 | 56073<br>−9463<br>333 011 | 56074<br>−9462<br>333 012 | 56075<br>−9461<br>333 013 | 56076<br>−9460<br>333 014 | 56077<br>−9459<br>333 015 | 56078<br>−9458<br>333 016 | 56079<br>−9457<br>333 017 |
| 1− | 56080<br>−9456<br>333 020 | 56081<br>−9455<br>333 021 | 56082<br>−9454<br>333 022 | 56083<br>−9453<br>333 023 | 56084<br>−9452<br>333 024 | 56085<br>−9451<br>333 025 | 56086<br>−9450<br>333 026 | 56087<br>−9449<br>333 027 | 56088<br>−9448<br>333 030 | 56089<br>−9447<br>333 031 | 56090<br>−9446<br>333 032 | 56091<br>−9445<br>333 033 | 56092<br>−9444<br>333 034 | 56093<br>−9443<br>333 035 | 56094<br>−9442<br>333 036 | 56095<br>−9441<br>333 037 |
| 2− | 56096<br>−9440<br>333 040 | 56097<br>−9439<br>333 041 | 56098<br>−9438<br>333 042 | 56099<br>−9437<br>333 043 | 56100<br>−9436<br>333 044 | 56101<br>−9435<br>333 045 | 56102<br>−9434<br>333 046 | 56103<br>−9433<br>333 047 | 56104<br>−9432<br>333 050 | 56105<br>−9431<br>333 051 | 56106<br>−9430<br>333 052 | 56107<br>−9429<br>333 053 | 56108<br>−9428<br>333 054 | 56109<br>−9427<br>333 055 | 56110<br>−9426<br>333 056 | 56111<br>−9425<br>333 057 |
| 3− | 56112<br>−9424<br>333 060 | 56113<br>−9423<br>333 061 | 56114<br>−9422<br>333 062 | 56115<br>−9421<br>333 063 | 56116<br>−9420<br>333 064 | 56117<br>−9419<br>333 065 | 56118<br>−9418<br>333 066 | 56119<br>−9417<br>333 067 | 56120<br>−9416<br>333 070 | 56121<br>−9415<br>333 071 | 56122<br>−9414<br>333 072 | 56123<br>−9413<br>333 073 | 56124<br>−9412<br>333 074 | 56125<br>−9411<br>333 075 | 56126<br>−9410<br>333 076 | 56127<br>−9409<br>333 077 |
| 4− | 56128<br>−9408<br>333 100 | 56129<br>−9407<br>333 101 | 56130<br>−9406<br>333 102 | 56131<br>−9405<br>333 103 | 56132<br>−9404<br>333 104 | 56133<br>−9403<br>333 105 | 56134<br>−9402<br>333 106 | 56135<br>−9401<br>333 107 | 56136<br>−9400<br>333 110 | 56137<br>−9399<br>333 111 | 56138<br>−9398<br>333 112 | 56139<br>−9397<br>333 113 | 56140<br>−9396<br>333 114 | 56141<br>−9395<br>333 115 | 56142<br>−9394<br>333 116 | 56143<br>−9393<br>333 117 |
| 5− | 56144<br>−9392<br>333 120 | 56145<br>−9391<br>333 121 | 56146<br>−9390<br>333 122 | 56147<br>−9389<br>333 123 | 56148<br>−9388<br>333 124 | 56149<br>−9387<br>333 125 | 56150<br>−9386<br>333 126 | 56151<br>−9385<br>333 127 | 56152<br>−9384<br>333 130 | 56153<br>−9383<br>333 131 | 56154<br>−9382<br>333 132 | 56155<br>−9381<br>333 133 | 56156<br>−9380<br>333 134 | 56157<br>−9379<br>333 135 | 56158<br>−9378<br>333 136 | 56159<br>−9377<br>333 137 |
| 6− | 56160<br>−9376<br>333 140 | 56161<br>−9375<br>333 141 | 56162<br>−9374<br>333 142 | 56163<br>−9373<br>333 143 | 56164<br>−9372<br>333 144 | 56165<br>−9371<br>333 145 | 56166<br>−9370<br>333 146 | 56167<br>−9369<br>333 147 | 56168<br>−9368<br>333 150 | 56169<br>−9367<br>333 151 | 56170<br>−9366<br>333 152 | 56171<br>−9365<br>333 153 | 56172<br>−9364<br>333 154 | 56173<br>−9363<br>333 155 | 56174<br>−9362<br>333 156 | 56175<br>−9361<br>333 157 |
| 7− | 56176<br>−9360<br>333 160 | 56177<br>−9359<br>333 161 | 56178<br>−9358<br>333 162 | 56179<br>−9357<br>333 163 | 56180<br>−9356<br>333 164 | 56181<br>−9355<br>333 165 | 56182<br>−9354<br>333 166 | 56183<br>−9353<br>333 167 | 56184<br>−9352<br>333 170 | 56185<br>−9351<br>333 171 | 56186<br>−9350<br>333 172 | 56187<br>−9349<br>333 173 | 56188<br>−9348<br>333 174 | 56189<br>−9347<br>333 175 | 56190<br>−9346<br>333 176 | 56191<br>−9345<br>333 177 |
| 8− | 56192<br>−9344<br>333 200 | 56193<br>−9343<br>333 201 | 56194<br>−9342<br>333 202 | 56195<br>−9341<br>333 203 | 56196<br>−9340<br>333 204 | 56197<br>−9339<br>333 205 | 56198<br>−9338<br>333 206 | 56199<br>−9337<br>333 207 | 56200<br>−9336<br>333 210 | 56201<br>−9335<br>333 211 | 56202<br>−9334<br>333 212 | 56203<br>−9333<br>333 213 | 56204<br>−9332<br>333 214 | 56205<br>−9331<br>333 215 | 56206<br>−9330<br>333 216 | 56207<br>−9329<br>333 217 |
| 9− | 56208<br>−9328<br>333 220 | 56209<br>−9327<br>333 221 | 56210<br>−9326<br>333 222 | 56211<br>−9325<br>333 223 | 56212<br>−9324<br>333 224 | 56213<br>−9323<br>333 225 | 56214<br>−9322<br>333 226 | 56215<br>−9321<br>333 227 | 56216<br>−9320<br>333 230 | 56217<br>−9319<br>333 231 | 56218<br>−9318<br>333 232 | 56219<br>−9317<br>333 233 | 56220<br>−9316<br>333 234 | 56221<br>−9315<br>333 235 | 56222<br>−9314<br>333 236 | 56223<br>−9313<br>333 237 |
| A− | 56224<br>−9312<br>333 240 | 56225<br>−9311<br>333 241 | 56226<br>−9310<br>333 242 | 56227<br>−9309<br>333 243 | 56228<br>−9308<br>333 244 | 56229<br>−9307<br>333 245 | 56230<br>−9306<br>333 246 | 56231<br>−9305<br>333 247 | 56232<br>−9304<br>333 250 | 56233<br>−9303<br>333 251 | 56234<br>−9302<br>333 252 | 56235<br>−9301<br>333 253 | 56236<br>−9300<br>333 254 | 56237<br>−9299<br>333 255 | 56238<br>−9298<br>333 256 | 56239<br>−9297<br>333 257 |
| B− | 56240<br>−9296<br>333 260 | 56241<br>−9295<br>333 261 | 56242<br>−9294<br>333 262 | 56243<br>−9293<br>333 263 | 56244<br>−9292<br>333 264 | 56245<br>−9291<br>333 265 | 56246<br>−9290<br>333 266 | 56247<br>−9289<br>333 267 | 56248<br>−9288<br>333 270 | 56249<br>−9287<br>333 271 | 56250<br>−9286<br>333 272 | 56251<br>−9285<br>333 273 | 56252<br>−9284<br>333 274 | 56253<br>−9283<br>333 275 | 56254<br>−9282<br>333 276 | 56255<br>−9281<br>333 277 |
| C− | 56256<br>−9280<br>333 300 | 56257<br>−9279<br>333 301 | 56258<br>−9278<br>333 302 | 56259<br>−9277<br>333 303 | 56260<br>−9276<br>333 304 | 56261<br>−9275<br>333 305 | 56262<br>−9274<br>333 306 | 56263<br>−9273<br>333 307 | 56264<br>−9272<br>333 310 | 56265<br>−9271<br>333 311 | 56266<br>−9270<br>333 312 | 56267<br>−9269<br>333 313 | 56268<br>−9268<br>333 314 | 56269<br>−9267<br>333 315 | 56270<br>−9266<br>333 316 | 56271<br>−9265<br>333 317 |
| D− | 56272<br>−9264<br>333 320 | 56273<br>−9263<br>333 321 | 56274<br>−9262<br>333 322 | 56275<br>−9261<br>333 323 | 56276<br>−9260<br>333 324 | 56277<br>−9259<br>333 325 | 56278<br>−9258<br>333 326 | 56279<br>−9257<br>333 327 | 56280<br>−9256<br>333 330 | 56281<br>−9255<br>333 331 | 56282<br>−9254<br>333 332 | 56283<br>−9253<br>333 333 | 56284<br>−9252<br>333 334 | 56285<br>−9251<br>333 335 | 56286<br>−9250<br>333 336 | 56287<br>−9249<br>333 337 |
| E− | 56288<br>−9248<br>333 340 | 56289<br>−9247<br>333 341 | 56290<br>9246<br>333 342 | 56291<br>−9245<br>333 343 | 56292<br>−9244<br>333 344 | 56293<br>−9243<br>333 345 | 56294<br>−9242<br>333 346 | 56295<br>−9241<br>333 347 | 56296<br>−9240<br>333 350 | 56297<br>−9239<br>333 351 | 56298<br>−9238<br>333 352 | 56299<br>−9237<br>333 353 | 56300<br>−9236<br>333 354 | 56301<br>−9235<br>333 355 | 56302<br>−9234<br>333 356 | 56303<br>−9233<br>333 357 |
| F− | 56304<br>−9232<br>333 360 | 56305<br>−9231<br>333 361 | 56306<br>−9230<br>333 362 | 56307<br>−9229<br>333 363 | 56308<br>−9228<br>333 364 | 56309<br>−9227<br>333 365 | 56310<br>−9226<br>333 366 | 56311<br>−9225<br>333 367 | 56312<br>−9224<br>333 370 | 56313<br>−9223<br>333 371 | 56314<br>−9222<br>333 372 | 56315<br>−9221<br>333 373 | 56316<br>−9220<br>333 374 | 56317<br>−9219<br>333 375 | 56318<br>−9218<br>333 376 | 56319<br>−9217<br>333 377 |

DECIMAL

 DECIMAL

OCTAL

| | −0 | −1 | −2 | −3 | −4 | −5 | −6 | −7 | −8 | −9 | −A | −B | −C | −D | −E | −F |
|---|---|---|---|---|---|---|---|---|---|---|---|---|---|---|---|---|
| **0−** | 56320<br>−9216<br>334 000 | 56321<br>−9215<br>334 001 | 56322<br>−9214<br>334 002 | 56323<br>−9213<br>334 003 | 56324<br>−9212<br>334 004 | 56325<br>−9211<br>334 005 | 56326<br>−9210<br>334 006 | 56327<br>−9209<br>334 007 | 56328<br>−9208<br>334 010 | 56329<br>−9207<br>334 011 | 56330<br>−9206<br>334 012 | 56331<br>−9205<br>334 013 | 56332<br>−9204<br>334 014 | 56333<br>−9203<br>334 015 | 56334<br>−9202<br>334 016 | 56335<br>−9201<br>334 017 |
| **1−** | 56336<br>−9200<br>334 020 | 56337<br>−9199<br>334 021 | 56338<br>−9198<br>334 022 | 56339<br>−9197<br>334 023 | 56340<br>−9196<br>334 024 | 56341<br>−9195<br>334 025 | 56342<br>−9194<br>334 026 | 56343<br>−9193<br>334 027 | 56344<br>−9192<br>334 030 | 56345<br>−9191<br>334 031 | 56346<br>−9190<br>334 032 | 56347<br>−9189<br>334 033 | 56348<br>−9188<br>334 034 | 56349<br>−9187<br>334 035 | 56350<br>−9186<br>334 036 | 56351<br>−9185<br>334 037 |
| **2−** | 56352<br>−9184<br>334 040 | 56353<br>−9183<br>334 041 | 56354<br>−9182<br>334 042 | 56355<br>−9181<br>334 043 | 56356<br>−9180<br>334 044 | 56357<br>−9179<br>334 045 | 56358<br>−9178<br>334 046 | 56359<br>−9177<br>334 047 | 56360<br>−9176<br>334 050 | 56361<br>−9175<br>334 051 | 56362<br>−9174<br>334 052 | 56363<br>−9173<br>334 053 | 56364<br>−9172<br>334 054 | 56365<br>−9171<br>334 055 | 56366<br>−9170<br>334 056 | 56367<br>−9169<br>334 057 |
| **3−** | 56368<br>−9168<br>334 060 | 56369<br>−9167<br>334 061 | 56370<br>−9166<br>334 062 | 56371<br>−9165<br>334 063 | 56372<br>−9164<br>334 064 | 56373<br>−9163<br>334 065 | 56374<br>−9162<br>334 066 | 56375<br>−9161<br>334 067 | 56376<br>−9160<br>334 070 | 56377<br>−9159<br>334 071 | 56378<br>−9158<br>334 072 | 56379<br>−9157<br>334 073 | 56380<br>−9156<br>334 074 | 56381<br>−9155<br>334 075 | 56382<br>−9154<br>334 076 | 56383<br>−9153<br>334 077 |
| **4−** | 56384<br>−9152<br>334 100 | 56385<br>−9151<br>334 101 | 56386<br>−9150<br>334 102 | 56387<br>−9149<br>334 103 | 56388<br>−9148<br>334 104 | 56389<br>−9147<br>334 105 | 56390<br>−9146<br>334 106 | 56391<br>−9145<br>334 107 | 56392<br>−9144<br>334 110 | 56393<br>−9143<br>334 111 | 56394<br>−9142<br>334 112 | 56395<br>−9141<br>334 113 | 56396<br>−9140<br>334 114 | 56397<br>−9139<br>334 115 | 56398<br>−9138<br>334 116 | 56399<br>−9137<br>334 117 |
| **5−** | 56400<br>−9136<br>334 120 | 56401<br>−9135<br>334 121 | 56402<br>−9134<br>334 122 | 56403<br>−9133<br>334 123 | 56404<br>−9132<br>334 124 | 56405<br>−9131<br>334 125 | 56406<br>−9130<br>334 126 | 56407<br>−9129<br>334 127 | 56408<br>−9128<br>334 130 | 56409<br>−9127<br>334 131 | 56410<br>−9126<br>334 132 | 56411<br>−9125<br>334 133 | 56412<br>−9124<br>334 134 | 56413<br>−9123<br>334 135 | 56414<br>−9122<br>334 136 | 56415<br>−9121<br>334 137 |
| **6−** | 56416<br>−9120<br>334 140 | 56417<br>−9119<br>334 141 | 56418<br>−9118<br>334 142 | 56419<br>−9117<br>334 143 | 56420<br>−9116<br>334 144 | 56421<br>−9115<br>334 145 | 56422<br>−9114<br>334 146 | 56423<br>−9113<br>334 147 | 56424<br>−9112<br>334 150 | 56425<br>−9111<br>334 151 | 56426<br>−9110<br>334 152 | 56427<br>−9109<br>334 153 | 56428<br>−9108<br>334 154 | 56429<br>−9107<br>334 155 | 56430<br>−9106<br>334 156 | 56431<br>−9105<br>334 157 |
| **7−** | 56432<br>−9104<br>334 160 | 56433<br>−9103<br>334 161 | 56434<br>−9102<br>334 162 | 56435<br>−9101<br>334 163 | 56436<br>−9100<br>334 164 | 56437<br>−9099<br>334 165 | 56438<br>−9098<br>334 166 | 56439<br>−9097<br>334 167 | 56440<br>−9096<br>334 170 | 56441<br>−9095<br>334 171 | 56442<br>−9094<br>334 172 | 56443<br>−9093<br>334 173 | 56444<br>−9092<br>334 174 | 56445<br>−9091<br>334 175 | 56446<br>−9090<br>334 176 | 56447<br>−9089<br>334 177 |
| **8−** | 56448<br>−9088<br>334 200 | 56449<br>−9087<br>334 201 | 56450<br>−9086<br>334 202 | 56451<br>−9085<br>334 203 | 56452<br>−9084<br>334 204 | 56453<br>−9083<br>334 205 | 56454<br>−9082<br>334 206 | 56455<br>−9081<br>334 207 | 56456<br>−9080<br>334 210 | 56457<br>−9079<br>334 211 | 56458<br>−9078<br>334 212 | 56459<br>−9077<br>334 213 | 56460<br>−9076<br>334 214 | 56461<br>−9075<br>334 215 | 56462<br>−9074<br>334 216 | 56463<br>−9073<br>334 217 |
| **9−** | 56464<br>−9072<br>334 220 | 56465<br>−9071<br>334 221 | 56466<br>−9070<br>334 222 | 56467<br>−9069<br>334 223 | 56468<br>−9068<br>334 224 | 56469<br>−9067<br>334 225 | 56470<br>−9066<br>334 226 | 56471<br>−9065<br>334 227 | 56472<br>−9064<br>334 230 | 56473<br>−9063<br>334 231 | 56474<br>−9062<br>334 232 | 56475<br>−9061<br>334 233 | 56476<br>−9060<br>334 234 | 56477<br>−9059<br>334 235 | 56478<br>−9058<br>334 236 | 56479<br>−9057<br>334 237 |
| **A−** | 56480<br>−9056<br>334 240 | 56481<br>−9055<br>334 241 | 56482<br>−9054<br>334 242 | 56483<br>−9053<br>334 243 | 56484<br>−9052<br>334 244 | 56485<br>−9051<br>334 245 | 56486<br>−9050<br>334 246 | 56487<br>−9049<br>334 247 | 56488<br>−9048<br>334 250 | 56489<br>−9047<br>334 251 | 56490<br>−9046<br>334 252 | 56491<br>−9045<br>334 253 | 56492<br>−9044<br>334 254 | 56493<br>−9043<br>334 255 | 56494<br>−9042<br>334 256 | 56495<br>−9041<br>334 257 |
| **B−** | 56496<br>−9040<br>334 260 | 56497<br>−9039<br>334 261 | 56498<br>−9038<br>334 262 | 56499<br>−9037<br>334 263 | 56500<br>−9036<br>334 264 | 56501<br>−9035<br>334 265 | 56502<br>−9034<br>334 266 | 56503<br>−9033<br>334 267 | 56504<br>−9032<br>334 270 | 56505<br>−9031<br>334 271 | 56506<br>−9030<br>334 272 | 56507<br>−9029<br>334 273 | 56508<br>−9028<br>334 274 | 56509<br>−9027<br>334 275 | 56510<br>−9026<br>334 276 | 56511<br>−9025<br>334 277 |
| **C−** | 56512<br>−9024<br>334 300 | 56513<br>−9023<br>334 301 | 56514<br>−9022<br>334 302 | 56515<br>−9021<br>334 303 | 56516<br>−9020<br>334 304 | 56517<br>−9019<br>334 305 | 56518<br>−9018<br>334 306 | 56519<br>−9017<br>334 307 | 56520<br>−9016<br>334 310 | 56521<br>−9015<br>334 311 | 56522<br>−9014<br>334 312 | 56523<br>−9013<br>334 313 | 56524<br>−9012<br>334 314 | 56525<br>−9011<br>334 315 | 56526<br>−9010<br>334 316 | 56527<br>−9009<br>334 317 |
| **D−** | 56528<br>−9008<br>334 320 | 56529<br>−9007<br>334 321 | 56530<br>−9006<br>334 322 | 56531<br>−9005<br>334 323 | 56532<br>−9004<br>334 324 | 56533<br>−9003<br>334 325 | 56534<br>−9002<br>334 326 | 56535<br>−9001<br>334 327 | 56536<br>−9000<br>334 330 | 56537<br>−8999<br>334 331 | 56538<br>−8998<br>334 332 | 56539<br>−8997<br>334 333 | 56540<br>−8996<br>334 334 | 56541<br>−8995<br>334 335 | 56542<br>−8994<br>334 336 | 56543<br>−8993<br>334 337 |
| **E−** | 56544<br>−8992<br>334 340 | 56545<br>−8991<br>334 341 | 56546<br>−8990<br>334 342 | 56547<br>−8989<br>334 343 | 56548<br>−8988<br>334 344 | 56549<br>−8987<br>334 345 | 56550<br>−8986<br>334 346 | 56551<br>−8985<br>334 347 | 56552<br>−8984<br>334 350 | 56553<br>−8983<br>334 351 | 56554<br>−8982<br>334 352 | 56555<br>−8981<br>334 353 | 56556<br>−8980<br>334 354 | 56557<br>−8979<br>334 355 | 56558<br>−8978<br>334 356 | 56559<br>−8977<br>334 357 |
| **F−** | 56560<br>−8976<br>334 360 | 56561<br>−8975<br>334 361 | 56562<br>−8974<br>334 362 | 56563<br>−8973<br>334 363 | 56564<br>−8972<br>334 364 | 56565<br>−8971<br>334 365 | 56566<br>−8970<br>334 366 | 56567<br>−8969<br>334 367 | 56568<br>−8968<br>334 370 | 56569<br>−8967<br>334 371 | 56570<br>−8966<br>334 372 | 56571<br>−8965<br>334 373 | 56572<br>−8964<br>334 374 | 56573<br>−8963<br>334 375 | 56574<br>−8962<br>334 376 | 56575<br>−8961<br>334 377 |

DECIMAL

🍎 DECIMAL

OCTAL

🍎 DECIMAL  −9216   BINARY  1101 1100   DECIMAL  56320   HEXADECIMAL ⬡ DC  OCTAL  334 000

FOURTH HEX DIGIT →  ← THIRD HEX DIGIT

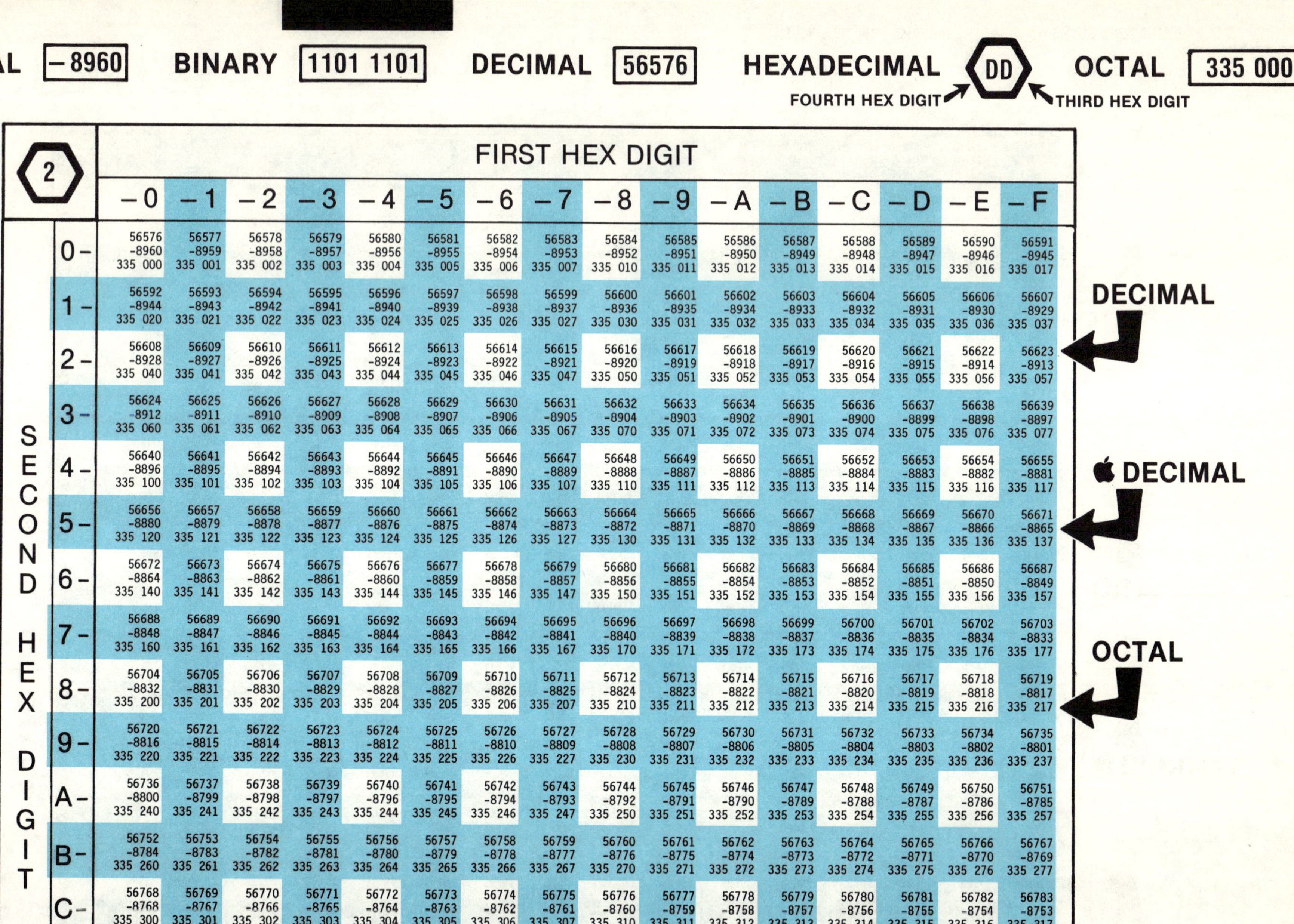

| 2 | FIRST HEX DIGIT | | | | | | | | | | | | | | | |
|---|---|---|---|---|---|---|---|---|---|---|---|---|---|---|---|---|
| | −0 | −1 | −2 | −3 | −4 | −5 | −6 | −7 | −8 | −9 | −A | −B | −C | −D | −E | −F |
| 0− | 56576<br>-8960<br>335 000 | 56577<br>-8959<br>335 001 | 56578<br>-8958<br>335 002 | 56579<br>-8957<br>335 003 | 56580<br>-8956<br>335 004 | 56581<br>-8955<br>335 005 | 56582<br>-8954<br>335 006 | 56583<br>-8953<br>335 007 | 56584<br>-8952<br>335 010 | 56585<br>-8951<br>335 011 | 56586<br>-8950<br>335 012 | 56587<br>-8949<br>335 013 | 56588<br>-8948<br>335 014 | 56589<br>-8947<br>335 015 | 56590<br>-8946<br>335 016 | 56591<br>-8945<br>335 017 |
| 1− | 56592<br>-8944<br>335 020 | 56593<br>-8943<br>335 021 | 56594<br>-8942<br>335 022 | 56595<br>-8941<br>335 023 | 56596<br>-8940<br>335 024 | 56597<br>-8939<br>335 025 | 56598<br>-8938<br>335 026 | 56599<br>-8937<br>335 027 | 56600<br>-8936<br>335 030 | 56601<br>-8935<br>335 031 | 56602<br>-8934<br>335 032 | 56603<br>-8933<br>335 033 | 56604<br>-8932<br>335 034 | 56605<br>-8931<br>335 035 | 56606<br>-8930<br>335 036 | 56607<br>-8929<br>335 037 |
| 2− | 56608<br>-8928<br>335 040 | 56609<br>-8927<br>335 041 | 56610<br>-8926<br>335 042 | 56611<br>-8925<br>335 043 | 56612<br>-8924<br>335 044 | 56613<br>-8923<br>335 045 | 56614<br>-8922<br>335 046 | 56615<br>-8921<br>335 047 | 56616<br>-8920<br>335 050 | 56617<br>-8919<br>335 051 | 56618<br>-8918<br>335 052 | 56619<br>-8917<br>335 053 | 56620<br>-8916<br>335 054 | 56621<br>-8915<br>335 055 | 56622<br>-8914<br>335 056 | 56623<br>-8913<br>335 057 |
| 3− | 56624<br>-8912<br>335 060 | 56625<br>-8911<br>335 061 | 56626<br>-8910<br>335 062 | 56627<br>-8909<br>335 063 | 56628<br>-8908<br>335 064 | 56629<br>-8907<br>335 065 | 56630<br>-8906<br>335 066 | 56631<br>-8905<br>335 067 | 56632<br>-8904<br>335 070 | 56633<br>-8903<br>335 071 | 56634<br>-8902<br>335 072 | 56635<br>-8901<br>335 073 | 56636<br>-8900<br>335 074 | 56637<br>-8899<br>335 075 | 56638<br>-8898<br>335 076 | 56639<br>-8897<br>335 077 |
| 4− | 56640<br>-8896<br>335 100 | 56641<br>-8895<br>335 101 | 56642<br>-8894<br>335 102 | 56643<br>-8893<br>335 103 | 56644<br>-8892<br>335 104 | 56645<br>-8891<br>335 105 | 56646<br>-8890<br>335 106 | 56647<br>-8889<br>335 107 | 56648<br>-8888<br>335 110 | 56649<br>-8887<br>335 111 | 56650<br>-8886<br>335 112 | 56651<br>-8885<br>335 113 | 56652<br>-8884<br>335 114 | 56653<br>-8883<br>335 115 | 56654<br>-8882<br>335 116 | 56655<br>-8881<br>335 117 |
| 5− | 56656<br>-8880<br>335 120 | 56657<br>-8879<br>335 121 | 56658<br>-8878<br>335 122 | 56659<br>-8877<br>335 123 | 56660<br>-8876<br>335 124 | 56661<br>-8875<br>335 125 | 56662<br>-8874<br>335 126 | 56663<br>-8873<br>335 127 | 56664<br>-8872<br>335 130 | 56665<br>-8871<br>335 131 | 56666<br>-8870<br>335 132 | 56667<br>-8869<br>335 133 | 56668<br>-8868<br>335 134 | 56669<br>-8867<br>335 135 | 56670<br>-8866<br>335 136 | 56671<br>-8865<br>335 137 |
| 6− | 56672<br>-8864<br>335 140 | 56673<br>-8863<br>335 141 | 56674<br>-8862<br>335 142 | 56675<br>-8861<br>335 143 | 56676<br>-8860<br>335 144 | 56677<br>-8859<br>335 145 | 56678<br>-8858<br>335 146 | 56679<br>-8857<br>335 147 | 56680<br>-8856<br>335 150 | 56681<br>-8855<br>335 151 | 56682<br>-8854<br>335 152 | 56683<br>-8853<br>335 153 | 56684<br>-8852<br>335 154 | 56685<br>-8851<br>335 155 | 56686<br>-8850<br>335 156 | 56687<br>-8849<br>335 157 |
| 7− | 56688<br>-8848<br>335 160 | 56689<br>-8847<br>335 161 | 56690<br>-8846<br>335 162 | 56691<br>-8845<br>335 163 | 56692<br>-8844<br>335 164 | 56693<br>-8843<br>335 165 | 56694<br>-8842<br>335 166 | 56695<br>-8841<br>335 167 | 56696<br>-8840<br>335 170 | 56697<br>-8839<br>335 171 | 56698<br>-8838<br>335 172 | 56699<br>-8837<br>335 173 | 56700<br>-8836<br>335 174 | 56701<br>-8835<br>335 175 | 56702<br>-8834<br>335 176 | 56703<br>-8833<br>335 177 |
| 8− | 56704<br>-8832<br>335 200 | 56705<br>-8831<br>335 201 | 56706<br>-8830<br>335 202 | 56707<br>-8829<br>335 203 | 56708<br>-8828<br>335 204 | 56709<br>-8827<br>335 205 | 56710<br>-8826<br>335 206 | 56711<br>-8825<br>335 207 | 56712<br>-8824<br>335 210 | 56713<br>-8823<br>335 211 | 56714<br>-8822<br>335 212 | 56715<br>-8821<br>335 213 | 56716<br>-8820<br>335 214 | 56717<br>-8819<br>335 215 | 56718<br>-8818<br>335 216 | 56719<br>-8817<br>335 217 |
| 9− | 56720<br>-8816<br>335 220 | 56721<br>-8815<br>335 221 | 56722<br>-8814<br>335 222 | 56723<br>-8813<br>335 223 | 56724<br>-8812<br>335 224 | 56725<br>-8811<br>335 225 | 56726<br>-8810<br>335 226 | 56727<br>-8809<br>335 227 | 56728<br>-8808<br>335 230 | 56729<br>-8807<br>335 231 | 56730<br>-8806<br>335 232 | 56731<br>-8805<br>335 233 | 56732<br>-8804<br>335 234 | 56733<br>-8803<br>335 235 | 56734<br>-8802<br>335 236 | 56735<br>-8801<br>335 237 |
| A− | 56736<br>-8800<br>335 240 | 56737<br>-8799<br>335 241 | 56738<br>-8798<br>335 242 | 56739<br>-8797<br>335 243 | 56740<br>-8796<br>335 244 | 56741<br>-8795<br>335 245 | 56742<br>-8794<br>335 246 | 56743<br>-8793<br>335 247 | 56744<br>-8792<br>335 250 | 56745<br>-8791<br>335 251 | 56746<br>-8790<br>335 252 | 56747<br>-8789<br>335 253 | 56748<br>-8788<br>335 254 | 56749<br>-8787<br>335 255 | 56750<br>-8786<br>335 256 | 56751<br>-8785<br>335 257 |
| B− | 56752<br>-8784<br>335 260 | 56753<br>-8783<br>335 261 | 56754<br>-8782<br>335 262 | 56755<br>-8781<br>335 263 | 56756<br>-8780<br>335 264 | 56757<br>-8779<br>335 265 | 56758<br>-8778<br>335 266 | 56759<br>-8777<br>335 267 | 56760<br>-8776<br>335 270 | 56761<br>-8775<br>335 271 | 56762<br>-8774<br>335 272 | 56763<br>-8773<br>335 273 | 56764<br>-8772<br>335 274 | 56765<br>-8771<br>335 275 | 56766<br>-8770<br>335 276 | 56767<br>-8769<br>335 277 |
| C− | 56768<br>-8768<br>335 300 | 56769<br>-8767<br>335 301 | 56770<br>-8766<br>335 302 | 56771<br>-8765<br>335 303 | 56772<br>-8764<br>335 304 | 56773<br>-8763<br>335 305 | 56774<br>-8762<br>335 306 | 56775<br>-8761<br>335 307 | 56776<br>-8760<br>335 310 | 56777<br>-8759<br>335 311 | 56778<br>-8758<br>335 312 | 56779<br>-8757<br>335 313 | 56780<br>-8756<br>335 314 | 56781<br>-8755<br>335 315 | 56782<br>-8754<br>335 316 | 56783<br>-8753<br>335 317 |
| D− | 56784<br>-8752<br>335 320 | 56785<br>-8751<br>335 321 | 56786<br>-8750<br>335 322 | 56787<br>-8749<br>335 323 | 56788<br>-8748<br>335 324 | 56789<br>-8747<br>335 325 | 56790<br>-8746<br>335 326 | 56791<br>-8745<br>335 327 | 56792<br>-8744<br>335 330 | 56793<br>-8743<br>335 331 | 56794<br>-8742<br>335 332 | 56795<br>-8741<br>335 333 | 56796<br>-8740<br>335 334 | 56797<br>-8739<br>335 335 | 56798<br>-8738<br>335 336 | 56799<br>-8737<br>335 337 |
| E− | 56800<br>-8736<br>335 340 | 56801<br>-8735<br>335 341 | 56802<br>-8734<br>335 342 | 56803<br>-8733<br>335 343 | 56804<br>-8732<br>335 344 | 56805<br>-8731<br>335 345 | 56806<br>-8730<br>335 346 | 56807<br>-8729<br>335 347 | 56808<br>-8728<br>335 350 | 56809<br>-8727<br>335 351 | 56810<br>-8726<br>335 352 | 56811<br>-8725<br>335 353 | 56812<br>-8724<br>335 354 | 56813<br>-8723<br>335 355 | 56814<br>-8722<br>335 356 | 56815<br>-8721<br>335 357 |
| F− | 56816<br>-8720<br>335 360 | 56817<br>-8719<br>335 361 | 56818<br>-8718<br>335 362 | 56819<br>-8717<br>335 363 | 56820<br>-8716<br>335 364 | 56821<br>-8715<br>335 365 | 56822<br>-8714<br>335 366 | 56823<br>-8713<br>335 367 | 56824<br>-8712<br>335 370 | 56825<br>-8711<br>335 371 | 56826<br>-8710<br>335 372 | 56827<br>-8709<br>335 373 | 56828<br>-8708<br>335 374 | 56829<br>-8707<br>335 375 | 56830<br>-8706<br>335 376 | 56831<br>-8705<br>335 377 |

# FIRST HEX DIGIT

Table 2 — Hexadecimal / Decimal / Octal conversion. Each cell lists DECIMAL (top), ● DECIMAL (middle, negative), and OCTAL (bottom). SECOND HEX DIGIT runs down the left.

| | −0 | −1 | −2 | −3 | −4 | −5 | −6 | −7 | −8 | −9 | −A | −B | −C | −D | −E | −F |
|---|---|---|---|---|---|---|---|---|---|---|---|---|---|---|---|---|
| **0−** | 56832<br>−8704<br>336 000 | 56833<br>−8703<br>336 001 | 56834<br>−8702<br>336 002 | 56835<br>−8701<br>336 003 | 56836<br>−8700<br>336 004 | 56837<br>−8699<br>336 005 | 56838<br>−8698<br>336 006 | 56839<br>−8697<br>336 007 | 56840<br>−8696<br>336 010 | 56841<br>−8695<br>336 011 | 56842<br>−8694<br>336 012 | 56843<br>−8693<br>336 013 | 56844<br>−8692<br>336 014 | 56845<br>−8691<br>336 015 | 56846<br>−8690<br>336 016 | 56847<br>−8689<br>336 017 |
| **1−** | 56848<br>−8688<br>336 020 | 56849<br>−8687<br>336 021 | 56850<br>−8686<br>336 022 | 56851<br>−8685<br>336 023 | 56852<br>−8684<br>336 024 | 56853<br>−8683<br>336 025 | 56854<br>−8682<br>336 026 | 56855<br>−8681<br>336 027 | 56856<br>−8680<br>336 030 | 56857<br>−8679<br>336 031 | 56858<br>−8678<br>336 032 | 56859<br>−8677<br>336 033 | 56860<br>−8676<br>336 034 | 56861<br>−8675<br>336 035 | 56862<br>−8674<br>336 036 | 56863<br>−8673<br>336 037 |
| **2−** | 56864<br>−8672<br>336 040 | 56865<br>−8671<br>336 041 | 56866<br>−8670<br>336 042 | 56867<br>−8669<br>336 043 | 56868<br>−8668<br>336 044 | 56869<br>−8667<br>336 045 | 56870<br>−8666<br>336 046 | 56871<br>−8665<br>336 047 | 56872<br>−8664<br>336 050 | 56873<br>−8663<br>336 051 | 56874<br>−8662<br>336 052 | 56875<br>−8661<br>336 053 | 56876<br>−8660<br>336 054 | 56877<br>−8659<br>336 055 | 56878<br>−8658<br>336 056 | 56879<br>−8657<br>336 057 |
| **3−** | 56880<br>−8656<br>336 060 | 56881<br>−8655<br>336 061 | 56882<br>−8654<br>336 062 | 56883<br>−8653<br>336 063 | 56884<br>−8652<br>336 064 | 56885<br>−8651<br>336 065 | 56886<br>−8650<br>336 066 | 56887<br>−8649<br>336 067 | 56888<br>−8648<br>336 070 | 56889<br>−8647<br>336 071 | 56890<br>−8646<br>336 072 | 56891<br>−8645<br>336 073 | 56892<br>−8644<br>336 074 | 56893<br>−8643<br>336 075 | 56894<br>−8642<br>336 076 | 56895<br>−8641<br>336 077 |
| **4−** | 56896<br>−8640<br>336 100 | 56897<br>−8639<br>336 101 | 56898<br>−8638<br>336 102 | 56899<br>−8637<br>336 103 | 56900<br>−8636<br>336 104 | 56901<br>−8635<br>336 105 | 56902<br>−8634<br>336 106 | 56903<br>−8633<br>336 107 | 56904<br>−8632<br>336 110 | 56905<br>−8631<br>336 111 | 56906<br>−8630<br>336 112 | 56907<br>−8629<br>336 113 | 56908<br>−8628<br>336 114 | 56909<br>−8627<br>336 115 | 56910<br>−8626<br>336 116 | 56911<br>−8625<br>336 117 |
| **5−** | 56912<br>−8624<br>336 120 | 56913<br>−8623<br>336 121 | 56914<br>−8622<br>336 122 | 56915<br>−8621<br>336 123 | 56916<br>−8620<br>336 124 | 56917<br>−8619<br>336 125 | 56918<br>−8618<br>336 126 | 56919<br>−8617<br>336 127 | 56920<br>−8616<br>336 130 | 56921<br>−8615<br>336 131 | 56922<br>−8614<br>336 132 | 56923<br>−8613<br>336 133 | 56924<br>−8612<br>336 134 | 56925<br>−8611<br>336 135 | 56926<br>−8610<br>336 136 | 56927<br>−8609<br>336 137 |
| **6−** | 56928<br>−8608<br>336 140 | 56929<br>−8607<br>336 141 | 56930<br>−8606<br>336 142 | 56931<br>−8605<br>336 143 | 56932<br>−8604<br>336 144 | 56933<br>−8603<br>336 145 | 56934<br>−8602<br>336 146 | 56935<br>−8601<br>336 147 | 56936<br>−8600<br>336 150 | 56937<br>−8599<br>336 151 | 56938<br>−8598<br>336 152 | 56939<br>−8597<br>336 153 | 56940<br>−8596<br>336 154 | 56941<br>−8595<br>336 155 | 56942<br>−8594<br>336 156 | 56943<br>−8593<br>336 157 |
| **7−** | 56944<br>−8592<br>336 160 | 56945<br>−8591<br>336 161 | 56946<br>−8590<br>336 162 | 56947<br>−8589<br>336 163 | 56948<br>−8588<br>336 164 | 56949<br>−8587<br>336 165 | 56950<br>−8586<br>336 166 | 56951<br>−8585<br>336 167 | 56952<br>−8584<br>336 170 | 56953<br>−8583<br>336 171 | 56954<br>−8582<br>336 172 | 56955<br>−8581<br>336 173 | 56956<br>−8580<br>336 174 | 56957<br>−8579<br>336 175 | 56958<br>−8578<br>336 176 | 56959<br>−8577<br>336 177 |
| **8−** | 56960<br>−8576<br>336 200 | 56961<br>−8575<br>336 201 | 56962<br>−8574<br>336 202 | 56963<br>−8573<br>336 203 | 56964<br>−8572<br>336 204 | 56965<br>−8571<br>336 205 | 56966<br>−8570<br>336 206 | 56967<br>−8569<br>336 207 | 56968<br>−8568<br>336 210 | 56969<br>−8567<br>336 211 | 56970<br>−8566<br>336 212 | 56971<br>−8565<br>336 213 | 56972<br>−8564<br>336 214 | 56973<br>−8563<br>336 215 | 56974<br>−8562<br>336 216 | 56975<br>−8561<br>336 217 |
| **9−** | 56976<br>−8560<br>336 220 | 56977<br>−8559<br>336 221 | 56978<br>−8558<br>336 222 | 56979<br>−8557<br>336 223 | 56980<br>−8556<br>336 224 | 56981<br>−8555<br>336 225 | 56982<br>−8554<br>336 226 | 56983<br>−8553<br>336 227 | 56984<br>−8552<br>336 230 | 56985<br>−8551<br>336 231 | 56986<br>−8550<br>336 232 | 56987<br>−8549<br>336 233 | 56988<br>−8548<br>336 234 | 56989<br>−8547<br>336 235 | 56990<br>−8546<br>336 236 | 56991<br>−8545<br>336 237 |
| **A−** | 56992<br>−8544<br>336 240 | 56993<br>−8543<br>336 241 | 56994<br>−8542<br>336 242 | 56995<br>−8541<br>336 243 | 56996<br>−8540<br>336 244 | 56997<br>−8539<br>336 245 | 56998<br>−8538<br>336 246 | 56999<br>−8537<br>336 247 | 57000<br>−8536<br>336 250 | 57001<br>−8535<br>336 251 | 57002<br>−8534<br>336 252 | 57003<br>−8533<br>336 253 | 57004<br>−8532<br>336 254 | 57005<br>−8531<br>336 255 | 57006<br>−8530<br>336 256 | 57007<br>−8529<br>336 257 |
| **B−** | 57008<br>−8528<br>336 260 | 57009<br>−8527<br>336 261 | 57010<br>−8526<br>336 262 | 57011<br>−8525<br>336 263 | 57012<br>−8524<br>336 264 | 57013<br>−8523<br>336 265 | 57014<br>−8522<br>336 266 | 57015<br>−8521<br>336 267 | 57016<br>−8520<br>336 270 | 57017<br>−8519<br>336 271 | 57018<br>−8518<br>336 272 | 57019<br>−8517<br>336 273 | 57020<br>−8516<br>336 274 | 57021<br>−8515<br>336 275 | 57022<br>−8514<br>336 276 | 57023<br>−8513<br>336 277 |
| **C−** | 57024<br>−8512<br>336 300 | 57025<br>−8511<br>336 301 | 57026<br>−8510<br>336 302 | 57027<br>−8509<br>336 303 | 57028<br>−8508<br>336 304 | 57029<br>−8507<br>336 305 | 57030<br>−8506<br>336 306 | 57031<br>−8505<br>336 307 | 57032<br>−8504<br>336 310 | 57033<br>−8503<br>336 311 | 57034<br>−8502<br>336 312 | 57035<br>−8501<br>336 313 | 57036<br>−8500<br>336 314 | 57037<br>−8499<br>336 315 | 57038<br>−8498<br>336 316 | 57039<br>−8497<br>336 317 |
| **D−** | 57040<br>−8496<br>336 320 | 57041<br>−8495<br>336 321 | 57042<br>−8494<br>336 322 | 57043<br>−8493<br>336 323 | 57044<br>−8492<br>336 324 | 57045<br>−8491<br>336 325 | 57046<br>−8490<br>336 326 | 57047<br>−8489<br>336 327 | 57048<br>−8488<br>336 330 | 57049<br>−8487<br>336 331 | 57050<br>−8486<br>336 332 | 57051<br>−8485<br>336 333 | 57052<br>−8484<br>336 334 | 57053<br>−8483<br>336 335 | 57054<br>−8482<br>336 336 | 57055<br>−8481<br>336 337 |
| **E−** | 57056<br>−8480<br>336 340 | 57057<br>−8479<br>336 341 | 57058<br>−8478<br>336 342 | 57059<br>−8477<br>336 343 | 57060<br>−8476<br>336 344 | 57061<br>−8475<br>336 345 | 57062<br>−8474<br>336 346 | 57063<br>−8473<br>336 347 | 57064<br>−8472<br>336 350 | 57065<br>−8471<br>336 351 | 57066<br>−8470<br>336 352 | 57067<br>−8469<br>336 353 | 57068<br>−8468<br>336 354 | 57069<br>−8467<br>336 355 | 57070<br>−8466<br>336 356 | 57071<br>−8465<br>336 357 |
| **F−** | 57072<br>−8464<br>336 360 | 57073<br>−8463<br>336 361 | 57074<br>−8462<br>336 362 | 57075<br>−8461<br>336 363 | 57076<br>−8460<br>336 364 | 57077<br>−8459<br>336 365 | 57078<br>−8458<br>336 366 | 57079<br>−8457<br>336 367 | 57080<br>−8456<br>336 370 | 57081<br>−8455<br>336 371 | 57082<br>−8454<br>336 372 | 57083<br>−8453<br>336 373 | 57084<br>−8452<br>336 374 | 57085<br>−8451<br>336 375 | 57086<br>−8450<br>336 376 | 57087<br>−8449<br>336 377 |

Right-margin keys: **DECIMAL** · ● **DECIMAL** · **OCTAL**

● DECIMAL  −8704   BINARY  1101 1110   DECIMAL  56832   HEXADECIMAL  ⬡ DE   OCTAL  336 000

FOURTH HEX DIGIT → ⬡ ← THIRD HEX DIGIT

DECIMAL — 8448 · BINARY 1101 1111 · DECIMAL 57088 · HEXADECIMAL DF · OCTAL 337 000

FOURTH HEX DIGIT → ← THIRD HEX DIGIT

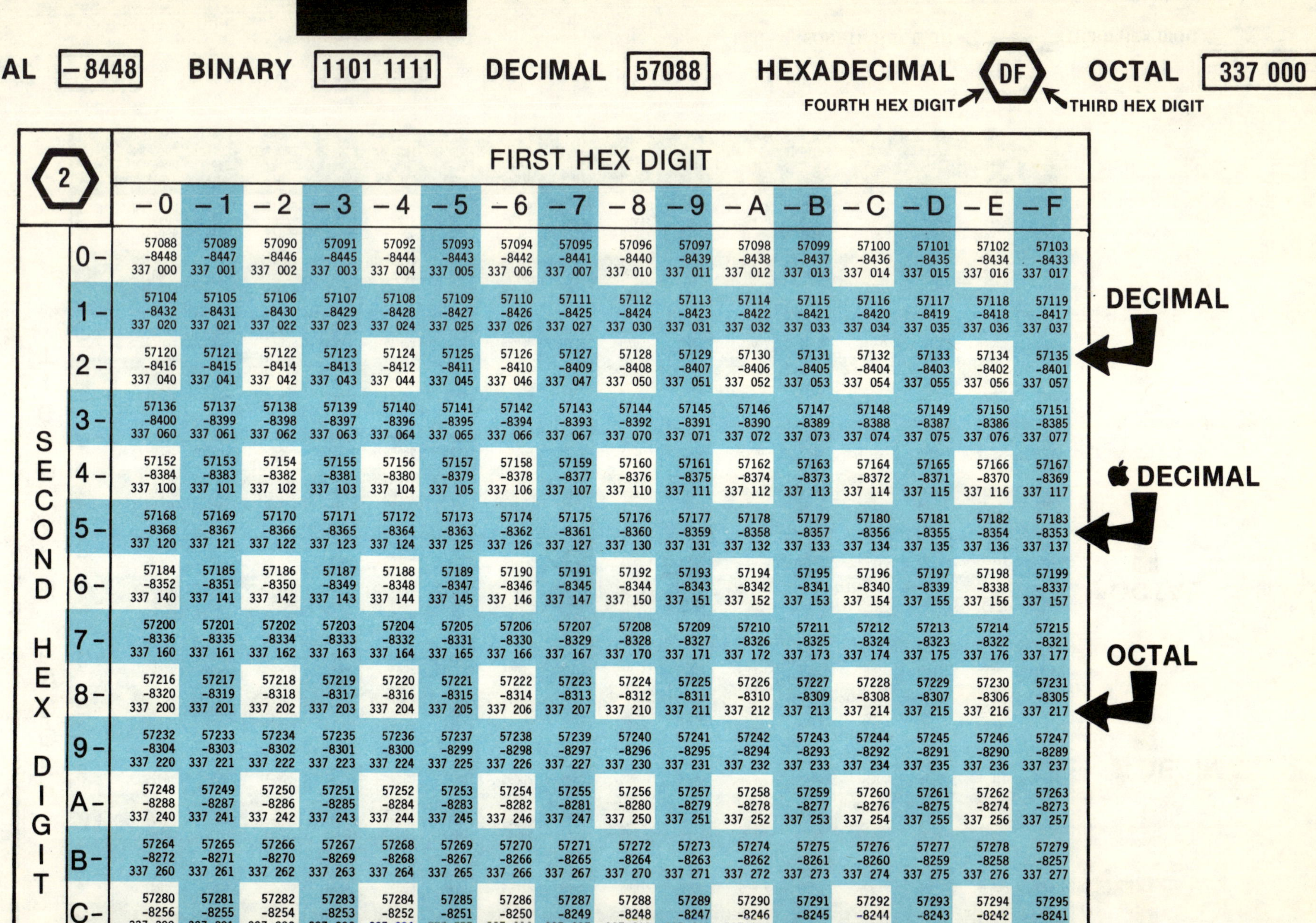

FIRST HEX DIGIT (②), SECOND HEX DIGIT rows. Each cell: decimal / negative decimal / octal.

| | −0 | −1 | −2 | −3 | −4 | −5 | −6 | −7 | −8 | −9 | −A | −B | −C | −D | −E | −F |
|---|---|---|---|---|---|---|---|---|---|---|---|---|---|---|---|---|
| 0− | 57088<br>−8448<br>337 000 | 57089<br>−8447<br>337 001 | 57090<br>−8446<br>337 002 | 57091<br>−8445<br>337 003 | 57092<br>−8444<br>337 004 | 57093<br>−8443<br>337 005 | 57094<br>−8442<br>337 006 | 57095<br>−8441<br>337 007 | 57096<br>−8440<br>337 010 | 57097<br>−8439<br>337 011 | 57098<br>−8438<br>337 012 | 57099<br>−8437<br>337 013 | 57100<br>−8436<br>337 014 | 57101<br>−8435<br>337 015 | 57102<br>−8434<br>337 016 | 57103<br>−8433<br>337 017 |
| 1− | 57104<br>−8432<br>337 020 | 57105<br>−8431<br>337 021 | 57106<br>−8430<br>337 022 | 57107<br>−8429<br>337 023 | 57108<br>−8428<br>337 024 | 57109<br>−8427<br>337 025 | 57110<br>−8426<br>337 026 | 57111<br>−8425<br>337 027 | 57112<br>−8424<br>337 030 | 57113<br>−8423<br>337 031 | 57114<br>−8422<br>337 032 | 57115<br>−8421<br>337 033 | 57116<br>−8420<br>337 034 | 57117<br>−8419<br>337 035 | 57118<br>−8418<br>337 036 | 57119<br>−8417<br>337 037 |
| 2− | 57120<br>−8416<br>337 040 | 57121<br>−8415<br>337 041 | 57122<br>−8414<br>337 042 | 57123<br>−8413<br>337 043 | 57124<br>−8412<br>337 044 | 57125<br>−8411<br>337 045 | 57126<br>−8410<br>337 046 | 57127<br>−8409<br>337 047 | 57128<br>−8408<br>337 050 | 57129<br>−8407<br>337 051 | 57130<br>−8406<br>337 052 | 57131<br>−8405<br>337 053 | 57132<br>−8404<br>337 054 | 57133<br>−8403<br>337 055 | 57134<br>−8402<br>337 056 | 57135<br>−8401<br>337 057 |
| 3− | 57136<br>−8400<br>337 060 | 57137<br>−8399<br>337 061 | 57138<br>−8398<br>337 062 | 57139<br>−8397<br>337 063 | 57140<br>−8396<br>337 064 | 57141<br>−8395<br>337 065 | 57142<br>−8394<br>337 066 | 57143<br>−8393<br>337 067 | 57144<br>−8392<br>337 070 | 57145<br>−8391<br>337 071 | 57146<br>−8390<br>337 072 | 57147<br>−8389<br>337 073 | 57148<br>−8388<br>337 074 | 57149<br>−8387<br>337 075 | 57150<br>−8386<br>337 076 | 57151<br>−8385<br>337 077 |
| 4− | 57152<br>−8384<br>337 100 | 57153<br>−8383<br>337 101 | 57154<br>−8382<br>337 102 | 57155<br>−8381<br>337 103 | 57156<br>−8380<br>337 104 | 57157<br>−8379<br>337 105 | 57158<br>−8378<br>337 106 | 57159<br>−8377<br>337 107 | 57160<br>−8376<br>337 110 | 57161<br>−8375<br>337 111 | 57162<br>−8374<br>337 112 | 57163<br>−8373<br>337 113 | 57164<br>−8372<br>337 114 | 57165<br>−8371<br>337 115 | 57166<br>−8370<br>337 116 | 57167<br>−8369<br>337 117 |
| 5− | 57168<br>−8368<br>337 120 | 57169<br>−8367<br>337 121 | 57170<br>−8366<br>337 122 | 57171<br>−8365<br>337 123 | 57172<br>−8364<br>337 124 | 57173<br>−8363<br>337 125 | 57174<br>−8362<br>337 126 | 57175<br>−8361<br>337 127 | 57176<br>−8360<br>337 130 | 57177<br>−8359<br>337 131 | 57178<br>−8358<br>337 132 | 57179<br>−8357<br>337 133 | 57180<br>−8356<br>337 134 | 57181<br>−8355<br>337 135 | 57182<br>−8354<br>337 136 | 57183<br>−8353<br>337 137 |
| 6− | 57184<br>−8352<br>337 140 | 57185<br>−8351<br>337 141 | 57186<br>−8350<br>337 142 | 57187<br>−8349<br>337 143 | 57188<br>−8348<br>337 144 | 57189<br>−8347<br>337 145 | 57190<br>−8346<br>337 146 | 57191<br>−8345<br>337 147 | 57192<br>−8344<br>337 150 | 57193<br>−8343<br>337 151 | 57194<br>−8342<br>337 152 | 57195<br>−8341<br>337 153 | 57196<br>−8340<br>337 154 | 57197<br>−8339<br>337 155 | 57198<br>−8338<br>337 156 | 57199<br>−8337<br>337 157 |
| 7− | 57200<br>−8336<br>337 160 | 57201<br>−8335<br>337 161 | 57202<br>−8334<br>337 162 | 57203<br>−8333<br>337 163 | 57204<br>−8332<br>337 164 | 57205<br>−8331<br>337 165 | 57206<br>−8330<br>337 166 | 57207<br>−8329<br>337 167 | 57208<br>−8328<br>337 170 | 57209<br>−8327<br>337 171 | 57210<br>−8326<br>337 172 | 57211<br>−8325<br>337 173 | 57212<br>−8324<br>337 174 | 57213<br>−8323<br>337 175 | 57214<br>−8322<br>337 176 | 57215<br>−8321<br>337 177 |
| 8− | 57216<br>−8320<br>337 200 | 57217<br>−8319<br>337 201 | 57218<br>−8318<br>337 202 | 57219<br>−8317<br>337 203 | 57220<br>−8316<br>337 204 | 57221<br>−8315<br>337 205 | 57222<br>−8314<br>337 206 | 57223<br>−8313<br>337 207 | 57224<br>−8312<br>337 210 | 57225<br>−8311<br>337 211 | 57226<br>−8310<br>337 212 | 57227<br>−8309<br>337 213 | 57228<br>−8308<br>337 214 | 57229<br>−8307<br>337 215 | 57230<br>−8306<br>337 216 | 57231<br>−8305<br>337 217 |
| 9− | 57232<br>−8304<br>337 220 | 57233<br>−8303<br>337 221 | 57234<br>−8302<br>337 222 | 57235<br>−8301<br>337 223 | 57236<br>−8300<br>337 224 | 57237<br>−8299<br>337 225 | 57238<br>−8298<br>337 226 | 57239<br>−8297<br>337 227 | 57240<br>−8296<br>337 230 | 57241<br>−8295<br>337 231 | 57242<br>−8294<br>337 232 | 57243<br>−8293<br>337 233 | 57244<br>−8292<br>337 234 | 57245<br>−8291<br>337 235 | 57246<br>−8290<br>337 236 | 57247<br>−8289<br>337 237 |
| A− | 57248<br>−8288<br>337 240 | 57249<br>−8287<br>337 241 | 57250<br>−8286<br>337 242 | 57251<br>−8285<br>337 243 | 57252<br>−8284<br>337 244 | 57253<br>−8283<br>337 245 | 57254<br>−8282<br>337 246 | 57255<br>−8281<br>337 247 | 57256<br>−8280<br>337 250 | 57257<br>−8279<br>337 251 | 57258<br>−8278<br>337 252 | 57259<br>−8277<br>337 253 | 57260<br>−8276<br>337 254 | 57261<br>−8275<br>337 255 | 57262<br>−8274<br>337 256 | 57263<br>−8273<br>337 257 |
| B− | 57264<br>−8272<br>337 260 | 57265<br>−8271<br>337 261 | 57266<br>−8270<br>337 262 | 57267<br>−8269<br>337 263 | 57268<br>−8268<br>337 264 | 57269<br>−8267<br>337 265 | 57270<br>−8266<br>337 266 | 57271<br>−8265<br>337 267 | 57272<br>−8264<br>337 270 | 57273<br>−8263<br>337 271 | 57274<br>−8262<br>337 272 | 57275<br>−8261<br>337 273 | 57276<br>−8260<br>337 274 | 57277<br>−8259<br>337 275 | 57278<br>−8258<br>337 276 | 57279<br>−8257<br>337 277 |
| C− | 57280<br>−8256<br>337 300 | 57281<br>−8255<br>337 301 | 57282<br>−8254<br>337 302 | 57283<br>−8253<br>337 303 | 57284<br>−8252<br>337 304 | 57285<br>−8251<br>337 305 | 57286<br>−8250<br>337 306 | 57287<br>−8249<br>337 307 | 57288<br>−8248<br>337 310 | 57289<br>−8247<br>337 311 | 57290<br>−8246<br>337 312 | 57291<br>−8245<br>337 313 | 57292<br>−8244<br>337 314 | 57293<br>−8243<br>337 315 | 57294<br>−8242<br>337 316 | 57295<br>−8241<br>337 317 |
| D− | 57296<br>−8240<br>337 320 | 57297<br>−8239<br>337 321 | 57298<br>−8238<br>337 322 | 57299<br>−8237<br>337 323 | 57300<br>−8236<br>337 324 | 57301<br>−8235<br>337 325 | 57302<br>−8234<br>337 326 | 57303<br>−8233<br>337 327 | 57304<br>−8232<br>337 330 | 57305<br>−8231<br>337 331 | 57306<br>−8230<br>337 332 | 57307<br>−8229<br>337 333 | 57308<br>−8228<br>337 334 | 57309<br>−8227<br>337 335 | 57310<br>−8226<br>337 336 | 57311<br>−8225<br>337 337 |
| E− | 57312<br>−8224<br>337 340 | 57313<br>−8223<br>337 341 | 57314<br>−8222<br>337 342 | 57315<br>−8221<br>337 343 | 57316<br>−8220<br>337 344 | 57317<br>−8219<br>337 345 | 57318<br>−8218<br>337 346 | 57319<br>−8217<br>337 347 | 57320<br>−8216<br>337 350 | 57321<br>−8215<br>337 351 | 57322<br>−8214<br>337 352 | 57323<br>−8213<br>337 353 | 57324<br>−8212<br>337 354 | 57325<br>−8211<br>337 355 | 57326<br>−8210<br>337 356 | 57327<br>−8209<br>337 357 |
| F− | 57328<br>−8208<br>337 360 | 57329<br>−8207<br>337 361 | 57330<br>−8206<br>337 362 | 57331<br>−8205<br>337 363 | 57332<br>−8204<br>337 364 | 57333<br>−8203<br>337 365 | 57334<br>−8202<br>337 366 | 57335<br>−8201<br>337 367 | 57336<br>−8200<br>337 370 | 57337<br>−8199<br>337 371 | 57338<br>−8198<br>337 372 | 57339<br>−8197<br>337 373 | 57340<br>−8196<br>337 374 | 57341<br>−8195<br>337 375 | 57342<br>−8194<br>337 376 | 57343<br>−8193<br>337 377 |

<table>
<tr><th>②</th><th colspan="16">FIRST HEX DIGIT</th><th></th></tr>
<tr><th>SECOND<br>HEX<br>DIGIT</th><th>−0</th><th>−1</th><th>−2</th><th>−3</th><th>−4</th><th>−5</th><th>−6</th><th>−7</th><th>−8</th><th>−9</th><th>−A</th><th>−B</th><th>−C</th><th>−D</th><th>−E</th><th>−F</th><th></th></tr>
<tr><td>0−</td><td>57344<br>−8192<br>340 000</td><td>57345<br>−8191<br>340 001</td><td>57346<br>−8190<br>340 002</td><td>57347<br>−8189<br>340 003</td><td>57348<br>−8188<br>340 004</td><td>57349<br>−8187<br>340 005</td><td>57350<br>−8186<br>340 006</td><td>57351<br>−8185<br>340 007</td><td>57352<br>−8184<br>340 010</td><td>57353<br>−8183<br>340 011</td><td>57354<br>−8182<br>340 012</td><td>57355<br>−8181<br>340 013</td><td>57356<br>−8180<br>340 014</td><td>57357<br>−8179<br>340 015</td><td>57358<br>−8178<br>340 016</td><td>57359<br>−8177<br>340 017</td><td>DECIMAL</td></tr>
<tr><td>1−</td><td>57360<br>−8176<br>340 020</td><td>57361<br>−8175<br>340 021</td><td>57362<br>−8174<br>340 022</td><td>57363<br>−8173<br>340 023</td><td>57364<br>−8172<br>340 024</td><td>57365<br>−8171<br>340 025</td><td>57366<br>−8170<br>340 026</td><td>57367<br>−8169<br>340 027</td><td>57368<br>−8168<br>340 030</td><td>57369<br>−8167<br>340 031</td><td>57370<br>−8166<br>340 032</td><td>57371<br>−8165<br>340 033</td><td>57372<br>−8164<br>340 034</td><td>57373<br>−8163<br>340 035</td><td>57374<br>−8162<br>340 036</td><td>57375<br>−8161<br>340 037</td><td></td></tr>
<tr><td>2−</td><td>57376<br>−8160<br>340 040</td><td>57377<br>−8159<br>340 041</td><td>57378<br>−8158<br>340 042</td><td>57379<br>−8157<br>340 043</td><td>57380<br>−8156<br>340 044</td><td>57381<br>−8155<br>340 045</td><td>57382<br>−8154<br>340 046</td><td>57383<br>−8153<br>340 047</td><td>57384<br>−8152<br>340 050</td><td>57385<br>−8151<br>340 051</td><td>57386<br>−8150<br>340 052</td><td>57387<br>−8149<br>340 053</td><td>57388<br>−8148<br>340 054</td><td>57389<br>−8147<br>340 055</td><td>57390<br>−8146<br>340 056</td><td>57391<br>−8145<br>340 057</td><td></td></tr>
<tr><td>3−</td><td>57392<br>−8144<br>340 060</td><td>57393<br>−8143<br>340 061</td><td>57394<br>−8142<br>340 062</td><td>57395<br>−8141<br>340 063</td><td>57396<br>−8140<br>340 064</td><td>57397<br>−8139<br>340 065</td><td>57398<br>−8138<br>340 066</td><td>57399<br>−8137<br>340 067</td><td>57400<br>−8136<br>340 070</td><td>57401<br>−8135<br>340 071</td><td>57402<br>−8134<br>340 072</td><td>57403<br>−8133<br>340 073</td><td>57404<br>−8132<br>340 074</td><td>57405<br>−8131<br>340 075</td><td>57406<br>−8130<br>340 076</td><td>57407<br>−8129<br>340 077</td><td></td></tr>
<tr><td>4−</td><td>57408<br>−8128<br>340 100</td><td>57409<br>−8127<br>340 101</td><td>57410<br>−8126<br>340 102</td><td>57411<br>−8125<br>340 103</td><td>57412<br>−8124<br>340 104</td><td>57413<br>−8123<br>340 105</td><td>57414<br>−8122<br>340 106</td><td>57415<br>−8121<br>340 107</td><td>57416<br>−8120<br>340 110</td><td>57417<br>−8119<br>340 111</td><td>57418<br>−8118<br>340 112</td><td>57419<br>−8117<br>340 113</td><td>57420<br>−8116<br>340 114</td><td>57421<br>−8115<br>340 115</td><td>57422<br>−8114<br>340 116</td><td>57423<br>−8113<br>340 117</td><td> DECIMAL</td></tr>
<tr><td>5−</td><td>57424<br>−8112<br>340 120</td><td>57425<br>−8111<br>340 121</td><td>57426<br>−8110<br>340 122</td><td>57427<br>−8109<br>340 123</td><td>57428<br>−8108<br>340 124</td><td>57429<br>−8107<br>340 125</td><td>57430<br>−8106<br>340 126</td><td>57431<br>−8105<br>340 127</td><td>57432<br>−8104<br>340 130</td><td>57433<br>−8103<br>340 131</td><td>57434<br>−8102<br>340 132</td><td>57435<br>−8101<br>340 133</td><td>57436<br>−8100<br>340 134</td><td>57437<br>−8099<br>340 135</td><td>57438<br>−8098<br>340 136</td><td>57439<br>−8097<br>340 137</td><td></td></tr>
<tr><td>6−</td><td>57440<br>−8096<br>340 140</td><td>57441<br>−8095<br>340 141</td><td>57442<br>−8094<br>340 142</td><td>57443<br>−8093<br>340 143</td><td>57444<br>−8092<br>340 144</td><td>57445<br>−8091<br>340 145</td><td>57446<br>−8090<br>340 146</td><td>57447<br>−8089<br>340 147</td><td>57448<br>−8088<br>340 150</td><td>57449<br>−8087<br>340 151</td><td>57450<br>−8086<br>340 152</td><td>57451<br>−8085<br>340 153</td><td>57452<br>−8084<br>340 154</td><td>57453<br>−8083<br>340 155</td><td>57454<br>−8082<br>340 156</td><td>57455<br>−8081<br>340 157</td><td></td></tr>
<tr><td>7−</td><td>57456<br>−8080<br>340 160</td><td>57457<br>−8079<br>340 161</td><td>57458<br>−8078<br>340 162</td><td>57459<br>−8077<br>340 163</td><td>57460<br>−8076<br>340 164</td><td>57461<br>−8075<br>340 165</td><td>57462<br>−8074<br>340 166</td><td>57463<br>−8073<br>340 167</td><td>57464<br>−8072<br>340 170</td><td>57465<br>−8071<br>340 171</td><td>57466<br>−8070<br>340 172</td><td>57467<br>−8069<br>340 173</td><td>57468<br>−8068<br>340 174</td><td>57469<br>−8067<br>340 175</td><td>57470<br>−8066<br>340 176</td><td>57471<br>−8065<br>340 177</td><td>OCTAL</td></tr>
<tr><td>8−</td><td>57472<br>−8064<br>340 200</td><td>57473<br>−8063<br>340 201</td><td>57474<br>−8062<br>340 202</td><td>57475<br>−8061<br>340 203</td><td>57476<br>−8060<br>340 204</td><td>57477<br>−8059<br>340 205</td><td>57478<br>−8058<br>340 206</td><td>57479<br>−8057<br>340 207</td><td>57480<br>−8056<br>340 210</td><td>57481<br>−8055<br>340 211</td><td>57482<br>−8054<br>340 212</td><td>57483<br>−8053<br>340 213</td><td>57484<br>−8052<br>340 214</td><td>57485<br>−8051<br>340 215</td><td>57486<br>−8050<br>340 216</td><td>57487<br>−8049<br>340 217</td><td></td></tr>
<tr><td>9−</td><td>57488<br>−8048<br>340 220</td><td>57489<br>−8047<br>340 221</td><td>57490<br>−8046<br>340 222</td><td>57491<br>−8045<br>340 223</td><td>57492<br>−8044<br>340 224</td><td>57493<br>−8043<br>340 225</td><td>57494<br>−8042<br>340 226</td><td>57495<br>−8041<br>340 227</td><td>57496<br>−8040<br>340 230</td><td>57497<br>−8039<br>340 231</td><td>57498<br>−8038<br>340 232</td><td>57499<br>−8037<br>340 233</td><td>57500<br>−8036<br>340 234</td><td>57501<br>−8035<br>340 235</td><td>57502<br>−8034<br>340 236</td><td>57503<br>−8033<br>340 237</td><td></td></tr>
<tr><td>A−</td><td>57504<br>−8032<br>340 240</td><td>57505<br>−8031<br>340 241</td><td>57506<br>−8030<br>340 242</td><td>57507<br>−8029<br>340 243</td><td>57508<br>−8028<br>340 244</td><td>57509<br>−8027<br>340 245</td><td>57510<br>−8026<br>340 246</td><td>57511<br>−8025<br>340 247</td><td>57512<br>−8024<br>340 250</td><td>57513<br>−8023<br>340 251</td><td>57514<br>−8022<br>340 252</td><td>57515<br>−8021<br>340 253</td><td>57516<br>−8020<br>340 254</td><td>57517<br>−8019<br>340 255</td><td>57518<br>−8018<br>340 256</td><td>57519<br>−8017<br>340 257</td><td></td></tr>
<tr><td>B−</td><td>57520<br>−8016<br>340 260</td><td>57521<br>−8015<br>340 261</td><td>57522<br>−8014<br>340 262</td><td>57523<br>−8013<br>340 263</td><td>57524<br>−8012<br>340 264</td><td>57525<br>−8011<br>340 265</td><td>57526<br>−8010<br>340 266</td><td>57527<br>−8009<br>340 267</td><td>57528<br>−8008<br>340 270</td><td>57529<br>−8007<br>340 271</td><td>57530<br>−8006<br>340 272</td><td>57531<br>−8005<br>340 273</td><td>57532<br>−8004<br>340 274</td><td>57533<br>−8003<br>340 275</td><td>57534<br>−8002<br>340 276</td><td>57535<br>−8001<br>340 277</td><td></td></tr>
<tr><td>C−</td><td>57536<br>−8000<br>340 300</td><td>57537<br>−7999<br>340 301</td><td>57538<br>−7998<br>340 302</td><td>57539<br>−7997<br>340 303</td><td>57540<br>−7996<br>340 304</td><td>57541<br>−7995<br>340 305</td><td>57542<br>−7994<br>340 306</td><td>57543<br>−7993<br>340 307</td><td>57544<br>−7992<br>340 310</td><td>57545<br>−7991<br>340 311</td><td>57546<br>−7990<br>340 312</td><td>57547<br>−7989<br>340 313</td><td>57548<br>−7988<br>340 314</td><td>57549<br>−7987<br>340 315</td><td>57550<br>−7986<br>340 316</td><td>57551<br>−7985<br>340 317</td><td></td></tr>
<tr><td>D−</td><td>57552<br>−7984<br>340 320</td><td>57553<br>−7983<br>340 321</td><td>57554<br>−7982<br>340 322</td><td>57555<br>−7981<br>340 323</td><td>57556<br>−7980<br>340 324</td><td>57557<br>−7979<br>340 325</td><td>57558<br>−7978<br>340 326</td><td>57559<br>−7977<br>340 327</td><td>57560<br>−7976<br>340 330</td><td>57561<br>−7975<br>340 331</td><td>57562<br>−7974<br>340 332</td><td>57563<br>−7973<br>340 333</td><td>57564<br>−7972<br>340 334</td><td>57565<br>−7971<br>340 335</td><td>57566<br>−7970<br>340 336</td><td>57567<br>−7969<br>340 337</td><td></td></tr>
<tr><td>E−</td><td>57568<br>−7968<br>340 340</td><td>57569<br>−7967<br>340 341</td><td>57570<br>−7966<br>340 342</td><td>57571<br>−7965<br>340 343</td><td>57572<br>−7964<br>340 344</td><td>57573<br>−7963<br>340 345</td><td>57574<br>−7962<br>340 346</td><td>57575<br>−7961<br>340 347</td><td>57576<br>−7960<br>340 350</td><td>57577<br>−7959<br>340 351</td><td>57578<br>−7958<br>340 352</td><td>57579<br>−7957<br>340 353</td><td>57580<br>−7956<br>340 354</td><td>57581<br>−7955<br>340 355</td><td>57582<br>−7954<br>340 356</td><td>57583<br>−7953<br>340 357</td><td></td></tr>
<tr><td>F−</td><td>57584<br>−7952<br>340 360</td><td>57585<br>−7951<br>340 361</td><td>57586<br>−7950<br>340 362</td><td>57587<br>−7949<br>340 363</td><td>57588<br>−7948<br>340 364</td><td>57589<br>−7947<br>340 365</td><td>57590<br>−7946<br>340 366</td><td>57591<br>−7945<br>340 367</td><td>57592<br>−7944<br>340 370</td><td>57593<br>−7943<br>340 371</td><td>57594<br>−7942<br>340 372</td><td>57595<br>−7941<br>340 373</td><td>57596<br>−7940<br>340 374</td><td>57597<br>−7939<br>340 375</td><td>57598<br>−7938<br>340 376</td><td>57599<br>−7937<br>340 377</td><td></td></tr>
</table>

 DECIMAL  −8192   BINARY  1110 0000   DECIMAL  57344   HEXADECIMAL  E0   OCTAL  340 000

FOURTH HEX DIGIT → ← THIRD HEX DIGIT

## FIRST HEX DIGIT

⬡ 2

| SECOND HEX DIGIT | -0 | -1 | -2 | -3 | -4 | -5 | -6 | -7 | -8 | -9 | -A | -B | -C | -D | -E | -F |
|---|---|---|---|---|---|---|---|---|---|---|---|---|---|---|---|---|
| 0- | 57600<br>-7936<br>341 000 | 57601<br>-7935<br>341 001 | 57602<br>-7934<br>341 002 | 57603<br>-7933<br>341 003 | 57604<br>-7932<br>341 004 | 57605<br>-7931<br>341 005 | 57606<br>-7930<br>341 006 | 57607<br>-7929<br>341 007 | 57608<br>-7928<br>341 010 | 57609<br>-7927<br>341 011 | 57610<br>-7926<br>341 012 | 57611<br>-7925<br>341 013 | 57612<br>-7924<br>341 014 | 57613<br>-7923<br>341 015 | 57614<br>-7922<br>341 016 | 57615<br>-7921<br>341 017 |
| 1- | 57616<br>-7920<br>341 020 | 57617<br>-7919<br>341 021 | 57618<br>-7918<br>341 022 | 57619<br>-7917<br>341 023 | 57620<br>-7916<br>341 024 | 57621<br>-7915<br>341 025 | 57622<br>-7914<br>341 026 | 57623<br>-7913<br>341 027 | 57624<br>-7912<br>341 030 | 57625<br>-7911<br>341 031 | 57626<br>-7910<br>341 032 | 57627<br>-7909<br>341 033 | 57628<br>-7908<br>341 034 | 57629<br>-7907<br>341 035 | 57630<br>-7906<br>341 036 | 57631<br>-7905<br>341 037 |
| 2- | 57632<br>-7904<br>341 040 | 57633<br>-7903<br>341 041 | 57634<br>-7902<br>341 042 | 57635<br>-7901<br>341 043 | 57636<br>-7900<br>341 044 | 57637<br>-7899<br>341 045 | 57638<br>-7898<br>341 046 | 57639<br>-7897<br>341 047 | 57640<br>-7896<br>341 050 | 57641<br>-7895<br>341 051 | 57642<br>-7894<br>341 052 | 57643<br>-7893<br>341 053 | 57644<br>-7892<br>341 054 | 57645<br>-7891<br>341 055 | 57646<br>-7890<br>341 056 | 57647<br>-7889<br>341 057 |
| 3- | 57648<br>-7888<br>341 060 | 57649<br>-7887<br>341 061 | 57650<br>-7886<br>341 062 | 57651<br>-7885<br>341 063 | 57652<br>-7884<br>341 064 | 57653<br>-7883<br>341 065 | 57654<br>-7882<br>341 066 | 57655<br>-7881<br>341 067 | 57656<br>-7880<br>341 070 | 57657<br>-7879<br>341 071 | 57658<br>-7878<br>341 072 | 57659<br>-7877<br>341 073 | 57660<br>-7876<br>341 074 | 57661<br>-7875<br>341 075 | 57662<br>-7874<br>341 076 | 57663<br>-7873<br>341 077 |
| 4- | 57664<br>-7872<br>341 100 | 57665<br>-7871<br>341 101 | 57666<br>-7870<br>341 102 | 57667<br>-7869<br>341 103 | 57668<br>-7868<br>341 104 | 57669<br>-7867<br>341 105 | 57670<br>-7866<br>341 106 | 57671<br>-7865<br>341 107 | 57672<br>-7864<br>341 110 | 57673<br>-7863<br>341 111 | 57674<br>-7862<br>341 112 | 57675<br>-7861<br>341 113 | 57676<br>-7860<br>341 114 | 57677<br>-7859<br>341 115 | 57678<br>-7858<br>341 116 | 57679<br>-7857<br>341 117 |
| 5- | 57680<br>-7856<br>341 120 | 57681<br>-7855<br>341 121 | 57682<br>-7854<br>341 122 | 57683<br>-7853<br>341 123 | 57684<br>-7852<br>341 124 | 57685<br>-7851<br>341 125 | 57686<br>-7850<br>341 126 | 57687<br>-7849<br>341 127 | 57688<br>-7848<br>341 130 | 57689<br>-7847<br>341 131 | 57690<br>-7846<br>341 132 | 57691<br>-7845<br>341 133 | 57692<br>-7844<br>341 134 | 57693<br>-7843<br>341 135 | 57694<br>-7842<br>341 136 | 57695<br>-7841<br>341 137 |
| 6- | 57696<br>-7840<br>341 140 | 57697<br>-7839<br>341 141 | 57698<br>-7838<br>341 142 | 57699<br>-7837<br>341 143 | 57700<br>-7836<br>341 144 | 57701<br>-7835<br>341 145 | 57702<br>-7834<br>341 146 | 57703<br>-7833<br>341 147 | 57704<br>-7832<br>341 150 | 57705<br>-7831<br>341 151 | 57706<br>-7830<br>341 152 | 57707<br>-7829<br>341 153 | 57708<br>-7828<br>341 154 | 57709<br>-7827<br>341 155 | 57710<br>-7826<br>341 156 | 57711<br>-7825<br>341 157 |
| 7- | 57712<br>-7824<br>341 160 | 57713<br>-7823<br>341 161 | 57714<br>-7822<br>341 162 | 57715<br>-7821<br>341 163 | 57716<br>-7820<br>341 164 | 57717<br>-7819<br>341 165 | 57718<br>-7818<br>341 166 | 57719<br>-7817<br>341 167 | 57720<br>-7816<br>341 170 | 57721<br>-7815<br>341 171 | 57722<br>-7814<br>341 172 | 57723<br>-7813<br>341 173 | 57724<br>-7812<br>341 174 | 57725<br>-7811<br>341 175 | 57726<br>-7810<br>341 176 | 57727<br>-7809<br>341 177 |
| 8- | 57728<br>-7808<br>341 200 | 57729<br>-7807<br>341 201 | 57730<br>-7806<br>341 202 | 57731<br>-7805<br>341 203 | 57732<br>-7804<br>341 204 | 57733<br>-7803<br>341 205 | 57734<br>-7802<br>341 206 | 57735<br>-7801<br>341 207 | 57736<br>-7800<br>341 210 | 57737<br>-7799<br>341 211 | 57738<br>-7798<br>341 212 | 57739<br>-7797<br>341 213 | 57740<br>-7796<br>341 214 | 57741<br>-7795<br>341 215 | 57742<br>-7794<br>341 216 | 57743<br>-7793<br>341 217 |
| 9- | 57744<br>-7792<br>341 220 | 57745<br>-7791<br>341 221 | 57746<br>-7790<br>341 222 | 57747<br>-7789<br>341 223 | 57748<br>-7788<br>341 224 | 57749<br>-7787<br>341 225 | 57750<br>-7786<br>341 226 | 57751<br>-7785<br>341 227 | 57752<br>-7784<br>341 230 | 57753<br>-7783<br>341 231 | 57754<br>-7782<br>341 232 | 57755<br>-7781<br>341 233 | 57756<br>-7780<br>341 234 | 57757<br>-7779<br>341 235 | 57758<br>-7778<br>341 236 | 57759<br>-7777<br>341 237 |
| A- | 57760<br>-7776<br>341 240 | 57761<br>-7775<br>341 241 | 57762<br>-7774<br>341 242 | 57763<br>-7773<br>341 243 | 57764<br>-7772<br>341 244 | 57765<br>-7771<br>341 245 | 57766<br>-7770<br>341 246 | 57767<br>-7769<br>341 247 | 57768<br>-7768<br>341 250 | 57769<br>-7767<br>341 251 | 57770<br>-7766<br>341 252 | 57771<br>-7765<br>341 253 | 57772<br>-7764<br>341 254 | 57773<br>-7763<br>341 255 | 57774<br>-7762<br>341 256 | 57775<br>-7761<br>341 257 |
| B- | 57776<br>-7760<br>341 260 | 57777<br>-7759<br>341 261 | 57778<br>-7758<br>341 262 | 57779<br>-7757<br>341 263 | 57780<br>-7756<br>341 264 | 57781<br>-7755<br>341 265 | 57782<br>-7754<br>341 266 | 57783<br>-7753<br>341 267 | 57784<br>-7752<br>341 270 | 57785<br>-7751<br>341 271 | 57786<br>-7750<br>341 272 | 57787<br>-7749<br>341 273 | 57788<br>-7748<br>341 274 | 57789<br>-7747<br>341 275 | 57790<br>-7746<br>341 276 | 57791<br>-7745<br>341 277 |
| C- | 57792<br>-7744<br>341 300 | 57793<br>-7743<br>341 301 | 57794<br>-7742<br>341 302 | 57795<br>-7741<br>341 303 | 57796<br>-7740<br>341 304 | 57797<br>-7739<br>341 305 | 57798<br>-7738<br>341 306 | 57799<br>-7737<br>341 307 | 57800<br>-7736<br>341 310 | 57801<br>-7735<br>341 311 | 57802<br>-7734<br>341 312 | 57803<br>-7733<br>341 313 | 57804<br>-7732<br>341 314 | 57805<br>-7731<br>341 315 | 57806<br>-7730<br>341 316 | 57807<br>-7729<br>341 317 |
| D- | 57808<br>-7728<br>341 320 | 57809<br>-7727<br>341 321 | 57810<br>-7726<br>341 322 | 57811<br>-7725<br>341 323 | 57812<br>-7724<br>341 324 | 57813<br>-7723<br>341 325 | 57814<br>-7722<br>341 326 | 57815<br>-7721<br>341 327 | 57816<br>-7720<br>341 330 | 57817<br>-7719<br>341 331 | 57818<br>-7718<br>341 332 | 57819<br>-7717<br>341 333 | 57820<br>-7716<br>341 334 | 57821<br>-7715<br>341 335 | 57822<br>-7714<br>341 336 | 57823<br>-7713<br>341 337 |
| E- | 57824<br>-7712<br>341 340 | 57825<br>-7711<br>341 341 | 57826<br>-7710<br>341 342 | 57827<br>-7709<br>341 343 | 57828<br>-7708<br>341 344 | 57829<br>-7707<br>341 345 | 57830<br>-7706<br>341 346 | 57831<br>-7705<br>341 347 | 57832<br>-7704<br>341 350 | 57833<br>-7703<br>341 351 | 57834<br>-7702<br>341 352 | 57835<br>-7701<br>341 353 | 57836<br>-7700<br>341 354 | 57837<br>-7699<br>341 355 | 57838<br>-7698<br>341 356 | 57839<br>-7697<br>341 357 |
| F- | 57840<br>-7696<br>341 360 | 57841<br>-7695<br>341 361 | 57842<br>-7694<br>341 362 | 57843<br>-7693<br>341 363 | 57844<br>-7692<br>341 364 | 57845<br>-7691<br>341 365 | 57846<br>-7690<br>341 366 | 57847<br>-7689<br>341 367 | 57848<br>-7688<br>341 370 | 57849<br>-7687<br>341 371 | 57850<br>-7686<br>341 372 | 57851<br>-7685<br>341 373 | 57852<br>-7684<br>341 374 | 57853<br>-7683<br>341 375 | 57854<br>-7682<br>341 376 | 57855<br>-7681<br>341 377 |

Right-margin labels (with arrows pointing to the table): DECIMAL · 󰀂 DECIMAL · OCTAL

| 2 | −0 | −1 | −2 | −3 | −4 | −5 | −6 | −7 | −8 | −9 | −A | −B | −C | −D | −E | −F |
|---|---|---|---|---|---|---|---|---|---|---|---|---|---|---|---|---|
| **FIRST HEX DIGIT** | | | | | | | | | | | | | | | | |
| 0− | 57856<br>−7680<br>342 000 | 57857<br>−7679<br>342 001 | 57858<br>−7678<br>342 002 | 57859<br>−7677<br>342 003 | 57860<br>−7676<br>342 004 | 57861<br>−7675<br>342 005 | 57862<br>−7674<br>342 006 | 57863<br>−7673<br>342 007 | 57864<br>−7672<br>342 010 | 57865<br>−7671<br>342 011 | 57866<br>−7670<br>342 012 | 57867<br>−7669<br>342 013 | 57868<br>−7668<br>342 014 | 57869<br>−7667<br>342 015 | 57870<br>−7666<br>342 016 | 57871<br>−7665<br>342 017 |
| 1− | 57872<br>−7664<br>342 020 | 57873<br>−7663<br>342 021 | 57874<br>−7662<br>342 022 | 57875<br>−7661<br>342 023 | 57876<br>−7660<br>342 024 | 57877<br>−7659<br>342 025 | 57878<br>−7658<br>342 026 | 57879<br>−7657<br>342 027 | 57880<br>−7656<br>342 030 | 57881<br>−7655<br>342 031 | 57882<br>−7654<br>342 032 | 57883<br>−7653<br>342 033 | 57884<br>−7652<br>342 034 | 57885<br>−7651<br>342 035 | 57886<br>−7650<br>342 036 | 57887<br>−7649<br>342 037 |
| 2− | 57888<br>−7648<br>342 040 | 57889<br>−7647<br>342 041 | 57890<br>−7646<br>342 042 | 57891<br>−7645<br>342 043 | 57892<br>−7644<br>342 044 | 57893<br>−7643<br>342 045 | 57894<br>−7642<br>342 046 | 57895<br>−7641<br>342 047 | 57896<br>−7640<br>342 050 | 57897<br>−7639<br>342 051 | 57898<br>−7638<br>342 052 | 57899<br>−7637<br>342 053 | 57900<br>−7636<br>342 054 | 57901<br>−7635<br>342 055 | 57902<br>−7634<br>342 056 | 57903<br>−7633<br>342 057 |
| 3− | 57904<br>−7632<br>342 060 | 57905<br>−7631<br>342 061 | 57906<br>−7630<br>342 062 | 57907<br>−7629<br>342 063 | 57908<br>−7628<br>342 064 | 57909<br>−7627<br>342 065 | 57910<br>−7626<br>342 066 | 57911<br>−7625<br>342 067 | 57912<br>−7624<br>342 070 | 57913<br>−7623<br>342 071 | 57914<br>−7622<br>342 072 | 57915<br>−7621<br>342 073 | 57916<br>−7620<br>342 074 | 57917<br>−7619<br>342 075 | 57918<br>−7618<br>342 076 | 57919<br>−7617<br>342 077 |
| 4− | 57920<br>−7616<br>342 100 | 57921<br>−7615<br>342 101 | 57922<br>−7614<br>342 102 | 57923<br>−7613<br>342 103 | 57924<br>−7612<br>342 104 | 57925<br>−7611<br>342 105 | 57926<br>−7610<br>342 106 | 57927<br>−7609<br>342 107 | 57928<br>−7608<br>342 110 | 57929<br>−7607<br>342 111 | 57930<br>−7606<br>342 112 | 57931<br>−7605<br>342 113 | 57932<br>−7604<br>342 114 | 57933<br>−7603<br>342 115 | 57934<br>−7602<br>342 116 | 57935<br>−7601<br>342 117 |
| 5− | 57936<br>−7600<br>342 120 | 57937<br>−7599<br>342 121 | 57938<br>−7598<br>342 122 | 57939<br>−7597<br>342 123 | 57940<br>−7596<br>342 124 | 57941<br>−7595<br>342 125 | 57942<br>−7594<br>342 126 | 57943<br>−7593<br>342 127 | 57944<br>−7592<br>342 130 | 57945<br>−7591<br>342 131 | 57946<br>−7590<br>342 132 | 57947<br>−7589<br>342 133 | 57948<br>−7588<br>342 134 | 57949<br>−7587<br>342 135 | 57950<br>−7586<br>342 136 | 57951<br>−7585<br>342 137 |
| 6− | 57952<br>−7584<br>342 140 | 57953<br>−7583<br>342 141 | 57954<br>−7582<br>342 142 | 57955<br>−7581<br>342 143 | 57956<br>−7580<br>342 144 | 57957<br>−7579<br>342 145 | 57958<br>−7578<br>342 146 | 57959<br>−7577<br>342 147 | 57960<br>−7576<br>342 150 | 57961<br>−7575<br>342 151 | 57962<br>−7574<br>342 152 | 57963<br>−7573<br>342 153 | 57964<br>−7572<br>342 154 | 57965<br>−7571<br>342 155 | 57966<br>−7570<br>342 156 | 57967<br>−7569<br>342 157 |
| 7− | 57968<br>−7568<br>342 160 | 57969<br>−7567<br>342 161 | 57970<br>−7566<br>342 162 | 57971<br>−7565<br>342 163 | 57972<br>−7564<br>342 164 | 57973<br>−7563<br>342 165 | 57974<br>−7562<br>342 166 | 57975<br>−7561<br>342 167 | 57976<br>−7560<br>342 170 | 57977<br>−7559<br>342 171 | 57978<br>−7558<br>342 172 | 57979<br>−7557<br>342 173 | 57980<br>−7556<br>342 174 | 57981<br>−7555<br>342 175 | 57982<br>−7554<br>342 176 | 57983<br>−7553<br>342 177 |
| 8− | 57984<br>−7552<br>342 200 | 57985<br>−7551<br>342 201 | 57986<br>−7550<br>342 202 | 57987<br>−7549<br>342 203 | 57988<br>−7548<br>342 204 | 57989<br>−7547<br>342 205 | 57990<br>−7546<br>342 206 | 57991<br>−7545<br>342 207 | 57992<br>−7544<br>342 210 | 57993<br>−7543<br>342 211 | 57994<br>−7542<br>342 212 | 57995<br>−7541<br>342 213 | 57996<br>−7540<br>342 214 | 57997<br>−7539<br>342 215 | 57998<br>−7538<br>342 216 | 57999<br>−7537<br>342 217 |
| 9− | 58000<br>−7536<br>342 220 | 58001<br>−7535<br>342 221 | 58002<br>−7534<br>342 222 | 58003<br>−7533<br>342 223 | 58004<br>−7532<br>342 224 | 58005<br>−7531<br>342 225 | 58006<br>−7530<br>342 226 | 58007<br>−7529<br>342 227 | 58008<br>−7528<br>342 230 | 58009<br>−7527<br>342 231 | 58010<br>−7526<br>342 232 | 58011<br>−7525<br>342 233 | 58012<br>−7524<br>342 234 | 58013<br>−7523<br>342 235 | 58014<br>−7522<br>342 236 | 58015<br>−7521<br>342 237 |
| A− | 58016<br>−7520<br>342 240 | 58017<br>−7519<br>342 241 | 58018<br>−7518<br>342 242 | 58019<br>−7517<br>342 243 | 58020<br>−7516<br>342 244 | 58021<br>−7515<br>342 245 | 58022<br>−7514<br>342 246 | 58023<br>−7513<br>342 247 | 58024<br>−7512<br>342 250 | 58025<br>−7511<br>342 251 | 58026<br>−7510<br>342 252 | 58027<br>−7509<br>342 253 | 58028<br>−7508<br>342 254 | 58029<br>−7507<br>342 255 | 58030<br>−7506<br>342 256 | 58031<br>−7505<br>342 257 |
| B− | 58032<br>−7504<br>342 260 | 58033<br>−7503<br>342 261 | 58034<br>−7502<br>342 262 | 58035<br>−7501<br>342 263 | 58036<br>−7500<br>342 264 | 58037<br>−7499<br>342 265 | 58038<br>−7498<br>342 266 | 58039<br>−7497<br>342 267 | 58040<br>−7496<br>342 270 | 58041<br>−7495<br>342 271 | 58042<br>−7494<br>342 272 | 58043<br>−7493<br>342 273 | 58044<br>−7492<br>342 274 | 58045<br>−7491<br>342 275 | 58046<br>−7490<br>342 276 | 58047<br>−7489<br>342 277 |
| C− | 58048<br>−7488<br>342 300 | 58049<br>−7487<br>342 301 | 58050<br>−7486<br>342 302 | 58051<br>−7485<br>342 303 | 58052<br>−7484<br>342 304 | 58053<br>−7483<br>342 305 | 58054<br>−7482<br>342 306 | 58055<br>−7481<br>342 307 | 58056<br>−7480<br>342 310 | 58057<br>−7479<br>342 311 | 58058<br>−7478<br>342 312 | 58059<br>−7477<br>342 313 | 58060<br>−7476<br>342 314 | 58061<br>−7475<br>342 315 | 58062<br>−7474<br>342 316 | 58063<br>−7473<br>342 317 |
| D− | 58064<br>−7472<br>342 320 | 58065<br>−7471<br>342 321 | 58066<br>−7470<br>342 322 | 58067<br>−7469<br>342 323 | 58068<br>−7468<br>342 324 | 58069<br>−7467<br>342 325 | 58070<br>−7466<br>342 326 | 58071<br>−7465<br>342 327 | 58072<br>−7464<br>342 330 | 58073<br>−7463<br>342 331 | 58074<br>−7462<br>342 332 | 58075<br>−7461<br>342 333 | 58076<br>−7460<br>342 334 | 58077<br>−7459<br>342 335 | 58078<br>−7458<br>342 336 | 58079<br>−7457<br>342 337 |
| E− | 58080<br>−7456<br>342 340 | 58081<br>−7455<br>342 341 | 58082<br>−7454<br>342 342 | 58083<br>−7453<br>342 343 | 58084<br>−7452<br>342 344 | 58085<br>−7451<br>342 345 | 58086<br>−7450<br>342 346 | 58087<br>−7449<br>342 347 | 58088<br>−7448<br>342 350 | 58089<br>−7447<br>342 351 | 58090<br>−7446<br>342 352 | 58091<br>−7445<br>342 353 | 58092<br>−7444<br>342 354 | 58093<br>−7443<br>342 355 | 58094<br>−7442<br>342 356 | 58095<br>−7441<br>342 357 |
| F− | 58096<br>−7440<br>342 360 | 58097<br>−7439<br>342 361 | 58098<br>−7438<br>342 362 | 58099<br>−7437<br>342 363 | 58100<br>−7436<br>342 364 | 58101<br>−7435<br>342 365 | 58102<br>−7434<br>342 366 | 58103<br>−7433<br>342 367 | 58104<br>−7432<br>342 370 | 58105<br>−7431<br>342 371 | 58106<br>−7430<br>342 372 | 58107<br>−7429<br>342 373 | 58108<br>−7428<br>342 374 | 58109<br>−7427<br>342 375 | 58110<br>−7426<br>342 376 | 58111<br>−7425<br>342 377 |

SECOND HEX DIGIT

DECIMAL →

 DECIMAL →

OCTAL →

 DECIMAL  −7680  BINARY  1110 0010  DECIMAL  57856  HEXADECIMAL  E2  OCTAL  342 000

FOURTH HEX DIGIT → E2 ← THIRD HEX DIGIT

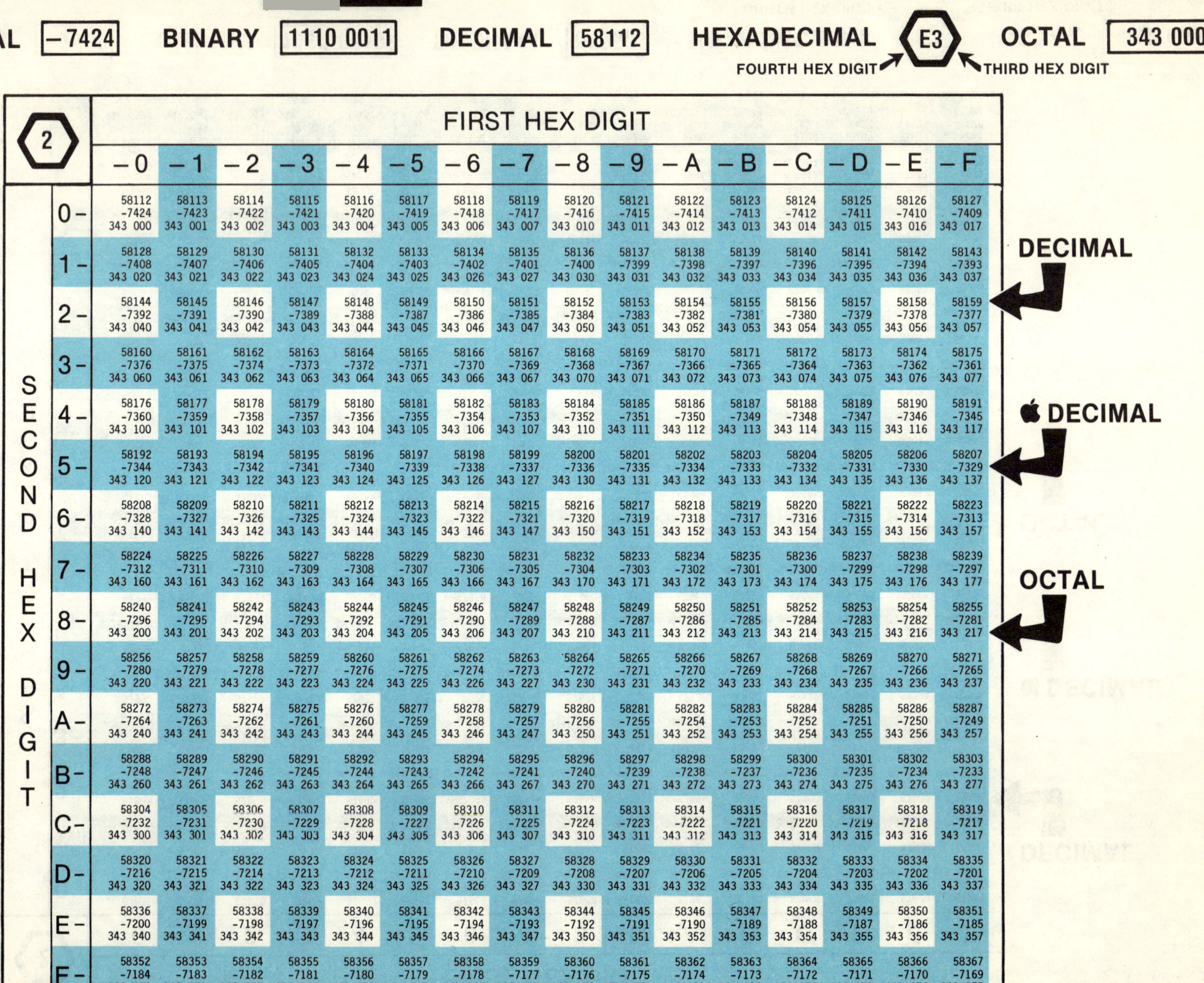

FIRST HEX DIGIT — SECOND HEX DIGIT — hexadecimal prefix 2 (each cell: decimal / signed decimal / octal)

| SECOND HEX DIGIT | −0 | −1 | −2 | −3 | −4 | −5 | −6 | −7 | −8 | −9 | −A | −B | −C | −D | −E | −F |
|---|---|---|---|---|---|---|---|---|---|---|---|---|---|---|---|---|
| 0− | 58112<br>−7424<br>343 000 | 58113<br>−7423<br>343 001 | 58114<br>−7422<br>343 002 | 58115<br>−7421<br>343 003 | 58116<br>−7420<br>343 004 | 58117<br>−7419<br>343 005 | 58118<br>−7418<br>343 006 | 58119<br>−7417<br>343 007 | 58120<br>−7416<br>343 010 | 58121<br>−7415<br>343 011 | 58122<br>−7414<br>343 012 | 58123<br>−7413<br>343 013 | 58124<br>−7412<br>343 014 | 58125<br>−7411<br>343 015 | 58126<br>−7410<br>343 016 | 58127<br>−7409<br>343 017 |
| 1− | 58128<br>−7408<br>343 020 | 58129<br>−7407<br>343 021 | 58130<br>−7406<br>343 022 | 58131<br>−7405<br>343 023 | 58132<br>−7404<br>343 024 | 58133<br>−7403<br>343 025 | 58134<br>−7402<br>343 026 | 58135<br>−7401<br>343 027 | 58136<br>−7400<br>343 030 | 58137<br>−7399<br>343 031 | 58138<br>−7398<br>343 032 | 58139<br>−7397<br>343 033 | 58140<br>−7396<br>343 034 | 58141<br>−7395<br>343 035 | 58142<br>−7394<br>343 036 | 58143<br>−7393<br>343 037 |
| 2− | 58144<br>−7392<br>343 040 | 58145<br>−7391<br>343 041 | 58146<br>−7390<br>343 042 | 58147<br>−7389<br>343 043 | 58148<br>−7388<br>343 044 | 58149<br>−7387<br>343 045 | 58150<br>−7386<br>343 046 | 58151<br>−7385<br>343 047 | 58152<br>−7384<br>343 050 | 58153<br>−7383<br>343 051 | 58154<br>−7382<br>343 052 | 58155<br>−7381<br>343 053 | 58156<br>−7380<br>343 054 | 58157<br>−7379<br>343 055 | 58158<br>−7378<br>343 056 | 58159<br>−7377<br>343 057 |
| 3− | 58160<br>−7376<br>343 060 | 58161<br>−7375<br>343 061 | 58162<br>−7374<br>343 062 | 58163<br>−7373<br>343 063 | 58164<br>−7372<br>343 064 | 58165<br>−7371<br>343 065 | 58166<br>−7370<br>343 066 | 58167<br>−7369<br>343 067 | 58168<br>−7368<br>343 070 | 58169<br>−7367<br>343 071 | 58170<br>−7366<br>343 072 | 58171<br>−7365<br>343 073 | 58172<br>−7364<br>343 074 | 58173<br>−7363<br>343 075 | 58174<br>−7362<br>343 076 | 58175<br>−7361<br>343 077 |
| 4− | 58176<br>−7360<br>343 100 | 58177<br>−7359<br>343 101 | 58178<br>−7358<br>343 102 | 58179<br>−7357<br>343 103 | 58180<br>−7356<br>343 104 | 58181<br>−7355<br>343 105 | 58182<br>−7354<br>343 106 | 58183<br>−7353<br>343 107 | 58184<br>−7352<br>343 110 | 58185<br>−7351<br>343 111 | 58186<br>−7350<br>343 112 | 58187<br>−7349<br>343 113 | 58188<br>−7348<br>343 114 | 58189<br>−7347<br>343 115 | 58190<br>−7346<br>343 116 | 58191<br>−7345<br>343 117 |
| 5− | 58192<br>−7344<br>343 120 | 58193<br>−7343<br>343 121 | 58194<br>−7342<br>343 122 | 58195<br>−7341<br>343 123 | 58196<br>−7340<br>343 124 | 58197<br>−7339<br>343 125 | 58198<br>−7338<br>343 126 | 58199<br>−7337<br>343 127 | 58200<br>−7336<br>343 130 | 58201<br>−7335<br>343 131 | 58202<br>−7334<br>343 132 | 58203<br>−7333<br>343 133 | 58204<br>−7332<br>343 134 | 58205<br>−7331<br>343 135 | 58206<br>−7330<br>343 136 | 58207<br>−7329<br>343 137 |
| 6− | 58208<br>−7328<br>343 140 | 58209<br>−7327<br>343 141 | 58210<br>−7326<br>343 142 | 58211<br>−7325<br>343 143 | 58212<br>−7324<br>343 144 | 58213<br>−7323<br>343 145 | 58214<br>−7322<br>343 146 | 58215<br>−7321<br>343 147 | 58216<br>−7320<br>343 150 | 58217<br>−7319<br>343 151 | 58218<br>−7318<br>343 152 | 58219<br>−7317<br>343 153 | 58220<br>−7316<br>343 154 | 58221<br>−7315<br>343 155 | 58222<br>−7314<br>343 156 | 58223<br>−7313<br>343 157 |
| 7− | 58224<br>−7312<br>343 160 | 58225<br>−7311<br>343 161 | 58226<br>−7310<br>343 162 | 58227<br>−7309<br>343 163 | 58228<br>−7308<br>343 164 | 58229<br>−7307<br>343 165 | 58230<br>−7306<br>343 166 | 58231<br>−7305<br>343 167 | 58232<br>−7304<br>343 170 | 58233<br>−7303<br>343 171 | 58234<br>−7302<br>343 172 | 58235<br>−7301<br>343 173 | 58236<br>−7300<br>343 174 | 58237<br>−7299<br>343 175 | 58238<br>−7298<br>343 176 | 58239<br>−7297<br>343 177 |
| 8− | 58240<br>−7296<br>343 200 | 58241<br>−7295<br>343 201 | 58242<br>−7294<br>343 202 | 58243<br>−7293<br>343 203 | 58244<br>−7292<br>343 204 | 58245<br>−7291<br>343 205 | 58246<br>−7290<br>343 206 | 58247<br>−7289<br>343 207 | 58248<br>−7288<br>343 210 | 58249<br>−7287<br>343 211 | 58250<br>−7286<br>343 212 | 58251<br>−7285<br>343 213 | 58252<br>−7284<br>343 214 | 58253<br>−7283<br>343 215 | 58254<br>−7282<br>343 216 | 58255<br>−7281<br>343 217 |
| 9− | 58256<br>−7280<br>343 220 | 58257<br>−7279<br>343 221 | 58258<br>−7278<br>343 222 | 58259<br>−7277<br>343 223 | 58260<br>−7276<br>343 224 | 58261<br>−7275<br>343 225 | 58262<br>−7274<br>343 226 | 58263<br>−7273<br>343 227 | 58264<br>−7272<br>343 230 | 58265<br>−7271<br>343 231 | 58266<br>−7270<br>343 232 | 58267<br>−7269<br>343 233 | 58268<br>−7268<br>343 234 | 58269<br>−7267<br>343 235 | 58270<br>−7266<br>343 236 | 58271<br>−7265<br>343 237 |
| A− | 58272<br>−7264<br>343 240 | 58273<br>−7263<br>343 241 | 58274<br>−7262<br>343 242 | 58275<br>−7261<br>343 243 | 58276<br>−7260<br>343 244 | 58277<br>−7259<br>343 245 | 58278<br>−7258<br>343 246 | 58279<br>−7257<br>343 247 | 58280<br>−7256<br>343 250 | 58281<br>−7255<br>343 251 | 58282<br>−7254<br>343 252 | 58283<br>−7253<br>343 253 | 58284<br>−7252<br>343 254 | 58285<br>−7251<br>343 255 | 58286<br>−7250<br>343 256 | 58287<br>−7249<br>343 257 |
| B− | 58288<br>−7248<br>343 260 | 58289<br>−7247<br>343 261 | 58290<br>−7246<br>343 262 | 58291<br>−7245<br>343 263 | 58292<br>−7244<br>343 264 | 58293<br>−7243<br>343 265 | 58294<br>−7242<br>343 266 | 58295<br>−7241<br>343 267 | 58296<br>−7240<br>343 270 | 58297<br>−7239<br>343 271 | 58298<br>−7238<br>343 272 | 58299<br>−7237<br>343 273 | 58300<br>−7236<br>343 274 | 58301<br>−7235<br>343 275 | 58302<br>−7234<br>343 276 | 58303<br>−7233<br>343 277 |
| C− | 58304<br>−7232<br>343 300 | 58305<br>−7231<br>343 301 | 58306<br>−7230<br>343 302 | 58307<br>−7229<br>343 303 | 58308<br>−7228<br>343 304 | 58309<br>−7227<br>343 305 | 58310<br>−7226<br>343 306 | 58311<br>−7225<br>343 307 | 58312<br>−7224<br>343 310 | 58313<br>−7223<br>343 311 | 58314<br>−7222<br>343 312 | 58315<br>−7221<br>343 313 | 58316<br>−7220<br>343 314 | 58317<br>−7219<br>343 315 | 58318<br>−7218<br>343 316 | 58319<br>−7217<br>343 317 |
| D− | 58320<br>−7216<br>343 320 | 58321<br>−7215<br>343 321 | 58322<br>−7214<br>343 322 | 58323<br>−7213<br>343 323 | 58324<br>−7212<br>343 324 | 58325<br>−7211<br>343 325 | 58326<br>−7210<br>343 326 | 58327<br>−7209<br>343 327 | 58328<br>−7208<br>343 330 | 58329<br>−7207<br>343 331 | 58330<br>−7206<br>343 332 | 58331<br>−7205<br>343 333 | 58332<br>−7204<br>343 334 | 58333<br>−7203<br>343 335 | 58334<br>−7202<br>343 336 | 58335<br>−7201<br>343 337 |
| E− | 58336<br>−7200<br>343 340 | 58337<br>−7199<br>343 341 | 58338<br>−7198<br>343 342 | 58339<br>−7197<br>343 343 | 58340<br>−7196<br>343 344 | 58341<br>−7195<br>343 345 | 58342<br>−7194<br>343 346 | 58343<br>−7193<br>343 347 | 58344<br>−7192<br>343 350 | 58345<br>−7191<br>343 351 | 58346<br>−7190<br>343 352 | 58347<br>−7189<br>343 353 | 58348<br>−7188<br>343 354 | 58349<br>−7187<br>343 355 | 58350<br>−7186<br>343 356 | 58351<br>−7185<br>343 357 |
| F− | 58352<br>−7184<br>343 360 | 58353<br>−7183<br>343 361 | 58354<br>−7182<br>343 362 | 58355<br>−7181<br>343 363 | 58356<br>−7180<br>343 364 | 58357<br>−7179<br>343 365 | 58358<br>−7178<br>343 366 | 58359<br>−7177<br>343 367 | 58360<br>−7176<br>343 370 | 58361<br>−7175<br>343 371 | 58362<br>−7174<br>343 372 | 58363<br>−7173<br>343 373 | 58364<br>−7172<br>343 374 | 58365<br>−7171<br>343 375 | 58366<br>−7170<br>343 376 | 58367<br>−7169<br>343 377 |

SECOND HEX DIGIT

| | −0 | −1 | −2 | −3 | −4 | −5 | −6 | −7 | −8 | −9 | −A | −B | −C | −D | −E | −F |
|---|---|---|---|---|---|---|---|---|---|---|---|---|---|---|---|---|
| 0- | 58368<br>−7168<br>344 000 | 58369<br>−7167<br>344 001 | 58370<br>−7166<br>344 002 | 58371<br>−7165<br>344 003 | 58372<br>−7164<br>344 004 | 58373<br>−7163<br>344 005 | 58374<br>−7162<br>344 006 | 58375<br>−7161<br>344 007 | 58376<br>−7160<br>344 010 | 58377<br>−7159<br>344 011 | 58378<br>−7158<br>344 012 | 58379<br>−7157<br>344 013 | 58380<br>−7156<br>344 014 | 58381<br>−7155<br>344 015 | 58382<br>−7154<br>344 016 | 58383<br>−7153<br>344 017 |
| 1- | 58384<br>−7152<br>344 020 | 58385<br>−7151<br>344 021 | 58386<br>−7150<br>344 022 | 58387<br>−7149<br>344 023 | 58388<br>−7148<br>344 024 | 58389<br>−7147<br>344 025 | 58390<br>−7146<br>344 026 | 58391<br>−7145<br>344 027 | 58392<br>−7144<br>344 030 | 58393<br>−7143<br>344 031 | 58394<br>−7142<br>344 032 | 58395<br>−7141<br>344 033 | 58396<br>−7140<br>344 034 | 58397<br>−7139<br>344 035 | 58398<br>−7138<br>344 036 | 58399<br>−7137<br>344 037 |
| 2- | 58400<br>−7136<br>344 040 | 58401<br>−7135<br>344 041 | 58402<br>−7134<br>344 042 | 58403<br>−7133<br>344 043 | 58404<br>−7132<br>344 044 | 58405<br>−7131<br>344 045 | 58406<br>−7130<br>344 046 | 58407<br>−7129<br>344 047 | 58408<br>−7128<br>344 050 | 58409<br>−7127<br>344 051 | 58410<br>−7126<br>344 052 | 58411<br>−7125<br>344 053 | 58412<br>−7124<br>344 054 | 58413<br>−7123<br>344 055 | 58414<br>−7122<br>344 056 | 58415<br>−7121<br>344 057 |
| 3- | 58416<br>−7120<br>344 060 | 58417<br>−7119<br>344 061 | 58418<br>−7118<br>344 062 | 58419<br>−7117<br>344 063 | 58420<br>−7116<br>344 064 | 58421<br>−7115<br>344 065 | 58422<br>−7114<br>344 066 | 58423<br>−7113<br>344 067 | 58424<br>−7112<br>344 070 | 58425<br>−7111<br>344 071 | 58426<br>−7110<br>344 072 | 58427<br>−7109<br>344 073 | 58428<br>−7108<br>344 074 | 58429<br>−7107<br>344 075 | 58430<br>−7106<br>344 076 | 58431<br>−7105<br>344 077 |
| 4- | 58432<br>−7104<br>344 100 | 58433<br>−7103<br>344 101 | 58434<br>−7102<br>344 102 | 58435<br>−7101<br>344 103 | 58436<br>−7100<br>344 104 | 58437<br>−7099<br>344 105 | 58438<br>−7098<br>344 106 | 58439<br>−7097<br>344 107 | 58440<br>−7096<br>344 110 | 58441<br>−7095<br>344 111 | 58442<br>−7094<br>344 112 | 58443<br>−7093<br>344 113 | 58444<br>−7092<br>344 114 | 58445<br>−7091<br>344 115 | 58446<br>−7090<br>344 116 | 58447<br>−7089<br>344 117 |
| 5- | 58448<br>−7088<br>344 120 | 58449<br>−7087<br>344 121 | 58450<br>−7086<br>344 122 | 58451<br>−7085<br>344 123 | 58452<br>−7084<br>344 124 | 58453<br>−7083<br>344 125 | 58454<br>−7082<br>344 126 | 58455<br>−7081<br>344 127 | 58456<br>−7080<br>344 130 | 58457<br>−7079<br>344 131 | 58458<br>−7078<br>344 132 | 58459<br>−7077<br>344 133 | 58460<br>−7076<br>344 134 | 58461<br>−7075<br>344 135 | 58462<br>−7074<br>344 136 | 58463<br>−7073<br>344 137 |
| 6- | 58464<br>−7072<br>344 140 | 58465<br>−7071<br>344 141 | 58466<br>−7070<br>344 142 | 58467<br>−7069<br>344 143 | 58468<br>−7068<br>344 144 | 58469<br>−7067<br>344 145 | 58470<br>−7066<br>344 146 | 58471<br>−7065<br>344 147 | 58472<br>−7064<br>344 150 | 58473<br>−7063<br>344 151 | 58474<br>−7062<br>344 152 | 58475<br>−7061<br>344 153 | 58476<br>−7060<br>344 154 | 58477<br>−7059<br>344 155 | 58478<br>−7058<br>344 156 | 58479<br>−7057<br>344 157 |
| 7- | 58480<br>−7056<br>344 160 | 58481<br>−7055<br>344 161 | 58482<br>−7054<br>344 162 | 58483<br>−7053<br>344 163 | 58484<br>−7052<br>344 164 | 58485<br>−7051<br>344 165 | 58486<br>−7050<br>344 166 | 58487<br>−7049<br>344 167 | 58488<br>−7048<br>344 170 | 58489<br>−7047<br>344 171 | 58490<br>−7046<br>344 172 | 58491<br>−7045<br>344 173 | 58492<br>−7044<br>344 174 | 58493<br>−7043<br>344 175 | 58494<br>−7042<br>344 176 | 58495<br>−7041<br>344 177 |
| 8- | 58496<br>−7040<br>344 200 | 58497<br>−7039<br>344 201 | 58498<br>−7038<br>344 202 | 58499<br>−7037<br>344 203 | 58500<br>−7036<br>344 204 | 58501<br>−7035<br>344 205 | 58502<br>−7034<br>344 206 | 58503<br>−7033<br>344 207 | 58504<br>−7032<br>344 210 | 58505<br>−7031<br>344 211 | 58506<br>−7030<br>344 212 | 58507<br>−7029<br>344 213 | 58508<br>−7028<br>344 214 | 58509<br>−7027<br>344 215 | 58510<br>−7026<br>344 216 | 58511<br>−7025<br>344 217 |
| 9- | 58512<br>−7024<br>344 220 | 58513<br>−7023<br>344 221 | 58514<br>−7022<br>344 222 | 58515<br>−7021<br>344 223 | 58516<br>−7020<br>344 224 | 58517<br>−7019<br>344 225 | 58518<br>−7018<br>344 226 | 58519<br>−7017<br>344 227 | 58520<br>−7016<br>344 230 | 58521<br>−7015<br>344 231 | 58522<br>−7014<br>344 232 | 58523<br>−7013<br>344 233 | 58524<br>−7012<br>344 234 | 58525<br>−7011<br>344 235 | 58526<br>−7010<br>344 236 | 58527<br>−7009<br>344 237 |
| A- | 58528<br>−7008<br>344 240 | 58529<br>−7007<br>344 241 | 58530<br>−7006<br>344 242 | 58531<br>−7005<br>344 243 | 58532<br>−7004<br>344 244 | 58533<br>−7003<br>344 245 | 58534<br>−7002<br>344 246 | 58535<br>−7001<br>344 247 | 58536<br>−7000<br>344 250 | 58537<br>−6999<br>344 251 | 58538<br>−6998<br>344 252 | 58539<br>−6997<br>344 253 | 58540<br>−6996<br>344 254 | 58541<br>−6995<br>344 255 | 58542<br>−6994<br>344 256 | 58543<br>−6993<br>344 257 |
| B- | 58544<br>−6992<br>344 260 | 58545<br>−6991<br>344 261 | 58546<br>−6990<br>344 262 | 58547<br>−6989<br>344 263 | 58548<br>−6988<br>344 264 | 58549<br>−6987<br>344 265 | 58550<br>−6986<br>344 266 | 58551<br>−6985<br>344 267 | 58552<br>−6984<br>344 270 | 58553<br>−6983<br>344 271 | 58554<br>−6982<br>344 272 | 58555<br>−6981<br>344 273 | 58556<br>−6980<br>344 274 | 58557<br>−6979<br>344 275 | 58558<br>−6978<br>344 276 | 58559<br>−6977<br>344 277 |
| C- | 58560<br>−6976<br>344 300 | 58561<br>−6975<br>344 301 | 58562<br>−6974<br>344 302 | 58563<br>−6973<br>344 303 | 58564<br>−6972<br>344 304 | 58565<br>−6971<br>344 305 | 58566<br>−6970<br>344 306 | 58567<br>−6969<br>344 307 | 58568<br>−6968<br>344 310 | 58569<br>−6967<br>344 311 | 58570<br>−6966<br>344 312 | 58571<br>−6965<br>344 313 | 58572<br>−6964<br>344 314 | 58573<br>−6963<br>344 315 | 58574<br>−6962<br>344 316 | 58575<br>−6961<br>344 317 |
| D- | 58576<br>−6960<br>344 320 | 58577<br>−6959<br>344 321 | 58578<br>−6958<br>344 322 | 58579<br>−6957<br>344 323 | 58580<br>−6956<br>344 324 | 58581<br>−6955<br>344 325 | 58582<br>−6954<br>344 326 | 58583<br>−6953<br>344 327 | 58584<br>−6952<br>344 330 | 58585<br>−6951<br>344 331 | 58586<br>−6950<br>344 332 | 58587<br>−6949<br>344 333 | 58588<br>−6948<br>344 334 | 58589<br>−6947<br>344 335 | 58590<br>−6946<br>344 336 | 58591<br>−6945<br>344 337 |
| E- | 58592<br>−6944<br>344 340 | 58593<br>−6943<br>344 341 | 58594<br>−6942<br>344 342 | 58595<br>−6941<br>344 343 | 58596<br>−6940<br>344 344 | 58597<br>−6939<br>344 345 | 58598<br>−6938<br>344 346 | 58599<br>−6937<br>344 347 | 58600<br>−6936<br>344 350 | 58601<br>−6935<br>344 351 | 58602<br>−6934<br>344 352 | 58603<br>−6933<br>344 353 | 58604<br>−6932<br>344 354 | 58605<br>−6931<br>344 355 | 58606<br>−6930<br>344 356 | 58607<br>−6929<br>344 357 |
| F- | 58608<br>−6928<br>344 360 | 58609<br>−6927<br>344 361 | 58610<br>−6926<br>344 362 | 58611<br>−6925<br>344 363 | 58612<br>−6924<br>344 364 | 58613<br>−6923<br>344 365 | 58614<br>−6922<br>344 366 | 58615<br>−6921<br>344 367 | 58616<br>−6920<br>344 370 | 58617<br>−6919<br>344 371 | 58618<br>−6918<br>344 372 | 58619<br>−6917<br>344 373 | 58620<br>−6916<br>344 374 | 58621<br>−6915<br>344 375 | 58622<br>−6914<br>344 376 | 58623<br>−6913<br>344 377 |

DECIMAL

 DECIMAL

OCTAL

 DECIMAL  −7168    BINARY  1110 0100    DECIMAL  58368    HEXADECIMAL  (E4)  OCTAL  344 000

FOURTH HEX DIGIT → (E4) ← THIRD HEX DIGIT

| 2 | −0 | −1 | −2 | −3 | −4 | −5 | −6 | −7 | −8 | −9 | −A | −B | −C | −D | −E | −F |
|---|---|---|---|---|---|---|---|---|---|---|---|---|---|---|---|---|
| **FIRST HEX DIGIT** → | | | | | | | | | | | | | | | | |
| 0- | 58624 / −6912 / 345 000 | 58625 / −6911 / 345 001 | 58626 / −6910 / 345 002 | 58627 / −6909 / 345 003 | 58628 / −6908 / 345 004 | 58629 / −6907 / 345 005 | 58630 / −6906 / 345 006 | 58631 / −6905 / 345 007 | 58632 / −6904 / 345 010 | 58633 / −6903 / 345 011 | 58634 / −6902 / 345 012 | 58635 / −6901 / 345 013 | 58636 / −6900 / 345 014 | 58637 / −6899 / 345 015 | 58638 / −6898 / 345 016 | 58639 / −6897 / 345 017 |
| 1- | 58640 / −6896 / 345 020 | 58641 / −6895 / 345 021 | 58642 / −6894 / 345 022 | 58643 / −6893 / 345 023 | 58644 / −6892 / 345 024 | 58645 / −6891 / 345 025 | 58646 / −6890 / 345 026 | 58647 / −6889 / 345 027 | 58648 / −6888 / 345 030 | 58649 / −6887 / 345 031 | 58650 / −6886 / 345 032 | 58651 / −6885 / 345 033 | 58652 / −6884 / 345 034 | 58653 / −6883 / 345 035 | 58654 / −6882 / 345 036 | 58655 / −6881 / 345 037 |
| 2- | 58656 / −6880 / 345 040 | 58657 / −6879 / 345 041 | 58658 / −6878 / 345 042 | 58659 / −6877 / 345 043 | 58660 / −6876 / 345 044 | 58661 / −6875 / 345 045 | 58662 / −6874 / 345 046 | 58663 / −6873 / 345 047 | 58664 / −6872 / 345 050 | 58665 / −6871 / 345 051 | 58666 / −6870 / 345 052 | 58667 / −6869 / 345 053 | 58668 / −6868 / 345 054 | 58669 / −6867 / 345 055 | 58670 / −6866 / 345 056 | 58671 / −6865 / 345 057 |
| 3- | 58672 / −6864 / 345 060 | 58673 / −6863 / 345 061 | 58674 / −6862 / 345 062 | 58675 / −6861 / 345 063 | 58676 / −6860 / 345 064 | 58677 / −6859 / 345 065 | 58678 / −6858 / 345 066 | 58679 / −6857 / 345 067 | 58680 / −6856 / 345 070 | 58681 / −6855 / 345 071 | 58682 / −6854 / 345 072 | 58683 / −6853 / 345 073 | 58684 / −6852 / 345 074 | 58685 / −6851 / 345 075 | 58686 / −6850 / 345 076 | 58687 / −6849 / 345 077 |
| 4- | 58688 / −6848 / 345 100 | 58689 / −6847 / 345 101 | 58690 / −6846 / 345 102 | 58691 / −6845 / 345 103 | 58692 / −6844 / 345 104 | 58693 / −6843 / 345 105 | 58694 / −6842 / 345 106 | 58695 / −6841 / 345 107 | 58696 / −6840 / 345 110 | 58697 / −6839 / 345 111 | 58698 / −6838 / 345 112 | 58699 / −6837 / 345 113 | 58700 / −6836 / 345 114 | 58701 / −6835 / 345 115 | 58702 / −6834 / 345 116 | 58703 / −6833 / 345 117 |
| 5- | 58704 / −6832 / 345 120 | 58705 / −6831 / 345 121 | 58706 / −6830 / 345 122 | 58707 / −6829 / 345 123 | 58708 / −6828 / 345 124 | 58709 / −6827 / 345 125 | 58710 / −6826 / 345 126 | 58711 / −6825 / 345 127 | 58712 / −6824 / 345 130 | 58713 / −6823 / 345 131 | 58714 / −6822 / 345 132 | 58715 / −6821 / 345 133 | 58716 / −6820 / 345 134 | 58717 / −6819 / 345 135 | 58718 / −6818 / 345 136 | 58719 / −6817 / 345 137 |
| 6- | 58720 / −6816 / 345 140 | 58721 / −6815 / 345 141 | 58722 / −6814 / 345 142 | 58723 / −6813 / 345 143 | 58724 / −6812 / 345 144 | 58725 / −6811 / 345 145 | 58726 / −6810 / 345 146 | 58727 / −6809 / 345 147 | 58728 / −6808 / 345 150 | 58729 / −6807 / 345 151 | 58730 / −6806 / 345 152 | 58731 / −6805 / 345 153 | 58732 / −6804 / 345 154 | 58733 / −6803 / 345 155 | 58734 / −6802 / 345 156 | 58735 / −6801 / 345 157 |
| 7- | 58736 / −6800 / 345 160 | 58737 / −6799 / 345 161 | 58738 / −6798 / 345 162 | 58739 / −6797 / 345 163 | 58740 / −6796 / 345 164 | 58741 / −6795 / 345 165 | 58742 / −6794 / 345 166 | 58743 / −6793 / 345 167 | 58744 / −6792 / 345 170 | 58745 / −6791 / 345 171 | 58746 / −6790 / 345 172 | 58747 / −6789 / 345 173 | 58748 / −6788 / 345 174 | 58749 / −6787 / 345 175 | 58750 / −6786 / 345 176 | 58751 / −6785 / 345 177 |
| 8- | 58752 / −6784 / 345 200 | 58753 / −6783 / 345 201 | 58754 / −6782 / 345 202 | 58755 / −6781 / 345 203 | 58756 / −6780 / 345 204 | 58757 / −6779 / 345 205 | 58758 / −6778 / 345 206 | 58759 / −6777 / 345 207 | 58760 / −6776 / 345 210 | 58761 / −6775 / 345 211 | 58762 / −6774 / 345 212 | 58763 / −6773 / 345 213 | 58764 / −6772 / 345 214 | 58765 / −6771 / 345 215 | 58766 / −6770 / 345 216 | 58767 / −6769 / 345 217 |
| 9- | 58768 / −6768 / 345 220 | 58769 / −6767 / 345 221 | 58770 / −6766 / 345 222 | 58771 / −6765 / 345 223 | 58772 / −6764 / 345 224 | 58773 / −6763 / 345 225 | 58774 / −6762 / 345 226 | 58775 / −6761 / 345 227 | 58776 / −6760 / 345 230 | 58777 / −6759 / 345 231 | 58778 / −6758 / 345 232 | 58779 / −6757 / 345 233 | 58780 / −6756 / 345 234 | 58781 / −6755 / 345 235 | 58782 / −6754 / 345 236 | 58783 / −6753 / 345 237 |
| A- | 58784 / −6752 / 345 240 | 58785 / −6751 / 345 241 | 58786 / −6750 / 345 242 | 58787 / −6749 / 345 243 | 58788 / −6748 / 345 244 | 58789 / −6747 / 345 245 | 58790 / −6746 / 345 246 | 58791 / −6745 / 345 247 | 58792 / −6744 / 345 250 | 58793 / −6743 / 345 251 | 58794 / −6742 / 345 252 | 58795 / −6741 / 345 253 | 58796 / −6740 / 345 254 | 58797 / −6739 / 345 255 | 58798 / −6738 / 345 256 | 58799 / −6737 / 345 257 |
| B- | 58800 / −6736 / 345 260 | 58801 / −6735 / 345 261 | 58802 / −6734 / 345 262 | 58803 / −6733 / 345 263 | 58804 / −6732 / 345 264 | 58805 / −6731 / 345 265 | 58806 / −6730 / 345 266 | 58807 / −6729 / 345 267 | 58808 / −6728 / 345 270 | 58809 / −6727 / 345 271 | 58810 / −6726 / 345 272 | 58811 / −6725 / 345 273 | 58812 / −6724 / 345 274 | 58813 / −6723 / 345 275 | 58814 / −6722 / 345 276 | 58815 / −6721 / 345 277 |
| C- | 58816 / −6720 / 345 300 | 58817 / −6719 / 345 301 | 58818 / −6718 / 345 302 | 58819 / −6717 / 345 303 | 58820 / −6716 / 345 304 | 58821 / −6715 / 345 305 | 58822 / −6714 / 345 306 | 58823 / −6713 / 345 307 | 58824 / −6712 / 345 310 | 58825 / −6711 / 345 311 | 58826 / −6710 / 345 312 | 58827 / −6709 / 345 313 | 58828 / −6708 / 345 314 | 58829 / −6707 / 345 315 | 58830 / −6706 / 345 316 | 58831 / −6705 / 345 317 |
| D- | 58832 / −6704 / 345 320 | 58833 / −6703 / 345 321 | 58834 / −6702 / 345 322 | 58835 / −6701 / 345 323 | 58836 / −6700 / 345 324 | 58837 / −6699 / 345 325 | 58838 / −6698 / 345 326 | 58839 / −6697 / 345 327 | 58840 / −6696 / 345 330 | 58841 / −6695 / 345 331 | 58842 / −6694 / 345 332 | 58843 / −6693 / 345 333 | 58844 / −6692 / 345 334 | 58845 / −6691 / 345 335 | 58846 / −6690 / 345 336 | 58847 / −6689 / 345 337 |
| E- | 58848 / −6688 / 345 340 | 58849 / −6687 / 345 341 | 58850 / −6686 / 345 342 | 58851 / −6685 / 345 343 | 58852 / −6684 / 345 344 | 58853 / −6683 / 345 345 | 58854 / −6682 / 345 346 | 58855 / −6681 / 345 347 | 58856 / −6680 / 345 350 | 58857 / −6679 / 345 351 | 58858 / −6678 / 345 352 | 58859 / −6677 / 345 353 | 58860 / −6676 / 345 354 | 58861 / −6675 / 345 355 | 58862 / −6674 / 345 356 | 58863 / −6673 / 345 357 |
| F- | 58864 / −6672 / 345 360 | 58865 / −6671 / 345 361 | 58866 / −6670 / 345 362 | 58867 / −6669 / 345 363 | 58868 / −6668 / 345 364 | 58869 / −6667 / 345 365 | 58870 / −6666 / 345 366 | 58871 / −6665 / 345 367 | 58872 / −6664 / 345 370 | 58873 / −6663 / 345 371 | 58874 / −6662 / 345 372 | 58875 / −6661 / 345 373 | 58876 / −6660 / 345 374 | 58877 / −6659 / 345 375 | 58878 / −6658 / 345 376 | 58879 / −6657 / 345 377 |

SECOND HEX DIGIT (rows) · FIRST HEX DIGIT (columns)

# FIRST HEX DIGIT

| (2) | −0 | −1 | −2 | −3 | −4 | −5 | −6 | −7 | −8 | −9 | −A | −B | −C | −D | −E | −F |
|---|---|---|---|---|---|---|---|---|---|---|---|---|---|---|---|---|
| **0−** | 58880<br>−6656<br>346 000 | 58881<br>−6655<br>346 001 | 58882<br>−6654<br>346 002 | 58883<br>−6653<br>346 003 | 58884<br>−6652<br>346 004 | 58885<br>−6651<br>346 005 | 58886<br>−6650<br>346 006 | 58887<br>−6649<br>346 007 | 58888<br>−6648<br>346 010 | 58889<br>−6647<br>346 011 | 58890<br>−6646<br>346 012 | 58891<br>−6645<br>346 013 | 58892<br>−6644<br>346 014 | 58893<br>−6643<br>346 015 | 58894<br>−6642<br>346 016 | 58895<br>−6641<br>346 017 |
| **1−** | 58896<br>−6640<br>346 020 | 58897<br>−6639<br>346 021 | 58898<br>−6638<br>346 022 | 58899<br>−6637<br>346 023 | 58900<br>−6636<br>346 024 | 58901<br>−6635<br>346 025 | 58902<br>−6634<br>346 026 | 58903<br>−6633<br>346 027 | 58904<br>−6632<br>346 030 | 58905<br>−6631<br>346 031 | 58906<br>−6630<br>346 032 | 58907<br>−6629<br>346 033 | 58908<br>−6628<br>346 034 | 58909<br>−6627<br>346 035 | 58910<br>−6626<br>346 036 | 58911<br>−6625<br>346 037 |
| **2−** | 58912<br>−6624<br>346 040 | 58913<br>−6623<br>346 041 | 58914<br>−6622<br>346 042 | 58915<br>−6621<br>346 043 | 58916<br>−6620<br>346 044 | 58917<br>−6619<br>346 045 | 58918<br>−6618<br>346 046 | 58919<br>−6617<br>346 047 | 58920<br>−6616<br>346 050 | 58921<br>−6615<br>346 051 | 58922<br>−6614<br>346 052 | 58923<br>−6613<br>346 053 | 58924<br>−6612<br>346 054 | 58925<br>−6611<br>346 055 | 58926<br>−6610<br>346 056 | 58927<br>−6609<br>346 057 |
| **3−** | 58928<br>−6608<br>346 060 | 58929<br>−6607<br>346 061 | 58930<br>−6606<br>346 062 | 58931<br>−6605<br>346 063 | 58932<br>−6604<br>346 064 | 58933<br>−6603<br>346 065 | 58934<br>−6602<br>346 066 | 58935<br>−6601<br>346 067 | 58936<br>−6600<br>346 070 | 58937<br>−6599<br>346 071 | 58938<br>−6598<br>346 072 | 58939<br>−6597<br>346 073 | 58940<br>−6596<br>346 074 | 58941<br>−6595<br>346 075 | 58942<br>−6594<br>346 076 | 58943<br>−6593<br>346 077 |
| **4−** | 58944<br>−6592<br>346 100 | 58945<br>−6591<br>346 101 | 58946<br>−6590<br>346 102 | 58947<br>−6589<br>346 103 | 58948<br>−6588<br>346 104 | 58949<br>−6587<br>346 105 | 58950<br>−6586<br>346 106 | 58951<br>−6585<br>346 107 | 58952<br>−6584<br>346 110 | 58953<br>−6583<br>346 111 | 58954<br>−6582<br>346 112 | 58955<br>−6581<br>346 113 | 58956<br>−6580<br>346 114 | 58957<br>−6579<br>346 115 | 58958<br>−6578<br>346 116 | 58959<br>−6577<br>346 117 |
| **5−** | 58960<br>−6576<br>346 120 | 58961<br>−6575<br>346 121 | 58962<br>−6574<br>346 122 | 58963<br>−6573<br>346 123 | 58964<br>−6572<br>346 124 | 58965<br>−6571<br>346 125 | 58966<br>−6570<br>346 126 | 58967<br>−6569<br>346 127 | 58968<br>−6568<br>346 130 | 58969<br>−6567<br>346 131 | 58970<br>−6566<br>346 132 | 58971<br>−6565<br>346 133 | 58972<br>−6564<br>346 134 | 58973<br>−6563<br>346 135 | 58974<br>−6562<br>346 136 | 58975<br>−6561<br>346 137 |
| **6−** | 58976<br>−6560<br>346 140 | 58977<br>−6559<br>346 141 | 58978<br>−6558<br>346 142 | 58979<br>−6557<br>346 143 | 58980<br>−6556<br>346 144 | 58981<br>−6555<br>346 145 | 58982<br>−6554<br>346 146 | 58983<br>−6553<br>346 147 | 58984<br>−6552<br>346 150 | 58985<br>−6551<br>346 151 | 58986<br>−6550<br>346 152 | 58987<br>−6549<br>346 153 | 58988<br>−6548<br>346 154 | 58989<br>−6547<br>346 155 | 58990<br>−6546<br>346 156 | 58991<br>−6545<br>346 157 |
| **7−** | 58992<br>−6544<br>346 160 | 58993<br>−6543<br>346 161 | 58994<br>−6542<br>346 162 | 58995<br>−6541<br>346 163 | 58996<br>−6540<br>346 164 | 58997<br>−6539<br>346 165 | 58998<br>−6538<br>346 166 | 58999<br>−6537<br>346 167 | 59000<br>−6536<br>346 170 | 59001<br>−6535<br>346 171 | 59002<br>−6534<br>346 172 | 59003<br>−6533<br>346 173 | 59004<br>−6532<br>346 174 | 59005<br>−6531<br>346 175 | 59006<br>−6530<br>346 176 | 59007<br>−6529<br>346 177 |
| **8−** | 59008<br>−6528<br>346 200 | 59009<br>−6527<br>346 201 | 59010<br>−6526<br>346 202 | 59011<br>−6525<br>346 203 | 59012<br>−6524<br>346 204 | 59013<br>−6523<br>346 205 | 59014<br>−6522<br>346 206 | 59015<br>−6521<br>346 207 | 59016<br>−6520<br>346 210 | 59017<br>−6519<br>346 211 | 59018<br>−6518<br>346 212 | 59019<br>−6517<br>346 213 | 59020<br>−6516<br>346 214 | 59021<br>−6515<br>346 215 | 59022<br>−6514<br>346 216 | 59023<br>−6513<br>346 217 |
| **9−** | 59024<br>−6512<br>346 220 | 59025<br>−6511<br>346 221 | 59026<br>−6510<br>346 222 | 59027<br>−6509<br>346 223 | 59028<br>−6508<br>346 224 | 59029<br>−6507<br>346 225 | 59030<br>−6506<br>346 226 | 59031<br>−6505<br>346 227 | 59032<br>−6504<br>346 230 | 59033<br>−6503<br>346 231 | 59034<br>−6502<br>346 232 | 59035<br>−6501<br>346 233 | 59036<br>−6500<br>346 234 | 59037<br>−6499<br>346 235 | 59038<br>−6498<br>346 236 | 59039<br>−6497<br>346 237 |
| **A−** | 59040<br>−6496<br>346 240 | 59041<br>−6495<br>346 241 | 59042<br>−6494<br>346 242 | 59043<br>−6493<br>346 243 | 59044<br>−6492<br>346 244 | 59045<br>−6491<br>346 245 | 59046<br>−6490<br>346 246 | 59047<br>−6489<br>346 247 | 59048<br>−6488<br>346 250 | 59049<br>−6487<br>346 251 | 59050<br>−6486<br>346 252 | 59051<br>−6485<br>346 253 | 59052<br>−6484<br>346 254 | 59053<br>−6483<br>346 255 | 59054<br>−6482<br>346 256 | 59055<br>−6481<br>346 257 |
| **B−** | 59056<br>−6480<br>346 260 | 59057<br>−6479<br>346 261 | 59058<br>−6478<br>346 262 | 59059<br>−6477<br>346 263 | 59060<br>−6476<br>346 264 | 59061<br>−6475<br>346 265 | 59062<br>−6474<br>346 266 | 59063<br>−6473<br>346 267 | 59064<br>−6472<br>346 270 | 59065<br>−6471<br>346 271 | 59066<br>−6470<br>346 272 | 59067<br>−6469<br>346 273 | 59068<br>−6468<br>346 274 | 59069<br>−6467<br>346 275 | 59070<br>−6466<br>346 276 | 59071<br>−6465<br>346 277 |
| **C−** | 59072<br>−6464<br>346 300 | 59073<br>−6463<br>346 301 | 59074<br>−6462<br>346 302 | 59075<br>−6461<br>346 303 | 59076<br>−6460<br>346 304 | 59077<br>−6459<br>346 305 | 59078<br>−6458<br>346 306 | 59079<br>−6457<br>346 307 | 59080<br>−6456<br>346 310 | 59081<br>−6455<br>346 311 | 59082<br>−6454<br>346 312 | 59083<br>−6453<br>346 313 | 59084<br>−6452<br>346 314 | 59085<br>−6451<br>346 315 | 59086<br>−6450<br>346 316 | 59087<br>−6449<br>346 317 |
| **D−** | 59088<br>−6448<br>346 320 | 59089<br>−6447<br>346 321 | 59090<br>−6446<br>346 322 | 59091<br>−6445<br>346 323 | 59092<br>−6444<br>346 324 | 59093<br>−6443<br>346 325 | 59094<br>−6442<br>346 326 | 59095<br>−6441<br>346 327 | 59096<br>−6440<br>346 330 | 59097<br>−6439<br>346 331 | 59098<br>−6438<br>346 332 | 59099<br>−6437<br>346 333 | 59100<br>−6436<br>346 334 | 59101<br>−6435<br>346 335 | 59102<br>−6434<br>346 336 | 59103<br>−6433<br>346 337 |
| **E−** | 59104<br>−6432<br>346 340 | 59105<br>−6431<br>346 341 | 59106<br>−6430<br>346 342 | 59107<br>−6429<br>346 343 | 59108<br>−6428<br>346 344 | 59109<br>−6427<br>346 345 | 59110<br>−6426<br>346 346 | 59111<br>−6425<br>346 347 | 59112<br>−6424<br>346 350 | 59113<br>−6423<br>346 351 | 59114<br>−6422<br>346 352 | 59115<br>−6421<br>346 353 | 59116<br>−6420<br>346 354 | 59117<br>−6419<br>346 355 | 59118<br>−6418<br>346 356 | 59119<br>−6417<br>346 357 |
| **F−** | 59120<br>−6416<br>346 360 | 59121<br>−6415<br>346 361 | 59122<br>−6414<br>346 362 | 59123<br>−6413<br>346 363 | 59124<br>−6412<br>346 364 | 59125<br>−6411<br>346 365 | 59126<br>−6410<br>346 366 | 59127<br>−6409<br>346 367 | 59128<br>−6408<br>346 370 | 59129<br>−6407<br>346 371 | 59130<br>−6406<br>346 372 | 59131<br>−6405<br>346 373 | 59132<br>−6404<br>346 374 | 59133<br>−6403<br>346 375 | 59134<br>−6402<br>346 376 | 59135<br>−6401<br>346 377 |

**SECOND HEX DIGIT** (row labels) · DECIMAL · ⌘ DECIMAL · OCTAL (right-margin arrow labels)

⌘ DECIMAL [−6656]  BINARY [1110 0110]  DECIMAL [58880]  HEXADECIMAL 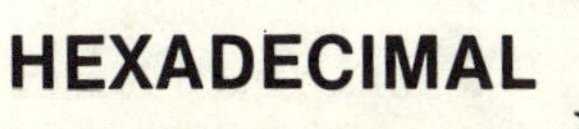 OCTAL [346 000]

FOURTH HEX DIGIT → ⬡ E6 ← THIRD HEX DIGIT

| ⬡2 | | FIRST HEX DIGIT | | | | | | | | | | | | | | |
|---|---|---|---|---|---|---|---|---|---|---|---|---|---|---|---|---|
| | | −0 | −1 | −2 | −3 | −4 | −5 | −6 | −7 | −8 | −9 | −A | −B | −C | −D | −E | −F |
| 0− | 59136<br>−6400<br>347 000 | 59137<br>−6399<br>347 001 | 59138<br>−6398<br>347 002 | 59139<br>−6397<br>347 003 | 59140<br>−6396<br>347 004 | 59141<br>−6395<br>347 005 | 59142<br>−6394<br>347 006 | 59143<br>−6393<br>347 007 | 59144<br>−6392<br>347 010 | 59145<br>−6391<br>347 011 | 59146<br>−6390<br>347 012 | 59147<br>−6389<br>347 013 | 59148<br>−6388<br>347 014 | 59149<br>−6387<br>347 015 | 59150<br>−6386<br>347 016 | 59151<br>−6385<br>347 017 |
| 1− | 59152<br>−6384<br>347 020 | 59153<br>−6383<br>347 021 | 59154<br>−6382<br>347 022 | 59155<br>−6381<br>347 023 | 59156<br>−6380<br>347 024 | 59157<br>−6379<br>347 025 | 59158<br>−6378<br>347 026 | 59159<br>−6377<br>347 027 | 59160<br>−6376<br>347 030 | 59161<br>−6375<br>347 031 | 59162<br>−6374<br>347 032 | 59163<br>−6373<br>347 033 | 59164<br>−6372<br>347 034 | 59165<br>−6371<br>347 035 | 59166<br>−6370<br>347 036 | 59167<br>−6369<br>347 037 |
| 2− | 59168<br>−6368<br>347 040 | 59169<br>−6367<br>347 041 | 59170<br>−6366<br>347 042 | 59171<br>−6365<br>347 043 | 59172<br>−6364<br>347 044 | 59173<br>−6363<br>347 045 | 59174<br>−6362<br>347 046 | 59175<br>−6361<br>347 047 | 59176<br>−6360<br>347 050 | 59177<br>−6359<br>347 051 | 59178<br>−6358<br>347 052 | 59179<br>−6357<br>347 053 | 59180<br>−6356<br>347 054 | 59181<br>−6355<br>347 055 | 59182<br>−6354<br>347 056 | 59183<br>−6353<br>347 057 |
| 3− | 59184<br>−6352<br>347 060 | 59185<br>−6351<br>347 061 | 59186<br>−6350<br>347 062 | 59187<br>−6349<br>347 063 | 59188<br>−6348<br>347 064 | 59189<br>−6347<br>347 065 | 59190<br>−6346<br>347 066 | 59191<br>−6345<br>347 067 | 59192<br>−6344<br>347 070 | 59193<br>−6343<br>347 071 | 59194<br>−6342<br>347 072 | 59195<br>−6341<br>347 073 | 59196<br>−6340<br>347 074 | 59197<br>−6339<br>347 075 | 59198<br>−6338<br>347 076 | 59199<br>−6337<br>347 077 |
| 4− | 59200<br>−6336<br>347 100 | 59201<br>−6335<br>347 101 | 59202<br>−6334<br>347 102 | 59203<br>−6333<br>347 103 | 59204<br>−6332<br>347 104 | 59205<br>−6331<br>347 105 | 59206<br>−6330<br>347 106 | 59207<br>−6329<br>347 107 | 59208<br>−6328<br>347 110 | 59209<br>−6327<br>347 111 | 59210<br>−6326<br>347 112 | 59211<br>−6325<br>347 113 | 59212<br>−6324<br>347 114 | 59213<br>−6323<br>347 115 | 59214<br>−6322<br>347 116 | 59215<br>−6321<br>347 117 |
| 5− | 59216<br>−6320<br>347 120 | 59217<br>−6319<br>347 121 | 59218<br>−6318<br>347 122 | 59219<br>−6317<br>347 123 | 59220<br>−6316<br>347 124 | 59221<br>−6315<br>347 125 | 59222<br>−6314<br>347 126 | 59223<br>−6313<br>347 127 | 59224<br>−6312<br>347 130 | 59225<br>−6311<br>347 131 | 59226<br>−6310<br>347 132 | 59227<br>−6309<br>347 133 | 59228<br>−6308<br>347 134 | 59229<br>−6307<br>347 135 | 59230<br>−6306<br>347 136 | 59231<br>−6305<br>347 137 |
| 6− | 59232<br>−6304<br>347 140 | 59233<br>−6303<br>347 141 | 59234<br>−6302<br>347 142 | 59235<br>−6301<br>347 143 | 59236<br>−6300<br>347 144 | 59237<br>−6299<br>347 145 | 59238<br>−6298<br>347 146 | 59239<br>−6297<br>347 147 | 59240<br>−6296<br>347 150 | 59241<br>−6295<br>347 151 | 59242<br>−6294<br>347 152 | 59243<br>−6293<br>347 153 | 59244<br>−6292<br>347 154 | 59245<br>−6291<br>347 155 | 59246<br>−6290<br>347 156 | 59247<br>−6289<br>347 157 |
| 7− | 59248<br>−6288<br>347 160 | 59249<br>−6287<br>347 161 | 59250<br>−6286<br>347 162 | 59251<br>−6285<br>347 163 | 59252<br>−6284<br>347 164 | 59253<br>−6283<br>347 165 | 59254<br>−6282<br>347 166 | 59255<br>−6281<br>347 167 | 59256<br>−6280<br>347 170 | 59257<br>−6279<br>347 171 | 59258<br>−6278<br>347 172 | 59259<br>−6277<br>347 173 | 59260<br>−6276<br>347 174 | 59261<br>−6275<br>347 175 | 59262<br>−6274<br>347 176 | 59263<br>−6273<br>347 177 |
| 8− | 59264<br>−6272<br>347 200 | 59265<br>−6271<br>347 201 | 59266<br>−6270<br>347 202 | 59267<br>−6269<br>347 203 | 59268<br>−6268<br>347 204 | 59269<br>−6267<br>347 205 | 59270<br>−6266<br>347 206 | 59271<br>−6265<br>347 207 | 59272<br>−6264<br>347 210 | 59273<br>−6263<br>347 211 | 59274<br>−6262<br>347 212 | 59275<br>−6261<br>347 213 | 59276<br>−6260<br>347 214 | 59277<br>−6259<br>347 215 | 59278<br>−6258<br>347 216 | 59279<br>−6257<br>347 217 |
| 9− | 59280<br>−6256<br>347 220 | 59281<br>−6255<br>347 221 | 59282<br>−6254<br>347 222 | 59283<br>−6253<br>347 223 | 59284<br>−6252<br>347 224 | 59285<br>−6251<br>347 225 | 59286<br>−6250<br>347 226 | 59287<br>−6249<br>347 227 | 59288<br>−6248<br>347 230 | 59289<br>−6247<br>347 231 | 59290<br>−6246<br>347 232 | 59291<br>−6245<br>347 233 | 59292<br>−6244<br>347 234 | 59293<br>−6243<br>347 235 | 59294<br>−6242<br>347 236 | 59295<br>−6241<br>347 237 |
| A− | 59296<br>−6240<br>347 240 | 59297<br>−6239<br>347 241 | 59298<br>−6238<br>347 242 | 59299<br>−6237<br>347 243 | 59300<br>−6236<br>347 244 | 59301<br>−6235<br>347 245 | 59302<br>−6234<br>347 246 | 59303<br>−6233<br>347 247 | 59304<br>−6232<br>347 250 | 59305<br>−6231<br>347 251 | 59306<br>−6230<br>347 252 | 59307<br>−6229<br>347 253 | 59308<br>−6228<br>347 254 | 59309<br>−6227<br>347 255 | 59310<br>−6226<br>347 256 | 59311<br>−6225<br>347 257 |
| B− | 59312<br>−6224<br>347 260 | 59313<br>−6223<br>347 261 | 59314<br>−6222<br>347 262 | 59315<br>−6221<br>347 263 | 59316<br>−6220<br>347 264 | 59317<br>−6219<br>347 265 | 59318<br>−6218<br>347 266 | 59319<br>−6217<br>347 267 | 59320<br>−6216<br>347 270 | 59321<br>−6215<br>347 271 | 59322<br>−6214<br>347 272 | 59323<br>−6213<br>347 273 | 59324<br>−6212<br>347 274 | 59325<br>−6211<br>347 275 | 59326<br>−6210<br>347 276 | 59327<br>−6209<br>347 277 |
| C− | 59328<br>−6208<br>347 300 | 59329<br>−6207<br>347 301 | 59330<br>−6206<br>347 302 | 59331<br>−6205<br>347 303 | 59332<br>−6204<br>347 304 | 59333<br>−6203<br>347 305 | 59334<br>−6202<br>347 306 | 59335<br>−6201<br>347 307 | 59336<br>−6200<br>347 310 | 59337<br>−6199<br>347 311 | 59338<br>−6198<br>347 312 | 59339<br>−6197<br>347 313 | 59340<br>−6196<br>347 314 | 59341<br>−6195<br>347 315 | 59342<br>−6194<br>347 316 | 59343<br>−6193<br>347 317 |
| D− | 59344<br>−6192<br>347 320 | 59345<br>−6191<br>347 321 | 59346<br>−6190<br>347 322 | 59347<br>−6189<br>347 323 | 59348<br>−6188<br>347 324 | 59349<br>−6187<br>347 325 | 59350<br>−6186<br>347 326 | 59351<br>−6185<br>347 327 | 59352<br>−6184<br>347 330 | 59353<br>−6183<br>347 331 | 59354<br>−6182<br>347 332 | 59355<br>−6181<br>347 333 | 59356<br>−6180<br>347 334 | 59357<br>−6179<br>347 335 | 59358<br>−6178<br>347 336 | 59359<br>−6177<br>347 337 |
| E− | 59360<br>−6176<br>347 340 | 59361<br>−6175<br>347 341 | 59362<br>−6174<br>347 342 | 59363<br>−6173<br>347 343 | 59364<br>−6172<br>347 344 | 59365<br>−6171<br>347 345 | 59366<br>−6170<br>347 346 | 59367<br>−6169<br>347 347 | 59368<br>−6168<br>347 350 | 59369<br>−6167<br>347 351 | 59370<br>−6166<br>347 352 | 59371<br>−6165<br>347 353 | 59372<br>−6164<br>347 354 | 59373<br>−6163<br>347 355 | 59374<br>−6162<br>347 356 | 59375<br>−6161<br>347 357 |
| F− | 59376<br>−6160<br>347 360 | 59377<br>−6159<br>347 361 | 59378<br>−6158<br>347 362 | 59379<br>−6157<br>347 363 | 59380<br>−6156<br>347 364 | 59381<br>−6155<br>347 365 | 59382<br>−6154<br>347 366 | 59383<br>−6153<br>347 367 | 59384<br>−6152<br>347 370 | 59385<br>−6151<br>347 371 | 59386<br>−6150<br>347 372 | 59387<br>−6149<br>347 373 | 59388<br>−6148<br>347 374 | 59389<br>−6147<br>347 375 | 59390<br>−6146<br>347 376 | 59391<br>−6145<br>347 377 |

SECOND HEX DIGIT

DECIMAL
 DECIMAL
OCTAL

## ⬡2 FIRST HEX DIGIT

SECOND HEX DIGIT

| | –0 | –1 | –2 | –3 | –4 | –5 | –6 | –7 | –8 | –9 | –A | –B | –C | –D | –E | –F |
|---|---|---|---|---|---|---|---|---|---|---|---|---|---|---|---|---|
| 0– | 59392<br>-6144<br>350 000 | 59393<br>-6143<br>350 001 | 59394<br>-6142<br>350 002 | 59395<br>-6141<br>350 003 | 59396<br>-6140<br>350 004 | 59397<br>-6139<br>350 005 | 59398<br>-6138<br>350 006 | 59399<br>-6137<br>350 007 | 59400<br>-6136<br>350 010 | 59401<br>-6135<br>350 011 | 59402<br>-6134<br>350 012 | 59403<br>-6133<br>350 013 | 59404<br>-6132<br>350 014 | 59405<br>-6131<br>350 015 | 59406<br>-6130<br>350 016 | 59407<br>-6129<br>350 017 |
| 1– | 59408<br>-6128<br>350 020 | 59409<br>-6127<br>350 021 | 59410<br>-6126<br>350 022 | 59411<br>-6125<br>350 023 | 59412<br>-6124<br>350 024 | 59413<br>-6123<br>350 025 | 59414<br>-6122<br>350 026 | 59415<br>-6121<br>350 027 | 59416<br>-6120<br>350 030 | 59417<br>-6119<br>350 031 | 59418<br>-6118<br>350 032 | 59419<br>-6117<br>350 033 | 59420<br>-6116<br>350 034 | 59421<br>-6115<br>350 035 | 59422<br>-6114<br>350 036 | 59423<br>-6113<br>350 037 |
| 2– | 59424<br>-6112<br>350 040 | 59425<br>-6111<br>350 041 | 59426<br>-6110<br>350 042 | 59427<br>-6109<br>350 043 | 59428<br>-6108<br>350 044 | 59429<br>-6107<br>350 045 | 59430<br>-6106<br>350 046 | 59431<br>-6105<br>350 047 | 59432<br>-6104<br>350 050 | 59433<br>-6103<br>350 051 | 59434<br>-6102<br>350 052 | 59435<br>-6101<br>350 053 | 59436<br>-6100<br>350 054 | 59437<br>-6099<br>350 055 | 59438<br>-6098<br>350 056 | 59439<br>-6097<br>350 057 |
| 3– | 59440<br>-6096<br>350 060 | 59441<br>-6095<br>350 061 | 59442<br>-6094<br>350 062 | 59443<br>-6093<br>350 063 | 59444<br>-6092<br>350 064 | 59445<br>-6091<br>350 065 | 59446<br>-6090<br>350 066 | 59447<br>-6089<br>350 067 | 59448<br>-6088<br>350 070 | 59449<br>-6087<br>350 071 | 59450<br>-6086<br>350 072 | 59451<br>-6085<br>350 073 | 59452<br>-6084<br>350 074 | 59453<br>-6083<br>350 075 | 59454<br>-6082<br>350 076 | 59455<br>-6081<br>350 077 |
| 4– | 59456<br>-6080<br>350 100 | 59457<br>-6079<br>350 101 | 59458<br>-6078<br>350 102 | 59459<br>-6077<br>350 103 | 59460<br>-6076<br>350 104 | 59461<br>-6075<br>350 105 | 59462<br>-6074<br>350 106 | 59463<br>-6073<br>350 107 | 59464<br>-6072<br>350 110 | 59465<br>-6071<br>350 111 | 59466<br>-6070<br>350 112 | 59467<br>-6069<br>350 113 | 59468<br>-6068<br>350 114 | 59469<br>-6067<br>350 115 | 59470<br>-6066<br>350 116 | 59471<br>-6065<br>350 117 |
| 5– | 59472<br>-6064<br>350 120 | 59473<br>-6063<br>350 121 | 59474<br>-6062<br>350 122 | 59475<br>-6061<br>350 123 | 59476<br>-6060<br>350 124 | 59477<br>-6059<br>350 125 | 59478<br>-6058<br>350 126 | 59479<br>-6057<br>350 127 | 59480<br>-6056<br>350 130 | 59481<br>-6055<br>350 131 | 59482<br>-6054<br>350 132 | 59483<br>-6053<br>350 133 | 59484<br>-6052<br>350 134 | 59485<br>-6051<br>350 135 | 59486<br>-6050<br>350 136 | 59487<br>-6049<br>350 137 |
| 6– | 59488<br>-6048<br>350 140 | 59489<br>-6047<br>350 141 | 59490<br>-6046<br>350 142 | 59491<br>-6045<br>350 143 | 59492<br>-6044<br>350 144 | 59493<br>-6043<br>350 145 | 59494<br>-6042<br>350 146 | 59495<br>-6041<br>350 147 | 59496<br>-6040<br>350 150 | 59497<br>-6039<br>350 151 | 59498<br>-6038<br>350 152 | 59499<br>-6037<br>350 153 | 59500<br>-6036<br>350 154 | 59501<br>-6035<br>350 155 | 59502<br>-6034<br>350 156 | 59503<br>-6033<br>350 157 |
| 7– | 59504<br>-6032<br>350 160 | 59505<br>-6031<br>350 161 | 59506<br>-6030<br>350 162 | 59507<br>-6029<br>350 163 | 59508<br>-6028<br>350 164 | 59509<br>-6027<br>350 165 | 59510<br>-6026<br>350 166 | 59511<br>-6025<br>350 167 | 59512<br>-6024<br>350 170 | 59513<br>-6023<br>350 171 | 59514<br>-6022<br>350 172 | 59515<br>-6021<br>350 173 | 59516<br>-6020<br>350 174 | 59517<br>-6019<br>350 175 | 59518<br>-6018<br>350 176 | 59519<br>-6017<br>350 177 |
| 8– | 59520<br>-6016<br>350 200 | 59521<br>-6015<br>350 201 | 59522<br>-6014<br>350 202 | 59523<br>-6013<br>350 203 | 59524<br>-6012<br>350 204 | 59525<br>-6011<br>350 205 | 59526<br>-6010<br>350 206 | 59527<br>-6009<br>350 207 | 59528<br>-6008<br>350 210 | 59529<br>-6007<br>350 211 | 59530<br>-6006<br>350 212 | 59531<br>-6005<br>350 213 | 59532<br>-6004<br>350 214 | 59533<br>-6003<br>350 215 | 59534<br>-6002<br>350 216 | 59535<br>-6001<br>350 217 |
| 9– | 59536<br>-6000<br>350 220 | 59537<br>-5999<br>350 221 | 59538<br>-5998<br>350 222 | 59539<br>-5997<br>350 223 | 59540<br>-5996<br>350 224 | 59541<br>-5995<br>350 225 | 59542<br>-5994<br>350 226 | 59543<br>-5993<br>350 227 | 59544<br>-5992<br>350 230 | 59545<br>-5991<br>350 231 | 59546<br>-5990<br>350 232 | 59547<br>-5989<br>350 233 | 59548<br>-5988<br>350 234 | 59549<br>-5987<br>350 235 | 59550<br>-5986<br>350 236 | 59551<br>-5985<br>350 237 |
| A– | 59552<br>-5984<br>350 240 | 59553<br>-5983<br>350 241 | 59554<br>-5982<br>350 242 | 59555<br>-5981<br>350 243 | 59556<br>-5980<br>350 244 | 59557<br>-5979<br>350 245 | 59558<br>-5978<br>350 246 | 59559<br>-5977<br>350 247 | 59560<br>-5976<br>350 250 | 59561<br>-5975<br>350 251 | 59562<br>-5974<br>350 252 | 59563<br>-5973<br>350 253 | 59564<br>-5972<br>350 254 | 59565<br>-5971<br>350 255 | 59566<br>-5970<br>350 256 | 59567<br>-5969<br>350 257 |
| B– | 59568<br>-5968<br>350 260 | 59569<br>-5967<br>350 261 | 59570<br>-5966<br>350 262 | 59571<br>-5965<br>350 263 | 59572<br>-5964<br>350 264 | 59573<br>-5963<br>350 265 | 59574<br>-5962<br>350 266 | 59575<br>-5961<br>350 267 | 59576<br>-5960<br>350 270 | 59577<br>-5959<br>350 271 | 59578<br>-5958<br>350 272 | 59579<br>-5957<br>350 273 | 59580<br>-5956<br>350 274 | 59581<br>-5955<br>350 275 | 59582<br>-5954<br>350 276 | 59583<br>-5953<br>350 277 |
| C– | 59584<br>-5952<br>350 300 | 59585<br>-5951<br>350 301 | 59586<br>-5950<br>350 302 | 59587<br>-5949<br>350 303 | 59588<br>-5948<br>350 304 | 59589<br>-5947<br>350 305 | 59590<br>-5946<br>350 306 | 59591<br>-5945<br>350 307 | 59592<br>-5944<br>350 310 | 59593<br>-5943<br>350 311 | 59594<br>-5942<br>350 312 | 59595<br>-5941<br>350 313 | 59596<br>-5940<br>350 314 | 59597<br>-5939<br>350 315 | 59598<br>-5938<br>350 316 | 59599<br>-5937<br>350 317 |
| D– | 59600<br>-5936<br>350 320 | 59601<br>-5935<br>350 321 | 59602<br>-5934<br>350 322 | 59603<br>-5933<br>350 323 | 59604<br>-5932<br>350 324 | 59605<br>-5931<br>350 325 | 59606<br>-5930<br>350 326 | 59607<br>-5929<br>350 327 | 59608<br>-5928<br>350 330 | 59609<br>-5927<br>350 331 | 59610<br>-5926<br>350 332 | 59611<br>-5925<br>350 333 | 59612<br>-5924<br>350 334 | 59613<br>-5923<br>350 335 | 59614<br>-5922<br>350 336 | 59615<br>-5921<br>350 337 |
| E– | 59616<br>-5920<br>350 340 | 59617<br>-5919<br>350 341 | 59618<br>-5918<br>350 342 | 59619<br>-5917<br>350 343 | 59620<br>-5916<br>350 344 | 59621<br>-5915<br>350 345 | 59622<br>-5914<br>350 346 | 59623<br>-5913<br>350 347 | 59624<br>-5912<br>350 350 | 59625<br>-5911<br>350 351 | 59626<br>-5910<br>350 352 | 59627<br>-5909<br>350 353 | 59628<br>-5908<br>350 354 | 59629<br>-5907<br>350 355 | 59630<br>-5906<br>350 356 | 59631<br>-5905<br>350 357 |
| F– | 59632<br>-5904<br>350 360 | 59633<br>-5903<br>350 361 | 59634<br>-5902<br>350 362 | 59635<br>-5901<br>350 363 | 59636<br>-5900<br>350 364 | 59637<br>-5899<br>350 365 | 59638<br>-5898<br>350 366 | 59639<br>-5897<br>350 367 | 59640<br>-5896<br>350 370 | 59641<br>-5895<br>350 371 | 59642<br>-5894<br>350 372 | 59643<br>-5893<br>350 373 | 59644<br>-5892<br>350 374 | 59645<br>-5891<br>350 375 | 59646<br>-5890<br>350 376 | 59647<br>-5889<br>350 377 |

DECIMAL

 DECIMAL

OCTAL

 DECIMAL –6144 BINARY 1110 1000 DECIMAL 59392 HEXADECIMAL E8 OCTAL 350 000

FOURTH HEX DIGIT THIRD HEX DIGIT

DECIMAL −5888    BINARY 1110 1001    DECIMAL 59648    HEXADECIMAL E9    OCTAL 351 000

FOURTH HEX DIGIT → E9 ← THIRD HEX DIGIT

**FIRST HEX DIGIT**

| ② | −0 | −1 | −2 | −3 | −4 | −5 | −6 | −7 | −8 | −9 | −A | −B | −C | −D | −E | −F |
|---|---|---|---|---|---|---|---|---|---|---|---|---|---|---|---|---|
| 0− | 59648<br>−5888<br>351 000 | 59649<br>−5887<br>351 001 | 59650<br>−5886<br>351 002 | 59651<br>−5885<br>351 003 | 59652<br>−5884<br>351 004 | 59653<br>−5883<br>351 005 | 59654<br>−5882<br>351 006 | 59655<br>−5881<br>351 007 | 59656<br>−5880<br>351 010 | 59657<br>−5879<br>351 011 | 59658<br>−5878<br>351 012 | 59659<br>−5877<br>351 013 | 59660<br>−5876<br>351 014 | 59661<br>−5875<br>351 015 | 59662<br>−5874<br>351 016 | 59663<br>−5873<br>351 017 |
| 1− | 59664<br>−5872<br>351 020 | 59665<br>−5871<br>351 021 | 59666<br>−5870<br>351 022 | 59667<br>−5869<br>351 023 | 59668<br>−5868<br>351 024 | 59669<br>−5867<br>351 025 | 59670<br>−5866<br>351 026 | 59671<br>−5865<br>351 027 | 59672<br>−5864<br>351 030 | 59673<br>−5863<br>351 031 | 59674<br>−5862<br>351 032 | 59675<br>−5861<br>351 033 | 59676<br>−5860<br>351 034 | 59677<br>−5859<br>351 035 | 59678<br>−5858<br>351 036 | 59679<br>−5857<br>351 037 |
| 2− | 59680<br>−5856<br>351 040 | 59681<br>−5855<br>351 041 | 59682<br>−5854<br>351 042 | 59683<br>−5853<br>351 043 | 59684<br>−5852<br>351 044 | 59685<br>−5851<br>351 045 | 59686<br>−5850<br>351 046 | 59687<br>−5849<br>351 047 | 59688<br>−5848<br>351 050 | 59689<br>−5847<br>351 051 | 59690<br>−5846<br>351 052 | 59691<br>−5845<br>351 053 | 59692<br>−5844<br>351 054 | 59693<br>−5843<br>351 055 | 59694<br>−5842<br>351 056 | 59695<br>−5841<br>351 057 |
| 3− | 59696<br>−5840<br>351 060 | 59697<br>−5839<br>351 061 | 59698<br>−5838<br>351 062 | 59699<br>−5837<br>351 063 | 59700<br>−5836<br>351 064 | 59701<br>−5835<br>351 065 | 59702<br>−5834<br>351 066 | 59703<br>−5833<br>351 067 | 59704<br>−5832<br>351 070 | 59705<br>−5831<br>351 071 | 59706<br>−5830<br>351 072 | 59707<br>−5829<br>351 073 | 59708<br>−5828<br>351 074 | 59709<br>−5827<br>351 075 | 59710<br>−5826<br>351 076 | 59711<br>−5825<br>351 077 |
| 4− | 59712<br>−5824<br>351 100 | 59713<br>−5823<br>351 101 | 59714<br>−5822<br>351 102 | 59715<br>−5821<br>351 103 | 59716<br>−5820<br>351 104 | 59717<br>−5819<br>351 105 | 59718<br>−5818<br>351 106 | 59719<br>−5817<br>351 107 | 59720<br>−5816<br>351 110 | 59721<br>−5815<br>351 111 | 59722<br>−5814<br>351 112 | 59723<br>−5813<br>351 113 | 59724<br>−5812<br>351 114 | 59725<br>−5811<br>351 115 | 59726<br>−5810<br>351 116 | 59727<br>−5809<br>351 117 |
| 5− | 59728<br>−5808<br>351 120 | 59729<br>−5807<br>351 121 | 59730<br>−5806<br>351 122 | 59731<br>−5805<br>351 123 | 59732<br>−5804<br>351 124 | 59733<br>−5803<br>351 125 | 59734<br>−5802<br>351 126 | 59735<br>−5801<br>351 127 | 59736<br>−5800<br>351 130 | 59737<br>−5799<br>351 131 | 59738<br>−5798<br>351 132 | 59739<br>−5797<br>351 133 | 59740<br>−5796<br>351 134 | 59741<br>−5795<br>351 135 | 59742<br>−5794<br>351 136 | 59743<br>−5793<br>351 137 |
| 6− | 59744<br>−5792<br>351 140 | 59745<br>−5791<br>351 141 | 59746<br>−5790<br>351 142 | 59747<br>−5789<br>351 143 | 59748<br>−5788<br>351 144 | 59749<br>−5787<br>351 145 | 59750<br>−5786<br>351 146 | 59751<br>−5785<br>351 147 | 59752<br>−5784<br>351 150 | 59753<br>−5783<br>351 151 | 59754<br>−5782<br>351 152 | 59755<br>−5781<br>351 153 | 59756<br>−5780<br>351 154 | 59757<br>−5779<br>351 155 | 59758<br>−5778<br>351 156 | 59759<br>−5777<br>351 157 |
| 7− | 59760<br>−5776<br>351 160 | 59761<br>−5775<br>351 161 | 59762<br>−5774<br>351 162 | 59763<br>−5773<br>351 163 | 59764<br>−5772<br>351 164 | 59765<br>−5771<br>351 165 | 59766<br>−5770<br>351 166 | 59767<br>−5769<br>351 167 | 59768<br>−5768<br>351 170 | 59769<br>−5767<br>351 171 | 59770<br>−5766<br>351 172 | 59771<br>−5765<br>351 173 | 59772<br>−5764<br>351 174 | 59773<br>−5763<br>351 175 | 59774<br>−5762<br>351 176 | 59775<br>−5761<br>351 177 |
| 8− | 59776<br>−5760<br>351 200 | 59777<br>−5759<br>351 201 | 59778<br>−5758<br>351 202 | 59779<br>−5757<br>351 203 | 59780<br>−5756<br>351 204 | 59781<br>−5755<br>351 205 | 59782<br>−5754<br>351 206 | 59783<br>−5753<br>351 207 | 59784<br>−5752<br>351 210 | 59785<br>−5751<br>351 211 | 59786<br>−5750<br>351 212 | 59787<br>−5749<br>351 213 | 59788<br>−5748<br>351 214 | 59789<br>−5747<br>351 215 | 59790<br>−5746<br>351 216 | 59791<br>−5745<br>351 217 |
| 9− | 59792<br>−5744<br>351 220 | 59793<br>−5743<br>351 221 | 59794<br>−5742<br>351 222 | 59795<br>−5741<br>351 223 | 59796<br>−5740<br>351 224 | 59797<br>−5739<br>351 225 | 59798<br>−5738<br>351 226 | 59799<br>−5737<br>351 227 | 59800<br>−5736<br>351 230 | 59801<br>−5735<br>351 231 | 59802<br>−5734<br>351 232 | 59803<br>−5733<br>351 233 | 59804<br>−5732<br>351 234 | 59805<br>−5731<br>351 235 | 59806<br>−5730<br>351 236 | 59807<br>−5729<br>351 237 |
| A− | 59808<br>−5728<br>351 240 | 59809<br>−5727<br>351 241 | 59810<br>−5726<br>351 242 | 59811<br>−5725<br>351 243 | 59812<br>−5724<br>351 244 | 59813<br>−5723<br>351 245 | 59814<br>−5722<br>351 246 | 59815<br>−5721<br>351 247 | 59816<br>−5720<br>351 250 | 59817<br>−5719<br>351 251 | 59818<br>−5718<br>351 252 | 59819<br>−5717<br>351 253 | 59820<br>−5716<br>351 254 | 59821<br>−5715<br>351 255 | 59822<br>−5714<br>351 256 | 59823<br>−5713<br>351 257 |
| B− | 59824<br>−5712<br>351 260 | 59825<br>−5711<br>351 261 | 59826<br>−5710<br>351 262 | 59827<br>−5709<br>351 263 | 59828<br>−5708<br>351 264 | 59829<br>−5707<br>351 265 | 59830<br>−5706<br>351 266 | 59831<br>−5705<br>351 267 | 59832<br>−5704<br>351 270 | 59833<br>−5703<br>351 271 | 59834<br>−5702<br>351 272 | 59835<br>−5701<br>351 273 | 59836<br>−5700<br>351 274 | 59837<br>−5699<br>351 275 | 59838<br>−5698<br>351 276 | 59839<br>−5697<br>351 277 |
| C− | 59840<br>−5696<br>351 300 | 59841<br>−5695<br>351 301 | 59842<br>−5694<br>351 302 | 59843<br>−5693<br>351 303 | 59844<br>−5692<br>351 304 | 59845<br>−5691<br>351 305 | 59846<br>−5690<br>351 306 | 59847<br>−5689<br>351 307 | 59848<br>−5688<br>351 310 | 59849<br>−5687<br>351 311 | 59850<br>−5686<br>351 312 | 59851<br>−5685<br>351 313 | 59852<br>−5684<br>351 314 | 59853<br>−5683<br>351 315 | 59854<br>−5682<br>351 316 | 59855<br>−5681<br>351 317 |
| D− | 59856<br>−5680<br>351 320 | 59857<br>−5679<br>351 321 | 59858<br>−5678<br>351 322 | 59859<br>−5677<br>351 323 | 59860<br>−5676<br>351 324 | 59861<br>−5675<br>351 325 | 59862<br>−5674<br>351 326 | 59863<br>−5673<br>351 327 | 59864<br>−5672<br>351 330 | 59865<br>−5671<br>351 331 | 59866<br>−5670<br>351 332 | 59867<br>−5669<br>351 333 | 59868<br>−5668<br>351 334 | 59869<br>−5667<br>351 335 | 59870<br>−5666<br>351 336 | 59871<br>−5665<br>351 337 |
| E− | 59872<br>−5664<br>351 340 | 59873<br>−5663<br>351 341 | 59874<br>−5662<br>351 342 | 59875<br>−5661<br>351 343 | 59876<br>−5660<br>351 344 | 59877<br>−5659<br>351 345 | 59878<br>−5658<br>351 346 | 59879<br>−5657<br>351 347 | 59880<br>−5656<br>351 350 | 59881<br>−5655<br>351 351 | 59882<br>−5654<br>351 352 | 59883<br>−5653<br>351 353 | 59884<br>−5652<br>351 354 | 59885<br>−5651<br>351 355 | 59886<br>−5650<br>351 356 | 59887<br>−5649<br>351 357 |
| F− | 59888<br>−5648<br>351 360 | 59889<br>−5647<br>351 361 | 59890<br>−5646<br>351 362 | 59891<br>−5645<br>351 363 | 59892<br>−5644<br>351 364 | 59893<br>−5643<br>351 365 | 59894<br>−5642<br>351 366 | 59895<br>−5641<br>351 367 | 59896<br>−5640<br>351 370 | 59897<br>−5639<br>351 371 | 59898<br>−5638<br>351 372 | 59899<br>−5637<br>351 373 | 59900<br>−5636<br>351 374 | 59901<br>−5635<br>351 375 | 59902<br>−5634<br>351 376 | 59903<br>−5633<br>351 377 |

SECOND HEX DIGIT (row labels)

DECIMAL ←    DECIMAL ←    OCTAL ←

## FIRST HEX DIGIT

(2)

| SECOND HEX DIGIT | −0 | −1 | −2 | −3 | −4 | −5 | −6 | −7 | −8 | −9 | −A | −B | −C | −D | −E | −F |
|---|---|---|---|---|---|---|---|---|---|---|---|---|---|---|---|---|
| 0− | 59904<br>−5632<br>352 000 | 59905<br>−5631<br>352 001 | 59906<br>−5630<br>352 002 | 59907<br>−5629<br>352 003 | 59908<br>−5628<br>352 004 | 59909<br>−5627<br>352 005 | 59910<br>−5626<br>352 006 | 59911<br>−5625<br>352 007 | 59912<br>−5624<br>352 010 | 59913<br>−5623<br>352 011 | 59914<br>−5622<br>352 012 | 59915<br>−5621<br>352 013 | 59916<br>−5620<br>352 014 | 59917<br>−5619<br>352 015 | 59918<br>−5618<br>352 016 | 59919<br>−5617<br>352 017 |
| 1− | 59920<br>−5616<br>352 020 | 59921<br>−5615<br>352 021 | 59922<br>−5614<br>352 022 | 59923<br>−5613<br>352 023 | 59924<br>−5612<br>352 024 | 59925<br>−5611<br>352 025 | 59926<br>−5610<br>352 026 | 59927<br>−5609<br>352 027 | 59928<br>−5608<br>352 030 | 59929<br>−5607<br>352 031 | 59930<br>−5606<br>352 032 | 59931<br>−5605<br>352 033 | 59932<br>−5604<br>352 034 | 59933<br>−5603<br>352 035 | 59934<br>−5602<br>352 036 | 59935<br>−5601<br>352 037 |
| 2− | 59936<br>−5600<br>352 040 | 59937<br>−5599<br>352 041 | 59938<br>−5598<br>352 042 | 59939<br>−5597<br>352 043 | 59940<br>−5596<br>352 044 | 59941<br>−5595<br>352 045 | 59942<br>−5594<br>352 046 | 59943<br>−5593<br>352 047 | 59944<br>−5592<br>352 050 | 59945<br>−5591<br>352 051 | 59946<br>−5590<br>352 052 | 59947<br>−5589<br>352 053 | 59948<br>−5588<br>352 054 | 59949<br>−5587<br>352 055 | 59950<br>−5586<br>352 056 | 59951<br>−5585<br>352 057 |
| 3− | 59952<br>−5584<br>352 060 | 59953<br>−5583<br>352 061 | 59954<br>−5582<br>352 062 | 59955<br>−5581<br>352 063 | 59956<br>−5580<br>352 064 | 59957<br>−5579<br>352 065 | 59958<br>−5578<br>352 066 | 59959<br>−5577<br>352 067 | 59960<br>−5576<br>352 070 | 59961<br>−5575<br>352 071 | 59962<br>−5574<br>352 072 | 59963<br>−5573<br>352 073 | 59964<br>−5572<br>352 074 | 59965<br>−5571<br>352 075 | 59966<br>−5570<br>352 076 | 59967<br>−5569<br>352 077 |
| 4− | 59968<br>−5568<br>352 100 | 59969<br>−5567<br>352 101 | 59970<br>−5566<br>352 102 | 59971<br>−5565<br>352 103 | 59972<br>−5564<br>352 104 | 59973<br>−5563<br>352 105 | 59974<br>−5562<br>352 106 | 59975<br>−5561<br>352 107 | 59976<br>−5560<br>352 110 | 59977<br>−5559<br>352 111 | 59978<br>−5558<br>352 112 | 59979<br>−5557<br>352 113 | 59980<br>−5556<br>352 114 | 59981<br>−5555<br>352 115 | 59982<br>−5554<br>352 116 | 59983<br>−5553<br>352 117 |
| 5− | 59984<br>−5552<br>352 120 | 59985<br>−5551<br>352 121 | 59986<br>−5550<br>352 122 | 59987<br>−5549<br>352 123 | 59988<br>−5548<br>352 124 | 59989<br>−5547<br>352 125 | 59990<br>−5546<br>352 126 | 59991<br>−5545<br>352 127 | 59992<br>−5544<br>352 130 | 59993<br>−5543<br>352 131 | 59994<br>−5542<br>352 132 | 59995<br>−5541<br>352 133 | 59996<br>−5540<br>352 134 | 59997<br>−5539<br>352 135 | 59998<br>−5538<br>352 136 | 59999<br>−5537<br>352 137 |
| 6− | 60000<br>−5536<br>352 140 | 60001<br>−5535<br>352 141 | 60002<br>−5534<br>352 142 | 60003<br>−5533<br>352 143 | 60004<br>−5532<br>352 144 | 60005<br>−5531<br>352 145 | 60006<br>−5530<br>352 146 | 60007<br>−5529<br>352 147 | 60008<br>−5528<br>352 150 | 60009<br>−5527<br>352 151 | 60010<br>−5526<br>352 152 | 60011<br>−5525<br>352 153 | 60012<br>−5524<br>352 154 | 60013<br>−5523<br>352 155 | 60014<br>−5522<br>352 156 | 60015<br>−5521<br>352 157 |
| 7− | 60016<br>−5520<br>352 160 | 60017<br>−5519<br>352 161 | 60018<br>−5518<br>352 162 | 60019<br>−5517<br>352 163 | 60020<br>−5516<br>352 164 | 60021<br>−5515<br>352 165 | 60022<br>−5514<br>352 166 | 60023<br>−5513<br>352 167 | 60024<br>−5512<br>352 170 | 60025<br>−5511<br>352 171 | 60026<br>−5510<br>352 172 | 60027<br>−5509<br>352 173 | 60028<br>−5508<br>352 174 | 60029<br>−5507<br>352 175 | 60030<br>−5506<br>352 176 | 60031<br>−5505<br>352 177 |
| 8− | 60032<br>−5504<br>352 200 | 60033<br>−5503<br>352 201 | 60034<br>−5502<br>352 202 | 60035<br>−5501<br>352 203 | 60036<br>−5500<br>352 204 | 60037<br>−5499<br>352 205 | 60038<br>−5498<br>352 206 | 60039<br>−5497<br>352 207 | 60040<br>−5496<br>352 210 | 60041<br>−5495<br>352 211 | 60042<br>−5494<br>352 212 | 60043<br>−5493<br>352 213 | 60044<br>−5492<br>352 214 | 60045<br>−5491<br>352 215 | 60046<br>−5490<br>352 216 | 60047<br>−5489<br>352 217 |
| 9− | 60048<br>−5488<br>352 220 | 60049<br>−5487<br>352 221 | 60050<br>−5486<br>352 222 | 60051<br>−5485<br>352 223 | 60052<br>−5484<br>352 224 | 60053<br>−5483<br>352 225 | 60054<br>−5482<br>352 226 | 60055<br>−5481<br>352 227 | 60056<br>−5480<br>352 230 | 60057<br>−5479<br>352 231 | 60058<br>−5478<br>352 232 | 60059<br>−5477<br>352 233 | 60060<br>−5476<br>352 234 | 60061<br>−5475<br>352 235 | 60062<br>−5474<br>352 236 | 60063<br>−5473<br>352 237 |
| A− | 60064<br>−5472<br>352 240 | 60065<br>−5471<br>352 241 | 60066<br>−5470<br>352 242 | 60067<br>−5469<br>352 243 | 60068<br>−5468<br>352 244 | 60069<br>−5467<br>352 245 | 60070<br>−5466<br>352 246 | 60071<br>−5465<br>352 247 | 60072<br>−5464<br>352 250 | 60073<br>−5463<br>352 251 | 60074<br>−5462<br>352 252 | 60075<br>−5461<br>352 253 | 60076<br>−5460<br>352 254 | 60077<br>−5459<br>352 255 | 60078<br>−5458<br>352 256 | 60079<br>−5457<br>352 257 |
| B− | 60080<br>−5456<br>352 260 | 60081<br>−5455<br>352 261 | 60082<br>−5454<br>352 262 | 60083<br>−5453<br>352 263 | 60084<br>−5452<br>352 264 | 60085<br>−5451<br>352 265 | 60086<br>−5450<br>352 266 | 60087<br>−5449<br>352 267 | 60088<br>−5448<br>352 270 | 60089<br>−5447<br>352 271 | 60090<br>−5446<br>352 272 | 60091<br>−5445<br>352 273 | 60092<br>−5444<br>352 274 | 60093<br>−5443<br>352 275 | 60094<br>−5442<br>352 276 | 60095<br>−5441<br>352 277 |
| C− | 60096<br>−5440<br>352 300 | 60097<br>−5439<br>352 301 | 60098<br>−5438<br>352 302 | 60099<br>−5437<br>352 303 | 60100<br>−5436<br>352 304 | 60101<br>−5435<br>352 305 | 60102<br>−5434<br>352 306 | 60103<br>−5433<br>352 307 | 60104<br>−5432<br>352 310 | 60105<br>−5431<br>352 311 | 60106<br>−5430<br>352 312 | 60107<br>−5429<br>352 313 | 60108<br>−5428<br>352 314 | 60109<br>−5427<br>352 315 | 60110<br>−5426<br>352 316 | 60111<br>−5425<br>352 317 |
| D− | 60112<br>−5424<br>352 320 | 60113<br>−5423<br>352 321 | 60114<br>−5422<br>352 322 | 60115<br>−5421<br>352 323 | 60116<br>−5420<br>352 324 | 60117<br>−5419<br>352 325 | 60118<br>−5418<br>352 326 | 60119<br>−5417<br>352 327 | 60120<br>−5416<br>352 330 | 60121<br>−5415<br>352 331 | 60122<br>−5414<br>352 332 | 60123<br>−5413<br>352 333 | 60124<br>−5412<br>352 334 | 60125<br>−5411<br>352 335 | 60126<br>−5410<br>352 336 | 60127<br>−5409<br>352 337 |
| E− | 60128<br>−5408<br>352 340 | 60129<br>−5407<br>352 341 | 60130<br>−5406<br>352 342 | 60131<br>−5405<br>352 343 | 60132<br>−5404<br>352 344 | 60133<br>−5403<br>352 345 | 60134<br>−5402<br>352 346 | 60135<br>−5401<br>352 347 | 60136<br>−5400<br>352 350 | 60137<br>−5399<br>352 351 | 60138<br>−5398<br>352 352 | 60139<br>−5397<br>352 353 | 60140<br>−5396<br>352 354 | 60141<br>−5395<br>352 355 | 60142<br>−5394<br>352 356 | 60143<br>−5393<br>352 357 |
| F− | 60144<br>−5392<br>352 360 | 60145<br>−5391<br>352 361 | 60146<br>−5390<br>352 362 | 60147<br>−5389<br>352 363 | 60148<br>−5388<br>352 364 | 60149<br>−5387<br>352 365 | 60150<br>−5386<br>352 366 | 60151<br>−5385<br>352 367 | 60152<br>−5384<br>352 370 | 60153<br>−5383<br>352 371 | 60154<br>−5382<br>352 372 | 60155<br>−5381<br>352 373 | 60156<br>−5380<br>352 374 | 60157<br>−5379<br>352 375 | 60158<br>−5378<br>352 376 | 60159<br>−5377<br>352 377 |

DECIMAL
 DECIMAL
OCTAL

 DECIMAL  −5632   BINARY  1110 1010   DECIMAL  59904   HEXADECIMAL  EA   OCTAL  352 000

FOURTH HEX DIGIT   THIRD HEX DIGIT

 DECIMAL  [−5376]   BINARY  [1110 1011]   DECIMAL  [60160]   HEXADECIMAL  (EB)  OCTAL  [353 000]

FOURTH HEX DIGIT →  ← THIRD HEX DIGIT

(2)

FIRST HEX DIGIT

| SECOND HEX DIGIT | −0 | −1 | −2 | −3 | −4 | −5 | −6 | −7 | −8 | −9 | −A | −B | −C | −D | −E | −F |
|---|---|---|---|---|---|---|---|---|---|---|---|---|---|---|---|---|
| 0− | 60160<br>−5376<br>353 000 | 60161<br>−5375<br>353 001 | 60162<br>−5374<br>353 002 | 60163<br>−5373<br>353 003 | 60164<br>−5372<br>353 004 | 60165<br>−5371<br>353 005 | 60166<br>−5370<br>353 006 | 60167<br>−5369<br>353 007 | 60168<br>−5368<br>353 010 | 60169<br>−5367<br>353 011 | 60170<br>−5366<br>353 012 | 60171<br>−5365<br>353 013 | 60172<br>−5364<br>353 014 | 60173<br>−5363<br>353 015 | 60174<br>−5362<br>353 016 | 60175<br>−5361<br>353 017 |
| 1− | 60176<br>−5360<br>353 020 | 60177<br>−5359<br>353 021 | 60178<br>−5358<br>353 022 | 60179<br>−5357<br>353 023 | 60180<br>−5356<br>353 024 | 60181<br>−5355<br>353 025 | 60182<br>−5354<br>353 026 | 60183<br>−5353<br>353 027 | 60184<br>−5352<br>353 030 | 60185<br>−5351<br>353 031 | 60186<br>−5350<br>353 032 | 60187<br>−5349<br>353 033 | 60188<br>−5348<br>353 034 | 60189<br>−5347<br>353 035 | 60190<br>−5346<br>353 036 | 60191<br>−5345<br>353 037 |
| 2− | 60192<br>−5344<br>353 040 | 60193<br>−5343<br>353 041 | 60194<br>−5342<br>353 042 | 60195<br>−5341<br>353 043 | 60196<br>−5340<br>353 044 | 60197<br>−5339<br>353 045 | 60198<br>−5338<br>353 046 | 60199<br>−5337<br>353 047 | 60200<br>−5336<br>353 050 | 60201<br>−5335<br>353 051 | 60202<br>−5334<br>353 052 | 60203<br>−5333<br>353 053 | 60204<br>−5332<br>353 054 | 60205<br>−5331<br>353 055 | 60206<br>−5330<br>353 056 | 60207<br>−5329<br>353 057 |
| 3− | 60208<br>−5328<br>353 060 | 60209<br>−5327<br>353 061 | 60210<br>−5326<br>353 062 | 60211<br>−5325<br>353 063 | 60212<br>−5324<br>353 064 | 60213<br>−5323<br>353 065 | 60214<br>−5322<br>353 066 | 60215<br>−5321<br>353 067 | 60216<br>−5320<br>353 070 | 60217<br>−5319<br>353 071 | 60218<br>−5318<br>353 072 | 60219<br>−5317<br>353 073 | 60220<br>−5316<br>353 074 | 60221<br>−5315<br>353 075 | 60222<br>−5314<br>353 076 | 60223<br>−5313<br>353 077 |
| 4− | 60224<br>−5312<br>353 100 | 60225<br>−5311<br>353 101 | 60226<br>−5310<br>353 102 | 60227<br>−5309<br>353 103 | 60228<br>−5308<br>353 104 | 60229<br>−5307<br>353 105 | 60230<br>−5306<br>353 106 | 60231<br>−5305<br>353 107 | 60232<br>−5304<br>353 110 | 60233<br>−5303<br>353 111 | 60234<br>−5302<br>353 112 | 60235<br>−5301<br>353 113 | 60236<br>−5300<br>353 114 | 60237<br>−5299<br>353 115 | 60238<br>−5298<br>353 116 | 60239<br>−5297<br>353 117 |
| 5− | 60240<br>−5296<br>353 120 | 60241<br>−5295<br>353 121 | 60242<br>−5294<br>353 122 | 60243<br>−5293<br>353 123 | 60244<br>−5292<br>353 124 | 60245<br>−5291<br>353 125 | 60246<br>−5290<br>353 126 | 60247<br>−5289<br>353 127 | 60248<br>−5288<br>353 130 | 60249<br>−5287<br>353 131 | 60250<br>−5286<br>353 132 | 60251<br>−5285<br>353 133 | 60252<br>−5284<br>353 134 | 60253<br>−5283<br>353 135 | 60254<br>−5282<br>353 136 | 60255<br>−5281<br>353 137 |
| 6− | 60256<br>−5280<br>353 140 | 60257<br>−5279<br>353 141 | 60258<br>−5278<br>353 142 | 60259<br>−5277<br>353 143 | 60260<br>−5276<br>353 144 | 60261<br>−5275<br>353 145 | 60262<br>−5274<br>353 146 | 60263<br>−5273<br>353 147 | 60264<br>−5272<br>353 150 | 60265<br>−5271<br>353 151 | 60266<br>−5270<br>353 152 | 60267<br>−5269<br>353 153 | 60268<br>−5268<br>353 154 | 60269<br>−5267<br>353 155 | 60270<br>−5266<br>353 156 | 60271<br>−5265<br>353 157 |
| 7− | 60272<br>−5264<br>353 160 | 60273<br>−5263<br>353 161 | 60274<br>−5262<br>353 162 | 60275<br>−5261<br>353 163 | 60276<br>−5260<br>353 164 | 60277<br>−5259<br>353 165 | 60278<br>−5258<br>353 166 | 60279<br>−5257<br>353 167 | 60280<br>−5256<br>353 170 | 60281<br>−5255<br>353 171 | 60282<br>−5254<br>353 172 | 60283<br>−5253<br>353 173 | 60284<br>−5252<br>353 174 | 60285<br>−5251<br>353 175 | 60286<br>−5250<br>353 176 | 60287<br>−5249<br>353 177 |
| 8− | 60288<br>−5248<br>353 200 | 60289<br>−5247<br>353 201 | 60290<br>−5246<br>353 202 | 60291<br>−5245<br>353 203 | 60292<br>−5244<br>353 204 | 60293<br>−5243<br>353 205 | 60294<br>−5242<br>353 206 | 60295<br>−5241<br>353 207 | 60296<br>−5240<br>353 210 | 60297<br>−5239<br>353 211 | 60298<br>−5238<br>353 212 | 60299<br>−5237<br>353 213 | 60300<br>−5236<br>353 214 | 60301<br>−5235<br>353 215 | 60302<br>−5234<br>353 216 | 60303<br>−5233<br>353 217 |
| 9− | 60304<br>−5232<br>353 220 | 60305<br>−5231<br>353 221 | 60306<br>−5230<br>353 222 | 60307<br>−5229<br>353 223 | 60308<br>−5228<br>353 224 | 60309<br>−5227<br>353 225 | 60310<br>−5226<br>353 226 | 60311<br>−5225<br>353 227 | 60312<br>−5224<br>353 230 | 60313<br>−5223<br>353 231 | 60314<br>−5222<br>353 232 | 60315<br>−5221<br>353 233 | 60316<br>−5220<br>353 234 | 60317<br>−5219<br>353 235 | 60318<br>−5218<br>353 236 | 60319<br>−5217<br>353 237 |
| A− | 60320<br>−5216<br>353 240 | 60321<br>−5215<br>353 241 | 60322<br>−5214<br>353 242 | 60323<br>−5213<br>353 243 | 60324<br>−5212<br>353 244 | 60325<br>−5211<br>353 245 | 60326<br>−5210<br>353 246 | 60327<br>−5209<br>353 247 | 60328<br>−5208<br>353 250 | 60329<br>−5207<br>353 251 | 60330<br>−5206<br>353 252 | 60331<br>−5205<br>353 253 | 60332<br>−5204<br>353 254 | 60333<br>−5203<br>353 255 | 60334<br>−5202<br>353 256 | 60335<br>−5201<br>353 257 |
| B− | 60336<br>−5200<br>353 260 | 60337<br>−5199<br>353 261 | 60338<br>−5198<br>353 262 | 60339<br>−5197<br>353 263 | 60340<br>−5196<br>353 264 | 60341<br>−5195<br>353 265 | 60342<br>−5194<br>353 266 | 60343<br>−5193<br>353 267 | 60344<br>−5192<br>353 270 | 60345<br>−5191<br>353 271 | 60346<br>−5190<br>353 272 | 60347<br>−5189<br>353 273 | 60348<br>−5188<br>353 274 | 60349<br>−5187<br>353 275 | 60350<br>−5186<br>353 276 | 60351<br>−5185<br>353 277 |
| C− | 60352<br>−5184<br>353 300 | 60353<br>−5183<br>353 301 | 60354<br>−5182<br>353 302 | 60355<br>−5181<br>353 303 | 60356<br>−5180<br>353 304 | 60357<br>−5179<br>353 305 | 60358<br>−5178<br>353 306 | 60359<br>−5177<br>353 307 | 60360<br>−5176<br>353 310 | 60361<br>−5175<br>353 311 | 60362<br>−5174<br>353 312 | 60363<br>−5173<br>353 313 | 60364<br>−5172<br>353 314 | 60365<br>−5171<br>353 315 | 60366<br>−5170<br>353 316 | 60367<br>−5169<br>353 317 |
| D− | 60368<br>−5168<br>353 320 | 60369<br>−5167<br>353 321 | 60370<br>−5166<br>353 322 | 60371<br>−5165<br>353 323 | 60372<br>−5164<br>353 324 | 60373<br>−5163<br>353 325 | 60374<br>−5162<br>353 326 | 60375<br>−5161<br>353 327 | 60376<br>−5160<br>353 330 | 60377<br>−5159<br>353 331 | 60378<br>−5158<br>353 332 | 60379<br>−5157<br>353 333 | 60380<br>−5156<br>353 334 | 60381<br>−5155<br>353 335 | 60382<br>−5154<br>353 336 | 60383<br>−5153<br>353 337 |
| E− | 60384<br>−5152<br>353 340 | 60385<br>−5151<br>353 341 | 60386<br>−5150<br>353 342 | 60387<br>−5149<br>353 343 | 60388<br>−5148<br>353 344 | 60389<br>−5147<br>353 345 | 60390<br>−5146<br>353 346 | 60391<br>−5145<br>353 347 | 60392<br>−5144<br>353 350 | 60393<br>−5143<br>353 351 | 60394<br>−5142<br>353 352 | 60395<br>−5141<br>353 353 | 60396<br>−5140<br>353 354 | 60397<br>−5139<br>353 355 | 60398<br>−5138<br>353 356 | 60399<br>−5137<br>353 357 |
| F− | 60400<br>−5136<br>353 360 | 60401<br>−5135<br>353 361 | 60402<br>−5134<br>353 362 | 60403<br>−5133<br>353 363 | 60404<br>−5132<br>353 364 | 60405<br>−5131<br>353 365 | 60406<br>−5130<br>353 366 | 60407<br>−5129<br>353 367 | 60408<br>−5128<br>353 370 | 60409<br>−5127<br>353 371 | 60410<br>−5126<br>353 372 | 60411<br>−5125<br>353 373 | 60412<br>−5124<br>353 374 | 60413<br>−5123<br>353 375 | 60414<br>−5122<br>353 376 | 60415<br>−5121<br>353 377 |

DECIMAL

DECIMAL

OCTAL

Each cell lists: DECIMAL / Ⓐ DECIMAL (negative) / OCTAL

|  | −0 | −1 | −2 | −3 | −4 | −5 | −6 | −7 | −8 | −9 | −A | −B | −C | −D | −E | −F |
|---|---|---|---|---|---|---|---|---|---|---|---|---|---|---|---|---|
| **0−** | 60416<br>−5120<br>354 000 | 60417<br>−5119<br>354 001 | 60418<br>−5118<br>354 002 | 60419<br>−5117<br>354 003 | 60420<br>−5116<br>354 004 | 60421<br>−5115<br>354 005 | 60422<br>−5114<br>354 006 | 60423<br>−5113<br>354 007 | 60424<br>−5112<br>354 010 | 60425<br>−5111<br>354 011 | 60426<br>−5110<br>354 012 | 60427<br>−5109<br>354 013 | 60428<br>−5108<br>354 014 | 60429<br>−5107<br>354 015 | 60430<br>−5106<br>354 016 | 60431<br>−5105<br>354 017 |
| **1−** | 60432<br>−5104<br>354 020 | 60433<br>−5103<br>354 021 | 60434<br>−5102<br>354 022 | 60435<br>−5101<br>354 023 | 60436<br>−5100<br>354 024 | 60437<br>−5099<br>354 025 | 60438<br>−5098<br>354 026 | 60439<br>−5097<br>354 027 | 60440<br>−5096<br>354 030 | 60441<br>−5095<br>354 031 | 60442<br>−5094<br>354 032 | 60443<br>−5093<br>354 033 | 60444<br>−5092<br>354 034 | 60445<br>−5091<br>354 035 | 60446<br>−5090<br>354 036 | 60447<br>−5089<br>354 037 |
| **2−** | 60448<br>−5088<br>354 040 | 60449<br>−5087<br>354 041 | 60450<br>−5086<br>354 042 | 60451<br>−5085<br>354 043 | 60452<br>−5084<br>354 044 | 60453<br>−5083<br>354 045 | 60454<br>−5082<br>354 046 | 60455<br>−5081<br>354 047 | 60456<br>−5080<br>354 050 | 60457<br>−5079<br>354 051 | 60458<br>−5078<br>354 052 | 60459<br>−5077<br>354 053 | 60460<br>−5076<br>354 054 | 60461<br>−5075<br>354 055 | 60462<br>−5074<br>354 056 | 60463<br>−5073<br>354 057 |
| **3−** | 60464<br>−5072<br>354 060 | 60465<br>−5071<br>354 061 | 60466<br>−5070<br>354 062 | 60467<br>−5069<br>354 063 | 60468<br>−5068<br>354 064 | 60469<br>−5067<br>354 065 | 60470<br>−5066<br>354 066 | 60471<br>−5065<br>354 067 | 60472<br>−5064<br>354 070 | 60473<br>−5063<br>354 071 | 60474<br>−5062<br>354 072 | 60475<br>−5061<br>354 073 | 60476<br>−5060<br>354 074 | 60477<br>−5059<br>354 075 | 60478<br>−5058<br>354 076 | 60479<br>−5057<br>354 077 |
| **4−** | 60480<br>−5056<br>354 100 | 60481<br>−5055<br>354 101 | 60482<br>−5054<br>354 102 | 60483<br>−5053<br>354 103 | 60484<br>−5052<br>354 104 | 60485<br>−5051<br>354 105 | 60486<br>−5050<br>354 106 | 60487<br>−5049<br>354 107 | 60488<br>−5048<br>354 110 | 60489<br>−5047<br>354 111 | 60490<br>−5046<br>354 112 | 60491<br>−5045<br>354 113 | 60492<br>−5044<br>354 114 | 60493<br>−5043<br>354 115 | 60494<br>−5042<br>354 116 | 60495<br>−5041<br>354 117 |
| **5−** | 60496<br>−5040<br>354 120 | 60497<br>−5039<br>354 121 | 60498<br>−5038<br>354 122 | 60499<br>−5037<br>354 123 | 60500<br>−5036<br>354 124 | 60501<br>−5035<br>354 125 | 60502<br>−5034<br>354 126 | 60503<br>−5033<br>354 127 | 60504<br>−5032<br>354 130 | 60505<br>−5031<br>354 131 | 60506<br>−5030<br>354 132 | 60507<br>−5029<br>354 133 | 60508<br>−5028<br>354 134 | 60509<br>−5027<br>354 135 | 60510<br>−5026<br>354 136 | 60511<br>−5025<br>354 137 |
| **6−** | 60512<br>−5024<br>354 140 | 60513<br>−5023<br>354 141 | 60514<br>−5022<br>354 142 | 60515<br>−5021<br>354 143 | 60516<br>−5020<br>354 144 | 60517<br>−5019<br>354 145 | 60518<br>−5018<br>354 146 | 60519<br>−5017<br>354 147 | 60520<br>−5016<br>354 150 | 60521<br>−5015<br>354 151 | 60522<br>−5014<br>354 152 | 60523<br>−5013<br>354 153 | 60524<br>−5012<br>354 154 | 60525<br>−5011<br>354 155 | 60526<br>−5010<br>354 156 | 60527<br>−5009<br>354 157 |
| **7−** | 60528<br>−5008<br>354 160 | 60529<br>−5007<br>354 161 | 60530<br>−5006<br>354 162 | 60531<br>−5005<br>354 163 | 60532<br>−5004<br>354 164 | 60533<br>−5003<br>354 165 | 60534<br>−5002<br>354 166 | 60535<br>−5001<br>354 167 | 60536<br>−5000<br>354 170 | 60537<br>−4999<br>354 171 | 60538<br>−4998<br>354 172 | 60539<br>−4997<br>354 173 | 60540<br>−4996<br>354 174 | 60541<br>−4995<br>354 175 | 60542<br>−4994<br>354 176 | 60543<br>−4993<br>354 177 |
| **8−** | 60544<br>−4992<br>354 200 | 60545<br>−4991<br>354 201 | 60546<br>−4990<br>354 202 | 60547<br>−4989<br>354 203 | 60548<br>−4988<br>354 204 | 60549<br>−4987<br>354 205 | 60550<br>−4986<br>354 206 | 60551<br>−4985<br>354 207 | 60552<br>−4984<br>354 210 | 60553<br>−4983<br>354 211 | 60554<br>−4982<br>354 212 | 60555<br>−4981<br>354 213 | 60556<br>−4980<br>354 214 | 60557<br>−4979<br>354 215 | 60558<br>−4978<br>354 216 | 60559<br>−4977<br>354 217 |
| **9−** | 60560<br>−4976<br>354 220 | 60561<br>−4975<br>354 221 | 60562<br>−4974<br>354 222 | 60563<br>−4973<br>354 223 | 60564<br>−4972<br>354 224 | 60565<br>−4971<br>354 225 | 60566<br>−4970<br>354 226 | 60567<br>−4969<br>354 227 | 60568<br>−4968<br>354 230 | 60569<br>−4967<br>354 231 | 60570<br>−4966<br>354 232 | 60571<br>−4965<br>354 233 | 60572<br>−4964<br>354 234 | 60573<br>−4963<br>354 235 | 60574<br>−4962<br>354 236 | 60575<br>−4961<br>354 237 |
| **A−** | 60576<br>−4960<br>354 240 | 60577<br>−4959<br>354 241 | 60578<br>−4958<br>354 242 | 60579<br>−4957<br>354 243 | 60580<br>−4956<br>354 244 | 60581<br>−4955<br>354 245 | 60582<br>−4954<br>354 246 | 60583<br>−4953<br>354 247 | 60584<br>−4952<br>354 250 | 60585<br>−4951<br>354 251 | 60586<br>−4950<br>354 252 | 60587<br>−4949<br>354 253 | 60588<br>−4948<br>354 254 | 60589<br>−4947<br>354 255 | 60590<br>−4946<br>354 256 | 60591<br>−4945<br>354 257 |
| **B−** | 60592<br>−4944<br>354 260 | 60593<br>−4943<br>354 261 | 60594<br>−4942<br>354 262 | 60595<br>−4941<br>354 263 | 60596<br>−4940<br>354 264 | 60597<br>−4939<br>354 265 | 60598<br>−4938<br>354 266 | 60599<br>−4937<br>354 267 | 60600<br>−4936<br>354 270 | 60601<br>−4935<br>354 271 | 60602<br>−4934<br>354 272 | 60603<br>−4933<br>354 273 | 60604<br>−4932<br>354 274 | 60605<br>−4931<br>354 275 | 60606<br>−4930<br>354 276 | 60607<br>−4929<br>354 277 |
| **C−** | 60608<br>−4928<br>354 300 | 60609<br>−4927<br>354 301 | 60610<br>−4926<br>354 302 | 60611<br>−4925<br>354 303 | 60612<br>−4924<br>354 304 | 60613<br>−4923<br>354 305 | 60614<br>−4922<br>354 306 | 60615<br>−4921<br>354 307 | 60616<br>−4920<br>354 310 | 60617<br>−4919<br>354 311 | 60618<br>−4918<br>354 312 | 60619<br>−4917<br>354 313 | 60620<br>−4916<br>354 314 | 60621<br>−4915<br>354 315 | 60622<br>−4914<br>354 316 | 60623<br>−4913<br>354 317 |
| **D−** | 60624<br>−4912<br>354 320 | 60625<br>−4911<br>354 321 | 60626<br>−4910<br>354 322 | 60627<br>−4909<br>354 323 | 60628<br>−4908<br>354 324 | 60629<br>−4907<br>354 325 | 60630<br>−4906<br>354 326 | 60631<br>−4905<br>354 327 | 60632<br>−4904<br>354 330 | 60633<br>−4903<br>354 331 | 60634<br>−4902<br>354 332 | 60635<br>−4901<br>354 333 | 60636<br>−4900<br>354 334 | 60637<br>−4899<br>354 335 | 60638<br>−4898<br>354 336 | 60639<br>−4897<br>354 337 |
| **E−** | 60640<br>−4896<br>354 340 | 60641<br>−4895<br>354 341 | 60642<br>−4894<br>354 342 | 60643<br>−4893<br>354 343 | 60644<br>−4892<br>354 344 | 60645<br>−4891<br>354 345 | 60646<br>−4890<br>354 346 | 60647<br>−4889<br>354 347 | 60648<br>−4888<br>354 350 | 60649<br>−4887<br>354 351 | 60650<br>−4886<br>354 352 | 60651<br>−4885<br>354 353 | 60652<br>−4884<br>354 354 | 60653<br>−4883<br>354 355 | 60654<br>−4882<br>354 356 | 60655<br>−4881<br>354 357 |
| **F−** | 60656<br>−4880<br>354 360 | 60657<br>−4879<br>354 361 | 60658<br>−4878<br>354 362 | 60659<br>−4877<br>354 363 | 60660<br>−4876<br>354 364 | 60661<br>−4875<br>354 365 | 60662<br>−4874<br>354 366 | 60663<br>−4873<br>354 367 | 60664<br>−4872<br>354 370 | 60665<br>−4871<br>354 371 | 60666<br>−4870<br>354 372 | 60667<br>−4869<br>354 373 | 60668<br>−4868<br>354 374 | 60669<br>−4867<br>354 375 | 60670<br>−4866<br>354 376 | 60671<br>−4865<br>354 377 |

**SECOND HEX DIGIT** (row labels, left side)

DECIMAL → (arrows point to decimal values)
Ⓐ DECIMAL → (arrows point to negative decimal values)
OCTAL → (arrows point to octal values)

---

 DECIMAL  −5120   BINARY  1110 1100   DECIMAL  60416   HEXADECIMAL  OCTAL  354 000

FOURTH HEX DIGIT → EC ← THIRD HEX DIGIT

**FIRST HEX DIGIT**

| ⬡2 | −0 | −1 | −2 | −3 | −4 | −5 | −6 | −7 | −8 | −9 | −A | −B | −C | −D | −E | −F |
|---|---|---|---|---|---|---|---|---|---|---|---|---|---|---|---|---|
| **0−** | 60672<br>−4864<br>355 000 | 60673<br>−4863<br>355 001 | 60674<br>−4862<br>355 002 | 60675<br>−4861<br>355 003 | 60676<br>−4860<br>355 004 | 60677<br>−4859<br>355 005 | 60678<br>−4858<br>355 006 | 60679<br>−4857<br>355 007 | 60680<br>−4856<br>355 010 | 60681<br>−4855<br>355 011 | 60682<br>−4854<br>355 012 | 60683<br>−4853<br>355 013 | 60684<br>−4852<br>355 014 | 60685<br>−4851<br>355 015 | 60686<br>−4850<br>355 016 | 60687<br>−4849<br>355 017 |
| **1−** | 60688<br>−4848<br>355 020 | 60689<br>−4847<br>355 021 | 60690<br>−4846<br>355 022 | 60691<br>−4845<br>355 023 | 60692<br>−4844<br>355 024 | 60693<br>−4843<br>355 025 | 60694<br>−4842<br>355 026 | 60695<br>−4841<br>355 027 | 60696<br>−4840<br>355 030 | 60697<br>−4839<br>355 031 | 60698<br>−4838<br>355 032 | 60699<br>−4837<br>355 033 | 60700<br>−4836<br>355 034 | 60701<br>−4835<br>355 035 | 60702<br>−4834<br>355 036 | 60703<br>−4833<br>355 037 |
| **2−** | 60704<br>−4832<br>355 040 | 60705<br>−4831<br>355 041 | 60706<br>−4830<br>355 042 | 60707<br>−4829<br>355 043 | 60708<br>−4828<br>355 044 | 60709<br>−4827<br>355 045 | 60710<br>−4826<br>355 046 | 60711<br>−4825<br>355 047 | 60712<br>−4824<br>355 050 | 60713<br>−4823<br>355 051 | 60714<br>−4822<br>355 052 | 60715<br>−4821<br>355 053 | 60716<br>−4820<br>355 054 | 60717<br>−4819<br>355 055 | 60718<br>−4818<br>355 056 | 60719<br>−4817<br>355 057 |
| **3−** | 60720<br>−4816<br>355 060 | 60721<br>−4815<br>355 061 | 60722<br>−4814<br>355 062 | 60723<br>−4813<br>355 063 | 60724<br>−4812<br>355 064 | 60725<br>−4811<br>355 065 | 60726<br>−4810<br>355 066 | 60727<br>−4809<br>355 067 | 60728<br>−4808<br>355 070 | 60729<br>−4807<br>355 071 | 60730<br>−4806<br>355 072 | 60731<br>−4805<br>355 073 | 60732<br>−4804<br>355 074 | 60733<br>−4803<br>355 075 | 60734<br>−4802<br>355 076 | 60735<br>−4801<br>355 077 |
| **4−** | 60736<br>−4800<br>355 100 | 60737<br>−4799<br>355 101 | 60738<br>−4798<br>355 102 | 60739<br>−4797<br>355 103 | 60740<br>−4796<br>355 104 | 60741<br>−4795<br>355 105 | 60742<br>−4794<br>355 106 | 60743<br>−4793<br>355 107 | 60744<br>−4792<br>355 110 | 60745<br>−4791<br>355 111 | 60746<br>−4790<br>355 112 | 60747<br>−4789<br>355 113 | 60748<br>−4788<br>355 114 | 60749<br>−4787<br>355 115 | 60750<br>−4786<br>355 116 | 60751<br>−4785<br>355 117 |
| **5−** | 60752<br>−4784<br>355 120 | 60753<br>−4783<br>355 121 | 60754<br>−4782<br>355 122 | 60755<br>−4781<br>355 123 | 60756<br>−4780<br>355 124 | 60757<br>−4779<br>355 125 | 60758<br>−4778<br>355 126 | 60759<br>−4777<br>355 127 | 60760<br>−4776<br>355 130 | 60761<br>−4775<br>355 131 | 60762<br>−4774<br>355 132 | 60763<br>−4773<br>355 133 | 60764<br>−4772<br>355 134 | 60765<br>−4771<br>355 135 | 60766<br>−4770<br>355 136 | 60767<br>−4769<br>355 137 |
| **6−** | 60768<br>−4768<br>355 140 | 60769<br>−4767<br>355 141 | 60770<br>−4766<br>355 142 | 60771<br>−4765<br>355 143 | 60772<br>−4764<br>355 144 | 60773<br>−4763<br>355 145 | 60774<br>−4762<br>355 146 | 60775<br>−4761<br>355 147 | 60776<br>−4760<br>355 150 | 60777<br>−4759<br>355 151 | 60778<br>−4758<br>355 152 | 60779<br>−4757<br>355 153 | 60780<br>−4756<br>355 154 | 60781<br>−4755<br>355 155 | 60782<br>−4754<br>355 156 | 60783<br>−4753<br>355 157 |
| **7−** | 60784<br>−4752<br>355 160 | 60785<br>−4751<br>355 161 | 60786<br>−4750<br>355 162 | 60787<br>−4749<br>355 163 | 60788<br>−4748<br>355 164 | 60789<br>−4747<br>355 165 | 60790<br>−4746<br>355 166 | 60791<br>−4745<br>355 167 | 60792<br>−4744<br>355 170 | 60793<br>−4743<br>355 171 | 60794<br>−4742<br>355 172 | 60795<br>−4741<br>355 173 | 60796<br>−4740<br>355 174 | 60797<br>−4739<br>355 175 | 60798<br>−4738<br>355 176 | 60799<br>−4737<br>355 177 |
| **8−** | 60800<br>−4736<br>355 200 | 60801<br>−4735<br>355 201 | 60802<br>−4734<br>355 202 | 60803<br>−4733<br>355 203 | 60804<br>−4732<br>355 204 | 60805<br>−4731<br>355 205 | 60806<br>−4730<br>355 206 | 60807<br>−4729<br>355 207 | 60808<br>−4728<br>355 210 | 60809<br>−4727<br>355 211 | 60810<br>−4726<br>355 212 | 60811<br>−4725<br>355 213 | 60812<br>−4724<br>355 214 | 60813<br>−4723<br>355 215 | 60814<br>−4722<br>355 216 | 60815<br>−4721<br>355 217 |
| **9−** | 60816<br>−4720<br>355 220 | 60817<br>−4719<br>355 221 | 60818<br>−4718<br>355 222 | 60819<br>−4717<br>355 223 | 60820<br>−4716<br>355 224 | 60821<br>−4715<br>355 225 | 60822<br>−4714<br>355 226 | 60823<br>−4713<br>355 227 | 60824<br>−4712<br>355 230 | 60825<br>−4711<br>355 231 | 60826<br>−4710<br>355 232 | 60827<br>−4709<br>355 233 | 60828<br>−4708<br>355 234 | 60829<br>−4707<br>355 235 | 60830<br>−4706<br>355 236 | 60831<br>−4705<br>355 237 |
| **A−** | 60832<br>−4704<br>355 240 | 60833<br>−4703<br>355 241 | 60834<br>−4702<br>355 242 | 60835<br>−4701<br>355 243 | 60836<br>−4700<br>355 244 | 60837<br>−4699<br>355 245 | 60838<br>−4698<br>355 246 | 60839<br>−4697<br>355 247 | 60840<br>−4696<br>355 250 | 60841<br>−4695<br>355 251 | 60842<br>−4694<br>355 252 | 60843<br>−4693<br>355 253 | 60844<br>−4692<br>355 254 | 60845<br>−4691<br>355 255 | 60846<br>−4690<br>355 256 | 60847<br>−4689<br>355 257 |
| **B−** | 60848<br>−4688<br>355 260 | 60849<br>−4687<br>355 261 | 60850<br>−4686<br>355 262 | 60851<br>−4685<br>355 263 | 60852<br>−4684<br>355 264 | 60853<br>−4683<br>355 265 | 60854<br>−4682<br>355 266 | 60855<br>−4681<br>355 267 | 60856<br>−4680<br>355 270 | 60857<br>−4679<br>355 271 | 60858<br>−4678<br>355 272 | 60859<br>−4677<br>355 273 | 60860<br>−4676<br>355 274 | 60861<br>−4675<br>355 275 | 60862<br>−4674<br>355 276 | 60863<br>−4673<br>355 277 |
| **C−** | 60864<br>−4672<br>355 300 | 60865<br>−4671<br>355 301 | 60866<br>−4670<br>355 302 | 60867<br>−4669<br>355 303 | 60868<br>−4668<br>355 304 | 60869<br>−4667<br>355 305 | 60870<br>−4666<br>355 306 | 60871<br>−4665<br>355 307 | 60872<br>−4664<br>355 310 | 60873<br>−4663<br>355 311 | 60874<br>−4662<br>355 312 | 60875<br>−4661<br>355 313 | 60876<br>−4660<br>355 314 | 60877<br>−4659<br>355 315 | 60878<br>−4658<br>355 316 | 60879<br>−4657<br>355 317 |
| **D−** | 60880<br>−4656<br>355 320 | 60881<br>−4655<br>355 321 | 60882<br>−4654<br>355 322 | 60883<br>−4653<br>355 323 | 60884<br>−4652<br>355 324 | 60885<br>−4651<br>355 325 | 60886<br>−4650<br>355 326 | 60887<br>−4649<br>355 327 | 60888<br>−4648<br>355 330 | 60889<br>−4647<br>355 331 | 60890<br>−4646<br>355 332 | 60891<br>−4645<br>355 333 | 60892<br>−4644<br>355 334 | 60893<br>−4643<br>355 335 | 60894<br>−4642<br>355 336 | 60895<br>−4641<br>355 337 |
| **E−** | 60896<br>−4640<br>355 340 | 60897<br>−4639<br>355 341 | 60898<br>−4638<br>355 342 | 60899<br>−4637<br>355 343 | 60900<br>−4636<br>355 344 | 60901<br>−4635<br>355 345 | 60902<br>−4634<br>355 346 | 60903<br>−4633<br>355 347 | 60904<br>−4632<br>355 350 | 60905<br>−4631<br>355 351 | 60906<br>−4630<br>355 352 | 60907<br>−4629<br>355 353 | 60908<br>−4628<br>355 354 | 60909<br>−4627<br>355 355 | 60910<br>−4626<br>355 356 | 60911<br>−4625<br>355 357 |
| **F−** | 60912<br>−4624<br>355 360 | 60913<br>−4623<br>355 361 | 60914<br>−4622<br>355 362 | 60915<br>−4621<br>355 363 | 60916<br>−4620<br>355 364 | 60917<br>−4619<br>355 365 | 60918<br>−4618<br>355 366 | 60919<br>−4617<br>355 367 | 60920<br>−4616<br>355 370 | 60921<br>−4615<br>355 371 | 60922<br>−4614<br>355 372 | 60923<br>−4613<br>355 373 | 60924<br>−4612<br>355 374 | 60925<br>−4611<br>355 375 | 60926<br>−4610<br>355 376 | 60927<br>−4609<br>355 377 |

*SECOND HEX DIGIT* (row labels)

DECIMAL • DECIMAL • OCTAL

# FIRST HEX DIGIT

| SECOND HEX DIGIT | −0 | −1 | −2 | −3 | −4 | −5 | −6 | −7 | −8 | −9 | −A | −B | −C | −D | −E | −F |
|---|---|---|---|---|---|---|---|---|---|---|---|---|---|---|---|---|
| **0−** | 60928<br>−4608<br>356 000 | 60929<br>−4607<br>356 001 | 60930<br>−4606<br>356 002 | 60931<br>−4605<br>356 003 | 60932<br>−4604<br>356 004 | 60933<br>−4603<br>356 005 | 60934<br>−4602<br>356 006 | 60935<br>−4601<br>356 007 | 60936<br>−4600<br>356 010 | 60937<br>−4599<br>356 011 | 60938<br>−4598<br>356 012 | 60939<br>−4597<br>356 013 | 60940<br>−4596<br>356 014 | 60941<br>−4595<br>356 015 | 60942<br>−4594<br>356 016 | 60943<br>−4593<br>356 017 |
| **1−** | 60944<br>−4592<br>356 020 | 60945<br>−4591<br>356 021 | 60946<br>−4590<br>356 022 | 60947<br>−4589<br>356 023 | 60948<br>−4588<br>356 024 | 60949<br>−4587<br>356 025 | 60950<br>−4586<br>356 026 | 60951<br>−4585<br>356 027 | 60952<br>−4584<br>356 030 | 60953<br>−4583<br>356 031 | 60954<br>−4582<br>356 032 | 60955<br>−4581<br>356 033 | 60956<br>−4580<br>356 034 | 60957<br>−4579<br>356 035 | 60958<br>−4578<br>356 036 | 60959<br>−4577<br>356 037 |
| **2−** | 60960<br>−4576<br>356 040 | 60961<br>−4575<br>356 041 | 60962<br>−4574<br>356 042 | 60963<br>−4573<br>356 043 | 60964<br>−4572<br>356 044 | 60965<br>−4571<br>356 045 | 60966<br>−4570<br>356 046 | 60967<br>−4569<br>356 047 | 60968<br>−4568<br>356 050 | 60969<br>−4567<br>356 051 | 60970<br>−4566<br>356 052 | 60971<br>−4565<br>356 053 | 60972<br>−4564<br>356 054 | 60973<br>−4563<br>356 055 | 60974<br>−4562<br>356 056 | 60975<br>−4561<br>356 057 |
| **3−** | 60976<br>−4560<br>356 060 | 60977<br>−4559<br>356 061 | 60978<br>−4558<br>356 062 | 60979<br>−4557<br>356 063 | 60980<br>−4556<br>356 064 | 60981<br>−4555<br>356 065 | 60982<br>−4554<br>356 066 | 60983<br>−4553<br>356 067 | 60984<br>−4552<br>356 070 | 60985<br>−4551<br>356 071 | 60986<br>−4550<br>356 072 | 60987<br>−4549<br>356 073 | 60988<br>−4548<br>356 074 | 60989<br>−4547<br>356 075 | 60990<br>−4546<br>356 076 | 60991<br>−4545<br>356 077 |
| **4−** | 60992<br>−4544<br>356 100 | 60993<br>−4543<br>356 101 | 60994<br>−4542<br>356 102 | 60995<br>−4541<br>356 103 | 60996<br>−4540<br>356 104 | 60997<br>−4539<br>356 105 | 60998<br>−4538<br>356 106 | 60999<br>−4537<br>356 107 | 61000<br>−4536<br>356 110 | 61001<br>−4535<br>356 111 | 61002<br>−4534<br>356 112 | 61003<br>−4533<br>356 113 | 61004<br>−4532<br>356 114 | 61005<br>−4531<br>356 115 | 61006<br>−4530<br>356 116 | 61007<br>−4529<br>356 117 |
| **5−** | 61008<br>−4528<br>356 120 | 61009<br>−4527<br>356 121 | 61010<br>−4526<br>356 122 | 61011<br>−4525<br>356 123 | 61012<br>−4524<br>356 124 | 61013<br>−4523<br>356 125 | 61014<br>−4522<br>356 126 | 61015<br>−4521<br>356 127 | 61016<br>−4520<br>356 130 | 61017<br>−4519<br>356 131 | 61018<br>−4518<br>356 132 | 61019<br>−4517<br>356 133 | 61020<br>−4516<br>356 134 | 61021<br>−4515<br>356 135 | 61022<br>−4514<br>356 136 | 61023<br>−4513<br>356 137 |
| **6−** | 61024<br>−4512<br>356 140 | 61025<br>−4511<br>356 141 | 61026<br>−4510<br>356 142 | 61027<br>−4509<br>356 143 | 61028<br>−4508<br>356 144 | 61029<br>−4507<br>356 145 | 61030<br>−4506<br>356 146 | 61031<br>−4505<br>356 147 | 61032<br>−4504<br>356 150 | 61033<br>−4503<br>356 151 | 61034<br>−4502<br>356 152 | 61035<br>−4501<br>356 153 | 61036<br>−4500<br>356 154 | 61037<br>−4499<br>356 155 | 61038<br>−4498<br>356 156 | 61039<br>−4497<br>356 157 |
| **7−** | 61040<br>−4496<br>356 160 | 61041<br>−4495<br>356 161 | 61042<br>−4494<br>356 162 | 61043<br>−4493<br>356 163 | 61044<br>−4492<br>356 164 | 61045<br>−4491<br>356 165 | 61046<br>−4490<br>356 166 | 61047<br>−4489<br>356 167 | 61048<br>−4488<br>356 170 | 61049<br>−4487<br>356 171 | 61050<br>−4486<br>356 172 | 61051<br>−4485<br>356 173 | 61052<br>−4484<br>356 174 | 61053<br>−4483<br>356 175 | 61054<br>−4482<br>356 176 | 61055<br>−4481<br>356 177 |
| **8−** | 61056<br>−4480<br>356 200 | 61057<br>−4479<br>356 201 | 61058<br>−4478<br>356 202 | 61059<br>−4477<br>356 203 | 61060<br>−4476<br>356 204 | 61061<br>−4475<br>356 205 | 61062<br>−4474<br>356 206 | 61063<br>−4473<br>356 207 | 61064<br>−4472<br>356 210 | 61065<br>−4471<br>356 211 | 61066<br>−4470<br>356 212 | 61067<br>−4469<br>356 213 | 61068<br>−4468<br>356 214 | 61069<br>−4467<br>356 215 | 61070<br>−4466<br>356 216 | 61071<br>−4465<br>356 217 |
| **9−** | 61072<br>−4464<br>356 220 | 61073<br>−4463<br>356 221 | 61074<br>−4462<br>356 222 | 61075<br>−4461<br>356 223 | 61076<br>−4460<br>356 224 | 61077<br>−4459<br>356 225 | 61078<br>−4458<br>356 226 | 61079<br>−4457<br>356 227 | 61080<br>−4456<br>356 230 | 61081<br>−4455<br>356 231 | 61082<br>−4454<br>356 232 | 61083<br>−4453<br>356 233 | 61084<br>−4452<br>356 234 | 61085<br>−4451<br>356 235 | 61086<br>−4450<br>356 236 | 61087<br>−4449<br>356 237 |
| **A−** | 61088<br>−4448<br>356 240 | 61089<br>−4447<br>356 241 | 61090<br>−4446<br>356 242 | 61091<br>−4445<br>356 243 | 61092<br>−4444<br>356 244 | 61093<br>−4443<br>356 245 | 61094<br>−4442<br>356 246 | 61095<br>−4441<br>356 247 | 61096<br>−4440<br>356 250 | 61097<br>−4439<br>356 251 | 61098<br>−4438<br>356 252 | 61099<br>−4437<br>356 253 | 61100<br>−4436<br>356 254 | 61101<br>−4435<br>356 255 | 61102<br>−4434<br>356 256 | 61103<br>−4433<br>356 257 |
| **B−** | 61104<br>−4432<br>356 260 | 61105<br>−4431<br>356 261 | 61106<br>−4430<br>356 262 | 61107<br>−4429<br>356 263 | 61108<br>−4428<br>356 264 | 61109<br>−4427<br>356 265 | 61110<br>−4426<br>356 266 | 61111<br>−4425<br>356 267 | 61112<br>−4424<br>356 270 | 61113<br>−4423<br>356 271 | 61114<br>−4422<br>356 272 | 61115<br>−4421<br>356 273 | 61116<br>−4420<br>356 274 | 61117<br>−4419<br>356 275 | 61118<br>−4418<br>356 276 | 61119<br>−4417<br>356 277 |
| **C−** | 61120<br>−4416<br>356 300 | 61121<br>−4415<br>356 301 | 61122<br>−4414<br>356 302 | 61123<br>−4413<br>356 303 | 61124<br>−4412<br>356 304 | 61125<br>−4411<br>356 305 | 61126<br>−4410<br>356 306 | 61127<br>−4409<br>356 307 | 61128<br>−4408<br>356 310 | 61129<br>−4407<br>356 311 | 61130<br>−4406<br>356 312 | 61131<br>−4405<br>356 313 | 61132<br>−4404<br>356 314 | 61133<br>−4403<br>356 315 | 61134<br>−4402<br>356 316 | 61135<br>−4401<br>356 317 |
| **D−** | 61136<br>−4400<br>356 320 | 61137<br>−4399<br>356 321 | 61138<br>−4398<br>356 322 | 61139<br>−4397<br>356 323 | 61140<br>−4396<br>356 324 | 61141<br>−4395<br>356 325 | 61142<br>−4394<br>356 326 | 61143<br>−4393<br>356 327 | 61144<br>−4392<br>356 330 | 61145<br>−4391<br>356 331 | 61146<br>−4390<br>356 332 | 61147<br>−4389<br>356 333 | 61148<br>−4388<br>356 334 | 61149<br>−4387<br>356 335 | 61150<br>−4386<br>356 336 | 61151<br>−4385<br>356 337 |
| **E−** | 61152<br>−4384<br>356 340 | 61153<br>−4383<br>356 341 | 61154<br>−4382<br>356 342 | 61155<br>−4381<br>356 343 | 61156<br>−4380<br>356 344 | 61157<br>−4379<br>356 345 | 61158<br>−4378<br>356 346 | 61159<br>−4377<br>356 347 | 61160<br>−4376<br>356 350 | 61161<br>−4375<br>356 351 | 61162<br>−4374<br>356 352 | 61163<br>−4373<br>356 353 | 61164<br>−4372<br>356 354 | 61165<br>−4371<br>356 355 | 61166<br>−4370<br>356 356 | 61167<br>−4369<br>356 357 |
| **F−** | 61168<br>−4368<br>356 360 | 61169<br>−4367<br>356 361 | 61170<br>−4366<br>356 362 | 61171<br>−4365<br>356 363 | 61172<br>−4364<br>356 364 | 61173<br>−4363<br>356 365 | 61174<br>−4362<br>356 366 | 61175<br>−4361<br>356 367 | 61176<br>−4360<br>356 370 | 61177<br>−4359<br>356 371 | 61178<br>−4358<br>356 372 | 61179<br>−4357<br>356 373 | 61180<br>−4356<br>356 374 | 61181<br>−4355<br>356 375 | 61182<br>−4354<br>356 376 | 61183<br>−4353<br>356 377 |

DECIMAL →

 DECIMAL →

OCTAL →

 DECIMAL  −4608    BINARY  1110 1110    DECIMAL  60928    HEXADECIMAL  ⬡ EE  OCTAL  356 000

FOURTH HEX DIGIT →  ← THIRD HEX DIGIT

 DECIMAL │ −4352 │ BINARY │ 1110 1111 │ DECIMAL │ 61184 │ HEXADECIMAL │ EF │ OCTAL │ 357 000

FOURTH HEX DIGIT → ← THIRD HEX DIGIT

(2)

**FIRST HEX DIGIT**

| SECOND HEX DIGIT | −0 | −1 | −2 | −3 | −4 | −5 | −6 | −7 | −8 | −9 | −A | −B | −C | −D | −E | −F |
|---|---|---|---|---|---|---|---|---|---|---|---|---|---|---|---|---|
| **0−** | 61184<br>−4352<br>357 000 | 61185<br>−4351<br>357 001 | 61186<br>−4350<br>357 002 | 61187<br>−4349<br>357 003 | 61188<br>−4348<br>357 004 | 61189<br>−4347<br>357 005 | 61190<br>−4346<br>357 006 | 61191<br>−4345<br>357 007 | 61192<br>−4344<br>357 010 | 61193<br>−4343<br>357 011 | 61194<br>−4342<br>357 012 | 61195<br>−4341<br>357 013 | 61196<br>−4340<br>357 014 | 61197<br>−4339<br>357 015 | 61198<br>−4338<br>357 016 | 61199<br>−4337<br>357 017 |
| **1−** | 61200<br>−4336<br>357 020 | 61201<br>−4335<br>357 021 | 61202<br>−4334<br>357 022 | 61203<br>−4333<br>357 023 | 61204<br>−4332<br>357 024 | 61205<br>−4331<br>357 025 | 61206<br>−4330<br>357 026 | 61207<br>−4329<br>357 027 | 61208<br>−4328<br>357 030 | 61209<br>−4327<br>357 031 | 61210<br>−4326<br>357 032 | 61211<br>−4325<br>357 033 | 61212<br>−4324<br>357 034 | 61213<br>−4323<br>357 035 | 61214<br>−4322<br>357 036 | 61215<br>−4321<br>357 037 |
| **2−** | 61216<br>−4320<br>357 040 | 61217<br>−4319<br>357 041 | 61218<br>−4318<br>357 042 | 61219<br>−4317<br>357 043 | 61220<br>−4316<br>357 044 | 61221<br>−4315<br>357 045 | 61222<br>−4314<br>357 046 | 61223<br>−4313<br>357 047 | 61224<br>−4312<br>357 050 | 61225<br>−4311<br>357 051 | 61226<br>−4310<br>357 052 | 61227<br>−4309<br>357 053 | 61228<br>−4308<br>357 054 | 61229<br>−4307<br>357 055 | 61230<br>−4306<br>357 056 | 61231<br>−4305<br>357 057 |
| **3−** | 61232<br>−4304<br>357 060 | 61233<br>−4303<br>357 061 | 61234<br>−4302<br>357 062 | 61235<br>−4301<br>357 063 | 61236<br>−4300<br>357 064 | 61237<br>−4299<br>357 065 | 61238<br>−4298<br>357 066 | 61239<br>−4297<br>357 067 | 61240<br>−4296<br>357 070 | 61241<br>−4295<br>357 071 | 61242<br>−4294<br>357 072 | 61243<br>−4293<br>357 073 | 61244<br>−4292<br>357 074 | 61245<br>−4291<br>357 075 | 61246<br>−4290<br>357 076 | 61247<br>−4289<br>357 077 |
| **4−** | 61248<br>−4288<br>357 100 | 61249<br>−4287<br>357 101 | 61250<br>−4286<br>357 102 | 61251<br>−4285<br>357 103 | 61252<br>−4284<br>357 104 | 61253<br>−4283<br>357 105 | 61254<br>−4282<br>357 106 | 61255<br>−4281<br>357 107 | 61256<br>−4280<br>357 110 | 61257<br>−4279<br>357 111 | 61258<br>−4278<br>357 112 | 61259<br>−4277<br>357 113 | 61260<br>−4276<br>357 114 | 61261<br>−4275<br>357 115 | 61262<br>−4274<br>357 116 | 61263<br>−4273<br>357 117 |
| **5−** | 61264<br>−4272<br>357 120 | 61265<br>−4271<br>357 121 | 61266<br>−4270<br>357 122 | 61267<br>−4269<br>357 123 | 61268<br>−4268<br>357 124 | 61269<br>−4267<br>357 125 | 61270<br>−4266<br>357 126 | 61271<br>−4265<br>357 127 | 61272<br>−4264<br>357 130 | 61273<br>−4263<br>357 131 | 61274<br>−4262<br>357 132 | 61275<br>−4261<br>357 133 | 61276<br>−4260<br>357 134 | 61277<br>−4259<br>357 135 | 61278<br>−4258<br>357 136 | 61279<br>−4257<br>357 137 |
| **6−** | 61280<br>−4256<br>357 140 | 61281<br>−4255<br>357 141 | 61282<br>−4254<br>357 142 | 61283<br>−4253<br>357 143 | 61284<br>−4252<br>357 144 | 61285<br>−4251<br>357 145 | 61286<br>−4250<br>357 146 | 61287<br>−4249<br>357 147 | 61288<br>−4248<br>357 150 | 61289<br>−4247<br>357 151 | 61290<br>−4246<br>357 152 | 61291<br>−4245<br>357 153 | 61292<br>−4244<br>357 154 | 61293<br>−4243<br>357 155 | 61294<br>−4242<br>357 156 | 61295<br>−4241<br>357 157 |
| **7−** | 61296<br>−4240<br>357 160 | 61297<br>−4239<br>357 161 | 61298<br>−4238<br>357 162 | 61299<br>−4237<br>357 163 | 61300<br>−4236<br>357 164 | 61301<br>−4235<br>357 165 | 61302<br>−4234<br>357 166 | 61303<br>−4233<br>357 167 | 61304<br>−4232<br>357 170 | 61305<br>−4231<br>357 171 | 61306<br>−4230<br>357 172 | 61307<br>−4229<br>357 173 | 61308<br>−4228<br>357 174 | 61309<br>−4227<br>357 175 | 61310<br>−4226<br>357 176 | 61311<br>−4225<br>357 177 |
| **8−** | 61312<br>−4224<br>357 200 | 61313<br>−4223<br>357 201 | 61314<br>−4222<br>357 202 | 61315<br>−4221<br>357 203 | 61316<br>−4220<br>357 204 | 61317<br>−4219<br>357 205 | 61318<br>−4218<br>357 206 | 61319<br>−4217<br>357 207 | 61320<br>−4216<br>357 210 | 61321<br>−4215<br>357 211 | 61322<br>−4214<br>357 212 | 61323<br>−4213<br>357 213 | 61324<br>−4212<br>357 214 | 61325<br>−4211<br>357 215 | 61326<br>−4210<br>357 216 | 61327<br>−4209<br>357 217 |
| **9−** | 61328<br>−4208<br>357 220 | 61329<br>−4207<br>357 221 | 61330<br>−4206<br>357 222 | 61331<br>−4205<br>357 223 | 61332<br>−4204<br>357 224 | 61333<br>−4203<br>357 225 | 61334<br>−4202<br>357 226 | 61335<br>−4201<br>357 227 | 61336<br>−4200<br>357 230 | 61337<br>−4199<br>357 231 | 61338<br>−4198<br>357 232 | 61339<br>−4197<br>357 233 | 61340<br>−4196<br>357 234 | 61341<br>−4195<br>357 235 | 61342<br>−4194<br>357 236 | 61343<br>−4193<br>357 237 |
| **A−** | 61344<br>−4192<br>357 240 | 61345<br>−4191<br>357 241 | 61346<br>−4190<br>357 242 | 61347<br>−4189<br>357 243 | 61348<br>−4188<br>357 244 | 61349<br>−4187<br>357 245 | 61350<br>−4186<br>357 246 | 61351<br>−4185<br>357 247 | 61352<br>−4184<br>357 250 | 61353<br>−4183<br>357 251 | 61354<br>−4182<br>357 252 | 61355<br>−4181<br>357 253 | 61356<br>−4180<br>357 254 | 61357<br>−4179<br>357 255 | 61358<br>−4178<br>357 256 | 61359<br>−4177<br>357 257 |
| **B−** | 61360<br>−4176<br>357 260 | 61361<br>−4175<br>357 261 | 61362<br>−4174<br>357 262 | 61363<br>−4173<br>357 263 | 61364<br>−4172<br>357 264 | 61365<br>−4171<br>357 265 | 61366<br>−4170<br>357 266 | 61367<br>−4169<br>357 267 | 61368<br>−4168<br>357 270 | 61369<br>−4167<br>357 271 | 61370<br>−4166<br>357 272 | 61371<br>−4165<br>357 273 | 61372<br>−4164<br>357 274 | 61373<br>−4163<br>357 275 | 61374<br>−4162<br>357 276 | 61375<br>−4161<br>357 277 |
| **C−** | 61376<br>−4160<br>357 300 | 61377<br>−4159<br>357 301 | 61378<br>−4158<br>357 302 | 61379<br>−4157<br>357 303 | 61380<br>−4156<br>357 304 | 61381<br>−4155<br>357 305 | 61382<br>−4154<br>357 306 | 61383<br>−4153<br>357 307 | 61384<br>−4152<br>357 310 | 61385<br>−4151<br>357 311 | 61386<br>−4150<br>357 312 | 61387<br>−4149<br>357 313 | 61388<br>−4148<br>357 314 | 61389<br>−4147<br>357 315 | 61390<br>−4146<br>357 316 | 61391<br>−4145<br>357 317 |
| **D−** | 61392<br>−4144<br>357 320 | 61393<br>−4143<br>357 321 | 61394<br>−4142<br>357 322 | 61395<br>−4141<br>357 323 | 61396<br>−4140<br>357 324 | 61397<br>−4139<br>357 325 | 61398<br>−4138<br>357 326 | 61399<br>−4137<br>357 327 | 61400<br>−4136<br>357 330 | 61401<br>−4135<br>357 331 | 61402<br>−4134<br>357 332 | 61403<br>−4133<br>357 333 | 61404<br>−4132<br>357 334 | 61405<br>−4131<br>357 335 | 61406<br>−4130<br>357 336 | 61407<br>−4129<br>357 337 |
| **E−** | 61408<br>−4128<br>357 340 | 61409<br>−4127<br>357 341 | 61410<br>−4126<br>357 342 | 61411<br>−4125<br>357 343 | 61412<br>−4124<br>357 344 | 61413<br>−4123<br>357 345 | 61414<br>−4122<br>357 346 | 61415<br>−4121<br>357 347 | 61416<br>−4120<br>357 350 | 61417<br>−4119<br>357 351 | 61418<br>−4118<br>357 352 | 61419<br>−4117<br>357 353 | 61420<br>−4116<br>357 354 | 61421<br>−4115<br>357 355 | 61422<br>−4114<br>357 356 | 61423<br>−4113<br>357 357 |
| **F−** | 61424<br>−4112<br>357 360 | 61425<br>−4111<br>357 361 | 61426<br>−4110<br>357 362 | 61427<br>−4109<br>357 363 | 61428<br>−4108<br>357 364 | 61429<br>−4107<br>357 365 | 61430<br>−4106<br>357 366 | 61431<br>−4105<br>357 367 | 61432<br>−4104<br>357 370 | 61433<br>−4103<br>357 371 | 61434<br>−4102<br>357 372 | 61435<br>−4101<br>357 373 | 61436<br>−4100<br>357 374 | 61437<br>−4099<br>357 375 | 61438<br>−4098<br>357 376 | 61439<br>−4097<br>357 377 |

DECIMAL

 DECIMAL

OCTAL

| ⬡ 2 | FIRST HEX DIGIT | | | | | | | | | | | | | | | |
|---|---|---|---|---|---|---|---|---|---|---|---|---|---|---|---|---|
| | −0 | −1 | −2 | −3 | −4 | −5 | −6 | −7 | −8 | −9 | −A | −B | −C | −D | −E | −F |
| 0− | 61440<br>-4096<br>360 000 | 61441<br>-4095<br>360 001 | 61442<br>-4094<br>360 002 | 61443<br>-4093<br>360 003 | 61444<br>-4092<br>360 004 | 61445<br>-4091<br>360 005 | 61446<br>-4090<br>360 006 | 61447<br>-4089<br>360 007 | 61448<br>-4088<br>360 010 | 61449<br>-4087<br>360 011 | 61450<br>-4086<br>360 012 | 61451<br>-4085<br>360 013 | 61452<br>-4084<br>360 014 | 61453<br>-4083<br>360 015 | 61454<br>-4082<br>360 016 | 61455<br>-4081<br>360 017 |
| 1− | 61456<br>-4080<br>360 020 | 61457<br>-4079<br>360 021 | 61458<br>-4078<br>360 022 | 61459<br>-4077<br>360 023 | 61460<br>-4076<br>360 024 | 61461<br>-4075<br>360 025 | 61462<br>-4074<br>360 026 | 61463<br>-4073<br>360 027 | 61464<br>-4072<br>360 030 | 61465<br>-4071<br>360 031 | 61466<br>-4070<br>360 032 | 61467<br>-4069<br>360 033 | 61468<br>-4068<br>360 034 | 61469<br>-4067<br>360 035 | 61470<br>-4066<br>360 036 | 61471<br>-4065<br>360 037 |
| 2− | 61472<br>-4064<br>360 040 | 61473<br>-4063<br>360 041 | 61474<br>-4062<br>360 042 | 61475<br>-4061<br>360 043 | 61476<br>-4060<br>360 044 | 61477<br>-4059<br>360 045 | 61478<br>-4058<br>360 046 | 61479<br>-4057<br>360 047 | 61480<br>-4056<br>360 050 | 61481<br>-4055<br>360 051 | 61482<br>-4054<br>360 052 | 61483<br>-4053<br>360 053 | 61484<br>-4052<br>360 054 | 61485<br>-4051<br>360 055 | 61486<br>-4050<br>360 056 | 61487<br>-4049<br>360 057 |
| 3− | 61488<br>-4048<br>360 060 | 61489<br>-4047<br>360 061 | 61490<br>-4046<br>360 062 | 61491<br>-4045<br>360 063 | 61492<br>-4044<br>360 064 | 61493<br>-4043<br>360 065 | 61494<br>-4042<br>360 066 | 61495<br>-4041<br>360 067 | 61496<br>-4040<br>360 070 | 61497<br>-4039<br>360 071 | 61498<br>-4038<br>360 072 | 61499<br>-4037<br>360 073 | 61500<br>-4036<br>360 074 | 61501<br>-4035<br>360 075 | 61502<br>-4034<br>360 076 | 61503<br>-4033<br>360 077 |
| 4− | 61504<br>-4032<br>360 100 | 61505<br>-4031<br>360 101 | 61506<br>-4030<br>360 102 | 61507<br>-4029<br>360 103 | 61508<br>-4028<br>360 104 | 61509<br>-4027<br>360 105 | 61510<br>-4026<br>360 106 | 61511<br>-4025<br>360 107 | 61512<br>-4024<br>360 110 | 61513<br>-4023<br>360 111 | 61514<br>-4022<br>360 112 | 61515<br>-4021<br>360 113 | 61516<br>-4020<br>360 114 | 61517<br>-4019<br>360 115 | 61518<br>-4018<br>360 116 | 61519<br>-4017<br>360 117 |
| 5− | 61520<br>-4016<br>360 120 | 61521<br>-4015<br>360 121 | 61522<br>-4014<br>360 122 | 61523<br>-4013<br>360 123 | 61524<br>-4012<br>360 124 | 61525<br>-4011<br>360 125 | 61526<br>-4010<br>360 126 | 61527<br>-4009<br>360 127 | 61528<br>-4008<br>360 130 | 61529<br>-4007<br>360 131 | 61530<br>-4006<br>360 132 | 61531<br>-4005<br>360 133 | 61532<br>-4004<br>360 134 | 61533<br>-4003<br>360 135 | 61534<br>-4002<br>360 136 | 61535<br>-4001<br>360 137 |
| 6− | 61536<br>-4000<br>360 140 | 61537<br>-3999<br>360 141 | 61538<br>-3998<br>360 142 | 61539<br>-3997<br>360 143 | 61540<br>-3996<br>360 144 | 61541<br>-3995<br>360 145 | 61542<br>-3994<br>360 146 | 61543<br>-3993<br>360 147 | 61544<br>-3992<br>360 150 | 61545<br>-3991<br>360 151 | 61546<br>-3990<br>360 152 | 61547<br>-3989<br>360 153 | 61548<br>-3988<br>360 154 | 61549<br>-3987<br>360 155 | 61550<br>-3986<br>360 156 | 61551<br>-3985<br>360 157 |
| 7− | 61552<br>-3984<br>360 160 | 61553<br>-3983<br>360 161 | 61554<br>-3982<br>360 162 | 61555<br>-3981<br>360 163 | 61556<br>-3980<br>360 164 | 61557<br>-3979<br>360 165 | 61558<br>-3978<br>360 166 | 61559<br>-3977<br>360 167 | 61560<br>-3976<br>360 170 | 61561<br>-3975<br>360 171 | 61562<br>-3974<br>360 172 | 61563<br>-3973<br>360 173 | 61564<br>-3972<br>360 174 | 61565<br>-3971<br>360 175 | 61566<br>-3970<br>360 176 | 61567<br>-3969<br>360 177 |
| 8− | 61568<br>-3968<br>360 200 | 61569<br>-3967<br>360 201 | 61570<br>-3966<br>360 202 | 61571<br>-3965<br>360 203 | 61572<br>-3964<br>360 204 | 61573<br>-3963<br>360 205 | 61574<br>-3962<br>360 206 | 61575<br>-3961<br>360 207 | 61576<br>-3960<br>360 210 | 61577<br>-3959<br>360 211 | 61578<br>-3958<br>360 212 | 61579<br>-3957<br>360 213 | 61580<br>-3956<br>360 214 | 61581<br>-3955<br>360 215 | 61582<br>-3954<br>360 216 | 61583<br>-3953<br>360 217 |
| 9− | 61584<br>-3952<br>360 220 | 61585<br>-3951<br>360 221 | 61586<br>-3950<br>360 222 | 61587<br>-3949<br>360 223 | 61588<br>-3948<br>360 224 | 61589<br>-3947<br>360 225 | 61590<br>-3946<br>360 226 | 61591<br>-3945<br>360 227 | 61592<br>-3944<br>360 230 | 61593<br>-3943<br>360 231 | 61594<br>-3942<br>360 232 | 61595<br>-3941<br>360 233 | 61596<br>-3940<br>360 234 | 61597<br>-3939<br>360 235 | 61598<br>-3938<br>360 236 | 61599<br>-3937<br>360 237 |
| A− | 61600<br>-3936<br>360 240 | 61601<br>-3935<br>360 241 | 61602<br>-3934<br>360 242 | 61603<br>-3933<br>360 243 | 61604<br>-3932<br>360 244 | 61605<br>-3931<br>360 245 | 61606<br>-3930<br>360 246 | 61607<br>-3929<br>360 247 | 61608<br>-3928<br>360 250 | 61609<br>-3927<br>360 251 | 61610<br>-3926<br>360 252 | 61611<br>-3925<br>360 253 | 61612<br>-3924<br>360 254 | 61613<br>-3923<br>360 255 | 61614<br>-3922<br>360 256 | 61615<br>-3921<br>360 257 |
| B− | 61616<br>-3920<br>360 260 | 61617<br>-3919<br>360 261 | 61618<br>-3918<br>360 262 | 61619<br>-3917<br>360 263 | 61620<br>-3916<br>360 264 | 61621<br>-3915<br>360 265 | 61622<br>-3914<br>360 266 | 61623<br>-3913<br>360 267 | 61624<br>-3912<br>360 270 | 61625<br>-3911<br>360 271 | 61626<br>-3910<br>360 272 | 61627<br>-3909<br>360 273 | 61628<br>-3908<br>360 274 | 61629<br>-3907<br>360 275 | 61630<br>-3906<br>360 276 | 61631<br>-3905<br>360 277 |
| C− | 61632<br>-3904<br>360 300 | 61633<br>-3903<br>360 301 | 61634<br>-3902<br>360 302 | 61635<br>-3901<br>360 303 | 61636<br>-3900<br>360 304 | 61637<br>-3899<br>360 305 | 61638<br>-3898<br>360 306 | 61639<br>-3897<br>360 307 | 61640<br>-3896<br>360 310 | 61641<br>-3895<br>360 311 | 61642<br>-3894<br>360 312 | 61643<br>-3893<br>360 313 | 61644<br>-3892<br>360 314 | 61645<br>-3891<br>360 315 | 61646<br>-3890<br>360 316 | 61647<br>-3889<br>360 317 |
| D− | 61648<br>-3888<br>360 320 | 61649<br>-3887<br>360 321 | 61650<br>-3886<br>360 322 | 61651<br>-3885<br>360 323 | 61652<br>-3884<br>360 324 | 61653<br>-3883<br>360 325 | 61654<br>-3882<br>360 326 | 61655<br>-3881<br>360 327 | 61656<br>-3880<br>360 330 | 61657<br>-3879<br>360 331 | 61658<br>-3878<br>360 332 | 61659<br>-3877<br>360 333 | 61660<br>-3876<br>360 334 | 61661<br>-3875<br>360 335 | 61662<br>-3874<br>360 336 | 61663<br>-3873<br>360 337 |
| E− | 61664<br>-3872<br>360 340 | 61665<br>-3871<br>360 341 | 61666<br>-3870<br>360 342 | 61667<br>-3869<br>360 343 | 61668<br>-3868<br>360 344 | 61669<br>-3867<br>360 345 | 61670<br>-3866<br>360 346 | 61671<br>-3865<br>360 347 | 61672<br>-3864<br>360 350 | 61673<br>-3863<br>360 351 | 61674<br>-3862<br>360 352 | 61675<br>-3861<br>360 353 | 61676<br>-3860<br>360 354 | 61677<br>-3859<br>360 355 | 61678<br>-3858<br>360 356 | 61679<br>-3857<br>360 357 |
| F− | 61680<br>-3856<br>360 360 | 61681<br>-3855<br>360 361 | 61682<br>-3854<br>360 362 | 61683<br>-3853<br>360 363 | 61684<br>-3852<br>360 364 | 61685<br>-3851<br>360 365 | 61686<br>-3850<br>360 366 | 61687<br>-3849<br>360 367 | 61688<br>-3848<br>360 370 | 61689<br>-3847<br>360 371 | 61690<br>-3846<br>360 372 | 61691<br>-3845<br>360 373 | 61692<br>-3844<br>360 374 | 61693<br>-3843<br>360 375 | 61694<br>-3842<br>360 376 | 61695<br>-3841<br>360 377 |

Left label: SECOND HEX DIGIT

Right-side labels: DECIMAL  •   DECIMAL  •  OCTAL

⬢ DECIMAL  −4096    BINARY  1111 0000    DECIMAL  61440    HEXADECIMAL  (F0)  OCTAL  360 000

FOURTH HEX DIGIT → (F0) ← THIRD HEX DIGIT

DECIMAL  -3840    BINARY  1111 0001    DECIMAL  61696    HEXADECIMAL  F1    OCTAL  361 000

FOURTH HEX DIGIT → F1 ← THIRD HEX DIGIT

## 2  FIRST HEX DIGIT

SECOND HEX DIGIT

| | -0 | -1 | -2 | -3 | -4 | -5 | -6 | -7 | -8 | -9 | -A | -B | -C | -D | -E | -F |
|---|---|---|---|---|---|---|---|---|---|---|---|---|---|---|---|---|
| 0- | 61696<br>-3840<br>361 000 | 61697<br>-3839<br>361 001 | 61698<br>-3838<br>361 002 | 61699<br>-3837<br>361 003 | 61700<br>-3836<br>361 004 | 61701<br>-3835<br>361 005 | 61702<br>-3834<br>361 006 | 61703<br>-3833<br>361 007 | 61704<br>-3832<br>361 010 | 61705<br>-3831<br>361 011 | 61706<br>-3830<br>361 012 | 61707<br>-3829<br>361 013 | 61708<br>-3828<br>361 014 | 61709<br>-3827<br>361 015 | 61710<br>-3826<br>361 016 | 61711<br>-3825<br>361 017 |
| 1- | 61712<br>-3824<br>361 020 | 61713<br>-3823<br>361 021 | 61714<br>-3822<br>361 022 | 61715<br>-3821<br>361 023 | 61716<br>-3820<br>361 024 | 61717<br>-3819<br>361 025 | 61718<br>-3818<br>361 026 | 61719<br>-3817<br>361 027 | 61720<br>-3816<br>361 030 | 61721<br>-3815<br>361 031 | 61722<br>-3814<br>361 032 | 61723<br>-3813<br>361 033 | 61724<br>-3812<br>361 034 | 61725<br>-3811<br>361 035 | 61726<br>-3810<br>361 036 | 61727<br>-3809<br>361 037 |
| 2- | 61728<br>-3808<br>361 040 | 61729<br>-3807<br>361 041 | 61730<br>-3806<br>361 042 | 61731<br>-3805<br>361 043 | 61732<br>-3804<br>361 044 | 61733<br>-3803<br>361 045 | 61734<br>-3802<br>361 046 | 61735<br>-3801<br>361 047 | 61736<br>-3800<br>361 050 | 61737<br>-3799<br>361 051 | 61738<br>-3798<br>361 052 | 61739<br>-3797<br>361 053 | 61740<br>-3796<br>361 054 | 61741<br>-3795<br>361 055 | 61742<br>-3794<br>361 056 | 61743<br>-3793<br>361 057 |
| 3- | 61744<br>-3792<br>361 060 | 61745<br>-3791<br>361 061 | 61746<br>-3790<br>361 062 | 61747<br>-3789<br>361 063 | 61748<br>-3788<br>361 064 | 61749<br>-3787<br>361 065 | 61750<br>-3786<br>361 066 | 61751<br>-3785<br>361 067 | 61752<br>-3784<br>361 070 | 61753<br>-3783<br>361 071 | 61754<br>-3782<br>361 072 | 61755<br>-3781<br>361 073 | 61756<br>-3780<br>361 074 | 61757<br>-3779<br>361 075 | 61758<br>-3778<br>361 076 | 61759<br>-3777<br>361 077 |
| 4- | 61760<br>-3776<br>361 100 | 61761<br>-3775<br>361 101 | 61762<br>-3774<br>361 102 | 61763<br>-3773<br>361 103 | 61764<br>-3772<br>361 104 | 61765<br>-3771<br>361 105 | 61766<br>-3770<br>361 106 | 61767<br>-3769<br>361 107 | 61768<br>-3768<br>361 110 | 61769<br>-3767<br>361 111 | 61770<br>-3766<br>361 112 | 61771<br>-3765<br>361 113 | 61772<br>-3764<br>361 114 | 61773<br>-3763<br>361 115 | 61774<br>-3762<br>361 116 | 61775<br>-3761<br>361 117 |
| 5- | 61776<br>-3760<br>361 120 | 61777<br>-3759<br>361 121 | 61778<br>-3758<br>361 122 | 61779<br>-3757<br>361 123 | 61780<br>-3756<br>361 124 | 61781<br>-3755<br>361 125 | 61782<br>-3754<br>361 126 | 61783<br>-3753<br>361 127 | 61784<br>-3752<br>361 130 | 61785<br>-3751<br>361 131 | 61786<br>-3750<br>361 132 | 61787<br>-3749<br>361 133 | 61788<br>-3748<br>361 134 | 61789<br>-3747<br>361 135 | 61790<br>-3746<br>361 136 | 61791<br>-3745<br>361 137 |
| 6- | 61792<br>-3744<br>361 140 | 61793<br>-3743<br>361 141 | 61794<br>-3742<br>361 142 | 61795<br>-3741<br>361 143 | 61796<br>-3740<br>361 144 | 61797<br>-3739<br>361 145 | 61798<br>-3738<br>361 146 | 61799<br>-3737<br>361 147 | 61800<br>-3736<br>361 150 | 61801<br>-3735<br>361 151 | 61802<br>-3734<br>361 152 | 61803<br>-3733<br>361 153 | 61804<br>-3732<br>361 154 | 61805<br>-3731<br>361 155 | 61806<br>-3730<br>361 156 | 61807<br>-3729<br>361 157 |
| 7- | 61808<br>-3728<br>361 160 | 61809<br>-3727<br>361 161 | 61810<br>-3726<br>361 162 | 61811<br>-3725<br>361 163 | 61812<br>-3724<br>361 164 | 61813<br>-3723<br>361 165 | 61814<br>-3722<br>361 166 | 61815<br>-3721<br>361 167 | 61816<br>-3720<br>361 170 | 61817<br>-3719<br>361 171 | 61818<br>-3718<br>361 172 | 61819<br>-3717<br>361 173 | 61820<br>-3716<br>361 174 | 61821<br>-3715<br>361 175 | 61822<br>-3714<br>361 176 | 61823<br>-3713<br>361 177 |
| 8- | 61824<br>-3712<br>361 200 | 61825<br>-3711<br>361 201 | 61826<br>-3710<br>361 202 | 61827<br>-3709<br>361 203 | 61828<br>-3708<br>361 204 | 61829<br>-3707<br>361 205 | 61830<br>-3706<br>361 206 | 61831<br>-3705<br>361 207 | 61832<br>-3704<br>361 210 | 61833<br>-3703<br>361 211 | 61834<br>-3702<br>361 212 | 61835<br>-3701<br>361 213 | 61836<br>-3700<br>361 214 | 61837<br>-3699<br>361 215 | 61838<br>-3698<br>361 216 | 61839<br>-3697<br>361 217 |
| 9- | 61840<br>-3696<br>361 220 | 61841<br>-3695<br>361 221 | 61842<br>-3694<br>361 222 | 61843<br>-3693<br>361 223 | 61844<br>-3692<br>361 224 | 61845<br>-3691<br>361 225 | 61846<br>-3690<br>361 226 | 61847<br>-3689<br>361 227 | 61848<br>-3688<br>361 230 | 61849<br>-3687<br>361 231 | 61850<br>-3686<br>361 232 | 61851<br>-3685<br>361 233 | 61852<br>-3684<br>361 234 | 61853<br>-3683<br>361 235 | 61854<br>-3682<br>361 236 | 61855<br>-3681<br>361 237 |
| A- | 61856<br>-3680<br>361 240 | 61857<br>-3679<br>361 241 | 61858<br>-3678<br>361 242 | 61859<br>-3677<br>361 243 | 61860<br>-3676<br>361 244 | 61861<br>-3675<br>361 245 | 61862<br>-3674<br>361 246 | 61863<br>-3673<br>361 247 | 61864<br>-3672<br>361 250 | 61865<br>-3671<br>361 251 | 61866<br>-3670<br>361 252 | 61867<br>-3669<br>361 253 | 61868<br>-3668<br>361 254 | 61869<br>-3667<br>361 255 | 61870<br>-3666<br>361 256 | 61871<br>-3665<br>361 257 |
| B- | 61872<br>-3664<br>361 260 | 61873<br>-3663<br>361 261 | 61874<br>-3662<br>361 262 | 61875<br>-3661<br>361 263 | 61876<br>-3660<br>361 264 | 61877<br>-3659<br>361 265 | 61878<br>-3658<br>361 266 | 61879<br>-3657<br>361 267 | 61880<br>-3656<br>361 270 | 61881<br>-3655<br>361 271 | 61882<br>-3654<br>361 272 | 61883<br>-3653<br>361 273 | 61884<br>-3652<br>361 274 | 61885<br>-3651<br>361 275 | 61886<br>-3650<br>361 276 | 61887<br>-3649<br>361 277 |
| C- | 61888<br>-3648<br>361 300 | 61889<br>-3647<br>361 301 | 61890<br>-3646<br>361 302 | 61891<br>-3645<br>361 303 | 61892<br>-3644<br>361 304 | 61893<br>-3643<br>361 305 | 61894<br>-3642<br>361 306 | 61895<br>-3641<br>361 307 | 61896<br>-3640<br>361 310 | 61897<br>-3639<br>361 311 | 61898<br>-3638<br>361 312 | 61899<br>-3637<br>361 313 | 61900<br>-3636<br>361 314 | 61901<br>-3635<br>361 315 | 61902<br>-3634<br>361 316 | 61903<br>-3633<br>361 317 |
| D- | 61904<br>-3632<br>361 320 | 61905<br>-3631<br>361 321 | 61906<br>-3630<br>361 322 | 61907<br>-3629<br>361 323 | 61908<br>-3628<br>361 324 | 61909<br>-3627<br>361 325 | 61910<br>-3626<br>361 326 | 61911<br>-3625<br>361 327 | 61912<br>-3624<br>361 330 | 61913<br>-3623<br>361 331 | 61914<br>-3622<br>361 332 | 61915<br>-3621<br>361 333 | 61916<br>-3620<br>361 334 | 61917<br>-3619<br>361 335 | 61918<br>-3618<br>361 336 | 61919<br>-3617<br>361 337 |
| E- | 61920<br>-3616<br>361 340 | 61921<br>-3615<br>361 341 | 61922<br>-3614<br>361 342 | 61923<br>-3613<br>361 343 | 61924<br>-3612<br>361 344 | 61925<br>-3611<br>361 345 | 61926<br>-3610<br>361 346 | 61927<br>-3609<br>361 347 | 61928<br>-3608<br>361 350 | 61929<br>-3607<br>361 351 | 61930<br>-3606<br>361 352 | 61931<br>-3605<br>361 353 | 61932<br>-3604<br>361 354 | 61933<br>-3603<br>361 355 | 61934<br>-3602<br>361 356 | 61935<br>-3601<br>361 357 |
| F- | 61936<br>-3600<br>361 360 | 61937<br>-3599<br>361 361 | 61938<br>-3598<br>361 362 | 61939<br>-3597<br>361 363 | 61940<br>-3596<br>361 364 | 61941<br>-3595<br>361 365 | 61942<br>-3594<br>361 366 | 61943<br>-3593<br>361 367 | 61944<br>-3592<br>361 370 | 61945<br>-3591<br>361 371 | 61946<br>-3590<br>361 372 | 61947<br>-3589<br>361 373 | 61948<br>-3588<br>361 374 | 61949<br>-3587<br>361 375 | 61950<br>-3586<br>361 376 | 61951<br>-3585<br>361 377 |

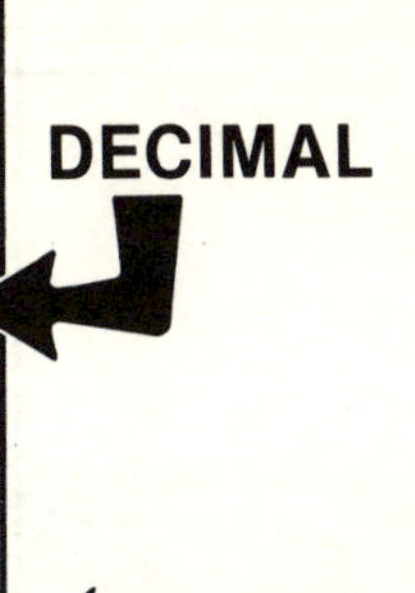


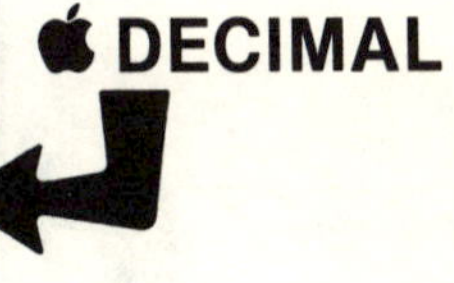


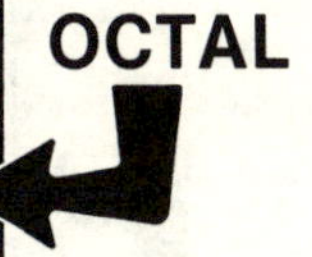

## FIRST HEX DIGIT

**SECOND HEX DIGIT**

| | −0 | −1 | −2 | −3 | −4 | −5 | −6 | −7 | −8 | −9 | −A | −B | −C | −D | −E | −F |
|---|---|---|---|---|---|---|---|---|---|---|---|---|---|---|---|---|
| **0−** | 61952<br>−3584<br>362 000 | 61953<br>−3583<br>362 001 | 61954<br>−3582<br>362 002 | 61955<br>−3581<br>362 003 | 61956<br>−3580<br>362 004 | 61957<br>−3579<br>362 005 | 61958<br>−3578<br>362 006 | 61959<br>−3577<br>362 007 | 61960<br>−3576<br>362 010 | 61961<br>−3575<br>362 011 | 61962<br>−3574<br>362 012 | 61963<br>−3573<br>362 013 | 61964<br>−3572<br>362 014 | 61965<br>−3571<br>362 015 | 61966<br>−3570<br>362 016 | 61967<br>−3569<br>362 017 |
| **1−** | 61968<br>−3568<br>362 020 | 61969<br>−3567<br>362 021 | 61970<br>−3566<br>362 022 | 61971<br>−3565<br>362 023 | 61972<br>−3564<br>362 024 | 61973<br>−3563<br>362 025 | 61974<br>−3562<br>362 026 | 61975<br>−3561<br>362 027 | 61976<br>−3560<br>362 030 | 61977<br>−3559<br>362 031 | 61978<br>−3558<br>362 032 | 61979<br>−3557<br>362 033 | 61980<br>−3556<br>362 034 | 61981<br>−3555<br>362 035 | 61982<br>−3554<br>362 036 | 61983<br>−3553<br>362 037 |
| **2−** | 61984<br>−3552<br>362 040 | 61985<br>−3551<br>362 041 | 61986<br>−3550<br>362 042 | 61987<br>−3549<br>362 043 | 61988<br>−3548<br>362 044 | 61989<br>−3547<br>362 045 | 61990<br>−3546<br>362 046 | 61991<br>−3545<br>362 047 | 61992<br>−3544<br>362 050 | 61993<br>−3543<br>362 051 | 61994<br>−3542<br>362 052 | 61995<br>−3541<br>362 053 | 61996<br>−3540<br>362 054 | 61997<br>−3539<br>362 055 | 61998<br>−3538<br>362 056 | 61999<br>−3537<br>362 057 |
| **3−** | 62000<br>−3536<br>362 060 | 62001<br>−3535<br>362 061 | 62002<br>−3534<br>362 062 | 62003<br>−3533<br>362 063 | 62004<br>−3532<br>362 064 | 62005<br>−3531<br>362 065 | 62006<br>−3530<br>362 066 | 62007<br>−3529<br>362 067 | 62008<br>−3528<br>362 070 | 62009<br>−3527<br>362 071 | 62010<br>−3526<br>362 072 | 62011<br>−3525<br>362 073 | 62012<br>−3524<br>362 074 | 62013<br>−3523<br>362 075 | 62014<br>−3522<br>362 076 | 62015<br>−3521<br>362 077 |
| **4−** | 62016<br>−3520<br>362 100 | 62017<br>−3519<br>362 101 | 62018<br>−3518<br>362 102 | 62019<br>−3517<br>362 103 | 62020<br>−3516<br>362 104 | 62021<br>−3515<br>362 105 | 62022<br>−3514<br>362 106 | 62023<br>−3513<br>362 107 | 62024<br>−3512<br>362 110 | 62025<br>−3511<br>362 111 | 62026<br>−3510<br>362 112 | 62027<br>−3509<br>362 113 | 62028<br>−3508<br>362 114 | 62029<br>−3507<br>362 115 | 62030<br>−3506<br>362 116 | 62031<br>−3505<br>362 117 |
| **5−** | 62032<br>−3504<br>362 120 | 62033<br>−3503<br>362 121 | 62034<br>−3502<br>362 122 | 62035<br>−3501<br>362 123 | 62036<br>−3500<br>362 124 | 62037<br>−3499<br>362 125 | 62038<br>−3498<br>362 126 | 62039<br>−3497<br>362 127 | 62040<br>−3496<br>362 130 | 62041<br>−3495<br>362 131 | 62042<br>−3494<br>362 132 | 62043<br>−3493<br>362 133 | 62044<br>−3492<br>362 134 | 62045<br>−3491<br>362 135 | 62046<br>−3490<br>362 136 | 62047<br>−3489<br>362 137 |
| **6−** | 62048<br>−3488<br>362 140 | 62049<br>−3487<br>362 141 | 62050<br>−3486<br>362 142 | 62051<br>−3485<br>362 143 | 62052<br>−3484<br>362 144 | 62053<br>−3483<br>362 145 | 62054<br>−3482<br>362 146 | 62055<br>−3481<br>362 147 | 62056<br>−3480<br>362 150 | 62057<br>−3479<br>362 151 | 62058<br>−3478<br>362 152 | 62059<br>−3477<br>362 153 | 62060<br>−3476<br>362 154 | 62061<br>−3475<br>362 155 | 62062<br>−3474<br>362 156 | 62063<br>−3473<br>362 157 |
| **7−** | 62064<br>−3472<br>362 160 | 62065<br>−3471<br>362 161 | 62066<br>−3470<br>362 162 | 62067<br>−3469<br>362 163 | 62068<br>−3468<br>362 164 | 62069<br>−3467<br>362 165 | 62070<br>−3466<br>362 166 | 62071<br>−3465<br>362 167 | 62072<br>−3464<br>362 170 | 62073<br>−3463<br>362 171 | 62074<br>−3462<br>362 172 | 62075<br>−3461<br>362 173 | 62076<br>−3460<br>362 174 | 62077<br>−3459<br>362 175 | 62078<br>−3458<br>362 176 | 62079<br>−3457<br>362 177 |
| **8−** | 62080<br>−3456<br>362 200 | 62081<br>−3455<br>362 201 | 62082<br>−3454<br>362 202 | 62083<br>−3453<br>362 203 | 62084<br>−3452<br>362 204 | 62085<br>−3451<br>362 205 | 62086<br>−3450<br>362 206 | 62087<br>−3449<br>362 207 | 62088<br>−3448<br>362 210 | 62089<br>−3447<br>362 211 | 62090<br>−3446<br>362 212 | 62091<br>−3445<br>362 213 | 62092<br>−3444<br>362 214 | 62093<br>−3443<br>362 215 | 62094<br>−3442<br>362 216 | 62095<br>−3441<br>362 217 |
| **9−** | 62096<br>−3440<br>362 220 | 62097<br>−3439<br>362 221 | 62098<br>−3438<br>362 222 | 62099<br>−3437<br>362 223 | 62100<br>−3436<br>362 224 | 62101<br>−3435<br>362 225 | 62102<br>−3434<br>362 226 | 62103<br>−3433<br>362 227 | 62104<br>−3432<br>362 230 | 62105<br>−3431<br>362 231 | 62106<br>−3430<br>362 232 | 62107<br>−3429<br>362 233 | 62108<br>−3428<br>362 234 | 62109<br>−3427<br>362 235 | 62110<br>−3426<br>362 236 | 62111<br>−3425<br>362 237 |
| **A−** | 62112<br>−3424<br>362 240 | 62113<br>−3423<br>362 241 | 62114<br>−3422<br>362 242 | 62115<br>−3421<br>362 243 | 62116<br>−3420<br>362 244 | 62117<br>−3419<br>362 245 | 62118<br>−3418<br>362 246 | 62119<br>−3417<br>362 247 | 62120<br>−3416<br>362 250 | 62121<br>−3415<br>362 251 | 62122<br>−3414<br>362 252 | 62123<br>−3413<br>362 253 | 62124<br>−3412<br>362 254 | 62125<br>−3411<br>362 255 | 62126<br>−3410<br>362 256 | 62127<br>−3409<br>362 257 |
| **B−** | 62128<br>−3408<br>362 260 | 62129<br>−3407<br>362 261 | 62130<br>−3406<br>362 262 | 62131<br>−3405<br>362 263 | 62132<br>−3404<br>362 264 | 62133<br>−3403<br>362 265 | 62134<br>−3402<br>362 266 | 62135<br>−3401<br>362 267 | 62136<br>−3400<br>362 270 | 62137<br>−3399<br>362 271 | 62138<br>−3398<br>362 272 | 62139<br>−3397<br>362 273 | 62140<br>−3396<br>362 274 | 62141<br>−3395<br>362 275 | 62142<br>−3394<br>362 276 | 62143<br>−3393<br>362 277 |
| **C−** | 62144<br>−3392<br>362 300 | 62145<br>−3391<br>362 301 | 62146<br>−3390<br>362 302 | 62147<br>−3389<br>362 303 | 62148<br>−3388<br>362 304 | 62149<br>−3387<br>362 305 | 62150<br>−3386<br>362 306 | 62151<br>−3385<br>362 307 | 62152<br>−3384<br>362 310 | 62153<br>−3383<br>362 311 | 62154<br>−3382<br>362 312 | 62155<br>−3381<br>362 313 | 62156<br>−3380<br>362 314 | 62157<br>−3379<br>362 315 | 62158<br>−3378<br>362 316 | 62159<br>−3377<br>362 317 |
| **D−** | 62160<br>−3376<br>362 320 | 62161<br>−3375<br>362 321 | 62162<br>−3374<br>362 322 | 62163<br>−3373<br>362 323 | 62164<br>−3372<br>362 324 | 62165<br>−3371<br>362 325 | 62166<br>−3370<br>362 326 | 62167<br>−3369<br>362 327 | 62168<br>−3368<br>362 330 | 62169<br>−3367<br>362 331 | 62170<br>−3366<br>362 332 | 62171<br>−3365<br>362 333 | 62172<br>−3364<br>362 334 | 62173<br>−3363<br>362 335 | 62174<br>−3362<br>362 336 | 62175<br>−3361<br>362 337 |
| **E−** | 62176<br>−3360<br>362 340 | 62177<br>−3359<br>362 341 | 62178<br>−3358<br>362 342 | 62179<br>−3357<br>362 343 | 62180<br>−3356<br>362 344 | 62181<br>−3355<br>362 345 | 62182<br>−3354<br>362 346 | 62183<br>−3353<br>362 347 | 62184<br>−3352<br>362 350 | 62185<br>−3351<br>362 351 | 62186<br>−3350<br>362 352 | 62187<br>−3349<br>362 353 | 62188<br>−3348<br>362 354 | 62189<br>−3347<br>362 355 | 62190<br>−3346<br>362 356 | 62191<br>−3345<br>362 357 |
| **F−** | 62192<br>−3344<br>362 360 | 62193<br>−3343<br>362 361 | 62194<br>−3342<br>362 362 | 62195<br>−3341<br>362 363 | 62196<br>−3340<br>362 364 | 62197<br>−3339<br>362 365 | 62198<br>−3338<br>362 366 | 62199<br>−3337<br>362 367 | 62200<br>−3336<br>362 370 | 62201<br>−3335<br>362 371 | 62202<br>−3334<br>362 372 | 62203<br>−3333<br>362 373 | 62204<br>−3332<br>362 374 | 62205<br>−3331<br>362 375 | 62206<br>−3330<br>362 376 | 62207<br>−3329<br>362 377 |

DECIMAL

⬤ DECIMAL

OCTAL

⬤ **DECIMAL** `−3584`   **BINARY** `1111 0010`   **DECIMAL** `61952`   **HEXADECIMAL** 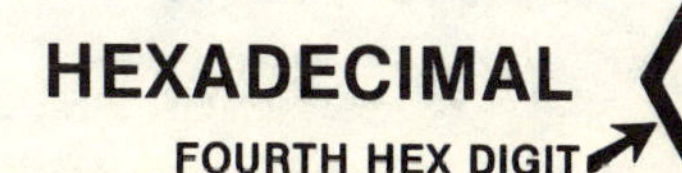 `F2`   **OCTAL** `362 000`

FOURTH HEX DIGIT → ← THIRD HEX DIGIT

 DECIMAL `−3328`  BINARY `1111 0011`  DECIMAL `62208`  HEXADECIMAL (F3) OCTAL `363 000`

FOURTH HEX DIGIT → ← THIRD HEX DIGIT

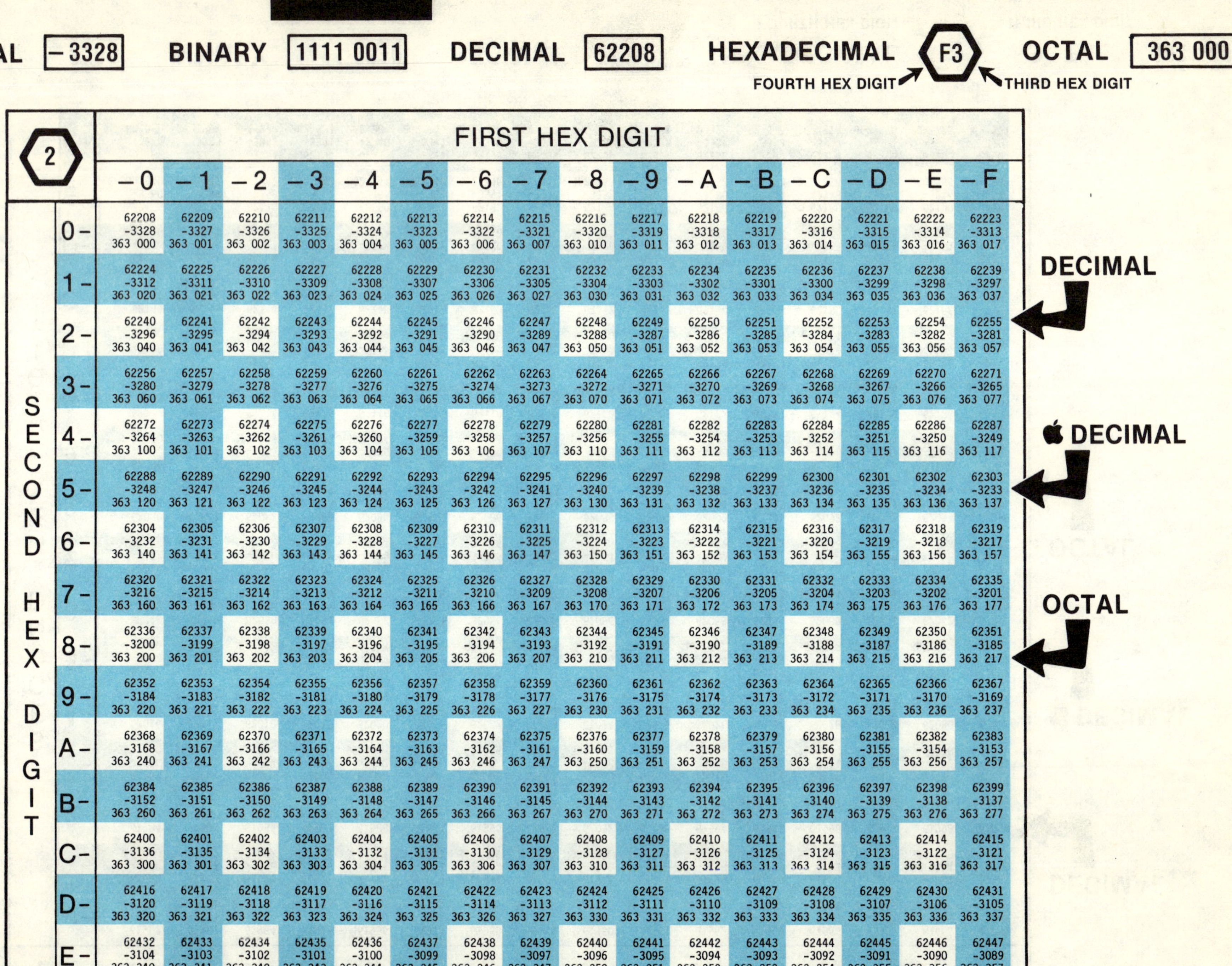



| (2) | −0 | −1 | −2 | −3 | −4 | −5 | −6 | −7 | −8 | −9 | −A | −B | −C | −D | −E | −F |
|---|---|---|---|---|---|---|---|---|---|---|---|---|---|---|---|---|
| **FIRST HEX DIGIT** ► | | | | | | | | | | | | | | | | |
| 0- | 62208<br>−3328<br>363 000 | 62209<br>−3327<br>363 001 | 62210<br>−3326<br>363 002 | 62211<br>−3325<br>363 003 | 62212<br>−3324<br>363 004 | 62213<br>−3323<br>363 005 | 62214<br>−3322<br>363 006 | 62215<br>−3321<br>363 007 | 62216<br>−3320<br>363 010 | 62217<br>−3319<br>363 011 | 62218<br>−3318<br>363 012 | 62219<br>−3317<br>363 013 | 62220<br>−3316<br>363 014 | 62221<br>−3315<br>363 015 | 62222<br>−3314<br>363 016 | 62223<br>−3313<br>363 017 |
| 1- | 62224<br>−3312<br>363 020 | 62225<br>−3311<br>363 021 | 62226<br>−3310<br>363 022 | 62227<br>−3309<br>363 023 | 62228<br>−3308<br>363 024 | 62229<br>−3307<br>363 025 | 62230<br>−3306<br>363 026 | 62231<br>−3305<br>363 027 | 62232<br>−3304<br>363 030 | 62233<br>−3303<br>363 031 | 62234<br>−3302<br>363 032 | 62235<br>−3301<br>363 033 | 62236<br>−3300<br>363 034 | 62237<br>−3299<br>363 035 | 62238<br>−3298<br>363 036 | 62239<br>−3297<br>363 037 |
| 2- | 62240<br>−3296<br>363 040 | 62241<br>−3295<br>363 041 | 62242<br>−3294<br>363 042 | 62243<br>−3293<br>363 043 | 62244<br>−3292<br>363 044 | 62245<br>−3291<br>363 045 | 62246<br>−3290<br>363 046 | 62247<br>−3289<br>363 047 | 62248<br>−3288<br>363 050 | 62249<br>−3287<br>363 051 | 62250<br>−3286<br>363 052 | 62251<br>−3285<br>363 053 | 62252<br>−3284<br>363 054 | 62253<br>−3283<br>363 055 | 62254<br>−3282<br>363 056 | 62255<br>−3281<br>363 057 |
| 3- | 62256<br>−3280<br>363 060 | 62257<br>−3279<br>363 061 | 62258<br>−3278<br>363 062 | 62259<br>−3277<br>363 063 | 62260<br>−3276<br>363 064 | 62261<br>−3275<br>363 065 | 62262<br>−3274<br>363 066 | 62263<br>−3273<br>363 067 | 62264<br>−3272<br>363 070 | 62265<br>−3271<br>363 071 | 62266<br>−3270<br>363 072 | 62267<br>−3269<br>363 073 | 62268<br>−3268<br>363 074 | 62269<br>−3267<br>363 075 | 62270<br>−3266<br>363 076 | 62271<br>−3265<br>363 077 |
| 4- | 62272<br>−3264<br>363 100 | 62273<br>−3263<br>363 101 | 62274<br>−3262<br>363 102 | 62275<br>−3261<br>363 103 | 62276<br>−3260<br>363 104 | 62277<br>−3259<br>363 105 | 62278<br>−3258<br>363 106 | 62279<br>−3257<br>363 107 | 62280<br>−3256<br>363 110 | 62281<br>−3255<br>363 111 | 62282<br>−3254<br>363 112 | 62283<br>−3253<br>363 113 | 62284<br>−3252<br>363 114 | 62285<br>−3251<br>363 115 | 62286<br>−3250<br>363 116 | 62287<br>−3249<br>363 117 |
| 5- | 62288<br>−3248<br>363 120 | 62289<br>−3247<br>363 121 | 62290<br>−3246<br>363 122 | 62291<br>−3245<br>363 123 | 62292<br>−3244<br>363 124 | 62293<br>−3243<br>363 125 | 62294<br>−3242<br>363 126 | 62295<br>−3241<br>363 127 | 62296<br>−3240<br>363 130 | 62297<br>−3239<br>363 131 | 62298<br>−3238<br>363 132 | 62299<br>−3237<br>363 133 | 62300<br>−3236<br>363 134 | 62301<br>−3235<br>363 135 | 62302<br>−3234<br>363 136 | 62303<br>−3233<br>363 137 |
| 6- | 62304<br>−3232<br>363 140 | 62305<br>−3231<br>363 141 | 62306<br>−3230<br>363 142 | 62307<br>−3229<br>363 143 | 62308<br>−3228<br>363 144 | 62309<br>−3227<br>363 145 | 62310<br>−3226<br>363 146 | 62311<br>−3225<br>363 147 | 62312<br>−3224<br>363 150 | 62313<br>−3223<br>363 151 | 62314<br>−3222<br>363 152 | 62315<br>−3221<br>363 153 | 62316<br>−3220<br>363 154 | 62317<br>−3219<br>363 155 | 62318<br>−3218<br>363 156 | 62319<br>−3217<br>363 157 |
| 7- | 62320<br>−3216<br>363 160 | 62321<br>−3215<br>363 161 | 62322<br>−3214<br>363 162 | 62323<br>−3213<br>363 163 | 62324<br>−3212<br>363 164 | 62325<br>−3211<br>363 165 | 62326<br>−3210<br>363 166 | 62327<br>−3209<br>363 167 | 62328<br>−3208<br>363 170 | 62329<br>−3207<br>363 171 | 62330<br>−3206<br>363 172 | 62331<br>−3205<br>363 173 | 62332<br>−3204<br>363 174 | 62333<br>−3203<br>363 175 | 62334<br>−3202<br>363 176 | 62335<br>−3201<br>363 177 |
| 8- | 62336<br>−3200<br>363 200 | 62337<br>−3199<br>363 201 | 62338<br>−3198<br>363 202 | 62339<br>−3197<br>363 203 | 62340<br>−3196<br>363 204 | 62341<br>−3195<br>363 205 | 62342<br>−3194<br>363 206 | 62343<br>−3193<br>363 207 | 62344<br>−3192<br>363 210 | 62345<br>−3191<br>363 211 | 62346<br>−3190<br>363 212 | 62347<br>−3189<br>363 213 | 62348<br>−3188<br>363 214 | 62349<br>−3187<br>363 215 | 62350<br>−3186<br>363 216 | 62351<br>−3185<br>363 217 |
| 9- | 62352<br>−3184<br>363 220 | 62353<br>−3183<br>363 221 | 62354<br>−3182<br>363 222 | 62355<br>−3181<br>363 223 | 62356<br>−3180<br>363 224 | 62357<br>−3179<br>363 225 | 62358<br>−3178<br>363 226 | 62359<br>−3177<br>363 227 | 62360<br>−3176<br>363 230 | 62361<br>−3175<br>363 231 | 62362<br>−3174<br>363 232 | 62363<br>−3173<br>363 233 | 62364<br>−3172<br>363 234 | 62365<br>−3171<br>363 235 | 62366<br>−3170<br>363 236 | 62367<br>−3169<br>363 237 |
| A- | 62368<br>−3168<br>363 240 | 62369<br>−3167<br>363 241 | 62370<br>−3166<br>363 242 | 62371<br>−3165<br>363 243 | 62372<br>−3164<br>363 244 | 62373<br>−3163<br>363 245 | 62374<br>−3162<br>363 246 | 62375<br>−3161<br>363 247 | 62376<br>−3160<br>363 250 | 62377<br>−3159<br>363 251 | 62378<br>−3158<br>363 252 | 62379<br>−3157<br>363 253 | 62380<br>−3156<br>363 254 | 62381<br>−3155<br>363 255 | 62382<br>−3154<br>363 256 | 62383<br>−3153<br>363 257 |
| B- | 62384<br>−3152<br>363 260 | 62385<br>−3151<br>363 261 | 62386<br>−3150<br>363 262 | 62387<br>−3149<br>363 263 | 62388<br>−3148<br>363 264 | 62389<br>−3147<br>363 265 | 62390<br>−3146<br>363 266 | 62391<br>−3145<br>363 267 | 62392<br>−3144<br>363 270 | 62393<br>−3143<br>363 271 | 62394<br>−3142<br>363 272 | 62395<br>−3141<br>363 273 | 62396<br>−3140<br>363 274 | 62397<br>−3139<br>363 275 | 62398<br>−3138<br>363 276 | 62399<br>−3137<br>363 277 |
| C- | 62400<br>−3136<br>363 300 | 62401<br>−3135<br>363 301 | 62402<br>−3134<br>363 302 | 62403<br>−3133<br>363 303 | 62404<br>−3132<br>363 304 | 62405<br>−3131<br>363 305 | 62406<br>−3130<br>363 306 | 62407<br>−3129<br>363 307 | 62408<br>−3128<br>363 310 | 62409<br>−3127<br>363 311 | 62410<br>−3126<br>363 312 | 62411<br>−3125<br>363 313 | 62412<br>−3124<br>363 314 | 62413<br>−3123<br>363 315 | 62414<br>−3122<br>363 316 | 62415<br>−3121<br>363 317 |
| D- | 62416<br>−3120<br>363 320 | 62417<br>−3119<br>363 321 | 62418<br>−3118<br>363 322 | 62419<br>−3117<br>363 323 | 62420<br>−3116<br>363 324 | 62421<br>−3115<br>363 325 | 62422<br>−3114<br>363 326 | 62423<br>−3113<br>363 327 | 62424<br>−3112<br>363 330 | 62425<br>−3111<br>363 331 | 62426<br>−3110<br>363 332 | 62427<br>−3109<br>363 333 | 62428<br>−3108<br>363 334 | 62429<br>−3107<br>363 335 | 62430<br>−3106<br>363 336 | 62431<br>−3105<br>363 337 |
| E- | 62432<br>−3104<br>363 340 | 62433<br>−3103<br>363 341 | 62434<br>−3102<br>363 342 | 62435<br>−3101<br>363 343 | 62436<br>−3100<br>363 344 | 62437<br>−3099<br>363 345 | 62438<br>−3098<br>363 346 | 62439<br>−3097<br>363 347 | 62440<br>−3096<br>363 350 | 62441<br>−3095<br>363 351 | 62442<br>−3094<br>363 352 | 62443<br>−3093<br>363 353 | 62444<br>−3092<br>363 354 | 62445<br>−3091<br>363 355 | 62446<br>−3090<br>363 356 | 62447<br>−3089<br>363 357 |
| F- | 62448<br>−3088<br>363 360 | 62449<br>−3087<br>363 361 | 62450<br>−3086<br>363 362 | 62451<br>−3085<br>363 363 | 62452<br>−3084<br>363 364 | 62453<br>−3083<br>363 365 | 62454<br>−3082<br>363 366 | 62455<br>−3081<br>363 367 | 62456<br>−3080<br>363 370 | 62457<br>−3079<br>363 371 | 62458<br>−3078<br>363 372 | 62459<br>−3077<br>363 373 | 62460<br>−3076<br>363 374 | 62461<br>−3075<br>363 375 | 62462<br>−3074<br>363 376 | 62463<br>−3073<br>363 377 |

SECOND HEX DIGIT

## ② FIRST HEX DIGIT

SECOND HEX DIGIT →

| | −0 | −1 | −2 | −3 | −4 | −5 | −6 | −7 | −8 | −9 | −A | −B | −C | −D | −E | −F |
|---|---|---|---|---|---|---|---|---|---|---|---|---|---|---|---|---|
| **0−** | 62464<br>−3072<br>364 000 | 62465<br>−3071<br>364 001 | 62466<br>−3070<br>364 002 | 62467<br>−3069<br>364 003 | 62468<br>−3068<br>364 004 | 62469<br>−3067<br>364 005 | 62470<br>−3066<br>364 006 | 62471<br>−3065<br>364 007 | 62472<br>−3064<br>364 010 | 62473<br>−3063<br>364 011 | 62474<br>−3062<br>364 012 | 62475<br>−3061<br>364 013 | 62476<br>−3060<br>364 014 | 62477<br>−3059<br>364 015 | 62478<br>−3058<br>364 016 | 62479<br>−3057<br>364 017 |
| **1−** | 62480<br>−3056<br>364 020 | 62481<br>−3055<br>364 021 | 62482<br>−3054<br>364 022 | 62483<br>−3053<br>364 023 | 62484<br>−3052<br>364 024 | 62485<br>−3051<br>364 025 | 62486<br>−3050<br>364 026 | 62487<br>−3049<br>364 027 | 62488<br>−3048<br>364 030 | 62489<br>−3047<br>364 031 | 62490<br>−3046<br>364 032 | 62491<br>−3045<br>364 033 | 62492<br>−3044<br>364 034 | 62493<br>−3043<br>364 035 | 62494<br>−3042<br>364 036 | 62495<br>−3041<br>364 037 |
| **2−** | 62496<br>−3040<br>364 040 | 62497<br>−3039<br>364 041 | 62498<br>−3038<br>364 042 | 62499<br>−3037<br>364 043 | 62500<br>−3036<br>364 044 | 62501<br>−3035<br>364 045 | 62502<br>−3034<br>364 046 | 62503<br>−3033<br>364 047 | 62504<br>−3032<br>364 050 | 62505<br>−3031<br>364 051 | 62506<br>−3030<br>364 052 | 62507<br>−3029<br>364 053 | 62508<br>−3028<br>364 054 | 62509<br>−3027<br>364 055 | 62510<br>−3026<br>364 056 | 62511<br>−3025<br>364 057 |
| **3−** | 62512<br>−3024<br>364 060 | 62513<br>−3023<br>364 061 | 62514<br>−3022<br>364 062 | 62515<br>−3021<br>364 063 | 62516<br>−3020<br>364 064 | 62517<br>−3019<br>364 065 | 62518<br>−3018<br>364 066 | 62519<br>−3017<br>364 067 | 62520<br>−3016<br>364 070 | 62521<br>−3015<br>364 071 | 62522<br>−3014<br>364 072 | 62523<br>−3013<br>364 073 | 62524<br>−3012<br>364 074 | 62525<br>−3011<br>364 075 | 62526<br>−3010<br>364 076 | 62527<br>−3009<br>364 077 |
| **4−** | 62528<br>−3008<br>364 100 | 62529<br>−3007<br>364 101 | 62530<br>−3006<br>364 102 | 62531<br>−3005<br>364 103 | 62532<br>−3004<br>364 104 | 62533<br>−3003<br>364 105 | 62534<br>−3002<br>364 106 | 62535<br>−3001<br>364 107 | 62536<br>−3000<br>364 110 | 62537<br>−2999<br>364 111 | 62538<br>−2998<br>364 112 | 62539<br>−2997<br>364 113 | 62540<br>−2996<br>364 114 | 62541<br>−2995<br>364 115 | 62542<br>−2994<br>364 116 | 62543<br>−2993<br>364 117 |
| **5−** | 62544<br>−2992<br>364 120 | 62545<br>−2991<br>364 121 | 62546<br>−2990<br>364 122 | 62547<br>−2989<br>364 123 | 62548<br>−2988<br>364 124 | 62549<br>−2987<br>364 125 | 62550<br>−2986<br>364 126 | 62551<br>−2985<br>364 127 | 62552<br>−2984<br>364 130 | 62553<br>−2983<br>364 131 | 62554<br>−2982<br>364 132 | 62555<br>−2981<br>364 133 | 62556<br>−2980<br>364 134 | 62557<br>−2979<br>364 135 | 62558<br>−2978<br>364 136 | 62559<br>−2977<br>364 137 |
| **6−** | 62560<br>−2976<br>364 140 | 62561<br>−2975<br>364 141 | 62562<br>−2974<br>364 142 | 62563<br>−2973<br>364 143 | 62564<br>−2972<br>364 144 | 62565<br>−2971<br>364 145 | 62566<br>−2970<br>364 146 | 62567<br>−2969<br>364 147 | 62568<br>−2968<br>364 150 | 62569<br>−2967<br>364 151 | 62570<br>−2966<br>364 152 | 62571<br>−2965<br>364 153 | 62572<br>−2964<br>364 154 | 62573<br>−2963<br>364 155 | 62574<br>−2962<br>364 156 | 62575<br>−2961<br>364 157 |
| **7−** | 62576<br>−2960<br>364 160 | 62577<br>−2959<br>364 161 | 62578<br>−2958<br>364 162 | 62579<br>−2957<br>364 163 | 62580<br>−2956<br>364 164 | 62581<br>−2955<br>364 165 | 62582<br>−2954<br>364 166 | 62583<br>−2953<br>364 167 | 62584<br>−2952<br>364 170 | 62585<br>−2951<br>364 171 | 62586<br>−2950<br>364 172 | 62587<br>−2949<br>364 173 | 62588<br>−2948<br>364 174 | 62589<br>−2947<br>364 175 | 62590<br>−2946<br>364 176 | 62591<br>−2945<br>364 177 |
| **8−** | 62592<br>−2944<br>364 200 | 62593<br>−2943<br>364 201 | 62594<br>−2942<br>364 202 | 62595<br>−2941<br>364 203 | 62596<br>−2940<br>364 204 | 62597<br>−2939<br>364 205 | 62598<br>−2938<br>364 206 | 62599<br>−2937<br>364 207 | 62600<br>−2936<br>364 210 | 62601<br>−2935<br>364 211 | 62602<br>−2934<br>364 212 | 62603<br>−2933<br>364 213 | 62604<br>−2932<br>364 214 | 62605<br>−2931<br>364 215 | 62606<br>−2930<br>364 216 | 62607<br>−2929<br>364 217 |
| **9−** | 62608<br>−2928<br>364 220 | 62609<br>−2927<br>364 221 | 62610<br>−2926<br>364 222 | 62611<br>−2925<br>364 223 | 62612<br>−2924<br>364 224 | 62613<br>−2923<br>364 225 | 62614<br>−2922<br>364 226 | 62615<br>−2921<br>364 227 | 62616<br>−2920<br>364 230 | 62617<br>−2919<br>364 231 | 62618<br>−2918<br>364 232 | 62619<br>−2917<br>364 233 | 62620<br>−2916<br>364 234 | 62621<br>−2915<br>364 235 | 62622<br>−2914<br>364 236 | 62623<br>−2913<br>364 237 |
| **A−** | 62624<br>−2912<br>364 240 | 62625<br>−2911<br>364 241 | 62626<br>−2910<br>364 242 | 62627<br>−2909<br>364 243 | 62628<br>−2908<br>364 244 | 62629<br>−2907<br>364 245 | 62630<br>−2906<br>364 246 | 62631<br>−2905<br>364 247 | 62632<br>−2904<br>364 250 | 62633<br>−2903<br>364 251 | 62634<br>−2902<br>364 252 | 62635<br>−2901<br>364 253 | 62636<br>−2900<br>364 254 | 62637<br>−2899<br>364 255 | 62638<br>−2898<br>364 256 | 62639<br>−2897<br>364 257 |
| **B−** | 62640<br>−2896<br>364 260 | 62641<br>−2895<br>364 261 | 62642<br>−2894<br>364 262 | 62643<br>−2893<br>364 263 | 62644<br>−2892<br>364 264 | 62645<br>−2891<br>364 265 | 62646<br>−2890<br>364 266 | 62647<br>−2889<br>364 267 | 62648<br>−2888<br>364 270 | 62649<br>−2887<br>364 271 | 62650<br>−2886<br>364 272 | 62651<br>−2885<br>364 273 | 62652<br>−2884<br>364 274 | 62653<br>−2883<br>364 275 | 62654<br>−2882<br>364 276 | 62655<br>−2881<br>364 277 |
| **C−** | 62656<br>−2880<br>364 300 | 62657<br>−2879<br>364 301 | 62658<br>−2878<br>364 302 | 62659<br>−2877<br>364 303 | 62660<br>−2876<br>364 304 | 62661<br>−2875<br>364 305 | 62662<br>−2874<br>364 306 | 62663<br>−2873<br>364 307 | 62664<br>−2872<br>364 310 | 62665<br>−2871<br>364 311 | 62666<br>−2870<br>364 312 | 62667<br>−2869<br>364 313 | 62668<br>−2868<br>364 314 | 62669<br>−2867<br>364 315 | 62670<br>−2866<br>364 316 | 62671<br>−2865<br>364 317 |
| **D−** | 62672<br>−2864<br>364 320 | 62673<br>−2863<br>364 321 | 62674<br>−2862<br>364 322 | 62675<br>−2861<br>364 323 | 62676<br>−2860<br>364 324 | 62677<br>−2859<br>364 325 | 62678<br>−2858<br>364 326 | 62679<br>−2857<br>364 327 | 62680<br>−2856<br>364 330 | 62681<br>−2855<br>364 331 | 62682<br>−2854<br>364 332 | 62683<br>−2853<br>364 333 | 62684<br>−2852<br>364 334 | 62685<br>−2851<br>364 335 | 62686<br>−2850<br>364 336 | 62687<br>−2849<br>364 337 |
| **E−** | 62688<br>−2848<br>364 340 | 62689<br>−2847<br>364 341 | 62690<br>−2846<br>364 342 | 62691<br>−2845<br>364 343 | 62692<br>−2844<br>364 344 | 62693<br>−2843<br>364 345 | 62694<br>−2842<br>364 346 | 62695<br>−2841<br>364 347 | 62696<br>−2840<br>364 350 | 62697<br>−2839<br>364 351 | 62698<br>−2838<br>364 352 | 62699<br>−2837<br>364 353 | 62700<br>−2836<br>364 354 | 62701<br>−2835<br>364 355 | 62702<br>−2834<br>364 356 | 62703<br>−2833<br>364 357 |
| **F−** | 62704<br>−2832<br>364 360 | 62705<br>−2831<br>364 361 | 62706<br>−2830<br>364 362 | 62707<br>−2829<br>364 363 | 62708<br>−2828<br>364 364 | 62709<br>−2827<br>364 365 | 62710<br>−2826<br>364 366 | 62711<br>−2825<br>364 367 | 62712<br>−2824<br>364 370 | 62713<br>−2823<br>364 371 | 62714<br>−2822<br>364 372 | 62715<br>−2821<br>364 373 | 62716<br>−2820<br>364 374 | 62717<br>−2819<br>364 375 | 62718<br>−2818<br>364 376 | 62719<br>−2817<br>364 377 |

← DECIMAL  
 DECIMAL  
← OCTAL

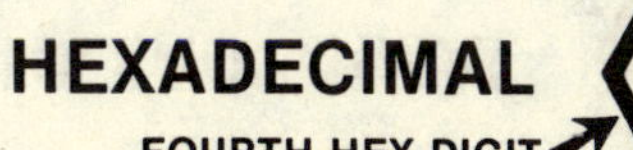

DECIMAL `−2816`  BINARY `1111 0101`  DECIMAL `62720`  HEXADECIMAL ⬡ **F5**  OCTAL `365 000`

FOURTH HEX DIGIT → **F5** ← THIRD HEX DIGIT

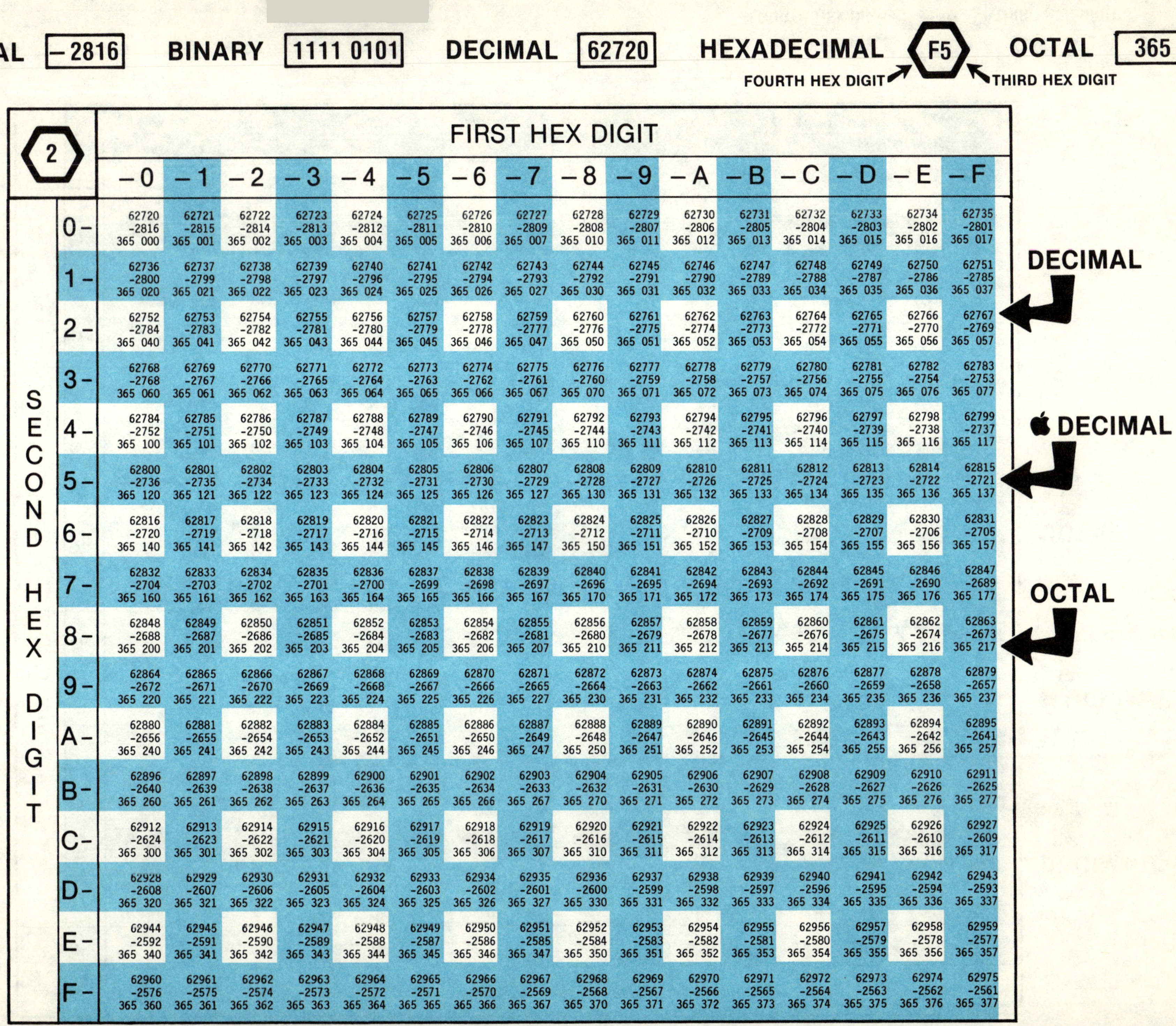



⬡ 2

FIRST HEX DIGIT

| SECOND HEX DIGIT | −0 | −1 | −2 | −3 | −4 | −5 | −6 | −7 | −8 | −9 | −A | −B | −C | −D | −E | −F |
|---|---|---|---|---|---|---|---|---|---|---|---|---|---|---|---|---|
| 0− | 62720<br>−2816<br>365 000 | 62721<br>−2815<br>365 001 | 62722<br>−2814<br>365 002 | 62723<br>−2813<br>365 003 | 62724<br>−2812<br>365 004 | 62725<br>−2811<br>365 005 | 62726<br>−2810<br>365 006 | 62727<br>−2809<br>365 007 | 62728<br>−2808<br>365 010 | 62729<br>−2807<br>365 011 | 62730<br>−2806<br>365 012 | 62731<br>−2805<br>365 013 | 62732<br>−2804<br>365 014 | 62733<br>−2803<br>365 015 | 62734<br>−2802<br>365 016 | 62735<br>−2801<br>365 017 |
| 1− | 62736<br>−2800<br>365 020 | 62737<br>−2799<br>365 021 | 62738<br>−2798<br>365 022 | 62739<br>−2797<br>365 023 | 62740<br>−2796<br>365 024 | 62741<br>−2795<br>365 025 | 62742<br>−2794<br>365 026 | 62743<br>−2793<br>365 027 | 62744<br>−2792<br>365 030 | 62745<br>−2791<br>365 031 | 62746<br>−2790<br>365 032 | 62747<br>−2789<br>365 033 | 62748<br>−2788<br>365 034 | 62749<br>−2787<br>365 035 | 62750<br>−2786<br>365 036 | 62751<br>−2785<br>365 037 |
| 2− | 62752<br>−2784<br>365 040 | 62753<br>−2783<br>365 041 | 62754<br>−2782<br>365 042 | 62755<br>−2781<br>365 043 | 62756<br>−2780<br>365 044 | 62757<br>−2779<br>365 045 | 62758<br>−2778<br>365 046 | 62759<br>−2777<br>365 047 | 62760<br>−2776<br>365 050 | 62761<br>−2775<br>365 051 | 62762<br>−2774<br>365 052 | 62763<br>−2773<br>365 053 | 62764<br>−2772<br>365 054 | 62765<br>−2771<br>365 055 | 62766<br>−2770<br>365 056 | 62767<br>−2769<br>365 057 |
| 3− | 62768<br>−2768<br>365 060 | 62769<br>−2767<br>365 061 | 62770<br>−2766<br>365 062 | 62771<br>−2765<br>365 063 | 62772<br>−2764<br>365 064 | 62773<br>−2763<br>365 065 | 62774<br>−2762<br>365 066 | 62775<br>−2761<br>365 067 | 62776<br>−2760<br>365 070 | 62777<br>−2759<br>365 071 | 62778<br>−2758<br>365 072 | 62779<br>−2757<br>365 073 | 62780<br>−2756<br>365 074 | 62781<br>−2755<br>365 075 | 62782<br>−2754<br>365 076 | 62783<br>−2753<br>365 077 |
| 4− | 62784<br>−2752<br>365 100 | 62785<br>−2751<br>365 101 | 62786<br>−2750<br>365 102 | 62787<br>−2749<br>365 103 | 62788<br>−2748<br>365 104 | 62789<br>−2747<br>365 105 | 62790<br>−2746<br>365 106 | 62791<br>−2745<br>365 107 | 62792<br>−2744<br>365 110 | 62793<br>−2743<br>365 111 | 62794<br>−2742<br>365 112 | 62795<br>−2741<br>365 113 | 62796<br>−2740<br>365 114 | 62797<br>−2739<br>365 115 | 62798<br>−2738<br>365 116 | 62799<br>−2737<br>365 117 |
| 5− | 62800<br>−2736<br>365 120 | 62801<br>−2735<br>365 121 | 62802<br>−2734<br>365 122 | 62803<br>−2733<br>365 123 | 62804<br>−2732<br>365 124 | 62805<br>−2731<br>365 125 | 62806<br>−2730<br>365 126 | 62807<br>−2729<br>365 127 | 62808<br>−2728<br>365 130 | 62809<br>−2727<br>365 131 | 62810<br>−2726<br>365 132 | 62811<br>−2725<br>365 133 | 62812<br>−2724<br>365 134 | 62813<br>−2723<br>365 135 | 62814<br>−2722<br>365 136 | 62815<br>−2721<br>365 137 |
| 6− | 62816<br>−2720<br>365 140 | 62817<br>−2719<br>365 141 | 62818<br>−2718<br>365 142 | 62819<br>−2717<br>365 143 | 62820<br>−2716<br>365 144 | 62821<br>−2715<br>365 145 | 62822<br>−2714<br>365 146 | 62823<br>−2713<br>365 147 | 62824<br>−2712<br>365 150 | 62825<br>−2711<br>365 151 | 62826<br>−2710<br>365 152 | 62827<br>−2709<br>365 153 | 62828<br>−2708<br>365 154 | 62829<br>−2707<br>365 155 | 62830<br>−2706<br>365 156 | 62831<br>−2705<br>365 157 |
| 7− | 62832<br>−2704<br>365 160 | 62833<br>−2703<br>365 161 | 62834<br>−2702<br>365 162 | 62835<br>−2701<br>365 163 | 62836<br>−2700<br>365 164 | 62837<br>−2699<br>365 165 | 62838<br>−2698<br>365 166 | 62839<br>−2697<br>365 167 | 62840<br>−2696<br>365 170 | 62841<br>−2695<br>365 171 | 62842<br>−2694<br>365 172 | 62843<br>−2693<br>365 173 | 62844<br>−2692<br>365 174 | 62845<br>−2691<br>365 175 | 62846<br>−2690<br>365 176 | 62847<br>−2689<br>365 177 |
| 8− | 62848<br>−2688<br>365 200 | 62849<br>−2687<br>365 201 | 62850<br>−2686<br>365 202 | 62851<br>−2685<br>365 203 | 62852<br>−2684<br>365 204 | 62853<br>−2683<br>365 205 | 62854<br>−2682<br>365 206 | 62855<br>−2681<br>365 207 | 62856<br>−2680<br>365 210 | 62857<br>−2679<br>365 211 | 62858<br>−2678<br>365 212 | 62859<br>−2677<br>365 213 | 62860<br>−2676<br>365 214 | 62861<br>−2675<br>365 215 | 62862<br>−2674<br>365 216 | 62863<br>−2673<br>365 217 |
| 9− | 62864<br>−2672<br>365 220 | 62865<br>−2671<br>365 221 | 62866<br>−2670<br>365 222 | 62867<br>−2669<br>365 223 | 62868<br>−2668<br>365 224 | 62869<br>−2667<br>365 225 | 62870<br>−2666<br>365 226 | 62871<br>−2665<br>365 227 | 62872<br>−2664<br>365 230 | 62873<br>−2663<br>365 231 | 62874<br>−2662<br>365 232 | 62875<br>−2661<br>365 233 | 62876<br>−2660<br>365 234 | 62877<br>−2659<br>365 235 | 62878<br>−2658<br>365 236 | 62879<br>−2657<br>365 237 |
| A− | 62880<br>−2656<br>365 240 | 62881<br>−2655<br>365 241 | 62882<br>−2654<br>365 242 | 62883<br>−2653<br>365 243 | 62884<br>−2652<br>365 244 | 62885<br>−2651<br>365 245 | 62886<br>−2650<br>365 246 | 62887<br>−2649<br>365 247 | 62888<br>−2648<br>365 250 | 62889<br>−2647<br>365 251 | 62890<br>−2646<br>365 252 | 62891<br>−2645<br>365 253 | 62892<br>−2644<br>365 254 | 62893<br>−2643<br>365 255 | 62894<br>−2642<br>365 256 | 62895<br>−2641<br>365 257 |
| B− | 62896<br>−2640<br>365 260 | 62897<br>−2639<br>365 261 | 62898<br>−2638<br>365 262 | 62899<br>−2637<br>365 263 | 62900<br>−2636<br>365 264 | 62901<br>−2635<br>365 265 | 62902<br>−2634<br>365 266 | 62903<br>−2633<br>365 267 | 62904<br>−2632<br>365 270 | 62905<br>−2631<br>365 271 | 62906<br>−2630<br>365 272 | 62907<br>−2629<br>365 273 | 62908<br>−2628<br>365 274 | 62909<br>−2627<br>365 275 | 62910<br>−2626<br>365 276 | 62911<br>−2625<br>365 277 |
| C− | 62912<br>−2624<br>365 300 | 62913<br>−2623<br>365 301 | 62914<br>−2622<br>365 302 | 62915<br>−2621<br>365 303 | 62916<br>−2620<br>365 304 | 62917<br>−2619<br>365 305 | 62918<br>−2618<br>365 306 | 62919<br>−2617<br>365 307 | 62920<br>−2616<br>365 310 | 62921<br>−2615<br>365 311 | 62922<br>−2614<br>365 312 | 62923<br>−2613<br>365 313 | 62924<br>−2612<br>365 314 | 62925<br>−2611<br>365 315 | 62926<br>−2610<br>365 316 | 62927<br>−2609<br>365 317 |
| D− | 62928<br>−2608<br>365 320 | 62929<br>−2607<br>365 321 | 62930<br>−2606<br>365 322 | 62931<br>−2605<br>365 323 | 62932<br>−2604<br>365 324 | 62933<br>−2603<br>365 325 | 62934<br>−2602<br>365 326 | 62935<br>−2601<br>365 327 | 62936<br>−2600<br>365 330 | 62937<br>−2599<br>365 331 | 62938<br>−2598<br>365 332 | 62939<br>−2597<br>365 333 | 62940<br>−2596<br>365 334 | 62941<br>−2595<br>365 335 | 62942<br>−2594<br>365 336 | 62943<br>−2593<br>365 337 |
| E− | 62944<br>−2592<br>365 340 | 62945<br>−2591<br>365 341 | 62946<br>−2590<br>365 342 | 62947<br>−2589<br>365 343 | 62948<br>−2588<br>365 344 | 62949<br>−2587<br>365 345 | 62950<br>−2586<br>365 346 | 62951<br>−2585<br>365 347 | 62952<br>−2584<br>365 350 | 62953<br>−2583<br>365 351 | 62954<br>−2582<br>365 352 | 62955<br>−2581<br>365 353 | 62956<br>−2580<br>365 354 | 62957<br>−2579<br>365 355 | 62958<br>−2578<br>365 356 | 62959<br>−2577<br>365 357 |
| F− | 62960<br>−2576<br>365 360 | 62961<br>−2575<br>365 361 | 62962<br>−2574<br>365 362 | 62963<br>−2573<br>365 363 | 62964<br>−2572<br>365 364 | 62965<br>−2571<br>365 365 | 62966<br>−2570<br>365 366 | 62967<br>−2569<br>365 367 | 62968<br>−2568<br>365 370 | 62969<br>−2567<br>365 371 | 62970<br>−2566<br>365 372 | 62971<br>−2565<br>365 373 | 62972<br>−2564<br>365 374 | 62973<br>−2563<br>365 375 | 62974<br>−2562<br>365 376 | 62975<br>−2561<br>365 377 |

**(2)** — FIRST HEX DIGIT

Each cell shows: decimal (top) / signed decimal (middle) / octal (bottom).

| SECOND HEX DIGIT | −0 | −1 | −2 | −3 | −4 | −5 | −6 | −7 | −8 | −9 | −A | −B | −C | −D | −E | −F |
|---|---|---|---|---|---|---|---|---|---|---|---|---|---|---|---|---|
| 0- | 62976<br>−2560<br>366 000 | 62977<br>−2559<br>366 001 | 62978<br>−2558<br>366 002 | 62979<br>−2557<br>366 003 | 62980<br>−2556<br>366 004 | 62981<br>−2555<br>366 005 | 62982<br>−2554<br>366 006 | 62983<br>−2553<br>366 007 | 62984<br>−2552<br>366 010 | 62985<br>−2551<br>366 011 | 62986<br>−2550<br>366 012 | 62987<br>−2549<br>366 013 | 62988<br>−2548<br>366 014 | 62989<br>−2547<br>366 015 | 62990<br>−2546<br>366 016 | 62991<br>−2545<br>366 017 |
| 1- | 62992<br>−2544<br>366 020 | 62993<br>−2543<br>366 021 | 62994<br>−2542<br>366 022 | 62995<br>−2541<br>366 023 | 62996<br>−2540<br>366 024 | 62997<br>−2539<br>366 025 | 62998<br>−2538<br>366 026 | 62999<br>−2537<br>366 027 | 63000<br>−2536<br>366 030 | 63001<br>−2535<br>366 031 | 63002<br>−2534<br>366 032 | 63003<br>−2533<br>366 033 | 63004<br>−2532<br>366 034 | 63005<br>−2531<br>366 035 | 63006<br>−2530<br>366 036 | 63007<br>−2529<br>366 037 |
| 2- | 63008<br>−2528<br>366 040 | 63009<br>−2527<br>366 041 | 63010<br>−2526<br>366 042 | 63011<br>−2525<br>366 043 | 63012<br>−2524<br>366 044 | 63013<br>−2523<br>366 045 | 63014<br>−2522<br>366 046 | 63015<br>−2521<br>366 047 | 63016<br>−2520<br>366 050 | 63017<br>−2519<br>366 051 | 63018<br>−2518<br>366 052 | 63019<br>−2517<br>366 053 | 63020<br>−2516<br>366 054 | 63021<br>−2515<br>366 055 | 63022<br>−2514<br>366 056 | 63023<br>−2513<br>366 057 |
| 3- | 63024<br>−2512<br>366 060 | 63025<br>−2511<br>366 061 | 63026<br>−2510<br>366 062 | 63027<br>−2509<br>366 063 | 63028<br>−2508<br>366 064 | 63029<br>−2507<br>366 065 | 63030<br>−2506<br>366 066 | 63031<br>−2505<br>366 067 | 63032<br>−2504<br>366 070 | 63033<br>−2503<br>366 071 | 63034<br>−2502<br>366 072 | 63035<br>−2501<br>366 073 | 63036<br>−2500<br>366 074 | 63037<br>−2499<br>366 075 | 63038<br>−2498<br>366 076 | 63039<br>−2497<br>366 077 |
| 4- | 63040<br>−2496<br>366 100 | 63041<br>−2495<br>366 101 | 63042<br>−2494<br>366 102 | 63043<br>−2493<br>366 103 | 63044<br>−2492<br>366 104 | 63045<br>−2491<br>366 105 | 63046<br>−2490<br>366 106 | 63047<br>−2489<br>366 107 | 63048<br>−2488<br>366 110 | 63049<br>−2487<br>366 111 | 63050<br>−2486<br>366 112 | 63051<br>−2485<br>366 113 | 63052<br>−2484<br>366 114 | 63053<br>−2483<br>366 115 | 63054<br>−2482<br>366 116 | 63055<br>−2481<br>366 117 |
| 5- | 63056<br>−2480<br>366 120 | 63057<br>−2479<br>366 121 | 63058<br>−2478<br>366 122 | 63059<br>−2477<br>366 123 | 63060<br>−2476<br>366 124 | 63061<br>−2475<br>366 125 | 63062<br>−2474<br>366 126 | 63063<br>−2473<br>366 127 | 63064<br>−2472<br>366 130 | 63065<br>−2471<br>366 131 | 63066<br>−2470<br>366 132 | 63067<br>−2469<br>366 133 | 63068<br>−2468<br>366 134 | 63069<br>−2467<br>366 135 | 63070<br>−2466<br>366 136 | 63071<br>−2465<br>366 137 |
| 6- | 63072<br>−2464<br>366 140 | 63073<br>−2463<br>366 141 | 63074<br>−2462<br>366 142 | 63075<br>−2461<br>366 143 | 63076<br>−2460<br>366 144 | 63077<br>−2459<br>366 145 | 63078<br>−2458<br>366 146 | 63079<br>−2457<br>366 147 | 63080<br>−2456<br>366 150 | 63081<br>−2455<br>366 151 | 63082<br>−2454<br>366 152 | 63083<br>−2453<br>366 153 | 63084<br>−2452<br>366 154 | 63085<br>−2451<br>366 155 | 63086<br>−2450<br>366 156 | 63087<br>−2449<br>366 157 |
| 7- | 63088<br>−2448<br>366 160 | 63089<br>−2447<br>366 161 | 63090<br>−2446<br>366 162 | 63091<br>−2445<br>366 163 | 63092<br>−2444<br>366 164 | 63093<br>−2443<br>366 165 | 63094<br>−2442<br>366 166 | 63095<br>−2441<br>366 167 | 63096<br>−2440<br>366 170 | 63097<br>−2439<br>366 171 | 63098<br>−2438<br>366 172 | 63099<br>−2437<br>366 173 | 63100<br>−2436<br>366 174 | 63101<br>−2435<br>366 175 | 63102<br>−2434<br>366 176 | 63103<br>−2433<br>366 177 |
| 8- | 63104<br>−2432<br>366 200 | 63105<br>−2431<br>366 201 | 63106<br>−2430<br>366 202 | 63107<br>−2429<br>366 203 | 63108<br>−2428<br>366 204 | 63109<br>−2427<br>366 205 | 63110<br>−2426<br>366 206 | 63111<br>−2425<br>366 207 | 63112<br>−2424<br>366 210 | 63113<br>−2423<br>366 211 | 63114<br>−2422<br>366 212 | 63115<br>−2421<br>366 213 | 63116<br>−2420<br>366 214 | 63117<br>−2419<br>366 215 | 63118<br>−2418<br>366 216 | 63119<br>−2417<br>366 217 |
| 9- | 63120<br>−2416<br>366 220 | 63121<br>−2415<br>366 221 | 63122<br>−2414<br>366 222 | 63123<br>−2413<br>366 223 | 63124<br>−2412<br>366 224 | 63125<br>−2411<br>366 225 | 63126<br>−2410<br>366 226 | 63127<br>−2409<br>366 227 | 63128<br>−2408<br>366 230 | 63129<br>−2407<br>366 231 | 63130<br>−2406<br>366 232 | 63131<br>−2405<br>366 233 | 63132<br>−2404<br>366 234 | 63133<br>−2403<br>366 235 | 63134<br>−2402<br>366 236 | 63135<br>−2401<br>366 237 |
| A- | 63136<br>−2400<br>366 240 | 63137<br>−2399<br>366 241 | 63138<br>−2398<br>366 242 | 63139<br>−2397<br>366 243 | 63140<br>−2396<br>366 244 | 63141<br>−2395<br>366 245 | 63142<br>−2394<br>366 246 | 63143<br>−2393<br>366 247 | 63144<br>−2392<br>366 250 | 63145<br>−2391<br>366 251 | 63146<br>−2390<br>366 252 | 63147<br>−2389<br>366 253 | 63148<br>−2388<br>366 254 | 63149<br>−2387<br>366 255 | 63150<br>−2386<br>366 256 | 63151<br>−2385<br>366 257 |
| B- | 63152<br>−2384<br>366 260 | 63153<br>−2383<br>366 261 | 63154<br>−2382<br>366 262 | 63155<br>−2381<br>366 263 | 63156<br>−2380<br>366 264 | 63157<br>−2379<br>366 265 | 63158<br>−2378<br>366 266 | 63159<br>−2377<br>366 267 | 63160<br>−2376<br>366 270 | 63161<br>−2375<br>366 271 | 63162<br>−2374<br>366 272 | 63163<br>−2373<br>366 273 | 63164<br>−2372<br>366 274 | 63165<br>−2371<br>366 275 | 63166<br>−2370<br>366 276 | 63167<br>−2369<br>366 277 |
| C- | 63168<br>−2368<br>366 300 | 63169<br>−2367<br>366 301 | 63170<br>−2366<br>366 302 | 63171<br>−2365<br>366 303 | 63172<br>−2364<br>366 304 | 63173<br>−2363<br>366 305 | 63174<br>−2362<br>366 306 | 63175<br>−2361<br>366 307 | 63176<br>−2360<br>366 310 | 63177<br>−2359<br>366 311 | 63178<br>−2358<br>366 312 | 63179<br>−2357<br>366 313 | 63180<br>−2356<br>366 314 | 63181<br>−2355<br>366 315 | 63182<br>−2354<br>366 316 | 63183<br>−2353<br>366 317 |
| D- | 63184<br>−2352<br>366 320 | 63185<br>−2351<br>366 321 | 63186<br>−2350<br>366 322 | 63187<br>−2349<br>366 323 | 63188<br>−2348<br>366 324 | 63189<br>−2347<br>366 325 | 63190<br>−2346<br>366 326 | 63191<br>−2345<br>366 327 | 63192<br>−2344<br>366 330 | 63193<br>−2343<br>366 331 | 63194<br>−2342<br>366 332 | 63195<br>−2341<br>366 333 | 63196<br>−2340<br>366 334 | 63197<br>−2339<br>366 335 | 63198<br>−2338<br>366 336 | 63199<br>−2337<br>366 337 |
| E- | 63200<br>−2336<br>366 340 | 63201<br>−2335<br>366 341 | 63202<br>−2334<br>366 342 | 63203<br>−2333<br>366 343 | 63204<br>−2332<br>366 344 | 63205<br>−2331<br>366 345 | 63206<br>−2330<br>366 346 | 63207<br>−2329<br>366 347 | 63208<br>−2328<br>366 350 | 63209<br>−2327<br>366 351 | 63210<br>−2326<br>366 352 | 63211<br>−2325<br>366 353 | 63212<br>−2324<br>366 354 | 63213<br>−2323<br>366 355 | 63214<br>−2322<br>366 356 | 63215<br>−2321<br>366 357 |
| F- | 63216<br>−2320<br>366 360 | 63217<br>−2319<br>366 361 | 63218<br>−2318<br>366 362 | 63219<br>−2317<br>366 363 | 63220<br>−2316<br>366 364 | 63221<br>−2315<br>366 365 | 63222<br>−2314<br>366 366 | 63223<br>−2313<br>366 367 | 63224<br>−2312<br>366 370 | 63225<br>−2311<br>366 371 | 63226<br>−2310<br>366 372 | 63227<br>−2309<br>366 373 | 63228<br>−2308<br>366 374 | 63229<br>−2307<br>366 375 | 63230<br>−2306<br>366 376 | 63231<br>−2305<br>366 377 |

DECIMAL

 DECIMAL

OCTAL

 DECIMAL  −2560   BINARY  1111 0110   DECIMAL  62976   HEXADECIMAL  F6   OCTAL  366 000

FOURTH HEX DIGIT ↗   ↖ THIRD HEX DIGIT

## FIRST HEX DIGIT

(2) SECOND HEX DIGIT

| | −0 | −1 | −2 | −3 | −4 | −5 | −6 | −7 | −8 | −9 | −A | −B | −C | −D | −E | −F |
|---|---|---|---|---|---|---|---|---|---|---|---|---|---|---|---|---|
| 0− | 63232<br>−2304<br>367 000 | 63233<br>−2303<br>367 001 | 63234<br>−2302<br>367 002 | 63235<br>−2301<br>367 003 | 63236<br>−2300<br>367 004 | 63237<br>−2299<br>367 005 | 63238<br>−2298<br>367 006 | 63239<br>−2297<br>367 007 | 63240<br>−2296<br>367 010 | 63241<br>−2295<br>367 011 | 63242<br>−2294<br>367 012 | 63243<br>−2293<br>367 013 | 63244<br>−2292<br>367 014 | 63245<br>−2291<br>367 015 | 63246<br>−2290<br>367 016 | 63247<br>−2289<br>367 017 |
| 1− | 63248<br>−2288<br>367 020 | 63249<br>−2287<br>367 021 | 63250<br>−2286<br>367 022 | 63251<br>−2285<br>367 023 | 63252<br>−2284<br>367 024 | 63253<br>−2283<br>367 025 | 63254<br>−2282<br>367 026 | 63255<br>−2281<br>367 027 | 63256<br>−2280<br>367 030 | 63257<br>−2279<br>367 031 | 63258<br>−2278<br>367 032 | 63259<br>−2277<br>367 033 | 63260<br>−2276<br>367 034 | 63261<br>−2275<br>367 035 | 63262<br>−2274<br>367 036 | 63263<br>−2273<br>367 037 |
| 2− | 63264<br>−2272<br>367 040 | 63265<br>−2271<br>367 041 | 63266<br>−2270<br>367 042 | 63267<br>−2269<br>367 043 | 63268<br>−2268<br>367 044 | 63269<br>−2267<br>367 045 | 63270<br>−2266<br>367 046 | 63271<br>−2265<br>367 047 | 63272<br>−2264<br>367 050 | 63273<br>−2263<br>367 051 | 63274<br>−2262<br>367 052 | 63275<br>−2261<br>367 053 | 63276<br>−2260<br>367 054 | 63277<br>−2259<br>367 055 | 63278<br>−2258<br>367 056 | 63279<br>−2257<br>367 057 |
| 3− | 63280<br>−2256<br>367 060 | 63281<br>−2255<br>367 061 | 63282<br>−2254<br>367 062 | 63283<br>−2253<br>367 063 | 63284<br>−2252<br>367 064 | 63285<br>−2251<br>367 065 | 63286<br>−2250<br>367 066 | 63287<br>−2249<br>367 067 | 63288<br>−2248<br>367 070 | 63289<br>−2247<br>367 071 | 63290<br>−2246<br>367 072 | 63291<br>−2245<br>367 073 | 63292<br>−2244<br>367 074 | 63293<br>−2243<br>367 075 | 63294<br>−2242<br>367 076 | 63295<br>−2241<br>367 077 |
| 4− | 63296<br>−2240<br>367 100 | 63297<br>−2239<br>367 101 | 63298<br>−2238<br>367 102 | 63299<br>−2237<br>367 103 | 63300<br>−2236<br>367 104 | 63301<br>−2235<br>367 105 | 63302<br>−2234<br>367 106 | 63303<br>−2233<br>367 107 | 63304<br>−2232<br>367 110 | 63305<br>−2231<br>367 111 | 63306<br>−2230<br>367 112 | 63307<br>−2229<br>367 113 | 63308<br>−2228<br>367 114 | 63309<br>−2227<br>367 115 | 63310<br>−2226<br>367 116 | 63311<br>−2225<br>367 117 |
| 5− | 63312<br>−2224<br>367 120 | 63313<br>−2223<br>367 121 | 63314<br>−2222<br>367 122 | 63315<br>−2221<br>367 123 | 63316<br>−2220<br>367 124 | 63317<br>−2219<br>367 125 | 63318<br>−2218<br>367 126 | 63319<br>−2217<br>367 127 | 63320<br>−2216<br>367 130 | 63321<br>−2215<br>367 131 | 63322<br>−2214<br>367 132 | 63323<br>−2213<br>367 133 | 63324<br>−2212<br>367 134 | 63325<br>−2211<br>367 135 | 63326<br>−2210<br>367 136 | 63327<br>−2209<br>367 137 |
| 6− | 63328<br>−2208<br>367 140 | 63329<br>−2207<br>367 141 | 63330<br>−2206<br>367 142 | 63331<br>−2205<br>367 143 | 63332<br>−2204<br>367 144 | 63333<br>−2203<br>367 145 | 63334<br>−2202<br>367 146 | 63335<br>−2201<br>367 147 | 63336<br>−2200<br>367 150 | 63337<br>−2199<br>367 151 | 63338<br>−2198<br>367 152 | 63339<br>−2197<br>367 153 | 63340<br>−2196<br>367 154 | 63341<br>−2195<br>367 155 | 63342<br>−2194<br>367 156 | 63343<br>−2193<br>367 157 |
| 7− | 63344<br>−2192<br>367 160 | 63345<br>−2191<br>367 161 | 63346<br>−2190<br>367 162 | 63347<br>−2189<br>367 163 | 63348<br>−2188<br>367 164 | 63349<br>−2187<br>367 165 | 63350<br>−2186<br>367 166 | 63351<br>−2185<br>367 167 | 63352<br>−2184<br>367 170 | 63353<br>−2183<br>367 171 | 63354<br>−2182<br>367 172 | 63355<br>−2181<br>367 173 | 63356<br>−2180<br>367 174 | 63357<br>−2179<br>367 175 | 63358<br>−2178<br>367 176 | 63359<br>−2177<br>367 177 |
| 8− | 63360<br>−2176<br>367 200 | 63361<br>−2175<br>367 201 | 63362<br>−2174<br>367 202 | 63363<br>−2173<br>367 203 | 63364<br>−2172<br>367 204 | 63365<br>−2171<br>367 205 | 63366<br>−2170<br>367 206 | 63367<br>−2169<br>367 207 | 63368<br>−2168<br>367 210 | 63369<br>−2167<br>367 211 | 63370<br>−2166<br>367 212 | 63371<br>−2165<br>367 213 | 63372<br>−2164<br>367 214 | 63373<br>−2163<br>367 215 | 63374<br>−2162<br>367 216 | 63375<br>−2161<br>367 217 |
| 9− | 63376<br>−2160<br>367 220 | 63377<br>−2159<br>367 221 | 63378<br>−2158<br>367 222 | 63379<br>−2157<br>367 223 | 63380<br>−2156<br>367 224 | 63381<br>−2155<br>367 225 | 63382<br>−2154<br>367 226 | 63383<br>−2153<br>367 227 | 63384<br>−2152<br>367 230 | 63385<br>−2151<br>367 231 | 63386<br>−2150<br>367 232 | 63387<br>−2149<br>367 233 | 63388<br>−2148<br>367 234 | 63389<br>−2147<br>367 235 | 63390<br>−2146<br>367 236 | 63391<br>−2145<br>367 237 |
| A− | 63392<br>−2144<br>367 240 | 63393<br>−2143<br>367 241 | 63394<br>−2142<br>367 242 | 63395<br>−2141<br>367 243 | 63396<br>−2140<br>367 244 | 63397<br>−2139<br>367 245 | 63398<br>−2138<br>367 246 | 63399<br>−2137<br>367 247 | 63400<br>−2136<br>367 250 | 63401<br>−2135<br>367 251 | 63402<br>−2134<br>367 252 | 63403<br>−2133<br>367 253 | 63404<br>−2132<br>367 254 | 63405<br>−2131<br>367 255 | 63406<br>−2130<br>367 256 | 63407<br>−2129<br>367 257 |
| B− | 63408<br>−2128<br>367 260 | 63409<br>−2127<br>367 261 | 63410<br>−2126<br>367 262 | 63411<br>−2125<br>367 263 | 63412<br>−2124<br>367 264 | 63413<br>−2123<br>367 265 | 63414<br>−2122<br>367 266 | 63415<br>−2121<br>367 267 | 63416<br>−2120<br>367 270 | 63417<br>−2119<br>367 271 | 63418<br>−2118<br>367 272 | 63419<br>−2117<br>367 273 | 63420<br>−2116<br>367 274 | 63421<br>−2115<br>367 275 | 63422<br>−2114<br>367 276 | 63423<br>−2113<br>367 277 |
| C− | 63424<br>−2112<br>367 300 | 63425<br>−2111<br>367 301 | 63426<br>−2110<br>367 302 | 63427<br>−2109<br>367 303 | 63428<br>−2108<br>367 304 | 63429<br>−2107<br>367 305 | 63430<br>−2106<br>367 306 | 63431<br>−2105<br>367 307 | 63432<br>−2104<br>367 310 | 63433<br>−2103<br>367 311 | 63434<br>−2102<br>367 312 | 63435<br>−2101<br>367 313 | 63436<br>−2100<br>367 314 | 63437<br>−2099<br>367 315 | 63438<br>−2098<br>367 316 | 63439<br>−2097<br>367 317 |
| D− | 63440<br>−2096<br>367 320 | 63441<br>−2095<br>367 321 | 63442<br>−2094<br>367 322 | 63443<br>−2093<br>367 323 | 63444<br>−2092<br>367 324 | 63445<br>−2091<br>367 325 | 63446<br>−2090<br>367 326 | 63447<br>−2089<br>367 327 | 63448<br>−2088<br>367 330 | 63449<br>−2087<br>367 331 | 63450<br>−2086<br>367 332 | 63451<br>−2085<br>367 333 | 63452<br>−2084<br>367 334 | 63453<br>−2083<br>367 335 | 63454<br>−2082<br>367 336 | 63455<br>−2081<br>367 337 |
| E− | 63456<br>−2080<br>367 340 | 63457<br>−2079<br>367 341 | 63458<br>−2078<br>367 342 | 63459<br>−2077<br>367 343 | 63460<br>−2076<br>367 344 | 63461<br>−2075<br>367 345 | 63462<br>−2074<br>367 346 | 63463<br>−2073<br>367 347 | 63464<br>−2072<br>367 350 | 63465<br>−2071<br>367 351 | 63466<br>−2070<br>367 352 | 63467<br>−2069<br>367 353 | 63468<br>−2068<br>367 354 | 63469<br>−2067<br>367 355 | 63470<br>−2066<br>367 356 | 63471<br>−2065<br>367 357 |
| F− | 63472<br>−2064<br>367 360 | 63473<br>−2063<br>367 361 | 63474<br>−2062<br>367 362 | 63475<br>−2061<br>367 363 | 63476<br>−2060<br>367 364 | 63477<br>−2059<br>367 365 | 63478<br>−2058<br>367 366 | 63479<br>−2057<br>367 367 | 63480<br>−2056<br>367 370 | 63481<br>−2055<br>367 371 | 63482<br>−2054<br>367 372 | 63483<br>−2053<br>367 373 | 63484<br>−2052<br>367 374 | 63485<br>−2051<br>367 375 | 63486<br>−2050<br>367 376 | 63487<br>−2049<br>367 377 |

DECIMAL →

DECIMAL →

OCTAL →

① **FIRST HEX DIGIT**

| SECOND HEX DIGIT | −0 | −1 | −2 | −3 | −4 | −5 | −6 | −7 | −8 | −9 | −A | −B | −C | −D | −E | −F |
|---|---|---|---|---|---|---|---|---|---|---|---|---|---|---|---|---|
| 0− | 63488<br>−2048<br>370 000 | 63489<br>−2047<br>370 001 | 63490<br>−2046<br>370 002 | 63491<br>−2045<br>370 003 | 63492<br>−2044<br>370 004 | 63493<br>−2043<br>370 005 | 63494<br>−2042<br>370 006 | 63495<br>−2041<br>370 007 | 63496<br>−2040<br>370 010 | 63497<br>−2039<br>370 011 | 63498<br>−2038<br>370 012 | 63499<br>−2037<br>370 013 | 63500<br>−2036<br>370 014 | 63501<br>−2035<br>370 015 | 63502<br>−2034<br>370 016 | 63503<br>−2033<br>370 017 |
| 1− | 63504<br>−2032<br>370 020 | 63505<br>−2031<br>370 021 | 63506<br>−2030<br>370 022 | 63507<br>−2029<br>370 023 | 63508<br>−2028<br>370 024 | 63509<br>−2027<br>370 025 | 63510<br>−2026<br>370 026 | 63511<br>−2025<br>370 027 | 63512<br>−2024<br>370 030 | 63513<br>−2023<br>370 031 | 63514<br>−2022<br>370 032 | 63515<br>−2021<br>370 033 | 63516<br>−2020<br>370 034 | 63517<br>−2019<br>370 035 | 63518<br>−2018<br>370 036 | 63519<br>−2017<br>370 037 |
| 2− | 63520<br>−2016<br>370 040 | 63521<br>−2015<br>370 041 | 63522<br>−2014<br>370 042 | 63523<br>−2013<br>370 043 | 63524<br>−2012<br>370 044 | 63525<br>−2011<br>370 045 | 63526<br>−2010<br>370 046 | 63527<br>−2009<br>370 047 | 63528<br>−2008<br>370 050 | 63529<br>−2007<br>370 051 | 63530<br>−2006<br>370 052 | 63531<br>−2005<br>370 053 | 63532<br>−2004<br>370 054 | 63533<br>−2003<br>370 055 | 63534<br>−2002<br>370 056 | 63535<br>−2001<br>370 057 |
| 3− | 63536<br>−2000<br>370 060 | 63537<br>−1999<br>370 061 | 63538<br>−1998<br>370 062 | 63539<br>−1997<br>370 063 | 63540<br>−1996<br>370 064 | 63541<br>−1995<br>370 065 | 63542<br>−1994<br>370 066 | 63543<br>−1993<br>370 067 | 63544<br>−1992<br>370 070 | 63545<br>−1991<br>370 071 | 63546<br>−1990<br>370 072 | 63547<br>−1989<br>370 073 | 63548<br>−1988<br>370 074 | 63549<br>−1987<br>370 075 | 63550<br>−1986<br>370 076 | 63551<br>−1985<br>370 077 |
| 4− | 63552<br>−1984<br>370 100 | 63553<br>−1983<br>370 101 | 63554<br>−1982<br>370 102 | 63555<br>−1981<br>370 103 | 63556<br>−1980<br>370 104 | 63557<br>−1979<br>370 105 | 63558<br>−1978<br>370 106 | 63559<br>−1977<br>370 107 | 63560<br>−1976<br>370 110 | 63561<br>−1975<br>370 111 | 63562<br>−1974<br>370 112 | 63563<br>−1973<br>370 113 | 63564<br>−1972<br>370 114 | 63565<br>−1971<br>370 115 | 63566<br>−1970<br>370 116 | 63567<br>−1969<br>370 117 |
| 5− | 63568<br>−1968<br>370 120 | 63569<br>−1967<br>370 121 | 63570<br>−1966<br>370 122 | 63571<br>−1965<br>370 123 | 63572<br>−1964<br>370 124 | 63573<br>−1963<br>370 125 | 63574<br>−1962<br>370 126 | 63575<br>−1961<br>370 127 | 63576<br>−1960<br>370 130 | 63577<br>−1959<br>370 131 | 63578<br>−1958<br>370 132 | 63579<br>−1957<br>370 133 | 63580<br>−1956<br>370 134 | 63581<br>−1955<br>370 135 | 63582<br>−1954<br>370 136 | 63583<br>−1953<br>370 137 |
| 6− | 63584<br>−1952<br>370 140 | 63585<br>−1951<br>370 141 | 63586<br>−1950<br>370 142 | 63587<br>−1949<br>370 143 | 63588<br>−1948<br>370 144 | 63589<br>−1947<br>370 145 | 63590<br>−1946<br>370 146 | 63591<br>−1945<br>370 147 | 63592<br>−1944<br>370 150 | 63593<br>−1943<br>370 151 | 63594<br>−1942<br>370 152 | 63595<br>−1941<br>370 153 | 63596<br>−1940<br>370 154 | 63597<br>−1939<br>370 155 | 63598<br>−1938<br>370 156 | 63599<br>−1937<br>370 157 |
| 7− | 63600<br>−1936<br>370 160 | 63601<br>−1935<br>370 161 | 63602<br>−1934<br>370 162 | 63603<br>−1933<br>370 163 | 63604<br>−1932<br>370 164 | 63605<br>−1931<br>370 165 | 63606<br>−1930<br>370 166 | 63607<br>−1929<br>370 167 | 63608<br>−1928<br>370 170 | 63609<br>−1927<br>370 171 | 63610<br>−1926<br>370 172 | 63611<br>−1925<br>370 173 | 63612<br>−1924<br>370 174 | 63613<br>−1923<br>370 175 | 63614<br>−1922<br>370 176 | 63615<br>−1921<br>370 177 |
| 8− | 63616<br>−1920<br>370 200 | 63617<br>−1919<br>370 201 | 63618<br>−1918<br>370 202 | 63619<br>−1917<br>370 203 | 63620<br>−1916<br>370 204 | 63621<br>−1915<br>370 205 | 63622<br>−1914<br>370 206 | 63623<br>−1913<br>370 207 | 63624<br>−1912<br>370 210 | 63625<br>−1911<br>370 211 | 63626<br>−1910<br>370 212 | 63627<br>−1909<br>370 213 | 63628<br>−1908<br>370 214 | 63629<br>−1907<br>370 215 | 63630<br>−1906<br>370 216 | 63631<br>−1905<br>370 217 |
| 9− | 63632<br>−1904<br>370 220 | 63633<br>−1903<br>370 221 | 63634<br>−1902<br>370 222 | 63635<br>−1901<br>370 223 | 63636<br>−1900<br>370 224 | 63637<br>−1899<br>370 225 | 63638<br>−1898<br>370 226 | 63639<br>−1897<br>370 227 | 63640<br>−1896<br>370 230 | 63641<br>−1895<br>370 231 | 63642<br>−1894<br>370 232 | 63643<br>−1893<br>370 233 | 63644<br>−1892<br>370 234 | 63645<br>−1891<br>370 235 | 63646<br>−1890<br>370 236 | 63647<br>−1889<br>370 237 |
| A− | 63648<br>−1888<br>370 240 | 63649<br>−1887<br>370 241 | 63650<br>−1886<br>370 242 | 63651<br>−1885<br>370 243 | 63652<br>−1884<br>370 244 | 63653<br>−1883<br>370 245 | 63654<br>−1882<br>370 246 | 63655<br>−1881<br>370 247 | 63656<br>−1880<br>370 250 | 63657<br>−1879<br>370 251 | 63658<br>−1878<br>370 252 | 63659<br>−1877<br>370 253 | 63660<br>−1876<br>370 254 | 63661<br>−1875<br>370 255 | 63662<br>−1874<br>370 256 | 63663<br>−1873<br>370 257 |
| B− | 63664<br>−1872<br>370 260 | 63665<br>−1871<br>370 261 | 63666<br>−1870<br>370 262 | 63667<br>−1869<br>370 263 | 63668<br>−1868<br>370 264 | 63669<br>−1867<br>370 265 | 63670<br>−1866<br>370 266 | 63671<br>−1865<br>370 267 | 63672<br>−1864<br>370 270 | 63673<br>−1863<br>370 271 | 63674<br>−1862<br>370 272 | 63675<br>−1861<br>370 273 | 63676<br>−1860<br>370 274 | 63677<br>−1859<br>370 275 | 63678<br>−1858<br>370 276 | 63679<br>−1857<br>370 277 |
| C− | 63680<br>−1856<br>370 300 | 63681<br>−1855<br>370 301 | 63682<br>−1854<br>370 302 | 63683<br>−1853<br>370 303 | 63684<br>−1852<br>370 304 | 63685<br>−1851<br>370 305 | 63686<br>−1850<br>370 306 | 63687<br>−1849<br>370 307 | 63688<br>−1848<br>370 310 | 63689<br>−1847<br>370 311 | 63690<br>−1846<br>370 312 | 63691<br>−1845<br>370 313 | 63692<br>−1844<br>370 314 | 63693<br>−1843<br>370 315 | 63694<br>−1842<br>370 316 | 63695<br>−1841<br>370 317 |
| D− | 63696<br>−1840<br>370 320 | 63697<br>−1839<br>370 321 | 63698<br>−1838<br>370 322 | 63699<br>−1837<br>370 323 | 63700<br>−1836<br>370 324 | 63701<br>−1835<br>370 325 | 63702<br>−1834<br>370 326 | 63703<br>−1833<br>370 327 | 63704<br>−1832<br>370 330 | 63705<br>−1831<br>370 331 | 63706<br>−1830<br>370 332 | 63707<br>−1829<br>370 333 | 63708<br>−1828<br>370 334 | 63709<br>−1827<br>370 335 | 63710<br>−1826<br>370 336 | 63711<br>−1825<br>370 337 |
| E− | 63712<br>−1824<br>370 340 | 63713<br>−1823<br>370 341 | 63714<br>−1822<br>370 342 | 63715<br>−1821<br>370 343 | 63716<br>−1820<br>370 344 | 63717<br>−1819<br>370 345 | 63718<br>−1818<br>370 346 | 63719<br>−1817<br>370 347 | 63720<br>−1816<br>370 350 | 63721<br>−1815<br>370 351 | 63722<br>−1814<br>370 352 | 63723<br>−1813<br>370 353 | 63724<br>−1812<br>370 354 | 63725<br>−1811<br>370 355 | 63726<br>−1810<br>370 356 | 63727<br>−1809<br>370 357 |
| F− | 63728<br>−1808<br>370 360 | 63729<br>−1807<br>370 361 | 63730<br>−1806<br>370 362 | 63731<br>−1805<br>370 363 | 63732<br>−1804<br>370 364 | 63733<br>−1803<br>370 365 | 63734<br>−1802<br>370 366 | 63735<br>−1801<br>370 367 | 63736<br>−1800<br>370 370 | 63737<br>−1799<br>370 371 | 63738<br>−1798<br>370 372 | 63739<br>−1797<br>370 373 | 63740<br>−1796<br>370 374 | 63741<br>−1795<br>370 375 | 63742<br>−1794<br>370 376 | 63743<br>−1793<br>370 377 |

DECIMAL

🍎 DECIMAL

OCTAL

🍎 **DECIMAL** │ −2048 │   **BINARY** │ 1111 1000 │   **DECIMAL** │ 63488 │   **HEXADECIMAL** ⬢ F8   **OCTAL** │ 370 000 │

FOURTH HEX DIGIT → ⬢ ← THIRD HEX DIGIT

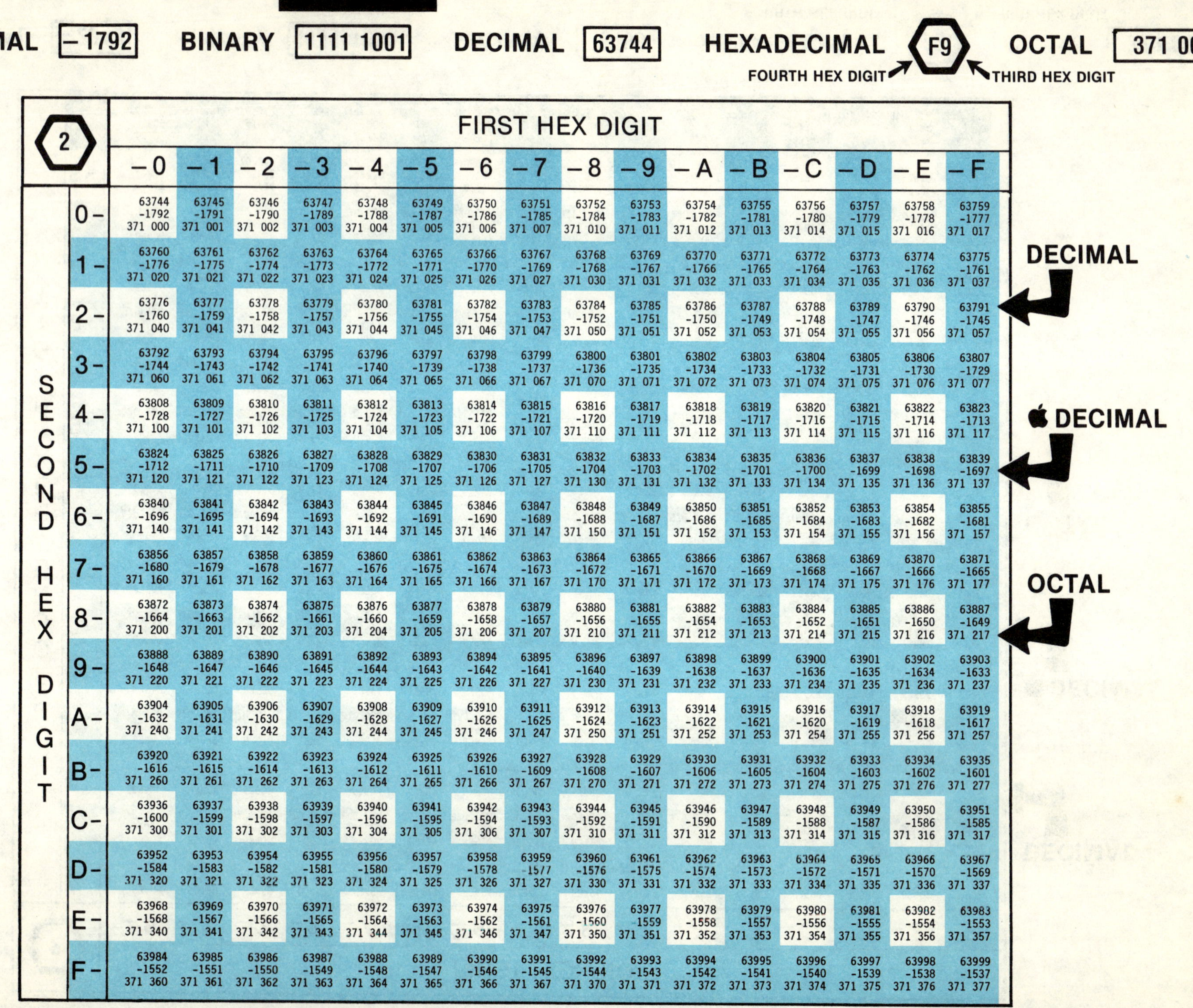


2

FIRST HEX DIGIT

| SECOND HEX DIGIT | −0 | −1 | −2 | −3 | −4 | −5 | −6 | −7 | −8 | −9 | −A | −B | −C | −D | −E | −F |
|---|---|---|---|---|---|---|---|---|---|---|---|---|---|---|---|---|
| 0− | 63744<br>−1792<br>371 000 | 63745<br>−1791<br>371 001 | 63746<br>−1790<br>371 002 | 63747<br>−1789<br>371 003 | 63748<br>−1788<br>371 004 | 63749<br>−1787<br>371 005 | 63750<br>−1786<br>371 006 | 63751<br>−1785<br>371 007 | 63752<br>−1784<br>371 010 | 63753<br>−1783<br>371 011 | 63754<br>−1782<br>371 012 | 63755<br>−1781<br>371 013 | 63756<br>−1780<br>371 014 | 63757<br>−1779<br>371 015 | 63758<br>−1778<br>371 016 | 63759<br>−1777<br>371 017 |
| 1− | 63760<br>−1776<br>371 020 | 63761<br>−1775<br>371 021 | 63762<br>−1774<br>371 022 | 63763<br>−1773<br>371 023 | 63764<br>−1772<br>371 024 | 63765<br>−1771<br>371 025 | 63766<br>−1770<br>371 026 | 63767<br>−1769<br>371 027 | 63768<br>−1768<br>371 030 | 63769<br>−1767<br>371 031 | 63770<br>−1766<br>371 032 | 63771<br>−1765<br>371 033 | 63772<br>−1764<br>371 034 | 63773<br>−1763<br>371 035 | 63774<br>−1762<br>371 036 | 63775<br>−1761<br>371 037 |
| 2− | 63776<br>−1760<br>371 040 | 63777<br>−1759<br>371 041 | 63778<br>−1758<br>371 042 | 63779<br>−1757<br>371 043 | 63780<br>−1756<br>371 044 | 63781<br>−1755<br>371 045 | 63782<br>−1754<br>371 046 | 63783<br>−1753<br>371 047 | 63784<br>−1752<br>371 050 | 63785<br>−1751<br>371 051 | 63786<br>−1750<br>371 052 | 63787<br>−1749<br>371 053 | 63788<br>−1748<br>371 054 | 63789<br>−1747<br>371 055 | 63790<br>−1746<br>371 056 | 63791<br>−1745<br>371 057 |
| 3− | 63792<br>−1744<br>371 060 | 63793<br>−1743<br>371 061 | 63794<br>−1742<br>371 062 | 63795<br>−1741<br>371 063 | 63796<br>−1740<br>371 064 | 63797<br>−1739<br>371 065 | 63798<br>−1738<br>371 066 | 63799<br>−1737<br>371 067 | 63800<br>−1736<br>371 070 | 63801<br>−1735<br>371 071 | 63802<br>−1734<br>371 072 | 63803<br>−1733<br>371 073 | 63804<br>−1732<br>371 074 | 63805<br>−1731<br>371 075 | 63806<br>−1730<br>371 076 | 63807<br>−1729<br>371 077 |
| 4− | 63808<br>−1728<br>371 100 | 63809<br>−1727<br>371 101 | 63810<br>−1726<br>371 102 | 63811<br>−1725<br>371 103 | 63812<br>−1724<br>371 104 | 63813<br>−1723<br>371 105 | 63814<br>−1722<br>371 106 | 63815<br>−1721<br>371 107 | 63816<br>−1720<br>371 110 | 63817<br>−1719<br>371 111 | 63818<br>−1718<br>371 112 | 63819<br>−1717<br>371 113 | 63820<br>−1716<br>371 114 | 63821<br>−1715<br>371 115 | 63822<br>−1714<br>371 116 | 63823<br>−1713<br>371 117 |
| 5− | 63824<br>−1712<br>371 120 | 63825<br>−1711<br>371 121 | 63826<br>−1710<br>371 122 | 63827<br>−1709<br>371 123 | 63828<br>−1708<br>371 124 | 63829<br>−1707<br>371 125 | 63830<br>−1706<br>371 126 | 63831<br>−1705<br>371 127 | 63832<br>−1704<br>371 130 | 63833<br>−1703<br>371 131 | 63834<br>−1702<br>371 132 | 63835<br>−1701<br>371 133 | 63836<br>−1700<br>371 134 | 63837<br>−1699<br>371 135 | 63838<br>−1698<br>371 136 | 63839<br>−1697<br>371 137 |
| 6− | 63840<br>−1696<br>371 140 | 63841<br>−1695<br>371 141 | 63842<br>−1694<br>371 142 | 63843<br>−1693<br>371 143 | 63844<br>−1692<br>371 144 | 63845<br>−1691<br>371 145 | 63846<br>−1690<br>371 146 | 63847<br>−1689<br>371 147 | 63848<br>−1688<br>371 150 | 63849<br>−1687<br>371 151 | 63850<br>−1686<br>371 152 | 63851<br>−1685<br>371 153 | 63852<br>−1684<br>371 154 | 63853<br>−1683<br>371 155 | 63854<br>−1682<br>371 156 | 63855<br>−1681<br>371 157 |
| 7− | 63856<br>−1680<br>371 160 | 63857<br>−1679<br>371 161 | 63858<br>−1678<br>371 162 | 63859<br>−1677<br>371 163 | 63860<br>−1676<br>371 164 | 63861<br>−1675<br>371 165 | 63862<br>−1674<br>371 166 | 63863<br>−1673<br>371 167 | 63864<br>−1672<br>371 170 | 63865<br>−1671<br>371 171 | 63866<br>−1670<br>371 172 | 63867<br>−1669<br>371 173 | 63868<br>−1668<br>371 174 | 63869<br>−1667<br>371 175 | 63870<br>−1666<br>371 176 | 63871<br>−1665<br>371 177 |
| 8− | 63872<br>−1664<br>371 200 | 63873<br>−1663<br>371 201 | 63874<br>−1662<br>371 202 | 63875<br>−1661<br>371 203 | 63876<br>−1660<br>371 204 | 63877<br>−1659<br>371 205 | 63878<br>−1658<br>371 206 | 63879<br>−1657<br>371 207 | 63880<br>−1656<br>371 210 | 63881<br>−1655<br>371 211 | 63882<br>−1654<br>371 212 | 63883<br>−1653<br>371 213 | 63884<br>−1652<br>371 214 | 63885<br>−1651<br>371 215 | 63886<br>−1650<br>371 216 | 63887<br>−1649<br>371 217 |
| 9− | 63888<br>−1648<br>371 220 | 63889<br>−1647<br>371 221 | 63890<br>−1646<br>371 222 | 63891<br>−1645<br>371 223 | 63892<br>−1644<br>371 224 | 63893<br>−1643<br>371 225 | 63894<br>−1642<br>371 226 | 63895<br>−1641<br>371 227 | 63896<br>−1640<br>371 230 | 63897<br>−1639<br>371 231 | 63898<br>−1638<br>371 232 | 63899<br>−1637<br>371 233 | 63900<br>−1636<br>371 234 | 63901<br>−1635<br>371 235 | 63902<br>−1634<br>371 236 | 63903<br>−1633<br>371 237 |
| A− | 63904<br>−1632<br>371 240 | 63905<br>−1631<br>371 241 | 63906<br>−1630<br>371 242 | 63907<br>−1629<br>371 243 | 63908<br>−1628<br>371 244 | 63909<br>−1627<br>371 245 | 63910<br>−1626<br>371 246 | 63911<br>−1625<br>371 247 | 63912<br>−1624<br>371 250 | 63913<br>−1623<br>371 251 | 63914<br>−1622<br>371 252 | 63915<br>−1621<br>371 253 | 63916<br>−1620<br>371 254 | 63917<br>−1619<br>371 255 | 63918<br>−1618<br>371 256 | 63919<br>−1617<br>371 257 |
| B− | 63920<br>−1616<br>371 260 | 63921<br>−1615<br>371 261 | 63922<br>−1614<br>371 262 | 63923<br>−1613<br>371 263 | 63924<br>−1612<br>371 264 | 63925<br>−1611<br>371 265 | 63926<br>−1610<br>371 266 | 63927<br>−1609<br>371 267 | 63928<br>−1608<br>371 270 | 63929<br>−1607<br>371 271 | 63930<br>−1606<br>371 272 | 63931<br>−1605<br>371 273 | 63932<br>−1604<br>371 274 | 63933<br>−1603<br>371 275 | 63934<br>−1602<br>371 276 | 63935<br>−1601<br>371 277 |
| C− | 63936<br>−1600<br>371 300 | 63937<br>−1599<br>371 301 | 63938<br>−1598<br>371 302 | 63939<br>−1597<br>371 303 | 63940<br>−1596<br>371 304 | 63941<br>−1595<br>371 305 | 63942<br>−1594<br>371 306 | 63943<br>−1593<br>371 307 | 63944<br>−1592<br>371 310 | 63945<br>−1591<br>371 311 | 63946<br>−1590<br>371 312 | 63947<br>−1589<br>371 313 | 63948<br>−1588<br>371 314 | 63949<br>−1587<br>371 315 | 63950<br>−1586<br>371 316 | 63951<br>−1585<br>371 317 |
| D− | 63952<br>−1584<br>371 320 | 63953<br>−1583<br>371 321 | 63954<br>−1582<br>371 322 | 63955<br>−1581<br>371 323 | 63956<br>−1580<br>371 324 | 63957<br>−1579<br>371 325 | 63958<br>−1578<br>371 326 | 63959<br>−1577<br>371 327 | 63960<br>−1576<br>371 330 | 63961<br>−1575<br>371 331 | 63962<br>−1574<br>371 332 | 63963<br>−1573<br>371 333 | 63964<br>−1572<br>371 334 | 63965<br>−1571<br>371 335 | 63966<br>−1570<br>371 336 | 63967<br>−1569<br>371 337 |
| E− | 63968<br>−1568<br>371 340 | 63969<br>−1567<br>371 341 | 63970<br>−1566<br>371 342 | 63971<br>−1565<br>371 343 | 63972<br>−1564<br>371 344 | 63973<br>−1563<br>371 345 | 63974<br>−1562<br>371 346 | 63975<br>−1561<br>371 347 | 63976<br>−1560<br>371 350 | 63977<br>−1559<br>371 351 | 63978<br>−1558<br>371 352 | 63979<br>−1557<br>371 353 | 63980<br>−1556<br>371 354 | 63981<br>−1555<br>371 355 | 63982<br>−1554<br>371 356 | 63983<br>−1553<br>371 357 |
| F− | 63984<br>−1552<br>371 360 | 63985<br>−1551<br>371 361 | 63986<br>−1550<br>371 362 | 63987<br>−1549<br>371 363 | 63988<br>−1548<br>371 364 | 63989<br>−1547<br>371 365 | 63990<br>−1546<br>371 366 | 63991<br>−1545<br>371 367 | 63992<br>−1544<br>371 370 | 63993<br>−1543<br>371 371 | 63994<br>−1542<br>371 372 | 63995<br>−1541<br>371 373 | 63996<br>−1540<br>371 374 | 63997<br>−1539<br>371 375 | 63998<br>−1538<br>371 376 | 63999<br>−1537<br>371 377 |

**②** FIRST HEX DIGIT — SECOND HEX DIGIT

DECIMAL / DECIMAL / OCTAL

| | −0 | −1 | −2 | −3 | −4 | −5 | −6 | −7 | −8 | −9 | −A | −B | −C | −D | −E | −F |
|---|---|---|---|---|---|---|---|---|---|---|---|---|---|---|---|---|
| 0- | 64000<br>-1536<br>372 000 | 64001<br>-1535<br>372 001 | 64002<br>-1534<br>372 002 | 64003<br>-1533<br>372 003 | 64004<br>-1532<br>372 004 | 64005<br>-1531<br>372 005 | 64006<br>-1530<br>372 006 | 64007<br>-1529<br>372 007 | 64008<br>-1528<br>372 010 | 64009<br>-1527<br>372 011 | 64010<br>-1526<br>372 012 | 64011<br>-1525<br>372 013 | 64012<br>-1524<br>372 014 | 64013<br>-1523<br>372 015 | 64014<br>-1522<br>372 016 | 64015<br>-1521<br>372 017 |
| 1- | 64016<br>-1520<br>372 020 | 64017<br>-1519<br>372 021 | 64018<br>-1518<br>372 022 | 64019<br>-1517<br>372 023 | 64020<br>-1516<br>372 024 | 64021<br>-1515<br>372 025 | 64022<br>-1514<br>372 026 | 64023<br>-1513<br>372 027 | 64024<br>-1512<br>372 030 | 64025<br>-1511<br>372 031 | 64026<br>-1510<br>372 032 | 64027<br>-1509<br>372 033 | 64028<br>-1508<br>372 034 | 64029<br>-1507<br>372 035 | 64030<br>-1506<br>372 036 | 64031<br>-1505<br>372 037 |
| 2- | 64032<br>-1504<br>372 040 | 64033<br>-1503<br>372 041 | 64034<br>-1502<br>372 042 | 64035<br>-1501<br>372 043 | 64036<br>-1500<br>372 044 | 64037<br>-1499<br>372 045 | 64038<br>-1498<br>372 046 | 64039<br>-1497<br>372 047 | 64040<br>-1496<br>372 050 | 64041<br>-1495<br>372 051 | 64042<br>-1494<br>372 052 | 64043<br>-1493<br>372 053 | 64044<br>-1492<br>372 054 | 64045<br>-1491<br>372 055 | 64046<br>-1490<br>372 056 | 64047<br>-1489<br>372 057 |
| 3- | 64048<br>-1488<br>372 060 | 64049<br>-1487<br>372 061 | 64050<br>-1486<br>372 062 | 64051<br>-1485<br>372 063 | 64052<br>-1484<br>372 064 | 64053<br>-1483<br>372 065 | 64054<br>-1482<br>372 066 | 64055<br>-1481<br>372 067 | 64056<br>-1480<br>372 070 | 64057<br>-1479<br>372 071 | 64058<br>-1478<br>372 072 | 64059<br>-1477<br>372 073 | 64060<br>-1476<br>372 074 | 64061<br>-1475<br>372 075 | 64062<br>-1474<br>372 076 | 64063<br>-1473<br>372 077 |
| 4- | 64064<br>-1472<br>372 100 | 64065<br>-1471<br>372 101 | 64066<br>-1470<br>372 102 | 64067<br>-1469<br>372 103 | 64068<br>-1468<br>372 104 | 64069<br>-1467<br>372 105 | 64070<br>-1466<br>372 106 | 64071<br>-1465<br>372 107 | 64072<br>-1464<br>372 110 | 64073<br>-1463<br>372 111 | 64074<br>-1462<br>372 112 | 64075<br>-1461<br>372 113 | 64076<br>-1460<br>372 114 | 64077<br>-1459<br>372 115 | 64078<br>-1458<br>372 116 | 64079<br>-1457<br>372 117 |
| 5- | 64080<br>-1456<br>372 120 | 64081<br>-1455<br>372 121 | 64082<br>-1454<br>372 122 | 64083<br>-1453<br>372 123 | 64084<br>-1452<br>372 124 | 64085<br>-1451<br>372 125 | 64086<br>-1450<br>372 126 | 64087<br>-1449<br>372 127 | 64088<br>-1448<br>372 130 | 64089<br>-1447<br>372 131 | 64090<br>-1446<br>372 132 | 64091<br>-1445<br>372 133 | 64092<br>-1444<br>372 134 | 64093<br>-1443<br>372 135 | 64094<br>-1442<br>372 136 | 64095<br>-1441<br>372 137 |
| 6- | 64096<br>-1440<br>372 140 | 64097<br>-1439<br>372 141 | 64098<br>-1438<br>372 142 | 64099<br>-1437<br>372 143 | 64100<br>-1436<br>372 144 | 64101<br>-1435<br>372 145 | 64102<br>-1434<br>372 146 | 64103<br>-1433<br>372 147 | 64104<br>-1432<br>372 150 | 64105<br>-1431<br>372 151 | 64106<br>-1430<br>372 152 | 64107<br>-1429<br>372 153 | 64108<br>-1428<br>372 154 | 64109<br>-1427<br>372 155 | 64110<br>-1426<br>372 156 | 64111<br>-1425<br>372 157 |
| 7- | 64112<br>-1424<br>372 160 | 64113<br>-1423<br>372 161 | 64114<br>-1422<br>372 162 | 64115<br>-1421<br>372 163 | 64116<br>-1420<br>372 164 | 64117<br>-1419<br>372 165 | 64118<br>-1418<br>372 166 | 64119<br>-1417<br>372 167 | 64120<br>-1416<br>372 170 | 64121<br>-1415<br>372 171 | 64122<br>-1414<br>372 172 | 64123<br>-1413<br>372 173 | 64124<br>-1412<br>372 174 | 64125<br>-1411<br>372 175 | 64126<br>-1410<br>372 176 | 64127<br>-1409<br>372 177 |
| 8- | 64128<br>-1408<br>372 200 | 64129<br>-1407<br>372 201 | 64130<br>-1406<br>372 202 | 64131<br>-1405<br>372 203 | 64132<br>-1404<br>372 204 | 64133<br>-1403<br>372 205 | 64134<br>-1402<br>372 206 | 64135<br>-1401<br>372 207 | 64136<br>-1400<br>372 210 | 64137<br>-1399<br>372 211 | 64138<br>-1398<br>372 212 | 64139<br>-1397<br>372 213 | 64140<br>-1396<br>372 214 | 64141<br>-1395<br>372 215 | 64142<br>-1394<br>372 216 | 64143<br>-1393<br>372 217 |
| 9- | 64144<br>-1392<br>372 220 | 64145<br>-1391<br>372 221 | 64146<br>-1390<br>372 222 | 64147<br>-1389<br>372 223 | 64148<br>-1388<br>372 224 | 64149<br>-1387<br>372 225 | 64150<br>-1386<br>372 226 | 64151<br>-1385<br>372 227 | 64152<br>-1384<br>372 230 | 64153<br>-1383<br>372 231 | 64154<br>-1382<br>372 232 | 64155<br>-1381<br>372 233 | 64156<br>-1380<br>372 234 | 64157<br>-1379<br>372 235 | 64158<br>-1378<br>372 236 | 64159<br>-1377<br>372 237 |
| A- | 64160<br>-1376<br>372 240 | 64161<br>-1375<br>372 241 | 64162<br>-1374<br>372 242 | 64163<br>-1373<br>372 243 | 64164<br>-1372<br>372 244 | 64165<br>-1371<br>372 245 | 64166<br>-1370<br>372 246 | 64167<br>-1369<br>372 247 | 64168<br>-1368<br>372 250 | 64169<br>-1367<br>372 251 | 64170<br>-1366<br>372 252 | 64171<br>-1365<br>372 253 | 64172<br>-1364<br>372 254 | 64173<br>-1363<br>372 255 | 64174<br>-1362<br>372 256 | 64175<br>-1361<br>372 257 |
| B- | 64176<br>-1360<br>372 260 | 64177<br>-1359<br>372 261 | 64178<br>-1358<br>372 262 | 64179<br>-1357<br>372 263 | 64180<br>-1356<br>372 264 | 64181<br>-1355<br>372 265 | 64182<br>-1354<br>372 266 | 64183<br>-1353<br>372 267 | 64184<br>-1352<br>372 270 | 64185<br>-1351<br>372 271 | 64186<br>-1350<br>372 272 | 64187<br>-1349<br>372 273 | 64188<br>-1348<br>372 274 | 64189<br>-1347<br>372 275 | 64190<br>-1346<br>372 276 | 64191<br>-1345<br>372 277 |
| C- | 64192<br>-1344<br>372 300 | 64193<br>-1343<br>372 301 | 64194<br>-1342<br>372 302 | 64195<br>-1341<br>372 303 | 64196<br>-1340<br>372 304 | 64197<br>-1339<br>372 305 | 64198<br>-1338<br>372 306 | 64199<br>-1337<br>372 307 | 64200<br>-1336<br>372 310 | 64201<br>-1335<br>372 311 | 64202<br>-1334<br>372 312 | 64203<br>-1333<br>372 313 | 64204<br>-1332<br>372 314 | 64205<br>-1331<br>372 315 | 64206<br>-1330<br>372 316 | 64207<br>-1329<br>372 317 |
| D- | 64208<br>-1328<br>372 320 | 64209<br>-1327<br>372 321 | 64210<br>-1326<br>372 322 | 64211<br>-1325<br>372 323 | 64212<br>-1324<br>372 324 | 64213<br>-1323<br>372 325 | 64214<br>-1322<br>372 326 | 64215<br>-1321<br>372 327 | 64216<br>-1320<br>372 330 | 64217<br>-1319<br>372 331 | 64218<br>-1318<br>372 332 | 64219<br>-1317<br>372 333 | 64220<br>-1316<br>372 334 | 64221<br>-1315<br>372 335 | 64222<br>-1314<br>372 336 | 64223<br>-1313<br>372 337 |
| E- | 64224<br>-1312<br>372 340 | 64225<br>-1311<br>372 341 | 64226<br>-1310<br>372 342 | 64227<br>-1309<br>372 343 | 64228<br>-1308<br>372 344 | 64229<br>-1307<br>372 345 | 64230<br>-1306<br>372 346 | 64231<br>-1305<br>372 347 | 64232<br>-1304<br>372 350 | 64233<br>-1303<br>372 351 | 64234<br>-1302<br>372 352 | 64235<br>-1301<br>372 353 | 64236<br>-1300<br>372 354 | 64237<br>-1299<br>372 355 | 64238<br>-1298<br>372 356 | 64239<br>-1297<br>372 357 |
| F- | 64240<br>-1296<br>372 360 | 64241<br>-1295<br>372 361 | 64242<br>-1294<br>372 362 | 64243<br>-1293<br>372 363 | 64244<br>-1292<br>372 364 | 64245<br>-1291<br>372 365 | 64246<br>-1290<br>372 366 | 64247<br>-1289<br>372 367 | 64248<br>-1288<br>372 370 | 64249<br>-1287<br>372 371 | 64250<br>-1286<br>372 372 | 64251<br>-1285<br>372 373 | 64252<br>-1284<br>372 374 | 64253<br>-1283<br>372 375 | 64254<br>-1282<br>372 376 | 64255<br>-1281<br>372 377 |

**⌘ DECIMAL** ⎣ −1536 ⎦  **BINARY** ⎣ 1111 1010 ⎦  **DECIMAL** ⎣ 64000 ⎦  **HEXADECIMAL** ⟨FA⟩ **OCTAL** ⎣ 372 000 ⎦

FOURTH HEX DIGIT → ⟨FA⟩ ← THIRD HEX DIGIT

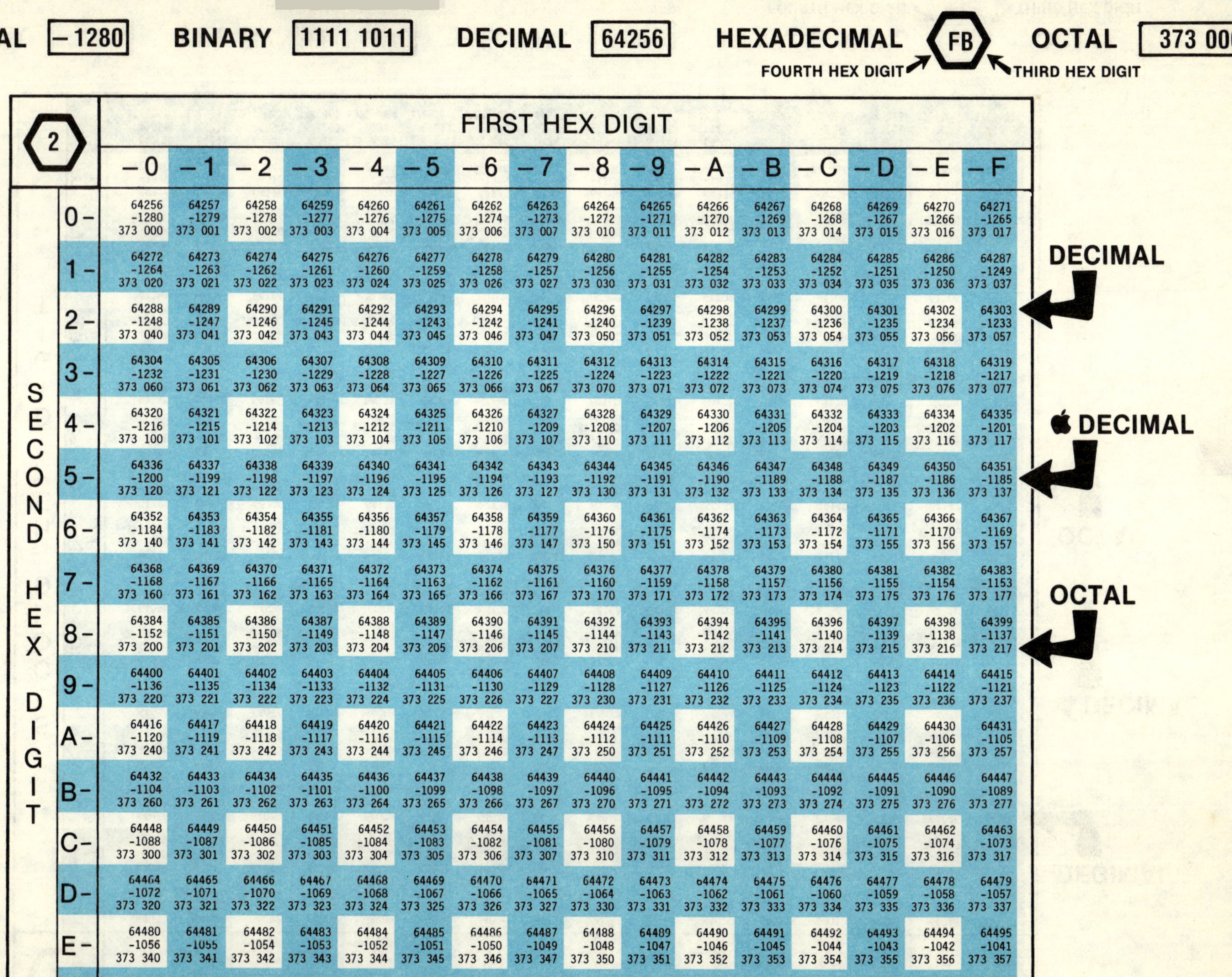

FIRST HEX DIGIT / SECOND HEX DIGIT conversion table ⟨2⟩ (Decimal / −Decimal / Octal)

| SECOND \ FIRST | −0 | −1 | −2 | −3 | −4 | −5 | −6 | −7 | −8 | −9 | −A | −B | −C | −D | −E | −F |
|---|---|---|---|---|---|---|---|---|---|---|---|---|---|---|---|---|
| 0- | 64256<br>−1280<br>373 000 | 64257<br>−1279<br>373 001 | 64258<br>−1278<br>373 002 | 64259<br>−1277<br>373 003 | 64260<br>−1276<br>373 004 | 64261<br>−1275<br>373 005 | 64262<br>−1274<br>373 006 | 64263<br>−1273<br>373 007 | 64264<br>−1272<br>373 010 | 64265<br>−1271<br>373 011 | 64266<br>−1270<br>373 012 | 64267<br>−1269<br>373 013 | 64268<br>−1268<br>373 014 | 64269<br>−1267<br>373 015 | 64270<br>−1266<br>373 016 | 64271<br>−1265<br>373 017 |
| 1- | 64272<br>−1264<br>373 020 | 64273<br>−1263<br>373 021 | 64274<br>−1262<br>373 022 | 64275<br>−1261<br>373 023 | 64276<br>−1260<br>373 024 | 64277<br>−1259<br>373 025 | 64278<br>−1258<br>373 026 | 64279<br>−1257<br>373 027 | 64280<br>−1256<br>373 030 | 64281<br>−1255<br>373 031 | 64282<br>−1254<br>373 032 | 64283<br>−1253<br>373 033 | 64284<br>−1252<br>373 034 | 64285<br>−1251<br>373 035 | 64286<br>−1250<br>373 036 | 64287<br>−1249<br>373 037 |
| 2- | 64288<br>−1248<br>373 040 | 64289<br>−1247<br>373 041 | 64290<br>−1246<br>373 042 | 64291<br>−1245<br>373 043 | 64292<br>−1244<br>373 044 | 64293<br>−1243<br>373 045 | 64294<br>−1242<br>373 046 | 64295<br>−1241<br>373 047 | 64296<br>−1240<br>373 050 | 64297<br>−1239<br>373 051 | 64298<br>−1238<br>373 052 | 64299<br>−1237<br>373 053 | 64300<br>−1236<br>373 054 | 64301<br>−1235<br>373 055 | 64302<br>−1234<br>373 056 | 64303<br>−1233<br>373 057 |
| 3- | 64304<br>−1232<br>373 060 | 64305<br>−1231<br>373 061 | 64306<br>−1230<br>373 062 | 64307<br>−1229<br>373 063 | 64308<br>−1228<br>373 064 | 64309<br>−1227<br>373 065 | 64310<br>−1226<br>373 066 | 64311<br>−1225<br>373 067 | 64312<br>−1224<br>373 070 | 64313<br>−1223<br>373 071 | 64314<br>−1222<br>373 072 | 64315<br>−1221<br>373 073 | 64316<br>−1220<br>373 074 | 64317<br>−1219<br>373 075 | 64318<br>−1218<br>373 076 | 64319<br>−1217<br>373 077 |
| 4- | 64320<br>−1216<br>373 100 | 64321<br>−1215<br>373 101 | 64322<br>−1214<br>373 102 | 64323<br>−1213<br>373 103 | 64324<br>−1212<br>373 104 | 64325<br>−1211<br>373 105 | 64326<br>−1210<br>373 106 | 64327<br>−1209<br>373 107 | 64328<br>−1208<br>373 110 | 64329<br>−1207<br>373 111 | 64330<br>−1206<br>373 112 | 64331<br>−1205<br>373 113 | 64332<br>−1204<br>373 114 | 64333<br>−1203<br>373 115 | 64334<br>−1202<br>373 116 | 64335<br>−1201<br>373 117 |
| 5- | 64336<br>−1200<br>373 120 | 64337<br>−1199<br>373 121 | 64338<br>−1198<br>373 122 | 64339<br>−1197<br>373 123 | 64340<br>−1196<br>373 124 | 64341<br>−1195<br>373 125 | 64342<br>−1194<br>373 126 | 64343<br>−1193<br>373 127 | 64344<br>−1192<br>373 130 | 64345<br>−1191<br>373 131 | 64346<br>−1190<br>373 132 | 64347<br>−1189<br>373 133 | 64348<br>−1188<br>373 134 | 64349<br>−1187<br>373 135 | 64350<br>−1186<br>373 136 | 64351<br>−1185<br>373 137 |
| 6- | 64352<br>−1184<br>373 140 | 64353<br>−1183<br>373 141 | 64354<br>−1182<br>373 142 | 64355<br>−1181<br>373 143 | 64356<br>−1180<br>373 144 | 64357<br>−1179<br>373 145 | 64358<br>−1178<br>373 146 | 64359<br>−1177<br>373 147 | 64360<br>−1176<br>373 150 | 64361<br>−1175<br>373 151 | 64362<br>−1174<br>373 152 | 64363<br>−1173<br>373 153 | 64364<br>−1172<br>373 154 | 64365<br>−1171<br>373 155 | 64366<br>−1170<br>373 156 | 64367<br>−1169<br>373 157 |
| 7- | 64368<br>−1168<br>373 160 | 64369<br>−1167<br>373 161 | 64370<br>−1166<br>373 162 | 64371<br>−1165<br>373 163 | 64372<br>−1164<br>373 164 | 64373<br>−1163<br>373 165 | 64374<br>−1162<br>373 166 | 64375<br>−1161<br>373 167 | 64376<br>−1160<br>373 170 | 64377<br>−1159<br>373 171 | 64378<br>−1158<br>373 172 | 64379<br>−1157<br>373 173 | 64380<br>−1156<br>373 174 | 64381<br>−1155<br>373 175 | 64382<br>−1154<br>373 176 | 64383<br>−1153<br>373 177 |
| 8- | 64384<br>−1152<br>373 200 | 64385<br>−1151<br>373 201 | 64386<br>−1150<br>373 202 | 64387<br>−1149<br>373 203 | 64388<br>−1148<br>373 204 | 64389<br>−1147<br>373 205 | 64390<br>−1146<br>373 206 | 64391<br>−1145<br>373 207 | 64392<br>−1144<br>373 210 | 64393<br>−1143<br>373 211 | 64394<br>−1142<br>373 212 | 64395<br>−1141<br>373 213 | 64396<br>−1140<br>373 214 | 64397<br>−1139<br>373 215 | 64398<br>−1138<br>373 216 | 64399<br>−1137<br>373 217 |
| 9- | 64400<br>−1136<br>373 220 | 64401<br>−1135<br>373 221 | 64402<br>−1134<br>373 222 | 64403<br>−1133<br>373 223 | 64404<br>−1132<br>373 224 | 64405<br>−1131<br>373 225 | 64406<br>−1130<br>373 226 | 64407<br>−1129<br>373 227 | 64408<br>−1128<br>373 230 | 64409<br>−1127<br>373 231 | 64410<br>−1126<br>373 232 | 64411<br>−1125<br>373 233 | 64412<br>−1124<br>373 234 | 64413<br>−1123<br>373 235 | 64414<br>−1122<br>373 236 | 64415<br>−1121<br>373 237 |
| A- | 64416<br>−1120<br>373 240 | 64417<br>−1119<br>373 241 | 64418<br>−1118<br>373 242 | 64419<br>−1117<br>373 243 | 64420<br>−1116<br>373 244 | 64421<br>−1115<br>373 245 | 64422<br>−1114<br>373 246 | 64423<br>−1113<br>373 247 | 64424<br>−1112<br>373 250 | 64425<br>−1111<br>373 251 | 64426<br>−1110<br>373 252 | 64427<br>−1109<br>373 253 | 64428<br>−1108<br>373 254 | 64429<br>−1107<br>373 255 | 64430<br>−1106<br>373 256 | 64431<br>−1105<br>373 257 |
| B- | 64432<br>−1104<br>373 260 | 64433<br>−1103<br>373 261 | 64434<br>−1102<br>373 262 | 64435<br>−1101<br>373 263 | 64436<br>−1100<br>373 264 | 64437<br>−1099<br>373 265 | 64438<br>−1098<br>373 266 | 64439<br>−1097<br>373 267 | 64440<br>−1096<br>373 270 | 64441<br>−1095<br>373 271 | 64442<br>−1094<br>373 272 | 64443<br>−1093<br>373 273 | 64444<br>−1092<br>373 274 | 64445<br>−1091<br>373 275 | 64446<br>−1090<br>373 276 | 64447<br>−1089<br>373 277 |
| C- | 64448<br>−1088<br>373 300 | 64449<br>−1087<br>373 301 | 64450<br>−1086<br>373 302 | 64451<br>−1085<br>373 303 | 64452<br>−1084<br>373 304 | 64453<br>−1083<br>373 305 | 64454<br>−1082<br>373 306 | 64455<br>−1081<br>373 307 | 64456<br>−1080<br>373 310 | 64457<br>−1079<br>373 311 | 64458<br>−1078<br>373 312 | 64459<br>−1077<br>373 313 | 64460<br>−1076<br>373 314 | 64461<br>−1075<br>373 315 | 64462<br>−1074<br>373 316 | 64463<br>−1073<br>373 317 |
| D- | 64464<br>−1072<br>373 320 | 64465<br>−1071<br>373 321 | 64466<br>−1070<br>373 322 | 64467<br>−1069<br>373 323 | 64468<br>−1068<br>373 324 | 64469<br>−1067<br>373 325 | 64470<br>−1066<br>373 326 | 64471<br>−1065<br>373 327 | 64472<br>−1064<br>373 330 | 64473<br>−1063<br>373 331 | 64474<br>−1062<br>373 332 | 64475<br>−1061<br>373 333 | 64476<br>−1060<br>373 334 | 64477<br>−1059<br>373 335 | 64478<br>−1058<br>373 336 | 64479<br>−1057<br>373 337 |
| E- | 64480<br>−1056<br>373 340 | 64481<br>−1055<br>373 341 | 64482<br>−1054<br>373 342 | 64483<br>−1053<br>373 343 | 64484<br>−1052<br>373 344 | 64485<br>−1051<br>373 345 | 64486<br>−1050<br>373 346 | 64487<br>−1049<br>373 347 | 64488<br>−1048<br>373 350 | 64489<br>−1047<br>373 351 | 64490<br>−1046<br>373 352 | 64491<br>−1045<br>373 353 | 64492<br>−1044<br>373 354 | 64493<br>−1043<br>373 355 | 64494<br>−1042<br>373 356 | 64495<br>−1041<br>373 357 |
| F- | 64496<br>−1040<br>373 360 | 64497<br>−1039<br>373 361 | 64498<br>−1038<br>373 362 | 64499<br>−1037<br>373 363 | 64500<br>−1036<br>373 364 | 64501<br>−1035<br>373 365 | 64502<br>−1034<br>373 366 | 64503<br>−1033<br>373 367 | 64504<br>−1032<br>373 370 | 64505<br>−1031<br>373 371 | 64506<br>−1030<br>373 372 | 64507<br>−1029<br>373 373 | 64508<br>−1028<br>373 374 | 64509<br>−1027<br>373 375 | 64510<br>−1026<br>373 376 | 64511<br>−1025<br>373 377 |

# FIRST HEX DIGIT

②

| SECOND HEX DIGIT | −0 | −1 | −2 | −3 | −4 | −5 | −6 | −7 | −8 | −9 | −A | −B | −C | −D | −E | −F |
|---|---|---|---|---|---|---|---|---|---|---|---|---|---|---|---|---|
| **0−** | 64512<br>−1024<br>374 000 | 64513<br>−1023<br>374 001 | 64514<br>−1022<br>374 002 | 64515<br>−1021<br>374 003 | 64516<br>−1020<br>374 004 | 64517<br>−1019<br>374 005 | 64518<br>−1018<br>374 006 | 64519<br>−1017<br>374 007 | 64520<br>−1016<br>374 010 | 64521<br>−1015<br>374 011 | 64522<br>−1014<br>374 012 | 64523<br>−1013<br>374 013 | 64524<br>−1012<br>374 014 | 64525<br>−1011<br>374 015 | 64526<br>−1010<br>374 016 | 64527<br>−1009<br>374 017 |
| **1−** | 64528<br>−1008<br>374 020 | 64529<br>−1007<br>374 021 | 64530<br>−1006<br>374 022 | 64531<br>−1005<br>374 023 | 64532<br>−1004<br>374 024 | 64533<br>−1003<br>374 025 | 64534<br>−1002<br>374 026 | 64535<br>−1001<br>374 027 | 64536<br>−1000<br>374 030 | 64537<br>−999<br>374 031 | 64538<br>−998<br>374 032 | 64539<br>−997<br>374 033 | 64540<br>−996<br>374 034 | 64541<br>−995<br>374 035 | 64542<br>−994<br>374 036 | 64543<br>−993<br>374 037 |
| **2−** | 64544<br>−992<br>374 040 | 64545<br>−991<br>374 041 | 64546<br>−990<br>374 042 | 64547<br>−989<br>374 043 | 64548<br>−988<br>374 044 | 64549<br>−987<br>374 045 | 64550<br>−986<br>374 046 | 64551<br>−985<br>374 047 | 64552<br>−984<br>374 050 | 64553<br>−983<br>374 051 | 64554<br>−982<br>374 052 | 64555<br>−981<br>374 053 | 64556<br>−980<br>374 054 | 64557<br>−979<br>374 055 | 64558<br>−978<br>374 056 | 64559<br>−977<br>374 057 |
| **3−** | 64560<br>−976<br>374 060 | 64561<br>−975<br>374 061 | 64562<br>−974<br>374 062 | 64563<br>−973<br>374 063 | 64564<br>−972<br>374 064 | 64565<br>−971<br>374 065 | 64566<br>−970<br>374 066 | 64567<br>−969<br>374 067 | 64568<br>−968<br>374 070 | 64569<br>−967<br>374 071 | 64570<br>−966<br>374 072 | 64571<br>−965<br>374 073 | 64572<br>−964<br>374 074 | 64573<br>−963<br>374 075 | 64574<br>−962<br>374 076 | 64575<br>−961<br>374 077 |
| **4−** | 64576<br>−960<br>374 100 | 64577<br>−959<br>374 101 | 64578<br>−958<br>374 102 | 64579<br>−957<br>374 103 | 64580<br>−956<br>374 104 | 64581<br>−955<br>374 105 | 64582<br>−954<br>374 106 | 64583<br>−953<br>374 107 | 64584<br>−952<br>374 110 | 64585<br>−951<br>374 111 | 64586<br>−950<br>374 112 | 64587<br>−949<br>374 113 | 64588<br>−948<br>374 114 | 64589<br>−947<br>374 115 | 64590<br>−946<br>374 116 | 64591<br>−945<br>374 117 |
| **5−** | 64592<br>−944<br>374 120 | 64593<br>−943<br>374 121 | 64594<br>−942<br>374 122 | 64595<br>−941<br>374 123 | 64596<br>−940<br>374 124 | 64597<br>−939<br>374 125 | 64598<br>−938<br>374 126 | 64599<br>−937<br>374 127 | 64600<br>−936<br>374 130 | 64601<br>−935<br>374 131 | 64602<br>−934<br>374 132 | 64603<br>−933<br>374 133 | 64604<br>−932<br>374 134 | 64605<br>−931<br>374 135 | 64606<br>−930<br>374 136 | 64607<br>−929<br>374 137 |
| **6−** | 64608<br>−928<br>374 140 | 64609<br>−927<br>374 141 | 64610<br>−926<br>374 142 | 64611<br>−925<br>374 143 | 64612<br>−924<br>374 144 | 64613<br>−923<br>374 145 | 64614<br>−922<br>374 146 | 64615<br>−921<br>374 147 | 64616<br>−920<br>374 150 | 64617<br>−919<br>374 151 | 64618<br>−918<br>374 152 | 64619<br>−917<br>374 153 | 64620<br>−916<br>374 154 | 64621<br>−915<br>374 155 | 64622<br>−914<br>374 156 | 64623<br>−913<br>374 157 |
| **7−** | 64624<br>−912<br>374 160 | 64625<br>−911<br>374 161 | 64626<br>−910<br>374 162 | 64627<br>−909<br>374 163 | 64628<br>−908<br>374 164 | 64629<br>−907<br>374 165 | 64630<br>−906<br>374 166 | 64631<br>−905<br>374 167 | 64632<br>−904<br>374 170 | 64633<br>−903<br>374 171 | 64634<br>−902<br>374 172 | 64635<br>−901<br>374 173 | 64636<br>−900<br>374 174 | 64637<br>−899<br>374 175 | 64638<br>−898<br>374 176 | 64639<br>−897<br>374 177 |
| **8−** | 64640<br>−896<br>374 200 | 64641<br>−895<br>374 201 | 64642<br>−894<br>374 202 | 64643<br>−893<br>374 203 | 64644<br>−892<br>374 204 | 64645<br>−891<br>374 205 | 64646<br>−890<br>374 206 | 64647<br>−889<br>374 207 | 64648<br>−888<br>374 210 | 64649<br>−887<br>374 211 | 64650<br>−886<br>374 212 | 64651<br>−885<br>374 213 | 64652<br>−884<br>374 214 | 64653<br>−883<br>374 215 | 64654<br>−882<br>374 216 | 64655<br>−881<br>374 217 |
| **9−** | 64656<br>−880<br>374 220 | 64657<br>−879<br>374 221 | 64658<br>−878<br>374 222 | 64659<br>−877<br>374 223 | 64660<br>−876<br>374 224 | 64661<br>−875<br>374 225 | 64662<br>−874<br>374 226 | 64663<br>−873<br>374 227 | 64664<br>−872<br>374 230 | 64665<br>−871<br>374 231 | 64666<br>−870<br>374 232 | 64667<br>−869<br>374 233 | 64668<br>−868<br>374 234 | 64669<br>−867<br>374 235 | 64670<br>−866<br>374 236 | 64671<br>−865<br>374 237 |
| **A−** | 64672<br>−864<br>374 240 | 64673<br>−863<br>374 241 | 64674<br>−862<br>374 242 | 64675<br>−861<br>374 243 | 64676<br>−860<br>374 244 | 64677<br>−859<br>374 245 | 64678<br>−858<br>374 246 | 64679<br>−857<br>374 247 | 64680<br>−856<br>374 250 | 64681<br>−855<br>374 251 | 64682<br>−854<br>374 252 | 64683<br>−853<br>374 253 | 64684<br>−852<br>374 254 | 64685<br>−851<br>374 255 | 64686<br>−850<br>374 256 | 64687<br>−849<br>374 257 |
| **B−** | 64688<br>−848<br>374 260 | 64689<br>−847<br>374 261 | 64690<br>−846<br>374 262 | 64691<br>−845<br>374 263 | 64692<br>−844<br>374 264 | 64693<br>−843<br>374 265 | 64694<br>−842<br>374 266 | 64695<br>−841<br>374 267 | 64696<br>−840<br>374 270 | 64697<br>−839<br>374 271 | 64698<br>−838<br>374 272 | 64699<br>−837<br>374 273 | 64700<br>−836<br>374 274 | 64701<br>−835<br>374 275 | 64702<br>−834<br>374 276 | 64703<br>−833<br>374 277 |
| **C−** | 64704<br>−832<br>374 300 | 64705<br>−831<br>374 301 | 64706<br>−830<br>374 302 | 64707<br>−829<br>374 303 | 64708<br>−828<br>374 304 | 64709<br>−827<br>374 305 | 64710<br>−826<br>374 306 | 64711<br>−825<br>374 307 | 64712<br>−824<br>374 310 | 64713<br>−823<br>374 311 | 64714<br>−822<br>374 312 | 64715<br>−821<br>374 313 | 64716<br>−820<br>374 314 | 64717<br>−819<br>374 315 | 64718<br>−818<br>374 316 | 64719<br>−817<br>374 317 |
| **D−** | 64720<br>−816<br>374 320 | 64721<br>−815<br>374 321 | 64722<br>−814<br>374 322 | 64723<br>−813<br>374 323 | 64724<br>−812<br>374 324 | 64725<br>−811<br>374 325 | 64726<br>−810<br>374 326 | 64727<br>−809<br>374 327 | 64728<br>−808<br>374 330 | 64729<br>−807<br>374 331 | 64730<br>−806<br>374 332 | 64731<br>−805<br>374 333 | 64732<br>−804<br>374 334 | 64733<br>−803<br>374 335 | 64734<br>−802<br>374 336 | 64735<br>−801<br>374 337 |
| **E−** | 64736<br>−800<br>374 340 | 64737<br>−799<br>374 341 | 64738<br>−798<br>374 342 | 64739<br>−797<br>374 343 | 64740<br>−796<br>374 344 | 64741<br>−795<br>374 345 | 64742<br>−794<br>374 346 | 64743<br>−793<br>374 347 | 64744<br>−792<br>374 350 | 64745<br>−791<br>374 351 | 64746<br>−790<br>374 352 | 64747<br>−789<br>374 353 | 64748<br>−788<br>374 354 | 64749<br>−787<br>374 355 | 64750<br>−786<br>374 356 | 64751<br>−785<br>374 357 |
| **F−** | 64752<br>−784<br>374 360 | 64753<br>−783<br>374 361 | 64754<br>−782<br>374 362 | 64755<br>−781<br>374 363 | 64756<br>−780<br>374 364 | 64757<br>−779<br>374 365 | 64758<br>−778<br>374 366 | 64759<br>−777<br>374 367 | 64760<br>−776<br>374 370 | 64761<br>−775<br>374 371 | 64762<br>−774<br>374 372 | 64763<br>−773<br>374 373 | 64764<br>−772<br>374 374 | 64765<br>−771<br>374 375 | 64766<br>−770<br>374 376 | 64767<br>−769<br>374 377 |

**DECIMAL** ←

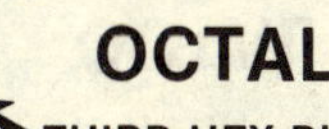 **DECIMAL** ←

**OCTAL** ←

---

 **DECIMAL** `−1024`   **BINARY** `1111 1100`   **DECIMAL** `64512`   **HEXADECIMAL** 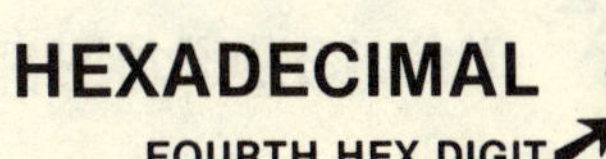 **OCTAL** `374 000`

FOURTH HEX DIGIT → FC ← THIRD HEX DIGIT

| (2) | −0 | −1 | −2 | −3 | −4 | −5 | −6 | −7 | −8 | −9 | −A | −B | −C | −D | −E | −F |
|---|---|---|---|---|---|---|---|---|---|---|---|---|---|---|---|---|
| **0−** | 64768<br>−768<br>375 000 | 64769<br>−767<br>375 001 | 64770<br>−766<br>375 002 | 64771<br>−765<br>375 003 | 64772<br>−764<br>375 004 | 64773<br>−763<br>375 005 | 64774<br>−762<br>375 006 | 64775<br>−761<br>375 007 | 64776<br>−760<br>375 010 | 64777<br>−759<br>375 011 | 64778<br>−758<br>375 012 | 64779<br>−757<br>375 013 | 64780<br>−756<br>375 014 | 64781<br>−755<br>375 015 | 64782<br>−754<br>375 016 | 64783<br>−753<br>375 017 |
| **1−** | 64784<br>−752<br>375 020 | 64785<br>−751<br>375 021 | 64786<br>−750<br>375 022 | 64787<br>−749<br>375 023 | 64788<br>−748<br>375 024 | 64789<br>−747<br>375 025 | 64790<br>−746<br>375 026 | 64791<br>−745<br>375 027 | 64792<br>−744<br>375 030 | 64793<br>−743<br>375 031 | 64794<br>−742<br>375 032 | 64795<br>−741<br>375 033 | 64796<br>−740<br>375 034 | 64797<br>−739<br>375 035 | 64798<br>−738<br>375 036 | 64799<br>−737<br>375 037 |
| **2−** | 64800<br>−736<br>375 040 | 64801<br>−735<br>375 041 | 64802<br>−734<br>375 042 | 64803<br>−733<br>375 043 | 64804<br>−732<br>375 044 | 64805<br>−731<br>375 045 | 64806<br>−730<br>375 046 | 64807<br>−729<br>375 047 | 64808<br>−728<br>375 050 | 64809<br>−727<br>375 051 | 64810<br>−726<br>375 052 | 64811<br>−725<br>375 053 | 64812<br>−724<br>375 054 | 64813<br>−723<br>375 055 | 64814<br>−722<br>375 056 | 64815<br>−721<br>375 057 |
| **3−** | 64816<br>−720<br>375 060 | 64817<br>−719<br>375 061 | 64818<br>−718<br>375 062 | 64819<br>−717<br>375 063 | 64820<br>−716<br>375 064 | 64821<br>−715<br>375 065 | 64822<br>−714<br>375 066 | 64823<br>−713<br>375 067 | 64824<br>−712<br>375 070 | 64825<br>−711<br>375 071 | 64826<br>−710<br>375 072 | 64827<br>−709<br>375 073 | 64828<br>−708<br>375 074 | 64829<br>−707<br>375 075 | 64830<br>−706<br>375 076 | 64831<br>−705<br>375 077 |
| **4−** | 64832<br>−704<br>375 100 | 64833<br>−703<br>375 101 | 64834<br>−702<br>375 102 | 64835<br>−701<br>375 103 | 64836<br>−700<br>375 104 | 64837<br>−699<br>375 105 | 64838<br>−698<br>375 106 | 64839<br>−697<br>375 107 | 64840<br>−696<br>375 110 | 64841<br>−695<br>375 111 | 64842<br>−694<br>375 112 | 64843<br>−693<br>375 113 | 64844<br>−692<br>375 114 | 64845<br>−691<br>375 115 | 64846<br>−690<br>375 116 | 64847<br>−689<br>375 117 |
| **5−** | 64848<br>−688<br>375 120 | 64849<br>−687<br>375 121 | 64850<br>−686<br>375 122 | 64851<br>−685<br>375 123 | 64852<br>−684<br>375 124 | 64853<br>−683<br>375 125 | 64854<br>−682<br>375 126 | 64855<br>−681<br>375 127 | 64856<br>−680<br>375 130 | 64857<br>−679<br>375 131 | 64858<br>−678<br>375 132 | 64859<br>−677<br>375 133 | 64860<br>−676<br>375 134 | 64861<br>−675<br>375 135 | 64862<br>−674<br>375 136 | 64863<br>−673<br>375 137 |
| **6−** | 64864<br>−672<br>375 140 | 64865<br>−671<br>375 141 | 64866<br>−670<br>375 142 | 64867<br>−669<br>375 143 | 64868<br>−668<br>375 144 | 64869<br>−667<br>375 145 | 64870<br>−666<br>375 146 | 64871<br>−665<br>375 147 | 64872<br>−664<br>375 150 | 64873<br>−663<br>375 151 | 64874<br>−662<br>375 152 | 64875<br>−661<br>375 153 | 64876<br>−660<br>375 154 | 64877<br>−659<br>375 155 | 64878<br>−658<br>375 156 | 64879<br>−657<br>375 157 |
| **7−** | 64880<br>−656<br>375 160 | 64881<br>−655<br>375 161 | 64882<br>−654<br>375 162 | 64883<br>−653<br>375 163 | 64884<br>−652<br>375 164 | 64885<br>−651<br>375 165 | 64886<br>−650<br>375 166 | 64887<br>−649<br>375 167 | 64888<br>−648<br>375 170 | 64889<br>−647<br>375 171 | 64890<br>−646<br>375 172 | 64891<br>−645<br>375 173 | 64892<br>−644<br>375 174 | 64893<br>−643<br>375 175 | 64894<br>−642<br>375 176 | 64895<br>−641<br>375 177 |
| **8−** | 64896<br>−640<br>375 200 | 64897<br>−639<br>375 201 | 64898<br>−638<br>375 202 | 64899<br>−637<br>375 203 | 64900<br>−636<br>375 204 | 64901<br>−635<br>375 205 | 64902<br>−634<br>375 206 | 64903<br>−633<br>375 207 | 64904<br>−632<br>375 210 | 64905<br>−631<br>375 211 | 64906<br>−630<br>375 212 | 64907<br>−629<br>375 213 | 64908<br>−628<br>375 214 | 64909<br>−627<br>375 215 | 64910<br>−626<br>375 216 | 64911<br>−625<br>375 217 |
| **9−** | 64912<br>−624<br>375 220 | 64913<br>−623<br>375 221 | 64914<br>−622<br>375 222 | 64915<br>−621<br>375 223 | 64916<br>−620<br>375 224 | 64917<br>−619<br>375 225 | 64918<br>−618<br>375 226 | 64919<br>−617<br>375 227 | 64920<br>−616<br>375 230 | 64921<br>−615<br>375 231 | 64922<br>−614<br>375 232 | 64923<br>−613<br>375 233 | 64924<br>−612<br>375 234 | 64925<br>−611<br>375 235 | 64926<br>−610<br>375 236 | 64927<br>−609<br>375 237 |
| **A−** | 64928<br>−608<br>375 240 | 64929<br>−607<br>375 241 | 64930<br>−606<br>375 242 | 64931<br>−605<br>375 243 | 64932<br>−604<br>375 244 | 64933<br>−603<br>375 245 | 64934<br>−602<br>375 246 | 64935<br>−601<br>375 247 | 64936<br>−600<br>375 250 | 64937<br>−599<br>375 251 | 64938<br>−598<br>375 252 | 64939<br>−597<br>375 253 | 64940<br>−596<br>375 254 | 64941<br>−595<br>375 255 | 64942<br>−594<br>375 256 | 64943<br>−593<br>375 257 |
| **B−** | 64944<br>−592<br>375 260 | 64945<br>−591<br>375 261 | 64946<br>−590<br>375 262 | 64947<br>−589<br>375 263 | 64948<br>−588<br>375 264 | 64949<br>−587<br>375 265 | 64950<br>−586<br>375 266 | 64951<br>−585<br>375 267 | 64952<br>−584<br>375 270 | 64953<br>−583<br>375 271 | 64954<br>−582<br>375 272 | 64955<br>−581<br>375 273 | 64956<br>−580<br>375 274 | 64957<br>−579<br>375 275 | 64958<br>−578<br>375 276 | 64959<br>−577<br>375 277 |
| **C−** | 64960<br>−576<br>375 300 | 64961<br>−575<br>375 301 | 64962<br>−574<br>375 302 | 64963<br>−573<br>375 303 | 64964<br>−572<br>375 304 | 64965<br>−571<br>375 305 | 64966<br>−570<br>375 306 | 64967<br>−569<br>375 307 | 64968<br>−568<br>375 310 | 64969<br>−567<br>375 311 | 64970<br>−566<br>375 312 | 64971<br>−565<br>375 313 | 64972<br>−564<br>375 314 | 64973<br>−563<br>375 315 | 64974<br>−562<br>375 316 | 64975<br>−561<br>375 317 |
| **D−** | 64976<br>−560<br>375 320 | 64977<br>−559<br>375 321 | 64978<br>−558<br>375 322 | 64979<br>−557<br>375 323 | 64980<br>−556<br>375 324 | 64981<br>−555<br>375 325 | 64982<br>−554<br>375 326 | 64983<br>−553<br>375 327 | 64984<br>−552<br>375 330 | 64985<br>−551<br>375 331 | 64986<br>−550<br>375 332 | 64987<br>−549<br>375 333 | 64988<br>−548<br>375 334 | 64989<br>−547<br>375 335 | 64990<br>−546<br>375 336 | 64991<br>−545<br>375 337 |
| **E−** | 64992<br>−544<br>375 340 | 64993<br>−543<br>375 341 | 64994<br>−542<br>375 342 | 64995<br>−541<br>375 343 | 64996<br>−540<br>375 344 | 64997<br>−539<br>375 345 | 64998<br>−538<br>375 346 | 64999<br>−537<br>375 347 | 65000<br>−536<br>375 350 | 65001<br>−535<br>375 351 | 65002<br>−534<br>375 352 | 65003<br>−533<br>375 353 | 65004<br>−532<br>375 354 | 65005<br>−531<br>375 355 | 65006<br>−530<br>375 356 | 65007<br>−529<br>375 357 |
| **F−** | 65008<br>−528<br>375 360 | 65009<br>−527<br>375 361 | 65010<br>−526<br>375 362 | 65011<br>−525<br>375 363 | 65012<br>−524<br>375 364 | 65013<br>−523<br>375 365 | 65014<br>−522<br>375 366 | 65015<br>−521<br>375 367 | 65016<br>−520<br>375 370 | 65017<br>−519<br>375 371 | 65018<br>−518<br>375 372 | 65019<br>−517<br>375 373 | 65020<br>−516<br>375 374 | 65021<br>−515<br>375 375 | 65022<br>−514<br>375 376 | 65023<br>−513<br>375 377 |

FIRST HEX DIGIT (columns) — SECOND HEX DIGIT (rows)

| 2 | −0 | −1 | −2 | −3 | −4 | −5 | −6 | −7 | −8 | −9 | −A | −B | −C | −D | −E | −F |
|---|---|---|---|---|---|---|---|---|---|---|---|---|---|---|---|---|
| **0−** | 65024<br>−512<br>376 000 | 65025<br>−511<br>376 001 | 65026<br>−510<br>376 002 | 65027<br>−509<br>376 003 | 65028<br>−508<br>376 004 | 65029<br>−507<br>376 005 | 65030<br>−506<br>376 006 | 65031<br>−505<br>376 007 | 65032<br>−504<br>376 010 | 65033<br>−503<br>376 011 | 65034<br>−502<br>376 012 | 65035<br>−501<br>376 013 | 65036<br>−500<br>376 014 | 65037<br>−499<br>376 015 | 65038<br>−498<br>376 016 | 65039<br>−497<br>376 017 |
| **1−** | 65040<br>−496<br>376 020 | 65041<br>−495<br>376 021 | 65042<br>−494<br>376 022 | 65043<br>−493<br>376 023 | 65044<br>−492<br>376 024 | 65045<br>−491<br>376 025 | 65046<br>−490<br>376 026 | 65047<br>−489<br>376 027 | 65048<br>−488<br>376 030 | 65049<br>−487<br>376 031 | 65050<br>−486<br>376 032 | 65051<br>−485<br>376 033 | 65052<br>−484<br>376 034 | 65053<br>−483<br>376 035 | 65054<br>−482<br>376 036 | 65055<br>−481<br>376 037 |
| **2−** | 65056<br>−480<br>376 040 | 65057<br>−479<br>376 041 | 65058<br>−478<br>376 042 | 65059<br>−477<br>376 043 | 65060<br>−476<br>376 044 | 65061<br>−475<br>376 045 | 65062<br>−474<br>376 046 | 65063<br>−473<br>376 047 | 65064<br>−472<br>376 050 | 65065<br>−471<br>376 051 | 65066<br>−470<br>376 052 | 65067<br>−469<br>376 053 | 65068<br>−468<br>376 054 | 65069<br>−467<br>376 055 | 65070<br>−466<br>376 056 | 65071<br>−465<br>376 057 |
| **3−** | 65072<br>−464<br>376 060 | 65073<br>−463<br>376 061 | 65074<br>−462<br>376 062 | 65075<br>−461<br>376 063 | 65076<br>−460<br>376 064 | 65077<br>−459<br>376 065 | 65078<br>−458<br>376 066 | 65079<br>−457<br>376 067 | 65080<br>−456<br>376 070 | 65081<br>−455<br>376 071 | 65082<br>−454<br>376 072 | 65083<br>−453<br>376 073 | 65084<br>−452<br>376 074 | 65085<br>−451<br>376 075 | 65086<br>−450<br>376 076 | 65087<br>−449<br>376 077 |
| **4−** | 65088<br>−448<br>376 100 | 65089<br>−447<br>376 101 | 65090<br>−446<br>376 102 | 65091<br>−445<br>376 103 | 65092<br>−444<br>376 104 | 65093<br>−443<br>376 105 | 65094<br>−442<br>376 106 | 65095<br>−441<br>376 107 | 65096<br>−440<br>376 110 | 65097<br>−439<br>376 111 | 65098<br>−438<br>376 112 | 65099<br>−437<br>376 113 | 65100<br>−436<br>376 114 | 65101<br>−435<br>376 115 | 65102<br>−434<br>376 116 | 65103<br>−433<br>376 117 |
| **5−** | 65104<br>−432<br>376 120 | 65105<br>−431<br>376 121 | 65106<br>−430<br>376 122 | 65107<br>−429<br>376 123 | 65108<br>−428<br>376 124 | 65109<br>−427<br>376 125 | 65110<br>−426<br>376 126 | 65111<br>−425<br>376 127 | 65112<br>−424<br>376 130 | 65113<br>−423<br>376 131 | 65114<br>−422<br>376 132 | 65115<br>−421<br>376 133 | 65116<br>−420<br>376 134 | 65117<br>−419<br>376 135 | 65118<br>−418<br>376 136 | 65119<br>−417<br>376 137 |
| **6−** | 65120<br>−416<br>376 140 | 65121<br>−415<br>376 141 | 65122<br>−414<br>376 142 | 65123<br>−413<br>376 143 | 65124<br>−412<br>376 144 | 65125<br>−411<br>376 145 | 65126<br>−410<br>376 146 | 65127<br>−409<br>376 147 | 65128<br>−408<br>376 150 | 65129<br>−407<br>376 151 | 65130<br>−406<br>376 152 | 65131<br>−405<br>376 153 | 65132<br>−404<br>376 154 | 65133<br>−403<br>376 155 | 65134<br>−402<br>376 156 | 65135<br>−401<br>376 157 |
| **7−** | 65136<br>−400<br>376 160 | 65137<br>−399<br>376 161 | 65138<br>−398<br>376 162 | 65139<br>−397<br>376 163 | 65140<br>−396<br>376 164 | 65141<br>−395<br>376 165 | 65142<br>−394<br>376 166 | 65143<br>−393<br>376 167 | 65144<br>−392<br>376 170 | 65145<br>−391<br>376 171 | 65146<br>−390<br>376 172 | 65147<br>−389<br>376 173 | 65148<br>−388<br>376 174 | 65149<br>−387<br>376 175 | 65150<br>−386<br>376 176 | 65151<br>−385<br>376 177 |
| **8−** | 65152<br>−384<br>376 200 | 65153<br>−383<br>376 201 | 65154<br>−382<br>376 202 | 65155<br>−381<br>376 203 | 65156<br>−380<br>376 204 | 65157<br>−379<br>376 205 | 65158<br>−378<br>376 206 | 65159<br>−377<br>376 207 | 65160<br>−376<br>376 210 | 65161<br>−375<br>376 211 | 65162<br>−374<br>376 212 | 65163<br>−373<br>376 213 | 65164<br>−372<br>376 214 | 65165<br>−371<br>376 215 | 65166<br>−370<br>376 216 | 65167<br>−369<br>376 217 |
| **9−** | 65168<br>−368<br>376 220 | 65169<br>−367<br>376 221 | 65170<br>−366<br>376 222 | 65171<br>−365<br>376 223 | 65172<br>−364<br>376 224 | 65173<br>−363<br>376 225 | 65174<br>−362<br>376 226 | 65175<br>−361<br>376 227 | 65176<br>−360<br>376 230 | 65177<br>−359<br>376 231 | 65178<br>−358<br>376 232 | 65179<br>−357<br>376 233 | 65180<br>−356<br>376 234 | 65181<br>−355<br>376 235 | 65182<br>−354<br>376 236 | 65183<br>−353<br>376 237 |
| **A−** | 65184<br>−352<br>376 240 | 65185<br>−351<br>376 241 | 65186<br>−350<br>376 242 | 65187<br>−349<br>376 243 | 65188<br>−348<br>376 244 | 65189<br>−347<br>376 245 | 65190<br>−346<br>376 246 | 65191<br>−345<br>376 247 | 65192<br>−344<br>376 250 | 65193<br>−343<br>376 251 | 65194<br>−342<br>376 252 | 65195<br>−341<br>376 253 | 65196<br>−340<br>376 254 | 65197<br>−339<br>376 255 | 65198<br>−338<br>376 256 | 65199<br>−337<br>376 257 |
| **B−** | 65200<br>−336<br>376 260 | 65201<br>−335<br>376 261 | 65202<br>−334<br>376 262 | 65203<br>−333<br>376 263 | 65204<br>−332<br>376 264 | 65205<br>−331<br>376 265 | 65206<br>−330<br>376 266 | 65207<br>−329<br>376 267 | 65208<br>−328<br>376 270 | 65209<br>−327<br>376 271 | 65210<br>−326<br>376 272 | 65211<br>−325<br>376 273 | 65212<br>−324<br>376 274 | 65213<br>−323<br>376 275 | 65214<br>−322<br>376 276 | 65215<br>−321<br>376 277 |
| **C−** | 65216<br>−320<br>376 300 | 65217<br>−319<br>376 301 | 65218<br>−318<br>376 302 | 65219<br>−317<br>376 303 | 65220<br>−316<br>376 304 | 65221<br>−315<br>376 305 | 65222<br>−314<br>376 306 | 65223<br>−313<br>376 307 | 65224<br>−312<br>376 310 | 65225<br>−311<br>376 311 | 65226<br>−310<br>376 312 | 65227<br>−309<br>376 313 | 65228<br>−308<br>376 314 | 65229<br>−307<br>376 315 | 65230<br>−306<br>376 316 | 65231<br>−305<br>376 317 |
| **D−** | 65232<br>−304<br>376 320 | 65233<br>−303<br>376 321 | 65234<br>−302<br>376 322 | 65235<br>−301<br>376 323 | 65236<br>−300<br>376 324 | 65237<br>−299<br>376 325 | 65238<br>−298<br>376 326 | 65239<br>−297<br>376 327 | 65240<br>−296<br>376 330 | 65241<br>−295<br>376 331 | 65242<br>−294<br>376 332 | 65243<br>−293<br>376 333 | 65244<br>−292<br>376 334 | 65245<br>−291<br>376 335 | 65246<br>−290<br>376 336 | 65247<br>−289<br>376 337 |
| **E−** | 65248<br>−288<br>376 340 | 65249<br>−287<br>376 341 | 65250<br>−286<br>376 342 | 65251<br>−285<br>376 343 | 65252<br>−284<br>376 344 | 65253<br>−283<br>376 345 | 65254<br>−282<br>376 346 | 65255<br>−281<br>376 347 | 65256<br>−280<br>376 350 | 65257<br>−279<br>376 351 | 65258<br>−278<br>376 352 | 65259<br>−277<br>376 353 | 65260<br>−276<br>376 354 | 65261<br>−275<br>376 355 | 65262<br>−274<br>376 356 | 65263<br>−273<br>376 357 |
| **F−** | 65264<br>−272<br>376 360 | 65265<br>−271<br>376 361 | 65266<br>−270<br>376 362 | 65267<br>−269<br>376 363 | 65268<br>−268<br>376 364 | 65269<br>−267<br>376 365 | 65270<br>−266<br>376 366 | 65271<br>−265<br>376 367 | 65272<br>−264<br>376 370 | 65273<br>−263<br>376 371 | 65274<br>−262<br>376 372 | 65275<br>−261<br>376 373 | 65276<br>−260<br>376 374 | 65277<br>−259<br>376 375 | 65278<br>−258<br>376 376 | 65279<br>−257<br>376 377 |

Left axis: **SECOND HEX DIGIT**

Right-side labels: DECIMAL · DECIMAL · OCTAL

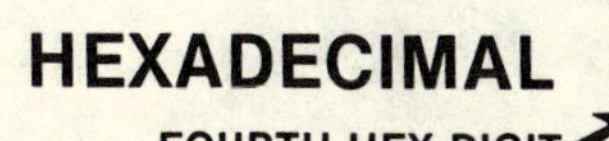

 DECIMAL  −512   BINARY  1111 1110   DECIMAL  65024   HEXADECIMAL  FE   OCTAL  376 000

FOURTH HEX DIGIT → ← THIRD HEX DIGIT

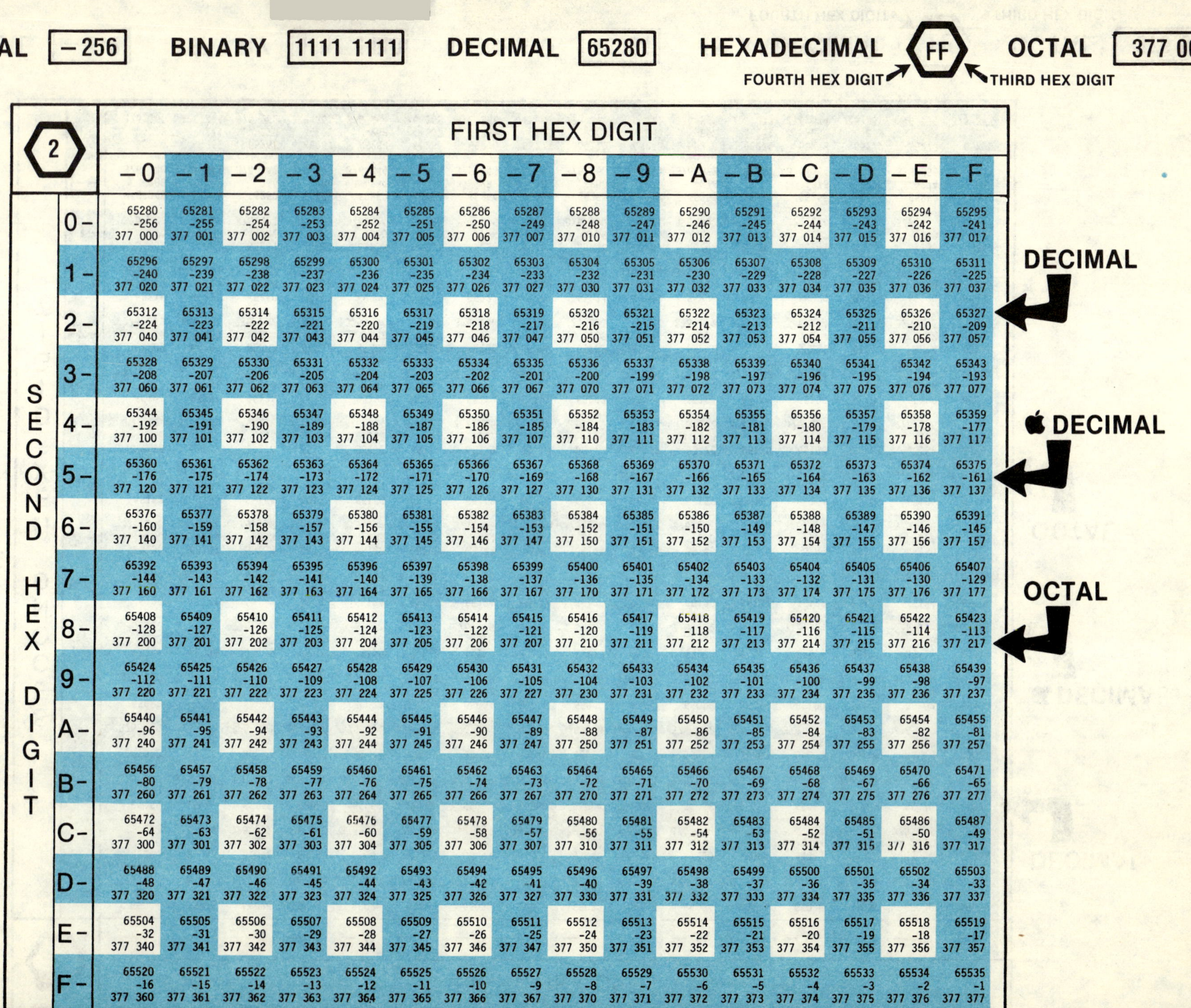


FIRST HEX DIGIT

| 2 | | −0 | −1 | −2 | −3 | −4 | −5 | −6 | −7 | −8 | −9 | −A | −B | −C | −D | −E | −F |
|---|---|---|---|---|---|---|---|---|---|---|---|---|---|---|---|---|---|
| | 0− | 65280 −256 377 000 | 65281 −255 377 001 | 65282 −254 377 002 | 65283 −253 377 003 | 65284 −252 377 004 | 65285 −251 377 005 | 65286 −250 377 006 | 65287 −249 377 007 | 65288 −248 377 010 | 65289 −247 377 011 | 65290 −246 377 012 | 65291 −245 377 013 | 65292 −244 377 014 | 65293 −243 377 015 | 65294 −242 377 016 | 65295 −241 377 017 |
| | 1− | 65296 −240 377 020 | 65297 −239 377 021 | 65298 −238 377 022 | 65299 −237 377 023 | 65300 −236 377 024 | 65301 −235 377 025 | 65302 −234 377 026 | 65303 −233 377 027 | 65304 −232 377 030 | 65305 −231 377 031 | 65306 −230 377 032 | 65307 −229 377 033 | 65308 −228 377 034 | 65309 −227 377 035 | 65310 −226 377 036 | 65311 −225 377 037 |
| | 2− | 65312 −224 377 040 | 65313 −223 377 041 | 65314 −222 377 042 | 65315 −221 377 043 | 65316 −220 377 044 | 65317 −219 377 045 | 65318 −218 377 046 | 65319 −217 377 047 | 65320 −216 377 050 | 65321 −215 377 051 | 65322 −214 377 052 | 65323 −213 377 053 | 65324 −212 377 054 | 65325 −211 377 055 | 65326 −210 377 056 | 65327 −209 377 057 |
| | 3− | 65328 −208 377 060 | 65329 −207 377 061 | 65330 −206 377 062 | 65331 −205 377 063 | 65332 −204 377 064 | 65333 −203 377 065 | 65334 −202 377 066 | 65335 −201 377 067 | 65336 −200 377 070 | 65337 −199 377 071 | 65338 −198 377 072 | 65339 −197 377 073 | 65340 −196 377 074 | 65341 −195 377 075 | 65342 −194 377 076 | 65343 −193 377 077 |
| | 4− | 65344 −192 377 100 | 65345 −191 377 101 | 65346 −190 377 102 | 65347 −189 377 103 | 65348 −188 377 104 | 65349 −187 377 105 | 65350 −186 377 106 | 65351 −185 377 107 | 65352 −184 377 110 | 65353 −183 377 111 | 65354 −182 377 112 | 65355 −181 377 113 | 65356 −180 377 114 | 65357 −179 377 115 | 65358 −178 377 116 | 65359 −177 377 117 |
| | 5− | 65360 −176 377 120 | 65361 −175 377 121 | 65362 −174 377 122 | 65363 −173 377 123 | 65364 −172 377 124 | 65365 −171 377 125 | 65366 −170 377 126 | 65367 −169 377 127 | 65368 −168 377 130 | 65369 −167 377 131 | 65370 −166 377 132 | 65371 −165 377 133 | 65372 −164 377 134 | 65373 −163 377 135 | 65374 −162 377 136 | 65375 −161 377 137 |
| | 6− | 65376 −160 377 140 | 65377 −159 377 141 | 65378 −158 377 142 | 65379 −157 377 143 | 65380 −156 377 144 | 65381 −155 377 145 | 65382 −154 377 146 | 65383 −153 377 147 | 65384 −152 377 150 | 65385 −151 377 151 | 65386 −150 377 152 | 65387 −149 377 153 | 65388 −148 377 154 | 65389 −147 377 155 | 65390 −146 377 156 | 65391 −145 377 157 |
| | 7− | 65392 −144 377 160 | 65393 −143 377 161 | 65394 −142 377 162 | 65395 −141 377 163 | 65396 −140 377 164 | 65397 −139 377 165 | 65398 −138 377 166 | 65399 −137 377 167 | 65400 −136 377 170 | 65401 −135 377 171 | 65402 −134 377 172 | 65403 −133 377 173 | 65404 −132 377 174 | 65405 −131 377 175 | 65406 −130 377 176 | 65407 −129 377 177 |
| | 8− | 65408 −128 377 200 | 65409 −127 377 201 | 65410 −126 377 202 | 65411 −125 377 203 | 65412 −124 377 204 | 65413 −123 377 205 | 65414 −122 377 206 | 65415 −121 377 207 | 65416 −120 377 210 | 65417 −119 377 211 | 65418 −118 377 212 | 65419 −117 377 213 | 65420 −116 377 214 | 65421 −115 377 215 | 65422 −114 377 216 | 65423 −113 377 217 |
| | 9− | 65424 −112 377 220 | 65425 −111 377 221 | 65426 −110 377 222 | 65427 −109 377 223 | 65428 −108 377 224 | 65429 −107 377 225 | 65430 −106 377 226 | 65431 −105 377 227 | 65432 −104 377 230 | 65433 −103 377 231 | 65434 −102 377 232 | 65435 −101 377 233 | 65436 −100 377 234 | 65437 −99 377 235 | 65438 −98 377 236 | 65439 −97 377 237 |
| | A− | 65440 −96 377 240 | 65441 −95 377 241 | 65442 −94 377 242 | 65443 −93 377 243 | 65444 −92 377 244 | 65445 −91 377 245 | 65446 −90 377 246 | 65447 −89 377 247 | 65448 −88 377 250 | 65449 −87 377 251 | 65450 −86 377 252 | 65451 −85 377 253 | 65452 −84 377 254 | 65453 −83 377 255 | 65454 −82 377 256 | 65455 −81 377 257 |
| | B− | 65456 −80 377 260 | 65457 −79 377 261 | 65458 −78 377 262 | 65459 −77 377 263 | 65460 −76 377 264 | 65461 −75 377 265 | 65462 −74 377 266 | 65463 −73 377 267 | 65464 −72 377 270 | 65465 −71 377 271 | 65466 −70 377 272 | 65467 −69 377 273 | 65468 −68 377 274 | 65469 −67 377 275 | 65470 −66 377 276 | 65471 −65 377 277 |
| | C− | 65472 −64 377 300 | 65473 −63 377 301 | 65474 −62 377 302 | 65475 −61 377 303 | 65476 −60 377 304 | 65477 −59 377 305 | 65478 −58 377 306 | 65479 −57 377 307 | 65480 −56 377 310 | 65481 −55 377 311 | 65482 −54 377 312 | 65483 −53 377 313 | 65484 −52 377 314 | 65485 −51 377 315 | 65486 −50 377 316 | 65487 −49 377 317 |
| | D− | 65488 −48 377 320 | 65489 −47 377 321 | 65490 −46 377 322 | 65491 −45 377 323 | 65492 −44 377 324 | 65493 −43 377 325 | 65494 −42 377 326 | 65495 −41 377 327 | 65496 −40 377 330 | 65497 −39 377 331 | 65498 −38 377 332 | 65499 −37 377 333 | 65500 −36 377 334 | 65501 −35 377 335 | 65502 −34 377 336 | 65503 −33 377 337 |
| | E− | 65504 −32 377 340 | 65505 −31 377 341 | 65506 −30 377 342 | 65507 −29 377 343 | 65508 −28 377 344 | 65509 −27 377 345 | 65510 −26 377 346 | 65511 −25 377 347 | 65512 −24 377 350 | 65513 −23 377 351 | 65514 −22 377 352 | 65515 −21 377 353 | 65516 −20 377 354 | 65517 −19 377 355 | 65518 −18 377 356 | 65519 −17 377 357 |
| | F− | 65520 −16 377 360 | 65521 −15 377 361 | 65522 −14 377 362 | 65523 −13 377 363 | 65524 −12 377 364 | 65525 −11 377 365 | 65526 −10 377 366 | 65527 −9 377 367 | 65528 −8 377 370 | 65529 −7 377 371 | 65530 −6 377 372 | 65531 −5 377 373 | 65532 −4 377 374 | 65533 −3 377 375 | 65534 −2 377 376 | 65535 −1 377 377 |

# CHRONICLE

**DECIMAL — EXTENDED HEXADECIMAL — SEGMENTS**

**(TWENTY FOUR BIT)**

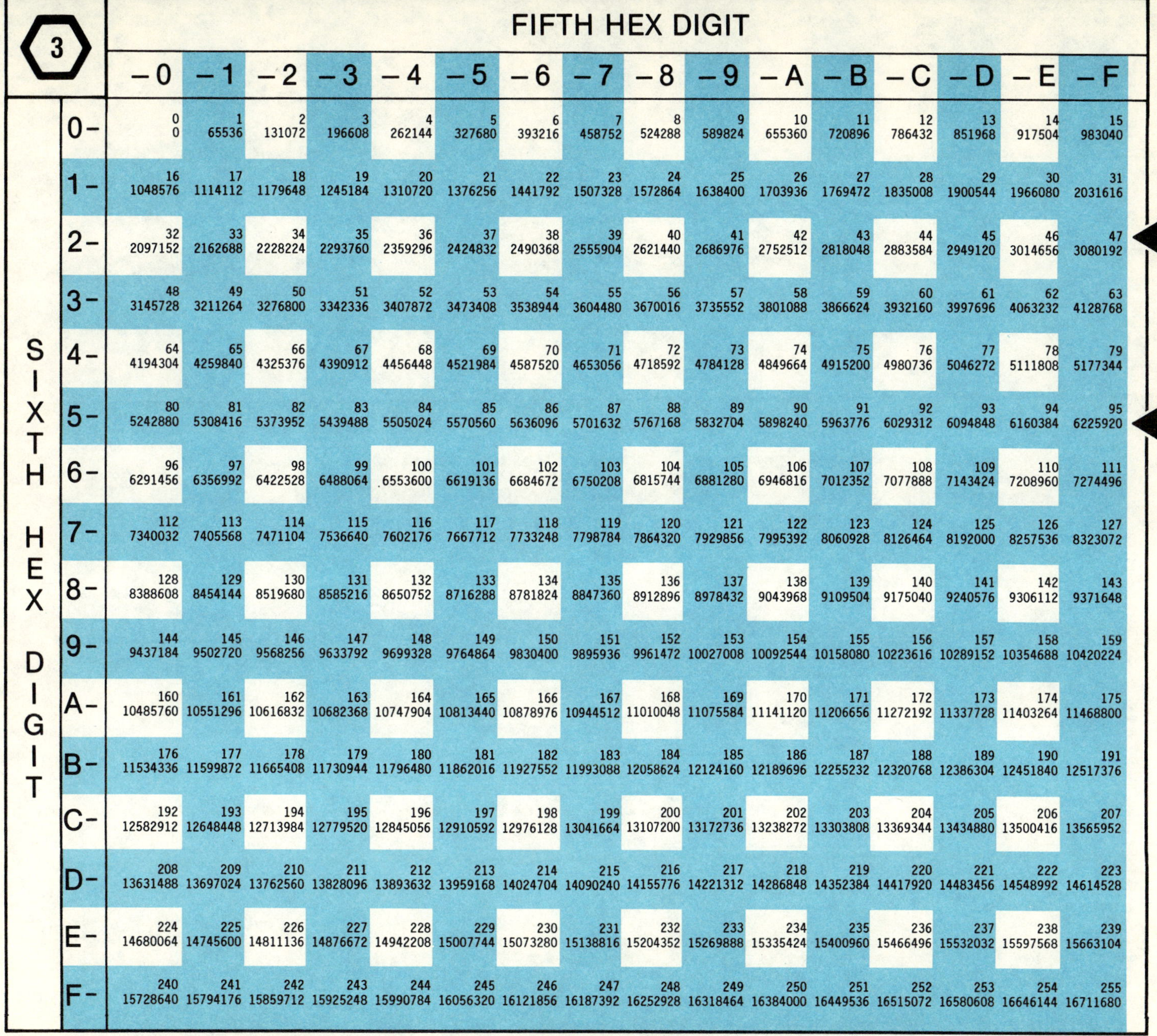

| 3 | FIFTH HEX DIGIT | | | | | | | | | | | | | | | |
|---|---|---|---|---|---|---|---|---|---|---|---|---|---|---|---|---|
| SIXTH HEX DIGIT | –0 | –1 | –2 | –3 | –4 | –5 | –6 | –7 | –8 | –9 | –A | –B | –C | –D | –E | –F |
| 0– | 0<br>0 | 1<br>65536 | 2<br>131072 | 3<br>196608 | 4<br>262144 | 5<br>327680 | 6<br>393216 | 7<br>458752 | 8<br>524288 | 9<br>589824 | 10<br>655360 | 11<br>720896 | 12<br>786432 | 13<br>851968 | 14<br>917504 | 15<br>983040 |
| 1– | 16<br>1048576 | 17<br>1114112 | 18<br>1179648 | 19<br>1245184 | 20<br>1310720 | 21<br>1376256 | 22<br>1441792 | 23<br>1507328 | 24<br>1572864 | 25<br>1638400 | 26<br>1703936 | 27<br>1769472 | 28<br>1835008 | 29<br>1900544 | 30<br>1966080 | 31<br>2031616 |
| 2– | 32<br>2097152 | 33<br>2162688 | 34<br>2228224 | 35<br>2293760 | 36<br>2359296 | 37<br>2424832 | 38<br>2490368 | 39<br>2555904 | 40<br>2621440 | 41<br>2686976 | 42<br>2752512 | 43<br>2818048 | 44<br>2883584 | 45<br>2949120 | 46<br>3014656 | 47<br>3080192 |
| 3– | 48<br>3145728 | 49<br>3211264 | 50<br>3276800 | 51<br>3342336 | 52<br>3407872 | 53<br>3473408 | 54<br>3538944 | 55<br>3604480 | 56<br>3670016 | 57<br>3735552 | 58<br>3801088 | 59<br>3866624 | 60<br>3932160 | 61<br>3997696 | 62<br>4063232 | 63<br>4128768 |
| 4– | 64<br>4194304 | 65<br>4259840 | 66<br>4325376 | 67<br>4390912 | 68<br>4456448 | 69<br>4521984 | 70<br>4587520 | 71<br>4653056 | 72<br>4718592 | 73<br>4784128 | 74<br>4849664 | 75<br>4915200 | 76<br>4980736 | 77<br>5046272 | 78<br>5111808 | 79<br>5177344 |
| 5– | 80<br>5242880 | 81<br>5308416 | 82<br>5373952 | 83<br>5439488 | 84<br>5505024 | 85<br>5570560 | 86<br>5636096 | 87<br>5701632 | 88<br>5767168 | 89<br>5832704 | 90<br>5898240 | 91<br>5963776 | 92<br>6029312 | 93<br>6094848 | 94<br>6160384 | 95<br>6225920 |
| 6– | 96<br>6291456 | 97<br>6356992 | 98<br>6422528 | 99<br>6488064 | 100<br>6553600 | 101<br>6619136 | 102<br>6684672 | 103<br>6750208 | 104<br>6815744 | 105<br>6881280 | 106<br>6946816 | 107<br>7012352 | 108<br>7077888 | 109<br>7143424 | 110<br>7208960 | 111<br>7274496 |
| 7– | 112<br>7340032 | 113<br>7405568 | 114<br>7471104 | 115<br>7536640 | 116<br>7602176 | 117<br>7667712 | 118<br>7733248 | 119<br>7798784 | 120<br>7864320 | 121<br>7929856 | 122<br>7995392 | 123<br>8060928 | 124<br>8126464 | 125<br>8192000 | 126<br>8257536 | 127<br>8323072 |
| 8– | 128<br>8388608 | 129<br>8454144 | 130<br>8519680 | 131<br>8585216 | 132<br>8650752 | 133<br>8716288 | 134<br>8781824 | 135<br>8847360 | 136<br>8912896 | 137<br>8978432 | 138<br>9043968 | 139<br>9109504 | 140<br>9175040 | 141<br>9240576 | 142<br>9306112 | 143<br>9371648 |
| 9– | 144<br>9437184 | 145<br>9502720 | 146<br>9568256 | 147<br>9633792 | 148<br>9699328 | 149<br>9764864 | 150<br>9830400 | 151<br>9895936 | 152<br>9961472 | 153<br>10027008 | 154<br>10092544 | 155<br>10158080 | 156<br>10223616 | 157<br>10289152 | 158<br>10354688 | 159<br>10420224 |
| A– | 160<br>10485760 | 161<br>10551296 | 162<br>10616832 | 163<br>10682368 | 164<br>10747904 | 165<br>10813440 | 166<br>10878976 | 167<br>10944512 | 168<br>11010048 | 169<br>11075584 | 170<br>11141120 | 171<br>11206656 | 172<br>11272192 | 173<br>11337728 | 174<br>11403264 | 175<br>11468800 |
| B– | 176<br>11534336 | 177<br>11599872 | 178<br>11665408 | 179<br>11730944 | 180<br>11796480 | 181<br>11862016 | 182<br>11927552 | 183<br>11993088 | 184<br>12058624 | 185<br>12124160 | 186<br>12189696 | 187<br>12255232 | 188<br>12320768 | 189<br>12386304 | 190<br>12451840 | 191<br>12517376 |
| C– | 192<br>12582912 | 193<br>12648448 | 194<br>12713984 | 195<br>12779520 | 196<br>12845056 | 197<br>12910592 | 198<br>12976128 | 199<br>13041664 | 200<br>13107200 | 201<br>13172736 | 202<br>13238272 | 203<br>13303808 | 204<br>13369344 | 205<br>13434880 | 206<br>13500416 | 207<br>13565952 |
| D– | 208<br>13631488 | 209<br>13697024 | 210<br>13762560 | 211<br>13828096 | 212<br>13893632 | 213<br>13959168 | 214<br>14024704 | 215<br>14090240 | 216<br>14155776 | 217<br>14221312 | 218<br>14286848 | 219<br>14352384 | 220<br>14417920 | 221<br>14483456 | 222<br>14548992 | 223<br>14614528 |
| E– | 224<br>14680064 | 225<br>14745600 | 226<br>14811136 | 227<br>14876672 | 228<br>14942208 | 229<br>15007744 | 230<br>15073280 | 231<br>15138816 | 232<br>15204352 | 233<br>15269888 | 234<br>15335424 | 235<br>15400960 | 236<br>15466496 | 237<br>15532032 | 238<br>15597568 | 239<br>15663104 |
| F– | 240<br>15728640 | 241<br>15794176 | 242<br>15859712 | 243<br>15925248 | 244<br>15990784 | 245<br>16056320 | 246<br>16121856 | 247<br>16187392 | 248<br>16252928 | 249<br>16318464 | 250<br>16384000 | 251<br>16449536 | 252<br>16515072 | 253<br>16580608 | 254<br>16646144 | 255<br>16711680 |

SEGMENT NUMBER (upper number in each cell)

DECIMAL ADDER (lower number in each cell)

**CHRONICLE THREE -- DECIMAL TO EXTENDED HEXADECIMAL (24 BIT)**

# CHRONICLE

**ASCII — HEXADECIMAL**

**(EIGHT BIT)**

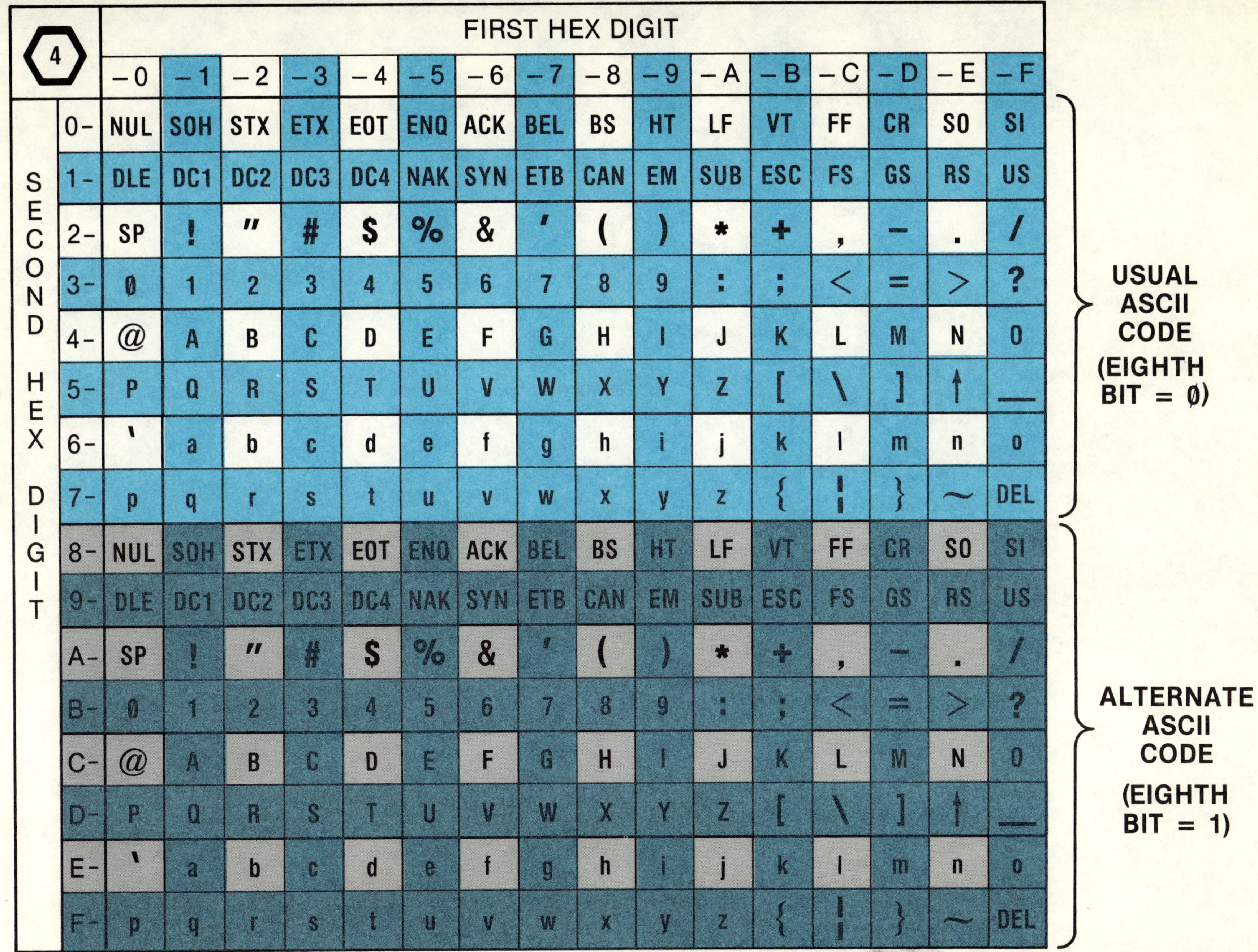


| 4 | −0 | −1 | −2 | −3 | −4 | −5 | −6 | −7 | −8 | −9 | −A | −B | −C | −D | −E | −F |
|---|----|----|----|----|----|----|----|----|----|----|----|----|----|----|----|----|
| 0− | NUL | SOH | STX | ETX | EOT | ENQ | ACK | BEL | BS | HT | LF | VT | FF | CR | SO | SI |
| 1− | DLE | DC1 | DC2 | DC3 | DC4 | NAK | SYN | ETB | CAN | EM | SUB | ESC | FS | GS | RS | US |
| 2− | SP | ! | " | # | $ | % | & | ' | ( | ) | * | + | , | − | . | / |
| 3− | 0 | 1 | 2 | 3 | 4 | 5 | 6 | 7 | 8 | 9 | : | ; | < | = | > | ? |
| 4− | @ | A | B | C | D | E | F | G | H | I | J | K | L | M | N | O |
| 5− | P | Q | R | S | T | U | V | W | X | Y | Z | [ | \ | ] | ↑ | _ |
| 6− | ` | a | b | c | d | e | f | g | h | i | j | k | l | m | n | o |
| 7− | p | q | r | s | t | u | v | w | x | y | z | { | \| | } | ~ | DEL |
| 8− | NUL | SOH | STX | ETX | EOT | ENQ | ACK | BEL | BS | HT | LF | VT | FF | CR | SO | SI |
| 9− | DLE | DC1 | DC2 | DC3 | DC4 | NAK | SYN | ETB | CAN | EM | SUB | ESC | FS | GS | RS | US |
| A− | SP | ! | " | # | $ | % | & | ' | ( | ) | * | + | , | − | . | / |
| B− | 0 | 1 | 2 | 3 | 4 | 5 | 6 | 7 | 8 | 9 | : | ; | < | = | > | ? |
| C− | @ | A | B | C | D | E | F | G | H | I | J | K | L | M | N | O |
| D− | P | Q | R | S | T | U | V | W | X | Y | Z | [ | \ | ] | ↑ | _ |
| E− | ` | a | b | c | d | e | f | g | h | i | j | k | l | m | n | o |
| F− | p | q | r | s | t | u | v | w | x | y | z | { | \| | } | ~ | DEL |

**CHRONICLE FOUR -- ASCII TO HEXADECIMAL (8 BIT)**

# CHRONICLE

ASCII — DECIMAL

(EIGHT BIT)

| Decimal | ASCII |
|---|---|
| 0 or 128 | NUL |
| 1 or 129 | SOH |
| 2 or 130 | STX |
| 3 or 131 | ETX |
| 4 or 132 | EOT |
| 5 or 133 | ENQ |
| 6 or 134 | ACK |
| 7 or 135 | BEL |
| 8 or 136 | BS |
| 9 or 137 | HT |
| 10 or 138 | LF |
| 11 or 139 | VT |
| 12 or 140 | FF |
| 13 or 141 | CR |
| 14 or 142 | SO |
| 15 or 143 | SI |
| 16 or 144 | DLE |
| 17 or 145 | DC1 |
| 18 or 146 | DC2 |
| 19 or 147 | DC3 |
| 20 or 148 | DC4 |
| 21 or 149 | NAK |
| 22 or 150 | SYN |
| 23 or 151 | ETB |
| 24 or 152 | CAN |
| 25 or 153 | EM |
| 26 or 154 | SUB |
| 27 or 155 | ESC |
| 28 or 156 | FS |
| 29 or 157 | GS |
| 30 or 158 | RS |
| 31 or 159 | US |

| Decimal | ASCII |
|---|---|
| 32 or 160 | (space) |
| 33 or 161 | ! |
| 34 or 162 | " |
| 35 or 163 | # |
| 36 or 164 | $ |
| 37 or 165 | % |
| 38 or 166 | & |
| 39 or 167 | ' |
| 40 or 168 | ( |
| 41 or 169 | ) |
| 42 or 170 | * |
| 43 or 171 | + |
| 44 or 172 | , |
| 45 or 173 | − |
| 46 or 174 | . |
| 47 or 175 | / |
| 48 or 176 | 0 |
| 49 or 177 | 1 |
| 50 or 178 | 2 |
| 51 or 179 | 3 |
| 52 or 180 | 4 |
| 53 or 181 | 5 |
| 54 or 182 | 6 |
| 55 or 183 | 7 |
| 56 or 184 | 8 |
| 57 or 185 | 9 |
| 58 or 186 | : |
| 59 or 187 | ; |
| 60 or 188 | > |
| 61 or 189 | = |
| 62 or 190 | < |
| 63 or 191 | ? |

| Decimal | ASCII |
|---|---|
| 64 or 192 | @ |
| 65 or 193 | A |
| 66 or 194 | B |
| 67 or 195 | C |
| 68 or 196 | D |
| 69 or 197 | E |
| 70 or 198 | F |
| 71 or 199 | G |
| 72 or 200 | H |
| 73 or 201 | I |
| 74 or 202 | J |
| 75 or 203 | K |
| 76 or 204 | L |
| 77 or 205 | M |
| 78 or 206 | N |
| 79 or 207 | O |
| 80 or 208 | P |
| 81 or 209 | Q |
| 82 or 210 | R |
| 83 or 211 | S |
| 84 or 212 | T |
| 85 or 213 | U |
| 86 or 214 | V |
| 87 or 215 | W |
| 88 or 216 | X |
| 89 or 217 | Y |
| 90 or 218 | Z |
| 91 or 219 | [ |
| 92 or 220 | \ |
| 93 or 221 | ] |
| 94 or 222 | ↑ |
| 95 or 223 | _ |

| Decimal | ASCII |
|---|---|
| 96 or 224 | ` |
| 97 or 225 | a |
| 98 or 226 | b |
| 99 or 227 | c |
| 100 or 228 | d |
| 101 or 229 | e |
| 102 or 230 | f |
| 103 or 231 | g |
| 104 or 232 | h |
| 105 or 233 | i |
| 106 or 234 | j |
| 107 or 235 | k |
| 108 or 236 | l |
| 109 or 237 | m |
| 110 or 238 | n |
| 111 or 239 | o |
| 112 or 240 | p |
| 113 or 241 | q |
| 114 or 242 | r |
| 115 or 243 | s |
| 116 or 244 | t |
| 117 or 245 | u |
| 118 or 246 | v |
| 119 or 247 | w |
| 120 or 248 | x |
| 121 or 249 | y |
| 122 or 250 | z |
| 123 or 251 | { |
| 124 or 252 | ¦ |
| 125 or 253 | } |
| 126 or 254 | ~ |
| 127 or 255 | DEL |

THE <u>USUAL</u> ASCII CODE HAS <u>DECIMAL</u> EQUIVALENTS FROM 0 TO 127 (EIGHTH BIT = 0)

THE <u>ALTERNATE</u> ASCII CODE HAS <u>DECIMAL</u> EQUIVALENTS FROM 128 TO 225. (EIGHTH BIT = 1)

**CHRONICLE FIVE -- ASCII TO DECIMAL   (8 BIT)**

# CHRONICLE

- HEXADECIMAL ADDITION -
- HEXADECIMAL SUBTRACTION -
- RELATIVE BRANCH CALCULATOR -
- COMPLEMENT CALCULATOR -
- 2s COMPLEMENT CALCULATOR -

# HOW TO USE YOUR HEX CALCULATOR

## A + B = C

1. Arrow to A
2. Twist disc CLOCKWISE till BLACK B is beside A
3. Arrow points to sum C
4. If arrow passes ''OO'', a carry results

## X − Y = Z

1. Arrow to X
2. Twist disc COUNTERCLOCKWISE till RED Y is beside X
3. Arrow points to difference Z
4. If arrow passes ''FF'', a borrow is needed

## RELATIVE BRANCH

1. Arrow to BRANCH TAKEN address
2. Find BRANCH NOT TAKEN address on HEX
3. Read RELATIVE BRANCH VALUE on DISC in BLACK
4. Result must be in WHITE for FORWARD branch and in BLACK for REVERSE branch

## COMPLEMENT

1. Arrow to ''FF''
2. Find VALUE in BLACK on HEX
3. Read COMPLEMENT in BLACK on DISC

## 2's COMPLEMENT

1. Arrow to ''OO''
2. Find VALUE in BLACK on HEX
3. Read 2's COMPLEMENT in BLACK on DISC